THE COMPLETE POETRY AND
SELECTED PROSE OF

John Donne

&

THE COMPLETE POETRY OF

William Blake

THE COMPLETE POETRY AND
SELECTED PROSE OF

John Donne

&

THE COMPLETE POETRY OF

William Blake

WITH AN INTRODUCTION BY

Robert Silliman Hillyer

THE MODERN LIBRARY

NEW YORK

>>

The poetry and prose of Donne are from the text of the Nonesuch Edition, edited by John Hayward. The poetry of Blake is from the Nonesuch Edition, edited by Geoffrey Keynes.

THE MODERN LIBRARY

IS PUBLISHED BY

RANDOM HOUSE, INC.

BENNETT A. CERF · DONALD S. KLOPFER · ROBERT K. HAAS

Manufactured in the United States of America
By H. Wolff

Contents

INTRODUCTION *by Robert Silliman Hillyer*

THE COMPLETE POETRY AND
SELECTED PROSE OF JOHN DONNE

THE POEMS

v

EPIGRAMS

Holy Sonnets

THE PROSE

PARADOXES AND PROBLEMES

THE COMPLETE POETRY OF
WILLIAM BLAKE

Introduction

BY ROBERT SILLIMAN HILLYER

I

CONVERSATIONAL poetry is as old as the recorded word. It differs from the more usual rhetorical style, for its speech is intimate. It does not rely so much on traditional symbols but creates them as it goes along; its phrasing is, as a rule, shorter and more closely fitted to the living voice; it can make sudden leaps to a sublimity toward which rhetoric would have to climb slowly, or, in unguarded moments, plunge into the pit of bathos. The rhetorical style has a past and delights us with verbal associations, whereas the aim of the conversational style is immediacy; the associations are personal. Some thousands of years ago a homesick Egyptian poet wrote: "I bathe in the river and speak to the fishes who are swimming northward where my country lies." A Chinese poet, of some eleven hundred years ago, having been dubiously honored with the governorship of a barbarous province, observed: "In this place I am satisfied with anyone who is even remotely human." These expressions of homesickness echo common experiences; they speak, freed of all the conventions of their period and tongue. But "I wandered lonely as a cloud" departs somewhat from immediacy and substitutes the beauty of the simile for the sting of directness. "She stood in tears amid the alien corn" is a triumph of the rhetorical style and demands, for its full effect, a knowledge of the story of Ruth. There is no hostility or invidious comparison between the two styles. Most poets have used them both to advantage. Often the two contrasting voices play against each other in a single composition. There is, I suppose, no better lyric example of the conversational style than Marvell's "To His Coy Mistress," yet the climax of it is magnificent rhetoric:

> But at my back I always hear
> Time's winged chariot hurrying near,
> And yonder, all before us, lie
> Deserts of vast eternity.

With what artistry the poet leads us from that passage back to the manner with which he began, until he can say, with almost colloquial flippancy:

> The grave's a fine and private place
> But none, I think, do there embrace.

Indeed, there are few poets who have limited themselves to one style or the other. Matthew Arnold's famous reference concerning Thomas Gray, "He never spoke out," shows the critic's reaction to a style which almost never deviates from high rhetoric and by that means wins its greatest triumphs. In the poetry of Robert Frost, on the contrary, the conversational style is almost unbroken. Late in the eighteenth century, when the rhetorical manner had so long reigned that it had grown imperial and soft, there were deliberate attempts, such as George Crabbe's against artificial themes, and Wordsworth's against artificial diction, to break it down. The same phenomenon, on a much smaller scale, took place in the early twentieth century, with the Imagist revolt against the abstractions of late Victorian rhetoric.

Among the few basic qualities shared by John Donne and William Blake, especially in their best-known work, was the recognition, by each for his own period, that the formal method needed shaking up. Two hundred years apart, each found himself at the end of a tremendous age, when no effort of fevered technique could invent ornament enough to hide the breaks in the Cyclopean wall.

In Donne's early years as poet, the conventions of the late Elizabethan lyric were already beginning to stifle the music. The thin and brittle tonelessness of the Cavalier song was to come. In the field of the sonnet, the Platonic radiance of Petrarch and Dante had been strained through the distorting glass of French and English minor sonneteers until there was no light left except from midnight oil. Renaissance vigor was dying out under a downpour of plaster nymphs and shepherds misbegotten from the Anthology. Eros had become Cupid; the Unicorn, an Indian ass; and Leda's swan, a goose. Shakespere's sonnet sequence, uneven in its grandeur, largely defied these conventions, though whether or not the sonnets really unlocked his heart is still as much of a riddle as when Wordsworth affirmed that they did and Browning insisted that they did not. Michael Drayton's sequence, second in quality only to Shakespere's—though it is unjustly represented as a rule by the excellence of a single sonnet—is largely free of baroque affectations. The speech, even when it is nervous or stammering, is direct and temperamental. With the exception of these two works, and occasional sonnets by Sidney, Spenser, Daniel, and Lodge, the Elizabethan sonnet was an irresistible challenge to reform. Love, the theme of so many uninspired performances, became wan with merely literary exercise. Drayton complained that no critic would suppose him sincere in passion after so many falsities toward the subject. "For God's sake, hold your tongue and let me love," cried Donne in exasperation at the chatter.

Donne's earliest lyrics show his desire to speak out in his own voice, to clear the air of echoes. For his lyric model he turned, indeed, to the complexity and stanzaic richness of the Elizabethan song, but the words were inspired by Eros, not Cupid. From this period of his life—his twenties—come the poems which justly excite the interest of the common reader. Later, he was to compose an occasional lyric masterpiece, like the familiar sonnet "Death be not proud" or the matchless "A Hymne to God the Father," but as time went on, much of his power was diverted into his sermons, and his poetic style conformed more closely to what was expected of it. His influence, too, had spread, and his manner of writing was no longer strange and wilful to the ears of its audience. By the end of the seventeenth century, his characteristics had themselves become a convention and in turn were overthrown.

Two hundred years after Donne, William Blake also found a prevalent style which called for revolt. It was different from the one Donne had attacked, but equally exhausted.

> How have you left the ancient love
> That bards of old enjoy'd in you!
> The languid strings do scarcely move!
> The sound is forc'd, the notes are few!

It was not a dying lyric tradition, but the opposite: the blunted satire and trite philosophy of the late heroic couplet. Pope's embroidery scissors had become shears fitter to clip a Flanders mare than the lovelock of a lady. With the exception of the work of George Crabbe and some of the melodious passages in Goldsmith's, the couplet was worn out. Nor had blank verse fared better in the heavy Miltonisms of Young's *Night Thoughts* and Thomson's *Seasons,* popular as these works were in their own period—and after. Public taste by the end of the century was set at an easy level, appropriate to the low vaultings of Hayley's *Triumphs of Temper,* a performance which, incidentally, Blake was at one time oddly called upon to admire.

Had Blake been born a decade or two later, it is just possible that he might have been swept along with the Romantic revolt to a position of some prominence, at least sufficient to be noticed by the condescension of Wordsworth (who, in fact, did admire Blake's *Songs*) or by the jibes of Byron. Blake, too, worked for verbal emancipation from the conventions of the past and saw the vision of human emancipation from the tyrannies of this world. Shelley would have approved the Liberty cap he affected during the early days of the French Revolution, and nearly all the Romantic poets would have applauded the bitter answers which, in the *Songs of Experience*, Blake set against the idylls of the *Songs of Innocence*. Innocence was Mankind in Eden—not Eden irrevocably lost but Eden to be redeemed by the individual soul welcoming free imagination and throwing off the time-corroded shackles of experience. Again, Coleridge, who also admired the *Songs* and paid several visits to their author, would not have found Blake's doctrines uncongenial to his speculations, nor would the Shelley of *Prometheus Unbound* or the Wordsworth of the *Ode on Intimations of Immortality*. But by the time the Romantics were in full cry, Blake's poetry was already committed to obscurity. Wordsworth might admire, Coleridge pay his respects, and Lamb speak of "one of the most extraordinary persons of the age," but physically the poet was old and tired, and spiritually he was far off from even the echoes of applause. His designs were better known among the few who could afford a small patronage.

Seeking thus a point of similarity between Donne and Blake, we begin with their common desire to escape from the stylistic fatigue of their periods, and to speak out. That common starting point only makes clearer the dissimilarity of their development. The reason lies, of course, in the almost opposing qualities of their temperaments and philosophies. Donne, working his way through a dark tangle of spiritual and material problems, became with worldly eminence more outwardly conforming. In the Church and in his Art his influence was strong. The theological pattern of which he was a spokesman was not broken until the Civil War, and his literary manner could not be ignored until the time of the Augustans—and even then, Pope honored his verses with a double recasting in a more correct, if less lively, mold. If we substitute Donne's name for Homer's we find an appropriate comment for such treatment in Blake's epigram:

> Thus Hayley on his Toilette seeing the soap,
> Cries, "Homer is very much improv'd by Pope."

That this improvement of Donne's verse would not have pleased his admirers in the mid-seventeenth century is obvious from the fact that toward the end of his life Donne was an acknowledged arbiter of style and of doctrine, the center of friendly esteem. But Blake, in his time, fought his way from one loneliness to another yet deeper, accompanied always by two loves of comfort and despair: of comfort, his wife Catherine, one of the major saints in the palace of art; and, of despair, the specter of unyielding want.

Lastly, since both Donne and Blake were dedicated to the science of

God, their visions of Man's redemption in God determine the full meaning of their art. Theology, based on tradition, logic, and faith spoke elo-
quently through Donne. Mysticism, that charts only the results of its
own exploration, sent Blake voyaging over the unpredictable. So divergent
are these points of view, that the following lines of Blake would have
applied to a man of Donne's intellect:

> The Vision of Christ that thou dost see
> Is my Vision's Greatest Enemy:
> Thine has a great hook nose like thine,
> Mine has a snub nose like to mine: . . .
> Both read the Bible day & night,
> But thou read'st black where I read white.

Where the source divides, the rivers must flow apart. So in mundane
matters, Donne's penitential homilies spoke for abstinence—abstinence
which, according to Blake, "sows sand all over the ruddy limbs and flaming hair." Donne deprecated gratification of desire, which, Blake main-
tained, planted fruits of life and beauty. Donne could stretch a point,
sometimes of mere rhetoric, to please an acquaintance; Blake denounced
unsparingly. They would never have got on together.

Yet they had at least one more taste in common. They were both, by
preference, city men. "Dr. Donne," said King James I, "I have invited
you to dinner; and, though you sit not down with me, yet I will carve to
you of a dish that I know you love well; for, knowing you love London, I
do therefore make you Dean of St. Paul's." As for Blake, his three years
in the country under Hayley's auspices were an experience dragged out
in boredom and terminated in horror. For both men, perhaps, the *urbs
mundi* was the best point of departure toward the *urbs beata*. Blake would
build Jerusalem in England's green and pleasant land, and Donne would
"consider the joy of our society, and conversation in heaven, since society
and conversation is one great element and ingredient into the joy which
we have in this world." It may be, indeed, that Faith, animating alike two
beings so unlike, might at last bring them together again at the same
Source; that the Imagination which played over Donne's theology might
speak out clearly to the Reason which ordered Blake's visions; that, by
some exquisite paradox of the spirit, they might find themselves face to
face, fellow artisans at work on the same City of God.

But of all these matters. the two poets know far more than we can
conjecture.

II

DONNE'S life was almost equally divided between the climax of the Elizabethan age and the first thirty years of the next century, the full turmoils of which he was not to witness. His early career was alienated by religion and diffidence from Elizabeth's Court; his later success was by favor of a Court and a Church already shaking and soon to be overthrown. This record, indeed, was a paradox. John Donne was brilliant, highly educated, well off, of respectable lineage on his father's side and distinguished family on his mother's. In the usual course of events he might have sought favor with the Queen's favorites, then, after her death, have fallen under the cloud with which James I enveloped so many from the former reign; or, like many others, have trimmed his sails to the new wind. If we were to regard only items of biography we should say, as indeed he was fond of persuading his friends: this man salvaged his misadventured youth through Faith and thus won the fruits of his maturity. But the annotator must read the text more carefully. Donne was far more worldly than is commonly supposed, but against any acceptance of ambitious compromise was pitted the need for a faith settled on logic. As the two forces of this world and the next were preparing for mortal combat, Donne fell in love, married, and took on responsibilities of which his twenty-eight years had in no way forewarned him. The one solution of the problem was a reconciliation between mundane and spiritual forces. He had been bred a Catholic, but it was the Anglican Church to which he must look for salvation. And again he sent the case back, as it were, to the jury for further deliberation. When at last he reached his decision and began his career at the age of forty-one, he and his wife had faced much bitter circumstance together.

Among his friends, during his later years, the Dean of St. Paul's deplored, and as much as he could, disclaimed, the young John Donne who had disported himself in the London of the 1590's. The Dean would gladly have seen the amorous lyrics of those days burnt. Or so he professed. But the perplexities that harried the young man harried the old one still. Beneath the amorous cynicism of the youth, as beneath the eloquent faith of the sage, moved the same impelling anxiety: Death. The war against his memories was merely a desire to rewrite the past in at least outward conformity to grace. So often he longed for the morning whence he had come. "And it is placed in the Lamentations, as though it were a lamentable negligence to have omitted it. *It is good for a man that he bear his yoke in his youth.* Rise as early as you can, you cannot be up before God: no, nor before God raise you . . . Though a man do sleep his forenoon, the Sun goes on its course, and comes to his Meridial splendor, though that man have not looked towards it." Nor did that youth who wrote "Busy old fool, unruly Sun . . ."

Having, as he supposed, failed his Master in the sunrise of his youth, he was impatient to run out and meet the dawn for which Death alone can provide the canvas. A few days before his death, he summoned Nicholas Stone, the sculptor, and entering his study he took off the daily garments of mortality and put on his winding sheet. Thus he posed, standing on a funeral urn, his face toward the East. And from this sketch was copied in marble the statue for his monument. Again, wherein lay the difference between this old, morbid man and the young one who amid thoughts of love left directions for his shrouding? Only in this: that the young man passed days of long study searching the answer to death's mystery; and the old man, persuaded that faith had at last provided it, could scarcely wait for Nature's final translation. Such was the main design, and all the rest was episode.

Among these episodes, sometimes the result of external need and sometimes from within his own temperament, Donne found enough to occupy him. As a child he was instructed by private tutors until at the age of twelve—precocious even for those days—he entered Oxford. After three years there he took up his studies at Cambridge. During this period he was still under Catholic influence. He pondered the logic of the medieval theologians with a mind already attuned to nice balances of doctrine. When he went up to London in 1590, he was prepared for the specialized legal training at Lincoln's Inn, where he began the study of the law in 1592. Had he lived in the days of antiquity, his love for learned argument for its own sake would have marked him as a young man of sophistical leanings; and doubtless the London of his time, drifting toward Puritan intolerance, would have rejected him socially and harried him officially could his mind have been read. But the fastidious and good-looking fellow who delighted in the company of well-bred ladies hid his secret preoccupations. His mind was, to a large extent, legalistic. We know the pattern today; it has always been familiar. Dialectic entranced adolescent Athenians no less than it does the modern law student worming his way through tomes bristling with inverted commas. And it entranced Donne.

By now, in his early twenties, he could have been angling for a minor post at Court. But the influence of the Catholic Church—possibly through his mother—was at work. His mother was of high lineage, the direct descendant of Sir Thomas More's sister. It is probable that she dwelt much on this interesting fact. It always receives some emphasis in accounts of Donne's life, as was the genealogical custom of the day, and we may surmise that the memory of a depleted grandeur added to his natural shyness. This was a time when men fitted for the hurly-burly of ambition made it their lifework to gain and keep a place. Everybody knew about everybody else. How, then, would it have gone with a poet who, with remembrance of a position rightly his, saw it snatched up by inglorious parvenus in an age of shifting social values? On the larger stage of history, the same conflict was going on as Robert Devereux stumbled to his ruin amid the snares laid by Robert Cecil and the new gentry. Donne's private answer to hopes so unacknowledged as scarcely to be called frustrate lies in the fourth *Satyre*. Here the fierce contempt for courtiers may be regarded as Donne's apologia to himself for failure in a contest in which he never actively engaged.

> . . . hast thou seen,
> O Sunne, in all thy journey, Vanitie,
> Such as swells the bladder of our court? I
> Thinke he which made your waxen garden, and
> Transported it from Italy to stand
> With us, at London, flouts our Presence, for
> Just such gay painted things, which no sappe, nor
> Tast have in them, ours are; And natural
> Some of the stocks are, their fruits, bastard all.

These parasites, kin to Michael Drayton's

> paltry, foolish, painted things
> That now in coaches trouble every street

were baseborn, the arrivists of an age (as Donne beheld it) of sycophancy.

These were the courtiers of Elizabeth. Donne's mother, like most single-hearted Catholics of the time, must have regarded this lady as an upstart Jezebel, who unjustly claimed power from God instead of submitting to His will. We may suspect that in the third *Satyre* Donne was not thinking merely of theology when he wrote

> Is not our Mistresse faire Religion,
> As worthy of all our Soules devotion,
> As vertue was to the first blinded age?

Such phrasing smacks too much of courtly eulogy to escape notice as an ironic twisting of it. The last decade of the reign was astir with double meanings, and the Queen herself complained to old William Lambarde, "I am Richard Second: Know ye not that?" But for all the promptings of his mother and the reserve of his own character, Donne was not entirely blind to the possibilities of his training. Some years later the Bishop of

Durham was to remind him of his expectation of state employment and his futile hopes at Court.

We know that the Court of Elizabeth was not haunted exclusively by such a bevy of human oddities as Donne attacked in his satire. That Court was regarded with hatred by fanatical Catholics of the day, including, probably, Donne's mother. She had seen to it that the tutors of his boyhood were Catholics; she may well have encouraged the Catholic friends of his youth who persuaded him to forego his academic license rather than swear allegiance to the Established Church, and it is hardly likely that in her household the Queen's Majesty was made to seem very majestic. In any case, Donne's conversion to the Anglican Church did not take place until the year after Elizabeth's death. Almost immediately he turned against the Roman Church with the violence of one who had long been waiting for revenge. Yet it is significant that to the end of his days he studied the works of the Fathers of the Church and that his theology accepted in the main only the tenets held by the two Churches in common, especially those doctrines having to do with the punishment and remission of sins.

No one can make windows into the hearts of men, and it is vain to speculate concerning the secret motives which resulted in Donne's conversion, his acceptance of Holy Orders in 1614, his elevation to the post of royal chaplain, and in 1621 to the post of Dean of St. Paul's. Ben Jonson no doubt was preening himself on his own comparative honesty when he remarked that he (Jonson) "hath a mind to be a churchman, and so he might have favour to make one sermon to the King; he careth not what thereafter should befall him, for he would not flatter though he saw death." We must admit that Donne saw enough God in the divinely right James I to satisfy even that conceited man; and one could build up a case against his sincerity, based on his own verse and prose in beslaverment of royalty, to set him in the company of the courtiers he had so despised in his youth. To do so, however, would involve a new interpretation of his character. Compromise there was, but hardly a spiritual surrender. It would be strange indeed, almost inhuman, if after so many years of poverty a prospect of security had not exercised attraction enough to warrant some formal payment. But the payment may be regarded as a rhetorical flourish. A legalistic mind could build up a case for the divine appointment of James Stuart, granting that most of that monarch's character were left out of consideration.

If, in these later years, Dr. Donne could not ravel from his life the gayer threads of youth that clung to the weaving, he could and did volubly regret them. Yet we are not disposed to accept unedited his memories of license. Every mature man would cancel some part of his greener years. "Men and women call one another inconstant, and accuse one another of having changed their minds, when, God knows, they have but changed the object of their eye, and seen a better white or red. An old man loves not the same sports that he did when he was young, nor a sick man the same meats that he did when he was well; but these men have not changed their minds; the old man hath changed his fancy, and the sick man his taste; neither his mind." With deeply religious or moral natures the change of taste is accompanied by an exaggeration—almost a glorification —of deeds not done but imagined.

Donne's early love affairs as echoed in his first lyrics are uncommonly literary, and the youth himself was described as of such promising features as could not harbor a vulgar soul, "not dissolute but very neat, a great visitor of ladies, a great frequenter of plays, a great writer of conceited verses." In other words, a fastidious young man about town, courtly, and romantically disposed toward *la princesse lointaine*—a conception of woman so extravagant as to result in cynicism. These were busy years also. In his twenties, Donne traveled on the Continent. He was a member of the Cadiz expedition led by Robert Devereux, Earl of Essex, and through these profitable indulgences, along with the purchase of many books, he managed to exhaust the funds he had acquired on coming of age. When he unquestionably fell in love, he was not financially eligible.

In 1600, while he was acting as secretary to Sir Thomas Egerton, he fell in love with Anne More, and in 1601 they were secretly married. The lady was the niece of Lady Egerton and daughter to Sir George More. For the effrontery of this overambitious mating, Donne was cast into Fleet prison for a short time and thereafter for seven years lived on very bad terms with his choleric father-in-law and very close terms with adversity. Izaak Walton speaks of Donne's marriage as "the remarkable error of his life," an opinion in which Donne seems to have concurred in spite of the sweet harmony of the marriage itself through years of dependence and squalor. Perhaps he was the more repentant because of the multiple responsibilities which he begat, in the persons of twelve children, seven of whom survived, and six of whom outlived their father. In spite of all hardship, the bond between husband and wife was strong and tender. Ten years after their marriage, Donne, who was at Amiens with Sir Robert Drury, had an occult vision of his wife. She was distraught, and was carrying in her arms the body of a dead child. At the moment of this apparition, the wife had in fact given birth to a stillborn infant and thereafter lay gravely ill. However one may account for such manifestations, they are vouchsafed only to those who, when they are separated,

> But thinke that wee
> Are but turn'd aside to sleepe;
> They who one another keepe
> Alive, n'er parted bee.

Anne lived to see Donne established in his career in the Church. By the time of her death in 1617, he had been three years a priest, royal chaplain to James I, and was already intimate at great houses, the minor courts of the period. From the beginning, his sermons inspired his hearers almost beyond their capacity for enthusiasm. He continued as poet, and in the graver key of his new instrument produced some memorable works, such as the philosophical *Progress of the Soul* and the two *Anniversaries*, the second of which ranks high in English sacred poetry. But the full attention of his genius was directed to prose cadence in which thunders the onrush of his long-tried faith. "A voice that carries with it a penetration (all shall hear it) and a persuasion (all shall believe it and be glad of it) and a power, a command (all shall obey it). Since that voice at the Creation, *Fiat*, Let there be a world, was never heard such a voice as this, *Surgite Mortui*, Arise ye dead. . . . this voice of the Archangel shall enable them to hear; the Archangel shall re-infuse the several souls into their bodies, and so they shall hear that voice, *Surgite Mortui*, Arise ye that were dead, and they shall arise."

But neither eloquence nor friends nor honors could heal Donne's fevers and ailing nerves. Worldly success, even in the Church, made him the victim of Court intrigue. At one time the King was prompted by gossip to suspect him of seditious complaints, and he was constantly on his mettle to maintain unscathed the dignity of his posts. Several attacks of severe illness assailed him. In 1624 he was too feeble to be considered for a bishopric that had been intended for him. The next year, when Charles I succeeded his father, Donne was again able to preach at Court, but from then on to its end, his life was checkered with shadow. There were fair days when he consumed the spirits of men in the ghostly fires of his rhetoric, and other days of retirement in the country houses of his friends and relatives when people supposed he had already died. Thus rumor outran the actual conclusion, and toward the end he could hardly wait to try in flight the charts which his faith had marked out for him, charts so dazzling as to hide their configurations in the revealed glory of their truth. "When I consider the past, and present, and future state of this body, in this world, I am able to conceive, able to express the worst that can befall it in nature, and the worst than can be inflicted upon it by man or fortune; But the least degree of glory that God hath prepared for that body in heaven, I am not able to express, not able to conceive."

Ben Jonson, who had a good deal, most of it sour, to say of his friend Donne, remarked to Drummond of Hawthornden that Donne wrote all his best pieces before he was twenty-five years old. These would include the love lyrics, the epigrams, the elegies, the satires, and some of the marriage songs. To a great extent, Jonson was anticipating the verdict of posterity. Most of the familiar poems of Donne are of early composition.

In regard to the love lyrics, John Dryden complained that Donne "perplexed the mind of the fair sex with nice speculations of philosophy when he should engage their hearts and entertain them with the softness of love." This extraordinary statement confirms our opinion that one age not only fails to understand another but actually does not see what the other intended. We are reminded of the eighteenth-century writer who wished to tear down a Gothic cathedral to make way for a neat Palladian structure. As for Donne, he was explaining love to himself, and perhaps it is better that he left the fair sex in a state of sad perplexity. The best love poetry is seldom a cajolery to sport. Nor is it likely that Donne, though he sometimes wrote like a Cavalier, had any such intention in mind. On the contrary, impulse alone seldom ruled him, however much the eagerness and warmth of his conversational style may give the illusion of their ascendancy. We do not find in his verses an unquestioning surrender followed by penitential afterthought as in Shakespeare's sonnet

> The expense of spirit in a waste of shame
> Is lust in action. . . .

The surrender and the questioning occur at the same time. The prevailing mood of these lyrics is an immediate clash between an emotion in progress and a running commentary by Donne's spirit, which sat, a patient looker-on, and viewed natural passions with supernatural irony. The result is a variety of emphasis, ranging from the cynicism of "Womans Constancy" to the transfiguration of "The Extasie."

The cynical note is usually the least convincing, in spite of the youthful poet's will to disbelieve.

> Goe, and catche a falling starre,
>   Get with child a mandrake roote,
> Tell me, where all past yeares are,
>   Or who cleft the Divil's foot,
> Teach me to hear Mermaids singing,
>   Or to keep off envies stinging,
>   And find
>   What wind
> Serves to advance an honest mind.

So begins the best known of the lyrics in this vein. The stanza form has an Elizabethan intricacy that is wholly beguiling. In passing, it should be pointed out that the two short lines must be read as equivalent—in time-length—to one long line, thus:

> And   f   i   n   d   What   w   i   n   d
> Serves   to   advance   an   honest   mind;

otherwise the music will be thrown out of measure. Besides the subtleties of sound, we find a catalogue of wonders that remind us of some of the items in Sir Thomas Browne's *Museum Clausum*: the hiding place of past years, the personage who cleft the Devil's foot, the song of the Mermaids, the unheard-of wind that serves to advance an honest mind. Throughout the song as a whole all themes are subordinated to that of woman's fickleness.

"The Indifferent" develops this subject even more elaborately. Here the lover can love anybody as long as she be not true. If she were true, her constancy would cloy his jaded appetite and give her an unfair advantage over him by making him her fixed subject; if she were only seeming true, then he would be again befooled. Venus assures him to his comfort and swears by "Love's sweetest part, Variety" that although there are two or three heretics who still practice faithfulness, she will dissuade them from it. All this combines in a pattern of delicate artificiality, but the general effect is brittle rather than resonant. To an extent it anticipated the shallowness of the Cavaliers. The inconstancy of women as a subject for nice wit is usually a sign of decadence; in a robust period, either of literary history or in the life of an individual author, it becomes merely farce. But Donne's conceited poems, read in the light of his other preoccupations, become significant. They are more than appears in paraphrase. They are not so much the cynicism of the disillusioned young lover as the recreations of despair. To bend one's best energies in the service of a trifling mood, however strong may be its momentary possession—this impulse toward spiritual suicide is known to most artists. Jean-Christophe, playing great music before an indifferent audience switches to "Malbrouck s'en va-t-en guerre" and shouts at them: "That's all you're worth." Drayton, to questions concerning his giddy metaphors, answers quite frankly: "I will resolve you: I am lunatic." And Donne's own answer is sufficiently clear in "The Triple Foole":

> I am two fooles, I know,
> For loving, and for saying so
>   In whining Poëtry;
> But where's that wiseman, that would not be I,
>   If she would not deny?

Then as th'earths inward narrow crooked lanes
Do purge sea waters fretfull salt away,
  I thought, if I could draw my paines,
Through Rimes vexation, I should them allay.
Griefe brought to numbers cannot be so fierce,
For, he tames it, that fetters it in verse.

  But when I had done so,
Some man, his art and voice to show,
  Doth Set and sing my paine,
And, by delighting many, frees againe
  Griefe, which verse did restraine.
To Love and Griefe tribute of Verse belongs,
But not of such as pleases when'tis read,
  Both are increased by such songs:
For both their triumphs so are published,
And I, which was two fooles, do so grow three;
Who are a little wise, the best fooles be.

"Who are a little wise, the best fooles be." Should we read this as equivalent to "A little learning is a dangerous thing?"—or, more likely, as a
suggestion that the disguise of wisdom is the more skilful kind of folly.
The latter is correct, for the burlesque of a minor style by a major artist
is always better than the original, and in its own terms.

The finest of Donne's love lyrics are also the most characteristic. Irony
is sometimes an ingredient, and the conversational style admits sudden
changes of mood or figure that in more rhetorical verse would have to be
prepared for. In "The Canonization," there is a basic and felicitous
wrenching of figurative use which, under the pressure of a less sensitive
hand (as with the nymphs, Muses, satyrs, and other pagan creatures who
prepare the entrance of St. Peter in "Lycidas") would become mere bad
taste. In "The Canonization" the objections to Love are so outbalanced
by its perfections—its single-heartedness amid confusion, its peace in a
warring world—that the lovers are canonized, not as saints of the Church
but as embodiments of the Platonic Idea:

And thus invoke us; You whom reverend love
  Made one anothers hermitage;
You, to whom love was peace, that now is rage;
  Who did the whole worlds soule contract, and drove
    Into the glasses of your eyes
    (So made such mirrors, and such spies,
  That they did all to you epitomize,)

> Countries, Townes, Courts: Beg from above
> A patterne of your love!

Thus, with growing maturity, the poet's emotional and physical selves began to balance more evenly. The cynicism and trifling of one who affected to be what he really was not, a sensualist, fell away as strand after strand of Donne's tangled feelings were gathered together and woven for at least a brief while in the pattern of his love for Anne More. He took, as it were, vacations from the new life in echoes of the old dalliance as he reclaimed his "buzzard love," or talked to some old lover's ghost, or at the familiar invitation to "come live with me and be my love" found himself no less ensnared than the fish in the crystal brooks. But the full tone of the best lyrics was grave and tender in its passion.

Now from the core of his being Love summoned Death, the figure who had always lurked in the background of Donne's thought and over whom no fantasy could spin the concealing web. Who gives himself wholly to Love must know Death too. First there is the knowledge of corruptible mortality, the dance of death, the foreknowledge of the skeleton by the flesh. This is the medieval theme whose minor music concludes the madrigal and is prelude for the dirge. *Timor mortis conturbat me*. Mine eyes dazzle; she died young. Like chimney sweepers, come to dust. He'll dig them up again. When thou must home to shades of underground. Love, the flesh; and Death, the bone. Such phrases multiply innumerably in the mind. The Elizabethan never gave himself up to the full sensualism of the Renaissance. The Gothic arch broke the Palladian façade, the sun suddenly went out as Corydon leaned toward Phyllis for a kiss. No new learning or study of the humanities penetrated the shadowy crypt beneath the library where the dust of the forbears passively awaited the dust of the sons. To a mind already medieval in cast, like Donne's, or later, Sir Thomas Browne's, these imaginings were irresistible. The theme of passing time sounds clearly in "The Anniversarie" and a few other early lyrics, but it is unimportant until in "The Funerall" Donne figuratively put on his shroud as actually he was to display himself in it shortly before his death.

> Who ever comes to shroud me, do not harme
>   Nor question much
> That subtile wreath of haire, which crowns my arme;
> The mystery, the signe you must not touch,
>   For'tis my outward Soule,
> Viceroy to that, which then to heaven being gone,
>   Will leave this to controule,
> And keep these limbes, her Provinces, from dissolution.

From there to the end of the lyric sequence, with the exception of echoes from the first part, the music resolves itself into a duet between Love and Death—or perhaps less a duet than a double voice from the one source. Again, in "The Relique," there is the admonition

> When my grave is broke up againe
> Some second ghest to entertaine, . . .
>   And he that digs it, spies
> A bracelet of bright haire about the bone,
>   Will he not let'us alone, . . .

The poem goes on, somewhat in the vein of "The Canonization," to speak of such love as a pattern worthy of a reliquary, something to be adored for its holiness in the perfection of love.

The poem is more closely autobiographical than most of the love lyrics. The last stanza refers to the obstacles in the path of his love for Anne More. Her father was legally empowered to keep them apart. At last, after their period of married chastity, Nature, "injured by late law" set them free. The bracelet was doubtless the memento of their love, woven from Anne's hair. As for the opening of the grave for the reception of a second guest, that was far from being mere symbol. Toward the end of the seventeenth century, Samuel Pepys, when he asked the sexton how room could be found for the corpse of a deceased relative, was told with a wink that the old ones could be "justled" together. There was a deal of graveyard justling as late as the early days of Queen Victoria, and there can be no doubt that these outward and visible symbols of death imparted a charnel mist to human activities. Even foolish, old, befuddled George II outdid himself in appropriate sentiment when he decreed that the corresponding sides of his own coffin and Queen Caroline's should be removed in order that his dust and hers might commingle in the tomb. From the grossest to the most sensitive minds, the idea of death, physical death, was a constant hanger-on at human festivities, a lurker in shadow behind the couch of love.

It seemed as though the sword-play of amorousness and repentance, of faith and doubt—the fury of all human contradictions—could sign no peace until the signatures were written in dust. Yet from these cypress groves of thought, Donne as the lover found a path back to the sunlight of clear spirit. In his "dialogue of one," "The Extasie," he transcended his art and his passion. It is, perhaps, his one contribution to the hymnology of pure mysticism, a fact which makes the title even more significant. It is a rephrasing of the mystical sentence: "Love, and the street stones will light their hidden lamps for you; when you see the light you are on the path home." Nor does it matter that he was to be driven back, by circum-

stance and the compromises of the world, to the dark territory whence
he had briefly emerged. In "The Extasie" the medieval admonition "Never
deny, when you return into the darkness, that you have seen the light"
was heeded and set down beyond denial.

> Where, like a pillow on a bed,
>   A Pregnant banke swell'd up, to rest
> The violets reclining head,
>   Sat we two, one anothers best. . . .
> And whil'st our soules negotiate there,
>   We like sepulchrall statues lay;
> All day, the same our postures were,
>   And wee said nothing, all the day.

The souls of the lovers meet; they are transplanted as one.

> A single violet transplant,
>   The strength, the colour, and the size,
> (All which before was poore, and scant,)
>   Redoubles still, and multiplies.

The bodies of the lovers are caught up and become the earthly text of the
spirit's meaning, the alloy necessary in Time to strengthen and give form
to the Eternal. So, in the final ecstasy, the body and soul are united, the
changing moment is held changeless.

> And if some lover, such as wee,
>   Have heard this dialogue of one,
> Let him still marke us, he shall see
>   Small change, when we'are to bodies gone.

In this transfiguration, that patient looker-on, Donne's spirit, is at last
persuaded from separation. All his nature moves in one harmony, perhaps
for the only instant in his life.

The moods of Donne's lyrics, as they mature toward unity, may be
summed up thus: A prevalent, somewhat artificial cynicism, with interludes of sheer tenderness; a contemplation of time and death, beginning,
roughly, with "The Anniversary"; then a gradual unifying of theme,
characterized by a deepening of the sense of mortality and relieved by
interludes in the earlier style; and lastly, "The Extasie," which stands
alone, not as a conclusion, but as a climax.

Donne's "Epigrams" were too highly praised by Drummond of Hawthornden, who spoke of them as the best to be found in English, but
wisely added that the English epigrammatists could not approach the ancients. With the ancients, especially of the Hellenistic and Roman periods,

the epigram was an independent form of art to which poets brought their best attention. In the Greek Anthology it reached the highest possibilities of concentrated expression and in later centuries exercised a strong influence on Renaissance poetry. But to Donne, as to most young poets of our tradition, the epigram was not even a moment's monument. It was, rather, a jotting down of a passing conceit, probably with some purpose of later expansion. Many of these notebook lines of Donne's were hastily composed and set down during the expedition against Cadiz; at least three of them, "A Burnt Ship," "Fall of a Wall," and "The Lier" include likely references to that event. Few of these poems have any distinction. Donne himself wrote far better epigrams in the course of longer poems, such as this couplet from the ninth *Elegy*, addressed to George Herbert's mother:

> No *Spring*, nor *Summer* Beauty hath such grace,
> As I have seen in one *Autumnal* face;

or, from *The First Anniversary*:

> There is no health; Physitians say that wee,
> At best, enjoy but a neutralitie;

or again, this strange anticipation of Mrs. Eddy's dogma:

> But Patient and Physician being free,
> As sin is nothing, let it no where be.

Among the pieces entitled *Epigrams*, only one holds more than a passing interest. In "A Burnt Ship" we have the tragic paradox:

> So all were lost, which in the ship were found,
> They in the sea being burnt, they in the burnt ship drown'd.

The five *Satyres* are, on the whole, merely vituperative. The issues they deal with were limited by Donne's own resentments and in any case are not sufficiently objective as portraits of characters to emerge from the passing interest of their day. Historically they have a certain interest as being early satires in the five-stress couplet; but what every critic seems to have ignored is the fact that Chaucer is clearly the first master of the satirical couplet in passages from his *Prologue*. In the satires, too, Donne's metrical roughness and impatient rhyming are conspicuous. "Donne for not keeping of accent deserved hanging," complained Jonson. We must add that the "keeping of accent" depends on the artistic intention. It has been pointed out that Donne's license may have been the result of the experiments in Classical quantity which engaged the Elizabethan poets in their more pedantic mood, and that the Classical writers themselves were wont to give an appropriately jagged effect to their verse when they were writing satire, as in what Saintsbury calls the "hideous hexameter" from Horace:

Non ego, namque parabilem amo Venerem facilemque.

In Donne's satirical verses we see the results of rage and haste as well as of deliberate effect. The first and fourth are somewhat akin in their attack on society in general and the Court in particular. Reading them, one would imagine Donne to be an atrabilious hermit rather than a man eager for friendship and a job at Court. The second *Satyre* opens with an attack on poetasters, reminding one in matter if not in manner of Pope's *Epistle to Dr. Arbuthnot*; but it shifts its grounds to bombard the lawyers, and the *Satyre* as a whole exhibits a lack of unified construction. The third *Satyre* is directed against the churches, from Puritanism to Catholicism, with veiled references, as has been noted, to the Queen as head of the Established Church. These first four *Satyres* are concerned with spheres of life in which Donne was personally involved, and the unrestrained bitterness of their hyperbole is as much a revelation of his own disappointments as of the society of the time. The fifth and last of the *Satyres,* presumably addressed to a more detached subject—the corruption of the judiciary—nevertheless exhumes the victims of the former onslaughts and subjects them to an after-drubbing.

We may say of Donne's technique in general that its harshness is justified when it is intentional. When it becomes mere self-indulgence, the result is a careless dissonance. Carrying the comparison further, we find in the work of those whom he influences a looseness of style usually uninformed by the vigor that redeemed his own metrical license. Even in the *Satyres,* it is obvious that if we grant the author's intention we must admit also its extemporary power. Pope "versified" the *Satyres* and took all the life out of them, just as he emasculated the couplets of Chaucer in his dainty revisions. Donne opens his fourth *Satyre* thus:

> Well, I may now receive, and die; My sinne
> Indeed is great, but I have beene in
> A Purgatorie, such as fear'd hell is
> A recreation to and scarse map of this.

Here is Pope's version of the same lines:

> Well, if it be my time to quit the stage,
> Adieu to all the follies of the age!
> I die in charity with fool and knave,
> Secure of peace at least beyond the grave.

Incidentally, it is strange that Pope, a Catholic, should have failed to include the reference to the last sacraments.

As time went on, Donne's style became smoother, more rhetorical. Among the earlier poems, we would note the Spenserian sweetness of the "Epithalamion made at Lincolnes Inne," composed when Donne was nineteen. Not only does this piece show his grasp of the more literary style, but it presages the tone of the later work, which conformed more nearly to the accepted idea of its intention. The epistles to his friends and patrons, for example, conceal sincerity in their adoption of conventional eulogy. The long philosophical poems, *"The First Anniversary"* and *"The Second Anniversary"* display a couplet chastened and polished in comparison with the *Satyres*. The tenth of the "Holy Sonnets" is justly known as one of the triumphs of the sonnet form in English. One of the latest poems, "A Hymne to God the Father" stands as the companion in gravity and power to "The Extasie" of the young lyrics. Those two poems are Donne's biography, his double epitaph.

In "A Hymne to God the Father," the ignoble device of punning is raised, as in many of Donne's poems, to noble usage. This rather frivolous Elizabethan trick was bent with varying success to the service of religious poetry in the seventeenth century. If in "A Hymne to God the Father" it links the author's name with the word of finality and thus becomes translated to divine song, in the conclusion to "The Crosse" it works, we may appropriately say, at cross-purposes and defeats all possibility of grandeur.

The same chance and mischance apply to the strained or "conceited" metaphors favored by Donne and his contemporaries. The term "metaphysical" is generally used to describe this style. *Metaphysical* is a word with small merit and so many meanings as to have no meaning at all. It should be dropped from the language—especially in criticism. Literally, it has to do with the conception of existence, with the living Universe and Man's place therein. Loosely, it has taken on, among others, such meanings as these: difficult, philosophical, obscure, ethereal, involved, supercilious, ingenious, fantastic, incongruous. A course in "metaphysics" in the Harvard of 1915 turned out to be merely a course in Freudian psychology. The consequences of such verbal corruption are many. For example, a most ill-assorted group of seventeenth-century poets are designated as metaphysical, but why, no two critics agree. When Dryden said that Donne "affects the metaphysics not only in his satires but in his amorous verses where nature only should reign," he meant, as he stated further, that the tone of Donne's lyrics was too intellectual, that Donne observed his own behavior objectively as a philosopher might, and, in noting it, had recourse to unusual metaphor. Such a usage lies near the scope of metaphysics, though very far from such true metaphysical poetry as that of Lucretius, Dante, or Bridges. Dr. Johnson placed the emphasis of the term on the figurative language when he defined the style as one in which "the most heterogeneous ideas are yoked by violence together." Since his time the usual associations of the word have had to do with metaphor and conceit rather than any larger philosophical problem involved in the work concerned. Only under such a nonsensical criterion could we find grouped together in a "school" poets so dissimilar as Sir John Suckling and George Herbert, to mention only the extremes. As John W. Hales suggests, if we must have a term based on the use of metaphor, then Ingenious or Fantastic were a better word than Metaphysical.

Donne was not, in the true sense of the word, a metaphysician. He was an analyst, a theologian, a logician. To those who would seek out for themselves the spaces between the stars, he gave this admonition: "Never hearken after the music of spheres, never hunt after the knowledge of higher secrets than appertain to thee . . . *Take heed what you hear* in derogation of either the State or the Church." And as poet he rises seldom above intellect into revelation. He lingers by the death bed and the charnel house—the bodily presences of death—in long contemplation of earthly corruption, before he ascends the last steps and opens the everlasting gates. His poetry has strength, fiber, roughness; it is a scar so newly healed that we can guess the direction of the lance. Above all, he is one of the few poets whose conversational passages ring with the authority of time and whose rhetoric is lively with the feeling of immediacy. He is the spokesman for one side, a troubled side, of human experience.

III

WHEN, as a little boy, William Blake saw the prophet Ezekiel under a tree amid a summer field, he was soundly trounced by his mother. Mrs. Blake, even though she was only the wife of a poor hosier, might have represented the eighteenth century trouncing the nonsense out of visionaries and enthusiasts. Blake was born in 1757. The century had passed its mid-point; it was growing old and somewhat frightened. At the top the fogram Court and the world of *ton* vied in dullness and superficiality; at the bottom the dregs of the race were astir with discontent. Between the two, the many strata of the middle class froze to the shape into which they had been poured, but they were without encouragement from above or support from beneath. They were held firm by dogma, a habitual mold left when the fires of conviction have gone out and the age is no longer fluid. Many restrictions that we think of as Victorian had their origin in the late eighteenth century. For example, conversation was squeamish. Farrington in his diary describes how an eccentric nobleman, forgetting that he was having tea with ladies, mentioned the "generation of bees"—a horrid phrase that caused some swooning. Fanny Burney was driven indoors by the oaths of sailors. Propriety, indeed, was the standard in politics, the Church, manners, and literature.

But this was also the age of Tom Paine in politics; and in religion, of the Wesley brothers and Methodism. This was the age that was soon to collapse in the French Revolution and the Napoleonic wars. Manners, indeed, held their own, but they were the etiquette of conformity, not courtesy from the heart. Poetry was murmuring in its sleep. Thomson, Gray and Collins had already shown tendencies that were later to be known as Romantic; Chatterton and Macpherson were dreaming of other and more heroic times. Crabbe, though employing the most impeccable couplets, summarized his own objections to artificiality:

> Must sleepy bards the flattering dream prolong,
> Mechanic echoes of the Mantuan song?
> From Truth and Nature shall we widely stray,
> Where Virgil, not where fancy, leads the way?

New voices, too, were astir in France and overheard in England. Being French, they were devoid of spiritual meaning, and their influence was confined to the more practical side of romanticism; that is, the reorganization of human society here and now. Blake, to whom everything must be seen *sub specie aeternitatis*, noted.

> Mock on, mock on, Voltaire, Rousseau;
> Mock on, mock on; 'tis all in vain!
> You throw the sand against the wind,
> And the wind blows it back again.

> And every sand becomes a gem
> Reflected in the beams divine;
> Blown back they blind the mocking eye,
> But still in Israel's paths they shine.

Blake could not compromise with materialism or cynicism. He found himself in a world which he described thus:

> When nations grow old, the Arts grow cold,
> And commerce settles on every tree;
> And the poor and the old can live upon gold,
> For all are born poor, aged sixty-three.

Beginning in that world, his first task was to transform it, to perceive in a dingy London sapling lights from the Tree of Life, to build Jerusalem in England's green and pleasant land. The miracle cannot be communicated or handed over complete. Only the key to the first door of many is available as a gift. From then on each "lost traveler" must go his own way.

> I will give you the end of a golden string,
>   Only wind it into a ball,
> It will lead you in at Heaven's gate
>   Built in Jerusalem's wall.

This one philosophy, consistent throughout Blake's entire life, is Mysticism. There is less understanding, and with cause, of this way of life than of any other. Bad poets use the word *mystic* as though it were a synonym for *mysterious*. Mysterious this revelation may be to those who have never experienced any hint of it. Furthermore, the actual enlightenment has been known to few though attempted by many. Lastly, the richer the fruits, the deeper the penetration, of the experience, so much greater becomes the difficulty of giving any expression to it in terms of human speech. "On these matters, let my lips guard a religious silence," said Herodotus, after witnessing the sacraments of Osiris. "The flight of the alone to the Alone," was Plotinus's description of the ecstasy. Perhaps this last comes as near to being a definition as we can hope for. Mysticism has as its path a gradual initiation of the individual soul through stage after stage of increasingly difficult conquest over material limitations which bar it from God. Some of these are softly lighted with encouragement; some, like the penultimate, the "dark night of the soul," seem the abyss of a cosmic despair. The goal is the union of the soul with God Himself, the reconciliation of all seeming divisions in the One,—the flight of the alone to the Alone. This is the Ecstasy.

We begin, however, as children of earth and time and space. There is much in the material world that must be transfigured, and the first transfiguration must take place within oneself. All mystics, of whatever period or nation, are bound toward the same final goal, but the paths there are diverse. An Oriental may withdraw into meditation; an Egyptian or a Catholic would acknowledge an outward and visible sign in the sacraments; and beyond such large acceptances of form lie the many lonely places where individuals have tried to work out their own salvation. Such solitaries seek kindred wisdom that they may select some hints and reject others. Thus Blake was at one time almost completely under the sway of Swedenborg, and heeded much from Jakob Böhme, Paracelsus, and other similar thinkers from various periods. That these writers had formulated much of their experience—as an alchemist might make a recipe for the true transmutation—weakened their main purpose from Blake's point of view. One cannot prove spiritual revelation by a formula. Blake would have agreed that the motto of the Evil One is "Organize It." The chaotic symbolism of his long *Prophetic Books*, which has proved misleading if not baffling to those who would interpret them, has often been cited as an example of his mental confusion; but in some instances he was avoiding the temptation to pretend that the inexplicable can be subjected to the last analysis. The lyrics are clear enough. They can be taken on the surface as songs and satires; or the "second voice," the symbolic meaning, can be interpreted at a not too cryptic level. They are sparks from the central fire. But the central fire itself dazzles beyond conjecture, let alone definition. As John Donne confessed that although he could describe the worst that can befall in Nature yet he was unable to express even the least degree of the glory of God, so Blake wrote of the Ecstasy at the end of his *Milton*:

> Terror struck in the Vale I stood at that immortal sound.
> My bones trembled, I fell outstretch'd upon the path
> A moment, and my Soul return'd into its mortal state
> To Resurrection & Judgment in the Vegetable Body,
> And my sweet Shadow of Delight stood trembling by my side.

Again, it is interesting to note in connection with this passage the similarity of mystical experience throughout the ages. Apuleius, a Roman initiate into the Mysteries of Isis, spoke of being "ravished throughout the Elements," and at "midnight" returning to his "proper place." Taken as a whole, the *Prophetic Books* are the record of Blake's life-long progress through the unfolding vistas of his revelation. But they are not devoid of opinions concerning less exalted ideas nor even of timely references, all gravely and sometimes incongruously fitted into the main design. The poetry brings to mind Bridges' description of Dante's book, which

> . . . mounted panting, and lieth now
> With all its earthly tangle by the throne of God.

It was the earthly tangle with which Blake had to deal before he could extricate his spirit for flight. And the more he considered it the more hostile became the snarls. In the first place, the descent of the soul into matter was itself the primal fall from innocence. Embodiment of an idea in practice, of imagination in a reasonable explanation, of Eternity in a physical universe, of the human soul in fleshly asceticism, of free behavior in a Puritanical code, of religion in a theology, of society in a monarchy—all these reversed salvation. The illusions of space and time are strong, but

> . . . all the Great
> Events of Time start forth and are conceived in such a Period,
> Within a Moment, a Pulsation of the Artery.

This restatement of the Oriental doctrine of the Eternal Now is difficult for ordinary conception. It might be illustrated thus: A man is walking through a series of walled courts. In each court he perceives only the objects within it. He opens a door, enters the next court, and the one he has left becomes merely a memory. The one ahead is in the future; it cannot be guessed at. But from a high window overlooking all the courts, the seer beholds them simultaneously. The court which to the walking man seems the only present reality is to the seer no more real than the court that the man has left behind or the one he is about to enter. In one flash the mystic experiences all, freed from the limitations which seem real to the groundling. We can find enlightenment in Blake's quatrain which introduces the *Auguries of Innocence*:

> To see a World in a Grain of Sand
> And a Heaven in a Wild Flower,
> Hold Infinity in the palm of your hand
> And Eternity in an hour.

Thus, the phenomena by which men live, and which have entangled the human soul in deadly illusion, must be re-examined; in fact, they must be reversed. Pragmatism will not do. The mere fact that something —a government, a code of morals, an inhibition—works in a society based on materialism shows its essential evil. It gives the man a feeling of security in terms of the cave; whereas he should be escaping from the cave into the sunlight. The Ten Commandments were written by the Devil. Traits that pass as virtues are just as apt to be disguises of evil. Thus, charity is merely a mask for existing injustice.

> Pity could be no more,
> If we did not make somebody poor;
> And Mercy no more could be,
> If all were as happy as we.

Prudery, asceticism, and all unnatural restraints inspire some of Blake's best epigrams:

> Abstinence sows sand all over
> The ruddy limbs and flaming hair,

But Desire Gratified
Plants fruits of life and beauty there.

The pitiable spectacle of the loveless—those afraid of love, those in-capable of love, those blasphemous against love—is caused by the main illusions and all their servants and vicars who govern this world. "Priests in black gowns" carry out the ugly commands of the Serpent that befouls the golden chapel of Love; they bind up in briars the joys of love. "The King and the Priest must be tied in a tether" before the virgin spirits can be united and freed by love's ecstasy. Free delight which dwells in the Eternal Now falls dead in the snares of convention set by Time.

He who binds to himself a joy
Does the winged life destroy;
But he who kisses the joy as it flies
Lives in eternity's sun rise.

Sexual love, that purest of joys, which sets the struggling body free from the entanglements of reason, gives to mortal life its flash of Eternity. In "The Sunflower," one of the most exquisite of the *Songs of Experience,* Blake goes to the core of his philosophy in behalf of divine pleasure.

Ah, Sun-flower! weary of time,
Who countest the steps of the Sun,
Seeking after that sweet golden clime
Where the traveller's journey is done:

Where the Youth pined away with desire,
And the pale Virgin shrouded in snow
Arise from their graves, and aspire
Where my Sun-flower wishes to go.

This perfection of lyric enchantment may be taken as it stands, or we may listen for the "second voice," the symbolic meaning. The sunflower is life rooted and imprisoned, the reflection of the Sun, the Source of Life. Thus turning with the Sun but unable to free itself, it seeks Eter-nity. So the Youth and the Virgin, who have been slain by their restraint, at last arise, and in the fulfillment of sexual delight aspire for one eternal moment beyond illusion.

Puritanism was, of course, repulsive to Blake. It was the code of Evil, a wicked imposture upheld first by the bloody hands of armies and later by jagged conventions. It was the instrument of the God of the Old Testament against the God of the New Testament, and cruelty and materialism were its fruits. Milton was at once the laureate of Puritanism and the English poet most admired by Blake. In the prophetic book of

Milton, Blake resolved this clash of allegiances by making Milton the central figure in the purification of the Poet from the wrongs which had deflected his genius from its proper course.

In politics, Blake was nominally the revolutionary; but he was firmly set against active participation by poets in the advancement of a merely external cause. As S. Foster Damon points out, in his discussion of Blake's attitude toward Milton, the political poet is apt to consider earthly conditions and codes as an end in themselves and to reduce deity to an abstraction. From any mystic's standpoint this procedure is the reverse of true revolution, which must have its source in the liberation of each individual toward spiritual freedom. The earthly reflection of such regeneration would follow as a matter of course. Milton, according to Blake, erred because "he was a mere politician busied about this world." Even Jesus "was wrong in suffering Himself to be crucified. He should not have attacked the Government. He had no business in such matters." In all his life Blake made only one major compromise with external affairs: that was his acceptance for three years of William Hayley's patronage, a period so fraught with anguish that Hayley came to serve, in Blake's mind, as a model for Satan.

Other individuals besides Hayley were used as models in Blake's work. The sinister John Scofield, in reality a low-witted soldier who haled Blake to court on a false charge of *lèse majesté,* appeared in *Jerusalem* as the wicked Accuser, the tool of war and religion. Robert Blake, William's younger brother, although he was assigned no specific part, became, after his death, symbolic in memory as the beloved inspiration in the regions of the spirit. And like the name of Boileau in Keats' *Sleep and Poetry,* the names of Johnson, Pope, and Dryden became synonymous, in Blake's epigrams, with the judicial criticism of the eighteenth century. In loose epigrams he paid his respects to all that he hated in the accepted standard of art and literature, religion and science.

Whether we find the protest in such extemporizations or in the noble music of such poems as "To the Muses" and the "Introduction" to the *Songs of Experience,* Blake was always in protest against the illusions of this world. His career as man, artist, and poet was unusually consistent. He was visionary as a child, rather alarmingly so in the case of Rylands, an engraver. His father had taken him to study with Rylands, but the boy shrank away. "Father, I do not like the man's look; he looks as if he would live to be hanged." So he was, twelve years later, but the coincidence is not so remarkable. Jonathan Swift once hindered a man from being pardoned for a rape because the man was a fiddler, therefore a rogue, and should hang for it. Coleridge's remark, after meeting Keats for the first time, "There is death in that hand," seems much more significant. In those days it was as psychic to prophesy the death of a healthy young man from natural causes as it was by hanging.

Too much has been made of Blake's occult experiences and visions; he made too much of them himself. It is probable that he saw the words of his poems flying through the room and that he drew from spectral originals; it is possible that these forms even appeared to the physical or outer eye; but he himself should have been the first to admit that such physical phenomena can have no significant bearing on Eternity. Another mystic, Arthur Machen, describes in his autobiography certain signs and wonders that befell him and concludes with the assurance that, amazing as they may seem, they were incalculably less important than an act of mercy done to a stray kitten. Furthermore, such emphasis on Blake's experiences has given far too much ammunition to hostile critics like G. K. Chesterton, for those who are hopelessly sane are always able to find evidences of insanity in their superiors. The truth is that Blake retained a childlike quality which, though it kept his perceptions fresh and his inventiveness fertile, yet distorted his sense of proportion. He moved toward his goals with a complete disregard of practical objection, which was at once his strength and his weakness. Also, he was fond of pranks, and if friends received with solemnity the news that he had just witnessed a fairy's funeral in the back garden, why should he doubt the apparition? We need not inquire, for with him the world of the imagination was the actual world.

And in spite of the trouncing he received as a child for beholding Ezekiel in the summer field, he was not the victim of an unsympathetic family. His father had sufficient insight to permit his four sons to develop with some independence. William had the further advantage with his parents that at this time the mystical doctrines of Emanuel Swedenborg were permeating the more impressionable classes very much as spiritism flourishes today. Doubtless Blake's first approach to Swedenborg was somewhat emotional. Here was a prophet acknowledged in the family circle who had had visions and followed them beyond the frontiers of scepticism. In short, here was a powerful ally for young William Blake. The physical world was crowded with hints and portents undreamed of in eighteenth-century philosophy, and someone else had borne witness to them. If the great revelation was accompanied by the small apparitions and innocent marvels of clairvoyance, these could provide exciting detail for poems and drawings. Modern criticism knows Swedenborg as a major scientist, one of the great physiologists and astronomers of all time, as well as an enlightened mystic of unusual clarity of communication. As Blake grew into maturity, he was deeply influenced by the Swedish philosopher, but, as his minute annotations and later comments show, with understanding came also disagreement and, to a great degree, disillusionment.

Swedenborg became his point of departure toward more extensive studies of religious and mystical, sometimes even occult, writings. Blake was a widely read man; besides his acquaintance with such appropriate authors as Plato, Paracelsus, Dante, Böhme, and Thomas Vaughan, he was influenced by the Elizabethans and by Milton, and, during the ill-fated three years under Hayley's patronage at the cottage in Felpham, his admiration for Homer incited him to study Greek. It is probable that a man of his impulsive nature would single out a few works to be marked, learned, and inwardly digested, and that many more would be explored merely through curiosity or the promptings of refutation. In the pictorial arts, his readings in Fuseli's translation of Winckelmann and his worship of Michangelo roused him in defense of "dear Mother Outline" against the balanced masses of such painters as Rubens or Reynolds. His annotations of Reynolds's *Discourses* open with the remark that "This Man was Hired to Depress Art" and continue in like vein.

The painters, writers and thinkers who failed to agree with his own cosmogony or principles of technique became the objects of his Gargantuan sense of humor that clubbed and drubbed with more than the violence of Blake's detested Dr. Johnson. The late Sir Walter Raleigh, in an essay which otherwise does him little credit, remarks of Blake's outbursts: "Let a prophet beware of satire. He may curse the adversaries of his faith; he may not laugh at them. Laughter, when it is employed as a weapon, is an appeal to common sense." Raleigh then proceeds to point out that the true visionary needs no such weapon; indeed, that its use is a confession of weakness, of personal vanity. As general criticism, all this is very wise, but what Raleigh fails to take into consideration is the age in which Blake lived. Blake was not contending for his own principles only; he was trying to pierce the enormous indifference that left visionaries (not primarily himself) to starve, and glutted the Hayleys, the Gainsboroughs, the Romneys, the bishops of the Established Church with adulation and luxury.

Certainly Blake had every reason to fight, and we note how the objects of his campaigns were permanent values, not private gains. Of these latter, he tasted few. There are not many in literary history who can approach, in fortitude and gaiety, the courage with which Blake and his wife passed their lives in poverty. From the material point of view, it was she who cheerfully bore the full weight of their necessity. The Blakes were as poor as anyone in the annals of literature, yet we know very little concerning the circumstances of their poverty. There is more than pathos in the following quatrain, in which Blake wryly applies the larger aspects of his philosophy to the shortcomings of his own external destiny:

> Since all the Riches of this World
> May be gifts from the Devil & Earthly Kings,
> I should suspect that I worship'd the Devil
> If I thank'd my God for Worldy things.

It may be truly said of Blake that he was nourished in joy of creating, and of Catherine, his wife, that she found her earthly satisfaction in being, as she believed, a faithful handmaid in the house of the Lord.

The earliest book of poems was the *Poetical Sketches*, published in 1783 when Blake was twenty-six. He had written these poems between the ages of twelve and twenty, and they are revelatory not only of his genius but also of the influences that were later to be more thoroughly assimilated: the Elizabethan lyric, the Shaksperian drama, the "Gothic" manner, Ossian, the unrhymed "Ode to Evening" of Collins, and, in at least one example ("To the Muses"), the high rhetoric of his period. The first six poems: "To Spring," "To Summer," "To Autumn," "To Winter," "To the Evening Star," and "To Morning" are unrhymed lyrics in five-stress meter. These are among the best, and the most famous of them, "To the Evening Star" is one of the finest of English lyrics. As in Tennyson's "Tears, idle tears," the music is at once so rich and so delicate that the absence of rhyme is unnoticed. One feels that no further music is necessary or even possible. The figures of speech, after the opening apostrophe, move toward their climax:

> . . . Let thy west wind sleep on
> The lake; speak silence with thy glimmering eyes,
> And wash the dusk with silver. . . .

There is a faint hint of ambiguity in the phrase "sleep on," which is not resolved until the next line. It holds the meaning in a drowsy suspense, very much as in Campion's superb lyric "Rose-cheek'd Laura, come," the word *still* in the line "But still moves delight" gives at once the sense of quiet, immobility, and timelessness. The figure "Speak silence with thy glimmering eyes, and wash the dusk with silver" is not merely the unutterable made eloquent, it is the happy blending of all the senses in one, a phase of mystical experience in which most men have shared at some time in their lives. The concluding four lines of the poem are as clear as a Greek pastoral. In these fourteen unrhymed lines are elements from almost the entire lyric range.

"Fair Elenor" shows a combination of the Gothic spirit, the folk ballad, and the charnel mood. It will not be forgotten that Blake's early

assignment as an engraver's apprentice was to sketch the tombs in Westminster Abbey, and to this fact we may attribute much of the Gothic
spirit of his work both in his drawings and his poetry. Certainly it would
explain the charnel touch in this particular lyric. The famous song,
"How sweet I roam'd from field to field" was written when he was fourteen. It is the first of a series of increasingly articulate thrusts at the
institution of marriage. We may well exclaim over the discrepancy between Blake's own marriage and his views on the institution in general,
but it was not in his temperament to permit a bit of personal luck to
soften his ideas against the darling bulwark of the Church and the State,
and which, on the larger scale, thwarted the free expression of sexual
joy. In the splendid "Mad Song" we find the familiar figure of the
"fiend in a cloud" driven to an extremity of pain by the light. This is not
only madness in the usual sense, it is the moment of frenzied despair when
mortal man understands the limitations of his state. Arthur Symons
remarks of "To the Muses" that "In these lines the eighteenth century
dies to music." Here Blake turns the rhetoric of the period against itself,
employing the gravest and most apostrophic style against the very manner in which it is written.

"An Imitation of Spenser" is chiefly interesting as an early indication
of Blake's weakness. Even the greatest of writers who work by the dictates of "inspiration" indulge themselves in occasional haste and care-
lessness. In this particular poem, it is obvious that an imitation of the
Spenserian stanza was intended. With the exception of a false rhyme in
line 3, the interlocking rhyme-scheme of the nine-line form is carried
out in the first stanza, but apparently the young poet at first failed to
notice that the Spenserian stanza calls for a six-stress line at the end.
This variation is, in fact, more important musically than the rhyme-
scheme or the number of lines. In the second, third, and sixth stanzas, the
terminal six-stress line appears. Stanza 2 is correctly Spenserian, stanzas 3
and 4 have only eight lines, stanza 5 is again correct but for the missing
foot at the end, and in stanza 6 the poet with intentional, but not Spenserian, artistry builds up a ten-line unit with a concluding couplet.
Pope's revision of Donne's second and fourth *Satyres* could not have
been farther from the intention of the original form. Some of this departure from the model was doubtless deliberate, but some was careless.
Critics of design, however much they admire Blake, find the same caprice
in his draughtsmanship. In his poetry, this tendency grew, and produced
in the long *Prophetic Books* certain avoidable confusions which only the
specialist can master, and effects of occasional power lost in pages of
verbal chaos. In such work, Blake was so violently at war with the Age
of Reason as to be equally guilty with it, though in the opposite direction.

The *Poetical Sketches* end with some dramatic fragments, only one of which, "King Edward the Third," proceeds beyond a prologue; and some pieces in poetic prose, which are more representative of a poet as youth than of Blake's genius in particular.

In the *Songs of Innocence and of Experience* "shewing the two contrary states of the human soul" are to be found the large majority of the poems familiar to the common reader. The strength of this work lies not only in the direct simplicity of its lyric melody, but also in those underlying harmonies which even if they are not interpreted rightly as symbols by the casual reader still yield their second voice to his enjoyment. This quality is the essence of symbolic writing: a double beauty in which the art is complete in itself, and made complete a second time on a deeper level of consciousness. "The Tyger" symbolically represents Wrath in the problem of Evil; it may, more specifically, have had some reference to that portion of wrath of which the French Revolution was an example during the period of its composition; yet "The Tyger" is also one of the best-loved "pure" lyrics in the language.

The scheme of these companion works, the *Songs of Innocence* and the *Songs of Experience*, was to show the contrast between the possibilities of life in the light of Eternity as a child might feel them and life as it unfolds amidst the material darkness of actuality. Two other poems that occur to us in this connection are Gray's "Ode on a Distant Prospect of Eton College," which opens with the idyllic picture of youth at play, continues with the melancholy prophecy of the ills that lie in wait, and concludes with the *carpe diem*:

> No more;—where ignorance is bliss,
> 'Tis folly to be wise,

and Wordsworth's "Ode on the Intimations of Immortality from Recollections of Early Childhood," wherein we find the vision of childhood in that radiant state of innocence which trails clouds of glory from eternity. Blake rises above the mundane view of fate described in Gray's poem, and carries Wordsworth's intimations to specific statements.

Hence, we have the voice of Experience, hard, bitter, rebellious, answering the songs of Innocence. *Innocence* is introduced by the piper, piping down the valleys wild, but *Experience* bids us

> Hear the voice of the Bard!
> Who Present, Past, & Future, sees;
> Whose ears have heard
> The Holy Word
> That walk'd among the ancient trees,

> Calling the lapsed Soul,
> And weeping in the evening dew;
> That might controll
> The starry pole,
> And fallen, fallen light renew!

At once we hear the prophetic note, and in "Earth's Answer," immediately following, we have the explanation for the bondage into which the Soul has fallen.

Thus the two voices speak back and forth. Many of the poems are matched. The "Lamb" of innocence becomes the "Tyger" of experience. The "Little Boy Lost" in the world of innocence is soon found wandering by God, disguised as his father; but in the corresponding poem, experience snares the little boy in depravity and death while his parents weep in vain. In the two "Holy Thursday" poems, we observe with the eye of innocence the radiant children singing at St. Paul's and well tended in their poverty; then, in the second poem, sounds the stern question: "Is this a holy thing to see?"—in a land of plenty so many children destitute?

> When the voices of children are heard on the green
> And laughing is heard on the hill,
> My heart is at rest within my breast
> And everything else is still.

sings the nurse in the *Songs of Innocence*, to which her grim sister replies in the *Songs of Experience*:

> When the voices of children are heard on the green
> And whisp'rings are in the dale,
> The days of my youth rise fresh in my mind,
> My face turns green and pale.

These children of experience suggest the horrible youngsters in Henry James's *The Turn of the Screw*. And so with the two chimney sweepers; the first a holy and delightful child, the second a grimy victim of a bad Church and a bad economic system. In spite of Blake's declared aloofness to specific political problems, a sturdy program of reform could be wrought from the contrasts of these moods.

But beyond all superficial evils lies the cause of all evil: the descent of spirit into matter. In the *Songs of Innocence*, Man is indeed the image of God.

> For Mercy has a human heart,
> Pity a human face,

And Love, the human form divine,
And Peace, the human dress.

But in *Experience,* God is the God of This World—Satan, none other:

A DIVINE IMAGE

Cruelty has a Human Heart,
And Jealousy a Human Face;
Terror the Human Form Divine,
And Secrecy the Human Dress.

And the summation of the whole experience is a protest against the descent into the flesh:

My mother groan'd! my father wept.
Into the dangerous world I leapt:
Helpless, naked, piping loud:
Like a fiend hid in a cloud.

Three of the *Songs of Innocence* had appeared in Blake's farcical satire, *An Island in the Moon.* This lunatic isle is a salon of the period, a burlesque of the circle of blue-stockings and faddists which Blake frequented during his late twenties. The humor has a Rabelaisian swagger quite in tone with some of the more exuberant passages of Sterne or Fielding. Blake's humor, when it was not too embittered for any laughter, is one of his less acknowledged traits, but is extremely important, nevertheless. No one could read the drunken scene in Chapter 9 of the *Island in the Moon* without a suspicion that the author would be delighted to make game of credulous folk, would, perhaps, not be averse to inventing an apparition or two for the consumption of adoring coteries.

Blake was shrewd. He saw people from behind his cloud much more clearly than they could see him, and it is hardly likely that there was any reciprocity of solemnity, however much the legendary "mad, naked Blake" might flourish with his immediate cult and their descendants. Some admirers, like Hayley, thought him an untutored genius with mild possibilities of conformity, some saw him as an engaging eccentric; some hallowed him as prophet—like Tatham, who, on conversion to evangelism burned his works—or, in later years, like Rossetti, who did not hesitate to rewrite passages he considered inferior. All such people Blake understood thoroughly. He convened them in the *Island in the Moon,* and, in the important prose work, *The Marriage of Heaven and Hell,* he included a few extravagances to shock them off his trail. It is not beyond likelihood that the difficulties and contradictions in the *Pro-*

phetic Books were not only, as is generally accepted, stylistic self-indulgence, but were again barricades against facile discovery by enthusiasts.

The *Prophetic Books* will always be a puzzle even to the specialist. A loose unrhymed verse, generally of six or seven stresses arranged with great syllabic freedom, is the vehicle of these prophecies. As a whole they represent the mystic's translation of earthly events in terms of Time and Space (*The French Revolution, America, Europe*) and, beyond Time and Space, the start and completion of the mystical release (*Thel, Tiriel, Urizen, Ahania, Los, Vala or the Four Zoas, Milton,* and *Jerusalem*). The theme of the mystical release moves through a series of spiritual records in the earlier *Prophetic Books* and is resolved through the *Four Zoas, Milton,* and *Jerusalem*—the most ambitious and by far the most difficult of Blake's epics. They are the account of a war to win back the human spirit from material bondage to Eternity. The soul has been lured by illusion into a sleep, a dark dream of being, over which presides the enemy, Reason (Urizen) and his various emanations and subordinates. It is Reason that confronts Love with the impossibility of its fulfilment, Reason that inspires in men the hatred, the tyrannies, the conventions, of the dust, and lulls them by earthly pleasures away from the joy of the spirit. He is the god of Systems, and so cunning is his logic he himself becomes entrapped in them. As defeat moves upon him, he becomes less and less articulate, and at last is merely a monster of ravening hate. The eventual triumph of the Spirit over its enemies is a radiance too dazzling to be described. It must always be borne in mind that this warfare, this cosmic experience, is beyond Time. Even while he seems to exist in the material world, Man has within him the moment of God.

The amateur of philosophy will at once recognize many similarities, either from natural congeniality or direct influence, with other revelations. Ancient Egyptian mysteries symbolized the same conflict, and taught two important doctrines that are embodied in the last three *Prophetic Books*: that there is no Hell, and that Evil is a necessary agent in the redemption and finally is redeemed in Eternity. Thus Set, the "Judas" of Egyptian theology, and Urizen, the "Satan" of Blake's vision, are both finally redeemed. The long warfare between Good and Evil, Light and Darkness, is also found in the Zoroastrian doctrine of the struggle between the good Ormuzd and the evil Ahriman. There are many other affinities of thought in these *Prophetic Books* with Buddhism, Platonism, neo-Platonism, Renaissance mysticism, and Swedenborgianism. The Christian doctrine of redemption through absolution appears in the *Jerusalem*. Professor S. F. Damon points out a new turn of thought in this last and important epic. Blake had always regarded the fall into

Matter as the unmitigable Evil. But in the *Jerusalem* "the Fall scattered many forces which, once given a body in which to work, can find again some purpose and eventually return to the zenith." Without the Fall, there could be no Redemption.

For the average reader, the *Prophetic Books* will serve rather as a trove for lyric selection than as a *de rerum natura* of mysticism. They rise to magnificent and stormy heights of rhetoric which may be heard without the philosopher's commentary. Anyone who tried to fashion a set theological scheme from them would find himself in the predicament of Urizen enmeshed in his own weavings. But with the knowledge of Blake's prevailing ideas as developed in these works, the shorter poems take on much more fullness and profundity. Nor should we, in contemplating Blake, depart too far from the echoes of the pure lyric of which he was one of the masters. He can be read for his music, his emotion, and his thought. Since his thought expressed itself so largely through symbols, we have the added quality of pictures, the sharp outlines of which become, in that mingling of the senses so familiar to the mystic, a thematic line, clear as a violin or the clearest of human voices.

When Blake died at the age of seventy, he was still working with full energy on a new set of drawings for Dante's *Divine Comedy*. At his death he left behind him a small group of disciples who understood very little about him, and his wife, the faithful Catherine who, having loved him most and served him best, probably understood him as well as could be. It was she who saw his leavetaking of this world in the ecstasy of his fulfilment.

IV

ONE could generalize through volumes concerning the interplay between works of literature and events of history, but footnotes would crowd the text off the page. We know how in periods of triumph the ticking of decay goes on underneath the arches, how years of complacency are jerked awake by the natural restlessness of man, and how an age of despair seeks escape "anywhere, anywhere out of the world." Such currents working against the main flow of event are often seen in literature and the arts. One could almost prognosticate the growing or waning popularity of a writer by watching the turn of the news. The more idiosyncratic the author, so much the stronger will be his attraction for a congenial age.

Donne and Blake are two of the most indicative poets in the language. Yet because of their dissimilarity, since one addresses the intellect and one the spirit, predominantly, they will always find an audience in years of indecision or dismay when material things are piled so high that they topple over and crush their worshippers. We die a physical as well as a spiritual death in the collapse of ponderable things. The cathedral that has become a mere museum invites the destroying bomb, and the body of man, emptied of spirit, presents nothing but its own vulnerability to the oncoming bullet. At such times dreams are strong, for there remains only the choice between the dream and oblivion.

John Donne's dream beyond oblivion was redemption in the Lord Jesus Christ, through communion with Him, the remission of sins, and the declaration of Faith. To an age like our own, perplexed almost beyond endurance, the bypaths through which he groped his way hold us most sympathetically, for we, too, are lost. To many who would reject his theological conclusions, he is still the master of self-analysis, of definition through metaphor. Lost in the anguish of his own doubting for so long, he is the subtle spokesman for the darker margins of consciousness.

Such angelic wrestling found an eager audience among the poets of his own time, as with ours, and its pious finale delighted the less frivolous. His influence extended even to the New World. An unusually good Colonial poet, Edward Taylor (whose work was edited and published by Mr. Thomas H. Johnson in 1939), was completely the disciple of Donne. Taylor's poems, composed in the last years of the seventeenth and the first quarter of the eighteenth century, are scarcely what one would expect from the pen of the Puritan minister who served the town of Westfield, Massachusetts, during the New England theocracy. They abound in High-Church echoes, and amid the austere countryside of our ancestors, Taylor wrote about the Altar and the smoke rising from censers.

In spite of the adulation in which Donne was held in his own century, he shrank to little more than a name in the two centuries that succeeded. To the eighteenth century he was known, if at all, as an early satirist, a harsh versifier, a literary curiosity to be "vastly improved by Pope." The Romantic Movement, delighted with its own turbulences, was foreign to him, and among the Victorians, only Robert Browning seems to have read and studied him with profitable care. In Humphrey Ward's great anthology of *English Poets,* John W. Hale begins his introduction thus: "Donne's contemporary reputation as a poet, and still more as a preacher, was immense; and a glance at his works would suffice to show that he did not deserve the contempt with which he was subsequently treated. But yet his chief interest is that he was the principal founder of a school which especially expressed and represented a certain bad taste of his day. Of his genius there can be no question; but it was perversely directed. One may almost invert Jonson's famous panegyric on Shakespeare, and say that Donne was not for all time but for an age." Such was the standard opinion in 1880. In Quiller-Couch's *Oxford Book of English Verse* (1900), Donne is proportionately better represented, but "The Extasie" is slashed without any indication that much of the poem has been omitted. His unearthly quality—the ghostly marriage of the fleshly and the incorporeal—was until recently passed over. Such a critic as Quiller-Couch apparently considered Donne's best to be the most conventionally lyric, and thus reduced "The Extasie" to a pleasantly pastoral love scene. Yet there are good reasons for Donne's relegation by critics of the late nineteenth century to the part of an interesting but slovenly lyric and satiric writer. The revival of interest in the Elizabethan song found Donne's phrasing muddy in comparison. His versification was weighed according to conventional standards and found wanting. As Blake said, in another connection: "Bring out number, weight, and measure in a year of dearth." Another inconvenience attached to Donne's poetry was its undependability. Anyone's daughter might easily chance on some gross impropriety such as "To his Mistris going to Bed."

Among his early critics of our own period, George Saintsbury ranks highest in appreciation of Donne's genius. His introductory essay to the poems in the Muses' Library was often recommended, in days when few read Donne's work, by the late Dean L. B. R. Briggs of Harvard, whose own excellent commentary was left unrecorded except in the memory of his hearers. The steady and serious enthusiasm for Donne during recent years has found expression in the criticism of Mr. T. S. Eliot, Professor Herbert J. C. Grierson, and of the contributors to Professor Theodore Spencer's collection, *A Garland for John Donne*. The best biography, however, is still Izaak Walton's. In spite of errors in detail (which have been set right by scholars) Walton's friendship and admiration for his subject, combined with the appropriate sweetness of his style, give us a living portrait that stands alone.

Now, with the tremors of history affrighting the spirit of the transitional era in which we live, interest in Donne has mounted to its highest level. No age of triumph or complacency would feel such need of him or such kinship with him. In our time the hysterias of change find their response in the nervousness, and their resolution in the nobility, of his writings both in verse and prose. Saintsbury has pointed out the degrees of opinion in which these are held: "It is almost necessary that those who do not like him should not like him at all; should be scarcely able to see how any decent and intelligent human being can like him. It is almost as necessary that those who do like him should either like him so much as to speak unadvisedly with their lips, or else curb and restrain the expression of their love for fear that it would seem on that side idolatry. But these are not the only dangers. Donne is eminently of that kind which lends itself to sham liking, to coterie worship, to a false enthusiasm; and here is another weapon in the hands of the infidels, and another stumbling-block for the feet of the true believers."

It would be impossible to list the modern poets who show direct or indirect influence from Donne, for it permeates the literary atmosphere. That much of the adulation heaped on his name is but "coterie worship" goes without saying. But on the whole, the attraction which this earthly, unearthly poet exercises over imagination springs from a desire to find refuge in the world of intellect from the world of things, and to rediscover beauties and strangenesses of idiom so long guarded against and excluded from our speech.

The same instinct in less meditative and perhaps more romantic form has led readers to Blake. Donne's poetry is analytical; Blake's is rhapsodic. Donne fashions the metaphor; Blake seizes on the symbol. Donne is companionable through a long period of uncertainty; Blake dismisses the sudden crisis. Donne accompanies us down the labyrinth of melancholy with promise of the light to come; Blake swears that the labyrinth is a myth. In the long routine of life's disappointments and half-accomplished passions, Donne has preceded us. In the unpredictable moment, Blake flashes from the air.

At the close of the last war, Blake and many other writers, lesser figures at least tinged with mysticism, found eager students. Emily Dickinson and Herman Melville came into their own. And down the rungs of the unsubstantial ladder, the whole occult world was astir. From the brilliant magic of Dr. Rudolf Steiner to the dreary and pathetic basements of spiritism, speculation proceeded according to the capacity of the minds involved. Every movement in human thought has degrees of manifestation, and what may exist as a fearfully difficult piece of spiritual discipline on the part of the few, may easily become a parlor game among the many. Blake and Freud, Ouspensky and Einstein, were names to bandy about the dinner party whence all the company might adjourn to the card table or the tipping table with equal seriousness of purpose. These were the years when the word *mystic* was stretched so far that it snapped; the years when history was ransacked to provide gaudy names for former incarnations, and, on a level inconceivably higher, the years when Blake's philosophy became recognized as a subject for careful study. Up to that period his symbols had been dealt with affectionately but somewhat impressionistically.

Blake's career in literary history was the reverse of Donne's, for he was ignored by the public of his own time and came into his heritage during the succeeding period. We must not, however, think of him as a recluse. Wordsworth, Coleridge, Lamb, and Southey were at least acquainted with his work, and in his later years he was master Seer to a number of ineffectual disciples, some of whom kept records of him as prophet, painter, or poet. Alexander Gilchrist's *Pictor Ignotus* was the first of the biographies. The interest of Swinburne and the members of the Pre-Raphaelite group spread the fame of his writings and his illustrations. Toward the end of the century everyone knew "The Tyger," "The Lamb," and "The Piper" and considered them charming. By the time Ward's *English Poets* appeared, Blake was sufficiently known to denote a period from "Addison to Blake." The twelve lyrics for the anthology were well selected, but J. Comyns Carr, who contributed the Introduction, found much if not all of Blake's poetry "infected with the suspicion of insanity" and with far juster acumen, deplored the obscurities encouraged by the "prophetic vagueness of the Ossianic verse."

W. B. Yeats, in his early enthusiasm, made a painstaking attempt to interpret all the symbols of Blake's poetry. Yeats was young and not very expert. Furthermore, he passed his impressionable years under the influence of a not very sound occultism embellished by such aesthetic influences as that of Ernest Dowson, to whose memory he clung, with misplaced loyalty, to the end of his days. On the meditative side, Yeats was more the magician than the initiate; he dallied much in the land of faery and frequently called on symbols merely to adorn a line of verse or startle his fellow-cultists. Yet when we consider the romantic mood with which Yeats approached symbolic usage, we must applaud the sensitiveness of his reactions to Blake even when he seemed to be taking infinite pains to arrive at a wrong conclusion. Although his editing was faulty, his general introduction to the poems in the Muses' Library edition of 1893 remains not only a fine clear piece of prose, but a just appreciation as well.

Through Yeats the knowledge of Blake's mysticism spread into the Celtic school and beyond. "A.E." and James Stephens both show their indebtedness, and Stephens's lines describing God seem almost a translation into verse of Blake's engraving, "The Ancient of Days":

> He was not satisfied;
>   His look was all dissatisfied.
> His beard swung on a wind far out of sight
> Behind the world's curve, and there was light
> Most fearful from His forehead, and He sighed . . .

By 1920 Blake's reputation was at the zenith. As always in such cases, the camp followers of enthusiasm, who invariably transform popularity into vogue, were so vociferous that one English poet complained of being put off "by posturing fools who . . . cackle all day of Blake." But happily, the poet was by then firmly established as one of the masters. In England and America, on the Continent, and even in Japan, the many facets of his genius received the most studious criticism. In 1924 appeared S. Foster Damon's *William Blake: His Philosophy and Symbols,* which remains, and seems destined to remain, the standard interpretation.

The direct influence of Blake on contemporary poets has been on the wane for the last few years. His simplicity is not enough. If one would absorb his manner, one would, to a large extent, have to share his spiritual convictions and his native subtlety. He is less adaptable to imitation, therefore, than Donne, for although his style is as easily recognized, his implications are more original. Emptied of such implications, poems like "The Piper" would seem almost as slight as R. L. Stevenson's *Child's Garden of Verses.* As for the *Prophetic Books,* an imitation of their method would induce merely the verbiage of spiritual whim, a fault from which, in fact, they themselves are not wholly free. The genius that informed Blake's poetry with its inimitable eloquence was his life itself, all concentrated in the Eternal Moment that provided at one flash the inspiration and the completed work.

John Donne and William Blake, the two poets included in this volume, complement each other. They both exorcise, though in such differing terms, the illusions of stupidity, greed, and cynicism from which we have fashioned the realm of our sorrow. They are two voices from another country concerning whose existence, now as never before, we need the assurance of the inspired and the wise.

Pomfret, Conn.
May, 1941

The Complete Poetry

and

Selected Prose of

John Donne

Songs and Sonets

THE GOOD-MORROW

I WONDER by my troth, what thou, and I
Did, till we lov'd? were we not wean'd till then?
But suck'd on countrey pleasures, childishly?
Or snorted we in the seaven sleepers den?
T'was so; But this, all pleasures fancies bee.
If ever any beauty I did see,
Which I desir'd, and got, t'was but a dreame of thee.

And now good morrow to our waking soules,
Which watch not one another out of feare;
For love, all love of other sights controules,
And makes one little roome, an every where.
Let sea-discoverers to new worlds have gone,
Let Maps to other, worlds on worlds have showne,
Let us possesse one world, each hath one, and is one.

My face is thine eye, thine in mine appeares,
And true plaine hearts doe in the faces rest,
Where can we finde two better hemispheares
Without sharpe North, without declining West?
What ever dyes, was not mixt equally;
If our two loves be one, or, thou and I
Love so alike, that none doe slacken, none can die.

SONG

GOE, and catche a falling starre,
    Get with child a mandrake roote,
Tell me, where all past yeares are,
    Or who cleft the Divels foot,

3

Teach me to heare Mermaides singing,
   Or to keep off envies stinging,
         And finde
         What winde
Serves to advance an honest minde.

If thou beest borne to strange sights,
   Things invisible to see,
Ride ten thousand daies and nights,
   Till age snow white haires on thee,
Thou, when thou retorn'st, wilt tell mee
All strange wonders that befell thee,
         And sweare
         No where
Lives a woman true, and faire.

If thou findst one, let mee know,
   Such a Pilgrimage were sweet;
Yet doe not, I would not goe,
   Though at next doore wee might meet,
Though shee were true, when you met her,
And last, till you write your letter,
         Yet shee
         Will bee
False, ere I come, to two, or three.

WOMANS CONSTANCY

N O W thou hast lov'd me one whole day,
To morrow when thou leav'st, what wilt thou say?
Wilt thou then Antedate some new made vow?
      Or say that now
We are not just those persons, which we were?
Or, that oathes made in reverentiall feare
Of Love, and his wrath, any may forsweare?
Or, as true deaths, true maryages untie,
So lovers contracts, images of those,
Binde but till sleep, deaths image, them unloose?
      Or, your owne end to Justifie,
For having purpos'd change, and falsehood; you
Can have no way but falsehood to be true?

Vaine lunatique, against these scapes I could
　　Dispute, and conquer, if I would,
　　　Which I abstaine to doe,
For by to morrow, I may thinke so too.

THE UNDERTAKING

I HAVE done one braver thing
　　Than all the *Worthies* did,
And yet a braver thence doth spring,
　　Which is, to keepe that hid.

It were but madnes now t'impart
　　The skill of specular stone,
When he which can have learn'd the art
　　To cut it, can finde none.

So, if I now should utter this,
　　Others (because no more
Such stuffe to worke upon, there is,)
　　Would love but as before.

But he who lovelinesse within
　　Hath found, all outward loathes,
For he who colour loves, and skinne,
　　Loves but their oldest clothes.

If, as I have, you also doe
　　Vertue'attir'd in woman see,
And dare love that, and say so too,
　　And forget the Hee and Shee;

And if this love, though placed so,
　　From prophane men you hide,
Which will no faith on this bestow,
　　Or, if they doe, deride:

Then you have done a braver thing
　　Than all the *Worthies* did;
And a braver thence will spring,
　　Which is, to keepe that hid.

THE SUNNE RISING

BUSIE old foole, unruly Sunne,
　　Why dost thou thus,
Through windowes, and through curtaines call on us?
Must to thy motions lovers seasons run?
　　　　Sawcy pedantique wretch, goe chide
　　　　Late schoole boyes, and sowre prentices,
　　Goe tell Court-huntsmen, that the King will ride,
　　Call countrey ants to harvest offices;
Love, all alike, no season knowes, nor clyme,
Nor houres, dayes, moneths, which are the rags of time.

　　　　Thy beames, so reverend, and strong
　　　　Why shouldst thou thinke?
I could eclipse and cloud them with a winke,
But that I would not lose her sight so long:
　　　　If her eyes have not blinded thine,
　　　　Looke, and to morrow late, tell mee,
　　Whether both the'India's of spice and Myne
　　Be where thou leftst them, or lie here with mee.
Aske for those Kings whom thou saw'st yesterday,
And thou shalt heare, All here in one bed lay.

　　　　She'is all States, and all Princes, I,
　　　　Nothing else is.
Princes doe but play us; compar'd to this,
All honor's mimique; All wealth alchimie.
　　　　Thou sunne art halfe as happy'as wee,
　　　　In that the world's contracted thus;
　　Thine age askes ease, and since thy duties bee
　　To warme the world, that's done in warming us.
Shine here to us, and thou art every where;
This bed thy center is, these walls, thy spheare.

THE INDIFFERENT

I CAN love both faire and browne,
Her whom abundance melts, and her whom want betraies,
Her who loves lonenesse best, and her who maskes and plaies,
Her whom the country form'd, and whom the town,

Her who beleeves, and her who tries,
Her who still weepes with spungie eyes,
And her who is dry corke, and never cries;
I can love her, and her, and you and you,
I can love any, so she be not true.

Will no other vice content you?
Wil it not serve your turn to do, as did your mothers?
Or have you all old vices spent, and now would finde out others?
Or doth a feare, that men are true, torment you?
Oh we are not, be not you so,
Let mee, and doe you, twenty know.
Rob mee, but binde me not, and let me goe.
Must I, who came to travaile thorow you,
Grow your fixt subject, because you are true?

Venus heard me sigh this song,
And by Loves sweetest Part, Variety, she swore,
She heard not this till now; and that it should be so no more.
She went, examin'd, and return'd ere long,
And said, alas, Some two or three
Poore Heretiques in love there bee,
Which thinke to stablish dangerous constancie.
But I have told them, since you will be true,
You shall be true to them, who'are false to you.

LOVES USURY

F O R every houre that thou will spare mee now,
     I will allow,
Usurious God of Love, twenty to thee,
When with my browne, my gray haires equall bee;
Till then, Love, let my body raigne, and let
Mee travell, sojourne, snatch, plot, have, forget,
Resume my last yeares relict: thinke that yet
     We'had never met.

Let mee thinke any rivalls letter mine,
     And at next nine
Keepe midnights promise; mistake by the way
The maid, and tell the Lady of that delay;

Onely let mee love none, no, not the sport;
From country grasse, to comfitures of Court,
Or cities quelque choses, let report
      My minde transport.

This bargaine's good; if when I'am old, I bee
      Inflam'd by thee,
If thine owne honour, or my shame, or paine,
Thou covet most, at that age thou shalt gaine.
Doe thy will then, then subject and degree,
And fruit of love, Love I submit to thee,
Spare mee till then, I'll beare it, though she bee
      One that loves mee.

THE CANONIZATION

F O R Godsake hold your tongue, and let me love,
      Or chide my palsie, or my gout,
My five gray haires, or ruin'd fortune flout,
   With wealth your state, your minde with Arts improve,
      Take you a course, get you a place,
      Observe his honour, or his grace,
Or the Kings reall, or his stamped face
    Contemplate, what you will, approve,
    So you will let me love.

Alas, alas, who's injur'd by my love?
    What merchants ships have my sighs drown'd?
Who saies my teares have overflow'd his ground?
    When did my colds a forward spring remove?
      When did the heats which my veines fill
      Adde one more to the plaguie Bill?
Soldiers finde warres, and Lawyers finde out still
    Litigious men, which quarrels move,
    Though she and I do love.

Call us what you will, wee are made such by love;
    Call her one, mee another flye,
We'are Tapers too, and at our owne cost die,
    And wee in us finde the'Eagle and the Dove.
    The Phœnix ridle hath more wit

By us, we two being one, are it.
So to one neutrall thing both sexes fit,
    Wee dye and rise the same, and prove
    Mysterious by this love.

Wee can dye by it, if not live by love,
    And if unfit for tombes and hearse
Our legend bee, it will be fit for verse;
    And if no peece of Chronicle wee prove,
        We'll build in sonnets pretty roomes;
        As well a well wrought urne becomes
The greatest ashes, as halfe-acre tombes,
    And by these hymnes, all shall approve
    Us *Canoniz'd* for Love:

And thus invoke us; You whom reverend love
    Made one anothers hermitage;
You, to whom love was peace, that now is rage;
    Who did the whole worlds soule contract, and **drove**
        Into the glasses of your eyes
        (So made such mirrors, and such spies,
That they did all to you epitomize,)
    Countries, Townes, Courts: Beg from above
    A patterne of your love!

THE TRIPLE FOOLE

I AM two fooles, I know,
For loving, and for saying so
    In whining Poëtry;
But where's that wiseman, that would not be I,
    If she would not deny?
Then as th'earths inward narrow crooked lanes
Do purge sea waters fretfull salt away,
    I thought, if I could draw my paines,
Through Rimes vexation, I should them allay.
Griefe brought to numbers cannot be so fierce,
For, he tames it, that fetters it in verse.

    But when I have done so,
Some man, his art and voice to show,

Doth Set and sing my paine,
And, by delighting many, frees againe
   Griefe, which verse did restraine.
To Love, and Griefe tribute of Verse belongs,
But not of such as pleases when'tis read,
   Both are increased by such songs:
For both their triumphs so are published,
And I, which was two fooles, do so grow three;
Who are a little wise, the best fooles bee.

LOVERS INFINITENESSE

I F yet I have not all thy love,
Deare, I shall never have it all,
I cannot breath one other sigh, to move,
Nor can intreat one other teare to fall,
And all my treasure, which should purchase thee,
Sighs, teares, and oathes, and letters I have spent.
Yet no more can be due to mee,
Than at the bargaine made was ment,
If then thy gift of love were partiall,
That some to mee, some should to others fall,
   Deare, I shall never have Thee All.

Or if then thou gavest mee all,
All was but All, which thou hadst then;
But if in thy heart, since, there be or shall,
New love created bee, by other men,
Which have their stocks intire, and can in teares,
In sighs, in oathes, and letters outbid mee,
This new love may beget new feares,
For, this love was not vowed by thee.
And yet it was, thy gift being generall,
The ground, thy heart is mine, what ever shall
   Grow there, deare, I should have it all.

Yet I would not have all yet,
Hee that hath all can have no more,
And since my love doth every day admit
New growth, thou shouldst have new rewards in store;
Thou canst not every day give me thy heart,

If thou canst give it, then thou never gavest it:
Loves riddles are, that though thy heart depart,
It stayes at home, and thou with losing savest it:
But wee will have a way more liberall,
Than changing hearts, to joyne them, so wee shall
  Be one, and one anothers All.

SONG

    SWEETEST love, I do not goe,
      For wearinesse of thee,
  Nor in hope the world can show
      A fitter Love for mee;
        But since that I
  Must dye at last, 'tis best,
  To use my selfe in jest
      Thus by fain'd deaths to dye;

  Yesternight the Sunne went hence,
      And yet is here to day,
  He hath no desire nor sense,
      Nor halfe so short a way:
        Then feare not mee,
  But beleeve that I shall make
  Speedier journeyes, since I take
      More wings and spurres than hee.

  O how feeble is mans power,
      That if good fortune fall,
  Cannot adde another houre,
      Nor a lost houre recall!
        But come bad chance,
  And wee joyne to'it our strength,
  And wee teach it art and length,
      It selfe o'r us to'advance.

  When thou sigh'st, thou sigh'st not winde,
      But sigh'st my soule away,
  When thou weep'st, unkindly kinde,
      My lifes blood doth decay.
        It cannot bee

That thou lov'st mee, as thou say'st,
If in thine my life thou waste,
    That art the best of mee.

Let not thy divining heart
    Forethinke me any ill,
Destiny may take thy part,
    And may thy feares fulfill;
      But thinke that wee
Are but turn'd aside to sleepe;
They who one another keepe
    Alive, ne'r parted bee.

THE LEGACIE

WHEN I dyed last, and, Deare, I dye
    As often as from thee I goe,
    Though it be but an houre agoe,
And Lovers houres be full eternity,
I can remember yet, that I
    Something did say, and something did bestow;
Though I be dead, which sent mee, I should be
Mine owne executor and Legacie.

I heard mee say, Tell her anon,
    That my selfe, (that is you, not I,)
    Did kill me, and when I felt mee dye,
I bid mee send my heart, when I was gone,
But I alas could there finde none,
    When I had ripp'd me, 'and search'd where hearts
      did lye;
It kill'd mee againe, that I who still was true,
In life, in my last Will should cozen you.

Yet I found something like a heart,
    But colours it, and corners had,
    It was not good, it was not bad,
It was intire to none, and few had part.
As good as could be made by art
    It seem'd; and therefore for our losses sad,
I meant to send this heart in stead of mine,
But oh, no man could hold it. for twas thine.

A FEAVER

O H doe not die, for I shall hate
   All women so, when thou art gone,
That thee I shall not celebrate,
   When I remember, thou wast one.

But yet thou canst not die, I know,
   To leave this world behinde, is death,
But when thou from this world wilt goe,
   The whole world vapors with thy breath.

Or if, when thou, the worlds soule, goest,
   It stay, tis but thy carkasse then,
The fairest woman, but thy ghost,
   But corrupt wormes, the worthyest men.

O wrangling schooles, that search what fire
   Shall burne this world, had none the wit
Unto this knowledge to aspire,
   That this her feaver might be it?

And yet she cannot wast by this,
   Nor long beare this torturing wrong,
For such corruption needfull is
   To fuell such a feaver long.

These burning fits but meteors bee,
   Whose matter in thee is soone spent.
Thy beauty,'and all parts, which are thee,
   Are unchangeable firmament.

Yet t'was of my minde, seising thee,
   Though it in thee cannot persever.
For I had rather owner bee
   Of thee one houre, than all else ever.

AIRE AND ANGELLS

T W I C E or thrice had I loved thee,
Before I knew thy face or name;

So in a voice, so in a shapelesse flame,
Angells affect us oft, and worship'd bee;
   Still when, to where thou wert, I came,
Some lovely glorious nothing I did see.
   But since my soule, whose child love is,
Takes limmes of flesh, and else could nothing doe,
   More subtile than the parent is,
Love must not be, but take a body too,
    And therefore what thou wert, and who,
      I bid Love aske, and now
That it assume thy body, I allow,
And fixe it selfe in thy lip, eye, and brow.

Whilst thus to ballast love, I thought,
And so more steddily to have gone,
With wares which would sinke admiration,
I saw, I had loves pinnace overfraught,
   Ev'ry thy haire for love to worke upon
Is much too much, some fitter must be sought;
   For, nor in nothing, nor in things
Extreme, and scatt'ring bright, can love inhere;
   Then as an Angell, face, and wings
Of aire, not pure as it, yet pure doth weare,
    So thy love may be my loves spheare;
      Just such disparitie
As is twixt Aire and Angells puritie,
'Twixt womens love, and mens will ever bee.

BREAKE OF DAY

'T I S true, 'tis day; what though it be?
O wilt thou therefore rise from me?
Why should we rise, because 'tis light?
Did we lie downe, because 'twas night?
Love which in spight of darknesse brought us hether,
Should in despight of light keepe us together.

Light hath no tongue, but is all eye;
If it could speake as well as spie,
This were the worst, that it could say,
That being well, I faine would stay,

And that I lov'd my heart and honor so,
That I would not from him, that had them, goe.

Must businesse thee from hence remove?
Oh, that's the worst disease of love,
The poore, the foule, the false, love can
Admit, but not the busied man.
He which hath businesse, and makes love, doth doe
Such wrong, as when a maryed man doth wooe.

THE ANNIVERSARIE

A L L Kings, and all their favorites,
  All glory of honors, beauties, wits,
The Sun it selfe, which makes times, as they passe,
Is elder by a yeare, now, than it was
When thou and I first one another saw:
All other things, to their destruction draw,
  Only our love hath no decay;
This, no to morrow hath, nor yesterday,
Running it never runs from us away,
But truly keepes his first, last, everlasting day.

  Two graves must hide thine and my coarse,
  If one might, death were no divorce.
Alas, as well as other Princes, wee,
(Who Prince enough in one another bee,)
Must leave at last in death, these eyes, and eares,
Oft fed with true oathes, and with sweet salt teares;
  But soules where nothing dwells but love
(All other thoughts being inmates) then shall prove
This, or a love increased there above,
When bodies to their graves, soules from their
    graves remove.

  And then wee shall be throughly blest,
  But wee no more, than all the rest;
Here upon earth, we'are Kings, and none but wee
Can be such Kings, nor of such subjects bee.
Who is so safe as wee? where none can doe
Treason to us, except one of us two.

True and false feares let us refraine,
Let us love nobly, and live, and adde againe
Yeares and yeares unto yeares, till we attaine
To write threescore: this is the second of our raigne.

A VALEDICTION: OF MY NAME, IN THE WINDOW

I

M Y name engrav'd herein,
Doth contribute my firmnesse to this glasse,
    Which, ever since that charme, hath beene
    As hard, as that which grav'd it, was;
Thine eye will give it price enough, to mock
        The diamonds of either rock.

II

        'Tis much that glasse should bee
As all confessing, and through-shine as I,
    'Tis more, that it shewes thee to thee,
    And cleare reflects thee to thine eye.
But all such rules, loves magique can undoe,
        Here you see mee, and I am you.

III

        As no one point, nor dash,
Which are but accessaries to this name,
    The showers and tempests can outwash,
    So shall all times finde mee the same;
You this intirenesse better may fulfill,
        Who have the patterne with you still.

IIII

        Or if too hard and deepe
This learning be, for a scratch'd name to teach,
    It, as a given deaths head keepe,
    Lovers mortalitie to preach,
Or thinke this ragged bony name to bee
        My ruinous Anatomie.

V

Then, as all my soules bee,
Emparadis'd in you, (in whom alone
　　I understand, and grow and see,)
　　The rafters of my body, bone
Being still with you, the Muscle, Sinew, and Veine,
　　　　Which tile this house, will come againe.

VI

Till my returne, repaire
And recompact my scattered body so.
　　As all the vertuous powers which are
　　Fix'd in the starres, are said to flow
Into such characters, as graved bee
　　　　When these starres have supremacie:

VII

So since this name was cut
When love and griefe their exaltation had,
　　No doore 'gainst this names influence shut;
　　As much more loving, as more sad,
'Twill make thee; and thou shouldst, till I returne,
　　　　Since I die daily, daily mourne.

VIII

When thy inconsiderate hand
Flings ope this casement, with my trembling name,
　　To looke on one, whose wit or land,
　　New battry to thy heart may frame,
Then thinke this name alive, and that thou thus
　　　　In it offendst my Genius.

IX

And when thy melted maid,
Corrupted by thy Lover's gold, and page,
　　His letter at thy pillow'hath laid,
　　Disputed it, and tam'd thy rage,
And thou begin'st to thaw towards him, for this,
　　　　May my name step in, and hide his.

X

And if this treason goe
To an overt act, and that thou write againe;
In superscribing, this name flow
Into thy fancy, from the pane.
So, in forgetting thou remembrest right,
And unaware to mee shalt write.

XI

But glasse, and lines must bee,
No meanes our firme substantiall love to keepe;
Neere death inflicts this lethargie,
And this I murmure in my sleepe;
Impute this idle talke, to that I goe,
For dying men talke often so.

TWICKNAM GARDEN

BLASTED with sighs, and surrounded with teares,
Hither I come to seeke the spring,
And at mine eyes, and at mine eares,
Receive such balmes, as else cure every thing;
But O, selfe traytor, I do bring
The spider love, which transubstantiates all,
And can convert Manna to gall,
And that this place may thoroughly be thought
True Paradise, I have the serpent brought.

'Twere wholsomer for mee, that winter did
Benight the glory of this place,
And that a grave frost did forbid
These trees to laugh, and mocke mee to my face;
But that I may not this disgrace
Indure, nor yet leave loving, Love let mee
Some senslesse peece of this place bee;
Make me a mandrake, so I may groane here,
Or a stone fountaine weeping out my yeare.

Hither with christall vyals, lovers come,
And take my teares, which are loves wine,

And try your mistresse Teares at home,
For all are false, that tast not just like mine;
  Alas, hearts do not in eyes shine,
Nor can you more judge womans thoughts by teares,
  Than by her shadow, what she weares.
O perverse sexe, where none is true but shee,
  Who's therefore true, because her truth kills mee.

A VALEDICTION: OF THE BOOKE

I'LL tell thee now (deare Love) what thou shalt doe
  To anger destiny, as she doth us,
  How I shall stay, though she Esloygne me thus
And how posterity shall know it too;
    How thine may out-endure
    Sybills glory, and obscure
    Her who from Pindar could allure,
  And her, through whose helpe *Lucan* is not lame,
And her, whose booke (they say) *Homer* did finde, and name.

Study our manuscripts, those Myriades
  Of letters, which have past twixt thee and mee,
  Thence write our Annals, and in them will bee
To all whom loves subliming fire invades,
    Rule and example found;
    There, the faith of any ground
    No schismatique will dare to wound,
  That sees, how Love this grace to us affords,
To make, to keep, to use, to be these his Records.

This Booke, as long-liv'd as the elements,
  Or as the worlds forme, this all-graved tome
  In cypher writ, or new made Idiome,
Wee for loves clergie only'are instruments:
    When this booke is made thus,
    Should againe the ravenous
    Vandals and Goths inundate us,
  Learning were safe; in this our Universe
Schooles might learne Sciences, Spheares Musick, Angels Verse.

Here Loves Divines, (since all Divinity
  Is love or wonder) may finde all they seeke,
  Whether abstract spirituall love they like,
Their Soules exhal'd with what they do not see,
      Or, loth so to amuze
      Faiths infirmitie, they chuse
      Something which they may see and use;
  For, though minde be the heaven, where love doth sit,
Beauty a convenient type may be to figure it.

Here more than in their bookes may Lawyers finde,
  Both by what titles Mistresses are ours,
  And how prerogative these states devours,
Transferr'd from Love himselfe, to womankinde,
      Who though from heart, and eyes,
      They exact great subsidies,
      Forsake him who on them relies,
  And for the cause, honour, or conscience give,
Chimeraes, vaine as they, or their prerogative.

Here Statesmen, (or of them, they which can reade,)
  May of their occupation finde the grounds:
  Love and their art alike it deadly wounds,
If to consider what 'tis, one proceed,
      In both they doe excell
      Who the present governe well,
      Whose weaknesse none doth, or dares tell;
  In this thy booke, such will their nothing see,
As in the Bible some can finde out Alchimy.

Thus vent thy thoughts; abroad I'll studie thee,
  As he removes farre off, that great heights takes;
  How great love is, presence best tryall makes,
But absence tryes how long this love will bee;
      To take a latitude
      Sun, or starres, are fitliest view'd
      At their brightest, but to conclude
  Of longitudes, what other way have wee,
But to marke when, and where the darke eclipses bee?

COMMUNITIE

G O O D wee must love, and must hate ill,
For ill is ill, and good good still,
   But there are things indifferent,
Which wee may neither hate, nor love,
But one, and then another prove,
   As wee shall finde our fancy bent.

If then at first wise Nature had
Made women either good or bad,
   Then some wee might hate, and some chuse,
But since shee did them so create,
That we may neither love, nor hate,
   Onely this rests, All, all may use.

If they were good it would be seene,
Good is as visible as greene,
   And to all eyes it selfe betrayes:
If they were bad, they could not last,
Bad doth it selfe, and others wast,
   So, they deserve nor blame, nor praise.

But they are ours as fruits are ours,
He that but tasts, he that devours,
   And he that leaves all, doth as well:
Chang'd loves are but chang'd sorts of meat,
And when hee hath the kernell eate,
   Who doth not fling away the shell?

LOVES GROWTH

I S C A R C E beleeve my love to be so pure
   As I had thought it was,
   Because it doth endure
Vicissitude, and season, as the grasse;
Me thinkes I lyde all winter, when I swore,
My love was infinite, if spring make'it more.
But if this medicine, love. which cures all sorrow

With more, not onely bee no quintessence,
But mixt of all stuffes, paining soule, or sense,
And of the Sunne his working vigour borrow,
Love's not so pure, and abstract, as they use
To say, which have no Mistresse but their Muse,
But as all else, being elemented too,
Love sometimes would contemplate, sometimes do.

And yet no greater, but more eminent,
        Love by the Spring is growne;
        As, in the firmament,
Starres by the Sunne are not inlarg'd, but showne.
Gentle love deeds, as blossomes on a bough,
From loves awakened root do bud out now.
If, as in water stir'd more circles bee
Produc'd by one, love such additions take,
Those like so many spheares, but one heaven make,
For, they are all concentrique unto thee.
And though each spring doe adde to love new heate,
As princes doe in times of action get
New taxes, and remit them not in peace,
No winter shall abate the springs encrease.

LOVES EXCHANGE

LOVE, any devill else but you,
Would for a given Soule give something too.
At Court your fellowes every day,
Give th'art of Riming, Huntsmanship, or Play,
For them which were their owne before;
Onely I have nothing which gave more,
But am, alas, by being lowly, lower.

I aske no dispensation now
To falsifie a teare, or sigh, or vow,
I do not sue from thee to draw
A *non obstante* on natures law,
These are prerogatives, they inhere
In thee and thine; none should forsweare
Except that hee *Loves* minion were.

Give mee thy weaknesse, make mee blinde,
Both wayes, as thou and thine, in eies and minde;
Love, let me never know that this
Is love, or, that love childish is.
Let me not know that others know
That she knowes my paines, lest that so
A tender shame make me mine owne new woe.

If thou give nothing, yet thou'art just,
Because I would not thy first motions trust;
Small townes which stand stiffe, till great shot
Enforce them, by warres law *condition* not.
Such in loves warfare is my case,
I may not article for grace,
Having put Love at last to shew this face.

This face, by which he could command
And change the Idolatrie of any land,
This face, which wheresoe'r it comes,
Can call vow'd men from cloisters, dead from tombes,
And melt both Poles at once, and store
Deserts with cities, and make more
Mynes in the earth, than Quarries were before.

For this, Love is enrag'd with mee,
Yet kills not. If I must example bee
To future Rebells; If th'unborne
Must learne, by my being cut up, and torne:
Kill, and dissect me, Love; for this
Torture against thine owne end is,
Rack't carcasses make ill Anatomies.

CONFINED LOVE

SOME man unworthy to be possessor
Of old or new love, himselfe being false or weake,
    Thought his paine and shame would be lesser,
If on womankind he might his anger wreake,
            And thence a law did grow,
            One might but one man know;
            But are other creatures so?

Are Sunne, Moone, or Starres by law forbidden,
To smile where they list, or lend away their light?
   Are birds divorc'd, or are they chidden
If they leave their mate, or lie abroad a-night?
         Beasts doe no joyntures lose
         Though they new lovers choose,
         But we are made worse than those.

   Who e'r rigg'd faire ship to lie in harbors,
And not to seeke new lands, or not to deale withall?
   Or built faire houses, set trees, and arbors,
Only to lock up, or else to let them fall?
         Good is not good, unlesse
         A thousand it possesse,
         But doth wast with greedinesse.

THE DREAME

DEARE love, for nothing lesse than thee
Would I have broke this happy dreame,
         It was a theame
For reason, much too strong for phantasie,
Therefore thou wakd'st me wisely; yet
My Dreame thou brok'st not, but continued'st it,
Thou art so truth, that thoughts of thee suffice,
To make dreames truths; and fables histories;
Enter these armes, for since thou thoughtst it best,
Not to dreame all my dreame, let's act the rest.

As lightning, or a Tapers light,
Thine eyes, and not thy noise wak'd mee;
         Yet I thought thee
(For thou lovest truth) an Angell, at first sight,
But when I saw thou sawest my heart,
And knew'st my thoughts, beyond an Angels art,
When thou knew'st what I dreamt, when thou knew'st when
Excesse of joy would wake me, and cam'st then,
I must confesse, it could not chuse but bee
Prophane, to thinke thee any thing but thee.

Comming and staying show'd thee, thee,
But rising makes me doubt, that now,
            Thou art not thou.
That love is weake, where feare's as strong as hee;
'Tis not all spirit, pure, and brave,
If mixture it of *Feare, Shame, Honor*, have.
Perchance as torches which must ready bee,
Men light and put out, so thou deal'st with mee,
Thou cam'st to kindle, goest to come; Then I
Will dreame that hope againe, but else would die.

A VALEDICTION: OF WEEPING

            L E T me powre forth
My teares before thy face, whil'st I stay here,
For thy face coines them, and thy stampe they beare,
And by this Mintage they are something worth,
            For thus they bee
            Pregnant of thee;
Fruits of much griefe they are, emblemes of more,
When a teare falls, that thou falls which it bore,
So thou and I are nothing then, when on a divers shore.
            On a round ball
A workeman that hath copies by, can lay
An Europe, Afrique, and an Asia,
And quickly make that, which was nothing, *All*,
            So doth each teare,
            Which thee doth weare,
A globe, yea world by that impression grow,
Till thy teares mixt with mine doe overflow
This world, by waters sent from thee, my heaven dissolved so.
            O more than Moone,
Draw not up seas to drowne me in thy spheare,
Weepe me not dead, in thine armes, but forbeare
To teach the sea, what it may doe too soone;
            Let not the winde
            Example finde,
To doe me more harme, than it purposeth;
Since thou and I sigh one anothers breath,
Who e'r sighes most, is cruellest, and hastes the others death.

LOVES ALCHYMIE

S O M E that have deeper digg'd loves Myne than I,
Say, where his centrique happinesse doth lie:
    I have lov'd, and got, and told,
But should I love, get, tell, till I were old,
I should not finde that hidden mysterie;
    Oh, 'tis imposture all:
And as no chymique yet th'Elixar got,
    But glorifies his pregnant pot,
    If by the way to him befall
Some odoriferous thing, or medicinall,
   So, lovers dreame a rich and long delight,
   But get a winter-seeming summers night.

Our ease, our thrift, our honor, and our day,
Shall we, for this vaine Bubles shadow pay?
    Ends love in this, that my man,
Can be as happy'as I can; If he can
Endure the short scorne of a Bridegroomes play?
    That loving wretch that sweares,
'Tis not the bodies marry, but the mindes,
    Which he in her Angelique findes,
   Would sweare as justly, that he heares,
In that dayes rude hoarse minstralsey, the spheares.
   Hope not for minde in women; at their best
   Sweetnesse and wit, they'are but *Mummy*, possest.

THE FLEA

M A R K E but this flea, and marke in this,
How little that which thou deny'st me is;
    It suck'd me first, and now sucks thee,
And in this flea, our two bloods mingled bee;
Thou know'st that this cannot be said
A sinne, nor shame, nor losse of maidenhead,
    Yet this enjoyes before it wooe,
   And pamper'd swells with one blood made of two,
   And this, alas, is more than wee would doe.

Oh stay, three lives in one flea spare,
Where wee almost, yea more than maryed are.
This flea is you and I, and this
Our mariage bed, and mariage temple is;
Though parents grudge, and you, w'are met,
And cloysterd in these living walls of Jet.
   Though use make you apt to kill mee,
    Let not to that, selfe murder added bee,
    And sacrilege, three sinnes in killing three.

Cruell and sodaine, hast thou since
Purpled thy naile, in blood of innocence?
Wherein could this flea guilty bee,
Except in that drop which it suckt from thee?
Yet thou triumph'st, and saist that thou
Find'st not thy selfe, nor mee the weaker now;
   'Tis true, then learne how false, feares bee;
    Just so much honor, when thou yeeld'st to mee,
    Will wast, as this flea's death tooke life from thee.

THE CURSE

W H O ever guesses, thinks, or dreames he knowes
Who is my mistris, wither by this curse;
   His only, and only his purse
   May some dull heart to love dispose,
And shee yeeld then to all that are his foes;
  May he be scorn'd by one, whom all else scorne,
  Forsweare to others, what to her he'hath sworne,
  With feare of missing, shame of getting, torne:

Madnesse his sorrow, gout his cramp, may hee
Make, by but thinking, who hath made him such:
   And may he feele no touch
   Of conscience, but of fame, and bee
Anguish'd, not that'twas sinne, but that'twas shee:
  In early and long scarcenesse may he rot,
  For land which had been his, if he had not
  Himselfe incestuously an heire begot:

May he dreame Treason, and beleeve, that hee
Meant to performe it, and confesse, and die,
    And no record tell why:
        His sonnes, which none of his may bee,
Inherite nothing but his infamie:
    Or may he so long Parasites have fed,
    That he would faine be theirs, whom he hath bred,
    And at the last be circumcis'd for bread:

The venom of all stepdames, gamsters gall,
What Tyrans, and their subjects interwish,
        What Plants, Myne, Beasts, Foule, Fish,
        Can contribute, all ill which all
Prophets, or Poets spake; And all which shall
    Be annex'd in schedules unto this by mee,
    Fall on that man; For if it be a shee
    Nature beforehand hath out-cursed mee.

THE MESSAGE

SEND home my long strayd eyes to mee,
    Which (Oh) too long have dwelt on thee;
    Yet since there they have learn'd such ill,
        Such forc'd fashions,
        And false passions,
            That they be
            Made by thee
    Fit for no good sight, keep them still.

Send home my harmlesse heart againe,
    Which no unworthy thought could staine;
    But if it be taught by thine
        To make jestings
        Of protestings,
            And crosse both
            Word and oath,
    Keepe it, for then 'tis none of mine.

Yet send me back my heart and eyes,
    That I may know, and see thy lyes,

And may laugh and joy, when thou
　　　　Art in anguish
　　　　And dost languish
　　　　　　For some one
　　　　　　That will none,
Or prove as false as thou art now.

A NOCTURNALL UPON S. LUCIES DAY,

Being the Shortest Day

TIS the yeares midnight, and it is the dayes,
Lucies, who scarce seaven houres herself unmaskes,
　　The Sunne is spent, and now his flasks
　　Send forth light squibs, no constant rayes;
　　　　The worlds whole sap is sunke:
The generall balme th'hydroptique earth hath drunk,
Whither, as to the beds-feet, life is shrunke,
Dead and enterr'd; yet all these seeme to laugh,
Compar'd with mee, who am their Epitaph.

Study me then, you who shall lovers bee
At the next world, that is, at the next Spring:
　　For I am every dead thing,
　　In whom love wrought new Alchimie.
　　　　For his art did expresse
A quintessence even from nothingnesse,
From dull privations, and leane emptinesse:
He ruin'd mee, and I am re-begot
Of absence, darknesse, death; things which are not.

All others, from all things, draw all that's good,
Life, soule, forme, spirit, whence they beeing have;
　　I, by loves limbecke, am the grave
　　Of all, that's nothing. Oft a flood
　　　　Have wee two wept, and so
Drownd the whole world, us two; oft did we grow
To be two Chaosses, when we did show
Care to ought else; and often absences
Withdrew our soules, and made us carcasses.

But I am by her death, (which word wrongs her)
Of the first nothing, the Elixer grown;
    Were I a man, that I were one,
    I needs must know; I should preferre,
       If I were any beast,
Some ends, some means; Yea plants, yea stones detest,
And love; All, all some properties invest;
If I an ordinary nothing were,
As shadow, a light, and body must be here.

But I am None; nor will my Sunne renew.
You lovers, for whose sake, the lesser Sunne
    At this time to the Goat is runne
    To fetch new lust, and give it you,
       Enjoy your summer all;
Since shee enjoyes her long nights festivall,
Let mee prepare towards her, and let mee call
This houre her Vigill, and her Eve, since this
Both the yeares, and the dayes deep midnight is.

WITCHCRAFT BY A PICTURE

    I FIXE mine eye on thine, and there
      Pitty my picture burning in thine eye,
    My picture drown'd in a transparent teare,
      When I looke lower I espie;
        Hadst thou the wicked skill
    By pictures made and mard, to kill,
How many wayes mightst thou performe thy will?

    But now I have drunke thy sweet salt teares,
      And though thou poure more I'll depart;
    My picture vanish'd, vanish feares,
      That I can be endamag'd by that art;
        Though thou retaine of mee
    One picture more, yet that will bee,
Being in thine owne heart, from all malice free.

THE BAITE

    COME live with mee, and bee my love,
    And wee will some new pleasures prove

Of golden sands, and christall brookes,
With silken lines, and silver hookes.

There will the river whispering runne
Warm'd by thy eyes, more than the Sunne.
And there the'inamor'd fish will stay,
Begging themselves they may betray.

When thou wilt swimme in that live bath,
Each fish, which every channell hath,
Will amorously to thee swimme,
Gladder to catch thee, than thou him.

If thou, to be so seene, beest loath,
By Sunne, or Moone, thou darknest both,
And if my selfe have leave to see,
I need not their light, having thee.

Let others freeze with angling reeds,
And cut their legges, with shells and weeds,
Or treacherously poore fish beset,
With strangling snare, or windowie net:

Let coarse bold hands, from slimy nest
The bedded fish in banks out-wrest,
Or curious traitors, sleavesilke flies
Bewitch poore fishes wandring eyes.

For thee, thou needst no such deceit,
For thou thy selfe art thine owne bait;
That fish, that is not catch'd thereby,
Alas, is wiser farre than I.

THE APPARITION

WHEN by thy scorne, O murdresse, I am dead,
And that thou thinkst thee free
From all solicitation from mee,
Then shall my ghost come to thy bed,
And thee, fain'd vestall, in worse armes shall see;
Then thy sicke taper will begin to winke,

And he, whose thou art then, being tyr'd before,
Will, if thou stirre, or pinch to wake him, thinke
         Thou call'st for more,
And in false sleepe will from thee shrinke,
And then poore Aspen wretch, neglected thou
Bath'd in a cold quicksilver sweat wilt lye
         A veryer ghost than I;
What I will say, I will not tell thee now,
Lest that preserve thee; and since my love is spent,
I'had rather thou shouldst painfully repent,
Than by my threatnings rest still innocent.

THE BROKEN HEART

H E is starke mad, who ever sayes,
     That he hath been in love an houre,
Yet not that love so soone decayes,
     But that it can tenne in lesse space devour;
Who will beleeve mee, if I sweare
That I have had the plague a yeare?
     Who would not laugh at mee, if I should say,
     I saw a flaske of *powder burne a day?*

Ah, what a trifle is a heart,
     If once into loves hands it come!
All other griefes allow a part
     To other griefes, and aske themselves but some;
They come to us, but us Love draws,
Hee swallows us, and never chawes:
     By him, as by chain'd shot, whole rankes doe dye,
     He is the tyran Pike, our hearts the Frye.

If 'twere not so, what did become
     Of my heart, when I first saw thee?
I brought a heart into the roome,
     But from the roome, I carried none with mee:
If it had gone to thee, I know
Mine would have taught thine heart to show
     More pitty unto mee: but Love, alas,
     At one first blow did shiver it as glasse.

Yet nothing can to nothing fall,
   Nor any place be empty quite,
Therefore I thinke my breast hath all
   Those peeces still, though they be not unite;
And now as broken glasses show
A hundred lesser faces, so
   My ragges of heart can like, wish, and adore,
   But after one such love, can love no more.

A VALEDICTION: FORBIDDING MOURNING

As virtuous men passe mildly away,
   And whisper to their soules, to goe,
Whilst some of their sad friends doe say,
   The breath goes now, and some say, no:

So let us melt, and make no noise,
   No teare-floods, nor sigh-tempests move,
T'were prophanation of our joyes
   To tell the layetie our love.

Moving of th'earth brings harmes and feares,
   Men reckon what it did and meant,
But trepidation of the spheares,
   Though greater farre, is innocent.

Dull sublunary lovers love
   (Whose soule is sense) cannot admit
Absence, because it doth remove
   Those things which elemented it.

But we by a love, so much refin'd,
   That our selves know not what it is,
Inter-assured of the mind,
   Care lesse, eyes, lips, and hands to misse.

Our two soules therefore, which are one,
   Though I must goe, endure not yet
A breach, but an expansion,
   Like gold to ayery thinnesse beate.

If they be two, they are two so
　　As stiffe twin compasses are two,
Thy soule the fixt foot, makes no show
　　To move, but doth, if th' other doe.

And though it in the center sit,
　　Yet when the other far doth rome,
It leanes, and hearkens after it,
　　And growes erect, as that comes home.

Such wilt thou be to mee, who must
　　Like th'other foot, obliquely runne;
Thy firmnes drawes my circle just,
　　And makes me end, where I begunne.

THE EXTASIE

W H E R E, like a pillow on a bed,
　　A Pregnant banke swel'd up, to rest
The violets reclining head,
　　Sat we two, one anothers best.
Our hands were firmely cimented
　　With a fast balme, which thence did spring,
Our eye-beames twisted, and did thred
　　Our eyes, upon one double string;
So to'entergraft our hands, as yet
　　Was all the meanes to make us one,
And pictures in our eyes to get
　　Was all our propagation.
As 'twixt two equall Armies, Fate
　　Suspends uncertaine victorie,
Our soules, (which to advance their state,
　　Were gone out,) hung 'twixt her, and mee.
And whil'st our soules negotiate there,
　　Wee like sepulchrall statues lay;
All day, the same our postures were,
　　And wee said nothing, all the day.
If any, so by love refin'd,
　　That he soules language understood,
And by good love were growen all minde,
　　Within convenient distance stood,

He (though he knew not which soul spake,
  Because both meant, both spake the same)
Might thence a new concoction take,
  And part farre purer than he came.
This Extasie doth unperplex
  (We said) and tell us what we love,
Wee see by this, it was not sexe,
  Wee see, we saw not what did move:
But as all severall soules containe
  Mixture of things, they know not what,
Love, these mixt soules, doth mixe againe,
  And makes both one, each this and that.
A single violet transplant,
  The strength, the colour, and the size,
(All which before was poore, and scant,)
  Redoubles still, and multiplies.
When love, with one another so
  Interinanimates two soules,
That abler soule, which thence doth flow,
  Defects of lonelinesse controules.
Wee then, who are this new soule, know,
  Of what we are compos'd, and made,
For, th'Atomies of which we grow,
  Are soules, whom no change can invade.
But O alas, so long, so farre
  Our bodies why doe wee forbeare?
They are ours, though they are not wee, Wee are
  The intelligences, they the spheares.
We owe them thankes, because they thus,
  Did us, to us, at first convay,
Yeelded their forces, sense, to us,
  Nor are drosse to us, but allay.
On man heavens influence workes not so,
  But that it first imprints the ayre,
Soe soule into the soule may flow,
  Though it to body first repaire.
As our blood labours to beget
  Spirits, as like soules as it can,
Because such fingers need to knit
  That subtile knot, which makes us man:

So must pure lovers soules descend
  T'affections, and to faculties,
Which sense may reach and apprehend,
  Else a great Prince in prison lies.
To'our bodies turne wee then, that so
  Weake men on love reveal'd may looke;
Loves mysteries in soules doe grow,
  But yet the body is his booke.
And if some lover, such as wee,
  Have heard this dialogue of one,
Let him still marke us, he shall see
  Small change, when we'are to bodies gone.

LOVES DEITIE

I LONG to talke with some old lovers ghost,
  Who dyed before the god of Love was borne:
I cannot thinke that hee, who then lov'd most,
  Sunke so low, as to love one which did scorne.
But since this god produc'd a destinie,
And that vice-nature, custome, lets it be;
  I must love her, that loves not mee.

Sure, they which made him god, meant not so much,
  Nor he, in his young godhead practis'd it.
But when an even flame two hearts did touch,
  His office was indulgently to fit
Actives to passives. Correspondencie
Only his subject was; It cannot bee
  Love, till I love her, that loves mee.

But every moderne god will now extend
  His vast prerogative, as far as Jove.
To rage, to lust, to write to, to commend,
  All is the purlewe of the God of Love.
Oh were wee wak'ned by this Tyrannie
To ungod this child againe, it could not bee
  I should love her, who loves not mee.

Rebell and Atheist too, why murmure I,
  As though I felt the worst that love could doe?

Love might make me leave loving, or might trie
  A deeper plague, to make her love mee too,
Which, since she loves before, I'am loth to see;
Falshood is worse than hate; and that must bee,
  If shee whom I love, should love mee.

LOVES DIET

T O what a combersome unwieldinesse
And burdenous corpulence my love had growne,
  But that I did, to make it lesse,
  And keepe it in proportion,
Give it a diet, made it feed upon
That which love worst endures, *discretion*.

Above one sigh a day I'allow'd him not,
Of which my fortune, and my faults had part;
  And if sometimes by stealth he got
  A she sigh from my mistresse heart,
And thought to feast on that, I let him see
'Twas neither very sound, nor meant to mee.

If he wroung from mee'a teare, I brin'd it so
With scorne or shame, that him it nourish'd not;
  If he suck'd hers, I let him know
  'Twas not a teare, which hee had got,
His drinke was counterfeit, as was his meat;
For, eyes which rowle towards all, weepe not, but sweat.

What ever he would dictate, I writ that,
But burnt my letters; When she writ to me,
  And that that favour made him fat,
  I said, if any title bee
Convey'd by this, Ah, what doth it availe,
To be the fortieth name in an entaile?

Thus I reclaim'd my buzard love, to flye
At what, and when, and how, and where I chuse;
  Now negligent of sport I lye,
  And now as other Fawkners use,
I spring a mistresse, sweare, write, sigh and weepe:
And the game kill'd, or lost, goe talke, and sleepe.

THE WILL

B E F O R E I sigh my last gaspe, let me breath,
Great love, some Legacies; Here I bequeath
Mine eyes to *Argus*, if mine eyes can see,
If they be blinde, then Love, I give them thee;
My tongue to Fame; to'Embassadours mine eares;
    To women or the sea, my teares.
Thou, Love, hast taught mee heretofore
By making mee serve her who'had twenty more,
That I should give to none, but such, as had too much
    before.

My constancie I to the planets give;
My truth to them, who at the Court doe live;
Mine ingenuity and opennesse,
To Jesuites; to Buffones my pensivenesse;
My silence to'any, who abroad hath beene;
    My mony to a Capuchin.
Thou Love taught'st me, by appointing mee
To love there, where no love receiv'd çan be,
Onely to give to such as have an incapacitie.

My faith I give to Roman Catholiques;
All my good works unto the Schismaticks
Of Amsterdam: my best civility
And Courtship, to an Universitie;
My modesty I give to souldiers bare;
    My patience let gamesters share.
Thou Love taughtst mee, by making mee
Love her that holds my love disparity,
Onely to give to those that count my gifts indignity.

I give my reputation to those
Which were my friends; Mine industrie to foes;
To Schoolemen I bequeath my doubtfulnesse;
My sicknesse to Physitians, or excesse;
To Nature, all that I in Ryme have writ;
    And to my company my wit.

Thou Love, by making mee adore
Her, who begot this love in mee before,
Taughtst me to make, as though I gave, when I did but
  restore.

To him for whom the passing bell next tolls,
I give my physick bookes; my writen rowles
Of Morall counsels, I to Bedlam give;
My brazen medals, unto them which live
In want of bread; To them which passe among
  All forrainers, mine English tongue.
Thou, Love, by making mee love one
Who thinkes her friendship a fit portion
For yonger lovers, dost my gifts thus disproportion.

Therefore I'll give no more; But I'll undoe
The world by dying; because love dies too.
Then all your beauties will be no more worth
Than gold in Mines, where none doth draw it forth;
And all your graces no more use shall have
  Than a Sun dyall in a grave.
Thou Love taughtst mee, by making mee
Love her, who doth neglect both mee and thee,
To'invent, and practise this one way, to'annihilate all
  three.

THE FUNERALL

W H O ever comes to shroud me, do not harme
  Nor question much
That subtile wreath of haire, which crowns my arme;
The mystery, the signe you must not touch,
  For'tis my outward Soule,
Viceroy to that, which then to heaven being gone,
  Will leave this to controule,
And keep these limbes, her Provinces, from dissolution.

For if the sinewie thread my braine lets fall
  Through every part,
Can tye those parts, and make mee one of all;

These haires which upward grew, and strength and art
    Have from a better braine,
Can better do'it; Except she meant that I
    By this should know my pain,
As prisoners then are manacled, when they'are condemn'd
    to die.

What ere shee meant by'it, bury it with me,
    For since I am
Loves martyr, it might breed idolatrie,
If into others hands these Reliques came;
    As'twas humility
To afford to it all that a Soule can doe,
    So,'tis some bravery,
That since you would save none of mee, I bury some of you

THE BLOSSOME

LITTLE think'st thou, poore flower,
    Whom I have watch'd sixe or seaven dayes,
And seene thy birth, and seene what every houre
Gave to thy growth, thee to this height to raise,
And now dost laugh and triumph on this bough,
    Little think'st thou
That it will freeze anon, and that I shall
To morrow finde thee falne, or not at all.

    Little think'st thou poore heart
    That labour'st yet to nestle thee,
And think'st by hovering here to get a part
In a forbidden or forbidding tree,
And hop'st her stiffenesse by long siege to bow:
    Little think'st thou,
That thou to morrow, ere that Sunne doth wake,
Must with this Sunne, and mee a journey take.

    But thou which lov'st to bee
    Subtile to plague thy selfe, wilt say,
Alas, if you must goe, what's that to mee?
Here lyes my businesse, and here I will stay:

You goe to friends, whose love and meanes present
        Various content
To your eyes, eares, and tongue, and every part.
If then your body goe, what need you a heart?

    Well then, stay here; but know,
        When thou hast stayd and done thy most;
    A naked thinking heart, that makes no show,
    Is to a woman, but a kinde of Ghost;
    How shall shee know my heart; or having none,
            Know thee for one?
    Practise may make her know some other part,
    But take my word, shee doth not know a Heart.

    Meet mee at London, then,
        Twenty dayes hence, and thou shalt see
    Mee fresher, and more fat, by being with men,
    Than if I had staid still with her and thee.
    For Gods sake, if you can, be you so too:
            I would give you
    There, to another friend, whom wee shall finde
    As glad to have my body, as my minde.

THE PRIMROSE, BEING AT MONTGOMERY CASTLE, UPON THE HILL, ON WHICH IT IS SITUATE

        UPON this Primrose hill,
            Where, if Heav'n would distill
        A shoure of raine, each severall drop might goe
        To his owne primrose, and grow Manna so;
        And where their forme, and their infinitie
            Make a terrestriall Galaxie,
            As the small starres doe in the skie:
        I walke to finde a true Love; and I see
        That'tis not a mere woman, that is shee,
        But must, or more, or lesse than woman bee.

            Yet know I not, which flower
            I wish; a sixe, or foure;

For should my true-Love lesse than woman bee,
She were scarce any thing; and then, should she
Be more than woman, shee would get above
          All thought of sexe, and thinke to move
          My heart to study her, and not to love;
Both these were monsters; Since there must reside
Falshood in woman, I could more abide,
She were by art, than Nature falsify'd.

          Live Primrose then, and thrive
          With thy true number five;
And women, whom this flower doth represent,
With this mysterious number be content;
Ten is the farthest number; if halfe ten
          Belonge unto each woman, then
          Each woman may take halfe us men;
Or if this will not serve their turne, Since all
Numbers are odde, or even, and they fall
First into this, five, women may take us all.

                THE RELIQUE

          WHEN my grave is broke up againe
          Some second ghest to entertaine,
          (For graves have learn'd that woman-head
          To be to more than one a Bed)
          And he that digs it, spies
A bracelet of bright haire about the bone,
          Will he not let'us alone,
And thinke that there a loving couple lies,
Who thought that this device might be some way
To make their soules, at the last busie day,
Meet at this grave, and make a little stay?

          If this fall in a time, or land,
          Where mis-devotion doth command,
          Then, he that digges us up, will bring
          Us, to the Bishop, and the King,
          To make us Reliques; then
Thou shalt be a Mary Magdalen, and I
          A something else thereby;

All women shall adore us, and some men;
And since at such time, miracles are sought,
I would have that age by this paper taught
What miracles wee harmlesse lovers wrought.

First, we lov'd well and faithfully,
Yet knew not what wee lov'd, nor why,
Difference of sex no more wee knew,
Than our Guardian Angells doe;
Comming and going, wee
Perchance might kisse, but not between those meales;
Our hands ne'r toucht the seales,
Which nature, injur'd by late law, sets free:
These miracles wee did; but now alas,
All measure, and all language, I should passe,
Should I tell what a miracle shee was.

THE DAMPE

WHEN I am dead, and Doctors know not why,
And my friends curiositie
Will have me cut up to survay each part,
When they shall finde your Picture in my heart,
You thinke a sodaine dampe of love
Will through all their senses move,
And worke on them as mee, and so preferre
Your murder, to the name of Massacre.

Poore victories! But if you dare be brave,
And pleasure in your conquest have,
First kill th'enormous Gyant, your *Disdaine*,
And let th'enchantresse *Honor*, next be slaine,
And like a Goth and Vandall rize,
Deface Records, and Histories
Of your owne arts and triumphs over men,
And without such advantage kill me then.

For I could muster up as well as you
My Gyants, and my Witches too,
Which are vast *Constancy*, and *Secretnesse*,

But these I neyther looke for, nor professe;
      Kill mee as Woman, let mee die
      As a meere man; doe you but try
Your passive valor, and you shall finde then,
Naked you'have odds enough of any man.

THE DISSOLUTION

SHEE is dead; And all which die
      To their first Elements resolve;
And wee were mutuall Elements to us,
      And made of one another.
My body then doth hers involve,
And those things whereof I consist, hereby
In me abundant grow, and burdenous,
      And nourish not, but smother.
My fire of Passion, sighes of ayre,
Water of teares, and earthly sad despaire,
      Which my materialls bee,
But neere worne out by loves securitie,
Shee, to my losse, both by her death repaire,
      And I might live long wretched so
But that my fire doth with my fuell grow.
      Now as those Active Kings
      Whose foraine conquest treasure brings,
Receive more, and spend more, and soonest breake:
This (which I am amaz'd that I can speake)
      This death, hath with my store
      My use encreas'd.
And so my soule more earnestly releas'd,
Will outstrip hers; As bullets flowen before
A latter bullet may o'rtake, the pouder being more.

A JEAT RING SENT

THOU are not so black, as my heart,
Nor halfe so brittle, as her heart, thou art;
What would'st thou say? shall both our properties by thee
      bee spoke?
Nothing more endlesse, nothing sooner broke?

Marriage rings are not of this stuffe;
　Oh, why should ought lesse precious, or lesse tough
Figure our loves? Except in thy name thou have bid it say,
　I'am cheap, and nought but fashion, fling me'away.

　Yet stay with mee since thou art come,
　Circle this fingers top, which did'st her thombe.
Be justly proud, and gladly safe, that thou dost dwell with
　　me,
　She that, Oh, broke her faith, would soon breake thee.

NEGATIVE LOVE

I NEVER stoop'd so low, as they
Which on an eye, cheeke, lip, can prey,
　Seldome to them, which soare no higher
　Than vertue or the minde to'admire,
For sense, and understanding may
　Know, what gives fuell to their fire:
My love, though silly, is more brave,
For may I misse, when ere I crave,
If I know yet, what I would have.

If that be simply perfectest
Which can by no way be exprest
　But *Negatives*, my love is so.
　To All, which all love, I say no.
If any who deciphers best,
　What we know not, our selves, can know,
Let him teach mee that nothing; This
As yet my ease, and comfort is,
Though I speed not, I cannot misse.

THE PROHIBITION

　TAKE heed of loving mee,
At least remember, I forbade it thee;
Not that I shall repaire my'unthrifty wast
Of Breath and Blood, upon thy sighes, and teares,

By being to thee then what to me thou wast;
But, so great Joy, our life at once outweares,
Then, lest thy love, by my death, frustrate bee,
If thou love mee, take heed of loving mee.

     Take heed of hating mee,
Or too much triumph in the Victorie.
Not that I shall be mine owne officer,
And hate with hate againe retaliate;
But thou wilt lose the stile of conquerour,
If I, thy conquest, perish by thy hate.
Then, lest my being nothing lessen thee,
If thou hate mee, take heed of hating mee.

     Yet, love and hate mee too,
So, these extreames shall neithers office doe;
Love mee, that I may die the gentler way;
Hate mee, because thy love is too great for mee;
Or let these two, themselves, not me decay;
So shall I, live, thy Stage, not triumph bee;
Lest thou thy love and hate and mee undoe,
To let mee live, O love and hate mee too.

THE EXPIRATION

s o, so, breake off this last lamenting kisse,
   Which sucks two soules, and vapors Both away,
Turne thou ghost that way, and let mee turne this,
   And let our selves benight our happiest day,
We ask'd none leave to love; nor will we owe
   Any, so cheape a death, as saying, Goe;

Goe; and if that word have not quite kil'd thee,
   Ease mee with death, by bidding mee goe too.
Oh, if it have, let my word worke on mee,
   And a just office on a murderer doe.
Except it be too late, to kill me so,
   Being double dead, going, and bidding, goe.

THE COMPUTATION

F O R the first twenty yeares, since yesterday,
   I scarce beleev'd, thou could'st be gone away,
For forty more, I fed on favours past,
   And forty'on hopes, that thou would'st, they might last.
Teares drown'd one hundred, and sighes blew out two,
   A thousand, I did neither thinke, nor doe,
   Or not divide, all being one thought of you;
   Or in a thousand more, forgot that too.
Yet call not this long life; But thinke that I
Am, by being dead, Immortall; Can ghosts die?

THE PARADOX

N O Lover saith, I love, nor any other
    Can judge a perfect Lover;
Hee thinkes that else none can, nor will agree
    That any loves but hee:
I cannot say I lov'd, for who can say
    Hee was kill'd yesterday?
Love with excesse of heat, more yong than old,
    Death kills with too much cold;
Wee dye but once, and who lov'd last did die,
    Hee that saith twice, doth lye:
For though hee seeme to move, and stirre a while,
    It doth the sense beguile.
Such life is like the light which bideth yet
    When the lights life is set,
Or like the heat, which fire in solid matter
    Leaves behinde, two houres after.
Once I lov'd and dy'd; and am now become
    Mine Epitaph and Tombe.
Here dead men speake their last, and so do I;
    Love-slaine, loe, here I lye.

FAREWELL TO LOVE

WHILST yet to prove,
I thought there was some Deitie in love
  So did I reverence, and gave
Worship; as Atheists at their dying houre
Call, what they cannot name, an unknowne power,
  As ignorantly did I crave:
     Thus when
Things not yet knowne are coveted by men,
  Our desires give them fashion, and so
As they waxe lesser, fall, as they sise, grow.

    But, from late faire
His highnesse sitting in a golden Chaire,
  Is not lesse cared for after three dayes
By children, than the thing which lovers so
Blindly admire, and with such worship wooe;
  Being had, enjoying it decayes:
     And thence,
What before pleas'd them all, takes but one sense,
  And that so lamely, as it leaves behinde
A kinde of sorrowing dulnesse to the minde.

    Ah cannot wee,
As well as Cocks and Lyons jocund be,
  After such pleasures? Unlesse wise
Nature decreed (since each such Act, they say,
Diminisheth the length of life a day)
  This, as shee would man should despise
     The sport,
Because that other curse of being short,
  And onely for a minute made to be
Eager desire, to raise posterity.

    Since so, my minde
Shall not desire what no man else can finde,
  I'll no more dote and runne
To pursue things which had indammag'd me.
And when I come where moving beauties be,

As men doe when the summers Sunne
    Growes great,
Though I admire their greatnesse, shun their heat;
    Each place can afford shadowes. If all faile,
'Tis but applying worme-seed to the Taile.

A LECTURE UPON THE SHADOW

STAND still, and I will read to thee
A Lecture, love, in Loves philosophy.
    These three houres that we have spent,
    Walking here, Two shadowes went
Along with us, which we our selves produc'd;
But, now the Sunne is just above our head,
    We doe those shadowes tread;
    And to brave clearnesse all things are reduc'd.
So whilst our infant loves did grow,
Disguises did, and shadowes, flow,
From us, and our cares; but, now 'tis not so.

That love hath not attain'd the high'st degree,
Which is still diligent lest others see.

Except our loves at this noone stay,
We shall new shadowes make the other way.
    As the first were made to blinde
    Others; these which come behinde
Will worke upon our selves, and blind our eyes.
If our loves faint, and westwardly decline;
    To me thou, falsely, thine,
    And I to thee mine actions shall disguise.
The morning shadowes weare away,
But these grow longer all the day,
But oh, loves day is short, if love decay.

Love is a growing, or full constant light;
And his first minute, after noone, is night.

SONNET. THE TOKEN

S E N D me some token, that my hope may live,
  Or that my easelesse thoughts may sleep and rest;
Send me some honey to make sweet my hive,
  That in my passion I may hope the best.
I beg noe ribbond wrought with thine owne hands,
  To knit our loves in the fantastick straine
Of new-toucht youth; nor Ring to shew the stands
  Of our affection, that as that's round and plaine,
So should our loves meet in simplicity.
  No, nor the Coralls which thy wrist infold,
Lac'd up together in congruity,
  To shew our thoughts should rest in the same hold;
No, nor thy picture, though most gracious,
  And most desir'd, because best like the best;
Nor witty Lines, which are most copious,
  Within the Writings which thou hast addrest.

Send me nor this, nor that, t'increase my store,
But swear thou thinkst I love thee, and no more.

SELFE LOVE

H E that cannot chuse but love,
  And strives against it still,
Never shall my fancy move;
  For he loves 'gaynst his will;
Nor he which is all his own,
  And can att pleasure chuse,
When I am caught he can be gone,
  And when he list refuse.
Nor he that loves none but faire,
  For such by all are sought;
Nor he that can for foul ones care,
  For his Judgement then is nought:
Nor he that hath wit, for he
  Will make me his jest or slave;
Nor a fool, for when others . . .,
  He can neither . . .

Nor he that still his Mistresse payes,
For she is thrall'd therefore:
Nor he that payes not, for he sayes
Within, shee's worth no more.
Is there then no kinde of men
Whom I may freely prove?
I will vent that humour then
In mine own selfe love.

Epigrams

HERO AND LEANDER

BOTH rob'd of aire, we both lye in one ground,
Both whom one fire had burnt, one water drownd.

PYRAMUS AND THISBE

TWO, by themselves, each other, love and feare
Slaine, cruell friends, by parting have joyn'd here.

NIOBE

BY childrens births, and death, I am become
So dry, that I am now mine owne sad tombe.

A BURNT SHIP

OUT of a fired ship, which, by no way
But drowning, could be rescued from the flame,
Some men leap'd forth, and ever as they came
Neere the foes ships, did by their shot decay;
So all were lost, which in the ship were found,
    They in the sea being burnt, they in the burnt
        ship drown'd.

FALL OF A WALL

UNDER an undermin'd, and shot-bruis'd wall
A too-bold Captaine perish'd by the fall,
Whose brave misfortune, happiest men envi'd,
That had a towne for tombe, his bones to hide.

A LAME BEGGAR

I AM unable, yonder beggar cries,
To stand, or move; if he say true, hee *lies*.

CALES AND GUYANA

I F you from spoyle of th'old worlds farthest end
To the new world your kindled valors bend,
What brave examples then do prove it trew
That one things end doth still beginne a new.

SIR JOHN WINGEFIELD

BEYOND th'old Pillers many have travailed
Towards the Suns cradle, and his throne, and bed.
A fitter Piller our Earle did bestow
In that late Island; for he well did know
Farther than Wingefield no man dares to goe.

A SELFE ACCUSER

YOUR mistris, that you follow whores, still taxeth you:
'Tis strange that she should thus confesse it, though'it be **true**.

A LICENTIOUS PERSON

THY sinnes and haires may no man equall call,
For, as thy sinnes increase, thy haires doe fall.

ANTIQUARY

I F in his Studie he hath so much care
To'hang all old strange things, let his wife beware.

DISINHERITED

T H Y father all from thee, by his last Will,
Gave to the poore; Thou hast good title still.

PHRYNE

T H Y flattering picture, *Phryne,* is like thee,
Onely in this, that you both painted be.

AN OBSCURE WRITER

P H I L O, with twelve yeares study, hath beene griev'd
To be understood; when will hee be beleev'd?

KLOCKIUS

K L O C K I U S so deeply hath sworn, ne'r more to come
In bawdie house, that hee dares not goe home.

RADERUS

W H Y this man gelded *Martiall* I muse,
Except himselfe alone his tricks would use,
As *Katherine,* for the Courts sake, put downe Stewes.

MERCURIUS GALLO-BELGICUS

L I K E *Esops* fellow-slaves, O *Mercury,*
Which could do all things, thy faith is; and I
Like *Esops* selfe, which nothing; I confesse
I should have had more faith, if thou hadst lesse;
Thy credit lost thy credit: 'Tis sinne to doe,
In this case, as thou wouldst be done unto,
To beleeve all: Change thy name: thou art like
Mercury in stealing, but lyest like a *Greeke.*

RALPHIUS

COMPASSION in the world againe is bred:
Ralphius is sick, the broker keeps his bed.

THE LIER

THOU in the fields walkst out thy supping howers
    And yet thou swear'st thou hast supp'd like a king:
Like Nebuchadnezar perchance with grass and flowers,
    A sallet worse than Spanish dyeting.

Elegies

1

JEALOSIE

FOND woman, which would'st have thy husband die,
And yet complain'st of his great jealosie;
If swolne with poyson, hee lay in'his last bed,
His body with a sere-barke covered,
Drawing his breath, as thick and short, as can
The nimblest crocheting Musitian,
Ready with loathsome vomiting to spue
His Soule out of one hell, into a new,
Made deafe with his poore kindreds howling cries,
Begging with few feign'd teares, great legacies,
Thou would'st not weepe, but jolly,'and frolicke bee,
As a slave, which to morrow should be free;
Yet weep'st thou, when thou seest him hungerly
Swallow his owne death, hearts-bane jealousie.
O give him many thanks, he'is courteous,
That in suspecting kindly warneth us.
Wee must not, as wee us'd, flout openly,
In scoffing ridles, his deformitie;
Nor at his boord together being satt,
With words, nor touch, scarce lookes adulterate.
Nor when he swolne, and pamper'd with great fare
Sits downe, and snorts, cag'd in his basket chaire,
Must wee usurpe his owne bed any more,
Nor kisse and play in his house, as before.
Now I see many dangers; for that is
His realme, his castle, and his diocesse.
But if, as envious men, which would revile
Their Prince, or coyne his gold, themselves exile

Into another countrie,'and doe it there,
Wee play'in another house, what should we feare?
There we will scorne his household policies,
His seely plots, and pensionary spies,
As the inhabitants of Thames right side
Do Londons Major; or Germans, the Popes pride.

II

THE ANAGRAM

MARRY, and love thy *Flavia*, for, she
Hath all things, whereby others beautious bee,
For, though her eyes be small, her mouth is great,
Though they be Ivory, yet her teeth be jeat,
Though they be dimme, yet she is light enough,
And though her harsh haire fall, her skinne is rough;
What though her cheeks be yellow, her haire's red,
Give her thine, and she hath a maydenhead.
These things are beauties elements, where these
Meet in one, that one must, as perfect, please.
If red and white and each good quality
Be in thy wench, ne'r aske where it doth lye.
In buying things perfum'd, we aske; if there
Be muske and amber in it, but not where.
Though all her parts be not in th'usuall place,
She'hath yet an Anagram of a good face.
If we might put the letters but one way,
In the leane dearth of words, what could we say?
When by the Gamut some Musitians make
A perfect song, others will undertake,
By the same Gamut chang'd, to equall it.
Things simply good, can never be unfit.
She's faire as any, if all be like her,
And if none be, then she is singular.
All love is wonder; if wee justly doe
Account her wonderfull, why not lovely too?
Love built on beauty, soone as beauty, dies,
Chuse this face, chang'd by no deformities.
Women are all like Angels; the faire be
Like those which fell to worse; but such as thee,

Like to good Angels, nothing can impaire:
'Tis lesse griefe to be foule, than to'have beene faire.
For one nights revels, silke and gold we chuse,
But, in long journeyes, cloth, and leather use.
Beauty is barren oft; best husbands say,
There is best land, where there is foulest way.
Oh what a soveraigne Plaister will shee bee,
If thy past sinnes have taught thee jealousie!
Here needs no spies, nor eunuches; her commit
Safe to thy foes; yea, to a Marmosit.
When Belgiaes citties, the round countries drowne,
That durty foulenesse guards, and armes the towne:
So doth her face guard her; and so, for thee,
Which, forc'd by businesse, absent oft must bee,
Shee, whose face, like clouds, turnes the day to night,
Who, mightier than the sea, makes Moores seem white,
Who, though seaven yeares, she in the Stews had laid,
A Nunnery durst receive, and thinke a maid,
And though in childbeds labour she did lie,
Midwifes would sweare,'twere but a tympanie,
Whom, if shee accuse her selfe, I credit lesse
Than witches, which impossibles confesse,
Whom Dildoes, Bedstaves, and her Velvet Glasse
Would be as loath to touch as Joseph was:
One like none, and lik'd of none, fittest were,
For, things in fashion every man will weare.

III

CHANGE

ALTHOUGH thy hand and faith, and good workes too,
Have seal'd thy love which nothing should undoe,
Yea though thou fall backe, that apostasie
Confirme thy love; yet much, much I feare thee.
Women are like the Arts, forc'd unto none,
Open to'all searchers, unpriz'd, if unknowne.
If I have caught a bird, and let him flie,
Another fouler using these meanes, as I,
May catch the same bird; and, as these things bee,

Women are made for men, not him, nor mee.
Foxes and goats; all beasts change when they please,
Shall women, more hot, wily, wild than these,
Be bound to one man, and did Nature then
Idly make them apter to'endure than men?
They'are our clogges, not their owne; if a man bee
Chain'd to a galley, yet the galley'is free;
Who hath a plow-land, casts all his seed corne there,
And yet allowes his ground more corne should beare;
Though Danuby into the sea must flow,
The sea receives the Rhene, Volga, and Po.
By nature, which gave it, this liberty
Thou lov'st, but Oh! canst thou love it and mee?
Likenesse glues love: and if that thou so doe,
To make us like and love, must I change too?
More than thy hate, I hate'it, rather let mee
Allow her change, than change as oft as shee,
And soe not teach, but force my'opinion
To love not any one, nor every one.
To live in one land, is captivitie,
To runne all countries, a wild roguery;
Waters stincke soone, if in one place they bide,
And in the vast sea are more putrifi'd:
But when they kisse one banke, and leaving this
Never looke backe, but the next banke doe kisse,
Then are they purest; Change'is the nursery
Of musicke, joy, life, and eternity.

IV

THE PERFUME

O N C E, and but once found in thy company,
All thy suppos'd escapes are laid on mee;
And as a thiefe at barre, is question'd there
By all the men, that have beene rob'd that yeare,
So am I, (by this traiterous meanes surpriz'd)
By thy Hydroptique father catechiz'd.
Though he had wont to search with glazed eyes,
As though he came to kill a Cockatrice,
Though he hath oft sworne, that he would remove

Thy beauties beautie, and food of our love,
Hope of his goods, if I with thee were seene,
Yet close and secret, as our soules, we'have beene.
Though thy immortall mother which doth lye
Still buried in her bed, yet will not dye,
Takes this advantage to sleepe out day-light,
And watch thy entries, and returnes all night,
And, when she takes thy hand, and would seeme kind,
Doth search what rings, and armelets she can finde,
And kissing notes the colour of thy face,
And fearing least thou'art swolne, doth thee embrace;
To trie if thou long, doth name strange meates,
And notes thy palenesse, blushing, sighs, and sweats;
And politiquely will to thee confesse
The sinnes of her owne youths ranke lustinesse;
Yet love these Sorceries did remove, and move
Thee to gull thine owne mother for my love.
Thy little brethren, which like Faiery Sprights
Oft skipt into our chamber, those sweet nights,
And kist, and ingled on thy fathers knee,
Were brib'd next day, to tell what they did see:
The grim eight-foot-high iron-bound serving-man,
That oft names God in oathes, and onely then,
He that to barre the first gate, doth as wide
As the great Rhodian Colossus stride,
Which, if in hell no other paines there were,
Makes mee feare hell, because he must be there:
Though by thy father he were hir'd to this,
Could never witnesse any touch or kisse.
But Oh, too common ill, I brought with mee
That, which betray'd mee to my enemie:
A loud perfume, which at my entrance cryed
Even at thy fathers nose, so were wee spied.
When, like a tyran King, that in his bed
Smelt gunpowder, the pale wretch shivered.
Had it beene some bad smell, he would have thought
That his owne feet, or breath, that smell had wrought.
But as wee in our Ile emprisoned,
Where cattell onely,'and diverse dogs are bred,
The pretious Unicornes, strange monsters call,
So thought he good, strange, that had none at all.
I taught my silkes, their whistling to forbeare,

Even my opprest shoes, dumbe and speechlesse were,
Onely, thou bitter sweet, whom I had laid
Next mee, mee traiterously hast betraid,
And unsuspected hast invisibly
At once fled unto him, and staid with mee.
Base excrement of earth, which dost confound
Sense, from distinguishing the sicke from sound;
By thee the seely Amorous sucks his death
By drawing in a leprous harlots breath;
By thee, the greatest staine to mans estate
Falls on us, to be call'd effeminate;
Though you be much lov'd in the Princes hall,
There, things that seeme, exceed substantiall.
Gods, when yee fum'd on altars, were pleas'd well,
Because you'were burnt, not that they lik'd your smell;
You'are loathsome all, being taken simply alone,
Shall wee love ill things joyn'd, and hate each one?
If you were good, your good doth soone decay;
And you are rare, that takes the good away.
All my perfumes, I give most willingly
To'embalme thy fathers corse; What? will hee die?

V

HIS PICTURE

HERE take my Picture; though I bid farewell,
Thine, in my heart, where my soule dwels, shall dwell.
'Tis like me now, but I dead, 'twill be more
When wee are shadowes both, than'twas before.
When weather-beaten I come backe; my hand,
Perhaps with rude oares torne, or Sun beams tann'd,
My face and brest of haircloth, and my head
With cares rash sodaine stormes, being o'rspread,
My body'a sack of bones, broken within,
And powders blew staines scatter'd on my skinne;
If rivall fooles taxe thee to'have lov'd a man,
So foule, and course, as, Oh, I may seeme then,
This shall say what I was: and thou shalt say,
Doe his hurts reach mee? doth my worth decay?
Or doe they reach his judging minde, that hee

Should now love lesse, what hee did love to see?
That which in him was faire and delicate,
Was but the milke, which in loves childish state
Did nurse it: who now is growne strong enough
To feed on that, which to disus'd tasts seemes **tough.**

VI

OH, LET MEE NOT SERVE

O H, let mee not serve so, as those men serve
Whom honours smoakes at once fatten and sterve;
Poorely enrich't with great mens words or lookes;
Nor so write my name in thy loving bookes
As those Idolatrous flatterers, which still
Their Princes stiles, with many Realmes fulfill
Whence they no tribute have, and where no sway.
Such services I offer as shall pay
Themselves, I hate dead names: Oh then let mee
Favorite in Ordinary, or no favorite bee.
When my Soule was in her owne body sheath'd,
Nor yet by oathes betroth'd, nor kisses breath'd
Into my Purgatory, faithlesse thee,
Thy heart seem'd waxe, and steele thy constancie:
So, carelesse flowers strow'd on the waters face,
The curled whirlepooles suck, smack, and embrace,
Yet drowne them; so, the tapers beamie eye
Amorously twinkling, beckens the giddie flie,
Yet burnes his wings; and such the devill is,
Scarce visiting them, who are intirely his
When I behold a streame, which, from the spring,
Doth with doubtfull melodious murmuring,
Or in a speechlesse slumber, calmely ride
Her wedded channels bosome, and then chide
And bend her browes, and swell if any bough
Do but stoop downe, or kisse her upmost brow:
Yet, if her often gnawing kisses winne
The traiterous banke to gape, and let her in,
She rusheth violently, and doth divorce
Her from her native, and her long-kept course,

And rores, and braves it, and in gallant scorne,
In flattering eddies promising retorne,
She flouts the channell, who thenceforth is drie;
Then say I; that is shee, and this am I.
Yet let not thy deepe bitternesse beget
Carelesse despaire in mee, for that will whet
My minde to scorne; and Oh, love dull'd with paine
Was ne'r so wise, nor well arm'd as disdaine.
Then with new eyes I shall survay thee,'and spie
Death in thy cheekes, and darknesse in thine eye.
Though hope bred faith and love: thus taught, I shall
As nations do from Rome, from thy love fall.
My hate shall outgrow thine, and utterly
I will renounce thy dalliance: and when I
Am the Recusant, in that resolute state,
What hurts it mee to be'excommunicate?

VII

NATURES LAY IDEOT

NATURES lay Ideot, I taught thee to love,
And in that sophistrie, Oh, thou dost prove
Too subtile: Foole, thou didst not understand
The mystique language of the eye nor hand:
Nor couldst thou judge the difference of the aire
Of sighes, and say, this lies, this sounds despaire:
Nor by the'eyes water call a maladie
Desperately hot, or changing feaverously.
I had not taught thee then, the Alphabet
Of flowers, how they devisefully being set
And bound up, might with speechlesse secrecie
Deliver arrands mutely, and mutually.
Remember since all thy words us'd to bee
To every suitor; *I, if my friends agree;*
Since, household charmes, thy husbands name to teach,
Were all the love trickes, that thy wit could reach;
And since, an houres discourse could scarce have made
One answer in thee, and that ill arraid
In broken proverbs, and torne sentences.

Thou are not by so many duties his,
That from the worlds Common having sever'd thee,
Inlaid thee, neither to be seene, nor see,
As mine: who have with amorous delicacies
Refin'd thee'into a blis-full Paradise.
Thy graces and good words my creatures bee;
I planted knowledge and lifes tree in thee,
Which Oh, shall strangers taste? Must I alas
Frame and enamell Plate, and drinke in Glasse?
Chafe waxe for others seales? breake a colts force
And leave him then, beeing made a ready horse?

VIII

THE COMPARISON

A S the sweet sweat of Roses in a Still,
As that which from chaf'd muskats pores doth trill,
As the Almighty Balme of th'early East,
Such are the sweat drops of my Mistris breast,
And on her [brow] her skin such lustre sets,
They seeme no sweat drops, but pearle coronets.
Ranke sweaty froth thy Mistresse's brow defiles,
Like spermatique issue of ripe menstruous boiles,
Or like the skumme, which, by needs lawlesse law
Enforc'd, Sanserra's starved men did draw
From parboild shooes, and bootes, and all the rest
Which were with any soveraigne fatnes blest,
And like vile lying stones in saffrond tinne,
Or warts, or wheales, they hang upon her skinne.
Round as the world's her head, on every side,
Like to the fatall Ball which fell on Ide,
Or that whereof God had such jealousie,
As, for the ravishing thereof we die.
Thy *head* is like a rough-hewne statue of jeat,
Where marks for eyes, nose, mouth, are yet scarce set;
Like the first Chaos, or flat seeming face
Of Cynthia, when th'earths shadowes her embrace.
Like Proserpines white beauty-keeping chest,
Or Joves best fortunes urne, is her faire breast.

Thine's like worme eaten trunkes, cloth'd in seals skin,
Or grave, that's dust without, and stinke within.
And like that slender stalke, at whose end stands
The wood-bine quivering, are her armes and hands.
Like rough bark'd elmboughes, or the russet skin
Of men late scurg'd for madnes, or for sinne,
Like Sun-parch'd quarters on the citie gate,
Such is thy tann'd skins lamentable state.
And like a bunch of ragged carrets stand
The short swolne fingers of thy gouty hand.
Then like the Chymicks masculine equall fire,
Which in the Lymbecks warme wombe doth inspire
Into th'earths worthlesse durt a soule of gold,
Such cherishing heat her best lov'd part doth hold.
Thine's like the dread mouth of a fired gunne,
Or like hot liquid metalls newly runne
Into clay moulds, or like to that Ætna
Where round about the grasse is burnt away.
Are not your kisses then as filthy, and more,
As a worme sucking an invenom'd sore?
Doth not thy fearefull hand in feeling quake,
As one which gath'ring flowers, still feares a snake?
Is not your last act harsh, and violent,
As when a Plough a stony ground doth rent?
So kisse good Turtles, so devoutly nice
Are Priests in handling reverent sacrifice,
And such in searching wounds the Surgeon is
As wee, when wee embrace, or touch, or kisse.
Leave her, and I will leave comparing thus,
She, and comparisons are odious.

I X

THE AUTUMNALL

N o *Spring,* nor *Summer* Beauty hath such grace,
   As I have seen in one *Autumnall* face.
Yong *Beauties* force our love, and that's a *Rape,*
   This doth but *counsaile,* yet you cannot scape.
If t'were a *shame* to love, here t'were no *shame,*
   Affection here takes *Reverences* name.

Were her first yeares the *Golden Age;* That's true,
  But now she's *gold* oft tried, and ever new.
That was her torrid and inflaming time,
  This is her tolerable *Tropique clyme.*
Faire eyes, who askes more heate than comes from hence,
  He in a fever wishes pestilence.
Call not these wrinkles, *graves;* If *graves* they were,
  They were *Loves graves;* for else he is no where.
Yet lies not Love *dead* here, but here doth sit
  Vow'd to this trench, like an *Anachorit.*
And here, till hers, which must be his *death,* come,
  He doth not digge a *Grave,* but build a *Tombe.*
Here dwells he, though he sojourne ev'ry where,
  In *Progresse,* yet his standing house is here.
Here, where still *Evening* is; not *noone,* nor *night;*
  Where no *voluptuousness,* yet all *delight.*
In all her words, unto all hearers fit,
  You may at *Revels,* you at *Counsaile,* sit.
This is loves timber, youth his under-wood;
  There he, as wine in *June,* enrages blood,
Which then comes seasonabliest, when our tast
  And appetite to other things, is past.
Xerxes strange *Lydian* love, the *Platane* tree,
  Was lov'd for age, none being so large as shee,
Or else because, being yong, nature did blesse
  Her youth with ages glory, *Barrennesse.*
If we love things long sought, *Age* is a thing
  Which we are fifty yeares in compassing.
If transitory things, which soone decay,
  Age must be lovelyest at the latest day.
But name not *Winter-faces,* whose skin's slacke;
  Lanke, as an unthrifts purse; but a soules sacke;
Whose *Eyes* seeke light within, for all here's shade;
  Whose *mouthes* are holes, rather worne out, than made;
Whose every tooth to a severall place is gone,
  To vexe their soules at *Resurrection;*
Name not these living *Deaths-heads* unto mee,
  For these, not *Ancient,* but *Antique* be.
I hate extreames; yet I had rather stay
  With *Tombes,* than *Cradles,* to weare out a day.

Since such loves naturall lation is, may still
   My love descend, and journey downe the hill,
Not panting after growing beauties, so,
   I shall ebbe out with them, who home-ward goe.

X

THE DREAME

I M A G E of her whom I love, more than she,
   Whose faire impression in my faithfull heart,
Makes mee her *Medall*, and makes her love mee,
   As Kings do coynes, to which their stamps impart
The value: goe, and take my heart from hence,
   Which now is growne too great and good for me:
Honours oppresse weake spirits, and our sense
   Strong objects dull; the more, the lesse wee see.
When you are gone, and *Reason* gone with you,
   Then *Fantasie* is Queene and Soule, and all;
She can present joyes meaner than you do;
   Convenient, and more proportionall.
So, if I dreame I have you, I have you,
   For, all our joyes are but fantasticall.
And so I scape the paine, for paine is true;
   And sleepe which locks up sense, doth lock out all.
After a such fruition I shall wake,
   And, but the waking, nothing shall repent;
And shall to love more thankfull Sonnets make,
   Than if more *honour, teares,* and *paines* were spent.
But dearest heart, and dearer image stay;
   Alas, true joyes at best are *dreame* enough;
Though you stay here you passe too fast away:
   For even at first lifes *Taper* is a snuffe.
Fill'd with her love, may I be rather grown
Mad with much *heart,* than *ideot* with none.

XI

THE BRACELET

Upon the losse of his Mistresses Chaine, for which
he made satisfaction

N O T that in colour it was like thy haire,
For Armelets of that thou maist let me weare:
Nor that thy hand is oft embrac'd and kist,
For so it had that good, which oft I mist:
Nor for that silly old moralitie,
That as these linkes were knit, our love should bee:
Mourne I that I thy seavenfold chaine have lost;
Nor for the luck sake; but the bitter cost.
O, shall twelve righteous Angels, which as yet
No leaven of vile soder did admit;
Nor yet by any way have straid or gone
From the first state of their Creation;
Angels, which heaven commanded to provide
All things to me, and be my faithfull guide;
To gaine new friends, t'appease great enemies;
To comfort my soule, when I lie or rise;
Shall these twelve innocents, by thy severe
Sentence (dread judge) my sins great burden beare?
Shall they be damn'd, and in the furnace throwne,
And punisht for offences not their owne?
They save not me, they doe not ease my paines,
When in that hell they'are burnt and tyed in chains.
Were they but Crownes of France, I cared not,
For, most of these, their naturall Countreys rot
I think possesseth, they come here to us,
So pale, so lame, so leane, so ruinous;
And howsoe'r French Kings most Christian be,
Their Crownes are circumcis'd most Jewishly.
Or were they Spanish Stamps, still travelling,
That are become as Catholique as their King,
Those unlickt beare-whelps, unfil'd pistolets
That (more than Canon shot) availes or lets;
Which negligently left unrounded, looke

Like many angled figures, in the booke
Of some great Conjurer that would enforce
Nature, as these doe justice, from her course;
Which, as the soule quickens head, feet and heart,
As streames, like veines, run through th'earth's every part,
Visit all Countries, and have slily made
Georgeous *France*, ruin'd, ragged and decay'd;
Scotland, which knew no State, proud in one day:
And mangled seventeen-headed *Belgia.*
Or were it such gold as that wherewithall
Almighty *Chymiques* from each minerall,
Having by subtle fire a soule out-pull'd;
Are dirtely and desperately gull'd:
I would not spit to quench the fire they'are in,
For, they are guilty of much hainous Sin.
But, shall my harmlesse angels perish? Shall
I lose my guard, my ease, my food, my all?
Much hope which they should nourish will be dead,
Much of my able youth, and lustyhead
Will vanish; if thou love let them alone,
For thou wilt love me lesse when they are gone;
And be content that some lowd squeaking Cryer
Well-pleas'd with one leane thred-bare groat, for hire,
May like a devill roare through every street;
And gall the finders conscience, if they meet.
Or let mee creepe to some dread Conjurer,
That with phantastique scheames fils full much paper;
Which hath divided heaven in tenements,
And with whores, theeves, and murderers stuft his rents,
So full, that though hee passe them all in sin,
He leaves himselfe no roome to enter in.
But if, when all his art and time is spent,
Hee say 'twill ne'r be found; yet be content;
Receive from him that doome ungrudgingly,
Because he is the mouth of destiny.
　　Thou say'st (alas) the gold doth still remaine,
Though it be chang'd, and put into a chaine;
So in the first falne angels, resteth still
Wisdome and knowledge; but,'tis turn'd to ill:
As these should doe good works; and should provide
Necessities; but now must nurse thy pride.

And they are still bad angels; Mine are none;
For, forme gives being, and their forme is gone:
Pitty these Angels; yet their dignities
Passe Vertues, Powers, and Principalities.
    But, thou art resolute; Thy will be done!
Yet with such anguish, as her onely sonne
The Mother in the hungry grave doth lay,
Unto the fire these Martyrs I betray.
Good soules, (for you give life to every thing)
Good Angels, (for good messages you bring)
Destin'd you might have beene to such an one,
As would have lov'd and worship'd you alone:
One that would suffer hunger, nakednesse,
Yea death, ere he would make your number lesse.
But, I am guilty of your sad decay;
May your few fellowes longer with me stay.
    But ô thou wretched finder whom I hate
So, that I almost pitty thy estate:
Gold being the heaviest metal amongst all,
May my most heavy curse upon thee fall:
Here fetter'd, manacled, and hang'd in chains,
First mayst thou bee; then chaind to hellish paines;
Or be with forraine gold brib'd to betray
Thy Countrey, and faile both of that and thy pay.
May the next thing thou stoop'st to reach, containe
Poyson, whose nimble fume rot thy moist braine;
Or libels, or some interdicted thing,
Which negligently kept, thy ruine bring.
Lust-bred diseases rot thee; and dwell with thee
Itchy desire, and no abilitie.
May all the evils that gold ever wrought;
All mischiefes that all devils ever thought;
Want after plenty; poore and gouty age;
The plagues of travellers; love; marriage
Afflict thee, and at thy lives last moment,
May thy swolne sinnes themselves to thee presen
    But, I forgive; repent thee honest man:
Gold is Restorative, restore it then:
But if from it thou beest loath to depart,
Because 'tis cordiall, would 'twere at thy heart.

XII

HIS PARTING FROM HER

S I N C E she must go, and I must mourn, come Night,
Environ me with darkness, whilst I write:
Shadow that hell unto me, which alone
I am to suffer when my Love is gone.
Alas the darkest Magick cannot do it,
Thou and greate Hell to boot are shadows to it.
Should *Cinthia* quit thee, *Venus*, and each starre,
It would not forme one thought dark as mine are.
I could lend thee obscureness now, and say,
Out of my self, There should be no more Day,
Such is already my felt want of sight,
Did not the fires within me force a light.
Oh Love, that fire and darkness should be mixt,
Or to thy Triumphs soe strange torments fixt!
Is't because thou thy self art blind, that wee
Thy Martyrs must no more each other see?
Or tak'st thou pride to break us on the wheel,
And view old Chaos in the Pains we feel?
Or have we left undone some mutual Rite,
Through holy fear, that merits thy despight?
No, no. The falt was mine, impute it to me,
Or rather to conspiring destinie,
Which (since I lov'd for forme before) decreed,
That I should suffer when I lov'd indeed:
And therefore now, sooner than I can say,
I saw the golden fruit, 'tis rapt away.
Or as I had watcht one drop in a vast stream,
And I left wealthy only in a dream.
Yet Love, thou'rt blinder than thy self in this,
To vex my Dove-like friend for my amiss:
And, where my own sad truth may expiate
Thy wrath, to make her fortune run my fate:
So blinded Justice doth, when Favorites fall,
Strike them, their house, their friends, their followers all.
Was't not enough that thou didst dart thy fires
Into our blouds, inflaming our desires,

And made'st us sigh and glow, and pant, and burn,
And then thy self into our flame did'st turn?
Was't not enough, that thou didst hazard us
To paths in love so dark, so dangerous:
And those so ambush'd round with household spies,
And over all, thy husbands towring eyes
That flam'd with oylie sweat of jealousie:
Yet went we not still on with Constancie?
Have we not kept our guards, like spie on spie?
Had correspondence whilst the foe stood by?
Stoln (more to sweeten them) our many blisses
Of meetings, conference, embracements, kisses?
Shadow'd with negligence our most respects?
Varied our language through all dialects,
Of becks, winks, looks, and often under-boards
Spoak dialogues with our feet far from our words?
Have we prov'd all these secrets of our Art,
Yea, thy pale inwards, and thy panting heart?
And, after all this passed Purgatory,
Must sad divorce make us the vulgar story?
First let our eyes be rivited quite through
Our turning brains, and both our lips grow to:
Let our armes clasp like Ivy, and our fear
Freese us together, that we may stick here,
Till Fortune, that would rive us, with the deed,
Strain her eyes open, and it make them bleed.
For Love it cannot be, whom hitherto
I have accus'd, should such a mischief doe.
Oh Fortune, thou'rt not worth my least exclame,
And plague enough thou hast in thy own shame.
Do thy great worst, my friend and I have armes,
Though not against thy strokes, against thy harmes.
Rend us in sunder, thou canst not divide
Our bodies so, but that our souls are ty'd,
And we can love by letters still and gifts,
And thoughts and dreams; Love never wanteth shifts.
I will not look upon the quickning Sun,
But straight her beauty to my sense shall run;
The ayre shall note her soft, the fire most pure;
Water suggest her clear, and the earth sure.
Time shall not lose our passages; the Spring
How fresh our love was in the beginning;

The Summer how it ripened in the eare;
And Autumn, what our golden harvests were.
The Winter I'll not think on to spite thee,
But count it a lost season, so shall shee.
And dearest Friend, since we must part, drown night
With hope of Day, burthens well born are light.
Though cold and darkness longer hang somewhere,
Yet *Phoebus* equally lights all the Sphere.
And what he cannot in like Portions pay,
The world enjoyes in Mass, and so we may.
Be then ever your self, and let no woe
Win on your health, your youth, your beauty: so
Declare your self base fortunes Enemy,
No less by your contempt than constancy:
That I may grow enamoured on your mind,
When my own thoughts I there reflected find.
For this to th'comfort of my Dear I vow,
My Deeds shall still be what my words are now;
The Poles shall move to teach me ere I start;
And when I change my Love, I'll change my heart;
Nay, if I wax but cold in my desire,
Think, heaven hath motion lost, and the world, fire:
Much more I could, but many words have made
That, oft, suspected which men would perswade;
Take therefore all in this: I love so true,
As I will never look for less in you.

XIII

JULIA

HARKE newes, ô envy, thou shalt heare descry'd
My *Julia;* who as yet was ne'r envy'd.
To vomit gall in slander, swell her vaines
With calumny, that hell it selfe disdaines,
Is her continuall practice; does her best,
To teare opinion even out of the brest
Of dearest friends, and (which is worse than vilde)
Sticks jealousie in wedlock; her owne childe

Scapes not the showres of envie, To repeate
The monstrous fashions, how, were, alive, to eate
Deare reputation. Would to God she were
But halfe so loath to act vice, as to heare
My milde reproofe. Liv'd *Mantuan* now againe,
That fœmall Mastix, to limme with his penne
This she *Chymera*, that hath eyes of fire,
Burning with anger, anger feeds desire,
Tongued like the night-crow, whose ill boding cries
Give out for nothing but new injuries,
Her breath like to the juice in *Tenarus*
That blasts the springs, though ne'r so prosperous,
Her hands, I know not how, us'd more to spill
The food of others, than her selfe to fill.
But oh her minde, that *Orcus,* which includes
Legions of mischiefs, countlesse multitudes
Of formlesse curses, projects unmade up,
Abuses yet unfashion'd, thoughts corrupt,
Mishapen Cavils, palpable untroths,
Inevitable errours, self-accusing oaths:
These, like those Atoms swarming in the Sunne,
Throng in her bosome for creation.
I blush to give her halfe her due; yet say,
No poyson's halfe so bad as *Julia*.

X I V

A TALE OF A CITIZEN AND HIS WIFE

I SING no harme good sooth to any wight,
To Lord or foole, Cuckold, begger or knight,
To peace-teaching Lawyer, Proctor, or brave
Reformed or reduced Captaine, Knave,
Officer, Jugler, or Justice of peace,
Juror or Judge; I touch no fat sowes grease,
I am no Libeller, nor will be any,
But (like a true man) say there are too many.
I feare not *ore tenus;* for my tale,
Nor Count nor Counsellour will redd or pale.
A citizen and his wife the other day

Both riding on one horse, upon the way
I overtooke, the wench a pretty peate,
And (by her eye) well fitting for the feate.
I saw the lecherous Citizen turne backe
His head, and on his wifes lip steale a smacke,
Whence apprehending that the man was kinde,
Riding before, to kisse his wife behinde,
To get acquaintance with him I began
To sort discourse fit for so fine a man:
I ask'd the number of the Plaguy Bill,
Ask'd if the Custome Farmers held out still,
Of the Virginian plot, and whether Ward
The traffique of the I[n]land seas had marr'd,
Whether the Brittaine *Burse* did fill apace,
And likely were to give th'Exchange disgrace;
Of new-built *Algate,* and the *More-field* crosses,
Of store of Bankerouts, and poore Merchants losses
I urged him to speake; But he (as mute
As an old Courtier worne to his last suite)
Replies with onely yeas and nayes; At last
(To fit his element) my theame I cast
On Tradesmens gaines; that set his tongue agoing:
Alas, good sir (quoth he) *There is no doing
In Court nor City now;* she smil'd and I,
And (in my conscience) both gave him the lie
In one met thought: but he went on apace,
And at the present time with such a face
He rail'd, as fray'd me; for he gave no praise,
To any but my Lord of *Essex* dayes;
Call'd those the age of action; true (quoth Hee)
There's now as great an itch of bravery,
And heat of taking up, but cold lay downe,
For, put to push of pay, away they runne;
Our onely City trades of hope now are
Bawd, Tavern-keeper, Whore and Scrivener;
The much of priviled'd kingsmen, and the store
Of fresh protections make the rest all poore;
In the first state of their Creation,
Though many stoutly stand, yet proves not one
A righteous pay-master. Thus ranne he on
In a continued rage: so void of reason
Seem'd his harsh talke, I sweat for feare of treason.

And (troth) how could I lesse? when in the prayer
For the protection of the wise Lord Major,
And his wise brethrens worships, when one prayeth,
He swore that none could say Amen with faith.
To get him off from what I glowed to heare,
(In happy time) an Angel did appeare,
The bright Signe of a lov'd and wel-try'd Inne,
Where many Citizens with their wives have bin
Well us'd and often; here I pray'd him stay,
To take some due refreshment by the way.
Looke how hee look'd that hid the gold (his hope)
And at's returne found nothing but a Rope,
So he on me, refus'd and made away,
Though willing she pleaded a weary day:
I found my misse, struck hands, and praid him tell
(To hold acquaintance still) where he did dwell;
He barely nam'd the street, promis'd the Wine,
But his kinde wife gave me the very Signe.

XV

THE EXPOSTULATION

T O make the doubt cleare, that no woman's true,
    Was it my fate to prove it strong in you?
Thought I, but one had breathed purest aire,
    And must she needs be false because she's faire?
Is it your beauties marke, or of your youth,
    Or your perfection, not to study truth?
Or thinke you heaven is deafe, or hath no eyes?
    Or those it hath, smile at your perjuries?
Are vowes so cheape with women, or the matter
    Whereof they are made, that they are writ in water,
And blowne away with winde? Or doth their breath
    (Both hot and cold at once) make life and death?
Who could have thought so many accents sweet
    Form'd into words, so many sighs should meete
As from our hearts, so many oathes, and teares
    Sprinkled among, (all sweeter by our feares
And the divine impression of stolne kisses,
    That seal'd the rest) should now prove empty blisses?

Did you draw bonds to forfet? signe to breake?
    Or must we reade you quite from what you speake,
And finde the truth out the wrong way? or must
    Hee first desire you false, would wish you just?
O I prophane, though most of women be
    This kinde of beast, my thought shall except thee;
My dearest love, though froward jealousie,
    With circumstance might urge thy'inconstancie,
Sooner I'll thinke the Sunne will cease to cheare
    The teeming earth, and *that* forget to beare,
Sooner that rivers will runne back, or Thames
    With ribs of Ice in June would bind his streames,
Or Nature, by whose strength the world endures,
    Would change her course, before you alter yours.
But O that treacherous breast to whom weake you
    Did trust our Counsells, and wee both may rue,
Having his falsehood found too late, 'twas hee
    That made me *cast* you guilty, and you me,
Whilst he, black wretch, betray'd each simple word
    Wee spake, unto the cunning of a third.
Curst may hee be, that so our love hath slaine,
    And wander on the earth, wretched as *Cain,*
Wretched as hee, and not deserve least pitty;
    In plaguing him, let misery be witty;
Let all eyes shunne him, and hee shunne each eye,
    Till hee be noysome as his infamie;
May he without remorse deny God thrice,
    And not be trusted more on his Soules price;
And after all selfe torment, when hee dyes,
    May Wolves teare out his heart, Vultures his eyes,
Swine eate his bowels, and his falser tongue
    That utter'd all, be to some Raven flung,
And let his carrion coarse be a longer feast
    To the Kings dogges, than any other beast.
Now have I curst, let us our love revive;
    In mee the flame was never more alive;
I could beginne againe to court and praise,
    And in that pleasure lengthen the short dayes
Of my lifes lease; like Painters that do take
    Delight, not in made worke, but whiles they make;
I could renew those times, when first I saw

Love in your eyes, that gave my tongue the law
To like what you lik'd; and at maskes and playes
     Commend the self same Actors, the same wayes;
Aske how you did, and often with intent
     Of being officious, be impertinent;
All which were such soft pastimes, as in these
     Love was as subtilly catch'd, as a disease;
But being got it is a treasure sweet,
     Which to defend is harder than to get:
And ought not be prophan'd on either part,
     For though'tis got by *chance,*'tis kept by *art*.

X V I

ON HIS MISTRIS

B Y our first strange and fatall interview,
By all desires which thereof did ensue,
By our long starving hopes, by that remorse
Which my words masculine perswasive force
Begot in thee, and by the memory
Of hurts, which spies and rivals threatned me,
I calmly beg: But by thy fathers wrath,
By all paines, which want and divorcement hath,
I conjure thee, and all the oathes which I
And thou have sworne to seale joynt constancy,
Here I unsweare, and overswear them thus,
Thou shalt not love by wayes so dangerous.
Temper, ô faire Love, loves impetuous rage,
Be my true Mistris still, not my faign'd Page;
I'll goe, and, by thy kinde leave, leave behinde
Thee, onely worthy to nurse in my minde,
Thirst to come backe; ô if thou die before,
My soule from other lands to thee shall soare.
Thy (else Almighty) beautie cannot move
Rage from the Seas, nor thy love teach them love,
Nor tame wilde Boreas harshnesse; Thou hast reade
How roughly hee in peeces shivered
Faire Orithea, whom he swore he lov'd.
Fall ill or good, 'tis madnesse to have prov'd

Dangers unurg'd; Feed on this flattery,
That absent Lovers one in th'other be.
Dissemble nothing, not a boy, nor change
Thy bodies habite, nor mindes; bee not strange
To thy selfe onely; All will spie in thy face
A blushing womanly discovering grace;
Richly cloath'd Apes, are call'd Apes, and as soone
Ecclips'd as bright we call the Moone the Moone.
Men of France, changeable Camelions,
Spittles of diseases, shops of fashions,
Loves fuellers, and the rightest company
Of Players, which upon the worlds stage be,
Will quickly know thee, and no lesse, alas!
Th'indifferent Italian, as we passe
His warme land, well content to thinke thee Page,
Will hunt thee with such lust, and hideous rage,
As *Lots* faire guests were vext. But none of these
Nor spungy hydroptique Dutch shall thee displease,
If thou stay here. O stay here, for, for thee
England is onely a worthy Gallerie,
To walke in expectation, till from thence
Our greatest King call thee to his presence.
When I am gone, dreame me some happinesse,
Nor let thy lookes our long hid love confesse,
Nor praise, nor dispraise me, nor blesse nor curse
Openly loves force, nor in bed fright thy Nurse
With midnights startings, crying out, oh, oh
Nurse, ô my love is slaine, I saw him goe
O'r the white Alpes alone; I saw him I,
Assail'd, fight, taken, stabb'd, bleed, fall, and die.
Augure me better chance, except dread *Jove*
Thinke it enough for me to'have had thy love.

XVII

VARIETY

THE heavens rejoyce in motion, why should I
Abjure my so much lov'd variety,
And not with many youth and love divide?
Pleasure is none, if not diversifi'd:

The sun that sitting in the chaire of light
Sheds flame into what else soever doth seem bright,
Is not contented at one Signe to Inne,
But ends his year and with a new beginnes.
All things doe willingly in change delight,
The fruitfull mother of our appetite:
Rivers the clearer and more pleasing are,
Where their fair spreading streames run wide and farr;
And a dead lake that no strange bark doth greet,
Corrupts it self and what doth live in it.
Let no man tell me such a one is faire,
And worthy all alone my love to share.
Nature in her hath done the liberall part
Of a kinde Mistresse, and imploy'd her art
To make her loveable, and I aver
Him not humane that would turn back from her:
I love her well, and would, if need were, dye
To doe her service. But followes it that I
Must serve her onely, when I may have choice
Of other beauties, and in change rejoice?
The law is hard, and shall not have my voice.
The last I saw in all extreames is faire,
And holds me in the Sun-beames of her haire;
Her nymph-like features such agreements have
That I could venture with her to the grave:
Another's brown, I like her not the worse,
Her tongue is soft and takes me with discourse:
Others, for that they well descended are,
Do in my love obtain as large a share;
And though they be not fair, 'tis much with mee
To win their love onely for their degree.
And though I faile of my required ends,
The attempt is glorious and it self commends.
How happy were our Syres in ancient time,
Who held plurality of loves no crime!
With them it was accounted charity
To stirre up race of all indifferently;
Kindreds were not exempted from the bands:
Which with the Persian still in usage stands.
Women were then no sooner asked than won,
And what they did was honest and well done.

But since this title honour hath been us'd,
Our weake credulity hath been abus'd;
The golden laws of nature are repeald,
Which our first Fathers in such reverence held;
Our liberty's revers'd, our Charter's gone,
And we're made servants to opinion,
A monster in no certain shape attir'd,
And whose originall is much desir'd,
Formlesse at first, but growing on it fashions,
And doth prescribe manners and laws to nations.
Here love receiv'd immedicable harmes,
And was dispoiled of his daring armes.
A greater want than is his daring eyes,
He lost those awfull wings with which he flies;
His sinewy bow, and those immortall darts
Wherewith he'is wont to bruise resisting hearts.
Onely some few strong in themselves and free
Retain the seeds of antient liberty,
Following that part of Love although deprest,
And make a throne for him within their brest,
In spight of modern censures him avowing
Their Soveraigne, all service him allowing.
Amongst which troop although I am the least,
Yet equall in perfection with the best,
I glory in subjection of his hand,
Nor ever did decline his least command:
For in whatever forme the message came
My heart did open and receive the same.
But time will in his course a point discry
When I this loved service must deny,
For our allegiance temporary is,
With firmer age returnes our liberties.
What time in years and judgement we repos'd,
Shall not so easily be to change dispos'd,
Nor to the art of severall eyes obeying;
But beauty with true worth securely weighing,
Which being found assembled in some one,
Wee'l love her ever, and love her alone.

XVIII

LOVES PROGRESS

WHO ever loves, if he do not propose
The right true end of love, he's one that goes
To sea for nothing but to make him sick:
Love is a bear-whelp born, if we o're lick
Our love, and force it new strange shapes to take,
We erre, and of a lump a monster make.
Were not a Calf a monster that were grown
Face'd like a man, though better than his own?
Perfection is in unitie: preferr
One woman first, and then one thing in her.
I, when I value gold, may think upon
The ductilness, the application,
The wholesomness, the ingenuitie,
From rust, from soil, from fire ever free:
But if I love it, 'tis because 'tis made
By our new nature (Use) the soul of trade.
    All these in women we might think upon
(If women had them) and yet love but one.
Can men more injure women than to say
They love them for that, by which they're not they?
Makes virtue woman? must I cool my bloud
Till I both be, and find one wise and good?
May barren Angels love so. But if we
Make love to woman; virtue is not she:
As beauty'is not nor wealth: He that strayes thus
From her to hers, is more adulterous,
Than if he took her maid. Search every sphear
And firmament, our *Cupid* is not there:
He's an infernal god and under ground,
With *Pluto* dwells, where gold and fire abound:
Men to such Gods, their sacrificing Coles
Did not in Altars lay, but pits and holes.
Although we see Celestial bodies move
Above the earth, the earth we Till and love:
So we her ayres contemplate, words and heart,
And virtues; but we love the Centrique part.
    Nor is the soul more worthy, or more fit

For love, than this, as infinite as it.
But in attaining this desired place
How much they erre; that set out at the face?
The hair a Forest is of Ambushes,
Of springes, snares, fetters and manacles:
The brow becalms us when 'tis smooth and plain,
And when 'tis wrinckled, shipwracks us again.
Smooth, 'tis a Paradice, where we would have
Immortal stay, and wrinkled 'tis our grave.
The Nose (like to the first Meridian) runs
Not 'twixt an East and West, but 'twixt two suns;
It leaves a Cheek, a rosie Hemisphere
On either side, and then directs us where
Upon the Islands fortunate we fall,
(Not faynte *Canaries,* but *Ambrosiall*)
Her swelling lips; To which when wee are come,
We anchor there, and think our selves at home,
For they seem all: there Syrens songs, and there
Wise Delphick Oracles do fill the ear;
There in a Creek where chosen pearls do swell,
The Remora, her cleaving tongue doth dwell.
These, and the glorious Promontory, her Chin
Ore past; and the streight *Hellespont* betweene
The *Sestos* and *Abydos* of her breasts,
(Not of two Lovers, but two Loves the neasts)
Succeeds a boundless sea, but yet thine eye
Some Island moles may scattered there descry;
And Sailing towards her *India,* in that way
Shall at her fair Atlantick Navell stay;
Though thence the Current be thy Pilot made,
Yet ere thou be where thou wouldst be embay'd,
Thou shalt upon another Forest set,
Where many Shipwrack, and no further get.
When thou art there, consider what this chace
Mispent by thy beginning at the face.
    Rather set out below; practice my Art,
Some Symetry the foot hath with that part
Which thou dost seek, and is thy Map for that
Lovely enough to stop, but not stay at:
Least subject to disguise and change it is;
Men say the Devil never can change his.

It is the Emblem that hath figured
Firmness; 'tis the first part that comes to bed.
Civilitie we see refin'd: the kiss
Which at the face began, transplanted is,
Since to the hand, since to the Imperial knee,
Now at the Papal foot delights to be:
If Kings think that the nearer way, and do
Rise from the foot, Lovers may do so too;
For as free Spheres move faster far than can
Birds, whom the air resists, so may that man
Which goes this empty and Ætherial way,
Than if at beauties elements he stay.
Rich Nature hath in women wisely made
Two purses, and their mouths aversely laid:
They then, which to the lower tribute owe,
That way which that Exchequer looks, must go:
He which doth not, his error is as great,
As who by Clyster gave the Stomack meat.

XIX

TO HIS MISTRIS GOING TO BED

COME, Madam, come, all rest my powers defie,
Until I labour, I in labour lie.
The foe oft-times having the foe in sight,
Is tir'd with standing though he never fight.
Off with that girdle, like heavens Zone glistering,
But a far fairer world incompassing.
Unpin that spangled breastplate which you wear,
That th'eyes of busie fooles may be stopt there.
Unlace your self, for that harmonious chyme,
Tells me from you, that now it is bed time.
Off with that happy busk, which I envie,
That still can be, and still can stand so nigh.
Your gown going off, such beautious state reveals,
As when from flowry meads th'hills shadow steales.
Off with that wyerie Coronet and shew
The haiery Diademe which on you doth grow:
Now off with those shooes, and then safely tread

In this loves hallow'd temple, this soft bed.
In such white robes, heaven's Angels us'd to be
Receavd by men; Thou Angel bringst with thee
A heaven like Mahomets Paradice; and though
Ill spirits walk in white, we easly know,
By this these Angels from an evil sprite,
Those set our hairs, but these our flesh upright.
    Licence my roaving hands, and let them go,
Before, behind, between, above, below.
O my America! my new-found-land,
My kingdome, safeliest when with one man man'd,
My Myne of precious stones, My Emperie,
How blest am I in this discovering thee!
To enter in these bonds, is to be free;
Then where my hand is set, my seal shall be.
    Full nakedness! All joyes are due to thee,
As souls unbodied, bodies uncloth'd must be,
To taste whole joyes. Gems which you women use
Are like Atlanta's balls, cast in mens views,
That when a fools eye lighteth on a Gem,
His earthly soul may covet theirs, not them.
Like pictures, or like books gay coverings made
For lay-men, are all women thus array'd;
Themselves are mystick books, which only wee
(Whom their imputed grace will dignifie)
Must see reveal'd. Then since that I may know;
As liberally, as to a Midwife, shew
Thy self: cast all, yea, this white lynnen hence,
There is no pennance due to innocence.
    To teach thee, I am naked first; why then
What needst thou have more covering than a man.

X X

LOVES WARR

TILL I have peace with thee, warr other Men,
And when I have peace, can I leave thee then?
All other Warrs are scrupulous; Only thou
O fayr free Citty, maist thyselfe allow
To any one: In Flanders, who can tell

Whether the Master presse; or men rebell?
Only we know, that which all Ideots say,
They beare most blows which come to part the fray.
France in her lunatique giddines did hate
Ever our men, yea and our God of late;
Yet she relyes upon our Angels well,
Which nere returne; no more than they which fell.
Sick Ireland is with a strange warr possest
Like to an Ague; now raging, now at rest;
Which time will cure: yet it must doe her good
If she were purg'd, and her head vayne let blood.
And Midas joyes our Spanish journeys give,
We touch all gold, but find no food to live.
And I should be in the hott parching clime,
To dust and ashes turn'd before my time.
To mew me in a Ship, is to inthrall
Mee in a prison, that weare like to fall;
Or in a Cloyster; save that there men dwell
In a calme heaven, here in a swaggering hell.
Long voyages are long consumptions,
And ships are carts for executions.
Yea they are Deaths; Is't not all one to flye
Into an other World, as t'is to dye?
Here lett mee warr; in these armes lett mee lye;
Here lett mee parle, batter, bleede, and dye.
Thyne armes imprison me, and myne armes thee,
Thy hart thy ransome is, take myne for mee.
Other men war that they their rest may gayne;
But wee will rest that wee may fight agayne.
Those warrs the ignorant, these th'experienc'd love,
There wee are alwayes under, here above.
There Engins farr off breed a just true feare,
Neere thrusts, pikes, stabs, yea bullets hurt not here.
There lyes are wrongs; here safe uprightly ly;
There men kill men, we'will make one by and by.
Thou nothing; I not halfe so much shall do
In these Warrs, as they may which from us two
Shall spring. Thousands wee see which travaile not
To warrs; But stay swords, armes, and shott
To make at home; And shall not I do then
More glorious service, staying to make men?

Heroicall Epistle

SAPHO TO PHILÆNIS

WHERE is that holy fire, which *Verse* is said
  To have? is that inchanting force decai'd?
Verse that drawes *Natures* workes, from *Natures* law,
  Thee, her best worke, to her worke cannot draw.
Have my teares quench'd my old *Poetique* fire;
  Why quench'd they not as well, that of *desire?*
Thoughts, my mindes creatures, often are with thee,
  But I, their maker, want their libertie.
Onely thine image, in my heart, doth sit,
  But that is waxe, and fires environ it.
My fires have driven, thine have drawne it hence;
  And I am rob'd of *Picture, Heart,* and *Sense.*
Dwells with me still mine irksome *Memory,*
  Which, both to keepe, and lose, grieves equally.
That tells me'how faire thou art: Thou art so faire,
  As, *gods,* when *gods* to thee I doe compare,
Are grac'd thereby; And to make blinde men see,
  What things *gods* are, I say they'are like to thee.
For, if we justly call each silly *man*
  A *little world,* What shall we call thee then?
Thou art not soft, and cleare, and strait, and faire,
  As *Down,* as *Stars, Cedars,* and *Lillies* are,
But thy right hand, and cheek, and eye, only
  Are like thy other hand, and cheek, and eye.
Such was my *Phao* awhile, but shall be never,
  As thou, wast, art, and, oh, maist be ever.
Here lovers sweare in their *Idolatrie,*
  That I am such; but *Griefe* discolors me.
And yet I grieve the lesse, lest *Griefe* remove
  My beauty, and make me'unworthy of thy love.

Plaies some soft boy with thee, oh there wants yet
    A mutuall feeling which should sweeten it.
His chinne, a thorny hairy unevennesse
    Doth threaten, and some daily change possesse.
Thy body is a naturall *Paradise,*
    In whose selfe, unmanur'd, all pleasure lies,
Nor needs *perfection;* why shouldst thou then
    Admit the tillage of a harsh rough man?
Men leave behinde them that which their sin showes,
    And are as theeves trac'd, which rob when it snows.
But of our dallyance no more signes there are,
    Than *fishes* leave in streames, or *Birds* in aire.
And betweene us all sweetnesse may be had;
    All, all that *Nature* yields, or *Art* can adde.
My two lips, eyes, thighs, differ from thy two,
    But so, as thine from one another doe;
And, oh, no more; the likenesse being such,
    Why should they not alike in all parts touch?
Hand to strange hand, lippe to lippe none denies;
    Why should they brest to brest, or thighs to thighs?
Likenesse begets such strange selfe flatterie,
    That touching my selfe, all seemes done to thee.
My selfe I embrace, and mine owne hands I kisse,
    And amorously thanke my selfe for this.
Me, in my glasse, I call thee; But alas,
    When I would kisse, teares dimme mine *eyes,* and *glasse.*
O cure this loving madnesse, and restore
    Me to mee; thee, my *halfe,* my *all,* my *more.*
So may thy cheekes red outweare scarlet dye,
    And their white, whitenesse of the *Galaxy,*
So may thy mighty, amazing beauty move
    Envy'in all *women,* and in all *men, love,*
And so be *change,* and *sicknesse,* farre from thee,
    As thou by comming neere, kep'st them from me.

Epithalamions or Marriage Songs

AN EPITHALAMION, OR MARRIAGE SONG

*on the Lady Elizabeth, and Count Palatine
being married on St. Valentines day*

I

HAILE Bishop Valentine, whose day this is,
    All the Aire is thy Diocis,
    And all the chirping Choristers
And other birds are thy Parishioners,
      Thou marryest every yeare
The Lirique Larke, and the grave whispering Dove,
The Sparrow that neglects his life for love,
The household Bird, with the red stomacher,
      Thou mak'st the black bird speed as soone,
As doth the Goldfinch, or the Halcyon;
The husband cocke lookes out, and straight is sped,
And meets his wife, which brings her feather-bed.
This day more cheerfully than ever shine,
This day, which might enflame thy self, Old Valentine.

II

Till now, Thou warmd'st with multiplying loves
    Two larkes, two sparrowes, or two Doves,
    All that is nothing unto this,
For thou this day couplest two Phœnixes;
      Thou mak'st a Taper see
What the sunne never saw, and what the Arke
(Which was of foules, and beasts, the cage, and park,)

89

Did not containe, one bed containes, through Thee,
      Two Phœnixes, whose joyned breasts
Are unto one another mutuall nests,
Where motion kindles such fires, as shall give
Young Phœnixes, and yet the old shall live.
Whose love and courage never shall decline,
But make the whole year through, thy day, O Valentine.

III

Up then faire Phœnix Bride, frustrate the Sunne,
      Thy selfe from thine affection
        Takest warmth enough, and from thine eye
All lesser birds will take their Jollitie.
        Up, up, faire Bride, and call,
Thy starres, from out their severall boxes, take
Thy Rubies, Pearles, and Diamonds forth, and make
Thy selfe a constellation, of them All,
      And by their blazing, signifie,
That a Great Princess falls, but doth not die;
Bee thou a new starre, that to us portends
Ends of much wonder; And be Thou those ends.
Since thou dost this day in new glory shine,
May all men date Records, from this thy Valentine.

IIII

Come forth, come forth, and as one glorious flame
      Meeting Another, growes the same,
        So meet thy Fredericke, and so
To an unseparable union growe.
      Since separation
Falls not on such things as are infinite,
Nor things which are but one, can disunite,
You'are twice inseparable, great, and one;
      Goe then to where the Bishop staies,
To make you one, his way, which divers waies
Must be effected; and when all is past,
And that you'are one, by hearts and hands made fast,
You two have one way left, your selves to'entwine,
Besides this Bishops knot, or Bishop Valentine.

V

But oh, what ailes the Sunne, that here he staies,
      Longer to day, than other daies?
      Staies he new light from these to get?
And finding here such store, is loth to set?
          And why doe you two walke,
So slowly pac'd in this procession?
Is all your care but to be look'd upon,
And be to others spectacle, and talke?
      The feast, with gluttonous delaies,
Is eaten, and too long their meat they praise,
The masquers come too late, and'I thinke, will stay,
Like Fairies, till the Cock crow them away.
Alas, did not Antiquity assigne
A night, as well as day, to thee, O Valentine?

VI

They did, and night is come; and yet wee see
      Formalities retarding thee.
      What meane these Ladies, which (as though
They were to take a clock in peeces,) goe
          So nicely about the Bride;
A Bride, before a good night could be said,
Should vanish from her cloathes, into her bed,
As Soules from bodies steale, and are spy'd.
      But now she is laid; What though shee bee?
Yet there are more delayes, For, where is he?
He comes, and passes through Spheare after Spheare,
First her sheetes, then her Armes, then any where.
Let not this day, then, but this night be thine,
Thy day was but the eve to this, O Valentine.

VII

Here lyes a shee Sunne, and a hee Moone here,
      She gives the best light to his Spheare,
      Or each is both, and all, and so
They unto one another nothing owe,
          And yet they doe, but are
So just and rich in that coyne which they pay,
That neither would, nor needs forbeare nor stay;
Neither desires to be spar'd, nor to spare,

They quickly pay their debt, and then
Take no acquittances, but pay again;
They pay, they give, they lend, and so let fall
No such occasion to be liberall.
More truth, more courage in these two do shine,
Than all thy turtles have, and sparrows, Valentine.

VIII

And by this act these two Phenixes
    Nature againe restored is,
    For since these two are two no more,
Ther's but one Phenix still, as was before.
    Rest now at last, and wee
As Satyres watch the Sunnes uprise, will stay
Waiting, when your eyes opened, let out day,
Onely desir'd, because your face wee see;
    Others neare you shall whispering speake,
And wagers lay, at which side day will breake,
And win by'observing, then, whose hand it is
That opens first a curtaine, hers or his;
This will be tryed to morrow after nine,
Till which houre, wee thy day enlarge, O Valentine

ECCLOGUE

1613. December 26

*Allophanes finding Idios in the country in Christmas time, reprehends
his absence from court, at the marriage of the Earle of Sommerset,
Idios gives an account of his purpose therein, and of his absence thence.*

ALLOPHANES
Unseasonable man, statue of ice,
    What could to countries solitude entice
Thee, in this yeares cold and decrepit time?
    Natures instinct drawes to the warmer clime
Even small birds, who by that courage dare,
    In numerous fleets, saile through their Sea, the aire.
What delicacie can in fields appeare,
    Whil'st Flora'herselfe doth a freeze jerkin weare?

Whil'st windes do all the trees and hedges strip
   Of leafes, to furnish roddes enough to whip
Thy madnesse from thee; and all springs by frost
   Have taken cold, and their sweet murmure lost;
If thou thy faults or fortunes would'st lament
   With just solemnity, do it in Lent;
At Court the spring already advanced is,
   The Sunne stayes longer up; and yet not his
The glory is, farre other, other fires.
   First, zeale to Prince and State; then loves desires
Burne in one brest, and like heavens two great lights,
   The first doth governe dayes, the other nights.
And then that early light, which did appeare
   Before the Sunne and Moone created were,
The princes favour is defus'd o'r all,
   From which all Fortunes, Names, and Natures fall;
Then from those wombes of starres, the Brides bright eyes,
   At every glance, a constellation flyes,
And sowes the Court with starres, and doth prevent
   In light and power, the all-ey'd firmament;
First her eyes kindle other Ladies eyes,
   Then from their beames their jewels lusters rise,
And from their jewels torches do take fire,
   And all is warmth, and light, and good desire;
Most other Courts, alas, are like to hell,
   Where in darke plotts, fire without light doth dwell:
Or but like Stoves, for lust and envy get
   Continuall, but artificiall heat;
Here zeale and love growne one, all clouds disgest,
   And make our Court an everlasting East.
And can'st thou be from thence?

IDIOS   No, I am there.
As heaven, to men dispos'd, is every where,
So are those Courts, whose Princes animate,
   Not onely all their house, but all their State.
Let no man thinke, because he is full, he hath all,
   Kings (as their patterne, God) are liberall
Not onely in fulnesse, but capacitie,
   Enlarging narrow men, to feele and see,
And comprehend the blessings they bestow.
   So, reclus'd hermits often times do know

More of heavens glory, than a worldling can.
    As man is of the world, the heart of man,
Is an epitome of Gods great booke
    Of creatures, and man need no farther looke;
So is the Country of Courts, where sweet peace doth,
    As their one common soule, give life to both,
I am not then from Court.

ALLOPHANES   Dreamer, thou art.
    Think'st thou fantastique that thou hast a part
In the East-Indian fleet, because thou hast
    A little spice, or Amber in thy taste?
Because thou art not frozen, art thou warme?
    Seest thou all good because thou seest no harme?
The earth doth in her inward bowels hold
    Stuffe well dispos'd, and which would faine be gold,
But never shall, except it chance to lye,
    So upward, that heaven gild it with his eye;
As, for divine things, faith comes from above,
    So, for best civill use, all tinctures move
From higher powers; From God religion springs,
    Wisdome, and honour from the use of Kings.
Then unbeguile thy selfe, and know with mee,
    That Angels, though on earth employd they bee,
Are still in heav'n, so is hee still at home
    That doth, abroad, to honest actions come.
Chide thy selfe then, O foole, which yesterday
    Might'st have read more than all thy books bewray;
Hast thou a history, which doth present
    A Court, where all affections do assent
Unto the Kings, and that, that Kings are just?
    And where it is no levity to trust?
Where there is no ambition, but to'obey,
    Where men need whisper nothing, and yet may;
Where the Kings favours are so plac'd, that all
    Finde that the King therein is liberall
To them, in him, because his favours bend
    To vertue, to the which they all pretend?
Thou hast no such; yet here was this, and more,
    An earnest lover, wise then, and before.

Our little Cupid hath sued Livery,
　　And is no more in his minority,
Hee is admitted now into that brest
　　Where the Kings Counsells and his secrets rest.
What hast thou lost, O ignorant man?

IDIOS   I knew
　　All this, and onely therefore I withdrew.
To know and feele all this, and not to have
　　Words to expresse it, makes a man a grave
Of his owne thoughts; I would not therefore stay
　　At a great feast, having no grace to say.
And yet I scap'd not here; for being come
　　Full of the common joy, I utter'd some;
Reade then this nuptiall song, which was not made
　　Either the Court or mens hearts to invade,
But since I'am dead, and buried, I could frame
　　No Epitaph, which might advance my fame
So much as this poor song, which testifies
　　I did unto that day some sacrifice.

EPITHALAMION

1

THE TIME OF THE MARRIAGE

T H O U are repriv'd old yeare, thou shalt not die,
Though thou upon thy death bed lye,
　　And should'st within five dayes expire,
Yet thou art rescu'd by a mightier fire,
　　Than thy old Soule, the Sunne,
When he doth in his largest circle runne.
The passage of the West or East would thaw,
And open wide their easie liquid jawe
To all our ships, could a Promethean art
Either unto the Northerne Pole impart
The fire of these inflaming eyes, or of this loving heart.

II

EQUALITY OF PERSONS

B U T undiscerning Muse, which heart, which eyes,
    In this new couple, dost thou prize,
      When his eye as inflaming is
As hers, and her heart loves as well as his?
      Be tryed by beauty, and then
The bridegroome is a maid, and not a man.
If by that manly courage they be tryed,
Which scornes unjust opinion; then the bride
Becomes a man. Should chance or envies Art
Divide these two, whom nature scarce did part?
Since both have both th'enflaming eyes, and both the loving
    heart.

III

RAISING OF THE BRIDEGROOME

T H O U G H it be some divorce to thinke of you
    Singly, so much one are you two,
      Yet let me here contemplate thee,
First cheerfull Bridegroome, and first let mee see,
      How thou prevent'st the Sunne,
And his red foming horses dost outrunne,
How, having laid downe in thy Soveraignes brest
All businesses, from thence to reinvest
Them, when these triumphs cease, thou forward art
To shew to her, who doth the like impart,
The fire of thy inflaming eyes, and of thy loving heart.

IIII

RAISING OF THE BRIDE

B U T now, to Thee, faire Bride, it is some wrong,
    To thinke thou wert in Bed so long,

Since Soone thou lyest downe first, tis fit
Thou in first rising should'st allow for it.
    Pouder thy Radiant haire,
Which if without such ashes thou would'st weare,
Thou, which to all which come to looke upon,
Art meant for Phœbus, would'st be Phaëton.
For our ease, give thine eyes th'unusual part
Of joy, a Teare; so quencht, thou maist impart,
To us that come, thy inflaming eyes, to him, thy loving heart.

V

HER APPARRELLING

T H U S thou descend'st to our infirmitie,
    Who can the Sun in water see.
      Soe dost thou, when in silke and gold,
Thou cloudst thy selfe; since wee which doe behold,
      Are dust, and wormes, 'tis just
Our objects be the fruits of wormes and dust;
Let every Jewell be a glorious starre,
Yet starres are not so pure, as their spheares are.
And though thou stoope, to'appeare to us in part,
Still in that Picture thou intirely art,
Which thy inflaming eyes have made within his loving heart.

VI

GOING TO THE CHAPPELL

N O W from your Easts you issue forth, and wee,
    As men which through a Cipres see
      The rising sun, doe thinke it two,
Soe, as you goe to Church, doe thinke of you,
      But that vaile being gone,
By the Church rites you are from thenceforth one.
The Church Triumphant made this match before,
And now the Militant doth strive no more;

Then, reverend Priest, who Gods Recorder art,
Doe, from his Dictates, to these two impart
All blessings, which are seene, or thought, by Angels eye or
    heart.

VII

THE BENEDICTION

BLEST payre of Swans, Oh may you interbring
    Daily new joyes, and never sing;
        Live, till all grounds of wishes faile,
Till honor, yea till wisedome grow so stale,
        That, new great heights to trie,
It must serve your ambition, to die;
Raise heires, and may here, to the worlds end, live
Heires from this King, to take thankes, you, to give,
Nature and grace doe all, and nothing Art.
May never age, or error overthwart
With any West, these radiant eyes, with any North, this
    heart.

VIII

FEASTS AND REVELLS

BUT you are over-blest. Plenty this day
    Injures; it causeth time to stay;
        The tables groane, as though this feast
Would, as the flood, destroy all fowle and beast.
        And were the doctrine new
That the earth mov'd, this day would make it true;
For every part to dance and revell goes.
They tread the ayre, and fal not where they rose.
Though six houres since, the Sunne to bed did part,
The masks and banquets will not yet impart
A sunset to these weary eyes, A Center to this heart.

IX

THE BRIDES GOING TO BED

W H A T mean'st thou Bride, this companie to keep?
　　To sit up, till thou faine wouldst sleep?
　　Thou maist not, when thou art laid, doe so.
Thy selfe must to him a new banquet grow,
　　　And you must entertaine
And doe all this daies dances o'er againe.
Know that if Sun and Moone together doe
Rise in one point, they doe not set so too;
Therefore thou maist, faire Bride, to bed depart,
Thou art not gone, being gone; where e'r thou art,
Thou leav'st in him thy watchfull eyes, in him thy loving
　　heart.

X

THE BRIDEGROOMES COMMING

A s he that sees a starre fall, runs apace,
　　And findes a gellie in the place,
　　So doth the Bridegroome haste as much,
Being told this starre is falne, and findes her such.
　　And as friends may looke strange,
By a new fashion, or apparrells change,
Their soules, though long acquainted they had beene,
These clothes, their bodies, never yet had seene;
Therefore at first shee modestly might start,
But must forthwith surrender every part,
As freely, as each to each before, gave either eye or heart.

XI

THE GOOD-NIGHT

N o w, as in Tullias tombe, one lampe burnt cleare,
　　Unchang'd for fifteene hundred yeare,

    May these love-lamps we here enshrine,
In warmth, light, lasting, equall the divine.
       Fire ever doth aspire,
And makes all like it selfe, turnes all to fire,
But ends in ashes, which these cannot doe,
For none of these is fuell, but fire too.
This is joyes bonfire, then, where loves strong Arts
Make of so noble individuall parts
One fire of foure inflaming eyes, and of two loving hearts.

    IDIOS
As I have brought this song, that I may doe
    A perfect sacrifice, I'll burne it too.

    ALLOPHANES
No Sir. This paper I have justly got,
    For, in burnt incense, the perfume is not
His only that presents it, but of all;
    What ever celebrates this Festivall
Is common, since the joy thereof is so.
    Nor may your selfe be Priest: But let me goe,
Backe to the Court, and I will lay'it upon
    Such Altars, as prize your devotion.

EPITHALAMION MADE AT LINCOLNES INNE

THE Sun-beames in the East are spred,
Leave, leave, faire Bride, your solitary bed,
    No more shall you returne to it alone,
It nourseth sadnesse, and your bodies print,
Like to a grave, the yielding downe doth dint;
    You and your other you meet there anon;
    Put forth, put forth that warme balme-breathing thigh,
Which when next time you in these sheets wil smother,
    There it must meet another,
        Which never was, but must be, oft, more nigh;
Come glad from thence, goe gladder than you came,
To day put on perfection, and a womans name.

Daughters of London, you which bee
Our Golden Mines, and furnish'd Treasurie,
  You which are Angels, yet still bring with you
Thousands of Angels on your mariage daies,
Help with your presence and devise to praise
  These rites, which also unto you grow due;
  Conceitedly dresse her, and be assign'd,
By you, fit place for every flower and jewell,
  Make her for love fit fewell
        As gay as Flora, and as rich as Inde;
So may shee faire, rich, glad, and in nothing lame,
To day put on perfection, and a womans name.

And you frolique Patricians,
Sonnes of these Senators wealths deep oceans,
  Ye painted courtiers, barrels of others wits,
Yee country men, who but your beasts love none,
Yee of those fellowships whereof hee's one,
  Of study and play made strange Hermaphrodits,
  Here shine; This Bridegroom to the Temple bring
Loe, in yon path which store of straw'd flowers graceth
  The sober virgin paceth;
        Except my sight faile, 'tis no other thing;
Weep not nor blush, here is no griefe nor shame,
To day put on perfection, and a womans name.

Thy two-leav'd gates faire Temple unfold,
And these two in thy sacred bosome hold,
  Till, mystically joyn'd, but one they bee;
Then may thy leane and hunger-starved wombe
Long time expect their bodies and their tombe,
  Long after their owne parents fatten thee.
  All elder claimes, and all cold barrennesse,
All yeelding to new loves bee far for ever,
  Which might these two dissever,
        All wayes all th'other may each one possesse;
For, the best Bride, best worthy of praise and fame,
To day puts on perfection, and a womans name.

Oh winter dayes bright much delight,
Not for themselves, but for they soon bring night;

Other sweets wait thee than these diverse meats,
Other disports than dancing jollities,
Other love tricks than glancing with the eyes,
   But that the Sun still in our halfe Spheare sweates;
     Hee flies in winter, but he now stands still.
Yet shadowes turne; Noone point he hath attain'd,
  His steeds nill bee restrain'd,
     But gallop lively downe the Westerne hill;
Thou shalt, when he hath runne the worlds half frame,
To night put on perfection, and a womans name.

The amorous evening starre is rose,
Why then should not our amorous starre inclose
  Her selfe in her wish'd bed? Release your strings
Musicians, and dancers take some truce
With these your pleasing labours, for great use
  As much wearinesse as perfection brings;
     You, and not only you, but all toyl'd beasts
Rest duly; at night all their toyles are dispensed;
But in their beds commenced
     Are other labours, and more dainty feasts;
She goes a maid, who, lest she turne the same
To night puts on perfection, and a womans name.

Thy virgins girdle now untie,
And in thy nuptiall bed (loves altar) lye
  A pleasing sacrifice; now dispossesse
Thee of these chaines and robes which were put on
T'adorne the day, not thee; for thou, alone,
  Like vertue'and truth, art best in nakednesse;
     This bed is onely to virginitie
A grave, but, to a better state, a cradle;
Till now thou wast but able
  To be what now thou art; then that by thee
No more be said, *I may bee,* but, *I am,*
To night put on perfection, and a womans name.

Even like a faithfull man content,
That this life for a better should be spent,
  So, shee a mothers rich stile doth preferre,
And at the Bridegroomes wish'd approach doth lye,

Like an appointed lambe, when tenderly
   The priest comes on his knees t'embowell her;
      Now sleep or watch with more joy; and O light
Of heaven, to morrow rise thou hot, and early;
This Sun will love so dearely
      Her rest, that long, long we shall want her sight;
Wonders are wrought, for shee which had no maime,
To night puts on perfection, and a womans name.

Satyres

I

A W A Y thou fondling motley humorist,
Leave mee, and in this standing woodden chest,
Consorted with these few bookes, let me lye
In prison, and here be coffin'd, when I dye;
Here are Gods conduits, grave Divines; and here
Natures Secretary, the Philosopher;
And jolly Statesmen, which teach how to tie
The sinewes of a cities mistique bodie;
Here gathering Chroniclers, and by them stand
Giddie fantastique Poëts of each land.
Shall I leave all this constant company,
And follow headlong, wild uncertaine thee?
First sweare by thy best love in earnest
(If thou which lov'st all, canst love any best)
Thou wilt not leave mee in the middle street,
Though some more spruce companion thou dost meet,
Not though a Captaine do come in thy way
Bright parcell gilt, with forty dead mens pay,
Not though a briske perfum'd piert Courtier
Deigne with a nod, thy courtesie to answer.
Nor come a velvet Justice with a long
Great traine of blew coats, twelve, or fourteen strong,
Wilt thou grin or fawne on him, or prepare
A speech to Court his beautious sonne and heire!
For better or worse take mee, or leave mee:
To take, and leave mee is adultery.
Oh monstrous, superstitious puritan,
Of refin'd manners, yet ceremoniall man,
That when thou meet'st one, with enquiring eyes
Dost search, and like a needy broker prize
The silke, and gold he weares, and to that rate
So high or low, dost raise thy formall hat:

That wilt comfort none, untill thou have knowne
What lands hee hath in hope, or of his owne,
As though all thy companions should make thee
Jointures, and marry thy deare company.
Why should'st thou (that dost not onely approve,
But in ranke itchie lust, desire, and love
The nakednesse and barenesse to enjoy,
Of thy plumpe muddy whore, or prostitute boy)
Hate vertue, though shee be naked, and bare?
At birth, and death, our bodies naked are;
And till our Soules be unapparrelled
Of bodies, they from blisse are banished.
Mans first blest state was naked, when by sinne
Hee lost that, yet hee was cloath'd but in beasts skin,
And in this course attire, which I now weare,
With God, and with the Muses I conferre.
But since thou like a contrite penitent,
Charitably warn'd of thy sinnes, dost repent
These vanities, and giddinesses, loe
I shut my chamber doore, and come, lets goe.
But sooner may a cheape whore, who hath beene
Worne by as many severall men in sinne,
As are black feathers, or musk-colour hose,
Name her childs right true father, 'mongst all those:
Sooner may one guesse, who shall beare away
The Infanta of London, Heire to an India;
And sooner may a gulling weather Spie
By drawing forth heavens Scheme tell certainly
What fashioned hats, or ruffes, or suits next yeare
Our subtile-witted antique youths will weare;
Than thou, when thou depart'st from mee, canst show
Whither, why, when, or with whom thou wouldst go.
But how shall I be pardon'd my offence
That thus have sinn'd against my conscience?
Now we are in the street; He first of all
Improvidently proud, creepes to the wall,
And so imprisoned, and hem'd in by mee
Sells for a little state his libertie;
Yet though he cannot skip forth now to greet
Every fine silken painted foole we meet,

He them to him with amorous smiles allures,
And grins, smacks, shrugs, and such an itch endures,
As prentises, or schoole-boyes which doe know
Of some gay sport abroad, yet dare not goe.
And as fidlers stop lowest, at highest sound,
So to the most brave, stoops hee nigh'st the ground.
But to a grave man, he doth move no more
Than the wise politique horse would heretofore,
Or thou O Elephant or Ape wilt doe,
When any names the King of Spaine to you.
Now leaps he upright, Joggs me, and cryes, Do you see
Yonder well favoured youth? Oh, 'tis hee
That dances so divinely; Oh, said I,
Stand still, must you dance here for company?
Hee droopt, wee went, till one (which did excell
Th'Indians, in drinking his Tobacco well)
Met us; they talk'd; I whispered, let'us goe,
'T may be you smell him not, truely I doe;
He heares not mee, but, on the other side
A many-coloured Peacock having spide,
Leaves him and mee; I for my lost sheep stay;
He followes, overtakes, goes on the way,
Saying, him whom I last left, all repute
For his device, in hansoming a sute,
To judge of lace, pinke, panes, print, cut, and pleate
Of all the Court, to have the best conceit;
Our dull Comedians want him, let him goe;
But Oh, God strengthen thee, why stoop'st thou so?
Why? he hath travayld; Long? No; but to me
(Which understand none,) he doth seeme to be
Perfect French, and Italian; I replyed,
So is the Poxe; He answered not, but spy'd
More men of sort, of parts, and qualities;
At last his Love he in a windowe spies,
And like light dew exhal'd, he flings from mee
Violently ravish'd to his lechery.
Many were there, he could command no more;
Hee quarrell'd, fought, bled; and turn'd out of dore
Directly came to mee hanging the head,
And constantly a while must keepe his bed.

II

S I R; though (I thanke God for it) I do hate
Perfectly all this towne, yet there's one state
In all ill things so excellently best,
That hate, toward them, breeds pitty towards the rest.
Though Poëtry indeed be such a sinne
As I thinke that brings dearth, and Spaniards in,
Though like the Pestilence and old fashion'd love,
Ridlingly it catch men; and doth remove
Never, till it be sterv'd out; yet their state
Is poore, disarm'd, like Papists, not worth hate.
One, (like a wretch, which at Barre judg'd as dead,
Yet prompts him which stands next, and cannot reade,
And saves his life) gives ideot actors meanes
(Starving himselfe) to live by his labor'd sceanes;
As in some Organ, Puppits dance above
And bellows pant below, which them do move.
One would move Love by rithmes; but witchcrafts charms
Bring not now their old feares, nor their old harmes:
Rammes, and slings now are seely battery,
Pistolets are the best Artillerie.
And they who write to Lords, rewards to get,
Are they not like singers at doores for meat?
And they who write, because all write, have still
That excuse for writing, and for writing ill;
But hee is worst, who (beggarly) doth chaw
Others wits fruits, and in his ravenous maw
Rankly digested, doth those things out-spue,
As his owne things; and they are his owne, 'tis true
For if one eate my meate, though it be knowne
The meate was mine, th'excrement is his owne:
But these do mee no harme, nor they which use
To out-swive Dildoes, and out-usure Jewes;
To out-drinke the sea, to out-sweare the Letanie;
Who with sinnes all kindes as familiar bee
As Confessors; and for whose sinfull sake,
Schoolemen new tenements in hell must make:
Whose strange sinnes, Canonists could hardly tell
In which Commandements large receit they dwell.

But these punish themselves; the insolence
Of Coscus onely breeds my just offence,
Whom time (which rots all, and makes botches poxe,
And plodding on, must make a calfe an oxe)
Hath made a Lawyer, which was (alas) of late
But a scarce Poët; jollier of this state,
Than are new benefic'd ministers, he throwes
Like nets, or lime-twigs, wheresoever he goes,
His title of Barrister, on every wench,
And wooes in language of the Pleas, and Bench:
A motion, Lady; Speake Coscus; I have beene
In love, ever since *tricesimo* of the Queene,
Continuall claimes I have made, injunctions got
To stay my rivals suit, that hee should not
Proceed; spare mee; In Hillary terme I went,
You said, If I return'd next size in Lent,
I should be in remitter of your grace;
In th'interim my letters should take place
Of affidavits: words, words, which would teare
The tender labyrinth of a soft maids eare,
More, more, than ten Sclavonians scolding, more
Than when winds in our ruin'd Abbeyes rore.
When sicke with Poëtrie, and possest with muse
Thou wast, and mad, I hop'd; but men which chuse
Law practise for meere gaine, bold soule, repute
Worse than imbrothel'd strumpets prostitute.
Now like an owlelike watchman, hee must walke
His hands still at a bill, now he must talke
Idly, like prisoners, which whole months will sweare
That onely suretiship hath brought them there,
And to every suitor lye in every thing,
Like a Kings favourite, yea like a King;
Like a wedge in a blocke, wring to the barre,
Bearing-like Asses; and more shamelesse farre
Than carted whores, lye, to the grave Judge; for
Bastardy abounds not in Kings titles, nor
Symonie and Sodomy in Churchmens lives,
As these things do in him; by these he thrives.
Shortly (as the sea) hee will compasse all our land;
From Scots, to Wight; from Mount, to Dover strand.
And spying heires melting with luxurie,
Satan will not joy at their sinnes, as hee.

For as a thrifty wench scrapes kitching-stuffe,
And barrelling the droppings, and the snuffe,
Of wasting candles, which in thirty yeare
(Relique-like kept) perchance buyes wedding geare;
Peecemeale he gets lands, and spends as much time
Wringing each Acre, as men pulling prime.
In parchments then, large as his fields, hee drawes
Assurances, bigge, as gloss'd civill lawes,
So huge, that men (in our times forwardnesse)
Are Fathers of the Church for writing lesse.
These hee writes not; nor for these written payes,
Therefore spares no length; as in those first dayes
When Luther was profest, He did desire
Short *Pater nosters,* saying as a Fryer
Each day his beads, but having left those lawes,
Addes to Christs prayer, the Power and glory clause.
But when he sells or changes land, he'impaires
His writings, and (unwatch'd) leaves out, *ses heires,*
As slily as any Commenter goes by
Hard words, or sense; or in Divinity
As controverters, in vouch'd Texts, leave out
Shrewd words, which might against them cleare the doubt.
Where are those spred woods which cloth'd heretofore
Those bought lands? not built, nor burnt within dore.
Where's th'old landlords troops, and almes? In great hals
Carthusian fasts, and fulsome Bachanalls
Equally I hate; meanes blesse; in rich mens homes
I bid kill some beasts, but no Hecatombs,
None starve, none surfet so; But (Oh) we allow,
Good workes as good, but out of fashion now,
Like old rich wardrops; but my words none drawes
Within the vast reach of th'huge statute lawes.

III

KINDE pitty chokes my spleene; brave scorn forbids
Those teares to issue which swell my eye-lids;
I must not laugh, nor weepe sinnes, and be wise,
Can railing then cure these worne maladies?
Is not our Mistresse faire Religion,

As worthy of all our Soules devotion,
As vertue was to the first blinded age?
Are not heavens joyes as valiant to asswage
Lusts, as earths honour was to them? Alas,
As wee do them in meanes, shall they surpasse
Us in the end, and shall thy fathers spirit
Meete blinde Philosophers in heaven, whose merit
Of strict life may be imputed faith, and heare
Thee, whom hee taught so easie wayes and neare
To follow, damn'd? O if thou dar'st, feare this;
This feare great courage, and high valour is.
Dar'st thou ayd mutinous Dutch, and dar'st thou lay
Thee in ships woodden Sepulchers, a prey
To leaders rage, to stormes, to shot, to dearth?
Dar'st thou dive seas, and dungeons of the earth?
Hast thou couragious fire to thaw the ice
Of frozen North discoueries? and thrise
Colder than Salamanders, like divine
Children in th'oven, fires of Spaine, and the line,
Whose countries limbecks to our bodies bee,
Canst thou for gaine beare? and must every hee
Which cryes not, Goddesse, to thy Mistresse, draw,
Or eate thy poysonous words? courage of straw!
O desperate coward, wilt thou seeme bold, and
To thy foes and his (who made thee to stand
Sentinell in his worlds garrison) thus yeeld,
And for the forbidden warres, leave th'appointed field?
Know thy foes: The foule Devill (whom thou
Strivest to please,) for hate, not love, would allow
Thee faine, his whole Realme to be quit; and as
The worlds all parts wither away and passe,
So the worlds selfe, thy other lov'd foe, is
In her decrepit wayne, and thou loving this,
Dost love a withered and worne strumpet; last,
Flesh (it selfes death) and joyes which flesh can taste,
Thou lovest; and thy faire goodly soule, which doth
Give this flesh power to taste joy, thou dost loath.
Seeke true religion. O where? Mirreus
Thinking her unhous'd here, and fled from us,
Seekes her at Rome; there, because hee doth know
That shee was there a thousand yeares agoe,

He loves her ragges so, as wee here obey
The statecloth where the Prince sate yesterday.
Crantz to such brave Loves will not be inthrall'd,
But loves her onely, who at Geneva is call'd
Religion, plaine, simple, sullen, yong,
Contemptuous, yet unhansome; As among
Lecherous humors, there is one that judges
No wenches wholsome, but course country drudges.
Graius stayes still at home here, and because
Some Preachers, vile ambitious bauds, and lawes
Still new like fashions, bid him thinke that shee
Which dwels with us, is onely perfect, hee
Imbraceth her, whom his Godfathers will
Tender to him, being tender, as Wards still
Take such wives as their Guardians offer, or
Pay valewes. Carelesse Phrygius doth abhorre
All, because all cannot be good, as one
Knowing some women whores, dares marry none.
Gracious loves all as one, and thinkes that so
As women do in divers countries goe
In divers habits, yet are still one kinde,
So doth, so is Religion; and this blind-
nesse too much light breeds; but unmoved thou
Of force must one, and forc'd but one allow;
And the right; aske thy father which is shee,
Let him aske his; though truth and falsehood bee
Neare twins, yet truth a little elder is;
Be busie to seeke her, beleeve mee this,
Hee's not of none, nor worst, that seekes the best.
To adore, or scorne an image, or protest,
May all be bad; doubt wisely; in strange way
To stand inquiring right, is not to stray;
To sleepe, or runne wrong, is. On a huge hill,
Cragged, and steep, Truth stands, and hee that will
Reach her, about must, and about must goe;
And what the hills suddennes resists, winne so;
Yet strive so, that before age, deaths twilight,
Thy Soule rest, for none can worke in that night.
To will, implyes delay, therefore now doe:
Hard deeds, the bodies paines; hard knowledge too
The mindes indeavours reach, and mysteries

Are like the Sunne, dazling, yet plaine to all eyes.
Keepe the truth which thou hast found; men do not stand
In so ill case here, that God hath with his hand
Sign'd Kings blanck-charters to kill whom they hate,
Nor are they Vicars, but hangman to Fate.
Foole and wretch, wilt thou let thy Soule be tyed
To mans lawes, by which she shall not be tryed
At the last day? Oh, will it then boot thee
To say a Philip, or a Gregory,
A Harry, or a Martin taught thee this?
Is not this excuse for mere contraries,
Equally strong? cannot both sides say so?
That thou mayest rightly obey power, her bounds know;
Those past, her nature, and name is chang'd; to be
Then humble to her is idolatrie.
As streames are, Power is; those blest flowers that dwell
At the rough streames calme head, thrive and do well,
But having left their roots, and themselves given
To the streames tyrannous rage, alas are driven
Through mills, and rockes, and woods, and at last, almost
Consum'd in going, in the sea are lost:
So perish Soules, which more chuse mens unjust
Power from God claym'd, than God himselfe to trust.

I V

WELL; I may now receive, and die; My sinne
Indeed is great, but I have beene in
A Purgatorie, such as fear'd hell is
A recreation to, and scarse map of this.
My minde, neither with prides itch, nor yet hath been
Poyson'd with love to see, or to bee seene,
I had no suit there, nor new suite to shew,
Yet went to Court; But as Glaze which did goe
To'a Masse in jest, catch'd, was faine to disburse
The hundred markes, which is the Statutes curse;
Before he scapt, So'it pleas'd my destinie
(Guilty of my sin of going), to thinke me
As prone to all ill, and of good as forget-
full, as proud, as lustfull, and as much in debt,

As vaine, as witlesse, and as false as they
Which dwell at Court, for once going that way.
Therefore I suffered this; Towards me did runne
A thing more strange, than on Niles slime, the Sunne
E'r bred; or all which into Noahs Arke came;
A thing, which would have pos'd Adam to name;
Stranger than seaven Antiquaries studies,
Than Africks Monsters, Guianaes rarities.
Stranger than strangers; One, who for a Dane,
In the Danes Massacre had sure beene slaine,
If he had liv'd then; And without helpe dies,
When next the Prentises 'gainst Strangers rise.
One, whom the watch at noone lets scarce goe by,
One, to whom, the examining Justice sure would cry,
Sir, by your priesthood tell me what you are.
His cloths were strange, though coarse; and black, though bare;
Sleeveless his jerkin was, and it had beene
Velvet, but 'twas now (so much ground was seene)
Become Tufftaffatie; and our children shall
See it plaine Rashe awhile, then nought at all.
This thing hath travail'd, and saith, speakes all tongues
And only knoweth what to all States belongs.
Made of th'Accents, and best phrase of all these,
He speakes one language; If strange meats displease,
Art can deceive, or hunger force my tast,
But Pedants motley tongue, souldiers bumbast,
Mountebankes drugtongue, nor the termes of law
Are strong enough preparatives, to draw
Me to beare this: yet I must be content
With his tongue, in his tongue, call'd complement:
In which he can win widdowes, and pay scores,
Make men speake treason, cosen subtlest whores,
Out-flatter favorites, or outlie either
Jovius, or both together.
He names mee, and comes to mee; I whisper, God!
How have I sinn'd, that thy wraths furious rod,
This fellow chuseth me? He saith, Sir,
I love your judgement; Whom doe you prefer,
For the best linguist? And I seelily
Said, that I thought Calepines Dictionarie;
Nay, but of men, most sweet Sir; Beza then,

Some other Jesuites, and two reverend men
Of our two Academies, I named; There
He stopt mee, and said; Nay, your Apostles were
Good pretty linguists, and so Panurge was;
Yet a poore gentleman, all these may passe
By travaile. Then, as if he would have sold
His tongue, he prais'd it, and such wonders told
That I was faine to say, If you'had liv'd, Sir,
Time enough to have beene Interpreter
To Babells bricklayers, sure the Tower had stood.
He adds, If of court life you knew the good,
You would leave lonenesse. I said, not alone
My lonenesse is, but Spartanes fashion,
To teach by painting drunkards, doth not last
Now; Aretines pictures have made few chast;
No more can Princes courts, though there be few
Better pictures of vice, teach me vertue;
He, like to a high strecht lute string squeakt, O Sir,
'Tis sweet to talke of Kings. At Westminster,
Said I, The man that keepes the Abbey tombes,
And for his price doth with who ever comes,
Of all our Harries, and our Edwards talke,
From King to King and all their kin can walke:
Your eares shall heare nought, but Kings; your eyes meet
Kings only; The way to it, is Kingstreet.
He smack'd, and cry'd, He's base, Mechanique, coarse,
So are all your Englishmen in their discourse.
Are not your Frenchmen neate? Mine? as you see,
I have but one Frenchman, looke, hee followes mee.
Certes they are neatly cloth'd; I, of this minde am,
Your only wearing is your Grogaram.
Not so Sir, I have more. Under this pitch
He would not flie; I chaff'd him; But as Itch
Scratch'd into smart, and as blunt iron ground
Into an edge, hurts worse: So, I (foole) found,
Crossing hurt mee; To fit my sullennesse,
He to another key, his stile doth addresse,
And askes, what newes? I tell him of new playes.
He takes my hand, and as a Still, which staies
A Sembriefe, 'twixt each drop, he nigardly,
As loth to enrich mee, so tells many a lie.

More than ten Hollensheads, or Halls, or Stowes,
Of triviall houshold trash he knowes; He knowes
When the Queene frown'd, or smil'd, and he knowes what
A subtle States-man may gather of that;
He knowes who loves; whom; and who by poyson
Hasts to an Offices reversion;
He knowes who'hath sold his land, and now doth beg
A licence, old iron, bootes, shooes, and egge-
shels to transport; Shortly boyes shall not play
At span-counter, or blow-point, but they pay
Toll to some Courtier; And wiser than all us,
He knowes what Ladie is not painted; Thus
He with home-meats tries me; I belch, spue, spit,
Looke pale, and sickly, like a Patient; Yet
He thrusts on more; And as if he'd undertooke
To say Gallo-Belgicus without booke
Speakes of all States, and deeds, that have been since
The Spaniards came, to the losse of Amyens.
Like a bigge wife, at sight of loathed meat,
Readie to travaile: So I sigh, and sweat
To heare this Makeron talke: In vaine; for yet,
Either my humour, or his owne to fit,
He like a priviledg'd spie, whom nothing can
Discredit, Libells now 'gainst each great man.
He names a price for every office paid;
He saith, our warres thrive ill, because delai'd;
That offices are entail'd, and that there are
Perpetuities of them, lasting as farre
As the last day; And that great officers,
Doe with the Pirates share, and Dunkirkers.
Who wasts in meat, in clothes, in horse, he notes;
Who loves whores, who boyes, and who goats.
I more amas'd than Circes prisoners, when
They felt themselves turne beasts, felt my selfe then
Becomming Traytor, and mee thought I saw
One of our Giant Statutes ope his jaw
To sucke me in; for hearing him, I found
That as burnt venome Leachers do grow sound
By giving others their soares, I might growe
Guilty, and he free: Therefore I did shew
All signes of loathing; But since I am in,
I must pay mine, and my forefathers sinne

To the last farthing; Therefore to my power
Toughly and stubbornly I beare this crosse; But the'houre
Of mercy now was come; He tries to bring
Me to pay a fine to scape his torturing,
And saies, Sir, can you spare me; I said, willingly;
Nay, Sir, can you spare me a crowne? Thankfully I
Gave it, as Ransome; But as fidlers, still,
Though they be paid to be gone, yet needs will
Thrust one more jigge upon you: so did hee
With his long complementall thankes vexe me.
But he is gone, thankes to his needy want,
And the prerogative of my Crowne: Scant
His thankes were ended, when I, (which did see
All the court fill'd with more strange things than hee)
Ran from thence with such or more haste, than one
Who feares more actions, doth make from prison.
At home in wholesome solitarinesse
My precious soule began, the wretchednesse
Of suiters at court to mourne, and a trance
Like his, who dreamt he saw hell, did advance
It selfe on mee, Such men as he saw there,
I saw at court, and worse, and more; Low feare
Becomes the guiltie, not the accuser; Then,
Shall I, nones slave, of high borne, or rais'd men
Feare frownes? And, my Mistresse Truth, betray thee
To th'huffing braggart, puft Nobility?
No, no, Thou which since yesterday hast beene
Almost about the whole world, hast thou seene,
O Sunne, in all thy journey, Vanitie,
Such as swells the bladder of our court? I
Thinke he which made your waxen garden, and
Transported it from Italy to stand
With us, at London, flouts our Presence, for
Just such gay painted things, which no sappe, nor
Tast have in them, ours are; And naturall
Some of the stocks are, their fruits, bastard all.
'Tis ten a clock and past; All whom the Mews,
Baloune, Tennis, Dyet, or the stewes,
Had all the morning held, now the second
Time made ready, that day, in flocks, are found
In the Presence, and I, (God pardon mee.)
As fresh, and sweet their Apparrells be, as bee

The fields they sold to buy them; For a King
Those hose are, cry the flatterers; And bring
Them next weeke to the Theatre to sell;
Wants reach all states; Me seemes they doe as well
At stage, as court; All are players; who e'r lookes
(For themselves dare not goe) o'r Cheapside books,
Shall finde their wardrops Inventory. Now,
The Ladies come; As Pirats, which doe know
That there came weak ships fraught with Cutchannel,
The men board them; and praise, as they thinke, well,
Their beauties; they the mens wits; Both are bought.
Why good wits ne'r weare scarlet gownes, I thought
This cause, These men, mens wits for speeches buy,
And women buy all reds which scarlets die.
He call'd her beauty limetwigs, her haire net;
She feares her drugs ill laid, her haire loose set.
Would not Heraclitus laugh to see Macrine,
From hat to shooe, himselfe at doore refine,
As if the Presence were a Moschite, and lift
His skirts and hose, and call his clothes to shrift,
Making them confesse not only mortall
Great staines and holes in them; but veniall
Feathers and dust, wherewith they fornicate:
And then by *Durers* rules survay the state
Of his each limbe, and with strings the odds trye
Of his neck to his legge, and wast to thighe.
So in immaculate clothes, and Symetrie
Perfect as circles, with such nicetie
As a young Preacher at his first time goes
To preach, he enters, and a Lady which owes
Him not so much as good will, he arrests,
And unto her protests protests protests
So much as at Rome would serve to have throwne
Ten Cardinalls into the Inquisition;
And whisperd by Jesu, so often, that A
Pursevant would have ravish'd him away
For saying of our Ladies psalter; But 'tis fit
That they each other plague, they merit it.
But here comes Glorious that will plague them both,
Who, in the other extreme, only doth
Call a rough carelessenesse, good fashion;
Whose cloak his spurres teare; whom he spits on

He cares not, His ill words doe no harme
To him; he rusheth in, as if arme, arme,
He meant to crie; And though his face be as ill
As theirs which in old hangings whip Christ, still
He strives to looke worse, he keepes all in awe;
Jeasts like a licenc'd foole, commands like law.
Tyr'd, now I leave this place, and but pleas'd so
As men which from gaoles to'execution goe,
Goe through the great chamber (why is it hung
With the seaven deadly sinnes?). Being among
Those Askaparts, men big enough to throw
Charring Crosse for a barre, men that doe know
No token of worth, but Queenes man, and fine
Living, barrells of beefe, flaggons of wine;
I shooke like a spyed Spie. Preachers which are
Seas of Wit and Arts, you can, then dare,
Drowne the sinnes of this place, for, for mee
Which am but a scarce brooke, it enough shall bee
To wash the staines away; Although I yet
With *Macchabees* modestie, the knowne merit
Of my worke lessen: yet some wise man shall,
I hope, esteeme my writs Canonicall.

V

THOU shalt not laugh in this leafe, Muse, nor they
Whom any pitty warmes; He which did lay
Rules to make Courtiers, (hee being understood
May make good Courtiers, but who Courtiers good?)
Frees from the sting of jests all who in extreme
Are wretched or wicked: of these two a theame
Charity and liberty give me. What is hee
Who Officers rage, and Suiters misery
Can write, and jest? If all things be in all,
As I thinke, since all, which were, are, and shall
Bee, be made of the same elements:
Each thing, each thing implyes or represents.
Then man is a world; in which, Officers
Are the vast ravishing seas; and Suiters,
Springs; now full, now shallow, now drye; which, to
That which drownes them, run: These selfe reasons do

Prove the world a man, in which, officers
Are the devouring stomacke, and Suiters
The excrements, which they voyd. All men are dust;
How much worse are Suiters, who to mens lust
Are made preyes? O worse than dust, or wormes meat,
For they do eate you now, whose selves wormes shall eate.
They are the mills which grinde you, yet you are
The winde which drives them; and a wastfull warre
Is fought against you, and you fight it; they
Adulterate lawe, and you prepare their way
Like wittals; th'issue your owne ruine is.
Greatest and fairest Empresse, know you this?
Alas, no more than Thames calme head doth know
Whose meades her armes drowne, or whose corne o'rflow:
You Sir, whose righteousnes she loves, whom I
By having leave to serve, am most richly
For service paid, authoriz'd, now beginne
To know and weed out this enormous sinne.
O Age of rusty iron! Some better wit
Call it some worse name, if ought equall it;
The iron Age *that* was, when justice was sold; now
Injustice is sold dearer farre. Allow
All demands, fees, and duties, gamsters, anon
The mony which you sweat, and sweare for, is gon
Into other hands: So controverted lands
Scape, like Angelica, the strivers hands.
If Law be the Judges heart, and hee
Have no heart to resist letter, or fee,
Where wilt thou appeale? powre of the Courts below
Flow from the first maine head, and these can throw
Thee, if they sucke thee in, to misery,
To fetters, halters; But if the injury
Steele thee to dare complaine, Alas, thou go'st
Against the stream, when upwards: when thou art most
Heavy and most faint; and in these labours they,
'Gainst whom thou should'st complaine, will in the way
Become great seas, o'r which, when thou shalt bee
Forc'd to make golden bridges, thou shalt see
That all thy gold was drown'd in them before;
All things follow their like, only who have may have more.
Judges are Gods; he who made and said them so,
Meant not that men should be forc'd to them to goe,

By meanes of Angels; When supplications
We send to God, to Dominations,
Powers, Cherubins, and all heavens Courts, if wee
Should pay fees as here, Daily bread would be
Scarce to Kings; so 'tis. Would it not anger
A Stoicke, a coward, yea a Martyr,
To see a Pursuivant come in, and call
All his cloathes, Copes; Bookes, Primers; and all
His Plate, Challices; and mistake them away,
And aske a fee for comming? Oh, ne'r may
Faire lawes white reverend name be strumpeted,
To warrant thefts: she is established
Recorder to Destiny, on earth, and shee
Speakes Fates words, and but tells us who must bee
Rich, who poore, who in chaires, who in jayles:
Shee is all faire, but yet hath foule long nailes,
With which she scracheth Suiters; In bodies
Of men, so in law, nailes are th'extremities,
So Officers stretch to more than Law can doe,
As our nailes reach what no else part comes to.
Why barest thou to yon Officer? Foole, Hath hee
Got those goods, for which erst men bar'd to thee?
Foole, twice, thrice, thou hast bought wrong, and now hungerly
Beg'st right; But that dole comes not till these dye.
Thou had'st much, and lawes Urim and Thummim trie
Thou wouldst for more; and for all hast paper
Enough to cloath all the great Carricks Pepper.
Sell that, and by that thou much more shalt leese,
Than Haman, when he sold his Antiquities.
O wretch that thy fortunes should moralize
Esops fables, and make tales, prophesies.
Thou'art the swimming dog whom shadows cosened,
And div'st, neare drowning, for what's vanished.

UPON MR. THOMAS CORYATS CRUDITIES

OH to what heighth will love of greatnesse drive
Thy leavened spirit, *Sesqui-superlative?*
Venice vast lake thou hadst seen, and wouldst seek then
Some vaster thing, and found'st a Curtizan.

That inland Sea having discovered well,
A Cellar gulfe, where one might saile to hell
From Heydelberg, thou longdst to see: And thou
This Booke, greater than all, producest now.
Infinite worke, which doth so far extend,
That none can study it to any end.
'Tis no one thing, it is not fruit nor roote;
Nor poorely limited with head or foot.
If man be therefore man, because he can
Reason, and laugh, thy booke doth halfe make man.
One halfe being made, thy modestie was such,
That thou on th'other half wouldst never touch.
When wilt thou be at full, great Lunatique?
Not till thou exceed the world? Canst thou be like
A prosperous nose-borne wenne, which sometimes growes
To be farre greater than the Mother-nose?
Goe then; and as to thee, when thou didst go,
Munster did Townes, and *Gesner* Authors show,
Mount now to *Gallo-belgicus;* appear
As deepe a States-man, as a Gazettier.
Homely and familiarly, when thou com'st back,
Talke of *Will, Conquerour,* and *Prester Jack.*
Go bashfull man, lest here thou blush to looke
Upon the progresse of thy glorious booke,
To which both Indies sacrifices send;
The West sent gold, which thou didst freely spend,
(Meaning to see't no more) upon the presse.
The East sends hither her deliciousnesse;
And thy leaves must imbrace what comes from thence,
The Myrrhe, the Pepper, and the Frankincense.
This magnifies thy leaves; but if they stoope
To neighbour wares, when Merchants do unhoope
Voluminous barrels; if thy leaves do then
Convey these wares in parcels unto men;
If for vast Tons of Currans, and of Figs,
Of Medicinall and Aromatique twigs,
Thy leaves a better method do provide,
Divide to pounds, and ounces sub-divide;
If they stoope lower yet, and vent our wares,
Home-*manufactures,* to thick popular Faires,
If *omni-praegnant* there, upon warme stalls,
They hatch all wares for which the buyer calls;

Then thus thy leaves we justly may commend,
That they all kinde of matter comprehend.
Thus thou, by means which th'Ancients never took,
A Pandect makest, and Universall Booke.
The bravest Heroes, for publike good,
Scattered in divers Lands their limbs and blood.
Worst malefactors, to whom men are prize,
Do publike good, cut in Anatomies;
So will thy booke in peeces: for a Lord
Which casts at Portescues, and all the board,
Provide whole books; each leafe enough will be
For friends to passe time, and keep company.
Can all carouse up thee? no, thou must fit
Measures; and fill out for the half-pint wit:
Some shall wrap pils, and save a friends life so,
Some shall stop muskets, and so kill a foe.
Thou shalt not ease the Criticks of next age
So much, at once their hunger to asswage:
Nor shall wit-pirats hope to finde thee lye
All in one bottome, in one Librarie.
Some Leaves may paste strings there in other books,
And so one may, which on another looks,
Pilfer, alas, a little wit from you;
But hardly* much; and yet I think this true;
As *Sibyls* was, your booke is mysticall,
For every peece is as much worth as all.
Therefore mine impotency I confesse,
The healths which my braine bears must be far lesse:
Thy Gyant-wit 'orethrowes me, I am gone;
And rather than read all, I would reade none.

IN EUNDEM MACARONICON

Quot, dos haec, Linguists perfetti, *Disticha* fairont,
Tot cuerdos *States-men, hic* livre fara *tuus.*
Es *sat* a my l'honneur estre hic inteso; Car *I leave*
L'honra, de personne nestre creduto, *tibi.*

Explicit Joannes Donne

* I meane from one page which shall paste strings in a booke.

Verse Letters to Severall Personages

THE STORME

THOU which art I, ('tis nothing to be soe)
Thou which art still thy selfe, by these shalt know
Part of our passage; And, a hand, or eye
By *Hilliard* drawne, is worth an history,
By a worse painter made; and (without ɩride)
When by thy judgment they are dignifi'd,
My lines are such: 'Tis the preheminence
Of friendship onely to'impute excellence.
England to whom we'owe, what we be, and have,
Sad that her sonnes did seeke a forraine grave
(For, Fates, or Fortunes drifts none can soothsay,
Honour and misery have one face and way.)
From out her pregnant intrailes sigh'd a winde
Which at th'ayres middle marble roome did finde
Such strong resistance, that it selfe it threw
Downeward againe; and so when it did view
How in the port, our fleet deare time did leese,
Withering like prisoners, which lye but for fees,
Mildly it kist our sailes, and, fresh and sweet,
As to a stomack sterv'd, whose insides meete,
Meate comes, it came; and swole our sailes, when wee
So joyd, as *Sara*'her swelling joy'd to see.
But 'twas but so kinde, as our countrimen,
Which bring friends one dayes way, and leave them then.
Then like two mighty Kings, which dwelling farre
Asunder, meet against a third to warre,
The South and West winds joyn'd, and, as they blew,
Waves like a rowling trench before them threw.

Sooner than you read this line, did the gale,
Like shot, not fear'd till felt, our sailes assaile;
And what at first was call'd a gust, the same
Hath now a stormes, anon a tempests name.
Jonas, I pitty thee, and curse those men,
Who when the storm rag'd most, did wake thee then;
Sleepe is paines easiest salve, and doth fulfill
All offices of death, except to kill.
But when I wakt, I saw, that I saw not;
Ay, and the Sunne, which should teach mee'had forgot
East, West, Day, Night, and I could onely say,
If'the world had lasted, now it had been day.
Thousands our noyses were, yet wee'mongst all
Could none by his right name, but thunder call:
Lightning was all our light, and it rain'd more
Than if the Sunne had drunke the sea before.
Some coffin'd in their cabbins lye,'equally
Griev'd that they are not dead, and yet must dye;
And as sin-burd'ned soules from graves will creepe,
At the last day, some forth their cabbins peepe:
And tremblingly'aske what newes, and doe heare so,
Like jealous husbands, what they would not know.
Some sitting on the hatches, would seeme there,
With hideous gazing to feare away feare.
Then note they the ships sicknesses, the Mast
Shak'd with this ague, and the Hold and Wast
With a salt dropsie clog'd, and all our tacklings
Snapping, like too-high-stretched treble strings.
And from our totterd sailes, ragges drop downe so,
As from one hang'd in chaines, a yeare agoe.
Even our Ordinance plac'd for our defence,
Strike to breake loose, and scape away from thence.
Pumping hath tir'd our men, and what's the gaine?
Seas into seas throwne, we suck in againe;
Hearing hath deaf'd our saylers; and if they
Knew how to heare, there's none knowes what to say.
Compar'd to these stormes, death is but a qualme,
Hell somewhat lightsome, and the'Bermuda calme.
Darknesse, lights elder brother, his birth-right
Claims o'er this world, and to heaven hath chas'd light.
All things are one, and that one none can be,
Since all formes, uniforme deformity

Doth cover, so that wee, except God say
Another *Fiat,* shall have no more day.
So violent, yet long these furies bee,
That though thine absence sterve me,'I wish not thee.

THE CALME

O U R storme is past, and that storms tyrannous rage,
A stupid calme, but nothing it, doth swage.
The fable is inverted, and farre more
A blocke afflicts, now, than a storke before.
Stormes chafe, and soon weare out themselves, or us;
In calmes, Heaven laughs to see us languish thus.
As steady'as I can wish, that my thoughts were,
Smooth as thy mistresse glasse, or what shines there,
The sea is now. And, as the Iles which wee
Seeke, when wee can move, our ships rooted bee.
As water did in stormes, now pitch runs out:
As lead, when a fir'd Church becomes one spout.
And all our beauty, and our trimme, decayes,
Like courts removing, or like ended playes.
The fighting place now seamens ragges supply;
And all the tackling is a frippery.
No use of lanthornes; and in one place lay
Feathers and dust, to day and yesterday.
Earths hollownesses, which the worlds lungs are,
Have no more winde than the upper valt of aire.
We can nor lost friends, nor sought foes recover,
But meteorlike, save that wee move not, hover.
Onely the Calenture together drawes
Deare friends, which meet dead in great fishes jawes:
And on the hatches as on Altars lyes
Each one, his owne Priest, and owne Sacrifice.
Who live, that miracle do multiply
Where walkers in hot Ovens, doe not dye.
If in despite of these, wee swimme, that hath
No more refreshing, than our brimstone Bath,
But from the sea, into the ship we turne,
Like parboyl'd wretches, on the coales to burne.
Like *Bajazet* encag'd, the shepheards scoffe,
Or like slacke sinew'd *Samson,* his haire off,

Languish our ships. Now, as a Miriade
Of Ants, durst th'Emperours lov'd snake invade,
The crawling Gallies, Sea-gaols, finny chips,
Might brave our Pinnaces, now bed-ridde ships.
Whether a rotten state, and hope of gaine,
Or to disuse mee from the queasie paine
Of being belov'd, and loving, or the thirst
Of honour, or faire death, out pusht mee first,
I lose my end: for here as well as I
A desperate may live, and a coward die.
Stagge, dogge, and all which from, or towards flies,
Is paid with life, or pray, or doing dyes.
Fate grudges us all, and doth subtly lay
A scourge,'gainst which wee all forget to pray,
He that at sea prayes for more winde, as well
Under the poles may begge cold, heat in hell.
What are wee then? How little more alas
Is man now, than before he was? he was
Nothing; for us, wee are for nothing fit;
Chance, or our selves still disproportion it.
Wee have no power, no will, no sense; I lye,
I should not then thus feele this miserie.

TO THE COUNTESSE OF HUNTINGTON

THAT unripe side of earth, that heavy clime
That gives us man up now, like *Adams* time
Before he ate; mans shape, that would yet bee
(Knew they not it, and fear'd beasts companie)
So naked at this day, as though man there
From Paradise so great a distance were,
As yet the newes could not arrived bee
Of *Adams* tasting the forbidden tree;
Depriv'd of that free state which they were in,
And wanting the reward, yet beare the sinne.
  But, as from extreme hights who downward looks,
Sees men at childrens shapes, Rivers at brookes,
And loseth younger formes; so, to your eye,
These (Madame) that without your distance lie,
Must either mist, or nothing seeme to be,
Who are at home but wits mere *Atomi*.

But, I who can behold them move, and stay,
Have found my selfe to you, just their midway;
And now must pitty them; for, as they doe
Seeme sick to me, just so must I to you.
Yet neither will I vexe your eyes to see
A sighing Ode, nor crosse-arm'd Elegie.
I come not to call pitty from your heart,
Like some white-liver'd dotard that would part
Else from his slipperie soule with a faint groane,
And faithfully, (without you smil'd) were gone.
I cannot feele the tempest of a frowne,
I may be rais'd by love, but not throwne down.
Though I can pittie those sigh twice a day,
I hate that thing whispers it selfe away.
Yet since all love is fever, who to trees
Doth talke, doth yet in loves cold ague freeze.
'Tis love, but, with such fatall weaknesse made,
That it destroyes it selfe with its owne shade.
Who first look'd sad, griev'd, pin'd, and shew'd his paine,
Was he that first taught women, to disdaine.

  As all things were one nothing, dull and weake,
Untill this raw disordered heape did breake,
And severall desires led parts away,
Water declin'd with earth, the ayre did stay,
Fire rose, and each from other but unty'd,
Themselves unprison'd were and purify'd:
So was love, first in vast confusion hid,
An unripe willingnesse which nothing did,
A thirst, an Appetite which had no ease,
That found a want, but knew not what would please.
What pretty innocence in those dayes mov'd!
Man ignorantly walk'd by her he lov'd;
Both sigh'd and enterchang'd a speaking eye,
Both trembled and were sick, both knew not why.
That naturall fearefulnesse that struck man dumbe,
Might well (those times consider'd) man become.
As all discoverers whose first assay
Findes but the place, after, the nearest way:
So passion is to womans love, about,
Nay, farther off, than when we first set out.
It is not love that sueth, or doth contend;
Love either conquers, or but meets a friend.

Man's better part consists of purer fire,
And findes it selfe allow'd, ere it desire.
Love is wise here, keepes home, gives reason sway,
And journeys not till it finde summer-way.
A weather-beaten Lover but once knowne,
Is sport for every girle to practise on.
Who strives through womans scornes, women to know,
Is lost, and seekes his shadow to outgoe;
It must be sicknesse, after one disdaine,
Though he be call'd aloud, to looke againe.
Let others sigh, and grieve; one cunning sleight
Shall freeze my Love to Christall in a night.
I can love first, and (if I winne) love still;
And cannot be remov'd, unlesse she will.
It is her fault if I unsure remaine,
Shee onely can untie, and binde againe.
The honesties of love with ease I doe,
But am no porter for a tedious woo.
     But (madame) I now thinke on you; and here
Where we are at our hights, you but appeare,
We are but clouds you rise from, our noone-ray
But a foule shadow, not your breake of day.
You are at first hand all that's faire and right,
And others good reflects but backe your light.
You are a perfectnesse, so curious hit,
That youngest flatteries doe scandall it.
For, what is more doth what you are restraine,
And though beyond, is downe the hill againe.
We'have no next way to you, we crosse to it:
You are the straight line, thing prais'd, attribute;
Each good in you's a light; so many a shade
You make, and in them are your motions made.
These are your pictures to the life. From farre
We see you move, and here your *Zani's* are:
So that no fountaine good there is, doth grow
In you, but our dimme actions faintly shew.
     Then finde I, if mans noblest part be love,
Your purest luster must that shadow move.
The soule with body, is a heaven combin'd
With earth, and for mans ease, but nearer joyn'd.
Where thoughts the starres of soule we understand,
We guesse not their large natures, but command.

And love in you, that bountie is of light,
That gives to all, and yet hath infinite.
Whose heat doth force us thither to intend,
But soule we finde too earthly to ascend,
'Till slow accesse hath made it wholy pure,
Able immortall clearnesse to endure.
Who dare aspire this journey with a staine,
Hath waight will force him headlong backe againe.
No more can impure man retaine and move
In that pure region of a worthy love,
Than earthly substance can unforc'd aspire,
And leave his nature to converse with fire:
Such may have eye, and hand; may sigh, may speak;
But like swoln bubles, when they are high'st they break.

   Though far removed Northerne fleets scarce finde
The Sunnes comfort; others thinke him too kinde.
There is an equall distance from her eye,
Men perish too farre off, and burne too nigh.
But as ayre takes the Sunne-beames equall bright
From the first Rayes, to his last opposite:
So able men, blest with a vertuous Love,
Remote or neare, or howsoe'r they move;
Their vertue breakes all clouds that might annoy,
There is no Emptinesse, but all is Joy.
He much profanes whom violent heats do move
To stile his wandring rage of passion, *Love*.
Love that imparts in every thing delight,
Is fain'd, which only tempts mans appetite.
Why love among the vertues is not knowne
Is, that love is them all contract in one.

TO SIR HENRY WOTTON

sir, more than kisses, letters mingle Soules;
For, thus friends absent speake. This ease controules
The tediousnesse of my life: But for these
I could ideate nothing, which could please,
But I should wither in one day, and passe
To'a bottle'of Hay, that am a locke of Grasse.
Life is a voyage, and in our lifes wayes
Countries, Courts, Townes are Rockes, or Remoraes;

They breake or stop all ships, yet our state's such,
That though than pitch they staine worse, wee must touch.
If in the furnace of the even line,
Or under th'adverse icy poles thou pine,
Thou know'st two temperate Regions girded in,
Dwell there: But Oh, what refuge canst thou winne
Parch'd in the Court, and in the country frozen?
Shall cities, built of both extremes, be chosen?
Can dung and garlike be'a perfume? or can
A Scorpion and Torpedo cure a man?
Cities are worst of all three; of all three
(O knottie riddle) each is worst equally.
Cities are Sepulchers; they who dwell there
Are carcases, as if such there were.
And Courts are Theaters, where some men play
Princes, some slaves, all to one end, and of one clay.
The Country is a desert, where no good,
Gain'd (as habits, not borne,) is understood.
There men become beasts, and prone to more evils;
In cities blockes, and in a lewd court, devills.
As in the first Chaos confusedly
Each elements qualities were in the'other three;
So pride, lust, covertize, being severall
To these three places, yet all are in all,
And mingled thus, their issue incestuous.
Falshood is denizon'd. Virtue is barbarous.
Let no man say there, Virtues flintie wall
Shall locke vice in mee, I'll do none, but know all.
Men are spunges, which to poure out, receive,
Who know false play, rather than lose, deceive.
For in best understandings, sinne beganne,
Angels sinn'd first, then Devills, and then man.
Onely perchance beasts sinne not; wretched wee
Are beasts in all, but white integritie.
I thinke if men, which in these places live
Durst looke for themselves, and themselves retrive,
They would like strangers greet themselves, seeing then
Utopian youth, growne old Italian.
  Be thou thine owne home, and in thy selfe dwell;
Inne any where, continuance maketh hell.
And seeing the snaile, which every where doth rome,
Carrying his owne house still, still is at home,

Follow (for he is easie pac'd) this snaile,
Bee thine owne Palace, or the world's thy gaole.
And in the worlds sea, do not like corke sleepe
Upon the waters face; nor in the deepe
Sinke like a lead without a line: but as
Fishes glide, leaving no print where they passe,
Nor making sound; so closely thy course goe,
Let men dispute, whether thou breathe, or no.
Onely'in this one thing, be no Galenist: To make
Courts hot ambitions wholesome, do not take
A dramme of Countries dulnesse; do not adde
Correctives, but as chymiques, purge the bad.
But, Sir, I advise not you, I rather doe
Say o'er those lessons, which I learn'd of you:
Whom, free from German schismes, and lightnesse
Of France, and faire Italies faithlesnesse,
Having from these suck'd all they had of worth,
And brought home that faith, which you carried forth,
I throughly love. But if my selfe, I have wonne
To know my rules, I have, and you have

DONNE.

TO SIR HENRY GOODYERE

W H O makes the Past, a patterne for next yeare,
   Turnes no new leafe, but still the same things reads,
Seene things, he sees againe, heard things doth heare,
   And makes his life, but like a paire of beads.

A Palace, when'tis that, which it should be,
   Leaves growing, and stands such, or else decayes:
But hee which dwels there, is not so; for hee
   Strives to urge upward, and his fortune raise;

So had your body'her morning, hath her noone,
   And shall not better; her next change is night:
But her faire larger guest, to'whom Sun and Moone
   Are sparkes, and short liv'd, claimes another right.

The noble Soule by age growes lustier,
   Her appetite, and her digestion mend,
Wee must not sterve, nor hope to pamper her
   With womens milke, and pappe unto the end.

Provide you manlyer dyet; you have seene
   All libraries, which are Schools, Camps, and Courts;
But aske your Garners if you have not beene
   In harvests, too indulgent to your sports.

Would you redeeme it? then your selfe transplant
   A while from hence. Perchance outlandish ground
Beares no more wit, than ours, but yet more scant
   Are those diversions there, which here abound.

To be a stranger hath that benefit,
   Wee can beginnings, but not habits choke.
Goe; whither? Hence; you get, if you forget;
   New faults, till they prescribe in us, are smoake.

Our soule, whose country'is heaven, and God her father,
   Into this world, corruptions sinke, is sent,
Yet, so much in her travaile she doth gather,
   That she returnes home, wiser than she went;

It payes you well, if it teach you to spare,
   And make you,'asham'd, to make your hawks praise, yours,
Which when herselfe she lessens in the aire,
   You then first say, that high enough she toures.

However, keepe the lively tast you hold
   Of God, love him as now, but feare him more,
And in your afternoones thinke what you told
   And promis'd him, at morning prayer before.

Let falshood like a discord anger you,
   Else be not froward. But why doe I touch
Things, of which none is in your practise new,
   And Tables, or fruit-trenchers teach as much;

But thus I make you keepe your promise Sir,
   Riding I had you, though you still staid there,
And in these thoughts, although you never stirre,
   You came with mee to Micham, and are here.

TO MR. ROWLAND WOODWARD

LIKE one who'in her third widdowhood doth professe
Her selfe a Nunne, tyed to retirednesse,
So'affects my muse now, a chast fallownesse;

Since shee to few, yet to too many hath showne
How love-song weeds, and Satyrique thornes are growne
Where seeds of better Arts, were early sown.

Though to use, and love Poëtrie, to mee,
Betroth'd to no'one Art, be no'adulterie;
Omissions of good, ill, as ill deeds bee.

For though to us it seeme, 'and be light and thinne,
Yet in those faithfull scales, where God throwes in
Mens workes, vanity weighs as much as sinne.

If our Soules have stain'd their first white, yet wee
May cloth them with faith, and deare honestie,
Which God Imputes, as native puritie.

There is no Vertue, but Religion:
Wise, valiant, sober, just, are names, which none
Want, which want not Vice-covering discretion.

Seeke wee then our selves in our selves; for as
Men force the Sunne with much more force to passe,
By gathering his beames with a christall glasse;

So wee, if wee into our selves will turne,
Blowing our sparkes of vertue, may outburne
The straw, which doth about our hearts sojourne.

You know, Physitians, when they would infuse
Into any'oyle, the Soules of Simples, use
Places, where they may lie still warme, to chuse.

So workes retirednesse in us; To rome
Giddily, and be every where, but at home,
Such freedome doth a banishment become.

Wee are but farmers of our selves, yet may,
If we can stocke our selves, and thrive, uplay
Much, much deare treasure for the great rent day.

Manure thy selfe then, to thy selfe be'approv'd,
And with vaine outward things be no more mov'd,
But to know, that I love thee'and would be lov'd.

TO SIR HENRY WOOTTON

H E R E ' S no more newes, than vertue,'I may as well　　2 1p.
Tell you *Cales*, or *Saint Michaels* tale for newes, as tell
That vice doth here habitually dwell.

Yet, as to'get stomachs, we walke up and downe,
And toyle to sweeten rest, so, may God frowne,
If, but to loth both, I haunt Court, or Towne.

For here no one is from the'extremitie
Of vice, by any other reason free,
But that the next to'him, is worse than hee.

In this worlds warfare, they whom rugged Fate,
(Gods Commissary,) doth so throughly hate,
As in'the Courts Squadron to marshall their state:

If they stand arm'd with seely honesty,
With wishing prayers, and neat integritie,
Like Indians'gainst Spanish hosts they bee.

Suspitious boldnesse to this place belongs,
And to'have as many eares as all have tongues;
Tender to know, tough to acknowledge wrongs.

Beleeve mee Sir, in my youths giddiest dayes,
When to be like the Court, was a playes praise,
Playes were not so like Courts, as Courts'are like playes.

Then let us at these mimicke antiques jeast,
Whose deepest projects, and egregious gests
Are but dull Moralls of a game at Chests.

But now'tis incongruity to smile,
Therefore I end; and bid farewell a while,
At Court; though *From Court,* were the better stile.

HENRICO WOTTONI IN HIBERNIA BELLIGERANTI

W E N T you to conquer? and have so much lost
Yourself, that what in you was best and most,
Respective friendship, should so quickly dye?
In publique gaine my share'is not such that I
Would lose your love for Ireland: better cheap
I pardon death (who though he do not reap
Yet gleanes hee many of our frends away)
Than that your waking mind should bee a prey
To lethargies. Lett shott, and boggs, and skeines
With bodies deale, as fate bids and restreynes;
Ere sicknesses attack, yong death is best,
Who payes before his death doth scape arrest.
Lett not your soule (at first with graces fill'd,
And since, and thorough crooked lymbecks, still'd
In many schools and courts, which quicken it,)
It self unto the Irish negligence submit.
I aske not labored letters which should weare
Long papers out: nor letters which should feare
Dishonest carriage: or a seers art:
Nor such as from the brayne come, but the hart.

TO THE COUNTESSE OF BEDFORD

MADAME,
R E A S O N is our Soules left hand, Faith her right,
By these wee reach divinity, that's you;
Their loves, who have the blessings of your light,
Grew from their reason, mine from faire faith grew.

But as, although a squint lefthandednesse
Be'ungracious, yet we cannot want that hand,
So would I, not to encrease, but to expresse
My faith. as I beleeve, so understand.

Therefore I study you first in your Saints,
Those friends, whom your election glorifies,
Then in your deeds, accesses, and restraints,
And what you reade, and what your selfe devize.

But soone, the reasons why you'are lov'd by all,
Grow infinite, and so passe reasons reach,
Then backe againe to'implicite faith I fall,
And rest on what the Catholique voice doth teach;

That you are good: and not one Heretique
Denies it: if he did, yet you are so.
For, rockes, which high top'd and deep rooted sticke,
Waves wash, not undermine, nor overthrow.

In every thing there naturally growes
A *Balsamum* to keepe it fresh, and new,
If'twere not injur'd by extrinsique blowes;
Your birth and beauty are this Balme in you.

But you of learning and religion,
And vertue,'and such ingredients, have made
A methridate, whose operation
Keepes off, or cures what can be done or said.

Yet, this is not your physicke, but your food,
A dyet fit for you; for you are here
The first good Angell, since the worlds frame stood,
That ever did in womans shape appeare.

Since you are then Gods masterpeece, and so
His Factor for our loves; do as you doe,
Make your returne home gracious; and bestow
This life on that; so make one life of two.
    For so God helpe mee,'I would not misse you there
    For all the good which you can do me here.

TO THE COUNTESSE OF BEDFORD

Madame,
y o u have refin'd mee, and to worthyest things
(Vertue, Art, Beauty, Fortune,) now I see
Rarenesse, or use, not nature value brings;
And such, as they are circumstanc'd, they bee.
    Two ills can ne're perplexe us, sinne to'excuse;
    But of two good things, we may leave and chuse.

Therefore at Court, which is not vertues clime,
(Where a transcendent height, (as, lownesse mee)
Makes her not be, or not show) all my rime
Your vertues challenge, which there rarest bee;
    For, as darke texts need notes: there some must bee
    To usher vertue, and say, *This is shee.*

So in the country'is beauty; to this place
You are the season (Madame) you the day,
   'Tis but a grave of spices, till your face
Exhale them, and a thick close bud display.
    Widow'd and reclus'd else, her sweets she'enshrines;
    As China, when the Sunne at Brasill dines.

Out from your chariot, morning breaks at night,
And falsifies both computations so;
Since a new world doth rise here from your light,
We your new creatures, by new recknings goe.
    This showes that you from nature lothly stray,
    That suffer not an artificiall day.

In this you'have made the Court the Antipodes,
And will'd your Delegate, the vulgar Sunne,
To doe profane autumnall offices,
Whilst here to you, wee sacrificers runne;
    And whether Priests, or Organs, you wee'obey,
    We sound your influence, and your Dictates say.

Yet to that Deity which dwels in you,
Your vertuous Soule, I now not sacrifice;
These are *Petitions,* and not *Hymnes;* they sue

But that I may survay the edifice.
 In all Religions as much care hath bin
 Of Temples frames, and beauty,'as Rites within.

As all which goe to Rome, doe not thereby
Esteeme religions, and hold fast the best,
But serve discourse, and curiosity,
With that which doth religion but invest,
 And shunne th'entangling laborinths of Schooles,
 And make it wit, to thinke the wiser fooles:

So in this pilgrimage I would behold
You as you'are vertues temple, not as shee,
What walls of tender christall her enfold,
What eyes, hands, bosome, her pure Altars bee;
 And after this survay, oppose to all
 Bablers of Chappels, you th'Escuriall.

Yet not as consecrate, but merely'as faire,
On these I cast a lay and country eye.
Of past and future stories, which are rare
I finde you all record, and prophecie.
 Purge but the booke of Fate, that it admit
 No sad nor guilty legends, you are it.

If good and lovely were not one, of both
You were the transcript, and originall,
The Elements, the Parent, and the Growth,
And every peece of you, is both their All:
 So'intire are all your deeds, and you, that you
 Must do the same thinge still; you cannot two.

But these (as nice thinne Schoole divinity
Serves heresie to furder or represse)
'Tast of Poëtique rage, or flattery,
And need not, where all hearts one truth professe;
 Oft from new proofes, and new phrase, new doubts grow,
 As strange attire aliens the men wee know.

Leaving then busie praise, and all appeale
To higher Courts, senses decree is true,
The Mine, the Magazine, the Commonweale,

The story of beauty,'in Twicknam is, and you.
  Who hath seene one, would both; As, who had bin
  In Paradise, would seeke the Cherubin.

TO SIR EDWARD HERBERT AT JULYERS

M A N is a lumpe, where all beasts kneaded bee,
    Wisdome makes him an Arke where all agree;
  The foole, in whom these beasts do live at jarre,
    Is sport to others, and a Theater;
  Nor scapes hee so, but is himselfe their prey,
    All which was man in him, is eate away,
  And now his beasts on one another feed,
    Yet couple'in anger, and new monsters breed.
  How happy'is hee, which hath due place assign'd
    To'his beasts, and disaforested his minde!
  Empail'd himselfe to keepe them out, not in;
    Can sow, and dares trust corne, where they have bin;
  Can use his horse, goate, wolfe, and every beast,
    And is not Asse himselfe to all the rest.
  Else, man not onely is the heard of swine,
    But he's those devills too, which did incline
  Them to a headlong rage, and made them worse:
    For man can adde weight to heavens heaviest curse.
  As Soules (they say) by our first touch, take in
    The poysonous tincture of Originall sinne,
  So, to the punishments which God doth fling,
    Our apprehension contributes the sting.
  To us, as to his chickins, he doth cast
    Hemlocke, and wee as men, his hemlocke taste;
  Wee do infuse to what he meant for meat,
    Corrosivenesse, or intense cold or heat.
  For, God no such specifique poyson hath
    As kills we know not how; his fiercest wrath
  Hath no antipathy, but may be good
    At least for physicke, if not for our food.
  Thus man, that might be'his pleasure, is his rod,
    And is his devill, that might be his God.
  Since then our businesse is, to rectifie
    Nature, to what she was, wee'are led awry

By them, who man to us in little show;
    Greater than due, no forme we can bestow
On him; for Man into himselfe can draw
    All; All his faith can swallow,'or reason chaw.
All that is fill'd, and all that which doth fill,
    All the round world, to man is but a pill,
In all it workes not, but it is in all
    Poysonous, or purgative, or cordiall,
For, knowledge kindles Calentures in some,
    And is to others icy *Opium*.
As brave as true, is that profession then
    Which you doe use to make; that you know man.
This makes it credible; you have dwelt upon
    All worthy bookes, and now are such an one.
Actions are authors, and of those in you
    Your friends finde every day a mart of new.

TO THE COUNTESSE OF BEDFORD

T'HAVE written then, when you writ, seem'd to mee
    Worst of spirituall vices, Simony,
And not t'have written then, seemes little lesse
    Than worst of civill vices, thanklessenesse.
In this, my debt I seem'd loath to confesse,
    In that, I seem'd to shunne beholdingnesse.
But 'tis not soe; *nothings*, as I am, may
    Pay all they have, and yet have all to pay.
Such borrow in their payments, and owe more
    By having leave to write so, than before.
Yet since rich mines in barren grounds are showne,
    May not I yeeld (not gold) but coale or stone?
Temples were not demolish'd, though prophane:
    Here *Peter Joves*, there *Paul* hath *Dian's* Fane.
So whether my hymnes you admit or chuse,
    In me you'have hallowed a Pagan Muse,
And denizend a stranger, who mistaught
    By blamers of the times they mard, hath sought
Vertues in corners, which now bravely doe
    Shine in the worlds best part, or all It; You.

I have beene told, that vertue'in Courtiers hearts
· Suffers an Ostracisme, and departs.
Profit, ease, fitnesse, plenty, bid it goe,
   But whither, only knowing you, I know;
Your (or you) vertue two vast uses serves,
   It ransomes one sex, and one Court preserves.
There's nothing but your worth, which being true,
   Is knowne to any other, not to you:
And you can never know it; To admit
   No knowledge of your worth, is some of it.
But since to you, your praises discords bee,
   Stoop, others ills to meditate with mee.
Oh! to confesse wee know not what we should,
   Is halfe excuse; wee know not what we would:
Lightnesse depresseth us, emptinesse fills,
   We sweat and faint, yet still goe downe the hills.
As new Philosophy arrests the Sunne,
   And bids the passive earth about it runne,
So wee have dull'd our minde, it hath no ends;
   Onely the bodie's busie, and pretends;
As dead low earth ecclipses and controules
   The quick high Moone: so doth the body, Soules.
In none but us, are such mixt engines found,
   As hands of double office: For, the ground
We till with them; and them to heav'n wee raise;
   Who prayer-lesse labours, or, without this, prayes,
Doth but one halfe, that's none; He which said, *Plough*
   And looke not back, to looke up doth allow.
Good seed degenerates, and oft obeyes
   The soyles disease, and into cockle strayes;
Let the minds thoughts be but transplanted so,
   Into the body,'and bastardly they grow.
What hate could hurt our bodies like our love?
   Wee (but no forraine tyrants could) remove
These not ingrav'd, but inborne dignities,
   Caskets of soules; Temples, and Palaces:
For, bodies shall from death redeemed bee,
   Soules but preserv'd, not naturally free.
As men to'our prisons, new soules to us are sent,
   Which learne vice there, and come in innocent.
First seeds of every creature are in us,
   What ere the world hath bad, or pretious,

Mans body can produce, hence hath it beene
  That stones, wormes, frogges, and snakes in man are
    seene:
But who ere saw, though nature can worke soe,
  That pearle, or gold, or corne in man did grow?
We'have added to the world Virginia,'and sent
  Two new starres lately to the firmament;
Why grudge wee us (not heaven) the dignity
  T'increase with ours, those faire soules company.
But I must end this letter, though it doe
  Stand on two truths, neither is true to you.
Vertue hath some perversenesse; For she will
  Neither beleeve her good, nor others ill.
Even in you, vertues best paradise,
  Vertue hath some, but wise degrees of vice.
Too many vertues, or too much of one
  Begets in you unjust suspition;
And ignorance of vice, makes vertue lesse,
  Quenching compassion of our wretchednesse.
But these are riddles; Some aspersion
  Of vice becomes well some complexion.
Statesmen purge vice with vice, and may corrode
  The bad with bad, a spider with a toad:
For so, ill thralls not them, but they tame ill
  And make her do much good against her will,
But in your Commonwealth, or world in you,
  Vice hath no office, or good worke to doe.
Take then no vitious purge, but be content
  With cordiall vertue, your knowne nourishment.

TO THE COUNTESSE OF BEDFORD

On New-yeares day

THIS twilight of two yeares, not past nor next,
  Some embleme is of mee, or I of this,
Who Meteor-like, of stuffe and forme perplext,
  Whose *what,* and *where,* in disputation is,
    If I should call mee *any thing,* should misse.

I summe the yeares, and mee, and finde mee not
 Debtor to th'old, nor Creditor to th'new,
That cannot say, My thankes I have forgot,
 Nor trust I this with hopes, and yet scarce true
 This bravery is, since these times shew'd mee you.

In recompence I would show future times
 What you were, and teach them to'urge towards such.
Verse embalmes vertue;'and Tombs, or Thrones of rimes,
 Preserve fraile transitory fame, as much
 As spice doth bodies from corrupt aires touch.

Mine are short-liv'd; the tincture of your name
 Creates in them, but dissipates as fast,
New spirits: for, strong agents with the same
 Force that doth warme and cherish, us doe wast;
 Kept hot with strong extracts, no bodies last:

So, my verse built of your just praise, might want
 Reason and likelihood, the firmest Base,
And made of miracle, now faith is scant,
 Will vanish soone, and so possesse no place,
 And you, and it, too much grace might disgrace.

When all (as truth commands assent) confesse
 All truth of you, yet they will doubt how I,
One corne of one low anthills dust, and lesse,
 Should name, know, or expresse a thing so high,
 And not an inch, measure infinity.

I cannot tell them, nor my selfe, nor you,
 But leave, lest truth b'endanger'd by my praise,
And turne to God, who knowes I thinke this true,
 And useth oft, when such a heart mis-sayes,
 To make it good, for, such a praiser prayes.

Hee will best teach you, how you should lay out
 His stock of *beauty, learning, favour, blood;*
He will perplex security with doubt,
 And cleare those doubts; hide from you,'and shew you
  good,
 And so increase your appetite and food;

Hee will teach you, that good and bad have not
   One latitude in cloysters, and in Court;
Indifferent there the greatest space hath got;
   Some pitty'is not good there, some vaine disport,
   On this side sinne, with that place may comport.

Yet he, as hee bounds seas, will fixe your houres,
   Which pleasure, and delight may not ingresse,
And though what none else lost, be truliest yours,
   Hee will make you, what you did not, possesse,
   By using others, not vice, but weakenesse.

He will make you speake truths, and credibly,
   And make you doubt, that others doe not so:
Hee will provide you keyes, and locks, to spie,
   And scape spies, to good ends, and hee will show
   What you may not acknowledge, what not know.

For your owne conscience, he gives innocence,
   But for your fame, a discreet warinesse,
And though to scape, than to revenge offence
   Be better, he showes both, and to represse
   Joy, when your state swells, *sadnesse* when'tis lesse.

From need of teares he will defend your soule,
   Or make a rebaptizing of one teare;
Hee cannot, (that's, he will not) dis-inroule
   Your name; and when with active joy we heare
   This private Ghospell, then'tis our New Yeare.

TO THE COUNTESSE OF HUNTINGDON

MADAME,

M A N to Gods image, *Eve,* to mans was made,
   Nor finde wee that God breath'd a soule in her,
Canons will not Church functions you invade,
   Nor lawes to civill office you preferre.

Who vagrant transitory Comets sees,
   Wonders, because they'are rare; But a new starre
Whose motion with the firmament agrees,
   Is miracle; for, there no new things are;

In woman so perchance milde innocence
    A seldome comet is, but active good
A miracle, which reason scapes, and sense;
    For, Art and Nature this in them withstood.

As such a starre, the *Magi* led to view
    The manger-cradled infant, God below:
By vertues beames by fame deriv'd from you,
    May apt soules, and the worst may, vertue know.

If the worlds age, and death be argued well
    By the Sunnes fall, which now towards earth doth bend,
Then we might feare that vertue, since she fell
    So low as woman, should be neare her end.

But she's not stoop'd, but rais'd; exil'd by men
    She fled to heaven, that's heavenly things, that's you;
She was in all men, thinly scatter'd then,
    But now amass'd, contracted in a few.

She guilded us: But you are gold, and Shee;
    Us she inform'd, but transubstantiates you;
Soft dispositions which ductile bee,
    Elixarlike, she makes not cleane, but new.

Though you a wifes and mothers name retaine,
    'Tis not a woman, for all are not soe,
But vertue having made you vertue,'is faine
    T'adhere in these names, her and you to show,

Else, being alike pure, wee should neither see;
    As, water being into ayre rarify'd,
Neither appeare, till in one cloud they bee,
    So, for our sakes you do low names abide;

Taught by great constellations, which being fram'd,
    Of the most starres, take low names, *Crab*, and *Bull*,
When single planets by the *Gods* are nam'd,
    You covet not great names, of great things full.

So you, as woman, one doth comprehend,
    And in the vaile of kindred others see;
To some ye are reveal'd, as in a friend,
    And as a vertuous Prince farre off, to mee.

To whom, because from you all vertues flow,
    And 'tis not none, to dare contemplate you,
I, which doe so, as your true subject owe
    Some tribute for that, so these lines are due.

If you can thinke these flatteries, they are,
    For then your judgement is below my praise,
If they were so, oft, flatteries worke as farre,
    As Counsels, and as farre th'endeavour raise.

So my ill reaching you might there grow good,
    But I remaine a poyson'd fountaine still;
But not your beauty, vertue, knowledge, blood
    Are more above all flattery, than my will.

And if I flatter any, 'tis not you
    But my owne judgement, who did long agoe
Pronounce, that all these praises should be true,
    And vertue should your beauty, 'and birth outgrow.

Now that my prophesies are all fulfill'd,
    Rather than God should not be honour'd too,
And all these gifts confess'd, which hee instill'd,
    Your selfe were bound to say that which I doe.

So I, but your Recorder am in this,
    Or mouth, or Speaker of the universe,
A ministeriall Notary, for 'tis
    Not I, but you and fame, that make this verse;

I was your Prophet in your yonger dayes,
And now your Chaplaine, God in you to praise.

TO MR. T. W.

A L L haile sweet Poet, more full of more strong fire,
    Than hath or shall enkindle any spirit,
    I lov'd what nature gave thee, but this merit
Of wit and Art I love not but admire;
Who have before or shall write after thee,
Their workes, though toughly laboured, will bee
Like infancie or age to mans firme stay,
Or earely and late twilights to mid-day.

Men say, and truly, that they better be
  Which be envyed than pittied: therefore I,
  Because I wish thee best, doe thee envie:
O wouldst thou, by like reason, pitty mee!
But care not for mee: I, that ever was
In Natures, and in Fortunes gifts, alas,
  (Before thy grace got in the Muses Schoole
  A monster) and a begger, am now a foole.

Oh how I grieve, that late borne modesty
  Hath got such root in easie waxen hearts,
  That men may not themselves, their owne good parts
Extoll, without suspect of surquedrie,
For, but thy selfe, no subject can be found
Worthy thy quill, nor any quill resound
  Thy worth but thine: how good it were to see
  A Poëm in thy praise, and writ by thee.

Now if this song be too'harsh for rime, yet, as
  The Painters bade god made a good devill,
  'Twill be good prose, although the verse be evill,
If thou forget the rime as thou dost passe.
Then write, that I may follow, and so bee
Thy debter, thy'eccho, thy foyle, thy zanee.
  I shall be thought, if mine like thine I shape,
  All the worlds Lyon, though I be thy Ape.

TO MR. T. W.

HASTE thee harsh verse, as fast as thy lame measure
  Will give thee leave, to him, my pain and pleasure.
I have given thee, and yet thou art too weake,
  Feete, and a reasoning soule and tongue to speake.
Plead for me, and so by thine and my labour
  I am thy Creator, thou my Saviour.
Tell him, all questions, which men have defended
  Both of the place and paines of hell, are ended;
And 'tis decreed our hell is but privation
  Of him, at least in this earths habitation:
And 'tis where I am, where in every street
  Infections follow, overtake, and meete:
Live I or die, by you my love is sent,
  And you'are my pawnes, or else my Testament.

TO MR. T. W.

PREGNANT again with th'old twins Hope, and Feare,
Oft have I askt for thee, both how and where
Thou wert, and what my hopes of letters were;

As in the streets sly beggars narrowly
Watch motions of the givers hand and eye,
And evermore conceive some hope thereby.

And now thy Almes is given, thy letter'is read,
The body risen againe, the which was dead
And thy poore starveling bountifully fed.

After this banquet my Soule doth say grace,
And praise thee for'it, and zealously imbrace
Thy love; though I thinke thy love in this case
   To be as gluttons, which say 'midst their meat,
   They love that best of which they most do eat.

TO MR. T. W.

AT once, from hence, my lines and I depart,
I to my soft still walks, they to my Heart;
I to the Nurse, they to the child of Art;

Yet as a firme house, though the Carpenter
Perish, doth stand: As an Embassadour
Lyes safe, how e'r his king be in danger:

So, though I languish, prest with Melancholy,
My verse, the strict Map of my misery,
Shall live to see that, for whose want I dye.

Therefore I envie them, and doe repent,
That from unhappy mee, things happy'are sent;
Yet as a Picture, or bare Sacrament,
   Accept these lines, and if in them there be
   Merit of love, bestow that love on mee.

TO MR. R. W.

ZEALOUSLY my Muse doth salute all thee,
Enquiring of that mistique trinitee
Whereof thou'and all to whom heavens do infuse
Like, fyer, are made; thy body, mind, and Muse.
Dost thou recover sicknes, or prevent?
Or is thy Mind travail'd with discontent?
Or art thou parted from the world and mee,
In a good skorn of the worlds vanitee?
Or is thy devout Muse retyr'd to sing
Upon her tender Elegiaque string?
Our Minds part not, joyne then thy Muse with myne,
For myne is barren thus devorc'd from thyne.

TO MR. R. W.

MUSE not that by thy Mind thy body is led:
For by thy Mind, my Mind's distempered.
So thy Care lives long, for I bearing part
It eates not only thyne, but my swolne hart.
And when it gives us intermission
We take new harts for it to feede upon.
But as a Lay Mans Genius doth controule
Body and mind; the Muse beeing the Soules Soule
Of Poets, that methinks should ease our anguish,
Although our bodyes wither and minds languish.
Wright then, that my griefes which thine got may bee
Cur'd by thy charming soveraigne melodee.

TO MR. C. B.

THY friend, whom thy deserts to thee enchaine,
   Urg'd by this unexcusable occasion,
   Thee and the Saint of his affection
Leaving behinde, doth of both wants complaine;
And let the love I beare to both sustaine
   No blott nor maime by this division,
   Strong is this love which ties our hearts in one,

And strong that love pursu'd with amorous paine;
But though besides thy selfe I leave behind
   Heavens liberall, and earths thrice-fairer Sunne,
   Going to where sterne winter aye doth wonne,
Yet, loves hot fires, which martyr my sad minde,
   Doe send forth scalding sighes, which have the Art
   To melt all Ice, but that which walls her heart.

TO MR. E. G.

E V E N as lame things thirst their perfection, so
The slimy rimes bred in our vale below,
Bearing with them much of my love and hart,
Fly unto that Parnassus, where thou art.
There thou oreseest London: Here I have beene,
By staying in London, too much overseene.
Now pleasures dearth our City doth posses,
Our Theaters are fill'd with emptines;
As lancke and thin is every street and way
As a woman deliver'd yesterday.
Nothing whereat to laugh my spleen espyes
But bearbaitings or Law exercise.
Therefore I'le leave it, and in the Country strive
Pleasure, now fled from London, to retrive.
Do thou so too: and fill not like a Bee
Thy thighs with hony, but as plenteously
As Russian Marchants, thy selfes whose vessel load,
And then at Winter retaile it here abroad.
Blesse us with Suffolks Sweets; and as it is
Thy garden, make thy hive and warehouse this.

TO MR. R. W.

I F, as mine is, thy life a slumber be,
   Seeme, when thou read'st these lines, to dreame of me,
Never did Morpheus nor his brother weare
   Shapes soe like those Shapes, whom they would appeare,
As this my letter is like me, for it
   Hath my name, words, hand, feet, heart, minde and wit;

It is my deed of gift of mee to thee,
   It is my Will, my selfe the Legacie.
So thy retyrings I love, yea envie,
   Bred in thee by a wise melancholy,
That I rejoyce, that unto where thou art,
   Though I stay here, I can thus send my heart,
As kindly'as any enamored Patient
   His Picture to his absent Love hath sent.

All newes I thinke sooner reach thee than mee;
   Heavens are Heavens, and Ships wing'd Angels be,
The which both Gospell, and sterne threatnings bring;
   Guyanaes harvest is nip'd in the spring,
I feare; And with us (me thinkes) Fate deales so
   As with the Jewes guide God did; he did show
Him the rich land, but bar'd his entry in:
   Oh, slownes is our punishment and sinne.
Perchance, these Spanish businesse being done,
   Which as the Earth betweene the Moone and Sun
Eclipse the light which Guyana would give,
   Our discontinued hopes we shall retrive:
But if (as all th'All must) hopes smoake away,
   Is not Almightie Vertue 'n India?
If men be worlds, there is in every one
   Some thing to answere in some proportion
All the worlds riches: And in good men, this,
   Vertue, our formes forme and our soules soule, is.

TO MR. R. W.

KINDLY I envy thy songs perfection
   Built of all th'elements as our bodyes are:
   That Litle of earth that is in it, is a faire
Delicious garden where all sweetes are sowne.
In it is cherishing fyer which dryes in mee
   Griefe which did drowne me: and halfe quench'd by it
   Are satirique fyres which urg'd me to have writt
In skorne of all: for now I admyre thee.
   And as Ayre doth fullfill the hollownes
   Of rotten walls; so it myne emptines,

Where tost and mov'd it did beget this sound
Which as a lame Eccho of thyne doth rebound.
    Oh, I was dead; but since thy song new Life did give,
I recreated, even by thy creature, live.

TO MR. S. B.

o T H O U which to search out the secret parts
    Of the India, or rather Paradise
    Of knowledge, hast with courage and advise
Lately launch'd into the vast Sea of Arts,
Disdaine not in thy constant travailing
    To doe as other Voyagers, and make
    Some turnes into lesse Creekes, and wisely take
Fresh water at the Heliconian spring;
I sing not, Siren like, to tempt; for I
    Am harsh; nor as those Scismatiques with you,
    Which draw all wits of good hope to their crew;
But seeing in you bright sparkes of Poetry,
    I, though I brought noe fuell, had desire
With these Articulate blasts to blow the fire.

TO MR. I. L.

o F that short Roll of friends writ in my heart
    Which with thy name begins, since their depart,
Whether in the English Provinces they be,
    Or drinke of Po, Sequan, or Danubie,
There's none that sometimes greets us not, and yet
    Your Trent is Lethe', that past, us you forget.
You doe not duties of Societies,
    If from the'embrace of a lov'd wife you rise,
View your fat Beasts, stretch'd Barnes, and labour'd fields,
    Eate, play, ryde, take all joyes which all day yeelds,
And then againe to your embracements goe:
    Some houres on us your frends, and some bestow
Upon your Muse, else both wee shall repent,
    I that my love, she that her guifts on you are spent.

TO MR. I. L.

BLEST are your North parts, for all this long time
    My Sun is with you, cold and darke'is our Clime;
Heavens Sun, which staid so long from us this yeare,
    Staid in your North (I thinke) for she was there,
And hether by kinde nature drawne from thence,
    Here rages, chafes, and threatens pestilence;
Yet I, as long as shee from hence doth staie,
    Thinke this no South, no Sommer, nor no day.
With thee my kinde and unkinde heart is run,
    There sacrifice it to that beauteous Sun:
And since thou art in Paradise and need'st crave
    No joyes addition, helpe thy friend to save.
So may thy pastures with their flowery feasts,
    As suddenly as Lard, fat thy leane beasts;
So may thy woods oft poll'd, yet ever weare
    A greene, and when thee list, a golden haire;
So may all thy sheepe bring forth Twins; and so
    In chace and race may thy horse all out goe;
So may thy love and courage ne'r be cold;
    Thy Sonne ne'r Ward; Thy lov'd wife ne'r seem old;
But maist thou wish great things, and them attaine,
    As thou telst her, and none but her, my paine.

TO MR. B. B.

IS not thy sacred hunger of science
    Yet satisfy'd? Is not thy braines rich hive
    Fulfil'd with hony which thou dost derive
From the Arts spirits and their Quintessence?
Then weane thy selfe at last, and thee withdraw
    From Cambridge thy old nurse, and, as the rest,
    Here toughly chew, and sturdily digest
Th'immense vast volumes of our common law;
And begin soone, lest my griefe grieve thee too,
    Which is, that that which I should have begun
    In my youthes morning, now late must be done;
And I as Giddy Travellers must doe,
    Which stray or sleepe all day, and having lost
    Light and strength, darke and tir'd must then ride post.

If thou unto thy Muse be marryed,
    Embrace her ever, ever multiply,
    Be far from me that strange Adulterie
To tempt thee and procure her widowhed.
My Muse, (for I had one,) because I'am cold,
    Divorc'd her selfe: the cause being in me,
    That I can take no new in Bigamye,
Not my will only but power doth withhold.
Hence comes it, that these Rymes which never had
    Mother, want matter, and they only have
    A little forme, the which their Father gave;
They are prophane, imperfect, oh, too bad
    To be counted Children of Poetry
    Except confirm'd and Bishoped by thee.

TO SIR H. W. AT HIS GOING AMBASSADOR TO VENICE

AFTER those reverend papers, whose soule is
    Our good and great Kings lov'd hand and fear'd name,
By which to you he derives much of his,
    And (how he may) makes you almost the same,

A Taper of his Torch, a copie writ
    From his Originall, and a faire beame
Of the same warme, and dazeling Sun, though it
    Must in another Sphere his vertue streame:

After those learned papers which your hand
    Hath stor'd with notes of use and pleasure too,
From which rich treasury you may command
    Fit matter whether you will write or doe:

After those loving papers, where friends send
    With glad griefe, to your Sea-ward steps, farewel,
Which thicken on you now, as prayers ascend
    To heaven in troupes at'a good mans passing bell:

Admit this honest paper, and allow
    It such an audience as your selfe would aske;
What you must say at Venice this meanes now,
    And hath for nature, what you have for taske:

To sweare much love, not to be chang'd before
   Honour alone will to your fortune fit;
Nor shall I then honour your fortune, more
   Than I have done your honour wanting it.

But'tis an easier load (though both oppresse)
   To want, than governe greatnesse, for wee are
In that, our owne and onely businesse,
   In this, wee must for others vices care;
'Tis therefore well your spirits now are plac'd
   In their last Furnace, in activity;
Which fits them (Schooles and Courts and Warres o'rpast)
   To touch and test in any best degree.

For mee, (if there be such a thing as I)
   Fortune (if there be such a thing as shee)
Spies that I beare so well her tyranny,
   That she thinks nothing else so fit for mee;

But though she part us, to heare my oft prayers
   For your increase, God is as neere mee here;
And to send you what I shall begge, his staires
   In length and ease are alike every where.

TO MRS. M. H.

MAD paper stay, and grudge not here to burne
   With all those sonnes whom my braine did create,
At least lye hid with mee, till thou returne
   To rags againe, which is thy native state.

What though thou have enough unworthinesse
   To come unto great place as others doe,
That's much; emboldens, pulls, thrusts I confesse,
   But'tis not all; Thou should'st be wicked too.

And, that thou canst not learne, or not of mee;
   Yet thou wilt goe? Goe, since thou goest to her
Who lacks but faults to be a Prince, for shee,
   Truth, whom they dare not pardon, dares preferre.

But when thou com'st to that perplexing eye
  Which equally claimes *love* and *reverence,*
Thou wilt not long dispute it, thou wilt die;
  And, having little now, have then no sense.

Yet when her warme redeeming hand, which is
  A miracle; and made such to worke more,
Doth touch thee (saples leafe) thou grow'st by this
  Her creature; glorify'd more than before.

Then as a mother which delights to heare
  Her early child mis-speake halfe uttered words,
Or, because majesty doth never feare
  Ill or bold speech, the Audience affords.

And then, cold speechlesse wretch, thou diest againe,
  And wisely; what discourse is left for thee?
For, speech of ill, and her, thou must abstaine,
  And is there any good which is not shee?

Yet maist thou praise her servants, though not her,
  And wit, and vertue,'and honour her attend,
And since they'are but her cloathes, thou shalt not erre,
  If thou her shape and beauty'and grace commend.

Who knowes thy destiny? when thou hast done,
  Perchance her Cabinet may harbour thee,
Whither all noble ambitious wits doe runne,
  A nest almost as full of Good as shee.

When thou are there, if any, whom wee know,
  Were sav'd before, and did that heaven partake,
When she revolves his papers, marke what show
  Of favour, she alone, to them doth make.

Marke, if to get them, she o'r skip the rest,
  Marke, if she read them twice, or kisse the name;
Marke, if she doe the same that they protest,
  Marke, if she marke whether her woman came.

Marke, if slight things be'objected, and o'r blowne,
  Marke, if her oathes against him be not still
Reserv'd, and that shee grieves she's not her owne,
  And chides the doctrine that denies Freewill.

I bid thee not doe this to be my spie;
  Nor to make my selfe her familiar;
But so much I doe love her choyce, that I
  Would faine love him that shall be lov'd of her.

TO THE COUNTESSE OF BEDFORD

HONOUR is so sublime perfection,
And so refinde; that when God was alone
And creaturelesse at first, himselfe had none;

But as of the elements, these which wee tread,
Produce all things with which wee'are joy'd or fed,
And, those are barren both above our head:

So from low persons doth all honour flow;
Kings, whom they would have honoured, to us show,
And but *direct* our honour, not *bestow*.

For when from herbs the pure part must be wonne
From grosse, by Stilling, this is better done
By despis'd dung, than by the fire or Sunne.

Care not then, Madame,'how low your prayers lye;
In labourers balads oft more piety
God findes, than in *Te Deums* melodie,

And, ordinance rais'd on Towers, so many mile
Send not their voice, nor last so long a while
As fires from th'earths low vaults in *Sicil* Isle.

Should I say I liv'd darker than were true,
Your radiation can all clouds subdue;
But one,'tis best light to contemplate you.

You, for whose body God made better clay,
Or tooke Soules stuffe such as shall late decay,
Or such as needs small change at the last day.

This, as an Amber drop enwraps a Bee,
Covering discovers your quicke Soule; that we
May in your through-shine front your hearts thoughts see.

You teach (though wee learne not) a thing unknowne
To our late times, the use of specular stone,
Through which all things within without were shown.

Of such were Temples; so and of such you are;
Beeing and *seeming* is your equall care,
And *vertues* whole *summe* is but *know* and *dare*.

But as our Soules of growth and Soules of sense
Have birthright of our reasons Soule, yet hence
They fly not from that, nor seeke presidence:

Natures first lesson, so, discretion
Must not grudge zeale a place, nor yet keepe none,
Not banish it selfe, nor religion.

Discretion is a wisemans Soule, and so
Religion is a Christians, and you know
How these are one; her *yea,* is not her *no.*

Nor may we hope to sodder still and knit
These two, and dare to breake them; nor must wit
Be colleague to religion, but be it.

In those poor types of God (round circles) so
Religious types, the peecelesse centers flow,
And are in all the lines which all wayes goe.

If either ever wrought in you alone
Or principally, then religion
Wrought your ends, and your wayes discretion.

Goe thither stil, goe the same way you went,
Who so would change, do covet or repent;
Neither can reach you, great and innocent.

TO THE COUNTESSE OF BEDFORD

Begun in France but never perfected

THOUGH I be *dead*, and buried, yet I have
(Living in you,) Court enough in my grave,
As oft as there I thinke my selfe to bee,
So many resurrections waken mee.

That thankfullnesse your favours have begot
   In mee, embalmes mee, that I doe not rot.
This season as 'tis Easter, as 'tis spring,
   Must both to growth and to confession bring
My thoughts dispos'd unto your influence; so,
   These verses bud, so these confessions grow.
First I confesse I have to others lent
   Your stock, and over prodigally spent
Your treasure, for since I had never knowne
   Vertue or beautie, but as they are growne
In you, I should not thinke or say they shine,
   (So as I have) in any other Mine.
Next I confesse this my confession,
   For, 'tis some fault thus much to touch upon
Your praise to you, where half rights seeme too much,
   And make your minds sincere complexion blush.
Next I confesse my'impenitence, for I
   Can scarce repent my first fault, since thereby
Remote low Spirits, which shall ne'r read you,
   May in lesse lessons finde enough to doe,
By studying copies, not Originals,
       Desunt cætera.

A LETTER TO THE LADY CAREY AND MRS. ESSEX RICHE, FROM AMYENS

Madame,
here where by All All Saints invoked are,
'Twere too much schisme to be singular,
And 'gainst a practise generall to warre.

Yet turning to Saincts, should my'humility
To other Saint than you directed bee,
That were to make my schisme, heresie.

Nor would I be a Convertite so cold,
As not to tell it; If this be too bold,
Pardons are in this market cheaply sold.

Where, because Faith is in too low degree,
I thought it some Apostleship in mee
To speake things which by faith alone I see.

That is, of you, who are a firmament
Of virtues, where no one is growne, or spent,
They'are your materials, not your ornament.

Others whom wee call vertuous, are not so
In their whole substance, but, their vertues grow
But in their humours, and at seasons show.

For when through tastlesse flat humilitie
In dow bak'd men some harmelessenes we see,
'Tis but his *flegme* that's *Vertuous*, and not Hee:

Soe is the Blood sometimes; who ever ran
To danger unimportun'd, he was then
No better than a *sanguine* Vertuous man.

So cloysterall men, who, in pretence of feare
All contributions to this life forbeare,
Have Vertue in *Melancholy*, and only there.

Spirituall *Cholerique* Crytiques, which in all
Religions find faults, and forgive no fall,
Have, through this zeale, Vertue but in their Gall.

We'are thus but parcel guilt; to Gold we'are growne
When Vertue is our Soules complexion;
Who knowes his Vertues name or place, hath none.

Vertue'is but aguish, when 'tis severall,
By occasion wak'd, and circumstantiall.
True vertue is *Soule*, Alwaies in all deeds *All*.

This Vertue thinking to give dignitie
To your soule, found there no infirmitie,
For, your soule was as good Vertue, as shee;

Shee therefore wrought upon that part of you
Which is scarce lesse than soule, as she could do,
And so hath made your beauty, Vertue too.

Hence comes it, that your Beauty wounds not hearts,
As Others, with prophane and sensuall Darts,
But as an influence, vertuous thoughts imparts.

But if such friends by the honor of your sight
Grow capable of this so great a light,
As to partake your vertues, and their might,

What must I thinke that influence must doe,
Where it findes sympathie and matter too,
Vertue, and beauty of the same stuffe, as you?

Which is, your noble worthie sister, shee
Of whom, if what in this my Extasie
And revelation of you both I see,

I should write here, as in short Galleries
The Master at the end large glasses ties,
So to present the roome twice to our eyes,

So I should give this letter length, and say
That which I said of you; there is no way
From either, but by the other, not to stray.

May therefore this be enough to testifie
My true devotion, free from flattery;
He that beleeves himselfe, doth never lie.

TO THE COUNTESSE OF SALISBURY

August, 1614

FAIRE, great, and good, since seeing you, wee see
What Heaven can doe, and what any Earth can be:
Since now your beauty shines, now when the Sunne
Growne stale, is to so low a value runne,
That his disshevel'd beames and scattered fires
Serve but for Ladies Periwigs and Tyres
In lovers Sonnets: you come to repaire
Gods booke of creatures, teaching what is faire.
Since now, when all is withered, shrunke, and dri'd,
All Vertues ebb'd out to a dead low tyde,
All the worlds frame being crumbled into sand,
Where every man thinks by himselfe to stand,
Integritie, friendship, and confidence,
(Ciments of greatnes) being vapor'd hence,

And narrow man being fill'd with little shares,
Court, Citie, Church, are all shops of small-wares,
All having blowne to sparkes their noble fire,
And drawne their sound gold-ingot into wyre;
All trying by a love of littlenesse
To make abridgments, and to draw to lesse,
Even that nothing, which at first we were;
Since in these times, your greatnesse doth appeare,
And that we learne by it, that man to get
Towards him that's infinite, must first be great.
Since in an age so ill, as none is fit
So much as to accuse, much lesse mend it,
(For who can judge, or witnesse of those times
Where all alike are guiltie of the crimes?)
Where he that would be good, is thought by all
A monster, or at best fantasticall:
Since now you durst be good, and that I doe
Discerne, by daring to contemplate you,
That there may be degrees of faire, great, good,
Through your light, largenesse, vertue understood:
If in this sacrifice of mine, be showne
Any small sparke of these, call it your owne.
And if things like these, have been said by mee
Of others; call not that Idolatrie.
For had God made man first, and man had seene
The third daies fruits, and flowers, and various greene,
He might have said the best that he could say
Of those faire creatures, which were made that day;
And when next day he had admir'd the birth
Of Sun, Moone, Stars, fairer than late-prais'd earth,
Hee might have said the best that he could say,
And not be chid for praising yesterday:
So though some things are not together true,
As, that another is worthiest, and, that you:
Yet, to say so, doth not condemne a man,
If when he spoke them, they were both true then.
How faire a proofe of this, in our soule growes?
Wee first have soules of growth, and sense, and those,
When our last soule, our soule immortall came,
Were swallowed into it, and have no name.
Nor doth he injure those soules, which doth cast
The power and praise of both them, on the last;

No more doe I wrong any; I adore
The same things now, which I ador'd before,
The subject chang'd, and measure; the same thing
In a low constable, and in the King
I reverence; His power to work on mee:
So did I humbly reverence each degree
Of faire, great, good; but more, now I am come
From having found their *walkes,* to find their *home.*
And as I owe my first soules thankes, that they
For my last soule did fit and mould my clay,
So am I debtor unto them, whose worth,
Enabled me to profit, and take forth
This new great lesson, thus to study you;
Which none, not reading others, first, could doe.
Nor lacke I light to read this booke, though I
In a dark Cave, yea in a Grave doe lie;
For as your fellow Angells, so you doe
Illustrate them who come to study you.
The first whom we in Histories doe finde
To have profest all Arts, was one borne blinde:
He lackt those eyes beasts have as well as wee,
Not those, by which Angels are seene and see;
So, though I'am borne without those eyes to live,
Which fortune, who hath none her selfe, doth give,
Which are, fit meanes to see bright courts and you,
Yet may I see you thus, as now I doe;
I shall by that, all goodnesse have discern'd,
And though I burne my librarie, be learn'd.

TO THE LADY BEDFORD

Y O U that are she and you, that's double shee,
   In her dead face, halfe of your selfe shall see;
Shee was the other part, for so they doe
   Which build them friendships, become one of two;
So two, that but themselves no third can fit,
   Which were to be so, when they were not yet;
Twinnes, though their birth *Cusco,* and *Musco* take,
   As divers starres one Constellation make,
Pair'd like two eyes, have equall motion, so
   Both but one meanes to see, one way to goe.

Had you dy'd first, a carcasse shee had beene;
　　And wee your rich Tombe in her face had seene;
She like the Soule is gone, and you here stay,
　　Not a live friend; but th'other halfe of clay;
And since you act that part, As men say, here
　　Lies such a Prince, when but one part is there,
And do all honour and devotion due
　　Unto the whole, so wee all reverence you;
For, such a friendship who would not adore
　　In you, who are all what both were before,
Not all, as if some perished by this,
　　But so, as all in you contracted is.
As of this all, though many parts decay,
　　The pure which elemented them shall stay;
And though diffus'd, and spread in infinite,
　　Shall recollect, and in one All unite:
So madame, as her Soule to heaven is fled,
　　Her flesh rests in the earth, as in the bed;
Her vertues do, as to their proper spheare,
　　Returne to dwell with you, of whom they were,
As perfect motions are all circular,
　　So they to you, their sea, whence lesse streames are.
Shee was all spices, you all metalls; so
　　In you two wee did both rich Indies know;
And as no fire, nor rust can spend or waste
　　One dramme of gold, but what was first shall last,
Though it bee forc'd in water, earth, salt, aire,
　　Expans'd in infinite, none will impaire;
So, to your selfe you may additions take,
　　But nothing can you lesse, or changed make.
Seeke not in seeking new, to seeme to doubt,
　　That you can match her, or not be without;
But let some faithfull booke in her roome be,
　　Yet but of *Judith* no such booke as shee.

An Anatomie of the World

THE FIRST ANNIVERSARY

TO THE PRAISE OF THE DEAD, AND THE ANATOMIE

WELL *dy'd the World, that we might live to see*
This world of wit, in his Anatomie:
No evill wants his good; so wilder heires
Bedew their Fathers Tombes, with forced teares,
Whose state requites their losse: whiles thus we gain,
Well may wee walke in blacks, but not complaine.
Yet how can I consent the world is dead
While this Muse lives? which in his spirits stead
Seemes to informe a World; and bids it bee,
In spight of losse or fraile mortalitie?
And thou the subject of this welborne thought,
Thrice noble maid, couldst not have found nor sought
A fitter time to yeeld to thy sad Fate,
Than whiles this spirit lives, that can relate
Thy worth so well to our last Nephews eyne,
That they shall wonder both at his and thine:
Admired match! where strives in mutuall grace
The cunning pencill, and the comely face:
A taske which thy faire goodnesse made too much
For the bold pride of vulgar pens to touch;

Enough is us to praise them that praise thee,
And say, that but enough those prayses bee,
Which hadst thou liv'd, had hid their fearfull head
From th'angry checkings of thy modest red:
Death barres reward and shame: when envy's gone,
And gaine, 'tis safe to give the dead their owne.
As then the wise Egyptians wont to lay
More on their Tombes than houses: these of clay,
But those of brasse, or marble were: so wee
Give more unto thy Ghost, than unto thee.
Yet what wee give to thee, thou gav'st to us,
And may'st but thanke thy selfe, for being thus:
Yet what thou gav'st, and wert, O happy maid,
Thy grace profest all due, where 'tis repayd.
So these high songs that to thee suited bin
Serve but to sound thy Makers praise, in thine,
Which thy deare soule as sweetly sings to him
Amid the Quire of Saints, and Seraphim,
As any Angels tongue can sing of thee;
The subjects differ, though the skill agree:
For as by infant-yeares men judge of age,
Thy early love, thy vertues, did presage
*What an high part thou bear'st in those best **songs**,*
Whereto no burden, nor no end belongs.
Sing on thou virgin Soule, whose lossfull gaine
Thy lovesick parents have bewail'd in vaine;
Never may thy Name be in our songs forgot,
Till wee shall sing thy ditty and thy note.

THE FIRST ANNIVERSARY

W H E N that rich Soule which to her heaven is gone,
Whom all do celebrate, who know they have one,
(For who is sure he hath a Soule, unlesse
It see, and judge, and follow worthinesse,
And by Deedes praise it? hee who doth not this,
May lodge an In-mate soule, but 'tis not his.)
When that Queene ended here her progresse time,
And, as t'her standing house to heaven did climbe,
Where loath to make the Saints attend her long,
She's now a part both of the Quire, and Song,

This World, in that great earthquake languished;
For in a common bath of teares it bled,
Which drew the strongest vitall spirits out:
But succour'd then with a perplexed doubt,
Whether the world did lose, or gaine in this,
(Because since now no other way there is,
But goodnesse, to see her, whom all would see,
All must endeavour to be good as shee,)
This great consumption to a fever turn'd,
And so the world had fits; it joy'd, it mourn'd;
And, as men thinke, that Agues physick are,
And th'Ague being spent, give over care,
So thou sicke World, mistak'st thy selfe to bee
Well, when alas, thou'rt in a Lethargie.
Her death did wound and tame thee then, and then
Thou might'st have better spar'd the Sunne, or Man.
That wound was deep, but 'tis more misery,
That thou hast lost thy sense and memory.
'Twas heavy then to heare thy voyce of mone,
But this is worse, that thou art speechlesse growne.
Thou hast forgot thy name, thou hadst; thou wast
Nothing but shee, and her thou hast o'rpast.
For as a child kept from the Font, untill
A prince, expected long, come to fulfill
The ceremonies, thou unnam'd had'st laid,
Had not her comming, thee her Palace made:
Her name defin'd thee, gave thee forme, and frame,
And thou forgett'st to celebrate thy name.
Some moneths she hath beene dead (but being dead,
Measures of times are all determined)
But long she'ath beene away, long, long, yet none
Offers to tell us who it is that's gone.
But as in states doubtfull of future heires,
When sicknesse without remedie empaires
The present Prince, they're loth it should be said,
The Prince doth languish, or the Prince is dead:
So mankinde feeling now a generall thaw,
A strong example gone, equall to law,
The Cyment which did faithfully compact,
And glue all vertues, now resolv'd, and slack'd,
Thought it some blasphemy to say sh'was dead,

Or that our weaknesse was discovered
In that confession; therefore spoke no more
Than tongues, the Soule being gone, the losse deplore.
But though it be too late to succour thee,
Sicke World, yea, dead, yea putrified, since shee
Thy'intrinsique balme, and thy preservative,
Can never be renew'd, thou never live,
I (since no man can make thee live) will try,
What wee may gaine by thy Anatomie.
Her death hath taught us dearely, that thou art
Corrupt and mortall in thy purest part.
Let no man say, the world it selfe being dead,
'Tis labour lost to have discovered
The worlds infirmities, since there is none
Alive to study this dissection;
For there's a kinde of World remaining still,
Though shee which did inanimate and fill
The world, be gone, yet in this last long night,
Her Ghost doth walke; that is, a glimmering light,
A faint weake love of vertue, and of good,
Reflects from her, on them which understood
Her worth; and though she have shut in all day,
The twilight of her memory doth stay;
Which, from the carcasse of the old world, free,
Creates a new world, and new creatures bee
Produc'd: the matter and the stuffe of this,
Her vertue, and the forme our practice is:
And though to be thus elemented, arme
These creatures, from home-borne intrinsique harme,
(For all assum'd unto this dignitie,
So many weedlesse Paradises bee,
Which of themselves produce no venemous sinne,
Except some forraine Serpent bring it in)
Yet, because outward stormes the strongest breake,
And strength it selfe by confidence growes weake,
This new world may be safer, being told
The dangers and diseases of the old:
For with due temper men doe then forgoe,
Or covet things, when they their true worth know.
There is no health; Physitians say that wee,
At best, enjoy but a neutralitie.
And can there be worse sicknesse, than to know

That we are never well, nor can be so?
Wee are borne ruinous: poor mothers cry,
That children come not right, nor orderly;
Except they headlong come and fall upon
An ominous precipitation.
How witty's ruine how importunate
Upon mankinde! it labour'd to frustrate
Even Gods purpose; and made woman, sent
For mans reliefe, cause of his languishment.
They were to good ends, and they are so still,
But accessory, and principall in ill;
For that first marriage was our funerall:
One woman at one blow, then kill'd us all,
And singly, one by one, they kill us now.
We doe delightfully our selves allow
To that consumption; and profusely blinde,
Wee kill our selves to propagate our kinde.
And yet we do not that; we are not men:
There is not now that mankinde, which was then,
When as, the Sunne and man did seeme to strive,
(Joynt tenants of the world) who should survive;
When, Stagge, and Raven, and the long-liv'd tree,
Compar'd with man, dy'd in minoritie;
When, if a slow pac'd starre had stolne away
From the observers marking, he might stay
Two or three hundred years to see't againe,
And then make up his observation plaine;
When, as the age was long, the sise was great;
Mans growth confess'd, and recompenc'd the meat;
So spacious and large, that every Soule
Did a faire Kingdome, and large Realme controule:
And when the very stature, thus erect,
Did that soule a good way towards heaven direct.
Where is this mankinde now? who lives to age,
Fit to be made *Methusalem* his page?
Alas, we scarce live long enough to try
Whether a true made clocke run right, or lie.
Old Grandsires talke of yesterday with sorrow,
And for our children wee reserve to morrow.
So short is life, that every peasant strives,
In a torne house, or field, to have three lives.

And as in lasting, so in length is man
Contracted to an inch, who was a spanne;
For had a man at first in forrests stray'd,
Or shipwrack'd in the Sea, one would have laid
A wager, that an Elephant, or Whale,
That met him, would not hastily assaile
A thing so equall to him: now alas,
The Fairies, and the Pigmies well may passe
As credible; mankinde decayes so soone,
We'are scarce our Fathers shadowes cast at noone:
Onely death addes t'our length: nor are wee growne
In stature to be men, till we are none.
But this were light, did our lesse volume hold
All the old Text; or had wee chang'd to gold
Their silver; or dispos'd into lesse glasse
Spirits of vertue, which then scatter'd was.
But 'tis not so: w'are not retir'd, but dampt;
And as our bodies, so our mindes are crampt:
'Tis shrinking, not close weaving that hath thus,
In minde, and body both bedwarfed us.
Wee seeme ambitious, Gods whole worke t'undoe;
Of nothing hee made us, and we strive too,
To bring our selves to nothing backe; and wee
Doe what wee can, to do't so soone as hee.
With new diseases on our selves we warre,
And with new Physicke, a worse Engin farre.
Thus man, this worlds Vice-Emperour, in whom
All faculties, all graces are at home;
And if in other creatures they appeare,
They're but mans Ministers, and Legats there,
To worke on their rebellions, and reduce
Them to Civility, and to mans use:
This man, whom God did wooe, and loth t'attend
Till man came up, did downe to man descend,
This man, so great, that all that is, is his,
Oh what a trifle, and poore thing he is!
If man were any thing, he's nothing now:
Helpe, or at least some time to wast, allow
T'his other wants, yet when he did depart
With her whom we lament, hee lost his heart.
She, of whom th'Ancients seem'd to prophesie,
When they call'd vertues by the name of *shee;*

Shee in whom vertue was so much refin'd,
That for Allay unto so pure a minde
Shee tooke the weaker Sex; shee that could drive
The poysonous tincture, and the staine of *Eve,*
Out of her thoughts, and deeds; and purifie
All, by a true religious Alchymie;
Shee, shee is dead; shee's dead: when thou knowest this,
Thou knowest how poore a trifling thing man is.
And learn'st thus much by our Anatomie,
The heart being perish'd, no part can be free.
And that except thou feed (not banquet) on
The supernaturall food, Religion,
Thy better Growth growes withered, and scant;
Be more than man, or thou'rt lesse than an Ant.
Then, as mankinde, so is the worlds whole frame
Quite out of joynt, almost created lame:
For, before God had made up all the rest,
Corruption entred, and deprav'd the best:
It seis'd the Angels, and then first of all
The world did in her cradle take a fall,
And turn'd her braines, and tooke a generall maime,
Wronging each joynt of th'universall frame.
The noblest part, man, felt it first; and then
Both beasts and plants, curst in the curse of man.
So did the world from the first houre decay,
That evening was beginning of the day,
And now the Springs and Sommers which we see,
Like sonnes of women after fiftie bee.
And new Philosophy calls all in doubt,
The Element of fire is quite put out;
The Sun is lost, and th'earth, and no mans wit
Can well direct him where to looke for it.
And freely men confesse that this world's spent,
When in the Planets, and the Firmament
They seeke so many new; then see that this
Is crumbled out againe to his Atomies.
'Tis all in peeces, all cohaerence gone;
All just supply, and all Relation:
Prince, Subject, Father, Sonne, are things forgot,
For every man alone thinkes he hath got
To be a Phœnix, and that then can bee
None of that kinde, of which he is, but hee.

This is the worlds condition now, and now
She that should all arts to reunion bow,
She that had all Magnetique force alone,
To draw, and fasten sundred parts in one;
She whom wise nature had invented then
When she obser'd that every sort of men
Did in their voyage in this worlds Sea stray,
And needed a new compasse for their way;
She that was best, and first originall
Of all faire copies, and the generall
Steward to Fate; she whose rich eyes, and breast
Guilt the West Indies, and perfum'd the East;
Whose having breath'd in this world, did bestow
Spice on those Iles, and bad them still smell so,
And that rich Indie which doth gold interre,
Is but as single money, coyn'd from her:
She to whom this world must it selfe refer,
As Suburbs, or the Microcosme of her,
Shee, shee is dead; shee's dead: when thou knowst this,
Thou knowst how lame a cripple this world is.
And learn'st thus much of our Anatomie,
That this worlds generall sicknesse doth not lie
In any humour, or one certaine part;
But as thou sawest it rotten at the heart,
Thou seest a Hectique feaver hath got hold
Of the whole substance, not to be contrould,
And that thou hast but one way, not t'admit
The worlds infection, to be none of it.
For the worlds subtilst immateriall parts
Feele this consuming wound, and ages darts.
For the worlds beauty is decai'd, or gone,
Beauty, that's colour, and proportion.
We thinke the heavens enjoy their Sphericall,
Their round proportion embracing all.
But yet their various and perplexed course,
Observ'd in divers ages, doth enforce
Men to finde out so many Eccentrique parts,
Such divers downe-right lines, such overthwarts,
As disproportion that pure forme: It teares
The Firmament in eight and forty sheires,
And in these Constellations then arise
New starres, and old doe vanish from our eyes:

As though heav'n suffered earthquakes, peace or war.
When new Towers rise, and old demolish't are.
They have impal'd within a Zodiake
The free-borne Sun, and keepe twelve Signes awake
To watch his steps; the Goat and Crab controule,
And fright him backe, who else to either Pole
(Did not these Tropiques fetter him) might runne:
For his course is not round; nor can the Sunne
Perfit a Circle, or maintaine his way
One inch direct; but where he rose to-day
He comes no more, but with a couzening line,
Steales by that point, and so is Serpentine:
And seeming weary with his reeling thus,
He meanes to sleepe, being now falne nearer us.
So, of the Starres which boast that they doe runne
In Circle still, none ends where he begun.
All their proportion's lame, it sinkes, it swels.
For of Meridians, and Parallels,
Man hath weav'd out a net, and this net throwne
Upon the Heavens, and now they are his owne.
Loth to goe up the hill, or labour thus
To goe to heaven, we make heaven come to us.
We spur, we reine the starres, and in their race
They're diversly content t'obey our pace.
But keepes the earth her round proportion still?
Doth not a Tenarif, or higher Hill
Rise so high like a Rocke, that one might thinke
The floating Moone would shipwrack there, and sinke?
Seas are so deepe, that Whales being strooke to day,
Perchance to morrow, scarse at middle way
Of their wish'd journies end, the bottome, die.
And men, to sound depths, so much line untie,
As one might justly thinke, that there would rise
At end thereof, one of th'Antipodies:
If under all, a Vault infernall bee,
(Which sure is spacious, except that we
Invent another torment, that there must
Millions into a straight hot roome be thrust)
Then solidnesse, and roundnesse have no place.
Are these but warts, and pock-holes in the face
Of th'earth? Thinke so: but yet confesse, in this
The worlds proportion disfigured is;

That those two legges whereon it doth rely,
Reward and punishment are bent awry.
And, Oh, it can no more be questioned,
That beauties best, proportion, is dead,
Since even griefe it selfe, which now alone
Is left us, is without proportion.
Shee by whose lines proportion should bee
Examin'd, measure of all Symmetree,
Whom had that Ancient seen, who thought soules made
Of Harmony, he would at next have said
That Harmony was shee, and thence infer,
That soules were but Resultances from her,
And did from her into our bodies goe,
As to our eyes, the formes from objects flow:
Shee, who if those great Doctors truly said
That the Arke to mans proportions was made,
Had been a type for that, as that might be
A type of her in this, that contrary
Both Elements, and Passions liv'd at peace
In her, who caus'd all Civill war to cease.
Shee, after whom, what forme soe'r we see,
Is discord, and rude incongruitie;
Shee, shee is dead, shee's dead; when thou knowst this,
Thou knowst how ugly a monster this world is:
And learn'st thus much by our Anatomie,
That here is nothing to enamour thee:
And that, not only faults in inward parts,
Corruptions in our braines, or in our hearts,
Poysoning the fountaines, whence our actions spring,
Endanger us: but that if every thing
Be not done fitly'and in proportion,
To satisfie wise, and good lookers on,
(Since most men be such as most thinke they bee)
They're lothsome to, by this Deformitee.
For good, and well, must in our actions meete;
Wicked is not much worse than indiscreet.
But beauties other second Element,
Colour, and lustre now, is as neere spent.
And had the world his just proportion,
Were it a ring still, yet the stone is gone.
As a compassionate Turcoyse which doth tell
By looking pale, the wearer is not well,

As gold falls sicke being stung with Mercury,
All the worlds parts of such complexion bee.
When nature was most busie, the first weeke,
Swadling the new borne earth, God seem'd to like
That she should sport her selfe sometimes, and play,
To mingle, and vary colours every day:
And then, as though shee could not make inow,
Himselfe his various Rainbow did allow.
Sight is the noblest sense of any one,
Yet sight hath only colour to feed on,
And colour is decai'd: summers robe growes
Duskie, and like an oft dyed garment showes.
Our blushing red, which us'd in cheekes to spred,
Is inward sunke, and only our soules are red.
Perchance the world might have recovered,
If she whom we lament had not beene dead:
But shee, in whom all white, and red, and blew
(Beauties ingredients) voluntary grew,
As in an unvext Paradise; from whom
Did all things verdure, and their lustre come,
Whose composition was miraculous,
Being all colour, all Diaphanous,
(For Ayre, and Fire but thick grosse bodies were,
And liveliest stones but drowsie, and pale to her,)
Shee, shee, is dead; shee's dead: when thou know'st this,
Thou know'st how wan a Ghost this our world is:
And learn'st thus much by our Anatomie,
That it should more affright, than pleasure thee.
And that, since all faire colour then did sinke,
'Tis now but wicked vanitie, to thinke
To colour vicious deeds with good pretence,
Or with bought colors to illude mens sense.
Nor in ought more this worlds decay appeares,
Than that her influence the heav'n forbeares,
Or that the Elements doe not feele this,
The father, or the mother barren is.
The cloudes conceive not raine, or doe not powre,
In the due birth, downe the balmy showre;
Th'Ayre doth not motherly sit on the earth,
To hatch her seasons, and give all things birth;
Spring-times were common cradles, but are tombes;
And false-conceptions fill the generall wombes;

Th'Ayre showes such Meteors, as none can see,
Not only what they meane, but what they bee;
Earth such new wormes, as would have troubled much
Th'Ægyptian *Mages* to have made more such.
What Artist now dares boast that he can bring
Heaven hither, or constellate any thing,
So as the influence of those starres may bee
Imprison'd in an Hearbe, or Charme, or Tree,
And doe by touch, all which those stars could doe?
The art is lost, and correspondence too.
For heaven gives little, and the earth takes lesse,
And man least knowes their trade and purposes.
If this commerce twixt heaven and earth were not
Embarr'd, and all this traffique quite forgot,
She, for whose losse we have lamented thus,
Would worke more fully, and pow'rfully on us:
Since herbes, and roots, by dying lose not all,
But they, yea Ashes too, are medicinall,
Death could not quench her vertue so, but that
It would be (if not follow'd) wondred at:
And all the world would be one dying Swan,
To sing her funerall praise, and vanish then.
But as some Serpents poyson hurteth not,
Except it be from the live Serpent shot,
So doth her vertue need her here, to fit
That unto us; shee working more than it.
But shee, in whom to such maturity
Vertue was growne, past growth, that it must die;
Shee, from whose influence all Impressions came,
But, by Receivers impotencies, lame,
Who, though she could not transubstantiate
All states to gold, yet guilded every state,
So that some Princes have some temperance;
Some Counsellers some purpose to advance
The common profit; and some people have
Some stay, no more than Kings should give, to crave;
Some women have some taciturnity,
Some nunneries some graines of chastitie.
She that did thus much, and much more could doe,
But that our age was Iron, and rustie too,
Shee, shee is dead; shee's dead; when thou knowst this,
Thou knowst how drie a Cinder this world is.

And learn'st thus much by our Anatomy,
That 'tis in vaine to dew, or mollifie
It with thy teares, or sweat, or blood: nothing
Is worth our travaile, griefe, or perishing,
But those rich joyes, which did possesse her heart,
Of which she's now partaker, and a part.
But as in cutting up a man that's dead,
The body will not last out, to have read
On every part, and therefore men direct
Their speech to parts, that are of most effect;
So the worlds carcasse would not last, if I
Were punctuall in this Anatomy;
Nor smels it well to hearers, if one tell
Them their disease, who faine would think they're well.
Here therefore be the end: And, blessed maid,
Of whom is meant what ever hath been said,
Or shall be spoken well by any tongue,
Whose name refines course lines, and makes prose song,
Accept this tribute, and his first yeares rent,
Who till his darke short tapers end be spent,
As oft as thy feast sees this widowed earth,
Will yearely celebrate thy second birth,
That is, thy death; for though the soule of man
Be got when man is made, 'tis borne but then
When man doth die; our body's as the wombe,
And, as a Mid-wife, death directs it home.
And you her creatures, whom she workes upon,
And have your last, and best concoction
From her example, and her vertue, if you
In reverence to her, do thinke it due,
That no one should her praises thus rehearse,
As matter fit for Chronicle, not verse;
Vouchsafe to call to minde that God did make
A last, and lasting'st peece, a song. He spake
To *Moses* to deliver unto all,
That song, because hee knew they would let fall
The Law, the Prophets, and the History,
But keepe the song still in their memory:
Such an opinion (in due measure) made
Me this great Office boldly to invade:
Nor could incomprehensiblenesse deterre
Mee, from thus trying to emprison her,

Which when I saw that a strict grave could doe,
I saw not why verse might not do so too.
Verse hath a middle nature: heaven keepes Soules,
The Grave keepes bodies, Verse the Fame enroules.

A FUNERALL ELEGIE

'T I S lost, to trust a Tombe with such a guest,
Or to confine her in a marble chest.
Alas, what's Marble, Jeat, or Porphyrie,
Priz'd with the Chrysolite of either eye,
Or with those Pearles, and Rubies, which she was?
Joyne the two Indies in one Tombe, 'tis glasse;
And so is all to her materials,
Though every inch were ten Escurials,
Yet she's demolish'd: can wee keepe her then
In works of hands, or of the wits of men?
Can these memorials, ragges of paper, give
Life to that name, by which name they must live?
Sickly, alas, short-liv'd, aborted bee
Those carcasse verses, whose soule is not shee.
And can shee, who no longer would be shee,
Being such a Tabernacle, stoop to be
In paper wrapt; or, when shee would not lie
In such a house, dwell in an Elegie?
But 'tis no matter; wee may well allow
Verse to live so long as the world will now,
For her death wounded it. The world containes
Princes for armes, and Counsellors for braines,
Lawyers for tongues, Divines for hearts, and more,
The Rich for stomackes, and for backes, the Poore;
The Officers for hands, Merchants for feet,
By which, remote and distant Countries meet.
But those fine spirits which do tune, and set
This Organ, are those peeces which beget
Wonder and love; and these were shee; and shee
Being spent, the world must needs decrepit bee;
For since death will proceed to triumph still,
He can finde nothing, after her, to kill,
Except the world it selfe, so great as shee.
Thus brave and confident may Nature bee,

Death cannot give her such another blow,
Because shee cannot such another show.
But must wee say she's dead? may't not be said
That as a sundred clocke is peecemeale laid,
Not to be lost, but by the makers hand
Repollish'd, without errour then to stand,
Or as the Affrique Niger streame enwombs
It selfe into the earth, and after comes
(Having first made a naturall bridge, to passe
For many leagues) farre greater than it was,
May't not be said, that her grave shall restore
Her, greater, purer, firmer, than before?
Heaven may say this, and joy in't, but can wee
Who live, and lacke her, here this vantage see?
What is't to us, alas, if there have beene
An Angell made a Thorne, or Cherubin?
Wee lose by't: and as aged men are glad
Being tastelesse growne, to joy in joyes they had,
So now the sick starv'd world must feed upon
This joy, that we had her, who now is gone.
Rejoyce then Nature, and this World, that you,
Fearing the last fires hastning to subdue
Your force and vigour, ere it were neere gone,
Wisely bestow'd and laid it all on one.
One, whose cleare body was so pure and thinne,
Because it need disguise no thought within.
'Twas but a through-light scarfe, her minde t'inroule;
Or exhalation breath'd out from her Soule.
One, whom all men who durst no more, admir'd:
And whom, who ere had worth enough, desir'd;
As when a Temple's built, Saints emulate
To which of them, it shall be consecrate.
But, as when heaven lookes on us with new eyes,
Those new starres every Artist exercise,
What place they should assigne to them they doubt,
Argue,'and agree not, till those starres goe out:
So the world studied whose this peece should be,
Till shee can be no bodies else, nor shee:
But like a Lampe of Balsamum, desir'd
Rather t'adorne, than last, she soone expir'd,
Cloath'd in her virgin white integritie,
For marriage, though it doe not staine, doth dye.

To scape th'infirmities which wait upon
Woman, she went away, before sh'was one;
And the worlds busie noyse to overcome,
Tooke so much death, as serv'd for *opium;*
For though she could not, nor could chuse to dye,
She'ath yeelded to too long an extasie:
Hee which not knowing her said History,
Should come to reade the booke of destiny,
How faire, and chast, humble, and high she'ad been,
Much promis'd, much perform'd, at not fifteene,
And measuring future things, by things before,
Should turne the leafe to reade, and reade no more,
Would thinke that either destiny mistooke,
Or that some leaves were torne out of the booke.
But 'tis not so; Fate did but usher her
To yeares of reasons use, and then inferre
Her destiny to her selfe, which liberty
She tooke but for thus much, thus much to die.
Her modestie not suffering her to bee
Fellow-Commissioner with Destinie,
She did no more but die; if after her
Any shall live, which dare true good prefer,
Every such person is her deligate,
T'accomplish that which should have beene her Fate.
They shall make up that Booke and shall have thanks
Of Fate, and her, for filling up their blankes.
For future vertuous deeds are Legacies,
Which from the gift of her example rise;
And 'tis in heav'n part of spirituall mirth,
To see how well the good play her, on earth.

The Progresse of the Soule

WHEREIN, BY OCCASION OF THE RELIGIOUS DEATH OF
MISTRESS ELIZABETH DRURY, THE INCOMMODITIES OF
THE SOULE IN THIS LIFE, AND HER EXALTATION IN
THE NEXT, ARE CONTEMPLATED

THE SECOND ANNIVERSARY

THE HARBINGER TO THE PROGRESSE

TWO *Soules move here, and mine (a third)* must move
Paces of admiration and of love;
Thy Soule (deare virgin) whose this tribute is,
Mov'd from this mortall Spheare to lively blisse;
And yet moves still, and still aspires to see
The worlds last day, thy glories full degree:
Like as those starres which thou o'r-lookest farre,
Are in their place, and yet still moved are:
No soule (whiles with the luggage of this clay
It clogged is) can follow thee halfe way;
Or see thy flight, which doth our thoughts outgoe
So fast, that now the lightning moves but slow:
But now thou are as high in heaven flowne
As heaven's from us; what soule besides thine **owne**
Can tell thy joyes, or say he can relate
Thy glorious Journals in that blessed state?
I envie thee (Rich soule) I envy thee,
Although I cannot yet thy glory see:
And thou (great spirit) which hers follow'd **hast**
So fast, as none can follow thine so fast;
So far, as none can follow thine so farre,
(And if this flesh did not the passage barre

Hadst caught her) let me wonder at thy flight
Which long agone hadst lost the vulgar sight,
And now mak'st proud the better eyes, that they
Can see thee less'ned in thine ayery way;
So while thou mak'st her soule by progresse knowne
Thou mak'st a noble progresse of thine owne,
From this worlds carkasse having mounted high
To that pure life of immortalitie;
Since thine aspiring thoughts themselves so raise
That more may not beseeme a creatures praise,
Yet still thou vow'st her more; and every yeare
Mak'st a new progresse, while thou wandrest here;
Still upward mount; and let thy Makers praise
Honor thy Laura, and adorne thy laies.
And since thy Muse her head in heaven shrouds,
Oh let her never stoope below the clouds:
And if those glorious sainted soules may know
Or what wee doe, or what wee sing below,
Those acts, those songs, shall still content them best
Which praise those awfull Powers that make them blest.

THE SECOND ANNIVERSARY

NOTHING could make me sooner to confesse
That this world had an everlastingnesse,
Than to consider, that a yeare is runne,
Since both this lower world's, and the Sunnes Sunne,
The Lustre, and the vigor of this All,
Did set; 'twere blasphemie to say, did fall.
But as a ship which hath strooke saile, doth runne
By force of that force which before, it wonne:
Or as sometimes in a beheaded man,
Though at those two Red seas, which freely ranne,
One from the Trunke, another from the Head,
His soule be sail'd, to her eternall bed,
His eyes will twinckle, and his tongue will roll,
As though he beckned, and cal'd backe his soule,
He graspes his hands, and he pulls up his feet,
And seemes to reach, and to step forth to meet
His soule; when all these motions which we saw,
Are but as Ice, which crackles at a thaw:

Or as a Lute, which in moist weather, rings
Her knell alone, by cracking of her strings:
So struggles this dead world, now shee is gone;
For there is motion in corruption.
As some daies are at the Creation nam'd,
Before the Sunne, the which fram'd daies, was fram'd,
So after this Sunne's set, some shew appeares,
And orderly vicissitude of yeares.
Yet a new deluge, and of *Lethe* flood,
Hath drown'd us all, All have forgot all good,
Forgetting her, the maine reserve of all.
Yet in this deluge, grosse and generall,
Thou seest me strive for life; my life shall bee,
To be hereafter prais'd, for praysing thee;
Immortall Maid, who though thou would'st refuse
The name of Mother, be unto my Muse
A Father, since her chast Ambition is,
Yearely to bring forth such a child as this.
These Hymnes may worke on future wits, and so
May great Grand children of thy prayses grow.
And so, though not revive, embalme and spice
The world, which else would putrifie with vice.
For thus, Man may extend thy progeny,
Untill man doe but vanish, and not die.
These Hymnes thy issue, may encrease so long,
As till Gods great *Venite* change the song.
Thirst for that time, O my insatiate soule,
And serve thy thirst, with Gods safe-sealing **Bowle**.
Be thirstie still, and drinke still till thou goe
To th'only Health, to be Hydroptique so.
Forget this rotten world; And unto thee
Let thine owne times as an old storie bee.
Be not concern'd: studie not why, nor when;
Doe not so much as not beleeve a man.
For though to erre, be worst, to try truths forth,
Is far more businesse, than this world is worth.
The world is but a carkasse; thou art fed
By it, but as a worme, that carkasse bred;
And why should'st thou, poore worme, consider more,
When this world will grow better than before,
Than those thy fellow wormes doe thinke upon
That carkasses last resurrection.

Forget this world, and scarce thinke of it so,
As of old clothes, cast off a yeare agoe.
To be thus stupid is Alacritie;
Men thus Lethargique have best Memory.
Look upward; that's towards her, whose happy state
We now lament not, but congratulate.
Shee, to whom all this world was but a stage,
Where all sat harkning how her youthfull age
Sould be emploi'd, because in all shee did,
Some Figure of the Golden times was hid.
Who could not lacke, what e'r this world could give,
Because shee was the forme, that made it live;
Nor could complaine, that this world was unfit
To be staid in, then when shee was in it;
Shee that first tried indifferent desires
By vertue, and vertue by religious fires,
Shee to whose person Paradise adher'd,
As Courts to Princes, shee whose eyes ensphear'd
Star-light enough, t'have made the South controule,
(Had shee beene there) the Star-full Northerne Pole,
Shee, shee is gone; she is gone; when thou knowest this,
What fragmentary rubbidge this world is
Thou knowest, and that it is not worth a thought;
He honors it too much that thinkes it nought.
Thinke then, my soule, that death is but a Groome,
Which brings a Taper to the outward roome,
Whence thou spiest first a little glimmering light,
And after brings it nearer to thy sight:
For such approaches doth heaven make in death.
Thinke thy selfe labouring now with broken breath,
And thinke those broken and soft Notes to bee
Division, and thy happyest Harmonie.
Thinke thee laid on thy death-bed, loose and slacke
And thinke that, but unbinding of a packe,
To take one precious thing, thy soule from thence.
Thinke thy selfe parch'd with fevers violence,
Anger thine ague more, by calling it
Thy Physicke; chide the slacknesse of the fit.
Thinke that thou hear'st thy knell, and think no more,
But that, as Bels cal'd thee to Church before,
So this, to the Triumphant Church, calls thee.
Thinke Satans Sergeants round about thee bee,

And thinke that but for Legacies they thrust;
Give one thy Pride, to'another give thy Lust:
Give them those sinnes which they gave thee before,
And trust th'immaculate blood to wash thy score.
Thinke thy friends weeping round, and thinke that they
Weepe but because they goe not yet thy way.
Thinke that they close thine eyes, and thinke in this,
That they confesse much in the world, amisse,
Who dare not trust a dead mans eye with that,
Which they from God, and Angels cover not.
Thinke that they shroud thee up, and think from thence
They reinvest thee in white innocence
Thinke that thy body rots, and (if so low,
Thy soule exalted so, thy thoughts can goe,)
Think thee a Prince, who of themselves create
Wormes which insensibly devoure their State.
Thinke that they bury thee, and thinke that right
Laies thee to sleepe but a Saint Lucies night.
Thinke these things cheerefully: and if thou bee
Drowsie or slacke, remember then that shee,
Shee whose Complexion was so even made,
That which of her Ingredients should invade
The other three, no Feare, no Art could guesse:
So far were all remov'd from more or lesse.
But as in Mithridate, or just perfumes,
Where all good things being met, no one presumes
To governe, or to triumph on the rest,
Only because all were, no part was best.
And as, though all doe know, that quantities
Are made of lines, and lines from Points arise,
None can these lines or quantities unjoynt,
And say this is a line, or this a point,
So though the Elements and Humors were
In her, one could not say, this governes there.
Whose even constitution might have wonne
Any disease to venter on the Sunne,
Rather than her: and make a spirit feare,
That hee to disuniting subject were.
To whose proportions if we would compare
Cubes, th'are unstable; Circles, Angular;
She who was such a chaine as Fate employes
To bring mankinde all Fortunes it enjoyes;

So fast, so even wrought, as one would thinke,
No Accident could threaten any linke;
Shee, shee embrac'd a sicknesse, gave it meat,
The purest blood, and breath, that e'r it eate;
And hath taught us, that though a good man hath
Title to heaven, and plead it by his Faith,
And though he may pretend a conquest, since
Heaven was content to suffer violence,
Yea though hee plead a long possession too,
(For they're in heaven on earth who heavens workes do)
Though hee had right and power and place, before,
Yet Death must usher, and unlocke the doore.
Thinke further on thy selfe my Soule, and thinke
How thou at first wast made but in a sinke;
Thinke that it argued some infirmitie,
That those two soules, which then thou foundst in me,
Thou fedst upon, and drewst into thee, both
My second soule of sense, and first of growth.
Thinke but how poore thou wast, how obnoxious;
Whom a small lumpe of flesh could poyson thus.
This curdled milke, this poore unlittered whelpe
My body, could, beyond escape or helpe,
Infect thee with Originall sinne, and thou
Couldst neither then refuse, nor leave it now.
Thinke that no stubborne sullen Anchorit,
Which fixt to a pillar, or a grave, doth sit
Bedded, and bath'd in all his ordures, dwels
So fowly as our Soules in their first-built Cels.
Thinke in how poore a prison thou didst lie
After, enabled but to suck and crie.
Thinke, when'twas growne to most,'twas a poore Inne,
A Province pack'd up in two yards of skinne,
And that usurp'd or threatened with the rage
Of sicknesses, or their true mother, Age.
But thinke that Death hath now enfranchis'd thee,
Thou hast thy'expansion now, and libertie;
Thinke that a rustie Peece, discharg'd, is flowne
In peeces, and the bullet is his owne,
And freely flies: This to thy Soule allow,
Thinke thy shell broke, thinke thy Soule hatch'd but now.
And think this slow-pac'd soule, which late did cleave
To'a body, and went but by the bodies leave,

Twenty, perchance, or thirty mile a day,
Dispatches in a minute all the way
Twixt heaven, and earth; she stayes not in the ayre,
To looke what Meteors there themselves prepare;
She carries no desire to know, nor sense,
Whether th'ayres middle region be intense;
For th'Element of fire, she doth not know,
Whether she past by such a place or no;
She baits not at the Moone, nor cares to trie
Whether in that new world, men live, and die.
Venus retards her not, to'enquire, how shee
Can, (*being one starre*) *Hesper,* and *Vesper* bee;
Hee that charm'd *Argus* eyes, sweet *Mercury,*
Workes not on her, who now is growne all eye;
Who, if she meet the body of the Sunne,
Goes through, not staying till his course be runne;
Who findes in *Mars* his Campe no corps of Guard;
Nor is by *Jove*, not by his father barr'd;
But ere she can consider how she went,
At once is at, and through the Firmament.
And as these starres were but so many beads
Strung on one string, speed undistinguish'd leads
Her through those Spheares, as through the beads, a string.
Whose quick succession makes it still one thing:
As doth the pith, which, lest our bodies slacke,
Strings fast the little bones of necke, and backe;
So by the Soule doth death string Heaven and Earth;
For when our Soule enjoyes this her third birth,
(Creation gave her one, a second, grace,)
Heaven is as neare, and present to her face,
As colours are, and objects, in a roome
Where darknesse was before, when Tapers come.
This must, my Soule, thy long-short Progresse bee;
To'advance these thoughts, remember then, that she,
She, whose faire body no such prison was,
But that a Soule might well be pleas'd to passe
An age in her; she whose rich beauty lent
Mintage to other beauties, for they went
But for so much as they were like to her;
Shee, in whose body (if we dare preferre
This low world, to so high a marke as shee,)
The Westerne treasure, Easterne spicerie,

Europe, and Afrique, and the unknowne rest
Were easily found, or what in them was best;
And when w'have made this large discoverie
Of all, in her some one part then will bee
Twenty such parts, whose plenty and riches is
Enough to make twenty such words as this;
Shee, whom had they knowne who did first betroth
The Tutelar Angels, and assign'd one, both
To Nations, Cities, and to Companies,
To Functions, Offices, and Dignities,
And to each severall man, to him, and him,
They would have given her one for every limbe;
She, of whose soule, if we may say, 'twas Gold,
Her body was th'Electrum, and did hold
Many degrees of that; wee understood
Her by her sight; her pure, and eloquent blood
Spoke in her cheekes, and so distinctly wrought,
That one might almost say, her body thought;
Shee, shee, thus richly and largely hous'd, is gone:
And chides us slow-pac'd snailes who crawle upon
Our prisons prison, earth, nor thinke us well,
Longer, than whil'st wee beare our brittle shell.
But 'twere but little to have chang'd our roome,
If, as we were in this our living Tombe
Oppress'd with ignorance, wee still were so.
Poore soule, in this thy flesh what dost thou know?
Thou know'st they selfe so little, as thou know'st not,
How thou didst die, nor how thou wast begot.
Thou neither know'st, how thou at first cam'st in,
Nor how thou took'st the poyson of mans sinne.
Nor dost thou, (though thou know'st, that thou art so)
By what way thou art made immortall, know.
Thou art too narrow, wretch, to comprehend
Even thy selfe: yea though thou wouldst but bend
To know thy body. Have not all soules thought
For many ages, that our body'is wrought
Of Ayre, and Fire, and other Elements?
And now they thinke of new ingredients,
And one Soule thinkes one, and another way
Another thinkes, and 'tis an even lay.
Knowst thou but how the stone doth enter in
The bladders cave, and never breake the skinne?

Know'st thou how blood, which to the heart doth flow,
Doth from one ventricle to th'other goe?
And for the putrid stuffe, which thou dost spit,
Know'st thou how thy lungs have attracted it?
There are no passages, so that there is
(For ought thou know'st) piercing of substances.
And of those many opinions which men raise
Of Nailes and Haires, dost thou know which to praise?
What hope have wee to know our selves, when wee
Know not the least things, which for our use be?
Wee see in Authors, too stiffe to recant,
A hundred controversies of an Ant;
And yet one watches, starves, freeses, and sweats,
To know but Catechismes and Alphabets
Of unconcerning things, matters of fact;
How others on our stage their parts did Act;
What *Cæsar* did, yea, and what *Cicero* said.
Why grasse is greene, or why our blood is red,
Are mysteries which none have reach'd unto.
In this low forme, poore soule, what wilt thou doe?
When wilt thou shake off this Pedantery,
Of being taught by sense, and Fantasie?
Thou look'st through spectacles; small things seeme great
Below; But up unto the watch-towre get,
And see all things despoyl'd of fallacies:
Thou shalt not peepe through lattices of eyes,
Nor heare through Labyrinths of eares, nor learne
By circuit, or collections to discerne.
In heaven thou straight know'st all, concerning it,
And what concernes it not, shalt straight forget.
There thou (but in no other schoole) maist bee
Perchance, as learned, and as full, as shee,
Shee who all libraries had throughly read
At home in her owne thoughts, and practised
So much good as would make as many more:
Shee whose examples they must all implore,
Who would or doe, or thinke well, and confesse
That all the vertuous Actions they expresse,
Are but a new, and worse edition
Of her some one thought, or one action:
She who in th'art of knowing Heaven, was growne
Here upon earth, to such perfection,

That she hath, ever since to Heaven she came,
(In a far fairer print,) but read the same:
Shee, shee not satisfied with all this waight,
(For so much knowledge, as would over-fraight
Another, did but ballast her) is gone
As well t'enjoy, as get perfection.
And cals us after her, in that shee tooke,
(Taking her selfe) our best, and worthiest booke.
Returne not, my Soule, from this extasie,
And meditation of what thou shalt bee,
To earthly thoughts, till it to thee appeare,
With whom thy conversation must be there.
With whom wilt thou converse? what station
Canst thou choose out, free from infection,
That will not give thee theirs, nor drinke in thine?
Shalt thou not finde a spungie slacke Divine
Drinke and sucke in th'instructions of Great men,
And for the word of God, vent them agen?
Are there not some Courts (and then, no things bee
So like as Courts) which, in this let us see,
That wits and tongues of Libellers are weake,
Because they do more ill, than these can speake?
The poyson's gone through all, poysons affect
Chiefly the chiefest parts, but some effect
In nailes, and haires, yea excrements, will show;
So lyes the poyson of sinne in the most low.
Up, up, my drowsie Soule, where thy new eare
Shall in the Angels songs no discord heare;
Where thou shalt see the blessed Mother-maid
Joy in not being that, which men have said.
Where she is exalted more for being good,
Than for her interest of Mother-hood.
Up to those Patriarchs, which did longer sit
Expecting Christ, than they'have enjoy'd him yet.
Up to those Prophets, which now gladly see
Their Prophesies growne to be Historie.
Up to th'Apostles, who did bravely runne
All the Suns course, with more light than the Sunne.
Up to those Martyrs, who did calmly bleed
Oyle to th'Apostles Lamps, dew to their seed.
Up to those Virgins, who thought, that almost
They made joyntenants with the Holy Ghost,

If they to any should his Temple give.
Up, up, for in that squadron there doth live
She, who hath carried thither new degrees
(As to their number) to their dignities.
Shee, who being to her selfe a State, injoy'd
All royalties which any State employ'd;
For shee made warres, and triumph'd; reason still
Did not o'rthrow, but rectifie her will:
And she made peace, for no peace is like this,
That beauty, and chastity together kisse:
She did high justice, for she crucified
Every first motion of rebellious pride:
And she gave pardons, and was liberall,
For, onely her selfe except, she pardon'd all:
Shee coy'nd, in this, that her impressions gave
To all our actions all the worth they have:
She gave protections! the thoughts of her brest
Satans rude Officers could ne'r arrest.
As these prerogatives being met in one,
Made her a soveraigne State; religion
Made her a Church; and these two made her all.
She who was all this All, and could not fall
To worse, by company, (for she was still
More Antidote, than all the world was ill,)
Shee, shee doth leaveit, and by Death, survive
All this, in Heaven; whither who doth not strive
The more, because shees there, he doth not know
That accidentall joyes in Heaven doe grow.
But pause, my soule; And study, ere thou fall
On accidentall joyes, th'essentiall.
Still before Accessories doe abide
A triall, must the principall be tride.
And what essentiall joy can'st thou expect
Here upon earth? what permanent effect
Of transitory causes? Dost thou love
Beauty? (And beauty worthy'st is to move)
Poore cousened cousenor, *that* she, and *that* thou,
Which did begin to love, are neither now;
You are both fluid, chang'd since yesterday;
Next day repaires, (but ill) last dayes decay.
Nor are, (although the river keepe the name)
Yesterdaies waters, and to daies the same

So flowes her face, and thine eyes, neither now
That Saint, nor Pilgrime, which your loving vow
Concern'd, remaines; but whil'st you thinke you bee
Constant, you'are hourely in inconstancie.
Honour may have pretence unto our love,
Because that God did live so long above
Without this Honour, and then lov'd it so,
That he at last made Creatures to bestow
Honour on him; not that he needed it,
But that, to his hands, man might grow more fit.
But since all Honours from inferiours flow,
(For they doe give it; Princes doe but shew
Whom they would have so honor'd) and that this
On such opinions, and capacities
Is built, as rise and fall, to more and lesse:
Alas, 'tis but a casuall happinesse.
Hath ever any man to'himselfe assign'd
This or that happiness to'arrest his minde,
But that another man which takes a worse,
Thinks him a foole for having tane that course?
They who did labour Babels tower to'erect,
Might have considered, that for that effect,
All this whole solid Earth could not allow
Nor furnish forth materialls enow;
And that this Center, to raise such a place,
Was farre too little, to have beene the Base;
No more affords this world, foundation
To erect true joy, were all the meanes in one.
But as the Heathen made them severall gods,
Of all Gods Benefits, and all his Rods,
(For as the Wine, and Corne, and Onions are
Gods unto them, so Agues bee, and Warre)
And as by changing that whole precious Gold
To such small Copper coynes, they lost the old,
And lost their only God, who ever must
Be sought alone, and not in such a thrust:
So much mankinde true happinesse mistakes;
No Joy enjoyes that man, that many makes.
Then, Soule, to thy first pitch worke up againe;
Know that all lines which circles doe containe,
For once that they the Center touch, doe touch
Twice the circumference; and be thou such;

Double on heaven thy thoughts on earth emploid;
All will not serve; Only who have enjoy'd
The sight of God, in fulnesse, can thinke it;
For it is both the object, and the wit.
This is essentiall joy, where neither hee
Can suffer diminution, nor wee;
'Tis such a full, and such a filling good;
Had th'Angels once look'd on him, they had stood.
To fill the place of one of them, or more,
Shee who wee celebrate, is gone before.
She, who had Here so much essentiall joy,
As no chance could distract, much lesse destroy;
Who with Gods presence was acquainted so,
(Hearing, and speaking to him) as to know
His face in any naturall Stone, or Tree,
Better than when in Images they bee:
Who kept by diligent devotion,
Gods Image, in such reparation,
Within her heart, that what decay was growne,
Was her first Parents fault, and not her owne:
Who being solicited to any act,
Still heard God pleading his safe precontract;
Who by a faithfull confidence, was here
Betroth'd to God, and now is married there;
Whose twilights were more cleare, than our mid-day;
Who dreamt devoutlier, than most use to pray;
Who being here fil'd with grace, yet strove to bee,
Both where more grace, and more capacitie
At once is given: she to Heaven is gone,
Who made this world in some proportion
A heaven, and here, became unto us all,
Joy, (as our joyes admit) essentiall.
But could this low world joyes essentiall touch,
Heavens accidentall joyes would passe them much.
How poor and lame, must then our casuall bee?
If thy Prince will his subjects to call thee
My Lord, and this doe swell thee, thou art then,
By being greater, growne to bee lesse Man.
When no Physitian of redresse can speake,
A joyfull casuall violence may breake
A dangerous Apostem in thy breast;
And whil'st thou joyest in this, the dangerous rest,

The bag may rise up, and so strangle thee.
What e'r was casuall, may ever bee.
What should the nature change? Or make the same
Certaine, which was but casuall, when it came?
All casuall joy doth loud and plainly say,
Only by comming, that it can away.
Only in Heaven joyes strength is never spent;
And accidental things are permanent.
Joy of a soules arrivall ne'r decaies;
For that soule ever joyes and ever staies.
Joy that their last great Consummation
Approaches in the resurrection;
When earthly bodies more celestiall
Shall be, than Angels were, for they could fall;
This kinde of joy doth every day admit
Degrees of growth, but none of losing it.
In this fresh joy, 'tis no small part, that shee,
Shee, in whose goodnesse, he that names degree,
Doth injure her; ('Tis losse to be cal'd best,
There where the stuffe is not such as the rest)
Shee, who left such a bodie, as even shee
Only in Heaven could learne, how it can bee
Made better; for shee rather was two soules,
Or like to full on both sides written Rols,
Where eyes might reade upon the outward skin,
As strong Records for God, as mindes within;
Shee, who by making full perfection grow,
Peeces a Circle, and still keeps it so,
Long'd for, and longing for it, to heaven is gone,
Where shee receives, and gives addition.
Here in a place, where mis-devotion frames
A thousand Prayers to Saints, whose very names
The ancient Church knew not, Heaven knows not yet:
And where, what lawes of Poetry admit,
Lawes of Religion have at least the same,
Immortall Maide, I might invoke thy name.
Could any Saint provoke that appetite,
Thou here should'st make me a French convertite.
But thou would'st not; nor would'st thou be content,
To take this, for my second yeares true Rent,
Did this Coine beare any other stampe, than his,
That gave thee power to doe, me, to say this.

Since his will is, that to posteritie,
Thou should'st for life, and death, a patterne bee,
And that the world should notice have of this,
The purpose, and th'authoritie is his;
Thou art the Proclamation; and I am
The Trumpet, at whose voyce the people came.

Epicedes and Obsequies upon the Deaths of Sundry Personages

ELEGIE ON THE UNTIMELY DEATH
OF THE
INCOMPARABLE PRINCE HENRY

LOOK to me, *Faith;* and look to my *Faith,* GOD:
For, both my *Centres* feel This *Period.*
Of *Waight,* one *Centre;* one of *Greatness* is:
And REASON is That *Centre;* FAITH is This.
For into our *Reason* flowe, and there doe end,
All that this naturall World doth comprehend;
Quotidian things, and Equi-distant hence,
Shut-in for Men in one *Circumference:*
But, for th'enormous *Greatnesses,* which are
So disproportion'd and so angulare,
As is GOD's *Essence, Place,* and *Providence,*
Where, How, when, What, Soules do, departed hence:
These *Things* (*Eccentrique* else) on Faith do strike;
Yet neither All, nor upon all alike:
For, *Reason,* put t'her best *Extension,*
Almost meetes *Faith,* and makes both *Centres* one:
And nothing ever came so neer to This,
As *Contemplation* of the PRINCE wee misse.
For, All that *Faith* could credit Mankinde *could,*
Reason still seconded that This PRINCE *would.*
If then, least Movings of the *Centre* make
(More than if whole Hell belcht) the World to shake,
What must This doo, *Centres* distracted so,
That Wee see not what to beleeve or knowe?
Was it not well believ'd, till now, that *Hee,*
Whose *Reputation* was an *Extasie*

On neighbour States; which knew not Why to wake
Till *Hee* discoverd what wayes *Hee* would take:
For *Whom* what *Princes* angled (when they tryed)
Mett a *Torpedo,* and were stupefied:
And Others studies, how *Hee* would be bent;
Was His great *Father's* greatest Instrument,
And activ'st spirit to convey and tye
This soule of *Peace* through CHRISTIANITIE?
Was it not well believ'd, that *Hee* would make
This *general Peace* th'eternall overtake?
And that *His* Times might have stretcht out so far
As to touch Those of which they *Emblems* are?
For, to confirm this just Belief, that Now
The *last Dayes* came, wee saw Heaven did allow
That but from *His* aspect and Exercise,
In *Peace*-full times, Rumors of *Warrs* should rise.
But *now* This *Faith* is *Heresie:* wee must
Still stay, and vexe our *Great-Grand-Mother,* DUST.
Oh! Is GOD prodigall? Hath he spent his store
Of Plagues on us? and only now, when more
Would ease us much, doth he grudge Miserie,
And will not lett's enjoy our *Curse,* to *Dye?*
As, for the Earth throw'n lowest downe of all,
'Twere an *Ambition* to desire to fall:
So God, in our *desire* to *dye,* dooth know
Our Plot for *Ease,* in beeing *Wretched* so.
Therefore *Wee* live: though such a Life we have
As but so manie *Mandrakes* on his Grave.
    What had *His growth* and *generation* donne?
When what wee are, his *putrefaction*
Sustains in us, Earth, which *Griefs* animate?
Nor hath our World now other *soule* than That.
And could *Grief* gett so high as Heav'n, that *Quire*
Forgetting This, their new Joy, would desire
(With grief to see him) *Hee* had staid belowe,
To rectifie Our *Errors* They foreknowe.
    Is th'other *Centre,* REASON, faster, then?
Where should wee look for That, now w'are not Men:
For, if our *Reason* be our *Connexion*
Of *Causes,* now to us there can be none.
For, as, if all the *Substances* were spent,
'Twere madness to enquire of *Accident:*

So is't to looke for *Reason,* HEE being gone,
The only *subject* REASON wrought upon.
    If *Faith* have such a *chaine,* whose divers Links
Industrious Man discerneth, as he thinks,
When Miracle dooth joine, and so steal-in
A new link Man knowes not where to begin:
At a much deader Fault must *Reason* bee,
Death having broke-off such a Link as *Hee.*
But, now, for us with busie *Proofs* to come
That w'have no *Reason,* would prove we had some:
So would just *Lamentations.* Therefore Wee
May safelier say, that Wee are dead, than *Hee.*
So, if our *Griefs* wee doo not well declare,
W'have double Excuse; *Hee* is not *dead,* We are.
Yet would not I dye yet; for though I bee
Too narrow, to think HIM, as *Hee* is HEE
(Our *Soule's* best Bayting and Mid-*period*
In her long *journey* of *Considering* GOD)
Yet (no Dishonor) I can reach Him *thus;*
As *Hee* embrac't the *Fires* of *Love* with us.
Oh! May I (*since* I live) but see or hear
That *Shee-Intelligence* which mov'd This *Sphear,*
I pardon Fate my Life. Who-e'r thou bee
Which hast the noble *Conscience,* Thou art *Shee.*
I conjure Thee by all the *Charmes Hee* spoke,
By th'Oathes which only you *Two* never broke,
By all the *Soules* you sigh'd; that if you see
These Lines, you wish I knew *Your Historie:*
So, much as *You Two mutual Heavens* were *here,*
I were an *Angel singing* what *You* were.

TO THE COUNTESS OF BEDFORD

MADAME,

I HAVE learn'd by those lawes wherein I am a little conversant, that hee
which bestowes any cost upon the dead, obliges him which is dead, but
not the heire; I do not therefore send this paper to your Ladyship, that
you should thanke mee for it, or thinke that I thanke you in it; your
favours and benefits to mee are so much above my merits, that they are
even above my gratitude, if that were to be judged by words which must

expresse it: But, Madame, since your noble brothers fortune being yours, the evidences also concerning it are yours, so his vertue being yours, the evidences concerning it, belong also to you, of which by your acceptance this may be one peace, in which quality I humbly present it, and as a testimony how intirely your familie possesseth

Your Ladieships most humble
and thankfull servant

JOHN DONNE

OBSEQUIES TO THE LORD HARRINGTON

Brother to the Lady Lucy, Countesse of Bedford

FAIRE soule, which wast, not onely, as all soules bee,
Then when thou wast infused, harmony,
But did'st continue so; and now dost beare
A part in Gods great organ, this whole Spheare:
If looking up to God; or downe to us,
Thou finde that any way is previous,
Twixt heav'n and earth, and that mans actions doe
Come to your knowledge, and affections too,
See, and with joy, mee to that good degree
Of goodnesse growne, that I can studie thee,
And, by these meditations refin'd,
Can unapparell and enlarge my minde,
And so can make by this soft extasie,
This place a map of heav'n, my selfe of thee.
Thou seest mee here at midnight, now all rest;
Times dead-low water; when all mindes devest
To morrows businesse, when the labourers have
Such rest in bed, that their last Church-yard grave,
Subject to change, will scarce be'a type of this,
Now when the clyent, whose last hearing is
To morrow, sleeps, when the condemned man,
(Who when hee opes his eyes, must shut them then
Againe by death,) although sad watch hee keepe,
Doth practice dying by a little sleepe,
Thou at this midnight seest mee, and as soone
As that Sunne rises to mee, midnight's noone,
All the world growes transparent, and I see
Through all, both Church and State, in seeing thee;

And I discerne by favour of this light,
My selfe, the hardest object of the sight.
God is the glasse; as thou when thou dost see
Him who sees all, seest all concerning thee,
So, yet unglorified, I comprehend
All, in these mirrors of thy wayes, and end.
Though God be our true glasse, through which we see
All, since the beeing of all things is hee,
Yet are the trunkes which doe to us derive
Things, in proportion fit, by perspective,
Deeds of good men; for by their living here,
Vertues, indeed remote, seeme to be neare.
But where can I affirme, or where arrest
My thoughts on his deeds? which shall I call best?
For fluid vertue cannot be look'd on,
Nor can endure a contemplation.
As bodies change, and as I do not weare
Those Spirits, humors, blood I did last yeare,
And, as if on a streame I fixe mine eye,
That drop, which I looked on, is presently
Pusht with more waters from my sight, and gone,
So in this sea of vertues, can no one
Bee'insisted on; vertues, as rivers, passe,
Yet still remaines that vertuous man there was;
And as if man feed on mans flesh, and so
Part of his body to another owe,
Yet at the last two perfect bodies rise,
Because God knowes where every Atome lyes;
So, if one knowledge were made of all those,
Who knew his minutes well, hee might dispose
His vertues into names, and ranks; but I
Should injure Nature, Vertue, and Destinie,
Should I divide and discontinue so,
Vertue, which did in one intirenesse grow.
For as, hee that would say, spirits are fram'd
Of all the purest parts that can be nam'd,
Honours not spirits halfe so much, as hee
Which sayes, they have no parts, but simple bee;
So is't of vertue; for a point and one
Are much entirer than a million.
And had Fate meant to have his vertues told,
It would have let him live to have beene old;

So, then that vertue in season, and then this,
We might have seene, and said, that now he is
Witty, now wise, now temperate, now just:
In good short lives, vertues are faine to thrust,
And to be sure betimes to get a place,
When they would exercise, lacke time, and space.
So was it in this person, forc'd to bee
For lack of time, his owne epitome:
So to exhibit in few yeares as much,
As all the long breath'd Chronicles can touch.
As when an Angell down from heav'n doth flye,
Our quick thought cannot keepe him company,
Wee cannot thinke, now hee is at the Sunne,
Now through the Moon, now he through th'aire doth run
Yet when he's come, we know he did repaire
To all twixt Heav'n and Earth, Sunne, Moon, and Aire;
And as this Angell in an instant knowes,
And yet wee know, this sodaine knowledge growes
By quick amassing severall formes of things,
Which he successively to order brings;
When they, whose slow-pac'd lame thoughts cannot goe
So fast as hee, thinke that he doth not so;
Just as a perfect reader doth not dwell,
On every syllable, nor stay to spell,
Yet without doubt, hee doth distinctly see
And lay together every A, and B;
So, in short liv'd good men, is'not understood
Each severall vertue, but the compound good;
For, they all vertues paths in that pace tread,
As Angells goe, and know, and as men read.
O why should then these men, these lumps of Balme
Sent hither, this worlds tempests to becalme,
Before by deeds they are diffus'd and spread,
And so make us alive, themselves be dead?
O Soule, O circle, why so quickly bee
Thy ends, thy birth and death, clos'd up in thee?
Since one foot of thy compasse still was plac'd
In heav'n, the other might securely'have pac'd
In the most large extent, through every path,
Which the whole world, or man the abridgment hath.
Thou knowst, that though the tropique circles have
(Yea and those small ones which the Poles engrave,)

All the same roundnesse, evennesse, and all
The endlessnesse of the equinoctiall;
Yet, when we come to measure distances,
How here, how there, the Sunne affected is,
When he doth faintly worke, and when prevaile,
Onely great circles, then can be our scale:
So, though thy circle to thy selfe expresse
All, tending to thy endlesse happinesse,
And wee, by our good use of it may trye,
Both how to live well young, and how to die,
Yet, since we must be old, and age endures
His Torrid Zone at Court, and calentures
Of hot ambitions, irrelegions ice,
Zeales agues, and hydroptique avarice,
Infirmities which need the scale of truth,
As well as lust, and ignorance of youth;
Why did'st thou not for these give medicines too,
And by thy doing tell us what to doe?
Though as small pocket-clocks, whose every wheele
Doth each mismotion and distemper feele,
Whose *hand* gets shaking palsies, and whose *string*
(His sinews) slackens, and whose *Soule,* the spring,
Expires, or languishes, whose pulse, the *flye,*
Either beates not, or beates unevenly,
Whose voice, the *Bell,* doth rattle, or grow dumbe,
Or idle,'as men, which to their last houres come,
If these clockes be not wound, or be wound still,
Or be not set, or set at every will;
So, youth is easiest to destruction,
If then wee follow all, or follow none.
Yet, as in great clocks, which in steeples chime,
Plac'd to informe whole towns, to'imploy their time,
An error doth more harme, being generall,
When, small clocks faults, only'on the wearer fall;
So worke the faults of age, on which the eye
Of children, servants, or the State relie.
Why wouldst not thou then, which hadst such a soule,
A clock so true, as might the Sunne controule,
And daily hadst him, who gave it thee,
Instructions, such as it could never be
Disordered, stay here, as a generall
And great Sun-dyall, to have set us All?

O why wouldst thou be any instrument
To this unnaturall course, or why consent
To this, not miracle, but Prodigie,
That when the ebbs, longer than flowings be,
Vertue, whose flood did with thy youth begin,
Should so much faster ebb out, than flow in?
Though her flood was blowne in, by thy first breath,
All is at once sunke in the whirle-poole death.
Which word I would not name, but that I see
Death, else a desert, growne a Court by thee.
Now I grow sure, that if a man would have
Good companie, his entry is a grave.
Mee thinkes all Cities now, but Anthills bee,
Where, when the severall labourers I see,
For children, house, Provision, taking paine,
They'are all but Ants, carrying eggs, straw, and grain;
And Church-yards are our cities, unto which
The most repaire, that are in goodnesse rich.
There is the best concourse, and confluence,
There are the holy suburbs, and from thence
Begins Gods City, New Jerusalem,
Which doth extend her utmost gates to them.
At that gate then Triumphant soule, dost thou
Begin thy Triumph; But since lawes allow
That at the Triumph day, the people may,
All that they will, 'gainst the Triumpher say,
Let me here use that freedome, and expresse
My griefe, though not to make thy Triumph lesse.
By law, to Triumphs none admitted bee,
Till they as Magistrates get victorie;
Though then to thy force, all youthes foes did yield,
Yet till fit time had brought thee to that field,
To which thy ranke in this state destin'd thee,
That there thy counsailes might get victorie,
And so in that capacite remove
All jealousies 'twixt Prince and subjects love,
Thou could'st no title, to this triumph have,
Thou didst intrude on death, usurp'dst a grave.
Then (though victoriously) thou hadst fought as yet
But with thine owne affections, with the heate
Of youths desires, and colds of ignorance,
But till thou should'st successefully advance

Thine armes 'gainst forraine enemies, which are
Both Envy, and acclamations popular,
(For, both these engines equally defeate,
Though by a divers Mine, those which are great,)
Till then thy War was but a civill War,
For which to Triumph, none admitted are.
No more are they, who though with good successe,
In a defensive war, their power expresse;
Before men triumph, the dominion
Must be *enlarg'd* and not *preserv'd* alone;
Why should'st thou then, whose battailes were to win
Thy selfe, from those straits nature put thee in,
And to deliver up to God that state,
Of which he gave thee the vicariate,
(Which is thy soule and body) as intire
As he, who takes endeavours, doth require,
But didst not stay, t'enlarge his kingdome too,
By making others, what thou didst, to doe;
Why shouldst thou Triumph now, when Heav'n no more
Hath got, by getting thee, than't had before?
For, Heav'n and thou, even when thou livedst here,
Of one another in possession were.
But this from Triumph most disables thee,
That, that place which is conquered, must bee
Left safe from present warre, and likely doubt
Of imminent commotions to breake out:
And hath he left us so? or can it bee
His territory was no more than Hee?
No, we were all his charge, the Diocis
Of ev'ry exemplar man, the whole world is,
And he was joyned in commission
With Tutelar Angels, sent to every one.
But though his freedome to upbraid, and chide
Him who Triumph'd, were lawfull, it was ty'd
With this, that it might never reference have
Unto the Senate, who this triumph gave;
Men might at Pompey jeast, but they might not
At that authoritie, by which he got
Leave to Triumph, before, by age, he might;
So, though, triumphant soule, I dare to write,
Mov'd with a reverentiall anger, thus,
That thou so earely wouldst abandon us;

Yet I am farre from daring to dispute
With that great soveraigntie, whose absolute
Prerogative hath thus dispens'd with thee,
'Gainst natures lawes, which just impugners bee
Of early triumphs; And I (though with paine)
Lessen our losse, to magnifie thy gaine
Of triumph, when I say, It was more fit,
That all men should lacke thee, than thou lack it.
Though then in our time, be not suffered
That testimonie of love, unto the dead,
To die with them, and in their graves be hid,
As Saxon wives, and French soldurii did;
And though in no degree I can expresse
Griefe in great Alexanders great excesse,
Who at his friends death, made whole townes devest
Their walls and bullwarks which became them best:
Doe not, faire soule, this sacrifice refuse,
That in thy grave I doe interre my Muse,
Who, by my griefe, great as thy worth, being cast
Behind hand, yet hath spoke, and spoke her last.

ELEGIE ON THE LADY MARCKHAM

MAN is the World, and death th'Ocean,
    To which God gives the lower parts of man.
This Sea invirons all, and though as yet
    God hath set markes, and bounds, twixt us and it,
Yet doth it rore, and gnaw, and still pretend,
    And breaks our bankes, when ere it takes a friend.
Then our land waters (teares of passion) vent;
    Our waters, then, above our firmament,
(Teares which our Soule doth for her sins let fall)
    Take all a brackish tast, and Funerall,
And even these teares, which should wash sin, are sin.
    We, after Gods *Noe*, drowne our world againe.
Nothing but man of all invenom'd things
    Doth worke upon itself, with inborne stings.
Teares are false Spectacles, we cannot see
    Through passions mist, what wee are, or what shee.

In her this sea of death hath made no breach,
　　But as the tide doth wash the slimie beach,
And leaves embroder'd workes upon the sand,
　　So is her flesh refin'd by deaths cold hand.
As men of China,'after an ages stay,
　　Do take up Porcelane, where they buried Clay;
So at this grave, her limbecke, which refines
　　The Diamonds, Rubies, Saphires, Pearles, and Mines,
Of which this flesh was, her soule shall inspire
　　Flesh of such stuffe, as God, when his last fire
Annuls this world, to recompence it, shall,
　　Make and name then, th'Elixar of this All.
They say, the sea, when it gaines, loseth too;
　　If carnall Death (the yonger brother) doe
Usurpe the body,'our soule, which subject is
　　To th'elder death, by sinne, is freed by this;
They perish both, when they attempt the just;
　　For, graves our trophies are, and both deaths' dust.
So, unobnoxious now, she'hath buried both;
　　For, none to death sinnes, that to sinne is loth,
Nor doe they die, which are not loth to die;
　　So hath she this, and that virginity.
Grace was in her extremely diligent,
　　That kept her from sinne, yet made her repent.
Of what small spots pure white complaines! Alas,
　　How little poyson cracks a christall glasse!
She sinn'd, but just enough to let us see
　　That God's word must be true, All, sinners be.
Soe much did zeale her conscience rarefie,
　　That, extreme truth lack'd little of a lye,
Making omissions, acts; laying the touch
　　Of sinne, on things that sometimes may be such.
As *Moses* Cherubines, whose natures doe
　　Surpasse all speed, by him are winged too:
So would her soule, already'in heaven, seeme then,
　　To clyme by teares, the common staires of men.
How fit she was for God, I am content
　　To speake, that Death his vaine haste may repent.
How fit for us, how even and how sweet,
　　How good in all her titles, and how meet,
To have reform'd this forward heresie,
　　That women can no parts of friendship bee;

How Morall, how Divine shall not be told,
 Lest they that heare her vertues, thinke her old:
And lest we take Deaths part, and make him glad
 Of such a prey, and to his tryumph adde.

ELEGIE ON MISTRIS BOULSTRED

DEATH I recant, and say, unsaid by mee
 What ere hath slip'd, that might diminish thee.
Spirituall treason, atheisme 'tis, to say,
 That any can thy Summons disobey.
Th'earths face is but thy Table; there are set
 Plants, cattell, men, dishes for Death to eate.
In a rude hunger now he millions drawes
 Into his bloody, or plaguy, or sterv'd jawes.
Now hee will seeme to spare, and doth more wast,
 Eating the best first, well preserv'd to last.
Now wantonly he spoiles, and eates us not,
 But breakes off friends, and lets us peecemeale rot.
Nor will this earth serve him; he sinkes the deepe
 Where harmlesse fish monastique silence keepe,
Who (were Death dead) by Roes of living sand,
 Might spunge that element, and make it land.
He rounds the aire, and breakes the hymnique notes
 In birds (Heavens choristers,) organique throats,
Which (if they did not dye) might seeme to bee
 A tenth ranke in the heavenly hierarchie.
O strong and long-liv'd death, how cam'st thou in?
 And how without Creation didst begin?
Thou hast, and shalt see dead, before thou dyest,
 All the foure Monarchies, and Antichrist.
How could I thinke thee nothing, that see now
 In all this All, nothing else is, but thou.
Our births and lives, vices, and vertues, bee
 Wastfull consumptions, and degrees of thee.
For, wee to live, our bellowes weare, and breath,
 Nor are wee mortall, dying, dead, but death.
And though thou beest, O mighty bird of prey,
 So much reclaim'd by God, that thou must lay
All that thou kill'st at his feet, yet doth he
 Reserve but few, and leaves the most to thee.

And of those few, now thou hast overthrowne
  One whom thy blow makes, not ours, nor thine own.
She was more stories high: hopelesse to come
  To her Soule, thou'hast offer'd at her lower roome.
Her Soule and body was a King and Court:
  But thou hast both of Captaine mist and fort.
As houses fall not, though the King remove,
  Bodies of Saints rest for their soules above.
Death gets 'twixt soules and bodies such a place
  As sinne insinuates 'twixt just men and grace,
Both worke a separation, no divorce.
  Her Soule is gone to usher up her corse,
Which shall be'almost another soule, for there
  Bodies are purer, than best Soules are here.
Because in her, her virtues did outgoe
  Her yeares, would'st thou, O emulous death, do so?
And kill her young to thy losse? must the cost
  Of beauty,'and wit, apt to doe harme, be lost?
What though thou found'st her proofe 'gainst sins of youth?
  Oh, every age a diverse sinne pursueth.
Thou should'st have stay'd, and taken better hold,
  Shortly, ambitious; covetous, when old,
She might have prov'd: and such devotion
  Might once have stray'd to superstition.
If all her vertues must have growne, yet might
  Abundant virtue'have bred a proud delight.
Had she persever'd just, there would have bin
  Some that would sinne, mis-thinking she did sinne.
Such as would call her friendship, love, and faine
  To sociablenesse, a name profane;
Or sinne, by tempting, or, not daring that,
  By wishing, though they never told her what.
Thus might'st thou'have slain more soules, had'st thou not crost
  Thy selfe, and to triumph, thine army lost.
Let though these wayes be lost, thou hast left one,
  Which is, immoderate griefe that she is gone.
But we may scape that sinne, yet weepe as much,
  Our teares are due, because we are not such.
Some teares, that knot of friends, her death must cost,
  Because the chaine is broke, though no linke lost.

ELEGIE

DEATH

LANGUAGE thou art too narrow, and too weake
    To ease us now; great sorrow cannot speake;
If we could sigh out accents, and weepe words,
    Griefe weares, and lessens, that tears breath affords.
Sad hearts, the lesse they seeme the more they are,
    (So guiltiest men stand mutest at the barre)
Not that they know not, feele not their estate,
    But extreme sense hath made them desperate.
Sorrow, to whom we owe all that we bee;
    Tyrant, in the fift and greatest Monarchy,
Was't, that she did possesse all hearts before,
    Thou hast kil'd her, to make thy Empire more?
Knew'st thou some would, that knew her not, lament,
    As in a deluge perish the'innocent?
Was't not enough to have that palace wonne,
    But thou must raze it too, that was undone?
Had'st thou staid there, and look'd out at her eyes,
    All had ador'd thee that now from thee flies,
For they let out more light, than they tooke in,
    They told not when, but did the day beginne.
She was too Saphirine, and cleare for thee;
    Clay, flint, and jeat now thy fit dwellings be;
Alas, shee was too pure, but not too weake;
    Who e'r saw Christall Ordinance but would break?
And if wee be thy conquest, by her fall
    Th'hast lost thy end, for in her perish all;
Or if we live, we live but to rebell,
    They know her better now, that knew her well.
If we should vapour out, and pine, and die;
    Since, shee first went, that were not miserie.
She chang'd our world with hers; now she is gone,
    Mirth and prosperity is oppression;
For of all morall vertues she was all,
    The Ethicks speake of vertues Cardinall.
Her soule was Paradise; the Cherubin
    Set to keepe it was grace, that kept out sinne.

Shee had no more than let in death, for wee
    All reape consumption from one fruitfull tree.
God tooke her hence, lest some of us should love
    Her, like that plant, him and his lawes above,
And when wee teares, hee mercy shed in this,
    To raise our mindes to heaven where now she is;
Who if her vertues would have let her stay
    Wee'had had a Saint, have now a holiday.
Her heart was that strange bush, where, sacred fire,
    Religion, did not consume, but'inspire
Such piety, so chast use of Gods day,
    That what we turne to *feast,* she turn'd to *pray,*
And did prefigure here, in devout tast,
    The rest of her high Sabaoth, which shall last.
Angels did hand her up, who next God dwell,
    (For she was of that order whence most fell)
Her body left with us, lest some had said,
    Shee could not die, except they saw her dead;
For from lesse vertue, and lesse beautiousnesse,
    The Gentiles fram'd them Gods and Goddesses.
The ravenous earth that now wooes her to be
    Earth too, will be a *Lemnia;* and the tree
That wraps that christall in a wooden Tombe,
    Shall be tooke up spruce, fill'd with diamond;
And we her sad glad friends all beare a part
    Of griefe, for all would waste a Stoicks heart.

ELEGIE ON THE L. C.

SORROW, who to this house scarce knew the way:
Is, Oh, heire of it, our All is his prey.
This strange chance claimes strange wonder, and to us
Nothing can be so strange, as to weepe thus.
'Tis well his lifes loud speaking workes deserve,
And give praise too, our cold tongues could not serve:
'Tis well, hee kept teares from our eyes before,
That to fit this deepe ill, we might have store.
Oh, if a sweet briar, climbe-up by'a tree,
If to a paradise that transplanted bee,
Or fell'd, and burnt for holy sacrifice,
Yet, that must wither, which by it did rise,

As wee for him dead: though no familie
Ere rigg'd a soule for heavens discoverie
With whom more Venturers more boldly dare
Venture their states, with him in joy to share.
Wee lose what all friends lov'd, him; he gaines now
But life by death, which worst foes would allow,
If hee could have foes, in whose practise grew
All vertues, whose names subtile Schoolmen knew.
What ease, can hope that wee shall see'him, beget,
When wee must die first, and cannot dye yet?
His children are his pictures, Oh they bee
Pictures of him dead, senselesse, cold as he.
Here needs no marble Tombe, since hee is gone,
He, and about him, his, are turn'd to stone.

AN HYMNE TO THE SAINTS, AND TO MARQUESSE HAMYLTON

To Sir Robert Carr.

Sir,

I PRESUME you rather try what you can doe in me, than what I can doe in verse; you know my uttermost when it was best, and even then I did best when I had least truth for my subjects. In this present case there is so much truth as it defeats all Poetry. Call therefore this paper by what name you will, and, if it bee not worthy of him, nor of you, nor of mee, smother it, and bee that the sacrifice. If you had commanded mee to have waited on his body to Scotland and preached there, I would have embraced the obligation with more alacrity; But, I thanke you that you would command me that which I was loath to doe, for, even that hath given a tincture of merit to the obedience of

Your poore friend and servant in Christ Jesus

J. D.

WHETHER that soule which now comes up to you
Fill any former ranke or make a new,
Whether it take a name nam'd there before,
Or be a name it selfe, and *order* more
Than was in heaven till now; (for may not hee
Bee so, if every severall Angell bee
A *kind* alone?) What ever order grow
Greater by him in heaven, wee doe not so.

One of your orders growes by his accesse;
But, by his losse grow all our *orders* lesse;
The name of *Father, Master, Friend*, the name
Of *Subject* and of *Prince*, in one are lame;
Faire mirth is dampt, and conversation black,
The *household* widdow'd, and the *garter* slack;
The *Chappell* wants an eare, *Councell* a tongue;
Story, a theame; and *Musicke* lacks a song;
Blest *order* that hath him! the losse of him
Gangred all *Orders* here; all lost a limbe.
Never made body such haste to confesse
What a soule was; All former comelinesse
Fled, in a minute, when the soule was gone,
And, having lost that beauty, would have none;
So fell our *Monasteries*, in one instant growne
Not to lesse houses, but, to heapes of stone;
So sent this body that faire forme it wore,
Unto the spheare of formes, and doth (before
His soule shall fill up his sepulchrall stone,)
Anticipate a Resurrection;
For, as in his fame, now, his soule is here,
So, in the forme thereof his bodie's there;
And if, faire soule, not with first *Innocents*
Thy station be, but with the *Pœnitents*,
(And, who shall dare to aske then when I am
Dy'd scarlet in the blood of that pure Lambe,
Whether that colour, which is scarlet then,
Were black or white before in eyes of men?)
When thou rememb'rest what sins thou didst finde
Amongst those many friends now left behinde,
And seest such sinners as they are, with thee
Got thither by repentance, Let it bee
Thy wish to wish all there, to wish them cleane;
Wish *him* a *David*, her a *Magdalen*.

Epitaphs

EPITAPH ON HIMSELFE

To the Countesse of Bedford

MADAME,
   THAT I might make your Cabinet my tombe,
     And for my fame which I love next my soule,
 Next to my soule provide the happiest roome,
     Admit to that place this last funerall Scrowle.
       Others by Wills give Legacies, but I
       Dying, of you doe beg a Legacie.

MY Fortune and my choice this custome break,
When we are senselesse grown to make stones speak,
Though no stone tell thee what I was, yet thou
In my graves inside see what thou art now:
Yet th'art not yet so good; till us death lay
To ripe and mellow there, w'are stubborne clay,
Parents make us earth, and soules dignifie
Us to be glasse, here to grow gold we lie;
Whilst in our soules sinne bred and pampered is,
Our soules become worme-eaten Carkasses.

OMNIBUS

MY Fortune and my choice this custome break,
When we are speechlesse grown, to make stones speak,
Though no stone tell thee what I was, yet thou
In my graves inside seest what thou art now:
Yet thou'art not yet so good, till death us lay
To ripe and mellow here, we are stubborne Clay.

Parents make us earth, and soules dignifie
Us to be glasse; here to grow gold we lie.
Whilst in our soules sinne bred and pamper'd is,
Our soules become wormeaten carkases;
So we our selves miraculously destroy.
Here bodies with lesse miracle enjoy
Such priviledges, enabled here to scale
Heaven, when the Trumpets ayre shall them exhale.
Heare this, and mend thy selfe, and thou mendst me,
By making me being dead, doe good to thee,
　　And thinke me well compos'd, that I could now
　　A last-sicke houre to syllables allow.

The Progresse of the Soule

EPISTLE

OTHERS at the Porches and entries of their Buildings set their Armes;
I, my picture; if any colours can deliver a minde so plaine, and flat, and
through-light as mine. Naturally at a new Author, I doubt, and sticke,
and doe not say quickly, good. I censure much and taxe; And this liberty
costs mee more than others, by how much my owne things are worse than
others. Yet I would not be so rebellious against my selfe, as not to doe it,
since I love it; nor so unjust to others, to do it *sine talione*. As long as I
give them as good hold upon mee, they must pardon mee my bitings. I
forbid no reprehender, but him that like the Trent Councell forbids not
bookes, but Authors, damning what ever such a name hath or shall write.
None writes so ill, that he gives not some thing exemplary, to follow, or
flie. Now when I beginne this booke, I have no purpose to come into any
mans debt; how my stocke will hold out I know not; perchance waste,
perchance increase in use; if I doe borrow any thing of Antiquitie, besides that I make account that I pay it to posterity, with as much and as
good: You shall still finde mee to acknowledge it, and to thanke not him
onely that hath digg'd out treasure for mee, but that hath lighted mee a
candle to the place. All which I will bid you remember, (for I will have
no such Readers as I can teach) as, that the Pithagorian doctrine doth
not onely carry one soule from man to man, nor man to beast, but indifferently to plants also: and therefore you must not grudge to finde
the same soule in an Emperour, in a Post-horse, and in a Mucheron, since
no unreadinesse in the soule, but an indisposition in the organs workes
this. And therefore though this soule could not move when it was a Melon,
yet it may remember, and now tell mee, at what lascivious banquet it was
serv'd. And though it could not speake, when it was a spider, yet it can
remember, and now tell me, who used it for poyson to attaine dignitie.
How ever the bodies have dull'd her other faculties, her memory hath
ever been her owne, which makes me so seriously deliver you by her relation all her passages from her first making when shee was that apple
which Eve eate, to this time when shee is hee, whose life you shall finde
in the end of this booke.

THE PROGRESSE OF THE SOULE

FIRST SONG

I

I SING the progresse of a deathlesse soule,
Whom Fate, which God made, but doth not controule,
Plac'd in most shapes; all times before the law
Yoak'd us, and when, and since, in this I sing.
And the great world to his aged evening;
From infant morne, through manly noone I draw.
What the gold Chaldee, or silver Persian saw,
Greeke brasse, or Roman iron, is in this one;
A worke t'outweare *Seths* pillars, bricke and stone,
   And (holy writt excepted) made to yeeld to none.

II

Thee, eye of heaven, this great Soule envies not,
By thy male force, is all wee have, begot.
In the first East, thou now beginst to shine,
Suck'st early balme, and Iland spices there,
And wilt anon in thy loose-rein'd careere
At Tagus, Po, Sene, Thames, and Danow dine,
And see at night thy Westerne land of Myne,
Yet hast thou not more nations seene than shee,
That before thee, one day beganne to bee,
   And thy fraile light being quench'd, shall long, long out live thee.

III

Nor, holy *Janus*, in whose soveraigne boate
The Church, and all the Monarchies did floate;
That swimming Colledge, and free Hospitall
Of all mankinde, that cage and vivarie
Of fowles, and beasts, in whose wombe, Destinie
Us, and our latest nephews did install
(From thence are all deriv'd, that fill this All,)
Did'st thou in that great stewardship embarke
So diverse shapes into that floating parke,
   As have beene moved, and inform'd by this heavenly sparke

IV

Great Destiny the Commissary of God,
That hast mark'd out a path and period
For every thing; who, where wee of-spring tooke,
Our wayes and ends seest at one instant; Thou
Knot of all causes, thou whose changelesse brow
Ne'r smiles nor frownes, O vouch thou safe to looke
And shew my story, in thy eternall booke:
That (if my prayer be fit) I may'understand
So much my selfe, as to know with what hand,
    How scant, or liberall this my lifes race is spand.

V

To my sixe lustres almost now outwore,
Except thy booke owe mee so many more,
Except my legend be free from the letts
Of steepe ambition, sleepie povertie,
Spirit-quenching sicknesse, dull captivitie,
Distracting businesse, and from beauties nets,
And all that calls from this, and to others whets,
O let me not launch out, but let mee save
Th'expense of braine and spirit; that my grave
    His right and due, a whole unwasted man may have.

VI

But if my dayes be long, and good enough,
In vaine this sea shall enlarge, or enrough
It selfe; for I will through the wave, and fome,
And shall, in sad lone wayes a lively spright,
Make my darke heavy Poëm light, and light.
For though through many streights, and lands I roame,
I launch at paradise, and I saile towards home;
The course I there began, shall here be staid,
Sailes hoised there, stroke here, and anchors laid
    In Thames, which were at Tigrys, and Euphrates waide.

VII

For the great soule which here amongst us now
Doth dwell, and moves that hand, and tongue, and brow,
Which, as the Moone the sea, moves us; to heare
Whose story, with long patience you will long;
(For 'tis the crowne, and last straine of my song)

This soule to whom *Luther,* and *Mahomet* were
Prisons of flesh; this soule which oft did teare,
And mend the wracks of th'Empire, and late Rome,
And liv'd when every great change did come,
    Had first in paradise, a low, but fatall roome.

VIII

Yet no low roome, nor than the greatest, lesse.
If (as devout and sharpe men fitly guesse)
That Crosse, our joy, and griefe, where nailes did tye
That All, which alwayes was all, every where;
Which could not sinne, and yet all sinnes did beare;
Which could not die, yet could not chuse but die;
Stood in the self same roome in Calvarie,
Where first grew the forbidden learned tree,
For on that tree hung in security
    This Soule, made by the Makers will from pulling free.

IX

Prince of the orchard, faire as dawning morne,
Fenc'd with the law, and ripe as soone as borne
That apple grew, which this Soule did enlive,
Till the then climing serpent, that now creeps
For that offence, for which all mankinde weepes,
Tooke it, and t'her whom the first man did wive
(Whom and her race, only forbiddings drive)
He gave it, she, t'her husband, both did eate;
So perished the eaters, and the meate:
    And wee (for treason taints the blood) thence die and sweat.

X

Man all at once was there by woman slaine,
And one by one we'are here slaine o'er againe
By them. The mother poison'd the well-head,
The daughters here corrupt us, Rivolets;
No smalnesse scapes, no greatnesse breaks their nets;
She thrust us out, and by them we are led
Astray, from turning, to whence we are fled.
Were prisoners Judges, t'would seeme rigorous,
Shee sinn'd, we beare; part of our paine is, thus
    To love them, whose fault to this painfull love yoak'd us.

XI

So fast in us doth this corruption grow,
That now wee dare aske why wee should be so.
Would God (disputes the curious Rebell) make
A law, and would not have it kept? Or can
His creatures will, crosse his? Of every man
For one, will God (and be just) vengeance take?
Who sinn'd? t'was not forbidden to the snake
Nor her, who was not then made; nor is't writ
That Adam cropt, or knew the apple; yet
    The worme and she, and he, and wee endure for it.

XII

But snatch mee heavenly Spirit from this vaine
Reckoning their vanities, lesse is their gaine
Than hazard still, to meditate on ill,
Though with good minde; their reasons, like those toyes
Of glassie bubbles, which the gamesome boyes
Stretch to so nice a thinnes through a quill
That they themselves breake, doe themselves spill:
Arguing is heretiques game, and Exercise
As wrastlers, perfects them; Not liberties
    Of speech, but silence; hands, not tongues, end heresies.

XIII

Just in that instant when the serpents gripe,
Broke the slight veines, and tender conduit-pipe,
Through which this soule from the trees root did draw
Life, and growth to this apple, fled away
This loose soule, old, one and another day.
As lightning, which one scarce dares say, he saw,
'Tis so soone gone, (and better proofe the law
Of sense, than faith requires) swiftly she flew
To a darke and foggie Plot; Her, her fates threw
    There through th'earths pores, and in a Plant hous'd her anew.

XIV

The plant thus abled, to it selfe did force
A place, where no place was; by natures course
As aire from water, water fleets away

From thicker bodies, by this root thronged so
His spungie confines gave him place to grow:
Just as in our streets, when the people stay
To see the Prince, and have so fill'd the way
That weesels scarce could passe, when she comes nere
They throng and cleave up, and a passage cleare,
    As if, for that time, their round bodies flatned were.

XV

His right arme he thrust out towards the East,
West-ward his left; th'ends did themselves digest
Into ten lesser strings, these fingers were:
And as a slumberer stretching on his bed,
This way he this, and that way scattered
His other legge, which feet with toes upbeare.
Grew on his middle parts, the first day, haire,
To show, that in loves businesse hee should still
A dealer bee, and be us'd well, or ill:
    His apples kindle, his leaves, force of conception kill.

XVI

A mouth, but dumbe, he hath; blinde eyes, deafe eares,
And to his shoulders dangle subtile haires;
A young *Colossus* there hee stands upright,
And as that ground by him were conquered
A leafie garland weares he on his head
Enchas'd with little fruits, so red and bright
That for them you would call your Loves lips white;
So, of a lone unhaunted place possest,
Did this soules second Inne, built by the guest,
    This living buried man, this quiet mandrake, rest.

XVII

No lustfull woman came this plant to grieve,
But 'twas because there was none yet but Eve:
And she (with other purpose) kill'd it quite;
Her sinne had now brought in infirmities,
And so her cradled child, the moist red eyes
Had never shut, nor slept since it saw light;
Poppie she knew, she knew the mandrakes might,

And tore up both, and so coold her childs blood;
Unvirtuous weeds might long unvex'd have stood;
  But hee's short liv'd, that with his death can doe most good.

XVIII

To an unfettered soules quick nimble haste
Are falling stars, and hearts thoughts, but slow pac'd:
Thinner than burnt aire flies this soule, and she
Whom foure new comming, and foure parting Suns
Had found, and left the Mandrakes tenant, runnes
Thoughtlesse of change, when her firme destiny
Confin'd, and enjayld her, that seem'd so free,
Into a small blew shell, the which a poore
Warme bird orespread, and sat still evermore,
  Till her inclos'd child kickt, and pick'd it selfe a dore.

XIX

Outcrept a sparrow, this soules moving Inne,
On whose raw armes stiffe feathers now begin,
As childrens teeth through gummes, to breake with paine,
His flesh is jelly yet, and his bones threds,
All a new downy mantle overspreads,
A mouth he opes, which would as much containe
As his late house, and the first houre speaks plaine,
And chirps alowd for meat. Meat fit for men
His father steales for him, and so feeds then
  One, that within a moneth, will beate him from his hen.

XX

In this worlds youth wise nature did make haste,
Things ripened sooner, and did longer last;
Already this hot cocke, in bush and tree,
In field and tent, oreflutters his next hen;
He asks her not, who did so last, nor when,
Nor if his sister, or his neece shee be;
Nor doth she pule for his inconstancie
If in her sight he change, nor doth refuse
The next that calls; both liberty doe use;
  Where store is of both kindes, both kindes may freely chuse.

XXI

Men, till they tooke laws which made freedome lesse,
Their daughters, and their sisters did ingresse;
Till now unlawful, therefore ill, 'twas not.
So jolly, that it can move, this soule is,
The body so free of his kindnesses,
That selfe-preserving it hath now forgot,
And slackneth so the soules, and bodies knot,
Which temperance streightens; freely on his she friends
He blood, and spirit, pith, and marrow spends,
　　Ill steward of himselfe, himselfe in three yeares ends.

XXII

Else might he long have liv'd; man did not know
Of gummie blood, which doth in holly grow,
How to make bird-lime, nor how to deceive
With faind calls, hid nets, or enwrapping snare,
The free inhabitants of the Plyant aire.
Man to beget, and woman to conceive
Askt not of rootes, nor of cock-sparrowes, leave:
Yet chuseth hee, though none of these he feares,
Pleasantly three, than streightned twenty yeares
　　To live, and to encrease his race, himselfe outweares.

XXIII

This cole with overblowing quench'd and dead,
The Soule from her too active organs fled
T'a brooke. A female fishes sandie Roe
With the males jelly, newly lev'ned was,
For they had intertouch'd as they did passe,
And one of those small bodies, fitted so,
This soule inform'd, and abled it to rowe
It selfe with finnie oares, which she did fit:
Her scales seem'd yet of parchment, and as yet
　　Perchance a fish, but by no name you could call it.

XXIV

When goodly, like a ship in her full trim,
A swan, so white that you may unto him
Compare all whitenesse, but himselfe to none,

Gilded along, and as he gilded watch'd,
And with his arched necke this poore fish catch'd.
It mov'd with state, as if to looke upon
Low things it scorn'd, and yet before that one
Could thinke he sought it, he had swallowed cleare
This, and much such, and unblam'd devour'd there
   All, but who too swift, too great, or well armed were.

XXV

Now swome a prison in a prison put,
And now this Soule in double walls was shut,
Till melted with the Swans digestive fire,
She left her house the fish, and vapour'd forth;
Fate not affording bodies of more worth
For her as yet, bids her againe retire
T'another fish, to any new desire
Made a new prey; For, he that can to none
Resistance make, nor complaint, sure is gone.
   Weaknesse invites, but silence feasts oppression.

XXVI

Pace with her native streame, this fish doth keepe,
And journeyes with her, towards the glassie deepe,
But oft retarded, once with a hidden net
Though with greate windowes, for when Need first taught
These tricks to catch food, then they were not wrought
As now, with curious greedinesse to let
None scape, but few, and fit for use, to get,
As, in this trap a ravenous pike was tane,
Who, though himselfe distrest, would faine have slain
   This wretch; So hardly are ill habits left again.

XXVII

Here by her smallnesse shee two deaths orepast,
Once innocence scap'd, and left the oppressor fast.
The net through-swome, she keepes the liquid path,
And whether she leape up sometimes to breath
And suck in aire, or finde it underneath,
Or working parts like mills or limbecks hath
To make the water thinne and airelike, faith

Cares not; but safe the Place she's come unto
Where fresh, with salt waves meet, and what to doe
   She knowes not, but betweene both makes a boord or two.

XXVIII

So farre from hiding her guests, water is,
That she showes them in bigger quantities
Than they are. Thus doubtfull of her way,
For game and not for hunger a sea Pie
Spied through this traiterous spectacle, from high,
The seely fish where it disputing lay,
And t'end her doubts and her, beares her away:
Exalted she'is, but to the exalters good,
As are by great ones, men which lowly stood.
   It's rais'd, to be the Raisers instrument and food.

XXIX

Is any kinde subject to rape like fish?
Ill unto man, they neither doe, nor wish:
Fishers they kill not, nor with noise awake,
They doe not hunt, nor strive to make a prey
Of beasts, nor their yong sonnes to beare away;
Foules they pursue not, nor do undertake
To spoile the nests industrious birds do make;
Yet them all these unkinde kinds feed upon,
To kill them is an occupation,
   And lawes make Fasts, and Lents for their destruction.

XXX

A sudden stiffe land-winde in that selfe houre
To sea-ward forc'd this bird, that did devour
The fish; he cares not, for with ease he flies,
Fat gluttonies best orator: at last
So long hee hath flowen, and hath flowen so fast
That many leagues at sea, now tir'd hee lyes,
And with his prey, that till then languisht, dies:
The soules no longer foes, two wayes did erre,
The fish I follow, and keepe no calender
   Of the other; he lives yet in some great officer.

XXXI

Into an embrion fish, our Soule is throwne,
And in due time throwne out againe, and growne
To such vastnesse as, if unmanacled
From Greece, Morea were, and that by some
Earthquake unrooted, loose Morea swome,
Or seas from Africks body had severed
And torne the hopefull Promontories head,
This fish would seeme these, and, when all hopes faile,
A great ship overset, or without saile
   Hulling, might (when this was a whelp) be like this whale.

XXXII

At every stroake his brazen finnes do take,
More circles in the broken sea they make
Than cannons voices, when the aire they teare:
His ribs are pillars, and his high arch'd roofe
Of barke that blunts best steele, is thunder-proofe:
Swimme in him swallow'd Dolphins, without feare,
And feele no sides, as if his vast wombe were
Some inland sea, and ever as hee went
Hee spouted rivers up, as if he ment
   To joyne our seas, with seas above the firmament.

XXXIII

He hunts not fish, but as an officer,
Stayes in his court, at his owne net, and there
All suitors of all sorts themselves enthrall;
So on his backe lyes this whale wantoning,
And in his gulfe-like throat, sucks every thing
That passeth neare. Fish chaseth fish, and all,
Flyer and follower, in this whirlepoole fall;
O might not states of more equality
Consist? and is it of necessity
   That thousand guiltlesse smals, to make one great, must die?

XXXIV

New drinkes he up seas, and he eates up flocks,
He justles Ilands, and he shakes firme rockes.
Now in a roomefull house this Soule doth float,

And like a Prince she sends her faculties
To all her limbes, distant as Provinces.
The Sunne hath twenty times both crab and goate
Parched, since first lanch'd forth this living boate;
'Tis greatest now, and to destruction
Nearest; There's no pause at perfection;
   Greatnesse a period hath, but hath no station.

XXXV

Two little fishes whom hee never harm'd,
Nor fed on their kinde, two not throughly arm'd
With hope that they could kill him, nor could doe
Good to themselves by his death (they did not eate
His flesh, nor suck those oyles, which thence outstreat)
Conspir'd against him, and it might undoe
The plot of all, that the plotters were two,
But that they fishes were, and could not speake.
How shall a Tyran wise strong projects breake,
   If wreches can on them the common anger wreake?

XXXVI

The flaile-finn'd Thresher, and steel-beak'd Sword-fish
Onely attempt to doe, what all doe wish.
The Thresher backs him, and to beate begins;
The sluggard Whale yeelds to oppression,
And t'hide himselfe from shame and danger, downe
Begins to sinke; the Swordfish upward spins,
And gores him with his beake; his staffe-like finnes,
So well the one, his sword the other plyes,
That now a scoffe, and prey, this tyran dyes,
   And (his owne dole) feeds with himselfe all companies.

XXXVII

Who will revenge his death? or who will call
Those to account, that thought, and wrought his fall?
The heires of slaine kings, wee see are often so
Transported with the joy of what they get,
That they, revenge and obsequies forget,
Nor will against such men the people goe,
Because h'is now dead, to whom they should show

Love in that act; Some kings by vice being growne
So needy of subjects love, that of their own
   They thinke they lose, if love be to the dead Prince shown.

XXXVIII

This Soule, now free from prison, and passion,
Hath yet a little indignation
That so small hammers should so soone downe beat
So great a castle. And having for her house
Got the streight cloyster of a wreched mouse
(As basest men that have not what to eate,
Nor enjoy ought, doe farre more hate the great
Than they, who good repos'd estates possesse)
This Soule, late taught that great things might by lesse
   Be slain, to gallant mischiefe doth herselfe addresse.

XXXIX

Natures great master-peece, an Elephant,
The onely harmlesse great thing; the giant
Of beasts; who thought, no more had gone, to make one wise
But to be just, and thankfull, loth to offend,
(Yet nature hath given him no knees to bend)
Himselfe he up-props, on himselfe relies,
And foe to none, suspects no enemies,
Still sleeping stood; vex'd not his fantasie
Blacke dreames; like an unbent bow, carelessly
   His sinewy Proboscis did remisly lie:

XL

In which as in a gallery this mouse
Walk'd, and surveid the roomes of this vast house,
And to the braine, the soules bedchamber, went,
And gnaw'd the life cords there; Like a whole towne
Cleane undermin'd, the slaine beast tumbled downe;
With him the murtherer dies, whom envy sent
To kill, not scape, (for, only hee that ment
To die, did ever kill a man of better roome,)
And thus he made his foe, his prey, and tombe:
   Who cares not to turn back, may any whither come.

XLI

Next, hous'd this Soule a Wolves yet unborne whelp,
Till the best midwife, Nature, gave it helpe,
To issue. It could kill, as soone as goe.
Abel, as white, and milde as his sheepe were,
(Who, in that trade, of Church, and kingdomes, there
Was the first type) was still infested soe,
With this wolfe, that it bred his losse and woe;
And yet his bitch, his sentinell attends
The flocke so neere, so well warnes and defends,
    That the wolfe, (hopelesse else) to corrupt her, intends.

XLII

Hee tooke a course, which since, successfully,
Great men have often taken, to espie
The counsels, or to breake the plots of foes.
To Abells tent he stealeth in the darke,
On whose skirts the bitch slept; ere she could barke,
Attach'd her with streight gripes, yet hee call'd those,
Embracements of love; to loves worke he goes,
Where deeds move more than words; nor doth she show,
Nor much resist, nor needs hee streighten so
    His prey, for, were shee loose, she would nor barke, nor goe.

XLIII

Hee hath engag'd her; his, she wholy bides;
Who not her owne, none others secrets hides.
If to the flocke he come, and Abell there,
She faines hoarse barkings, but she biteth not,
Her faith is quite, but not her love forgot.
At last a trap, of which some every where
Abell had plac'd, ends all his losse, and feare,
By the Wolves death; and now just time it was
That a quicke soule should give life to that masse
    Of blood in Abells bitch, and thither this did passe.

XLIV

Some have their wives, their sisters some begot,
But in the lives of Emperours you shall not
Reade of a lust the which may equall this;
This wolfe begot himselfe, and finished

What he began alive, when hee was dead;
Sonne to himselfe, and father too, hee is
A ridling lust, for which Schoolemen would misse
A proper name. The whelpe of both these lay
In Abels tent, and with soft Moaba,
   His sister, being yong, it us'd to sport and play.

XLV

Hee soone for her too harsh, and churlish grew,
And Abell (the dam dead) would use this new
For the field. Being of two kindes thus made,
He, as his dam, from sheepe drove wolves away,
And as his Sire, he made them his owne prey.
Five yeares he liv'd, and cosened with his trade,
Then hopelesse that his faults were hid, betraid
Himself by flight, and by all followed,
From dogges, a wolfe; from wolves, a dogge he fled;
   And, like a spie to both sides false, he perished.

XLVI

It quicknd next a toyfull Ape, and so
Gamesome it was, that it might freely goe
From tent to tent, and with the children play.
His organs now so like theirs hee doth finde,
That why he cannot laugh, and speake his minde,
He wonders. Much with all, most he doth stay
With Adams fift daughter *Siphatecia*,
Doth gaze on her, and, where she passeth, passe,
Gathers her fruits, and tumbles on the grasse,
   And wisest of that kinde, the first true lover was.

XLVII

He was the first that more desir'd to have
One than another; first that ere did crave
Love by mute signes, and had no power to speake;
First that could make love faces, or could doe
The valters sombersalts, or us'd to wooe
With hoiting gambolls, his owne bones to breake
To make his mistresse merry; or to wreake
Her anger on himselfe. Sinnes against kinde
They easily doe, that can let feed their minde
   With outward beauty; beauty they in boyes and beasts do find.

XLVIII

By this misled, too low things men have prov'd,
And too high; beasts and angels have beene lov'd.
This Ape, though else through-vaine, in this was wise,
He reach'd at things too high, but open way
There was, and he knew not she would say nay;
His toyes prevaile not, likelier meanes he tries,
He gazeth on her face with teare-shot eyes,
And up lifts subtly with his russet pawe
Her kidskinne apron without feare or awe
    Of Nature; Nature hath no gaole, though shee hath law.

XLIX

First she was silly and knew not what he ment.
That vertue, by his touches, chaft and spent,
Succeeds an itchie warmth, that melts her quite;
She knew not first, nowe cares not what he doth,
And willing halfe and more, more than halfe loth,
She neither puls nor pushes, but outright
Now cries, and now repents; when *Tethlemite*
Her brother, enterd, and a great stone threw
After the Ape, who, thus prevented, flew.
    This house thus batter'd downe, the Soule possest a new.

L

And whether by this change she lose or win,
She comes out next, where the Ape would have gone in.
Adam and *Eve* had mingled bloods, and now
Like Chimiques equall fires, her temperate wombe
Had stew'd and form'd it: and part did become
A spungie liver, that did richly allow,
Like a free conduit, on a high hils brow,
Life-keeping moisture unto every part;
Part hardned it selfe to a thicker heart,
    Whose busie furnaces lifes spirits do impart.

LI

Another part became the well of sense,
The tender well-arm'd feeling braine, from whence,
Those sinowie strings which do our bodies tie,

Are raveld out; and fast there by one end,
Did this Soule limbes, these limbes a soule attend;
And now they joyn'd; keeping some quality
Of every past shape, she knew treachery,
Rapine, deceit, and lust, and ills enow
To be a woman. *Themech* she is now,
  Sister and wife to *Caine, Caine* that first did plow.

LII

Who ere thou beest that read'st this sullen Writ,
Which just so much courts thee, as thou dost it,
Let me arrest thy thoughts; wonder with mee,
Why plowing, building, ruling and the rest,
Or most of those arts, whence our lives are blest,
By cursed *Cains* race invented be,
And blest *Seth* vext us with Astronomie.
Ther's nothing simply good, nor ill alone,
Of every quality comparison,
  The onely measure is, and judge, opinion.

TO E. OF D. WITH SIX HOLY SONNETS

S E E Sir, how as the Suns hot Masculine flame
   Begets strange creatures on Niles durty slime,
   In me, your fatherly yet lusty Ryme
(For, these songs are their fruits) have wrought the same;
But though the ingendring force from whence they came
   Bee strong enough, and nature doe admit
   Seaven to be borne at once, I send as yet
But six; they say, the seaventh hath still some maime.
   I choose your judgement, which the same degree
   Doth with her sister, your invention, hold,
As fire these drossie Rymes to purifie,
   Or as Elixar, to change them to gold;
You are that Alchimist which alwaies had
Wit, whose one spark could make good things of bad.

TO THE LADY MAGDALEN HERBERT:
OF ST. MARY MAGDALEN

H E R of your name, whose fair inheritance
   Bethina was, and jointure Magdalo:
An active faith so highly did advance,
   That she once knew, more than the Church did know,
The Resurrection; so much good there is
   Deliver'd of her, that some Fathers be
Loth to believe one Woman could do this;
   But, think these Magdalens were two or three.
Increase their number, Lady, and their fame:
   To their Devotion, add your Innocence;
Take so much of th'example, as of the name;
   The latter half; and in some recompence
That they did harbour Christ himself, a Guest,
   Harbour these Hymns, to his dear name addrest.

HOLY SONNETS

I. LA CORONA

DEIGNE *at my hands this crown of prayer and praise,*
Weav'd in my low devout melancholie,
Thou which of good, hast, yea art treasury,
All changing unchang'd Antient of dayes;
But doe not, with a vile crowne of fraile bayes,
Reward my muses white sincerity,
But what thy thorny crowne gain'd, that give mee,
A crowne of Glory, which doth flower alwayes;
The ends crowne our workes, but thou crown'st our ends,
For, at our end begins our endlesse rest;
The first last end, now zealously possest,
With a strong sober thirst, my soule attends.
'Tis time that heart and voice be lifted high,
Salvation to all that will is nigh.

2. ANNUNCIATION

Salvation to all that will is nigh;
That All, which alwayes is All every where,
Which cannot sinne, and yet all sinnes must beare,
Which cannot die, yet cannot chuse but die,
Loe, faithfull Virgin, yeelds himselfe to lye
In prison, in thy wombe; and though he there
Can take no sinne, nor thou give, yet he'will weare
Taken from thence, flesh, which deaths force may trie.
Ere by the spheares time was created, thou
Wast in his minde, who is thy Sonne, and Brother;
Whom thou conceiv'st, conceiv'd; yea thou art now
Thy Makers maker, and thy Fathers mother;
Thou'hast light in darke; and shutst in little roome,
Immensity cloysterd in thy deare wombe.

3. NATIVITIE

Immensity cloystered in thy deare wombe,
Now leaves his welbelov'd imprisonment,
There he hath made himselfe to his intent

Weake enough, now into our world to come;
But Oh, for thee, for him, hath th'Inne no roome?
Yet lay him in this stall, and from the Orient,
Starres, and wisemen will travell to prevent
Th'effect of *Herods* jealous generall doome.
Seest thou, my Soule, with thy faiths eyes, how he
Which fils all place, yet none holds him, doth lye?
Was not his pity towards thee wondrous high,
That would have need to be pittied by thee?
Kisse him, and with him into Egypt goe,
With his kinde mother, who partakes thy woe.

4. TEMPLE

With his kinde mother who partakes thy woe,
Joseph turne backe; see where your child doth sit,
Blowing, yea blowing out those sparks of wit,
Which himselfe on the Doctors did bestow;
The Word but lately could not speake, and loe
It sodenly speakes wonders, whence comes it,
That all which was, and all which should be writ,
A shallow seeming child, should deeply know?
His Godhead was not soule to his manhood,
Nor had time mellowed him to this ripenesse,
But as for one which hath a long taske, 'tis good,
With the Sunne to beginne his businesse,
He in his ages morning thus began
By miracles exceeding power of man.

5. CRUCIFYING

By miracles exceeding power of man,
Hee faith in some, envie in some begat,
For, what weake spirits admire, ambitious, hate;
In both affections many to him ran,
But Oh! the worst are most, they will and can,
Alas, and do, unto the immaculate,
Whose creature Fate is, now prescribe a Fate,
Measuring selfe-lifes infinity to'a span,
Nay to an inch. Loe, where condemned hee
Beares his owne crosse, with paine, yet by and by
When it beares him, he must beare more and die.
Now thou art lifted up, draw mee to thee,

And at thy death giving such liberall dole,
Moyst, with one drop of thy blood, my dry soule.

6. RESURRECTION

Moyst with one drop of thy blood, my dry soule
Shall (though she now be in extreme degree
Too stony hard, and yet too fleshly,) bee
Freed by that drop, from being starv'd, hard, or foule,
And life, by this death abled, shall controule
Death, whom thy death slue; nor shall to mee
Feare of first or last death, bring miserie,
If in thy little booke my name thou enroule,
Flesh in that long sleep is not putrified,
But made that there, of which, and for which 'twas;
Nor can by other meanes be glorified.
May then sinnes sleep, and deaths soone from me passe,
That wak't from both, I againe risen may
Salute the last, and everlasting day.

7. ASCENTION

Salute the last and everlasting day,
Joy at the uprising of this Sunne, and Sonne,
Yee whose just teares, or tribulation
Have purely washt, or burnt your drossie clay;
Behold the Highest, parting hence away,
Lightens the darke clouds, which hee treads upon,
Nor doth hee by ascending, show alone,
But first hee, and hee first enters the way.
O strong Ramme, which hast batter'd heaven for mee,
Mild Lambe, which with thy blood, hast mark'd the path;
Bright Torch, which shin'st, that I the way may see
Oh, with thy owne blood quench thy owne just wrath,
And if thy holy Spirit, my Muse did raise,
Deigne at my hands this crown of prayer and praise.

Holy Sonnets

I

T H O U hast made me, And shall thy worke decay?
Repaire me now, for now mine end doth haste,
I runne to death, and death meets me as fast,
And all my pleasures are like yesterday;
I dare not move my dimme eyes any way,
Despaire behind, and death before doth cast
Such terrour, and my feeble flesh doth waste
By sinne in it, which it t'wards hell doth weigh;
Onely thou art above, and when towards thee
By thy leave I can looke, I rise againe;
But our old subtle foe so tempteth me,
That not one houre my selfe I can sustaine;
Thy Grace may wing me to prevent his art,
And thou like Adamant draw mine iron heart.

II

A S due by many titles I resigne
My selfe to thee, O God, first I was made
By thee, and for thee, and when I was decay'd
Thy blood bought that, the which before was thine;
I am thy sonne, made with thy selfe to shine,
Thy servant, whose paines thou hast still repaid,
Thy sheepe, thine Image, and, till I betray'd
My selfe, a temple of thy Spirit divine;
Why doth the devill then usurpe on mee?
Why doth he steale, nay ravish that's thy right?
Except thou rise and for thine owne worke fight,
Oh I shall soone despaire, when I doe see
That thou lov'st mankind well, yet wilt'not chuse me,
And Satan hates mee, yet is loth to lose mee.

III

O MIGHT those sighes and teares returne againe
Into my breast and eyes, which I have spent,
That I might in this holy discontent
Mourne with some fruit, as I have mourn'd in vaine;
In mine Idolatry what showres of raine
Mine eyes did waste? what griefs my heart did rent?
That sufferance was my sinne; now I repent;
'Cause I did suffer I must suffer paine.
Th'hydroptique drunkard, and night-scouting thiefe,
The itchy Lecher, and selfe tickling proud
Have the remembrance of past joyes, for reliefe
Of comming ills. To (poore) me is allow'd
No ease; for, long, yet vehement griefe hath beene
Th'effect and cause, the punishment and sinne.

IV

OH my blacke Soule! now thou art summoned
By sicknesse, deaths herald, and champion;
Thou art like a pilgrim, which abroad hath done
Treason, and durst not turne to whence hee is fled,
Or like a thiefe, which till deaths doome be read,
Wisheth himselfe delivered from prison;
But damn'd and hal'd to execution,
Wisheth that still he might be imprisoned.
Yet grace, if thou repent, thou canst not lacke;
But who shall give thee that grace to beginne?
Oh make thy selfe with holy mourning blacke,
And red with blushing, as thou art with sinne;
Or wash thee in Christs blood, which hath this might
That being red, it dyes red soules to white.

V

I AM a little world made cunningly
Of Elements, and an Angelike spright,
But black sinne hath betraid to endlesse night
My worlds both parts, and (oh) both parts must die.
You which beyond that heaven which was most high
Have found new sphears, and of new lands can write,
Powre new seas in mine eyes, that so I might

Drowne my world with my weeping earnestly,
Or wash it if it must be drown'd no more:
But oh it must be burnt! alas the fire
Of lust and envie have burnt it heretofore,
And made it fouler; Let their flames retire,
And burne me ô Lord, with a fiery zeale
Of thee and thy house, which doth in eating heale.

VI

THIS is my playes last scene, here heavens appoint
My pilgrimages last mile; and my race
Idly, yet quickly runne, hath this last pace,
My spans last inch, my minutes latest point,
And gluttonous death, will instantly unjoynt
My body, and soule, and I shall sleepe a space,
But my'ever-waking part shall see that face,
Whose feare already shakes my every joynt;
Then, as my soule, to'heaven her first seate, takes flight,
And earth-borne body, in the earth shall dwell,
So, fall my sinnes, that all may have their right,
To where they're bred, and would presse me, to hell.
Impute me righteous, thus purg'd of evill,
For thus I leave the world, the flesh, the devill.

VII

AT the round earths imagin'd corners, blow
Your trumpets, Angells, and arise, arise
From death, you numberlesse infinities
Of soules, and to your scattred bodies goe,
All whom the flood did, and fire shall o'erthrow,
All whom warre, dearth, age, agues, tyrannies,
Despaire, law, chance, hath slaine, and you whose eyes,
Shall behold God, and never tast deaths woe.
But let them sleepe, Lord, and mee mourne a space,
For, if above all these, my sinnes abound,
'Tis late to aske abundance of thy grace,
When wee are there; here on this lowly ground,
Teach mee how to repent; for that's as good
As if thou'hadst seal'd my pardon, with thy blood.

VIII

I F faithfull soules be alike glorifi'd
As Angels, then my fathers soul doth see,
And adds this even to full felicitie,
That valiantly I hels wide mouth o'stride:
But if our mindes to these soules be descry'd
By circumstances, and by signes that be
Apparent in us, not immediately,
How shall my mindes white truth by them be try'd?
They see idolatrous lovers weepe and mourne,
And vile blasphemous Conjurers to call
On Jesus name, and Pharisaicall
Dissemblers feigne devotion. Then turne
O pensive soule, to God, for he knowes best
Thy true griefe, for he put it in my breast.

IX

I F poysonous mineralls, and if that tree,
Whose fruit threw death on else immortall us,
If lecherous goats, if serpents envious
Cannot be damn'd; Alas; why should I bee?
Why should intent or reason, borne in mee,
Make sinnes, else equall, in mee more heinous?
And mercy being easie, and glorious
To God; in his sterne wrath, why threatens hee?
But who am I, that dare dispute with thee
O God? Oh! of thine onely worthy blood,
And my teares, make a heavenly Lethean flood,
And drowne in it my sinnes black memorie;
That thou remember them, some claime as debt,
I thinke it mercy if thou wilt forget.

X

DEATH be not proud, though some have called thee
Mighty and dreadfull, for, thou art not soe,
For, those, whom thou think'st, thou dost overthrow,
Die not, poore death, nor yet canst thou kill mee.
From rest and sleepe, which but thy pictures bee,
Much pleasure, then from thee, much more must flow,
And soonest our best men with thee doe goe,

Rest of their bones, and soules deliverie.
Thou art slave to Fate, Chance, kings, and desperate men,
And dost with poyson, warre, and sicknesse dwell,
And poppie, or charmes can make us sleepe as well,
And better than thy stroake; why swell'st thou then?
One short sleepe past, wee wake eternally,
And death shall be no more; death, thou shalt die.

XI

S P I T in my face you Jewes, and pierce my side,
Buffet, and scoffe, scourge, and crucifie mee,
For I have sinn'd, and sinn'd, and onely hee,
Who could do no iniquitie, hath dyed:
But by my death can not be satisfied
My sinnes, which passe the Jewes impiety:
They kill'd once an inglorious man, but I
Crucifie him daily, being now glorified.
Oh let mee then, his strange love still admire:
Kings pardon, but he bore our punishment.
And *Jacob* came cloth'd in vile harsh attire
But to supplant, and with gainfull intent:
God cloth'd himselfe in vile mans flesh, that so
Hee might be weake enough to suffer woe.

XII

W H Y are wee by all creatures waited on?
Why doe the prodigall elements supply
Life and food to mee, being more pure than I,
Simple, and further from corruption?
Why brook'st thou, ignorant horse, subjection?
Why dost thou bull, and bore so seelily
Dissemble weaknesse, and by'one mans stroke die,
Whose whole kinde, you might swallow and feed upon?
Weaker I am, woe is mee, and worse than you,
You have not sinn'd, nor need be timorous.
But wonder at a greater wonder, for to us
Created nature doth these things subdue,
But their Creator, whom sin, nor nature tyed,
For us, his Creatures, and his foes, hath dyed.

XIII

WHAT if this present were the worlds last night?
Marke in my heart, O Soule, where thou dost dwell,
The picture of Christ crucified, and tell
Whether that countenance can thee affright,
Teares in his eyes quench the amazing light,
Blood fills his frownes, which from his pierc'd head fell.
And can that tongue adjudge thee unto hell,
Which pray'd forgivenesse for his foes fierce spight?
No, no; but as in my idolatrie
I said to all my profane mistresses,
Beauty, of pitty, foulnesse onely is
A signe of rigour: so I say to thee,
To wicked spirits are horrid shapes assign'd,
This beauteous forme assures a pitious minde.

XIV

BATTER my heart, three person'd God; for, you
As yet but knocke, breathe, shine, and seeke to mend,
That I may rise, and stand, o'erthrow mee,'and bend
Your force, to breake, blowe, burn and make me new
I, like an usurpt towne, to'another due,
Labour to'admit you, but Oh, to no end,
Reason your viceroy in mee, mee should defend,
But is captiv'd, and proves weake or untrue.
Yet dearely'I love you,'and would be loved faine,
But am bethroth'd unto your enemie:
Divorce mee,'untie, or breake that knot againe,
Take mee to you, imprison mee, for I
Except you'enthrall mee, never shall be free,
Nor ever chast, except you ravish mee.

XV

WILT thou love God, as he thee? then digest,
My Soule, this wholsome meditation,
How God the Spirit, by Angels waited on
In heaven, doth make his Temple in thy brest.
The Father having begot a Sonne most blest,
And still begetting, (for he ne'r begonne)
Hath deign'd to chuse thee by adoption,
Coheire to'his glory,'and Sabbaths endlesse rest;

And as a robb'd man, which by search doth finde
His stolne stuffe sold, must lose or buy'it againe·
The Sonne of glory came downe, and was slaine,
Us whom he'had made, and Satan stolne, to unbinde.
'Twas much, that man was made like God before,
But, that God should be made like man, much more.

XVI

FATHER, part of his double interest
Unto thy kingdome, thy Sonne gives to mee,
His joynture in the knottie Trinitie
Hee keepes, and gives to me his deaths conquest.
This Lambe, whose death, with life the world hath blest,
Was from the worlds beginning slaine, and he
Hath made two Wills, which with the Legacie
Of his and thy kingdome, doe thy Sonnes invest.
Yet such are thy laws, that men argue yet
Whether a man those statutes can fulfill;
None doth; but all-healing grace and spirit
Revive againe what law and letter kill.
Thy lawes abridgement, and thy last command
Is all but love; Oh let this last Will stand!

XVII

SINCE she whom I lov'd hath payd her last debt
To Nature, and to hers, and my good is dead,
And her Soule early into heaven ravished,
Wholly on heavenly things my mind is sett.
Here the admyring her my mind did whett
To seeke thee God; so streames do shew their head;
But though I have found thee, and thou my thirst hast fed,
A holy thirsty dropsy melts mee yett.
But why should I begg more Love, when as thou
Dost wooe my soule for hers; offring all thine:
And dost not only feare least I allow
My Love to Saints and Angels things divine,
But in thy tender jealousy dost doubt
Least the World, Fleshe, yea Devill putt thee out.

XVIII

s h o w me deare Christ, thy Spouse, so bright and clear.
What! is it She, which on the other shore
Goes richly painted? or which rob'd and tore
Laments and mournes in Germany and here?
Sleepes she a thousand, then peepes up one yeare?
Is she selfe truth and errs? now new, now outwore?
Doth she, and did she, and shall she evermore
On one, on seaven, or on no hill appeare?
Dwells she with us, or like adventuring knights
First travaile we to seeke and then make Love?
Betray kind husband thy spouse to our sights,
And let myne amorous soule court thy mild Dove,
Who is most trew, and pleasing to thee, then
When she'is embrac'd and open to most men.

XIX

o h, to vex me, contraryes meet in one:
Inconstancy unnaturally hath begott
A constant habit; that when I would not
I change in vowes, and in devotione.
As humorous is my contritione
As my prophane Love, and as soone forgott:
As ridlingly distemper'd, cold and hott,
As praying, as mute; as infinite, as none.
I durst not view heaven yesterday; and to day
In prayers, and flattering speaches I court God:
To morrow I quake with true feare of his rod.
So my devout fitts come and go away
Like a fantastique Ague: save that here
Those are my best dayes, when I shake with feare.

THE CROSSE

s i n c e Christ embrac'd the Crosse it selfe, dare I
His image, th'image of his Crosse deny?
Would I have profit by the sacrifice,
And dare the chosen Altar to despise?
It bore all other sinnes, but is it fit
That it should beare the sinne of scorning it?
Who from the picture would avert his eye,

How would he flye his paines, who there did dye?
From mee, no Pulpit, nor misgrounded law,
Nor scandall taken, shall this Crosse withdraw,
It shall not, for it cannot; for, the losse
Of this Crosse, were to mee another Crosse;
Better were worse, for, no affliction,
No Crosse is so extreme, as to have none.
Who can blot out the Crosse, with th'instrument
Of God, dew'd on mee in the Sacrament?
Who can deny mee power, and liberty
To stretch mine armes, and mine owne Crosse to be?
Swimme, and at every stroake, thou art thy Crosse;
The Mast and yard make one, where seas do tosse;
Looke downe, thou spiest out Crosses in small things;
Looke up thou seest birds rais'd on crossed wings;
All the Globes frame, and spheares, is nothing else
But the Meridians crossing Parallels.
Materiall Crosses then, good physicke bee,
But yet spirituall have chiefe dignity.
These for extracted chimique medicine serve,
And cure much better, and as well preserve;
Then are you your own physicke, or need none,
When Still'd, or purg'd by tribulation.
For when that Crosse ungrudg'd, unto you stickes,
Then are you to your selfe, a Crucifixe.
As perchance, Carvers do not faces make,
But that away, which hid them there, do take.
Let Crosses, soe, take what hid Christ in thee,
And be his image, or not his, but hee.
But, as oft Alchimists doe coyners prove,
So may a selfe-dispising, get selfe-love;
And then as worst surfets, of best meates bee,
Soe is pride, issued from humility,
For, 'tis no child, but monster; therefore Crosse
Your joy in crosses, else, 'tis double losse,
And crosse thy senses, else, both they, and thou
Must perish soone, and to destruction bowe.
For if the'eye seeke good objects, and will take
No crosse from bad, wee cannot scape a snake.
So with harsh, hard, sowre, stinking, crosse the rest,
Make them indifferent all; call nothing best.

But most the eye needs crossing, that can rome,
And move; To th'other th'objects must come home.
And crosse thy heart: for that in man alone
Points downewards, and hath palpitation.
Crosse those dejections, when it downeward tends,
And when it to forbidden heights pretends.
And as the braine through bony walls doth vent
By sutures, which a Crosses forme present,
So when thy braine workes, ere thou utter it,
Crosse and correct concupiscence of witt.
Be covetous of Crosses, let none fall.
Crosse no man else, but crosse thy selfe in all.
Then doth the Crosse of Christ worke fruitfully
Within our hearts, when wee love harmlessly
That Crosses pictures much, and with more care
That Crosses children, which our Crosses are.

RESURRECTION, IMPERFECT

SLEEP sleep old Sun, thou canst not have repast
As yet, the wound thou took'st on friday last;
Sleepe then, and rest; The world may beare thy stay,
A better Sun rose before thee to day,
Who, not content to'enlighten all that dwell
On the earths face, as thou, enlightned hell,
And made the darke fires languish in that vale,
As, at thy presence here, our fires grow pale.
Whose body having walk'd on earth, and now
Hasting to Heaven, would, that he might allow
Himselfe unto all stations, and fill all,
For these three daies become a minerall;
Hee was all gold when he lay downe, but rose
All tincture, and doth not alone dispose
Leaden and iron wills to good, but is
Of power to make even sinfull flesh like his.
Had one of those, whose credulous pietie
Thought, that a Soule one might descerne and see
Goe from a body,'at this sepulcher been,
And, issuing from the sheet, this body seen,
He would have justly thought this body a soule,
If not of any man, yet of the whole.

                    Desunt cætera

UPON THE ANNUNTIATION AND PASSION

Falling upon one day. 1608

T A M E L Y, fraile body,'abstaine to day; to day
My soule eates twice, Christ hither and away.
She sees him man, so like God made in this,
That of them both a circle embleme is,
Whose first and last concurre; this doubtfull day
Of feast or fast, Christ came, and went away.
Shee sees him nothing twice at once, who'is all;
Shee sees a Cedar plant it selfe, and fall,
Her Maker put to making, and the head
Of life, at once, not yet alive, yet dead.
She sees at once the virgin mother stay
Reclus'd at home, Publique at Golgotha;
Sad and rejoyc'd shee's seen at once, and seen
At almost fiftie, and at scarce fifteene.
At once a Sonne is promis'd her, and gone,
Gabriell gives Christ to her, He her to John;
Not fully a mother, Shee's in Orbitie,
At once receiver and the legacie.
All this, and all betweene, this day hath showne,
Th'Abridgement of Christs story, which makes one
(As in plaine Maps, the furthest West is East)
Of the'Angels *Ave,*'and *Consummatum est.*
How well the Church, Gods Court of faculties
Deales, in some times, and seldome joyning these!
As by the selfe-fix'd Pole wee never doe
Direct our course, but the next starre thereto,
Which showes where the'other is, and which we say
(Because it strayes not farre) doth never stray;
So God by his Church, neerest to him, wee know,
And stand firme, if wee by her motion goe;
His Spirit, as his fiery Pillar doth
Leade, and his Church, as cloud; to one end both.
This Church, by letting these daies joyne, hath shown
Death and conception in mankinde is one;
Or'twas in him the same humility,
That he would be a man, and leave to be:

Or as creation he hath made, as God,
With the last judgement, but one period,
His imitating Spouse would joyne in one
Manhoods extremes: He shall come, he is gone:
Or as though one blood drop, which thence did fall,
Accepted, would have serv'd, he yet shed all;
So though the least of his paines, deeds, or words,
Would busie a life, she all this day affords;
This treasure then, in grosse, my Soule uplay,
And in my life retaile it every day.

GOOD FRIDAY, 1613. RIDING WESTWARD

LET mans Soule be a Spheare, and then, in this,
The intelligence that moves, devotion is,
And as the other Spheares, by being growne
Subject to forraigne motions, lose their owne,
And being by others hurried every day,
Scarce in a yeare their naturall forme obey:
Pleasure or businesse, so, our Soules admit
For their first mover, and are whirld by it.
Hence is't, that I am carryed towards the West
This day, when my Soules forme bends toward the East.
There I should see a Sunne, by rising set,
And by that setting endlesse day beget;
But that Christ on this Crosse, did rise and fall,
Sinne had eternally benighted all.
Yet dare I'almost be glad, I do not see
That spectacle of too much weight for mee.
Who sees Gods face, that is selfe life, must dye;
What a death were it then to see God dye?
It made his owne Lieutenant Nature shrinke,
It made his footstoole crack, and the Sunne winke.
Could I behold those hands which span the Poles,
And tune all spheares at once, peirc'd with those holes?
Could I behold that endlesse height which is
Zenith to us, and our Antipodes,
Humbled below us? or that blood which is
The seat of all our Soules, if not of his,
Made durt of dust, or that flesh which was worne
By God, for his apparell, rag'd, and torne?

If on these things I durst not looke, durst I
Upon his miserable mother cast mine eye,
Who was Gods partner here, and furnish'd thus
Halfe of that Sacrifice, which ransom'd us?
Though these things, as I ride, be from mine eye,
They'are present yet unto my memory,
For that looks towards them; and thou look'st towards mee,
O Saviour, as thou hang'st upon the tree;
I turne my backe to thee, but to receive
Corrections, till thy mercies bid thee leave.
O thinke mee worth thine anger, punish mee,
Burne off my rusts, and my deformity,
Restore thine Image, so much, by thy grace,
That thou may'st know mee, and I'll turne my face.

THE LITANIE

I. THE FATHER

FATHER of Heaven, and him, by whom
It, and us for it, and all else, for us
      Thou madest, and govern'st ever, come
   And re-create mee, now growne ruinous:
         My heart is by dejection, clay,
         And by selfe-murder, red.
From this red earth, O Father, purge away
All vicious tinctures, that new fashioned
I may rise up from death, before I'm dead.

II. THE SONNE

   O Sonne of God, who seeing two things,
Sinne, and death crept in, which were never made,
   By bearing one, tryed'st with what stings
The other could thine heritage invade;
         O be thou nail'd unto my heart,
         And crucified againe,
Part not from it, though it from thee would part,
But let it be, by applying so thy paine,
Drown'd in thy blood, and in thy passion slaine.

III. THE HOLY GHOST

O Holy Ghost, whose temple I
Am, but of mudde walls, and condensed dust,
And being sacrilegiously
Halfe wasted with youths fires, of pride and lust,
Must with new stormes be weatherbeat;
Double in my heart thy flame,
Which let devout sad teares intend; and let
(Though this glasse lanthorne, flesh, do suffer maime)
Fire, Sacrifice, Priest, Altar be the same.

IV. THE TRINITY

O Blessed glorious Trinity,
Bones to Philosophy, but milke to faith,
Which, as wise serpents, diversly
Most slipperinesse, yet most entanglings hath,
As you distinguish'd undistinct
By power, love, knowledge bee,
Give mee a such selfe different instinct
Of these; let all mee elemented bee,
Of power, to love, to know, you unnumbr'd three.

V. THE VIRGIN MARY

For that faire blessed Mother-maid,
Whose flesh redeem'd us; that she-Cherubin,
Which unlock'd Paradise, and made
One claime for innocence, and disseiz'd sinne,
Whose wombe was a strange heav'n for there
God cloth'd himselfe, and grew,
Our zealous thankes wee poure. As her deeds were
Our helpes, so are her prayers; nor can she sue
In vaine, who hath such titles unto you.

VI. THE ANGELS

And since this life our nonage is,
And wee in Wardship to thine Angels be,
Native in heavens faire Palaces,
Where we shall be but denizen'd by thee,
As th'earth conceiving by the Sunne,
Yeelds faire diversitie,
Yet never knowes which course that light doth run,

So let mee study, that mine actions bee
Worthy their sight, though blinde in how they see.

VII. THE PATRIARCHES

And let thy Patriarches Desire
(Those great Grandfathers of thy Church, which saw
   More in the cloud, than wee in fire,
Whom Nature clear'd more, than us Grace and Law,
     And now in Heaven still pray, that wee
      May use our new helpes right,)
Be satisfy'd, and fructifie in mee;
Let not my minde be blinder by more light
Nor Faith, by Reason added, lose her sight.

VIII. THE PROPHETS

Thy Eagle-sighted Prophets too,
Which were thy Churches Organs, and did sound
   That harmony, which made of two
One law, and did unite, but not confound;
     Those heavenly Poëts which did see
      Thy will, and it expresse
In rythmique feet, in common pray for mee,
That I by them excuse not my excesse
In seeking secrets, or Poëtiquenesse.

IX. THE APOSTLES

And thy illustrious Zodiacke
Of twelve Apostles, which ingirt this All,
   (From whom whosoever do not take
Their light, to darke deep pits, throw downe, and fall,)
     As through their prayers, thou'hast let mee know
      That their bookes are divine;
May they pray still, and be heard, that I goe
Th'old broad way in applying; O decline
Mee, when my comment would make thy word mine.

X. THE MARTYRS

And since thou so desirously
Did'st long to die, that long before thou could'st,
   And long since thou no more couldst dye,

Thou in thy scatter'd mystique body wouldst
          In Abel dye, and ever since
              In thine; let their blood come
To begge for us, a discreet patience
Of death, or of worse life: for Oh, to some
Not to be Martyrs, is a martyrdome.

XI. THE CONFESSORS

Therefore with thee triumpheth there
A Virgin Squadron of white Confessors,
      Whose bloods betroth'd, not marryed were,
Tender'd, not taken by those Ravishers:
              They know, and pray, that wee may know,
              In every Christian
Hourly tempestuous persecutions grow;
Tentations martyr us alive; A man
Is to himselfe a Dioclesian.

XII. THE VIRGINS

The cold white snowie Nunnery,
Which, as thy mother, their high Abbesse, sent
      Their bodies backe againe to thee,
As thou hadst lent them, cleane and innocent,
          Though they have not obtain'd of thee,
          That or thy Church, or I,
Should keep, as they, our first integrity;
Divorce thou sinne in us, or bid it die,
And call chast widowhead Virginitie.

XIII. THE DOCTORS

Thy sacred Academie above
Of Doctors, whose paines have unclasp'd, and taught
      Both bookes of life to us (for love
To know thy Scriptures tells us, we are wrote
          In thy other booke) pray for us there
          That what they have misdone
Or mis-said, wee to that may not adhere;
Their zeale may be our sinne. Lord let us runne
Meane waies, and call them stars, but not the Sunne.

XIV

And whil'st this universall Quire,
That Church in triumph, this in warfare here,
  Warm'd with one all-partaking fire
Of love, that none be lost, which cost thee deare,
        Prayes ceaslesly,'and thou hearken too,
        (Since to be gratious
Our taske is treble, to pray, beare, and doe)
Heare this prayer Lord: O Lord deliver us
From trusting in those prayers, though powr'd out thus.

XV

From being anxious, or secure,
Dead clods of sadnesse, or light squibs of mirth,
  From thinking, that great courts immure
All, or no happinesse, or that this earth
        Is only for our prison fram'd,
        Or that thou art covetous
To them thou lovest, or that they are maim'd
From reaching this worlds sweet, who seek thee thus,
With all their might, Good Lord deliver us.

XVI

From needing danger, to bee good,
From owing thee yesterdaies teares to day,
  From trusting so much to thy blood,
That in that hope, wee wound our soule away,
        From bribing thee with Almes, to excuse
        Some sinne more burdenous,
From light affecting, in religion, newes,
From thinking us all soule, neglecting thus
Our mutuall duties, Lord deliver us.

XVII

From tempting Satan to tempt us,
By our connivence, or slack companie,
  From measuring ill by vitious,
Neglecting to choake sins spawne, Vanitie,
        From indiscreet humilitie,
        Which might be scandalous,

And cast reproach on Christianitie,
From being spies, or to spies pervious,
From thirst, or scorne of fame, deliver us.

XVIII

Deliver us for thy descent
Into the Virgin, whose wombe was a place
Of middle kind; and thou being sent
To'ungratious us, staid'st at her full of grace;
And through thy poore birth, where first thou
Glorifiedst Povertie,
And yet soone after riches didst allow,
By accepting Kings gifts in the Epiphanie,
Deliver, and make us, to both waies free.

XIX

And through that bitter agonie,
Which is still the agonie of pious wits,
Disputing what distorted thee,
And interrupted evennesse, with fits;
And through thy free confession
Though thereby they were then
Made blind, so that thou might'st from them have gone,
Good Lord deliver us, and teach us when
Wee may not, and we may blinde unjust men.

XX

Through thy submitting all, to blowes
Thy face, thy clothes to spoile; thy fame to scorne,
All waies, which rage, or Justice knowes,
And by which thou could'st shew, that thou wast born;
And through thy gallant humblenesse
Which thou in death did'st shew,
Dying before thy soule they could expresse,
Deliver us from death, by dying so,
To this world, ere this world doe bid us goe.

XXI

When senses, which thy souldiers are,
Wee arme against thee, and they fight for sinne,
When want, sent but to tame, doth warre
And worke despaire a breach to enter in,

When plenty, Gods image, and seale
    Makes us Idolatrous,
And love it, not him, whom it should reveale,
When wee are mov'd to seeme religious
Only to vent wit, Lord deliver us.

XXII

In Churches, when the'infirmitie
Of him which speakes, diminishes the Word,
    When Magistrates doe mis-apply
To us, as we judge, lay or ghostly sword,
        When plague, which is thine Angell, raignes,
        Or wars, thy Champions, swaie,
When Heresie, thy second deluge, gaines;
In th'houre of death, th'Eve of last judgement day,
Deliver us from the sinister way.

XXIII

Heare us, O heare us Lord; to thee
A sinner is more musique, when he prayes,
    Than spheares, or Angells praises bee,
In Panegyrique Allelujaes;
        Heare us, for till thou heare us, Lord
        We know not what to say;
Thine eare to'our sighes, teares, thoughts gives voice and word.
O Thou who Satan heard'st in Jobs sicke day,
Heare thy selfe now, for thou in us dost pray.

XXIV

That wee may change to evennesse
This intermitting aguish Pietie;
    That snatching cramps of wickednesse
And Apoplexies of fast sin, may die;
        That musique of thy promises,
        Not threats in Thunder may
Awaken us to our just offices;
What in thy booke, thou dost, or creatures say,
That we may heare, Lord heare us, when wee pray.

XXV

That our eares sicknesse wee may cure,
And rectifie those Labyrinths aright,
    That wee, by harkning, not procure
Our praise, nor others dispraise so invite,
        That wee get not a slipperinesse,
            And senslesly decline,
·From hearing bold wits jeast at Kings excesse,
To'admit the like of majestie divine,
That we may locke our eares, Lord open thine.

XXVI

That living law, the Magistrate,
Which to give us, and make us physicke, doth
    Our vices often aggravate,
That Preachers taxing sinne, before her growth,
        That Satan, and invenom'd men
            Which well, if we starve, dine,
When they doe most accuse us, may see then
Us, to amendment, heare them; thee decline:
That we may open our eares, Lord lock thine.

XXVII

That learning, thine Ambassador,
From thine allegeance wee never tempt,
    That beauty, paradises flower
For physicke made, from poyson be exempt,
        That wit, borne apt high good to doe,
            By dwelling lazily
Or Natures nothing, be not nothing too,
That our affections kill us not, nor dye,
Heare us, weake ecchoes, O thou eare, and cry.

XXVIII

Sonne of God heare us, and since thou
By taking our blood, owest it us againe,
    Gaine to thy self, or us allow;
And let not both us and thy selfe be slaine;

O Lambe of God, which took'st our sinne
Which could not stick to thee,
O let it not returne to us againe,
But Patient and Physition being free,
As sinne is nothing, let it no where be.

UPON THE TRANSLATION OF THE PSALMES

By Sir Philip Sydney, and the Countesse of Pembroke His Sister

ETERNALL God, (for whom who ever dare
Seeke new expressions, doe the Circle square,
And thrust into strait corners of poore wit
Thee, who art cornerlesse and infinite)
I would but blesse thy Name, not name thee now;
(And thy gifts are as infinite as thou:)
Fixe we our prayses therefore on this one,
That, as thy blessed Spirit fell upon
These Psalmes first Author in a cloven tongue;
(For 'twas a double power by which he sung
The highest matter in the noblest forme;)
So thou hast cleft that spirit, to performe
That worke againe, and shed it, here, upon
Two, by their bloods, and by thy Spirit one;
A Brother and a Sister, made by thee
The Organ, where thou art the Harmony.
Two that make one *John Baptists* holy voyce,
And who that Psalme, *Now let the Iles rejoyce*,
Have both translated, and apply'd it too,
Both told us what, and taught us how to doe.
They shew us Ilanders our joy, our King,
They tell us *why*, and teach us *how* to sing;
Make all this All, three Quires, heaven, earth, and sphears;
The first, Heaven, hath a song, but no man heares,
The Spheares have Musick, but they have no tongue,
Their harmony is rather danc'd than sung;
But our third Quire, to which the first gives eare,
(For, Angels learne by what the Church does here)
This Quire hath all. The Organist is hee
Who hath tun'd God and Man, the Organ we:
The songs are these, which heavens high holy Muse
Whisper'd to *David, David* to the Jewes:

And *Davids* Successors, in holy zeale,
In formes of joy and art doe re-reveale
To us so sweetly and sincerely too,
That I must not rejoyce as I would doe
When I behold that these Psalmes are become
So well attyr'd abroad, so ill at home,
So well in Chambers, in thy Church so ill,
As I can scarce call that reform'd untill
This be reform'd; Would a whole State present
A lesser gift than some one man hath sent?
And shall our Church, unto our Spouse and King
More hoarse, more harsh than any other, sing?
For *that* we pray, we praise thy name for *this*,
Which, by this *Moses* and this *Miriam*, is
Already done; and as those Psalmes we call
(Though some have other Authors) *Davids* all:
So though some have, some may some Psalmes translate,
We thy Sydnean Psalmes shall celebrate,
And, till we come th'Extemporall song to sing,
(Learn'd the first hower, that we see the King,
Who hath translated those translators) may
These their sweet learned labours, all the way
Be as our tuning, that, when hence we part,
We may fall in with them, and sing our part.

TO MR. TILMAN AFTER HE HAD TAKEN ORDERS

T H O U, whose diviner soule hath caus'd thee now
To put thy hand unto the holy Plough,
Making Lay-scornings of the Ministry,
Not an impediment, but victory;
What bringst thou home with thee? how is thy mind
Affected since the vintage? Dost thou finde
New thoughts and stirrings in thee? and as Steele
Toucht with a Loadstone, dost new motions feele?
Or, as a Ship after much paine and care,
For Iron and Cloth brings home rich Indian ware,
Hast thou thus traffiqu'd, but with farre more gaine
Of noble goods, and with lesse time and paine?
Thou art the same materials, as before,

Onely the stampe is changed; but no more.
And as new crowned Kings alter the face,
But not the monies substance; so hath grace
Chang'd onely Gods old Image by Creation,
To Christs new stampe, at this thy Coronation;
Or, as we paint Angels with wings, because
They beare Gods message, and proclaime his lawes,
Since thou must doe the like, and so must move,
Art thou new feather'd with cœlestiall love?
Deare, tell me where thy purchase lies, and shew
What thy advantage is above, below.
But if thy gainings doe surmount expression,
Why doth the foolish world scorne that profession,
Whose joye passe speech? Why do they think unfit
That Gentry should joyne families with it?
As if their day were onely to be spent
In dressing, Mistressing and complement;
Alas poore joyes, but poorer men, whose trust
Seemes richly placed in sublimed dust;
(For, such are cloathes and beauty, which though gay,
Are, at the best, but of sublimed clay.)
Let then the world thy calling disrespect,
But goe thou on, and pitty their neglect.
What function is so noble, as to bee
Embassadour to God and destinie?
To open life, to give kingdomes to more
Than Kings give dignities; to keepe heavens doore?
Maries prerogative was to beare Christ, so
'Tis preachers to convey him, for they doe
As Angels out of clouds, from Pulpits speake;
And blesse the poore beneath, the lame, the weake.
If then th'Astronomers, whereas they spie
A new-found Starre, their Opticks magnifie,
How brave are those, who with their Engine, can
Bring man to heaven, and heaven againe to man?
These are thy titles and preheminences,
In whom must meet Gods graces, mens offences,
And so the heavens which beget all things here,
And the earth our mother, which these things doth beare,
Both these in thee, are in thy Calling knit,
And make thee now a blest Hermaphrodite.

A HYMNE TO CHRIST

At the Authors Last Going into Germany

I N what torne ship soever I embarke,
That ship shall be my embleme of thy Arke;
What sea soever swallow mee, that flood
Shall be to mee an embleme of thy blood;
Though thou with clouds of anger do disguise
Thy face; yet through that maske I know those eyes,
   Which, though they turne away sometimes,
      They never will despise.

I sacrifice this Iland unto thee,
And all whom I lov'd there, and who lov'd mee;
When I have put our seas twixt them and mee,
Put thou thy sea betwixt my sinnes and thee.
As the trees sap doth seeke the root below
In winter, in my winter now I goe,
   Where none but thee, th'Eternall root
      Of true Love I may know.

Nor thou nor thy religion dost controule,
The amorousnesse of an harmonious Soule,
But thou would'st have that love thy selfe: As thou
Art jealous, Lord, so I am jealous now,
Thou lov'st not, till from loving more, thou free
My soule: Who ever gives, takes libertie:
   O, if thou car'st not whom I love
      Alas, thou lov'st not mee.

Seale then this bill of my Divorce to All,
On whom those fainter beames of love did fall;
Marry those loves, which in youth scattered bee
On Fame, Wit, Hopes (false mistresses) to thee.
Churches are best for Prayer, that have least light:
To see God only, I goe out of sight:
   And to scape stormy dayes, I chuse
      An Everlasting night.

THE LAMENTATIONS OF JEREMY

For the most part according to Tremelius

CHAPTER I

H O W sits this citie, late most populous,
　　Thus solitary, and like a widdow thus!
Amplest of Nations, Queene of Provinces
　　She was, who now this tributary is!

Still in the night shee weepes, and her teares fall
　　Downe by her cheeks along, and none of all
Her lovers comfort her; Perfidiously
　　Her friends have dealt, and now are enemie.

Unto great bondage, and affliction
　　Juda is captive led; Those nations
With whom shee dwells, no place of rest afford,
　　In streights shee meets her Persecutors sword.

Emptie are the gates of Sion, and her waies
　　Mourne, because none come to her solemne dayes.
Her Priests doe groane, her maides are comfortless,
　　And shee's unto her selfe a bitternesse.

Her foes are growne her head, and live at Peace,
　　Because when her transgressions did increase,
The Lord strooke her with sadnesse: Th'enemie
　　Doth drive her children to captivitie.

From Sions daughter is all beauty gone,
　　Like Harts, which seeke for Pasture, and find none,
Her Princes are, and now before the foe
　　Which still pursues them, without strength they go.

Now in her daies of Teares, Jerusalem
　　(Her men slaine by the foe, none succouring them)
Remembers what of old, shee esteemed most,
　　Whilest her foes laugh at her, for what she hath lost.

Jerusalem hath sinn'd, therefore is shee
　　Remov'd, as women in uncleannesse bee;
Who honor'd, scorne her, for her foulnesse they
　　Have seene; her selfe doth groane, and turne away.

Her foulnesse in her skirts was seene, yet she
   Remembered not her end; Miraculously
Therefore she fell, none comforting: Behold
   O Lord my affliction, for the Foe growes bold.

Upon all things where her delight hath beene,
   The foe hath stretch'd his hand, for shee hath seene
Heathen, whom thou command'st, should not doe so,
   Into her holy Sanctuary goe.

And all her people groane, and seeke for bread;
   And they have given, only to be fed,
All precious things, wherein their pleasure lay:
   How cheape I'am growne, O Lord, behold, and weigh.

All this concerns not you, who passe by mee,
   O see, and marke if any sorrow bee
Like to my sorrow, which Jehova hath
   Done to mee in the day of his fierce wrath?

That fire, which by himselfe is governed
   He hath cast from heaven on my bones, and spred
A net before my feet, and mee o'rthrowne,
   And made me languish all the day alone.

His hand hath of my sinnes framed a yoake
   Which wreath'd, and cast upon my neck, hath broke
My strength. The Lord unto those enemies
   Hath given mee, from whom I cannot rise.

He under foot hath troden in my sight
   My strong men; He did company invite
To breake my young men; he the winepresse hath
   Trod upon Juda's daughter in his wrath.

For these things doe I weepe, mine eye, mine eye
   Casts water out; For he which should be nigh
To comfort mee, is now departed farre;
   The foe prevailes, forlorne my children are.

There's none, though *Sion* do stretch out her hand,
   To comfort her, it is the Lords command
That *Jacobs* foes girt him. *Jerusalem*
   Is as an uncleane woman amongst them.

But yet the Lord is just, and righteous still,
    I have rebell'd against his holy will;
O heare all people, and my sorrow see,
    My maides, my young men in captivitie.

I called for my *lovers* then, but they
    Deceiv'd mee, and my Priests, and Elders lay
Dead in the citie; for they sought for meat
    Which should refresh their soules, they could not get.

Because I am in streights, *Jehova* see
    My heart o'rturn'd, my bowells muddy bee,
Because I have rebell'd so much, as fast
    The sword without, as death within, doth wast.

Of all which heare I mourne, none comforts mee,
    My foes have heard my griefe, and glad they be,
That thou hast done it; But thy promis'd day
    Will come, when, as I suffer, so shall they.

Let all their wickednesse appeare to thee,
    Doe unto them, as thou hast done to mee,
For all my sinnes: The sighs which I have had
    Are very many, and my heart is sad.

CHAPTER II

H O W over Sions daughter hath God hung
    His wraths thicke cloud! and from heaven hath flung
To earth the beauty of *Israel,* and hath
    Forgot his foot-stoole in the day of wrath!

The Lord unsparingly hath swallowed
    All Jacob's dwellings, and demolished
To ground the strengths of *Juda,* and prophan'd
    The Princes of the Kingdome, and the land.

In heat of wrath, the horne of *Israel* hee
    Hath cleane cut off, and lest the enemie
Be hindred, his right hand he doth retire,
    But is towards *Jacob,* All-devouring fire.

Like to an enemie he bent his bow,
    His right hand was in posture of a foe,
To kill what *Sions* daughter did desire,
    'Gainst whom his wrath, he poured forth, like fire.

For like an enemie *Jehova* is,
　Devouring *Israel,* and his Palaces,
Destroying holds, giving additions
　To *Juda's* daughters lamentations.

Like to a garden hedge he hath cast downe
　The place where was his congregation,
And *Sions* feasts and sabbaths are forgot;
　Her King, her Priest, his wrath regardeth not.

The Lord forsakes his Altar, and detests
　His Sanctuary, and in the foes hand rests
His Palace, and the walls, in which their cries
　Are heard, as in the true solemnities.

The Lord hath cast a line, so to confound
　And levell *Sions* walls unto the ground;
He drawes not back his hand, which doth oreturne
　The wall, and Rampart, which together mourne.

Their gates are sunke into the ground, and hee
　Hath broke the barres; their King and Princes bee
Amongst the heathen, without law, nor there
　Unto their Prophets doth the Lord appeare.

There *Sions Elders* on the ground are plac'd,
　And silence keepe; Dust on their heads they cast,
In sackcloth have they girt themselves, and low
　The Virgins towards ground, their heads do throw.

My bowells are growne muddy, and mine eyes
　Are faint with weeping: and my liver lies
Pour'd out upon the ground, for miserie
　That sucking children in the streets doe die.

When they had cryed unto their Mothers, where
　Shall we have bread, and drinke? they fainted there,
And in the streets like wounded persons lay
　Till 'twixt their mothers breasts they went away.

Daughter Jerusalem, Oh what may bee
　A witnesse, or comparison for thee?
Sion, to ease thee, what shall I name like thee?
　Thy breach is like the sea, what help can bee?

For thee vaine foolish things thy Prophets sought,
    Thee, thine iniquities they have not taught,
Which might disturne thy bondage: but for thee
    False burthens, and false causes they would see.

The passengers doe clap their hands, and hisse,
    And wag their head at thee, and say, Is this
That citie, which so many men did call
    Joy of the earth, and perfectest of all?

Thy foes doe gape upon thee, and they hisse,
    And gnash their teeth, and say, Devoure wee this,
For this is certainly the day which wee
    Expected, and which now we finde, and see.

The Lord hath done that which he purposed,
    Fulfill'd his word of old determined;
He hath throwne downe, and not spar'd, and thy foe
    Made glad above thee, and advanc'd him so.

But now, their hearts against the Lord do call,
    Therefore, O walls of *Sion,* let teares fall
Downe like a river, day and night; take thee
    No rest, but let thine eye incessant be.

Arise, cry in the night, poure, for thy sinnes,
    Thy heart, like water, when the watch begins;
Lift up thy hands to God, lest children dye,
    Which, faint for hunger, in the streets doe lye.

Behold O Lord, consider unto whom
    Thou hast done this; what, shall the women come
To eate their children of a spanne? shall thy
    Prophet and Priest be slaine in Sanctuary?

On ground in streets, the yong and old do lye,
    My virgins and yong men by sword do dye;
Them in the day of try wrath thou hast slaine,
    Nothing did thee from killing them containe.

As to a solemne feast, all whom I fear'd
    Thou call'st about mee; when his wrath appear'd,
None did remaine or scape, for those which I
    Brought up, did perish by mine enemie.

CHAPTER III

I AM the man which have affliction seene,
  Under the rod of Gods wrath having beene,
He hath led mee to darknesse, not to light,
  And against mee all day, his hand doth fight.

Hee hath broke my bones, worne out my flesh and skinne,
  Built up against mee; and hath girt mee in
With hemlocke, and with labour; and set mee
  In darke, as they who dead for ever bee.

Hee hath hedg'd me lest I scape, and added more
  To my steele fetters, heavier than before.
When I crie out, he out shuts my prayer: And hath
  Stop'd with hewn stone my way, and turn'd my path.

And like a Lion hid in secrecie,
  Or Beare which lyes in wait, he was to mee.
He stops my way, teares me, made desolate,
  And hee makes mee the marke he shooteth at.

Hee made the children of his quiver passe
  Into my reines, I with my people was
All the day long, a song and mockery.
  Hee hath fill'd mee with bitternesse, and he

Hath made me drunke with wormewood. He hath burst
  My teeth with stones, and covered mee with dust;
And thus my Soule farre off from peace was set,
  And my prosperity I did forget.

My strength, my hope (unto my selfe I said)
  Which from the Lord should come, is perished.
But when my mournings I do thinke upon,
  My wormwood, hemlocke, and affliction,

My Soule is humbled in remembring this;
  My heart considers, therefore, hope there is.
'Tis Gods great mercy we'are not utterly
  Consum'd, for his compassions do not die;

For every morning they renewed bee,
  For great, O Lord, is thy fidelity.
The Lord is, saith my Soule, my portion,
  And therefore in him will I hope alone.

The Lord is good to them, who on him relie,
 And to the Soule that seeks him earnestly.
It is both good to trust, and to attend
 (The Lords salvation) unto the end:

'Tis good for one his yoake in youth to beare;
 He sits alone, and doth all speech forbeare,
Because he hath borne it. And his mouth he layes
 Deepe in the dust, yet then in hope he stayes.

He gives his cheekes to whosoever will
 Strike him, and so he is reproched still.
For, not for ever doth the Lord forsake,
 But when he'hath strucke with sadnes, hee doth take

Compassion, as his mercy'is infinite;
 Nor is it with his heart, that he doth smite;
That underfoot the prisoners stamped bee,
 That a mans right the Judge himselfe doth see

To be wrung from him, That he subverted is
 In his just cause; the Lord allowes not this.
Who then will say, that ought doth come to passe,
 But that which by the Lord commanded was?

Both good and evill from his mouth proceeds;
 Why then grieves any man for his misdeeds?
Turne wee to God, by trying out our wayes;
 To him in heaven, our hands with hearts upraise.

Wee have rebell'd, and falne away from thee,
 Thou pardon'st not; Usest no clemencie;
Pursuest us, kill'st us, coverest us with wrath,
 Cover'st thy selfe with clouds, that our prayer hath

No power to passe. And thou hast made us fall
 As refuse, and off-scouring to them all.
All our foes gape at us. Feare and a snare
 With ruine, and with waste, upon us are.

With watry rivers doth mine eye oreflow
 For ruine of my peoples daughter so;
Mine eye doth drop downe teares incessantly,
 Untill the Lord looke downe from heaven to see.

And for my citys daughters sake, mine eye
  Doth breake mine heart. Causles mine enemy,
Like a bird chac'd me. In a dungeon
  They have shut my life, and cast on me a stone.

Waters flow'd o'r my head, then thought I, I am
  Destroy'd; I called Lord, upon thy name
Out of the pit. And thou my voice didst heare;
  Oh from my sigh, and crye, stop not thine eare.

Then when I call'd upon thee, thou drew'st nere
  Unto mee, and said'st unto mee, do you feare.
Thou Lord my Soules cause handled hast, and thou
  Rescud'st my life. O Lord do thou judge now,

Thou heardst my wrong. Their vengeance all they have
    wrought;
  How they reproach'd, thou hast heard, and what
    they thought,
What their lips uttered, which against me rose,
  And what was ever whisper'd by my foes.

I am their song, whether they rise or sit,
  Give them rewards Lord, for their working fit,
Sorrow of heart, thy curse. And with thy might
  Follow, and from under heaven destroy them quite.

CHAPTER IV

H O W is the gold become so dimme? How is
  Purest and finest gold thus chang'd to this?
The stones which were stones of the Sanctuary,
  Scattered in corners of each street do lye.

The pretious sonnes of Sion, which should bee
  Valued at purest gold, how do wee see
Low rated now, as earthen Pitchers, stand,
  Which are the worke of a poore Potters hand.

Even the Sea-calfes draw their brests, and give
  Sucke to their young; my peoples daughters live,
By reason of the foes great cruelnesse,
  As do the Owles in the vast Wildernesse.

And when the sucking child doth strive to draw,
   His tongue for thirst cleaves to his upper jaw.
And when for bread the little children crye,
   There is no man that doth them satisfie.

They which before were delicately fed,
   Now in the streets forlorne have perished,
And they which ever were in scarlet cloath'd,
   Sit and embrace the dunghills which they loath'd.

The daughters of my people have sinned more,
   Than did the towne of *Sodome* sinne before;
Which being at once destroy'd, there did remaine
   No hands amongst them, to vexe them againe.

But heretofore purer her Nazarite
   Was than the snow, and milke was not so white;
As carbuncles did their pure bodies shine,
   And all their polish'dnesse was Saphirine.

They are darker now than blacknes, none can know
   Them by the face, as through the streets they goe,
For now their skin doth cleave unto the bone,
   And withered, is like to dry wood growne.

Better by sword than famine 'tis to dye;
   And better through pierc'd, than through penury.
Women by nature pitifull have eate
   Their children drest with their owne hand for meat.

Jehova here fully accomplish'd hath
   His indignation, and powr'd forth his wrath,
Kindled a fire in *Sion,* which hath power
   To eate, and her foundations to devour.

Nor would the Kings of the earth, nor all which live
   In the inhabitable world beleeve,
That any adversary, any foe
   Into *Jerusalem* should enter so.

For the Priests sins, and Prophets, which have shed
   Blood in the streets, and the just murthered:

Which when those men, whom they made blinde, did stray
   Thorough the streets, defiled by the way

With blood, the which impossible it was
   Their garments should scape touching, as they passe,
Would cry aloud, depart defiled men,
   Depart, depart, and touch us not: and then

They fled, and strayd, and with the *Gentiles* were,
   Yet told their friends, they should not long dwell there;
For this they are scattered by Jehovahs face
   Who never will regard them more; No grace

Unto their old men shall the foe afford,
   Nor, that they are Priests, redeeme them from the sword.
And wee as yet, for all these miseries
   Desiring our vaine helpe, consume our eyes:

And such a nation as cannot save,
   We in desire and speculation have.
They hunt our steps, that in the streets wee feare
   To goe: our end is now approached neere,

Our dayes accomplish'd are, this the last day.
   Eagles of heaven are not so swift as they
Which follow us, o'r mountaine tops they flye
   At us, and for us in the desart lye.

The annointed Lord, breath of our nostrils, hee
   Of whom we said, under his shadow, wee
Shall with more ease under the Heathen dwell,
   Into the pit which these men digged, fell.

Rejoyce *O Edoms daughter*, joyfull bee
   Thou which inhabitst *Huz*, for unto thee
This cup shall passe, and thou with drunkennesse
   Shalt fill thy selfe, and shew thy nakednesse.

And then thy sinnes *O Sion*, shall be spent,
   The Lord will not leave thee in banishment.
Thy sinnes *O Edoms daughter*, hee will see,
   And for them, pay thee with captivitie.

CHAPTER V

REMEMBER, O Lord, what is fallen on us;
 See, and marke how we are reproached thus,
For unto strangers our possession
 Is turn'd, our houses unto Aliens gone,

Our mothers are become as widowes, wee
 As Orphans all, and without father be;
Waters which are our owne, wee drunke, and pay,
 And upon our owne wood a price they lay.

Our persecutors on our necks do sit,
 They make us travaile, and not intermit,
We stretch our hands unto th'*Egyptians*
 To get us bread; and to the *Assyrians*.

Our Fathers did these sinnes, and are no more,
 But wee do beare the sinnes they did before.
They are but servants, which do rule us thus,
 Yet from their hands none would deliver us.

With danger of our life our bread wee gat;
 For in the wildernesse, the sword did wait.
The tempests of this famine wee liv'd in,
 Black as an Oven colour'd had our skinne:

In *Judaes* cities they the maids abus'd
 By force, and so women in *Sion* us'd.
The Princes with their hands they hung; no grace
 Nor honour gave they to the Elders face.

Unto the mill our yong men carried are,
 And children fell under the wood they bare.
Elders, the gates; youth did their songs forbeare,
 Gone was our joy; our dancings, mournings were.

Now is the crowne falne from our head; and woe
 Be unto us, because we'have sinned so.
For this our hearts do languish, and for this
 Over our eyes a cloudy dimnesse is.

Because mount *Sion* desolate doth lye,
  And foxes there do goe at libertie:
But thou O Lord art ever, and thy throne
  From generation, to generation.

Why should'st thou forget us eternally?
  Or leave us thus long in this misery?
Restore us Lord to thee, that so we may
  Returne, and as of old, renew our day.

For oughtest thou, O Lord, despise us thus,
  And to be utterly enrag'd at us?

HYMNE TO GOD MY GOD, IN MY SICKNESSE

SINCE I am comming to that Holy roome,
  Where, with thy Quire of Saints for evermore,
I shall be made thy Musique; As I come
  I tune the Instrument here at the dore,
  And what I must doe then, thinke here before.

Whilst my Physitians by their love are growne
  Cosmographers, and I their Mapp, who lie
Flat on this bed, that by them may be showne
  That this is my South-west discoverie
  Per fretum febris, by these streights to die,

I joy, that in these straits, I see my West;
  For, though theire currants yeeld returne to none,
What shall my West hurt me? As West and East
  In all flatt Maps (and I am one) are one,
  So death doth touch the Resurrection.

Is the Pacifique Sea my home? Or are
  The Easterne riches? Is *Jerusalem?*
Anyan, and *Magellan,* and *Gibraltare,*
  All streights, and none but streights, are wayes to them,
  Whether where *Japhet* dwelt, or *Cham,* or *Sem.*

We thinke that *Paradise* and *Calvarie,*
  Christs Crosse, and *Adams* tree, stood in one place;

Looke Lord, and finde both *Adams* met in me;
　As the first *Adams* sweat surrounds my face,
　May the last *Adams* blood my soule embrace.

So, in his purple wrapp'd receive mee Lord,
　By these his thornes give me his other Crowne;
And as to others soules I preach'd thy word,
　Be this my Text, my Sermon to mine owne,
　Therfore that he may raise the Lord throws down.

A HYMNE TO GOD THE FATHER

I

W I L T thou forgive that sinne where I begunne,
　Which is my sin, though it were done before?
Wilt thou forgive those sinnes, through which I runne,
　And do run still: though still I do deplore?
　　When thou hast done, thou hast not done,
　　　For, I have more.

II

Wilt thou forgive that sinne by which I'have wonne
　Others to sinne? and, made my sinne their doore?
Wilt thou forgive that sinne which I did shunne
　A yeare, or two: but wallowed in, a score?
　　When thou hast done, thou hast not done,
　　　For, I have more.

III

I have a sinne of feare, that when I have spunne
　My last thred, I shall perish on the shore;
Sweare by thy selfe, that at my death thy sonne
　Shall shine as he shines now, and heretofore;
　　And, having done that, Thou haste done,
　　　I feare no more.

DE LIBRO CUM MUTUARETUR IMPRESSO;
DOMI À PUERIS FRUSTATIM LACERATO; ET
POST REDDITO MANUSCRIPTO

Doctissimo Amicissimoque V.

D. D. Andrews

PARTURIUNT madido quae nixu praela, recepta,
　　Sed quae scripta manu, sunt veneranda magis.
Qui liber in pluteos, blattis cinerique relictos,
　　Si modo sit praeli sanguine tinctus, abit;
Accedat calamo scriptus, reverenter habetur,
　　Involat et veterum scrinia summa Patrum.
Dicat Apollo modum; Pueros infundere libro
　　Nempe vetustatem canitiemque novo.
Nil mirum, medico pueros de semine natos,
　　Haec nova fata libro posse dedisse novo.
Si veterem faciunt pueri, qui nuperus, Annon
　　Ipse Pater Juvenem me dabit arte senem?
Hei miseris senibus! nos vertit dura senectus
　　Omnes in pueros, neminem at in Juvenem.
Hoc tibi servasti praestandum, Antique Dierum,
　　Quo viso, et vivit, et juvenescit Adam.
Interea, infirmae fallamus taedia vitae,
　　Libris, et Coelorum aemulâ amicitiâ.
Hos inter, qui a te mihi redditus iste libellus,
　　Non mihi tam charus, tam meus, ante fuit.

EPIGRAMMA

Transiit in Sequanam Moenus; Victoris in aedes;
　　Et Francofurtum, te revehente, meat.

AMICISSIMO, ET MERITISSIMO
BEN. JOHNSON

In Vulponem

QUOD arte ausus es hic tuâ, Poeta,
Si auderent hominum Deique juris
Consulti, veteres sequi aemularierque,
O omnes saperemus ad salutem.
His sed sunt veteres araneosi;
Tam nemo veterum est sequutor, ut tu
Illos quod sequeris novator audis.
Fac tamen quod agis; tuique primâ
Libri canitie induantur horâ:
Nam chartis pueritia est neganda,
Nascanturque senes, oportet, illi
Libri, queis dare vis perennitatem.
Priscis, ingenium facit, laborque
Te parem; hos superes, ut et futuros,
Ex nostrâ vitiositate sumas,
Quâ priscos superamus, et futuros.

TO MR. GEORGE HERBERT,

With one of my seals, of the anchor and Christ

QUI prius assuetus Serpentum fasce Tabellas
    Signare, (haec nostrae symbola parva Domus)
Adscitus domui Domini, patrioque relicto
    Stemmate, nanciscor stemmata jure nova.
Hinc mihi Crux primo quae fronti impressa lavacro,
    Finibus extensis, anchora facta patet.
Anchorae in effigiem Crux tandem desinit ipsam,
    Anchora fit tandem Crux tolerata diu.
Hoc tamen ut fiat, Christo vegetatur ab ipso
    Crux, et ab Affixo, est Anchora facta, Jesu.
Nec Natalitiis penitus serpentibus orbor,
    Non ita dat Deus, ut auferat ante data.

Quâ sapiens, Dos est; Quâ terram lambit et ambit,
    Pestis; At in nostra fit Medicina Cruce,
Serpens; fixa Cruci si sit Natura; Crucique
    A fixo, nobis, Gratia tota fluat.
Omnia cum Crux sint, Crux Anchora facta, sigillum
    Non tam dicendum hoc quam Catechismus erit.
Mitto nec exigua, exiguâ sub imagine, dona,
    Pignora amicitiae, et munera; Vota, preces.
Plura tibi accumulet, sanctus cognominis, Ille
    Regia qui flavo Dona sigillat Equo.

A S H E A F E of Snakes used heretofore to be
My Seal, The Crest of our poore Family.
Adopted in Gods Family, and so
Our old Coat lost, unto new armes I go.
The Crosse (my seal at Baptism) spred below,
Does, by that form, into an Anchor grow.
Crosses grow Anchors; Bear, as thou shouldst do
Thy Crosse, and that Crosse grows an Anchor too.
But he that makes our Crosses Anchors thus,
Is Christ, who there is crucifi'd for us.
Yet may I, with this, my first Serpents hold,
God gives new blessings, and yet leaves the old;
The Serpent, may, as wise, my pattern be;
My poison, as he feeds on dust, that's me.
And as he rounds the Earth to murder sure,
My death he is, but on the Crosse, my cure.
Crucifie nature then, and then implore
All Grace from him, crucified there before;
When all is Crosse, and that Crosse Anchor grown,
This Seal's a Catechism, not a Seal alone.
Under that little Seal great gifts I send,
[Wishes,] and prayers, pawns, and fruits of a friend.
And may that Saint which rides in our great Seal,
To you, who bear his name, great bounties deal.

TRANSLATED OUT OF GAZÆUS, *VOTA AMICO FACTA.* FOL. 160

G O D grant thee thine own wish, and grant thee mine,
Thou, who dost, best friend, in best things outshine;

May thy soul, ever chearfull, nere know cares,
Nor thy life, ever lively, know gray haires.
Nor thy hand, ever open, know base holds,
Nor thy purse, ever plump, know pleits, or folds.
Nor thy tongue, ever true, know a false thing,
Nor thy word, ever mild, know quarrelling.
Nor thy works, ever equall, know disguise,
Nor thy fame, ever pure, know contumelies.
Nor thy prayers, know low objects, still Divine;
God grant thee thine own wish, and grant thee mine.

Paradoxes and Problems

A DEFENCE OF WOMENS INCONSTANCY

THAT Women are *Inconstant,* I with any man confess, but that *Inconstancy* is a bad quality, I against any man will maintain: For every thing as it is one better than another, so is it fuller of *change;* The *Heavens* themselves continually turn, the *Stars* move, the *Moon* changeth; *Fire* whirleth, *Aire* flyeth, *Water* ebbs and flowes, the face of the *Earth* altereth her looks, *time* staies not; the Colour that is most light, will take most dyes: so in Men, they that have the most reason are the most inalterable in their designes, and the darkest or most ignorant, do seldomest change; therefore Women changing more than Men, have also more *Reason.* They cannot be immutable like stocks, like stones, like the Earths dull Center; Gold that lyeth still, rusteth; Water, corrupteth; Aire that moveth not, poysoneth; then why should that which is the perfection of other things, be imputed to Women as greatest imperfection? Because thereby they deceive Men. Are not your wits pleased with those jests, which cozen your expectation? You can call it pleasure to be beguil'd in troubles, and in the most excellent toy in the world, you call it Treachery: I would you had your *Mistresses* so constant, that they would never change, no not so much as their *smocks,* then should you see what sluttish vertue, *Constancy* were. *Inconstancy* is a most commendable and cleanly quality, and Women in this quality are far more absolute than the Heavens, than the Stars, Moon, or any thing beneath it; for long observation hath pickt certainty out of their mutability. The Learned are so well acquainted with the Stars, Signes and Planets, that they make them but Characters, to read the meaning of the Heaven in his own forehead. Every simple fellow can bespeak of the change of the *Moon* a great while beforehand: but I would fain have the learnedst man so skilfull, as to tell when the simplest Woman meaneth to vary. Learning affords no rules to know, much less

277

knowledge to rule the minde of a Woman: For as *Philosophy* teacheth us, that *Light things do always tend upwards,* and *heavy things decline downward;* Experience teacheth us otherwise, that the disposition of a *Light* Woman, is to fall down, the nature of women being contrary to all Art and Nature. Women are like *Flies,* which feed among us at our Table, or *Fleas* sucking our very blood, who leave not our most retired places free from their familiarity, yet for all their fellowship will they never be tamed nor commanded by us. Women are like the *Sun,* which is violently carried one way, yet hath a proper course contrary: so though they, by the mastery of some over-ruling churlish husbands, are forced to his Byas, yet have they a motion of their own, which their husbands never know of: It is the nature of nice and fastidious mindes to know things only to be weary of them: Women by their slye *changeableness,* and pleasing doubleness, prevent even the mislike of those, for they can never be so well known, but that there is still more unknown. Every woman is a *Science;* for he that plods upon a woman all his life long, shall at length finde himself short of the knowledge of her: they are born to take down the pride of wit, and ambition of wisdom, making *fools* wise in the adventuring to win them, *wisemen* fools in conceit of losing their labours; *witty* men stark mad, being confounded with their uncertainties. *Philosophers* write against them for spight, not desert, that having attained to some knowledge in all other things, in them only they know nothing, but are meerly ignorant: *Active* and *Experienced* men rail against them, because they love in their liveless and decrepit age, when all goodness leaves them. These envious *Libellers* ballad against them, because having nothing in themselves able to deserve their love, they maliciously discommend all they cannot obtain, thinking to make men believe they know much, because they are able to dispraise much, and rage against *Inconstancy,* when they were never admitted into so much favour as to be forsaken. In mine opinion such men are happie that women are *Inconstant,* for so may they chance to be beloved of some excellent woman (when it comes to their turn) out of their *Inconstancy* and mutability, though not out of their own desert. And what reason is there to clog any woman with one man, be he never so singular? Women had rather, and it is far better and more Judicial to enjoy all the vertues in several men, than but some of them in one, for otherwise they lose their taste, like divers sorts of meat minced together in one dish: and to have all excellencies in one man (if it were possible) is *Confusion* and *Diversity.* Now who can deny, but such as are obstinately bent to undervalue their worth, are those that have not soul enough to comprehend their excellency, Women being the most excellent Creatures, in that Man is able to subject all things else, and to grow wise in every thing, but still persists a fool in Woman? The greatest *Scholler,* if he once take a wife, is found so unlearned, that he must begin his *Horn-book*, and all is by *Inconstancy*. To conclude therefore; this name of *Inconstancy*, which hath so much been poysoned with slanders, ought to be changed into *variety*, for the which the world is so delightfull, *and a Woman for that the most delightfull thing in this world.*

II

THAT WOMEN OUGHT TO PAINT

Foulness is Lothsome: can that be so which helps it? who forbids his beloved to gird in her waste? to mend by shooing her uneven lameness? to burnish her teeth? or to perfume her breath? yet that the *Face* be more precisely regarded, it concerns more: For as open confessing sinners are always punished, but the wary and concealing offenders without witness do it also without punishment; so the secret parts needs the less respect; but of the *Face,* discovered to all Examinations and surveys, there is not too nice a Jealousie. Nor doth is only draw the busie Eyes, but it is subject to the divinest touch of all, to kissing, the strange and mystical union of souls. If she should prostitute her self to a more unworthy man than thy self, how earnestly and justly wouldst thou exclaim, that for want of this easier and ready way of repairing, to betray her body to ruine and deformity (the tyrannous *Ravishers,* and sodain *Deflourers* of all women) what a hainous adultery is it! What thou lovest in her *face* is *colour,* and *painting* gives that, but thou hatest it, not because it is, but because thou knowest it. Fool, whom Ignorance makes happy, the Stars, the Sun, the Skye whom thou admirest, alas, have no *colour,* but are fair, because they seem to be coloured: If this seeming will not satisfie thee in her, thou hast good assurance of her *colour,* when thou seest her *lay* it on. If her *face* be *painted* on a Board or Wall, thou wilt love it, and the Board, and the Wall: Canst thou loath it then when it speaks, smiles, and kisses, because it is *painted?* Are we not more delighted with seeing Birds, Fruits, and Beasts *painted* than we are with Naturals? And do we not with pleasure behold the *painted* shape of Monsters and Devils, whom true, we durst not regard? We repair the ruines of our houses, but first cold tempests warn us of it, and bites us through it; we mend the wrack and stains of our Apparell, but first our eyes, and other bodies are offended; but by this providence of Women, this is prevented. If in *Kissing* or *breathing* upon her, the *painting* fall off, thou art angry; wilt thou be so, if it stick on? Thou didst love her; if thou beginnest to hate her, then 'tis because she is not *painted*. If thou wilt say now, thou didst hate her before, thou didst hate her and love her together. Be constant in something, and love her who shews her great *love* to thee, in taking this pains to seem *lovely* to thee.

IV

THAT GOOD IS MORE COMMON THAN EVIL

I HAVE not been so pittifully tired with any *vanity,* as with silly *Old Mens* exclaiming against these times, and extolling their own: Alas! they betray themselves, for if the *times* be *changed,* their manners have changed them. But their senses are to *pleasures,* as *sick mens* tastes are to *Liquors;* for indeed no *new thing* is done in the *world,* all things are what, and as they were, and *Good* is as ever it was, more plenteous, and must of necessity be *more common than Evil,* because it hath this for *nature* and *perfection* to be *common.* It makes *Love* to all *Natures,* all, all affect it. So that in the *Worlds* early *Infancy,* there was a time when nothing was *Evill,* but if this World shall suffer *dotage* in the extreamest *Crookednesse* thereof, there shall be no time when nothing shall be *good.* It dares appear and spread, and glister in the *World,* but *Evill* buries it self in night and darkness, and is chastised and suppressed when *Good* is cherished and rewarded. And as *Imbroderers, Lapidaries,* and other *Artisans,* can by all things adorn their works; for by adding better things, the better they shew in [*Lustre*] and in *Eminency;* so *Good* doth not only prostrate her *Amiablenesse* to all, but refuses no end, no not of her utter contrary *Evill,* that she may be the more *common* to us. For *Evill Manners* are *Parents* of *good Lawes;* and in every *Evill* there is an *excellency,* which (in common speech) we call *good.* For the fashions of *habits,* for our moving in *gestures,* for phrases in our *speech,* we say they are *good* as long as they were used, that is, as long as they were *common;* and we eat, we walk, only when it is, or seems *good* to do so. All *fair,* all *profitable,* all *vertuous,* is, *good,* and these three things I think embrace all things, but their utter *contraries;* of which also *fair* may be *rich* and *vertuous; poor,* may be *vertuous* and *fair; vitious,* may be *fair* and *rich;* so that *Good* hath this good means to be *common,* that some subjects she can possess entirely; and in subjects poysoned with *Evill,* she can humbly stoop to accompany the *Evill.* And of *Indifferent* things many things are become perfectly good by being *Common,* as *Customs* by use are made binding *Lawes.* But I remember nothing that is therefore *ill,* because it is *Common,* but *Women,* of whom also: *They that are most Common, are the best of that Occupation they profess.*

VI

THAT IT IS POSSIBLE TO FINDE SOME VERTUE IN SOME WOMEN

I A M not of that seard *Impudence* that I dare defend *Women*, or pronounce them good; yet we see *Physitians* allow some *vertue* in every *poyson*. Alas! why should we except *Women?* since certainly, they are good for *Physicke* at least, so as some *wine* is good for a *feaver*. And though they be the *Occasioners* of many sins, they are also the *Punishers* and *Revengers* of the same sins: For I have seldom seen one which consumes his *substance* and *body* upon them, escape *diseases*, or *beggery;* and this is their *Justice*. And if *suum cuique dare*, be the fulfilling of all *Civil Justice*, they are *most just;* for they deny that which is theirs to no man.

Tanquam non liceat nulla puella negat.

And who may doubt of great wisdome in them, that doth but observe with how much labour and cunning our *Justicers* and other *dispensers* of the *Laws* studie to imbrace them: and how zealously our *Preachers* dehort men from them, only by urging their *subtilties* and *policies*, and *wisdom*, which are in them? Or who can deny them a good measure of *Fortitude*, if he consider how *valiant men* they have overthrown, and being themselves overthrown, how much and how patiently they *bear?* And though they be most *intemperate*, I care not, for I undertook to furnish them with *some vertue*, not with *all*. *Necessity*, which makes even bad things good, prevails also for them, for we must say of them, as of some sharp pinching *Laws:* If men were free from *infirmities*, they were needless. These or none must serve for *reasons*, and it is my great happiness that *Examples* prove not *Rules*, for to confirm this *Opinion*, the World yields not *one Example*.

VIII

THAT NATURE IS OUR WORST GUIDE

S H A L L she be *guide* to all *Creatures*, which is her self one? Or if she also have a *guide*, shall any *Creature* have a better guide than we? The affections of *lust* and *anger*, yea even to *erre* is natural, shall we follow these? Can she be a good *guide* to us, which hath *corrupted* not us only but her self? was not the first *Man*, by the desire of *knowledge*, corrupted even in the *whitest integrity* of *Nature?* And did not *Nature*, (if *Nature* did any thing) infuse into him this desire of *knowledge*, and so this *Corruption* in him, into us? If by *Nature* we shall understand our *essence*, our *definition* [*our reasonableness*], then this being alike common to all (the *Idiot* and the *Wizard* being equally *reasonable*) why should not all men having equally all one *nature*, follow one course? Or if we shall understand our *inclinations;* alas! how unable a guide is that which follows the *temperature* of our slimie *bodies!* For we cannot say that we derive our *inclinations*, our *mindes*, or *soules* from our *Parents* by any way: to say that it is *all from all*, is *errour* in *reason*, for then with the first nothing remains; or is a *part from all*, is *errour* in *experience*, for then this *part* equally imparted to many children, would like *Gavell-kind lands*, in few generations become nothing: or to say it by *communication*, is *errour* in *Divinity*, for to communicate the *ability* of communicating *whole essence* with any but God, is utterly *blasphemy*. And if thou hit thy *Fathers nature* and *inclination*, he also had his *Fathers*, and so climbing up, all comes of one man, and have one *nature*, all shall imbrace one course; but that cannot be, therefore our *Complexions* and whole *Bodies*, we inherit from *Parents;* our *inclinations* and minds follow that: For our *mind* is heavy in our *bodies afflictions*, and rejoyceth in our *bodies pleasure:* how then shall this *nature* governe us, that is governed by the worst part of us? *Nature though oft chased away, it will return;* 'tis true, but those *good motions* and *inspirations* which be our guides must be *wooed, courted*, and *welcomed*, or else they abandon us. And that old *Axiome, nihil invita, &c.* must not be said thou *shalt*, but thou *wilt* doe nothing against *Nature*; so *unwilling* he notes us to curbe our *natural appetites*. We call our *bastards* alwayes our *naturall issue*, and we define a *Foole* by nothing so ordinary, as by the name of *naturall*. And that poore knowledge whereby we conceive what *rain* is, what *wind*, what *thunder*, we call *Metaphysicke, supernaturall;* such *small* things, such *no* things do we allow to our pliant *Natures* apprehension. Lastly, by following her, we lose the pleasant, and lawfull *Commodities* of this *life*, for we shall drinke water and eate rootes, and those not sweet and delicate, as now by Mans *art* and *industry* they are made: we shall lose all the necessities of *societies, lawes, arts,* and *sciences*, which are all the workemanship of *Man:* yea we shall lack the last *best refuge* of misery, *death*, because *no death is naturall:* for if yee will not dare to call all *death violent* (though I see not why *sicknesses* be not *violences*) yet *causes* of all *deaths* proceed of the *defect* of that which *nature* made perfect, and would preserve, and therefore all against *nature*.

X

THAT A WISE MAN IS KNOWN BY MUCH LAUGHING

Ridi, si sapis, ô puella ride; If thou beest *wise, laugh:* for since the *powers* of *discourse*, and *Reason*, and *laughter*, be equally *proper* unto Man only, why shall not he be only most *wise*, which hath most use of *laughing*, as well as he which hath most of *reasoning* and *discoursing*? I always did, and shall understand that *Adage;*

Per risum multum possis cognoscere stultum,

That by much *laughing* thou maist know there is a *fool*, not, that the *laughers* are *fools*, but that among them there is some *fool*, at whom *wise men* laugh: which moved *Erasmus* to put this as his first *Argument* in the mouth of his *Folly*, that *she made Beholders laugh:* for *fools* are the most laughed at, and laugh the least themselves of any. And *Nature* saw this *faculty* to be so necessary in man, that she hath been content that by *more causes* we should be importuned to *laugh*, than to the *exercise* of any other *power;* for things in themselves utterly *contrary*, beget this effect; for we *laugh* both at *witty* and *absurd* things: At both which sorts I have seen men *laugh so long*, and *so earnestly*, that at last they have *wept* that they could laugh no more. And therefore the *Poet* having described the *quietnesse* of a *wise retired man*, saith in one, what we have said before in many lines; *Quid facit Canius tuus? ridet.* We have received that even the *extremity* of *laughing*, yea of *weeping* also, hath been accounted *wisdom:* and that *Democritus* and *Heraclitus*, the *lovers* of these *Extreams*, have been called *lovers of Wisdom*. Now among our *wise men*, I doubt not but many would be found, who would laugh at *Heraclitus* weeping, none which weep at *Democritus* laughing. At the hearing of *Comedies* or other *witty* reports, I have noted some, which not understanding *jests*, &c. have yet chosen this as the best means to seem *wise* and *understanding*, to *laugh* when their *Companions laugh;* and I have presumed them *ignorant*, whom I have seen *unmoved*. A *fool* if he come into a *Princes Court*, and see a *gay* man leaning at the wall, so *glistering*, and so *painted* in many *colours* that he is hardly discerned from one of the *Pictures* in the *Arras*, hanging his *body* like an *Iron-bound chest*, girt in and thick *ribb'd* with *broad gold laces*, may (and commonly doth) envy him. But alas! shall a *wise man*, which may not only not *envy*, but not *pitty* this *Monster*, do nothing? Yes, let him *laugh*. And if one of these *hot cholerick firebrands*, which nourish themselves by *quarrelling*, and kindling others, spit upon a *fool* one *sparke* of *disgrace*, he, like a *thatcht house* quickly burning, may be *angry;* but the *wise man*, as *cold* as the *Salamander*, may not only not be *angry* with him, but not be *sorry* for him; therefore let him *laugh:* so he shall be known a Man, because he can *laugh*, a *wise Man* that he knows at *what* to laugh, and a *valiant Man* that he *dares* laugh: for he that *laughs* is justly reputed more *wise*, than at whom it is *laughed*. And hence I think proceeds that which in these later *formal* times I have much noted; that now when our *superstitious civilitie* of *manners* is become a mutuall *tickling flattery* of one another, almost every man affecteth an *humour* of *jesting*, and is content to be *deject*, and to *deform* himself, yea become *fool* to no other *end* that I can spie, but to give his *wise Companion* occasion to *laugh;* and to shew themselves in *promptness* of *laughing* is so great in *wise men*, that I think all *wise men*, if any *wise men* do read this *Paradox*, will *laugh* both at it and me.

XI

THAT THE GIFTS OF THE BODY ARE BETTER THAN THOSE OF THE MINDE

I S A Y again, that the *body* makes the *minde*, not that it created it a *minde*, but *forms* it a *good* or a *bad minde;* and this *minde* may be confounded with *soul* without any violence or injustice to *Reason* or *Philosophy:* then the *soul* it seems is enabled by our *Body*, not this by it. My *Body* licenseth my *soul* to *see* the worlds *beauties* through mine *eyes:* to *hear* pleasant things through mine *ears;* and affords it apt *Organs* for the conveiance of all perceivable *delight*. But alas! my *soul* cannot make any *part*, that is not of it self disposed to *see* or *hear*, though without doubt she be as able and as willing to see *behinde as before*. Now if my *soul* would say, that she enables any part to taste these *pleasures*, but is her selfe only delighted with those rich *sweetnesses* which her *inward eyes* and *senses* apprehend, shee should dissemble; for I see her often solaced with *beauties*, which shee sees through mine *eyes*, and with *musicke* which through mine *eares* she heares. This *perfection* then my *body* hath, that it can impart to my *minde* all his *pleasures;* and my *mind* hath still many, that she can neither teach my *indisposed* part her *faculties*, nor to the best *espoused* parts shew it *beauty* of *Angels*, of *Musicke*, of *Spheres*, whereof she boasts the *contemplation*. Are *Chastity*, *Temperance*, and *Fortitude* gifts of the *minde?* I appeale to *Physitians* whether the *cause* of these be not in the *body; health* is the gift of the *body,* and *patience* in sicknesse *the gift of the *minde:* then who will say that *patience* is as good a happinesse, as *health,* when wee must be extremely *miserable* to purchase this *happinesse.* And for nourishing of *civill societies* and *mutuall love* amongst men, which is our *chief end* while we are men; I say, this *beauty, presence,* and *proportion* of the *body,* hath a more *masculine* force in begetting this *love,* than the *vertues* of the *minde:* for it strikes us *suddenly,* and possesseth us *immoderately;* when to know those *vertues* requires some *Judgement* in him which shall discerne, a *long time* and *conversation* between them. And even at last how much of our *faith* and *beleefe* shall we be driven to bestow, to assure our selves that these *vertues* are not *counterfeited:* for it is the same to *be,* and *seem vertuous,* because that he that hath *no verture,* can *dissemble* none, but he which hath a *little,* may *gild* and *enamell,* yea and transforme much *vice* into *vertue:* For allow a man to be *discreet* and *flexible* to *complaints,* which are great *vertuous* gifts of the *minde,* this *discretion* will be to him the *soule* and *Elixir* of all *vertues,* so that touched with this, even *pride* shall be made *humility;* and *Cowardice,* honourable and wise *valour.* But in things seen there is not this danger, for the *body* which thou lovest and esteemest *faire,* is *faire:* certainly if it be not *faire* in *perfection,* yet it is *faire* in the same *degree* that thy *Judgment* is good. And in a *faire body,* I do seldom suspect a *disproportioned minde,* and as seldome hope for a good, in a *deformed.* When I see a *goodly house,* I assure my selfe of a *worthy possessour,* from a *ruinous weather-beaten building* I turn away, because it seems either stuffed with *varlets* as a *Prison,* or handled by an *unworthy* and *negligent tenant,* that so suffers the *wast* thereof. And truly the gifts of *Fortune,* which are *riches,* are only *handmaids,* yea *Pandars* of the *bodies pleasure;* with their service we nourish *health,* and preserve *dainty,* and wee buy *delights;* so that *vertue* which must be loved for *it selfe,* and respects no *further end,* is indeed *nothing:* And *riches,* whose *end* is the *good* of the *body,* cannot be so *perfectly good,* as the *end* whereto it levels.

XII

THAT VIRGINITY IS A VERTUE

I C A L L not that *Virginity a vertue,* which resideth onely in the *Bodies integrity;* much lesse if it be with a purpose of perpetuall keeping it: for then it is a most inhumane vice—But I call that *Virginity a vertue* which is willing and desirous to yield it selfe upon honest and lawful terms, when just reason requireth; and until then, is kept with a modest chastity of

Body and Mind. Some perchance will say that *Virginity* is in us by *Nature*, and therefore no *vertue*. True, as it is in us by *Nature*, it is neither a *Vertue* nor *Vice*, and is onely in the body: (as in Infants, Children, and such as are incapable of parting from it) But that *Virginity* which is in Man or Woman of perfect age, is not in them by *Nature: Nature* is the greatest enemy to it, and with most subtile allurements seeks the over-throw of it, continually beating against it with her *Engines*, and giving such forcible assaults to it, that it is a strong and more than ordinary *vertue* to hold out till marriage. *Ethick* Philosophy saith, *That no Vertue is corrupted, or is taken away by that which is good:* Hereupon some may say, that *Virginity* is therefore no *vertue*, being taken away by marriage. *Virginity* is no otherwise taken away by marriage, than is the light of the starres by a greater light (the light of the Sun:) or as a lesse Title is taken away by a greater (an Esquire by being created an Earle:) yet *Virginity* is a *vertue*, and hath her Throne in the middle: The extreams are, in *Excesse*, to violate it before marriage; in *Defect*, not to marry. In ripe years as soon as reason perswades and opportunity admits, These extreams are equally removed from the mean: The excesse proceeds from *Lust*, the defect from *Peevishness*, *Pride* and *Stupidity*. There is an old Proverb, That, *they that dy maids, must lead Apes in Hell*. An Ape is a ridiculous and an unprofitable Beast, whose flesh is not good for meat, nor its back for burden, nor is it commodious to keep an house: and perchance for the unprofitablenesse of this Beast did this proverb come up: For surely nothing is more unprofitable in the Commonwealth of *Nature*, than they that dy old maids, because they refuse to be used to that end for which they were only made. The Ape bringeth forth her young, for the most part by twins; that which she loves best, she killeth by pressing it too hard; so foolish maids soothing themselves with a false conceit of *vertue*, in fond obstinacie, live and die maids; and so not onely kill in themselves the *vertue* of *Virginity*, and of a *Vertue* make it a *Vice*, but they also accuse their parents in condemning marriage. If this appli-cation hold not touch, yet there may be an excellent one gathered from an Apes tender love to Conies in keeping them from the Weasel and Ferret. From this similitude of an Ape and an old Maid did the foresaid proverb first arise. But alas, there are some old Maids that are *Virgins* much against their wills, and fain would change their *Virgin-life* for a *Married:* such if they never have had any offer of fit Husbands, are in some sort excusable, and their willingnesse, their desire to marry, and their forbearance from all dishonest, and unlawfull copulation, may be a kind of inclination to *vertue*, although not *Vertue* it selfe. This *Vertue* of *Virginity* (though it be small and fruitlesse) it is an extraordinary, and no common *Vertue*. All other *Vertues* lodge in the *Will* (it is the *Will* that makes them vertues.) But it is the unwillingness to keep it, the desire to forsake it, that makes this a *vertue*. As in the naturall generation and formation made of the seed in the womb of a woman, the body is joynted and organized about the 28th day, and so it begins to be no more an *Embrion*, but capable as a matter prepared to its form to receive the soule, which faileth not to insinuate and innest it selfe into the body about the fortieth day; about the third month it hath motion and sense: Even so *Virginity* is an *Embrion*, an unfashioned lump, till it attain to a certain time, which is about twelve years of age in women, fourteen in men, and then it beginneth to have the soule of *Love* infused into it, and to become a *vertue:* There is also a certain limited time when it ceaseth to be a *vertue,* which in men is about fourty, in women about thirty years of age: yea, the loss of so much time makes their *Virginity* a *Vice,* were not their endeavour wholly bent, and their desires altogether fixt upon marriage: In Harvest time do we not account it a great vice of sloath and negligence in a Husband-man, to overslip a week or ten dayes after his fruits are fully ripe; May we not much more account it a more heynous vice, for a *Virgin* to let her Fruit (*in potentia*) consume and rot to nothing, and to let the *vertue* of her *Virginity* degenerate into *Vice,* (for *Virginity* ever kept is ever lost.) Avarice is the greatest deadly sin next Pride: it takes more pleasure in hoording Treasure than in making use of it, and will neither let the possessor nor others take benefit by it during the Misers life; yet it remains intire, and when the Miser dies must come to som body. *Virginity* ever kept, is a vice far worse than Avarice, it will neither let the possessor nor others take benefit by it, nor can it be bequeathed to any: with long keeping it decayes and withers, and becomes corrupt and nothing worth. Thus seeing that *Virginity* becomes a vice in defect, by exceeding a limited time; I counsell all female *Virgins* to make choyce of some *Paracelsian* for their Physitian, to prevent the death of that *Vertue:* The *Paracelsians* (curing like by like) say, That if the lives of living Creatures could be taken down, they would make us immortall. By this Rule, female *Virgins* by a discreet marriage should swallow down into their *Virginity* another *Virginity,* and devour such a life and spirit into their womb, that it might make them, as it were, immortall here on earth, besides their perfect immortality in heaven: And that *Vertue* which otherwise would putrifie and corrupt, shall then be compleat; and shall be recorded in Heaven, and enrolled here on Earth; and the name of *Virgin* shal be exchanged for a farre more honorable name, *A Wife.*

PROBLEMES

II

WHY PURITANS MAKE LONG SERMONS?

I T needs not for *perspicuousness,* for God knows they are plain enough: nor do all of them use *Sem-brief-Accents,* for some of them have *Crotchets* enough. It may be they intend not to rise like *glorious Tapers* and *Torches,* but like *Thin-wretched-sick-watching-Candles,* which *languish* and are in a Divine *Consumption* from the first minute, yea in their *snuff,* and *stink,* when others are in their more profitable *glory.* I have thought sometimes, that out of conscience, they allow *long measure* to *course ware.* And sometimes, that *usurping* in that *place* a *liberty* to *speak freely* of *Kings,* they would *reigne* as long as they could. But now I think they do it out of a *zealous* imagination, that, *It is their duty to Preach on till their Auditory wake.*

VI

WHY HATH THE COMMON OPINION AFFORDED WOMEN SOULES?

I T is agreed that we have not so much from them as any *part* of either our *mortal soules* of *sense* or *growth;* and we deny *soules* to others equall to them in all but in *speech* for which they are beholding to their *bodily instruments:* For perchance an *Oxes* heart, or a *Goates,* or a *Foxes,* or a *Serpents* would speake just so, if it were in the *breast,* and could move that *tongue* and *jawes.* Have they so many *advantages* and *means* to hurt us (for, ever their *loving* destroyed us) that we dare not *displease* them, but give them what they will? And so when some call them *Angels,* some Goddesses, and the [*Peputian*] *Hereticks* made them *Bishops,* we descend so much with the stream, to allow them *Soules?* Or do we some-what (in this dignifying of them) flatter *Princes* and *great Personages* that are so much governed by them? Or do we in that *easiness* and *prodigality,* wherein we daily lose our own *souls* to we care not whom, so labour to perswade our selves, that sith a *woman* hath a *soul,* a *soul* is no great matter? Or do we lend them *souls* but for use, since they for our sakes, give their *souls* again, and their *bodies* to boot? Or perchance because the *Devil* (who is all *soul*) doth most *mischief,* and for convenience and pro-portion, because they would come *nearer* him, we allow them some souls: and so as the *Romans* naturalized some *Provinces* in revenge, and made them *Romans,* only for the *burthen* of the *Common-wealth;* so we have given *women* souls only to make them capable of *Damnation?*

IX

WHY IS VENUS-STAR MULTINOMINOUS, CALLED BOTH *HESPERUS* AND *VESPER?*

T H E *Moone* hath as many *names,* but not as she is a *starre,* but as she hath divers *governments;* but *Venus* is *multinominous* to give example to her *prostitute disciples,* who so often, either to *renew* or *refresh* them selves towards *lovers,* or to *disguise* themselves from *Magistrates,* are to take *new names.* It may be she takes *new names* after her many *functions,* for as she is *Supreme* Monarch of all *Sunnes* at large (which is *lust*) so is she joyned in Commission with all *Mythologicks,* with *Juno, Diana,* and all others for *Marriage.* It may be because of the divers *names* to her self, for her *Affections* have more *names* than any *vice; scilicet: Pollution, Fornication, Adultery, Lay-Incest, Church-Incest, Rape, Sodomy, Mastupration, Masturbation,* and a thousand others. Perchance her divers *names* shewed her appliableness to divers men, for *Neptune* distilled and wet her in *Love,* the *Sunne* warms and melts her, *Mercury* perswaded and swore her, *Jupiters* authority secured, and *Vulcan* hammer'd her. As *Hesperus* she presents you with her *bonum utile,* because it is *wholesomest* in the *Morning:* As *Vesper* with her *bonum delectabile,* because it is *pleasantest* in the *Evening.* And because *industrious* men rise and endure with the *Sunne* in their *civill* businesses, this starre cals them up a little before, and remembers them again a little after for her business; for certainly,

Venit Hesperus, ite capellae:

was spoken to *lovers* in the persons of *Goats.*

XI

WHY DOTH THE POXE SOE MUCH AFFECT TO UNDERMINE THE NOSE?

Paracelsus perchance saith true, That every Disease hath his Exaltation in some part certaine. But why this in the Nose? Is there so much mercy in this desease, that it provides that one should not smell his own stinck? Or hath it but the common fortune, that being begot and bred in obscurest and secretest places, because therefore his serpentine crawling and insinuation should not be suspected, nor seen, he comes soonest into great place, and is more able to destroy the worthiest member, than a Disease better born? Perchance as mice defeat Elephants by knawing their *Proboscis,* which is their Nose, this wretched Indian Vermine practiseth to do the same upon us. Or as the ancient furious Custome and Connivency of some Lawes, that one might cut off their Nose whome he deprehended in Adulterie, was but a Tipe of this; And that now more charitable lawes having taken away all Revenge from particular hands, this common Magistrate and Executioner is come to doe the same Office invisibly? Or by withdrawing this conspicuous part, the Nose, it warnes us from all adventuring upon that Coast; for it is as good a marke to take in a flag, as to hang one out. Possibly heate, which is more potent and active than cold, thought her selfe injured, and the Harmony of the world out of tune, when cold was able to shew the high-way to Noses in *Muscovia,* except she found the meanes to doe the same in other countries. Or because by the consent of all, there is an Analogy, Proportion and affection between the Nose and that part where this disease is first contracted, and therefore *Heliogabalus* chose not his Minions in the Bath but by the Nose; And *Albertus* had a knavish meaning when he prefered great Noses; And the licentious Poet was *Naso Poeta.* I think this reason is nearest truth, That the Nose is most compassionate with this part: Except this be nearer, that it is reasonable that this Disease in particular should affect the most eminent and perspicuous part, which in general doth affect to take hold of the most eminent and conspicuous men.

XVI

WHY ARE COURTIERS SOONER ATHEISTS THAN MEN OF OTHER CONDITIONS?

I s it because as *Physitians* contemplating Nature, and finding many abstruse things subject to the search of Reason, think therfore that all is so; so they (seeing mens destinies, mad[e] at Court, neck[s] [put] out [in] joynt there, *War, Peace, Life* and *Death* derived from thence) climb no higher? Or doth a familiarity with greatness, and daily conversation and acquaintance with it breed a contempt of all greatness? Or because that they see that opinion or need of one another, and fear makes the degrees of servants, Lords and Kings, do they think that God likewise for such Reason hath been mans Creator? Perchance it is because they see Vice prosper best there, and, burthened with sinne, doe they not, for their ease, endeavour to put off the feare and Knowledge of God, as facinorous men deny Magistracy? Or are the most Atheists in that place, because it is the foole that said in his heart, There is no God.

Miscellaneous Prose

NEWES FROM THE VERY COUNTREY

T H A T it is a fripery of Courtiers, Merchants and others, which have been
in fashion, and are very neere worne out. That Justices of peace have the
felling of underwoods, but the Lords have the great falls.

That Jesuits are like Apricocks, heretofore here and there one succour'd
in a great man's house, and cost deare, now you may have them for nothing in every cottage.

That every great vice is a Pike in a pond, that devoures vertues and lesse
vices.

That it is wholsomest getting a stomacke, by walking on your own
ground: and the thriftiest laying of it at another's table.

That debtors are in *London* close prisoners, and here have the libertie of
the house.

That *Atheists* in affliction, like blind beggars, are forced to aske though
they know not of whom.

That there are (God be thanked) not two such acres in all the country,
as the *Exchange* and *Westminster-hall*.

That only Christmas Lords know their ends.

That weomen are not so tender fruit, but that they doe as well and beare
as well upon beds, as plashed against walls.

That our carts are never worse employed, than when they are wayted on
by coaches.

That sentences in Authors, like haires in an horse-taile, concurre in one
roote of beauty and strength, but being pluckt out one by one, serve only
for springes and snares.

That both want and abundance equally advance a rectified man from the
world, as cotton and stones are both good casting for an hawke.

That I am sure there is none of the forbidden fruit left, because we doe
not all eat thereof.

That our best three pilde mischiefe comes from beyond the sea, and rides
post through the country, but his errand is to Court.

That next to no wife and children, your owne wife and children are best pastime, anothers wife and your children worse, your wife and anothers children worst.

That Statesmen hunt their fortunes, and are often at default: Favorites course her and are ever in view.

That intemperance is not so unwholesome heere, for none ever saw Sparrow sicke of the pox.

That here is no trechery nor fidelity, but it is because here are no secrets.

That Court motions are up and down, ours circular; theirs like squibs cannot stay at the highest, nor return to the place which they rose from, but vanish and weare out in the way, Ours are like mill-wheels busie without changing place; they have peremptorie fortunes, we vicissitudes.

THE CHARACTER OF A SCOT AT THE FIRST SIGHT

A T his first appearing in the *Charterhouse,* an Olive coloured Velvet suit owned him, which since became mous-colour, A pair of unskour'd stockings-gules, One indifferent shooe, his band of *Edenburgh,* and cuffs of *London,* both strangers to his shirt, a white feather in a hat that had bin sod, one onely cloak for the rain, which yet he made serve him for all weathers: A Barren-half-acre of Face, amidst whereof an eminent Nose advanced himself, like the new Mount at *Wansted,* over-looking his Beard, and all the wilde Countrey thereabouts; He was tended enough, but not well; for they were certain dumb creeping Followers, yet they made way for their Master, the Laird. At the first presentment his Breeches were his Sumpter, and his Packets, Trunks, Cloak-bags, Portmanteaus and all; He then grew a Knight-wright, and there is extant of his ware at 100 l. 150 l. and 200 l. price. Immediately after this, he shifteth his suit, so did his Whore, and to a Bear-baiting they went, whither I followed them not, but *Tom. Thorney* did.

THE TRUE CHARACTER OF A DUNCE

H E hath a soule drowned in a lumpe of flesh, or is a peece of earth that *Prometheus* put not halfe his proportion of fire into. A thing that hath neither edge of desire, nor feeling of affection in it; the most dangerous creature for confirming an Atheist, who would sweare his soule were nothing but the bare temperature of his body. He sleepes as hee goes, and his thoughts seldome reach an inch further than his eies. The most part of the faculties of his soule lie fallow, or are like the restive Jades, that no spur can drive forwards towards the pursuit of any worthy designes. One of the most unprofitable of Gods creatures being as he is, a thing put cleane besides the right use, made fit for the cart and the flayle; and by mischance intangled amongst books and papers. A man cannot tell possibly what hee is now good for, save to move up and downe and fill roome, or to serve as *animatum instrumentum* for others to worke withall in base imployments, or to be foile for better wits, or to serve (as they say Monsters doe) to set out the varietie of nature, and ornament of the universe. Hee is meere nothing of himselfe, neither eats, nor drinkes, nor goes, nor spits, but by Imitation, for all which he hath set-formes and fashions, which he never varies, but stickes to with the like plodding constancie, that a mill-horse followes his trace. But the Muses and the Graces are his hard Mistresses, though he daily invocate them, though he sacrifice *Hecatombs,* they still look asquint. You shall note him oft (besides his dull eye, and lowring head, and a certain clammy benummed pace) by a faire displaied beard, a night cap, and a gowne, whose very wrinckles proclaime him the true *Genius* of formalitie. But of all others, his discourse, and compositions best speake him, both of them are much of one stuffe and fashion. He speaks just what his bookes or last company said unto him, without varying one whit, and very seldome understands himselfe. You may know by his discourse where he was last: for what he heard or read yesterday, hee now dischargeth his memory or Note-booke of, not his understanding, for it never came there. What hee hath, he flings abroad at all adventures without accomodating it to time, place, persons, or occasions. He commonly loseth himselfe in his tale, and flutters up and downe windlesse without recovery, and whatsoever next presents it selfe, his heavy conceit seizeth upon, and goeth along with, how ever *Heterogeneall* to his matter in hand. His Jests are either old flead *Proverbs,* or leane-sterv'd-hackney-*Apophthegmes,* or poore verball quips, outworne by Servingmen, Tapsters, and Milkemaids, even laid aside by Balladers. He assents to all men that bring any shadow of reason, and you may make him when he speakes most Dogmatically, even with one breath, to averre poore contradictions. His compositions differ onely *terminorum positione,* from dreames; nothing but rude heaps of immaterial, incoherent, drossie, rubbish stuffe, promiscuously thrust up together. Enough to infuse dulnesse and barrennesse of conceit into him that is so prodigall of his eares as to give the hearing. Enough to make a mans memory ake with suffering such durty stuffe cast into it. As unwelcome to any true conceit, as sluttish morsels, or wallowish potions to a nice stomacke, which whiles he empties himselfe of, it stickes in his teeth, nor can hee bee delivered without sweat, and sighes, and hems, and coughs, enough to shake his Grandams teeth out of her head. He spits, and scratches, and spawles, and turnes like sick men from one elbow to another, and deserves as much pitty during his torture, as men in fits of *Tertian fevers* or selfe-lashing Penitentiaries. In a word, rippe him quite asunder, and examine every shred of him, you shall find him to bee just nothing, but the subject of nothing; the object of contempt; yet such as hee is you must take him, for there is no hope he should ever become better.

AN ESSAY OF VALOUR

I AM of opinion, that nothing is so potent either to procure, or merit Love, as Valour, and I am glad I am so, for thereby I shall doe my selfe much ease. Because valour never needs much wit to maintain it. To speak of it in it selfe, It is a quality which he that hath, shall have least need of: so the best league betweene Princes, is a mutuall feare of each other. It teacheth a man to value his reputation as his life, and chiefely to hold the lie insufferable, though being alone hee findes no hurt it doth him. It leaves it selfe to others censures. For he that brags of his owne, disswades others from beleeving it. It feareth a Sword no more than an Ague, It alwaies makes good the owner, for though he be generally held a foole, hee shall seldome heare so much by word of mouth; and that inlargeth him more than any spectacles, for it maketh a little fellow be called a *Tall-man*. It yeelds the wall to none but a woman, whose weaknesse is her prerogative; or a man seconded with a woman, as an Usher which alwaies goes before his betters. It makes a man become the witnesse of his owne wordes, and stand to what ever he hath said, and thinketh it a reproach to commit his reviling unto the Law. It furnisheth youth with action, and age with discourse, and both by futures; for a man must ever boast himself in the present tense. And to come neerer home, nothing drawes a woman like to it, for valour towards men, is an Embleme of an Ability towards women, a good quality signifies a better: Nothing is more behoovefull for that Sexe; for from it they receive protection, and we free from the danger of it: Nothing makes a shorter cut to obteyning, for a man of armes is alwaies void of ceremonie, which is the wall that stands betwixt *Piramus* and *Thisbe,* that is, Man and Woman, for there is no pride in women but that which rebounds from our owne basenesse (as cowards grow valiant upon those that are more cowards) so that onely by our pale asking, we teach them to deny. And by our shamefac'tnesse, wee put them in minde to bee modest: whereas indeed it is cunning Rhetoricke to perswade the hearers that they are that already, which he would have them to be. This kinde of bashfulness is far from men of valour, and especially from souldiers, for such are ever men (without doubt) forward, and confident, losing no time lest they should lose opportunity, which is the best Factor for a Lover. And because they know women are given to dissemble; they will never beleeve them when they deny. Whilome before this age of wit, and wearing black broke in upon us, there was no way knowne to win a Lady, but by Tilting, Tournying, and Riding through Forrests, in which time these slender striplings with little legs, were held but of strength enough to marie their widowes. And even in our daies there can be given no reason of the inundation of servingmen upon their mistresses, but onely that usually they carry their Mistrisses weapons, and his valour. To bee counted handsome, just, learned, or well favoured; all this carries no danger with it, but it is to bee admitted to the title of valiant Acts, at least the venturing of his mortality, and al women take delight to hold him safe in their armes, who hath escaped thither through many dangers. To speak at once, man hath a privilege in valour; In clothes and good faces we but imitate women, and many of that sexe will not thinke much (as far as an answer goes) to dissemble wit too. So then these neat youths, these women in mens apparell, are too neere a woman to bee beloved of her, they bee both of a Trade, but be of grim aspect, and such a one a Glass dares take, and she will desire him for newnesse and variety. A skar in a mans face is the same that a mole in a womans, and a mole in a womans, is a Jewell set in white to make it seeme more white; For a skar in a man is a marke of honour, and no blemish; for 'tis a skarre and a blemish in a Souldier to be without one. Now as for all things else, which are to procure Love, as a good face, wit, cloathes, or a good body; each of them I confesse may worke somewhat for want of a better, that is, *if valour be not their Ryvall*. A good face availes nothing if it be in a coward that is bashfull, the utmost of it is to be kissed, which rather increaseth than quencheth Appetite. Hee that sendes her guifts, sends her word also that he is a man of small guifts otherwise: for wooing by signes and tokens, implies the author dumbe. And if *Ovid* who writ the Law of Love, were alive (as hee is extant) would allow it as good a diversitie, that gifts should bee sent as gratuities, not as bribes. Wit getteth rather promise than Love. Wit is not to bee seene: and no woman takes advice of any in her loving; but of her own eies, and her wayting womans: Nay which is worse, wit is not to be felt, and so no good Bed fellow: Wit applied to a woman makes her dissolve her sympering, and discover her teeth with laughter, and this is surely a purge for love; for the beginning of love is a kind of foolish melancholly. As for the man that makes his Taylor his Bawd, and hopes to inveagle his love with such a coloured suite, surely the same deepely hazards the losse of her favour upon every change of his cloathes. So likewise for the other that courts her silently with a good Body, let me certifie him that his cloathes depend upon the comlinesse of his body, and so both upon opinion. Shee that hath beene seduced by apparell, let me give her to wit, that men alwaies put off their cloathes before they goe to bed. And let her that hath been enamoured of her servants body, understand, that if she saw him in a skinne of cloath, that is, in a Suit made to the patterne of his body, she would see slender cause to love him ever after. There is no cloathes sit so well in a womans eye, as a Suit of steele, though not of the fashion, and no man so soone surpriseth a womans affections, as he that is the subject of all whispering, and hath alwaies twenty stories of his owne deedes depending upon him. Mistake me not, I understand not by valour, one that never fights, but when he is backed with drinke or anger, or hissed on with beholders, nor one that is desperate, nor one that takes away a Servingmans weapons, when perchance it cost him his Quarters wages, nor yet one that weares a privie coat of defence and therein is confident for then such as made Bucklers would bee counted the Catalines of the Commonwealth. I intend one of an even Resolution grounded upon reason: which is alwaies even, having his power restrained by the Law of not doing wrong. But now I remember I am for valour, and therefore must bee a man of few words.

PREFACE TO ΒΙΑΘΑΝΑΤΟΣ

*Declaring the Reasons, the Purpose, the way, and
the end of the author.*

BEZA, a man as eminent and illustrious, in the full glory and Noone of Learning, as others were in the dawning, and Morning, when any, the least sparkle was notorious, confesseth of himself, that only for the anguish of a Scurffe, which over-ranne his head, he had once drown'd himselfe from the Miller's bridge in Paris, if his Uncle by chance had not then come that way; I have often such a sickly inclination. And, whether it be, because I had my first breeding and conversation with men of suppressed and afflicted Religion, accustomed to the despite of death, and hungry of an imagin'd Martyrdome; Or that the common Enemie find that doore worst locked against him in mee; Or that there bee a perplexitie and flexibility in the doctrine it selfe; Or because my Conscience ever assures me, that no rebellious grudging at Gods gifts, nor other sinfull concurrence accompanies these thoughts in me, or that a brave scorn, or that a faint cowardlinesse beget it, whensoever any affliction assails me, mee thinks I have the keyes of my prison in mine owne hand, and no remedy presents it selfe so soone to my heart, as mine own sword. Often Meditation of this hath wonne me to a charitable interpretation of their action, who dy so: and provoked me a little to watch and exagitate their reasons, which pronounce so peremptory judgements upon them.

A devout and godly man, hath guided us well, and rectified our uncharitablenesse in such cases, by this remembrance, [Scis lapsum etc. *Thou knowest this mans fall, but thou knowest not his wrastling; which perchance was such, that almost his very fall is justified and accepted of God.*] For, to this end, saith one, [*God hath appointed us tentations, that we might have some excuse for our sinnes, when he calls us to account.*]

An uncharitable mis-interpreter unthriftily demolishes his own house, and repaires not another. He loseth without any gaine or profit to any. and, as Tertullian comparing and making equall, him which provokes another, and him who will be provoked by another, sayes, [*There is no difference, but that the provoker offended first, And that is nothing, because in evill there is no respect of Order or Prioritie.*] So wee may soone become as ill as any offendor, if we offend in a severe increpation of the fact. For, Climachus in his Ladder of Paradise, places these two steps very neere one another, when hee sayes, [*Though in the world it were possible for thee, to escape all defiling by actuall sinne, yet by judging and condemning those who are defiled, thou art defiled.*] In this thou are defiled, as *Basil* notes, [*That in comparing others sinnes, thou canst not avoid excusing thine owne*] Especially this is done, if thy zeale be too fervent in the reprehension of others: For, as in most other Accidents, so in this also, Sinne hath the nature of Poyson, that [*It enters easiest, and works fastest upon cholerique constitutions.*] It is good counsell of the Pharises stiled, [*Ne judices proximum, donec ad ejus locum pertingas.*] Feele and wrastle with such tentations as he hath done, and thy zeale will be tamer. For, [*Therefore* (saith the Apostle) *it became Christ to be like us, that he might be mercifull.*] If therefore after a Christian protestation of an innocent purpose herein, And after a submission of all which is said, not only to every Christian Church, but to every Christian man, and after an entreaty, that the Reader will follow this advice of Tabaeus, [*Qui litigant, sint ambo in conspectu tuo mali et rei,*] and trust neither me, nor the adverse part, but the Reasons, there be any scandall in this enterprise of mine, it is Taken, not Given. And though I know, that the malitious prejudged man, and the lazy affectors of ignorance, will use the same calumnies and obtrectations toward me, (for the voyce and sound of the Snake and Goose is all one) yet because I thought, that as in the poole of *Bethsaida*, there was no health till the water was troubled, so the best way to finde the truth in this matter, was to debate and vexe it, (for [We must as well dispute de veritate, *as* pro veritate,]) I abstained not for feare of mis-interpretation from this undertaking. Our stomachs are not now so tender, and queasie, after so long feeding upon solid Divinity, nor we so umbragious and startling, having been so long enlightened in Gods pathes, that wee should thinke any truth strange to us, or relapse into that childish age, in which a Councell in France forbad *Aristotles Metaphysiques*, and punished with Excommunication the excribing, reading, or having that booke.

Contemplative and bookish men, must of necessitie be more quarrelsome than others, because they contend not about matter of fact, nor can determine their controversies by any certaine witnesses, nor judges. But as long as they goe towards peace, that is Truth, it is no matter which way. The tutelare Angels resisted one another in *Persia*, but neither resisted Gods revealed purpose. *Hierome* and *Gregorie* seem to be of opinion, that *Solomon* is damned; *Ambrose* and *Augustine*, that he is saved: All Fathers, all zealous of Gods glory. At the same time when the *Romane* Church canonized *Becket*, the Schooles of *Paris* disputed whether hee could be saved; both Catholique Judges, and of reverend authoritie. And after so many Ages of a devout and religious celebrating the memory of Saint *Hierome*, *Causaeus* hath spoken so dangerously, that *Campian* saies, hee pronounceth him to be as deepe in hell as the Devil. But in all such intricacies, where both opinions seem equally to conduce to the honor of God, his Justice being as much advanced in the one, as his Mercie in the other, it seemes reasonable to me, that this turne the scales, if on either side there appeare charity towards the poore soul departed. The Church in her Hymnes and Antiphones, doth often salute the Nayles and the Crosse, with Epithets of sweetnesse, and thanks; But the Speare which pierced Christ when he was dead, it ever calles *dirum Mucronem*.

This pietie, I protest againe, urges me in this discourse; and what infirmity soever my reasons may have, yet I have comfort in Trismegistus Axiome, [*Qui pius est, summè Philosophatur.*] And therefore without any disguising, or curious and libellous concealing, I present and object it, to all of candour, and indifferencie, to escape that just taxation, [*Novum malitiae genus est, et intemperantis, scribere quod occultes.*] For as, when *Ladislaus* tooke occasion of the great schisme, to corrupt the nobility in Rome, and hoped thereby to possesse the towne, to their seven Governours whom they called *Sapientes* they added three more, whom they called *Bonos*, and confided in them; So doe I wish, and as much as I can, effect, that to those many learned and subtile men which have travelled in this point, some charitable and compassionate men might be added.

If therefore, of Readers, which *Gorionides* observes to be of foure sorts, [Spunges which attract all without distinguishing; Howre-glasses, which receive and powre out as fast; Bagges which retaine onely the dregges of the Spices, and let the Wine escape; And Sives, which retaine the best onely], I finde some of the last sort, I doubt not but they may bee hereby enlightened. And as the eyes of *Eve*, were opened by the taste of the Apple, though it bee said before that shee saw the beauty of the tree, So the digesting of this may, though not present faire objects, yet bring them to see the nakednesse and deformity of their owne reasons, founded upon a rigorous suspition, and winne them to be of that temper, which *Chrisostome* commends, [*He which suspects benignly would faine be deceived, and bee overcome, and is piously glad, when he findes it to be false, which he did uncharitably suspect.*] And it may have as much vigour (as one observes of another Author) as the Sunne in March; it may stirre and dissolve humors, though not expell them; for that must bee the worke of a stronger power.

Every branch which is excerpted from other authors, and engrafted here, is not written for the readers faith, but for illustration and comparison. Because I undertooke the declaration of such a proposition as was controverted by many, and therefore was drawne to the citation of many authorities, I was willing to goe all the way with company, and to take light from others, as well in the journey as at the journeys end. If therefore in multiplicity of not necessary citations there appeare vanity, or ostentation, or digression my honesty must make my excuse and compensation, who acknowledge as Pliny doth [*That to chuse rather to be taken in a theft, than to give every man due,* is obnoxii animi, et infelicis ingenii.] I did it the rather because scholastique and artificiall men use this way of instructing; and I made account that I was to deal with such, because I presume that naturall men are at least enough inclinable of themselves to this doctrine.

This my way; and my end is to remove scandall. For certainly God often punisheth a sinner much more severely, because others have taken occasion of sinning by his fact. If therefore wee did correct in our selves this easines of being scandalized, how much easier and lighter might we make the punishment of many transgressors! for God in his judgement hath almost made us his assistants, and counsellors, how far he shall punish; and our interpretation of anothers sinne doth often give the measure to Gods Justice or Mercy.

If therefore, since [*disorderly long haire which was pride and wantonnesse in* Absolon, *and squallor and horridnes in* Nebuchodonozor *was vertue and strength in* Samson, *and sanctification in* Samuel,] these severe men will not allow to indifferent things the best construction they are capable of, nor pardon my inclination to do so, they shall pardon me this opinion, that their severity proceeds from a self-guiltines, and give me leave to apply that of *Ennodius*, [*That it is the nature of stiffe wickednesse, to think that of others, which themselves deserve and it is all the comfort the guilty have, not to find any innocent.*]

THE THIRD PART

Of the

LAW OF GOD.

Distinction 1.   Sect. 1

That light which issues from the Moone, doth best represent and expresse that which in our selves we call the light of Nature; for as that in the Moone is permanent and ever there, and yet it is unequall, various, pale, and languishing, So is our light of Nature changeable. For being at the first kindling at full, it wayned presently, and by departing farther and farther from God, declined by generall sinne, to almost a totall Eclipse: till God comming neerer to us, first by the Law, and then by Grace, enlightened and repayred it againe, conveniently to his ends, and further exercise of his Mercy and Justice. And then those Artificiall Lights, which our selves make for our use and service here, as Fires, Tapers, and such, resemble the light of Reason, as wee have in our Second part accepted that Word. For though the light of these Fires and Tapers be not so naturall, as the Moone, yet because they are more domestique, and obedient to us, wee distinguish particular objects better by them, than by the Moone; So by the Arguments, and Deductions, and Conclusions, which our selves beget and produce, as being more serviceable and under us, because they are our creatures, particular cases are made more cleare and evident to us; for these we can behold withall, and put them to any office, and examine, and prove their truth, or likelihood, and make them answere as long as wee will aske; whereas the light of Nature, with a solemne and supercilious Majestie, will speake but once, and give no Reason, nor endure Examination.

But because of these two kindes of light, the first is too weake, and the other false, (for onely colour is the object of sight, and we not trust candlelight to discerne Colours) we have therefore the Sunne, which is the Fountaine and Treasure of all created light, for an Embleme of that third best light of our understanding, which is the Word of God. [*Mandatum lucerna, et Lex Lux*] sayes *Solomon*. But yet as weake credulous men thinke sometimes they see two or three Sunnes, when they see none but Meteors, or other apparances; so are many transported with like facilitie or dazeling, that for some opinions which they maintaine, they think they have the light and authority of Scripture, when, God knowes, truth, which is the light of Scriptures, is Diametrally under them, and removed in the farthest distance that can bee. If any small place of Scripture mis-appeare to them to bee of use for justifying any opinion of theirs; then (as the Word of God hath that precious nature of gold, that a little quantity thereof, by reason of a faithfull tenacity and ductilenesse, will be brought to cover 10000 times as much of any other metall,) they extend it so farre, and labour, and beat it, to such a thinnesse, as it is scarce any longer the Word of God, only to give their other reasons a little tincture and colour of gold, though they have lost all their waight and estimation.

But since the Scripture it self teaches, [*That no Prophecie in the Scripture, is of private interpretation,*] the whole Church may not be bound and concluded by the fancie of one, or of a few, who being content to enslumber themselves in an opinion, and lazy prejudice, dreame arguments to establish, and authorize that.

A professed interpreter of Dreames, tells us, [*That no Dreame of a private man may be interpreted to signifie a publique businesse.*] This I say because of those places of Scriptures, which are aledged for the Doctrine which we now examine, scarce any one, (except the Precept, *Thou shalt not kill*) is offered by any two Authors. But to one, one place, to another, another seemes directly to governe in the point, and to me, (to allow Truth her naturall and comely boldnesse) no place, but that seemes to looke towards it.

And therefore in going over all those sentences, which I have gathered from many Authors, and presenting convenient answers and interpretations thereof, I will forbeare the names of those Authors, who produced them so impertinently, least I should seeme to discover their nakednesse, or insimulate them even of prevarication.

If any Divine shall thinke the cause, or persons injured herein, and esteeme me so much worth reducing to the other opinion, as to apply an answer hereunto, with the same Charitie which provoked me, and which, I thanke God hath accompanied me from the beginning, I beseech him, to take thus much advantage from me and my instruction, that he will doe it without bitternesse. He shall see the way the better, and shew it the better and saile through it the better, if he raise no stormes.

Such men, as they are [*Fishers of men*], so may they also hunt us into their nets, for our good. But there is perchance, some mystique interpretation belonging to that Canon which allowes Clergy men to hunt; for they may doe it by Nets and Snares, but not by Dogges; for clamour and biting are forbidden them.

And I have been sorry to see, that even *Beza* himselfe, writing against an Adversary, and a cause equally and extreamly obnoxious, onely by allowing too much fuell to his zeale, enraged against the man, and neglecting, or but prescribing in the cause, hath with lesse thoroughnesse and satisfaction, than either became his learning and watchfulnesse, or answered his use and custome, given an answer to *Ochius* booke of *Polygamy.*

FIVE PRAYERS

FROM

ESSAYS IN DIVINITY

I

O ETERNALL and Almighty power, which being infinite, hast enabled a limited creature, Faith, to comprehend thee; And being, even to Angels but a passive Mirror and looking-glasse, art to us an Active guest and domestick, (for thou hast said, *I stand at the door and knock, if any man hear me, and open the doore, I will come in unto him, and sup with him, and he with me*), and so thou dwellst in our hearts; And not there only, but even in our mouths; for though thou beest greater and more remov'd, yet humbler and more communicable than the Kings of *Egypt,* or *Roman* Emperours, which disdain'd their particular distinguishing Names, for *Pharaoh* and *Caesar,* names of confusion; hast contracted thine immensity, and shut thy selfe within Syllables, and accepted a Name from us; O keep and defend my tongue from misusing that Name in lightnesse, passion, or falshood; and my heart, from mistaking thy Nature, by an inordinate preferring thy Justice before thy Mercy, or advancing this before that. And as, though thy self hadst no beginning thou gavest a beginning to all things in which thou wouldst be served and glorified; so, though this soul of mine, by which I partake thee, begin not now, yet let this minute, O God, this happy minute of thy visitation, be the beginning of her conversion, and shaking away confusion, darknesse, and barrennesse; and let her now produce Creatures, thoughts, words, and deeds agreeable to thee. And let her not produce them, O God, out of any contemplation, or (I cannot say, *Idæa*), but *Chimera* of my worthinesse, either because I am a man and no worme, and within the pale of thy

Church, and not in the wild forrest, and enlightned with some glimmerings of Naturall knowledge; but meerely out of Nothing: Nothing preexistent in her selfe, but by power of thy Divine will and word. By which, as thou didst so make Heaven, as thou didst not neglect Earth, and madest them answerable and agreeable to one another, so let my Soul's Creatures have that temper and Harmony, that they be not by a misdevout consideration of the next life, stupidly and trecherously negligent of the offices and duties which thou enjoynest amongst us in this life; nor so anxious in these, that the other (which is our better business, though this also must be attended) be the less endeavoured. Thou hast, O God, denyed even to Angells, the ability of arriving from one Extreme to another, without passing the mean way between. Nor can we pass from the prison of our Mothers womb, to thy palace, but we must walk (in that pace whereto thou hast enabled us) through the street of this life, and not sleep at the first corner, nor in the midst. Yet since my soul is sent immediately from thee, let me (for her return) rely, not principally, but wholly upon thee and thy word: and for this body, made of preordained matter, and instruments, let me so use the materiall means of her sustaining, that I neither neglect the seeking, nor grudge the missing of the Conveniences of this life: And that for fame, which is a mean Nature between them, I so esteem opinion, that I despise not others thoughts of me, since most men are such, as most men think they be: nor so reverence it, that I make it alwayes the rule of my Actions. And because in this world my Body was first made, and then my Soul, but in the next my soul shall be first, and then my body, In my Exterior and morall conversation let my first and presentest care be to give them satisfaction with whom I am mingled, because they may be scandaliz'd, but thou, which seest hearts, canst not: But for my faith, let my first relation be to thee, because of that thou art justly jealous, which they cannot be. Grant these requests, O God, if I have asked fit things fitly, and as many more, under the same limitations, as are within that prayer which (as thy *Manna*, which was meat for all tasts, and served to the appetite of him which took it, and was that which every man would) includes all which all can aske, *Our Father which art, etc.*

II

O ETERNALL God, as thou didst admit thy faithfull servant *Abraham*, to make the granting of one petition an incouragement and rise to another, and gavest him leave to gather upon thee from fifty to ten; so I beseech thee, that since by thy grace, I have thus long meditated upon thee, and spoken of thee, I may now speak to thee. As thou hast enlightened and enlarged me to contemplate thy greatness, so, O God, descend thou and stoop down to see my infirmities and the Egypt in which I live; and (If thy good pleasure be such) hasten mine *Exodus* and deliverance, for I desire to be, disolved, and be with thee. O Lord, I most humbly acknowledge and confess thine infinite Mercy, that when thou hadst almost broke the staff of bread, and called a famine of thy word almost upon all the world, then thou broughtest me into this Egypt, where thou hadst appointed thy stewards to husband thy blessings, and to feed thy flock. Here also, O God, thou hast multiplied thy children in me, by begetting and cherishing in me reverent devotions, and pious affections towards thee, but that mine own corruption, mine own *Pharaoh* hath ever smothered and strangled them. And thou hast put me in my way towards thy land of promise, thy Heavenly *Canaan,* by removing me from the Egypt of frequented and populous, glorious places, to a more solitary and desart retiredness, where I may more safely feed upon both thy Mannaes, thy self in thy Sacrament, and that other, which is true Angells food, contemplation of thee. O Lord, I most humbly acknowledge and confess, that I feel in me so many strong effects of thy Power, as only for the Ordinariness and frequency thereof, they are not Miracles. For hourly thou rectifiest my lameness, hourly thou restorest my sight, and hourly not only deliverest me from the Egypt, but raisest me from the death of sin. My sin, O God, hath not only caused thy descent hither, and passion here; but by it I am become that hell into which thou descendedst after thy Passion; yea, after thy glorification: for hourly thou in thy Spirit descendest into my heart, to overthrow there Legions of spirits of Disobedience, and Incredulity, and Murmuring. O Lord, I most humbly acknowledge and confesse, that by thy Mercy I have a sense of thy Justice; for not onely those afflictions with which it pleaseth thee to exercise mee, awaken me to consider how terrible thy severe justice is; but even the rest and security which thou affordest mee, puts me often into fear, that thou reservest and sparest me for a greater measure of punishment. O Lord, I most humbly acknowledge and confesse, that I have understood sin, by understanding thy laws and judgments; but have done against thy known and revealed will. Thou hast set up many candlesticks, and kindled many lamps in mee; but I have either blown them out, or carried them to guide me in by and forbidden ways. Thou hast given mee a desire of knowledge, and some meanes to it, and some possession of it; and I have armed my self with thy weapons against thee: Yet, O God, have mercy upon me, for thine own sake have mercy upon me. Let not sin and me be able to exceed thee, nor to defraud thee, nor to frustrate thy purposes: But let me, in despite of Me, be of so much use to thy glory, that by thy mercy to my sin, other sinners may see how much sin thou canst pardon. Thus show mercy to many in one: And shew thy power and al-mightinesse upon thy self, by casting manacles upon thine own hands, and calling back those Thunder-bolts which thou hadst thrown against me. Show thy Justice upon the common Seducer and Devourer of us all: and show us so much of thy Judgments, as may instruct, not condemn us. Hear us, O God, hear us, for this contrition which thou hast put into us, who come to thee with that watch-word, by which thy Son hath assured us of access. *Our Father which art in Heaven, &c.*

III

O ETERNALL God, who art not only first and last, but in whom, first and last is all one, who art not only all Mercy, and all Justice, but in whom Mercy and Justice is all one; who in the height of thy Justice, wouldst not spare thine own, and only most innocent Son; and yet in the depth of thy mercy, would'st not have the wretched'st liver come to destruction; Behold us, O God, here gathered together in thy fear, according to thine ordinance, and in confidence of thy promise, that when two or three are gathered together in thy name, thou wilt be in the midst of them, and grant them their petitions. We confess O God, that we are not worthy so much as to confess: less to be heard, least of all to be pardoned our manifold sins and transgressions against thee. We have betrayed thy Temples to prophaness, our bodies to sensuality, thy fortresses to thine enemy, our soules to Satan. We have armed him with thy munition to fight against thee, by surrendring our eyes, and eares, all our senses, all our faculties to be exercised and wrought upon, and tyrannized by him. Vanities and disguises have covered us, and thereby we are naked; licenciousness hath inflam'd us, and thereby we are frozen; voluptuousness hath fed us, and thereby we are sterved, the fancies and traditions of men have taught and instructed us, and thereby we are ignorant. These distempers, thou only, O God, who art true, and perfect harmonie, canst tune, and rectify, and set in order again. Doe so then, O most Merciful Father, for thy most innocent Sons sake: and since he hath spread his armes upon the cross, to receive the whole world, O Lord, shut out none of us (who are now fallen before the throne of thy Majesty and thy Mercy) from the benefit of his merits; but with as many of us, as begin their conversion and newness of life, this minute, this minute, O God, begin thou thy account with them, and put all that is past out of thy remembrance. Accept our humble thanks for all thy Mercies; and, continue and enlarge them upon the whole Church, etc.

IV

O MOST glorious and most gracious God, into whose presence our own consciences make us afraid to come, and from whose presence we cannot

hide our selves, hide us in the wounds of thy Son, our Saviour Christ
Jesus; And though our sins be as red as scarlet, give them there another
redness, which may be acceptable in thy sight. We renounce, O Lord, all
our confidence in this world; for this world passeth away, and the lusts
thereof: Wee renounce all our confidence in our own merits for we have
done nothing in respect of that which we might have done; neither could
we ever have done any such thing, but that still we must have remained
unprofitable servants to thee: we renounce all confidence, even in our
own confessions, and accusations of our self; for our sins are above
number, if we would reckon them; above weight and measure, if we would
weigh and measure them; and past finding out, if we would seek them in
those dark corners, in which we have multiplied them against thee: yea
we renounce all confidence even in our repentances; for we have found
by many lamentable experiences that we never perform our promises to
thee, never perfect our purposes in our selves, but relapse again and again
into those sins which again and again we have repented. We have no
confidence in this world, but in him who hath taken possession of the
next world for us, by sitting down at thy right hand. We have no confidence in our merits, but in him, whose merits thou hast been pleased to
accept for us, and to apply to us, we have: no confidence in our own
confessions and repentances, but in that blessed Spirit, who is the Author
of them, and loves to perfect his own works and build upon his own
foundations, we have: Accept them therefore, O Lord, for their sakes
whose they are; our poor endeavours, for thy glorious Sons sake, who
gives them their root, and so they are his; our poor beginnings of sanctification, for thy blessed Spirits sake, who gives their growth, and so they
are his: and for thy Sons sake, in whom only our prayers are acceptable
to thee: and for thy Spirits sake which is now in us, and must be so whensoever we do pray acceptably to thee; accept our humble prayers for, etc.

v

O ETERNALL and most merciful God, against whom, as we know and
acknowledge that we have multiplied contemptuous and rebellious sins,
so we know and acknowledge too, that it were a more sinfull contempt and
rebellion, than all those, to doubt of thy mercy for them; have mercy
upon us: In the merits and mediation of thy Son, our Saviour Christ Jesus,
be mercifull unto us. Suffer not, O Lord, so great a waste, as the effusion
of his blood, without any return to thee suffer not the expence of so rich
a treasure, as the spending of his life, without any purchace to thee; but
as thou didst empty and evacuate his glory here upon earth, glorify us
with that glory which his humiliation purchased for us in the kingdom of
Heaven. And as thou didst empty that Kingdome of thine, in a great part,

by the banishment of those Angels, whose pride threw them into ever-lasting ruine, be pleased to repair that Kingdom, which their fall did so far depopulate, by assuming us into their places, and making us rich with their confiscations. And to that purpose, O Lord, make us capable of that succession to thine Angels there; begin in us here in this life an angelicall purity, an angelicall chastity, an angelicall integrity to thy service, an Angelical acknowledgment that we alwaies stand in thy presence, and should direct all our actions to thy glory. Rebuke us not, O Lord, in thine anger, that we have not done so till now; but enable us now to begin that great work; and imprint in us an assurance that thou receivest us now graciously, as reconciled, though enemies; and fatherly, as children, though prodigals; and powerfully, as the God of our Salvation, though our own consciences testifie against us. Continue and enlarge thy blessings upon the whole Church, etc.

Insultus Morbi
Primus;

The first alteration, The first
grudging of the sicknesse.

I

VARIABLE, and therfore miserable condition of Man; this minute
I was well, and am ill, this minute. I am surpriz'd with a sodaine change,
and alteration to worse, and can impute it to no cause, nor call it by any
name. We study *Health,* and we deliberate upon our *meats,* and *drink,*
and *ayre,* and *exercises,* and we hew, and wee polish every stone, that goes
to that building; and so our *Health* is a long and regular work; But in
a minute a Canon batters all, overthrowes all, demolishes all; a *Sicknes*
unprevented for all our diligence, unsuspected for all our curiositie; nay,
undeserved, if we consider only *disorder,* summons us, seizes us, possesses
us, destroyes us in an instant. O miserable condition of Man, which was
not imprinted by *God,* who as hee is *immortall* himselfe, had put a *coale,*
a *beame* of *Immortalitie* into us, which we might have blowen into a *flame,*
but blew it out, by our first sinne; wee beggard our selves by hearkning
after false riches, and infatuated our selves by hearkning after false
knowledge. So that now, we doe not onely die, but die upon the Rack, die
by the torment of sicknesse; nor that onely, but are preafflicted, super-
afflicted with these jelousies and suspitions, and apprehensions of *Sicknes,*
before we can cal it a sicknes; we are not sure we are ill; one hand askes
the other by the pulse, and our eye asks our urine, how we do. O multiplied
misery! we die, and cannot enjoy death, because wee die in this torment of
sicknes; we art tormented with sicknes, and cannot stay till the torment
come, but preapprehensions and presages, prophecy those torments,
which induce that *death* before either come; and our dissolution is conceived in these *first changes, quickned* in the *sicknes* it selfe, and *borne* in
death, which beares date from these first changes. Is this the honour
which Man hath by being a *litle world,* That he hath these *earthquakes*
in him selfe, sodaine shakings; these *lightnings,* sodaine flashes; these
thunders, sodaine noises; these *Eclypses,* sodain offuscations, and dark-
nings of his senses; these *Blazing stars,* sodaine fiery exhalations; these
Rivers of blood, sodaine red waters? Is he a *world* to himselfe onely
therefore, that he hath inough in himself, not only to destroy, and execute
himselfe, but to presage that execution upon himselfe; to assist the sicknes,
to antidate the sicknes, to make the sicknes the more irremediable, by
sad apprehensions, and as if he would make a fire the more vehement,

by sprinkling water upon the coales, so to wrap a hote fever in cold Melancholy, least the fever alone should not destroy fast enough, without this contribution, nor perfit the work (which is *destruction*) except we joynd an artificiall sicknes, of our owne *melancholy*, to our natural, our unnaturall fever. O perplex'd discomposition, O ridling distemper, O miserable condition of Man!

Actio Laesa.   *The strength, and the function of the Senses, and other faculties change and faile.*

II

T H E *Heavens* are not the less constant, because they move continually, because they move continually one and the same way. The *Earth* is not the more constant, because it lyes stil continually, because continually it changes, and melts in al parts thereof. *Man*, who is the noblest part of the *Earth*, melts so away, as if he were a *statue*, not of *Earth*, but of *Snowe*. We see his owne *Envie* melts him, he growes leane with that; he will say, anothers *beautie* melts him; but he feels that a *Fever* doth not melt him like *snow*, but powr him out like *lead*, like *iron*, like *brasse* melted in a furnace: It doth not only *melt* him, but *calcine* him, reduce him to *Atomes*, and to *ashes;* not to *water*, but to *lime*. And how quickly? Sooner than thou canst receive an answer, sooner than thou canst conceive the question; *Earth* is the *center* of my *Bodie*, *Heaven* is the *center* of my *Soule;* these two are the naturall places of those two; but those goe not to these two in an equall pace: My *body* falls downe without pushing, my *Soule* does not go up without pulling: *Ascension* is my *Soules* pace and measure, but *precipitation* my *bodies:* And, even *Angells*, whose home is *Heaven*, and who are winged too, yet had a *Ladder* to goe to *Heaven*, by steps. The *Sunne* who goes so many miles in a minut, the *Starres* of the *Firmament*, which go so very many more, goe not so fast, as my *body* to the *earth*. In the same instant that I feele the first attempt of the disease, I feele the victory; In the twinckling of an eye, I can scarse see, instantly the tast is insipid, and fatuous; instantly the appetite is dull and desirelesse: instantly the knees are sinking and strengthlesse; and in an instant, sleepe, which is the *picture*, the *copie* of *death*, is taken away, that the *Originall*, *Death* it selfe may succeed, and that so I might have death to the life. It was part of *Adams* punishment, *In the sweat of thy browes thou shalt eate thy bread:* it is multiplied to me, I have earned bread in the sweat of my browes, in the labor of my calling, and I have it; and I sweat againe, and againe, from the brow, to the sole of the foot, but I eat no bread, I tast no sustenance: Miserable distribution of *Mankind,* where one halfe lackes meat, and the other stomacke.

Decubitus sequitur tandem. *The Patient takes his bed.*

III

WEE attribute but one priviledge and advantage to Mans body, above other moving creatures, that he is not as others, groveling, but of an erect, of an upright form, naturally built, and disposed to the contemplation of *Heaven*. Indeed it is a thankfull forme, and recompences that *soule,* which gives it, with carrying that soule so many foot higher, towards *heaven*. Other creatures look to the *earth;* and even that is no unfit object, no unfit contemplation for *Man;* for thither hee must come; but because, *Man* is not to stay there, as other creatures are, *Man* in his naturall forme, is carried to the contemplation of that place, which is his *home, Heaven*. This is *Mans* prerogative; but what state hath he in this *dignitie?* A fever can fillip him downe, a fever can depose him; a fever can bring that head, which yesterday caried a *crown* of gold, five foot towards a *crown* of glory, as low as his own foot, today. When *God* came to breath into *Man* the breath of life, he found him flat upon the ground; when he comes to withdraw that breath from him againe, hee prepares him to it, by laying him flat upon his bed. Scarse any prison so close, that affords not the prisoner two, or three steps. The *Anchorites* that barqu'd themselves up in hollowe trees, and immur'd themselves in hollow walls; that perverse man, that barrell'd himselfe in a Tubb, all could stand, or sit, and enjoy some change of posture. A sicke bed, is a grave; and all that the patient saies there, is but a varying of his owne *Epitaph*. Every nights bed is a *Type* of the *grave:* At night wee tell our servants at what houre wee will rise; here we cannot tell our selves, at what day, what week, what moneth. Here the head lies as low as the foot; the *Head* of the people, as lowe as they, whome those feete trod upon; And that hande that signed Pardons, is too weake to begge his owne, if he might have it for lifting up that hand: Strange fetters to the feete, strange Manacles to the hands, when the feete, and handes are bound so much the faster, by how much the coards are slacker; So much the lesse able to doe their Offices, by how much more the Sinews and Ligaments are the looser. In the *Grave* I may speak through the stones, in the voice of my friends, and in the accents of those wordes, which their love may afford my memory; Here I am mine owne *Ghost,* and rather affright my beholders, than instruct them; they conceive the worst of me now, and yet feare worse; they give me for dead now, and yet wonder how I doe, when they wake at midnight, and aske how I doe to morrow. Miserable and, (though common to all) inhuman *posture*, where I must practise my lying in the *grave*, by lying still, and not practise my *Resurrection*, by rising any more.

Medicusque vocatur.   *The Phisician is sent for.*

IV

I T is too little to call *Man* a *little World;* Except *God*, Man is a *diminutive* to nothing. Man consistes of more pieces, more parts, than the world; than the world doeth, nay than the world is. And if those pieces were extended, and stretched out in Man, as they are in the world, Man would bee the *Gyant,* and the Worlde the *Dwarfe,* the World but the *Map,* and the Man the *World.* If all the *Veines* in our bodies, were extended to *Rivers,* and all the *Sinewes,* to *Vaines of Mines,* and all the *Muscles,* that lye upon one another, to *Hilles,* and all the *Bones* to *Quarries* of stones, and all the other pieces, to the proportion of those which correspond to them in the world, the *Aire* would be too litle for this *Orbe* of Man to move in, the firmament would bee but enough for this *Starre;* for, as the whole world hath nothing, to which something in man doth not answere, so hath man many pieces, of which the whole world hath no representation. Inlarge this Meditation upon this *great world, Man,* so farr, as to consider the immensitie of the creatures this world produces; our *creatures* are our *thoughts, creatures* that are borne *Gyants;* that reach from *East* to *West,* from *Earth* to *Heaven,* that doe not onely bestride all the *Sea,* and *Land,* but span the *Sunn and Firmament* at once; My thoughts reach all, comprehend all. Inexplicable mistery; I their *Creator* am in a close prison, in a sicke bed, any where, and any one of my *Creatures,* my *thoughts,* is with the *Sunne,* and beyond the *Sunne,* overtakes the *Sunne,* and overgoes the *Sunne* in one pace, one steppe, everywhere. And then as the other *world* produces *Serpents,* and *Vipers,* malignant, and venimous creatures, and *Wormes,* and *Caterpillars,* that endeavour to devoure that world which produces them, and *Monsters* compiled and complicated of divers parents, and kinds, so this world, our selves, produces all these in us, in producing *diseases,* and *sicknesses,* of all those sort; venimous, and infectious diseases, feeding and consuming diseases, and manifold and entangled diseases, made up of many several ones. And can the other world name so many *venimous,* so many consuming, so many monstrous creatures, as we can diseases, of all these kindes? O miserable abundance, O beggarly riches! how much doe wee lacke of having *remedies* for everie disease, when as yet we have not *names* for them? But wee have a *Hercules* against these *Gyants*, these *Monsters;* that is, the *Phisician;* hee musters up al the forces of the other world, to succour this; all Nature to relieve Man. We *have* the *Phisician*, but we *are not* the *Phisician*. Heere we shrinke in our proportion, sink in our dignitie, in respect of verie meane creatures, who are *Phisicians* to themselves. The *Hart* that is pursued and wounded, they say, knowes an Herbe, which being eaten, throwes off the arrow: A strange kind of *vomit*. The *dog* that pursues it, though hee bee subject to sicknes, even *proverbially*, knowes his *grasse* that recovers him. And it may be true, that the *Drugger* is as neere to *Man*, as to other *creatures*, it may be that obvious and present *Simples*, easie to bee had, would cure him; but the *Apothecary* is not so neere him, nor the *Phisician* so neere him, as they two are to other creatures; Man hath not that *innate instinct*, to apply these naturall medicines to his present danger, as those inferiour creatures have; he is not his owne *Apothecary*, his owne *Phisician*, as they are. Call back therefore thy Meditation again, and bring it downe; whats become of mans great extent and proportion, when himselfe shrinkes himselfe, and consumes himselfe to a handfull of dust? whats become of his soaring thoughts, his compassing thoughts, when himselfe brings himselfe to the ignorance, to the thoughtlessnesse of the *Grave?* His *diseases* are his owne, but the *Phisician* is not; hee hath them at home, but hee must send for the *Phisician*.

Solus adest. *The Phisician comes.*

V

A s *Sicknes* is the greatest misery, so the greatest misery of sicknes, is *solitude;* when the infectiousnes of the disease deterrs them who should assist, from comming; even the *Phisician* dares scarse come. *Solitude* is a torment which is not threatned in *hell* it selfe. Meere *vacuitie*, the first *Agent, God*, the first *instrument* of *God, Nature*, will not admit; Nothing can be utterly *emptie*, but so neere a degree towards *Vacuitie*, as *Solitude*, to bee but one, they love not. When I am dead, and my body might infect, they have a remedy, they may bury me; but when I am but sick, and might infect, they have no remedy, but their absence, and my solitude. It is an *excuse* to them that are *great*, and pretend, and yet are loth to come; it is an *inhibition* to those who would truly come, because they may be made instruments, and pestiducts, to the infection of others, by their comming. And it is an *Outlawry*, an *Excommunication* upon the *Patient*, and seperats him from all offices not onely of *Civilitie*, but of *working Charitie*. A long sicknesse will weary friends at last, but a pestilentiall sicknes averts them from the beginning. *God* himself would admit a *figure* of *Society*, as there is a plurality of persons in *God*, though there bee but one *God*; and all his externall actions testifie a love of *Societie*, and *communion*. In *Heaven* there are *Orders* of *Angels*, and *Armies* of *Martyrs*, and *in that house, many mansions*; in *Earth, Families, Cities, Churches, Colleges*, all *plurall things*; and lest either of these should not be company enough alone, there is an association of both, a *Communion of Saints*, which makes the *Militant*, and *Triumphant Church*, one Parish; So that *Christ*, was not out of his *Dioces*, when hee was upon the *Earth*, nor out of his *Temple*, when he was in our flesh. *God*, who sawe that all that hee made, was good, came not so neer seeing a *defect* in any of his works, as when he saw that it was not good, for man to bee *alone*, therefore *hee made him a helper*; and one that should helpe him so, as to increase the *number*, and give him *her owne*, and *more societie*. *Angels*, who do not propagate, nor multiply, were made at the first in an abundant number; and so were starres: But for the things of this world, their blessing was, *Encrease*; for I think, I need not aske leave to think, that there is no *Phenix*; nothing singular, nothing alone: Men that inhere upon *Nature* only, are so far from thinking, that there is anything *singular* in this world, as that they will scarce thinke, that this world it selfe is *singular*, but that every *Planet*, and every *Starre*, is another *world* like this; They finde reason to conceive, not onely a *pluralitie* in every *Species* in the world, but a *pluralitie of worlds*; so that the abhorrers of *Solitude*, are not solitary; for *God*, and *Nature*, and *Reason* concurre against it. Now a man may counterfeyt the *Plague* in a *vowe*, and mistake a *Disease* for *Religion*; by such a retiring, and recluding of himselfe from all men, as to doe good to no man, to converse with no man. *God* hath two *Testaments*, two *Wils*; but this is a *Scedule*, and not of his, a *Codicill*, and not of his, not in the *body* of his *Testaments*, but *interlin'd*, and *postscrib'd* by others, that the way to the *Communion of Saints*, should be by such a *solitude*, as excludes all doing of good here. That is a *disease* of the *mind*; as the height of an infectious disease of the body, is *solitude*, to be left alone: for this makes an infectious bed, equall, nay worse than a *grave*, that thogh in both I be equally alone, in my bed I *know* it, and *feele* it, and shall not in my *grave*: and this too, that in my bedd, my soule is still in an infectious body, and shall not in my grave bee so.

Metuit.   *The Phisician is afraid.*

VI

I OBSERVE the *Phisician,* with the same diligence, as hee the *disease;* I see hee *feares,* and I feare with him: I overtake him, I overrun him in his feare, and I go the faster, because he makes his pace slow; I feare the more, because he disguises his fear, and I see it with the more sharpnesse, because hee would not have me see it. He knowes that his *feare* shall not disorder the practise, and exercise of his *Art,* but he knows that my *fear* may disorder the effect, and working of his practise. As the ill affections of the *spleene,* complicate, and mingle themselves with every infirmitie of the body, so doth *feare* insinuat it self in every *action,* or *passion* of the *mind;* and as the *wind* in the body will counterfet any disease, and seem the *stone,* and seem the *Gout,* so feare will counterfet any disease of the *Mind;* It shall seeme *love,* a love of having, and it is but a *fear,* a jealous, and suspitious feare of loosing; It shall seem *valor* in despising, and undervaluing danger, and it is but *feare,* in an overvaluing of *opinion,* and *estimation,* and a feare of loosing that. A man that is not afraid of a *Lion* is afraid of a *Cat;* not afraid of *starving,* and yet is afraid of some *joynt of meat* at the table, presented to feed him; not afraid of the sound of *Drummes,* and *Trumpets,* and *Shot,* and those, which they seeke to drowne, the last cries of men, and is afraid of some particular *harmonious instrument;* so much afraid, as that with any of these the *enemy* might drive this man, otherwise valiant enough, out of the field. I know not, what fear is, nor I know not what it is that I fear now; I feare not the hastening of my *death,* and yet I do fear the increase of the *disease;* I should belie *Nature,* if I should deny that I feared this, and if I should say that I feared *death,* I should belye *God;* My weaknesse is from *Nature,* who hath but her *Measure,* my strength is from *God,* who pos-sesses, and distributes infinitely. As then every cold ayre, is not a *dampe,* every *shivering* is not a *stupefaction,* so every *feare,* is not a *fearefulnes,* every declination is not a running away, every debating is not a resolving, every wish, that it were not thus, is not a murmuring, nor a dejection though it bee thus; but as my *Phisicians* fear puts not him from his *practise,* neither doth mine put me, from receiving from *God,* and *Man,* and *my selfe, spirituall,* and *civill,* and *morall* assistances, and consolations.

Socios sibi jungier instat.   *The Phisician desires to have*
                                          others joyned with him.

VII

THERE is *more feare*, therefore *more cause*. If the *Phisician* desire help,
the burden grows great: There is a growth of the *Disease* then; But
there must bee an *Autumne* to; But whether an *Autumne* of the *disease*
or *mee*, it is not my part to choose: but if it bee of *mee*, it is of *both;* My
disease cannot *survive mee*, I may *overlive* it. Howsoever, his desiring of
others, argues his *candor*, and his *ingenuitie;* if the danger be *great*, he
justifies his proceedings, and he *disguises* nothing, that calls in *witnesses;*
And if the danger bee not *great*, hee is not *ambitious*, that is so readie to
divide the thankes, and the honour of that work, which he begun alone,
with others. It diminishes not the dignitie of a *Monarch*, that hee derive
part of his care upon others; *God* hath not made many *Suns*, but he hath
made many *bodies*, that *receive*, and *give* light. The *Romanes* began
with *one King;* they came to *two Consuls;* they returned in extremities,
to *one Dictator:* whether in *one*, or *many*, the *Soveraigntie* is the same,
in all *States*, and the danger is not the more, and the providence is the
more, where there are more *Phisicians;* as the State is the happier, where
businesses are carried by more counsels, than can bee in one breast, how
large soever. *Diseases* themselves hold *Consultations*, and conspire how
they may multiply, and joyn with one another, and *exalt* one anothers
force, so; and shal we not call *Phisicians*, to *consultations? Death* is in
an olde mans dore, he appeares, and tels him so, and *death* is at a young
mans *backe*, and saies nothing; *Age* is a *sicknesse*, and *Youth* is an
ambush; and we need so many *Phisicians*, as may make up a *Watch*, and
spie every inconvenience. There is scarce any thing, that hath not killed
some body; a *haire*, a *feather* hath done it; Nay, that which is our best
Antidote against it, hath donn it; the best *Cordiall* hath bene *deadly
poyson;* Men have dyed of *Joy*, and allmost forbidden their friends to
weepe for them, when they have seen them dye laughing. Even that Tiran
Dyonisius (I thinke the same, that suffered so much after) who could
not die of that sorrow, of that high fal, from a *King* to a *wretched private
man*, dyed of so poore a *Joy*, as to be declard by the *people* at a *Theater*,
that hee was a good *Poet*. We say often that a *Man may live of a litle;*
but, alas, of how much lesse may a Man dye! And therfore the more assistants, the better; who comes to a day of hearing, in a cause of any im-
portance, with one *Advocate?* In our *Funerals*, we our selves have no interest; there wee cannot *advise*, we cannot *direct:* And though some *Nations*,
(the *Egiptians* in particular) built themselves better *tombs*, than *houses*,

because they were to dwell *longer* in them; yet, amongst our selves, the greatest *Man of Stile,* whom we have had, *The Conqueror,* was left, as soone as his soule left him, not only without persons to assist at his *grave,* but without a *grave.* Who will keepe us then, we know not; As long as we can, let us admit as much *helpe* as wee can; Another, and another *Phisician,* is not another, and another *Indication,* and *Symptom* of *death,* but another, and another *Assistant,* and *Proctor* of *life:* Nor doe they so much feed the imagination with apprehension of *danger,* as the under-standing with *comfort;* Let not one bring *Learning,* another *Diligence,* another *Religion,* but every one bring all, and, as many Ingredients enter into a Receit, so may many men make the Receit. But why doe I exer-cise my Meditation so long upon this, of having plentifull helpe in time of need? Is not my Meditation rather to be enclined another way, to condole, and commiserate their distresse, who have *none?* How many are sicker (perchance) than I, and laid on their wofull straw at home (if that corner be a home) and have no more hope of helpe, though they die, than of preferment, though they live? Nor doe no more expect to see a *Phisician* then, than to bee an *Officer* after; of whome, the first that takes knowledge, is the *Sexten* that buries them; who buries them in *oblivion* too? For they doe but fill up the number of the dead in the Bill, but we shall never heare their *Names,* till wee reade them in the Booke of life, with our owne. How many are sicker (perchance) than I, and thrown into *Hospitals,* where, (as a fish left upon the Sand, must stay the tide) they must stay the *Phisicians* houre of visiting, and then can bee but *visited?* How many are sicker (perchaunce) than all we, and have not this *Hospitall* to cover them, not this straw, to lie in, to die in, but have their *Grave-stone* under them, and breathe out then soules in the eares, and in the eies of passengers, harder than their bed, the flint of the street? That taste of no part of our *Phisick,* but a *sparing dyet;* to whom ordinary porridge would bee *Julip* enough, the refuse of our servants, *Bezar* enough, and the off-scouring of our Kitchen tables, *Cordiall* enough. O my *soule,* when thou art not enough awake, to blesse thy *God* enough for his plentifull mercy, in affoording thee many *Helpers,* remem-ber how many lacke them, and helpe them to them, or to those other things, which they lacke as much as them.

Et Rexi ipse   *The King sends his*
suum mittit.   *owne Phisician.*

VIII

s t i l l when we return to that *Meditation,* that *Man* is a *World,* we find new *discoveries.* Let him be a *world,* and him self will be the *land,* and *misery* the *sea*. His misery (for misery is his, his own; of the happinesses of this world hee is but *Tenant*, but of misery the *Free-holder;* of happines he is but the *farmer*, but the *usufructuary*, but of misery, the *Lord*, the *proprietary*) his misery, as the *sea*, swells above all the hilles, and reaches to the remotest parts of this *earth, Man;* who of himselfe is but *dust*, and coagulated and kneaded into earth, by *teares;* his *matter* is *earth*, his *forme, misery*. In this *world*, that is *Mankinde*, the highest ground, the eminentest *hils*, are *Kings;* and have they line, and lead enough to fadome this *sea*, and say, My misery is but this deepe? Scarce any misery equal to *sicknesse;* and they are subject to that equally, with their lowest subject. A glasse is not the lesse brittle, because a *Kings* face is represented in it; nor a King the lesse brittle, because *God* is represented in him. They have *Phisicians* continually about them, and therfore *sicknesses*, or the worst of sicknesses, continuall feare of it. Are they *gods?* He that calld them so, cannot flatter. They are *Gods*, but *sicke gods;* and *God* is presented to us under many human affections, as far as *infirmities; God* is called *Angry*, and *Sorry*, and *Weary*, and *Heavy;* but never a *sicke God:* for then hee might *die* like men, as our *gods* do. The worst that they could say in reproch, and scorne of the *gods* of the *Heathen*, was, that perchance they were *asleepe;* but *Gods* that are so sicke, as that they cannot sleepe, are in an infirmer condition. A *God*, and need a *Phisician?* A *Jupiter* and need an *Æsculapius?* that must have *Rheubarbe* to purge his *choller*, lest he be too angry, and *Agarick* to purge his *flegme*, lest he be too drowsie; that as *Tertullian* saies of the *Ægyptian gods*, *plants* and *herbes, That God was beholden to Man, for growing in his Garden*, so wee must say of these gods, *Their eternity*, (*an eternity* of three score and ten yeares) is in the *Apothecaryes* shop, and not in the *Metaphoricall Deity*. But their *Deitye* is better expressed in their *humility*, than in their *heighth;* when abounding and overflowing, as *God*, in means of doing good, they descend, as *God*, to a communication of their abundances with men, according to their necessities, then they are *Gods*. No man is well, that understands not, that values not his being well; that hath not a cheerefulnesse, and a joy in it; and whosoever hath this *Joy*, hath a desire to communicate, to propagate that, which occasions his happinesse, and his *Joy*, to others; for every man loves witnesses of his happinesse; and the best witnesses, are experimentall witnesses; they who have tasted of that in themselves, which makes us happie: It consummates therefore, it perfits the happinesse of *Kings*, to confer, to transfer, honor, and riches, and (as they can) health, upon those that need them.

Medicamina   *Upon their Consultation,*
scribunt.   *they prescribe.*

IX

T H E Y have seene me, and heard mee, arraign'd mee in these fetters, and
receiv'd the *evidence;* I have cut up mine *Anatomy,* dissected my selfe,
and they are gon to *read* upon me. O how manifold, and perplexed a
thing, nay, how wanton and various a thing is *ruine* and *destruction!*
God presented to *David* three kinds, *War, Famine,* and *Pestilence;*
Satan left out these, and brought in, *fires from heaven,* and *windes from*
the wildernes. [As] if there were no *ruine* but *sicknes,* wee see, the Masters of that *Art,* can scarce *number,* nor *name* all sicknesses; every thing
that *disorders* a faculty, and the function of that is a sicknesse: The
names wil not serve them which are given from the *place affected,* the
Plurisie is so; nor from the *effect* which it works, the *falling sicknes* is so;
they cannot have names enow, from *what it does,* nor *where it is,* but
they must extort names from what *it is like,* what it *resembles,* and but
in some one thing, or els they would lack names; for the *Wolf,* and the
Canker, and the *Polypus* are so; and that question, *whether there be*
more names or things, is as perplexd in sicknesses, as in any thing else;
except it be easily resolvd upon that side, that there are more *sicknesses*
than *names.* If *ruine* were reduc'd to that one way, that Man could perish
noway but by *sicknes,* yet his danger were infinit; and if *sicknes* were
reduc'd to that one way, that there were no *sicknes* but a *fever,* yet the
way were infinite still; for it would overlode, and oppress any naturall,
disorder and discompose any artificiall *Memory,* to deliver the *names* of
severall *fevers;* how intricate a worke then have they, who are gone to
consult, which of these *sicknesses* mine is, and then which of these *fevers,*
and then what it would do, and then how it may be countermind. But
even in *ill,* it is a degree of *good,* when the *evil* wil admit *consultation.*
In many *diseases,* that which is but an *accident,* but a *symptom* of the
main *disease,* is so violent, that the *Phisician* must attend the cure of
that, though hee pretermit (so far as to intermit) the cure of the *disease*
it self. Is it not so in *States* too? somtimes the insolency of those that are
great, put[s] the people into *commotions;* the great disease, and the
greatest danger to the *Head,* is the *insolency of the great ones;* and yet,
they execute *Martial law,* they come to present executions upon the
people, whose commotion was indeed but a *symptom,* but an *accident* of
the maine *disease;* but this *sympton,* grown so violent, would allow no
time for a *consultation.* Is it not so in the accidents of the *diseases* of our

mind too? Is it not evidently so in our *affections*, in our *passions?* If a *cholerick* man be ready to strike, must I goe about to purge his *choler*, or to breake the blow? But where there is room for *consultation*, things are not desperate. They *consult;* so there is nothing *rashly, inconsideratly* done; and then they *prescribe*, they *write*, so there is nothing *covertly, disguisedly, unavowedly* done. In *bodily diseases* it is not alwaies so; sometimes, as soon as the *Phisicians* foote is in the *chamber*, his *knife* is in the patients *arme;* the disease would not allow a *minutes* forbearing of *blood*, nor *prescribing* of other remedies. In States and matter of government it is so too; they are somtimes surprizd with such *accidents*, as that the *Magistrat* asks not what may be done by *law*, but does that, which must *necessarily* be don in that case. But it is a degree of *good*, in *evill*, a degree that carries hope and comfort in it, when we may have recourse to that which is *written*, and that the proceedings may be apert, and ingenuous, and candid, and avowable, for that gives satisfaction, and acquiescence. They who have received my *Anatomy* of my selfe, *consult*, and end their *consultation* in *prescribing*, and in prescribing *Phisick;* proper and convenient remedy: for if they should come in again, and chide mee, for some disorder, that had occasion'd, and inducd, or that had hastned and exalted this *sicknes*, or if they should begin to write now rules for my *dyet*, and *exercise* when I were well, this were to *antidate*, or to *postdate* their *Consultation*, not to give *Phisicke*. It were rather a vexation, than a reliefe, to tell a condemnd prisoner, you might have liv'd if you had done this; and if you can get pardon, you shal do wel, to take this, or this course hereafter. I am glad they know (I have hid nothing from them) glad they consult, (they hide nothing from one another) glad they write (they hide nothing from the world) glad that they write and prescribe *Phisick*, that there are *remedies* for the present case.

Lentè et Serpenti satagunt occurrere Morbo.	*They find the Disease to steale on insensibly, and endeavour to meet with it so.*

X

ᴛ ʜ ɪ s is *Natures nest of Boxes;* The Heavens containe the *Earth*, the *Earth, Cities, Cities, Men.* And all these are *Concentrique;* the common *center* to them all, is *decay, ruine;* only that is *Eccentrique*, which was never made; only that place, or garment rather, which we can *imagine*, but not *demonstrate*, That light, which is the very emanation of the light of *God*, in which the Saints shall dwell, with which the *Saints* shall be appareld, only that bends not to this *Center*, to *Ruine;* that which was not made of *Nothing*, is not threatned with this annihilation. All other things are; even *Angels*, even our *soules;* they move upon the same *poles*, they bend to the same *Center;* and if they were not made immortall by *preservation*, their *Nature* could not keep them from sinking to this *center*, *Annihilation*. In all these (the *frame of the heavens*, the *States upon earth*, and *Men in them*, comprehend all) Those are the greatest mischifs, which are least discerned; the most insensible in their *wayes* come to bee the most sensible in their *ends*. The *Heavens* have had their *Dropsie*, they drownd the world, and they shall have their *Fever*, and burn the world. Of the *dropsie*, the flood, the world had a foreknowledge 120 yeares before it came; and so some made provision against it, and were saved; the *fever* shall break out in an instant, and consume all; The *dropsie* did no harm to the *heavens*, from whence it fell, it did not put out those *lights*, it did not quench those *heates;* but the *fever*, the fire shall burne the *furnace* it selfe, annihilate those *heavens*, that breath it out; Though the *Dog-Starre* have a pestilent breath, an infectious exhalation, yet because we know when it wil rise, we clothe our selves, and wee diet our selves, and we shadow our selves to a sufficient prevention; but *Comets* and *blazing starres*, whose effects, or significations no man can interrupt or frustrat, no man foresaw: no *Almanack* tells us, when a *blazing starre* will break out, the matter is carried up in secret; no *Astrologer* tels us when the effects will be accomplished, for thats a secret of a higher spheare, than the other; and that which is most *secret*, is most *dangerous*. It is so also here in the *societies* of men, in *States*, and *Commonwealths*. Twentie *rebellious drums* make not so dangerous a noise, as a few *whisperers*, and secret plotters in corners. The *Canon* doth not so much hurt against a wal, as a *Myne* under the wall; nor a thousand enemies that threaten, so much as a few that take an *oath* to say *nothing*. *God* knew many heavy sins of the people, in the wildernes and after, but still he charges them with that one, with *Murmuring, murmuring* in their *hearts*, secret disobediences, secret repugnances against his declar'd wil; and these are the most deadly, the most pernicious. And it is so too, with the *diseases* of the *body;* and that is my case. The *pulse*, the *urine*, the *sweat*, all have sworn to say nothing, to give no *Indication*, of any dangerous *sicknesse*. My forces are not enfeebled, I find no decay in my strength; my provisions are not cut off, I find no abhorring in mine appetite; my counsels are not corrupted or infatuated, I find no false apprehensions, to work upon mine understanding; and yet they see, that invisibly, and I feele, that insensibly the *disease* prevailes. The *disease* hath established a *Kingdome,* an *Empire* in mee, and will have certaine *Arcana Imperii, secrets of State,* by which it will proceed, and not be bound to *declare* them. But yet against those secret conspiracies in the State, the *Magistrate* hath the *rack;* and against the insensible diseases, *Phisicians* have their *examiners;* and those these employ now.

Nobilibusque trahunt, a cincto Corde, venenum, Succis et Gemmis, et quæ generosa, Ministrant Ars, et Natura, instillant.	*They use Cordials, to keep the venim and Malignitie of the disease from the Heart.*

XI

WHENCE can wee take a better argument, a clearer demonstration, that all the *Greatnes* of this world, is built upon *opinion* of others, and hath in itself no *reall being,* nor power of subsistence, than from the *heart of man?* It is always in *action,* and *motion,* still busie, still pretending to doe all, to furnish all the powers, and faculties with all that they have; But if an enemy dare rise up against it, it is the soonest endangered, the soonest defeated of any part. The *Braine* will hold out longer than it, and the *Liver* longer than that; They will endure a *Siege;* but an unnatural heat, a rebellious heat, will blow up the *heart,* like a *Myne,* in a *minute.* But howsoever, since the *Heart* hath the *birthright* and *Primogeniture,* and that it is *Natures eldest Sonne* in us, the part which is first borne to life in man, and that the other parts, as *younger brethren,* and servants in this family, have a dependance upon it, it is reason that the principall care bee had of it, though it bee not the strongest part; as the *eldest* is oftentimes not the strongest of the family. And since the *Braine,* and *Liver,* and *Heart,* hold not a *Triumvirate* in *Man,* a *Soveraigntie* equally shed upon them all, for his *well-being,* as thě foure *Elements* doe, for his very *being,* but the *Heart* alone is in the *Principalitie,* and in the *Throne,* as *King,* the rest as *Subjects,* though in eminent *Place* and *Office,* must contribute to that, as *Children* to their *Parents,* as all persons to all kinds of *Superiours,* though oftentimes, those *Parents,* or those *Superiours,* bee not of stronger parts, than themselves, that serve and obey them that are weaker; Neither doth this Obligation fall upon us, by second *Dictates* of *Nature,* by *Consequences* and *Conclusions* arising out of *Nature,* or deriv'd from *Nature,* by *Discourse,* (as many things binde us even by the Law of *Nature,* and yet not by the *primarie* Law of *Nature;* as all Lawes of *Proprietie* in that which we possesse, are of the Law of *Nature,* which law is, *To give every one his owne,* and yet in the *primarie* law of Nature there was no *Proprietie,* no *Meum* and *Tuum,* but an universall *Com-*

munitie over all; So the Obedience of *Superiours,* is of the law of *Nature,* and yet in the *primarie* law of *Nature,* there was no *Superioritie,* no *Magistracie;*) but this contribution of assistance of all to the *Soveraigne,* of all parts to the *Heart,* is from the very *first dictates of Nature;* which is, in the first place, to have care of our owne *Preservation,* to look first to ourselves; for therefore doth the *Phisician* intermit the present care of *Braine,* or *Liver,* because there is a possibilitie that they may subsist, though there bee not a present and a particular care had of them, but there is no possibilitie that they can subsist, if the *Heart* perish: and so, when we seem to begin with others, in such assistances, indeed wee doe beginne with ourselves, and wee ourselves are principally in our contemplation; and so all these officious, and mutual assistances are but *complements* towards others, and our true end is *ourselves.* And this is the reward of the paines of *Kings;* sometimes they neede the power of law, to be obey'd; and when they seeme to be obey'd *voluntarily,* they who doe it, doe it for their owne sakes. O how little a thing is all the *greatnes of man,* and through how false glasses doth he make shift to *multiply it,* and *magnifie* it to himselfe! And yet this is also another misery of this *King of man,* the *Heart,* which is also applyable to the *Kings of this world, great men,* that the venime and poyson of every pestilentiall disease directs itself to the *Heart,* affects that (pernicious affection,) and the *malignity* of ill men, is also directed upon the *greatest,* and the *best;* and not only *greatnesse,* but *goodnesse* looses the vigour of beeing an *Antidote,* or *Cordiall* against it. And as the noblest, and most generous *Cordialls* that *Nature* or *Art* afford, or can prepare, if they be often taken, and made *familiar,* become no *Cordialls,* nor have any extraordinary operation, so the greatest *Cordiall* of the *Heart,* patience, if it bee much exercis'd, exalts the *venim* and the *malignity* of the *Enemy,* and the more we suffer, the more wee are insulted upon. When *God* had made this *Earth* of *nothing,* it was but a little helpe, that he had, to make other things of this *Earth:* nothing can be neerer nothing, than this *Earth;* and yet how little of this *Earth* is the *greatest Man!* Hee thinkes he treads upon the *Earth,* that all is under his feete, and the *Braine* that thinkes so, is but *Earth;* his highest Region, the flesh that covers that, is but *earth;* and even the toppe of that, that, wherein so many *Absolons* take so much pride, is but a bush growing upon that *Turfe of Earth.* How little of the world is the *Earth!* And yet that is all that *Man hath,* or *is.* How little of a *Man* is the *Heart,* and yet it is all, by which he *is;* and this continually subject, not only to forraine poysons, conveyed by others, but to intestine poysons, bred in ourselves by pestilentiall sicknesses. O who, if before hee had a beeing, he could have sense of this miserie, would buy a being here upon these conditions?

Spirante Columbâ	*They apply Pidgeons, to*
Suppositâ pedibus, Revocantur	*draw the vapors from*
ad ima vapores.	*the Head.*

XII

W H A T will not kill a man if a *vapor* will? How great an *Elephant,* how small a *Mouse* destroys! To dye by a *bullet* is the *Souldiers dayly bread;* but few men dye by *haile-shot:* A man is more worth, than to bee sold for *single money;* a *life* to be valued above a *trifle.* If this were a violent shaking of the Ayre by *Thunder,* or by *Canon,* in that case the *Ayre* is condensed above the thicknesse of *water,* of *water* baked into *Ice,* almost *petrified,* almost made stone, and no wonder that kills; but that that which is but a *vapor,* and a *vapor* not forced, but breathed, should kill, that our *Nourse* should overlay us, and *Ayre* that nourishes us, should destroy us, but that it is a *halfe Atheisme* to murmure against *Nature,* who is *Gods immediate commissioner,* who would not think himselfe miserable to bee put into the hands of *Nature,* who does not only set him up for a *marke* for others to shoote at, but delights herselfe to blow him up like a glasse, till shee see him breake, even with her owne breath? nay, if this infectious *vapor* were sought for, or travail'd to, as *Plinie* hunted after the *vapor* of *Ætna,* and dared and challenged *Death,* in the forme of a vapor, to doe his worst, and felt the worst, he dyed; or if this *vapor* were met withall in an *ambush,* and we surprized with it, out of a long shutt *Well,* or out of a new opened *Myne,* who would lament, who would accuse, when we had nothing to accuse, none to lament against but *Fortune,* who is lesse than a *vapor:* But when our selves are the *Well,* that breaths out this exhalation, the *Oven* that spits out this fiery smoke, the *Myne* that spues out this suffocating, and strangling *dampe,* who can ever after this, aggravate his sorrow, by this *Circumstance,* That it was his *Neighbor,* his *familiar Friend,* his *Brother,* that destroyed him, and destroyed him with a whispering, and a calumniating breath, when wee our selves doe it to our selves by the same meanes, kill our selves with our owne *vapors?* Or if these occasions of this selfe-destruction, had any contribution from our owne *Wils,* any assistance from our owne *intentions,* nay from our own *errors,* we might divide the rebuke, and chide our selves as much as them. *Fevers* upon wilful distempers of drinke, and surfets, *Consumptions* upon intemperances, and licentiousnes, *Madnes* upon misplacing, or over-bending our naturall faculties, proceed from our selves, and so, as that our selves are in the plot, and wee are not onely *passive,* but *active* too, to our owne destruction; But what have I done, either to *breed*, or to *breath* these *vapors?* They tell me it is my *Melancholy;* Did I infuse, did I drinke in *Melancholly* into my selfe? It is my *thoughtfulnesse;* was I not made to *thinke?* It is my *study;* doth not my *Calling* call for that? I have don nothing, wilfully, perversly toward it, yet must suffer in it, die by it; There are too many *Examples* of men, that have bin their own *executioners*, and that have made hard shift to bee so; some have alwayes had *poyson* about them, in a *hollow ring* upon their finger, and some in their *Pen* that they used to write with: some have beat out their *braines* at the wal of their prison, and some have eate the *fire* out of their chimneys: and one is said to have come neerer our case than so, to have strangled himself, though his hands were bound, by crushing his throat between his knees; But I doe nothing upon my selfe, and yet am mine owne *Executioner*. And we have heard of *death* upon small occasions, and by scornefull *instruments:* a *pinne*, a *combe*, a *haire*, pulled, hath gangred, and killd; But when I have said, a *vapour*, if I were asked again, what is a *vapour*, I could not tell, it is so insensible a thing; so neere *nothing* is that that reduces us to *nothing*. But extend this *vapour*, rarifie it; from so narow a roome, as our *Naturall bodies*, to any *Politike body*, to a *State*. That which is *fume* in us, is in a *State, Rumor*, and these *vapours* in us, which wee consider here pestilent and infectious fumes, are in a State *infectious rumors*, detracting and dishonourable *Calumnies, Libels*. The *Heart* in that *body* is the *King;* and the *Braine*, his *Councell;* and the whole *Magistracie*, that ties all together, is the *Sinewes*, which proceed from thence; and the *life* of all is *Honour*, and just *respect*, and due *reverence;* and therfore, when these *vapors*, these venimous *rumors*, are directed against these *Noble parts*, the whole body suffers. But yet for all their priviledges, they are not priviledged from our *misery;* that as the *vapours* most pernitious to us, arise in our owne bodies, so do the most dishonorable *rumours*, and those that wound a *State* most, arise at home. What ill *ayre*, that I could have met in the street, what *Channell*, what *Shambles*, what *Dunghill*, what *vault*, could have hurt mee so much, as these home-bredd *vapours?* What *Fugitive*, what *Almes-man of any forraine State*, can doe so much harme as a *Detracter*, a *Libeller*, a scornefull *Jester* at home? For, as they that write of *poysons*, and of creatures naturally disposed to the ruine of Man, do as well mention the *Flea*, as the *Viper*, because the *Flea*, though hee kill none, hee does all the harme hee can; so even these libellous and licentious *Jesters* utter the venim they have, though sometimes *vertue*, and alwaies *power*, be a good *Pigeon* to draw this *vapor* from the *Head*, and from doing any deadly harme there.

Ingeniumque malum, numeroso
   stigmate, fassus
Pellitur . ad pectus, Morbique
   Suburbia, Morbus.

The Sicknes declares the
infection and malignity
thereof by spots.

XIII

WEE say, that the world is made of *sea,* and *land,* as though they were
equal; but we know that ther is more *sea* in the *Western,* than in the
Eastern Hemisphere: We say that the *Firmament* is full of *starres,* as
though it were equally full; but we know, that there are more *stars* under
the *Northerne,* than under the *Southern Pole.* We say, the *Elements* of
man are *misery,* and *happinesse,* as though he had an equal proportion of
both, and the dayes of man vicissitudinary, as though he had as many
good daies, as *ill,* and that he liv'd under a perpetuall *Equinoctial night,*
and *day* equall, good and ill fortune in the same measure. But it is far
from that; hee *drinkes misery,* and he *tastes happinesse;* he *mowes misery,*
and he *gleanes happinesse;* he *journies in misery,* he does but *walke in
happinesse;* and which is worst, his misery is *positive,* and *dogmaticall,*
his happinesse is but *disputable,* and *problematicall;* All men call *Misery,*
Misery, but Happinesse changes the name, by the taste of man. In this
accident that befalls mee now, that this sicknesse declares itself by *Spots,*
to be a malignant, and pestilentiall disease, if there be a *comfort* in the
declaration, that therby the *Phisicians* see more cleerely what to doe,
there may bee as much *discomfort* in this, That the malignitie may bee so
great, as that all that they can doe, shall doe *nothing;* That an enemy
declares himselfe, then, when he is able to subsist, and to pursue, and to
atchive his ends, is no great comfort. In intestine Conspiracies, *voluntary*
Confessions doe more good, than Confessions upon the *Rack;* in these
Infections, when *Nature* her selfe confesses, and cries out by these outward declarations, which she is able to put forth of her selfe, they minister
comfort; but when all is by strength of *Cordials,* it is but a *Confession*
upon the Racke, by which though wee come to knowe the malice of that
man, yet wee doe not knowe whether there bee not as much malice in his
heart then, as before his confession; we are sure of his *Treason,* but not
of his *Repentance;* sure of *him,* but not of *his Complices.* It is a faint
comfort to know the worst, when the worst is *remedilesse;* and a weaker
than that, to know *much ill,* and not to know, that that is the worst. A
woman is comforted with the birth of her *Son,* her body is eased of a
burthen; but if shee could *prophetically* read his *History,* how *ill a man,*

perchance how *ill a sonne,* he would prove, shee should receive a greater burthen into her *Mind.* Scarce any purchase that is not clogged with secret *encumbrances;* scarce any *happines* that hath not in it so much of the *nature* of false and base money, as that the *Allay* is more than the *Metall.* Nay, is it not so, (at least much towards it) even in the exercise of *Vertues?* I must bee poore, and want, before I can exercise the vertue of *Gratitude;* miserable, and in torment, before I can exercise the vertue of *patience;* How deepe do we dig, and for how coarse gold? And what other *Touchstone* have we of our *gold,* but *comparison?* Whether we be as happy, as others, or as ourselves at other times; O poore stepp toward being well, when these *spots* do only tell us, that we are worse, than we were sure of before.

Idque notant Criticis, Medici
     evenisse Diebus.

The Phisicians observe these accidents to have fallen upon the criticall dayes.

XIV

I WOULD not make *Man* worse than hee is, Nor his Condition more miserable than it is. But could I though I would? As a man cannot *flatter God,* nor over prayse him, so a man cannot *injure* Man, nor undervalue him. Thus much must necessarily be presented to his remembrance, that those *false Happinesses,* which he hath in this World, have their *times,* and their *seasons,* and their *critical dayes,* and they are *Judged,* and *Denominated* according to the times, when they befall us. What poore *Elements* are our *happinesses* made of, if *Tyme, Tyme* which wee can scarce consider to be *any thing,* be an essential part of our happines! All things are done in some *place;* but if we consider *Place* to be no more, but the next hollow *Superficies* of the *Ayre, Alas,* how thinne, and fluid a thing is *Ayre,* and how thinne a *filme* is a *Superficies,* and a *Superficies* of *Ayre!* All things are done in *time* too; but if we consider *Tyme* to be but the *Measure of Motion,* and howsoever it may seeme to have three *stations, past, present,* and *future,* yet the *first* and *last* of these *are* not (one is not, now, and the other is not yet) and that which you call *present,* is not *now* the same that it was, when you began to call it so in this *Line,* (before you sound that word, *present,* or that *Monosyllable, now,* the present, and the *Now* is past), if this *Imaginary halfe-nothing, Tyme,* be of the Essence of our *Happinesses,* how can they be thought *durable? Tyme* is not so; How can they bee thought to be? *Tyme* is not so; not so, considered in any of the *parts* thereof. If we consider *Eternity,* into that, *Tyme* never entred; *Eternity* is not an everlasting flux of *Tyme;* but *Tyme* is a short *parenthesis* in a longe *period;* and *Eternity* had been the same, as it is, though time had never beene; If we consider, not *Eternity,* but *Perpetuity,* not that which had no *Tyme* to beginne in, but which shall outlive *Tyme* and be, when *Tyme shall bee no more,* what *A Minute* is the life of the Durablest *Creature,* compared to that! And what a Minute is Mans life in respect of the *Sunnes,* or of a Tree! and yet how little of our *life* is *Occasion, opportunity* to receyve good in; and how litle of that *occasion,* doe wee apprehend, and lay hold of! How busie and perplexed a *Cobweb,* is the *Happinesse* of Man here, that must bee made up with a *Watchfulnesse,* to lay hold upon *Occasion,* which is but a little peece of that, which is *Nothing, Tyme!* And yet the best things are *Nothing* without that. *Honors, Pleasures, Possessions,* presented to us, out of time, in our decrepit, and distasted, and unapprehensive *Age,* loose their *Office,* and loose their *Name;* They are not *Honors* to us, that shall never appeare, nor come abroad into the Eyes of the people, to receive *Honor,* from them who give it: Nor *pleasures* to us, who have lost our sense to taste them; nor *possessions* to us, who are departing from the possession of them. Youth is their *Criticall Day;* that *Judges* them, that *Denominates* them, that *inanimates,* and *informes* them, and makes them *Honors,* and *Pleasures,* and *Possessions;* and when they come in an unapprehensive *Age,* they come as a *Cordial* when the bell rings out, as a *Pardon,* when the Head is off. We rejoyce in the Comfort of *fire,* but does any man cleave to it at *Midsomer;* Wee are glad of the freshnesse, and coolenes of a *Vault,* but does any man keepe his *Christmas* there; or are the pleasures of the *Spring* acceptable in *Autumne?* If happinesse be in the *season,* or in the *Clymate,* how much happier then are *Birdes* than *Men,* who can change the *Climate,* and accompanie, and enjoy the same season ever.

Intereà insomnes noctes Ego　　　　　　　　*I sleepe not day*
　　duco, Diesque.　　　　　　　　　　　　　　*nor night.*

XV

N A T U R A L L men have conceived a twofold use of *sleepe;* That it is a *refreshing* of the body in this life; That it is a *preparing* of the *soule* for the next; That it is a *feast,* and it is the *grace* at that *feast;* That it is our *recreation,* and cheeres us, and it is our *Catechisme* and instructs us; wee lie downe in a hope, that wee shall rise the stronger; and we lie downe in a knowledge, that wee may rise no more. *Sleepe* is an *Opiate* which gives us *rest,* but such an *Opiate,* as perchance, being under it, we shall wake no more. But though naturall men, who have induced secondary and figurative considerations, have found out this second, this *emblematicall* use of *sleepe,* that it should be a *representation of death, God,* who wrought and perfected his worke, before *Nature* began, (for *Nature* was but his *Apprentice,* to learne in the first *seven daies,* and now is his *foreman,* and works next under him) *God,* I say, intended *sleepe* onely for the *refreshing* of man by bodily rest, and not for a *figure of death,* for he intended not *death* it selfe then. But *Man* having induced *death* upon himselfe, *God* hath taken *Mans Creature, death,* into his hand, and mended it; and whereas it hath in itselfe a fearefull forme and aspect, so that Man is afraid of his own *Creature, God* presents it to him, in a *familiar,* in an *assiduous,* in an *agreeable* and *acceptable* forme, in *sleepe,* that so when hee awakes from *sleepe,* and saies to himselfe, shall I bee no otherwise when I am dead, than I was even now, when I was asleep, hee may bee ashamed of his waking *dreames,* and of his *Melancholique* fancying out a horrid and an affrightfull figure of that *death* which is so like sleepe. As then wee need *sleepe* to live out our *threescore and ten yeeres,* so we need *death,* to live that *life* which we cannot *out-live.* And as *death* being our *enemie, God* allowes us to defend ourselves against it (for wee *victuall* ourselves against *death, twice* every day, as often as we *eat*) so *God* having so sweetned *death* unto us as hee hath in *sleepe,* wee put ourselves into our *enemies* hands *once* every day; so farre, as *sleepe* is *death;* and *sleepe* is as much *death,* as *meat* is *life.* This then is the *misery* of my *sicknesse,* That death as it is produced from mee, and is mine owne *Creature,* is now before mine *Eyes,* but in that forme, in which *God* hath mollified it to us, and made it acceptable, in *sleepe,* I cannot see it: how many *prisoners,* who have even hollowed themselves their *graves* upon that *Earth,* on which they have lien long under heavie fetters, yet at this *houre* are *asleepe,* though they bee yet working upon their owne *graves* by their owne *waight!* Hee that hath seene his *friend* die to *day,* or knowes hee shall see it to *morrow,* yet will sinke into a sleepe betweene. I cannot; and oh, if I be entring now into *Eternitie,* where there shall bee no more distinction of *houres,* why is it al my businesse now *to tell Clocks?* why is none of the heavinesse of my *heart,* dispensed into mine *Eye-lids,* that they might fall as my heart doth? And why, since I have lost my delight in all objects, cannot I discontinue the facultie of seeing them, by closing mine *eyes* in *sleepe?* But why rather being entring into that presence, where I shall wake continually and never sleepe more, doe I not interpret my continuall waking here, to bee a *parasceve,* and a *preparation* to that?

Et properare meum clamant,
  è Turre propinqua,
Obstreperæ Campanæ aliorum
  in funere, funus.

*From the Bells of the Church
adjoyning, I am daily remembred of my buriall in the
funeralls of others.*

XVI

W E have a *Convenient Author,* who writ a *Discourse of Bells,* when hee
was prisoner in *Turky.* How would hee have enlarged himselfe if he had
beene my *fellow-prisoner* in this *sicke bed,* so neere to that *Steeple,* which
never ceases, no more than the *harmony of the spheres,* but is more heard.
When the *Turkes* took *Constantinople,* they melted the *Bells* into *Ordnance;* I have heard both *Bells* and *Ordnance,* but never been so much
affected with those, as with these *Bells.* I have *lien* near a *Steeple,* in which
there are said to be more than *thirty Bels;* And neere another, where there
is one so bigge, as that the *Clapper* is said to weigh more than *six hundred pound,* yet never so affected as here. Here the *Bells* can scarse
solemnise the funerall of any person, but that I knew him, or knew that
he was my *Neighbour:* we dwelt in houses neere to one another before,
but now hee is gone into that house, into which I must follow him. There
is a way of correcting the *Children* of great persons, that other *Children*
are corrected in their *behalfe,* and in their *names,* and this workes upon
them, who indeed had more deserved it. And when these *Bells* tell me,
that now one, and now another is buried, must not I acknowledge, that
they have the *correction* due to me, and paid the *debt* that I owe? There
is a story of a *Bell* in a *Monastery* which, when any of the house was sicke
to death, rung alwaies *voluntarily,* and they knew the inevitablenesse of
the danger by that. It rung once, when no man was sick; but the next day
one of the house, fell from the *steeple,* and died, and the *Bell* held the
reputation of a *Prophet* still. If these *Bells* that warne to a *Funerall* now,
were appropriated to none, may not I, by the houre of the *Funerall,* supply? How many men that stand at an *execution,* if they would aske, for
what dies that man, should heare their owne faults condemned, and see
themselves executed, by *Atturney?* We scarce heare of any man *preferred,*
but wee thinke of our selves, that wee might very well have beene that
Man; Why might not I have beene that *Man,* that is carried to his *grave*
now? Could I fit my selfe, to *stand,* or *sit* in any mans *place,* and not to
lie in any mans *grave?* I may lacke much of the *good parts* of the meanest,
but I lacke nothing of the *mortality* of the weakest; They may have
acquired better *abilities* than I, but I was borne to as many *infirmities* as
they. To be an *Incumbent* by lying down in a *grave,* to be a *Doctor* by

teaching *Mortification* by *Example*, by *dying*, though I may have *seniors*, others may be *elder* than I, yet I have proceeded apace in a good *University*, and gone a great way in a little time, by the furtherance of a vehement *Fever;* and whomsoever these *Bells* bring to the ground to day, if hee and I had beene compared yesterday, perchance I should have been thought likelier to come to this preferment, then, than he. *God* hath kept the power of *death* in his owne hands, lest any man should *bribe death*. If man knew the *gaine of death*, the *ease of death*, he would solicite, he would provoke *death* to assist him, by any hand, which he might use. But as when men see many of their owne professions preferd, it ministers a hope that that may light upon them; so when these hourely *Bells* tell me of so many *funerals* of men like me, it presents, if not a *desire* that it may, yet a *comfort* whensoever mine shall come.

Nunc lento sonitu dicunt,
 Morieris.

Now, this Bell tolling softly for another, saies to me, Thou must die.

XVII

PERCHANCE hee for whom this *Bell* tolls, may be so ill, as that he knowes not it tolls for him; And perchance I may thinke my selfe so much better than I am, as that they who are about mee, and see my state, may have caused it to toll for mee, and I know not that. The *Church* is *Catholike, universall,* so are all her *Actions; All* that she does, belongs to *all.* When she *baptizes a child,* that action concernes mee; for that child is thereby connected to that *Head* which is my *Head* too, and engraffed into that *body,* whereof I am a *member.* And when she *buries a Man,* that action concernes me: All *mankinde* is of one *Author,* and is one *volume;* when one Man dies, one *Chapter* is not *torne* out of the *booke,* but *translated* into a better *language;* and every *Chapter* must be so *translated;* God emploies several *translators;* some peeces are translated by *age,* some by *sicknesse,* some by *warre,* some by *justice;* but *Gods* hand is in every *translation;* and his hand shall binde up all our scattered leaves againe, for that *Librarie* where every *booke* shall lie open to one another: As therefore the *Bell* that rings to a *Sermon,* calls not upon the *Preacher* onely, but upon the *Congregation* to come; so this *Bell* calls us all: but how much more mee, who am brought so neere the *doore* by this *sicknesse.* There was a *contention* as farre as a *suite,* (in which both *pietie* and *dignitie, religion,* and *estimation,* were mingled) which of the religious *Orders* should ring to *praiers* first in the *Morning;* and it was *deter-*

mined, that *they should ring first that rose earliest.* If we understand aright the *dignitie* of this *Belle* that tolls for our *evening prayer,* wee would bee glad to make it ours, by rising early, in that *application,* that it might bee ours, as wel as his, whose indeed it is. The *Bell* doth toll for him that *thinkes* it doth; and though it *intermit* againe, yet from that *minute,* that that occasion wrought upon him, hee is united to *God.* Who casts not up his *Eye* to the *Sunne* when it rises? but who takes off his *Eye* from a *Comet* when that breakes out? Who bends not his *eare* to any *bell,* which upon any occasion rings? but who can remove it from that *bell,* which is passing a *peece of himselfe* out of this *world?* No man is an *Iland,* intire of it selfe; every man is a peece of the *Continent,* a part of the *maine;* if a *Clod* bee washed away by the *Sea, Europe* is the lesse, as well as if a *Promontorie* were, as well as if a *Mannor* of thy *friends* or of *thine owne* were; any mans *death* diminishes *me,* because I am involved in *Man-kinde;* And therefore never send to know for whom the *bell* tolls; It tolls for *thee.* Neither can we call this a *begging* of *Miserie* or a *borrowing* of *Miserie,* as though we were not miserable enough of our selves, but must fetch in more from the next house, in taking upon us the *Miserie* of our *Neighbours.* Truly it were an excusable *covetousnesse* if wee did; for *affliction* is a *treasure,* and scarce any man hath *enough* of it. No man hath *affliction* enough that is not matured, and ripened by it, and made fit for *God* by that *affliction.* If a man carry *treasure* in *bullion,* or in a *wedge* of *gold,* and have none coined into *currant Monies,* his *treasure* will not defray him as he travells. *Tribulation* is *Treasure* in the *nature* of it, but it is not *currant money* in the *use* of it, except wee get nearer and nearer our *home, Heaven,* by it. Another man may be sicke too, and sick to *death,* and this *affliction* may lie in his *bowels,* as *gold* in a *Mine,* and be of no use to him; but this *bell,* that tells me of his *affliction,* digs out, and applies that *gold* to *mee:* if by this consideration of anothers danger, I take mine owne into contemplation, and so secure my selfe, by making my recourse to my *God,* who is our onely securitie.

At inde
Mortuus es, Sonitu celeri,
  pulsuque agitato.

The Bell rings out, and tells me in him, that I am dead.

XVIII

T H E *Bell* rings out; the *pulse* thereof is changed; the *tolling* was a *faint,* and *intermitting pulse,* upon one side; this *stronger,* and argues *more* and *better life.* His *soule* is gone out; and as a Man, who had a lease of 1000. *yeeres* after the expiration of a short one, or an inheritance after the *life* of a man in a *consumption*, he is now entred into the possession of his *better estate*. His *soule* is gone; *whither?* Who saw it *come in*, or who saw it *goe out? No body;* yet every body is sure, he *had one*, and *hath none*. If I will aske meere *Philosophers*, what the *soule* is, I shall finde amongst them, that will tell me, it is nothing, but the *temperament* and *harmony*, and *just and equall composition of the Elements in the body*, which pro-duces all those *faculties* which we ascribe to the *soule;* and so, in it selfe is *nothing*, no *seperable substance*, that overlives the *body*. They see the *soule* is nothing else in other *Creatures*, and they affect an *impious humil-itie*, to think *as low* of *Man*. But if my *soule* were no more than the soul of a *beast*, I could not thinke so; that *soule* that can *reflect* upon it selfe, *consider* it selfe, is *more* than so. If I will aske, not meere *Philosophers*, but *mixt men, Philosophicall Divines, how* the *soule*, being a *separate substance*, enters into *Man*, I shall finde some that will tell me, that it is by *generation*, and *procreation* from *parents*, because they thinke it hard, to charge the *soule* with the guiltiness of *originall* sinne, if the *soule* were infused into a *body*, in which it must necessarily grow *foule*, and contract *originall sinne*, whether it *will* or *no;* and I shall finde some that will tell mee, that it is by *immediate infusion from God*, because they think it hard, to *maintaine* an *immortality* in such a *soule*, as should be begotten, and derived with the *body* from *mortall parents*. If I will aske, not a *few men*, but almost *whole bodies, whole Churches*, what becomes of the *soules* of the *righteous*, at the *departing* thereof from the *body*, I shall bee told by some, *That they attend an expiation, a purification in a place of tor-ment;* By some, that *they attend the fruition of the sight of God, in a place of rest; but yet, but of expectation;* By some, *that they passe to an immediate possession of the presence of God. S. Augustine* studied the *nature* of the *soule*, as much as anything, but the *salvation of the soule;* and he sent an expresse *Messenger* to Saint *Hierome*, to consult of some things concerning the *soule:* But he satisfies himselfe with this: *Let the departure of my soule to salvation be evident to my faith, and I care the lesse, how darke the entrance of my soule, into my body, bee to my reason.* It is the *going out*, more than the *comming in*, that concernes us. This *soule*, this Bell tells me, is *gone out; Whither?* Who shall tell mee that? I know not *who it is;* much less *what he was;* The condition of the man, and the course of his life, which should tell mee *whither* hee is gone, I know not. I was not there in his *sicknesse*, nor at his *death;* I saw not his *way*, nor his *end*, nor can aske them, who did, thereby to *conclude*, or *argue*, whither he is gone. But yet I have one neerer mee than all these; mine owne *Charity;* I aske that; and that tels me, *He is gone to everlasting rest*, and *joy*, and *glory:* I owe him a good *opinion;* it is but *thankfull charity* in mee, because I received *benefit* and *instruc-*

tion from him when his *Bell* told: and I, being made the fitter to *pray*, by that disposition, wherein I was assisted by his occasion, did *pray* for him; and I *pray* not without *faith;* so I doe *charitably*, so I do *faithfully* beleeve, that that *soule* is gone to everlasting *rest*, and *joy*, and *glory*. But for the *body*, how poore a wretched thing is *that?* wee cannot expresse it *so fast*, as it growes *worse* and *worse*. That *body* which scarce *three minutes* since was such a *house*, as that that *soule*, which made but one step from thence to *Heaven*, was scarse thorowly content, to leave that for *Heaven:* that *body* hath lost the *name* of a *dwelling house*, because none dwells in it, and is making haste to lose the name of a *body*, and dissolve to *putrefaction*. Who would not bee affected, to see a cleere and sweet *River* in the *Morning*, grow a *kennell* of muddy land water by *noone*, and condemned to the saltnesse of the *Sea* by *night?* And how lame a *picture*, how faint a *representation* is that, of the precipitation of mans body to *dissolution! Now* all the parts built up, and knit by a lovely *soule*, *now* but a *statue* of *clay*, and *now*, these limbs melted off, as if that *clay* were but *snow;* and now, the whole *house* is but a *handfull* of *sand*, so much *dust*, and but a *pecke* of *rubbidge*, so much *bone*. If *he*, who, as this *Bell* tells mee, is gone now, were some *excellent Artificer*, who comes to him for a *clocke*, or for a *garment* now? or for *counsaile*, if hee were a *Lawyer?* If a *Magistrate*, for *Justice? Man*, before hee hath his *immortall soule*, hath a *soule* of *sense*, and a *soule* of *vegetation* before that: This *immortall soule* did not forbid other soules, to be in us before, but when this *soule* departs, it carries all with it; no more *vegetation*, no more *sense:* such a *Mother in law* is the *Earth*, in respect of our *naturall mother;* in her *wombe* we *grew;* and when she was delivered of us, wee were planted in some *place*, in some *calling* in the *world;* In the wombe of the *earth*, wee *diminish*, and when shee is *deliverd* of us, our *grave opened* for another, wee are not *transplanted*, but *transported*, our *dust* blowne away with *prophane dust*, with *every wind*.

Oceano tandem emenso, aspicienda resurgit Terra; vident, justis, medici, jam cocta mederi se posse, indiciis.	*At last, the Physitians, after a long and stormie voyage, see land; They have so good signes of the concoction of the disease, as that they may safely proceed to purge.*

XIX

A L L this while the *Physitians* themselves have beene *patients*, patiently attending when they should see any *land* in this *Sea*, any *earth*, any *cloud*, any *indication* of *concoction* in these waters. Any *disorder* of mine, any *pretermission* of theirs, exalts the disease, accelerates the rages of it; no *diligence* accelerates the *concoction*, the *maturitie* of the *disease;* they must stay till the *season* of the sicknesse come, and till it be ripened of it selfe, and then they may put to their hand, to *gather* it before it *fall* off, but they cannot hasten the *ripening.* Why should wee looke for it in a *disease,* which is the *disorder,* the *discord,* the *irregularitie,* the *commotion,* and *rebellion* of the *body?* It were scarce a *disease,* if it could bee *ordered,* and made obedient to our *times.* Why should wee looke for that in *disorder,* in a *disease,* when we cannot have it in *Nature,* who is so *regular,* and so *pregnant,* so forward to bring her worke to perfection, and to light? Yet we cannot awake the *July-flowers* in *January,* nor retard the *flowers* of the *spring* to *autumne.* We cannot bid the *fruits* come in *May,* nor the *leaves* to sticke on in *December.* A *woman* that is weake cannot put off her *ninth moneth* to a *tenth,* for her *deliverie,* and say shee will stay till shee bee *stronger;* nor a *Queene* cannot hasten it to a *seventh,* that shee may bee ready for some other pleasure. *Nature* (if we looke for *durable* and *vigorous* effects) will not admit *preventions,* nor *anticipations,* nor *obligations* upon her; for they are *precontracts,* and she will bee left to her *libertie. Nature* would not be spurred, nor forced to mend her pace; nor *power,* the *power of man; greatnesse* loves not that kinde of *violence* neither. There are of *them* that will *give,* that will *do justice,* that will *pardon,* but they have their owne *seasons* for al these, and he that knowes not *them,* shall *starve* before that gift come, and *ruine,* before the Justice, and *dye* before the pardon save him: some *tree* beares no fruit, except much *dung* be laid about it; and *Justice* comes not from some, till they bee richly manured: some *trees* require much *visiting,* much *watring,* much *labour;* and some men give not their *fruits* but upon *importunitie;* some *trees* require *incision,* and *pruning,* and *lopping;* some men must bee *intimidated* and *syndicated* with *Commissions,* before they will deliver the fruits of *Justice;* some *trees* require the *early* and the *often* accesse of the *Sunne;* some men *open* not, but upon the *favours* and *letters* of *Court mediation;* some *trees* must bee *housd* and kept within doores; some men locke up, not onely their liberalitie, but their *Justice,* and their *compassion,* till the sollicitation of a *wife,* or a *sonne,* or a *friend,* or a *servant* turne the *key. Reward* is the *season* of one man, and *importunitie* of another; *feare* the *season* of one man, and *favour* of another; *friendship* the *season* of one man, and *naturall affection* of another; and hee that knowes not their *seasons,* nor cannot *stay* them, must lose the *fruits;* As *Nature* will not, so *power* and *greatnesse* will not bee put to change their *seasons;* and shall wee looke for this *Indulgence* in a *disease,* or thinke to shake it off before it bee *ripe?* All this while, therefore, we are but upon a *defensive warre*, and that is but a *doubtfull state;* especially where they who are *besieged* doe know the *best* of their *defences*, and doe not know the *worst* of their *enemies power;* when they cannot mend their *works within*, and the *enemie* can increase his *numbers without*. O how many farre more miserable, and farre more worthy to be lesse miserable than I, are besieged with this *sicknesse*, and lacke their *Sentinels*, their *Physitians* to *watch*, and lacke their *munition*, their *cordials* to *defend*, and perish before the *enemies* weaknesse might invite them to *sally*, before the *disease* shew any *declination*, or admit any way of *working* upon it selfe! In me the *siege* is so farre slackned, as that we may come to *fight*, and so die in the *field*, if I *die*, and not in a *prison*.

Id agunt.   *Upon these Indications of digested matter, they proceed to purge.*

XX

THOUGH *counsel* seeme rather to consist of *spirituall parts*, then *action*, yet *action* is the *spirit* and the *soule* of *counsell*. *Counsels* are not alwaies determined in *Resolutions;* wee cannot alwaies say, *this was concluded;* *actions* are alwaies determined in *effects;* wee can say *this was done*. Then have *Lawes* their *reverence*, and their *majestie*, when we see the *Judge* upon the *Bench* executing them. Then have *counsels of warre* their *impressions*, and their *operations*, when we see the *seale* of an *Armie* set to them. It was an ancient way of celebrating the *memorie* of such as deserved well of the *State*, to afford them that kinde of *statuarie representation*, which was then called *Hermes;* which was, *the head and shoulders of a man, standing upon a Cube*, but those *shoulders* without *armes* and *hands*. All together it figured a *constant supporter of the State*, by his *counsell:* But in this *Hieroglyphique*, which they made without *hands*, they passe their consideration no farther, but that the *Counsellor* should bee without *hands*, so farre as *not to reach out his hand to forraigne tentations of bribes, in matters of Counsell*, and that it was not necessary, that the *head* should employ *his owne hand;* that *the same men* should serve in the *execution*, which assisted in the *Counsell;* but that there should not belong *hands* to every *head*, *action* to every *counsell*, was never intended, so much as in *figure*, and *representation*. For, as *Matrimonie* is scarce to bee called *Matrimonie*, where there is a *resolution* against the *fruits of matrimonie*, against the having of *Children*, so *counsels* are not *counsels*, but *illusions*, where there is from the beginning no purpose to execute the determinations of those *counsels*. The *arts* and *sciences* are most properly referred to the *head;* that is their proper *Element* and *Spheare;* but yet the *art* of *proving, Logique,* and the *art* of *perswading, Rhetorique,* are deduced to the *hand,* and *that* expressed by a *hand* contracted into a *fist,* and *this* by a *hand* enlarged, and expanded; and evermore the *power of man,* and the *power of God* himselfe is expressed so, *All things are in his hand;* neither is *God* so often presented to us, by names that carry our consideration upon *counsell,* as upon *execution* of *counsell;* he is oftener called the *Lord of Hosts,* than by all other *names,* that may be referred to the other signification. Hereby therefore wee take into our *meditation,* the slipperie condition of *man,* whose *happinesse,* in any kinde, the defect of *any one thing,* conducing to that *happinesse,* may *ruine;* but it must have *all the peeces* to make it up. Without *counsell,* I had not got thus farre; without *action* and *practise,* I should goe no farther towards *health.* But what is the present necessary *action?* purging: A *withdrawing,* a violating of *Nature, a farther weakening: O deare price,* and O *strange* way of *addition,* to doe it by *substraction;* of *restoring* Nature, to *violate Nature;* of *providing strength,* by *increasing weaknesse! Was I not sicke* before? And is it a *question* of *comfort* to be asked now, Did *your Physicke make you sicke?* Was that it that my *Physicke* promised, to make me *sicke?* This is another *step,* upon which we may stand, and see farther into the *miserie of man,* the *time,* the *season* of his *Miserie;* It must bee done *now: O over-cunning, over-watchfull, over-diligent,* and *over-sociable misery of man,* that seldome comes alone, but then when it may accompanie other *miseries,* and so put one another into the higher *exaltation,* and better *heart!* I am ground even to an *attenuation,* and must proceed to *evacuation,* all waies to exinanition and annihilation.

Atque annuit Ille,	*God prospers their practise,*
Qui, per eos, clamat, Linquas	*and he, by them, calls*
jam, Lazare, lectum.	*Lazarus out of his tombe, mee out of my bed.*

XXI

I F man had beene left *alone* in this *world,* at first, shall I thinke, that he would not have *fallen?* If there had beene no *Woman,* would not man have served, to have beene his own *Tempter?* When I see him now, subject to infinite weaknesses, fall into *infinite sinne,* without any *forraine tentations,* shall I thinke, hee would have had *none,* if hee had beene *alone? God* saw that Man needed a *Helper,* if hee should bee well; but to make *Woman* ill, the *Devill* saw, that there needed no *third.* When *God,* and *wee* were *alone*, in *Adam*, that was not enough; when the *Devill* and wee were *alone*, in *Eve*, it was enough. O what a *Giant* is *Man*, when he fights against himselfe, and what a *Dwarfe* when hee *needs*, or *exercises* his owne assistance for himselfe! I cannot *rise* out of my bed, till the *Physitian enable* mee, nay I cannot tel, that I am able to rise, till *hee* tell me so. I *doe* nothing, I *know* nothing of myselfe: how little, and how impotent a peece of the *world*, is any *Man* alone! and how much lesse a peece of *himselfe* is *that Man!* So little, as that when it falls out, (as it falls out in some cases) that more *misery*, and more *oppression*, would be an *ease* to a *man*, he cannot give himselfe that *miserable addition*, of *more misery;* a *man* that is *pressed to death*, and might be eased by more *weights*, cannot lay those more *weights* upon himselfe: Hee can sinne *alone*, and suffer *alone*, but not *repent*, not bee *absolved*, without *another*. Another tels mee, *I may rise;* and *I doe* so. But is every *raising* a *preferment?* or is every present *preferment* a *station?* I am readier to fall to the *Earth*, now I am up, than I was when I *lay* in the bed: O *perverse way, irregular motion* of *Man;* even *rising* it selfe is the way to *Ruine*. How many *men* are raised, and then doe not *fill* the place they are raised to? No *corner* of any place can bee *empty;* there can be no *vacuity;* If that *Man* doe not fill the place, *other men* will; complaints of his *insufficiency* will *fill* it; Nay, such an abhorring is there in *Nature*, of *vacuity*, that if there be but an *imagination* of not *filling*, in any *man*, that which is but *imagination* neither, will *fill* it, that is *rumor* and *voice*, and it will be *given out*, (upon no ground, but *Imagination*, and no man knowes *whose imagination*) that hee is *corrupt* in his place, or *insufficient* in his place, and another prepared to *succeed* him in his place. A man *rises*, sometimes, and *stands* not, because hee doth not, or is not beleeved to *fill* his place; and sometimes he *stands* not, because hee *overfills* his place: Hee may bring so much *vertue*, so much *Justice*, so much *integrity* to the place, as shall *spoile* the place, *burthen* the place; his *integrity* may bee a *Libell* upon his *Predecessor*, and cast an *infamy* upon him, and a *burthen* upon his *successor*, to proceede by *example*, and to bring the place itselfe to an *under-value*, and the *market* to an *uncertainty*. I am *up*, and I seeme to *stand*, and I goe *round;* and I am a new *Argument* of the *new Philosophie*, That the *Earth* moves round; why may I not beleeve, that the *whole earth* moves in a *round motion*, though that seeme to mee to *stand*, when as I seeme to *stand* to my *Company*, and yet am carried, in a giddy, and *circular motion*, as I *stand?* Man hath no *center* but *misery; there* and onely *there*, hee is *fixt*, and sure to finde himselfe. How little soever hee bee *raised*, he *moves*, and moves in a *circle*, giddily; and as in the *Heavens*, there are but a few *Circles*, that goe about the whole world, but many *Epicircles*, and other lesser *Circles*, but yet *Circles*, so of those men, which are *raised*, and put into *Circles*, few of them move from *place* to *place*, and passe through many and beneficiall places, but fall into little *Circles*, and, within a step or two, are at their *end*, and not so well, as they were in the *Center*, from which they were *raised*. Every thing serves to *exemplifie*, to *illustrate* mans *misery*. But I need goe no farther, than *my selfe*: for a long time, I was not able to *rise*; At last, I must bee *raised* by others; and now I am *up*, I am ready to sinke *lower* than before.

| Sit morbi fomes tibi cura; | *The Physitians consider the root and occasion, the embers, and coales, and fuell of the disease, and seek to purge or correct that.* |

XXII

H O W *ruinous* a *farme* hath *man* taken, in taking *himselfe!* How ready is the *house* every day to fall downe, and how is all the *ground* overspread with *weeds, all the* body with *diseases!* where not onely every *turfe*, but every *stone*, beares *weeds;* not onely every *muscle* of the *flesh*, but every *bone* of the *body*, hath some *infirmitie;* every little *flint* upon the *face* of this *soile*, hath some *infectious weede*, every *tooth* in our *head*, such a paine as a *constant man* is afraid of, and yet *ashamed* of that *feare*, of that sense of the paine. How *deare*, and how *often* a *rent* doth Man pay for this *farme!* hee paies *twice a day*, in *double meales*, and how little time he hath to *raise his rent!* How many *holy daies* to call him from his labour! Every day is *halfe-holy day*, halfe spent in *sleepe*. What *reparations*, and *subsidies*, and *contributions* he is put to, besides his *rent!* What *medicines*, besides his *diet!* and what *Inmates* he is *faine* to take in, besides his owne *familie*, what *infectious diseases*, from *other men! Adam* might have had *Paradise* for *dressing* and *keeping* it; and *then* his *rent* was not *improved* to such a *labour*, as would have made his *brow sweat;* and yet he gave it over; how farre greater a *rent* doe wee pay for this farme, this *body*, who pay *our selves*, who pay the *farme it selfe*, and cannot *live* upon it! Neither is our *labour* at an end, when wee have cut downe some *weed*, as soone as it sprung up, corrected some *violent* and dangerous *accident* of a *disease*, which would have destroied *speedily;* nor when wee have pulled up that *weed*, from the very *root*, recovered *entirely* and *soundly*, from that *particular disease;* but the whole *ground* is of an *ill nature*, the whole soile *ill disposed;* there are inclinations, there is a propensenesse to *diseases* in the *body,* out of which without any other *disorder,* *diseases* will grow, and so wee are put to a continuall labour upon this *farme,* to a continuall studie of the whole *complexion* and *constitution* of our *body.* In the *distempers* and *diseases* of *soiles, sourenesse, drinesse, weeping,* any kinde of *barrennesse,* the *remedy* and the *physicke,* is, for a great part, sometimes in *themselves;* sometime[s] the very *situation* releeves them; the *hanger* of a *hill,* will purge and vent his owne *malignant moisture;* and the burning of the upper *turfe* of some ground (as *health* from *cauterizing*) puts a *new* and a *vigorous youth* into that *soile,* and there rises a kinde of *Phœnix* out of the *ashes,* a *fruitfulnesse* out of that which was *barren* before, and *by that,* which is the barrennest of all, *ashes.* And where the *ground* cannot give it selfe *Physicke,* yet it receives *Physicke* from other grounds, from other soiles, which are not the worse, for having contributed that helpe to them, from *Marle* in other *hils,* or from *slimie sand* in other *shoares: grounds* helpe *themselves,* or hurt not other *grounds,* from whence they receive *helpe.* But I have taken a *farme* at this *hard rent,* and upon those *heavie covenants,* that it can afford it selfe no *helpe;* (no part of my *body,* if it were cut off, would *cure* another part; in some cases it might *preserve* a sound part, but in no case *recover* an infected) and, if my *body* may have any *Physicke,* any *Medicine* from another *body,* one *Man* from the flesh of another *Man* (as by Mummy, or any such *composition,*) it must bee from a man that is dead, and not, as in other *soiles,* which are never the worse for contributing their *Marle,* or their fat slime to my *ground.* There is nothing in the same *man,* to helpe *man,* nothing in *mankind* to helpe *one another* (in this sort, by way of *Physicke*) but that hee who *ministers* the *helpe,* is in as ill case, as he that *receives* it would have beene, if he had not had it; for hee from whose *body* the *Physicke* comes, is *dead.* When therefore I tooke this *farme,* undertooke this body, I undertooke to *draine,* not a *marish,* but a *moat,* where there was, not water *mingled* to offend, but all was *water;* I under-tooke to *perfume dung,* where no one part, but all was equally *unsavory;* I undertooke to make such a thing *wholsome,* as was not *poison* by any manifest quality, *intense heat,* or *cold,* but *poison* in the *whole substance,* and in the *specifique forme* of it. To cure the *sharpe accidents* of *diseases,* is a great worke; to cure the *disease it selfe* is a greater; but to cure the *body,* the *root,* the *occasion* of *diseases,* is a worke reserved for the great *Phisitian,* which he doth never any other way, but by *glorifying* these *bodies* in the next world.

Metusque, relabi.   *They warne mee of the fearefull*
                                     danger of relapsing.

XXIII

I T is not in *mans body*, as it is in the *Citie*, that when the *Bell* hath rung, to cover your *fire*, and rake up the *embers*, you may lie downe and sleepe without feare. Though you have by *physicke* and *diet*, raked up the *embers* of your *disease*, stil there is a feare of a *relapse;* and the *greater* danger is in that. Even in *pleasures*, and in *paines*, there is a *propriety*, a *Meum* and *Tuum;* and a man is most affected with that *pleasure* which is *his, his* by former enjoying and experience, and most intimidated with those *paines* which are *his, his* by a wofull sense of them, in former afflictions. A *covetous* person, who hath preoccupated all his senses, filled all his capacities, with the *delight* of *gathering*, wonders how any man can have *any taste* of *any pleasure* in *any opennesse*, or *liberalitie;* So also in *bodily paines*, in a fit of the *stone*, the Patient wonders why any man should call the *Gout* a *paine:* And hee that hath felt neither, but the *tooth-ach*, is as much afraid of a fit of that, as either of the other, of either of the other. *Diseases*, which we never *felt* in our selves, come but to a *compassion* of others that have endured them; Nay, *compassion* it selfe comes to no great *degree*, if wee have not felt in some *proportion*, in *our selves*, that which wee lament and condole in another. But when wee have had those torments in their *exaltation, our selves*, wee tremble at a relapse. When wee must *pant* through all those *fierie heats*, and *saile* thorow all those *overflowing sweats*, when wee must *watch* through all those long *nights*, and *mourne* through all those long *daies*, (*daies* and *nights*, so *long*, as that *Nature* her selfe shall seeme to be *perverted*, and to have put the *longest day*, and the *longest night*, which should bee *six moneths* asunder, into one *naturall, unnaturall day*) when wee must stand at the same *barre*, expect the returne of *Physitians* from their *consultations*, and not bee sure of the same *verdict*, in any good *Indications*, when we must goe the same *way* over againe, and not see the same *issue*, this is a *state*, a *condition*, a *calamitie*, in respect of which, any other *sicknesse*, were a *convalescence*, and any *greater, lesse*. It addes to the *affliction*, that *relapses* are, (and for the most part justly) imputed to *our selves*, as occasioned by some *disorder* in us; and so we are not onely *passive*, but *active*, in our owne *ruine;* we doe not onely stand under a *falling house*, but *pull* it downe upon us; and wee are not onely *executed*, (that implies *guiltinesse*) but wee are *executioners*, (that implies *dishonor*) and *executioners* of *our selves*, (and that implies *impietie*). And wee fall from that *comfort* which wee might have in our first *sicknesse,* from that *meditation, Alas, how generally miserable is Man, and how subject to diseases,* (for in that it is some degree of *comfort,* that wee are but in the state *common* to all) we fall, I say, to this *discomfort,* and *selfe accusing,* and *selfe condemning; Alas, how unprovident, and in that, how unthankfull to God and his instruments am I, in making so ill use of so great benefits, in destroying so soone, so long a worke, in relapsing, by my disorder, to that from which they had delivered mee;* and so my *meditation* is fearefully transferred from the *body* to the *minde,* and from the consideration of the *sicknesse* to that sinne, that *sinful carelessnes,* by which I have occasioned my *relapse.* And amongst the many *weights* that aggravate a *relapse,* this also is one, that a *relapse* proceeds with a more violent dispatch, and more *irremediably,* because it finds the *Countrie weakned,* and *depopulated* before. Upon a *sicknesse,* which as yet appeares not, wee can scarce fix a *feare,* because wee know not what to feare; but as *feare* is the *busiest,* and *irksomest affection,* so is a *relapse* (which is still *ready to come*) into that, which is but newly gone, the *nearest object,* the *most immediate* exercise of that *affection* of *feare.*

Sermons

FROM A SERMON PREACHED TO THE KING'S MAJESTIE AT WHITEHALL

24 FEBR. 1625.

I

F O R the first *generall sale* by *Adam,* wee complaine now that *Land* will not sell; that 20. is come to 15. yeares purchase; but doe wee not take too late a *Medium,* too low a time to reckon by? How cheape was *Land* at first, how cheape were *we?* what was *Paradise* sold for? What was *Heaven,* what was *Mankinde* sold for? *Immortalitie* was sold, and what yeares Purchase was that worth? *Immortalitie* is our *Eternitie; God* hath another manner of *eternitie* in *him;* He hath a *whole eternall day;* an *eternall afternoone,* and an *eternall forenoone* too; for as he shall have no *end,* so hee never had *beginning;* we have an *eternall afternoone* in our *immortalitie;* we shall no more see an *end,* than *God* hath seene a *beginning;* and *Millions* of yeares, multiplied by *Millions,* make not up a *Minute* to this *Eternitie,* this *Immortalitie.* When *Dives* values a *droppe* of water at so high a price, what would he give for a *River?* How poore a *Clod* of Earth is a *Mannor!* how poore an *inch,* a *Shire!* how poore a *spanne,* a *Kingdome!* how poore a *pace,* the whole *world!* and yet how prodigally we sell *Paradise, Heaven, Soules, Consciences, Immortalitie, Eternitie,* for a *few Graines* of this *Dust!* What had *Eve* for *Heaven;* so little, as that the *Holy Ghost* will not let us know, what she had, not what kinde of *Fruite;* yet something *Eve* had. What had *Adam* for *Heaven?* but a satisfaction that hee had pleased an *Ill wife,* as St. *Hierome* states his fault, that he eate that Fruite, *Ne contristaretur Delicias suas,* least he should cast her, whom he lov'd so much, into an inordinate dejection; but if he *satisfied* her, and his owne *Uxoriousnesse,* any *satisfaction* is not *nothing.* But what had *I* for *Heaven? Adam* sinnd, and *I* suffer; I *forfeited* before I had any *Possession,* or could claime any *Interest;* I had a *Punishment,* before I had a *being,* And *God* was displeased with *me* before *I* was *I;* I was built up scarse 50. years ago, in my Mothers womb, and I was cast down,

343

almost 6000 years agoe, in *Adams* loynes; I was *borne* in the last *Age* of
the world, and *dyed* in the first. How and how justly do we cry out against
a Man, that hath sold a *Towne*, or sold an *Army*. And *Adam* sold the
World. He sold *Abraham*, and *Isaac* and *Jacob*, and all the *Patriarchs*, and
all the *Prophets*. He sold *Peter*, and *Paul*, and both their *Regiments*, both
the glorious *Hemispheres* of the World, The *Jewes*, and the *Gentiles*. He
sold *Evangelists*, and *Apostles*, and *Disciples*, and the *Disciple whom the
Lord loved*, and the *beloved Mother of the Lord, her selfe*, say what they
will to the contrary. And if *Christ* had not provided for himselfe, by a
miraculous Generation, Adam had sold *him:* If *Christ* had bene conceivd
in *Originall sinne*, hee must have dyed for *himselfe*, nay, he could not have
dyed for *himselfe*, but must have needed another *Saviour*. It is in that
Contemplation, as hee was descended from *Adam*, that St. *Paul* sayes of
himselfe, *Venundatus, I am carnall, sold under sinne*. For though St.
Augustine, and some others of the *Fathers*, doe sometimes take the
Apostle, in that place, to speake of himselfe, as in the person of a *naturall
Man*, (that every Man considered in *nature, is sold under sinne*, but the
Supernaturall, the *Sanctified* Man is not so) yet St. *Augustine* himselfe,
in his latest, and gravest Bookes, and particularly in his *Retractations*,
returnes to this sense of these words, That no man, in what measure soever
Sanctified, can so emancipate himselfe from that *Captivitie*, to which
Adam hath enthralld him, but that, as hee is enwrapped in *Originall* sinne,
hee is *solde under sinne*. And both S. *Hierome*, and S. *Ambrose*, (both
which, seeme in other places, to goe an other way, That onely they are
sold under sinne, which have abandond, and prostituted themselves to
particular sinnes,) doe yet returne to this sense, That because the *Embers*,
the *Spaune*, the *leaven* of *Originall sinne*, remaines, by *Adams* sale, in the
best, the best are sold under sinne.

So the *Jewes* were, and so were *we* sold by *Adam*, to *Originall sinne*,
very *cheape;* but in the *second sale*, as wee are sold to *actuall*, and *habituall sinnes*, by *our selves, cheaper;* for so, sayes this *Prophet, You have
sold your selves for nothing: Our selves*, that is *all our selves;* o[u]r
bodies to intemperance, and ryot, and licenciousnes, and our *soules* to a
greedines of sinne; and all this for *nothing*, for *sinne* it selfe, for which
wee sell our selves, is but a *privation*, and *privations* are *nothing*. *What
fruit had you of those things, whereof you are now ashamed, sayes the
Apostle;* here is *Barrennesse* and *shame; Barrennesse* is a *privation* of
fruit, shame is a *privation* of that *confidence*, which a good *Conscience*
administers, and when the *Apostle* tells them, they sold themselves for
barrennesse and shame, it was for *privation*, for *nothing*. The *Adulterer
waits for the twy-light*, sayes *Job*. The *Twy-light* comes, and serves his
turne; and *sin*, to night looks like a *Purchase*, like a *Treasure;* but aske

this *sinner* to *morrow,* and he hath sold *himselfe* for *nothing;* for *debility* in his *limnes,* for *darknesse* in his understanding, for *emptinesse* in his purse, for *absence of grace* in his Soule; and *Debilitie,* and *Darkenes,* and *emptinesse,* and *Absence,* are *privations,* and *privations* are *nothing.* All the name of *Substance* or *Treasure* that *sinne* takes, is that in the *Apostle, Thesaurizastis Iram Dei, You have treasured up the wrath of God, against the day of wrath:* And this is a fearefull *privation,* of the *grace* of *God* here, and of the *Face* of *God* hereafter; a *privation* so much worse than *nothing,* as that they upon whom it falls, would faine be *nothing,* and cannot.

2

As some *Schoolemasters* have usd that *Discipline,* to correct the Children of great Persons, whose personall correction they finde reason to forbeare, by correcting other Children in their *names,* and in their *sight,* and have wrought upon *good Natures,* that way, So did *Almightie God* correct the *Jewes* in the *Ægyptians;* for the *ten plagues of Ægypt,* were as *Moses Decem Verba,* as the *Ten Commandements to Israel,* that they should not provoke GOD. Every *Judgement* that falls upon another, should be a *Catechisme* to me. But when this *Discipline* prevaild not upon them, *God sold* them away, *gave* them away, *cast* them away, in the tempest, in the whirlewinde, in the inundation of his indignation, and scatterd them as so much dust in a windy day, as so many broken strawes upon a wrought Sea. With one *word, One Fiat,* (*Let there bee a world,*) nay with one *thought* of *God* cast toward it, (for *Gods* speaking in the *Creation,* was but a *thinking,*) *God* made all of *Nothing.* And is any one *rationall Ant,* (The wisest *Phylosopher* is no more) Is any *roaring Lyon,* (the most ambitious and devouring Prince is no more) Is any *hive of Bees,* (The wisest *Councels,* and *Parliaments* are no more) Is any of these so estab-[l]ishd, as that, that *God* who by a *word,* by a *thought,* made them of *nothing,* cannot by recalling that *word,* and withdrawing that *thought,* in sequestring his *Providence,* reduce them to *nothing* againe? That *Man,* that *Prince,* that *State* thinks Past-board Canon-proofe, that thinkes Power, or Policy a Rampart, when the *Ordinance* of *God* is planted against it. *Navyes* will not keepe off *Navies,* if *God* be not the *Pilot,* Nor *Walles* keepe out *Men,* if *God* be not the *Sentinell.* If they could, if wee were walld with a *Sea* of fire and brimstone without, and walld with Brasse within, yet we cannot ciel the Heavens with a roofe of Brasse, but that *God* can come downe in *Thunder* that way, Nor pave the Earth with a floare of Brasse, but that God can come up in *Earthquakes* that way. *God* can call up *Damps,* and *Vapors* from below, and powre down putride *defluxions* from above, and bid them meet and condense into a *plague,* a *plague* that shall not be onely uncureable, uncontrollable, unexorable, but undisputable, unexaminable, unquestionable; A *plague* that shall not onely not admit a *remedy,* when it is come, but not give a *reason* how it did come. If God had not set a marke upon *Cain,* every Man, any Man, any thing might have killd him. Hee apprehended that of himselfe, and was afraid, when we know of none, by name, in the world, but his Father, and Mother: But, as Saint *Hierome* exalts this consideration, *Cains* owne Conscience tells him, *Catharma sum, Anathema sum,* I am the *plague* of the world, and I must dye, to deliver it, *Catharma sum.* I am a *separated Vagabond,* not an *Anachorit* shut up betweene two walls, but shut out from all, *Anathema sum.* As long as the *Cherubim,* and the fiery Sword is at the Gate, *Adam* cannot returne to *Paradise;* as long as the Testimonies of GODS anger lye at the dore of the *Conscience,* no man can returne to peace there. If *God* sell away a Man, give him away, give way to him, by withdrawing his Providence, he shall but neede (as the *Prophet* sayes) *Sibilare Muscam,* to hisse, to whisper for the *Fly,* for the *Bee,* for the *Hornet,* for *Forraigne Incumbrances;* nay, hee shall not neede to hisse, to whisper for them; for at home, *Locusts* shall swarme in his *Gardens,* and *Frogs in his bed-chamber,* and *hailstones, as big as talents,* (as they are measured in the *Revelation*) shall breake, as well the coverd, and the armd, as the bare, and naked head; as well the *Mytred,* and the *Turband,* and the *crownd* head, that lifts it selfe up against GOD, lyes open to him, as his that must not put on his Hat, as his that hath no Hat to put on; when as that head, which being exalted here, submits it selfe to that GOD, that exalted it, GOD shall crowne, with multiplied crownes here, and having so crownd that head with Crownes here, hee shall crowne those crownes, with the Head of all, *Christ Jesus,* and all that is his, hereafter.

FROM A SERMON OF COMMEMORATION OF THE LADY DANVERS, LATE WIFE OF SIR JOHN DANVERS.

1627

THE PRAYER BEFORE THE SERMON

O ETERNALL, *and most* Glorious God, *who sometimes in thy* Justice, *dost* give the dead bodies of the Saints, to be meat unto the Fowles of the Heaven, *and the* flesh of thy Saints unto the beasts of the Earth, *so that* their bloud is shed like water, and there is none to burie them, *Who sometimes,* sel'st thy People for nought, *and dost* not increase thy wealth, by their price, *and yet never leav'st us without that knowledge, That* precious in thy sight is the death of thy Saints, *inable us, in life and death, seriously to consider the value, the price of a* Soule. *It is precious, ô* Lord, *because thine Image is stampt, and imprinted upon it; Precious, because the bloud of thy* Sonne *was paid for it; Precious, because thy blessed* Spirit, *the* Holy Ghost *workes upon it, and tries it, by his divers fires; And precious, because it is enter'd into thy* Revenue, *and made a part of thy* Treasure. *Suffer us not therefore, ô* Lord, *so to undervalue our selves, nay, so to impoverish thee, as to give away those soules, thy soules, thy deare and precious soules, for nothing, and all the world is nothing, if the* Soule *must be given for it. We know, ô* Lord, *that our* Rent, *due to thee, is our* Soule; *and the* day *of our* death, *is the* day, *and our* Death-bed *the* place, *where this* Rent *is to bee paid. And wee know too, that hee that hath* sold *his* soule *before, for unjust gaine, or* given away *his* soule *before, in the society and fellowship of sinne, or* lent away *his* soule, *for a time, by a* lukewarmnesse, *and* temporizing, *to the dishonor of thy name, to the weaking of thy cause, to the discouraging of thy Servants, he comes to that* day, *and to that* place, *his* Death, *and* Death-bed, *without any* Rent *in his hand, without any* soule, *to this purpose, to surrender it unto thee. Let therefore ô* Lord, *the same hand which is to receive them then, preserve these* soules *till then; Let that mouth, that breath'd them into us, at first, breath alwaies upon them, whilst they are in us, and sucke them into it selfe, when they depart from us. Preserve our soules ô* Lord, *because they belong to thee; and preserve our* bodies, *because they belong to those* soules. *Thou alone, dost steere our Boat, through all our Voyage, but hast a more especiall care of it, a more watchfull eye upon it, when it comes to a narrow currant, or to a dangerous fall of waters. Thou hast a care of the preservation of these* bodies, *in all the waies of our life; But in the* Straights of Death, *open thine eyes wider, and enlarge thy providence towards us, so farre, that no* Fever *in the* body, *may shake the* soule, *no* Apoplexie *in the* body, *dampe or benumbe the* soule, *nor any paine, or* agonie *of the* body, *presage future torments to the* soule. *But so make thou our bed in all our sicknesse, that being us'd to thy hand, wee may be content with any bed of thy making; Whether thou bee pleas'd to change our* feathers *into* flockes, *by withdrawing the conveniences of this life, or to change our* flockes *into* dust, *even the* dust *of the* Grave, *by withdrawing us out of this life. And though thou divide man and wife, mother and child, friend and friend, by the hand of* Death, *yet stay them that stay, and send them away that goe, with this consolation, that though we part at divers daies, and by divers waies, here, yet wee shall all meet at one place, and at one day, a day that no night shall determine, the day of the glorious* Resurrection. *Hasten that day, ô* Lord, *for their sakes, that beg it at thy hands, from under the* Altar *in* Heaven; *Hasten it for our sakes,*

that groane under the manifold incombrances of these mortall bodies;
Hasten it for her sake, whom wee have lately laid downe, in this thy holy
ground; *And hasten it for thy* Son Christ Jesus *sake, to whom then, and
not till then, all things shall bee absolutely* subdu'd. *Seale to our* soules
*now an assurance of thy gracious purpose towards us in that day, by
accepting this daies service, at our hands. Accept our humble thankes, for
all thy benefits, spirituall, and temporall, already bestowed upon us, and
accept our humble prayers for the continuance and enlargement of them.
Continue, and enlarge them, ô* God *upon thine* universall Church, *dispersed, etc.*

I   [p. 12]

FIRST then, to shake the constancy of a Christian, there will alwaies be
Scorners, Jesters, Scoffers, and *Mockers at Religion;* The *Period* and
Consummation of the *Christian Religion,* the *Judgement day,* the *second
comming of Christ,* will alwaies be subject to *scornes.* And many times a
scorne cuts deeper than a *sword. Lucian* wounded *Religion* more by making *Jests* at it, than *Arius,* or *Pelagius,* or *Nestorius,* with making *Arguments* against it. For, against those profest *Heretikes,* and against their
studied *Arguments,* which might seeme to have some weight, it well
beseem'd those grave and Reverend *Fathers* of the *Church,* to call their
Councels, and to take into their serious consideration those *Arguments,*
and solemnly to conclude, and determine, and decree in the point. But it
would ill have become those reverend persons, to have cal'd their Councels,
or taken into their so serious considerations, *Epigrams,* and *Satyres,* and
Libells, and *scurrill* and *scornfull jests,* against any point of *Religion;*
Scornes and *Jests* are easilier apprehended, and understood by vulgar and
ordinary capacities, than *Arguments* are; and then, learned men are not
so earnest, nor so diligent to overthrow, and confute a *Jest,* or *Scornee,* as
they are, an Argument; and so they passe more uncontrol'd, and prevaile
further, and live longer, than *Arguments* doe. It is the height of *Jobs*
complaint, that contemptible persons made *Jests* upon him. And it is the
depth of *Samsons* calamity, that when the *Philistins hearts were merry,*
then they cald for *Samson, to make them sport.* So to the *Israelites* in
Babylon, when they were in that heavinesse, that every breath they
breath'd was a *sigh,* their enemies cal'd, *to sing them a song.* And so they
proceeded with him, who fulfil'd in himselfe alone, all *Types,* and *Images,*
and *Prophesies* of sorrowes, who was (as the Prophet calls him) *Vir dolorum,* A man compos'd, and elemented of sorrowes, our *Lord* and *Saviour
Christ Jesus;* For, They *platted a crowne of thornes upon his head, and
they put a reed into his hand, and they bowed the knee before him, and
mockt him.* Truly, the conniving at several *Religions,* (as dangerous as

it is) is not so *dishonourable* to *God*, as the suffering of *Jesters* at *Religion:* That may induce *heresie;* but this *does* establish *Atheisme.* And as that is the publike mischiefe, so, for the private, there lies much danger in this, that hee that gives himselfe the liberty, of *jesting* at *Religion,* shall finde it hard, to take up at last; as, when *Julian* the *Apostate* had received his Deathes-wound, and could not chuse but confesse, that that wound came from the hand, and power of *Christ,* yet he confest it, in a Phrase of *Scorne, Vicisti Galilæe, The day is thine, O Galilean,* and no more; It is not, Thou hast accomplish't thy purpose, *O my God, nor O my Maker, nor O my Redeemer,* but, in a stile of contempt, *Vicisti Galilæe,* and no more.

2

[p. 27]

It is a fearefull thing to fall into the hands of the living God, if I doe but fall into his hands, in a fever in my bed, or in a tempest at Sea, or in a discontent at home; But, *to fall into the hands of the living God,* so, as that, that *living God,* enters into *Judgement,* with mee, and passes a finall, and irrevocable Judgement upon mee, this is a Consternation of all my spirits, an Extermination of all my succours. I consider, what *God* did with one word; with one *Fiat* he made all; And, I know, he can doe as much with another word; With one *Pereat,* he can destroy all; As hee *spake, and it was done, he commanded and all stood fast;* so he can *speak,* and all shall bee *undone; command,* and all shall *fall in peeces.* I consider, that I may bee surpriz'd by *that day,* the *day of Judgement.* Here Saint *Peter* saies, *The day of the Lord wil come as a Thiefe.* And Saint *Paul* saies, we cannot be ignorant of it, *Your selves know perfectly, that the day of the Lord so commeth as a Thiefe.* And, as the *Judgement* it selfe, so the *Judge* himselfe saies of himselfe, *I will come upon thee as a Thiefe.* He saies, *he will,* and he *does* it. For it is not, *Ecce veniam,* but *Ecce venio, Behold I doe come upon thee as a Thiefe;* There, the *future,* which might imply a *dilatorinesse,* is reduc'd to an infallible *present;* It is so sure, that he *will* doe it, that he is said, to *have* done it already. I consider, *hee will come as a Thiefe,* and then, *as a Thiefe in the night;* And I doe not only not know *when* that night shall be, (For, himselfe, as he is the Son of man, knowes not that) but I doe not only not know *what* night, that is, *which* night, but not *what* night, that is, *what kinde* of night he meanes. It is said so often, so often repeated, that *he will come as a Thiefe in the night,* as that hee may meane all kinde of *nights.* In my night of *Ignorance* hee may come; and hee may come in my night of *Wantonnesse;* In my night of inordinate and sinfull *melancholy,* and *suspicion* of his *mercy,* hee may come; and he may come in the night of so *stupid,* or so *raging a sicknesse,* as that he shall not *come* by *comming;* Not come so, as that I shall receive him in the *absolution* of his *Minister,* or receive him in the participation of his *body* and his *bloud* in the *Sacrament.* So hee may come upon mee, as *such a Thiefe,* in *such a night;* nay, when all these nights of *Ignorance,* of *Wantonnesse,* of *Desperation,* of *Sicknesse,* of *Stupiditie,* of *Rage,* may bee upon mee all at once. I consider, that the *Holy Ghost* meant to make a deepe impression of a great *terror* in me, when he came to that expression, *That the Heavens should passe away,* Cum stridore, *with a great noise, and the Elements melt with fervent heat, and the earth, and the workes that are therein,* shall be burnt up; And when he adds in *Esay, The Lord will come with fire, and with his Chariots, like a whirlewind, to render his anger, with fury; for by fire, and by his sword will the Lord plead with all flesh.* So when hee proceeds in *Joel, a day of darknesse, and gloominesse; and yet a fire devoureth before them, and a flame burneth behind them.* And so in *Daniel* also, *His Throne a fiery flame, and his wheeles a burning fire, and a fiery streame issuing from him.* I consider too, that with this *streame* of *fire,* from him, there shall bee a *streame,* a deluge, a floud of teares, from us; and all that *floud,* and *deluge* of teares, shall not put out one coale, nor quench one sparke of that fire. *Behold, hee commeth with clouds, and every eye shall see him;* And, *plangent omnes, All the kindreds of the earth shall waile and lament,* and weepe and howle *because of him.* I consider, that I shall *looke* upon him then, and see all my *Sinnes, Substance,* and *Circumstance* of sin, *Waight,* and *measure* of sinne, *hainousnesse,* and *continuance* of sinne, all my sinnes imprinted in his wounds; and how shall I bee affected then, confounded then to see him so mangled with my sinnes? But then I consider againe, that I shall looke upon him againe, and not see all my sinnes in his wounds; My *forgotten* sinnes, mine *unconsidered, unconfest, unrepented* sinnes, I shall not see there; And how shall I bee affected then, when I shall stand in *Judgement,* under the guiltinesse of some sins, not buried in the wounds, not drown'd in the bloud of my *Saviour? Many,* and *many,* and *very many, infinite,* and *infinitely infinite,* are the *terrours* of that day.

3   [p. 75]

For, if we consider *God* in the *present,* to day, now, *God* hath had as long a *forenoone,* as he shall have *an afternoone; God* hath beene *God,* as many millions of millions of generations, already, as hee shall be hereafter; but if we consider *man* in the *present,* to day, now, how short a *forenoone* hath any man had; if 60. if 80. yeeres, yet, *few and evill have his daies beene.* Nay if we take man *collectively, entirely, altogether,* all mankind, how short a *forenoone* hath man had? It is not yet 6000. yeeres, since man had his first *being.* But if we consider him in his *Afternoone,* in his *future state,* in his *life* after *death,* if every minute of his 6000 yeeres, were multipli'd by so many millions of *Ages,* all would amount to nothing, meerely nothing, in respect of that *Eternity,* which hee is to dwell in. We can expresse mans *Afternoone,* his future Perpetuity, his Everlastingnesse, but one way; But it is a faire way, a noble way; This; That how late a *Beginning* soever *God* gave Man, Man shall no more see an *end,* no more die, than *God* himselfe, that gave him life.

4   [p. 106]

But as it is said of old *Cosmographers,* that when they had said all that they knew of a *Countrey,* and yet much more was to be said, they said that the rest of those countries were possest with *Giants,* or *Witches,* or *Spirits,* or *Wilde beasts,* so that they could pierce no farther into that Countrey, so when wee have travell'd as farre as wee can, with safetie, that is, as farre as *Ancient,* or *Moderne Expositors* lead us, in the *discoverie* of these *new Heavens,* and *new Earth,* yet wee must say at last, that it is a *Countrey* inhabited with *Angells,* and *Arch-angells,* with *Cherubins,* and *Seraphins,* and that wee can looke no farther into it, with these eyes. Where it is *locally,* wee enquire not; We rest in this, that it is the habitation prepar'd for the blessed *Saints of God; Heavens,* where the *Moone* is more glorious than our *Sunne,* and the *Sunne* as glorious as *Hee* that made it; For it is he himselfe, the *Sonne* of God, the *Sunne* of *glorie.* A *new Earth,* where all their *waters* are *milke,* and all their *milke, honey;* where all their *grasse* is *corne,* and all their *corne, Manna;* where all their *glebe,* all their *clods* of earth are *gold,* and all their *gold* of innumerable *carats;* Where all their *minutes* are *ages,* and all their *ages, Eternity;* Where every thing, is every minute, in the highest exaltation, as good as it can be, and yet super-exalted, and infinitely multiplied, by every minutes addition; every minute, *infinitely* better, than ever it was before. Of these *new heavens,* and this *new earth* we must say at last, that wee can say nothing; For, the *eye of Man hath not seene, nor eare heard, nor heart conceiv'd, the State of this place.* We limit, and determine our consideration with that *Horizon,* with which the *Holy Ghost* hath limited us, that it is that *new Heavens,* and *new Earth, wherein dwelleth Righteousnesse.*

Here then the *Holy Ghost* intends the same *new Heavens,* and *new Earth,* which he does in the *Apocalyps,* and describes there, by another name, the *new Jerusalem.* But here, the *Holy Ghost* does not proceed, as there, to enamour us of the place, by a promise of improvement of those things, which wee *have,* and *love* here; but by a promise of that, which here wee have not at all. There, and elsewhere, the *holy Ghost* applies himselfe, to the natural affections of men. To those that are affected with *riches,* he saies, that *that new City shall be all of gold,* and in the *foundations, all manner of precious stones;* To those that are affected with *beauty,* hee promises an everlasting association, with that beautifull Couple, that faire Paire, which spend their time, in that contemplation, and that protestation, *Ecce tu pulchra dilecta mea; Ecce tu Pulcher; Behold thou art faire, my Beloved,* saies he; and then, she replies, *Behold thou art faire too;* noting the mutuall complacencie betweene *Christ* and his *Church* there. To those which delight in *Musicke,* hee promises continuall *singing,* and every minute, a *new song;* To those, whose thoughts are exerciz'd upon *Honour,* and *Titles, Civill,* or *Ecclesiasticall,* hee promises *Priesthood,* and if that be not honour enough, *a Royall Priesthood;* And to those, who looke after *military honor, Triumph* after their *victory,* in the *Militant Church;* And to those, that are carried with sumptuous, and magnifique *feasts,* a *Mariage supper* of the *Lambe,* where, not onely all the rarities of the whole world, but the whole world it selfe shall be serv'd in; The whole world shall bee brought to that *fire,* and serv'd at that *Table.* But here, the *holy Ghost* proceeds not that way, by improvement of things, which wee *have,* and *love* here; *riches,* or *beauty,* or *musicke,* or *honour,* or *feasts;* but by an everlasting possession of that, which wee hunger, and thirst, and pant after, here, and cannot compasse, that is, *Justice,* or *Righteousnesse;* for, both those, our present word denotes, and both those wee want here, and shall have both, for ever, in these *new Heavens,* and *new Earth.*

5   [p. 135]

And for her, some sicknesses, in the declination of her yeeres, had opened her to an overflowing of *Melancholie;* Not that she ever lay under that *water,* but yet, had sometimes, some high Tides of it; and, though this distemper would sometimes cast a cloud, and some halfe damps upon her naturall cheerfulnesse, and sociablenesse, and sometimes induce darke, and sad apprehensions, *Neverthel··· ·,* who ever heard, or say in her, any such effect of *Melancholy* as to murmure, or repine, or dispute upon any of *Gods* proceedings, or to lodge a Jelousie, or Suspition of his mercy, and goodnesse towards her, and all hers? The *Wit* of our time is *Prophanesse; Neverthelesse,* shee, that lov'd *that,* hated *this;* Occasionall *Melancholy* had taken some hold in her; *Neverthelesse,* that never Ecclipst, never interrupted her cheerfull confidence, and assurance in *God.*

Our second word denotes the *person; We, Neverthelesse We;* And, here in this consideration, *Neverthelesse shee.* This may seeme to promise some picture, some Character of her *person.* But, shee was no stranger to them that heare me now; nor scarce to any that may heare of this hereafter, which you heare now, and therefore, much needes not, to that purpose. Yet, to that purpose, of her *person,* and *personall circumstances,* thus much I may *remember* some, and *informe* others, That from that *Worthy family,* whence she had her originall extraction, and birth, she suckt that love of *hospitality,* (*hospitality,* which hath celebrated that *family,* in many Generations, successively) which dwelt in her, to her end. But in that *ground,* her Fathers *family,* shee grew not many yeeres. Transplanted young from thence, by mariage, into another *family* of *Honour,* as a flower that doubles and multiplies by transplantation, she multiplied into *ten Children; Job's* number; and *Job's* distribution, (as shee, her selfe would very often remember) *seven sonnes,* and *three daughters.* And, in this ground, shee grew not many yeeres more, than were necessary, for the producing of so many plants. And being then left to chuse her owne ground in her *Widow-hood,* having at home establisht, and increast the estate, with a faire, and noble Addition, proposing to her selfe, as her principall care, the education of her *children,* to advance that, shee came with them, and dwelt with them, in the *Universitie;* and recompenc't to them, the losse of a *Father,* in giving them *two mothers;* her owne personal care, and the advantage of that place; where shee contracted a friendship, with divers reverend persons, of eminency, and estimation there; which continued to their ends. And as this was her greatest *businesse,* so she made this state, a large *Period;* for in this state of *widowhood,* shee continued *twelve yeeres.* And then, returning to a *second mariage,* that *second mariage* turnes us to the consideration of another *personall circumstance;* that is, the *naturall endowments of her person;* Which were such, as that, (though her *vertues* were his principall *object*) yet, even these her *personall,* and *natural endowments,* had their part, in drawing, and fixing the affections of such a person, as by his *birth,* and *youth,* and *interest in great favours in Court,* and *legall proximity* to great possessions in the world, might justly have promist him acceptance, in what *family* soever, or upon what *person* soever, hee had directed, and plac't his Affections. He plac't them here; neither *diverted* then, nor *repented* since. For, as the well tuning of an *Instrument,* makes *higher* and *lower* strings, of one sound, so the inequality of their yeeres, was thus reduc't to an evennesse, that shee had a *cheerfulnesse,* agreeable to his *youth,* and he a *sober staidnesse,* conformable to her *more yeeres.* So that, I would not consider her, at so much more than *forty,* nor him, at so much lesse than *thirty,* at that time, but, as their *persons* were made *one,* and their *fortunes* made one, by *mariage,* so I would put their yeeres into *one number,* and finding a *sixty* betweene them, thinke them *thirty* a peece; for, as twins of one houre, they liv'd. *God,* who joyn'd them, then, having also separated them now, may make their *yeeres* even, this other

way too; by giving him, as many yeeres after her going out of this World,
as he had given her, before his comming into it; and then, as many more,
as *God* may receive *Glory,* and the World, *Benefit* by that Addition; That
so, as at their first meeting, she was, at their last meeting, he may bee the
elder person.

To this consideration of her *person* then, belongs this, that *God* gave
her such a *comelinesse,* as, though shee were not *proud* of it, yet she was so
content with it, as not to goe about to mend it, by any *Art.* And for her
Attire, (which is another *personall circumstance*) it was never *sumptuous,*
never *sordid;* But alwayes agreeable to her *quality,* and agreeable to her
company; Such as shee might, and such, as others, such as shee was, did
weare. For, in such things of *indifferency* in themselves, many times, a
singularity may be a little worse, than a fellowship in that, which is not
altogether so good. It may be *worse,* nay, it may be a *worse pride,* to weare
worse things, than others doe. Her *rule* was *mediocrity.*

And, as to the consideration of the *house,* belongs the consideration of
the *furniture* too, so, in these *personall circumstances,* we consider her
fortune, her *estate.* Which was in a faire, and noble proportion, deriv'd
from her *first husband,* and fairely, and nobly dispenc'd, by her selfe, with
the allowance of her *second.* In which shee was one of *Gods* true *Stewards,*
and *Almoners* too. There are dispositions, which had rather *give presents,*
than *pay debts;* and rather doe good to *strangers,* than to those, that are
neerer to them. But *shee* alwayes thought the care of her family, a *debt,*
and upon that, for the *provision,* for the *order,* for the *proportions,* in a
good largenesse, she plac't her first thoughts, of that kinde. For, for our
families, we are *Gods Stewards;* For those without, we are his *Almoners.*
In which office, shee gave not at some *great dayes,* or some solemne goings
abroad, but, as *Gods true Almoners,* the *Sunne,* and *Moone,* that passe
on, in a continuall doing of good, as shee receiv'd her *daily bread* from
God, so *daily,* she distributed, and imparted it, to others. In which office,
though she never turn'd her face from those, who in a strict inquisition,
might be call'd idle, and vagrant Beggers, yet shee ever look't first, upon
them, who *labour'd,* and whose *labours* could not overcome the *difficulties,*
nor bring in the *necessities* of this life; and to the *sweat* of their *browes,*
shee contributed, even her *wine,* and her *oyle,* and any thing that was, and
any thing, that might be, if it were not, prepar'd for her owne table. And
as her house was a *Court,* in the conversation of the best, and an *Almes-
house,* in feeding the poore, so was it also an *Hospitall,* in ministring
releefe to the *sicke.* And truly, the love of doing good in this kind, of
ministring to the sicke, was the *hony,* that was spread over all her bread;
the *Aire,* the *Perfume,* that breath'd over all her house; The disposition
that dwelt in those her children, and those her kindred, which dwelt with

her, so bending this way, that the *studies* and *knowledge* of *one*, the *hand* of another, and *purse* of all, and a *joynt-facility*, and *opennesse*, and *accessiblenesse* to persons of the meanest quality, concur'd in this blessed *Act* of *Charity*, to *minister releefe to the sicke*. Of which, my selfe, who, at that time, had the favour to bee admitted into that *family*, can, and must testifie this, that when the late heavy *visitation* fell hotly upon this *Towne*, when every doore was shut up, and, lest *Death* should enter into the house, every house was made a *Sepulchre* of them that were in it, then, then, in that time of *infection*, divers persons visited with that *infection*, had their releefe, and releefe *appliable to that very infection*, from this house.

Now when I have said thus much (rather thus little) of her *person*, as of a *house*, That the *ground* upon which it was built, was the *family* where she was *borne*, and then, where she was *married*, and then, the time of her *widowhood*, and lastly, her *last mariage*, And that the *house* it selfe, was those faire *bodily endowments*, which *God* had bestow'd upon her, And the *furniture* of that *house*, the *fortune*, and the *use* of that *fortune*, of which *God* had made her *Steward* and *Almoner*, when I shall also have said, that the *Inhabitants* of this *house*, (rather the *servants*, for they did but wait upon *Religion* in her) were those married couples, of *morall vertues*, *Conversation* married with a *Retirednesse*, *Facility* married with a *Reservednesse*, *Alacrity* married with a *Thoughtfulnesse*, and *Largenesse* married with a *Providence*, I may have leave to depart from this consideration of her *person*, and *personall circumstances*, lest by insisting longer upon them, I should seeme to pretend, to say all the good, that might bee said of her; But that's not in my *purpose;* yet, onely therefore, because it is not in my *power;* For I would doe her all *right*, and all you that good, if I could, to say all. But, I haste to an end, in consideration of some things, that appertaine more expresly to me, than these *personall*, or *civill*, or *morall* things doe.

In those, the next is, the *Secundum promissa*, That shee govern'd her selfe, *according to his promises;* his promises, laid downe in his *Scriptures*. For, as the *rule* of all her *civill Actions*, was *Religion*, so, the *rule* of her *Religion*, was the *Scripture;* And, her *rule*, for her particular understanding of the *Scripture*, was the *Church*. Shee never diverted towards the *Papist*, in undervaluing the *Scripture;* nor towards the *Separatist*, in undervaluing the *Church*. But in the *doctrine*, and *discipline* of that *Church*, in which, *God* seal'd her, to himselfe, in *Baptisme*, shee brought up her children, she assisted her family, she dedicated her soule to *God* in her life, and surrendered it to him in her death; And, in that forme of *Common Prayer*, which is ordain'd by that *Church*, and to which shee had accustom'd her selfe, with her family, twice every day, she joyn'd with that company, which was about her *death-bed,* in answering to every part thereof, which the Congregation is directed to answer to, with a *cleere understanding,* with a *constant memory,* with a *distinct voyce,* not two houres before she died.

According to this promise, that is, the will of *God* manifested in the *Scriptures,* She *expected;* She expected this, that she hath received; *Gods Physicke,* and *Gods Musicke;* a *Christianly death.* For, *death,* in the *old Testament* was a *Commination;* but in the *new Testament, death* is a *Promise;* When there was a *Super-dying,* a *death* upon the *death,* a *Morte* upon the *Morieris,* a *Spirituall* death after the *bodily,* then wee died *according to Gods threatning;* Now, when by the *Gospell,* that *second death* is taken off, though wee die still, yet we die *according to his Promise;* That's a part of his *mercy,* and his *Promise,* which his *Apostle* gives us from him, That wee shall *all bee changed:* For, after that *promise,* that *change,* follows that triumphant *Acclamation, O death where is thy sting, O grave where is thy victory?* Consider us fallen in *Adam,* and wee are miserable, that wee must die; But consider us restor'd, and redintegrated in *Christ,* wee were more miserable if wee might not die; Wee lost the *earthly Paradise* by death then; but wee get not *Heaven,* but by *death,* now. This shee expected till it came, and embrac't it when it came. How may we thinke, shee was joy'd to see that face, that *Angels* delight to looke upon, the face of her *Saviour,* that did not abhor the face of his fearfullest *Messenger,* Death? Shee shew'd no feare of his face, in any change of her owne; but died without any change of *countenance,* or *posture;* without any *strugling,* any *disorder;* but her *Death-bed* was as quiet, as her *Grave.* To another *Magdalen, Christ* said upon earth, *Touch me not, for I am not ascended.* Being ascended now, to his glory, and she being gone up to him, after shee had awaited his leisure, so many yeeres, as that more, would soone have growne to bee *vexation,* and *sorrow,* as her last words here, were, *I submit my will to the will of God;* so wee doubt not, but the first word which she heard there, was that *Euge,* from her *Saviour, Well done good and faithfull servant; enter into thy masters joy.*

Shee expected that; dissolution of body, and soule; and rest in both, from the incumbrances, and tentations of this world. But yet, shee is in *expectation* still; Still a *Reversionarie;* And a *Reversionary* upon a long life; The whole world must die, before she come to a *possession* of this *Reversion;* which is a *Glorified body in the Resurrection.* In which *expectation,* she returns to her former *charity;* shee will not have that, till *all wee* shall have it, as well as shee; She eat not her morsels alone, in her life, (as *Job* speakes); Shee lookes not for the *glory* of the *Resurrection* alone, after her death. But when *all wee,* shall have beene mellow'd in the earth. many yeeres, or chang'd in the *Aire,* in the twinkling of an eye, (*God* knowes which) That *body* upon which you tread now, That *body* which now, whilst I speake, is mouldring, and crumbling into lesse, and lesse dust, and so hath some *motion*, though no *life*, That *body*, which was the *Tabernacle* of a *holy Soule*, and a *Temple* of the *holy Ghost*, That *body* that was eyes to the blinde, and hands, and feet to the lame, whilst it liv'd, and being dead, is so still, by having beene so *lively* an example, to teach others, to be so, That *body* at last, shall have her last expectation satisfied, and dwell *bodily*, with that *Righteousnesse*, in these *new Heavens*, and *new Earth*, for *ever*, and *ever*, and *ever*, and *infinite*, and *super infinite evers*. Wee end all, with the *valediction* of the *Spouse* to *Christ: His left hand is under my head, and his right embraces mee*, was the *Spouses* valediction, and *goodnight* to *Christ* then, when she laide her selfe downe to sleepe in the strength of his *Mandrakes*, and in the power of his *Spices*, as it is exprest there; that is, in the *influence* of his *mercies*. Beloved, every good *Soule* is the *Spouse* of *Christ*. And this good *Soule*, being thus laid downe to sleepe in his peace, *His left hand under her head*, gathering, and composing, and preserving her *dust*, for *future Glory, His right hand embracing her*, assuming, and establishing her *soule* in present *Glory*, in his *name*, and in her *behalfe*, I say that, to *all you*, which *Christ* sayes there, in the behalfe of that *Spouse, Adjuro vos, I adjure you, I charge you, O daughters of Jerusalem, that yee wake her not, till she please*. The words are directed to the *daughters*, rather than to the *sons* of *Jerusalem*, because for the most part, the aspersions that women receive, either in *Morall* or *Religious* actions, proceed from women themselves. Therfore, *Adjuro vos*, I charge you, O ye daughters of *Jerusalem*, wake her not. Wake her not, with any *halfe calumnies*, with any *whisperings;* But if you wil wake her, wake her, and keepe her awake with an active imitation, of her *Morall*, and her *Holy vertues*. That so her *example* working upon you, and the number of *Gods Saints*, being, the sooner, by this blessed *example*, fulfil'd, wee may all meet, and meet quickly in that *kingdome*, which *hers*, and *our Saviour*, hath purchac't for us all, with the inestimable price of his incorruptible bloud.

PASSAGES FROM SIX SERMONS, 1634

II

Preached to the King at the Court [April 1629]

I   [pp. 11-14]

GOD himself made all that he made, according to a pattern. God had deposited and laid up in himself certain forms, patterns, *Ideas* of every thing that he made. He made nothing, of which he had not preconceived the form, and predetermined in himself, I will make it thus. And when he had made any thing, he saw that it was good; Good, because it answered the pattern, the image; Good, because it was like to that. And therefore though of other creatures God pronounced they were good, because they were presently like their pattern, that is, like that form which was in him for them: yet of man, he forebore to say that he was good; because his conformitie to his pattern was to appeare after in his subsequent actions. Now as God made man after another pattern, and therefore we have a dignitie above all, that we had another manner of creation than the rest: so have we a comfort above all, that we have another manner of administration than the rest. God exercises another manner of providence upon man, than upon other creatures. *A sparrow falls not without God,* sayes Christ: yet no doubt God works otherwise in the fall of eminent persons, than in the fall of sparrows; *for ye are of more value than many sparrows,* sayes Christ there of every man: and some men single, are of more value than many men. God doth not thank the ant, for her industrie and good husbandrie in providing for her self. God doth not reward the foxes, for concurring with *Samson* in his revenge. God doth not fee the lion, which was his executioner upon the Prophet which had disobeyed his commandment; nor those two she-bears, which slew the petulant children, who had calumniated and reproached *Elisha*. God doth not fee them before, nor thank them after, nor take knowledge of their service: But for those men that served Gods execution upon the idolaters of the golden calf, it is pronounced in their behalf, that therein they consecrated themselves unto God; and for that service God made that Tribe, the Tribe of Levi, his portion, his clergie, his consecrated Tribe: So, *Quia fecisti hoc,* sayes God to Abraham, *By my self I have sworn, because thou hast done this thing, and hast not witheld thy sonne, thine onely sonne: that in blessing I will blesse thee, and in multiplying I will multiply thee.* So neither is God angrie with the dog that turns to his vomit; nor with the sow, that after her washing wallows in the mire. But of man in that case he sayes, *It is impossible for those who were once enlightned, if they fall away, to renew themselves again by repentance.* The creatures live under his law, but a law imposed thus, This they shall do, this they must do: Man lives under another manner of law, This you shall do, that is, This you should do, This I would have you do. And, *Fac hoc, Do this, and you shall live;* disobey, and you shall die: but yet the choice is yours; choose you this day life or death. So that this is Gods administration in the creature, that he hath imprinted in them an instinct, and so he hath something to preserve in them: In man, his administration is this, that he hath imprinted in him a facultie of will and election, and hath something to reward in him. That instinct in the creature God leaves to the naturall working thereof in it self: but the freewill of man God visits and assists with his grace, to do supernaturall things. When the creature doth an extraordinary action above the nature thereof (as when Balaams asse spake) the creature exercises no facultie, no will in it self; but God forced it to that it did. When man doth any thing conducing to supernaturall ends, though the work be Gods, the will of man is not meerly passive. The will of man is but Gods agent; but still an agent it is, and an agent in another manner than the tongue of the beast. For the will considered as a will (and grace never destroyes nature; nor, though it make a dead will a live will, or an ill will a good will, doth it make the will no will) might refuse or omit that it does. So that because we are created by another pattern, we are governed by another law, and another providence.

2

[pp. 22-23]

We should wonder to see a mother in the midst of many sweet children, passing her time in making babies and puppets for her own delight. We should wonder to see a man, whose chambers and galleries were full of curious master-pieces, thrust in a village-fayre, to look upon sixpenie pictures and three-farthing prints. We have all the image of God at home; and we all make babies, fancies of honour in our ambitions. The master-piece is our own, in our own bosome; and we thrust in countrey-fayres, that is, we endure the distempers of any unseasonable weather, in night-journeys and watchings; we endure the oppositions, and scorns, and triumphs of a rivall and competitour, that seeks with us, and shares with us. We endure the guiltinesse and reproach of having deceived the trust, which a confident friend reposes in us, and solicite his wife or daughter. We endure the decay of fortune, of bodie, of soul, of honour, to possesse lower pictures; pictures that are not originals, not made by that hand of God, Nature; but artificial beauties: and for that bodie we give a soul; and for that drug which might have been bought where they bought it, for a shilling, we give an estate. The image of God is more worth than all substances; and we give it for colours, for dreams, for shadows.

III

Preached at a Marriage

[pp. 16-17]

FIRST then, as in the former part, the secular marriage, for the persons there, we considered first Adam and Eve; and after, every man and woman, and this couple in particular: so in this spirituall marriage, we consider first Christ and his Church, for the persons; but more particu-

larly, Christ and my soul. And can these persons meet? In such a distance,
and in such a disparagement, can these persons meet? The Sonne of God,
and the sonne of man? When I consider Christ to be *Germen Jehovæ*, the
bud and blossome, the fruit and off-spring of Jehovah, Jehovah himself;
and my self, before he took me in hand, to be, not a potters vessel of earth,
but that earth of which the potter might make a vessel if he would, and
break it if he would, when he had made it: when I consider Christ to have
been from before all beginnings, and to be still the image of the Father,
the same stamp upon the same metall; and my selfe a piece of rusty copper,
in which those lines of the image of God, which were imprinted in me, in
my creation, are defaced, and worn, and washed, and burnt, and ground
away by my many, and many, and many sinnes: when I consider Christ
in his circle, in glorie with his Father, before he came into this world,
establishing a glorious Church when he was in this world, and glorifying
that Church, with that glorie which himself had before, when he went out
of this world; and then consider my self in my circle, I came into this
world washed in mine own tears, and either out of compunction for my
self, or compassion for others, I passe through this world, as through a
valley of tears, where tears settle and swell; and when I passe out of this
world, I leave their eyes, whose hands close mine, full of tears too: Can
these persons, this image of God, this God himself, this glorious God, and
this vessel of earth, this earth it self, this inglorious worm of the earth,
meet without disparagement?

IV

Preached to the Nobility

[pp. 3-7]

In finem dilexit eos, saith S. *John, He loved them to the end*, not for any
particular end, for any use of his own, but to their end *Qui erant in mundo*,
saith *Cyril, ad distinctionem Angelorum;* he loved them in the world, and
not Angels: he loved not onely them who were in a confirmed estate of
mutuall loving of him too, but even them who were themselves conceived
in sinne, and then conceived all their purposes in sinne too; them who
could have no cleansing but in his bloud, and when they were cleansed in
his bloud, their own clothes would defile them again; them, who by nature
are not able to love him at all; and when by grace they are brought to love
him, can expresse their love no other way, but to be glad that he was betrayed, and scourged, and scorned, and nailed, and crucified; and to be
glad, that if all this were not alreadie done, it might be done yet; and to
long and to wish, if Christ were not crucified, to have him crucified now
(which is a strange manner of expressing love) those men he loved, and

loved to the end; men, and not Angels; and then men, *Ad distinctionem mortuorum,* saith *Chrysostome:* not onely the Patriarchs who were departed out of the world, who had loved him so well, as to take his word for their salvation, and had lived and died in a faithfull contemplation of a future promise, which they never saw performed; but those who were the partakers of the performance of all those promises; those, into the midst of whom he came in person; those, upon whom he wrought by his piercing doctrine and powerfull miracles; those, who for all this loved not him, he loved, *Et in finem,* he loved them to the end. It is much he should love them *in fine,* at their end; that he should look graciously on them at last; that when their sunne sets, their eyes faint, his sonne of grace should arise, and his East should be brought to their West; that then, in the shadow of death, the Lord of life should quicken and inanimate their hearts; that when their last bell tolls, and calls them to their first and last judgement, which to this purpose is all one; for the passing bell and the Angels trump sound but one note: *Surgite qui dormitis in pulvere, Arise ye that sleep in the dust,* which is the voice of the Angels; and, *Surgite qui vigilatis in plumis, Arise ye that cannot sleep in feathers,* for the pangs of death, which is the voice of the bell, is in effect but one voice: for God at the generall judgement shall never reverse any particular judgement formerly given: that God should then come to thy bedside *Ad sibilandum populum suum,* as the Prophet *Ezechiel* saith, to hisse softly for his childe, to speak comfortably in his eare, to whisper gently to his departing soul, and to drown and overcome with this soft musick of his all the clangour of the Angels trumpets, all the horrour of the ringing bell, all the cries and vociferations of a distressed, and distracted, and scattering family; yea, all the accusations of his own conscience, and all the triumphant acclamations of the devil himself: that God should love a man thus *in fine,* at his end, and return to him then though he had suffered him to go astray before, is a great testimonie of the inexpressible love. But this love is not *in fine, in the end;* but *in finem, to the end.* He leaves them not uncalled at the first, he leaves them not unaccompanied in the way, he leaves them not unrecompensed at the last. That God, who is Almighty, Alpha and Omega, First and Last, that God is also Love it self; and therefore this Love is Alpha and Omega, First and Last too. Consider Christs proceeding with *Peter* in the ship, in the storm: First he suffered him to be in some danger in the storm, but then he visits him with that strong assurance, *Noli timere, Be not afraid, it is I:* any testimonie of his presence rectifies all. This puts *Peter* into that spirituall confidence and courage, *Jube me venire, Lord bid me come to thee;* he hath a desire to be with Christ, but yet stayes his bidding: he puts not himself into an unnecessarie danger, without commandment: Christ bids him, and *Peter* comes: but yet, though Christ were in his sight, and even in the actuall exercise of his love to him, so soon as he saw a gust, a storm, *Timuit, He was afraid;* and Christ lets him fear, and lets him sink, and lets him crie, but he directs his fear and his crie to the right end: *Domine, salvum me fac; Lord, save me;* and thereupon he stretched forth his hand and saved him. God doth not raise his children to honour and great estate, and then leave them, and expose them to be subjects and exercises of the malice of others; neither doth he make them mightie and then leave them, *ut glorietur in malo qui potens est,* that he should think it a glorie to do harm: he doth not impoverish and dishonour his children, and then leave them unsensible of that doctrine, that patience is as great a blessing as abundance. God gives not his people health, and then leaves them to a boldnesse in surfeting; nor beautie, and then leaves them to a confidence, and opening themselves to all sollicitations; nor valour, and then leaves them to a spirituous, quarrelsomenesse: God makes no patterns of his works, nor models of his houses; he makes whole pieces, and perfect houses: he puts his children into good wayes, and he directs and protects them in those wayes; for this is the constancie and perseverance of the love of Christ Jesus to us, as he is called in this Text *a stone.*

PASSAGES FROM EIGHTY SERMONS. 1640

SERMON I

St. Paul's. Christmas Day. 1622

[p. 10]

I F you will reconcile things in heaven, and earth, with things in hell, that is a reconciling out of this Text. If you will mingle the service of God, and the service of this world, there is no reconciling of God and Mammon in this Text. If you will mingle a true religion, and a false religion, there is no reconciling of God and Belial in this Text. For the adhering of persons born within the Church of Rome, to the Church of Rome, our law sayes nothing to them if they come; But for reconciling to the Church of Rome, by persons born within the Allegeance of the King, or for perswading of men to be so reconciled, our law hath called by an infamous and Capitall name of Treason, and yet every Tavern, and Ordinary is full of such Traitors. Every place from jest to earnest is filled with them; from the very stage to the death-bed; At a Comedy they will perswade you, as you sit, as you laugh, And in your sicknesse they will perswade you, as you lye, as you dye. And not only in the bed of sicknesse, but in the bed of wantonnesse they perswade too; and there may be examples of women, that have thought it a fit way to gain a soul, by prostituting themselves, and by entertaining unlawfull love, with a purpose to convert a servant, which is somewhat a strange Topique, to draw arguments of religion from. Let me see a Dominican and a Jesuit reconciled, in doctrinall papistry, for freewill and predestination, Let me see a French papist and an Italian papist reconciled in State-papistry, for the Popes jurisdiction, Let me see the Jesuits, and the secular priests reconciled in England, and when they are reconciled to one another, let them presse reconciliation to their Church. To end all, Those men have their bodies from the earth, and they have their soules from heaven; and so all things in earth and heaven are reconciled: but they have their Doctrine from the Devill; and for things in hell, there is no peace made, and with things in hell, there is no reconciliation to be had by the blood of his Crosse, except we will tread that blood under our feet, and make a mock of Christ Jesus, and crucifie the Lord of Life againe.

SERMON II

St. Paul's. Christmas Day in the evening. 1624

[pp. 12-13]

T H E aire is not so full of Moats, of Atomes, as the Church is of Mercies; and as we can suck in no part of aire, but we take in those Moats, those Atomes; so here in the Congregation we cannot suck in a word from the preacher, we cannot speak, we cannot sigh a prayer to God, but that that whole breath and aire is made of mercy. But we call not upon you from this Text, to consider Gods ordinary mercy, that which he exhibites to all in the ministery of his Church; nor his miraculous mercy, his extraordinary deliverances of States and Churches but we call upon particular Consciences, by occasion of this Text, to call to minde Gods occasionall mercies to them; such mercies as a regenerate man will call mercies, though a naturall man would call them accidents, or occurrences, or contingencies; A man wakes at midnight full of unclean thoughts, and he heares a passing Bell; this is an occasionall mercy, if he call that his own knell, and consider how unfit he was to be called out of the world then, how unready to receive that voice, *Foole, this night they shall fetch away thy soule.* The adulterer, whose eye waites for the twy-light, goes forth, and casts his eyes upon forbidden houses, and would enter, and sees a *Lord have mercy upon us* upon the doore; this is an occasionall mercy, if this bring him to know that they who lie sick of the plague within, passe through a furnace, but by Gods grace, to heaven; and hee without, carries his own furnace to hell, his lustfull loines to everlasting perdition. What an occasional!

mercy had *Balaam,* when his Asse Catechized him: What an occasionall mercy had one Theefe, when the other catechized him so, *Art not thou afraid being under the same condemnation?* What an occasionall mercy had all they that saw that, when the Devil himself fought for the name of Jesus, and wounded the sons of *Sceva* for exorcising in the name of Jesus, with that indignation, with that increpation, *Jesus we know, and Paul we know, but who are ye?* If I should declare what God hath done (done occasionally) for my soule, where he instructed me for feare of falling, where he raised me when I was fallen, perchance you would rather fixe your thoughts upon my illnesse, and wonder at that, than at Gods goodnesse, and glorifie him in that; rather wonder at my sins, than at his mercies, rather consider how ill a man I was, than how good a God he is. If I should inquire upon what occasion God elected me, and writ my name in the book of Life, I should sooner be afraid that it were not so, than finde a reason why it should be so. God made Sun and Moon to distinguish seasons, and day, and night, and we cannot have the fruits of the earth but in their seasons: But God hath made no decree to distinguish the seasons of his mercies; In paradise, the fruits were ripe, the first minute, and in heaven it is alwaies Autumne, his mercies are ever in their maturity. We ask *panem quotidianam,* our daily bread, and God never sayes you should have come yesterday, he never sayes you must againe to morrow, but *to day if you will heare his voice,* to day he will heare you. If some King of the earth have so large an extent of Dominion, in North, and South, as that he hath Winter and Summer together in his Dominions, so large an extent East and West, as that he hath day and night together in his Dominions, much more hath God mercy and judgement together: He brought light out of darknesse, not out of a lesser light; he can bring thy Summer out of Winter, though thou have no Spring; though in the wayes of fortune, or understanding, or conscience, thou have been benighted till now, wintred and frozen, clouded and eclypsed, damped and benummed, smothered and stupefied till now, now God comes to thee, not as in the dawning of the day, not as in the bud of the spring, but as the Sun at noon to illustrate all shadowes, as the sheaves in harvest, to fill all penuries, all occasions invite his mercies, and all times are his seasons.

SERMON III

St. Paul's. Christmas Day. 1625

I   [p. 20]

WEE are met here to celebrate the generation of Christ Jesus; but *Generationem ejus quis enarrabit,* sayes the Prophet, *who shall declare his*

generation, his age? For, for essentiall generation, by which he is the
Son of God, the Angels, who are almost 6000. yeares elder than we, are
no nearer to that generation of his, than if they had been made but yesterday: Eternity hath no such distinctions, no limits, no periods, no seasons, no moneths, no yeares, no dayes; *Methusalem,* who was so long
lived, was no elder in respect of eternity, than *Davids* son by *Berseba,*
that dyed the first week. The first *Fiat* in the Creation of *Adam,* and the
last note of the blowing of the Trumpets to judgement, though there be
between these (as it is ordinarily received) 2000. yeares of nature, between the Creation, and the giving of the Law by *Moses,* and 2000. yeares
of the Law between that, and the comming of Christ, and 2000. yeares of
Grace and Gospell between Christ first, and his second comming, yet this
Creation and this Judgement are not a minute asunder in respect of
eternity, which hath no minutes. Whence then arises all our vexation and
labour, all our anxieties and anguishes, all our suits and pleadings, for long
leases, for many lives, for many yeares purchase in this world, when, if
we be in our way to the eternall King of the eternall kingdome, Christ
Jesus, all we are not yet, all the world shall never be a minute old; *Gen-*
erationem ejus quis enarrabit, what tongue can declare, what heart can
conceive his generation which was so long before any heart or tongue was
made? But we come not now to consider that eternall generation, not
Christ meerly as the Son of God, but the Son of *Mary* too: And that generation the Holy Ghost hath told us, was in *the fulnesse of time: When*
the fulnesse of time was come, God sent forth, &c.

2   [p. 21]

    How much misery is presaged to us, when we come so generally weep-
ing into the world, that, perchance, in the whole body of history we reade
but of one childe, *Zoroaster* that laughed at his birth: What miserable
revolutions and changes, what downfals, what break-necks, and precipita-
tions may we justly think our selves ordained to, if we consider, that in our
comming into this world out of our mothers womb, we doe not make account that a childe comes right, except it come with the head forward,
and thereby prefigure that headlong falling into calamities which it must
suffer after? Though therefore the dayes of the Martyrs, which are for
our example celebrated in the Christian Church, be ordinarily called
natalitia Martyrum, the birth-day of the Martyrs, yet that is not intended of their birth in this world, but of their birth in the next; when,
by death their soules were new delivered of their prisons here, and they
newly born into the kingdome of heaven; that day, upon that reason, the
day of their death was called their birth-day, and celebrated in the Church
by that name. Onely to Christ Jesus, *the fulnesse of time* was at his

birth; not because he also had not a painfull life to passe through, but because the work of our redemption was an intire work, and all that Christ said, or did, or suffered, concurred to our salvation, as well his mothers swathing him in little clouts, as *Josephs* shrowding him in a funerall sheete; as well his cold lying in the Manger, as his cold dying upon the Crosse; as well the *puer natus,* as the *consummatum est;* as well his birth, as his death is said to have been *the fulnesse of time.*

SERMON IV

St. Paul's. Christmas Day. 1626.

[pp. 38-39]

M Y body is my prison; and I would be so obedient to the Law, as not to break prison; I would not hasten my death by starving, or macerating this body: But if this prison be burnt down by continuall feavers, or blowen down with continuall vapours, would any man be so in love with that ground upon which that prison stood, as to desire rather to stay there, than to go home? Our prisons are fallen, our bodies are dead to many former uses; Our palate dead in a tastlesnesse; Our stomach dead in an indigestiblenesse; our feete dead in a lamenesse, and our invention in a dulnesse, and our memory in a forgetfulnesse; and yet, as a man that should love the ground, where his prison stood, we love this clay, that was a body in the dayes of our youth, and but our prison then, when it was at best; wee abhorre the graves of our bodies; and the body, which, in the best vigour thereof, was but the grave of the soule, we over-love. *Pharaohs* Butler, and his Baker went both out of prison in a day; and in both cases, *Joseph,* in the interpretation of their dreames, calls that, (their very discharge out of prison) a lifting up of their heads, a kinde of preferment: Death raises every man alike, so far, as that it delivers every man from his prison, from the incumbrances of this body: both Baker and Butler were delivered of their prison; but they passed into divers states after, one to the restitution of his place, the other to an ignominious execution. Of thy prison thou shalt be delivered whether thou wilt or no; thou must die; Foole, this night thy soule may be taken from thee; and then, what thou shalt be to morrow, prophecy upon thy selfe, by that which thou hast done to day; If thou didst depart from that Table in peace, thou canst depart from this world in peace. And the peace of that Table is, to come to it *in pace desiderii,* with a contented minde, and with an enjoying of those temporall blessings which thou hast, without macerating thy self, without usurping upon others, without murmuring at God; And to be at that Table, *in pace cogitationum*, in the peace of the Church, without the spirit of contradiction, or inquisition, without uncharitablenesse towards others, without curiosity in thy selfe: And then to come from that Table *in pace domestica,* with a bosome peace, in thine own Conscience, in that seale of thy reconciliation, in that Sacrament; that so, riding at that Anchor, and in that calme, whether God enlarge thy voyage, by enlarging thy life, or put thee into the harbour, by the breath, by the breathlesnesse of Death, either way, East or West, thou maist depart in peace, according to his word, that is, as he shall be pleased to manifest his pleasure upon thee.

SERMON V

St. Paul's. Christmas Day. 1627

[pp. 44-45]

MAN is but earth; Tis true; but earth is the center. That man who dwels upon himself, who is alwaies conversant in himself, rests in his true center. Man is a celestial creature too, a heavenly creature; and that man that dwels upon himselfe, that hath his conversation in himselfe, hath his conversation in heaven. If you weigh any thing in a scale, the greater it is, the lower it sinkes; as you grow greater and greater in the eyes of the world, sinke lower and lower in your owne. If thou ask thy self *Quis ego,* what am I? and beest able to answer thy selfe, why now I am a man of title, of honour, of place, of power, of possessions, a man fit for a Chronicle, a man considerable in the Heralds Office, goe to the Heralds Office, the spheare and element of Honour, and thou shalt finde those men as busie there, about the consideration of Funerals, as about the consideration of Creations; thou shalt finde that office to be as well the Grave, as the Cradle of Honour; And thou shalt finde in that Office as many Records of attainted families, and escheated families, and empoverished and forgotten, and obliterate families, as of families newly erected and presently celebrated. In what heighth soever, any of you that sit here, stand at home, there is some other in some higher station than yours, that weighs you downe: And he that stands in the highest of subordinate heighths, nay in the highest supreme heighth in this world, is weighed downe, by that, which is nothing; for what is any Monarch to the whole world? and the whole world is but that; but what? but nothing.

GOD, who vouchsafed to be made Man for man, for man vouchsafes also
to doe all the offices of man towards man. He is our Father, for he made
us: Of what? Of clay; So God is *Figulus,* so in the Prophet; so in the
Apostle, God is our Potter. God stamped his Image upon us, and so God
is *Statuarius,* our Minter, our Statuary. God clothed us, and so is
vestiarius; he hath opened his wardrobe unto us. God gave us all the
fruits of the earth to eate, and so is *œconomus,* our Steward. God poures
his oyle, and his wine into our wounds, and so is *Medicus,* and *Vicinus,*
that Physitian, that Neighbour, that Samaritan intended in the Parable.
God plants us, and waters and weeds us, and gives the increase; and so
God is *Hortulanus,* our Gardiner. God builds us up into a Church, and so
God is *Architectus,* our Architect, our Builder; God watches the City
when it is built; and so God is *Speculator,* our Sentinell. God fishes for men,
(for all his *Johns,* and his *Andrews,* and his *Peters,* are but the nets that he
fishes withall) God is the fisher of men; And here, in this Chapter, God in
Christ is our Shepheard. The book of *Job* is a representation of God, in a
Tragique-Comedy, lamentable beginnings comfortably ended: The book
of the Canticles is a representation of God in Christ, as a Bridegroom in
a Marriage-song, in an Epithalamion: God in Christ is represented to us,
in divers formes, in divers places, and this Chapter is his Pastorall. The
Lord is our Shepheard, and so called, in more places, than by any other
name; and in this Chapter, exhibits some of the offices of a good Shepheard. Be pleased to taste a few of them. First, he sayes, *The good Shepheard comes in at the doore,* the right way. If he come in at the window,
that is, alwayes clamber after preferment; If he come in at vaults, and
cellars, that is, by clandestin, and secret contracts with his Patron, he
comes not the right way: When he is in the right way, *His sheep heare
his voyce:* first there is a voyce, He is heard; Ignorance doth not silence
him, nor lazinesse, nor abundance of preferment; nor indiscreet, and
distempered zeale does not silence him; (for to induce, or occasion a
silencing upon our selves, is as ill as the ignorant, or the lazie silence).
There is a voyce, and (sayes that Text) [it] is his voyce, not alwayes
another in his roome; for (as it is added in the next verse) *The sheep
know his voyce,* which they could not doe, if they heard it not often, if
they were not used to it. And then, for the best testimony, and consummation of all. he sayes, *The good Shepheard gives his life for his sheep.* Every

good Shepheard gives his life, that is, spends his life, weares out his life for his sheep: of which this may be one good argument, That there are not so many crazie, so many sickly men, men that so soon grow old in any profession, as in ours.

2 [p. 63]

What eye can fixe it self upon East and West at once? And he must see more than East and West, that sees God, for God spreads infinitely beyond both: God alone is all; not onely all that is, but all that is not, all that might be, if he would have it be. God is too large, too immense, and then man is too narrow, too little to be considered; for, who can fixe his eye upon an Atome? and he must see a lesse thing than an Atome, that sees man, for man is nothing. First, for the incomprehensiblenesse of God, the understanding of man, hath a limited, a determined latitude; it is an intelligence able to move that Spheare which it is fixed to, but could not move a greater: I can comprehend *naturam naturatam*, created nature, but for that *natura naturans*, God himselfe, the understanding of man cannot comprehend. I can see the Sun in a looking-glasse, but the nature, and the whole working of the Sun I cannot see in that glasse. I can see God in the creature, but the nature, the essence, the secret purposes of God, I cannot see there. There is *defatigatio in intellectualibus*, sayes the saddest and soundest of the Hebrew Rabbins, the soule may be tired, as well as the body, and the understanding dazeled, as well as the eye.

3 [pp. 64-65]

Let man be something; how poore, and inconsiderable a ragge of this world, is man! Man, whom *Paracelsus* would have undertaken to have made, in a Limbeck, in a Furnace: Man, who, if they were altogether, all the men, that ever were, and are, and shall be, would not have the power of one Angel in them all, whereas all the Angels, (who, in the Schoole are conceived to be more in number, than, not onely all the Species, but all the individualls of this lower world) have not in them all, the power of one finger of Gods hand: Man, of whom when *David* had said, (as the lowest diminution that he could put upon him) *I am a worme and no man,* He might have gone lower, and said, I am a man and no worm; for man is so much lesse than a worm, as that wormes of his own production, shall feed upon his dead body in the grave, and an immortall worm gnaw his conscience in the torments of hell.

4 [pp. 70-71]

There is Ayre enough in the world, to give breath to every thing, though everything does not breathe. If a tree, or a stone doe not breathe, it is not because it wants ayre, but because it wants meanes to receive it, or to returne it. All egges are not hatched that the hen sits upon; neither could Christ himselfe get all the chickens that were hatched, to come, and to stay under his wings. That man that is blinde, or that will winke, shall see no more sunne upon S. *Barnabies* day, than upon S. *Lucies;* no more in the summer, than in the winter solstice. And therefore as there is *copiosa redemptio,* a plentifull redemption brought into the world by the death of Christ, so (as S. *Paul* found it in his particular conversion) there is *copiosa lux,* a great and a powerful light exhibited to us, that we might see, and lay hold of this life, in the Ordinances of the Church, in the Confessions, and Absolutions, and Services, and Sermons, and Sacraments of the Church; Christ came *ut daret,* that he might bring life into the world, by his death, and then he instituted his Church; *ut haberent,* that by the meanes thereof this life might be infused into us, and infused so, as the last word of our Text delivers it, *Abundantiùs, I came, that they might have life more abundantly.*

Dignaris Domine, ut eis, quibus debita dimittis, te, promissionibus tuis, debitorem facias; This, O Lord, is thine abundant proceedings; First thou forgivest me my debt to thee, and then thou makest thy selfe a debter to me by thy large promises; and after all, performest those promises more largely than thou madest them. Indeed, God can doe nothing scantly, penuriously, singly. Even his maledictions, (to which God is ever loth to come) his first commination was plurall, it was death, and death upon death, *Morte morieris.* Death may be plurall; but this benediction of life cannot admit a singular; *Chajim,* which is the word for *life,* hath no singular number. This is the difference betweene Gods Mercy, and his Judgements, that sometimes his Judgements may be plurall, complicated, enwrapped in one another, but his Mercies are alwayes so, and cannot be otherwise; he gives them *abundantiùs, more abundantly.*

5

[p. 75]

Humiliation is the beginning of sanctification; and as without this, without holinesse, no man shall see God, though he pore whole nights upon the Bible; so without that, without humility, no man shall heare God speake to his soule, though hee heare three two-houres Sermons every day. But if God bring thee to that humiliation of soule and body here, hee will emprove, and advance thy sanctification *abundantiùs,* more abundantly, and when he hath brought it to the best perfection, that this life is capable of, he will provide another *abundantiùs,* another man[n]er of abundance in the life to come; which is the last beating of the pulse of this text, the last panting of the breath thereof, our anhelation, and panting after the joyes, and glory, and eternity of the kingdome of

Heaven; of which, though, for the most part, I use to dismisse you, with saying something, yet it is alwaies little that I can say thereof; at this time, but this, that if all the joyes of all the Martyrs, from *Abel* to him that groanes now in the Inquisition, were condensed into one body of joy, (and certainly the joyes that the Martyrs felt at their deaths, would make up a far greater body, than their sorrowes would doe,) (for though it bee said of our great Martyr, or great Witnesse, as S. *John* calls Christ Jesus) to whom, all other Martyrs are but sub-martyrs, witnesses that testifie his testimony, *Non dolor sicut dolor ejus,* there was never sorrow like unto his sorrow, it is also true, *Non gaudium sicut gaudium ejus,* There was never joy like unto that joy which was set before him, when he endured the crosse;) If I had all this joy of all these Martyrs, (which would, no doubt, be such a joy, as would worke a liquefaction, a melting of my bowels) yet I shall have it *abundantiùs,* a joy more abundant, than even this superlative joy, in the world to come. What a dimme vespers of a glorious festivall, what a poore halfe-holyday, is *Methusalems* nine hundred yeares, to eternity! what a poore account hath that man made, that saies, this land hath beene in my name, and in my Ancestors from the Conquest! what a yesterday is that? not six hundred yeares. If I could beleeve the transmigration of soules, and thinke that my soule had beene successively in some creature or other, since the Creation, what a yesterday is that? not six thousand yeares. What a yesterday for the past, what a to morrow for the future, is any terme, that can be comprehendred in Cyphar or Counters! But as, how abundant a life soever any man hath in this world for temporall abundances, I have life more abundantly than hee, if I have the spirituall life of grace, so what measure soever I have of this spirituall life of grace, in this world, I shall have that more abundantly in Heaven, for there, my terme shall bee a terme for three lives; for those three, that as long as the Father, and the Son, and the holy Ghost live, I shall not dye.

SERMON IX

Candlemas Day. Feb. 2 [1616/7 *or* 1622/3]

I [p. 90]

T H A T soule, that is accustomed to direct her selfe to God, upon every occasion, that, as a flowre at Sun-rising, conceives a sense of God, in every beame of his, and spreads and dilates it selfe towards him, in a thankful-nesse, in every small blessing that he sheds upon her; that soule, that as a flowre at the Suns declining, contracts and gathers in, and shuts up her selfe, as though she had received a blow, when soever she heares her Saviour wounded by a oath, or blasphemy, or execration; that soule, who, whatsoever string be strucken in her, base or treble, her high or her low estate, is ever tun'd toward God, that soule prayes sometimes when it does not know that it prayes. I heare that man name God, and aske him what said you, and perchance he cannot tell; but I remember, that he casts forth some of those *ejaculationes animæ*, (as S. *Augustine:* calls them) some of those darts of a devout soule, which, though they have not particular deliberations, and be not formall prayers, yet they are the *indicia*, pregnant evidences and blessed fruits of a religious custome; much more it is true, which S. *Bernard* saies there, of them, *Deus audit*, God heares that voice of the heart, which the heart it selfe heares not, that is, at first considers not. Those occasionall and transitory prayers, and those fixed and stationary prayers, for which, many times, we binde our selves to private prayer at such a time, are payments of this debt, in such peeces, and in such summes, as God, no doubt, accepts at our hands. But yet the solemne dayes of payment, are the Sabbaths of the Lord, and the place of this payment, is the house of the Lord, where, as *Tertullian* expresses it, *Agmine facto*, we muster our forces together, and besiege God; that is, not taking up every tatter'd fellow, every sudden ragge or fragment of speech, that rises from our tongue, or our affections, but mustering up those words, which the Church hath levied for that service, in the Confessions, and Absolutions, and Collects, and Litanies of the Church, we pay this debt, and we receive our acquittance.

2 [pp. 95-96]

Begin therefore to pay these debts to thy selfe betimes; for, as we told you at beginning, some [of] you are too tender at noone, some at evening. Even at your noon and warmest Sun-shine of prosperity, you owe your selves a true information, how you came by that prosperity, who gave it you, and why he gave it. Let not the Olive boast of her own fatnesse, nor the Fig-tree of her own sweetnesse, nor the Vine of her own fruitfulnesse, for we were all but Brambles. Let no man say, I could not misse a fortune, for I have studied all my youth; How many men have studied more nights, than he hath done hours, and studied themselves blinde, and mad in the Mathematiques, and yet withers in beggery in a corner? Let him never adde, But I studied in a usefull and gainfull profession; How many have done so too, and yet never compassed the favour of a Judge? And how many that have had all that, have struck upon a Rock, even at full Sea, and perished there? In their Grandfathers and great Grandfathers, in a few generations, whosoever is greatest now, must say, With this Staffe came I over Jordan; nay, without any staffe came I over Jordan, for he had in them at first, a beginning of nothing. As for spiritual happinesse, *Non volentis, nec currentis, sed miserentis Dei,* It is not in him that would run, nor in him that doth, but only in God that prospers his course; so for the things of this world, it is in vain to rise early, and to lie down late, and to eat the bread of sorrow, for, *nisi Dominus ædificaverit, nisi Dominus custodierit,* except the Lord build the house, they labour in vaine; except the Lord keep the City, the watchman waketh but in vain. Come not therefore to say, I studied more than my fellows, and therefore am richer than my fellowes, but say, God that give me my contemplations at first, gave me my practice after, and hath given me his blessing now. How many men have worn their braines upon other studies and spent their time and themselves therein? how many men have studied more in thine own profession, and yet, for diffidence in themselves, or some disfavour from others, have not had thy practice? How many men have been equall to thee, in study, in practice, and in getting too, and yet upon a wanton confidence, that that world would alwayes last, or upon the burden of many children, and an expensive breeding of them, or for other reasons, which God hath found in his wayes, are left upon the sand at last, in a low fortune? whilest the Sun shines upon thee in all these, pay thy self the debt, of knowing whence, and why all this came, for else thou canst not know how much, or how little is thine, nor thou canst not come to restore that which is none of thine, but unjustly wrung from others. Pay therefore this debt of surveying thine estate, and then pay thy selfe thine own too, by a chearfull enjoying and using that which is truly thine, and doe not deny nor defraud thy selfe of those things which are thine, and so become a wretched debtor, to thy back, or to thy belly, as though the world had not enough, or God knew not what were enough for thee.

Pay this debt to thy selfe of looking into thy debts, of surveying, of severing, of serving thy selfe with that which is truly thine, at thy noone, in the best of thy fortune, and in the strength of thine understanding; that when thou commest to pay thy other, thy last debt to thy self, which is, to open a doore out of this world, by the dissolution of body and soule, thou have not all thy money to tell over when the Sun is ready to set, all the account to make of every bag of money, and of every quillet of land, whose it is, and whether it be his that looks for it from thee, or his from whom it was taken by thee; whether it belong to thine heire, that weepes joyfull tears behinde the curtain, or belong to him that weeps true, and bloody teares, in the hole in a prison. There will come a time, when that land that thou leavest shall not be his land, when it shall be no bodies land, when it shall be no land, for the earth must perish; there will be a time when there shall be no Mannors, no Acres in the world, and yet there shall lie Mannors and Acres upon thy soul, when land shall be no more, when time shall be no more, and thou passe away, not into the land of the living, but of eternal death. Then the Accuser will be ready to inter-line the schedules of thy debts, thy sins, and insert false debts, by abusing an over-tendernesse, which may be in thy conscience then, in thy last sicknesse, in thy death-bed: Then he will be ready to adde a cyphar more to thy debts, and make hundreds thousands, and abuse the faintnesse which may be in thy conscience then, in thy last sicknesse, in thy death-bed. Then he will be ready to abuse even thy confidence in God, and bring thee to think, that as a Pirate ventures boldly home, though all that he hath be stoln, if he be rich enough to bribe for a pardon; so, howsoever those families perish whom thou hast ruined, and those whole parishes whom thou hast depopulated, thy soule may goe confidently home too, if thou bribe God then, with an Hospitall or a Fellowship in a Colledge, or a Legacy to any pious use in apparance, and in the eye of the world.

SERMON XIII

To the King, in Lent. April 20th, 1630

[p. 129]

MEN of this world do sometimes repaire, and recompence those men whom they have oppressed before, but this is an after recompence; Gods first intention even when he destroyes is to preserve, as a Physitians first intention, in the most distastfull physick, is health; even Gods demolitions are super-edifications, his Anatomies, his dissections are so many re-compactings, so many resurrections; God windes us off the Skein, that he may weave us up into the whole peece, and he cuts us out of the whole peece into peeces, that he may make us up into a whole garment.

But for all these humiliations, and confessions, *Job* doth not wave his protestation; *My righteousnesse I hold fast, and my heart shall not re-proach me as long as I live.* Not that I shall never sin, but never leave any sin unrepented; And then, my heart cannot reproach me of a repented sin, without reproaching God himself. *The Sun must not set upon my anger;* much lesse will I let the Sun set upon the anger of God towards me, or sleep in an unrepented sin. Every nights sleep is a *Nunc dimittis;* then the Lord lets his servant depart in peace. Thy lying down is a valediction, a parting, a taking leave, (shall I say so?) a shaking hands with God; and, when thou shakest hands with God, let those hands be clean. Enter into thy grave, thy metaphoricall, thy quotidian grave, thy bed, as thou entredst into the Church at first, by Water, by Baptisme; Re-baptise thy self every night, in *Jobs Snow water*, in holy tears that may cool the inordinate lusts of thy heart, and with-hold uncleane abuses of those hands even in that thy grave, thy Bed; And evermore remember *Jobs* fear and jealousie in that place, That *when he had washed himself in Snow water, Abominabuntur me vestimenta mea, Mine own clothes will make me foul again.* Thy flesh is thy clothes; and to this mischievous purpose of fouling thy hands with thine own clothes, thou hast most clothes on when thou art naked; Then, in that nakednesse, thou art in most danger of fouling thy hands with thine own clothes. Miserable man! that couldest have no use of hands, nor any other organ of sense, if there were no other creature but thy self, and yet, if there were no other creature but thy self, couldest sin upon thy self, and foule thy hands with thine own hands. How much more then, if thou strike with those hands, by oppression in thy office, or shut up those hands, and that which is due to another, in them! Sleep with cleane hands, either kept cleane all day, by integrity; or washed cleane, at night, by repentance; and whensoever thou wakest, though all *Jobs* messengers thunder about thee, and all *Jobs* friends multiply misinterpretations against thee, yet *Jobs* protestation shall be thy protestation, what end soever God have in this proceeding, *It is not for any injustice in my hands,* and the other part of his protestation too, *Also my prayer is pure.*

SERMON XV

At Whitehall. 1st Friday in Lent. March 8. 1621/2

I   [pp. 147-148]

DOTH not man die even in his birth? The breaking of prison is death, and what is our birth, but a breaking of prison? As soon as we were clothed by God, our very apparell was an Embleme of death. In the skins of dead beasts, he covered the skins of dying men. As soon as God set us on work, our very occupation was an Embleme of death; It was to digge the earth; not to digge pitfals for other men, but graves for our selves. Hath any man here forgot to day, that yesterday is dead? And the Bell tolls for to day, and will ring out anon; and for as much of every one of us, as appertaines to this day. *Quotidiè morimur, et tamen nos esse æternos putamus,* sayes S. *Hierome;* We die every day, and we die all the day long; and because we are not absolutely dead, we call that an eternity, an eternity of dying: And is there comfort in that state? why, that is the state of hell it self, Eternall dying, and not dead.

But for this there is enough said, by the Morall man; (that we may respite divine proofes, for divine points anon, for our severall Resurrections) for this death is meerly naturall, and it is enough that the morall man sayes, *Mors lex, tributum, officium mortalium.* First it is *lex,* you were born under that law, upon that condition to die: so it is a rebellious thing not to be content to die, it opposes the Law. Then it is *Tributum,* an imposition which nature the Queen of this world layes upon us, and which she will take, when and where she list; here a yong man, there an old man, here a happy, there a miserable man; And so it is a seditious thing not to be content to die, it opposes the prerogative. And lastly, it is *officium,* men are to have their turnes, to take their time, and then to give way by death to successors; and so it is *Incivile, inofficiosum,* not to be content to die, it opposes the frame and form of government. It comes equally to us all, and makes us all equall when it comes. The ashes of an Oak in the Chimney, are no Epitaph of that Oak, to tell me how high or how large that was; It tels me not what flocks it sheltered while it stood, nor what men it hurt when it fell. The dust of great persons graves is speechlesse too, it sayes nothing, it distinguishes nothing: As soon the dust of a wretch whom thou wouldest not, as of a Prince whom thou couldest not look upon, will trouble thine eyes, if the winde blow it thither; and when a whirle-winde hath blowne the dust of the Church-yard into the Church, and the man sweeps out the dust of the Church into the Church-yard, who will undertake to sift those dusts again, and to pronounce, This is the Patrician, this is the noble flowre, and this the yeomanly, this the Plebeian bran.

2   [pp. 148-149]

Death hangs upon the edge of every persecutors sword; and upon the sting of every calumniators, and accusers tongue. In the Bull of Phalaris, in the Bulls of Basan, in the Bulls of Babylon, the shrewdest Bulls of all, in temporall, in spirituall persecutions, ever since God put an enmity between Man, and the Serpent, from the time of *Cain* who began in a murther, to the time of Anti-christ, who proceeds in Massacres, Death hath adhered to the enemy, and so is an enemy.

Death hath a Commission, *Stipendium peccati mors est, The reward of sin is Death,* but where God gives a Supersedeas, upon that Commission, *Vivo Ego, nolo mortem, As I live saith the Lord, I would have no sinner dye,* not dye the second death, yet Death proceeds to that execution: And whereas the enemy, whom he adheres to, the Serpent himselfe, hath power but *In calcaneo,* upon the heele, the lower, the mortall part, the body of man, *Death is come up into our windowes,* saith the Prophet, into our best lights, our understandings, and benights us there, either with ignorance, before sin, or with senselesnesse after: And a Sheriffe that should burne him, who were condemned to be hanged, were a murderer, though that man must have dyed: To come in by the doore, by the way of sicknesse upon the body, is, but to come in at the window by the way of sin, is not deaths Commission; God opens not that window.

3 [p. 149]

Death is the last, and in that respect the worst enemy. In an enemy, that appeares at first, when we are or may be provided against him, there is some of that, which we call Honour: but in the enemie that reserves himselfe unto the last, and attends our weake estate, there is more danger. Keepe it, where I intend it, in that which is my spheare, the Conscience: If mine enemie meet me betimes in my youth, in an object of tentation, (so *Josephs* enemie met him in *Potifars* Wife) yet if I doe not adhere to this enemy, dwell upon a delightfull meditation of that sin, if I doe not fuell, and foment that sin, assist and encourage that sin, by high diet, wanton discourse, other provocation, I shall have reason on my side, and I shall have grace on my side, and I shall have the History of a thousand that have perished by that sin, on my side; Even Spittles will give me souldiers to fight for me, by their miserable example against that sin; nay perchance sometimes the vertue of that woman, whom I sollicite, will assist me. But when I lye under the hands of that enemie, that hath reserved himselfe to the last, to my last bed, then when I shall be able to stir no limbe in any other measure than a Feaver or a Palsie shall shake them, when everlasting darknesse shall have an inchoation in the present dimnesse of mine eyes, and the everlasting gnashing in the present chattering of my teeth, and the everlasting worme in the present gnawing of the Agonies of my body, and anguishes of my minde, when the last enemie shall watch my remedilesse body, and my disconsolate soule there, there, where not the Physitian, in his way, perchance not the Priest in his, shall be able to give any assistance, And when he hath sported himselfe with my misery upon that stage, my death-bed, shall shift the Scene, and throw me from that bed, into the grave, and there triumph over me, God knowes, how many generations, till the Redeemer, my Redeemer, the Redeemer of all me, body, as well as soule, come againe; As death is *Novissimus hostis,* the enemy which watches me, at my last weaknesse, and shall hold me, when I shall be no more, till that Angel come, *Who shall say, and sweare that time shall be no more,* in that consideration, in that apprehension, he is the powerfullest, the fearfullest enemy; and yet even there this enemy *Abolebitur,* he shall be destroyed.

SERMON XIX

St. Paul's. Easter day in the evening. March 28. 1624

1   [pp. 185-186]

B U T when the Church was newly conceived, and then lay like the egge
of a Dove, and a Gyants foot over it, like a worm, like an ant, and hill
upon hill whelmed upon it, nay, like a grain of corn between the upper
and lower Mill-stone, ground to dust between Tyrans and Heretiques,
when as she bled in her Cradle, in those children whom *Herod* slew, so
she bled upon her crutches, in those decrepit men whom former persecutions and tortures had creepled before, when East and West joyned
hands to crush her, and hands, and brains, joyned execution to consultation to annihilate her; in this wane of the Moon God gave her an instant
fulnesse; in this exinanition, instant glory; in this grave, an instant Resurrection.

2   [p. 190]

That soule, which being borne free, is made a slave to this body, by
comming to it; It must act, but what this body will give it leave to act,
according to the Organs, which this body affords it; and if the body be
lame in any limme, the soule must be lame in her operation, in that limme
too; It must doe, but what the body will have it doe, and then it must
suffer, whatsoever that body puts it to, or whatsoever any others will put
that body to: If the body oppresse it selfe with Melancholy, the soule
must be sad; and if other men oppresse the body with injury, the soule
must be sad too; Consider, (it is too, immense a thing to consider it) reflect
but one thought, but upon this one thing in the soule, here, and hereafter,
In her grave, the body, and in her Resurrection in Heaven; That is the
knowledge of the soule.

Here saies S. *Augustine,* when the soule considers the things of this
world, *Non veritate certior, sed consuetudine securior;* She rests upon
such things as she is not sure are true, but such as she sees, are ordinarily
received and accepted for truths: so that the end of her knowledge is
not Truth, but opinion, and the way, not Inquisition, but ease: But saies
he, when she proceeds in this life, to search into heavenly things,
Verberatur luce veritatis, The beames of that light are too strong for
her, and they sink her, and cast her downe, *Et ad familiaritatem tene-
brarum suarum, non electione sed fatigatione convertitur;* and so she
returnes to her owne darknesse, because she is most familiar, and best
acquainted with it; *Non electione,* not because she loves ignorance, but

because she is weary of the trouble of seeking out the truth, and so swallowes even any Religion to escape the paine of debating, and disputing; and in this lazinesse she sleeps out her lease, her terme of life, in this death, in this grave, in this body.

But then in her Resurrection, her measure is enlarged, and filled at once; There she reads without spelling, and knowes without thinking, and concludes without arguing; she is at the end of her race, without running; In her triumph, without fighting; In her Haven, without sayling: A freeman, without any prentiship; at full yeares, without any wardship; and a Doctor, without any proceeding: She knowes truly, and easily, and immediately, and entirely, and everlastingly; Nothing left out at first, nothing worne out at last, that conduces to her happinesse. What a death is this life! what a resurrection is this death! For though this world be a sea, yet (which is most strange) our Harbour is larger than the sea; Heaven infinitely larger than this world. For, though that be not true, which *Origen* is said to say, That at last all shall be saved, nor that evident, which *Cyril* of Alexandria saies, That without doubt the number of them that are saved, is far greater than of them that perish, yet surely the number of them, with whom we shall have communion in Heaven, is greater than ever lived at once upon the face of the earth: And of those who lived in our time, how few did we know? and of those whom we did know, how few did we care much for? In Heaven we shall have Communion of Joy and Glory with all, alwaies; *Ubi non intrat inimicus, nec amicus exit,* Where never any man shall come in that loves us not, nor go from us that does.

SERMON XXI

St. Paul's. Easter Day in the Evening. April 9th, 1626

[pp. 211-212]

T H U S it is, when a soule is scattered upon the daily practice of any one predominant, and habituall sin; but when it is indifferently scattered upon all, how much more is it so? In him, that swallowes sins in the world, as he would doe meats at a feast; passes through every dish, and never askes Physitian the nature, the quality, the danger, the offence of any dish: That baits at every sin that rises, and poures himselfe into every sinfull mold he meets: That knowes not when he began to spend his soule, nor where, nor upon what sin he laid it out; no, nor whether he have, whether ever he had any soule, or no; but hath lost his soule so long agoe, in rusty, and in incoherent sins, (not sins that produced one another, as in *Davids* case, and yet that is a fearfull state, that concatenation of sins, that pedigree of sins) but in sins which he embraces, meerely out of an easinesse to sin, and not out of a love, no, nor out of a tentation to that sin in particular) that in these incoherent sins hath so scattered his soule, as that he hath not soule enough left, to seek out the rest. And therefore *David* makes it the Title of the whole Psalme, *Domine ne disperdas, O Lord doe not scatter us:* And he begins to expresse his sense of Gods Judgements, in the next Psalme, so, *O Lord thou hast cast us out, thou hast scattered us, turn again unto us;* for even from this aversion, there may be conversion, and from this last and lowest fall, a resurrection. But how?

In the generall resurrection upon naturall death, God shall work upon this dispersion of our scattered dust, as in the first fall, which is the Divorce, by way of Re-union, and in the second, which is Putrifaction, by way of Re-efformation; so in this third, which is Dispersion, by way of Re-collection; where mans buried flesh hath brought forth grasse, and that grasse fed beasts, and those beasts fed men, and those men fed other men, God that knowes in which Boxe of his Cabinet all this seed Pearle lies, in what corner of the world every atome, every graine of every mans dust sleeps, shall recollect that dust, and then recompact that body, and then re-inanimate that man, and that is the accomplishment of all.

SERMON XXII

St. Paul's. Easter Day. March 25th, 1627

1   [p. 215]

†HERE is nothing that God hath established in a constant course of nature, and which therefore is done every day, but would seeme a Miracle, and exercise our admiration, if it were done but once; Nay, the ordinary things in Nature, would be greater miracles, than the extraordinary, which we admire most, if they were done but once; The standing still of the Sun, for *Josuahs* use, was not, in it selfe, so wonderfull a thing, as that so vast and immense a body as the Sun, should run so many miles, in a minute; The motion of the Sun were a greater wonder than the standing still, if all were to begin againe; And onely the daily doing takes off the admiration. But then God having, as it were, concluded himself in a course of nature, and written downe in the booke of Creatures, Thus and thus all things shall be carried, though he glorifie himselfe sometimes, in doing a miracle, yet there is in every miracle, a silent chiding of the world, and a tacite reprehension of them, who require, or who need miracles.

Now what was this that they qualified and dignified by that addition, *The better Resurrection?* Is it called better, in that it is better than this life, and determined in that comparison, and degree of betternesse, and no more? Is it better than those honours, and preferments which that King offered them, and determined in that comparison, and no more? Or better than other men shall have at the last day, (for all men shall have a Resurrection) and determined in that? Or, as S. *Chrysostome* takes it, is it but a better Resurrection than that in the former part of this Text, where dead children are restored to their mothers alive again? Is it but a better Resurrection in some of these senses? Surely better in a higher sense than any of these; It is a supereminent degree of glory, a larger measure of glory, than every man, who in a generall happinesse, is made partaker of the Resurrection of the righteous, is made partaker of.

Beloved, There is nothing so little in heaven, as that we can expresse it; but if wee could tell you the fulnesse of a soul there, what that fulnesse is; the infinitenesse of that glory there, how far that infinitenesse goes; the Eternity of that happinesse there, how long that happinesse lasts; if we could make you know all this, yet this *Better Resurrection* is a heaping, even of that Fulnesse, and an enlarging, even of that Infinitenesse, and an extention, even of that eternity of happinesse; For, all these, this Fulnesse, this Infinitenesse, this Eternity are in all the Resurrections of the Righteous, and this is a *better Resurrection;* We may almost say, it is something more than Heaven; for, all that have any Resurrection to life, have all heaven; And something more than God; for, all that have any Resurrection to life, have all God; and yet these shall have a better Resurrection. Amorous soule, ambitious soule, covetous soule, voluptuous soule, what wouldest thou have in heaven? What doth thy holy amorousnesse, thy holy covetousnesse, thy holy ambition, and voluptuousnesse most carry thy desire upon? Call it what thou wilt; think it what thou canst; think it something that thou canst not think; and all this thou shalt have, if thou have any Resurrection unto life; and yet there is a *Better Resurrection.* When I consider what I was in my parents loynes (a substance unworthy of a word, unworthy of a thought) when I consider what I am now, (a Volume of diseases bound up together, a dry cynder, if I look for naturall, for radicall moisture, and yet a Spunge, a bottle of overflowing Rheumes, if I consider accidentall; an aged childe, a gray-headed Infant, and but the ghost of mine own youth) When I consider what I shall be at last, by the hand of death, in my grave, (first, but Putrifaction, and then, not so much as Putrifaction, I shall not be able to send forth so much as an ill ayre, not any ayre at all, but shall

be all insipid, tastelesse, savourlesse dust; for a while, all wormes, and
after a while, not so much as wormes, sordid, senselesse, nameless dust)
When I consider the past, and present, and future state of this body, in
this world, I am able to conceive, able to expresse the worst that can befall
it in nature, and the worst that can be inflicted upon it by man, or fortune; But the least degree of glory that God hath prepared for that body
in heaven, I am not able to expresse, not able to conceive.

SERMON XXIII

St. Paul's. Easter Day. April 13th, 1628

I   [pp. 226-227]

THE whole frame of the world is the Theatre, and every creature the
stage, the *medium,* the glasse in which we may see God. *Moses made the
Laver in the Tabernacle, of the looking glasses of women:* Scarce can you
imagine a vainer thing (except you will except the vaine lookers on, in
that action) than the looking glasses of women; and yet *Moses* brought
the looking-glasses of women to a religious use, to shew them that came
in, the spots of dirt which they had taken by the way, that they might
wash themselves cleane before they passed any farther.

There is not so poore a creature but may be thy glasse to see God in.
The greatest flat glasse that can be made, cannot represent any thing
greater than it is: If every gnat that flies were an Arch-angell, all that
could but tell me, that there is a God; and the poorest worme that creeps,
tells me that. If I should aske the Basilisk, how camest thou by those
killing eyes, he would tell me, Thy God made me so; And if I should aske
the Slow-worme, how camest thou to be without eyes, he would tell me,
Thy God made me so. The Cedar is no better a glasse to see God in, than
the Hyssope upon the wall; all things that are, are equally removed from
being nothing; and whatsoever hath any beeing, is by that very beeing,
a glasse in which we see God, who is the roote, and the fountaine of all
beeing. The whole frame of nature is the Theatre, the whole Volume of
creatures is the glasse, and the light of nature, reason, is our light, which
is another Circumstance.

2   [p. 227]

God affords no man the comfort, the false comfort of Atheism: He will
not allow a pretending Atheist the power to flatter himself, so far, as
seriously to thinke there is no God. He must pull out his own eyes, and
see no creature, before he can say, he sees no God; He must be no man,

and quench his reasonable soule, before he can say to himselfe, there is
no God. The difference betweene the Reason of man, and the Instinct of
the beast is this, That the beast does but know, but the man knows that
he knows. The bestiall Atheist will pretend that he knows there is no
God; but he cannot say, that hee knows, that he knows it; for, his knowledge will not stand the battery of an argument from another, nor of a
ratiocination from himselfe. He dares not aske himselfe who is it that I
pray to, in a sudden danger, if there be no God? Nay he dares not aske,
who is it that I sweare by, in a sudden passion if there be no God? Whom
do I tremble at, and sweat under, at midnight, and whom do I curse by
next morning, if there be no God?

3   [p. 230]

He that asks me what heaven is, meanes not to heare me, but to silence
me; He knows I cannot tell him; When I meet him there, I shall be able
to tell him, and then he will be as able to tell me; yet then we shall be
but able to tell one another, This, this that we enjoy is heaven, but the
tongues of Angels, the tongues of glorified Saints, shall not be able to
expresse what that heaven is; for, even in heaven our faculties shall be
finite. Heaven is not a place that was created; for, all place that was
created, shall be dissolved. God did not plant a Paradise for himself, and
remove to that, as he planted a Paradise for *Adam,* and removed him to
that; But God is still where he was before the world was made. And in
that place, where there are more Suns than there are Stars in the Firmament, (for all the Saints are Suns) And more light in another Sun, The
S[o]n of righteousnesse, the Son of Glory, the Son of God, than in all
them, in that illustration, that emanation, that effusion of beams of glory,
which began not to shine 6000. yeares ago, but 6000. millions of millions
ago, had been 6000. millions of millions before that, in those eternall, in
those uncreated heavens, shall we see God.

SERMON XXVI

St. Paul's. Easter Day. [1622]

1   [p. 257]

T H E dead heare not Thunder, nor feele they an Earthquake. If the Canon
batter that Church walls, in which they lye buryed, it wakes not them,
nor does it shake or affect them, if that dust, which they are, be thrown
out, but yet there is a voyce, which the dead shall heare; *The dead shall*
heare the voyce of the Son of God (sayes the Son of God himself) *and*

they that heare shall live; And that is the voyce of our Text. It is here called a clamour, a vociferation, a shout, and varied by our Translators, and Expositors, according to the origination of the word, to be *clamor hortatorius,* and *suasorius,* and *jussorius,* A voyce that carries with it a penetration, (all shall heare it) and a perswasion, (all shall beleeve it, and be glad of it) and a power, a command, (all shall obey it). Since that voyce at the Creation, *Fiat,* Let there be a world, was never heard such a voyce as this, *Surgite mortui,* Arise ye dead. That was spoken to that that was meerely nothing, and this to them, who in themselves shall have no co-operation, no concurrence to the hearing or answering this voyce.

The power of this voyce is exalted in that it is said to be the *voyce of the Archangel.* Though legions of Angels, millions of Angels shall be employed about the Resurrection, to recollect their scattered dust, and recompact their ruined bodies, yet those bodies so recompact, shall not be able to heare a voyce. They shall be then but such bodies, as they were when they were laid downe in the grave, when, though they were intire bodies, they could not heare the voice of the mourner. But this voyce of the Archangel shall enable them to heare; The Archangel shall re-infuse the severall soules into their bodies, and so they shall heare that voyce, *Surgite mortui,* Arise ye that were dead, and they shall arise.

2   [p. 265]

The Hypocrite hath a Being, and, in God, but it is not with God, *Qua cor longé, With his lips he honours God, but removes his heart far from him.* And God sends him after his heart, that he may keep him at that distance, (as S. *Gregory* reads and interprets that place of *Esay*) *Redite prævaricatores ad cor,* Return O sinners, follow your own heart, and then I am sure you and I shall never meet. Our Saviour Christ delivers this distance plainly, *Discedite à me, Depart from me, ye cursed, into everlasting fire.* Where the first part of the sentence is incomparably the heaviest, the departing worse than the fire; the intensenesse of that fire, the ayre of that brimstone, the anguish of that worm, the discord of that howling, and gnashing of teeth, is no comparable, no considerable part of the torment, in respect of the privation of the sight of God, the banishment from the presence of God, an absolute hopelesnesse, an utter impossibility of ever comming to that, which sustaines the miserable in this world, that thought I see no Sun here, I shall see the Son of God there.

3   [p. 266]

How barren a thing is Arithmetique! (and yet Arithmetique will tell you, how many single graines of sand, will fill this hollow Vault to the Firmament) How empty a thing is Rhetorique! (and yet Rhetorique will

make absent and remote things present to your understanding) How weak
a thing is poetry! (and yet Poetry is a counterfait Creation, and makes
things that are not, as though they were) How infirme, how impotent are
all assistances, if they be put to expresse this Eternity!

SERMON XXVII

*To the Lords upon Easter Day at the Communion, the King being
dangerously sick at New-Market. March 28, 1619*

[p. 267]

W E E are all conceived in close Prison; in our Mothers wombes, we are
close Prisoners all; when we are borne, we are borne but to the liberty of
the house; Prisoners still, though within larger walls; and then all our life
is but a going out to the place of Execution, to death. Now was there ever
any man seen to sleep in the Cart, between New-gate, and Tyborne? between the Prison, and the place of Execution, does any man sleep? And
we sleep all the way; from the womb to the grave we are never throughly
awake; but passe on with such dreames, and imaginations as these, I may
live as well, as another, and why should I dye, rather than another? but
awake, and tell me, sayes this Text, *Quis homo?* who is that other that
thou talkest of? *What man is he that liveth, and shall not see death?*

SERMON XXXIV

St. Paul's. Whitsunday. [1623]

I

[p. 338]

I N the great Ant-hill of the whole world, I am an Ant; I have my part in
the Creation, I am a Creature; But there are ignoble Creatures. God comes
nearer; In the great field of clay, of red earth, that man was made of, and
mankind, I am a clod; I am a man, I have my part in the Humanity; But
Man was worse than annihilated again. When satan in that serpent was
come, as *Hercules* with his club into a potters shop, and had broke all the
vessels, destroyed all mankind, And the gracious promise of a Messias to
redeeme all mankind, was shed and spread upon all, I had my drop of that
dew of Heaven, my sparke of that fire of heaven, in the universall promise, in which I was involved; But this promise was appropriated after,
in a particular Covenant, to one people, to the Jewes, to the seed of *Abraham*. But for all that I have my portion there; for all that professe Christ

Jesus are by a spirituall engrafting, and transmigration, and transplantation, in and of that stock, and that seed of *Abraham;* and I am one of
those. But then, of those who doe professe Christ Jesus, some grovell still
in the superstitions they were fallen into, and some are raised, by Gods
good grace, out of them; and I am one of those; God hath afforded me my
station, in that Church, which is departed from Babylon.

Now, all this while, my soule is in a cheerefull progresse; when I consider what God did for Goshen in Egypt, for a little parke in the midst
of a forest; what he did for Jury, in the midst of enemies, as a shire that
should stand out against a Kingdome round about it: How many San-
cerras he hath delivered from famins, how many Genevas from plots, and
machinations against her; all this while my soule is in a progresse: But
I am at home when I consider Buls of excommunications, and solicitations
of Rebellions, and pistols and poysons, and the discoveries of those; There
is our *Nos, We,* testimonies that we are in the favour, and care of God;
We, our Nation, we, our Church; There I am at home; but I am in my
Cabinet at home, when I consider, what God hath done for me, and my
soule; There is the *Ego,* the particular, the individuall, I.

2   [pp. 340-341]

The holy Ghost could not expresse more danger to a man, than when he
calls him *Filium sæculi, The childe of this world;* Nor a worse disposition,
than when he cals him, *Filium diffidentiæ, The childe of diffidence, and
distrust in God;* Nor a worse pursuer of that ill disposition, than when he
calls him *Filium diaboli,* (as S. *Peter* calls *Elymas*) *The childe of the
devill;* Nor a worse possessing of the devill, than when he calls him *Filium
perditionis, The childe of perdition;* Nor a worse execution of all this,
than when he calls him *Filium gehennæ, The childe of hell:* The childe of
this world, The childe of desperation, The childe of the devill, The childe
of perdition, The childe of hell, is a high expressing, a deep aggravating
of his damnation; That his damnation is not only his purchase, as he
hath acquired it, but it is his inheritance, he is the childe of damnation.
So it is also a high exaltation, when the holy Ghost draws our Pedegree
from any good thing, and calls us the children of that: As, when he cals
us *Filios lucis, The children of light,* that we have seen the day-star arise,
when he cals us *Filios sponsi, The children of the bride-chamber,* begot
in lawfull marriage upon the true Church, these are faire approaches to
the highest title of all, to be *Filii Dei, The children of God;* and not children of God, *Per filiationem vestigii,* (so every creature is a childe of God)
by having an Image, and impression of God, in the very Beeing thereof,
but *children* so, as that we are *heires,* and *heires* so, as that we are *Co-*

heires with Christ, as it follows in the next verse, and is implyed in this name, *Children of God.*

Heires of heaven, which is not a Gavel-kinde, every son, every man alike; but it is an universall primogeniture, every man full, so full, as that every man hath all, in such measure, as that there is nothing in heaven, which any man in heaven wants. Heires of the joyes of heaven; Joy in a continuall dilatation of thy heart, to receive augmentation of that which is infinite, in the accumulation of essentiall and accidentall joy. Joy in a continuall melting of indissoluble bowels, in joyfull, and yet compassionate beholding thy Saviour; Rejoycing at thy being there, and almost lamenting (in a kinde of affection, which we can call by no name) that thou couldst not come thither, but by those wounds, which are still wounds, though wounds glorified. Heires of the joy, and heires of the glory of heaven; where if thou look down, and see Kings fighting for Crownes, thou canst look off as easily, as from boyes at stool-ball for points here; And from Kings triumphing after victories, as easily, as a Philosopher from a Pageant of children here. Where thou shalt not be subject to any other title of Dominion in others, but *Jesus of Nazareth King of the Jews,* nor ambitious of any other title in thy selfe, but that which thou possessest, *To be the childe of God.* Heires of joy, heires of glory, and heires of the eternity of heaven; Where, in the possession of this joy, and this glory, The Angels which were there almost 6000. yeares before thee, and so prescribe, and those soules which shall come at Christs last comming, and so enter but then, shall not survive thee, but they, and thou, and all, shall live as long as he that gives you all that life, as God himselfe.

SERMON XXXVI

St. Paul's. Whitsunday. [1625]

I [p. 353]

H E A V E N is Glory, and heaven is Joy; we cannot tell which most; we cannot separate them; and this comfort is joy in the Holy Ghost. This makes all *Jobs* states alike; as rich in the first Chapter of his Booke, where all is suddenly lost, as in the last, where all is abundantly restored. This consolation from the Holy Ghost makes my mid-night noone, mine Executioner a Physitian, a stake and pile of Fagots, a Bone-fire of triumph; this consolation makes a Satyr, and Slander, and Libell against me, a Panegyrique, and an Elogy in my praise; It makes a *Tolle* an *Ave,* a *Væ* an *Euge,* a *Crucifige* an *Hosanna;* It makes my death-bed, a mariage-bed, and my Passing-bell, an Epithalamion.

2   [p. 357]

As the world is the whole frame of the world, God hath put into it a
reproofe, a rebuke, lest it should seem eternall, which is, a sensible decay
and age in the whole frame of the world, and every piece thereof. The
seasons of the yeare irregular and distempered; the Sun fainter, and languishing; men lesse in stature, and shorter-lived. No addition, but only
every yeare, new sorts, new species of wormes, and flies, and sicknesses,
which argue more and more putrefaction of which they are engendred.
And the Angels of heaven, which did so familiarly converse with men in
the beginning of the world, though they may not be doubted to perform
to us still their ministeriall assistances, yet they seem so far to have deserted this world, as that they do not appeare to us, as they did to those
our Fathers. S. *Cyprian* observed this in his time, when writing to *Deme-
trianus,* who imputed all those calamities which afflicted the world then,
to the impiety of the Christians who would not joyne with them in the
worship of their gods, *Cyprian* went no farther for the cause of these
calamities, but *Ad senescentem mundum,* To the age and impotency of
the whole world; And therefore, says he, *Imputent senes Christianis,
quòd minùs valeant in senectutem;* Old men were best accuse Christians,
that they are more sickly in their age, than they were in their youth; Is
the fault in our religion, or in their decay? *Canos in pueris videmus, nec
ætas in senectute desinit, sed incipit à senectute;* We see gray haires in
children, and we do not die old, and yet we are borne old. Lest the world
(as the world signifies the whole frame of the world) should glorifie it
selfe, or flatter, and abuse us with an opinion of eternity, we may admit
usefully (though we do not conclude peremptorily) this observation to be
true, that there is a reproofe, a rebuke born in it, a sensible decay and
mortality of the whole world.

SERMON XXXVII

St. Paul's. Whitsunday. [1626]

[pp. 365-366]

WHEN the Holy Ghost hath brought us into the Ark from whence we
may see all the world without, sprawling and gasping in the flood, (the
flood of sinfull courses in the world, and of the anger of God) when we
can see this violent flood, (the anger of God) break in at windowes, and
there devoure the licentious man in his sinfull embracements, and make
his bed of wantonnesse his death-bed; when we can see this flood (the

anger of God) swell as fast as the ambitious man swels, and pursue him through all his titles, and at last suddenly, and violently wash him away in his owne blood, not alwayes in a vulgar, but sometimes in an ignominious death; when we shall see this flood (the flood of the anger of God) over-flow the valley of the voluptuous mans gardens, and orchards, and follow him into his Arbours, and Mounts, and Terasses, and carry him from thence into a bottomlesse Sea, which no Plummer can sound, (no heavy sadnesse relieve him) no anchor take hold of, (no repentance stay his tem-pested and weather-beaten conscience) when wee finde our selves in this Ark, where we have first taken in the fresh water of Baptisme; and then the Bread, and Wine, and Flesh, of the Body and Blood of Christ Jesus, Then are we reproved, forbidden all scruple, then are we convinced, That as *the twelve Apostles shall sit upon twelve seats, and judge the twelve Tribes at the last day;* So doth the Holy Ghost make us Judges of all the world now, and inables us to pronounce that sentence; That all but they, who have sincerely accepted the Christian Religion, are still *sub peccato,* under sin, and without remedy. For we must not waigh God with leaden, or iron, or stone waights; how much land, or metall, or riches he gives one man more than another, but how much grace in the use of these, or how much patience in the want, or in the losse of these, we have above others.

SERMON XL

Lincoln's Inn. Sunday after Trinity. [1621]

[p. 398]

THE Lord then, the Son of God, had a *Sitio* in heaven, as well as upon the Crosse; He thirsted our salvation there, and in the midst of the fellow-ship of the Father from whom he came, and of the Holy Ghost, who came from him and the Father, and all the Angels, who came (by a lower way) from them all, he desired the conversation of Man, for Mans sake; He that was God *The Lord* became *Christ,* a man, and he that was *Christ,* became *Jesus,* no man, a dead man, to save man: To save man, all wayes, in all his parts, And to save all men, in all parts of the world: To save his soule from hell, where we should have felt pains, and yet been dead, then when we felt them; and seen horrid spectacles, and yet been in darknes and blindnes, then when we saw them; And suffered unsufferable tor-ments, and yet have told over innumerable ages in suffering them: To save this soule from that hell, and to fill that capacity which it hath, and give it a capacity which it hath not, to comprehend the joyes and glory of Heaven, this *Christ* became *Jesus.* To save this body from the condemnation of everlasting corruption, where the wormes that we breed are our betters, because they have a life, where the dust of dead Kings is blowne into the street, and the dust of the street blowne into the River, and the muddy River tumbled into the Sea, and the Sea remaunded into all the veynes and channels of the earth; to save this body from everlasting dissolution, dispersion, dissipation, and to make it in a glorious Resurrection, not onely a Temple of the holy Ghost, but a Companion of the holy Ghost in the kingdome of heaven, This *Christ* became this *Jesus.* To save this man, body and soule together, from the punishments due to his former sinnes, and to save him from falling into future sinnes by the assistance of his Word preached, and his Sacraments administred in the Church, which he purchased by his bloud, is this person, The *Lord,* the *Christ,* become this *Jesus,* this Saviour. To save so, All wayes, In soule, in body, in both; And also to save all men. For, to exclude others from that Kingdome, is a tyrannie, an usurpation; and to exclude thy selfe, is a sinfull, and a rebellious melancholy. But as melancholy in the body is the hardest humour to be purged, so is the melancholy in the soule, the distrust of thy salvation too. Flashes of presumption a calamity will quench, but clouds of desperation calamities thicken upon us; But even in this inordinate dejection thou exaltest thy selfe above God, and makest thy worst better than his best, thy sins larger than his mercy.

SERMON XLIV

St. Dunstan's in the West. Trinity Sunday. May 20th, 1627

[pp. 440-441]

B U T have the Saints of God no Vacation? doe they never cease? nay, as the word imports, *Requiem non habent,* They have no *Rest.* Beloved, God himselfe rested not, till the seventh day; be thou content to stay for thy Sabbath, till thou maist have an eternall one. If we understand this, of rest meerly, of bodily rest, the Saints of God are least likely to have it, in this life; For, this life, is (to them especially, above others) a businesse, and a perplext businesse, a warfare, and a bloody warfare, a voyage, and a tempestuous voyage. If we understand this rest to be Cessation, Intermission, the Saints in heaven have none of that, in this service. It is a labour that never wearies, to serve God there. As the Sun is no wearier now, than when he first set out, six thousand yeares since; As that Angel, which God hath given to protect thee, is not weary of his office, for all thy perversenesses, so, howsoever God deale with thee, be not thou weary

of bearing thy part, in his Quire here in the Militant Church. God will
have low voyces, as well as high; God will be glorified *De profundis*, as
well as *In excelsis;* God will have his tribute of praise, out of our adversity,
as well as out of our prosperity.

SERMON XLV

Preached on All-Saints Day

[p. 450]

IF the calamities of the world, or the heavy consideration of thine own
sins, have benummed and benighted thy soule in the vale of darknesse,
and in the shadow of death; If thou thinke to wrastle and bustle through
these strong stormes, and thick clouds, with a strong hand; If thou thinke
thy money, thy bribes shall conjure thee up stronger spirits than those
that oppose thee; If thou seek ease in thy calamities, that way to shake
and shipwrack thine enemies; In these crosse winds, in these counter-
mines, (to oppresse as thou art oppressed) all this is but a turning to the
North, to blow away and scatter these sadnesses, with a false, an illusory,
and a sinfull comfort. If thou thinke to ease thy selfe in the contemplation of thine honour, thine offices, thy favour, thy riches, thy health, this
is but a turning to the South, the Sun-shine of worldly prosperity. If
thou sinke under thy afflictions, and canst not finde nourishment (but
poyson) in Gods corrections, nor justice (but cruelty) in his judgements,
nor mercy (but slacknesse) in his forbearance till now; If thou suffer thy
soule to set in a cloud, a dark cloud of ignorance of Gods providence and
proceedings, or in a darker, of diffidence of his performance towards thee,
this is a turning to the West, and all these are perverse and awry. But
turne to the East, and to the Angel that comes from thence, The Ministery
of the Gospel of Christ Jesus in his Church; It is true, thou mayst find
some dark places in the Scriptures; and, *Est silentii species obscuritas,* To
speake darkly and obscurely is a kinde of silence, I were as good not be
spoken to, as not be made to understand that which is spoken, yet fixe
thy selfe upon this Angel of the East, the preaching of the Word, the
Ordinance of God, and thine understanding shall be enlightned, and thy
beliefe established, and thy conscience thus far unburthened, that though
the sins which thou hast done, cannot be undone, yet neither shalt thou
bee undone by them; There, where thou art afraid of them, in judgement,
they shall never meet thee; but as in the round frame of the World, the
farthest West is East, where the West ends, the East begins, So in thee

(who art a World too) thy West and thy East shall joyne, and when thy Sun, thy soule comes to set in thy death-bed, the Son of Grace shall suck it up into glory.

SERMON XLVI

St. Paul's. The Sunday after the Conversion of S. Paul.
January 30th, 1624/5

[pp. 463-464]

I TAKE no farther occasion from this Circumstance, but to arme you with consolation, how low soever God be pleased to cast you, Though it be to the earth, yet he does not so much cast you downe, in doing that, as bring you home. Death is not a banishing of you out of this world; but it is a visitation of your kindred that lie in the earth; neither are any nearer of kin to you, than the earth it selfe, and the wormes of the earth. You heap earth upon your soules, and encumber them with more and more flesh, by a superfluous and luxuriant diet; You adde earth to earth in new purchases, and measure not by Acres, but by Manors, nor by Manors, but by Shires; And there is a little Quillet, a little Close, worth all these, A quiet Grave. And therefore, when thou readest, That God makes thy bed in thy sicknesse, rejoyce in this, not onely that he makes that bed, where thou dost lie, but that bed where thou shalt lie; That that God, that made the whole earth, is now making thy bed in the earth, a quiet grave, where thou shalt sleep in peace, till the Angels Trumpet wake thee at the Resurrection, to that Judgement where thy peace shall be made before thou commest, and writ, and sealed, in the blood of the Lamb.

Saul falls to the earth; So farre; But he falls no lower. God brings his servants to a great lownesse here; but he brings upon no man a perverse sense, or a distrustfull suspition of falling lower hereafter; His hand strikes us to the earth, by way of humiliation; But it is not his hand, that strikes us into hell, by way of desperation. Will you tell me, that you have observed and studied Gods way upon you all your life, and out of that can conclude what God meanes to doe with you after this life? That God took away your Parents in your infancy, and left you Orphanes then, That he hath crossed you in all your labours in your calling, ever since, That he hath opened you to dishonours, and calumnies, and mis-interpretations, in things well intended by you, That he hath multiplied sicknesses upon you, and given you thereby an assurance of a miserable, and a short life, of few, and evill dayes, nay, That he hath suffered you to fall into sins, that you your selves have hated, To con-

tinue in sins, that you your selves have been weary of, To relapse into
sins, that you your selves have repented; And will you conclude out of
this that God had no good purpose upon you, that if ever he had meant
to doe you good, he would never have gone thus farre, in heaping of
evills upon you? Upon what doest thou ground this? upon thy selfe?
Because thou shouldest not deal thus with any man, whom thou mean'st
well to? How poore, how narrow, how impious a measure of God, is this,
that he must doe, as thou wouldest doe, if thou wert God! God hath not
made a week without a Sabbath; no tentation, without an issue; God
inflicts no calamity, no cloud, no eclipse, without light, to see ease in it,
if the patient will look upon that which God hath done to him, in other
cases, or to that which God hath done to others, at other times. *Saul fell
to the ground,* but he fell no lower; God brings us to humiliation, but not
to desperation.

   He fell; he fell to the ground, And *he fell blinde;* for so it is evident in
the story. Christ had said to the Pharisees, *I came into the world, that they
which see, might be made blinde;* And the Pharisees ask him, *Have you
been able to doe so upon us? Are we blinde?* Here Christ gives them an
example; a reall, a literall, an actuall example; *Saul,* a Pharisee, is made
blinde. He that will fill a vessell with wine, must take out the water; He
that will fill a covetous mans hand with gold, must take out the silver that
was there before, sayes S. *Chrysostome.* Christ, who is about to infuse
new light into *Saul,* withdrawes that light that was in him before; That
light, by which *Saul* thought he saw all before, and thought himselfe a
competent Judge, which was the onely true Religion, and that all others
were to be persecuted, even to death, that were not of his way. *Stultus
factus est omnis homo à scientia,* sayes God in the Prophet, Every man
that trusts in his owne wit, is a foole. But *let him become a foole, that he
may be wise,* sayes the Apostle; Let him be so, in his own eyes, and God
will give him better eyes, better light, better understanding. *Saul* was
struck blinde, but it was a blindnesse contracted from light; It was a
light that struck him blinde, as you see in his story. This blindnesse which
we speak of, which is a sober and temperate abstinence from the immoderate study, and curious knowledge of this world, this holy simplicity
of the soule, is not a darknesse, a dimnesse, a stupidity in the understanding, contracted by living in a corner, it is not an idle retiring into a
Monastery, or into a Village, or a Country solitude, it is not a lazy affectation of ignorance; not darknesse, but a greater light, must make us blinde.

   The sight, and the Contemplation of God, and our present benefits
by him, and our future interest in him, must make us blinde to the world
so, as that we look upon no face, no pleasure, no knowledge, with such an
Affection, such an Ambition, such a Devotion, as upon God, and the

wayes to him. *Saul* had such a blindnesse, as came from light; we must affect no other simplicity, than arises from the knowledge of God, and his Religion. And then, *Saul* had such a blindnesse, as that he fell with it. There are birds, that when their eyes are cieled, still soare up, and up, till they have spent all their strength. Men blinded with the lights of this world, soare still into higher places, or higher knowledges, or higher opinions; but the light of heaven humbles us, and layes flat that soule, which the leaven of this world had puffed and swelled up. That powerfull 'ight felled *Saul;* but after he was fallen, his owne sight was restored to him againe; *Ananias* saies to him, *Brother Saul, receive thy sight.* To those men, who imploy their naturall faculties to the glory of God, and their owne, and others edification, God shall afford an exaltation of those naturall faculties; In those, who use their learning, or their wealth, or their power, well, God shall increase that power, and that wealth, and that learning, even in this world.

SERMON XLVIII

St. Paul's. In the evening. Upon the day of St. Paul's Conversion.
January 25, 1628/9

I   [p. 483]

ALAS, they, we, men of this world, wormes of this dunghil, whether Basilisks or blind wormes, whether Scarabs or Silkworms, whether high or low in the world, have no minds to change. The Platonique Philosophers did not only acknowledge *Animam in homine,* a soule in man, but *Mentem in anima,* a minde in the soul of man. They meant by the minde, the superiour faculties of the soule, and we never come to exercise them. Men and women call one another inconstant, and accuse one another of having changed their minds, when, God knowes, they have but changed the object of their eye, and seene a better white or red. An old man loves not the same sports that he did when he was young, nor a sicke man the same meats that hee did when hee was well: But these men have not changed their mindes; The old man hath changed his fancy, and the sick man his taste; neither his minde.

2   [p. 486]

Poore intricated soule! Riddling, perplexed, labyrinthicall soule! Thou couldest not say, that thou beleevest not in God, if there were no God; Thou couldest not beleeve in God, if there were no God; If there were no God, thou couldest not speake, thou couldest not thinke, not a word, not a thought, no not against God; Thou couldest not blaspheme the Name of God, thou couldest not sweare, if there were no God: For, all thy faculties, how ever depraved, and perverted by thee, are from him; and except thou canst seriously beleeve, that thou art nothing, thou canst not beleeve that there is no God. If I should aske thee at a Tragedy, where thou shouldest see him that had drawne blood, lie weltring, and surrounded in his owne blood, Is there a God now? If thou couldst answer me, No, These are but Inventions, and Representations of men, and I beleeve a God never the more for this; If I should ask thee at a Sermon, where thou shouldest heare the Judgements of God formerly denounced, and executed, re-denounced, and applied to present occasions, Is there a God now? If thou couldest answer me, No, These are but Inventions of State, to souple and regulate Congregations, and keep people in order, and I beleeve a God never the more for this; Bee as confident as thou canst, in company; for company is the Atheists Sanctuary; I respit thee not till the day of Judgement, when I may see thee upon thy knees, upon thy face, begging of the hills, that they would fall downe and cover thee from the fierce wrath of God, to aske thee then, Is there a God now? I respit thee not till the day of thine own death, when thou shalt have evidence enough, that there is a God, though no other evidence, but to finde a Devill, and evidence enough, that there is a Heaven, though no other evidence, but to feele Hell; To aske thee then, Is there a God now? I respit thee but a few houres, but six houres, but till midnight. Wake then; and then darke, and alone, Heare God aske thee then, remember that I asked thee now, Is there a God? and if thou darest, say No.

SERMON XLIX

St. Paul's. Conversion of St. Paul. January 25, 1629/30

[pp. 495-496]

BUT stop we the floodgates of this consideration; it would melt us into teares. End we all with this, That we have all, all these, Sadduces and Pharisees in our owne bosomes: Sadduces that deny spirits; carnall apprehensions that are apt to say, Is your God all Spirit, and hath bodily eyes to see sin? All Spirit, and hath bodily hands to strike for a sinne? Is your soule all spirit, and hath a fleshly heart to feare? All spirit, and hath sensible sinews to feele a materiall fire? Was your God, who is all Spirit, wounded when you quarrelled? or did your soule, which is all spirit, drink when you were drunk? Sins of presumption, and carnall confidence are our Sadduces; and then our Pharisees are our sins of separation, of division, of diffidence and distrust in the mercies of our God; when we are apt to say, after a sin, Cares God, who is all Spirit, for my eloquent prayers, or for my passionate teares? Is the giving of my goods to the poore, or of my body to the fire, any thing to God who is all Spirit? My spirit, and nothing but my spirit, my soule, and nothing but my soule, must satisfie the justice, the anger of God, and be separated from him for ever. My Sadduce, my Presumption suggests, that there is no spirit, no soule to suffer for sin; and my Pharisee, my Desperation suggests, That my soule must perish irremediably, irrecoverably, for every sinne that my body commits.

Now if I go S. *Pauls* way, to put a dissention between these my *Sadduces,* and my *Pharisees,* to put a jealousie between my presumption and my desperation, to make my presumption see, that my desperation lies in wait for her; and to consider seriously, that my presumption will end in desperation, I may, as S. *Paul* did in the Text, scape the better for that. But if, without farther troubling these *Sadduces* and these *Pharisees,* I be content to let them agree, and to divide my life between them, so as that my presumption shall possesse all my youth, and desperation mine age, I have heard my sentence already, *The end of this man will be worse than his beginning,* How much soever God be incensed with me, for my presumption at first, he will be much more inexorable for my desperation at last. And therefore interrupt the prescription of sin; break off the correspondence of Sin; unjoynt the dependency of sin upon sin. Bring every single sin, as soon as thou committest it, into the presence of thy God, upon those two legs, Confession, and Detestation, and thou shalt see, that, as, though an intire Iland stand firme in the Sea, yet a single clod of earth cast into the Sea, is quickly washt into nothing; so, howsoever thine habituall, and customary, and concatenated sins, sin enwrapped and complicated in sin, sin entrenched and barricadoed in sin, sin screwed up, and riveted with sin, may stand out, and wrastle even with the mercies of God, in the blood of Christ Jesus; yet if thou bring every single sin into the sight of God, it will be but as a clod of earth, but as a graine of dust in the Ocean. Keep thy sins then from mutuall intelligence; That they doe not second one another, induce occasion, and then support and disguise one another, and then, neither shall the body of sin ever oppresse thee, nor the exhalations, and damps, and vapors of thy sad soule, hang between thee, and the mercies of thy God; But thou shalt live in the light and serenity of a peaceable conscience here, and die in a faire possibility of a present melioration and improvement of that light. All thy life thou shalt be preserved, in an Orientall light, an Easterne light, a rising and a growing light, the light of grace; and at thy death thou shalt be super-illustrated, with a Meridionall light, a South light, the light of glory. And be this enough for the explication, and application of these words, and their complication with the day; for the justifying of S. *Pauls* Stratagem in himselfe, and the exemplifying, and imitation thereof in us. *Amen.*

SERMON LII

Preached upon the Penitentiall Psalmes. [1627/8?]

[p. 526]

YET I am loath to depart my selfe, loath to dismisse you from this ayre of Paradise, of Gods comming, and returning to us. Therefore we consider againe, that as God came long agoe, six thousand years agoe, in nature, when we were created in *Adam,* and then in nature returned to us, in the generation of our Parents: so our Saviour Christ Jesus came to us long agoe, sixteene hundred yeares agoe, in grace, and yet in grace returnes to us, as often as he assembles us, in these holy Convocations. He came to us then, as the Wisemen came to him, with treasure, and gifts, and gold, and incense, and myrrhe; As having an ambition upon the soules of men, he came with that abundant treasure to purchase us. And as to them who live upon the Kings Pension, it is some comfort to heare that the Exchequer is full, that the Kings moneyes are come in: so is it to us, to know that there is enough in Gods hands, paid by his Son, for the discharge of all our debts; He gave enough for us all at that comming; But it is his returning to us, that applyes to us, and derives upon us in particular, the benefit of this generall satisfaction. When he returns to us in the dispensation and distribution of his graces, in his Word and Sacraments; When he calls upon us to come to the receipt; When the greater the summe is, the gladder he is of our comming, that where sinne abounds, grace might abound too; When we can pursue this Prayer, *Revertere Domine,* Returne O Lord in grace, in more and more grace, and when we are in possession of a good measure of that grace, we can pray againe, *Revertere Domine,* Returne O Lord in glory, Come Lord Jesus, come quickly; When we are so rectified by his Ordinances here, that in a sincerity of soule, we are not onely contented, but desirous to depart from hence, then have we religiously followed our example, that man according to Gods heart, *David,* in this prayer of his. If Christ have not beene thus fully in thine heart, before, this is his comming; entertaine him now: If he have been there and gone againe, this is his returning;

blesse him for that: And meet him, and love him, and embrace him, as often as he offers himselfe to thy soule, in these his Ordinances: With every day a Sunday, and every meale a Sacrament, and every discourse a Homily, and he shall shine upon thee in all dark wayes, and rectifie thee in all ragged wayes, and direct thee in all crosse wayes, and stop thee in all doubtfull wayes, and returne to thee in every corner, and relieve thee in every danger, and arme thee against even himselfe, by advancing thy worke, in which thou besiegest him, that is, this Prayer, and enabling thee to prevaile upon him, as in this first Petition, *Revertere Domine, O Lord returne,* so in that which followes next, *Eripe animam, Deliver my soule.*

SERMON LIII

Preached upon the Penitentiall Psalmes. [1627/8?]

[p. 531]

IT may well be inquired, why Death seemed so terrible to the good and godly men of those times, as that evermore we see them complaine of shortnesse of life, and of the neerenesse of death. Certainely the rule is true, in naturall, and in civill, and in divine things, as long as wee are in this World, *Nolle meliorem, est corruptio primæ habitudinis,* That man is not well, who desires not to be better; It is but our corruption here, that makes us loth to hasten to our incorruption there. And besides, many of the Ancients, and all the later Casuists of the other side, and amongst our owne men, *Peter Martyr,* and *Calvin,* assigne certain cases, in which it hath *Rationem boni,* The nature of Good, and therefore is to be embraced, to wish our dissolution and departure out of this world; and yet, many good and godly men have declared this lothnesse to dye. Beloved, waigh Life and Death one against another, and the balance will be even; Throw the glory of God into either balance, and that turnes the scale. S. *Paul* could not tell which to wish, Life or Death; There the balance was even; Then comes in the glory of God, the addition of his soule to that Quire, that spend all their time, eternity it selfe, only in glorifying God, and that turnes the scale, and then, he comes to his *Cupio dissolvi,* To *desire to be dissolved, and to be with Christ.* But then, he puts in more of the same waight in the other scale, he sees that it advances Gods glory more, for him to stay, and labour in the building of Gods Kingdome here, and so adde more soules than his owne to that state, than only to enjoy that Kingdome in himself, and that turnes the scale againe, and so he is content *to live.*

Whitehall. To the King upon the occasion of the Fast. April 5th, 1628

I   [pp. 540-541]

TENTATIONS take hold of us sometimes after our teares, after our repentance, but seldome or never in the act of our repentance, and in the
very shedding of our teares; At least *Libidinum pompa,* The victory, the
triumph of lust breaks not in upon us, in a bed, so dissolved, so surrounded,
so macerated with such teares. Thy bed is a figure of thy grave; Such as
thy grave receives thee at death, it shall deliver thee up to Judgement at
last; Such as thy bed receives thee at night, it shall deliver thee in the
morning: If thou sleepe without calling thy selfe to an account, thou wilt
wake so, and walke so, and proceed so, without ever calling thy selfe to
an account, till Christ Jesus call thee in the Clouds. It is not intended,
that thou shouldest afflict thy selfe so grievously, as some over-doing
Penitents, to put chips, and shels, and splints, and flints, and nayles, and
rowels of spurres in thy bed, to wound and macerate thy body so. The
inventions of men, are not intended here; But here is a precept of God,
implied in this precedent and practise of *David,* That as long as the sense
of a former sinne, or the inclination to a future oppresses thee, thou must
not close thine eyes, thou must not take thy rest, till, as God married thy
body and soule together in the Creation, and shall at last crowne thy
body and soule together in the Resurrection, so they may also rest together here, that as thy body rests in thy bed, thy soule may rest in the
peace of thy Conscience, and that thou never say to thy head, Rest upon
this pillow, till thou canst say to thy soule, Rest in this repentance, in this
peace.

2   [p. 542]

Against this Vermination, (as the Originall denotes) against this gnawing of the worme, that may bore through, and sink the strongest vessell
that sailes in the seas of the world, there is no other varnish, no other
liniment, no other medicament, no other pitch nor rosin against this
worme, but the bloud of Christ Jesus: And therefore whensoever this
worme, this apprehension of Gods future indignation, reserved for the
Judgement, bites upon thee, be sure to present to it the bloud of thy
Saviour: Never consider the judgement of God for sin alone, but in the
company of the mercies of Christ. It is but the hissing of the Serpent, and
the whispering of Satan, when he surprises thee in a melancholy midnight
of dejection of spirit, and layes thy sins before thee then; Looke not upon

thy sins so inseparably, that thou canst not see Christ too: Come not to
a confession to God, without consideration of the promises of his Gospel;
Even the sense and remorse of sin is a dangerous consideration, but when
the cup of salvation stands by me, to keep me from fainting. *David* himselfe could not get off when he would; but (as he complaines there, which
is the last act of his sorrow to be considered in this, which is all his part,
and all our first part) *Inveteravit, He waxed old because of all his enemies.*

3   [p. 544]

Now, *Stipendium peccati mors est,* There is the punishment for sin,
The reward of sin is death. If there remaine no death, there remaines no
punishment: *For the reward of sin is death,* And death complicated in it
selfe, death wrapped in death; and what is so intricate, so intangling as
death? Who ever got out of a winding sheet? It is death agravated by it
selfe, death waighed downe by death: And what is so heavy as death?
Who ever threw off his grave stone? It is death multiplied by it selfe;
And what is so infinite as death? Who ever told over the dayes of death?
It is *Morte morieris,* A Double death, Eternall, and Temporary. Temporall, and Spirituall death. Now, the Temporary, the Naturall death,
God never takes away from us, he never pardons that punishment, because he never takes away that sin that occasioned it, which is Originall
sin; To what Sanctification soever a man comes, Originall sin lives to his
last breath. And therefore, *Statutum est,* That Decree stands, *Semel mori,*
that every man must dye once; but for any *Bis mori,* for twice dying,
for eternall death upon any man, as man, if God consider him not as an
impotent sinner, there is no such invariable Decree; for, that death
being also the punishment for actuall sin, if he take away the cause, the
sin, he takes away that effect, that death also; for this death it selfe,
eternall death, we all agree that it is taken away with the sin; And then
for other calamities in this life, which we call *Morticulas,* Little deaths,
the children, the issue, the off-spring, the propagation of death, if we
would speak properly, no Affliction, no Judgement of God in this life,
hath in it exactly the nature of a punishment; not onely not the nature
of satisfaction, but not the nature of a punishment. We call not Coyn,
base Coyne, till the Allay be more than the pure metall: Gods Judgements are not punishments, except there be more anger than love, more
Justice than Mercy in them; and that is never; for *Miserationes ejus super
omnia opera,* His mercies are above all his works: In his first work, in
the Creation, his *Spirit,* the Holy Ghost, *moved upon the face of the
waters;* and still upon the face of all our waters, (as waters are emblemes
of tribulation in all the Scriptures) his Spirit, the Spirit of comfort,
moves too; and as the waters produced the first creatures in the Creation,

so tribulations offer us the first comforts; sooner than prosperity does. God excutes no judgement upon man in this life, but in mercy; either in mercy to that person, in his sense thereof, if he be sensible, or at least in mercy to his Church, in the example thereof, if he be not: There is no person to whom we can say, that Gods Corrections are Punishments, any otherwise than Medicinall, and such, as he may receive amendment by, that receives them; Neither does it become us in any case, to say God layes this upon him, because he is so ill, but because he may be better.

SERMON LVII

Preached upon the Penitentiall Psalmes (Ps. xxxii)

[p. 579]

THE hand of God shall grow heavy upon a silent sinner, in his body, in his health; and if he conceive a comfort, that for all his sicknesse, he is rich, and therefore cannot fayle of helpe and attendance, there comes another worme, and devours that, faithlessnesse in persons trusted by him, oppressions in persons that have trusted him, facility in undertaking for others, corrupt Judges, heavy adversaries, tempests and Pirats at Sea, unseasonable or ill Markets at land, costly and expensive ambitions at Court, one worme or other shall devoure his riches, that he eased himselfe upon. If he take up another Comfort, that though health and wealth decay, though he be poore and weake, yet he hath learning, and philosophy, and morall constancy, and he can content himselfe with himselfe, he can make his study a Court, and a few Books shall supply to him the society and the conversation of many friends, there is another worme to devoure this too, the hand of divine Justice shall grow heavy upon him, in a sense of an unprofitable retirednesse, in a disconsolate melancholy, and at last, in a stupidity, tending to desperation.

SERMON LXII

Preached upon the Penitentiall Psalmes (Ps. xxxii)

[p. 623]

FOR, certainly, no man is so inclinable to submit himselfe to any burden of labour, of danger, of cost, of dishonour, of law, of sicknesse, as the licentious man is; He refuses none, to come to his ends. Neither is there any tree so loaded with boughs, any one sin that hath so many branches, so many species as this. Shedding of blood we can limit in murder, and manslaughter, and a few more; and other sins in as few names. In this sin of lust, the sexe, the quality, the distance, the manner, and a great many other circumstances, create new names to the sin, and make it a sin of another kinde. And as the sin is a Mule, to beare all these loads, so the sinner in this kind is so too, and (as we finde an example in the Nephew of a Pope) delights to take as many loads of this sin upon him, as he could; to vary, and to multiply the kindes of this sin in one act, He would not satisfie his lust by a fornication, or adultery, or incest, (these were vulgar) but upon his own sex; and that not upon an ordinary person, but in their account, upon a Prince; And he, a spirituall Prince, A Cardinall; And all this, not by solicitation, but by force: for thus he compiled his sins, He ravished a Cardinall. This is the sin, in which men pack up as much sin as they can, and as though it were a shame to have too little, they belie their own pack, they bragge of sins in this kinde, which they never did, as S. *Augustine* with a holy and penitent ingenuity confesses of himselfe.

SERMON LXIII

Preached upon the Penitentiall Psalmes (Ps. xxxii)

[pp. 630-632]

N o w the pride of the wicked is to conceale their sorrowes, that God might receive no glory by the discovery of them. And therefore if we should goe about to number their sorrowes, they would have their victory still, and still say to themselves, yet for all his cunning he hath mist; they would ever have some bosome-sorrowes, which we could not light upon. Yet we shall not easily misse, nor leave out any, if we remember those men, that even this false and imaginary joy, which they take in concealing their sorrow and affliction, is a new affliction, a new cause of sorrow. We shall make up the number apace, if we remember these men, that all their new sins, and all their new shifts, to put away their sorrowes, are sorrowfull things, and miserable comforters; if their conscience doe present all their sins, the number growes great; And if their own conscience have forgotten them, if God forget nothing that they have thought, or said, or done, in all their lives, are not their occasions of sorrow the more for their forgetting, the more for Gods remembering? *Judgements are prepared for the scorners,* sayes *Solomon,* God foresaw their wickednesse from before all times, and even then set himselfe on work, *To prepare judgements for them;* And as they are *Prepared* before, so *affliction followeth sinners,* sayes the same Wise King; It *followes* them, and it knowes how to *overtake* them; eyther by the sword of the Magistrate, or by that

which is nearer them, Diseases in their owne bodies, accelerated and complicated by their sins. And then, as affliction is *Prepared,* and *Followes,*
and *Overtakes,* so sayes that wise King still, *There shall be no end of
plagues to the evill man;* We know the beginning of their plagues; they
are *Prepared* in Gods Decree, as soone as God saw their sins; we know
their continuance, they shall *Follow,* and they shall *Overtake;* Their end
we doe not know, we cannot know, for they have none. Thus they are
Many.

And if we consider farther, the manifold Topiques, and places, from
which the sorrowes of the wicked arise, That every inch of their ground
is overgrown with that venomous weed, that every place, and every part
of time, and every person buddes out a particular occasion of sorrow to
him, that he can come into no chamber, but he remembers, In such a
place as this, I sinned thus, That he cannot heare a Clock strike, but he
remembers At this hour I sinned thus, That he cannot converse with
few persons, but he remembers, With such a person I sinned thus, And if
he dare goe no farther than to himselfe, he can look scarcely upon any
limb of his body, but in that he sees some infirmity, or some deformity,
that he imputes to some sin, and must say, By this sin, this is thus: When
he can open the Bible in no place, but if he meet a judgement, he must
say, *Vindicta mihi,* This vengeance belongs to me; and if he meet a
mercy, he must say, *Quid mihi?* What have I to doe to take this mercy
into my mouth? In this deluge of occasions of sorrow, I must not say with
God to *Abraham,* Look up to heaven, and number the Starres, (for this
man cannot look up to heaven) but I must say, Continue thy dejected
look, and look downe to the earth, thy earth, and number the graines of
dust there, and the sorrowes of the wicked are more than they. *Many are
the sorrowes;* And as the word as naturally denotes, *Great; Great sorrowes are upon the wicked.*

That Pill will choak one man, which will slide down with another
easily, and work well. That sorrow, that affliction would strangle the
wicked, which would purge, and recover the godly. The coare of *Adams*
apple is still in their throat, which the blood of the Messias hath washt
away in the righteous; *Adams* disobedience works in them still, and therefore Gods Physick, the affliction, cannot work. So they are great to them,
as *Cains* punishment was to him, greater than he could beare, because
he could not ease himselfe upon the consideration of Gods purpose, in
laying that punishment upon him. But it is not onely their indisposition,
and impatience, that makes their sorrowes and afflictions great; They
are truly so in themselves; as the Holy Ghost expresses it, *Is not destruction to the wicked, and strange punishment to the workers of iniquity?*
A punishment, which we cannot tell how to measure, how to waigh, how

to call, *A strange punishment;* Greater than former examples have presented. There the greatnesse is exprest in the Word; And in *Esay* it is exprest in the action; *When the scourge shall run over you, and passe thorow you, Eritis in conculcationem, You shall be trodden to dust;* Which is, as the Prophet cals it there, *Flagellum inundans,* An affliction that overflowes, and surrounds all, as a deluge, a flood, that shall wash away from thee, even the water of thy Baptisme, and all the power of that, And wash away from thee the blood of thy Saviour, and all his offers of grace to worthy receivers; A flood that shall carry away the Ark it selfe out of thy sight, and leave thee no apprehension of reparation by Gods institution in his Church; A flood that shall dissolve, and wash thee thy selfe into water; Thy sorrowes shall scatter thee into drops, into teares, upon a carnall sense of thy torment, And into drops, into incoherent doubts, and perplexities, and scruples, in understanding, and conscience, and into desperation at last. And this is the Greatnesse: *Solutis doloribus inferni,* In another sense then *David* speaks that of Christ; There it is, that the sorrowes of hell were loosed, that is, were slacked, dissolved by him: But here it is that the sorrowes of hell are loosed, that is, let loose upon thee; and when thou shalt heare Christ say from the Crosse, *Behold and see, if ever there were any sorrow like my sorrow,* thou shalt finde thy sorrow like his in the Greatnesse, and nothing like his in the Goodnesse: Christ bore that sorrow, that every man might rejoyce, and thou wouldest be the more sorry, if every man had not as much cause of desperate sorrow, as thou hast.

Many, and great are the sor[r]owes of the wicked, and then *eternall* too, which is more than intimated, in that the Originall hath neither of those particles of supplement, which are in our Translations, no such (*shall come*) no such (*shall be*) nor no (*shall*) at all; but onely, *Many sorrowes to the wicked,* Many and great now, more and greater hereafter, All for ever, if they amend not.

It is not, They have had sorrowes, but they are overblown; nor that they have them, but patience shall outweare them; nor that they shall have them, but they have a breathing time to gather strength before hand; But as it was in the beginning, is now, and ever shall be, Sorrowes upon them, and upon them for ever. Whatsoever any man conceives for ease in this case, it is a false conception; *You shall conceive chaffe and bring forth stubble.* And this stubble is your vaine hope of a determination of this sorrow; But the wicked shall not be able to lodge such a hope, though this hope, if they could apprehend it, would be but an aggravating of their sorrowes in the end. It is eternall, no determination of time afforded to it. For, *They shall bee as the burning of lime, and as thornes cut up shall they bee burnt in the fire. Who amongst us shall dwell with the devouring fire? Who amongst us shall dwell with that ever-lasting burning?* It is a *devouring fire,* and yet it is an *everlasting burning.* The Prophet asks, *Who can dwell there?* In that intensenesse who can last? They that must, and that is, All the wicked. *Fire is kindled in my wrath,* saith God; Yet may not teares quench it? Teares might, if they could be had; But *It shall burne to the bottome of hell,* saith God there. And *Dives* that could not procure a drop of water to coole his tongue there, can much lesse procure a repentant teare in that place: There, as S. *John* speakes, *Plagues shall come in one day;* Death, and Sorrow, and Famine. But it is in a long day; Short for the suddennesse of comming, for that is come already, which for any thing we know, may come this minute, before we be at an end of this point, or at a period of this sentence: So it is sudden in comming, but long for the enduring. For it is that day, when *They shall be burnt with fire, for strong is the Lord God, that will condemne them.* That is argument enough of the vehemence of that fire, that the *Lord God,* who is called the *strong God,* makes it a Master-piece of his strength, to make that fire.

Art thou able to dispute out this *Fire,* and to prove that there can be no reall, no materiall fire in Hell, after the dissolution of all materiall things created? If thou be not able to argue away the immortality of thine owne soule, but that that soule must last, nor to argue away the eternity of God himselfe, but that that must last, thou hast but little ease, in making shift to give a figurative interpretation to that fire, and to say, It may be a torment, but it cannot be a fire, since it must be an everlasting torment; nor to give a figurative signification to the *Worme,* and to say, It may bee a paine, a remorse, but it can bee no worme after the generall dissolution, since that Conscience, in which that remorse, and anguish shall ever live, must live ever: If there bee a figure in the names, and words, of *Fire* and *Wormes,* there is an indisputable reality in the sorrow, in the torment, and in the manifoldnesse, and in the weightinesse, and in the everlastingnesse thereof. For in the inchoation of these sorrowes, in this life, and in the consummation of them, in the life to come, *The sorrowes of the wicked are many,* and *great,* and *eternall.*

SERMON LXIV

Preached upon the Penitentiall Psalmes (Ps. li)

[pp. 641-642]

I T is therefore but an imperfect comfort for any man to say, I have overcome tentations to great sins, and my sins have beene but of infirmity, not of malice. For herein, more than in any other contemplation appeares the greatnesse, both of thy danger, and of thy transgression. For, consider what a dangerous, and slippery station thou art in, if after a victory over Giants, thou mayest be overcome by Pigmees; If after thy soule hath beene Canon proofe against strong tentations, she be slaine at last by a Pistoll; And after she hath swom over a tempestuous Sea, shee drowne at last, in a shallow and standing ditch. And as it showes the greatnesse of thy danger, so it aggravates the greatnesse of thy fault; That after thou hast had the experience, that by a good husbanding of those degrees of grace, which God hath afforded thee, thou hast beene able to stand out the great batteries of strong tentations, and seest by that, that thou art much more able to withstand tentations to lesser sins, if thou wilt, yet by disarming thy selfe, by devesting thy garisons, by discontinuing thy watches, meerely by inconsideration, thou sellest thy soule for nothing, for little pleasure, little profit, thou frustratest thy Saviour of that purchase, which he bought with his precious blood, and thou enrichest the Devils treasure as much, with thy single money, thy frequent small sins, as another hath done with his talent; for, as God was well pleased with the widowes two farthings, so is the Devill well pleased, with the negligent mans lesser sins. O who can be confident in his footing, or in his hold, when *David,* that held out so long, fell, and if we consider but himselfe, irrecoverably, where the temper was weake, and afar off?

SERMON LXV

St. Paul's. 'The first of the Prebend of Cheswick's five Psalmes.'
May 8, 1625

[p. 660]

THE Applause of the people is vanity, Popularity is vanity. At how deare a rate doth that man buy the peoples affections, that payes his owne head for their hats! How cheaply doth he sell his Princes favour, that hath nothing for it, but the peoples breath! And what age doth not see some examples of so ill merchants of their owne honours and lives too! How many men, upon confidence of that flattering gale of winde, the breath and applause of the people, have taken in their anchors, (that is, departed from their true, and safe hold, The right of the Law, and the favour of the Prince) and as soone as they hoysed their sailes, (that is, entred into any by-action) have found the wind in their teeth, that is, Those people whom they trusted in, armed against them! And as it is in Civill, and Secular, so it is in Ecclesiasticall, and Spirituall things too.

How many men, by a popular hunting after the applause of the people, in their manner of preaching, and humouring them in their distempers, have made themselves incapable of preferment in the Church where they tooke their Orders, and preached themselves into a necessity of running away into forraine parts, that are receptacles of seditious and schismaticall Separatists, and have been put there, to learne some trade, and become Artificers for their sustentation? The same people that welcommed Christ, from the Mount of Olives, into Jerusalem, upon Sunday, with their *Hosannaes to the Sonne of David,* upon Friday mocked him in Jerusalem, with their *Haile King of the Jews,* and blew him out of Jerusalem to Golgotha, with the pestilent breath, with the tempestuous whirlwind of their *Crucifiges.* And of them, who have called the Master Beelzebub, what shall any servant looke for? *Surely men of low degree are vanity.*

And then, under the same oath, and asseveration, *Surely,* as surely as the other, *men of high degree are a lie.* Doth *David* meane these men, whom he calls *a lie,* to be any lesse than those whom hee called *vanity?* Lesse than vanity, than emptinesse, than nothing, nothing can be; And low, and high are to this purpose, and in this consideration, (compared with God, or considered without God) equally nothing. He that hath the largest patrimony, and space of earth, in the earth, must heare me say, That all that was nothing; And if he ask, But what was this whole Kingdom, what all Europe, what all the World? It was all, not so much as another nothing, but all one and the same nothing as thy dunghill was.

SERMON LXVI

St. Paul's. 'The second of my Prebend Sermons upon my five Psalmes.'
Jan. 29, 1625/6

I [pp. 664-666]

ALL our life is a continuall burden, yet we must not groane; A continuall squeasing, yet we must not pant; And as in the tendernesse of our child-hood, we suffer, and yet are whipt if we cry, so we are complained of, if we complaine, and made delinquents if we call the times ill. And that which adds waight to waight, and multiplies the sadnesse of this con-sideration, is this, That still the best men have had most laid upon them. As soone as I heare God say, that he hath found *an upright man, that fears God, and eschews evill,* in the next lines I finde a Commission to Satan, to bring in Sabeans and Chaldeans upon his cattell, and servants, and fire and tempest upon his children, and loathsome diseases upon himselfe. As soone as I heare God say, That he hath found *a man accord-*

ing to his own heart, I see his sonnes ravish his daughters, and then murder
one another, and then rebell against the Father, and put him into straites
for his life. As soone as I heare God testifie of Christ at his Baptisme,
This is my beloved Sonne in whom I am well pleased, I finde that Sonne
of his *led up by the Spirit, to be tempted of the Devill.* And after I heare
God ratifie the same testimony againe, at his Transfiguration, (*This is
my beloved Sonne, in whom I am well pleased*) I finde that beloved Sonne
of his, deserted, abandoned, and given over to Scribes, and Pharisees,
and Publicans, and Herodians, and Priests, and Souldiers, and people, and
Judges, and witnesses, and executioners, and he that was called the beloved Sonne of God, and made partaker of the glory of heaven, in this
world, in his Transfiguration, is made now the Sewer of all the corruption, of all the sinnes of this world, as no Sonne of God, but a meere
man, as no man, but a contemptible worme. As though the greatest weaknesse in this world, were man, and the greatest fault in man were to be
good, man is more miserable than other creatures, and good men more
miserable than any other men.

2

Let me wither and weare out mine age in a discomfortable, in an unwholesome, in a penurious prison, and so pay my debts with my bones,
and recompence the wastfulnesse of my youth, with the beggery of mine
age; Let me wither in a spittle under sharpe, and foule, and infamous
diseases, and so recompence the wantonnesse of my youth, with that loathsomnesse in mine age; yet, if God with-draw not his spirituall blessings,
his Grace, his Patience, If I can call my suffering his Doing, my passion
his Action, All this that is temporall, is but a caterpiller got into one
corner of my garden, but a mill-dew fallen upon one acre of my Corne;
The body of all, the substance of all is safe, as long as the soule is safe.
But when I shall trust to that, which wee call a good spirit, and God shall
deject, and empoverish, and evacuate that spirit, when I shall rely upon
a morall constancy, and God shall shake, and enfeeble, and enervate,
destroy and demolish that constancy; when I shall think to refresh my
selfe in the serenity and sweet ayre of a good conscience, and God shall
call up the damps and vapours of hell it selfe, and spread a cloud of diffidence, and an impenetrable crust of desperation upon my conscience;
when health shall flie from me, and I shall lay hold upon riches to succour
me, and comfort me in my sicknesse, and riches shall flie from me, and
I shall snatch after favour, and good opinion, to comfort me in my
poverty; when even this good opinion shall leave me, and calumnies and
misinformations shall prevaile against me; when I shall need peace, because there is none but thou, O Lord, that should stand for me, and then

shall finde, that all the wounds that I have, come from thy hand, all the
arrowes that stick in me, from thy quiver; when I shall see, that because
I have given my selfe to my corrupt nature, thou hast changed thine; and
because I am all evill towards thee, therefore thou hast given over being
good towards me; When it comes to this height, that the fever is not in
the humors, but in the spirits, that mine enemy is not an imaginary
enemy, fortune, nor a transitory enemy, malice in great persons, but a
reall, and an irresistible, and an inexorable, and an everlasting enemy,
The Lord of Hosts himselfe, The Almighty God himselfe, the Almighty
God himselfe onely knowes the waight of this affliction, and except hee
put in that *pondus gloriæ*, that exceeding waight of an eternall glory, with
his owne hand, into the other scale, we are waighed downe, we are swallowed up, irreparably, irrevocably, irrecoverably, irremediably.

SERMON LXVII

*St. Paul's. 'In Vesperis.' 'The third of my Prebend Sermons upon my
five Psalmes.' Nov. 5th,* 1626

[p. 677]

UPON this earth, a man cannot possibly make one step in a straight, and
a direct line. The earth it selfe being round, every step wee make upon
it, must necessarily bee a segment, an arch of a circle. But yet though
no piece of a circle be a straight line, yet if we take any piece, nay if wee
take the whole circle, there is no corner, no angle in any piece, in any
intire circle. A perfect rectitude we cannot have in any wayes in this
world; In every Calling there are some inevitable tentations. But, though
wee cannot make up our circle of a straight line, (that is impossible to
humane frailty) yet wee may passe on, without angles, and corners, that
is, without disguises in our Religion, and without the love of craft, and
falsehood, and circumvention in our civill actions. A Compasse is a necessary thing in a Ship, and the helpe of that Compasse brings the Ship home
safe, and yet that Compasse hath some variations, it doth not looke
directly North; Neither is that starre which we call the North-pole, or
by which we know the North-pole, the very Pole it selfe; but we call it
so, and we make our uses of it, and our conclusions by it, as if it were so,
because it is the neerest starre to that Pole. He that comes as neere up-
rightnesse, as infirmities admit, is an upright man, though he have some
obliquities. To God himselfe we may alwayes go in a direct line, a straight,
a perpendicular line; For God is verticall to me, over my head now, and
verticall now to them, that are in the East, and West-Indies; To our

Antipodes, to them that are under our feet, God is verticall, over their heads, then when he is over ours.

SERMON LXVIII

St. Paul's. 'The fourth of my Prebend Sermons upon my five Psalmes.'
Jan. 28*th*, 1626/7

[p. 694]

T H O U G H death be but a sleepe, yet it is a sleepe that an Earth-quake cannot wake; And yet there is a Trumpet that will, when that hand of God, that gathered dust to make these bodies, shall crumble these bodies into dust againe, when that soule that evaporated it selfe in unnecessary disputations in this world, shall make such fearfull and distempered con-clusions, as to see God onely by absence, (never to see him face to face) And to know God onely by ignorance, (never to know him *sicuti est,* as he is) (for he is All mercy) And to possesse immortality, and impossibility of dying onely in a continuall dying; when, as a Cabinet whose key were lost, must be broken up, and torne in pieces, before the Jewell that was laid up in it, can be taken out; so thy body, (the Cabinet of thy soule) must be shaked and shivered by violent sicknesse, before that soule can goe out, And when it is thus gone out, must answer for all the imperfec-tions of that body, which body polluted it, And yet, though this soule be such a loser by that body, it is not perfectly well, nor fully satisfied, till it be reunited to that body againe; when thou remembrest, (and, oh, never forget it) that Christ himselfe *was heavy in his soule unto Death,* That Christ himselfe came to a *Si possible, If it be possible, let this Cup passe;* That he came to a *Quare dereliquisti,* a bitter sense of Gods dere-liction, and forsaking of him, when thou considerest all this, compose thy selfe for death, but thinke it not a light matter to dye. Death made the Lyon of Judah to roare; and doe not thou thinke, that that which we call going away like a Lambe, doth more testifie a conformity with Christ, than a strong sense, and bitter agony, and colluctation with death, doth. Christ gave us the Rule, in the Example; He taught us what we should doe, by his doing it; And he pre-admitted a fearfull apprehension of death. A Lambe is a Hieroglyphique of Patience, but not of stupidity. And death was Christs *Consummatum est,* All ended in death; yet he had sense of death; How much more doth a sad sense of our transmigration belong to us, to whom death is no *Consummatum est,* but an *In principio;* our account, and our everlasting state begins but then.

SERMON LXIX

St. Paul's. 'The fifth of my Prebend Sermons upon my five Psalmes.'
[1627]

1 [p. 702]

WHEN I look upon God, as I am bid to doe in this Text, in those terrible Judgements, which he hath executed upon some men, and see that there is nothing between mee and the same Judgement, (for I have sinned the same sinnes, and God is the same God) I am not able of my selfe to dye that glasse, that spectacle, thorow which I looke upon this God, in what colour I will; whether this glasse shall be black, through my despaire, and so I shall see God in the cloud of my sinnes, or red in the blood of Christ Jesus, and I shall see God in a Bath of the blood of his Sonne, whether I shall see God as a Dove with an Olive branch, (peace to my soule) or as an Eagle, a vulture to prey, and to prey everlastingly upon mee, whether in the deepe floods of Tribulation, spirituall or temporall, I shall see God as an Arke to take mee in, or as a Whale to swallow mee; and if his Whale doe swallow mee, (the Tribulation devour me) whether his purpose bee to restore mee, or to consume me, I, I of my selfe cannot tell. I cannot look upon God, in what line I will, nor take hold of God, by what handle I will; Hee is a terrible God, I take him so; And then I cannot discontinue, I cannot breake off this terriblenesse, and say, Hee hath beene terrible to that man, and there is an end of his terror; it reaches not to me. Why not to me? In me there is no merit, nor shadow of merit; In God there is no change, nor shadow of change. I am the same sinner, he is the same God; still the same desperate sinner, still the same terrible God.

2 [pp. 702-703]

The true feare of God is true wisedome. It is true Joy; *Rejoice in trembling,* saith *David;* There is no rejoycing without this feare; there is no Riches without it; *Reverentia Jehovæ,* The feare of the Lord is his treasure, and that is the best treasure. Thus farre we are to goe; *Let us serve God with reverence, and godly feare,* (godly feare is but a Reverence, it is not a Jealousie, a suspition of God.) And let us doe it upon the reason that followes in the same place, *For our God is a consuming fire,* There is all his terriblenesse; he is *a consuming fire* to his enemies, but he is *our God;* and God is love: And therefore to conceive a cruell God, a God that hated us, even to damnation, before we were, (as some, who have departed from the sense and modesty of the Ancients,

have adventured to say) or to conceive a God so cruell, as that at our
death, or in our way, he will afford us no assurance, that hee is ours, and
we his, but let us live and die in anxiety and torture of conscience, in
jealousie and suspition of his good purpose towards us in the salvation of
our soules, (as those of the Romane Heresie teach) to conceive such a
God as from all eternity meant to damne me, or such a God as would
never make me know, and be sure that I should bee saved, this is not to
professe God to be terrible in his works; For, his Actions are his works,
and his Scriptures are his works, and God hath never done, or said any
thing to induce so terrible an opinion of him.

SERMON LXX

Whitehall.   April 8th, 1621

I   [pp. 711-712]

W E need not quarrell the words of the Poet, *Tu quamcunque; Deus tibi
fortunaverit horam, Grata sume manu,* Thanke God for any good fortune,
since the Apostle sayes too, that *Godlinesse hath the promise of this life;*
The godly man shall be fortunate, God will blesse him with good fortune
here; but still it is fortune, and chance, in the sight and reason of man,
and therefore he hath but found, whatsoever he hath in that kinde. It is
intimated in the very word which we use for all worldly things; It is
Inventarium, an Inventory; we found them here, and here our successors
finde them, when we are gone from hence. *Jezabel* had an estimation of
beauty, and she thought to have drawne the King with that beauty, but
she found it, she found it in her box, and in her wardrope, she was not
truly fayre. *Achitophel* had an estimation of wisedome in Counsell, I know
not how he found it; he counselled by an example, which no man would
follow, he hanged himselfe. Thou wilt not be drawne to confesse, that a
man that hath an office is presently wiser than thou, or a man that is
Knighted, presently valianter than thou. Men have preferment for those
parts, which other men, equall to them in the same things, have not, and
therefore they doe but finde them; And to things that are but found, what
is our title? *Nisi reddantur, rapina est,* sayes the Law, If we restore not
that which we finde, it is robbery. S. *Augustine* hath brought it nearer,
Qui alienum negat, si posset, tolleret, He that confesseth not that which
he hath found of another mans, if he durst, he would have taken it by
force. For that which we have found in this world, our calling is the owner,
our debts are the owner, our children are the owner; our lusts, our super-

fluities are no owners: of all the rest, God is the owner, and to this purpose, the poore is God.

2   [p. 714]

We know the receipt, the capacity of the ventricle, the stomach of man,
how much it can hold; and wee know the receipt of all the receptacles of
blood, how much blood the body can have; so wee do of all the other
conduits and cisterns of the body; But this infinite Hive of honey, this
insatiable whirlpoole of the covetous mind, no Anatomy, no dissection
hath discovered to us. When I looke into the larders, and cellars, and
vaults, into the vessels of our body for drink, for blood, for urine, they
are pottles, and gallons; when I looke into the furnaces of our spirits, the
ventricles of the heart and of the braine, they are not thimbles; for spirituall things, the things of the next world, we have no roome; for temporall things, the things of this world, we have no bounds. How then shall
this over-eater bee filled with his honey?

SERMONS LXXI AND LXXII

*The Hague. 'Since in my sicknesse at Abrey-hatche in Essex, 1630,
revising my short notes of that Sermon, I digested them into these two.'*
Dec. 19th, 1619

I   [p. 725. Sermon lxxi]

EVEN that murmuring at poverty, is a net; leave that. Leave thy superfluous desire of having the riches of this world; though thou mayest flatter
thy selfe, that thou desirest to have onely that thou mightest leave it, that
thou mightest employ it charitably, yet it might prove a net, and stick
too close about thee to part with it. *Multa relinquitis, si desideriis renun-
ciatis,* You leave your nets, if you leave your over-earnest greedinesse of
catching; for, when you doe so, you doe not onely fish with a net, (that
is, lay hold upon all you can compasse) but, (which is strange) you fish
for a net, even that which you get proves a net to you, and hinders you in
the following of Christ, and you are lesse disposed to follow him, when
you have got your ends, than before. He that hath least, hath enough to
waigh him down from heaven, by an inordinate love of that little which
he hath, or in an inordinate and murmuring desire of more. And he that
hath most, hath not too much to give for heaven; *Tantum valet regnum
Dei, quantum tu vales,* Heaven is alwayes so much worth, as thou art
worth. A poore man may have heaven for a penny, that hath no greater
store; and, God lookes, that he to whom he hath given thousands, should

lay out thousands upon the purchase of heaven. The market changes, as the plenty of money changes; Heaven costs a rich man more than a poore, because he hath more to give. But in this, rich and poore are both equall, that both must leave themselves without nets, that is, without those things, which, in their own Consciences they know, retard the following of Christ. Whatsoever hinders my present following, that I cannot follow to day, whatsoever may hinder my constant following, that I cannot follow to morrow, and all my life, is a net, and I am bound to leave that.

And these are the pieces that constitute our first part, the circumstances that invest these persons, *Peter*, and *Andrew*, in their former condition, before, and when Christ called them.

2   [pp. 729-730. Sermon lxxii]

So early, so primary a sin is pride, as that, out of every mercy, and blessing, which God affords us, (and, *His mercies are new every morning*) we gather Pride; wee are not the more thankfull for them, and yet we are the prouder of them. Nay, we gather Pride, not onely out of those things, which mend and improve us, (Gods blessings and mercies) but out of those actions of our own, that destroy and ruine us, we gather pride; sins overthrow us, demolish us, destroy and ruine us, and yet we are proud of our sinnes. How many men have we heard boast of their sinnes; and, (as S. *Augustine* confesses of himselfe) belie themselves, and boast of more sinnes than ever they committed? Out of every thing, out of nothing sin grows. Therefore was this commandment in our text, *Sequere, Follow*, come after, well placed first, for we are come to see even children strive for place and precedency, and mothers are ready to goe to the Heralds to know how Cradles shall be ranked, which Cradle shall have the highest place; Nay, even in the wombe, there was contention for precedency; *Jacob* tooke hold of his brother *Esaus* heele, and would have been borne before him.

And as our pride begins in our Cradle, it continues in our graves and Monuments. It was a good while in the primitive Church, before any were buried in the Church; The best contented themselves with the Church-yards. After, a holy ambition, (may we call it so) a holy Pride brought them *ad Limina*, to the Church-threshold, to the Church-doore, because some great Martyrs were buried in the Porches, and devout men desired to lie near them, as one Prophet did to lie neare another, (*Lay my bones besides his bones.*) But now, persons whom the Devill kept from Church all their lives, Separatists, Libertines, that never came to any Church, And persons, whom the Devill brought to Church all their lives, (for, such as come meerly out of the obligation of the Law, and to redeem that vexation, or out of custome, or company, or curiosity or a perverse and sinister affection to the particular Preacher, though they come to Gods house, come upon the Devils invitation) Such as one Devill, that is, worldly respect, brought to Church in their lives, another Devill, that is, Pride and vain-glory, brings to Church after their deaths, in an affectation of high places, and sumptuous Monuments in the Church. And such as have given nothing at all to any pious uses, or have determined their almes and their dole which they have given, in that one day of their funerall, and no farther, have given large annuities, perpetuities, for new painting their tombes, and for new flags, and scutcheons, every certaine number of yeares.

O the earlinesse! O the latenesse! how early a Spring, and no Autumne! how fast a growth, and no declination, of this branch of this sin. Pride, against which, this first word of ours, *Sequere, Follow,* come after, is opposed! this love of place, and precedency, it rocks us in our Cradles, it lies down with us in our graves. There are diseases proper to certaine things, Rots to sheepe, Murrain to cattell. There are diseases proper to certaine places, as the Sweat was to us. There are diseases proper to cer- taine times, as the plague is in divers parts of the Eastern Countryes, where they know assuredly, when it will begin and end. But for this infec- tious disease of precedency, and love of place, it is run over all places, as well Cloysters as Courts, And over all men, as well spirituall as temporall, And over all times, as well the Apostles as ours.

3

[p. 733. Sermon lxxii]

Forraine crosses, other mens merits are not mine; spontaneous and vol- untary crosses, contracted by mine owne sins, are not mine; neither are devious, and remote, and unnecessary crosses, my crosses. Since I am bound to take up my crosse, there must be a crosse that is mine to take up; that is, a crosse prepared for me by God, and laid in my way, which is tentations or tribulations in my calling; and I must not go out of my way to seeke a crosse; for, so it is not mine, nor laid for my taking up. I am not bound to hunt after a persecution, nor to stand it, and not flye, nor to affront a plague, and not remove, nor to open my selfe to an injury, and not defend. I am not bound to starve my selfe by inordinate fasting, nor to teare my flesh by inhumane whippings, and flagellations. I am bound to take up my Crosse; and that is onely mine which the hand of God hath laid for me, that is, in the way of my Calling, tentations and tribulations incident to that.

'Preached to the King in my Ordinary Wayting at Whitehall.'
April 30th, 1626

[pp. 747-748]

G O D hath a progresse house, a removing house here upon earth, His house of prayer; At this houre, God enters into as many of these houses, as are opened for his service at this houre: But his standing house, his house of glory, is that in Heaven, and that he promises them. God himselfe dwelt in Tents in this world, and he gives them a House in Heaven. A House, in the designe and survay whereof, the Holy Ghost himselfe is figurative, the Fathers wanton, and the School-men wilde. The Holy Ghost, in describing this House, fills our contemplation with foundations, and walls, and gates, of gold, of precious stones, and all materialls, that we can call precious. The Holy Ghost is figurative; And the Fathers are wanton in their spirituall elegancies, such as that of S. *Augustins,* (if that booke be his) *Hiems horrens, Æstas torrens,* And, *Virent prata, vernant sata,* and such other harmonious, and melodious, and mellifluous cadences of these waters of life. But the School-men are wild; for as one Author, who is afraid of admitting too great a hollownesse in the Earth, lest then the Earth might not be said to be solid, pronounces that Hell cannot possibly be above three thousand miles in compasse, (and then one of the torments of Hell will be the throng, for their bodies must be there, in their dimensions, as well as their soules) so when the School-men come to measure this house in heaven, (as they will measure it, and the Master, God, and all his Attributes, and tell us how Allmighty, and how Infinite he is) they pronounce, that every soule in that house shall have more roome to it selfe, than all this world is. We know not that; nor see we that the consolation lyes in that; we rest in this, that it is a House, It hath a foundation, no Earth-quake shall shake it, It hath walls, no Artillery shall batter it, It hath a roofe, no tempest shall pierce it. It is a house that affords security, and that is one beame; And it is *Domus patris,* His Fathers house, a house in which he hath interest, and that is another beame of his Consolation.

It was his Fathers, and so his; And his, and so ours; for we are not joynt purchasers of Heaven with the Saints, but we are co-heires with Christ Jesus. We have not a place there, because they have done more than enough for themselves, but because he hath done enough for them and us too. By death we are gathered to our Fathers in nature; and by death, through his mercy, gathered to his Father also. Where we shall have a full satisfaction, in that wherein S. *Philip* placed all satisfaction, *Ostende nobis patrem, Lord, shew us thy Father, and it is enough.* We shall see his Father, and see him made ours in him.

And then a third beame of this Consolation is, That in this house of his Fathers, thus by him made ours, there are *Mansions;* In which word, the Consolation is not placed, (I doe not say, that there is not truth in it) but the Consolation is not placed in this, That some of these Mansions are below, some above staires, some better seated, better lighted, better vaulted, better fretted, better furnished than others; but onely in this, That they are *Mansions;* which word, in the Originall, and Latin, and our Language, signifies a *Remaining,* and denotes the perpetuity, the ever-lastingnesse of that state. A state but of one Day, because no Night shall over-take, or determine it, but such a Day, as is not of a thousand yeares, which is the longest measure in the Scriptures, but of a thousand millions of millions of generations: *Qui nec præceditur hesterno, nec excluditur crastino,* A day that hath no *pridie,* nor *postridie,* yesterday doth not usher it in, nor to morrow shall not drive it out. *Methusalem,* with all his hundreds of yeares, was but a Mushrome of a nights growth, to this day, And all the foure Monarchies, with all their thousands of yeares, And all the powerfull Kings, and all the beautifull Queenes of this world, were but as a bed of flowers, some gathered at six, some at seven, some at eight, All in one Morning, in respect of this Day. In all the two thousand yeares of Nature, before the Law given by *Moses,* And the two thousand yeares of Law, before the Gospel given by Christ, And the two thousand of Grace, which are running now, (of which last houre we have heard three quarters strike, more than fifteen hundred of this last two thousand spent) In all this six thousand, and in all those which God may be pleased to adde, *In domo patris,* In this House of his Fathers, there was never heard quarter clock to strike, never seen minute glasse to turne. No time lesse than it selfe would serve to expresse this time, which is intended in this word *Mansions;* which is also exalted with another beame, that they are *Multa, In my Fathers House there are many Mansions.*

In this Circumstance, an Essentiall, a Substantiall Circumstance, we would consider the joy of our society, and conversation in heaven, since society and conversation is one great element and ingredient into the joy, which we have in this world. We shall have an association with Christ himselfe; for *where he is,* it is his promise, *that we also shall be.* We shall have an association with the Angels, and such a one, as we shall be such as they. We shall have an association with the Saints, and not onely so, to be such as they, but to be they: And with all *who come from the East, and from the West, and from the North, and from the South, and sit down with Abraham, and Isaac, and Jacob in the kingdome of heaven.* Where we shall be so far from being enemies to one another, as that we shall not be strangers to one another: And so far from envying one another, as that all that every one hath, shall be every others possession: where all soules shall be so intirely knit together, as if all were but one soule, and God so intirely knit to every soule, as if there were as many Gods as soules.

SERMON LXXIV

Whitehall.   April 30th, 1620

[p. 753]

F O R the first temporall blessing of peace, we may consider the lovelinesse, the amiablenesse of that, if we looke upon the horror and gastlinesse of warre: either *in Effigie,* in that picture of warre, which is drawn in every leafe of our own Chronicles, in the blood of so many Princes, and noble families, or if we look upon warre it selfe, at that distance where it cannot hurt us, as God had formerly kindled it amongst our neighbours, and as he hath transferred it now to remoter Nations, whilest we enjoy yet a Goshen in the midst of all those Egypts. In all Cities, disorderly and facinorous men, covet to draw themselves into the skirts and suburbs of those Cities, that so they may be the nearer the spoyle, which they make upon passengers. In all Kingdomes that border upon other Kingdomes, and in Islands which have no other border but the Sea, particular men, who by dwelling in those skirts and borders, may make their profit of spoile, delight in hostility, and have an adversenesse and detestation of peace: but it is not so within: they who till the earth, and breed up cattell, and imploy their industry upon Gods creatures, according to Gods ordinance, feele the benefit and apprehend the sweetnesse, and pray for the continuance of peace.

SERMON LXXV

Whitehall.   April 15*th,* 1628

[p. 765]

B U T if the whole space to the Firmament were filled with sand, and we had before us *Clavius* his number, how many thousands would be; If all that space were filled with water, and so joyned the waters above with the waters below the Firmament, and we had the number of all those drops of water; And then had every single sand, and every single drop multiplied by the whole number of both, we were still short of numbring the benefits of God, as God; But then, of God in Christ, infinitely, super-infinitely short. To have been once nothing, and to be now co-heire with the Son of God, is such a Circle, such a Compasse, as that no revolutions in this world, to rise from the lowest to the highest, or to fall from the highest to the lowest, can be called or thought any Segment, any Arch, any Point in respect of this Circle; To have once been nothing, and now to be co-heires with the Son of God: That Son of God, who if there had been but one soule to have been saved, would have dyed for that; nay, if all soules had been to be saved, but one, and that that onely had sinned, he would not have contented himselfe with all the rest, but would have dyed for that. And there is the goodnesse, the liberality of our King, our God, our Christ, our Jesus.

SERMON LXXVI

'To the Earle of Carlile, and his Company, at Sion.'   [*After* 1622]

[pp. 776-777]

T H A T God should let my soule fall out of his hand, into a bottomlesse pit and roll an unremoveable stone upon it, and leave it to that which it finds there, (and it shall finde that there, which it never imagined, till it came thither) and never thinke more of that soule, never have more to doe with it. That of that providence of God, that studies the life of every weed, and worme, and ant, and spider, and toad, and viper, there should never, never any beame flow out upon me; that that God, who looked upon me, when I was nothing, and called me when I was not, as though I had been, out of the womb and depth of darknesse, will not looke upon me now, when, though a miserable, and a banished, and a damned creature, yet I am his creature still, and contribute something to his glory, even in my damnation; that that God, who hath often looked upon me in my foulest uncleannesse, and when I had shut out the eye of the day, the Sunne, and the eye of the night, the Taper, and the eyes of all the world, with cur-taines and windowes and doores, did yet see me, and see me in mercy, by making me see that he saw me, and sometimes brought me to a present remorse, and (for that time) to a forbearing of that sinne, should so turne himselfe from me, to his glorious Saints and Angels, as that no Saint nor Angel, nor Christ Jesus himselfe, should ever pray him to look towards me, never remember him, that such a soule there is; that that God, who hath so often said to my soule, *Quare morieris?* Why wilt thou die? and so often sworne to my soule, *Vivit Dominus,* As the Lord liveth, I would not have thee dye, but live, will nether let me dye, nor let me live, but dye and everlasting life, and live an everlasting death; that that God, who, when he could not get into me, by standing, and knocking, by his ordinary meanes of entring, by his Word, his mercies, hath applied his judgements, and hath shaked the house, this body, with agues and palsies, and set this house on fire, with fevers and calentures, and frighted the Master of the house, my soule, with horrors, and heavy apprehensions, and so made an entrance into me; That that God should frustrate all his owne purposes and practises upon me, and leave me, and cast me away, as though I had cost him nothing, that this God at last, should let this soule goe away, as a smoake, as a vapour, as a bubble, and that then this soule cannot be a smoake, a vapour, nor a bubble, but must lie in darknesse, as long as the Lord of light is light it selfe, and never sparke of that light reach to my soule; What Tophet is not Paradise, what Brimstone is not Amber, what gnashing is not a comfort, what gnawing of the worme is not a tickling, what torment is not a marriage bed to this damnation, to be secluded eternally, eternally, eternally from the sight of God? Especially to us, for as the perpetuall losse of that is most heavy, with which we have been best acquainted, and to which wee have been most accustomed; so shall this damnation, which consists in the losse of the sight and presence of God, be heavier to us than others, because God hath so graciously, and so evidently, and so diversly appeared to us, in his pillar of fire, in the light of prosperity, and in the pillar of the Cloud, in hiding himselfe for a while from us; we that have seene him in all the parts of this Commission, in his Word, in his Sacraments, and in good example, and not beleeved, shall be further removed from his sight, in the next world, than they to whom he never appeared in this. But *Vincenti et credenti*, to him that beleeves aright, and overcomes all tentations to a wrong beliefe, God shall give the accomplishment of fulnesse, and fulnesse of joy, and joy rooted in glory, and glory established in eternity, and this eternity is God; To him that beleeves and overcomes, God shall give himselfe in an everlasting presence and fruition, *Amen.*

SERMON LXXIX

St. Pauls. [*c.* 1620-22]

I [pp. 809-810]

N O W if we looke for this early mercy from God, we must rise betimes too, and meet God early. God hath promised to give *Matutinam stellam*, the Morning-star; but they must be up betimes in the morning, that will take the Morning-star. He himselfe who is it, hath told us who is this Morning star; *I Jesus am the bright and Morning starre.* God will give us Jesus: Him, and all his, all his teares, all his blood, all his merits: But to whom, and upon what conditions? That is expressed there, *Vincenti dabo, To him that overcometh I will give the Morning-star*. Our life is a warfare, our whole life; It is not onely with lusts in our youth, and ambitions in our middle yeares, and indevotions in our age, but with agonies in our body, and tentations in our spirit upon our death-bed, that we are to fight; and he cannot be said to overcome, that fights not out the whole battell. If he enter not the field in the morning, that is, apply not himselfe to Gods service in his youth, If hee continue not to the Evening, If hee faint in the way, and grow remisse in Gods service, for collaterall respects, God will overcome his cause, and his glory shall stand fast, but that man can scarce be said to have overcome.

It is the counsell of the Wise man, *Prevent the Sunne to give thanks to God, and at the day-spring pray unto him*. You see still, how these two duties are marshalled, and disposed; First Praise, and then Prayer, but both early: And it is placed in the Lamentations, as though it were a lamentable negligence to have omitted it, *It is good for a man, that he beare his yoake in his youth*. Rise as early as you can, you cannot be up before God; no, nor before God raise you: Howsoever you prevent this Sunne, the Sunne of the Firmament, yet the Sonne of Heaven hath prevented you, for without his preventing Grace you could not stirre. Have any of you slept out their Morning, resisted his private motions to private Prayer at home, neglected his callings so? Though a man doe sleepe out his forenoone, the Sunne goes on his course, and comes to his Meridionall splendor, though that man have not looked towards it. That Sonne which hath risen to you at home, in those private motions, hath gone on his course, and hath shined out here, in this house of God, upon Wednesday, and upon Friday, and upon every day of holy Convocation; All this, at home, and here, yee have slept out and neglected. Now, upon the Sabbath, and in these holy Exercises, this Sonne shines out as at noone, the Grace of God is in the Exaltation, exhibited in the powerfullest and effectuallest way of his Ordinance, and if you will but awake now, rise now, meet God now, now at noone, God will call even this early. Have any of you slept out the whole day, and are come in that drowsinesse to your evening, to the closing of your eyes, to the end of your dayes? Yet rise now, and God shall call even this an early rising; If you can make shift to deceive your owne soules and say, We never heard God call us; If you neglected your former callings so, as that you have forgot that you have been called; yet, is there one amongst you, that denies that God calls him now? If he neglect this calling now, to morrow he may forget that he was called to day, or remember it with such terror, and shall blow a dampe, and a consternation upon his soule, and a lethargy worse than his former sleepe; but if he will wake now, and rise now, though this be late in his evening,

in his age, yet God shall call this early. Bee but able to say with *Esay*
this night, *My soule hath desired thee in the night,* and thou maist be
bold to say with *David* to morrow morning, *Satura nos mane, Satisfie us
early with thy mercy,* and he shall doe it.

But yet no prayer of ours, howsoever made in the best disposition, in
the best testimony of a rectified conscience, must limit God his time, or
appoint him, in what morning, or what houre in the morning, God shall
come to our deliverance. The Sonne of man was not the lesse the Sonne of
God, nor the lesse a beloved Sonne, though God hid from him the knowledge of the day of the generall Judgement. Thou art not the lesse the
servant of God, nor the lesse rewarded by him, though he keepe from
thee the knowledge of thy deliverance from any particular calamity. All
Gods deliverances are in the morning, because there is a perpetuall night,
and an invincible darknesse upon us, till he deliver us. God is the God of
that Climate, where the night is six Moneths long, as well as of this, where
it is but halfe so many houres. The highest Hill hinders not the roundnesse of the earth, the earth is round for all that hill; The lowest vaults,
and mines hinder not the solidnesse of the earth, the earth is solid for all
that; Much lesse hath a yeare, or ten yeares, or all our threescore and ten,
any proportion at all to eternity; And therefore God comes early in a sort
to me though I lose abundance of my reward by so long lingring, if he
come not till hee open me the gate of heaven, by the key of death. There
are Indies at my right hand, in the East; but there are Indies at my left
hand too, in the West. There are testimonies of Gods love to us, in our
East, in our beginnings; but if God continue tribulation upon us to our
West, to our ends, and give us the light of his presence then, if he appeare
to us at our transmigration, certainly he was favourable to us all our peregrination, and though he shew himselfe late, hee was our friend early.
The Prayer is, that he would come early, but it is, if it be rightly formed,
upon both these conditions; first, that I rise early to meet him, and then
that I magnifie his houre as early, whensoever he shall be pleased to come.

2   [pp. 814-816]

God shall never take from me, my *Shamach,* my internal gladnesse and
consolation, in his undeceivable and undeceiving Spirit, that he is mine,
and I am his; And this joy, this gladnesse, in my way, and in my end,
shall establish me; for that is that which is intended in the next, and last
word, *Omnibus diebus,* we shall *Rejoyce and be Glad all our dayes.*

Nothing but this testimony, *That the Spirit beares witnesse with my
spirit,* that upon my prayer, so conditioned, of praise, and prayer, I shall
still prevaile with God, could imprint in me, this *joy, all my dayes.* The
seales of his favour, in outward blessings, fayle me in the dayes of ship-

wracke, in the dayes of fire, in the dayes of displacing my potent friends, or raysing mine adversaries; In such dayes I cannot rejoyce, and be glad. The seales of his favour, in inward blessings, and holy cheerfulnesse, fayle me in a present remorse after a sinne newly committed. But yet in the strength of a Christian hope, as I can pronounce out of the grounds of Nature, in an Eclipse of the Sunne, that the Sunne shall returne to his splendor againe, I can pronounce out of the grounds of Gods Word, (and Gods Word is much better assurance, than the grounds of Nature, for God can and does shake the grounds of Nature by Miracles, but no Jo [t] of his Word shall ever perish) that I shall returne againe on my hearty penitence, if I delay it not, and rejoyce and be glad all my dayes, that is, what kinde of day soever overtake me. In the dayes of our youth, when the joyes of this world take up all the roome, there shall be roome for this holy Joy, that my recreations were harmlesse, and my conversation innocent; and certainly to be able to say, that in my recreations, in my conversation, I neither ministred occasion of tentation to another, nor exposed my selfe to tentations from another, is a faire beame of this rejoycing in the dayes of my youth. In the dayes of our Age, when we become incapable, insensible of the joyes of this world, yet this holy joy shall season us, not with a sinfull delight in the memory of our former sinnes, but with a rejuveniscence, a new and a fresh youth, in being come so neere to another, to an immortall life. In the dayes of our mirth, and of laughter, this holy joy shall enter; And as the Sunne may say to the starres at Noone, How frivoulous and impertinent a thing is your light now? So this joy shall say *unto laughter, Thou art mad, and unto mirth, what dost thou?* And in the mid-night of sadnesse, and dejection of spirit, this joy shall shine out, and chide away that sadnesse, with *Davids* holy charme, *My soule, why art thou cast downe, why art thou disquieted within me?* In those dayes, which *Job* speaks of, *Prævenerunt me dies afflictionis meæ, Miseries are come upon me before their time;* My intemperances have hastned age, my riotousnesse hath hastned poverty, my neglecting of due officiousnesse and respect towards great persons hath hastned contempt upon me, Afflictions which I suspected not, thought not of, have prevented my feares; and then in those dayes, which *Job* speaks of againe, *Possident me dies afflictionis,* Studied and premeditated plots and practises swallowe mee, possesse me intirely, In all these dayes, I shall not onely have a *Zoar* to flie to, if I can get out of *Sodom,* joy, if I can overcome my sorrow; There shall not be a *Goshen* bordering upon my Egypt, joy, if I can passe beyond, or besides my sorrow, but I shall have a *Goshen* in my *Egypt,* nay my very *Egypt* shall be my *Goshen,* I shall not onely have joy, though I have sorrow, but therefore; my very sorrow shall be the occasion of joy; I shall not onely have a Sabbath after my six dayes labor, but *Omnibus diebus,* a Sabbath shall enlighten every day, and inanimate every minute of every day: And as my soule is as well in my foot, as in my hand, though all the waight and oppression lie upon the foot, and all action upon the hand, so these beames of joy shall appeare as well in my pillar of cloud, as in theirs of fire; in my adversity, as well as in their prosperity; And when their Sun shall set at Noone, mine shall rise at midnight; they shall have damps in their glory, and I joyfull exaltions in my dejections.

And to end with the end of all, *In die mortis,* In the day of my death, and that which is beyond the end of all, and without end in it selfe, The day of Judgement, If I have the testimony of a rectified conscience, that I have accustomed my selfe to that accesse to God, by prayer, and such prayer, as though it have had a body of supplication, and desire of future things, yet the soule and spirit of that prayer, that is, my principall intention in that prayer, hath been praise and thanksgiving, If I be involved in S. *Chrysostoms* Patent, *Orantes, non natura, sed dispensatione Angeli fiunt,* That those who pray so, that is, pray by way of praise, (which is the most proper office of Angels) as they shall be better than Angels in the next world, (for they shall be glorifying spirits, as the Angels are, but they shall also be glorified bodies, which the Angels shall never bee) so in this world they shall be as Angels, because they are employed in the office of Angels, to pray by way of praise, If, as S. *Basil* reads those words of that Psalme, not *spiritus meus,* but *respiratio mea laudet Dominum,* Not onely my spirit, but my very breath, not my heart onely, but my tongue, and my hands bee accustomed to glorifie God, *In die mortis,* in the day of my death, when a mist of sorrow, and of sighes shall fill my chamber, and a cloude exhaled and condensed from teares, shall bee the curtaines of my bed, when those that love me, shall be sorry to see mee die, and the devill himselfe that hates me, sorry to see me die so, in the favour of God; And *In die Judicii,* In the day of Judgement, when as all Time shall cease, so all measures shall cease; The joy, and the sorrow that shall be then, shall be eternall, no end, and infinite, no measure, no limitation, when every circumstance of sinne shall aggravate the condemnation of the unrepentant sinner, and the very substance of my sinne shall bee washed away, in the blood of my Saviour, when I shall see them, who sinned for my sake, perish eternally, because they proceeded in that sinne, and I my selfe, who occasioned their sin received into glory, because God upon my prayer, and repentance had satisfied me early with his mercy, early, that is, before my transmigration, *In omnibus diebus,* In all these dayes, the dayes of youth, and the wantonnesses of that, the dayes of age, and the tastlesnesse of that, the dayes of mirth, and the sportfulnesse of that, and of inordinate melancholy, and the disconsolate-

nesse of that, the days of such miseries, as astonish us with their suddennesse, and of such as aggravate their owne waight with a heavy expectation; In the day of Death, which pieces up that circle, and in that day
which enters another circle that hath no pieces, but is one equall everlastingnesse, the day of Judgement, Either I shall rejoyce, be able to
declare my faith, and zeale to the assistance of others, or at least be glad
in mine owne heart, in a firme hope of mine owne salvation.

SERMON LXXX

*'Preached at the funeral of Sir William Cokayne, Knight,
Alderman of London.' Dec. 12th, 1626*

I

JOH. II. 21

Lord, if thou hadst been here, my brother had not died.

[pp. 816-817]

G o D made the first Marriage, and man made the first Divorce; God married the Body and Soule in the Creation, and man divorced the Body and
Soule by death through sinne, in his fall. God doth not admit, not justifie,
not authorize such Super-inductions upon such Divorces, as some have
imagined; That the soule departing from one body, should become the
soule of another body, in a perpetuall revolution and transmigration of
soules through bodies, which hath been the giddinesse of some Philosophers to think; Or that the body of the dead should become the body
of an evill spirit, that that spirit might at his will, and to his purposes
informe, and inanimate that dead body; God allowes no such Super-inductions, no such second Marriages upon such divorces by death, no such
disposition of soule or body, after their dissolution by death. But because
God hath made the band of Marriage indissoluble but by death, farther
than man can die, this divorce cannot fall upon man; As farre as man
is immortall, man is a married man still, still in possession of a soule, and
a body too; And man is for ever immortall in both; Immortall in his soule
by Preservation, and immortall in his body by Reparation in the Resurrection. For, though they be separated *à Thoro et Mensa,* from Bed and
Board, they are not divorced; Though the soule be at the *Table of the
Lambe,* in Glory, and the body but at the table of *the Serpent, in dust;*
Though the soule be *in lecto florido,* in that bed which is alwayes green,

in an everlasting spring, in *Abrahams Bosome;* And the body but in that
green-bed, whose covering is but a yard and a halfe of Turfe, and a Rugge
of grasse, and the sheet but a winding sheet, yet they are not divorced;
they shall returne to one another againe, in an inseparable re-union in the
Resurrection.

2   [p. 818]

How imperfect is all our knowledge! What one thing doe we know perfectly? Whether wee consider Arts, or Sciences, the servant knows but
according to the proportion of his Masters knowledge in that Art, and the
Scholar knows but according to the proportion of his Masters knowledge
in that Science; Young men mend not their sight by using old mens Spectacles; and yet we looke upon Nature, but with *Aristotles* Spectacles, and
upon the body of man, but with *Galens,* and upon the frame of the world,
but with *Ptolomies* Spectacles. Almost all knowledge is rather like a child
that is embalmed to make Mummy, than that is nursed to make a Man;
rather conserved in the stature of the first age, than growne to be greater;
And if there be any addition to knowledge, it is rather a new knowledge,
than a greater knowledge; rather a singularity in a desire of proposing
something that was not knowne at all before, than an emproving, an
advancing, a multiplying of former inceptions; and by that meanes, no
knowledge comes to be perfect. One Philosopher thinks he is dived to the
bottome, when he sayes, he knows nothing but this, That he knows nothing; and yet another thinks, that he hath expressed more knowledge than
he, in saying, That he knows not so much as that, That he knows nothing.
S. *Paul* found that to be all knowledge. To know Christ; And Mahomet
thinks himselfe wise therefore, because he knows not, acknowledges not
Christ, as S. *Paul* does. Though a man knew not, that every sin casts
another shovell of Brimstone upon him in Hell, yet if he knew that every
riotous feast cuts off a year, and every wanton night seaven years of his
seventy in this world, it were some degree towards perfection in knowledge. He that purchases a Mannor, will thinke to have an exact Survey
of the Land: But who thinks of taking so exact a survey of his Conscience,
how that money was got, that purchased that Mannor? We call that
a mans meanes, which he hath; But that is truly his meanes, what way he
came by it. And yet how few are there, (when a state comes to any great
proportion) that know that; that know what they have, what they are
worth? We have seen great Wills, dilated into glorious uses, and into
pious uses, and then too narrow an estate to reach to it; And we have seen
Wills, where the Testator thinks he hath bequeathed all, and he hath
not knowne halfe of his own worth. When thou knowest a wife, a sonne, a
servant, a friend no better, but that that wife betrayes thy bed, and that

sonne thine estate, and that servant thy credit, and that friend thy secret, what canst thou say thou knowest? But we must not insist upon this Consideration of knowledge; for, though knowledge be of a spirituall nature, yet it is but as a terrestriall Spirit, conversant upon Earth; Spirituall things, of a more rarified nature than knowledge, even faith it selfe, and all that grows from that in us, falls within this Rule, which we have in hand, That even in spirituall things, nothing is perfect.

3   [p. 820]

When we consider with a religious seriousnesse the manifold weaknesses of the strongest devotions in time of Prayer, it is a sad consideration. I throw my selfe downe in my Chamber, and I call in, and invite God, and his Angels thither, and when they are there, I neglect God and his Angels, for the noise of a Flie, for the ratling of a Coach, for the whining of a doore; I talke on, in the same posture of praying; Eyes lifted up; knees bowed downe; as though I prayed to God; and, if God, or his Angels should aske me, when I thought last of God in that prayer, I cannot tell: Sometimes I finde that I had forgot what I was about, but when I began to forget it, I cannot tell. A memory of yesterdays pleasures, a feare of to morrows dangers, a straw under my knee, a noise in mine eare, a light in mine eye, an any thing, a nothing, a fancy, a Chimera in my braine, troubles me in my prayer. So certainely is there nothing, nothing in spirituall things, perfect in this world.

4   [pp. 823-826]

I need not call in new Philosophy, that denies a settlednesse, an acquiescence in the very body of the Earth, but makes the Earth to move in that place, where we thought the Sunne had moved; I need not that helpe, that the Earth it selfe is in Motion, to prove this, That nothing upon Earth is permanent; The Assertion will stand of it selfe, till some man assigne me some instance, something that a man may relie upon, and find permanent. Consider the greatest Bodies upon Earth, The Monarchies; Objects, which one would thinke, Destiny might stand and stare at, but not shake; Consider the smallest bodies upon Earth, The haires of our head, Objects, which one would thinke, Destiny would not observe, or could not discerne; And yet, Destiny, (to speak to a naturall man) And God, (to speake to a Christian) is no more troubled to make a Monarchy ruinous, than to make a haire gray. Nay, nothing needs be done to either, by God, or Destiny; A Monarchy will ruine, as a haire will grow gray, of it selfe. In the Elements themselves, of which all sub-elementary things are composed, there is no acquiescence, but a vicissitudinary transmutation into one another; Ayre condensed becomes water, a more solid body,

And Ayre rarified becomes fire, a body more disputable, and in-apparent.
It is so in the Conditions of men too; A Merchant condensed, kneaded
and packed up in a great estate, becomes a Lord; And a Merchant rarified, blown up by a perfidious Factor, or by a riotous Sonne, evaporates
into ayre, into nothing, and is not seen. And if there were any thing permanent and durable in this world, yet we got nothing by it, because howsoever that might last in it selfe, yet we could not last to enjoy it; If our
goods were not amongst Moveables, yet we our selves are; if they could
stay with us, yet we cannot stay with them; which is another Consideration in this part.

The world is a great Volume, and man the Index of that Booke; Even
in the body of man, you may turne to the whole world; This body is an
Illustration of all Nature; Gods recapitulation of all that he had said
before in his *Fiat lux*, and *Fiat firmamentum*, and in all the rest, said or
done, in all the six dayes. Propose this body to thy consideration in the
highest exaltation thereof; as it is the *Temple of the Holy Ghost:* Nay,
not in a Metaphor, or comparison of a Temple, or any other similitudinary
thing, but as it was really and truly the very body of God, in the person
of Christ, and yet this body must wither, must decay, must languish, must
perish. When *Goliah* had armed and fortified this body, And *Jezabel* had
painted and perfumed this body, And *Dives* had pampered and larded
this body, As God said to *Ezekiel*, when he brought him to the *dry bones,
Fili hominis, Sonne of Man doest thou thinke these bones can live?* They
said in their hearts to all the world, Can these bodies die? And they are
dead. *Jezabels* dust is not Ambar, nor *Goliahs* dust *Terra sigillata,* Medicinall; nor does the Serpent, whose meat they are both, finde any better
relish in *Dives* dust, than in *Lazarus.* But as in our former part, where
our foundation was, That in nothing, no spirituall thing, there was any
perfectnesse, which we illustrated in the weaknesses of Knowledge, and
Faith, and Hope, and Charity, yet we concluded, that for all those defects,
God accepted those their religious services; So in this part, where our
foundation is, That nothing in temporall things is permanent, as we have
illustrated that, by the decay of that which is Gods noblest piece in Nature,
The body of man; so we shall also conclude that, with this goodnesse of
God, that for all this dissolution, and putrefaction, he affords this Body
a Resurrection.

The Gentils, and their Poets, describe the sad state of Death so, *Nox
una obeunda,* That it is one everlasting Night; To them, a Night; But to
a Christian, it is *Dies Mortis,* and *Dies Resurrectionis,* The day of Death,
and The day of Resurrection; We die in the light; in the sight of Gods
presence, and we rise in the light, in the sight of his very Essence. Nay,
Gods corrections, and judgements upon us in this life, are still expressed

so, *Dies visitationis*, still it is a Day, though a *Day of visitation;* and still
we may discerne God to be in the action. The *Lord of Life* was the first
that named *Death; Morte morieris*, sayes God, Thou shalt die the Death.
I doe the lesse feare, or abhorre Death, because I finde it in his mouth;
Even a malediction hath a sweetnesse in his mouth; for there is a blessing
wrapped up in it; a mercy in every correction, a Resurrection upon every
Death. When *Jezabels* beauty, exalted to that height which it had by art
or higher than that, to that height which it had in her own opinion, shall
be infinitely multiplied upon every Body; And as God shall know no man
from his own Sonne, so as not to see the very righteousnesse of his own
Sonne upon that man; So the Angels shall know no man from Christ, so
as not to desire to looke upon that mans face, because the most deformed
wretch that is there, shall have the very beauty of Christ himselfe; So
shall *Goliahs* armour, and *Dives* fulnesse, be doubled, and redoubled upon
us. And every thing that we can call good, shall first be infinitely exalted
in the goodnesse, and then infinitely multiplied in the proportion, and
againe infinitely extended in the duration. And since we are in an action
of preparing this dead Brother of ours to that state, (for the Funerall is
the Easter-eve, The Buriall is the depositing of that man for the Resurrection) As we have held you, with Doctrine of Mortification, by extend-
ing the Text, from *Martha* to this occasion; so shall we dismisse you with
Consolation, by a like occasionall inverting the Text, from passion in
Martha's mouth, *Lord, if thou hadst been here, my Brother had not dyed*,
to joy in ours, *Lord, because thou wast here, our Brother is not dead.*

The Lord was with him in all these steps; with him in his life; with him
in his death; He is with him in his funerals, and he shall be with him in
his Resurrection; and therefore, because the Lord was with him, our
Brother is not dead. He was with him in the beginning of his life, in this
manifestation, That though he were of Parents of a good, of a great Estate,
yet his possibility and his expectation from them, did not slacken his own
industry; which is a Canker that eats into, nay that hath eat up many a
family in this City, that relying wholly upon what the Father hath done,
the Sonne does nothing for himselfe. And truly, it falls out too often, that
he that labours not for more, does not keepe his own. God imprinted in
him an industrious disposition, though such hopes from such parents
might have excused some slacknesse, and God prospered his industry so,
as that when his Fathers estate came to a distribution by death, he needed
it not. God was with him, as with *David* in a Dilatation, and then in a
Repletion; God enlarged him, and then he filled him; He gave him a large
and a comprehensive understanding, and with it, A publique heart; And
such as perchance in his way of education, and in our narrow and contracted times, in which every man determines himselfe in himselfe, and

scarce looks farther, it would be hard to finde many Examples of such largenesse. You have, I thinke, a phrase of Driving a Trade; And you have, I know, a practise of Driving away Trade, by other use of money; And you have lost a man, that drove a great Trade, the right way in making the best use of our home-commodity. To fetch in Wine, and Spice, and Silke, is but a drawing of Trade; The right driving of trade, is, to vent our owne outward; And yet, for the drawing in of that, which might justly seeme most behoofefull, that is, of Arts, and Manufactures, to be imployed upon our owne Commodity within the Kingdome, he did his part, diligently, at least, if not vehemently, if not passionately. This City is a great Theater, and he Acted great and various parts in it; And all well; And when he went higher, (as he was often heard in Parliaments, at Councell tables, and in more private accesses to the late King of ever blessed memory) as, for that comprehension of those businesses, which he pretended to understand, no man doubts, for no man lacks arguments and evidences of his ability therein, So for his manner of expressing his intentions, and digesting and uttering his purposes, I have sometimes heard the greatest Master of Language and Judgement, which these times, or any other did, or doe, or shall give, (that good and great King of ours) say of him, That he never heard any man of his breeding, handle businesses more rationally, more pertinently, more elegantly, more perswasively; And when his purpose was, to do a grace to a Preacher, of very good abilities, and good note in his owne Chappell, I have heard him say, that his language, and accent, and manner of delivering himselfe, was like this man. This man hath God accompanied all his life; and by performance thereof seemes to have made that Covenant with him, which he made to *Abraham, Multiplicabote vehementer, I will multiply thee exceedingly.* He multiplied his estate so, as was fit to endow many and great Children; and he multiplied his Children so, both in their number, and in their quality, as they were fit to receive a great Estate. God was with him all the way, In *a Pillar of Fire,* in the brightnesse of prosperity, and in the *Pillar of Clouds* too, in many darke, and sad, and heavy crosses: So great a Ship, required a great Ballast, So many blessings, many crosses; And he had them, and sailed on his course the steadier for them; The *Cloud* as well as the *Fire,* was a *Pillar* to him; His crosses, as well as his blessings established his assurance in God; And so, in all the course of his life, *The Lord was here,* and therefore *our Brother is not dead;* not dead in the evidences and testimonies of life; for he, whom the world hath just cause to celebrate, for things done, when he was alive, is alive still in their celebration.

The Lord was here, that is, with him at his death too. He was served with the Processe here in the City, but his cause was heard in the Country;

Here he sickned, There he languished, and dyed there. In his sicknesse there, those that assisted him, are witnesses, of his many expressings, of a religious and a constant heart towards God, and of his pious joyning with them, even in the holy declaration of kneeling, then, when they, in favour of his weaknesse, would disswade him from kneeling. I must not defraud him of this testimony for my selfe, that into this place where we are now met, I have observed him to enter with much reverence, and compose himselfe in this place with much declaration of devotion. And truly it is that reverence, which those persons who are of the same ranke that he was in the City, that reverence that they use in this place, when they come hither, is that that makes us, who have now the administration of this Quire, glad, that our Predecessors, but a very few yeares before our time, (and not before all our times neither) admitted these Honourable and worshipfull Persons of this City, to sit in this Quire, so, as they do upon Sundayes: The Church receives an honour in it; But the honour is more in their reverence, than in their presence; though in that too: And they receive an honour, and an ease in it; and therefore they do piously towards God, and prudently for themselves, and gratefully towards us, in giving us, by their reverent comportment here, so just occasion of continuing that honour, and that ease to them here, which to lesse reverend, and unrespective persons, we should be lesse willing to doe. To returne to him in his sicknesse; He had but one dayes labour, and all the rest were Sabbaths, one day in his sicknesse he converted to businesse; Thus; He called his family, and friends together; Thankfully he acknowledged Gods manifold blessings, and his own sins as penitently: And then, to those who were to have the disposing of his estate, joyntly with his Children, he recommended his servants, and the poore, and the Hospitals, and the Prisons, which, according to his purpose, have beene all taken into consideration; And after this (which was his Valediction to the world) he seemed alwaies loath to returne to any worldly businesse, His last Commandement to Wife and Children was Christs last commandement to his Spouse the Church, in the Apostles, *To love one another.* He blest them, and the Estate devolved upon them, unto them: And by Gods grace shall prove as true a Prophet to them in that blessing, as he was to himselfe, when in entring his last bed, two dayes before his Death, he said, *Help me off with my earthly habit, and let me go to my last bed.* Where, in the second night after, he said, *Little know ye what paine I feele this night, yet I know, I shall have joy in the morning;* And in that morning he dyed. The forme in which he implored his Saviour, was evermore, towards his end, this, *Christ Jesus, which dyed on the Crosse, forgive me my sins; He have mercy upon me:* And his last and dying words were the repetition of the name of Jesus; And when he had not strength to utter that name distinctly and perfectly, they might heare it from within him, as from a man a far off; even then, when his hollow and remote naming of Jesus, was rather a certifying of them, that he was with his Jesus, than a prayer that he might come to him. And so *The Lord was here*, here with him in his Death; and because *the Lord was here, our Brother is not dead;* not dead in the eyes and eares of God; for as the blood of *Abel* speaks yet, so doth the zeale of Gods Saints; and their last prayers (though we heare them not) God continues still; and they pray in Heaven, as the Martyrs under the Altar, even till the Resurrection.

He is with him now too; Here in his Funerals. Buriall, and Christian Buriall, and Solemne Buriall are all evidences, and testimonies of Gods presence. God forbid we should conclude, or argue an absence of God, from the want of Solemne Buriall, or Christian Buriall, or any Buriall; But neither must we deny it, to be an evidence of his favour and presence, where he is pleased to afford these. So God makes that the seale of all his blessings to *Abraham, That he should be buried in a good age;* God established *Jacob* with that promise, *That his Son Joseph should have care of his Funerals:* And *Joseph* does cause his servants, *The Physitians, to embalme him, when he was dead.* Of Christ it was Prophecied, *That he should have a glorious Buriall;* And therefore Christ interprets well that profuse, and prodigall piety of the Woman that poured out the Oyntment upon him, *That she did it to Bury him;* And so shall *Joseph* of Arimathea be ever celebrated, for his care in celebrating Christs Funerals. If we were to send a Son, or a friend, to take possession of any place in Court, or forraine parts, we would send him out in the best equipage: Let us not grudge to set downe our friends, in the Anti-chamber of Heaven, the Grave, in as good manner, as without vaine-gloriousnesse, and wastfulnesse we may; And, in inclining them, to whom that care belongs, to expresse that care as they doe this day, *The Lord is with him,* even in this Funerall; And because *The Lord is here, our brother is not dead;* Not dead in the memories and estimation of men.

And lastly, that we may have God present in all his Manifestations, *Hee that was, and is, and is to come,* was with him, in his life and death, and is with him in this holy Solemnity, and shall bee with him againe in the Resurrection. God sayes to *Jacob, I will goe downe with thee into Egypt, and I will also surely bring thee up againe.* God goes downe with a good man into the Grave, and will surely bring him up againe. When? The Angel promised to returne to *Abraham* and *Sarah,* for the assurance of the birth of *Isaac, according to the time of life;* that is, in such time, as by nature a woman may have a childe. God will returne to us in the Grave, *according to the time of life;* that is, in such time, as he, by his gracious Decree, hath fixed for the Resurrection. And in the meane time, no more than the God-head departed from the dead body of our Saviour, in the grave, doth his power, and his presence depart from our dead bodies in that darknesse; But that which *Moses* said to the whole Congregation, I say to you all, both to you that heare me, and to him that does not, *All ye that did cleave unto the Lord your God, are alive, every one of you, this day;* Even hee, whom wee call dead, is alive this day. In the presence of God, we lay him downe; In the power of God, he shall rise; In the person of Christ, he is risen already. And so into the same hands that have received his soule, we commend his body; beseeching his blessed Spirit, that as our charity enclines us to hope confidently of his good estate, our faith may assure us of the same happinesse, in our owne behalfe; And that for all our sakes, but especially for his own glory, he will be pleased to hasten the consummation of all, in that kingdome which that Son of God hath purchased for us, with the inestimable price of his incorruptible blood. *Amen.*

PASSAGES FROM *FIFTY SERMONS.* 1649

SERMON I

At the Earl of Bridgewaters house in London at the marriage of his daughter. Nov. 19th, 1627

[p. 3]

THERE are so many evidences of the immortality of the soule, even to a naturall mans *reason,* that it required not an Article of the Creed, to fix this notion of the Immortality of the soule. But the Resurrection of the *Body* is discernible by no other light, but that of *Faith,* nor could be fixed by any lesse assurance than an *Article* of the *Creed.* Where be all the splinters of that Bone, which a shot hath shivered and scattered in the Ayre? Where be all the Atoms of that flesh, which a *Corrasive* hath eat away, or a *Consumption* hath breath'd, and exhal'd away from our arms, and other Limbs? In what wrinkle, in what furrow, in what bowel of the earth, ly all the graines of the ashes of a body burnt a thousand years since? In what corner, in what ventricle of the sea, lies all the jelly of a Body drowned in the *generall flood?* What cohaerence, what sympathy, what dependence maintaines any relation, any correspondence, between that arm that was lost in Europe, and that legge that was lost in Afrique or Asia, scores of yeers between? One humour of our dead body produces worms, and those worms suck and exhaust all other humour, and then all dies, and all dries, and molders into dust, and that dust is blowen into the River, and that puddled water tumbled into the sea, and that ebs and flows in infinite revolutions, and still, still God knows in what *Cabinet* every *seed-Pearle* lies, in what part of the world every graine of every mans dust lies; and, *sibilat populum suum,* (as his Prophet speaks in another case) he whispers, he hisses, he beckens for the bodies of his Saints, and in the twinckling of an eye, that body that was scattered over all the elements, is sate down at the right hand of God, in a glorious resurrection. A Dropsie hath extended me to an enormous corpulency, and unwieldinesse; a Consumption hath attenuated me to a feeble macilency and leannesse, and God raises me a body, such as it should have been, if these infirmities had not interven'd and deformed it.

SERMON XIV

Lincolns Inne [*after* 1616]

[pp. 113-114]

Corruption in the skin, says *Job;* In the outward beauty, These be the Records of velim, these be the parchmins, the endictments, and the evidences that shall condemn many of us, at the last day, our *own skins;* we have the book of God, the Law, written in our own hearts; we have the image of God imprinted in our own souls; wee have the character, and seal of God stamped in us, in our baptism; and, all this is bound up in this velim, in this parchmin, in this skin of ours, and we neglect book, and image, and character, and seal, and all for the covering. It is not a clear case, if we consider the originall words properly, *That Jesabel did paint;* and yet all translators, and expositors have taken a just occasion, out of the ambiguity of those words, to cry down that abomination of painting. It is not a clear case, if we consider the propriety of the words, That *Absolon was hanged by the hair of the head;* and yet the Fathers and others have made use of that indifferency, and verisimilitude, to explode that abomination, of cherishing and curling haire, to the enveagling, and ensnaring, and entangling of others; *Judicium patietur æternum,* says *Saint Hierome,* Thou are guilty of a murder, though no body die; *Quia vinum attulisti, si fuisset qui bibisset;* Thou hast poyson'd a cup, if any would drink, thou hast prepar'd a tentation, if any would swallow it. *Tertullian* thought he had done enough, when he had writ his book *De Habitu muliebri,* against the excesse of women in clothes, but he was fain to adde another with more vehemence, *De cultu fœminarum,* that went beyond their clothes to their skin. And he concludes, *Illud ambitionis crimen,* there's vain-glory in their excesse of clothes, but,

Hoc prostitutionis, there's prostitution in drawing the eye to the skin. *Pliny* says, that when their thin silke stuffes were first invented at Rome, *Excogitatum ad fœminas denudandas;* It was but an invention that women might go naked in clothes, for their skins might bee seen through those clothes, those thinne stuffes: Our women are not so carefull, but they expose their nakednesse professedly, and paint it, to cast bird-lime for the passengers eye. Beloved, good dyet makes the best Complexion, and a good Conscience is a continuall feast; A cheerfull heart makes the best blood, and peace with God is the true cheerfulnesse of heart. Thy Saviour neglected his skin so much, as that at last, he scarse had any; all was torn with the whips, and scourges; and thy skin shall come to that absolute corruption, as that, though a hundred years after thou art buryed, one may find thy bones, and say, this was a *tall* man, this was a *strong* man, yet we shall soon be past saying, upon any relique of thy skinne, This was a *fair* man; Corruption seises the skinne, all outward beauty quickly, and so it does the body, the whole frame and constitution, which is another consideration; *After my skinne, my Body.*

If the whole body were an eye, or an ear, where were the body, says Saint *Paul;* but, when of the whole body there is neither eye nor ear, nor any member left, where is the body? And what should an eye do there, where there is nothing to be seen but loathsomnesse; or a nose there, where there is nothing to be smelt, but putrefaction; or an ear, where in the grave they doe not praise God? Doth not that body that boasted but yesterday of that priviledge above all creatures, that it onely could goe upright, lie to day as flat upon the earth as the body of a horse, or of a dogge? And doth it not to morrow lose his other priviledge, of looking up to heaven? Is it not farther remov'd from the eye of heaven, the Sunne, than any dogge, or horse, by being cover'd with the earth, which they are not? Painters have presented to us with some horrour, the *sceleton,* the frame of the bones of a mans body; but the state of a body, in the dissolution of the grave, no pencil can present to us. Between that excrementall jelly that thy body is made of at first, and that jelly which thy body dissolves to at last; there is not so noysome, so putrid a thing in nature. This skinne, (this outward beauty) this body, (this whole constitution) must be destroy'd, says *Job,* in the next place.

The word is well chosen, by which all this is expressed, in this text, *Nakaph,* which is a word of as heavy a signification, to expresse an utter abolition, and annihilation, as perchance can be found in all the Scriptures. *Tremellius* hath mollifyed it in his translation; there is but one *Confodere,* to pierce. And yet it is such a piercing, such a sapping, such an undermining, such a demolishing of a fort or Castle, as may justly remove us from any high valuation, or any great confidence, in that skinne, and in that body, upon which this *Confoderint* must fall. But, in the great Bible it is *Contriverint,* Thy *skinne,* and thy *body* shall be *ground* away, trod away upon the ground. Aske where that iron is that is ground off of a knife, or axe; Aske that marble that is worn off of the threshold in the Church-porch by continuall treading, and with that iron, and with that marble, thou mayst finde thy Fathers skinne, and body; *Contrita sunt,* The knife, the marble, the skinne, the body are ground away, trod away, they are destroy'd, who knows the revolutions of dust? Dust upon the Kings high-way, and dust upon the Kings grave, are both, or neither, Dust Royall, and may change places; who knows the revolutions of dust? Even in the dead body of Christ Jesus himself, one dram of the decree of his Father, one sheet, one sentence of the prediction of the Prophets preserv'd his body from corruption, and incineration, more than all *Josephs* new tombs, and fine linnen, and great proportion of spices could have done. O, who can expresse this inexpressible mystery? The soul of Christ Jesus, which took no harm by him, contracted no Originall sin, in coming to him, was guilty of no more sin, when it went out, than when it came from the breath and bosome of God; yet this soul left this body in death. And the Divinity, the Godhead, incomparably better than that soul, which soul was incomparably better than all the Saints, and Angels in heaven, that Divinity, that God-head did not forsake the body, though it were dead. If we might compare things infinite in themselves; it was nothing so much, that God did assume mans nature, as that God did still cleave to that man, then when he was no man, in the separation of body and soul, in the grave. But fall we from incomprehensible mysteries; for, there is mortification enough, (and mortification is vivification, and aedification) in this obvious consideration; *skinne and body,* beauty and substance must be destroy'd; And, *Destroyed by wormes,* which is another descent in this humiliation, and exinanition of man, in death; *After my skinne, wormes shall destroy this body.*

I will not insist long upon this, because it is not in the Originall; In the Originall there is no mention of *wormes.* But because in other places of *Job* there is, (*They shall lye down alike in the dust, and the* worms *shall cover them*) (*The* womb *shall forget them, and the* worm *shall feed sweetly on them;* and because the word *Destroying* is presented in that form and number, *Contriverint,* when *they* shall destroy, *they* and no other persons, no other creatures named) both our later translations, (for indeed, our first translation hath no mention of *wormes*) and so very many others, even *Tremellius* that adheres most to the letter of the Hebrew, have filled up this place, with that addition, *Destroyed by worms.* It makes the destruction the more contemptible; Thou that wouldest not admit the beames of the Sunne upon thy skinne, and yet hast admitted the spirit of lust, and unchast solicitations to breath upon thee, in execrable oathes, and blasphemies, to vicious purposes; Thou, whose body hath (as farre as it can) putrefyed and corrupted even the body of thy Saviour, in an unworthy receiving thereof, in this *skinne*, in this *body*, must be the food of worms, the prey of destroying worms. After a low birth thou mayst passe an honourable life, after a sentence of an ignominious death, thou mayst have an honourable end; But, in the grave canst thou make these worms silke worms? They were bold and early worms that eat up *Herod* before he dyed; They are bold and ever-lasting worms, which after thy skinne and body is destroyed, shall remain as long as God remains, in an eternall gnawing of thy conscience; long, long after the destroying of skinne and body, by bodily worms.

SERMON XIX

Lincolns Inne [*after* 1616]

1   [pp. 155-156]

AFTER wee have parled with a tentation, debating whether we should embrace it or no, and entertain'd some discourse with it, though some tendernesse, some remorse, make us turn our back upon it, and depart a little from it, yet the arrow overtakes us; some *reclinations*, some *retrospects* we have, a little of *Lots wife* is in us, a little *sociablenesse*, and *conversation*, a little point of *honour*, not to be false to former promises, a little *false gratitude*, and thankfulnesse, in respect of former obligations, a little of the *compassion* and *charity* of Hell, that another should not be miserable, for want of *us*, a little of this, which is but the good nature of the *Devill*, arrests us, stops us, fixes us, till the arrow, the tentation shoot us in the back, even when wee had a purpose of departing from that sin, and kils us over again.

2   [p. 158]

Every tentation, every tribulation is not *deadly*. But their multiplicity disorders us, discomposes us, unsettles us, and so hazards us. Not onely every *periodicall* variation of our years, *youth* and *age*, but every day hath a divers arrow, every hours of the day, a divers tentation. An old man wonders then, how an arrow from an eye could wound him, when he was young, and how *love* could make him doe those things which hee did *then;* And an arrow from the tongue of inferiour people, that which we make shift to call *honour*, wounds him deeper now; and *ambition* makes him doe as strange things now, as *love* did then; A fair day shoots arrows

of *visits,* and *comedies,* and *conversation,* and so wee goe abroad: and a
foul day shoots arrows of *gaming,* or *chambering,* and *wantonnesse,* and
so we stay at home.

SERMON XX

Lincolns Inne [after 1616]

1   [p. 166]

F I R E and Aire, Water and Earth, are not the Elements of man; Inward
decay, and outward violence, bodily pain, and sorrow of heart may be
rather styled his Elements; And though he be destroyed by these, yet
he consists of nothing but these. As the good qualities of all creatures are
not for their own use, (for the *Sun* sees not his own glory, nor the *Rose*
smells not her own breath: but all their good is for *man*) so the ill conditions of the creature, are not directed upon themselves, (the Toad poisons
not it selfe, nor does the Viper bite it self) but all their ill powrs down
upon *man.* As though man could be a *Microcosm,* a world in himself, no
other way, except all the misery of the world fell upon him.

2   [pp. 168-169]

Behold God hath walled us with mud walls, and wet mud walls, that
waste away faster, than God meant at first, they should. And by sinnes,
this flesh, that is but the loame and plaster of thy Tabernacle, thy body,
that, all, that, *that* in the intire substance is corrupted. Those Gummes,
and spices, which should embalme thy flesh, when thou art dead, are spent
upon that diseased body whilest thou art alive: Thou seemest, in the
eye of the world, to walk in *silks,* and thou doest but walke in *sear-cloth;*
Thou hast a desire to please some *eyes,* when thou hast much to doe, not
to displease every *Nose;* and thou wilt solicite an adulterous entrance into
their beds, who, if they should but see thee goe into thine own bed, would
need no other mortification, nor answer to thy solicitation. Thou pursuest
the works of the flesh, and hast none, for thy flesh is but dust held together
by plaisters; Dissolution and putrefaction is gone over thee alive; Thou
hast over liv'd thine own death, and art become thine own ghost, and
thine own hell; *No soundnesse in all thy flesh;* and yet beyond all these,
beyond the generall miserable condition of man, and the highest of
humane miseries, sicknesse, and sicknesse over all the parts, and so over
them all, as that it hath putrefied them all, there is another degree, which
followes in our Text, and *David* calls *Trouble, There is no soundnesse in
my flesh, nor rest in my bones.*

Lincolns Inne [*after* 1616]

[p. 181]

F O R, this plurality, this multiplicity of sin, hath found first a spunginesse in the soul, an aptnesse to receive any liquor, to embrace any sin, that is offered to it; and after a while, a hunger and thirst in the soul, to hunt, and pant and draw after a tentation, and not to be able to endure any *vacuum,* any discontinuance, or intermission of sinne: and hee will come to think it a melancholique thing, still to stand in fear of Hell; a sordid, a *yeomanly* thing, still to be plowing, and weeding, and worming a conscience; a mechanicall thing, still to be removing logs, or filing iron, still to be busied in removing occasions of tentation, or filing and clearing particular actions: and, at last he will come to that case, which S. *Augustine* out of an abundant ingenuity, and tendernesse, and compunction, confesses of himself, *Ne vituperarer, vitiosior fiebam,* I was fain to sin, lest I should lose my credit, and be under-valued; *Et ubi non suberat, quo admisso, aequarer perditis,* when I had no means to doe some sins, whereby I might be equall to my fellow, *Fingebam me fecisse quod non feceram, ne viderer abjectior, quo innocentior,* I would bely myself, and say I had done that, which I never did, lest I should be undervalued for not having done it. *Audiebam eos exaltantes flagitia,* sayes that tender blessed Father, I saw it was thought wit, to make Sonnets of their own sinnes, *Et libebat facere, non libidine facti, sed libidine laudis,* I sinn'd, not for the pleasure I had in the sin, but for the pride that I had to write feelingly of it. O what a *Leviathan* is sin, how vast, how immense a body! And then, what a spawner, how numerous! Between these two, the *denying* of sins, which we have done, and the *bragging* of sins, which we have not done, what a space, what a compasse is there, for millions of millions of sins!

Lincolns Inne [*after* 1616]

I [p. 194]

T H E covetous man lies still, and attends his *quarter days,* and studies the endorsements of his bonds, and he wonders that the ambitious man can endure the shufflings and thrustings of Courts, and can measure his happinesse by the smile of a greater man: And, he that does so, wonders

as much, that this covetous man can date his happinesse by an Almanack,
and soch revolutions, and though he have quick returns of receipt, yet
scarce affords himself bread to live till that day come, and though all
his joy be in his bonds, yet denies himself a candles end to look upon them.
Hilly ways are wearisome ways, and tire the ambitious man; Carnall
pleasures are *dirty ways,* and tire the licentious man; Desires of gain, are
thorny ways, and tire the covetous man; Aemulations of higher men, are
dark and *blinde ways,* and tire the envious man; Every way, that is out
of the way, wearies us; But, *lassati sumus; sed lassis non datur requies;*
we labour, and have no rest, when we have done; we are wearied with our
sins, and have no satisfaction in them; we goe to bed to night, weary of
our sinfull labours, and we will rise freshly to morrow, to the same sinfull
labours again; And when a sinner does so little remember *yesterday,*
how little does he consider to *morrow?* He that forgets what he hath *done,*
foresees not what he shall suffer: so sin is a burden; it crookens us, it
wearies us.

2   [p. 196]

They were *sins, his sins, many sinnes,* the *sinnes of the world;* and then,
as in his Type, *David, Supergressæ,* his sins, these sins *were got above*
him, And not as *Davids,* or *ours,* by an insensible growth, and swelling
of a Tide in course of time, but this inundation of all the sins of all places,
and times, and persons, was upon him in an instant, in a minute; in such
a point as admits, and requires a subtile, and a serious consideration; for
it is *eternity;* which though it doe infinitely exceed all *time,* yet is in this
consideration, lesse than any part of time, that it is *indivisible,* eternity
is so; and though it last for ever, is all at once, eternity is so. And from
this point, this *timelesse time,* time that is all *time,* time that is no *time,*
from all eternity, all the sins of the-world were gone over him.

SERMON XXVI

To the King at White-Hall.
The first Sunday in Lent [1626/7?]

I   [p. 219]

WHAT can be certain in this world, if even the mercy of God admit a
variation? what can be endlesse here, if even the mercy of God receive a
determination? and *sin* doth vary the nature, *sin* doth determine even the
infinitenesse of the mercy of God himself, for though *The childe shall die*
a hundred yeares old, yet *the sinner being a hundred years old shall be*

accursed. Disconsolate soul, dejected spirit, bruised and broken, ground and trodden, attenuated, evaporated, annihilated heart come back; heare thy *reprieve,* and sue for thy *pardon;* God will not take thee away in thy sins, thou shalt have time to repent, *The childe shall die a hundred years old.* But then lame and decrepit soul, gray and inveterate sinner, behold the full ears of corn blasted with a mildew, behold this long day shutting up in such a night, as shall never see light more, the night of death; in which, the deadliest pang of thy *Death* will be thine *Immortality:* In this especially shalt thou die, that thou canst not die, when thou art dead; but must live dead for ever: for *The sinner being a hundred yeers old, shall be accursed,* he shall be so for ever.

2 [p. 219]

God antidates no malediction: Till there be a sinner, there is no malediction; nay not till there be an *invetcrate* sinner; *A sinner of a hundred yeares,* at least, such a sinner, as would be so, if God would spare him a hundred yeares here. And upon such a sinner, God thunders out this Prosternation, this Consternation, in this one word of our Text, which involves and inwraps all kinds of miseries, feeblenesse in body, infatuation in mind, evacuation of power, dishonour in fame, eclipses in favour, ruine in fortune, dejection in spirit, *He shall be accursed.* Where, because in this second part we are in the Region and Sphear of maledictions, we cannot consider this future, *He shall be,* as a future of favour, a prorogation, a deferring of the malediction: *He shall be,* is not, he shall be hereafter, but not yet: but it is *a future of continuation; He shall be accursed,* that is, he shall be so *for ever.*

3 [p. 222]

Long life is a blessing, as it is an image of eternity: as Kings are blessings, because they are Images of God. And as to speak properly, a King that possest the whole earth, hath no proportion at all to God, (he is not a dramme, not a grain, not an atome to God) so neither if a thousand *Methusalems* were put in one life, had that long life any proportion to eternity; for *Finite* and *Infinite* have no proportion to one another. But yet when we say so, That the King is *nothing* to *God,* we speak then between God and the King; and we say that, onely to assist the Kings Religious humiliation of himself in the presence of God. But when we speak between the King and our selves his Subjects, there we raise our selves to a just reverence of him, by taking knowledge that he is the Image of God to us. So though *long life* be nothing to eternity, yet because we need such *Glasses* and such *Images,* as God shews us himself in the King, so he shewes us his eternitie in a long life.

4   [p. 227]

How men do bear it, we know not; what passes between God and those men, upon whom the curse of God lieth, in their dark *horrours at midnight*, they would not have us know, because it is part of their curse, to envy God that glory. But we may consider in some part the insupportablenesse of that weight, if we proceed but so farre, as to accommodate to God, that which is ordinarily said of naturall things. *Corruptio optimi pessima;* when the best things change their nature, they become worst. When God, who is all sweetnesse, shall have learned frowardnesse from us, as *David* speaks; and being all rectitude, shall have learned perversenesse and crookednesse from us, as *Moses* speaks; and being all providence, shall have learned negligence from us: when God who is all Blessing, hath learned to curse of us, and being of himself spread as an universall Hony-combe over All, takes in an impression, a tincture, an infusion of gall from us, what extraction of Wormwood can be so bitter, what exaltation of fire can be so raging, what multiplying of talents can be so heavy, what stifnesse of destiny can be so inevitable, what confection of gnawing worms, of gnashing teeth, of howling cries, of scalding brimstone, of palpable darknesse, can be so, so insupportable, so inexpressible, so inimaginable, as the curse and malediction of God? *And therefore* let not us by our works provoke, nor by our words teach God to curse.

5   [p. 227]

This is the *Anathema Maran-atha,* accursed *till the Lord come;* and when the Lord cometh, he cometh not to reverse, nor to alleviate, but to ratifie and aggravate that curse. As soon as Christ curst the *fig-tree,* it withered, and it never recovered: for saith that Gospell, he curst it *In æternum,* for ever. In the course of our sinne, the *Holy Ghost* hath put here a number of yeares, a hundred yeares: We sinne long, as long as we can, but yet sinne hath an end. But in this curse of God in the Text, there is no number; it is an *indefinite* future; *He shall be accursed:* A mile of cyphers or figures, added to the former hundred, would not make up a minute of this eternity. Men have calculated how many particular graines of sand, would fill up all the vast space between the Earth and the Firmament: and we find, that a few lines of cyphers will designe and expresse that number. But if every grain of sand were that number, and multiplied again by that number, yet all that, all that inexpressible, inconsiderable number, made not up one minute of this eternity; neither would this curse, be a minute the shorter for having been indured so many Generations, as there were grains of sand in that number.

6 [p. 228]

But we are now in the work of an houre, and no more. If there be a minute of sand left, (There is not) If there be a minute of patience left, heare me say, This minute that is left, is that eternitie which we speake of; upon this minute dependeth that eternity: And this minute, God is in this Congregation, and puts his eare to every one of your hearts, and hearkens what you will bid him say to yourselves: whether he shall blesse you for your acceptation, or curse you for your refusall of him this minute: for this minute makes up your *Century*, your hundred yeares, your eternity, because it may be your last minute. We need not call that a *Fable*, but a *Parable*, where we heare, That a Mother to still her froward childe told him, she would cast him to the Wolf, the Wolf should have him; and the Wolf which was at the doore, and within hearing, waited, and hoped he should have the childe indeed: but the childe being still'd, and the Mother pleased, then she saith, so shall we kill the Wolf, the Wolf shall have none of my childe, and then the Wolf stole away. No metaphor, no comparison is too high, none too low, too triviall, to imprint in you a sense of Gods everlasting goodnesse towards you. God bids your Mother the Church, and us her Servants for your Souls, to denounce his judgements upon your sinnes, and we do it; and the executioner *Satan*, beleeves us, before you beleeve us, and is ready on his part. Be you also ready on your part, to lay hold upon those conditions, which are annext to all Gods maledictions, Repentance of former, *preclusion* against *future sinnes*, and we shall be alwayes ready, on our part to assist you with the *Power* of our *Intercession*, to deliver you with the *Keies* of our *Absolution*, and to establish you with the *seales* of *Reconciliation*, and so disappoint that *Wolf*, that roaring *Lion*, that seeks whom he may devour: Go in Peace, and be this your Peace, to know this, *Maledictus qui pendet in Cruce*, God hath laid the whole curse belonging to us upon him, that hangs upon the Crosse; But *Benedictus qui pendet in pendentem;* To all them that hang upon him, that hangeth there, God offereth now, all those blessings, which he that hangeth there hath purchased with the inestimable price of his Incorruptible blood; And to this glorious *Sonne* of God, who hath *suffered* all this, and to the most Almighty *Father*, who hath *done* all this, and to the *blessed Spirit of God*, who offereth now to *apply* all this, be ascribed by us, and by the whole Church, All power, praise, might, majesty, glory, and dominion, now and for evermore *Amen*.

SERMON XXVII

To the King at Whitehall, May 6th, 1627

1   [p. 230]

THE first thing that God made, was *light;* The last thing, that he hath
reserved to doe, is the manifestation, of the light of his Essence in our
Glorification. And for Publication of himselfe here, by the way, he hath
constituted a *Church,* in a Visibility, in an eminency, *as a City upon a hill;*
And in this Church, his Ordinance is Ordinance indeed; his Ordinance
of preaching batters the soule, and by that breach, the Spirit enters; His
Ministers are an *Earth-quake,* and shake an earthly soule; They are the
sonnes of thunder, and scatter a cloudy conscience; They are as the fall
of waters, and carry with them whole Congregations; 3000 at a Sermon,
5000 at a Sermon, a whole City, such a City as Nineveh at a Sermon; and
they are as the roaring of a Lion, where the Lion of the tribe of Juda, cries
down the Lion that seekes whom he may devour; that is, Orthodoxall
and fundamentall truths, are established against clamorous, and vocifer-
ant innovations. Therefore what Christ tels us in the darke, he bids us
speake in the light; and what he saies in our eare, he bids us preach on
the house-top. Nothing is Gospell, not *Evangelium* good message, if it be
not put into a Messengers mouth, and delivered by him; nothing is con-
ducible to his end, nor available to our salvation, except it be avowable
doctrine, doctrine that may be spoke alowd, though it awake them, that
sleep in their sinne, and make them the more froward, for being so awaked.

God hath made all things in a *Roundnesse,* from the round superficies
of this earth, which we tread here, to the round convexity of those heavens,
which (as long as they shal have any beeing) shall be our footstool, when
we come to heaven, God hath wrapped up all things in Circles, and then
a Circle hath no *Angles;* there are no *Corners* in a Circle.

2   [p. 235]

This whisperer wounds thee, and with a stilletta of gold, he strangles
thee with scarfes of silk, he smothers thee with the down of Phœnixes, he
stifles thee with a perfume of Ambar, he destroys thee by praising thee,
overthrows thee by exalting thee, and undoes thee by trusting thee; By
trusting thee with those secrets that bring thee into a desperate perplexity,
Aut alium accusare in subsidium tui, (as the Patriarch, and Oracle of
Statesmen, *Tacitus,* says) Either to betray another, that pretends to have
trusted thee, or to perish thy selfe, for the saving of another, that plotted
to betray thee. And therefore, if you can heare a good Organ at Church,

and have the musique of a domestique peace at home, peace in thy walls, peace in thy bosome, never hearken after the musique of sphears, never hunt after the knowledge of higher secrets, than appertaine to thee; But since Christ hath made you *Regale Sacerdotium,* Kings and Priests, in your proportion, *Take heed what you hear,* in derogation of either the State, or the Church.

SERMON XXX

'*To the Countesse of Bedford, then at Harrington House,*' *Jan. 7th,* 1620/1

[p. 270]

L O O K E upon the *water,* and we are as that, and as that spilt upon the ground: Looke to the *earth,* and we are not like that, but we are earth it self: At our Tables we feed upon the dead, and in the Temple we tread upon the dead: and when we meet in a Church, God hath made many *echoes,* many testimonies of our death, in the walls, and in the windowes, and he onely knowes, whether he will not make another testimony of our mortality, of the youngest amongst us, before we part, and make the very *place of our buriall,* our *death-bed.*

SERMON XXXI

I

[pp. 275-276]

H O W different are the wayes of God, from the ways of man! the eyes of God from the eyes of man! and the wayes and eyes of a godly man, from the eyes, and wayes of a man of this world! We looke still upon high persons, and after high places, and from those heights, we thinke, we see far; but he that will see this object, must lye low; it is best discerned in the dark, in a heavy, and a calamitous fortune. The naturall way is *upward;* I can better know a man upon the top of a steeple, than if he were halfe that depth in a well; but yet for higher objects, I can better see the stars of heaven, in the bottome of a well, than if I stood upon the highest steeple upon earth. If I twist a cable of infinite fadomes in length, if there be no ship to ride by it, nor anchor to hold by it, what use is there of it? If Mannor thrust Mannor, and title flow into title, and bags powre out into chests, if I have no anchor, (*faith in Christ*) if I have not a ship to carry to a haven, (a soule to save) what's my long cable to me? If I adde number to number, a span, a mile long, if at the end of all that long line of numbers, there be nothing that notes, *pounds,* or *crownes,* or *shillings;* what's that long number, but so many millions of millions of nothing? If my span of life become a mile of life, my penny a pound, my pint a gallon, my acre a sheere; yet if there be nothing of the next world at the end, so much peace of conscience, so much joy, so much glory, still all is but *nothing* multiplied, and that is still nothing at all. 'Tis the *end* that qualifies all; and what kinde of man I shall be at my end, upon my *death-bed,* what trembling hands, and what lost legs, what deafe eares, and what gummy eyes, I shall have then, I know; and the nearer I come to that disposition, in my life, (the more *mortified* I am) the better I am disposed to see this object, future glory. God made the Sun, and Moon, and Stars, glorious lights for man to see by; but mans infirmity requires *spectacles;* and affliction does that office. Gods meaning was, that by the sun-shine of prosperity, and by the beames of honour, and temporall blessings, a man should see farre into him; but I know not how he is come to need *spectacles;* scarce any man sees much in this matter, till affliction shew it him.

2 [p. 278]

How many times go we to Comedies, to Masques, to places of great and noble resort, nay even to Church onely to see the company? If I had no other errand to heaven, but the *communion of Saints,* the fellowship of the faithfull, [T]o see that flock of *Lambs,* Innocent, unbaptized *children,* recompensed with the twice-baptized *Martyrs,* (baptized in *water,* and baptized in their owne *blood*) and that middle sort, the children baptized in blood, and not in the water, that rescued Christ Jesus, by their death, under *Herod;* to see the *Prophets* and the *Evangelists,* and not know one from the other, by their writings, for they all write the same things (for *prophecy* is but *antidated Gospell,* and *Gospell* but *postdated prophecy;*) to see holy *Matrons* saved by the bearing, and bringing up of children, and holy *Virgins,* saved by restoring their bodies in the integrity, that they received them, sit all upon one seate; to see *Princes,* and *Subjects* crowned all with one crowne, and *rich* and *poore* inherit one portion; to see this scene, this Court, this Church, this Catholique Church, not onely *Easterne* and *Westerne,* but *Militant* and *Triumphant* Church, all in one roome together, to see this *Communion of Saints,* this fellowship of the faithful, is worth all the paynes, that that sight costs us in this world.

'Denmark house, some few days before the body of King James was removed from thence, to his buriall,' April 26, 1625

[pp. 300-304]

H E R E, at your coming hither now, you have *two glasses,* wherein you may see your selves from head to foot; One in the Text, your *Head, Christ Jesus,* represented unto you, in the name and person of *Solomon, Behold King Solomon crowned, &c.* And another, under your feet, in the dissolution of this great *Monarch,* our *Royall Master,* now layd lower by death than any of us, his Subjects and servants.

First then, behold your selves in that first glasse, *Behold King Solomon; Solomon* the sonne of *David,* but not the Son of *Bathsheba,* but of a better mother, the most blessed *Virgin Mary.* For, *Solomon,* in this text, is not a *proper* Name, but an *Appellative;* a significative word: *Solomon* is *pacificus,* the *Peacemaker,* and our peace is made in, and by Christ Jesus: and he is that *Solomon,* whom we are called upon to see here. Now, as Saint *Paul* says, that *he would know nothing but Christ,* (that's his first abridgement) and then he would know nothing of Christ, but *him crucifyed,* (and that's the re-abridgement) so we seek no other glasse, to see our selves in, but Christ, nor any other thing in this glasse, but his *Humiliation.* What need we? Even that, his lowest humiliation, his death, is expressed here, in three words of exaltation, It is a *Crown,* it is a *Mariage,* it is the *gladnesse of heart: Behold King Solomon crowned,* &c.

The Crown, which we are called to see him crowned with, *his mother* put upon him; The Crown which his *Father gave him,* was that glory, wherewith he was glorifyed, with the Father, *from all eternity,* in his *divine nature:* And the Crown wherewith his Father crowned his *Humane nature,* was the glory given to that, in his *Ascension. His Mother* could give him no such Crown: she her selfe had no Crown, but that, which *he* gave her. The Crown that *she* gave him, was that substance, that he received from her, *our flesh,* our *nature,* our *humanity;* and this, *Athanasius,* and this, Saint *Ambrose,* calls the *Crown,* wherewith *his mother crowned him,* in this text, his infirm, his humane nature. Or, *the Crown wherewith his Mother crowned him,* was that Crown, to which, that infirme nature which he tooke from her, submitted him, which was his *passion,* his *Crown of thornes;* for so *Tertullian,* and divers others take this Crown of his, from her, to be his *Crown of thorns: Woe to the Crown of pride, whose beauty is a fading flower,* says the Prophet; But blessed be this Crown of Humiliation, whose flower cannot fade. Then was there truly

a *Rose* amongst *Thorns,* when through his Crown of *Thorns,* you might
see his title, *Jesus Nazarenus:* for, in that very name *Nazarenus,* is involved the signification of a *flower;* the very word signifies *a flower.*
Esay's flower in the Crown of pride fades, and is removed; This flower
in the Crown of Thornes fades not, nor could be removed; for, for all the
importunity of the Jews, *Pilate* would not suffer *that title* to be removed,
or to be changed; still *Nazarenus* remained, and still a rose amongst
thorns. You know the curse of the earth, *Thorns and thistles shall it bring
forth unto thee;* It did so to our *Solomon* here, it brought forth thornes to
Christ, and he made a *Crown* of those thorns, not onely for *himself,* but
for us too, *Omnes aculei mortis, in Dominici Corporis tolerantia, obtusi
sunt,* All the thorns of life and death, are broken, or blunted upon the
head of our *Solomon,* and now, even our *thorns,* make up *our Crown,* our
tribulation in life, our dissolution in death, conduce to our glory: *Behold
him crowned with his Mothers Crown,* for even that brought him to his
Fathers Crown, his humiliation to exaltation, his passion to glory.

Behold your *Solomon, your Saviour* again, and you shall see another
beam of Comfort, in your tribulations from his; for even this *Humiliation* of his, is called his *Espousals,* his *marriage, Behold him crowned in
the day of his Espousals.* His Spouse is the *Church,* His marriage is the
uniting of himselfe to this Spouse, in his becomming *Head of the Church.*
The great City, the heavenly Jerusalem, is called *The Bride,* and *The
Lambs wife,* in the *Revelation:* And he is the *Head* of this body, the
Bridegroom of this Bride, the Head of this Church, as he is *The first-
borne of the Dead;* Death, that dissolves all ours, made up this marriage.
His Death is his Marriage, and upon his Death flowed out from his side,
those two *Elements of the Church, water* and *bloud;* The Sacraments of
Baptisme, and of the *Communion* of himself. Behold then this *Solomon
crowned* and *married;* both words of *Exaltation,* and *Exultation,* and
both by *Death;* and trust him for working the same effects upon thee;
That thou (*though by Death*) shalt be *crowned* with a Crown of Glory,
and *married* to him, in whose right and merit thou shalt have that Crown.

And *Behold* him once again, and you shall see not a *beam,* but a *stream*
of comfort; for this day, which is the day of death, he calls here *The day
of the gladnesse of his heart. Behold him crowned in the day of the gladnesse of his heart.* The fulnesse, the compasse, the two *Hemispheres* of
Heaven, are often designed to us, in these two names, *Joy* and *Glory:* If
the *Crosse* of Christ, the *Death* of Christ, present us both these, how
neare doth it bring, how fully doth it deliver Heaven it self to us in this
life? And then we heare the Apostle say, *We see Jesus, for the suffering
of Death, crowned with Honour and Glory:* There is *half* Heaven got by
Death, Glory. And then, *for the joy that was set before him, he indured*

the Crosse; There is the *other half, Joy;* All Heaven purchased by Death. And therefore, *if any man suffer as a Christian, let him not be ashamed,* saith the *Apostle;* but *let him glorifie God, In isto Nomine,* as the *vulgate* read it; *In that behalfe,* as *we translate it.* But, *In isto Nomine,* saith S. *Augustine:* Let us glorifie God, in that Name; *Non solum in nomine Christiani, sed Chri[sti]ani patientis,* not onely because he is a *Christian* in his *Baptisme,* but a Christian in a *second Baptisme,* a *Baptisme of bloud;* not onely as he hath received Christ, in accepting his *Institution,* but because he hath conformed himself to Christ, in fulfilling his *sufferings.* And therefore, though we admit *naturall* and *humane sorrow,* in the calamities which overtake us, and surround us in this life: (for as *all glasses* will gather drops and tears from externall causes, so this very glasse which we looke upon now, our *Solomon* in the Text, our *Saviour,* had those *sadnesses of heart* toward his Passion, and *Agonies* in his passion) yet *count it all Joy when you fall into tentations,* saith the Apostle: *All Joy,* that is, both the *interest,* and the *principall,* hath the *earnest* and the *bargain;* for if you can conceive joy in your tribulations in this world, how shall that joy be multiplied unto you, when no tribulation shall be mingled with it? There is not a better evidence, nor a more binding earnest of everlasting Joy in the next world, than to find *Joy of heart* in the *tribulations* of this; fixe thy self therefore upon this first glasse, this *Solomon,* thy Saviour, *Behold King Solomon crownd,* &c. and by conforming thy self to his *holy sadnesse,* and *humiliation,* thou shalt also become like him, in his Joy, and Glory.

But then the hand of God, hath *not set up,* but *laid down another Glasse,* wherein thou maist see thy self; a glasse that reflects thy self, and nothing but thy selfe. Christ, who was the other glasse, *is like thee in every thing,* but not absolutely, for *sinne* is *excepted:* but in this glasse presented now (*The Body of our Royall,* but *dead Master and Soveraigne*) we cannot, we doe not except sinne. Not onely the greatest man is subiect to *naturall infirmities,* (Christ himself was so) but the holiest man is subiect to *Originall and Actuall sinne,* as thou art, and so a fit glasse for thee, to see thy self in. *Jeat* showes a man his face, as well as *Crystall:* nay, a Crystall glasse will not show a man his face, except it be steeled, except it be darkned on the backside: Christ as he was a pure *Crystall* glasse, as he was *God,* had not been a glasse for us, to have seen our selves in, except he had been *steeled, darkened with our humane nature;* Neither was he ever so throughly darkened, as that he could present us wholly to our selves, because he had no *sinne,* without seeing of which we do not see our selves. Those therefore that are like thee in all things, subiect to humane *infirmities,* subject to *sinnes,* and yet are translated, and *translated by Death,* to everlasting *Joy,* and *Glory,* are nearest and clearest glasses for thee, to see thy self in; and such is this glasse, which God hath proposed to thee, in this house. And therefore, change the word of the Text, in a letter or two, from *Egredimini*, to *Ingredimini;* never goe forth tc see, but *Go in and see a Solomon crowned with his mothers crown, &c.* And when you shall find that hand that has signed to one of you a *Patent* for *Title,* to another for *Pension,* to another for *Pardon,* to another for *Dispensation, Dead:* That hand that settled Possessions by his *Seale,* in the *Keeper,* and rectified *Honours* by the *sword,* in his *Marshall,* and distributed relief to the *Poore,* in his *Almoner,* and *Health* to the *Diseased,* by his *immediate Touch,* Dead: That Hand that ballanced his *own three Kingdomes* so equally, as that none of them complained of one another, nor of him; and carried the *Keyes* of all the Christian world, and locked up, and let out *Armies* in their due season, Dead; how poore, how faint, how pale, how momenta[r]y, how transitory, how empty, how frivolous, how Dead things, must you necessarily thinke *Titles,* and *Possessions,* and *Favours,* and all, when you see that Hand, which was the *hand of Destinie,* of *Christian Destinie,* of the *Almighty God,* lie dead! It was not so *hard* a hand when we touched it last, nor so *cold* a hand when we kissed it last: That hand which was wont to *wipe all teares from all our eyes,* doth now but presse and squeaze us as so many spunges, filled one with one, another with another cause of teares. Teares that can have no other banke to bound them, but the declared and manifested *will of God:* For, till our teares flow to that heighth, that they might be called a *murmuring* against the declared will of God, it is against our Allegiance, it is *Disloyaltie,* to give our teares any stop, any termination, any measure. It was a great part of *Anna's prayse, That she departed not from the Temple, day nor night;* visit Gods Temple often in the day, meet him in his owne House, and depart not from his *Temples,* (The *dead bodies* of his Saints are his Temples still) even at *midnight;* at midnight remember them, who resolve into dust, and make them thy glasses to see thy self in. Looke now especially upon him whom God hath presented to thee now, and with as much cheerfulnesse as ever thou heardst him say, *Remember my Favours, or remember my Commandements;* heare him say now with the wise man, *Remember my Judgement, for thine also shall be so; yesterday for me, and to day for thee;* He doth not say *to morrow,* but *to Day, for thee.* Looke upon him as a beame of that Sunne, as an abridgement of that *Solomon* in the Text; for every Christian truely reconciled to God, and *signed* with his hand in the *Absolution,* and *sealed* with his bloud in the *Sacrament,* (and this was his case) is a beame, and an abridgement of *Christ* himselfe. *Behold him* therefore, *Crowned with the Crown that his Mother gives him: His Mother, The Earth.* In ancient times, when they used to reward Souldiers with particular kinds of *Crowns,* there was a great dignity *in Corona graminea,* in a Crown of Grasse: That denoted a Conquest, or a Defence of that land. He that hath but *Coronan Gramineam,* a turfe of grasse in *a Church yard,* hath a Crown from his *Mother,* and even in that buriall taketh *seisure* of the *Resurrection,* as by a turfe of grasse men give seisure of land. *He is crowned in the day of his Marriage;* for though it be a day of *Divorce* of us from him, and of *Divorce* of his body from his soul, yet neither of these Divorces breake the Marriage: His *soule* is married to him that made it, and his body and soul shall meet again, and all we, both then in that Glory where we shall acknowledge, that there is no way to this *Marriage,* but this *Divorce,* nor to *Life,* but by *Death.* And lastly, he is *Crowned in the day of the Gladnesse of his heart:* He leaveth that heart, which was accustomed to the halfe joyes of the earth, in the earth; and he hath enlarged his heart to a greater capacity of Joy, and Glory, and God hath filled it according to that new capacity. And therefore, to end all with the Apostles words, *I would not have you to be ignorant, Brethren, concerning them, which are asleepe, that ye sorrow not, as others that have no hope; for if ye beleeve that Jesus died, and rose again, even so them also, which sleepe in him, will God bring with him.* But when you have performed this *Ingredimini,* that you have gone in, and mourned upon him, and performed the *Egredimini,* you have gone forth, and laid his Sacred body, in Consecrated Dust, and come them to another *Egredimini,* to a going forth in many severall wayes: some to the service of their *new Master,* and some to the enjoying of their Fortunes conferred by their old; some to the raising of new *Hopes,* some to the burying of old, and all; some to new, and busie endeavours in Court, some to contented retirings in the Countrey; let none of us, goe so farre from him, or from one another, in any of our wayes, but that all we that have served him, may meet once a day, the first time we see the Sunne, in the eares of almighty God, with humble and hearty prayer, that he will be pleased to hasten that day, in which it shall be *an addition,* even to the joy of that place, as perfect as it is, and as infinite as it is, to see that face againe, and to see those eyes open there, which we have seen closed here. Amen

SERMON XXXVI

St. Pauls.   Christmas-day.   1621

[pp. 324-327]

T H E *reason* therefore of Man, must first be satisfied; but the way of such satisfaction must be *this,* to make him see, That this World, a frame of

so much harmony, so much concinnitie and conveniencie, and such a correspondence, and subordination in the parts thereof, must necessarily
have had a workeman, for nothing can make it selfe: That no such workeman would deliver over a frame, and worke, of so much Majestie, to be
governed by *Fortune*, casually, but would still retain the Administration
thereof in his owne hands: That if he doe so, if he made the World, and
sustaine it still by his watchfull Providence, there belongeth a worship
and service to him, for doing so: That therefore he hath certainly revealed
to man, what kinde of worship, and service, shall be acceptable to him:
That this manifestation of his Will, must be permanent, it must be *written*,
there must be a *Scripture*, which is his *Word* and his *Will:* And that therefore, from that Scripture, from that Word of God, all Articles of our Beliefe
are to bee drawne.

If then his *Reason* confessing all this, aske farther proofe, how he shall
know that *these Scriptures* accepted by the Christian Church, are the
true Scriptures, let him bring any other Booke which pretendeth to be
the Word of God, into comparison with these; It is true, we have not a
Demonstration; not such an Evidence as that one and two, are three, to
prove these to be Scriptures of God; God hath not proceeded in that manner, to drive our Reason into a pound, and to force it by a peremptory
necessitie to accept these for Scriptures, for then, here had been no exercise of our *Will*, and our assent, if we could not have resisted. But yet
these Scriptures have so orderly, so sweet, and so powerfull a working
upon the reason, and the understanding, as if any third man, who were
utterly discharged of all preconceptions and anticipations in matter of
Religion, one who were altogether neutrall, disinteressed, unconcerned in
either party, nothing towards a *Turke*, and as little toward a *Christian*,
should heare a *Christian* pleade for his Bible, and a *Turke* for his Alcoran,
and should weigh the evidence of both; the Majesty of the *Style*, the
punctuall accomplishment of the *Prophecies*, the harmony and concurrence of the *foure Evangelists*, the consent and unanimity of the *Christian
Church* ever since, and many other such reasons, he would be drawne to
such an Historicall, such a Gramaticall, such a Logicall beliefe of our Bible,
as to preferre it before any other, that could be pretended to be the Word
of God. He would believe it, and he would know *why* he did so. For let
no man thinke that *God* hath given him so much ease here, as to save
him by believing he knoweth not what, or why. *Knowledge* cannot save
us, but we cannot be saved without Knowledge; Faith is not on this side
Knowledge, but beyond it; we must necessarily come to *Knowledge* first,
though we must not stay at it, when we are come thither. For, a regenerate Christian, being now a *new Creature*, hath also *a new facultie of Reason:* and so believeth the Mysteries of Religion, out of another Reason,

than as a meere natural Man, he believed naturall and morall things. He believeth them for their own sake, by *Faith*, though he take *Knowledge* of them before, by that common Reason, and by those humane Arguments, which worke upon other men, in naturall or morall things. Divers men may walke by the Sea side, and the same beames of the Sunne giving light to them all, one gathereth by the benefit of that light pebles, or speckled shells, for curious vanitie, and another gathers precious Pearle, or medicinall Ambar, by the same light. So the common light of reason illumins us all; but one imployes this light upon the searching of impertinent vanities, another by a better use of the same light, finds out the Mysteries of Religion: and when he hath found them, loves them, not for the lights sake, but for the naturall and true worth of the thing it self. Some men by the benefit of this light of Reason, have found out things profitable and usefull to the whole world; As in particular, *Printing*, by which the learning of the whole world is communicable to one another, and our minds and our inventions, our wits and compositions may trade and have commerce together, and we may participate of one anothers understandings, as well as of our Clothes, and Wines, and Oyles, and other Merchandize: So by the benefit of this light of reason, they have found out *Artillery*, by which warres come to quicker ends than heretofore, and the great expence of bloud is avoyded: for the numbers of men slain now, since the invention of Artillery, are much lesse than before, when the sword was the executioner. Others, by the benefit of this light have searched and found the secret corners of gaine, and profit, wheresoever they lie. They have found wherein the weaknesse of another man consisteth, and made their profit of that, by circumventing him in a bargain: They have found his riotous, and wastefull inclination, and they have fed and fomented that disorder, and kept open that leake, to their advantage, and the others ruine. They have found where was the easiest, and the most accessible way, to sollicite the Chastitie of a woman, whether *Discourse, Musicke,* or *Presents,* and according to that discovery, they have pursued *hers,* and *their* own eternall destruction. By the benefit of this light, men see through the darkest, and most impervious places that are, that is, *Courts of Princes,* and the greatest *Officers* in Courts; and can submit themselves to second, and to advance the humours of men in great place, and so make their profit of the weakenesses which they have discovered in these great men. All the wayes, both of *Wisdome,* and of *Craft* lie open to this light, this light of naturall reason: But when they have gone all these wayes by the benefit of this light, they have got no further, than to have walked by a tempestuous Sea, and to have gathered pebles, and speckled cockle shells. Their light seems to be great out of the same reason, that a Torch in a misty night, seemeth greater than in a clear, because it hath kindled and inflamed much thicke and grosse Ayre round about it. So the light and wisedome of worldly men, seemeth great, because he hath kindled an admiration, or an applause in Aiery flatterers, not because it is so in deed.

But, if thou canst take this light of reason that is in thee, this poore snuffe, that is almost out in thee, thy faint and dimme knowledge of God, that riseth out of this light of nature, if thou canst in those embers, those cold ashes, finde out one small coale, and wilt take the paines to kneell downe, and blow that coale with thy devout *Prayers,* and light thee a *little candle,* (a *desire* to reade that Booke, which they call the Scriptures, and the Gospell, and the Word of God;) If with that little candle thou canst creep humbly into low and poore places, if thou canst finde thy Saviour in a *Manger,* and in his *swathing clouts,* in his humiliation, and blesse God for that beginning, if thou canst finde him flying into Egypt, and finde in thy selfe a disposition to accompany him in a persecution, in a banishment, if not a bodily banishment, a locall banishment, yet a *reall, a spirituall banishment,* a banishment from those sinnes, and that sinne-full conversation, which thou hast loved more than thy *Parents,* or *Countrey,* or thine owne body, which perchance thou hast consumed, and destroyed with that sinne; if thou canst finde him contenting and containing himselfe at home in his fathers house, and not breaking out, no not about the worke of our salvation, till the due time was come, when it was to be done. And if according to that example, thou canst contain thy selfe in that station and vocation in which God hath planted thee, and not, through a hasty and precipitate *zeale,* breake out to an imaginary, and intempestive, and unseasonable *Reformation,* either in *Civill* or *Ecclesiasticall* businesse, which belong not to thee; if with this little poore light, these *first degrees* of *Knowledge* and *Faith,* thou canst follow him into the *Garden,* and gather up some of the droppes of his precious Bloud and sweat, which he shed for thy soule, if thou canst follow him to *Jerusalem,* and pick up some of those *teares,* which he shed upon that City, and upon thy soule; if thou canst follow him to the place of his scourging, and to his crucifying, and provide thee some of that balme, which must cure thy soule; if after all this, thou canst turne this little light inward, and canst thereby discerne where thy diseases, and thy wounds, and thy corruptions are, and canst apply those teares, and blood and balme to them, (all this is, That if thou attend the light of naturall reason, and cherish that, and exalt that, so that that bring thee to a *love of the Scriptures,* and that *love to a beleefe* of the truth thereof, and that *historicall faith* to a *faith of application, of appropriation,* that as all those things were certainly done, so they were certainly done *for thee*) thou shalt never envy the lustre and glory of the great lights of worldly men, which are great by the infirmity of others, or by their own opinion, great because others think them great, or because they think themselves so, but thou shalt finde, that howsoever they magnifie their lights, their wit, their learning, their industry, their fortune, their favour, and *sacrifice to their owne nets*, yet thou shalt see, that thou by thy small light has gathered *Pearle* and *Amber*, and they by their great lights nothing but shels and pebles; they have determined the light of nature, upon the booke of nature, this world, and thou hast carried the light of nature higher, thy naturall reason, and even *humane arguments*, have brought thee to reade the Scriptures, and to that *love*, God hath set to the seale of *faith*. Their light shall set at noone; even in their heighth, some heavy crosse shall cast a damp upon their soule, and cut off all their succours, and devest them of all comforts, and thy light shall grow up, from a *faire hope*, to a modest assurance and *infiallibility*, that that light shall never go out, nor the *works of darknesse*, nor the *Prince of darknesse* ever prevaile upon thee, but as thy light of *reason* is exalted by *faith* here, so thy light of *faith* shall be exalted into the light of *glory*, and fruition in the Kingdome of heaven. Before the sunne was made, there was *a light* which did that office of distinguishing night and day; but when the sunne was created, that did all the offices of the former light, and more. *Reason* is that first, and primogeniall light, and goes no farther in a naturall man; but in a man regenerate by faith, that light does all that reason did, *and more;* and all his *Morall*, and *Civill*, and *Domestique*, and indifferent actions, (though they be never done *without Reason*) yet their principall scope, and marke is the glory of God, and though they seeme but *Morall*, or *Civill*, or *domestique*, yet they have a deeper tincture, a heavenly nature, a relation *to God*, in them.

SERMON XXXVIII

St. Pauls. Oct. 13th, 1622

[p. 352]

A PAINTER can cardly diminish or contract an Elephant into so little a forme, but that that Elephant, when it is at the least, will still be greater than an Ant at the life, and the greatest. Sinne hath diminished man shrowdly, and brought him into a narrower compasse; but yet, his *naturall immortality*, (his soule cannot dye) and his *spirituall possibility*, even to the last gaspe, of spending that immortality in the kingdome of glory, and living for ever with God, (for otherwise, our immortality were the heaviest part of our curse) exalt this valley, this clod of earth, to a noble

heigth. How ill husbands then of this dignity are we by *sinne*, to forfeit it by submitting our selves to inferior things! either to *gold*, than which every worme, (because a worme hath life, and gold hath none) is in nature, more estimable, and more precious: Or, to that which is lesse than gold, to *Beauty*; for there went neither labour, nor study, nor cost to the making of that; (the Father cannot diet himselfe so, nor the mother so, as to be sure of a faire child) but it is a thing that hapned by chance, wheresoever it is; and, as there are Diamonds of divers waters, so men enthrall themselves in one clime to a black, in another to a white beauty. To that which is lesse than *gold* or *Beauty, voice, opinion, fame, honour,* we sell our selves. And though the good opinion of good men, by good ways, be worth our study, yet popular applause, and the voice of inconsiderate men, is too cheape a price to set our selves at. And yet, it is hardly got too; for as a ship that lies in harbour within land, sometimes needs most of the points of the Compasse, to bring her forth: so if a man surrender himselfe wholly to the opinion of other men, and have not his *Criterium,* his touchstone within him, he will need both *North* and *South,* all the points of the Compasse, the breath of all men; because, as there are contrary Elements in every body, so there are contrary factions in every place, and when one side cries him up, the other will depresse him, and he shall, (if not *shipwrack*) lie *still.* But yet we doe forfeit our dignity, for that which is lesse than all, than *Gold,* than *Beauty,* than *Honour;* for *sinne;* sinne which is but a privation, (as darknesse is but a privation) and privations are nothing.

SERMON XL

St. Pauls.

I

[p. 366]

I BRING not a *Star-chamber* with me up into the Pulpit, to punish a *forgery,* if you counterfeit a zeale in coming hither now; nor an *Exchequer,* to punish usurious contracts, though made in the Church; nor a high *Commission,* to punish incontinencies, if they be promoted by wanton interchange of looks, in this place. Onely by my prayers, which he hath promised to accompany and prosper in his service, I can diffuse his overshadowing Spirit over all the corners of this Congregation, and pray that *Publican,* that stands below afar off, and dares not lift his eyes to heaven, to receive a chearfull confidence, that his sinnes are forgiven him; and pray that *Pharisee,* that stands above, and onely thanks God, that he is not like other men, to believe himself to be, if not a rebellious, yet an unprofitable servant. I can only tell them, that neither of them is in the right way of reconciliation to God, *Nec qui impugnant gratiam, nec qui superbè gratias agunt,* neither he who by a diffidence hinders the working of Gods grace, nor he that thanks God in such a fashion, as though all that he had received, were not of meer mercy, but between a *debt* and a *benefit,* and that he had either merited before, or paid God after, in pious works, for all, and for more than he hath received at Gods hand.

2 [p. 370]

What an Organe hath that man tuned, how hath he brought all things in the world to a Comfort, and what a blessed Anthem doth he sing to that Organe, that is at peace with God! His Rye-bread is *Manna,* and his Beefe is *Quailes,* his day-labours are thrustings at the narrow gate into Heaven, and his night watchings are extasies and evocations of his soule into the presence and communion of Saints, his sweat is *Pearls,* and his bloud is *Rubies,* it is at peace with God. No man that is at suite in himselfe, no man that carrieth a *Westminster* in his bosome, and is *Plaintiffe* and *Defendant* too, no man that serveth himself with [a] Process out of his owne Conscience, for every nights pleasure that he taketh, in the morning, and for every dayes pound that he getteth, in the evening, hath any of the pleasure, or profit, that may be had in this life; nor any that is not at peace with God. That peace we bring you; how will you receive us?

3 [p. 372]

Amongst *naturall Creatures,* because howsoever they differ in bignesse, yet they have some proportion to one another, we consider that some very little creatures, contemptible in themselves, are yet called enemies to great creatures, as the Mouse is to the Elephant. (For the greatest Creature is not *Infinite,* nor the least is not *Nothing.*) But shall man, betweene whom and nothing, there went but a word, *Let us make Man,* That Nothing, which is infinitely lesse than a Mathematicall point, than an imaginary Atome, shall this Man, this yesterdayes Nothing, this to morrow worse than Nothing, be capable of that honour, that *dishonourable honour,* that confounding honour, to be the enemy of God, of God who is not onely a multiplied Elephant, millions of Elephants multiplied into one, but a multiplied World, a multiplied All, All that can be conceived by us, infinite many times over; Nay, (if we may dare to say so,) a multiplied God, a God that hath the Millions of the Heathens gods in himselfe alone, shall this man be an enemy to this God? Man cannot be allowed so high a sinne as enmity with God. The Devil himselfe is but a *slave* to God, and shall Man be called his enemy? It is true, if we consider the infinite disproportion between them, he cannot; but to many sad purposes, and in many heavy applications Man is an enemy to God. *Job* could goe no higher in expressing his misery, *Why hidest thou thy face, and holdest me for thine enemy?* and againe, *Behold, he findeth occasions against me, and counteth me for his enemy.* So Man is an enemy to God; And then to adhere to an enemy, is to become an enemy; for Man to adhere to Man, to ascribe any thing to the power of his *naturall faculties,* to thinke of any beame of clearnesse in his own understanding, or any line of rectitude in his owne will, this is to accumulate and multiply enmities against God, and to assemble and muster up more, and more m[e]n, to fight against God.

SERMON XLII

St. Pauls. In the Evening. Nov. 23rd, 1628

[p. 390]

HE that oppresses the poor, digs in a dunghill for wormes; And he departs from that posture, which God, in nature gave him, that is, *erect,* to look upward; for his eye is always down, upon them, *that lie in the dust,* under his feet. Certainly, he that seares up himselfe, and makes himselfe insensible of the cries, and curses of the poor here in this world, does but prepare himselfe for the *howlings,* and *gnashings of teeth,* in the world to come. It is the Serpents taste, the Serpents diet, *Dust shalt thou eate all the days of thy life;* and he feeds but on dust, that oppresses the poor. And as there is evidently, more *inhumanity,* more violation of *nature,* in this oppression, than in emulation, so may there well seem to be more *impiety,* and more violation of *God* himselfe, by that word, which the holy Ghost chooses in the next place, which is *Reproach, He that oppresses the poor, reproaches his Maker.*

SERMON XLIV

St. Paul's Crosse. Nov. 22nd, 1629

I   [p. 416]

BELOVED, there is an *inward Joy,* there is an *outward dignity* and reverence, that accompanies *Riches,* and the *Godly,* the righteous man is not incapable of these; Nay, they belong rather to him, than to the ungodly: *Non decent stultum divitiæ,* (as the Vulgate reades that place) *Riches doe not become a fool.* But because, for all that, though Riches doe not *become* a fool, yet *fools doe become rich;* our Translations read that place thus: *joy, pleasure, delight, is not seemly for a fool;* Though the fool, the ungodly man, may bee rich, yet a right joy, a holy delight in riches, belongs onely to the wise, to the righteous. The Patriarchs in the Old Testament, many examples in the New, are testimonies to us of the compatibility of riches, and righteousnesse; that they may, that they have often met in one person. For, is fraud, and circumvention so sure a way, of attaining Gods blessings, as industry, and conscientiousnesse is? Or is God so likely to concurre with the fraudulent, the deceitfull man, as with the laborious, and religious? Was not *Ananias,* with his disguises, more suddenly destroyed, than *Job,* and more irrecoverably? And cannot a *Star-chamber,* or an *Exchequer,* leave an ungodly man as poor, as a *storm at sea,* in a ship-wracke, or a *fire at land,* in a lightning, can doe the godly? Murmure not, be not scandalized, nor offended in him, if God hath exposed the riches of this world, as well, rather to the godly, than the wicked.

2 [pp. 420-422]

Blessednesse it selfe, is God himselfe; our blessednesse is our possession; our union with God. In what consists this? A great limbe of the Schoole with their *Thomas,* place this blessednesse, this union with God, *In visione,* in this, That in heaven *I shall see God,* see God essentially, *God face to face,* God as he is. We do not see one another so, in this world; In this world we see but outsides; In heaven I shall see God, and God essentially. But then another great branch of the Schoole, with their *Scotus,* place this blessednesse, this union with God, *in Amore,* in this, that in heaven, I shall love God. Now love presumes knowledge; for *Amari nisi nota non possunt,* we can love nothing, but that which we do, or think we do understand. There, in heaven, I shall *know* God, so, as that I shall be admitted, not onely to an *Adoration* of God, to an *admiration* of God, to a *prosternation,* and reverence before God, but to an *affection,* to an office, of more familiarity towards God, of more equality with God, I shall *love* God. But even love it selfe, as noble a passion as it is, is but a paine, except we enjoy that we love; and therefore another branch of the Schoole, with their *Aureolus,* place this blessednesse, this union of our souls with God, *in Gaudio,* in our joy, that is, in our enjoying of God. In this world we enjoy nothing; enjoying presumes perpetuity; and here, all things are fluid, transitory: There I shall enjoy, and possesse for ever, God himself. But yet, every one of these, to *see* God, or to *love* God, or to *enjoy* God, have seemed to some too narrow to comprehend this blessednesse, beyond which, nothing can be proposed; and therefore another limbe of the Schoole, with their *Bonaventure,* place this blessednesse *in all these* together. And truly, if any of those did exclude any of these, so, as that I might *see* God, and not *love* him, or *love* God, and not *enjoy* him, it could not well be called *blessednesse;* but he that hath any one of these, hath every one, all: And therefore the greatest part concurre, and safely, *In visione,* That vision is *beatification,* to see God, as he is, is that blessednesse.

There then, in heaven, I shall have *continuitatem Intuendi;* It is not onely *vision,* but *Intuition,* not onely a seeing, but a beholding, a contemplating of God, and that *in Continuitate,* I shall have an un-interrupted, an un-intermitted, an un-discontinued sight of God; I shall looke, and never looke off; not looke, and looke againe, as here, but looke, and looke still, for that is, *Continuitas intuendi.* There my soule shall have *Inconcussam quietem;* we need owe *Plato* nothing; but we may thank *Plato* for this expression, if he meant so much by this *Inconcussa quies,* That in heaven my soule shall sleep, not onely without trouble, and startling, but without rocking, without any other help, than that peace, which is in it selfe; My soule shall be thoroughly awake, and thoroughly asleep too; still busie, active, diligent, and yet still at rest. But the Apostle will exceed the Philosopher, St. *Paul* will exceed *Plato,* as he does when he sayes, *I shall be unus spiritus cum Deo,* I shall be still but the servant of my God, and yet I shall be *the same spirit with that God.* When? *Dies quem tanquam supremum reformidas, æterni natalis est,* sayes the Morall mans Oracle, *Seneca.* Our last day is our first day, our *Saturday* is our *Sunday,* our *Eve* is our *Holyday,* our *sun-setting* is our *morning,* the day of our death, is the first day of our eternall life. The next day after that, which is the day of judgement, *Veniet dies, quae me mihi revelabit,* comes that day that shall show me to my selfe; here I never saw my selfe, but in disguises: There, Then, I shall see my selfe, and see God too. *Totam lucem, et Totus lux aspiciam;* I shall see the whole light; Here I see some parts of the ayre enlightned by the Sunne, but I do not see the whole light of the Sunne; There I shal see God intirely, all God, *totam lucem,* and *totus lux,* I my self shal be al light to see that light by. Here, I have one faculty enlightned, and another left in darknesse; mine *understanding* sometimes cleared, my *will,* at the same time perverted. There, I shall be all light, no shadow upon me; my soule invested with the *light of joy,* and my body in the *light of glory.* How glorious is God, as he looks down upon us, through the Sunne! How glorious in that glasse of his! How glorious is God, as he looks out amongst us through *the King!* How glorious in that Image of his! How glorious is God, as he calls up our eyes to him, in the beauty, and splendor, and service of the Church! How glorious in that spouse of his! But how glorious shall I conceive this light to be, *cum suo loco viderim,* when I shall see it, in his owne place. In that Spheare, which though a Spheare, is a Center too; In that place, which, though a place, is all, and every where. I shall see it, in the face of that God, who is all face, all manifestation, all Innotescence to me, (for, *facies Dei est, qua Deus nobis innotescit,* that's Gods face to us, by which God manifests himselfe to us) I shall see this light in his face, who is all face, and yet all hand, all application, and communication, and delivery of all himselfe to all his Saints. This is *Beatitudo in Auge,* blessednesse in the Meridionall height, blessednesse in the South point, in a perpetuall Summer solstice, beyond which nothing can be proposed, to see God so, Then, There. And yet the farmers of heaven and hell, the merchants of soules, *the Romane Church,* make this blessednesse, but an under degree, but a kinde of apprentiship; after they have beatified, declared a man to be blessed in the fruition of God in heaven, if that man, in that inferiour state doe good service to that Church, that they see much profit will rise, by the devotion, and concurrence of men, to the worship of that person, then they will proceed to a *Canonization;* and so, he that in his *Novitiat,* and years of probation was but blessed *Ignatius,* and blessed *Xaxier,* is lately become Saint *Xavier,* and Saint *Ignatius.* And so they pervert the right order, and method, which is first to come to *Sanctification,* and then to *Beatification,* first to holinesse, and then to blessednesse. And in this method, our blessed God bee pleased to proceed with us, by the operation of his holy Spirit, to bring us to *Sanctification* here, and by the merits and intercession of his glorious Sonne, to *Beatification* hereafter. That so not being offended in him, but resting in those meanes and seales, of reconciliation, which thou hast instituted in thy Church, wee may have life, and life more abundantly, life of grace here, and life of glory there, in that kingdome, which thy Sonne, our Saviour Christ Jesus hath purchased for us, with the inestimable price of his incorruptible bloud. *Amen.*

SERMON XLVII

St. Dunstans. 'Upon the commemoration of a Parishioner, a Benefactor to that Parish.' [*after* 1624]

I [pp. 442-443]

PEACE is a blessed state, but it must be the peace of God; for, *Simeon* and *Levi* are brethren, they agree well enough together; but they are instruments of evill; and, in that case, the better agreement, the worse. So, war is a fearfull state; but not so, if it be the war of God, undertaken for his cause, or by his Word. Many times, a State suffers by the security of a Peace, and gains by the watchfulness of a War. Wo be to that man that is so at peace, as that the spirit fights not against the flesh in him; and wo to them too, who would make them friends, or reconcile them, betweene whom, God hath perpetuated an everlasting war, The seed of the woman, and the seed of the Serpent, Christ and *Beliall*, Truth and Superstition. Till God proclaimed a warre between them, the Serpent did easily overthrow them, but therefore God brought it to a war, that man might stand upon his guard. And so it was a Mercy.

But the greatest mercy is in the last, and that which belongs most directly, (though all conduce pertinently and usefully to our present occasion;) *Dust shalt thou eat all the days of thy life.* He must eat dust, that is, our bodies, and carnall affections; Hee was at a richer diet, he was in better pasture before; before, he fed upon souls too; But for that his head was bruised, in the promise of a Messias, who delivers our souls from his tyranny; But the dust, the body, that body, which for all the precious ransome, and the rich, and large mercy of the Messias, must die, that dust is left to the Serpent, to Satan, that is, to that dissolution, and that putrefaction, which he hath induced upon man, in death. He eats but our dust, in our death, when he hath brought us to that; that is a mercy; nay he eats up our dust before our death, which is a greater mercy; our carnal affections, our concupiscencies are eaten up, and devoured by him; and so, even his eating is a sweeping, a cleansing, a purging of us. Many times we are the better for his tentations. My discerning a storm, makes me put on a cloak. My discerning a tentation, makes me see my weaknesse, and fly to my strength. Nay, I am somtimes the safer, and the readier for a victory, by having been overcome by him. The sense, and the remorse of a sin, after I have fallen into it, puts me into a better state, and establishes better conditions between God and me than were before, when I felt no tentations to sin.

2   [p. 445]

In this state of dust, and so in the territory of the Serpent, the Tyrant of the dead, lies this dead brother of ours, and hath lien some years, who occasions our meeting now, and yearly upon this day, and whose soul, we doubt not, is in the hands of God, who is the God of the living. And having gathered a good *Gomer* of Manna, a good measure of temporall blessings in this life, and derived a fair measure thereof, upon them, whom nature and law directed it upon, (and in whom we beseech God to blesse it) hath also distributed something to the poor of this Parish, yearly, this day, and something to a meeting for the conserving of neighbourly love, and something for this exercise. In which, no doubt, his intention was not so much to be yearly remembred himself, as that his posterity, and his neighbours might be yearly remembred to doe as he had done. For, this is

truly to glorifie God in his Saints, to sanctifie our selves in their examples;
To celebrate them, is to imitate them. For, as it is probably conceived, and
agreeably to Gods Justice, that they that write wanton books, or make
wanton pictures, have additions of torment, as often as other men are corrupted with their books, or their pictures: so may they, who have left
permanent examples of good works, well be beleeved, to receive additions
of glory and joy, when others are led by that to do the like: And so, they
who are extracted, and derived from him, and they who dwelt about him,
may assist their own happiness, and enlarge his, by following his good
example in good proportions. Amen.

PASSAGES FROM TWENTY-SIX SERMONS

SERMON IV

Whitehall. Before the King. Feb. 16th, 1620/21

[pp. 57-58]

I T is not enough to hear Sermons; it is not enough to live a morall honest
life; but take it in the midst, and that extends to all; for there is no believing without hearing, nor working without believing. Be pleased to consider
this great work of believing, in the matter, what it was that was to be
believed: That that Jesus, whose age they knew, must be antidated so far,
as that they must believe him to be elder than *Abraham:* That that Jesus,
whose Father and Mother, and Brothers and Sisters, they knew, must be
believed to be of another Family, and to have a Father in another place;
and yet he to be as old as his Father; And to have another proceeding
from him, and yet he to be no older than that person who proceeded from
him: That that Jesus, whom they knew to be that Carpenters Son, and
knew his work, must be believ'd to have set up a frame, that reached to
heaven, out of which no man could, and in which any man might be saved:
was it not as easie to believe, that those teares which they saw upon his
cheeks, were Pearles; that those drops of Blood, which they saw upon his
back were Rubies; That that spittle, which they saw upon his face, was
ennamel: that those hands which they saw buffet him, were reached out
to place him in a Throne: And that that Voyce which they heard cry,
Crucifige, Crucifie him, was a *Vivat Rex, Long live Jesus of Nazareth King
of the Jewes;* As to believe that from that man, that worm, and no man,
ingloriously traduced as a Conjuror, ingloriously apprehended as a Thief,
ingloriously executed a Traytor; they should look for glory, and all glory,
and everlasting glory? And from that melancholick man, who was never

seen to laugh in all his life, and *whose soul was heavy unto death;* they
should look for joy, and all joy, and everlasting joy: And for salvation,
and everlasting salvation from him, who could not save himself from the
Ignominy, from the Torment, from the Death of the Crosse?

SERMON V

Whitehall. To the King. Feb. 12th, 1629/30

[p. 61]

I HAVE seen Minute-glasses; Glasses so short-liv'd. If I were to preach
upon this Texte, to such a glass, it were enough for half the Sermon;
enough to show the worldly man his Treasure, and the Object of his heart
(*for, where your Treasure is, there will your Heart be also*) to call his
eye to that Minute-glass, and to tell him, There flows, there flies your
Treasure, and your Heart with it. But if I had a Secular Glass, a Glass
that would run an age; if the two Hemispheres of the World were composed in the form of such a Glass, and all the World calcin'd and burnt to
ashes, and all the ashes, and sands, and atoms of the World put into that
Glass, it would not be enough to tell the godly man what his Treasure,
and the Object of his Heart is. A Parrot, or a Stare, docile Birds, and of
pregnant imitation, will sooner be brought to relate to us the wisdom of
a Council Table, than any *Ambrose,* or any *Chrysostome,* Men that have
Gold and Honey in their Names, shall tell us what the Sweetness, what
the Treasure of Heaven is, and what that mans peace, that hath set his
Heart upon that Treasure.

SERMON VI

Whitehall. April 21st, 1616

[pp. 82-83]

HOW desperate a state art thou in, if nothing will convert thee, but a
speedie execution, after which, there is no possibility, no room left for a
Conversion! God is *the Lord of hosts,* and he can proceed by Martial
Law: he can hang thee upon the next tree; he can choak thee with a crum,
with a drop, at a voluptuous feast; he can sink down the Stage and the
Player, The bed of wantonness, and the wanton actor, into the jaws of
the earth, into the mouth of hell: he can surprise thee, even in the act
of sin; and dost thou long for such a speedy execution, for such an expedition? Thou canst not lack Examples, that he hath done so upon others,

and will no proof serve thee, but a speedy judgement upon thy self? Scatter
thy thoughts no farther then; contract them in thy self, and consider Gods
speedy execution upon thy soul, and upon thy body, and upon thy soul
and body together. Was not Gods judgement executed speedily enough
upon thy soul, when in the same instant that it was created, and conceiv'd,
and infus'd, it was put to a necessity of contracting Original sin, and so
submitted to the penalty of *Adam's* disobedience, the first minute? Was
not Gods judgement speedily enough executed upon thy body, if before
it had any temporal life, it had a spiritual death; a sinful conception,
before any inanimation? If hereditary diseases from thy parents, Gouts
and Epilepsies, were in thee, before the diseases of thine own purchase,
the effects of thy licentiousness and thy riot; and that from the first
minute that thou beganst to live, thou beganst to die too? Are not the
judgements of God speedily enough executed upon thy soul and body
together, every day, when as soon as thou commitst a sin, thou ar[t]
presently left to thine Impenitence, to thine Insensibleness, and Obduration? Nay, the judgement is more speedy than so: for, that very sin it
self, was a punishment of thy former sins.

SERMON XV

Whitehall. Feb. 29, 1627/8

I [p. 205]

H E that will dy with Christ upon Good-Friday, must hear his own bell
toll all Lent; he that will be partaker of his passion at last, must conform
himself to his discipline of prayer and fasting before. Is there any man,
that in his chamber hears a bell toll for another man, and does not kneel
down to pray for that dying man? and then when his charity breaths out
upon another man, does he not also reflect upon himself, and dispose himself as if he were in the state of that dying man? We begin to hear Christs
bell toll now, and is not our bell in the chime? We must be in his grave,
before we come to his resurrection, and we must be in his death-bed before
we come to his grave: we must do as he did, fast and pray, before we can
say as he said, that *In manus tuas,* Into thy hands O Lord I commend my
Spirit. You would not go into a Medicinal Bath without some preparatives; presume not upon that Bath, the blood of Christ Jesus, in the Sacrament then, without preparatives neither. Neither say to your selves, we
shall have preparatives enough, warnings enough, many more Sermons
before it come to that, and so it is too soon yet; you are not sure you
shall have more; not sure you shall have all this; not sure you shall be

affected with any. If you be, when you are, remember that as in that good
Custome in these Cities, you hear cheerful street musick in the winter
mornings, but yet there was a sad and doleful bell-man, that wak'd you,
and call'd upon you two or three hours before that musick came; so for
all that blessed musick which the servants of God shall present to you in
this place, it may be of use, that a poor bell-man wak'd you before, and
though but by his noyse, prepared you for their musick.

2   [pp. 216 (214)-219]

Here I shall only present to you two Pictures, two pictures in little:
two pictures of dying men; and every man is like one of these, and may
know himself by it; he that dies in the Bath of a peaceable, and he that
dies upon the wrack of a distracted conscience. When the devil imprints
in a man, *a mortuum me esse non curo,* I care not though I were dead,
it were but a candle blown out, and there were an end of it all, where the
Devil imprints that imagination: God will imprint an *Emori nolo,* a loath-
ness to die, and fearful apprehension at his transmigration: As God expresses the bitterness of death, in an ingemination, *morte morietur,* in a
conduplication of deaths, he shall die, and die, die twice over; So
ægrotando ægrotabit, in sicknesse he shall be sick, twice sick, body-sick
and soul-sick too, sense-sick and conscience-sick together; when, as the
sinnes of his body have cast sicknesses and death upon his Soule, so the
inordinate sadnesse of his Soule, shall aggravate and actuate the sicknesse
of his body. His Physitian ministers, and wonders it works not; He imputes that to flegme, and ministers against that, and wonders again that
it works not: He goes over all the humors, and all his Medicines, and
nothing works, for there lies at his Patients heart a dampe that hinders
the concurrence of all his faculties, to the intention of the Physitian, or
the virtue of the Physick. Loose not, O blessed Apostle, thy question upon
this Man, *O Death where is thy Sting? O Grave where is thy victory?* for
the sting of Death is in every limb of his body, and his very body, is a
victorious grave upon his Soule: And as his Carcas and his Coffin shall
lie equally insensible in his grave, so his Soule, which is but a Carcas,
and his body, which is but a Coffin of that Carcas, shall be equally miserable upon his Death-bed; And Satan's Commissions upon him shall not
be signed by Succession, as upon *Job,* first against his goods, and then
his Servants, and then his children, and then himselfe; but not at all upon
his life; but he shall apprehend all at once, Ruine upon himselfe and all
his, ruine upon himselfe and all him, even upon his life; both his lives,
the life of this, and the life of the next world too. Yet a drop would
redeeme a shoure, and a Sigh now a Storme then: Yet a teare from the
eye, would save the bleeding of the heart, and a word from the mouth

now, a roaring, or (which may be worse) a silence of consternation, of stupefaction, or obduration at that last houre. Truly, if the death of the wicked ended in Death, yet to scape that manner of death were worthy a Religious life. To see the house fall, and yet be afraid to goe out of it; To leave an injur'd world, and meet an incensed God; To see oppression and wrong in all thy professions, and to foresee ruine and wastefulnesse in all thy Posterity; and Lands gotten by one sin in the Father, molder away by another in the Sonne; to see true figures of horror, and ly, and fancy worse; To begin to see thy sins but then, and finde every sin (at first sight) in the proportion of a Gyant, able to crush thee into despair; To see the Blood of Christ, imputed, not to thee, but to thy Sinnes; To see Christ crucified, and not crucifyed for thee, but crucified by thee; To heare this blood speake, not better things, than the blood of *Abel,* but lowder for vengeance than the blood of *Abel* did; This is his picture that hath been Nothing, that hath done nothing, that hath proposed no *Stephen,* No Law to regulate, No example to certifie his Conscience: But to him that hath done this, Death is but a Sleepe.

Many have wondred at that note of Saint *Chrysostom's,* That till Christ's time death was called death, plainly, literally death, but after Christ, death was called but sleepe; for, indeede, in the old-Testament before Christ, I thinke there is no one metaphor so often used, as Sleepe for Death, and that the Dead are said to Sleepe: Therefore wee wonder sometimes, that Saint *Chrysostome* should say so: But this may be that which that holy Father intended in that Note, that they in the old-Testament, who are said to have slept in Death, are such as then, by Faith, did apprehend, and were fixed upon Christ; such as were all the good men of the old-Testament, and so there will not bee many instances against Saint *Chrysostome's* note, That to those that die in Christ, Death is but a Sleepe; to all others, Death is Death, literally Death. Now of this dying Man, that dies in Christ, that dies the Death of the Righteous, that embraces Death as a Sleepe, must wee give you a Picture too.

There is not a minute left to do it; not a minutes sand; Is there a minutes patience? Bee pleased to remember that those Pictures which are deliver'd in a minute, from a print upon a paper, had many dayes, weeks, Moneths time for the graving of those Pictures in the Copper; So this Picture of that dying Man, that dies in Christ, that dies the death of the Righteous, that embraces Death as a Sleepe, was graving all his life; All his publique actions were the lights, and all his private the shadowes of this Picture. And when this Picture comes to the Presse, this Man to the streights and agonies of Death, thus he lies, thus he looks, this he is. His understanding and his will is all one faculty; He understands Gods purpose upon him, and he would not have God's purpose turned any other way; hee sees God will dissolve him, and he would faine be dissolved, to be with Christ; His understanding and his will is all one faculty; His memory and his foresight are fixt, and concentred upon one object, upon goodnesse; Hee remembers that hee hath proceeded in the sinceritie of a good Conscience in all the wayes of his calling, and he foresees that his good name shall have the Testimony, and his Posterity the support of the good men of this world; His sicknesse shall be but a fomentation to supple and open his Body for the issuing of his Soule; and his Soule shall goe forth, not as one that gave over his house, but as one that travelled to see and learne better Architecture, and meant to returne and re-edifie that house, according to those better Rules: And as those thoughts which possesse us most awake, meete us againe when we are asleepe; So his holy-thoughts, having been alwaies conversant upon the directing of his family, the education of his Children, the discharge of his place, the safety of the State, the happinesse of the King all his life; when he is faln asleepe in Death, all his Dreames in that blessed Sleepe, all his devotions in heaven shall be upon the same Subjects, and he shal solicite him that sits upon the Throne, and the Lamb, God for Christ Jesus sake, to blesse all these with his particular blessings: for, so God giveth his beloved sleep, so as that they enjoy the next world and assist this.

So then, the Death of the Righteous is a sleepe; first, as it delivers them to a present rest. Now men sleepe not well fasting; Nor does a fasting Conscience, a Conscience that is not nourish'd with a Testimony of having done well, come to this Sleepe; but *dulcis somnus operanti*, The sleepe of a labouring man is sweete. To him that laboureth in his calling, even this sleepe of Death is welcome. *When thou lyest downe thou shalt not be afraid,* saith *Salomon;* when thy Physician sayes, Sir, you must keepe your bed, thou shalt not be afraid of that sick-bed; And then it followes, *And thy sleepe shall be sweet unto thee;* Thy sicknesse welcome, and thy death too; for, in those two *David* seems to involve all, *I will both lay me downe in Peace and sleep;* imbrace patiently my death-bed and Death it selfe.

So then this death is a sleepe, as it delivers us to a present Rest; And then, lastly, it is so also as it promises a future waiting in a glorious Resurrection. To the wicked it is far from both: Of them God sayes, *I will make them drunke, and they shall sleepe a perpetuall sleepe and not awake;* They shall have no part in the *Second Resurrection.* But for them that have slept in Christ, as Christ sayd of *Lazarus,* Lazarus *Sleepeth, but I goe that I may wake him out of sleep,* he shall say to his father; Let me goe that I may wake them who have slept so long in expectation of my coming: And *Those that sleep in Jesus Christ* (saith the Apostle) *will bring God with him;* not only fetch them out of the dust when he comes, but bring them with him, that is, declare that they have beene in his hands ever since they departed out of this world. They shall awake as *Jacob* did, and say as *Jacob* said, *Surely the Lord is in this place,* and *this is no other but the house of God, and the gate of heaven,* And into that gate they shall enter, and in that house they shall dwell, where there shall be no Cloud nor Sun, no darknesse nor dazling, but one equall light, no noyse nor silence, but one equall musick, no fears nor hopes, but one equal pos-session, no foes nor friends, but an equall communion and Identity, no ends nor beginnings; but one equall eternity. Keepe us Lord so awake in the duties of our Callings, that we may thus sleepe in thy Peace, and wake in thy glory, and change that infallibility which thou affordest us here, to an Actuall and undeterminable possession of that Kingdome which thy Sonne our Saviour Christ Jesus hath purchased for us, with the inestimable price of his incorruptible Blood. *Amen.*

SERMON XXI

St. Dunstans. 'The First Sermon after Our Dispersion by the Sickness.' Jan. 15th, 1625/6

1   [p. 295]

M E N whose lust carried them into the jaws of infection in lewd houses, and seeking one sore perished with another; men whose rapine and covet-ousness broke into houses, and seeking the Wardrobes of others, found their own winding-sheet, in the infection of that house where they stole their own death; men who sought no other way to divert sadness, but strong drink in riotous houses, and there drank up *Davids* cup of Maledic-tion, the cup of Condemned men, of death, in the infection of that place. For these men that died in their sins, that sinned in their dying, that sought and hunted after death so sinfully, we have little comfort of such men, in the phrase of this Text, *They were dead;* for they are dead still: As *Moses* said of the *Egyptians,* I am afraid we may say of these men, *We shall see them no more for ever.*

2   [pp. 297-298]

As between two men of equal age, if one sleep, and the other wake all night, yet they rise both of an equal age in the morning; so they who shall have slept out a long night of many ages in the grave, and they who shall be caught up in the clouds, to meet the Lord Jesus in the aire, at the last day, shall enter all at once in their bodies into Heaven. No antiquity, no seniority for their bodies; neither can their souls who went before, be said to have been there a minute before ours, because we shall all be in a place that reckons not by minutes. Clocks and Sun-dials were but a late invention upon earth; but the Sun it self, and the earth it self, was but a late invention in heaven. God had been an infinite, a super-infinite, an unimaginable space, millions of millions of unimaginable spaces in heaven, before the Creation. And our afternoon shall be as long as Gods forenoon; for, as God never saw beginning, so we shall never see end; but they whom we tread upon now, and we whom others shall tread upon hereafter, shall meet at once, where, though we were dead, dead in our several houses, dead in a sinful *Egypt,* dead in our family, dead in our selves, dead in the Grave, yet we shall be received, with that consolation, and glorious consolation, you were dead, but are alive. *Enter ye blessed into the Kingdom, prepared for you, from the beginning. Amen.*

SERMON XXIV

Paul's Cross. 'To the Lords of the Council, and other Honorable Persons. It being the Anniversary of the King's coming to the Crown, and his Majesty being then gone into Scotland.' March 24th, 1616/7

[pp. 332-333]

s o also must he that affects this pureness of heart, and studies the preserving of it, sweep down every cobweb that hangs about it. Scurrile and obscene language; yea, mis-interpretable words, such as may bear an ill sense; pleasurable conversation, and all such little entanglings, which though he think too weak to hold him, yet they foul him. And let him that is subject to these *smaller sins,* remember, that as a spider builds always where he knows there is most access and haunt of flies, so the Devil that hath cast these light cobwebs into thy heart, knows that that heart is made of vanities and levities; and he that gathers into his treasure whatsoever thou wast'st out of thine, how negligent soever thou be, he keeps thy reckoning exactly, and will produce against thee at last as many lascivious glaunces as shall make up an Adultery, as many covetous wishes as shall make up a Robery, as many angry words as shall make up a Murder; and thou shalt have dropt and crumbled away thy soul, with as much irrecoverableness, as if thou hadst poured it out all at once; and thy merry sins, thy laughing sins, shall grow to be crying sins, even in the ears of God; and though thou drown thy soul here, drop after drop, it shall not burn spark after spark, but have all the fire, and all at once, and all eternally, in one intire and intense torment.

SERMON XXV

The Spital. April 22, 1622

O U R God is not out of breath, because he hath blown one tempest, and swallowed a Navy: Our God hath not burnt out his eyes, because he hath looked upon a Train of Powder: In the light of Heaven, and in the darkness of hell, he sees alike; he sees not onely all Machinations of hands, when things come to action; but all Imaginations of hearts, when they are in their first Consultations; past, and present, and future, distinguish not his *Quando;* all is one time to him: Mountains and Vallies, Sea and Land, distinguish not his *Ubi;* all is one place to him: *When I begin,* says God to *Eli, I will make an end;* not onely that all Gods purposes shall have their certain end, but that even then, when he begins, he makes an end: from the very beginning, imprints an infallible assurance, that whom he loves, he loves to the end: as a Circle is printed all at once, so his beginning and ending is all one.

The drowning of the first world, and the repairing that again; the burning of this world, and establishing another in heaven, do not so much strain a mans Reason, as the Creation, a Creation of all out of nothing. For, for the repairing of the world after the Flood, compared to the Creation, it was eight to nothing; eight persons to begin a world upon, then; but in the Creation, none. And for the glory which we receive in the next world, it is (in some sort) as the stamping of a print upon a Coyn; the metal is there already, a body and a soul to receive glory; but at the Creation, there was no soul to receive glory, no body to receive a soul, no stuff, no matter, to make a body of. The less any thing is, the less we know it: how invisible, how [un]intelligible a thing then, is this *Nothing!* We say in the School, *Deus cognoscibilior Angelis,* We have better means to know the nature of God, than of Angels, because God hath appeared and manifested himself more in actions, than Angels have done: we know what they are, by knowing what they have done; and it is very little that is related to us what Angels have done: what then is there that can bring this Nothing to our understanding? what hath that done? A Leviathan, a Whale, from a grain of Spawn; an Oke from a buried Akehorn, is a great; but a great world from nothing, is a strange improvement. We wonder to see a man rise from nothing to a great Estate; but that Nothing is but nothing in comparison; but absolutely nothing, meerly

nothing, is more incomprehensible than any thing, than all things together. It is a state (if a man may call it a state) that the Devil himself in the midst of his torments, cannot wish.

3   [p. 385]

The light of the knowledge of the glory of this world, is a good, and a
great peece of learning. To know, that all the glory of man, is as the flower
of grass: that even the glory, and all the glory, of man, of all mankind,
is but a flower, and but as a flower; somewhat less than the Proto-type,
than the Original, than the flower it self; and all this but as the flower
of grass neither, no very beautiful flower to the eye, no very fragrant
flower to the smell: To know, that for the glory of *Moab, Auferetur*, it
shall be contemned, consumed; and for the glory of *Jacob* it self, *Attenu-
rbitur*, It shall be extenuated, that the glory of Gods enemies shall be
brought to nothing, and the glory of his servants shall be brought low in
this word: To know how near nothing, how meer nothing, all the glory of
this world is, is a good, a great degree of learning.

4   [pp. 389-392]

Some things the Angels do know by the dignity of their Nature, by their
Creation, which we know not; as we know many things which inferior
Creatures do not; and such things all the Angels, good and bad know.
Some things they know by the Grace of their confirmation, by which they
have more given them, than they had by Nature in their Creation; and
those things only the Angels that stood, but all they, do know. Some
things they know by Revelation, when God is pleased to manifest them
unto them; and so some of the Angels know that, which the rest, though
confirm'd, doe not know. By Creation, they know as his Subjects; by Confirmation, they know as his servants; by Revelation, they know as his
Councel. Now, *Erimus sicut Angeli*, says Christ, *There we shall be as the
Angels:* The knowledge which I have by Nature, shall have no Clouds;
here it hath: that which I have by Grace, shall have no reluctation, no
resistance; here it hath: That which I have by Revelation, shall have no
suspition, no jealousie; here it hath: sometimes it is hard to distinguish
between a respiration from God, and a suggestion from the Devil. There
our curiosity shall have this noble satisfaction, we shall know how the
Angels know, by knowing as they know. We shall not pass from Author,
to Author, as in a Grammar School, nor from Art to Art, as in an University; but, as that General which Knighted this whole Army, God shall
Create us all Doctors in a minute. That great Library, those infinite Volumes of the Books of Creatures, shall be taken away, quite away, no more
Nature; those reverend Manuscripts, written with Gods own hand, the

Scriptures themselves, shall be taken away, quite away; no more preaching, no more reading of the Scriptures, and that great School-Mistress, Experience, and Observation shall be remov'd, no new thing to be done, and in an instant, I shall know more, than they all could reveal unto me. I shall know, not only as I know already, that a Bee-hive, that an Ant-hill is the same Book in *Decimo sexto,* as a Kingdom is in *Folio.* That a flower that lives but a day, is an abridgment of that King, that lives out his threescore and ten yeers; but I shall know too, that all these Ants, and Bees, and Flowers, and Kings, and Kingdoms, howsoever they may be Examples, and Comparisons to one another, yet they are all as nothing, altogether thing, less than nothing, infinitely less than nothing, to that which shall then be the subject of my knowledge, for, *it is the knowledge of the glory of God.*

DEATH'S DUEL

OR, A CONSOLATION TO THE SOULE, AGAINST THE DYING LIFE, AND LIVING DEATH OF THE BODY

Delivered in a Sermon at White-Hall, before the Kings Majesty, in the beginning of Lent [Feb. 25], 1630, Being his last Sermon, and called by his Majesties household The Doctors Owne Funerall Sermon

TO THE READER

[Preface to the 1st edition (1632) by Richard Redmer, the publisher.]

This Sermon was, by Sacred Authoritie, stiled the Authors owne funeral Sermon. Most fitly: whether wee respect the time, or the matter. It was preached not many dayes before his death; as if, having done this, there remained nothing for him to doe, but to die: And the matter is, of Death; the occasion and subject of all funerall Sermons. It hath beene observed of this Reverent Man, That his Faculty in Preaching continually encreased: and, That as hee exceeded others at first; so, at last hee exceeded himselfe. This is his last Sermon; I will not say, it is therefore his best; because, all his were excellent. Yet thus much: A dying Mans words, if they concerne our selves, doe usually make the deepest impression, as being spoken most feelingly, and with least affectation. Now, whom doth it not concerne to learn, both the danger, and benefit of death? Death is every mans enemy, and intends hurt to all; though to many, hee be occasion of greatest goods. This enemy wee must all combate dying;

whom hee living did almost conquer; having discovered the utmost of his power, the utmost of his crueltie. May wee make such use of this and other the like preparatives. That neither death, whensoever it shall come, may seeme terrible; nor life tedious, how long soever it shall last.   R.

PSALME 68. VERS. 20.   *In finè.*

And unto God the (LORD) *belong the issues of death.*
i.e. *From death.*

BUILDINGS stand by the benefit of their *foundations* that susteine and *support* them, and of their *butteresses* that comprehend and *embrace* them, and of their *contignations* that knit and *unite* them: The *foundations* suffer them not to *sinke*, the *butteresses* suffer them not to *swerve*, and the *contignation* and knitting suffers them not to *cleave;* The body of our building is in the former part of this verse: It is this; hee that *is our God* is the *God of salvation; ad salutes*, of salvations in the plurall, so it is in the originall; the *God* that gives us spirituall and temporall salvation too. But of this *building*, the *foundation*, the *butteresses*, the *contignations* are in this part of the *verse*, which constitutes *our text*, and in the three divers *acceptations* of the words amongst our expositors. *Unto God the Lord belong the issues from death.* For *first* the *foundation* of this *building*, (that our *God* is the *God of all salvations*) is laid in this; That *unto* this *God the Lord belong the issues of death*, that is, it is in his power to give us an *issue* and deliverance, even then when wee are brought to the jawes and teeth of death, and to the lippes of that whirlepoole, the grave. And so in this acceptation, this *exitus mortis*, this *issue of death* is *liberatio à morte, a deliverance from death*, and this is the most obvious and most ordinary acceptation of these words, and that upon which our *translation* laies hold, *The issues from death.* And then *secondly* the butteresses that comprehend and settle this building, That hee that is *our God*, is the *God of* all *salvations*, are thus raised; *Unto God the Lord belong the issues of death*, that is, the disposition and *manner of our death:* what kinde of *issue* and *transmigration* wee shall have out of this world, whether prepared or sudden, whether violent or naturall, whether in our perfect senses or shaken and disordered by sicknes; there is no condemnation to bee argued out of that, no Judgement to bee made upon that, for howsoever they dye, *precious in his sight is the death of his saints*, and with him are *the issues of death*, the *wayes* of our *departing* out of this *life* are in his *hands*. And so in this *sense* of the *words*, this *exitus mortis*, the *issue of death*, is *liberatio in morte, A deliverance in death;* Not that God will *deliver us* from *dying*, but that hee will *have a care* of us in the *houre of death*, of what kinde soever our passage be. And in this *sense* and acceptation of the *words*, the naturall frame and contexture doth well and pregnantly administer unto us; And then *lastly* the *contignation* and knitting of this building, that hee that is *our God* is the *God of all salvations*, consists in this, *Unto this God the Lord belong the issues of death*, that is, that this *God* the *Lord* having *united* and knit *both natures in one*, and being *God*, having also *come* into this *world*, in our *flesh*, he could have no other meanes to save us, he could have no other *issue* out of this world, nor *returne* to his former *glory*, but by *death;* And so in this sense, this *exitus mortis*, this *issue of death*, is *liberatio per mortem*, a *deliverance by death*, by the death of this *God* our *Lord Christ Jesus*. And this is Saint *Augustines* acceptation of the words, and those many and great persons that have adhered to him. In all these three lines then, we shall looke upon these words; *First*, as the *God* of *power*, the *Almighty Father* rescues his servants from the jawes of death: *And then* as the *God* of *mercy*, the glorious *Sonne* rescued us, by taking upon himselfe this *issue of death: And then* betweene these two, as the *God* of *comfort*, the *holy Ghost* rescues us from all discomfort by his blessed impressions before hand, that what manner of death soever be ordeined for us, yet this *exitus mortis* shall bee *introitus in vitam*, our *issue in death* shall be an *entrance into everlasting life*. And these three considerations, our deliverance *à morte, in morte, per mortem, from death, in death, and by death*, will abundantly doe all the offices of the *foundations*, of the *butteresses*, of the *contignation* of this our *building;* That he that is our *God*, is the *God of all salvations*, because *unto* this *God the Lord belong the issues of death*.

First, then, we consider this *exitus mortis*, to bee *liberatio à morte*, that with *God* the *Lord* are the *issues of death*, and therefore in all our deaths, and deadly calamities of this life, wee may justly *hope* of a good *issue* from him. And all our *periods* and *transitions* in this life, are so many passages *from death* to *death;* our very *birth* and entrance into this life, is *exitus à morte*, an *issue from death*, for in our mothers *wombe* wee are *dead so*, as that wee doe *not know* wee *live*, not so much as wee doe in our *sleepe*, neither is there any *grave* so close, or so *putrid* a *prison*, as the *wombe* would be unto us, if we stayed in it *beyond* our time, or dyed there *before* our time. In the *grave* the *wormes* doe not kill us, wee *breed* and *feed*, and then *kill* those wormes which wee our selves produc'd. In the wombe the dead *child* kills the *Mother* that conceived it, and is a murtherer, nay a *parricide*, even after it is dead. And if wee bee not dead so in the *wombe*, so as that being dead wee kill her that gave us our first life, our life of *vegetation*, yet wee are dead so, as *Davids Idols* are dead. In the *wombe* wee have *eyes and see not, eares and heare not;* There in the wombe wee are fitted for *workes of darknes,* all the while deprived of light: And there in the *wombe* wee are taught *cruelty,* by being *fed with blood,* and may be *damned,* though we be *never borne.* Of our very making in the *wombe, David* sayes, *I am wonderfully and fearefully made,* and, *Such knowledge is too excellent for me,* for even that *is the Lords doing,* and it *is wonderfull in our eyes; Ipse fecit nos,* it is *hee that hath made us, and not wee our selves* nor our parents neither; *Thy hands have made me and fashioned me round about,* saith *Job,* and (as the *originall word is) thou hast taken paines about me,* and *yet,* says he, *thou doest destroy me.* Though I bee the *Master-peece* of the greatest *Master (man* is so), yet if thou doe no more forme, if thou leave me where thou madest mee, destruction will follow. The *wombe* which should be the *house of life,* becomes *death* it selfe, if *God* leave us there. That which God threatens so often, the *shutting of the womb,* is not so *heavy,* nor so discomfortable a *curse* in the *first,* as in the *latter* shutting, nor in the shutting of *barrennes,* as in the shutting of *weakenes,* when *children are come to the birth,* and there is not *strength to bring forth.*

It is the *exaltation of misery,* to *fall* from a *neare hope* of *happines.* And in that vehement imprecation, the *Prophet* expresses the highest of *Gods* anger, *give them ô Lord, what wilt thou give them?* give them a *miscarying wombe.* Therefore as soone as wee are men, (that is, *inanimated,* quickened in the *womb*) thogh we cannot our selves, our parents have reason to say in our behalf, *wretched man that he is, who shall deliver* him *from this body of death?* for even the *wombe* is a *body of death,* if there bee no deliverer. It must be he that said to *Jeremy,* Before *I formed thee I knew thee,* and *before thou camest out of the wombe I sanctified thee.* Wee are not sure that there was no kinde of shippe nor boate to fish in, nor to passe by, till *God* prescribed *Noah* that absolute *form* of *the Arke.* That word which the *holy Ghost* by *Moses* useth for the *Arke,* is common to all kinde of *boates, Thebah,* and is the same word that *Moses* useth for the *boate* that he was *exposed in, That his mother layed him in an arke of bulrushes.* But we are sure that *Eve* had no *Midwife* when she was *delivered* of *Cain,* therefore shee might well say, *possedi virum à Domino, I have gotten a man from the Lord,* wholly, entirely from the Lord; It is the *Lord* that *enabled* me to *conceive, The Lord* that *infus'd* a *quickening soule* into that conception, the *Lord* that *brought into the world* that which himself *had quickened,* without all this might *Eve* say, My *body had bene* but *the house of death,* and *Domini Domini sunt exitus mortis,* to *God the Lord belong the issues of death.*

But then this *exitus a morte,* is but *introitus in mortem,* this *issue,* this deliverance *from* that *death,* the death of the *wombe,* is an *entrance,* a delivering over to *another death*, the manifold deathes of this *world*. Wee have a winding sheete in our Mothers wombe, which growes with us from our conception, and wee come into the world, wound up in that *winding sheet*, for wee come to *seeke a grave;* And as prisoners discharg'd of actions may lie for fees, so when the *wombe* hath discharg'd us, yet we are bound to it by *cordes* of flesh by such a *string*, as that wee cannot goe thence, nor stay there; wee celebrate our owne funeralls with cries, even at our birth; as though our *threescore and ten years life* were spent in our mothers labour, and our circle made up in the first point thereof, we begge our *Baptisme*, with another *Sacrament*, with *teares;* And we come into a world that lasts many ages, but wee last not; *in domo Patris*, says our *Saviour*, speaking of *heaven, multæ mansiones*, there *are many mansions*, divers and durable, so that if a man cannot possesse a *martyrs* house, (he hath shed no blood for *Christ*) yet hee may have a *Confessors*, he hath bene ready to glorifie *God* in the *shedding of his blood*. And if a woman cannot possesse a *virgins house* (she hath embrac'd the *holy state* of *mariage*) yet she may have a *matrons* house, she hath brought forth and brought up *children in the feare of God*. *In domo patris, in my fathers house*, in heaven there *are many mansions;* but here upon earth the *sonne of man hath not where to lay his head*, sayes he himselfe. *Nonne terram dedit filiis hominum?* how then hath *God given this earth* to the *sonnes of men?* hee hath *given* them *earth* for their *materialls* to bee made of earth, and hee hath given them *earth* for their *grave* and sepulture, to *returne* and resolve to *earth*, but not for their *possession: Here wee have no continuing citty*, nay no *cottage* that continues, nay no persons, no bodies that continue. Whatsoever moved Saint *Jerome* to call the journies of the *Israelites*, in the *wildernes*, mansions; The *word* (the word is *Nasang*) signifies but a *journey*, but a peregrination. Even the *Israel of God* hath no mansions; but journies, pilgrimages in this life. By that measure did *Jacob* measure his life to *Pharaoh;* the dayes of the years *of my pilgrimage*. And though the *Apostle* would not say *morimur*, that, whilst wee *are in the body* wee *are dead*, yet hee sayes, *Peregrinamur*, whilest wee are *in the body*, wee are but in *a pilgrimage*, and wee are *absent from the Lord*; hee might have said *dead*, for this whole *world* is but an *universall churchyard*, but one *common grave*, and the life and motion that the greatest persons have in it, is but as the shaking of buried bodies in the grave, by an *earth-quake*. That which we call life, is but *Hebdomada mortium*, a *weeke of deaths*, seaven dayes, seaven periods of our life spent in dying, *a dying seaven times over;* and there is an end. *Our birth dies* in *infancy*, and our *infancy* dies in *youth*, and *youth* and the rest die in *age*, and *age* also dies, and *determines all*. Nor doe all these, youth out of infancy, or age out of youth arise so, as a *Phœnix* out of the *ashes* of another *Phœnix* formerly *dead*, but as a *waspe* or a *serpent* out of a *caryon*, or as a *Snake* out of *dung*. Our *youth* is *worse* than our *infancy*, and our *age worse* than our *youth*. Our *youth* is *hungry and thirsty*, after those *sinnes*, which our *infancy knew not;* And our *age* is *sory* and *angry*, that it *cannot pursue* those *sinnes* which our *youth did;* and besides, al the way, so many deaths, that is, so many deadly calamities accompany every condition, and every period of this life, as that death it selfe would bee an ease to them that suffer them: Upon this sense doth *Job* wish that *God had not given him* an *issue* from the *first death*, from the *wombe, Wherefore hast thou brought me* forth *out of the wombe? O that I had given up the Ghost, and no eye seene me! I should have beene as though I had not beene.* And not only the impatient *Israelites* in their murmuring (*would to God wee had died by the hand of the Lord in the land of Egypt*) but *Eliah* himselfe, when he *fled* from *Jesabell*, and went for his life, as that text sayes, under the *Juniper tree*, requested that *hee might die*, and said, *it is enough now, O Lord, take away my life.* So *Jonah* justifies his impatience, nay his anger towards *God* himselfe. *Now ô Lord take, I beseech thee, my life from mee, for it is better to die than to live.* And when *God* asked him, *doest thou well to be angry for this*, he replies, *I doe well to be angry, even unto death.* How much worse a death than death, is this life, which so good men would so often change for death! But if my case bee as Saint *Paules* case, *quotidiè morior*, that *I die dayly*, that something heavier than death falls upon me every day; If my case be *Davids* case, *tota die mortificamur; all the day long wee are killed*, that not onely every day, but every houre of the day some thing heavier than death falls upon me, though that bee true of me, *Conceptus in peccatis*, I *was shapen* in *iniquity, and in sinne did my mother conceive me*, (there I dyed one death), though that be true of me (*Natus filius iræ*) I *was borne* not onely the child of sinne, but *the child of wrath*, of the wrath of *God* for sinne, which is a heavier death; Yet *Domini Domini sunt exitus mortis*, with *God the Lord are the issues of death*, and after a *Job*, and a *Joseph*, and a *Jeremie*, and a *Daniel*, I cannot doubt of a deliverance. And if no other deliverance conduce more to his glory and my good, yet he hath the *keys of death*, and hee can let me out at that dore, that is, deliver me from the manifold deaths of this world, the *omni die* and the *tota die*, the *every days death* and *every houres death*, by that *one death*, the *finall dissolution* of body and soule, the end of all. But then is that the end of all? Is that dissolution of body and soule, the last death that the body shall suffer? (for of spirituall death wee speake not now) It is not. Though this be *exitus à morte*, It is *introitus in mortem;* though it bee an *issue from* the manifold *deaths* of this *world*, yet it is an *entrance* into the *death of corruption* and *putrefaction* and *vermiculation* and *incineration*, and dispersion in and from the *grave*, in which every dead man dies over againe. It was a *prerogative* peculiar to *Christ*, not to die this death, *not to see corruption:* what gave him this privilege? Not *Josephs* great proportion of *gummes and spices*, that might have preserved his body from corruption and *incineration* longer than he needed it, longer than *three dayes*, but would not have done it for ever: what preserved him then? did his exemption and *freedome from originall sinne* preserve him from this corruption and *incineration?* 'tis true that original sinne hath induced this corruption and *incineration* upon us; If wee had not sinned in *Adam, mortality had not put on immortality*, (as the *Apostle* speakes) nor, *corruption had not put on incorruption*, but we had had our *transmigration* from this to the other world, without any *mortality*, any *corruption at all*. But yet since Christ took *sinne* upon him, so farre as made him *mortall*, he had it so farre too, as might have made him see this corruption and *incineration*, though he had no *originall sinne* in himself; what preserv'd him then? Did the *hypostaticall union* of both *natures, God* and *Man*, preserve him from this corruption and *incineration?* 'tis true that this was a most powerfull *embalming*, to be embalmd with the *divine nature* itselfe, to bee embalmd with *eternity,* was able to preserve him from corruption and *incineration* for ever. And he was embalmd so, embalmd with the *divine nature* it selfe, even in his *body* as well as in his *soule;* for the *Godhead*, the *divine nature* did not depart, but remained still *united* to his *dead body* in the *grave;* But yet for al this powerful *embalming*, this *hypostaticall union* of both natures, we see *Christ* did *die;* and for all this *union* which made him *God* and *Man*, hee became no man (for the *union* of the *body* and *soule* makes the man, and hee whose soule and body are separated by *death* as long as that state lasts is properly no man.) And therefore as in him the dissolution of *body* and *soule* was no *dissolution* of the *hypostaticall union;* so is there nothing that constraines us to say, that though the *flesh* of *Christ* had *seene corruption* and *incineration* in the grave, this had bene any *dissolution* of the *hypostaticall union*, for the divine *nature*, the Godhead might have remained with all the *Elements* and *principles* of *Christs* body, as well as it did with the two *constitutive* parts of his *person*, his *body* and his *soul*. This *incorruption* then was not in *Josephs gummes* and *spices*, nor was it in *Christs* innocency, and *exemption* from *originall sin*, nor was it (that is, it is not necessary to say it was) in the *hypostaticall union*. But this *incorruptiblenes* of his *flesh* is most conveniently plac'd in that, *Non dabis, thou wilt not suffer thy holy one to see corruption*. Wee looke no further for *causes* or *reasons* in the *mysteries of religion*, but to the *will* and pleasure of *God: Christ* himselfe limited his *inquisition* in that *ita est, even so Father, for so it seemeth good in thy sight*. *Christs* body did *not see corruption*, therefore, because *God* had *decreed* it shold not. The humble soule (and onely the humble soule is the religious soule) rests himselfe upon *Gods* purposes and the decrees of *God,* which he hath declared and manifested not such as are *conceived* and imagined in our selves, though upon some probability, some *veresimilitude.* So in our present case *Peter* proceeds in his *Sermon* at *Jerusalem,* and so *Paul* in *his* at *Antioch.* They preached *Christ* to have *bene risen* without seeing *corruption* not onely because *God* had *decreed* it, but because he had *manifested* that *decree* in his *Prophet.* Therefore doth Saint *Paul* cite by speciall number the *second Psalme* for that *decree;* And therefore both Saint *Peter* and S. *Paul* cite for it that place in the 16. *Psalme,* for when *God* declares his *decree* and purpose in the expresse words of his *Prophet,* or when he declares it in the reall execution of the decree, then he makes it ours, then he manifests it to us. And therfore as the *Mysteries* of our *Religion,* are *not* the *objects* of *our reason,* but *by faith we rest* on *Gods decree* and purpose, (It is so ô *God,* because it is *thy will,* it should be so) so *Gods decrees* are ever to be considered in the *manifestation* thereof. All *manifestation* is either in the *word* of *God,* or in the *execution* of the *decree;* And when these two concur and meete, it is the strongest *demonstration* that can bee: when therefore I finde those *markes* of *adoption* and *spiritual filiation,* which are delivered in the *word* of *God* to be upon me, when I finde that reall *execution* of his *good purpose* upon me, as that *actually* I doe *live* under the *obedience,* and under the *conditions* which are *evidences* of *adoption* and *spiritual filiation;* Then so long as I see these *markes* and live so; I may safely comfort my selfe in a *holy certitude* and a *modest infallibility* of my *adoption. Christ* determines himself in that, the purpose of *God* was manifest to him: S. *Peter* and S. *Paul* determine themselves in those two wayes of knowing the *purpose* of *God,* the *word* of *God* before, the *execution* of the *decree* in the *fulnes of time.* It was *prophecyed before,* say they, and it *is performed now, Christ is risen* without seeing corruption. Now this which is so singularly peculiar to him, that *his flesh should not see corruption,* at his *second coming,* his coming to *Judgement,* shall extend to all that are then alive, their flesh shall not *see corruption,* because as th' *Apostle* sayes, and sayes as *a secret,* as *a mystery; Behold I shew you a mistery, we shall not all sleepe,* (that is, not continue in the state of the dead in the grave), *but wee shall all be changed in an instant,* we shall have a *dissolution,* and in the *same instant* a *redintegration,* a *recompacting* of *body* and *soule,* and that shall be truely a death and truely a resurrection, but no sleeping in corruption; But for us that die now and sleepe in the state of the dead, we must al passe this *posthume* death, this *death* after *death,* nay this death after buriall, this *dissolution* after *dissolution,* this *death* of *corruption* and *putrifaction,* of *vermiculation* and *incineration,* of *dissolution* and *dispersion* in and *from* the *grave,* when these bodies that have beene the *children* of *royall parents*, and the *parents* of *royall children*, must say with *Job, Corruption thou art my father*, and *to the Worme thou art my mother and my sister. Miserable riddle*, when the *same worme* must bee *my mother*, and *my sister*, and *my selfe. Miserable incest*, when I must bee *maried* to my *mother* and my *sister*, and bee both *father* and *mother* to my *owne mother* and *sister, beget* and *beare* that *worme* which is all that *miserable penury;* when my *mouth* shall be *filled* with *dust*, and the *worme* shall *feed*, and *feed sweetely* upon me, when the *ambitious* man shall have *no satisfaction, if* the *poorest alive* tread upon him, nor the *poorest* receive any *contentment* in being made *equall* to *Princes*, for they *shall bee equall* but *in dust*. One dyeth at his full strength, being wholly at ease and in quiet, and another dies in the *bitternes of his soul*, and never *eates* with *pleasure*, but they lye downe *alike* in *the dust*, and the *worme covers them;* In *Job* and in *Esay*, it *covers them and is spred under them*, the worme is spred *under thee*, and the worme *covers thee*, There's the *Mats* and the *Carpets* that *lie under*, and there's the *State* and the *Canapye*, that *hangs over* the greatest of the sons of men; Even those bodies that were *the temples of the holy Ghost*, come to this *dilapidation*, to ruine, to rubbidge, to dust, even the *Israel of the Lord*, and *Jacob* himselfe hath no other specification, no other denomination, but that *vermis Jacob*, thou *worme of Jacob*. Truely the consideration of this *posthume death*, this death after buriall, that after *God*, (with whom are the *issues of death*) hath delivered me from the *death* of the *wombe*, by bringing mee into the *world*, and from the manifold *deaths* of the *world*, by laying me in the *grave*, I must die againe in an *Incineration* of this *flesh*, and in a dispersion of that dust. That that *Monarch*, who spred over many nations alive, must in his dust lie in a corner of that *sheete of lead*, and there, but so long as that lead will laste, and that privat and *retir'd man*, that thought himselfe his owne for ever, and never came forth, must in his dust of the grave bee published, and (such are the *revolutions* of the *graves*) bee mingled with the dust of every high way, and of every dunghill, and swallowed in every puddle and pond: This is the most inglorious and contemptible *vilification*, the most deadly and peremptory *nullification* of man, that wee can consider; *God* seemes to have caried the declaration of his *power* to a great height, when hee sets the *Prophet Ezechiel* in the *valley of drye bones*, and says, *Sonne of man can these bones live?* as though it had bene impossible, and yet they did; The *Lord* layed *Sinewes upon them, and flesh*, and *breathed into them*, and *they did live:* But in that case there were *bones* to bee *seene*, something visible, of which it might be said, can this thing live? But in this death of *incineration*, and dispersion of dust, wee see *nothing* that wee call *that mans;* If we say, can this dust live? perchance it *cannot*, it may bee the meere *dust* of the *earth*, which never did live, never shall. It may be the dust of that mans *worme*, which did live, but shall no more. It may bee the dust of *another* man, that concernes not him of whom it is askt. This death of *incineration* and dispersion, is, to naturall *reason*, the most *irrecoverable death* of all, and yet *Domini Domini sunt exitus mortis, unto God the Lord belong the issues of death*, and by *recompacting* this *dust* into the *same body*, and *reinanimating* the *same body* with the *same soule*, hee shall in a blessed and glorious *resurrection* give mee such an *issue from* this *death*, as shal never passe into any other *death*, but establish me into a life that shall last as long as the *Lord of life* himself.

And so have you that that belongs to the *first acceptation* of these words, (*unto God the Lord belong the issues of death*) That though from the *wombe* to the *grave* and in the grave it selfe wee passe from *death* to *death*, yet, as *Daniel* speakes, the *Lord our God is able to deliver us, and hee will deliver us*.

And so wee passe unto our *second accommodation* of *these words* (*unto God the Lord belong the issues of death*) That it *belongs* to *God*, and *not* to *man* to *passe a judgement* upon us at our death, or to conclude a dereliction on *Gods* part upon the manner thereof.

Those *indications* which the *Physitians* receive, and those *presagitions* which they give for *death* or *recovery* in the *patient*, they receive and they give out of the grounds and the *rules of their art:* But we have no such rule or art to give a *presagition* of *spirituall death* and damnation upon any such *indication* as wee see in any *dying man;* wee see often enough to be sory, but not to despaire; wee may bee deceived both wayes; wee use to comfort our selfe in the death of *a friend,* if it be testified that he went away like a *Lambe,* that is, without any *reluctation.* But, *God* knowes, that [he] may bee accompanied with a *dangerous damp* and *stupefaction,* and *insensibility* of his *present state.* Our blessed *Saviour* suffered *coluctations* with *death,* and a *sadnes even in his soule to death,* and an *agony* even to a *bloody sweate* in his *body,* and *expostulations* with *God,* and *exclamations* upon the crosse. He was a *devout man,* who said upon his death bed, or dead turfe (for hee was an *Heremit*) *septuaginta annis Domino servivisti, et mori times? hast thou served a good Master threescore and ten yeares,* and *now art thou loath to goe into his presence?* yet *Hilarion* was loath; *Barlaam* was a *devout* man (an *Heremit* too) that said that day hee died. *Cogita te hodie cœpisse servire Domino, et hodie finiturum. Consider this to be the first days service that ever thou didst thy Master,* to glorifie him in a Christianly and a constant death, *and if thy first day* be *thy last day too, how soone dost thou come* to *receive thy wages?* yet *Barlaam* could have beene content to have staid longer for it: Make no *ill conclusions* upon any mans *loathnes* to *die,* for the *mercies* of

God worke *momentarily* in minutes, and many times *insensibly* to *by-standers* or any other than the party departing. And then upon *violent deaths* inflicted, as upon malefactors, *Christ* himselfe hath forbidden us by his owne death to make any *ill conclusion;* for his owne *death* had those impressions in it; He was *reputed,* he was *executed* as a *malefactor,* and no doubt many of them who concurred to his death, did beleeve him to bee so; Of *sudden death* there are scarce examples to be found in the *scriptures* upon *good men,* for *death* in *battaile* cannot be called *sudden death;* But *God* governes not by *examples,* but by *rules,* and therefore make no *ill conclusion* upon *sudden death* nor upon *distempers* neither, though perchance accompanied with some *words of diffidence* and distrust in the *mercies of God:* The *tree lies as it falles* its true, but it is *not* the *last stroake* that *fells* the *tree,* nor the *last word* nor *gaspe* that *qualifies* the *soule.* Stil *pray* wee for a *peaceable life* against *violent death,* and for *time* of *repentance* against *sudden death,* and for *sober* and *modest assurance* against *distemperd* and *diffident death,* but never make *ill conclusions* upon persons overtaken with such deaths; *Domini Domini sunt exitus mortis, to God the Lord belong the issues of death.* And *he* received *Sampson,* who went out of this world in *such* a *manner* (consider it *actively,* consider it *passively* in his *owne death,* and in those whom he *slew* with himselfe) as was subject to interpretation hard enough. Yet the *holy Ghost* hath moved S. *Paul* to celebrate *Sampson* in his *great Catalogue,* and so doth all the *Church:* Our *criticall* day is *not* the *very day* of our *death:* but the whole course of our life. I thanke him that *prayes* for me when the *Bell* tolles, but I thank him much more that *Catechises* mee, or *preaches* to mee, or *instructs mee how to live. Fac hoc et vives, there's* my securitie, the mouth of the *Lord hath said it, doe this and thou shalt live:* But *though I doe it,* yet I *shall die too,* die a bodily, a naturall death. But *God* never mentions, never seems to consider that death, the bodily, the naturall death. *God* doth not say, live well and thou shalt die well, that is, an easie, a quiet death; But *live well here,* and thou shalt *live well for ever.* As the first part of a sentence peeces wel with the last, and never respects, never hearkens after the *parenthesis* that comes betweene, so doth a *good life* here flowe into an *eternall life,* without any consideration, what *manner* of *death* wee dye: But whether the *gate* of *my prison* be *opened* with an *oyld key* (by a gentle and *preparing sicknes*), *or* the gate bee *hewen downe* by a *violent death, or* the gate bee *burnt downe* by a *raging* and *frantique feaver, a gate into heaven* I *shall have,* for *from the Lord is the cause of my life,* and *with God the Lord* are the *issues of death.* And further wee cary not this *second acceptation* of the *words,* as this *issue of death is liberatio in morte, Gods care* that the *soule be safe,* what *agonies* soever the *body suffers* in the *houre* of *death.*

But passe to our *third part* and last part; as this *issue of death* is *liberatio per mortem*, a *deliverance by the death* of another, by the death of Christ. *Sufferentiam Job audiisti, et vidisti finem Domini*, sayes Saint *James* 5. 11. *You have heard of the patience of Job*, says he, All this while you have done that, for in every man, calamitous, miserable man, a *Job* speakes; Now *see the end of the Lord*, saith that *Apostle*, which is not that end that the *Lord* propos'd to himselfe (*salvation to us*) nor the end which he proposes to us (*conformitie to him*) but *see the end of the Lord*, sayes he, The end, *that the Lord* himselfe *came to, Death* and a painefull and a shamefull death. But why did he die? and why die so? *Quia Domini Domini sunt exitus mortis* (as Saint *Augustine* interpreting this *text* answeres that question) because *to* this *God our Lord belong'd the issues of death. Quid apertius diceretur?* sayes hee there, what can bee more obvious, more manifest than this sense of these words. In the former part of this verse, it is said; *He that is our God, is the God of salvation, Deus salvos faciendi*, so hee reads it, the *God* that must save us. Who can that be, sayes he, but *Jesus?* for *therefore* that *name* was *given him*, because he was to *save us*. And to this *Jesus*, sayes he, this *Saviour, belong the issues of death; Nec oportuit eum de hac vita alios exitus habere quam mortis*. Being come into this life in our mortal nature, *He could not goe out of it* any other way *but by death. Ideo dictum*, sayes he, *therefore it is said*, To *God the Lord belong the issues of death; ut ostenderetur moriendo nos salvos facturum*, to *shew that his way to save us was to die.* And from this *text* doth Saint *Isodore* prove, that *Christ* was *truely Man*, (which as many *sects* of *heretiques denied*, as that he was *truely God*) because to him, though he were *Dominus Dominus* (as the *text* doubles it) *God* the *Lord*, yet to *him*, to *God the Lord belong'd the issues of death, oportuit eum pati* more can not be said, than *Christ* himselfe sayes of himselfe; *These things Christ ought to suffer*, hee had no other way but by death: So then *this part* of our *Sermon* must needes be a *passion Sermon;* since all his *life* was a *continuall passion*, all *our Lent* may well bee a *continuall good Friday. Christs* painefull life tooke off none of the paines of his death, hee felt not the lesse then for having felt so much before. Nor will any thing that shall be said before, lessen, but rather inlarge the devotion, to that which shall be said of his passion at the time of due *solemnization* thereof. *Christ* bled not a droppe the lesse at the last, for having bled at his *Circumcision* before, nor wil you shed a teare the lesse then, if you shed some now. And therefore bee now content to consider with mee how to *this God the Lord belong'd the issues of death*. That *God*, this *Lord*, the *Lord* of *life could die*, is a strange contemplation; That the *red Sea* could bee *drie*, That the *Sun* could *stand still*, that an *Oven* could be *seaven times heat* and *not burne*, That *Lions* could be *hungry* and *not bite,* is strange, *miraculously strange,* but *supermiraculous* that *God could die;* but that *God would die* is an *exaltation* of that. But even of that also it is a *superexaltation,* that *God shold die, must die,* and *non exitus* (said S. *Augustine*), *God* the *Lord had no issue but by death,* and *oportuit pati,* (says *Christ* himself), all this *Christ ought to suffer,* was bound to suffer; *Deus ultionum Deus* says *David, God* is the *God of revenges,* he wold *not passe* over the *sinne of man* unrevenged, unpunished. But then *Deus ultionum liberè egit* (sayes *that place*) The *God of revenges workes freely,* he *punishes,* he *spares whome he will.* And wold he *not spare himselfe?* he would not: *Dilectio fortis ut mors, love is strong as death,* stronger, it drew in death that naturally is not welcom. *Si possibile,* says *Christ, if it be possible, let this Cup passe,* when his *love expressed in a former decree* with his *Father,* had *made it impossible.* Many *waters quench not love, Christ* tried many; He was *Baptized* out of his *love,* and his love determined not there. He *mingled blood* with *water* in his *agony* and that determined not his love; hee *wept pure blood,* all his blood at all his eyes, at all his pores, in his *flagellation* and *thornes* (*to the Lord our God belong'd the issues of blood*) and these *expressed,* but these did *not quench his love.* Hee *would not* spare, nay he *could not spare himselfe.* There was nothing more free, more voluntary, more spontaneous than the death of *Christ.* 'Tis true, *libere egit,* he *died voluntarily,* but yet when we consider the *contract* that had passed betweene his *Father* and *him,* there was an *oportuit,* a kind of *necessity* upon him. All this *Christ ought to suffer.* And when shall we *date* this *obligation,* this *oportuit,* this *necessity?* when shall wee say *that begun?* Certainly this *decree* by which *Christ was to suffer* all this, was an *eternall decree,* and was there any thing before that, that was eternall? *Infinite love, eternall love;* be pleased to follow this home, and to consider it seriously, that what liberty soever wee can *conceive* in *Christ,* to die or not to die, this *necessity of dying,* this *decree* is as *eternall* as that *liberty;* and yet how small a matter made hee of this *necessity* and this *dying?* His *Father* cals it but *a bruise,* and but a *bruising of his heele* (*the serpent shall bruise his heele*) and yet that was that, the *serpent* should *practise* and *compasse* his *death.* Himselfe calls it but a *Baptisme,* as though he were to bee the better for it. *I have a Baptisme to be Baptized with,* and he was in paine till it was accomplished, and yet this *Baptisme* was *his death.* The *holy Ghost* calls it *Joy* (for *the Joy which was set before him hee indured the Crosse*) which was not a *joy* of his reward after his passion, but a joy that filled him even in the middest of those torments, and arose from him; when *Christ* calls his *Calicem, a Cuppe,* and no worse (*can ye drink of my Cuppe*) he speakes not odiously, not with detestation of it: Indeed it was a *Cup, salus mundo, a health to all the world.* And *quid retribuam,* says *David, what shall I render to the Lord?* answere you with *David, accipiam Calicem,* I *will take the Cup of salvation,* take it, that *Cup* is *salvation,* his *passion,* if not into your *present imitation,* yet into your *present contemplation.* And behold how that *Lord* that was *God,* yet *could die, would die, must die,* for your *salvation.* That *Moses* and *Elias talkt with Christ* in the *transfiguration,* both Saint *Mathew* and Saint *Marke* tell us, but what they talkt of onely S. *Luke, Dicebant excessum ejus,* says he, *they talkt of his decease,* of *his death* which *was to be accomplished* at *Jerusalem,* The *word* is of his *Exodus,* the very word of our *text, exitus,* his *issue by death. Moses* who in his *Exodus* had *prefigured* this *issue of our Lord,* and in passing *Israel* out of *Egypt* through the *red Sea,* had foretold in that actuall *prophesie, Christ passing of mankind through* the *sea* of his *blood.* And *Elias,* whose *Exodus* and *issue out of* this *world* was a *figure* of *Christs ascension,* had no doubt a great satisfaction in *talking* with our *blessed Lord de excessu ejus,* of the *full consummation* of *all this* in *his death,* which was to bee *accomplished* at *Jerusalem.* Our *meditation* of his *death* should be more *viscerall* and affect us more because it is of a thing already done. The ancient *Romans* had a certain tendernesse and detestation of the name of death, they could not name death, no, not in their wills. There they could not say *Si mori contigerit,* but *si quid humanitus contingat,* not if, or when I die, but when the course of nature is accomplished upon me. To us that speake daily of the *death* of *Christ,* (he was *crucified, dead* and *buried*) can the memory or the mention of our owne *death* bee irkesome or bitter? There are in these latter times amongst us, that name death freely enough, and the death of *God,* but in *blasphemous oathes* and *execrations.* Miserable men, who shall therefore bee said never to have named *Jesus,* because they have named him *too often.* And therefore heare *Jesus* say, *Nescivi vos,* I *never knew you,* because they made themselves *too familiar* with him. *Moses* and *Elias* talkt with *Christ* of his *death,* only, in *a holy* and *joyfull sense* of the *benefit* which *they* and *all* the world were to *receive by that. Discourses* of *Religion* should not be *out* of *curiosity,* but to *edification.* And then they talkt with *Christ* of his *death* at that time, when he was in the greatest *height of glory* that ever he admitted in this world, that is, his *transfiguration.* And wee are afraid to speake to the *great men* of this world of their *death,* but nourish in them a *vaine imagination* of *immortality,* and *immutability.* But *bonum est nobis esse hic* (as Saint *Peter* said there) It *is good to dwell here,* in this *consideration* of his *death,* and therefore *transferre* wee our *tabernacle* (our *devotions*) through some of those *steps* which *God* the *Lord* made to his *issue of death* that *day.* Take in the *whole day* from the *houre* that *Christ received* the *passeover* upon *Thursday, unto* the *houre* in which hee *died* the *next day.* Make *this* present *day* that *day* in thy *devotion*, and consider what *hee did*, and remember what *you have done*. Before hee *instituted* and *celebrated* the *Sacrament*, (which was *after* the *eating of the passeover*) hee proceeded to that *act* of *humility*, to *wash his disciples feete*, even *Peters, who* for a while *resisted* him; In thy *preparation* to the holy and blessed *Sacrament*, hast thou with a sincere *humility* sought a *reconciliation* with all the *world*, even with those that have been *averse* from it, and *refused* that *reconciliation* from thee? If so and not else thou hast spent that *first part* of his *last day*, in a *conformity* with him. After the *Sacrament* hee spent the time till night in *prayer*, in *preaching*, in *Psalmes;* Hast thou considered that a *worthy receaving* of the *Sacrament* consists in a *continuation* of *holinesse after*, as wel as in a *preparation* before? If so, thou hast therein also *conformed* thy selfe to him, so *Christ* spent his time till night; *At night* hee *went into the garden* to *pray*, and he prayed *prolixius* he spent *much time* in *prayer.* How much? Because it is literally expressed, that he *prayed there three severall times*, and that *returning to his Disciples* after his *first prayer*, and *finding them asleepe* said, *could ye not watch with me one houre*, it is collected that he *spent three houres* in *prayer.* I dare scarce aske thee *whither* thou *wentest*, or *how* thou *disposedst* of *thy self*, when it *grew darke* and after *last night:* If that time were spent in a *holy recommendation* of thy self to *God*, and a *submission* of *thy will* to *his*, It was spent in a *conformity* to him. In that *time* and in those *prayers* was *his agony* and *bloody sweat.* I will *hope* that thou didst *pray*, but not *every ordinary* and *customary prayer*, but *prayer actually* accompanied with *shedding of teares*, and *dispositively* in a readines to *shed blood* for *his glory* in *necessary cases*, puts thee into a *conformity* with him; About midnight he was *taken* and *bound with a kisse.* Art thou not *too conformable* to him in that? Is not that *too literally*, too exactly *thy case?* at *midnight* to have *bene taken and bound with a kisse?* from thence he was *caried back* to *Jerusalem*, first to *Annas*, then to *Caiphas*, and (as late as it was) then hee was *examined* and *buffeted*, and *delivered over* to the custody of those *officers*, from whome he received all those *irrisions*, and *violences*, the *covering of his face*, the *spitting upon his face*, the *blasphemies of words*, and the *smartnes of blowes* which that *Gospell* mentions. In which compasse fell that *Gallicinium*, that *crowing of the Cock* which *called up Peter* to his *repentance.* How thou passedst all that time last night thou knowest. If thou didst any thing that needed *Peters teares*, and hast *not shed them*, let me be thy *Cock*, doe it now, Now thy *Master* (in the unworthiest of his servants) *lookes back upon thee*, doe it now; *Betimes*, in the morning, so soone as it was day, the *Jewes held a counsell* in the *high Priests hall*, and *agreed upon their evidence* against him, and then caried him to *Pilate*, who was to be his *Judge;* diddest thou *accuse* thy selfe when thou *wakedst this morning,* and wast thou content even with *false accusations* (that is) rather to *suspect actions* to have beene sin, which were not, than to *smother* and *justify* such as were *truly sins?* then thou spentst that *houre* in *conformity* to him: *Pilate* found *no evidence against him,* and therefore to ease himselfe, and to passe a *complement* upon *Herod, Tetrarch* of *Galilee,* who was at that time at *Jerusalem* (because *Christ* being a *Galilean* was of *Herods jurisdiction*) *Pilat sent him* to *Herod,* and rather as a *madman* than a *malefactor, Herod* remaunded him (*with scornes*) to *Pilat* to proceed against him; And this was about *eight* of the *clock.* Hast thou been content to come to this *Inquisition,* this examination, this agitation, this cribration, this pursuit of thy *conscience,* to *sift* it, to follow it from the *sinnes* of thy *youth* to thy *present sinnes,* from the *sinnes* of thy *bed,* to the *sinnes* of thy *boorde,* and from the *substance* to the *circumstance* of thy *sinnes?* That's *time spent* like thy *Saviours. Pilat* wold have *saved Christ,* by using the *priviledge* of *the day* in his behalfe, because that *day* one *prisoner was to be delivered,* but they *choose Barrabas.* Hee would have *saved* him *from death,* by *satisfying their fury,* with *inflicting* other *torments* upon him, *scourging* and *crowning with thornes,* and *loading* him with many *scornefull* and *ignominous contumelies;* But they regarded him not, they pressed a *crucifying.* Hast thou gone about to *redeeme thy sinne,* by *fasting,* by *Almes,* by *disciplines* and *mortifications,* in way of *satisfaction* to the *Justice* of *God?* that will not serve, that's not the right way, *wee presse* an utter *Crucifying* of that *sinne* that governes thee; and that *conformes* thee to *Christ.* Towards *noone Pilat* gave *judgement,* and they made such *hast* to execution, as that *by noone* hee was *upon the Crosse.* There now hangs that *sacred Body* upon the *Crosse, rebaptized* in his owne *teares* and *sweat* and *embalmed* in his *owne blood alive.* There are those *bowells of compassion,* which are so conspicuous, so manifested, as that you may *see them through his wounds.* There those *glorious eyes* grew faint in their light: so as the *Sun ashamed* to survive them, *departed with his light too.* And then that *Sonne of God,* who was *never from us,* and yet had now come a *new way unto* us in *assuming our nature,* delivers that *soule* (which was *never out* of his *Fathers hands*) by a *new way,* a *voluntary emission* of it into his Fathers hands; For though to this *God our Lord, belong'd these issues of death,* so that considered in his owne contract, he *must* necessarily *die,* yet at *no breach* or *battery,* which they had made upon his *sacred Body,* issued his soule, but *emisit,* hee *gave up the Ghost,* and as *God breathed a soule into* the *first Adam,* so this *second Adam breathed his soule into God, into the hands of God.* There wee leave you in that *blessed dependancy*, to *hang* upon *him* that *hangs* upon the *Crosse*, there *bath* in his *teares*, there *suck* at his *woundes*, and *lie downe in peace* in his *grave*, till hee vouchsafe you a *resurrection*, and an *ascension* into that *Kingdome*, which hee *hath purchas'd for you*, with the *inestimable price* of his *incorruptible blood*. Amen.

The Complete Poetry

of

William Blake

Poetical Sketches

Printed 1783

MISCELLANEOUS POEMS

TO SPRING

O THOU with dewy locks, who lookest down
Thro' the clear windows of the morning, turn
Thine angel eyes upon our western isle,
Which in full choir hails thy approach, O Spring!

The hills tell each other, and the list'ning
Vallies hear; all our longing eyes are turned
Up to thy bright pavillions: issue forth,
And let thy holy feet visit our clime.

Come o'er the eastern hills, and let our winds
Kiss thy perfumed garments; let us taste
Thy morn and evening breath; scatter thy pearls
Upon our love-sick land that mourns for thee.

O deck her forth with thy fair fingers; pour
Thy soft kisses on her bosom; and put
Thy golden crown upon her languish'd head,
Whose modest tresses were bound up for thee!

TO SUMMER

O THOU, who passest thro' our vallies in
Thy strength, curb thy fierce steeds, allay the heat
That flames from their large nostrils! thou, O Summer,

493

Oft pitched'st here thy golden tent, and oft
Beneath our oaks hast slept, while we beheld
With joy thy ruddy limbs and flourishing hair.

Beneath our thickest shades we oft have heard
Thy voice, when noon upon his fervid car
Rode o'er the deep of heaven; beside our springs
Sit down, and in our mossy vallies, on
Some bank beside a river clear, throw thy
Silk draperies off, and rush into the stream:
Our vallies love the Summer in his pride.

Our bards are fam'd who strike the silver wire:
Our youth are bolder than the southern swains:
Our maidens fairer in the sprightly dance:
We lack not songs, nor instruments of joy,
Nor echoes sweet, nor waters clear as heaven,
Nor laurel wreaths against the sultry heat.

TO AUTUMN

O AUTUMN, laden with fruit, and stained
With the blood of the grape, pass not, but sit
Beneath my shady roof; there thou may'st rest,
And tune thy jolly voice to my fresh pipe;
And all the daughters of the year shall dance!
Sing now the lusty song of fruits and flowers.

"The narrow bud opens her beauties to
The sun, and love runs in her thrilling veins;
Blossoms hang round the brows of morning, and
Flourish down the bright cheek of modest eve,
Till clust'ring Summer breaks forth into singing,
And feather'd clouds strew flowers round her head.

The spirits of the air live on the smells
Of fruit; and joy, with pinions light, roves round
The gardens, or sits singing in the trees."
Thus sang the jolly Autumn as he sat;
Then rose, girded himself, and o'er the bleak
Hills fled from our sight; but left his golden load.

TO WINTER

O WINTER! bar thine adamantine doors:
The north is thine; there hast thou built thy dark
Deep-founded habitation. Shake not thy roofs,
Nor bend thy pillars with thine iron car.

He hears me not, but o'er the yawning deep
Rides heavy; his storms are unchain'd, sheathed
In ribbed steel; I dare not lift mine eyes,
For he hath rear'd his sceptre o'er the world.

Lo! now the direful monster, whose skin clings
To his strong bones, strides o'er the groaning rocks:
He withers all in silence, and his hand
Unclothes the earth, and freezes up frail life.

He takes his seat upon the cliffs; the mariner
Cries in vain. Poor little wretch! that deal'st
With storms, till heaven smiles, and the monster
Is driv'n yelling to his caves beneath mount Hecla.

TO THE EVENING STAR

THOU fair-hair'd angel of the evening,
Now, whilst the sun rests on the mountains, light
Thy bright torch of love; thy radiant crown
Put on, and smile upon our evening bed!
Smile on our loves, and, while thou drawest the
Blue curtains of the sky, scatter thy silver dew
On every flower that shuts its sweet eyes
In timely sleep. Let thy west wind sleep on
The lake; speak silence with thy glimmering eyes,
And wash the dusk with silver. Soon, full soon,
Dost thou withdraw; then the wolf rages wide,
And the lion glares thro' the dun forest:
The fleeces of our flocks are cover'd with
Thy sacred dew: protect them with thine influence.

TO MORNING

O HOLY virgin! clad in purest white,
Unlock heav'n's golden gates, and issue forth;
Awake the dawn that sleeps in heaven; let light
Rise from the chambers of the east, and bring
The honied dew that cometh on waking day.
O radiant morning, salute the sun,
Rouz'd like a huntsman to the chace, and, with
Thy buskin'd feet, appear upon our hills.

FAIR ELENOR

THE bell struck one, and shook the silent tower;
The graves give up their dead: fair Elenor
Walk'd by the castle gate, and looked in.
A hollow groan ran thro' the dreary vaults.

She shriek'd aloud, and sunk upon the steps
On the cold stone her pale cheeks. Sickly smells
Of death issue as from a sepulchre,
And all is silent but the sighing vaults.

Chill death withdraws his hand, and she revives;
Amaz'd, she finds herself upon her feet,
And, like a ghost, thro' narrow passages
Walking, feeling the cold walls with her hands.

Fancy returns, and now she thinks of bones,
And grinning skulls, and corruptible death,
Wrap'd in his shroud; and now fancies she hears
Deep sighs, and sees pale sickly ghosts gliding.

At length, no fancy, but reality
Distracts her. A rushing sound, and the feet
Of one that fled, approaches—Ellen stood,
Like a dumb statue, froze to stone with fear.

The wretch approaches, crying, "The deed is done;
Take this, and send it by whom thou wilt send;

It is my life—send it to Elenor:—
He's dead, and howling after me for blood!

"Take this," he cry'd; and thrust into her arms
A wet napkin, wrap'd about; then rush'd
Past, howling: she receiv'd into her arms
Pale death, and follow'd on the wings of fear.

They pass'd swift thro' the outer gate; the wretch,
Howling, leap'd o'er the wall into the moat,
Stifling in mud. Fair Ellen pass'd the bridge,
And heard a gloomy voice cry, "Is it done?"

As the deer wounded, Ellen flew over
The pathless plain; as the arrows that fly
By night, destruction flies, and strikes in darkness.
She fled from fear, till at her house arriv'd.

Her maids await her; on her bed she falls,
That bed of joy, where erst her lord hath press'd:
"Ah, woman's-fear!" she cry'd; "Ah, cursed duke!
Ah, my dear lord! ah, wretched Elenor!

"My lord was like a flower upon the brows
Of lusty May! Ah, life is frail as flower!
O ghastly death! withdraw thy cruel hand,
Seek'st thou that flow'r to deck thy horrid temples?

"My lord was like a star, in highest heav'n
Drawn down to earth by spells and wickedness;
My lord was like the opening eyes of day,
When western winds creep softly o'er the flowers:

"But he is darken'd; like the summer's noon,
Clouded; fall'n like the stately tree, cut down;
The breath of heaven dwelt among his leaves.
O Elenor, weak woman, fill'd with woe"

Thus having spoke, she raised up her head,
And saw the bloody napkin by her side,
Which in her arms she brought; and now, tenfold
More terrified, saw it unfold itself.

Her eyes were fix'd; the bloody cloth unfolds,
Disclosing to her sight the murder'd head
Of her dear lord, all ghastly pale, clotted
With gory blood; it groan'd, and thus it spake:

"O Elenor, I am thy husband's head,
Who, sleeping on the stones of yonder tower,
Was 'reft of life by the accursed duke!
A hired villain turn'd my sleep to death!

"O Elenor, beware the cursed duke;
O give not him thy hand now I am dead;
He seeks thy love, who, coward, in the night,
Hired a villain to bereave my life."

She sat with dead cold limbs, stiffen'd to stone;
She took the gory head up in her arms;
She kiss'd the pale lips; she had no tears to shed;
She hugg'd it to her breast, and groan'd her last.

SONG

H O W sweet I roam'd from field to field,
    And tasted all the summer's pride,
'Till I the prince of love beheld,
    Who in the sunny beams did glide!

He shew'd me lilies for my hair,
    And blushing roses for my brow;
He led me through his gardens fair,
    Where all his golden pleasures grow.

With sweet May dews my wings were wet,
    And Phœbus fir'd my vocal rage;
He caught me in his silken net,
    And shut me in his golden cage.

He loves to sit and hear me sing,
    Then, laughing, sports and plays with me;
Then stretches out my golden wing,
    And mocks my loss of liberty.

SONG

M Y silks and fine array,
  My smiles and languish'd air,
By love are driv'n away;
  And mournful lean Despair
Brings me yew to deck my grave:
Such end true lovers have.

His face is fair as heav'n,
  When springing buds unfold;
O why to him was't giv'n,
  Whose heart is wintry cold?
His breast is love's all worship'd tomb,
Where all love's pilgrims come.

Bring me an axe and spade,
  Bring me a winding sheet;
When I my grave have made,
  Let winds and tempests beat:
Then down I'll lie, as cold as clay.
True love doth pass away!

SONG

L O V E and harmony combine,
And around our souls intwine,
While thy branches mix with mine,
And our roots together join.

Joys upon our branches sit,
Chirping loud, and singing sweet;
Like gentle streams beneath our feet
Innocence and virtue meet.

Thou the golden fruit dost bear,
I am clad in flowers fair;
Thy sweet boughs perfume the air,
And the turtle buildeth there.

There she sits and feeds her young,
Sweet I hear her mournful song;
And thy lovely leaves among,
There is love: I hear his tongue.

There his charming nest doth lay,
There he sleeps the night away;
There he sports along the day,
And doth among our branches play.

SONG

I LOVE the jocund dance,
  The softly-breathing song,
Where innocent eyes do glance,
  And where lisps the maiden's tongue.

I love the laughing vale,
  I love the echoing hill,
Where mirth does never fail,
  And the jolly swain laughs his fill.

I love the pleasant cot,
  I love the innocent bow'r,
Where white and brown is our lot,
  Or fruit in the mid-day hour.

I love the oaken seat,
  Beneath the oaken tree,
Where all the old villagers meet,
  And laugh our sports to see.

I love our neighbours all,
  But, Kitty, I better love thee;
And love them I ever shall;
  But thou art all to me.

SONG

MEMORY, hither come,
  And tune your merry notes;
And, while upon the wind
  Your music floats,

I'll pore upon the stream,
Where sighing lovers dream,
And fish for fancies as they pass
Within the watery glass.

I'll drink of the clear stream,
And hear the linnet's song;
And there I'll lie and dream
The day along:
And, when night comes, I'll go
To places fit for woe,
Walking along the darken'd valley
With silent Melancholy.

MAD SONG

THE wild winds weep,
And the night is a-cold;
Come hither, Sleep,
And my griefs unfold:
But lo! the morning peeps
Over the eastern steeps,
And the rustling birds of dawn
The earth do scorn.

Lo! to the vault
Of paved heaven,
With sorrow fraught
My notes are driven:
They strike the ear of night,
Make weep the eyes of day;
They make mad the roaring winds,
And with tempests play.

Like a fiend in a cloud,
With howling woe,
After night I do croud,
And with night will go;
I turn my back to the east,
From whence comforts have increas'd;
For light doth seize my brain
With frantic pain.

SONG

FRESH from the dewy hill, the merry year
Smiles on my head, and mounts his flaming car;
Round my young brows the laurel wreathes a shade,
And rising glories beam around my head.

My feet are wing'd, while o'er the dewy lawn
I meet my maiden, risen like the morn:
Oh bless those holy feet, like angels' feet;
Oh bless those limbs, beaming with heav'nly light!

Like as an angel glitt'ring in the sky
In times of innocence and holy joy;
The joyful shepherd stops his grateful song
To hear the music of an angel's tongue.

So when she speaks, the voice of Heaven I hear:
So when we walk, nothing impure comes near;
Each field seems Eden, and each calm retreat;
Each village seems the haunt of holy feet.

But that sweet village, where my black-ey'd maid
Closes her eyes in sleep beneath night's shade,
Whene'er I enter, more than mortal fire
Burns in my soul, and does my song inspire.

SONG

WHEN early morn walks forth in sober grey,
Then to my black ey'd maid I haste away;
When evening sits beneath her dusky bow'r,
And gently sighs away the silent hour,
The village bell alarms, away I go,
And the vale darkens at my pensive woe.

To that sweet village, where my black ey'd maid
Doth drop a tear beneath the silent shade,
I turn my eyes; and, pensive as I go,
Curse my black stars, and bless my pleasing woe.

Oft when the summer sleeps among the trees,
Whisp'ring faint murmurs to the scanty breeze,
I walk the village round; if at her side
A youth doth walk in stolen joy and pride,
I curse my stars in bitter grief and woe,
That made my love so high, and me so low.

O should she e'er prove false, his limbs I'd tear,
And throw all pity on the burning air;
I'd curse bright fortune for my mixed lot,
And then I'd die in peace, and be forgot.

TO THE MUSES

WHETHER on Ida's shady brow,
   Or in the chambers of the East,
The chambers of the sun, that now
   From antient melody have ceas'd;

Whether in Heav'n ye wander fair,
   Or the green corners of the earth,
Or the blue regions of the air,
   Where the melodious winds have birth;

Whether on chrystal rocks ye rove,
   Beneath the bosom of the sea
Wand'ring in many a coral grove,
   Fair Nine, forsaking Poetry!

How have you left the antient love
   That bards of old enjoy'd in you!
The languid strings do scarcely move!
   The sound is forc'd, the notes are few!

GWIN, KING OF NORWAY

COME, Kings, and listen to my song:
   When Gwin, the son of Nore,
Over the nations of the North
   His cruel sceptre bore,

The Nobles of the land did feed
  Upon the hungry Poor;
They tear the poor man's lamb, and drive
  The needy from their door!

"The land is desolate; our wives
  And children cry for bread;
Arise, and pull the tyrant down!
  Let Gwin be humbled!"

Gordred the giant rous'd himself
  From sleeping in his cave;
He shook the hills, and in the clouds
  The troubl'd banners wave.

Beneath them roll'd, like tempests black,
  The num'rous sons of blood;
Like lions' whelps, roaring abroad,
  Seeking their nightly food.

Down Bleron's hills they dreadful rush,
  Their cry ascends the clouds;
The trampling horse, and clanging arms
  Like rushing mighty floods!

Their wives and children, weeping loud,
  Follow in wild array,
Howling like ghosts, furious as wolves
  In the bleak wintry day.

"Pull down the tyrant to the dust,
  Let Gwin be humbled,"
They cry, "and let ten thousand lives
  Pay for the tyrant's head."

From tow'r to tow'r the watchmen cry:
  "O Gwin, the son of Nore,
Arouse thyself! the nations, black
  Like clouds, come rolling o'er!"

Gwin rear'd his shield, his palace shakes,
  His chiefs come rushing round;
Each, like an awful thunder cloud,
  With voice of solemn sound:

Like reared stones around a grave
   They stand around the King;
Then suddenly each seiz'd his spear,
   And clashing steel does ring.

The husbandman does leave his plow.
   To wade thro' fields of gore;
The merchant binds his brows in steel,
   And leaves the trading shore;

The shepherd leaves his mellow pipe,
   And sounds the trumpet shrill;
The workman throws his hammer down
   To heave the bloody bill.

Like the tall ghost of Barraton,
   Who sports in stormy sky,
Gwin leads his host, as black as night,
   When pestilence does fly,

With horses and with chariots—
   And all his spearmen bold
March to the sound of mournful song,
   Like clouds around him roll'd.

Gwin lifts his hand—the nations halt;
   "Prepare for war," he cries——
"Gordred appears!—his frowning brow
   Troubles our northern skies."

The armies stand, like balances
   Held in th' Almighty's hand:
"Gwin, thou hast fill'd thy measure up,
   Thou'rt swept from out the land."

And now the raging armies rush'd,
   Like warring mighty seas;
The Heav'ns are shook with roaring war,
   The dust ascends the skies!

Earth smokes with blood, and groans, and shakes
   To drink her children's gore,
A sea of blood; nor can the eye
   See to the trembling shore!

And on the verge of this wild sea
  Famine and death doth cry;
The cries of women and of babes
  Over the field doth fly.

The King is seen raging afar,
  With all his men of might,
Like blazing comets, scattering death
  Thro' the red fev'rous night.

Beneath his arm like sheep they die,
  And groan upon the plain;
The battle faints, and bloody men
  Fight upon hills of slain.

Now death is sick, and riven men
  Labour and toil for life;
Steed rolls on steed, and shield on shield,
  Sunk in the sea of strife!

The god of war is drunk with blood;
  The earth doth faint and fail;
The stench of blood makes sick the heav'ns;
  Ghosts glut the throat of hell!

O what have Kings to answer for,
  Before that awful throne!
When thousand deaths for vengeance cry,
  And ghosts accusing groan!

Like blazing comets in the sky,
  That shake the stars of light,
Which drop like fruit unto the earth
  Thro' the fierce burning night;

Like these did Gwin and Gordred meet,
  And the first blow decides;
Down from the brow unto the breast
  Gordred his head divides!

Gwin fell; the Sons of Norway fled,
  All that remain'd alive;
The rest did fill the vale of death,
  For them the eagles strive.

   The river Dorman roll'd their blood
     Into the northern sea,
  Who mourn'd his sons, and overwhelm'd
     The pleasant south country.

AN IMITATION OF SPENSER

GOLDEN Apollo, that thro' heaven wide
  Scatter'st the rays of light and truth's beams!
In lucent words my darkling verses dight,
  And wash my earthy mind in thy clear streams,
  That wisdom may descend in fairy dreams:
All while the jocund hours in thy train
  Scatter their fancies at thy poet's feet;
And when thou yields to night thy wide domain,
Let rays of truth enlight his sleeping brain.

For brutish Pan in vain might thee assay
  With tinkling sounds to dash thy nervous verse,
Sound without sense; yet in his rude affray,
  (For ignorance is Folly's leasing nurse,
  And love of Folly needs none other curse;)
Midas the praise hath gain'd of lengthen'd ears,
  For which himself might deem him ne'er the worse
To sit in council with his modern peers,
  And judge of tinkling rhimes, and elegances terse.

And thou, Mercurius, that with winged brow
  Dost mount aloft into the yielding sky,
And thro' Heav'n's halls thy airy flight dost throw,
  Entering with holy feet to where on high
  Jove weighs the counsel of futurity;
Then, laden with eternal fate, dost go
  Down, like a falling star, from autumn sky,
  And o'er the surface of the silent deep dost fly:

If thou arrivest at the sandy shore,
  Where nought but envious hissing adders dwell,
Thy golden rod, thrown on the dusty floor,
  Can charm to harmony with potent spell;
  Such is sweet Eloquence, that does dispel

Envy and Hate, that thirst for human gore;
　And cause in sweet society to dwell
　Vile savage minds that lurk in lonely cell.

O Mercury, assist my lab'ring sense,
　That round the circle of the world would fly!
As the wing'd eagle scorns the tow'ry fence
　Of Alpine hills round his high aery,
　And searches thro' the corners of the sky,
Sports in the clouds to hear the thunder's sound,
　And sees the winged lightnings as they fly;
Then, bosom'd in an amber cloud, around
　Plumes his wide wings, and seeks Sol's palace high.

And thou, O warrior maid invincible,
　Arm'd with the terrors of Almighty Jove!
Pallas, Minerva, maiden terrible,
　Lov'st thou to walk the peaceful solemn grove,
　In solemn gloom of branches interwove?
Or bear'st thy Egis o'er the burning field,
　Where, like the sea, the waves of battle move?
Or have thy soft piteous eyes beheld
　The weary wanderer thro' the desert rove?
　Or does th' afflicted man thy heav'nly bosom move?

BLIND-MAN'S BUFF

WHEN silver Snow decks Susan's cloaths,
And jewel hangs at th' shepherd's nose,
The blushing bank is all my care,
With hearth so red, and walls so fair;
"Heap the sea-coal; come, heap it higher,
The oaken log lay on the fire:"
The well-wash'd stools, a circling row,
With lad and lass, how fair the show!
The merry can of nut-brown ale,
The laughing jest, the love-sick tale,
'Till, tir'd of chat, the game begins.
The lasses prick the lads with pins;
Roger from Dolly twitch'd the stool,
She, falling, kiss'd the ground, poor fool!

She blush'd so red, with side-long glance
At hob-nail Dick, who griev'd the chance.
But now for Blind-man's Buff they call;
Of each incumbrance clear the hall——
Jenny her silken 'kerchief folds,
And blear-ey'd Will the black lot holds;
Now laughing, stops, with "Silence! hush!"
And Peggy Pout gives Sam a push.——
The Blind-man's arms, extended wide,
Sam slips between:——"O woe betide
Thee, clumsy Will!"——but titt'ring Kate
Is pen'd up in the corner strait!
And now Will's eyes beheld the play;
He thought his face was t'other way.——
"Now, Kitty, now; what chance hast thou,
Roger so near thee? Trips, I vow!"
She catches him—then Roger ties
His own head up—but not his eyes;
For thro' the slender cloth he sees,
And runs at Sam, who slips with ease
His clumsy hold, and, dodging round,
Sukey is tumbled on the ground!——
"See what it is to play unfair!
Where cheating is, there's mischief there."
But Roger still pursues the chace,——
"He sees! he sees!" cries softly, Grace;
"O Roger, thou, unskill'd in art,
Must, surer bound, go thro' thy part!"
Now Kitty, pert, repeats the rhymes,
And Roger turns him round three times;
Then pauses ere he starts——but Dick
Was mischief bent upon a trick:
Down on his hands and knees he lay,
Directly in the Blind-man's way——
Then cries out, "Hem!" Hodge heard, and ran
With hood-wink'd chance—sure of his man;
But down he came.—Alas, how frail
Our best of hopes, how soon they fail!
With crimson drops he stains the ground;
Confusion startles all around!
Poor piteous Dick supports his head,
And fain would cure the hurt he made;

But Kitty hasted with a key,
And down his back they strait convey
The cold relief—the blood is stay'd,
And Hodge again holds up his head.
Such are the fortunes of the game,
And those who play should stop the same
By wholesome laws, such as—all those
Who on the blinded man impose
Stand in his stead; as, long a-gone,
When men were first a nation grown,
Lawless they liv'd—till wantonness
And liberty began t'increase,
And one man lay in another's way;
Then laws were made to keep fair play.

KING EDWARD THE THIRD

PERSONS

KING EDWARD.
THE BLACK PRINCE.
QUEEN PHILIPPA.
DUKE OF CLARENCE.
SIR JOHN CHANDOS.
SIR THOMAS DAGWORTH.

SIR WALTER MANNY.
LORD AUDLEY.
LORD PERCY.
BISHOP.
WILLIAM, *Dagworth's Man.*
PETER BLUNT, *a common Soldier*

SCENE: *The Coast of France.* KING EDWARD *and Nobles before it.*

THE ARMY

KING. O thou, to whose fury the nations are
But as dust, maintain thy servant's right!
Without thine aid, the twisted mail, and spear,
And forged helm, and shield of seven times beaten brass,
Are idle trophies of the vanquisher.
When confusion rages, when the field is in a flame,
When the cries of blood tear horror from heav'n,
And yelling death runs up and down the ranks,
Let Liberty, the charter'd right of Englishmen,
Won by our fathers in many a glorious field,
Enerve my soldiers; let Liberty

Blaze in each countenance, and fire the battle.
The enemy fight in chains, invisible chains, but heavy;
Their minds are fetter'd; then how can they be free?
While, like the mounting flame,
We spring to battle o'er the floods of death,
And these fair youths, the flow'r of England,
Vent'ring their lives in my most righteous cause.
O sheathe their hearts with triple steel, that they
May emulate their father's virtues!
And thou, my son, be strong; thou fightest for a crown
That death can never ravish from thy brow,
A crown of glory; but from thy very dust
Shall beam a radiance, to fire the breasts
Of youth unborn! Our names are written equal
In fame's wide trophied hall; 'tis ours to gild
The letters, and to make them shine with gold
That never tarnishes: whether Third Edward,
Or the Prince of Wales, or Montacute, or Mortimer,
Or ev'n the least by birth, shall gain the brightest fame,
Is in his hand to whom all men are equal.
The world of men are like the num'rous stars,
That beam and twinkle in the depth of night,
Each clad in glory according to his sphere;—
But we, that wander from our native seats,
And beam forth lustre on a darkling world,
Grow larger as we advance! and some perhaps
The most obscure at home, that scarce were seen
To twinkle in their sphere, may so advance,
That the astonish'd world, with up-turn'd eyes,
Regardless of the moon, and those that once were bright,
Stand only for to gaze upon their splendor!
          [*He here knights the* PRINCE, *and other young Nobles.*
Now let us take a just revenge for those
Brave Lords, who fell beneath the bloody axe
At Paris. Thanks, noble Harcourt, for 'twas
By your advice we landed here in Brittany—
A country not yet sown with destruction,
And where the fiery whirlwind of swift war
Has not yet swept its desolating wing.——
Into three parties we divide by day,
And separate march, but join again at night:
Each knows his rank, and Heav'n marshal all.
                                        [*Exeunt.*

SCENE: *English Court.* LIONEL, DUKE OF CLARENCE; QUEEN
PHILIPPA, LORDS, BISHOP, *etc.*

CLARENCE. My lords, I have, by the advice of her
Whom I am doubly bound to obey, my Parent
And my Sovereign, call'd you together.
My task is great, my burden heavier than
My unfledg'd years;
Yet, with your kind assistance, Lords, I hope
England shall dwell in peace; that while my father
Toils in his wars, and turns his eyes on this
His native shore, and sees commerce fly round
With his white wings, and sees his golden London,
And her silver Thames, throng'd with shining spires
And corded ships, her merchants buzzing round
Like summer bees, and all the golden cities
In his land overflowing with honey,
Glory may not be dimm'd with clouds of care.
Say, Lords, should not our thoughts be first to commerce?
My Lord Bishop, you would recommend us agriculture?

BISHOP. Sweet Prince! the arts of peace are great,
And no less glorious than those of war,
Perhaps more glorious in the philosophic mind.
When I sit at my home, a private man,
My thoughts are on my gardens, and my fields,
How to employ the hand that lacketh bread.
If Industry is in my diocese,
Religion will flourish; each man's heart
Is cultivated, and will bring forth fruit:
This is my private duty and my pleasure.
But as I sit in council with my prince,
My thoughts take in the gen'ral good of the whole,
And England is the land favour'd by Commerce;
For Commerce, tho' the child of Agriculture,
Fosters his parent, who else must sweat and toil,
And gain but scanty fare. Then, my dear Lord,
Be England's trade our care; and we, as tradesmen,
Looking to the gain of this our native land.

CLARENCE. O my good Lord, true wisdom drops like honey
From your tongue, as from a worship'd oak!
Forgive, my Lords, my talkative youth, that speaks

Not merely what my narrow observation has
Pick'd up, but what I have concluded from your lessons:
Now, by the Queen's advice, I ask your leave
To dine to-morrow with the Mayor of London:
If I obtain your leave, I have another boon
To ask, which is, the favour of your company;
I fear Lord Percy will not give me leave.

    PERCY. Dear Sir, a prince should always keep his state,
And grant his favours with a sparing hand,
Or they are never rightly valued.
These are my thoughts, yet it were best to go;
But keep a proper dignity, for now
You represent the sacred person of
Your father; 'tis with princes as 'tis with the sun,
If not sometimes o'er-clouded, we grow weary
Of his officious glory.

    CLARENCE. Then you will give me leave to shine sometimes,
My Lord?

    LORD. Thou hast a gallant spirit, which I fear
Will be imposed on by the closer sort!   *[Aside.*

    CLARENCE. Well, I'll endeavour to take
Lord Percy's advice; I have been used so much
To dignity, that I'm sick on't.

    QUEEN PHILIPPA. Fie, Fie, Lord Clarence; you proceed not to business,
But speak of your own pleasures.
I hope their Lordships will excuse your giddiness.

    CLARENCE. My Lords, the French have fitted out many
Small ships of war, that, like to ravening wolves,
Infest our English seas, devouring all
Our burden'd vessels, spoiling our naval flocks.
The merchants do complain, and beg our aid.

    PERCY. The merchants are rich enough;
Can they not help themselves?

    BISHOP. They can, and may; but how to gain their will,
Requires our countenance and help.

    PERCY. When that they find they must, my Lord, they will:
Let them but suffer awhile, and you shall see
They will bestir themselves.

    BISHOP. Lord Percy cannot mean that we should suffer
This disgrace; if so, we are not sovereigns
Of the sea; our right, that Heaven gave
To England, when at the birth of nature

She was seated in the deep, the Ocean ceas'd
His mighty roar; and, fawning, play'd around
Her snowy feet, and own'd his lawful Queen.
Lord Percy, if the heart is sick, the head
Must be aggriev'd; if but one member suffer,
The heart doth fail. You say, my Lord, the merchants
Can, if they will, defend themselves against
These rovers: this is a noble scheme,
Worthy the brave Lord Percy, and as worthy
His generous aid to put it into practice.

 PERCY. Lord Bishop, what was rash in me, is wise
In you; I dare not own the plan. 'Tis not
Mine. Yet will I, if you please,
Quickly to the Lord Mayor, and work him onward
To this most glorious voyage, on which cast
I'll set my whole estate.
But we will bring these Gallic rovers under.

 QUEEN PHILIPPA. Thanks, brave Lord Percy; you have the thanks
Of England's Queen, and will, ere long, of England.   [*Exeunt.*

SCENE: *At Cressy.* SIR THOMAS DAGWORTH *and* LORD AUDLEY, *meeting.*

 AUDLEY. Good morrow, brave Sir Thomas; the bright morn
Smiles on our army, and the gallant sun
Springs from the hills like a young hero
Into the battle, shaking his golden locks
Exultingly; this is a promising day.

 DAGWORTH. Why, my Lord Audley, I don't know.
Give me your hand, and now I'll tell you what
I think you do not know—Edward's afraid of Philip.

 AUDLEY. Ha, Ha, Sir Thomas! you but joke;
Did you e'er see him fear? At Blanchetaque,
When almost singly he drove six thousand
French from the ford, did he fear then?

 DAGWORTH. Yes, fear; that made him fight so.

 AUDLEY. By the same reason I might say, 'tis fear
That makes you fight.

 DAGWORTH. Mayhap you may; look upon Edward's face—
No one can say he fears. But when he turns
His back, then I will say it to his face,
He is afraid; he makes us all afraid.

I cannot bear the enemy at my back.
Now here we are at Cressy; where, to-morrow,
To-morrow we shall know. I say, Lord Audley,
That Edward runs away from Philip.
   AUDLEY. Perhaps you think the Prince too is afraid?
   DAGWORTH. No; God forbid! I'm sure he is not—
He is a young lion. O I have seen him fight,
And give command, and lightning has flashed
From his eyes across the field; I have seen him
Shake hands with death, and strike a bargain for
The enemy; he has danc'd in the field
Of battle, like the youth at morrice play.
I'm sure he's not afraid, nor Warwick, nor none,
None of us but me; and I am very much afraid.
   AUDLEY. Are you afraid too, Sir Thomas?
I believe that as much as I believe
The King's afraid; but what are you afraid of?
   DAGWORTH. Of having my back laid open; we turn
Our backs to the fire till we shall burn our skirts.
   AUDLEY. And this, Sir Thomas, you call fear? Your fear
Is of a different kind than from the King's;
He fears to turn his face, and you to turn your back.—
I do not think, Sir Thomas, you know what fear is.

Enter SIR JOHN CHANDOS.

   CHANDOS. Good morrow, Generals; I give you joy:
Welcome to the fields of Cressy. Here we stop,
And wait for Philip.
   DAGWORTH. I hope so.
   AUDLEY. There, Sir Thomas; do you call that fear?
   DAGWORTH. I don't know; perhaps he takes it by fits.
Why, noble Chandos, look you here—
One rotten sheep spoils the whole flock;
And if the bell-weather is tainted, I wish
The Prince may not catch the distemper too.
   CHANDOS. Distemper, Sir Thomas! what distemper?
I have not heard.
   DAGWORTH. Why, Chandos, you are a wise man,
I know you understand me; a distemper
The King caught here in France of running away.
   AUDLEY. Sir Thomas, you say you have caught it too.
   DAGWORTH. And so will the whole army; 'tis very catching,

For when the coward runs, the brave man totters.
Perhaps the air of the country is the cause.—
I feel it coming upon me, so I strive against it;
You yet are whole, but after a few more
Retreats, we all shall know how to retreat
Better than fight.—To be plain, I think retreating
Too often, takes away a soldier's courage.

CHANDOS. Here comes the King himself; tell him your thoughts
Plainly, Sir Thomas.

DAGWORTH. I've told him before, but his disorder
Makes him deaf.

Enter KING EDWARD *and* BLACK PRINCE.

KING. Good morrow, Generals; when English courage fails,
Down goes our right to France;
But we are conquerors every where; nothing
Can stand our soldiers; each man is worthy
Of a triumph. Such an army of heroes
Ne'er shouted to the Heav'ns, nor shook the field.
Edward, my son, thou art
Most happy, having such command; the man
Were base who were not fir'd to deeds
Above heroic, having such examples.

PRINCE. Sire! with respect and deference I look
Upon such noble souls, and wish myself
Worthy the high command that Heaven and you
Have given me. When I have seen the field glow,
And in each countenance the soul of war
Curb'd by the manliest reason, I have been wing'd
With certain victory; and 'tis my boast,
And shall be still my glory, I was inspir'd
By these brave troops.

DAGWORTH. Your Grace had better make
Them all Generals.

KING. Sir Thomas Dagworth, you must have your joke,
And shall, while you can fight as you did at
The Ford.

DAGWORTH. I have a small petition to your Majesty.

KING. What can Sir Thomas Dagworth ask, that Edward
Can refuse?

DAGWORTH. I hope your Majesty cannot refuse so great
A trifle; I've gilt your cause with my best blood,
And would again, were I not forbid

By him whom I am bound to obey; my hands
Are tied up, my courage shrunk and wither'd,
My sinews slacken'd, and my voice scarce heard;
Therefore I beg I may return to England.

KING. I know not what you could have ask'd, Sir Thomas,
That I would not have sooner parted with
Than such a soldier as you have been, and such a friend;
Nay, I will know the most remote particulars
Of this your strange petition; that, if I can,
I still may keep you here.

DAGWORTH. Here on the fields of Cressy we are settled,
'Till Philip springs the tim'rous covey again.
The Wolf is hunted down by causeless fear;
The Lion flees, and fear usurps his heart,
Startled, astonish'd at the clam'rous Cock;
The Eagle, that doth gaze upon the sun,
Fears the small fire that plays about the fen;
If, at this moment of their idle fear,
The Dog doth seize the Wolf, the Forester the Lion,
The Negro in the crevice of the rock
Doth seize the soaring Eagle; undone by flight,
They tame submit: such the effect flight has
On noble souls. Now hear its opposite:
The tim'rous Stag starts from the thicket wild,
The fearful Crane springs from the splashy fen,
The shining Snake glides o'er the bending grass,
The Stag turns head! and bays the crying Hounds;
The Crane o'ertaken, fighteth with the Hawk;
The Snake doth turn, and bite the padding foot;
And, if your Majesty's afraid of Philip,
You are more like a Lion than a Crane:
Therefore I beg I may return to England.

KING. Sir Thomas, now I understand your mirth,
Which often plays with Wisdom for its pastime,
And brings good counsel from the breast of laughter.
I hope you'll stay, and see us fight this battle,
And reap rich harvest in the fields of Cressy;
Then go to England, tell them how we fight,
And set all hearts on fire to be with us.
Philip is plum'd, and thinks we flee from him,
Else he would never dare to attack us. Now,
Now the quarry's set! and Death doth sport

In the bright sunshine of this fatal day.

DAGWORTH. Now my heart dances, and I am as light
As the young bridegroom going to be married.
Now must I to my soldiers, get them ready,
Furbish our armours bright, new plume our helms,
And we will sing, like the young housewives busied
In the dairy; my feet are wing'd, but not
For flight, an please your grace.

KING. If all my soldiers are as pleas'd as you,
'Twill be a gallant thing to fight or die;
Then I can never be afraid of Philip.

DAGWORTH. A raw-bon'd fellow t'other day pass'd by me;
I told him to put off his hungry looks—
He answer'd me, "I hunger for another battle."
I saw a little Welchman with a fiery face;
I told him he look'd like a candle half
Burn'd out; he answer'd, he was "pig enough
To light another pattle." Last night, beneath
The moon I walk'd abroad, when all had pitch'd
Their tents, and all were still;
I heard a blooming youth singing a song
He had compos'd, and at each pause he wip'd
His drooping eyes. The ditty was, "if he
Return'd victorious, he should wed a maiden
Fairer than snow, and rich as midsummer."
Another wept, and wish'd health to his father.
I chid them both, but gave them noble hopes.
These are the minds that glory in the battle,
And leap and dance to hear the trumpet sound.

KING. Sir Thomas Dagworth, be thou near our person;
Thy heart is richer than the vales of France:
I will not part with such a man as thee.
If Philip came arm'd in the ribs of death,
And shook his mortal dart against my head,
Thou'dst laugh his fury into nerveless shame!
Go now, for thou art suited to the work,
Throughout the camp; enflame the timorous,
Blow up the sluggish into ardour, and
Confirm the strong with strength, the weak inspire,
And wing their brows with hope and expectation:
Then to our tent return, and meet to council.   [*Exit* DAGWORTH.

CHANDOS. That man's a hero in his closet, and more

A hero to the servants of his house
Than to the gaping world; he carries windows
In that enlarged breast of his, that all
May see what's done within.

PRINCE. He is a genuine Englishman, my Chandos,
And hath the spirit of Liberty within him.
Forgive my prejudice, Sir John; I think
My Englishmen the bravest people on
The face of the earth.

CHANDOS. Courage, my Lord, proceeds from self-dependence:
Teach man to think he's a free agent,
Give but a slave his liberty, he'll shake
Off sloth, and build himself a hut, and hedge
A spot of ground; this he'll defend; 'tis his
By right of nature: thus set in action,
He will still move onward to plan conveniences,
'Till glory fires his breast to enlarge his castle,
While the poor slave drudges all day, in hope
To rest at night.

KING. O Liberty, how glorious art thou!
I see thee hov'ring o'er my army, with
Thy wide-stretch'd plumes; I see thee
Lead them on to battle;
I see thee blow thy golden trumpet, while
Thy sons shout the strong shout of victory!
O noble Chandos! think thyself a gardener,
My son a vine, which I commit unto
Thy care; prune all extravagant shoots, and guide
Th' ambitious tendrils in the paths of wisdom;
Water him with thy advice, and Heav'n
Rain fresh'ning dew upon his branches. And,
O Edward, my dear son! learn to think lowly of
Thyself, as we may all each prefer other—
'Tis the best policy, and 'tis our duty.   [*Exit* KING EDWARD.

PRINCE. And may our duty, Chandos, be our pleasure.
Now we are alone, Sir John, I will unburden,
And breathe my hopes into the burning air,
Where thousand deaths are posting up and down,
Commission'd to this fatal field of Cressy;
Methinks I see them arm my gallant soldiers,
And gird the sword upon each thigh, and fit
Each shining helm, and string each stubborn bow,

And dance to the neighing of our steeds.
Methinks the shout begins, the battle burns;
Methinks I see them perch on English crests,
And roar the wild flame of fierce war upon
The thronged enemy! In truth, I am too full;
It is my sin to love the noise of war.
Chandos, thou seest my weakness; strong nature
Will bend or break us; my blood, like a springtide,
Does rise so high, to overflow all bounds
Of moderation; while Reason, in his
Frail bark, can see no shore or bound for vast
Ambition. Come, take the helm, my Chandos,
That my full-blown sails overset me not
In the wild tempest; condemn my 'vent'rous youth,
That plays with danger, as the innocent child
Unthinking plays upon the viper's den.
I am a coward in my reason, Chandos;

    CHANDOS. You are a man, my prince, and a brave man,
If I can judge of actions; but your heat
Is the effect of youth, and want of use;
Use makes the armed field and noisy war
Pass over as a summer cloud, unregarded,
Or but expected as a thing of course.
Age is contemplative; each rolling year
Brings forth fruit to the mind's treasure-house;
While vacant youth doth crave and seek about
Within itself, and findeth discontent:
Then, tir'd of thought, impatient takes the wing,
Seizes the fruits of time, attacks experience,
Roams round vast Nature's forest; where no bounds
Are set, the swiftest may have room, the strongest
Find prey; till tir'd at length, sated and tired
With the changing sameness, old variety,
We sit us down, and view our former joys
With distaste and dislike.

    PRINCE. Then if we must tug for experience,
Let us not fear to beat round Nature's wilds,
And rouze the strongest prey; then if we fall,
We fall with glory; I know the wolf
Is dangerous to fight, not good for food,
Nor is the hide a comely vestment; so
We have our battle for our pains. I know

That youth has need of age to point fit prey,
And oft the stander-by shall steal the fruit
Of th' other's labour. This is philosophy;
These are the tricks of the world; but the pure soul
Shall mount on native wings, disdaining
Little sport, and cut a path into the heaven of glory,
Leaving a track of light for men to wonder at.
I'm glad my father does not hear me talk;
You can find friendly excuses for me, Chandos;
But do you not think, Sir John, that if it please
Th' Almighty to stretch out my span of life,
I shall with pleasure view a glorious action,
Which my youth master'd.

   CHANDOS. Considerate age, my Lord, views motives,
And not acts; when neither warbling voice
Nor trilling pipe is heard, nor pleasure sits
With trembling age; the voice of Conscience then,
Sweeter than music in a summer's eve,
Shall warble round the snowy head, and keep
Sweet symphony to feather'd angels, sitting
As guardians round your chair; then shall the pulse
Beat slow, and taste, and touch, and sight, and sound, and smell,
That sing and dance round Reason's fine-wrought throne,
Shall flee away, and leave him all forlorn;
Yet not forlorn if Conscience is his friend.   [*Exeunt*.

SCENE *in* SIR THOMAS DAGWORTH'S *Tent*. DAGWORTH *and*
WILLIAM, *his Man*.

   DAGWORTH. Bring hither my armour, William;
Ambition is the growth of ev'ry clime.
   WILLIAM. Does it grow in England, Sir?
   DAGWORTH. Aye, it grows most in lands most cultivated.
   WILLIAM. Then it grows most in France; the vines here
Are finer than any we have in England.
   DAGWORTH. Aye, but the oaks are not.
   WILLIAM. What is the tree you mentioned? I don't think
I ever saw it.
   DAGWORTH. Ambition.
   WILLIAM. Is it a little creeping root that grows in ditches?
   DAGWORTH. Thou dost not understand me, William.

It is a root that grows in every breast;
Ambition is the desire or passion that one man
Has to get before another in any pursuit after glory;
But I don't think you have any of it.

WILLIAM. Yes, I have; I have a great ambition to know every thing, Sir.

DAGWORTH. But when our first ideas are wrong, what follows must all be wrong of course; 'tis best to know a little, and to know that little aright.

WILLIAM. Then, Sir, I should be glad to know if it was not ambition that brought over our King to France to fight for his right?

DAGWORTH. Tho' the knowledge of that will not profit thee much, yet I will tell you that it was ambition.

WILLIAM. Then if ambition is a sin, we are all guilty in coming with him, and in fighting for him.

DAGWORTH. Now, William, thou dost thrust the question home; but I must tell you, that guilt being an act of the mind, none are guilty but those whose minds are prompted by that same ambition.

WILLIAM. Now I always thought that a man might be guilty of doing wrong, without knowing it was wrong.

DAGWORTH. Thou art a natural philosopher, and knowest truth by instinct, while reason runs aground, as we have run our argument. Only remember, William, all have it in their power to know the motives of their own actions, and 'tis a sin to act without some reason.

WILLIAM. And whoever acts without reason, may do a great deal of harm without knowing it.

DAGWORTH. Thou art an endless moralist.

WILLIAM. Now there's a story come into my head, that I will tell your honour, if you'll give me leave.

DAGWORTH. No, William, save it till another time; this is no time for story-telling; but here comes one who is as entertaining as a good story.

Enter PETER BLUNT

PETER. Yonder's a musician going to play before the King; it's a new song about the French and English, and the Prince has made the minstrel a 'squire, and given him I don't know what, and I can't tell whether he don't mention us all one by one; and he is to write another about all us that are to die, that we may be remembered in Old England, for all our blood and bones are in France; and a great deal more that we shall all hear by and by; and I came to tell your honour, because you love to hear war-songs.

DAGWORTH. And who is this minstrel, Peter, do'st know?

PETER. O aye, I forgot to tell that; he has got the same name as Sir John Chandos, that the prince is always with—the wise man, that knows us all as well as your honour, only e'nt so good natur'd.

DAGWORTH. I thank you, Peter, for your information, but not for your compliment, which is not true; there's as much difference between him and me, as between glittering sand and fruitful mould; or shining glass and a wrought diamond, set in rich gold, and fitted to the finger of an emperor: such is that worthy Chandos.

PETER. I know your honour does not think any thing of yourself, but every body else does.

DAGWORTH. Go, Peter, get you gone; flattery is delicious, even from the lips of a babbler. [*Exit* PETER.

WILLIAM. I never flatter your honour.

DAGWORTH. I don't know that.

WILLIAM. Why you know, Sir, when we were in England at the tournament at Windsor, and the Earl of Warwick was tumbled over, you ask'd me if he did not look well when he fell? and I said, No, he look'd very foolish; and you was very angry with me for not flattering you.

DAGWORTH. You mean that I was angry with you for not flattering the Earl of Warwick. [*Exeunt.*

SCENE: SIR THOMAS DAGWORTH's *Tent.* SIR THOMAS
DAGWORTH—*to him*

Enter SIR WALTER MANNY.

SIR WALTER. Sir Thomas Dagworth, I have been weeping
Over the men that are to die to-day.

DAGWORTH. Why, brave Sir Walter, you or I may fall.

SIR WALTER. I know this breathing flesh must lie and rot,
Cover'd with silence and forgetfulness.—
Death wons in cities' smoke, and in still night,
When men sleep in their beds, walketh about!
How many in walled cities lie and groan,
Turning themselves upon their beds,
Talking with death, answering his hard demands!
How many walk in darkness, terrors are round
The curtains of their beds, destruction is
Ready at the door! How many sleep
In earth, cover'd with stones and deathy dust,
Resting in quietness, whose spirits walk
Upon the clouds of heaven, to die no more!
Yet death is terrible, tho' borne on angels' wings!
How terrible then is the field of death,
Where he doth rend the vault of heaven,

And shake the gates of hell!
O Dagworth, France is sick! the very sky,
Tho' sunshine light it, seems to me as pale
As the pale fainting man on his death-bed,
Whose face is shewn by light of sickly taper!
It makes me sad and sick at very heart,
Thousands must fall to-day!

DAGWORTH. Thousands of souls must leave this prison-house
To be exalted to those heavenly fields,
Where songs of triumph, palms of victory,
Where peace, and joy, and love, and calm content,
Sit singing in the azure clouds, and strew
Flowers of heaven's growth over the banquet-table;
Bind ardent Hope upon your feet like shoes,
Put on the robe of preparation,
The table is prepar'd in shining heaven,
The flowers of immortality are blown;
Let those that fight, fight in good stedfastness,
And those that fall shall rise in victory.

SIR WALTER. I've often seen the burning field of war,
And often heard the dismal clang of arms;
But never, till this fatal day of Cressy,
Has my soul fainted with these views of death!
I seem to be in one great charnel-house,
And seem to scent the rotten carcases!
I seem to hear the dismal yells of death,
While the black gore drops from his horrid jaws:
Yet I not fear the monster in his pride.——
But O the souls that are to die to-day!

DAGWORTH. Stop, brave Sir Walter; let me drop a tear,
Then let the clarion of war begin;
I'll fight and weep, 'tis in my country's cause;
I'll weep and shout for glorious liberty.
Grim war shall laugh and shout, deck'd in tears,
And blood shall flow like streams across the meadows,
That murmur down their pebbly channels, and
Spend their sweet lives to do their country service:
Then shall England's verdure shoot, her fields shall smile,
Her ships shall sing across the foaming sea,
Her mariners shall use the flute and viol,
And rattling guns, and black and dreary war,

Shall be no more.

 Sir Walter. Well, let the trumpet sound, and the drum beat;
Let war stain the blue heavens with bloody banners,
I'll draw my sword, nor ever sheath it up
'Till England blow the trump of victory,
Or I lay stretch'd upon the field of death!   [*Exeunt.*

Scene, *in the Camp. Several of the Warriors met at the King's Tent*
   with a Minstrel, *who sings the following song:*

O Sons of Trojan Brutus, cloath'd in war,
Whose voices are the thunder of the field,
Rolling dark clouds o'er France, muffling the sun
In sickly darkness like a dim eclipse,
Threatening as the red brow of storms, as fire
Burning up nations in your wrath and fury!

Your ancestors came from the fires of Troy,
(Like lions rouz'd by light'ning from their dens,
Whose eyes do glare against the stormy fires)
Heated with war, fill'd with the blood of Greeks,
With helmets hewn, and shields covered with gore,
In navies black, broken with wind and tide!

They landed in firm array upon the rocks
Of Albion; they kiss'd the rocky shore;
"Be thou our mother, and our nurse," they said;
"Our children's mother, and thou shalt be our grave;
The sepulchre of ancient Troy, from whence
Shall rise cities, and thrones, and arms, and awful pow'rs."

Our fathers swarm from the ships. Giant voices
Are heard from the hills, the enormous sons
Of Ocean run from rocks and caves: wild men,
Naked and roaring like lions, hurling rocks,
And wielding knotty clubs, like oaks entangled
Thick as a forest, ready for the axe.

Our fathers move in firm array to battle;
The savage monsters rush like roaring fire;
Like as a forest roars, with crackling flames,

When the red lightning, borne by furious storms,
Lights on some woody shore; the parched heavens
Rain fire into the molten raging sea!

The smoaking trees are strewn upon the shore,
Spoil'd of their verdure! O how oft have they
Defy'd the storm that howled o'er their heads!
Our fathers, sweating, lean on their spears, and view
The mighty dead: giant bodies streaming blood,
Dread visages frowning in silent death!

Then Brutus spoke, inspir'd; our fathers sit
Attentive on the melancholy shore:——
Hear ye the voice of Brutus—"The flowing waves
Of time come rolling o'er my breast," he said;
"And my heart labours with futurity:
Our sons shall rule the empire of the sea.

"Their mighty wings shall stretch from east to west,
Their nest is in the sea; but they shall roam
Like eagles for the prey; nor shall the young
Crave or be heard; for plenty shall bring forth,
Cities shall sing, and vales in rich array
Shall laugh, whose fruitful laps bend down with fulness.

"Our sons shall rise from thrones in joy,
Each one buckling on his armour; Morning
Shall be prevented by their swords gleaming,
And Evening hear their song of victory!
Their towers shall be built upon the rocks,
Their daughters shall sing, surrounded with shining spears!

"Liberty shall stand upon the cliffs of Albion,
Casting her blue eyes over the green ocean;
Or, tow'ring, stand upon the roaring waves,
Stretching her mighty spear o'er distant lands;
While, with her eagle wings, she covereth
Fair Albion's shore, and all her families."

PROLOGUE
INTENDED FOR A DRAMATIC PIECE OF
KING EDWARD THE FOURTH

O FOR a voice like thunder, and a tongue
To drown the throat of war!—When the senses
Are shaken, and the soul is driven to madness,
Who can stand? When the souls of the oppressed
Fight in the troubled air that rages, who can stand?
When the whirlwind of fury comes from the
Throne of God, when the frowns of his countenance
Drive the nations together, who can stand?
When Sin claps his broad wings over the battle,
And sails rejoicing in the flood of Death;
When souls are torn to everlasting fire,
And fiends of Hell rejoice upon the slain,
O who can stand? O who hath caused this?
O who can answer at the throne of God?
The Kings and Nobles of the Land have done it!
Hear it not, Heaven, thy Ministers have done it!

PROLOGUE TO KING JOHN

JUSTICE hath heaved a sword to plunge in Albion's breast; for Albion's
sins are crimson dy'd, and the red scourge follows her desolate sons! Then
Patriot rose; full oft did Patriot rise, when Tyranny hath stain'd fair
Albion's breast with her own children's gore. Round his majestic feet
deep thunders roll; each heart does tremble, and each knee grows slack.
The stars of heaven tremble: the roaring voice of war, the trumpet, calls
to battle! Brother in brother's blood must bathe, rivers of death! O land,
most hapless! O beauteous island, how forsaken! Weep from thy silver
fountains; weep from thy gentle rivers! The angel of the island
weeps! Thy widowed virgins weep beneath thy shades! Thy aged fathers
gird themselves for war! The sucking infant lives to die in battle; the
weeping mother feeds him for the slaughter! The husbandman doth leave
his bending harvest! Blood cries afar! The land doth sow itself! The
glittering youth of courts must gleam in arms! The aged senators their
ancient swords assume! The trembling sinews of old age must work the
work of death against their progeny; for Tyranny hath stretch'd his

purple arm, and "blood," he cries; "the chariots and the horses, the noise of shout, and dreadful thunder of the battle heard afar!"—Beware, O Proud! thou shalt be humbled; thy cruel brow, thine iron heart is smitten, though lingering Fate is slow. O yet may Albion smile again, and stretch her peaceful arms, and raise her golden head, exultingly! Her citizens shall throng about her gates, her mariners shall sing upon the sea, and myriads shall to her temples crowd! Her sons shall joy as in the morning! Her daughters sing as to the rising year!

A WAR SONG TO ENGLISHMEN

PREPARE, prepare the iron helm of war,
Bring forth the lots, cast in the spacious orb;
Th' Angel of Fate turns them with mighty hands,
And casts them out upon the darken'd earth!
     Prepare, prepare.

Prepare your hearts for Death's cold hand! prepare
Your souls for flight, your bodies for the earth!
Prepare your arms for glorious victory!
Prepare your eyes to meet a holy God!
     Prepare, prepare.

Whose fatal scroll is that? Methinks 'tis mine!
Why sinks my heart, why faultereth my tongue?
Had I three lives, I'd die in such a cause,
And rise, with ghosts, over the well-fought field.
     Prepare, prepare.

The arrows of Almighty God are drawn!
Angels of Death stand in the low'ring heavens!
Thousands of souls must seek the realms of light,
And walk together on the clouds of heaven!
     Prepare, prepare.

Soldiers, prepare! Our cause is Heaven's cause;
Soldiers, prepare! Be worthy of our cause:
Prepare to meet our fathers in the sky:
Prepare, O troops, that are to fall to-day!
     Prepare, prepare.

Alfred shall smile, and make his harp rejoice;
The Norman William, and the learned Clerk,
And Lion Heart, and black-brow'd Edward with
His loyal queen shall rise, and welcome us!
Prepare, prepare.

THE COUCH OF DEATH

THE veiled Evening walked solitary down the western hills, and Silence reposed in the valley; the birds of day were heard in their nests, rustling in brakes and thickets; and the owl and bat flew round the darkening trees: all is silent when Nature takes her repose.—In former times, on such an evening, when the cold clay breathed with life, and our ancestors, who now sleep in their graves, walked on the stedfast globe, the remains of a family of the tribes of Earth, a mother and a sister were gathered to the sick bed of a youth: Sorrow linked them together, leaning on one another's necks alternately—like lilies, dropping tears in each other's bosom, they stood by the bed like reeds bending over a lake, when the evening drops trickle down. His voice was low as the whisperings of the woods when the wind is asleep, and the visions of Heaven unfold their visitation. "Parting is hard, and death is terrible; I seem to walk through a deep valley, far from the light of day, alone and comfortless! The damps of death fall thick upon me! Horrors stare me in the face! I look behind, there is no returning; Death follows after me; I walk in regions of Death, there no tree is; without a lantern to direct my steps, without a staff to support me."—Thus he laments through the still evening, till the curtains of darkness were drawn! Like the sound of a broken pipe, the aged woman raised her voice. "O my son, my son, I know but little of the path thou goest! But lo, there is a God, who made the world; stretch out thy hand to Him." The youth replied, like a voice heard from a sepulchre, "My hand is feeble, how should I stretch it out? My ways are sinful, how should I raise mine eyes? My voice hath used deceit, how should I call on Him who is Truth? My breath is loathsome, how should he not be offended? If I lay my face in the dust, the grave opens its mouth for me; if I lift up my head, sin covers me as a cloak! O my dear friends, pray ye for me! Stretch forth your hands, that my helper may come! Through the void space I walk between the sinful world and eternity! Beneath me burns eternal fire! O for a hand to pluck me forth!" As the voice of an omen heard in the silent valley, when the few inhabitants cling trembling together: as the voice of the Angel of Death, when the thin beams of the moon give a faint light, such was this young man's voice to his friends!

Like the bubbling waters of the brook in the dead of night, the aged woman raised her cry, and said, "O Voice, that dwellest in my breast, can I not cry, and lift my eyes to Heaven? Thinking of this, my spirit is turned within me into confusion! O my child, my child! is thy breath infected? So is mine. As the deer wounded, by the brooks of water, so the arrows of sin stick in my flesh; the poison hath entered into my marrow." —Like rolling waves, upon a desert short, sighs succeeded sighs; they covered their faces, and wept! The youth lay silent—his mother's arm was under his head; he was like a cloud tossed by the winds, till the sun shine, and the drops of rain glisten, the yellow harvest breathes, and the thankful eyes of the villagers are turned up in smiles. The traveller that hath taken shelter under an oak, eyes the distant country with joy! Such smiles were seen upon the face of the youth; a visionary hand wiped away his tears, and a ray of light beamed around his head! All was still. The moon hung not out her lamp, and the stars faintly glimmered in the summer sky; the breath of night slept among the leaves of the forest; the bosom of the lofty hill drank in the silent dew, while on his majestic brow the voice of Angels is heard, and stringed sounds ride upon the wings of night. The sorrowful pair lift up their heads, hovering Angels are around them, voices of comfort are heard over the Couch of Death, and the youth breathes out his soul with joy into eternity.

CONTEMPLATION

W H O is this, that with unerring step dares tempt the wilds, where only Nature's foot hath trod? 'Tis Contemplation, daughter of the grey Morning! Majestical she steppeth, and with her pure quill on every flower writeth Wisdom's name. Now lowly bending, whispers in mine ear, "O man, how great, how little thou! O man, slave of each moment, lord of eternity! seest thou where Mirth sits on the painted cheek? doth it not seem ashamed of such a place, and grow immoderate to brave it out? O what an humble garb true Joy puts on! Those who want Happiness must stoop to find it; it is a flower that grows in every vale. Vain foolish man, that roams on lofty rocks, where, 'cause his garments are swoln with wind, he fancies he is grown into a giant! Lo then, Humility, take it, and wear it in thine heart; lord of thyself, thou then art lord of all. Clamour brawls along the streets, and destruction hovers in the city's smoak; but on these plains, and in these silent woods, true joys descend! here build thy nest; here fix thy staff; delights blossom around; numberless beauties blow; the green grass springs in joy, and the nimble air kisses the leaves; the brook stretches its arms along the velvet meadow, its silver inhabitants sport and play; the youthful sun joys like a hunter roused to the chace: he rushes up the sky, and lays hold on the immortal coursers of day; the sky glitters with the jingling trappings! Like a triumph, season follows season, while the airy music fills the world with joyful sounds." I answered, "Heavenly goddess! I am wrapped in mortality, my flesh is a prison, my bones the bars of death; Misery builds over our cottage roofs, and Discontent runs like a brook. Even in childhood Sorrow slept with me in my cradle; he followed me up and down in the house when I grew up; he was my school-fellow: thus he was in my steps and in my play, till he became to me as my brother. I walked through dreary places with him, and in church-yards; and I oft found myself sitting by Sorrow on a tombstone!"

SAMSON

SAMSON, the strongest of the children of men, I sing; how he was foiled by woman's arts, by a false wife brought to the gates of death! O Truth, that shinest with propitious beams, turning our earthly night to heavenly day, from presence of the Almighty Father! thou visitest our darkling world with blessed feet, bringing good news of Sin and Death destroyed! O white-robed Angel, guide my timorous hand to write as on a lofty rock with iron pens the words of truth, that all who pass may read.—Now Night, noon-tide of damned spirits, over the silent earth spreads her pavilion, while in dark council sat Philista's lords; and where strength failed, black thoughts in ambush lay. Their helmed youth and aged warriors in dust together lie, and Desolation spreads his wings over the land of Palestine; from side to side the land groans, her prowess lost, and seeks to hide her bruised head under the mists of night, breeding dark plots. For Dalila's fair arts have long been tried in vain; in vain she wept in many a treacherous tear. "Go on, fair traitress; do thy guileful work; ere once again the changing moon her circuit hath performed, thou shalt overcome, and conquer him by force unconquerable, and wrest his secret from him. Call thine alluring arts and honest-seeming brow, the holy kiss of love, and the transparent tear; put on fair linen, that with the lily vies, purple and silver; neglect thy hair, to seem more lovely in thy loose attire; put on thy country's pride, deceit; and eyes of love decked in mild sorrow, and sell thy Lord for gold."—For now, upon her sumptuous couch reclined, in gorgeous pride, she still intreats, and still she grasps his vigorous knees with her fair arms.—"Thou lov'st me not! thou'rt war, thou art not love! O foolish Dalila! O weak woman! it is death cloathed in flesh thou lovest, and thou hast been incircled in his arms!—Alas, my Lord, what am I calling thee? Thou art my God! To thee I pour my tears for sacrifice morning and evening: My days are covered with sorrow, shut up, darkened. By night I am deceived! Who says that thou wast born of mortal kind? Destruction was thy father, a lioness suckled thee, thy young hands tore human limbs, and gorged human flesh! Come hither, Death; art thou not Samson's servant? 'Tis Dalila that calls, thy master's wife; no, stay, and let thy master do the deed: one blow of that strong arm would ease my pain; then should I lay at quiet, and have rest. Pity forsook thee at thy birth! O Dagon furious, and all ye gods of Palestine, withdraw your hand! I am but a weak woman. Alas, I am wedded to your enemy! I will go mad, and tear my crisped hair; I'll run about, and pierce the ears o' th' gods! O Samson, hold me not; thou lovest me not! Look not upon me with those deathful eyes! Thou wouldst my death, and death approaches fast."—Thus, in false tears, she bath'd his feet, and thus she day by day oppressed his soul: he seemed a mountain, his brow among the clouds; she seemed a silver stream, his feet embracing. Dark thoughts rolled to and fro in his mind, like thunder clouds troubling the sky; his visage was troubled; his soul was distressed.—"Though I should tell her all my heart, what can I fear? Though I should tell this secret of my birth, the utmost may be warded off as well when told as now." She saw him moved, and thus resumes her wiles.—"Samson, I'm thine; do with me what thou wilt; my friends are enemies; my life is death; I am a traitor to my nation, and despised; my joy is given into the hands of him who hates me, using deceit to the wife of his bosom. Thrice hast thou mocked me, and grieved my soul. Didst thou not tell me with green withes to bind thy nervous arms, and after that, when I had found thy falsehood, with new ropes to bind thee fast? I knew thou didst but mock me. Alas, when in thy sleep I bound thee with them to try thy truth, I cried, 'The Philistines be upon thee, Samson!' Then did suspicion wake thee; how didst thou rend the feeble ties! Thou fearest nought, what shouldst thou fear? Thy power is more than mortal, none can hurt thee; thy bones are brass, they sinews are iron! Ten thousand spears are like the summer grass; an army of mighty men are as flocks in the vallies; what canst thou fear? I drink my tears like water; I live upon sorrow! O worse than wolves and tygers, what canst thou give when such a trifle is denied me? But O at last thou mockest me, to shame my over-fond inquiry! Thou toldest me to weave thee to the beam by thy strong hair; I did even that to try thy truth: but when I cried, 'The Philistines be upon thee!' then didst thou leave me to bewail that Samson loved me not."—He sat, and inward griev'd; he saw and lov'd the beauteous suppliant, nor could conceal aught that might appease her; then, leaning on her bosom, thus he spoke: "Hear, O Dalila! doubt no more of Samson's love; for that fair breast was made the ivory palace of my inmost heart, where it shall lie at rest; for sorrow is the lot of all of woman born: for care was I brought forth, and labour is my lot: nor matchless might, nor wisdom, nor every gift enjoyed, can from the heart of man hide sorrow.—Twice was my birth foretold from heaven, and twice a sacred vow enjoined me that I should drink no wine, nor eat of any unclean thing, for holy unto Israel's God I am, a Nazarite even from my mother's womb. Twice was it told, that it might not be broken. 'Grant me a son, kind Heaven,' Manoa cried; but Heaven refused! Childless he mourned, but thought his God knew best. In solitude, though not obscure, in Israel he lived, till venerable age came on: his flocks increased, and plenty crowned his board: beloved, revered of man! But God hath other joys in store. Is burdened Israel his grief? The son of his old age shall set it free! The venerable sweetner of his life receives the promise first from Heaven. She saw the maidens play, and blessed their innocent mirth; she blessed each new-joined pair; but from her the long-wished deliverer shall spring. Pensive, alone she sat within the house, when busy day was fading, and calm evening, time for contemplation, rose from the forsaken east, and drew the curtains of heaven; pensive she sat, and thought on Israel's grief, and silent prayed to Israel's God; when lo, an angel from the fields of light entered the house! His form was manhood in the prime, and from his spacious brow shot terrors through the evening shade! But mild he hailed her——'Hail, highly favoured!' said he, 'for lo, thou shalt conceive, and bear a son, and Israel's strength shall be upon his shoulders, and he shall be called Israel's Deliverer! Now therefore drink no wine, and eat not any unclean thing, for he shall be a Nazarite to God.'—Then as a neighbour, when his evening tale is told, departs, his blessing leaving, so seemed he to depart: she wondered with exceeding joy, nor knew he was an angel. Manoa left his fields to sit in the house, and take his evening's rest from labour—the sweetest time that God has allotted mortal man. He sat, and heard with joy, and praised God who Israel still doth keep. The time rolled on, and Israel groaned oppressed. The sword was bright, while the plow-share rusted, till hope grew feeble, and was ready to give place to doubting: then prayed Manoa —'O Lord, thy flock is scattered on the hills! The wolf teareth them, Oppression stretches his rod over our land, our country is plowed with swords, and reaped in blood! The echoes of slaughter reach from hill to hill! Instead of peaceful pipe, the shepherd bears a sword; the ox goad is turned into a spear! O when shall our Deliverer come? The Philistine riots on our flocks, our vintage is gathered by bands of enemies! Stretch forth thy hand, and save.'——Thus prayed Manoa. The aged woman walked into the field, and lo, again the angel came! Clad as a traveller fresh risen on his journey; she ran and called her husband, who came and talked with him.——'O man of God,' said he, 'thou comest from far! Let us detain thee while I make ready a kid, that thou mayest sit and eat, and tell us of thy name and warfare; that when thy sayings come to pass, we may honour thee.' The Angel answered, 'My name is wonderful; enquire not after it, seeing it is a secret: but, if thou wilt, offer an offering unto the Lord.' "

Songs of Innocence and of Experience

SHEWING THE TWO CONTRARY STATES OF THE
HUMAN SOUL

SONGS OF INNOCENCE

INTRODUCTION

PIPING down the valleys wild,
Piping songs of pleasant glee,
On a cloud I saw a child,
And he laughing said to me:

"Pipe a song about a Lamb!"
So I piped with a merry chear.
"Piper, pipe that song again;"
So I piped: he wept to hear.

"Drop thy pipe, thy happy pipe;
Sing thy songs of happy chear:"
So I sung the same again,
While he wept with joy to hear.

"Piper, sit thee down and write
In a book, that all may read."
So he vanish'd from my sight,
And I pluck'd a hollow reed,

And I made a rural pen,
And I stain'd the water clear,
And I wrote my happy songs
Every child may joy to hear.

THE SHEPHERD

H O W sweet is the Shepherd's sweet lot!
From the morn to the evening he strays;
He shall follow his sheep all the day,
And his tongue shall be filled with praise.

For he hears the lamb's innocent call,
And he hears the ewe's tender reply;
He is watchful while they are in peace,
For they know when their Shepherd is nigh.

THE ECCHOING GREEN

T H E Sun does arise,
And make happy the skies;
The merry bells ring
To welcome the Spring;
The skylark and thrush,
The birds of the bush,
Sing louder around
To the bells' chearful sound,
While our sports shall be seen
On the Ecchoing Green.

Old John, with white hair,
Does laugh away care,
Sitting under the oak,
Among the old folk.
They laugh at our play,
And soon they all say:
"Such, such were the joys
When we all, girls & boys,
In our youth time were seen
On the Ecchoing Green."

Till the little ones, weary,
No more can be merry;
The sun does descend,
And our sports have an end.

Round the laps of their mothers
Many sisters and brothers,
Like birds in their nest,
Are ready for rest,
And sport no more seen
On the darkening Green.

THE LAMB

LITTLE Lamb, who made thee?
Dost thou know who made thee?
Gave thee life, & bid thee feed
By the stream & o'er the mead;
Gave thee clothing of delight,
Softest clothing, wooly, bright;
Gave thee such a tender voice,
Making all the vales rejoice?
Little Lamb, who made thee?
Dost thou know who made thee?

Little Lamb, I'll tell thee,
Little Lamb, I'll tell thee:
He is called by thy name,
For he calls himself a Lamb.
He is meek, & he is mild;
He became a little child.
I a child, & thou a lamb,
We are called by his name.
Little Lamb, God bless thee!
Little Lamb, God bless thee!

THE LITTLE BLACK BOY

MY mother bore me in the southern wild,
And I am black, but O! my soul is white;
White as an angel is the English child,
But I am black, as if bereav'd of light.

My mother taught me underneath a tree,
And sitting down before the heat of day,
She took me on her lap and kissed me,
And pointing to the east, began to say:

"Look on the rising run: there God does live,
And gives his light, and gives his heat away;
And flowers and trees and beasts and men receive
Comfort in morning, joy in the noonday.

"And we are put on earth a little space,
That we may learn to bear the beams of love;
And these black bodies and this sunburnt face
Is but a cloud, and like a shady grove.

"For when our souls have learn'd the heat to bear,
The cloud will vanish; we shall hear his voice,
Saying: 'Come out from the grove, my love & care,
And round my golden tent like lambs rejoice.' "

Thus did my mother say, and kissed me;
And thus I say to little English boy:
When I from black and he from white cloud free,
And round the tent of God like lambs we joy,

I'll shade him from the heat, till he can bear
To lean in joy upon our father's knee;
And then I'll stand and stroke his silver hair,
And be like him, and he will then love me.

THE BLOSSOM

MERRY, Merry Sparrow!
Under leaves so green
A happy Blossom
Sees you swift as arrow
Seek your cradle narrow
Near my Bosom.

Pretty, Pretty Robin!
Under leaves so green
A happy Blossom
Hears you sobbing, sobbing,
Pretty, Pretty Robin,
Near my Bosom.

THE CHIMNEY SWEEPER

WHEN my mother died I was very young,
And my father sold me while yet my tongue
Could scarcely cry " 'weep! 'weep! 'weep! 'weep!"
So your chimneys I sweep, & in soot I sleep.

There's little Tom Dacre, who cried when his head,
That curl'd like a lamb's back, was shav'd: so I said
"Hush, Tom! never mind it, for when your head's bare
You know that the soot cannot spoil your white hair."

And so he was quiet, & that very night,
As Tom was a-sleeping, he had such a sight!
That thousands of sweepers, Dick, Joe, Ned, & Jack,
Were all of them lock'd up in coffins of black.

And by came an Angel who had a bright key,
And he open'd the coffins & set them all free;
Then down a green plain leaping, laughing, they run,
And wash in a river, and shine in the Sun.

Then naked & white, all their bags left behind,
They rise upon clouds and sport in the wind;
And the Angel told Tom, if he'd be a good boy,
He'd have God for his father, & never want joy.

And so Tom awoke; and we rose in the dark,
And got with our bags & our brushes to work.
Tho' the morning was cold, Tom was happy & warm;
So if all do their duty they need not fear harm.

THE LITTLE BOY LOST

"FATHER! father! where are you going?
O do not walk so fast.
Speak, father, speak to your little boy,
Or else I shall be lost."

The night was dark, no father was there;
The child was wet with dew;
The mire was deep, & the child did weep,
And away the vapour flew.

THE LITTLE BOY FOUND

THE little boy lost in the lonely fen,
Led by the wand'ring light,
Began to cry; but God, ever nigh,
Appear'd like his father in white.

He kissed the child & by the hand led
And to his mother brought,
Who in sorrow pale, thro' the lonely dale,
Her little boy weeping sought.

LAUGHING SONG

WHEN the green woods laugh with the voice of joy,
And the dimpling stream runs laughing by;
When the air does laugh with our merry wit,
And the green hill laughs with the noise of it;

When the meadows laugh with lively green,
And the grasshopper laughs in the merry scene,
When Mary and Susan and Emily
With their sweet round mouths sing "Ha, Ha, He!"

When the painted birds laugh in the shade,
Where our table with cherries and nuts is spread,
Come live & be merry, and join with me,
To sing the sweet chorus of "Ha, Ha, He!"

A CRADLE SONG

SWEET dreams, form a shade
O'er my lovely infant's head;
Sweet dreams of pleasant streams
By happy, silent, moony beams.

Sweet sleep, with soft down
Weave thy brows an infant crown.
Sweep sleep, Angel mild,
Hover o'er my happy child.

Sweet smiles, in the night
Hover over my delight;
Sweet smiles, Mother's smiles,
All the livelong night beguiles.

Sweet moans, dovelike sighs,
Chase not slumber from thy eyes.
Sweet moans, sweeter smiles,
All the dovelike moans beguiles.

Sleep, sleep, happy child,
All creation slept and smil'd;
Sleep, sleep, happy sleep,
While o'er thee thy mother weep.

Sweet babe, in thy face
Holy image I can trace.
Sweet babe, once like thee,
Thy maker lay and wept for me,

Wept for me, for thee, for all,
When he was an infant small
Thou his image ever see,
Heavenly face that smiles on thee,

Smiles on thee, on me, on all;
Who became an infant small.
Infant smiles are his own smiles;
Heaven & earth to peace beguiles.

THE DIVINE IMAGE

T o Mercy, Pity, Peace, and Love
All pray in their distress;
And to these virtues of delight
Return their thankfulness.

For Mercy, Pity, Peace, and Love
Is God, our father dear,
And Mercy, Pity, Peace, and Love
Is Man, his child and care.

For Mercy has a human heart,
Pity a human face,
And Love, the human form divine,
And Peace, the human dress.

Then every man, of every clime,
That prays in his distress,
Prays to the human form divine,
Love, Mercy, Pity, Peace.

And all must love the human form,
In heathen, turk, or jew;
Where Mercy, Love, & Pity dwell
There God is dwelling too.

HOLY THURSDAY

'T W A S on a Holy Thursday, their innocent faces clean,
The children walking two & two, in red & blue & green,
Grey-headed beadles walk'd before, with wands as white as snow,
Till into the high dome of Paul's they like Thames' waters flow.

O what a multitude they seem'd, these flowers of London town!
Seated in companies they sit with radiance all their own.
The hum of multitudes was there, but multitudes of lambs,
Thousands of little boys & girls raising their innocent hands.

Now like a mighty wind they raise to heaven the voice of song,
Or like harmonious thunderings the seats of Heaven among.
Beneath them sit the aged men, wise guardians of the poor;
Then cherish pity, lest you drive an angel from your door.

NIGHT

T H E sun descending in the west,
The evening star does shine;
The birds are silent in their nest,
And I must seek for mine.

The moon like a flower
In heaven's high bower,
With silent delight
Sits and smiles on the night.

Farewell, green fields and happy groves,
Where flocks have took delight.
Where lambs have nibbled, silent moves
The feet of angels bright;
Unseen they pour blessing
And joy without ceasing,
On each bud and blossom,
And each sleeping bosom.

They look in every thoughtless nest,
Where birds are cover'd warm;
They visit caves of every beast,
To keep them all from harm.
If they see any weeping
That should have been sleeping,
They pour sleep on their head,
And sit down by their bed.

When wolves and tygers howl for prey,
They pitying stand and weep;
Seeking to drive their thirst away,
And keep them from the sheep;
But if they rush dreadful,
The angels, most heedful,
Receive each mild spirit,
New worlds to inherit.

And there the lion's ruddy eyes
Shall flow with tears of gold,
And pitying the tender cries,
And walking round the fold,
Saying "Wrath, by his meekness,
And by his health, sickness
Is driven away
From our immortal day.

"And now beside thee, bleating lamb,
I can lie down and sleep;
Or think on him who bore thy name,
Graze after thee and weep.
For, wash'd in life's river,
My bright mane for ever
Shall shine like the gold
As I guard o'er the fold."

SPRING

SOUND the Flute!
Now it's mute.
Birds delight
Day and Night;
Nightingale
In the dale,
Lark in Sky,
Merrily,
Merrily, Merrily, to welcome in the Year.

Little Boy,
Full of joy;
Little Girl,
Sweet and small;
Cock does crow,
So do you;
Merry voice,
Infant noise,
Merrily, Merrily, to welcome in the Year.

Little Lamb,
Here I am;
Come and lick
My white neck;
Let me pull
Your soft Wool;
Let me kiss
Your soft face:
Merrily, Merrily, we welcome in the Year.

NURSE'S SONG

WHEN the voices of children are heard on the green
And laughing is heard on the hill,
My heart is at rest within my breast
    And everything else is still.

"Then come home, my children, the sun is gone down
And the dews of night arise;
Come, come, leave off play, and let us away
Till the morning appears in the skies.

"No, no, let us play, for it is yet day
And we cannot go to sleep;
Besides, in the sky the little birds fly
And the hills are all cover'd with sheep.

"Well, well, go & play till the light fades away
And then go home to bed."
The little ones leaped & shouted & laugh'd
    And all the hills ecchoed.

INFANT JOY

"I HAVE no name:
I am but two days old."
What shall I call thee?
"I happy am,
Joy is my name."
Sweet joy befall thee!

Pretty joy!
Sweet joy but two days old,
Sweet joy I call thee:
Thou dost smile,
I sing the while,
Sweet joy befall thee!

A DREAM

ONCE a dream did weave a shade
O'er my Angel-guarded bed,
That an Emmet lost its way
Where on grass methought I lay.

Troubled, 'wilder'd, and forlorn,
Dark, benighted, travel-worn,
Over many a tangled spray,
All heart-broke I heard her say:

"O, my children! do they cry?
Do they hear their father sigh?
Now they look abroad to see:
Now return and weep for me."

Pitying, I drop'd a tear;
But I saw a glow-worm near,
Who replied: "What wailing wight
Calls the watchman of the night?

"I am set to light the ground,
While the beetle goes his round:
Follow now the beetle's hum;
Little wanderer, hie thee home."

ON ANOTHER'S SORROW

CAN I see another's woe,
And not be in sorrow too?
Can I see another's grief,
And not seek for kind relief?

Can I see a falling tear,
And not feel my sorrow's share?
Can a father see his child
Weep, nor be with sorrow fill'd?

Can a mother sit and hear
An infant groan an infant fear?
No, no! never can it be!
Never, never can it be!

And can he who smiles on all
Hear the wren with sorrows small,
Hear the small bird's grief & care,
Hear the woes that infants bear,

And not sit beside the nest,
Pouring pity in their breast;
And not sit the cradle near,
Weeping tear on infant's tear;

And not sit both night & day,
Wiping all our tears away?
O, no! never can it be!
Never, never can it be!

He doth give his joy to all;
He becomes an infant small;
He becomes a man of woe;
He doth feel the sorrow too.

Think not thou canst sigh a sigh
And thy maker is not by;
Think not thou canst weep a tear
And thy maker is not near.

O! he gives to us his joy
That our grief he may destroy;
Till our grief is fled & gone
He doth sit by us and moan.

SONGS OF EXPERIENCE

INTRODUCTION

HEAR the voice of the Bard!
Who Present, Past, & Future, sees;
Whose ears have heard
The Holy Word
That walk'd among the ancient trees,

Calling the lapsed Soul,
And weeping in the evening dew;
That might controll
The starry pole,
And fallen, fallen light renew!

"O Earth, O Earth, return!
Arise from out the dewy grass;
Night is worn,
And the morn
Rises from the slumberous mass.

"Turn away no more;
Why wilt thou turn away?
The starry floor,
The wat'ry shore,
Is giv'n thee till the break of day."

EARTH'S ANSWER

EARTH rais'd up her head
From the darkness dread & drear.
Her light fled,
Stony dread!
And her locks cover'd with grey despair.

"Prison'd on wat'ry shore,
Starry Jealousy does keep my den:
Cold and hoar,
Weeping o'er,
I hear the father of the ancient men.

"Selfish father of men!
Cruel, jealous, selfish fear!
Can delight,
Chain'd in night,
The virgins of youth and morning bear?

"Does spring hide its joy
When buds and blossoms grow?
Does the sower
Sow by night,
Or the plowman in darkness plow?

"Break this heavy chain
That does freeze my bones around.
Selfish! vain!
Eternal bane!
That free Love with bondage bound."

THE CLOD AND THE PEBBLE

"LOVE seeketh not Itself to please,
Nor for itself hath any care,
But for another gives its ease,
And builds a Heaven in Hell's despair."

So sung a little Clod of Clay
Trodden with the cattle's feet,
But a Pebble of the brook
Warbled out these metres meet:

"Love seeketh only Self to please,
To bind another to Its delight,
Joys in another's loss of ease,
And builds a Hell in Heaven's despite."

HOLY THURSDAY

IS this a holy thing to see
In a rich and fruitful land,
Babes reduc'd to misery,
Fed with cold and usurous hand?

Is that trembling cry a song?
Can it be a song of joy?
And so many children poor?
It is a land of poverty!

And their sun does never shine,
And their fields are bleak & bare,
And their ways are fill'd with thorns:
It is eternal winter there.

For where-e'er the sun does shine,
And where-e'er the rain does fall,
Babe can never hunger there,
Nor poverty the mind appall.

THE LITTLE GIRL LOST

IN futurity
I prophetic see
That the earth from sleep
(Grave the sentence deep)

Shall arise and seek
For her maker meek;
And the desart wild
Become a garden mild.
          *   *   *
In the southern clime,
Where the summer's prime
Never fades away,
Lovely Lyca lay.

Seven summers old
Lovely Lyca told;
She had wander'd long
Hearing wild birds' song.

"Sweet sleep, come to me
Underneath this tree.
Do father, mother weep,
Where can Lyca sleep?

"Lost in desart wild
Is your little child.
How can Lyca sleep
If her mother weep?

"If her heart does ake
Then let Lyca wake;
If my mother sleep,
Lyca shall not weep.

"Frowning, frowning night,
O'er this desart bright
Let thy moon arise
While I close my eyes."

Sleeping Lyca lay
While the beasts of prey,
Come from caverns deep,
View'd the maid asleep.

The kingly lion stood
And the virgin view'd,
Then he gamboll'd round
O'er the hallow'd ground.

Leopards, tygers, play
Round her as she lay,
While the lion old
Bow'd his mane of gold

And her bosom lick,
And upon her neck
From his eyes of flame
Ruby tears there came;

While the lioness
Loos'd her slender dress,
And naked they convey'd
To caves the sleeping maid.

THE LITTLE GIRL FOUND

ALL the night in woe
Lyca's parents go
Over vallies deep,
While the desarts weep.

Tired and woe-begone,
Hoarse with making moan,
Arm in arm seven days
They trac'd the desert ways.

Seven nights they sleep
Among shadows deep,
And dream they see their child
Starv'd in desert wild.

Pale, thro' pathless ways
The fancied image strays
Famish'd, weeping, weak,
With hollow piteous shriek.

Rising from unrest,
The trembling woman prest
With feet of weary woe:
She could no further go.

In his arms he bore
Her, arm'd with sorrow sore;
Till before their way
A couching lion lay.

Turning back was vain:
Soon his heavy mane
Bore them to the ground.
Then he stalk'd around,

Smelling to his prey;
But their fears allay
When he licks their hands,
And silent by them stands.

They look upon his eyes
Fill'd with deep surprise,
And wondering behold
A spirit arm'd in gold.

On his head a crown,
On his shoulders down
Flow'd his golden hair.
Gone was all their care.

"Follow me," he said;
"Weep not for the maid;
In my palace deep
Lyca lies asleep."

Then they followed
Where the vision led,
And saw their sleeping child
Among tygers wild.

To this day they dwell
In a lonely dell;
Nor fear the wolvish howl
Nor the lions' growl.

THE CHIMNEY SWEEPER

A LITTLE black thing among the snow,
Crying " 'weep! 'weep!" in notes of woe!
"Where are thy father & mother? say?"
"They are both gone up to the church to pray.

"Because I was happy upon the heath,
And smil'd among the winter's snow,
They clothed me in the clothes of death,
And taught me to sing the notes of woe.

"And because I am happy & dance & sing,
They think they have done me no injury,
And are gone to praise God & his Priest & King,
Who make up a heaven of our misery."

NURSE'S SONG

WHEN the voices of children are heard on the green
And whisp'rings are in the dale,
The days of my youth rise fresh in my mind,
My face turns green and pale.

Then come home, my children, the sun is gone down,
And the dews of night arise;
Your spring & your day are wasted in play,
And your winter and night in disguise.

THE SICK ROSE

O ROSE, thou art sick!
The invisible worm
That flies in the night,
In the howling storm,

Has found out thy bed
Of crimson joy,
And his dark secret love
Does thy life destroy.

THE FLY

LITTLE Fly,
Thy summer's play
My thoughtless hand
Has brush'd away.

Am not I
A fly like thee?
Or art not thou
A man like me?

For I dance,
And drink, & sing,
Till some blind hand
Shall brush my wing.

If thought is life
And strength & breath,
And the want
Of thought is death;

Then am I
A happy fly,
If I live
Or if I die.

THE ANGEL

I DREAMT a Dream! what can it mean?
And that I was a maiden Queen,
Guarded by an Angel mild:
Witless woe was ne'er beguil'd!

And I wept both night and day,
And he wip'd my tears away,
And I wept both day and night,
And hid from him my heart's delight.

So he took his wings and fled;
Then the morn blush'd rosy red;
I dried my tears, & arm'd my fears
With ten thousand shields and spears.

Soon my Angel came again:
I was arm'd, he came in vain;
For the time of youth was fled,
And grey hairs were on my head

THE TYGER

TYGER! Tyger! burning bright
In the forests of the night,
What immortal hand or eye
Could frame thy fearful symmetry?

In what distant deeps or skies
Burnt the fire of thine eyes?
On what wings dare he aspire?
What the hand dare sieze the fire?

And what shoulder, & what art,
Could twist the sinews of thy heart?
And when thy heart began to beat,
What dread hand? & what dread feet?

What the hammer? what the chain?
In what furnace was thy brain?
What the anvil? what dread grasp
Dare its deadly terrors clasp?

When the stars threw down their spears,
And water'd heaven with their tears,
Did he smile his work to see?
Did he who made the Lamb make thee?

Tyger! Tyger! burning bright
In the forests of the night,
What immortal hand or eye
Dare frame thy fearful symmetry?

MY PRETTY ROSE-TREE

A FLOWER was offer'd to me,
Such a flower as May never bore;
But I said "I've a Pretty Rose-tree,"
And I passed the sweet flower o'er.

Then I went to my Pretty Rose-tree,
To tend her by day and by night;
But my Rose turn'd away with jealousy,
And her thorns were my only delight.

AH! SUN-FLOWER

A H, Sun-flower! weary of time,
Who countest the steps of the Sun,
Seeking after that sweet golden clime
Where the traveller's journey is done:

Where the Youth pined away with desire
And the pale Virgin shrouded in snow
Arise from their graves, and aspire
Where my Sun-flower wishes to go.

THE LILLY

T H E modest Rose puts forth a thorn,
The humble Sheep a threat'ning horn;
While the Lilly white shall in Love delight,
Nor a thorn, nor a threat, stain her beauty bright.

THE GARDEN OF LOVE

I W E N T to the Garden of Love,
And saw what I never had seen:
A Chapel was built in the midst,
Where I used to play on the green.

And the gates of this Chapel were shut,
And "Thou shalt not" writ over the door;
So I turn'd to the Garden of Love
That so many sweet flowers bore;

And I saw it was filled with graves,
And tomb-stones where flowers should be;
And Priests in black gowns were walking their rounds,
And binding with briars my joys & desires.

THE LITTLE VAGABOND

D E A R Mother, dear Mother, the Church is cold,
But the Ale-house is healthy & pleasant & warm;
Besides I can tell where I am used well,
Such usage in Heaven will never do well.

But if at the Church they would give us some Ale,
And a pleasant fire our souls to regale,
We'd sing and we'd pray all the live-long day,
Nor ever once wish from the Church to stray.

Then the Parson might preach, & drink, & sing,
And we'd be as happy as birds in the spring;
And modest Dame Lurch, who is always at Church,
Would not have bandy children, nor fasting, nor birch.

And God, like a father rejoicing to see
His children as pleasant and happy as he,
Would have no more quarrel with the Devil or the Barrel,
But kiss him, & give him both drink and apparel.

LONDON

I WANDER thro' each charter'd street,
Near where the charter'd Thames does flow,
And mark in every face I meet
Marks of weakness, marks of woe.

In every cry of every Man,
In every Infant's cry of fear,
In every voice, in every ban,
The mind-forg'd manacles I hear.

How the Chimney-sweeper's cry
Every black'ning Church appalls;
And the hapless Soldier's sigh
Runs in blood down Palace walls.

But most thro' midnight streets I hear
How the youthful Harlot's curse
Blasts the new born Infant's tear,
And blights with plagues the Marriage hearse.

THE HUMAN ABSTRACT

PITY would be no more
If we did not make somebody Poor;
And Mercy no more could be
If all were as happy as we.

And mutual fear brings peace,
Till the selfish loves increase:
Then Cruelty knits a snare,
And spreads his baits with care.

He sits down with holy fears,
And waters the ground with tears;
Then Humility takes its root
Underneath his foot.

Soon spreads the dismal shade
Of Mystery over his head;
And the Catterpiller and Fly
Feed on the Mystery.

And it bears the fruit of Deceit,
Ruddy and sweet to eat;
And the Raven his nest has made
In its thickest shade.

The Gods of the earth and sea
Sought thro' Nature to find this Tree;
But their search was all in vain:
There grows one in the Human Brain.

INFANT SORROW

M Y mother groan'd! my father wept.
Into the dangerous world I leapt:
Helpless, naked, piping loud:
Like a fiend hid in a cloud.

Struggling in my father's hands,
Striving against my swadling bands,
Bound and weary I thought best
To sulk upon my mother's breast.

A POISON TREE

I W A S angry with my friend:
I told my wrath, my wrath did end.
I was angry with my foe:
I told it not, my wrath did grow.

And I water'd it in fears,
Night & morning with my tears;
And I sunned it with smiles,
And with soft deceitful wiles.

And it grew both day and night,
Till it bore an apple bright;
And my foe beheld it shine,
And he knew that it was mine,

And into my garden stole
When the night had veil'd the pole:
In the morning glad I see
My foe outstretch'd beneath the tree.

A LITTLE BOY LOST

"NOUGHT loves another as itself,
Nor venerates another so,
Nor is it possible to Thought
A greater than itself to know:

"And Father, how can I love you
Or any of my brothers more?
I love you like the little bird
That picks up crumbs around the door."

The Priest sat by and heard the child,
In trembling zeal he siez'd his hair:
He led him by his little coat,
And all admir'd the Priestly care.

And standing on the altar high,
"Lo! what a fiend is here!" said he,
"One who sets reason up for judge
Of our most holy Mystery."

The weeping child could not be heard,
The weeping parents wept in vain;
They strip'd him to his little shirt,
And bound him in an iron chain;

And burn'd him in a holy place,
Where many had been burn'd before:
The weeping parents wept in vain.
Are such things done on Albion's shore?

A LITTLE GIRL LOST

Children of the future Age
Reading this indignant page,
Know that in a former time
Love! sweet Love! was thought a crime.

IN the Age of Gold,
Free from winter's cold,
Youth and maiden bright
To the holy light,
Naked in the sunny beams delight.

Once a youthful pair,
Fill'd with softest care,
Met in garden bright
Where the holy light
Had just remov'd the curtains of the night.

There, in rising day,
On the grass they play;
Parents were afar,
Strangers came not near,
And the maiden soon forgot her fear.

Tired with kisses sweet,
They agree to meet
When the silent sleep
Waves o'er heaven's deep,
And the weary tired wanderers weep.

To her father white
Came the maiden bright;
But his loving look,
Like the holy book,
All her tender limbs with terror shook.

"Ona! pale and weak!
To thy father speak:
O, the trembling fear!
O, the dismal care!
That shakes the blossoms of my hoary hair."

TO TIRZAH

[Probably added about 1801]

WHATE'ER is Born of Mortal Birth
Must be consumed with the Earth
To rise from Generation free:
Then what have I to do with thee?

The Sexes sprung from Shame & Pride,
Blow'd in the morn; in evening died;
But Mercy chang'd Death into Sleep;
The Sexes rose to work & weep.

Thou, Mother of my Mortal part,
With cruelty didst mould my Heart,
And with false self-deceiving tears
Didst bind my Nostrils, Eyes, & Ears:

Didst close my Tongue in senseless clay,
And me to Mortal Life betray.
The Death of Jesus set me free:
Then what have I to do with thee?

THE SCHOOLBOY

I LOVE to rise in a summer morn
When the birds sing on every tree;
The distant huntsman winds his horn,
And the sky-lark sings with me.
O! what sweet company.

But to go to school in a summer morn,
O! it drives all joy away;
Under a cruel eye outworn,

The little ones spend the day
In sighing and dismay.

Ah! then at times I drooping sit,
And spend many an anxious hour,
Nor in my book can I take delight,
Nor sit in learning's bower,
Worn thro' with the dreary shower.

How can the bird that is born for joy
Sit in a cage and sing?
How can a cnild, when fears annoy,
But droop his tender wing,
And forget his youthful spring?

O! father & mother, if buds are nip'd
And blossoms blown away,
And if the tender plants are strip'd
Of their joy in the springing day,
By sorrow and care's dismay,

How shall the summer arise in joy,
Or the summer fruits appear?
Or how shall we gather what griefs destroy,
Or bless the mellowing year,
When the blasts of winter appear?

THE VOICE OF THE ANCIENT BARD

YOUTH of delight, come hither,
And see the opening morn,
Image of truth new born.
Doubt is fled, & clouds of reason,
Dark disputes & artful teazing.
Folly is an endless maze,
Tangled roots perplex her ways.
How many have fallen there!
They stumble all night over bones of the dead,
And feel they know not what but care,
And wish to lead others, when they should be led.

A DIVINE IMAGE

CRUELTY has a Human Heart,
And Jealousy a Human Face;
Terror the Human Form Divine,
And Secrecy the Human Dress.

The Human Dress is forged Iron,
The Human Form a fiery Forge,
The Human Face a Furnace seal'd,
The Human Heart is hungry Gorge.

Poems and Fragments

POEMS WRITTEN IN A COPY OF "POETICAL SKETCHES"

Composed about 1787

SONG 1ST BY A SHEPHERD

WELCOME, stranger, to this place,
Where joy doth sit on every bough,
Paleness flies from every face;
We reap not what we do not sow.

Innocence doth like a rose
Bloom on every maiden's cheek;
Honour twines around her brows,
The jewel health adorns her neck.

SONG 2ND BY A YOUNG SHEPHERD

WHEN the trees do laugh with our merry wit,
And the green hills laugh with the noise of it,
When the meadows laugh with lively green
And the grasshopper laughs in the merry scene,

When the greenwood laughs with the voice of joy,
And the dimpling stream runs laughing by,
When Edessa, and Lyca, and Emilie,
With their sweet round mouths sing ha, ha, he,

When the painted Birds laugh in the shade,
Where our table with cherries and nuts is spread;
Come live and be merry and join with me
To sing the sweet chorus of ha, ha, he.

SONG BY AN OLD SHEPHERD

W H E N silver snow decks Sylvio's clothes
And jewel hangs at shepherd's nose,
We can abide life's pelting storm
That makes our limbs quake, if our hearts be warm.

Whilst Virtue is our walking-staff
And Truth a lantern to our path,
We can abide life's pelting storm
That makes our limbs quake, if our hearts be warm.

Blow, boisterous wind, stern winter frown,
Innocence is a winter's gown;
So clad, we'll abide life's pelting storm
That makes our limbs quake, if our hearts be warm.

POEMS FROM MSS.

Written about 1793

❉

NEVER seek to tell thy love
Love that never told can be;
For the gentle wind does move
Silently, invisibly.

I told my love, I told my love,
I told her all my heart,
Trembling, cold, in ghastly fears—
Ah, she doth depart.

Soon as she was gone from me
A traveller came by
Silently, invisibly—
O, was no deny.

❉

I LAID me down upon a bank
Where love lay sleeping.
I heard among the rushes dank
Weeping, Weeping.

Then I went to the heath & the wild
To the thistles & thorns of the waste
And they told me how they were beguil'd,
Driven out, & compel'd to be chaste.

❧

I SAW a chapel all of gold
That none did dare to enter in,
And many weeping stood without,
Weeping, mourning, worshipping.

I saw a serpent rise between
The white pillars of the door,
And he forc'd & forc'd & forc'd,
Down the golden hinges tore.

And along the pavement sweet,
Set with pearls & rubies bright,
All his slimy length he drew,
Till upon the altar white

Vomiting his poison out
On the bread & on the wine.
So I turn'd into a sty
And laid me down among the swine.

❧

I ASKED a thief to steal me a peach:
He turned up his eyes.
I ask'd a lithe lady to lie her down:
Holy & meek she cries.

As soon as I went an angel came:
He wink'd at the thief
And smil'd at the dame,
And without one word spoke
Had a peach from the tree,
And 'twixt earnest & joke
Enjoy'd the Lady.

I HEARD an Angel singing
When the day was springing,
"Mercy, Pity, Peace
Is the world's release."

Thus he sung all day
Over the new mown hay,
Till the sun went down
And haycocks looked brown.

I heard a Devil curse
Over the heath & the furze,
"Mercy could be no more,
If there was nobody poor,

"And pity no more could be,
If all were as happy as we."
At his curse the sun went down,
And the heavens gave a frown.

Down pour'd the heavy rain
Over the new reap'd grain,
And Miseries' increase
Is Mercy, Pity, Peace.

A CRADLE SONG

SLEEP, Sleep, beauty bright
Dreaming o'er the joys of night.
Sleep, Sleep: in thy sleep
Little sorrows sit & weep.

Sweet Babe, in thy face
Soft desires I can trace
Secret joys & secret smiles
Little pretty infant wiles.

As thy softest limbs I feel
Smiles as of the morning steal
O'er thy cheek & o'er thy breast
Where thy little heart does rest.

O, the cunning wiles that creep
In thy little heart asleep.
When thy little heart does wake,
Then the dreadful lightnings break.

From thy cheek & from thy eye
O'er the youthful harvests nigh
Infant wiles & infant smiles
Heaven & Earth of peace beguiles.

❋

I FEAR'D the fury of my wind
Would blight all blossoms fair & true;
And my sun it shin'd & shin'd
And my wind it never blew.

But a blossom fair or true
Was not found on any tree;
For all blossoms grew & grew
Fruitless, false, tho' fair to see.

❋

WHY should I care for the men of Thames,
Or the cheating waves of charter'd streams,
Or shrink at the little blasts of fear
That the hireling blows into my ear?

Tho' born on the cheating banks of Thames,
Tho' his waters bathed my infant limbs,
The Ohio shall wash his stains from me:
I was born a slave, but I go to be free.

INFANT SORROW

MY mother groan'd, my father wept;
Into the dangerous world I leapt,
Helpless, naked, piping loud,
Like a fiend hid in a cloud.

Struggling in my father's hands
Striving against my swaddling bands,
Bound & weary, I thought best
To sulk upon my mother's breast.

When I saw that rage was vain,
And to sulk would nothing gain,
Turning many a trick & wile,
I began to soothe & smile.

And I sooth'd day after day
Till upon the ground I stray;
And I smil'd night after night,
Seeking only for delight.

And I saw before me shine
Clusters of the wand'ring vine,
And many a lovely flower & tree
Stretch'd their blossoms out to me.

My father then with holy look,
In his hands a holy book,
Pronounc'd curses on my head
And bound me in a mirtle shade.

[*First draft of "Infant Sorrow" in the* Songs of Experience;
see p. 559.]

IN A MIRTLE SHADE

W H Y should I be bound to thee,
O my lovely mirtle tree?
Love, free love, cannot be bound
To any tree that grows on ground.

O, how sick & weary I
Underneath my mirtle lie.
Like to dung upon the ground
Underneath my mirtle bound.

Oft my mirtle sigh'd in vain
To behold my heavy chain;
Oft my father saw us sigh,
And laugh'd at our simplicity.

So I smote him & his gore
Stain'd the roots my mirtle bore.
But the time of youth is fled,
And grey hairs are on my head.

*

SILENT, Silent Night
Quench the holy light
Of thy torches bright.

For possess'd of Day
Thousand spirits stray
That sweet joys betray

Why should joys be sweet
Used with deceit
Nor with sorrows meet?

But an honest joy
Does itself destroy
For a harlot coy.

*

O LAPWING, thou fliest around the heath,
Nor seest the net that is spread beneath.
Why dost thou not fly among the corn fields?
They cannot spread nets where a harvest yields.

*

THOU hast a lap full of seed,
And this is a fine country.
Why dost thou not cast thy seed
And live in it merrily?

Shall I cast it on the sand
And turn it into fruitful land?
For on no other ground
Can I sow my seed
Without tearing up
Some stinking weed.

LONDON

I WANDER thro' each dirty street,
Near where the dirty Thames does flow,
And mark in every face I meet
Marks of weakness, marks of woe.

In every cry of every man,
In every infant's cry of fear,
In every voice, in every ban,
The mind forg'd manacles I hear.

How the chimney sweeper's cry
Blackens o'er the churches' walls,
And the hapless soldier's sigh
Runs in blood down palace walls.

But most the midnight harlot's curse
From every dismal street I hear,
Weaves around the marriage hearse
And blasts the new born infant's tear.

[First draft of "London" in the Songs of Experience;
see p. 558.*]*

TO NOBODADDY

WHY art thou silent & invisible,
Father of Jealousy?
Why dost thou hide thy self in clouds
From every searching Eye?

Why darkness & obscurity
In all thy words & laws,
That none dare eat the fruit but from
The wily serpent's jaws?
Or is it because Secresy gains females' loud
    applause?

ARE not the joys of morning sweeter
Than the joys of night?
And are the vig'rous joys of youth
Ashamed of the light?

Let age & sickness silent rob
The vineyards in the night;
But those who burn with vig'rous youth
Pluck fruits before the light.

THE TYGER

TYGER, Tyger, burning bright
In the forests of the night,
What immortal hand or eye
Dare frame thy fearful symmetry?

Burnt in distant deeps or skies
The cruel fire of thine eyes?
On what wings dare he aspire?
What the hand dare sieze the fire?

And what shoulder & what art
Could twist the sinews of thy heart?
And when thy heart began to beat
What dread hand & what dread feet

Could fetch it from the furnace deep
And in thy horrid ribs dare steep
In the well of sanguine woe?
In what clay & in what mould
Were thy eyes of fury roll'd?

Where the hammer? Where the chain?
In what furnace was thy brain?
What the anvil? What dread grasp
Dare its deadly terrors clasp?

When the stars threw down their spears
And water'd heaven with their tears
Dare he laugh his work to see?
Dare he who made the lamb make thee?

Tyger, Tyger, burning bright
In the forests of the night,
What immortal hand or eye
Dare frame thy fearful symmetry?

[*First draft of "The Tyger" in the* Songs of **Experience**;
see p. 555.]

THE HUMAN IMAGE

PITY could be no more,
If we did not make somebody poor;
And Mercy no more could be,
If all were as happy as we.

And mutual fear brings Peace,
Till the selfish Loves increase;
Then Cruelty knits a snare,
And spreads his baits with care.

He sits down with holy fears
And waters the ground with tears;
Then humility takes its root
Underneath his foot.

Soon spreads the dismal shade
Of Mystery over his head;
And the caterpiller & fly
Feed on the Mystery.

And it bears the fruit of deceit,
Ruddy & sweet to eat;
And the raven his nest has made
In its thickest shade.

The Gods of the Earth & Sea
Sought thro' nature to find this tree;
But their search was all in vain:
Till they sought in the human brain.

They said this mystery never shall cease;
The priest promotes war & the soldier peace.

. . .

There souls of men are bought & sold,
And milk-fed infancy for gold;
And youth to slaughter houses led,
And beauty for a bit of bread.

[*First draft of "The Human Abstract" in the* Songs of Experience;
see p. 558.]

✳

LOVE to faults is always blind,
Always is to joy inclin'd,
Lawless, wing'd, & unconfin'd,
And breaks all chains from every mind.

Deceit to secresy confin'd,
Lawful, cautious, & refin'd;
To every thing but interest blind,
And forges fetters for the mind.

THE WILD FLOWER'S SONG

AS I wander'd the forest,
The green leaves among,
I heard a wild flower
Singing a song:

"I slept in the dark
In the silent night,
I murmur'd my fears
And I felt delight.

"In the morning I went
As rosy as morn
To seek for new Joy,
But I met with scorn."

SOFT SNOW

I WALKED abroad in a snowy day:
I ask'd the soft snow with me to play:
She play'd & she melted in all her prime,
And the winter call'd it a dreadful crime.

AN ANCIENT PROVERB

REMOVE away that black'ning church:
Remove away that marriage hearse:
Remove away that place of blood:
You'll quite remove the ancient curse.

TO MY MIRTLE

TO a lovely mirtle bound,
Blossoms show'ring all around,
O, how sick & weary I
Underneath my mirtle lie.
Why should I be bound to thee,
O, my lovely mirtle tree?

✻

" NOUGHT loves another as itself,
Nor venerates another so,
Nor is it possible to Thought
A greater than itself to know.

"Then, father, I cannot love you
Nor any of my brothers more.
I love myself: so does the bird
That picks up crumbs around the door."

The Priest sat by and heard the child.
In trembling zeal he siez'd his hair:
The mother follow'd, weeping loud:
"O, that I such a fiend should bear."

And standing on the altar high:
"Lo, what a fiend is here," said he,
"One who sets reason up for judge
Of our most holy mystery."

The weeping child could not be heard;
The weeping parents wept in vain.
They bound his little ivory limbs
In a cruel Iron chain.

They burn'd him in a holy fire,
Where many had been burn'd before.
The weeping parents wept in vain.
Are Such things done on Albion's shore?

[*First draft of "A Little Boy Lost" in* Songs of Experience; *see p.* 560.]

MERLIN'S PROPHECY

T H E harvest shall flourish in wintry weather
When two virginities meet together:

The King & the Priest must be tied in a tether
Before two virgins can meet together.

DAY

T H E Sun arises in the East,
Cloth'd in robes of blood & gold;
Swords & spears & wrath increast
All around his bosom roll'd,
Crown'd with warlike fires & raging desires.

THE MARRIAGE RING

"C O M E hither my sparrows,
My little arrows.
If a tear or a smile
Will a man beguile,

If an amorous delay
Clouds a sunshiny day,
If the step of a foot
Smites the heart to its root,
'Tis the marriage ring
Makes each fairy a king."

So a fairy sung.
From the leaves I sprung.
He leap'd from the spray
To flee away.
But in my hat caught
He soon shall be taught.
Let him laugh, let him cry,
He's my butterfly;
For I've pull'd out the sting
Of the marriage ring.

❈

THE sword sung on the barren heath,
The sickle in the fruitful field:
The sword he sung a song of death,
But could not make the sickle yield.

❈

ABSTINENCE sows sand all over
The ruddy limbs & flaming hair,
But Desire Gratified
Plants fruits of life & beauty there.

❈

IN a wife I would desire
What in whores is always found—
The lineaments of Gratified desire.

IF you trap the moment before it's ripe,
The tears of repentance you'll certainly wipe;
But if once you let the ripe moment go
You can never wipe off the tears of woe.

ETERNITY

HE who binds to himself a joy
Does the winged life destroy;
But he who kisses the joy as it flies
Lives in eternity's sun rise.

THE QUESTION ANSWER'D

WHAT is it men in women do require?
The lineaments of Gratified Desire.
What is it women do in men require?
The lineaments of Gratified Desire.

LACEDEMONIAN INSTRUCTION

"COME hither, my boy, tell me what thou seest there."
"A fool tangled in a religious snare."

RICHES

THE countless gold of a merry heart,
The rubies & pearls of a loving eye,
The indolent never can bring to the mart,
Nor the secret hoard up in his treasury.

AN ANSWER TO THE PARSON

"WHY of the sheep do you not learn peace?"
"Because I don't want you to shear my fleece."

THE look of love alarms
Because 'tis fill'd with fire;
But the look of soft deceit
Shall win the lover's hire.

❊

WHICH are beauties sweetest dress?
Soft deceit & idleness,
These are beauties sweetest dress.

MOTTO TO THE SONGS OF INNOCENCE
& OF EXPERIENCE

THE Good are attracted by Men's perceptions,
And think not for themselves;
Till Experience teaches them to catch
And to cage the Fairies & Elves.

And then the Knave begins to snarl
And the Hypocrite to howl;
And all his good Friends shew their private ends,
And the Eagle is known from the Owl.

❊

HER whole Life is an Epigram, smart, smooth, & neatly pen'd,
Platted quite neat to catch applause with a sliding noose at the end.

❊

AN old maid early—e'er I knew
Ought but the love that on me grew;
And now I'm cover'd o'er & o'er
And wish that I had been a whore.

O, I cannot, cannot find
The undaunted courage of a Virgin Mind,
For Early I in love was crost,
Before my flower of love was lost.

❋

"LET the Brothels of Paris be opened
With many an alluring dance
To awake the Pestilence thro' the city,"
Said the beautiful Queen of France.

The King awoke on his couch of gold,
As soon as he heard these tidings told:
"Arise & come, both fife & drum,
And the Famine shall eat both crust & crumb."

Then he swore a great & solemn Oath:
"To kill the people I am loth,
But If they rebel, they must go to hell:
They shall have a Priest & a passing bell."

Then old Nobodaddy aloft
Farted & belch'd & cough'd,
And said, "I love hanging & drawing & quartering
Every bit as well as war & slaughtering.
Damn praying & singing,
Unless they will bring in
The blood of ten thousand by fighting or swinging."

The Queen of France just touched this Globe,
And the Pestilence darted from her robe;
But our good Queen quite grows to the ground,
And a great many suckers grow all around.

Fayette beside King Lewis stood;
He saw him sign his hand;
And soon he saw the famine rage
About the fruitful land.

Fayette beheld the Queen to smile
And wink her lovely eye;
And soon he saw the pestilence
From street to street to fly.

Fayette beheld the King & Queen
In tears & iron bound;
But mute Fayette wept tear for tear,
And guarded them around.

Fayette, Fayette, thou'rt bought & sold,
And sold is thy happy morrow;
Thou gavest the tears of Pity away
In exchange for the tears of sorrow.

Who will exchange his own fire side
For the steps of another's door?
Who will exchange his wheaten loaf
For the links of a dungeon floor?

O, who would smile on the wintry seas,
& Pity the stormy roar?
Or who will exchange his new born child
For the dog at the wintry door?

✻

WHEN Klopstock England defied,
Uprose William Blake in his pride;
For old Nobodaddy aloft
Farted & Belch'd & cough'd;
Then swore a great oath that made heaven quake,
And call'd aloud to English Blake.
Blake was giving his body ease
At Lambeth beneath the poplar trees.
From his seat then started he,
And turned him round three times three.
The Moon at that sight blush'd scarlet red,
The stars threw down their cups & fled,
And all the devils that were in hell
Answered with a ninefold yell.
Klopstock felt the intripled turn,

And all his bowels began to churn,
And his bowels turned round three times three,
And lock'd in his soul with a ninefold key,
That from his body it ne'er could be parted
Till to the last trumpet it was farted.
Then again old Nobodaddy swore
He ne'er had seen such a thing before,
Since Noah was shut in the ark,
Since Eve first chose her hellfire spark,
Since 'twas the fashion to go naked,
Since the old anything was created,
And so feeling, he beg'd me to turn again
And ease poor Klopstock's ninefold pain.
If Blake could do this when he rose up from a shite,
What might he not do if he sat down to write?

❉

A FAIRY leapt upon my knee
Singing & dancing merrily;
I said, "Thou thing of patches, rings,
Pins, Necklaces, & such like things,
Disguiser of the Female Form,
Thou paltry, gilded, poisonous worm!"
Weeping, he fell upon my thigh,
And thus in tears did soft reply:
"Knowest thou not, O Fairies' Lord!
How much by us Contemn'd, Abhorr'd,
Whatever hides the Female form
That cannot bear the Mental storm?
Therefore in Pity still we give
Our lives to make the Female live;
And what would turn into disease
We turn to what will joy & please."

LINES FOR THE ILLUSTRATIONS TO GRAY'S POEMS

Written about 1800

AROUND the Springs of Gray my wild root weaves.
Traveller repose & Dream among my leaves.

TO MRS. ANNA FLAXMAN

A LITTLE Flower grew in a lonely Vale.
Its form was lovely but its colours pale.
One standing in the Porches of the Sun,
When his Meridian Glories were begun,
Leap'd from the steps of fire & on the grass
Alighted where this little flower was.
With hands divine he mov'd the gentle Sod
And took the Flower up in its native Clod;
Then planting it upon a Mountain's brow—
" 'Tis your own fault if you don't flourish now."

POEMS FROM MSS.

Written about 1800-1803

MY Spectre around me night & day
Like a Wild beast guards my way.
My Emanation far within
Weeps incessantly for my Sin.

A Fathomless & boundless deep,
There we wander, there we weep;
On the hungry craving wind
My Spectre follows thee behind.

He scents thy footsteps in the snow,
Wheresoever thou dost go
Thro' the wintry hail & rain.
When wilt thou return again?

Dost thou not in Pride & scorn
Fill with tempests all my morn,
And with jealousies & fears
Fill my pleasant nights with tears?

Seven of my sweet loves thy knife
Has bereaved of their life.
Their marble tombs I built with tears
And with cold & shuddering fears.

Seven more loves weep night & day
Round the tombs where my loves lay,
And seven more loves attend each night
Around my couch with torches bright.

And seven more Loves in my bed
Crown with wine my mournful head,
Pitying & forgiving all
Thy transgressions, great & small.

When wilt thou return & view
My loves, & them to life renew?
When wilt thou return & live?
When wilt thou pity as I forgive?

"Never, Never, I return:
Still for Victory I burn.
Living, thee alone I'll have
And when dead I'll be thy Grave.

"Thro' the Heaven & Earth & Hell
Thou shalt never never quell:
I will fly & thou pursue,
Night & Morn the flight renew."

Till I turn from Female Love,
And root up the Infernal Grove,
I shall never worthy be
To Step into Eternity.

And, to end thy cruel mocks,
Annihilate thee on the rocks,
And another form create
To be subservient to my Fate.

Let us agree to give up Love,
And root up the infernal grove;
Then shall we return & see
The worlds of happy Eternity.

& Throughout all Eternity
I forgive you, you forgive me.
As our dear Redeemer said:
"This the Wine & this the Bread."

[Additional stanzas]

O'er my Sins thou sit & moan:
Hast thou no sins of thy own?
O'er my Sins thou sit & weep,
And lull thy own Sins fast asleep.

What Transgressions I commit
Are for thy Transgressions fit.
They thy Harlots, thou their slave,
And my Bed becomes their Grave.

Poor pale pitiable form
That I follow in a Storm,
Iron tears & groans of lead
Bind around my aking head.

❊

WHEN a Man has Married a Wife, he finds out whether
Her knees & elbows are only glewed together.

ON THE VIRGINITY OF THE VIRGIN MARY
& JOHANNA SOUTHCOTT

WHATE'ER is done to her she cannot know,
And if you'll ask her she will swear it so.
Whether 'tis good or evil none's to blame:
No one can take the pride, no one the shame.

❊

MOCK on, Mock on Voltaire, Rousseau:
Mock on, Mock on: 'tis all in vain!
You throw the sand against the wind,
And the wind blows it back again.

And every sand becomes a Gem
Reflected in the beams divine;
Blown back they blind the mocking Eye,
But still in Israel's paths they shine.

The Atoms of Democritus
And Newton's Particles of light
Are sands upon the Red sea shore,
Where Israel's tents do shine so bright.

MORNING

To find the Western path
Right thro' the Gates of Wrath
I urge my way;
Sweet Mercy leads me on:
With soft repentant moan
I see the break of day.

The war of swords & spears
Melted by dewy tears
Exhales on high;
The Sun is freed from fears
And with soft grateful tears
Ascends the sky.

✳

TERROR in the house does roar,
But Pity stands before the door.

✳

EACH Man is in his Spectre's power
Untill the arrival of that hour,
When his Humanity awake
And cast his own Spectre into the Lake.

And there to Eternity aspire
The selfhood in a flame of fire
Till then the Lamb of God . . .

THE BIRDS

He. WHERE thou dwellest, in what Grove,
Tell me, Fair one, tell me, love;
Where thou thy charming Nest dost build,
O thou pride of every field!

She. Yonder stands a lonely tree,
There I live & mourn for thee.
Morning drinks my silent tear,
And evening winds my sorrows bear.

He. O thou Summer's harmony,
I have liv'd & mourn'd for thee.
Each day I mourn along the wood,
And night hath heard my sorrows loud.

She. Dost thou truly long for me?
And am I thus sweet to thee?
Sorrow now is at an End,
O my Lover & my Friend!

He. Come, on wings of joy we'll fly
To where my Bower hangs on high!
Come, & make thy calm retreat
Among green leaves & blossoms sweet!

Poems written about 1803

THE SMILE

THERE is a Smile of Love,
And there is a Smile of Deceit,
And there is a Smile of Smiles
In which these two Smiles meet.

And there is a Frown of Hate,
And there is a Frown of Disdain,
And there is a Frown of Frowns
Which you strive to forget in vain,

For it sticks in the Heart's deep Core
And it sticks in the deep Back bone;
And no Smile that ever was smil'd,
But only one Smile alone,

That betwixt the Cradle & Grave
It only once Smil'd can be;
But, when it once is Smil'd,
There's an end to all Misery.

THE GOLDEN NET

THREE Virgins at the break of day:
"Whither, young Man, whither away?
Alas for woe! alas for woe!"
They cry, & tears for ever flow.
The one was Cloth'd in flames of fire,
The other Cloth'd in iron wire,
The other Cloth'd in tears & sighs
Dazling bright before my Eyes.
They bore a Net of golden twine
To hang upon the branches fine.
Pitying I wept to see the woe
That Love & Beauty undergo,
To be consum'd in burning Fires
And in ungratified desires,
And in tears cloth'd Night & day
Melted all my Soul away.
When they saw my Tears, a Smile
That did Heaven itself beguile,
Bore the Golden Net aloft
As on downy Pinions soft
Over the Morning of my day.
Underneath the Net I stray,
Now intreating Burning Fire,
Now intreating Iron Wire,
Now Intreating Tears & Sighs.
O when will the morning rise?

THE MENTAL TRAVELLER

I TRAVEL'D thro' a Land of Men,
A Land of Men & Women too,
And heard & saw such dreadful things
As cold Earth wanderers never knew.

For there the Babe is born in joy
That was begotten in dire woe;
Just as we Reap in joy the fruit
Which we in bitter tears did sow.

And if the Babe is born a Boy
He's given to a Woman Old,
Who nails him down upon a rock,
Catches his shrieks in cups of gold.

She binds iron thorns around his head,
She pierces both his hands & feet,
She cuts his heart out at his side
To make it feel both cold & heat.

Her fingers number every Nerve,
Just as a Miser counts his gold;
She lives upon his shrieks & cries,
And she grows young as he grows old.

Till he becomes a bleeding youth,
And she becomes a Virgin bright;
Then he rends up his Manacles
And binds her down for his delight.

He plants himself in all her Nerves,
Just as a Husbandman his mould;
And she becomes his dwelling place
And Garden fruitful seventy fold.

An aged Shadow, soon he fades,
Wand'ring round an Earthly Cot,
Full filled all with gems & gold
Which he by industry had got.

And these are the gems of the Human Soul,
The rubies & pearls of a lovesick eye,
The countless gold of the akeing heart,
The martyr's groan & the lover's sigh.

They are his meat, they are his drink;
He feeds the Beggar & the Poor
And the wayfaring Traveller:
For ever open is his door.

His grief is their eternal joy;
They make the roofs & walls to ring;
Till from the fire on the hearth
A little Female Babe does spring.

And she is all of solid fire
And gems & gold, that none his hand
Dares stretch to touch her Baby form,
Or wrap her in his swaddling-band.

But She comes to the Man she loves,
If young or old, or rich or poor;
They soon drive out the aged Host,
A Beggar at another's door.

He wanders weeping far away,
Untill some other take him in;
Oft blind & age-bent, sore distrest,
Untill he can a Maiden win.

And to allay his freezing Age
The Poor Man takes her in his arms;
The Cottage fades before his sight,
The Garden & its lovely Charms.

The Guests are scatter'd thro' the land,
For the Eye altering alters all;
The Senses roll themselves in fear,
And the flat Earth becomes a Ball;

The stars, sun, Moon, all shrink away,
A desart vast without a bound,
And nothing left to eat or drink,
And a dark desart all around.

The honey of her Infant lips,
The bread & wine of her sweet smile,
The wild game of her roving Eye,
Does him to Infancy beguile;

For as he eats & drinks he grows
Younger & younger every day;
And on the desart wild they both
Wander in terror & dismay.

Like the wild Stag she flees away,
Her fear plants many a thicket wild;
While he pursues her night & day,
By various arts of Love beguil'd,

By various arts of Love & Hate,
Till the wide desart planted o'er
With Labyrinths of wayward Love,
Where roam the Lion, Wolf & Boar,

Till he becomes a wayward Babe,
And she a weeping Woman Old.
Then many a Lover wanders here;
The Sun & Stars are nearer roll'd.

The trees bring forth sweet Extacy
To all who in the desart roam;
Till many a City there is Built,
And many a pleasant Shepherd's home.

But when they find the frowning Babe,
Terror strikes thro' the region wide:
They cry "The Babe! the Babe is Born!"
And flee away on Every side.

For who dare touch the frowning form,
His arm is wither'd to its root;
Lions, Boars, Wolves, all howling flee,
And every Tree does shed its fruit.

And none can touch that frowning form,
Except it be a Woman Old;
She nails him down upon the Rock,
And all is done as I have told.

THE LAND OF DREAMS

AWAKE, awake, my little Boy!
Thou wast thy Mother's only joy;
Why dost thou weep in thy gentle sleep?
Awake! thy Father does thee keep.

"O, what Land is the Land of Dreams?
What are its Mountains & what are its Streams?
O Father, I saw my Mother there,
Among the Lillies by waters fair.

"Among the Lambs, clothed in white,
She walk'd with her Thomas in sweet delight.
I wept for joy, like a dove I mourn;
O! when shall I again return?"

Dear Child, I also by pleasant Streams
Have wander'd all Night in the Land of Dreams;
But tho' calm & warm the waters wide,
I could not get to the other side.

"Father, O Father! what do we here
In this Land of unbelief & fear?
The Land of Dreams is better far,
Above the light of the Morning Star."

MARY

SWEET Mary, the first time she ever was there,
Came into the Ball room among the Fair;
The young Men & Maidens around her throng,
And these are the words upon every tongue:

"An Angel is here from the heavenly climes,
Or again does return the golden times;
Her eyes outshine every brilliant ray,
She opens her lips—'tis the Month of May."

Mary moves in soft beauty & conscious delight
To augment with sweet smiles all the joys of the Night,
Nor once blushes to own to the rest of the Fair
That sweet Love & Beauty are worthy our care.

In the Morning the Villagers rose with delight
And repeated with pleasure the joys of the night,
And Mary arose among Friends to be free,
But no Friend from henceforward thou, Mary, shalt see.

Some said she was proud, some call'd her a whore,
And some, when she passed by, shut to the door;
A damp cold came o'er her, her blushes all fled;
Her lillies & roses are blighted & shed.

"O, why was I born with a different Face?
Why was I not born like this Envious Race?
Why did Heaven adorn me with bountiful hand,
And then set me down in an envious Land?

"To be weak as a Lamb & smooth as a dove,
And not to raise Envy, is call'd Christian Love;
But if you raise Envy your Merit's to blame
For planting such spite in the weak & the tame.

"I will humble my Beauty, I will not dress fine,
I will keep from the Ball, & my Eyes shall not shine;
And if any Girl's Lover forsakes her for me,
I'll refuse him my hand & from Envy be free."

She went out in Morning attir'd plain & neat;
"Proud Mary's gone Mad," said the Child in the Street;
She went out in Morning in plain neat attire,
And came home in Evening bespatter'd with mire.

She trembled & wept, sitting on the Bed side;
She forgot it was Night, & she trembled & cried;
She forgot it was Night, she forgot it was Morn,
Her soft Memory imprinted with Faces of Scorn,

With Faces of Scorn & with Eyes of disdain
Like foul Fiends inhabiting Mary's mild Brain;
She remembers no Face like the Human Divine.
All Faces have Envy, sweet Mary, but thine;

And thine is a Face of sweet Love in despair,
And thine is a Face of mild sorrow & care,
And thine is a Face of wild terror & fear
That shall never be quiet till laid on its bier.

THE CRYSTAL CABINET

THE Maiden caught me in the Wild,
Where I was dancing merrily;
She put me into her Cabinet
And Lock'd me up with a golden Key.

This Cabinet is form'd of Gold
And Pearl & Crystal shining bright,
And within it opens into a World
And a little lovely Moony Night.

Another England there I saw,
Another London with its Tower,
Another Thames & other Hills,
And another pleasant Surrey Bower,

Another Maiden like herself,
Translucent, lovely, shining clear,
Threefold each in the other clos'd—
O, what a pleasant trembling fear!

O, what a smile! a threefold Smile
Fill'd me, that like a flame I burn'd;
I bent to Kiss the lovely Maid,
And found a Threefold Kiss return'd.

I strove to seize the inmost Form
With ardor fierce & hands of flame,
But burst the Crystal Cabinet,
And like a Weeping Babe became—

A weeping Babe upon the wild,
And Weeping Woman pale reclin'd,
And in the outward air again
I fill'd with woes the passing Wind.

THE GREY MONK

"I DIE, I DIE !" the Mother said,
"My Children die for lack of Bread.
What more has the merciless Tyrant said?"
The Monk sat down on the Stony Bed.

The blood red ran from the Grey Monk's side,
His hands & feet were wounded wide,
His Body bent, his arms & knees
Like to the roots of ancient trees.

His eye was dry; no tear could flow:
A hollow groan first spoke his woe.
He trembled & shudder'd upon the Bed,
At length with a feeble cry he said:

"When God commanded this hand to write
In the studious hours of deep midnight,
He told me the writing I wrote should prove
The Bane of all that on Earth I lov'd.

"My Brother starv'd between two Walls,
His Children's Cry my Soul appalls;
I mock'd at the wrack & griding chain,
My bent body mocks their torturing pain.

"Thy Father drew his sword in the North,
With his thousands strong he marched forth;
Thy Brother has arm'd himself in Steel
To avenge the wrongs thy Children feel.

"But vain the Sword & vain the Bow,
They never can work War's overthrow.
The Hermit's Prayer & the Widow's tear
Alone can free the World from fear.

"For a Tear is an Intellectual Thing,
And a Sigh is the Sword of an Angel King,
And the bitter groan of the Martyr's woe
Is an Arrow from the Almightie's Bow.

"The hand of Vengeance found the Bed
To which the Purple Tyrant fled;
The iron hand crush'd the Tyrant's head
And became a Tyrant in his stead."

AUGURIES OF INNOCENCE

TO see a World in a Grain of Sand
And a Heaven in a Wild Flower,
Hold Infinity in the palm of your hand
And Eternity in an hour.

A Robin Red breast in a Cage
Puts all Heaven in a Rage.
A dove house fill'd with doves & Pigeons
Shudders Hell thro' all its regions.
A dog starv'd at his Master's Gate
Predicts the ruin of the State.
A Horse misus'd upon the Road
Calls to Heaven for Human blood.
Each outcry of the hunted Hare
A fibre from the Brain does tear.
A Skylark wounded in the wing,
A Cherubim does cease to sing.
The Game Cock clip'd & arm'd for fight
Does the Rising Sun affright.
Every Wolf's & Lion's howl
Raises from Hell a Human Soul.
The wild deer, wand'ring here & there,
Keeps the Human Soul from Care.
The Lamb misus'd breeds Public strife
And yet forgives the Butcher's Knife.
The Bat that flits at close of Eve
Has left the Brain that won't Believe.
The Owl that calls upon the Night
Speaks the Unbeliever's fright.
He who shall hurt the little Wren
Shall never be belov'd by Men.
He who the Ox to wrath has mov'd
Shall never be by Woman lov'd.
The wanton Boy that kills the Fly

Shall feel the Spider's enmity.
He who torments the Chafer's sprite
Weaves a Bower in endless Night.
The Catterpiller on the Leaf
Repeats to thee thy Mother's grief.
Kill not the Moth nor Butterfly,
For the Last Judgment draweth nigh.
He who shall train the Horse to War
Shall never pass the Polar Bar.
The Beggar's Dog & Widow's Cat,
Feed them & thou wilt grow fat.
The Gnat that sings his Summer's song
Poison gets from Slander's tongue.
The poison of the Snake & Newt
Is the sweat of Envy's Foot.
The Poison of the Honey Bee
Is the Artist's Jealousy.
The Prince's Robes & Beggar's Rags
Are Toadstools on the Miser's Bags.
A truth that's told with bad intent
Beats all the Lies you can invent.
It is right it should be so;
Man was made for Joy and Woe;
And when this we rightly know
Thro' the World we safely go,
Joy & Woe are woven fine,
A Clothing for the Soul divine;
Under every grief & pine
Runs a joy with silken twine.
The Babe is more than swadling Bands;
Throughout all these Human Lands
Tools were made, & Born were hands,
Every Farmer Understands.
Every Tear from Every Eye
Becomes a Babe in Eternity;
This is caught by Females bright
And return'd to its own delight.
The Bleat, the Bark, Bellow & Roar
Are Waves that Beat on Heaven's Shore.
The Babe that weeps the Rod beneath
Writes Revenge in realms of death.
The Beggar's Rags, fluttering in Air,

Does to Rags the Heavens tear.
The Soldier, arm'd with Sword & Gun,
Palsied strikes the Summer's Sun.
The poor Man's Farthing is worth more
Than all the Gold on Afric's Shore.
One Mite wrung from the Labrer's hands
Shall buy & sell the Miser's Lands:
Or, if protected from on high,
Does that whole Nation sell & buy.
He who mocks the Infant's Faith
Shall be mock'd in Age & Death.
He who shall teach the Child to Doubt
The rotting Grave shall ne'er get out.
He who respects the Infant's faith
Triumphs over Hell & Death.
The Child's Toys & the Old Man's Reasons
Are the Fruits of the Two seasons.
The Questioner, who sits so sly,
Shall never know how to Reply.
He who replies to words of Doubt
Doth put the Light of Knowledge out.
The Strongest Poison ever known
Came from Caesar's Laurel Crown.
Nought can deform the Human Race
Like to the Armour's iron brace.
When Gold & Gems adorn the Plow
To Peaceful Arts shall Envy Bow.
A Riddle or the Cricket's Cry
Is to Doubt a fit Reply.
The Emmet's Inch & Eagle's Mile
Make Lame Philosophy to smile.
He who Doubts from what he sees
Will ne'er Believe, do what you Please.
If the Sun & Moon should doubt,
They'd immediately Go out.
To be in a Passion you Good may do,
But no Good if a Passion is in you.
The Whore & Gambler, by the State
Licenc'd, build that Nation's Fate.
The Harlot's cry from Street to Street
Shall weave Old England's winding Sheet.
The Winner's Shout, the Loser's Curse,

Dance before dead England's Hearse.
Every Night & every Morn
Some to Misery are Born.
Every Morn & every Night
Some are Born to sweet delight.
Some are Born to sweet delight,
Some are Born to Endless Night.
We are led to Believe a Lie
When we see not Thro' the Eye
Which was Born in a Night to perish in a Night
When the Soul Slept in Beams of Light.
God Appears & God is Light
To those poor Souls who dwell in Night,
But does a Human Form Display
To those who Dwell in Realms of day.

LONG JOHN BROWN & LITTLE MARY BELL

LITTLE Mary Bell had a Fairy in a Nut,
Long John Brown had the Devil in his Gut;
Long John Brown lov'd Little Mary Bell,
And the Fairy drew the Devil into the Nut-shell.

Her Fairy Skip'd out & her Fairy Skip'd in;
He laugh'd at the Devil saying "Love is a Sin."
The Devil he raged & and Devil he was wroth,
And the Devil enter'd into the Young Man's broth.

He was soon in the Gut of the loving Young Swain,
For John eat & drank to drive away Love's pain;
But all he could do he grew thinner & thinner,
Tho' he eat & drank as much as ten Men for his dinner.

Some said he had a Wolf in his stomach day & night,
Some said he had the Devil & they guess'd right;
The Fairy skip'd about in his Glory, Joy & Pride,
And he laugh'd at the Devil till poor John Brown died.

Then the Fairy skip'd out of the old Nut-shell,
And woe & alack for Pretty Mary Bell!
For the Devil crept in when the Fairy skip'd out,
And there goes Miss Bell with her fusty old Nut.

WILLIAM BOND

I WONDER whether the Girls are mad,
And I wonder whether they mean to kill,
And I wonder if William Bond will die,
For assuredly he is very ill.

He went to Church in a May morning
Attended by Fairies, one, two & three;
But the Angels of Providence drove them away,
And he return'd home in Misery.

He went not out to the Field nor Fold,
He went not out to the Village nor Town,
But he came home in a black, black cloud,
And took to his Bed & there lay down.

And an Angel of Providence at his Feet,
And an Angel of Providence at his Head,
And in the midst a Black, Black Cloud,
And in the midst the Sick Man on his Bed.

And on his Right hand was Mary Green,
And on his Left hand was his Sister Jane,
And their tears fell thro' the black, black Cloud
To drive away the sick man's pain.

"O William, if thou dost another Love,
Dost another Love better than poor Mary,
Go & take that other to be thy Wife,
And Mary Green shall her servant be."

"Yes, Mary, I do another Love,
Another I Love far better than thee,
And Another I will have for my Wife;
Then what have I to do with thee?

"For thou art Melancholy Pale,
And on thy Head is the cold Moon's shine,
But she is ruddy & bright as day,
And the sun beams dazzle from her eyne."

Mary trembled & Mary chill'd
And Mary fell down on the right hand floor,
That William Bond & his Sister Jane
Scarce could recover Mary more.

When Mary woke & found her Laid
On the Right hand of her William dear,
On the Right hand of his loved Bed,
And saw her William Bond so near,

The Fairies that fled from William Bond
Danced around her Shining Head;
They danced over the Pillow white,
And the Angels of Providence left the Bed.

I thought Love liv'd in the hot sun shine,
But O, he lives in the Moony light!
I thought to find Love in the heat of day,
But sweet Love is the Comforter of Night.

Seek Love in the Pity of other's Woe,
In the gentle relief of another's care,
In the darkness of night & the winter's snow,
In the naked & outcast, Seek Love there!

DEDICATION OF THE ILLUSTRATIONS TO BLAIR'S GRAVE

Printed 1808

TO THE QUEEN

THE Door of Death is made of Gold,
That Mortal Eyes cannot behold;
But, when the Mortal Eyes are clos'd,
And cold and pale the Limbs repos'd,
The Soul awakes; and, wond'ring, sees
In her mild Hand the golden Keys:
The Grave is Heaven's golden Gate,
And rich and poor around it wait;
O Shepherdess of England's Fold,
Behold this Gate of Pearl and Gold!

To dedicate to England's Queen
The Visions that my Soul has seen,
And, by Her kind permission, bring
What I have borne on solemn Wing
From the vast regions of the Grave,
Before Her Throne my Wings I wave;
Bowing before my Sov'reign's Feet,
"The Grave produc'd these Blossoms sweet
In mild repose from Earthly strife;
The Blossoms of Eternal Life!"

POEMS FROM MSS.

Written about 1810

❋

THE Angel that presided o'er my birth
Said, "Little creature, form'd of Joy & Mirth,
Go love without the help of any Thing on Earth."

❋

IF it is True, what the Prophets write,
That the heathen Gods are all stocks & stones,
Shall we, for the sake of being Polite,
Feed them with the juice of our marrow bones?

And if Bezaleel & Aholiab drew
What the Finger of God pointed to their View,
Shall we suffer the Roman & Grecian Rods
To compell us to worship them as Gods?

They stole them from the Temple of the Lord,
And Worshipp'd them that they might make
     Inspired Art Abhorr'd.

The Wood & Stone were call'd The Holy Things
And their Sublime Intent given to their Kings,
All the Atonements of Jehovah spurn'd,
And Criminals to Sacrifices Turn'd.

❋

I WILL tell you what Joseph of Arimathea
Said to my Fairy—was it not very queer?
Pliny & Trajan! what are you here?
Come listen to Joseph of Arimathea:
Listen patient, & when Joseph has done
'Twill make a fool laugh & a Fairy Fun.

❧

GROWN old in Love from Seven till Seven times Seven
I oft have wish'd for Hell for Ease from Heaven.

❧

WHY was Cupid a Boy
And why a boy was he?
He should have been a Girl
For ought that I can see.

For he shoots with his bow,
And the Girl shoots with her Eye,
And they both are merry & glad
And laugh when we do cry.

And to make Cupid a Boy
Was the Cupid Girl's mocking plan;
For a boy can't interpret the thing
Till he is become a man.

And then he's so pierc'd with cares
And wounded with arrowy smarts,
That the whole business of his life
Is to pick out the heads of the darts.

'Twas the Greeks' love of war
Turn'd Love into a Boy,
And Woman into a Statue of Stone—
And away flew every Joy.

❧

SINCE all the Riches of this World
May be gifts from the Devil & Earthly Kings,
I should suspect that I worship'd the Devil
If I thank'd my God for Worldly things.

❧

TO Chloe's breast young Cupid slily stole,
But he crept in at Myra's pocket hole.

❧

NAIL his neck to the Cross: nail it with a nail.
Nail his neck to the Cross: ye all have power over his tail.

❧

THE Caverns of the Grave I've seen,
And these I shew'd to England's Queen.
But now the Caves of Hell I view:
Who shall I dare to shew them to?
What mighty Soul in Beauty's form
Shall dauntless View the Infernal Storm?
Egremont's Countess can controll
The flames of Hell that round me roll.
If she refuse, I still go on
Till the Heavens & Earth are gone,
Still admir'd by Noble minds,
Follow'd by Envy on the winds,
Re-engrav'd Time after Time,
Ever in their youthful prime,
My designs unchang'd remain.
Time may rage but rage in vain.
Far above Time's troubled Fountains
On the Great Atlantic Mountains,
In my Golden House on high,
There they Shine Eternally.

❧

I ROSE up at the dawn of day—
Get thee away! get thee away!
Pray'st thou for Riches? away! away!
This is the Throne of Mammon grey.

Said I, "this sure is very odd.
I took it to be the Throne of God.
For every Thing besides I have:
It is only for Riches that I can crave.

"I have Mental Joy & Mental Health
And Mental Friends & Mental wealth;
I've a Wife I love & that loves me;
I've all but Riches Bodily.

"I am in God's presence night & day,
And he never turns his face away.
The accuser of sins by my side does stand
And he holds my money bag in his hand.

"For my worldly things God makes him pay,
And he'd pay more if to him I would pray;
And so you may do the worst you can do:
Be assur'd Mr. devil I won't pray to you.

"Then If for Riches I must not Pray,
God knows I little of Prayers need say.
So as a Church is known by its Steeple,
If I pray it must be for other People.

"He says, if I do not worship him for a God,
I shall eat coarser food & go worse shod;
So as I don't value such things as these,
You must do, Mr. devil, just as God please."

The Everlasting Gospel

THERE is not one Moral Virtue that Jesus Inculcated but Plato & Cicero
did Inculcate before him; what then did Christ Inculcate? Forgiveness
of Sins. This alone is the Gospel, & this is the Life & Immortality brought
to light by Jesus, Even the Covenant of Jehovah, which is This: If you
forgive one another your Trespasses, so shall Jehovah forgive you, That
he himself may dwell among you; but if you Avenge, you Murder the
Divine Image, & he cannot dwell among you; because you Murder him
he arises again, & you deny that he is Arisen, & are blind to Spirit.

1

If Moral Virtue was Christianity,
Christ's Pretensions were all Vanity,
And Cai[a]phas & Pilate, Men
Praise Worthy, & the Lion's Den
And not the Sheepfold, Allegories
Of God & Heaven & their Glories.
The Moral Christian is the Cause
Of the Unbeliever & his Laws.
The Roman Virtues, Warlike Fame,
Take Jesus' & Jehovah's Name;
For what is Antichrist but those
Who against Sinners Heaven close
With Iron bars, in Virtuous State,
And Rhadamanthus at the Gate?

2

What can this Gospel of Jesus be?
What Life & Immortality,
What was it that he brought to Light
That Plato & Cicero did not write?
The Heathen Deities wrote them all,
These Moral Virtues, great & small.

What is the Accusation of Sin
But Moral Virtues' deadly Gin?
The Moral Virtues in their Pride
Did o'er the World triumphant ride
In Wars & Sacrifice for Sin,
And Souls to Hell ran trooping in.
The Accuser, Holy God of All
This Pharisaic Worldly Ball,
Amidst them in his Glory Beams
Upon the Rivers & the Streams.
Then Jesus rose & said to Me,
"Thy Sins are all forgiven thee."
Loud Pilate Howl'd, loud Cai[a]phas yell'd,
When they the Gospel Light beheld.
It was when Jesus said to Me,
"Thy Sins are all forgiven thee."
The Christian trumpets loud proclaim
Thro' all the World in Jesus' name
Mutual forgiveness of each Vice,
And oped the Gates of Paradise.
The Moral Virtues in Great fear
Formed the Cross & Nails & Spear,
And the Accuser standing by
Cried out, "Crucify! Crucify!
Our Moral Virtues ne'er can be,
Nor Warlike pomp & Majesty;
For Moral Virtues all begin
In the Accusations of Sin,
And all the Heroic Virtues End
In destroying the Sinners' Friend.
Am I not Lucifer the Great,
And you my daughters in Great State,
The fruit of my Mysterious Tree
Of Good & Evil & Misery
And Death & Hell, which now begin
On everyone who Forgives Sin?"

a

THE Vision of Christ that thou dost see
Is my Vision's Greatest Enemy:
Thine has a great hook nose like thine,
Mine has a snub nose like to mine:

Thine is the friend of All Mankind,
Mine speaks in parables to the Blind:
Thine loves the same world that mine hates,
Thy Heaven doors are my Hell Gates.
Socrates taught what Meletus
Loath'd as a Nation's bitterest Curse,
And Caiaphas was in his own Mind
A benefactor to Mankind:
Both read the Bible day & night,
But thou read'st black where I read white.

b

Was Jesus gentle, or did he
Give any marks of Gentility?
When twelve years old he ran away
And left his Parents in dismay.
When after three days' sorrow found,
Loud as Sinai's trumpet sound:
"No Earthly Parents I confess—
My Heavenly Father's business!
Ye understand not what I say,
And, angry, force me to obey."
Obedience is a duty then,
And favour gains with God & Men.
John from the Wilderness loud cried;
Satan gloried in his Pride.
"Come," said Satan, "come away,
I'll soon see if you'll obey!
John for disobedience bled,
But you can turn the stones to bread.
God's high king & God's high Priest
Shall Plant their Glories in your breast
If Caiaphas you will obey,
If Herod you with bloody Prey
Feed with the sacrifice, & be
Obedient, fall down, worship me."
Thunders & lightnings broke around,
And Jesus' voice in thunders' sound:
"Thus I seize the Spiritual Prey.
Ye smiters with disease, make way.
I come your King & God to seize.
Is God a smiter with disease?"

The God of this World raged in vain:
He bound Old Satan in his Chain,
And bursting forth, his furious ire
Became a Chariot of fire.
Throughout the land he took his course,
And traced diseases to their source:
He curs'd the Scribe & Pharisee,
Trampling down Hipocrisy:
Where'er his Chariot took its way,
There Gates of death let in the day,
Broke down from every Chain & Bar;
And Satan in his Spiritual War
Drag'd at his Chariot wheels: loud howl'd
The God of this World: louder roll'd
The Chariot Wheels & louder still
His voice was heard from Zion's hill,
And in his hand the Scourge shone bright;
He scourg'd the Merchant Canaanite
From out the Temple of his Mind,
And in his Body tight does bind
Satan & all his Hellish Crew;
And thus with wrath he did subdue
The Serpent Bulk of Nature's dross,
Till He had nail'd it to the Cross,
He took on Sin in the Virgin's Womb,
And put it off on the Cross & Tomb
To be Worship'd by the Church of Rome.

_c_

Was Jesus Humble? or did he
Give any proofs of Humility?
When but a Child he ran away
And left his Parents in dismay.
When they had wonder'd three days long
These were the words upon his Tongue:
"No Earthly Parents I confess:
I am doing my Father's business."
When the rich learned Pharisee
Came to consult him secretly,
Upon his heart with Iron pen
He wrote, "Ye must be born again."
He was too Proud to take a bribe:

He spoke with authority, not like a Scribe.
He says with most consummate Art,
"Follow me, I am meek & lowly of heart,"
As that is the only way to Escape
The Miser's net & the Glutton's trap.
He who loves his Enemies, hates his Friends;
This is surely not what Jesus intends;
He must mean the meer love of Civility,
And so he must mean concerning Humility;
But he acts with triumphant, honest pride,
And this is the Reason Jesus died.
If he had been Antichrist, Creeping Jesus,
He'd have done anything to please us:
Gone sneaking into the Synagogues
And not used the Elders & Priests like Dogs,
But humble as a Lamb or an Ass,
Obey himself to Caiaphas.
God wants not Man to humble himself:
This is the Trick of the Ancient Elf.
Humble toward God, Haughty toward Man,
This is the Race that Jesus ran,
And when he humbled himself to God,
Then descended the cruel rod.
"If thou humblest thyself, thou humblest me;
Thou also dwelst in Eternity.
Thou art a Man, God is no more,
Thine own Humanity learn to adore
And thy Revenge Abroad display
In terrors at the Last Judgment day.
God's Mercy & Long Suffering
Are but the Sinner to Judgment to bring.
Thou on the Cross for them shalt pray
And take Revenge at the last Day.

"Do what you will, this Life's a Fiction
And is made up of Contradiction."

d

Was Jesus Humble? or did he
Give any Proofs of Humility?
Boast of high Things with Humble tone,
And give with Charity a Stone?

When but a Child he ran away
And left his Parents in dismay.
When they had wander'd three days long
These were the words upon his tongue:
"No Earthly Parents I confess:
I am doing my Father's business."
When the rich learned Pharisee
Came to consult him secretly,
Upon his heart with Iron pen
He wrote, "Ye must be born again."
He was too Proud to take a bribe;
He spoke with authority, not like a Scribe.
He says with most consummate Art,
"Follow me, I am meek & lowly of heart,"
As that is the only way to escape
The Miser's net & the Glutton's trap.
What can be done with such desperate Fools
Who follow after the Heathen Schools?
I was standing by when Jesus died;
What I call'd Humility, they call'd Pride.
He who loves his Enemies betrays his Friends;
This surely is not what Jesus intends,
But the sneaking Pride of Heroic Schools,
And the Scribes' & Pharisees' Virtuous Rules;
For he acts with honest, triumphant Pride,
And this is the cause that Jesus died.
He did not die with Christian Ease,
Asking pardon of his Enemies:
If he had, Caiaphas would forgive:
Sneaking submission can always live.
He had only to say that God was the devil,
And the devil was God, like a Christian Civil:
Mild Christian regrets to the devil confess
For affronting him thrice in the Wilderness;
He had soon been bloody Caesar's Elf,
And at last he would have been Caesar himself.
Like dr. Priestly & Bacon & Newton—
Poor Spiritual Knowledge is not worth a button!
For thus the Gospel Sir Isaac confutes:
"God can only be known by his Attributes;
And as for the Indwelling of the Holy Ghost
Or of Christ & his Father, it's all a boast

And Pride & Vanity of the imagination,
That disdains to follow this World's Fashion."
To teach doubt & Experiment
Certainly was not what Christ meant.
What was he doing all that time,
From twelve years old to manly prime?
Was he then Idle, or the Less
About his Father's business?
Or was his wisdom held in scorn
Before his wrath began to burn
In Miracles throughout the Land,
That quite unnerv'd Caiaphas' hand?
If he had been Antichrist, Creeping Jesus,
He'd have done anything to please us—
Gone sneaking into Synagogues
And not us'd the Elders & Priests like dogs,
But Humble as a Lamb or Ass
Obey'd himself to Caiaphas.
God wants not Man to Humble himself:
This is the trick of the ancient Elf.
This is the Race that Jesus ran:
Humble to God, Haughty to Man,
Cursing the Rulers before the People
Even to the temple's highest Steeple;
And when he Humbled himself to God,
Then descended the Cruel Rod.
"If thou humblest thyself, thou humblest me;
Thou also dwell'st in Eternity.
Thou art a Man, God is no more,
Thy own humanity learn to adore,
For that is my Spirit of Life.
Awake, arise to Spiritual Strife
And thy Revenge abroad display
In terrors at the Last Judgment day
God's Mercy & Long Suffering
Is but the Sinner to Judgment to bring.
Thou on the Cross for them shalt pray
And take Revenge at the Last Day.
This Corporeal life's a fiction
And is made up of Contradiction."
Jesus replied & thunders hurl'd:
"I never will Pray for the World.

Once I did so when I pray'd in the Garden;
I wish'd to take with me a Bodily Pardon."
Can that which was of woman born
In the absence of the Morn,
When the Soul fell into Sleep
And Archangels round it weep,
Shooting out against the Light
Fibres of a deadly night,
Reasoning upon its own dark Fiction,
In doubt which is Self Contradiction?
Humility is only doubt,
And does the Sun & Moon blot out,
Rooting over with thorns & stems
The buried Soul & all its Gems.
This Life's dim Windows of the Soul
Distorts the Heavens from Pole to Pole
And leads you to Believe a Lie
When you see with, not thro', the Eye
That was born in a night to perish in a night,
When the Soul slept in the beams of Light.
Was Jesus Chaste? or did he, &c.

                    e

Was Jesus Chaste? or did he
Give any Lessons of Chastity?
The morning blush'd fiery red:
Mary was found in Adulterous bed;
Earth groan'd beneath, & Heaven above
Trembled at discovery of Love.
Jesus was sitting in Moses' Chair,
They brought the trembling Woman There.
Moses commands she be stoned to death,
What was the sound of Jesus' breath?
He laid His hand on Moses' Law:
The Ancient Heavens, in Silent Awe
Writ with Curses from Pole to Pole,
All away began to roll:
The Earth trembling & Naked lay
In secret bed of Mortal Clay,
On Sinai felt the hand divine
Putting back the bloody shrine,

And she heard the breath of God
As she heard by Eden's flood:
"Good & Evil are no more!
Sinai's trumpets, cease to roar!
Cease, finger of God, to write!
The Heavens are not clean in thy Sight,
Thou art Good, and thou Alone;
Nor may the sinner cast one stone.
To be Good only, is to be
A God or else a Pharisee.
Thou Angel of the Presence Divine
That didst create this Body of Mine,
Wherefore hast thou writ these Laws
And Created Hell's dark jaws?
My Presence I will take from thee:
A Cold Leper thou shalt be.
Tho' thou wast so pure & bright
That Heaven was Impure in thy Sight,
Tho' thy Oath turn'd Heaven Pale,
Tho' thy Covenant built Hell's Jail,
Tho' thou didst all to Chaos roll
With the Serpent for its soul,
Still the breath Divine does move
And the breath Divine is Love.
Mary, Fear Not! Let me see
The Seven Devils that torment thee:
Hide not from my Sight thy Sin,
That forgiveness thou maist win.
Has no Man Condemned thee?"
"No Man, Lord:" "then what is he
Who Shall Accuse thee? Come Ye forth,
Fallen fiends of Heav'nly birth
That have forgot your Ancient love
And driven away my trembling Dove.
You shall bow before her feet;
You shall lick the dust for Meat;
And tho' you cannot Love, but Hate,
Shall be beggars at Love's Gate.
What was thy love? Let me see it;
Was it love or dark deceit?"
"Love too long from Me has fled;

'Twas dark deceit, to Earn my bread;
'Twas Covet, or 'twas Custom, or
Some trifle not worth caring for;
That they may call a shame & Sin
Love's temple that God dwelleth in,
And hide in secret hidden shrine
The Naked Human form divine,
And render that a Lawless thing
On which the Soul Expands its wing.
But this, O Lord, this was my Sin
When first I let these devils in
In dark pretence to Chastity:
Blaspheming Love, blaspheming thee.
Thence Rose Secret Adulteries,
And thence did Covet also rise.
My sin thou hast forgiven me,
Canst thou forgive my Blasphemy?
Canst thou return to this dark Hell,
And in my burning bosom dwell?
And canst thou die that I may live?
And canst thou Pity & forgive?"
Then Roll'd the shadowy Man away
From the Limbs of Jesus, to make them his prey,
An Ever devouring appetite
Glittering with festering venoms bright,
Crying, "Crucify this cause of distress,
Who don't keep the secrets of holiness!
All Mental Powers by Diseases we bind,
But he heals the deaf & the dumb & the Blind.
Whom God has afflicted for Secret Ends,
He Comforts & Heals & calls them Friends."
But, when Jesus was Crucified,
Then was perfected his glitt'ring pride:
In three Nights he devour'd his prey,
And still he devours the Body of Clay;
For dust & Clay is the Serpent's meat,
Which never was made for Man to Eat.

ƒ

I am sure this Jesus will not do
Either for Englishman or Jew.

g

Seeing this False Christ, In fury & Passion
I made my Voice heard all over the Nation.
What are those, &c.[1]

h

This was spoke by My Spectre to Voltaire, Bacon, &c.

Did Jesus teach doubt? or did he
Give any lessons of Philosophy,
Charge Visionaries with decieving,
Or call Men wise for not Believing?

i

Was Jesus Born of a Virgin Pure
With narrow Soul & looks demure?
If he intended to take on Sin
The Mother should an Harlot been,
Just such a one as Magdalen
With seven devils in her Pen;
Or were Jew Virgins still more Curst,
And more sucking devils nurst?
Or what was it which he took on
That he might bring Salvation?
A Body subject to be Tempted,
From neither pain nor grief Exempted?
Or such a body as might not feel
The passions that with Sinners deal?
Yes, but they say he never fell.
Ask Caiaphas; for he can tell.
"He mock'd the Sabbath, & he mock'd
The Sabbath's God, & he unlock'd
The Evil spirits from their Shrines,
And turn'd Fishermen to Divines;
O'erturn'd the Tent of Secret Sins,
& its Golden cords & Pins—
'Tis the Bloody Shrine of War
Pinn'd around from Star to Star,
Halls of justice, hating Vice,
Where the devil Combs his lice.

[1] The rest of this passage is lost.

He turn'd the devils into Swine
That he might tempt the Jews to dine;
Since which, a Pig has got a look
That for a Jew may be mistook.
'Obey your parents.'—What says he?
'Woman, what have I to do with thee?
No Earthly Parents I confess:
I am doing my Father's Business.'
He scorn'd Earth's Parents, scorn'd Earth's God,
And mock'd the one & the other's Rod;
His Seventy Disciples sent
Against Religion & Government:
They by the Sword of Justice fell
And him their Cruel Murderer tell.
He left his Father's trade to roam
A wand'ring Vagrant without Home;
And thus he others' labour stole
That he might live above Controll.
The Publicans & Harlots he
Selected for his Company,
And from the Adulteress turn'd away
God's righteous Law, that lost its Prey."

Didactic and Symbolical Works

THERE IS NO NATURAL RELIGION

FIRST SERIES

Etched about 1788

T H E *Argument*. Man has no notion of moral fitness but from Education. Naturally he is only a natural organ subject to Sense.

I. Man cannot naturally Perceive but through his natural or bodily organs.

II. Man by his reasoning power can only compare & judge of what he has already perciev'd.

II. From a perception of only 3 senses or 3 elements none could deduce a fourth or fifth.

IV. None could have other than natural or organic thoughts if he had none but organic perceptions.

V. Man's desires are limited by his perceptions, none can desire what he has not perciev'd.

VI. The desires & perceptions of man, untaught by any thing but organs of sense, must be limited to objects of sense.

Conclusion. If it were not for the Poetic or Prophetic character the Philosophic & Experimental would soon be at the ratio of all things, & stand still, unable to do other than repeat the same dull round over again.

THERE IS NO NATURAL RELIGION

SECOND SERIES

Etched about 1788

I. Man's perceptions are not bounded by organs of perception; he perceives more than sense (tho' ever so acute) can discover.

II. Reason, or the ratio of all we have already known, is not the same that it shall be when we know more.

III. [*This proposition has been lost.*]

IV. The bounded is loathed by its possessor. The same dull round, even of a universe, would soon become a mill with complicated wheels.

V. If the many become the same as the few when possess'd, More! More! is the cry of a mistaken soul; less than All cannot satisfy Man.

VI. If any could desire what he is incapable of possessing, despair must be his eternal lot.

VII. The desire of Man being Infinite, the possession is Infinite & himself Infinite.

Application. He who sees the Infinite in all things, sees God. He who sees the Ratio only, sees himself only.

Therefore God becomes as we are, that we may be as he is.

ALL RELIGIONS ARE ONE

Etched about 1788

The Voice of one crying in the Wilderness

1 HE *Argument.* As the true method of knowledge is experiment, the true faculty of knowing must be the faculty which experiences. This faculty I treat of.

PRINCIPLE 1st. That the Poetic Genius is the true Man, and that the body or outward form of Man is derived from the Poetic Genius. Likewise that the forms of all things are derived from their Genius, which by the Ancients was call'd an Angel & Spirit & Demon.

PRINCIPLE 2d. As all men are alike in outward form, So (and with the same infinite variety) all are alike in the Poetic Genius.

PRINCIPLE 3d. No man can think, write, or speak from his heart, but he must intend truth. Thus all sects of Philosophy are from the Poetic Genius adapted to the weaknesses of every individual.

PRINCIPLE 4th. As none by traveling over known lands can find out the unknown, So from already acquired knoweldge Man could not acquire more: therefore an universal Poetic Genius exists.

PRINCIPLE 5th. The Religions of all Nations are derived from each Nation's different reception of the Poetic Genius, which is every where call'd the Spirit of Prophecy.

PRINCIPLE 6th. The Jewish & Christian Testaments are An original derivation from the Poetic Genius; this is necessary from the confined nature of bodily sensation.

PRINCIPLE 7th. As all men are alike (tho' infinitely various), So all Religions &, as all similars, have one source.

The true Man is the source, he being the Poetic Genius.

TIRIEL

Written about 1789

I

AND Aged Tiriel stood before the Gates of his beautiful palace
With Myratana, once the Queen of all the western plains;
But now his eyes were dark'ned & his wife fading in death.
They stood before their once delightful palace, & thus the Voice
Of aged Tiriel arose, that his sons might hear in their gates:

"Accursed race of Tiriel! behold your father;
Come forth & look on her that bore you! come, you accursed sons!
In my weak arms I here have borne your dying mother.
Come forth, sons of the Curse, come forth! see the death of Myratana!"

His sons ran from their gates & saw their aged parents stand,
And thus the eldest son of Tiriel rais'd his mighty voice:

"Old man! unworthy to be call'd the father of Tiriel's race!
For every one of those thy wrinkles, each of those grey hairs
Are cruel as death & as obdurate as the devouring pit!
Why should thy sons care for thy curses, thou accursed man?
Were we not slaves till we rebel'd? Who cares for Tiriel's curse?
His blessing was a cruel curse. His curse may be a blessing."

He ceast: the aged man rais'd up his right hand to the heavens,
His left supported Myratana, shrinking in pangs of death:
The orbs of his large eyes he open'd, & thus his voice went forth:

"Serpents, not sons, wreathing around the bones of Tiriel!
Ye worms of death, feasting upon your aged parent's flesh!
Listen! & hear your mother's groans! No more accursed Sons
She bears; she groans not at the birth of Heuxos or Yuva.

These are the groans of death, ye serpents! These are the groans of death!
Nourish'd with milk, ye serpents, nourish'd with mother's tears & cares!
Look at my eyes, blind as the orbless scull among the stones!
Look at my bald head! Hark! listen, ye serpents, listen!
What, Myratana! What, my wife! O Soul! O Spirit! O fire!
What, Myratana! art thou dead? Look here, ye serpents, look!
The serpents sprung from her own bowels have drain'd her dry as this.
Curse on your ruthless heads, for I will bury her even here!"

So saying, he began to dig a grave with his aged hands;
But Heuxos call'd a Son of Zazel to dig their mother a grave.

"Old Cruelty, desist! & let us dig a grave for thee.
Thou hast refus'd our charity, thou hast refus'd our food,
Thou hast refus'd our clothes, our beds, our houses for thy dwelling,
Chusing to wander like a Son of Zazel in the rocks.
Why dost thou curse? is not the curse now come upon your head?
Was it not you enslav'd the sons of Zazel? & they have curs'd,
And now you feel it. Dig a grave, & let us bury our mother.

"There, take the body, cursed sons! & may the heavens rain wrath
As thick as northern fogs around your gates, to choke you up!
That you may lie as now your mother lies, like dogs cast out,
The stink of your dead carcases annoying man & beast,
Till your white bones are bleach'd with age for a memorial.
No! your remembrance shall perish; for, when your carcases
Lie stinking on the earth, the buriers shall arise from the east,
And not a bone of all the sons of Tiriel remain.
Bury your mother! but you cannot bury the curse of Tiriel."

He ceast & darkling o'er the mountains sought his pathless way.

2

He wander'd day & night: to him both day and night were dark.
The sun he felt, but the bright moon was now a useless globe:
O'er mountains & thro' vales of woe the blind & aged man
Wander'd, till he that leadeth all led him to the vales of Har.

And Har & Heva, like two children, sat beneath the Oak:
Mnetha, now aged, waited on them & brought them food & clothing,
But they were as the shadow of Har & as the years forgotten.
Playing with flowers & running after birds they spent the day,
And in the night like infants slept, delighted with infant dreams.

Soon as the blind wanderer enter'd the pleasant gardens of Har,
They ran weeping, like frighted infants, for refuge in Mnetha's arms.
The blind man felt his way & cried: "Peace to these open doors!
Let no one fear, for poor blind Tiriel hurts none but himself.
Tell me, O friends, where am I now & in what pleasant place?"

"This is the valley of Har," said Mnetha, "& this the tent of Har.
Who art thou, poor blind man, that takest the name of Tiriel on thee?
Tiriel is king of all the west: who art thou? I am Mnetha,
And this is Har & Heva, trembling like infants by my side."

"I know Tiriel is king of the west, & there he lives in joy.
No matter who I am; O Mnetha, if you hast any food,
Give it me, for I cannot stay; my journey is far from hence."

Then Har said: "O my mother Mnetha, venture not so near him;
For he is the king of rotten wood & of the bones of death;
He wanders without eyes & passes thro' thick walls & doors.
Thou shalt not smite my mother Mnetha, O thou eyeless man!

"A wanderer, I beg for food: you see I cannot weep:
I cast away my staff, the kind companion of my travel,
And I kneel down that you may see I am a harmless man."

He kneeled down, & Mnetha said: "Come, Har & Heva, rise!
He is an innocent old man & hungry with his travel."

Then Har arose & laid his hand upon old Tiriel's head.

"God bless thy poor bald pate! God bless thy hollow winking eyes!
God bless thy shrivel'd beard! God bless thy many-wrinkled forehead!
Thou hast no teeth, old man, & thus I kiss thy sleek bald head.
Heva, come kiss his bald head, for he will not hurt us, Heva."

Then Heva came & took old Tiriel in her mother's arms.

"Bless thy poor eyes, old man, & bless the old father of Tiriel!
Thou art my Tiriel's old father; I know thee thro' thy wrinkles,
Because thou smellest like the fig-tree, thou smellest like ripe figs.
How didst thou lose thy eyes, old Tiriel? bless thy wrinkled face!"

Mnetha said: "Come in, aged wanderer! tell us of thy name.
Why shouldest thou conceal thyself from those of thine own flesh?"

"I am not of this region," said Tiriel dissemblingly,
"I am an aged wanderer, once father of a race
Far in the north; but they were wicked & were all destroy'd,
And I their father sent an outcast. I have told you all.
Ask me no more, I pray, for grief hath seal'd my precious sight."

"O Lord!" said Mnetha, "how I tremble! are there then more people,
More human creatures on this earth, beside the sons of Har?"

"No more," Tiriel, "but I, remain on all this globe,
And I remain an outcast; hast thou any thing to drink?"

Then Mnetha gave him milk & fruits, & they sat down together.

3

They sat & eat, & Har & Heva smil'd on Tiriel.

"Thou art a very old old man, but I am older than thou.
How came thine hair to leave thy forehead? how came thy face so brown?
My hair is very long, my beard doth cover all my breast.
God bless thy piteous face! to count the wrinkles in thy face
Would puzzle Mnetha: bless thy face! for thou art Tiriel."

"Tiriel I never saw but once: I sat with him & eat;
He was as chearful as a prince & gave me entertainment;
But long I staid not at his palace, for I am forc'd to wander."

"What! wilt thou leave us too?" said Heva: "thou shalt not leave us too,
For we have many sports to shew thee & many songs to sing,
And after dinner we will walk into the cage of Har,
And thou shalt help us to catch birds & gather them ripe cherries.
Then let thy name be Tiriel & never leave us more."

"If thou dost go," said Har, "I wish thine eyes may see thy folly.
My sons have left me; did thine leave thee? O, 'twas very cruel!"

"No! venerable man," said Tiriel, "ask me not such things,
For thou dost make my heart to bleed: my sons were not like thine,
But worse. O never ask me more, or I must flee away!"

"Thou shalt not go," said Heva, "till thou hast seen our singing birds,
And heard Har sing in the great cage & slept upon our fleeces.
Go not! for thou art so like Tiriel that I love thine head,
Tho' it is wrinkled like the earth parch'd with the summer heat."

Then Tiriel rose up from the seat & said: "God bless these tents!
My Journey is o'er rocks & mountains, not in pleasant vales:
I must not sleep nor rest, because of madness & dismay."

And Mnetha said: "Thou must not go to wander dark, alone;
But dwell with us & let us be to thee instead of eyes,
And I will bring thee food, old man, till death shall call thee hence."

Then Tiriel frown'd & answer'd: "Did I not command you, saying,
'Madness & deep dismay possess the heart of the blind man,
The wanderer who seeks the woods, leaning upon his staff?' "

Then Mnetha, trembling at his frowns, led him to the tent door
And gave to him his staff & blest him: he went on his way.

But Har & Heva stood & watch'd him till he enter'd the wood,
And then they went & wept to Mnetha: but they soon forgot their tears.

4

Over the weary hills the blind man took his lonely way;
To him the day & night alike was dark & desolate;
But far he had not gone when Ijim from his woods came down,
Met him at entrance of the forest in a dark & lonely way.

"Who art thou, Eyeless wretch, that thus obstruct'st the lion's path?
Ijim shall rend thy feeble joints, thou tempter of dark Ijim!
Thou hast the form of Tiriel, but I know thee well enough.
Stand from my path, foul fiend! is this the last of thy deceits,
To be a hypocrite & stand in shape of a blind beggar?"

The blind man heard his brother's voice & kneel'd down on his knee.

"O Brother Ijim, if it is thy voice that speaks to me,
Smite not thy brother Tiriel, tho' weary of his life.
My sons have smitten me already; and, if thou smitest me,
The curse that rolls over their heads will rest itself on thine.
'Tis now seven years since in my palace I beheld thy face."

"Come, thou dark fiend, I dare thy cunning! know that Ijim scorns
To smite thee in the form of helpless age & eyeless policy.
Rise up! for I discern thee & I dare thy eloquent tongue.
Come! I will lead thee on thy way & use thee as a scoff."

"O Brother Ijim, thou beholdest wretched Tiriel:
Kiss me, my brother, & then leave me to wander desolate!"

"No! artful fiend, but I will lead thee; dost thou want to go?
Reply not, lest I bind thee with the green flags of the brook.
Ay! now thou art discover'd, I will use thee like a slave."

When Tiriel heard the words of Ijim, he sought not to reply:
He knew 'twas vain, for Ijim's words were as the voice of Fate.

And they went on together, over hills, thro' woody dales,
Blind to the pleasures of the sight & deaf to warbling birds:
All day they walk'd & all the night beneath the pleasant Moon,
Westwardly journeying, till Tiriel grew weary with his travel.

"O Ijim, I am faint & weary, for my knees forbid
To bear me further: urge me not, lest I should die with travel.
A little rest I crave, a little water from a brook,
Or I shall soon discover that I am a mortal man,
And you will lose your once lov'd Tiriel: alas! how faint I am!"

"Impudent fiend!" said Ijim, "hold thy glib & eloquent tongue!
Tiriel is a king, & thou the tempter of dark Ijim.
Drink of this running brook & I will bear thee on my shoulders."

He drank, & Ijim rais'd him up & bore him on his shoulders:
All day he bore him, & when evening drew her solemn curtain,
Enter'd the gates of Tiriel's palace & stood & call'd aloud:

"Heuxos, come forth! I here have brought the fiend that troubles Ijim.
Look! know'st thou aught of this grey beard, or of these blinded eyes?"

Heuxos & Lotho ran forth at the sound of Ijim's voice,
And saw their aged father borne upon his mighty shoulders.
Their eloquent tongues were dumb, & sweat stood on their trembling
    limbs:
They knew 'twas vain to strive with Ijim; they bow'd & silent stood.

"What, Heuxos! call thy father, for I mean to sport to-night.
This is the hypocrite that sometimes roars a dreadful lion;
Then I have rent his limbs & left him rotting in the forest
For birds to eat; but I have scarce departed from the place,

But like a tyger he would come: & so I rent him too.
Then like a river he would seek to drown me in his waves;
But soon I buffetted the torrent: anon like to a cloud
Fraught with the swords of lightning; but I brav'd the vengeance too.
Then he would creep like a bright serpent till around my neck.
While I was sleeping, he would twine: I squeez'd his pois'nous soul.
Then like a toad, or like a newt, would whisper in my ears;
Or like a rock stood in my way, or like a pois'nous shrub.
At last I caught him in the form of Tiriel, blind & old,
And so I'll keep him! fetch your father, fetch forth Myratana!"

They stood confounded, and Thus Tiriel rais'd his silver voice:

"Serpents, not sons, why do you stand? fetch hither Tiriel!
Fetch hither Myratana! & delight yourselves with scoffs;
For poor blind Tiriel is return'd, & this much-injur'd head
Is ready for your bitter taunts: come forth, sons of the curse!"

Mean time the other sons of Tiriel ran around their father,
Confounded at the terrible strength of Ijim: they knew 'twas vain,
Both spear & shield were useless & the coat of iron mail,
When Ijim stretch'd his mighty arm; the arrow from his limbs
Rebounded & the piercing sword broke on his naked flesh.

"Then is it true, Heuxos, that thou hast turn'd thy aged parent
To be the sport of wintry winds?" said Ijim, "is this true?
It is a lie & I am like the tree torn by the wind,
Thou eyeless fiend, & you dissemblers! Is this Tiriel's house?
It is as false as Matha & as dark as vacant Orcus.
Escape, ye fiends! for Ijim will not lift his hand against ye."

So saying, Ijim gloomy turn'd his back, & silent sought
The secret forests & all night wander'd in desolate ways.

5

And aged Tiriel stood & said: "Where does the thunder sleep?
Where doth he hide his terrible head? & his swift & fiery daughters,
Where do they shroud their fiery wings & the terrors of their hair?
Earth, thus I stamp thy bosom! rouse the earthquake from his den,
To raise his dark & burning visage thro' the cleaving ground,
To thrust these towers with his shoulders! let his fiery dogs
Rise from the center, belching flames & roarings, dark smoke!

Where art thou, Pestilence, that bathest in fogs & standing lakes?
Rise up thy sluggish limbs & let the loathsomest of poisons
Drop from thy garments as thou walkest, wrapt in yellow clouds!
Here take thy seat in this wide court; let it be strown with dead;
And sit & smile upon these cursed sons of Tiriel!
Thunder & fire & pestilence, hear you not Tiriel's curse?"

He ceast: the heavy clouds confus'd roll'd round the lofty towers,
Discharging their enormous voices at the father's curse.
The earth trembled; fires belched from the yawning clefts;
And when the shaking ceast, a fog possest the accursed clime.

The cry was great in Tiriel's palace: his five daughters ran
And caught him by the garments, weeping with cries of bitter woe.

"Aye, now you feel the curse, you cry! but may all ears be deaf
As Tiriel's, & all eyes as blind as Tiriel's to your woes!
May never stars shine on your roofs! may never sun nor moon
Visit you, but eternal fogs hover around your wails!
Hela, my youngest daughter, you shall lead me from this place,
And let the curse fall on the rest & wrap them up together!"

He ceast, & Hela led her father from the noisom place.
In haste they fled, while all the sons & daughters of Tiriel,
Chain'd in thick darkness, utter'd cries of mourning all the night;
And in the morning, Lo! an hundred men in ghastly death!
The four daughters stretch'd on the marble pavement, silent all,
Fall'n by the pestilence!—the rest moped round in guilty fears;
And all the children in their beds were cut off in one night.
Thirty of Tiriel's sons remain'd, to wither in the palace,
Desolate, Loathed, Dumb, Astonish'd, waiting for black death.

6

And Hela led her father thro' the silent of the night,
Astonish'd, silent, till the morning beams began to spring.

"Now, Hela, I can go with pleasure & dwell with Har & Heva,
Now that the curse shall clean devour all those guilty sons.
This is the right & ready way; I know it by the sound
That our feet make. Remember, Hela, I have sav'd thee from death;
Then be obedient to thy father, for the curse is taken off thee.
I dwelt with Myratana five years in the desolate rock,

And all that time we waited for the fire to fall from heaven,
Or for the torrents of the sea to overwhelm you all.
But now my wife is dead & all the time of grace is past:
You see the parent's curse. Now lead me where I have commanded."

"O leagued with evil spirits, thou accursed man of sin!
True, I was born thy slave! who ask'd thee to save me from death?
'Twas for thy self, thou cruel man, because thou wantest eyes."

"True, Hela, this is the desert of all those cruel ones.
Is Tiriel cruel? look! his daughter & his youngest daughter
Laughs at affection, glories in rebellion, scoffs at Love.
I have not eat these two days; lead me to Har & Heva's tent,
Or I will wrap thee up in such a terrible father's curse
That thou shalt feel worms in thy marrow creeping thro' thy bones.
Yet thou shalt lead me! Lead me, I command, to Har & Heva!"

"O cruel! O destroyer! O consumer! O avenger!
To Har & Heva I will lead thee: then would that they would curse!
Then would they curse as thou hast cursed! but they are not like thee!
O! they are holy & forgiving, fill'd with loving mercy,
Forgetting the offences of their most rebellious children,
Or else thou wouldest not have liv'd to curse thy helpless children."

"Look on my eyes, Hela, & see, for thou hast eyes to see,
The tears swell from my stony fountains: wherefore do I weep?
Wherefore from my blind orbs art thou not seiz'd with pois'nous stings?
Laugh, serpent, youngest venomous reptile of the flesh of Tiriel!
Laugh! for thy father Tiriel shall give thee cause to laugh,
Unless thou lead me to the tent of Har, child of the curse!"

"Silence thy evil tongue, thou murderer of thy helpless children!
I lead thee to the tent of Har; not that I mind thy curse,
But that I feel they will curse thee & hang upon thy bones
Fell shaking agonies, & in each wrinkle of that face
Plant worms of death to feast upon the tongue of terrible curses."

"Hela, my daughter, listen! thou art the daughter of Tiriel.
Thy father calls. Thy father lifts his hand unto the heavens,
For thou hast laughed at my tears & curst thy aged father.
Let snakes rise from thy bedded locks & laugh among thy curls!"

He ceast: her dark hair upright stood, while snakes infolded round
Her madding brows: her shrieks appall'd the soul of Tiriel.

"What have I done, Hela, my daughter? fear'st thou now the curse,
Or wherefore dost thou cry? Ah, wretch, to curse thy aged father!
Lead me to Har & Heva, & the curse of Tiriel
Shall fail. If thou refuse, howl in the desolate mountains!"

7

She, howling, led him over mountains & thro' frighted vales,
Till to the caves of Zazel they approach'd at even tide.
Forth from their caves old Zazel & his sons ran; when they saw
Their tyrant prince blind, & his daughter howling & leading him,
They laugh'd & mocked; some threw dirt & stones as they pass'd by;

But when Tiriel turn'd around & rais'd his awful voice,
Some fled away; but Zazel stood still, & thus begun:

'Bald tyrant, wrinkled, cunning, listen to Zazel's chains!
'Twas thou that chain'd thy brother Zazel! where are now thine eyes?
Shout, beautiful daughter of Tiriel! thou singest a sweet song!
Where are you going? come & eat some roots & drink some water
Thy crown is bald, old man; the sun will dry thy brains away,
And thou wilt be as foolish as thy foolish brother Zazel."

The blind man heard, & smote his breast, & trembling passed on.
They threw dirt after them, till to the covert of a wood
The howling maiden led her father, where wild beasts resort,
Hoping to end her woes; but from her cries the tygers fled.
All night they wander'd thro' the wood, & when the sun arose,
They enter'd on the mountains of Har: at Noon the happy tents
Were frighted by the dismal cries of Hela on the mountains.

But Har & Heva slept fearless as babes on loving breasts.
Mnetha awoke: she ran & stood at the tent door, & saw
The aged wanderer led towards the tents; she took her bow,
And chose her arrows, then advanc'd to meet the terrible pair.

8

And Mnetha hasted & met them at the gate of the lower garden.

"Stand still. or from my bow receive a sharp & winged death!"

Then Tiriel stood, saying: "What soft voice threatens such bitter things?
Lead me to Har & Heva; I am Tiriel, king of the west."

And Mnetha led them to the tent of Har, and Har & Heva
Ran to the door; when Tiriel felt the ankles of aged Har,
He said: "O weak mistaken father of a lawless race,
Thy laws, O Har, & Tiriel's wisdom, end together in a curse.
Why is one law given to the lion & the patient Ox? [1]
And why men bound beneath the heavens in a reptile form,
A worm of sixty winters creeping on the dusky ground?
The child springs from the womb; the father ready stands to form
The infant head, while the mother idle plays with her dog on her couch:
The young bosom is cold for lack of mother's nourishment, & milk
Is cut off from the weeping mouth: with difficulty & pain
The little lids are lifted & the little nostrils open'd:
The father forms a whip to rouze the sluggish senses to act
And scourges off all youthful fancies from the new-born man.
Then walks the weak infant in sorrow, compell'd to number footsteps
Upon the sand. And when the drone has reach'd his crawling length,

Black berries appear that poison all round him, Such was Tiriel,[2]
Compell'd to pray repugnant & to humble the immortal spirit
Till I am subtil as a serpent in a paradise,
Consuming all, both flowers & fruits, insects & warbling birds.
And now my paradise is fall'n & a drear sandy plain
Returns my thirsty hissings in a curse on thee, O Har.
Mistaken father of a lawless race, my voice is past."

He ceast, outstretch'd at Har & Heva's feet in awful death.

[1] *Followed by twelve lines deleted:*
Dost thou not see that men cannot be formed all alike,
Some nostril'd wide, breathing out blood; some close shut up
In silent deceit, poisons inhaling from the morning rose,
With daggers hid beneath their lips & poison in their tongue;
Or eyed with little sparks of Hell & with infernal brands
Flinging flames of discontent & plagues of dark despair;
Or those whose mouths are graves, whose teeth the gates of eternal death.
Can wisdom be put in a silver rod, or love in a golden bowl?
Is the son of a king warmed without wool? or does he cry with a voice
Of thunder? does he look upon the sun & laugh or stretch
His little hands unto the depths of the sea, to bring forth
The deadly cunning of the scaly tribe & spread it to the morning?

[2] *Followed by one line deleted:*
Hypocrisy, the idiot's wisdom & the wise man's folly.

THE BOOK OF THEL

Etched 1789

THEL'S MOTTO

Does the Eagle know what is in the pit?
Or wilt thou go ask the Mole?
Can Wisdom be put in a silver rod?
Or Love in a golden bowl?

I

THE daughters of the Seraphim led round their sunny flocks,
All but the youngest: she in paleness sought the secret air,
To fade away like morning beauty from her mortal day:
Down by the river of Adona her soft voice is heard,
And thus her gentle lamentation falls like morning dew:

"O life of this our spring! why fades the lotus of the water,
Why fade these children of the spring, born but to smile & fall?
Ah! Thel is like a wat'ry bow, and like a parting cloud;
Like a reflection in a glass; like shadows in the water;
Like dreams of infants, like a smile upon an infant's face;
Like the dove's voice; like transient day; like music in the air.
Ah! gentle may I lay me down, and gentle rest my head,
And gentle sleep the sleep of death, and gentle hear the voice
Of him that walketh in the garden in the evening time."

The Lilly of the valley, breathing in the humble grass,
Answer'd the lovely maid and said: "I am a wat'ry weed,
And I am very small and love to dwell in lowly vales;
So weak, the gilded butterfly scarce perches on my head.
Yet I am visited from heaven, and he that smiles on all
Walks in the valley and each morn over me spreads his hand,
Saying, 'Rejoice, thou humble grass, thou new-born lilly flower,
Thou gentle maid of silent valleys and of modest brooks;
For thou shalt be clothed in light, and fed with morning manna,
Till summer's heat melts thee beside the fountains and the springs
To flourish in eternal vales,' Then why should Thel complain?
Why should the mistress of the vales of Har utter a sigh?"

She ceas'd & smil'd in tears, then sat down in her silver shrine.

Thel answer'd: "O thou little virgin of the peaceful valley,
Giving to those that cannot crave, the voiceless, the o'ertired;
Thy breath doth nourish the innocent lamb, he smells thy milky garments,
He crops thy flowers while thou sittest smiling in his face,
Wiping his mild and meekin mouth from all contagious taints.
Thy wine doth purify the golden honey; thy perfume,
Which thou dost scatter on every little blade of grass that springs,
Revives the milked cow, & tames the fire-breathing steed.
But Thel is like a faint cloud kindled at the rising sun:
I vanish from my pearly throne, and who shall find my place?"

"Queen of the vales," the Lilly answer'd, "ask the tender cloud,
And it shall tell thee why it glitters in the morning sky,
And why it scatters its bright beauty thro' the humid air.
Descend, O little Cloud, & hover before the eyes of Thel."

The Cloud descended, and the Lilly bow'd her modest head
And went to mind her numerous charge among the verdant grass.

II

"O little Cloud," the virgin said, "I charge thee tell to me
Why thou complainest not when in one hour thou fade away:
Then we shall seek thee, but not find. Ah! Thel is like to thee:
I pass away: yet I complain, and no one hears my voice."

The Cloud then shew'd his golden head & his bright form emerg'd,
Hovering and glittering on the air before the face of Thel.

"O virgin, know'st thou not our steeds drink of the golden springs
Where Luvah doth renew his horses? Look'st thou on my youth,
And fearest thou, because I vanish and am seen no more,
Nothing remains? O maid, I tell thee, when I pass away
It is to tenfold life, to love, to peace and raptures holy:
Unseen descending, weigh my light wings upon balmy flowers,
And court the fair-eyed dew to take me to her shining tent:
The weeping virgin, trembling kneels before the risen sun,
Till we arise link'd in a golden band and never part,
But walk united, bearing food to all our tender flowers."

"Dost thou, O little Cloud? I fear that I am not like thee,
For I walk thro' the vales of Har, and smell the sweetest flowers,
But I feed not the little flowers; I hear the warbling birds,
But I feed not the warbling birds; they fly and seek their food:
But Thel delights in these no more, because I fade away;
And all shall say, 'Without a use this shining woman liv'd,
Or did she only live to be at death the food of worms?'"

The Cloud reclin'd upon his airy throne and answer'd thus:

"Then if thou art the food of worms, O virgin of the skies,
How great thy use, how great thy blessing! Every thing that lives
Lives not alone nor for itself. Fear not, and I will call
The weak worm from its lowly bed, and thou shalt hear its voice.
Come forth, worm of the silent valley, to thy pensive queen."

The helpless worm arose, and sat upon the Lilly's leaf,
And the bright Cloud sail'd on, to find his partner in the vale.

III

Then Thel astonish'd view'd the Worm upon its dewy bed.

"Art thou a Worm? Image of weakness, art thou but a Worm?
I see thee like an infant wrapped in the Lilly's leaf.
Ah! weep not, little voice, thou canst not speak, but thou canst weep.
Is this a Worm? I see thee lay helpless & naked, weeping,
And none to answer, none to cherish thee with mother's smiles."

The Clod of Clay heard the Worm's voice & rais'd her pitying head:
She bow'd over the weeping infant, and her life exhal'd
In milky fondness: then on Thel she fix'd her humble eyes.

"O beauty of the vales of Har! we live not for ourselves.
Thou seest me the meanest thing, and so I am indeed.
My bosom of itself is cold, and of itself is dark;
But he, that loves the lowly, pours his oil upon my head,
And kisses me, and binds his nuptial bands around my breast,
And says: 'Thou mother of my children, I have loved thee
And I have given thee a crown that none can take away.'
But how this is, sweet maid, I know not, and I cannot know;
I ponder, and I cannot ponder; yet I live and love."

The daughter of beauty wip'd her pitying tears with her white veil,
And said: "Alas! I knew not this, and therefore did I weep.
That God would love a Worm I knew, and punish the evil foot
That wilful bruis'd its helpless form; but that he cherish'd it
With milk and oil I never knew, and therefore did I weep;
And I complain'd in the mild air, because I fade away,
And lay me down in thy cold bed, and leave my shining lot."

"Queen of the vales," the matron Clay answer'd, "I heard thy sighs,
And all thy moans flew o'er my roof, but I have call'd them down.
Wilt thou, O Queen, enter my house? 'Tis given thee to enter
And to return: fear nothing, enter with thy virgin feet."

IV

The eternal gates' terrific porter lifted the northern bar:
Thel enter'd in & saw the secrets of the land unknown.
She saw the couches of the dead, & where the fibrous roots
Of every heart on earth infixes deep its restless twists:
A land of sorrowes & of tears where never smile was seen.

She wander'd in the land of clouds thro' valleys dark, list'ning
Dolours & lamentations; waiting oft beside a dewy grave
She stood in silence, list'ning to the voices of the ground,
Till to her own grave plot she came, & there she sat down,
And heard this voice of sorrow breathed from the hollow pit.

"Why cannot the Ear be closed to its own destruction?
Or the glist'ning Eye to the poison of a smile?
Why are Eyelids stor'd with arrows ready drawn,
Where a thousand fighting men in ambush lie?
Or an Eye of gifts & graces show'ring fruits & coined gold?
Why a Tongue impress'd with honey from every wind?
Why an Ear, a whirlpool fierce to draw creations in?
Why a Nostril wide inhaling terror, trembling, & affright?
Why a tender curb upon the youthful burning boy?
Why a little curtain of flesh on the bed of our desire?"

The Virgin started from her seat, & with a shriek
Fled back unhinder'd till she came into the vales of Har.

THE FRENCH REVOLUTION

A Poem in Seven Books

BOOK THE FIRST

Printed 1791

T H E dead brood over Europe, the cloud and vision descends over chearful
France;

O cloud well appointed! Sick, sick, the Prince on his couch, wreath'd
in dim

And appalling mist, his strong hand outstretch'd, from his shoulder down
the bone

Runs aching cold into the scepter, too heavy for mortal grasp, no more

To be swayed by visible hand, nor in cruelty bruise the mild flourishing
mountains.

Sick the mountains, and all their vineyards weep, in the eyes of the kingly
mourner;

Pale is the morning cloud in his visage. Rise, Necker! the ancient dawn
calls us

To awake from slumbers of five thousand years. I awake, but my soul
is in dreams;

From my window I see the old mountains of France, like aged men, fading away.

Troubled, leaning on Necker, descends the King to his chamber of council;
shady mountains

In fear utter voices of thunder; the woods of France embosom the sound;

Clouds of wisdom prophetic reply, and roll over the palace roof heavy.

Forty men, each conversing with woes in the infinite shadows of his soul,

Like our ancient fathers in regions of twilight, walk, gathering round
the King;

Again the loud voice of France cries to the morning; the morning
prophecies to its clouds.

For the Commons convene in the Hall of the Nation. France shakes!
And the heavens of France

Perplex'd vibrate round each careful countenance! Darkness of old times
around them

Utters loud despair, shadowing Paris; her grey towers groan, and the Bastile trembles.

In its terrible towers the Governor stood, in dark fogs list'ning the horror;

A thousand his soldiers, old veterans of France, breathing red clouds of power and dominion.

Sudden seiz'd with howlings, despair, and black night, he stalk'd like a lion from tower

To tower; his howlings were heard in the Louvre; from court to court restless he dragg'd

His strong limbs; from court to court curs'd the fierce torment unquell'd,

Howling and giving the dark command; in his soul stood the purple plague,

Tugging his iron manacles, and piercing through the seven towers dark and sickly,

Panting over the prisoners like a wolf gorg'd; and the den nam'd Horror held a man

Chain'd hand and foot, round his neck an iron band, bound to the impregnable wall.

In his soul was the serpent coil'd round in his heart, hid from the light, as in a cleft rock:

And the man was confin'd for a writing prophetic: in the tower nam'd Darkness was a man

Pinion'd down to the stone floor, his strong bones scarce cover'd with sinews; the iron rings

Where forg'd smaller as the flesh decay'd, a mask of iron on his face hid the lineaments

Of ancient Kings, and the frown of the eternal lion was hid from the oppressed earth.

In the tower named Bloody, a skeleton yellow remained in its chains on its couch

Of stone, once a man who refus'd to sign papers of abhorrence; the eternal worm

Crept in the skeleton. In the den nam'd Religion, a loathsome sick woman bound down

To a bed of straw; the seven diseases of earth, like birds of prey, stood on the couch

And fed on the body. She refus'd to be whore to the Minister, and with a knife smote him.

In the tower nam'd Order, an old man, whose white beard cover'd the stone floor like weeds

On margin of the sea, shrivel'd up by heat of day and cold of night; his den was short

And narrow as a grave dug for a child, with spider's webs wove, and
with slime

Of ancient horrors cover'd, for snakes and scorpions are his companions;
harmless they breathe

His sorrowful breath: he, by conscience urg'd, in the city of Paris rais'd
a pulpit,

And taught wonders to darken'd souls. In the den nam'd Destiny a strong
man sat,

His feet and hands cut off, and his eyes blinded; round his middle a
chain and a band

Fasten'd into the wall; fancy gave him to see an image of despair in
his den,

Eternally rushing round, like a man on his hands and knees, day and
night without rest:

He was friend to the favourite. In the seventh tower, nam'd the tower
of God, was a man

Mad, with chains loose, which he dragg'd up and down; fed with hopes
year by year, he pined

For liberty; vain hopes! his reason decay'd, and the world of attraction
in his bosom

Center'd, and the rushing of chaos overwhelm'd his dark soul. He was
confin'd

For a letter of advice to a King, and his ravings in winds are heard over
Versailles.

But the dens shook and trembled: the prisoners look up and assay to
shout; they listen,

Then laugh in the dismal den, then are silent, and a light walks round
the dark towers:

For the Commons convene in the Hall of the Nation, like spirits of fire
in the beautiful

Porches of the Sun, to plant beauty in the desart craving abyss, they gleam

On the anxious city; all children new-born first behold them; tears are
fled,

And they nestle in earth-breathing bosoms. So the city of Paris, their
wives and children,

Look up to the morning Senate, and visions of sorrow leave pensive streets.

But heavy brow'd jealousies lower o'er the Louvre, and terrors of ancient
Kings

Descend from the gloom and wander thro' the palace, and weep round
the King and his Nobles.

While loud thunders roll, troubling the dead, Kings are sick throughout
  all the earth.
The voice ceas'd: the Nation sat: And the triple forg'd fetters of times
  were unloos'd.
The voice ceas'd: the Nation sat: but ancient darkness and trembling
  wander thro' the palace.

As in day of havock and routed battle, among thick shades of discontent,
On the soul-skirting mountains of sorrow, cold waving the Nobles fold
  round the King;
Each stern visage lock'd up as with strong bands of iron, each strong
  limb bound down as with marble,
In flames of red wrath burning, bound in astonishment a quarter of an
  hour.

Then the King glow'd: his Nobles fold round, like the sun of old time
  quench'd in clouds;
In their darkness the King stood; his heart flam'd, and utter'd a with'ring
  heat, and these words burst forth:

"The nerves of five thousand years' ancestry tremble, shaking the heavens
  of France;
Throbs of anguish beat on brazen war foreheads, they descend and look
  into their graves.
I see thro' darkness, thro' clouds rolling round me, the spirits of ancient
  Kings
Shivering over their bleached bones; round them their counsellors look
  up from the dust,
Crying: 'Hide from the living! Our bonds and our prisoners shout in
  the open field,
Hide in the nether earth! Hide in the bones! Sit obscured in the hollow
  scull!
Our flesh is corrupted, and we wear away. We are not numbered among
  the living. Let us hide
In stones, among roots of trees. The prisoners have burst their dens.
Let us hide; let us hide in the dust; and plague and wrath and tempest
  shall cease.'"

He ceas'd, silent pond'ring; his brows folded heavy, his forehead was in
  affliction.
Like the central fire, from the window he saw his vast armies spread over
  the hills,

Breathing red fires from man to man, and from horse to horse: then his bosom
Expanded like starry heaven; he sat down: his Nobles took their ancient seats.

Then the ancientest Peer, Duke of Burgundy, rose from the Monarch's right hand, red as wines
From his mountains; an odor of war, like a ripe vineyard, rose from his garments,
And the chamber became as a clouded sky; o'er the council he stretch'd his red limbs,
Cloth'd in flames of crimson; as a ripe vineyard stretches over sheaves of corn,
The fierce Duke hung over the council; around him croud, weeping in his burning robe,
A bright cloud of infant souls; his words fall like purple autumn on the sheaves:

"Shall this marble built heaven become a clay cottage, this earth an oak stool, and these mowers
From the Atlantic mountains mow down all this great starry harvest of six thousand years?
And shall Necker, the hind of Geneva, stretch out his crook'd sickle o'er fertile France
Till our purple and crimson is faded to russet, and the kingdoms of earth bound in sheaves,
And the ancient forests of chivalry hewn, and the joys of the combat burnt for fuel;
Till the power and dominion is rent from the pole, sword and scepter from sun and moon,
The law and gospel from fire and air, and eternal reason and science
From the deep and the solid, and man lay his faded head down on the rock
Of eternity, where the eternal lion and eagle remain to devour?
This to prevent—urg'd by cries in day, and prophetic dreams hovering in night,
To enrich the lean earth that craves, furrow'd with plows, whose seed is departing from her—
Thy Nobles have gather'd thy starry hosts round this rebellious city,
To rouze up the ancient forests of Europe, with clarions of cloud breathing war,

To hear the horse neigh to the drum and trumpet, and the trumpet and war shout reply.

Stretch the hand that beckons the eagles of heaven; they cry over Paris, and wait

Till Fayette point his finger to Versailles; the eagles of heaven must have their prey!"

He ceas'd the burn'd silent; red clouds roll round Necker; a weeping is heard o'er the palace.

Like a dark cloud Necker paus'd, and like thunder on the just man's buriel day he paus'd;

Silent sit the winds, silent the meadows, while the husbandman and woman of weakness

And bright children look after him into the grave, and water his clay with love,

Then turn towards pensive fields; so Necker paus'd, and his visage was cover'd with clouds.

The King lean'd on his mountains, then lifted his head and look'd on his armies, that shone

Through heaven, tinging morning with beams of blood; then turning to Burgundy, troubled:

"Burgundy, thou wast born a lion! My soul is o'ergrown with distress

For the Nobles of France, and dark mists roll round me and blot the writing of God

Written in my bosom. Necker rise! leave the kingdom, thy life is surrounded with snares.

We have call'd an Assembly, but not to destroy; we have given gifts, not to the weak;

I hear rushing of muskets, and bright'ning of swords, and visages redd'ning with war,

Frowning and looking up from brooding villages and every dark'ning city.

Ancient wonders frown over the kingdom, and cries of women and babes are heard,

And tempests of doubt roll around me, and fierce sorrows, because of the Nobles of France.

Depart! answer not! for the tempest must fall, as in years that are passed away."

Dropping a tear the old man his place left, and when he was gone out

He set his face toward Geneva to flee; and the women and children of the city

Knell'd round him and kissed his garments and wept: he stood a short
  space in the street,
Then fled; and the whole city knew he was fled to Geneva, and the
  Senate heard it.

But the Nobles burn'd wrathful at Necker's departure, and wreath'd
  their clouds and waters
In dismal volumes, as, risen from beneath, the Archbishop of Paris arose
In the rushing of scales and hissing of flames and rolling of sulphurous
  smoke:

"Harken Monarch of France, to the terrors of heaven, and let thy soul
  drink of my counsel!
Sleeping at midnight in my golden tower, the repose of the labours of
  men
Wav'd its solemn cloud over my head. I awoke; a cold hand passed over
  my limbs, and behold
An aged form, white as snow, hov'ring in mist, weeping in the uncertain light.
Dim the form almost faded, tears fell down the shady cheeks; at his
  feet, many cloth'd
In white robes; strewn in air, censers and harps; silent they lay pros-
  trated;
Beneath, in the awful void, myriads descending and weeping thro' dis-
  mal winds;
Endless the shady train shiv'ring descended from the gloom where the
  aged form wept.
At length, trembling, the vision, sighing in a low voice like the voice of the
  grasshopper, whisper'd:
'My groaning is heard in the abbeys, and God, so long worshipp'd,
  departs as a lamp
Without oil; for a curse is heard hoarse thro' the land from a godless race
Descending to beasts; they look downward and labour and forget my
  holy law;
The sound of prayer fails from lips of flesh, and the holy hymn from
  thicken'd tongues;
For the bars of Chaos are burst; her millions prepare their fiery way
Thro' the orbed abode of the holy dead, to root up and pull down and
  remove,
And Nobles and Clergy shall fail from before me, and my cloud and
  vision be no more;
The mitre become black, the crown vanish, and the scepter and ivory staff

Of the ruler wither among bones of death; they shall consume from the
thistly field,

And the sound of the bell, and voice of the sabbath, and singing of the
holy choir

Is turn'd into songs of the harlot in day, and cries of the virgin in night.

They shall drop at the plow and faint at the harrow, unredeem'd, uncon-
fess'd, unpardon'd;

The priest rot in his surplice by the lawless lover, the holy beside the
accursed,

The King, frowning in purple, beside the grey plowman, and their worms
embrace together.'

The voice ceas'd: a groan shook my chamber; I slept, for the cloud of
repose returned,

But morning dawn'd heavy upon me. I rose to bring my Prince heaven
utter'd counsel.

Hear my counsel, O King, and send forth thy Generals; the command
of Heaven is upon thee!

Then do thou command, O King, to shut up this Assembly in their final
home;

Let thy soldiers possess this city of rebels, that threaten to bathe their
feet

In the blood of Nobility, trampling the heart and the head; let the
Bastile devour

These rebellious seditious; seal them up, O Anointed, in everlasting
chains."

He sat down: a damp cold pervaded the Nobles, and monsters of worlds
unknown

Swam round them, watching to be delivered; When Aumont, whose chaos-
born soul

Eternally wand'ring a Comet and swift-falling fire, pale enter'd the
chamber.

Before the red Council he stood, like a man that returns from hollow
graves:

"Awe-surrounded, alone thro' the army, a fear and a with'ring blight
blown by the north,

The Abbé de Sieyes from the Nation's Assembly, O Princes and Generals
of France,

Unquestioned, unhindered! awe-struck are the soldiers; a dark shadowy
man in the form

Of King Henry the Fourth walks before him in fires; the captains like
men bound in chains

Stood still as he pass'd: he is come to the Louvre, O King, with a message to thee!

The strong soldiers tremble, the horses their manes bow, and the guards of thy palace are fled!"

Up rose awful in his majestic beams Bourbon's strong Duke; his proud sword from his thigh

Drawn, he threw on the Earth! the Duke of Bretagne and the Earl of Bourgogne

Rose inflam'd, to and fro in the chamber, like thunderclouds ready to burst.

"What! damp all our fires, O spectre of Henry?" said Bourbon, "and rend the flames

From the head of our King? Rise, Monarch of France! command me, and I will lead

This army of superstition at large, that the ardor of noble souls, quenchless,

May yet burn in France, nor our shoulders be plow'd with the furrows of poverty."

Then Orleans, generous as mountains, arose and unfolded his robe, and put forth

His benevolent hand, looking on the Archbishop who, changed as pale as lead,

Would have risen but could not: his voice issued harsh grating; instead of words harsh hissings

Shook the chamber; he ceas'd abash'd. Then Orleans spoke; all was silent.

He breath'd on them, and said: "O princes of fire, whose flames are for growth, not consuming,

Fear not dreams, fear not visions, nor be you dismay'd with sorrows which flee at the morning!

Can the fires of Nobility ever be quench'd, or the stars by a stormy night?

Is the body diseas'd when the members are healthful? can the man be bound in sorrow

Whose ev'ry function is fill'd with its fiery desire? can the soul whose brain and heart

Cast their rivers in equal tides thro' the great Paradise, languish because the feet,

Hands, head, bosom, and parts of love follow their high breathing joy?

And can Nobles be bound when the people are free, or God weep when his children are happy?

Have you never seen Fayette's forehead, or Mirabeau's eyes, or the
  shoulders of Target,
Or Bailly the strong foot of France, or Clermont the terrible voice? and
  your robes
Still retain their own crimson: mine never yet faded, for fire delights in
  its form.
But go! merciless man! enter into the infinite labyrinth of another's brain
Ere thou measure the circle that he shall run. Go, thou cold recluse, into
  the fires
Of another's high flaming rich bosom, and return unconsum'd, and write
  laws.
If thou canst not do this, doubt thy theories; learn to consider all men
  as thy equals,
Thy brethren, and not as thy foot or thy hand, unless thou first fearest
  to hurt them."

The Monarch stood up; the strong Duke his sword to its golden scabbard
  return'd;
The Nobles sat round like clouds on the mountains, when the storm is
  passing away:
"Let the Nation's Ambassador come among Nobles, like incense of the
  valley!"

Aumont went out and stood in the hollow porch, his ivory wand in his
  hand;
A cold orb of disdain revolv'd round him, and covered his soul with
  snows eternal.
Great Henry's soul shuddered, a whirlwind and fire tore furious from his
  angry bosom;
He indignant departed on horses of heav'n. Then the Abbé de Sieyes
  rais'd his feet
On the steps of the Louvre; like a voice of God following a storm, the
  Abbé follow'd
The pale fires of Aumont into the chamber; as a father that bows to his
  son,
Whose rich fields inheriting spread their old glory, so the voice of the
  people bowed
Before the ancient seat of the kingdom and mountains to be renewed.

"Hear, O Heavens of France, the voice of the people arising from valley
  and hill,

O'erclouded with power. Hear the voice of vallies, the voice of meek cities,

Mourning oppressed on village and field, till the village and field is a waste.

For the husbandman weeps at blights of the fife, and blasting of trumpets consume

The souls of mild France; the pale mother nourishes her child to the deadly slaughter.

When the heavens were seal'd with a stone, and the terrible sun clos'd in an orb, and the moon

Rent from the nations, and each star appointed for watchers of night,

The millions of spirits immortal were bound in the ruins of sulphur, heaven

To wander enslav'd; black, deprest in dark ignorance, kept in awe with the whip

To worship terrors, bred from the blood of revenge and breath of desire

In beastial forms, or more terrible men; till the dawn of our peaceful morning,

Till dawn, till morning, till the breaking of clouds, and swelling of winds, and the universal voice;

Till man raise his darken'd limbs out of the caves of night: his eyes and his heart

Expand: where is Space? where, O Sun, is thy dwelling? where thy tent, O faint slumb'rous Moon?

Then the valleys of France shall cry to the soldier: 'Throw down thy sword and musket,

And run and embrace the meek peasant.' Her Nobles shall hear and shall weep, and put off

The red robe of terror, the crown of oppression, the shoes of contempt, and unbuckle

The girdle of war from the desolate earth; then the Priest in his thund'rous cloud

Shall weep, bending to earth, embracing the valleys, and putting his hand to the plow,

Shall say: 'No more I curse thee; but now I will bless thee: No more in deadly black

Devour thy labour; nor lift up a cloud in thy heavens, O laborious plow,

That the wild raging millions, that wander in forests, and howl in law blasted wastes,

Strength madden'd with slavery, honesty bound in the dens of superstition,

May sing in the village, and shout in the harvest, and woo in pleasant gardens

Their once savage loves, now beaming with knowledge, with gentle awe adorned;

And the saw, and the hammer, the chisel, the pencil, the pen, and the instruments

Of heavenly song sound in the wilds once forbidden, to teach the laborious plowman

And shepherd, deliver'd from clouds of war, from pestilence, from night-fear, from murder,

From falling, from stifling, from hunger, from cold, from slander, discontent and sloth,

That walk in beasts and birds of night, driven back by the sandy desart,

Like pestilent fogs round cities of men; and the happy earth sing in its course,

The mild peaceable nations be opened to heav'n, and men walk with their fathers in bliss.'

Then hear the first voice of the morning: 'Depart, O clouds of night, and no more

Return; be withdrawn cloudy war, troops of warriors depart, nor around our peaceable city

Breathe fires; but ten miles from Paris let all be peace, nor a soldier be seen!' "

He ended: the wind of contention arose, and the clouds cast their shadows; the Princes,

Like the mountains of France, whose aged trees utter an awful voice, and their branches

Are shatter'd, till gradual a murmur is heard descending into the valley,

Like a voice in the vineyards of Burgundy when grapes are shaken on grass,

Like the low voice of the labouring man, instead of the shout of joy;

And the palace appear'd like a cloud driven abroad; blood ran down the ancient pillars.

Thro' the cloud a deep thunder, the Duke of Burgundy, delivers the King's command:

"Seest thou yonder dark castle, that moated around, keeps this city of Paris in awe?

Go command yonder tower, saying: 'Bastile, depart! and take thy shadowy course;

Overstep the dark river, thou terrible tower, and get thee up into the country ten miles.

And thou black southern prison, move along the dusky road to Versailles; there

Frown on the gardens; and if it obey and depart, then the King will disband

This war-breathing army; but if it refuse, let the Nation's Assembly thence learn

That this army of terrors, that prison of horrors, are the bands of the murmuring kingdom."

Like the morning star arising above the black waves, when a shipwreck'd soul sighs for morning,

Thro' the ranks, silent, walk'd the Ambassador back to the Nation's Assembly, and told

The unwelcome message; silent they heard; then a thunder roll'd round loud and louder;

Like pillars of ancient halls and ruins of times remote, they sat.

Like a voice from the dim pillars Mirabeau rose; the thunders subsided away;

A rushing of wings around him was heard as he brighten'd, and cried out aloud:

"Where is the General of the Nation?" The walls re-echo'd: "Where is the General of the Nation?"

Sudden as the bullet wrapp'd in his fire, when brazen cannons rage in the field,

Fayette sprung from his seat saying, "Ready!" Then bowing like clouds, man toward man, the Assembly

Like a council of ardors seated in clouds, bending over the cities of men,

And over the armies of strife, where their children are marshall'd together to battle,

They murmuring divide; while the wind sleeps beneath, and the numbers are counted in silence,

While they vote the removal of War, and the pestilence weighs his red wings in the sky.

So Fayette stood silent among the Assembly, and the votes were given, and the numbers numb'red;

And the vote was that Fayette should order the army to remove ten miles from Paris.

The aged sun rise appall'd from dark mountains, and gleams a dusky
  beam
On Fayette; but on the whole army a shadow, for a cloud on the eastern
  hills
Hover'd, and stretch'd across the city, and across the army, and across
  the Louvre.
Like a flame of fire he stood before dark ranks, and before expecting
  captains:
On pestilent vapours around him flow frequent spectres of religious men,
  weeping
In winds; driven out of the abbeys, their naked souls shiver in keen open
  air;
Driven out by the fiery cloud of Voltaire, and thund'rous rocks of
  Rousseau,
They dash like foam against the ridges of the army, uttering a faint
  feeble cry.

Gleams of fire streak the heavens, and of sulphur the earth, from Fayette
  as he lifted his hand;
But silent he stood, till all the officers rush round him like waves
Round the shore of France, in day of the British flag, when heavy cannons
Affright the coasts, and the peasant looks over the sea and wipes a tear;
Over his head the soul of Voltaire shone fiery; and over the army Rous-
  seau his white cloud
Unfolded, on souls of war, living terrors, silent list'ning toward Fayette.
His voice loud inspir'd by liberty, and by spirits of the dead, thus
  thunder'd:

"The Nation's Assembly command that the Army remove ten miles from
  Paris;
Nor a soldier be seen in road or in field, till the Nation command return."

Rushing along iron ranks glittering, the officers each to his station
Depart, and the stern captain strokes his proud steed, and in front of
  his solid ranks
Waits the sound of trumpet; captains of foot stand each by his cloudy
  drum:
Then the drum beats, and the steely ranks move, and trumpets rejoice
  in the sky.
Dark cavalry, like clouds fraught with thunder, ascend on the hills, and
  bright infantry, rank
Behind rank, to the soul shaking drum and shrill fife, along the roads
  glitter like fire.

The noise of trampling, the wind of trumpets, smote the palace walls with a blast,

Pale and cold sat the King in midst of his peers, and his noble heart sunk, and his pulses

Suspended their motion; a darkness crept over his eyelids, and chill cold sweat

Sat round his brows faded in faint death; his peers pale, like mountains of the dead

Cover'd with dews of night, groaning, shaking forests and floods. The cold newt,

And snake, and damp toad on the kingly foot crawl, or croak on the awful knee,

Shedding their slime; in folds of the robe the crown'd adder builds and hisses

From stony brows; shaken the forests of France, sick the kings of the nations,

And the bottoms of the world were open'd, and the graves of arch-angels unseal'd:

The enormous dead lift up their pale fires and look over the rocky cliffs.

A faint heat from their fires reviv'd the cold Louvre; the frozen blood reflow'd.

Awful up rose the king; him the peers follow'd; they saw the courts of the Palace

Forsaken, and Paris without a soldier, silent; for the noise was gone up

And follow'd the army, and the Senate in peace sat beneath morning's beam.

END OF THE FIRST BOOK

THE MARRIAGE OF HEAVEN AND HELL

Etched about 1793

THE ARGUMENT

RINTRAH roars & shakes his fires in the burden'd air;
Hungry clouds swag on the deep.

Once meek, and in a perilous path,
The just man kept his course along

The vale of death.
Roses are planted where thorns grow,
And on the barren heath
Sing the honey bees.

Then the perilous path was planted,
And a river and a spring
On every cliff and tomb,
And on the bleached bones
Red clay brought forth;

Till the villain left the paths of ease,
To walk in perilous paths, and drive
The just man into barren climes.

Now the sneaking serpent walks
In mild humility,
And the just man rages in the wilds
Where lions roam.
Rintrah roars & shakes his fires in the burden'd **air**;
Hungry clouds swag on the deep.

❊

As a new heaven is begun, and it is now thirty-three years since its advent, the Eternal Hell revives. And lo! Swedenborg is the Angel sitting at the tomb: his writings are the linen clothes folded up. Now is the dominion of Edom, & the return of Adam into Paradise. See Isaiah xxxiv & xxxv Chap.

Without Contraries is no progression. Attraction and Repulsion, Reason and Energy, Love and Hate, are necessary to Human existence.

From these contraries spring what the religious call Good & Evil. Good is the passive that obeys Reason. Evil is the active springing from Energy.

Good is Heaven. Evil is Hell.

THE VOICE OF THE DEVIL

ALL Bibles or sacred codes have been the causes of the following Errors:

1. That Man has two real existing principles: Viz: a Body & a Soul.
2. That Energy, call'd Evil, is alone from the body; & that Reason, call'd Good, is alone from the Soul.

3. That God will torment Man in Eternity for following his Energies.

But the following Contraries to these are True:

1. Man has no Body distinct from his Soul; for that call'd Body is a portion of Soul discern'd by the five Senses, the chief inlets of Soul in this age.

2. Energy is the only life, and is from the Body; and Reason is the bound or outward circumference of Energy.

3. Energy is Eternal Delight.

*

THOSE who restrain desire, do so because theirs is weak enough to be restrained; and the restrainer or reason usurps its place & governs the unwilling.

And being restrain'd, it by degrees becomes passive, till it is only the shadow of desire.

The history of this is written in Paradise Lost, & the Governor or Reason is call'd Messiah.

And the original Archangel, or possessor of the command of the heavenly host, is call'd the Devil or Satan, and his children are call'd Sin & Death.

But in the Book of Job, Milton's Messiah is call'd Satan.

For this history has been adopted by both parties.

It indeed appear'd to Reason as if Desire was cast out; but the Devil's account is, that the Messiah fell, & formed a heaven of what he stole from the Abyss.

This is shewn in the Gospel, where he prays to the Father to send the comforter, or Desire, that Reason may have Ideas to build on; the Jehovah of the Bible being no other than he who dwells in flaming fire.

Know that after Christ's death, he became Jehovah.

But in Milton, the Father is Destiny, the Son a Ratio of the five senses, & the Holy-ghost Vacuum!

Note: The reason Milton wrote in fetters when he wrote of Angels & God, and at liberty when of Devils & Hell, is because he was a true Poet and of the Devil's party without knowing it.

A MEMORABLE FANCY

AS I was walking among the fires of hell, delighted with the enjoyments of Genius, which to Angels look like torment and insanity, I collected some of their Proverbs; thinking that as the sayings used in a nation mark its character, so the Proverbs of Hell show the nature of Infernal wisdom better than any description of buildings or garments.

When I came home: on the abyss of the five senses, where a flat sided steep frowns over the present world, I saw a mighty Devil folded in black clouds, hovering on the sides of the rock: with corroding fires he wrote the following sentence now percieved by the minds of men, & read by them on earth:

How do you know but ev'ry Bird that cuts the airy way,
Is an immense world of delight, clos'd by your senses five?

PROVERBS OF HELL

IN seed time learn, in harvest teach, in winter enjoy.
Drive your cart and your plow over the bones of the dead.
The road of excess leads to the palace of wisdom.
Prudence is a rich, ugly old maid courted by Incapacity.
He who desires but acts not, breeds pestilence.
The cut worm forgives the plow.
Dip him in the river who loves water.
A fool sees not the same tree that a wise man sees.
He whose face gives no light, shall never become a star.
Eternity is in love with the productions of time.
The busy bee has no time for sorrow.
The hours of folly are measur'd by the clock; but of wisdom, no clock can measure.
All wholesome food is caught without a net or a trap.
Bring out number, weight & measure in a year of dearth.
No bird soars too high, if he soars with his own wings.
A dead body revenges not injuries.
The most sublime act is to set another before you.
If the fool would persist in his folly he would become wise.
Folly is the cloke of knavery.
Shame is Pride's cloke.
Prisons are built with stones of Law, Brothels with bricks of Religion.
The pride of the peacock is the glory of God.
The lust of the goat is the bounty of God.
The wrath of the lion is the wisdom of God.
The nakedness of woman is the work of God.
Excess of sorrow laughs. Excess of joy weeps.

The roaring of lions, the howling of wolves, the raging of the stormy sea, and the destructive sword, are portions of eternity, too great for the eye of man.

The fox condemns the trap, not himself.

Joys impregnate. Sorrows bring forth.

Let man wear the fell of the lion, women the fleece of the sheep.

The bird a nest, the spider a web, man friendship.

The selfish, smiling fool, & the sullen, frowning fool shall be both thought wise, that they may be a rod.

What is now proved was once only imagin'd.

The rat, the mouse, the fox, the rabbet watch the roots; the lion, the tyger, the horse, the elephant watch the fruits.

The cistern contains: the fountain overflows.

One thought fills immensity.

Always be ready to speak your mind, and a base man will avoid you.

Every thing possible to be believ'd is an image of truth.

The eagle never lost so much time as when he submitted to learn of the crow.

The fox provides for himself, but God provides for the lion.

Think in the morning. Act in the noon. Eat in the evening. Sleep in the night.

He who has suffer'd you to impose on him, knows you.

As the plow follows words, so God rewards prayers.

The tygers of wrath are wiser than the horses of instruction.

Expect poison from the standing water.

You never know what is enough unless you know what is more than enough.

Listen to the fool's reproach! it is a kingly title!

The eyes of fire, the nostrils of air, the mouth of water, the beard of earth.

The weak in courage is strong in cunning.

The apple tree never asks the beech how he shall grow; nor the lion, the horse, how he shall take his prey.

The thankful reciever bears a plentiful harvest.

If others had not been foolish, we should be so.

The soul of sweet delight can never be defil'd.

When thou seest an Eagle, thou seest a portion of Genius; lift up thy head!

As the caterpiller chooses the fairest leaves to lay her eggs on, so the priest lays his curse on the fairest joys.

To create a little flower is the labour of ages.

Damn braces. Bless relaxes.

The best wine is the oldest, the best water the newest.

Prayers plow not! Praises reap not!

Joys laugh not! Sorrows weep not!

The head Sublime, the heart Pathos, the genitals Beauty, the hands & feet Proportion.

As the air to a bird or the sea to a fish, so is contempt to the contemptible.

The crow wish'd every thing was black, the owl that every thing was white.

Exuberance is Beauty.

If the lion was advised by the fox, he would be cunning.

Improvement makes strait roads; but the crooked roads without Improvement are roads of Genius.

Sooner murder an infant in its cradle than nurse unacted desires.

Where man is not, nature is barren.

Truth can never be told so as to be understood, and not be believ'd.

Enough! or Too much.

❀

THE ancient Poets animated all sensible objects with Gods or Geniuses, calling them by the names and adorning them with the properties of woods, rivers, mountains, lakes, cities, nations, and whatever their enlarged & numerous senses could percieve.

And particularly they studied the genius of each city & country, placing it under its mental deity;

Till a system was formed, which some took advantage of, & enslav'd the vulgar by attempting to realize or abstract the mental deities from their objects: thus began Priesthood;

Choosing forms of worship from poetic tales.

And at length they pronounc'd that the Gods had order'd such things.

Thus men forgot that All deities reside in the human breast.

A MEMORABLE FANCY

THE Prophets Isaiah and Ezekiel dined with me, and I asked them how they dared so roundly to assert that God spoke to them; and whether they did not think at the time that they would be misunderstood, & so be the cause of imposition.

Isaiah answer'd: "I saw no God, nor heard any, in a finite organical perception; but my senses discov'd the infinite in everything, and as I was then perswaded, & remain confirm'd, that the voice of honest indignation is the voice of God, I cared not for consequences, but wrote."

Then I asked: "does a firm perswasion that a thing is so, make it so?"

He replied: "All poets believe that it does, & in ages of imagination this firm perswasion removed mountains; but many are not capable of a firm perswasion of any thing."

Then Ezekiel said: "The philosophy of the east taught the first principles of human perception: some nations held one principle for the origin, and some another: we of Israel taught that the Poetic Genius (as you now call it) was the first principle and all the others merely derivative, which was the cause of our despising the Priests & Philosophers of other countries, and prophecying that all Gods would at last be proved to originate in ours & to be the tributaries of the Poetic Genius; it was this that our great poet, King David, desired so fervently & invokes so pathetic'ly, saying by this he conquers enemies & governs kingdoms; and we so loved our God, that we cursed in his name all the deities of surrounding nations, and asserted that they had rebelled: from these opinions the vulgar came to think that all nations would at last be subject to the jews."

"This," said he, "like all firm perswasions, is come to pass; for all nations believe the jews' code and worship the jews' god, and what greater subjection can be?"

I heard this with some wonder, & must confess my own conviction. After dinner I ask'd Isaiah to favour the world with his lost works; he said none of equal value was lost. Ezekiel said the same of his.

I also asked Isaiah what made him go naked and barefoot three years? he answer'd: "the same that made our friend Diogenes, the Grecian."

I then asked Ezekiel why he eat dung, & lay so long on his right & left side? he answer'd, "the desire of raising other men into a perception of the infinite: this the North American tribes practise, & is he honest who resists his genius or conscience only for the sake of present ease or gratification?"

❄

T H E ancient tradition that the world will be consumed in fire at the end of six thousand years is true, as I have heard from Hell.

For the cherub with his flaming sword is hereby commanded to leave his guard at tree of life; and when he does, the whole creation will be consumed and appear infinite and holy, whereas it now appears finite & corrupt.

This will come to pass by an improvement of sensual enjoyment.

But first the notion that man has a body distinct from his soul is to be expunged; this I shall do by printing in the infernal method, by corrosives, which in Hell are salutary and medicinal, melting apparent surfaces away, and displaying the infinite which was hid.

If the doors of perception were cleansed every thing would appear to man as it is, infinite.

For man has closed himself up, till he sees all things thro' narrow chinks of his cavern.

A MEMORABLE FANCY

I WAS in a Printing house in Hell, & saw the method in which knowledge is transmitted from generation to generation.

In the first chamber was a Dragon-Man, clearing away the rubbish from a cave's mouth; within, a number of Dragons were hollowing the cave.

In the second chamber was a Viper folding round the rock & the cave, and others adorning it with gold, silver and precious stones.

In the third chamber was an Eagle with wings and feathers of air: he caused the inside of the cave to be infinite; around were numbers of Eagle-like men who built palaces in the immense cliffs.

In the fourth chamber were Lions of flaming fire, raging around & melting the metals into living fluids.

In the fifth chamber were Unnam'd forms, which cast the metals into the expanse.

There they were receiv'd by Men who occupied the sixth chamber, and took the forms of books & were arranged in libraries.

❋

THE Giants who formed this world into its sensual existence, and now seem to live in it in chains, are in truth the causes of its life & the sources of all activity; but the chains are the cunning of weak and tame minds which have power to resist energy; according to the proverb, the weak in courage is strong in cunning.

Thus one portion of being is the Prolific, the other the Devouring: to the Devourer it seems as if the producer was in his chains; but it is not so, he only takes portions of existence and fancies that the whole.

But the Prolific would cease to be Prolific unless the Devourer, as a sea, received the excess of his delights.

Some will say: "Is not God alone the Prolific?" I answer: "God only Acts & Is, in existing beings or Men."

These two classes of men are always upon earth, & they should be enemies: whoever tries to reconcile them seeks to destroy existence.

Religion is an endeavour to reconcile the two.

Note: Jesus Christ did not wish to unite, but to seperate them, as in the Parable of sheep and goats! & he says: "I came not to send Peace, but a Sword."

Messiah or Satan or Tempter was formerly thought to be one of the Antediluvians who are our Energies.

A MEMORABLE FANCY

A N Angel came to me and said: "O pitiable foolish young man! O horrible! O dreadful state! consider the hot burning dungeon thou art preparing for thyself to all eternity, to which thou art going in such career."

I said: "Perhaps you will be willing to shew me my eternal lot, & we will contemplate together upon it, and see whether your lot or mine is most desirable."

So he took me thro' a stable & thro' a church & down into the church vault, at the end of which was a mill: thro' the mill we went, and came to a cave: down the winding cavern we groped our tedious way, till a void boundless as a nether sky appear'd beneath us, & we held by the roots of trees and hung over this immensity; but I said: "if you please, we will commit ourselves to this void, and see whether providence is here also: if you will not, I will:" but he answer'd: "do not presume, O young man, but as we here remain, behold thy lot which will soon appear when the darkness passes away."

So I remain'd with him, sitting in the twisted root of an oak; he was suspended in a fungus, which hung with the head downward into the deep.

By degrees we beheld the infinite Abyss, fiery as the smoke of a burning city; beneath us, at an immense distance, was the sun, black but shining; round it were fiery tracks on which revolv'd vast spiders, crawling after their prey, which flew, or rather swum, in the infinite deep, in the most terrific shapes of animals sprung from corruption; & the air was full of them, & seem'd composed of them: these are Devils, and are called Powers of the air. I now asked my companion which was my eternal lot? he said: "between the black & white spiders."

But now, from between the black & white spiders, a cloud and fire burst and rolled thro' the deep, black'ning all beneath, so that the nether deep grew black as a sea, & rolled with a terrible noise; beneath us was nothing now to be seen but a black tempest, till looking east between the clouds & the waves, we saw a cataract of blood mixed with fire, and not many stones' throw from us appear'd and sunk again the scaly fold of a monstrous serpent; at last, to the east, distant about three degrees, appear'd a fiery crest above the waves; slowly it reared like a ridge of golden rocks, till we discover'd two globes of crimson fire, from which the sea fled away in clouds of smoke; and now we saw it was the head of Leviathan; his forehead was divided into streaks of green & purple like those on a tyger's forehead: soon we saw his mouth & red gills hang just above the raging foam, tinging the black deep with beams of blood, advancing toward us with all the fury of a spiritual existence.

My friend the Angel climb'd up from his station into the mill: I remain'd alone; & then this appearance was no more, but I found myself sitting on a pleasant bank beside a river by moonlight, hearing a harper, who sung to the harp; & his theme was: "The man who never alters his opinion is like standing water, & breeds reptiles of the mind."

But I arose and sought for the mill, & there I found my Angel, who, surprised, asked me how I escaped?

I answer'd: "All that we saw was owing to your metaphysics; for when you ran away, I found myself on a bank by moonlight hearing a harper. But now we have seen my eternal lot, shall I shew you yours?" he laugh'd at my proposal; but I by force suddenly caught him in my arms, & flew westerly thro' the night, till we were elevated above the earth's shadow; then I flung myself with him directly into the body of the sun; here I clothed myself in white, & taking in my hand Swedenborg's volumes, sunk from the glorious clime, and passed all the planets till we came to saturn: here I stay'd to rest, & then leap'd into the void between saturn & the fixed stars.

"Here," said I, "is your lot, in this space—if space it may be call'd." Soon we saw the stable and the church, & I took him to the altar and open'd the Bible, and lo! it was a deep pit, into which I descended, driving the Angel before me; soon we saw seven houses of brick; one we enter'd; in it were a number of monkeys, baboons, & all of that species, chain'd by the middle, grinning and snatching at one another, but withheld by the shortness of their chains: however, I saw that they sometimes grew numerous, and then the weak were caught by the strong, and with a grinning aspect, first coupled with, & then devour'd, by plucking off first one limb and then another, till the body was left a helpless trunk; this, after grinning & kissing it with seeming fondness, they devour'd too; and here & there I saw one savourily picking the flesh off his own tail; as the stench terribly annoy'd us both, we went into the mill, & I in my hand brought the skeleton of a body, which in the mill was Aristotle's Analytics.

So the Angel said: "thy phantasy has imposed upon me, & thou oughtest to be ashamed."

I answer'd: "we impose on one another, & it is but lost time to converse with you whose works are only Analytics."

❉

OPPOSITION is true Friendship.[1]

❉

I HAVE always found that Angels have the vanity to speak of themselves as the only wise; this they do with a confident insolence sprouting from systematic reasoning.

Thus Swedenborg boasts that what he writes is new: tho' it is only the Contents or Index of already publish'd books.

A man carried a monkey about for a shew, & because he was a little wiser than the monkey, grew vain, and conciev'd himself as much wiser than seven men. It is so with Swedenborg: he shews the folly of churches, & exposes hypocrites, till he imagines that all are religious, & himself the single one on earth that ever broke a net.

Now hear a plain fact: Swedenborg has not written one new truth. Now hear another: he has written all the old falsehoods.

And now hear the reason. He conversed with Angels who are all religious, & conversed not with Devils who all hate religion, for he was incapable thro' his conceited notions.

Thus Swedenborg's writings are a recapitulation of all superficial opinions, and an analysis of the more sublime—but no further.

Have now another plain fact. Any man of mechanical talents may, from the writings of Paracelsus or Jacob Behmen, produce ten thousand volumes of equal value with Swedenborg's, and from those of Dante or Shakespear an infinite number.

But when he has done this, let him not say that he knows better than his master, for he only holds a candle in sunshine.

A MEMORABLE FANCY

ONCE I saw a Devil in a flame of fire, who arose before an Angel that sat on a cloud, and the Devil utter'd these words:

"The worship of God is: Honouring his gifts in other men, each ac-

[1] This sentence has been obliterated in some copies of the original.

cording to his genius, and loving the greatest men best: those who envy or calumniate great men hate God; for there is no other God."

The Angel hearing this became almost blue; but mastering himself he grew yellow, & at last white, pink, & smiling, and then replied:

"Thou Idolater! is not God One? & is not he visible in Jesus Christ? and has not Jesus Christ given his sanction to the law of ten commandments? and are not all other men fools, sinners, & nothings?"

The Devil answer'd: "bray a fool in a morter with wheat, yet shall not his folly be beaten out of him; if Jesus Christ is the greatest man, you ought to love him in the greatest degree; now hear how he has given his sanction to the law of ten commandments: did he not mock at the sabbath and so mock the sabbath's God? murder those who were murder'd because of him? turn away the law from the woman taken in adultery? steal the labor of others to support him? bear false witness when he omitted making a defence before Pilate? covet when he pray'd for his disciples, and when he bid them shake off the dust of their feet against such as refused to lodge them? I tell you, no virtue can exist without breaking these ten commandments. Jesus was all virtue, and acted from impulse, not from rules."

When he had so spoken, I beheld the Angel, who stretched out his arms, embracing the flame of fire, & he was consumed and arose as Elijah.

Note: This Angel, who is now become a Devil, is my particular friend; we often read the Bible together in its infernal or diabolical sense, which the world shall have if they behave well.

I have also The Bible of Hell, which the world shall have whether they will or no.

❧

O N E Law for the Lion & Ox is Oppression.

A SONG OF LIBERTY

I

T H E Eternal Female groan'd! it was heard over all the Earth.

2. Albion's coast is sick, silent; the American meadows faint!

3. Shadows of Prophecy shiver along by the lakes and the rivers, and mutter across the ocean: France, rend down thy dungeon!

4. Golden Spain, burst the barriers of old Rome!

5. Cast thy keys, O Rome, into the deep down falling, even to eternity down falling.

6. And weep.

7. In her trembling hand she took the new born terror, howling.

8. On those infinite mountains of light, now barr'd out by the atlantic sea, the new born fire stood before the starry king!

9. Flag'd with grey brow'd snows and thunderous visages, the jealous wings wav'd over the deep.

10. The speary hand burned aloft, unbuckled was the shield; forth went the hand of jealousy among the flaming hair, and hurl'd the new born wonder thro' the starry night.

11. The fire, the fire is falling!

12. Look up! look up! O citizen of London, enlarge thy countenance! O Jew, leave counting gold! return to thy oil and wine. O African! black African! (go, winged thought, widen his forehead.)

13. The fiery limbs, the flaming hair, shot like the sinking sun into the western sea.

14. Wak'd from his eternal sleep, the hoary element roaring fled away.

15. Down rush'd, beating his wings in vain, the jealous king; his grey brow'd councellors, thunderous warriors, curl'd veterans, among helms, and shields, and chariots, horses, elephants, banners, castles, slings, and rocks.

16. Falling, rushing, ruining! buried in the ruins, on Urthona's dens;

17. All night beneath the ruins; then, their sullen flames faded, emerge round the gloomy king.

18. With thunder and fire, leading his starry hosts thro' the waste wilderness, he promulgates his ten commands, glancing his beamy eyelids over the deep in dark dismay,

19. Where the son of fire in his eastern cloud, while the morning plumes her golden breast,

20. Spurning the clouds written with curses, stamps the stony law to dust, loosing the eternal horses from the dens of night, crying:

EMPIRE IS NO MORE! AND NOW THE LION
& WOLF SHALL CEASE.

CHORUS

Let the Priests of the Raven of dawn no longer, in deadly black, with hoarse note curse the sons of joy. Nor his accepted brethren—whom, tyrant, he calls free—lay the bound or build the roof. Nor pale religious letchery call that virginity that wishes but acts not!

For every thing that lives is Holy.

VISIONS OF THE DAUGHTERS OF ALBION

The Eye sees more than the Heart knows

Etched 1793

THE ARGUMENT

I LOVED Theotormon,
And I was not ashamed;
I trembled in my virgin fears,
And I hid in Leutha's vale!

I plucked Leutha's flower,
And I rose up from the vale;
But the terrible thunders tore
My virgin mantle in twain.

VISIONS

ENSLAV'D, the Daughters of Albion weep; a trembling lamentation
Upon their mountains; in their valleys, sighs toward America.

For the soft soul of America, Oothoon, wander'd in woe,
Along the vales of Leutha seeking flowers to comfort her;
And thus she spoke to the bright Marygold of Leutha's vale:

"Art thou a flower? art thou a nymph? I see thee now a flower,
Now a nymph! I dare not pluck thee from thy dewy bed!"

The Golden nymph replied: "Pluck thou my flower, Oothoon the mild!
Another flower shall spring, because the soul of sweet delight
Can never pass away." She ceas'd, & clos'd her golden shrine.

Then Oothoon pluck'd the flower, saying: "I pluck thee from thy bed,
Sweet flower, and put thee here to glow between my breasts,
And thus I turn my face to where my whole soul seeks."

Over the waves she went in wing'd exulting swift delight,
And over Theotormon's reign took her impetuous course.

Bromion rent her with his thunders; on his stormy bed
Lay the faint maid, and soon her woes appall'd his thunders hoarse.

Bromion spoke: "Behold this harlot here on Bromion's bed,
And let the jealous dolphins sport around the lovely maid!
Thy soft American plains are mine, and mine thy north & south:
Stampt with my signet are the swarthy children of the sun;
They are obedient, they resist not, they obey the scourge;
Their daughters worship terrors and obey the violent.
Now thou maist marry Bromion's harlot, and protect the child
Of Bromion's rage, that Oothoon shall put forth in nine moons' time."

Then storms rent Theotormon's limbs: he roll'd his waves around
And folded his black jealous waters round the adulterate pair.
Bound back to back in Bromion's caves, terror & meekness dwell:

At entrance Theotormon sits, wearing the threshold hard
With secret tears; beneath him sound like waves on a desart shore
The voice of slaves beneath the sun, and children bought with money,
That shiver in religious caves beneath the burning fires
Of lust, that belch incessant from the summits of the earth.

Oothoon weeps not; she cannot weep! her tears are locked up;
But she can howl incessant writhing her soft snowy limbs
And calling Theotormon's Eagles to prey upon her flesh.

"I call with holy voice! Kings of the sounding air,
Rend away this defiled bosom that I may reflect
The image of Theotormon on my pure transparent breast."

The Eagles at her call descend & rend their bleeding prey:
Theotormon severely smiles; her soul reflects the smile,
As the clear spring, mudded with feet of beasts, grows pure & smiles.

The Daughters of Albion hear her woes, & eccho back her sighs.

"Why does my Theotormon sit weeping upon the threshold,
And Oothoon hovers by his side, perswading him in vain?
I cry: arise, O Theotormon! for the village dog
Barks at the breaking day; the nightingale has done lamenting;
The lark does rustle in the ripe corn, and the Eagle returns
From nightly prey and lifts his golden beak to the pure east,

Shaking the dust from his immortal pinions to awake
The sun that sleeps too long. Arise, my Theotormon, I am pure
Because the night is gone that clos'd me in its deadly black.
They told me that the night & day were all that I could see;
They told me that I had five senses to inclose me up,
And they inclos'd my infinite brain into a narrow circle,
And sunk my heart into the Abyss, a red, round globe, hot burning,
Till all from life I was obliterated and erased.
Instead of morn arises a bright shadow, like an eye
In the eastern cloud; instead of night a sickly charnel house:
That Theotormon hears me not! to him the night and morn
Are both alike; a night of sighs, a morning of fresh tears,
And none but Bromion can hear my lamentations.

"With what sense is it that the chicken shuns the ravenous hawk?
With what sense does the tame pigeon measure out the expanse?
With what sense does the bee form cells? have not the mouse & frog
Eyes and ears and sense of touch? yet are their habitations
And their pursuits as different as their forms and as their joys.
Ask the wild ass why he refuses burdens, and the meek camel
Why he loves man: is it because of eye, ear, mouth, or skin,
Or breathing nostrils? No, for these the wolf and tyger have.
Ask the blind worm the secrets of the grave, and why her spires
Love to curl round the bones of death; and ask the rav'nous snake
Where she gets poison, & the wing'd eagle why he loves the sun;
And then tell me the thoughts of man, that have been hid of old.

"Silent I hover all the night, and all day could be silent
If Theotormon once would turn his loved eyes upon me.
How can I be defil'd when I reflect thy image pure?
Sweetest the fruit that the worm feeds on, & the soul prey'd on by woe,
The new wash'd lamb ting'd with the village smoke, & the bright swan
By the red earth of our immortal river. I bathe my wings,
And I am white and pure to hover round Theotormon's breast."

Then Theotormon broke his silence, and he answered:—
"Tell me what is the night or day to one o'erflow'd with woe?
Tell me what is a thought, & of what substance is it made?
Tell me what is a joy, & in what gardens do joys grow?
And in what rivers swim the sorrows? and upon what mountains
Wave shadows of discontent? and in what houses dwell the wretched,
Drunken with woe forgotten, and shut up from cold despair?

"Tell me where dwell the thoughts forgotten till thou call them forth?
Tell me where dwell the joys of old? & where the ancient loves,
And when they will renew again, & the night of oblivion past,
That I might traverse times & spaces far remote, and bring
Comforts into a present sorrow and a night of pain?
Where goest thou, O thought? to what remote land is thy flight?
If thou returnest to the present moment of affliction
Wilt thou bring comforts on thy wings, and dews and honey and balm,
Or poison from the desart wilds, from the eyes of the envier?"

Then Bromion said, and shook the cavern with his lamentation:

"Thou knowest that the ancient trees seen by thine eyes have fruit,
But knowest thou that trees and fruits flourish upon the earth
To gratify senses unknown? trees, beasts and birds unknown;
Unknown, not unperciev'd, spread in the infinite microscope,
In places yet unvisited by the voyager, and in worlds
Over another kind of seas, and in atmospheres unknown:
Ah! are there other wars beside the wars of sword and fire?
And are there other sorrows beside the sorrows of poverty?
And are there other joys beside the joys of riches and ease?
And is there not one law for both the lion and the ox?
And is there not eternal fire and eternal chains
To bind the phantoms of existence from eternal life?"

Then Oothoon waited silent all the day and all the night;
But when the morn arose, her lamentation renew'd.
The Daughters of Albion hear her woes, & eccho back her sighs.

"O Urizen! Creator of men! mistaken Demon of heaven!
Thy joys are tears, thy labour vain to form men to thine image.
How can one joy absorb another? are not different joys
Holy, eternal, infinite? and each joy is a Love.

"Does not the great mouth laugh at a gift, & the narrow eyelids mock
At the labour that is above payment? and wilt thou take the ape
For thy councellor, or the dog for a schoolmaster to thy children?
Does he who contemns poverty and he who turns with abhorrence
From usury feel the same passion, or are they moved alike?
How can the giver of gifts experience the delights of the merchant?
How the industrious citizen the pains of the husbandman?
How different far the fat fed hireling with hollow drum,

Who buys whole corn fields into wastes, and sings upon the heath!
How different their eye and ear! how different the world to them!
With what sense does the parson claim the labour of the farmer?
What are his nets & gins & traps; & how does he surround him
With cold floods of abstraction, and with forests of solitude,
To build him castles and high spires, where kings & priests may dwell;
Till she who burns with youth, and knows no fixed lot, is bound
In spells of law to one she loaths? and must she drag the chain
Of life in weary lust? must chilling, murderous thoughts obscure
The clear heaven of her eternal spring; to bear the wintry rage
Of a harsh terror, driv'n to madness, bound to hold a rod
Over her shrinking shoulders all the day, & all the night
To turn the wheel of false desire, and longings that wake her womb
To the abhorred birth of cherubs in the human form,
That live a pestilence & die a meteor, & are no more;
Till the child dwell with one he hates, and do the deed he loaths,
And the impure scourge force his seed into its unripe birth
Ere yet his eyelids can behold the arrows of the day?

"Does the whale worship at thy footsteps as the hungry dog;
Or does he scent the mountain prey because his nostrils wide
Draw in the ocean? does his eye discern the flying cloud
As the raven's eye? or does he measure the expanse like the vulture?
Does the still spider view the cliffs where eagles hide their young;
Or does the fly rejoice because the harvest is brought in?
Does not the eagle scorn the earth & despise the treasures beneath?
But the mole knoweth what is there, & the worm shall tell it thee.
Does not the worm erect a pillar in the mouldering church yard
And a palace of eternity in the jaws of the hungry grave?
Over his porch these words are written: 'Take thy bliss, O **Man**!
And sweet shall be thy taste, & sweet thy infant joys renew!'

"Infancy! fearless, lustful, happy, nestling for delight
In laps of pleasure: Innocence! honest, open, seeking
The vigorous joys of morning light; open to virgin bliss.
Who taught thee modesty, subtil modesty, child of night & sleep?
When thou awakest wilt thou dissemble all thy secret joys,
Or wert thou not awake when all this mystery was disclos'd?
Then com'st thou forth a modest virgin, knowing to dissemble,
With nets found under thy night pillow, to catch virgin joy
And brand it with the name of whore, & sell it in the night,
In silence, ev'n without a whisper, and in seeming sleep.

Religious dreams and holy vespers light thy smoky fires:
Once were thy fires lighted by the eyes of honest morn.
And does my Theotormon seek this hypocrite modesty,
This knowing, artful, secret, fearful, cautious, trembling hypocrite?
Then is Oothoon a whore indeed! and all the virgin joys
Of life are harlots, and Theotormon is a sick man's dream;
And Oothoon is the crafty slave of selfish holiness.

"But Oothoon is not so: a virgin fill'd with virgin fancies,
Open to joy and to delight where ever beauty appears;
If in the morning sun I find it, there my eyes are fix'd
In happy copulation; if in evening mild, wearied with work,
Sit on a bank and draw the pleasures of this free born joy.

"The moment of desire! the moment of desire! The virgin
That pines for man shall awaken her womb to enormous joys
In the secret shadows of her chamber: the youth shut up from
The lustful joy shall forget to generate & create an amorous image
In the shadows of his curtains and in the folds of his silent pillow.
Are not these the places of religion, the rewards of continence,
The self enjoyings of self denial? why dost thou seek religion?
Is it because acts are not lovely that thou seekest solitude
Where the horrible darkness is impressed with reflections of desire?

"Father of Jealousy, be thou accursed from the earth!
Why hast thou taught my Theotormon this accursed thing?
Till beauty fades from off my shoulders, darken'd and cast out,
A solitary shadow wailing on the margin of non-entity.

"I cry: Love! Love! Love! happy happy Love! free as the mountain wind!
Can that be Love that drinks another as a sponge drinks water,
That clouds with jealousy his nights, with weepings all the day,
To spin a web of age around him, grey and hoary, dark,
Till his eyes sicken at the fruit that hangs before his sight?
Such is self-love that envies all, a creeping skeleton
With lamplike eyes watching around the frozen marriage bed.

"But silken nets and traps of adamant will Oothoon spread,
And catch for thee girls of mild silver, or of furious gold.
I'll lie beside thee on a bank & view their wanton play
In lovely copulation, bliss on bliss, with Theotormon:
Red as the rosy morning, lustful as the first born beam,

Oothoon shall view his dear delight, nor e'er with jealous cloud
Come in the heaven of generous love, nor selfish blightings bring.

"Does the sun walk in glorious raiment on the secret floor
Where the cold miser spreads his gold; or does the bright cloud drop
On his stone threshold? does his eye behold the beam that brings
Expansion to the eye of pity? or will he bind himself
Beside the ox to thy hard furrow? does not that mild beam blot
The bat, the owl, the glowing tyger, and the king of night?
The sea fowl takes the wintry blast for a cov'ring to her limbs,
And the wild snake the pestilence to adorn him with gems & gold;
And trees & birds & beasts & men behold their eternal joy.
Arise, you little glancing wings, and sing your infant joy!
Arise, and drink your bliss, for every thing that lives is holy!"

Thus every morning wails Oothoon; but Theotormon sits
Upon the margin'd ocean conversing with shadows dire.
The Daughters of Albion hear her woes, & eccho back her sighs.

AMERICA

A Prophecy

Etched 1793

PRELUDIUM

T H E shadowy Daughter of Urthona stood before red Orc,
When fourteen suns had faintly journey'd o'er his dark abode:
His food she brought in iron baskets, his drink in cups of iron:
Crown'd with a helmet & dark hair the nameless female stood;
A quiver with its burning stores, a bow like that of night,
When pestilence is shot from heaven: no other arms she need!
Invulnerable tho' naked, save where clouds roll round her loins
Their awful folds in the dark air: silent she stood as night;
For never from her iron tongue could voice or sound arise,
But dumb till that dread day when Orc assay'd his fierce embrace.

"Dark Virgin," said the hairy youth, "thy father stern, abhorr'd,
Rivets my tenfold chains while still on high my spirit soars;
Sometimes an eagle screaming in the sky, sometimes a lion
Stalking upon the mountains, & sometimes a whale, I lash

The raging fathomless abyss; anon a serpent folding
Around the pillars of Urthona, and round thy dark limbs
On the Canadian wilds I fold; feeble my spirit folds,
For chain'd beneath I rend these caverns: when thou bringest food
I howl my joy, and my red eyes seek to behold thy face—
In vain! these clouds roll to & fro, & hide thee from my sight."

Silent as despairing love, and strong as jealousy,
The hairy shoulders rend the links; free are the wrists of fire;
Round the terrific loins he seiz'd the panting, struggling womb;
It joy'd: she put aside her clouds & smiled her first-born smile,
As when a black cloud shews its lightnings to the silent deep.

Soon as she saw the terrible boy, then burst the virgin cry:

"I know thee, I have found thee, & I will not let thee go:
Thou art the image of God who dwells in darkness of Africa,
And thou art fall'n to give me life in regions of dark death.
On my American plains I feel the struggling afflictions
Endur'd by roots that writhe their arms into the nether deep.
I see a Serpent in Canada who courts me to his love,
In Mexico an Eagle, and a Lion in Peru;
I see a Whale in the South-sea, drinking my soul away.
O what limb rending pains I feel! thy fire & my frost
Mingle in howling pains, in furrows by the lightnings rent.
This is eternal death, and this the torment long foretold."

A PROPHECY

THE Guardian Prince of Albion burns in his nightly tent:
Sullen fires across the Atlantic glow to America's shore,
Piercing the souls of warlike men who rise in silent night.
Washington, Franklin, Paine & Warren, Gates, Hancock & Green
Meet on the coast glowing with blood from Albion's fiery Prince.

Washington spoke: "Friends of America! look over the Atlantic sea;
A bended bow is lifted in heaven, & a heavy iron chain
Descends, link by link, from Albion's cliffs across the sea, to bind
Brothers & sons of America till our faces pale and yellow,
Heads deprest, voices weak, eyes downcast, hands work-bruis'd,
Feet bleeding on the sultry sands, and the furrows of the whip
Descend to generations that in future times forget."

The strong voice ceas'd, for a terrible blast swept over the heaving sea:
The eastern cloud rent: on his cliffs stood Albion's wrathful Prince,
A dragon form, clashing his scales: at midnight he arose,
And flam'd red meteors round the land of Albion beneath;
His voice, his locks, his awful shoulders, and his glowing eyes
Appear to the Americans upon the cloudy night.
Solemn heave the Atlantic waves between the gloomy nations,
Swelling, belching from its deeps red clouds & raging fires.
Albion is sick! America faints! enrag'd the Zenith grew.
As human blood shooting its veins all round the orbed heaven,
Red rose the clouds from the Atlantic in vast wheels of blood,
And in the red clouds rose a Wonder o'er the Atlantic sea,
Intense! naked! a Human fire, fierce glowing, as the wedge
Of iron heated in the furnace: his terrible limbs were fire
With myriads of cloudy terrors, banners dark & towers
Surrounded: heat but not light went thro' the murky atmosphere.

The King of England looking westward trembles at the vision.

Albion's Angel stood beside the Stone of night, and saw
The terror like a comet, or more like the planet red
That once enclos'd the terrible wandering comets in its sphere.
Then, Mars, thou wast our center, & the planets three flew round
Thy crimson disk: so e'er the Sun was rent from thy red sphere.
The Spectre glow'd his horrid length staining the temple long
With beams of blood; & thus a voice came forth, and shook the temple:

"The morning comes, the night decays, the watchmen leave their stations;
The grave is burst, the spices shed, the linen wrapped up;
The bones of death, the cov'ring clay, the sinews shrunk & dry'd
Reviving shake, inspiring move, breathing, awakening,
Spring like redeemed captives when their bonds & bars are burst.
Let the slave grinding at the mill run out into the field,
Let him look up into the heavens & laugh in the bright air;
Let the inchained soul, shut up in darkness and in sighing,
Whose face has never seen a smile in thirty weary years,
Rise and look out; his chains are loose, his dungeon doors are open;
And let his wife and children return from the oppressor's scourge.
They look behind at every step & believe it is a dream,
Singing: 'The Sun has left his blackness & has found a fresher morning,
And the fair Moon rejoices in the clear & cloudless night;
For Empire is no more, and now the Lion & Wolf shall cease.'"

In thunders ends the voice. Then Albion's Angel wrathful burnt
Beside the Stone of Night, and like the Eternal Lion's howl
In famine & war, reply'd: "Art thou not Orc, who serpent-form'd
Stands at the gate of Enitharmon to devour her children?
Blasphemous Demon, Antichrist, hater of Dignities,
Lover of wild rebellion, and transgressor of God's Law,
Why dost thou come to Angel's eyes in this terrific form?"

The Terror answer'd: "I am Orc, wreath'd round the accursed tree:
The times are ended; shadows pass, the morning 'gins to break;
The fiery joy, that Urizen perverted to ten commands,
What night he led the starry hosts thro' the wide wilderness,
That stony law I stamp to dust; and scatter religion abroad
To the four winds as a torn book, & none shall gather the leaves;
But they shall rot on desart sands, & consume in bottomless deeps,
To make the desarts blossom, & the deeps shrink to their fountains,
And to renew the fiery joy, and burst the stony roof;
That pale religious letchery, seeking Virginity,
May find it in a harlot, and in coarse-clad honesty
The undefil'd, tho' ravish'd in her cradle night and morn;
For everything that lives is holy, life delights in life;
Because the soul of sweet delight can never be defil'd.
Fires inwrap the earthly globe, yet man is not consum'd;
Amidst the lustful fires he walks; his feet become like brass,
His knees and thighs like silver, & his breast and head like gold."

"Sound! sound! my loud war-trumpets, & alarm my Thirteen Angels!
Loud howls the eternal Wolf! the eternal Lion lashes his tail!
America is darken'd; and my punishing Demons, terrified,
Crouch howling before their caverns deep, like skins dry'd in the wind.
They cannot smite the wheat, nor quench the fatness of the earth; They
cannot smite with sorrows, nor subdue the plow and spade;
They cannot wall the city, nor moat round the castle of princes;
They cannot bring the stubbed oak to overgrow the hills;
For terrible men stand on the shores, & in their robes I see
Children take shelter from the lightnings: there stands Washington
And Paine and Warren with their foreheads rear'd toward the east.
But clouds obscure my aged sight. A vision from afar!
Sound! sound! my loud war-trumpets, & alarm my thirteen Angels!
Ah vision from afar! Ah rebel form that rent the ancient
Heavens! Eternal Viper, self-renew'd, rolling in clouds,
I see thee in thick clouds and darkness on America's shore,

Writhing in pangs of abhorred birth; red flames the crest rebellious
And eyes of death; the harlot womb, oft opened in vain,
Heaves in enormous circles: now the times are return'd upon thee,
Devourer of thy parent, now thy unutterable torment renews.
Sound! sound! my loud war-trumpets, & alarm my thirteen Angels!
Ah terrible birth! a young one bursting! where is the weeping mouth,
And where the mother's milk? instead, those ever-hissing jaws
And parched lips drop with fresh gore: now roll thou in the clouds;
Thy mother lays her length outstretch'd upon the shore beneath.
Sound! sound! my loud war-trumpets, & alarm my thirteen Angels!
Loud howls the eternal Wolf! the eternal Lion lashes his tail!"

Thus wept the Angel voice, & as he wept, the terrible blasts
Of trumpets blew a loud alarm across the Atlantic deep.
No trumpets answer; no reply of clarions or of fifes:
Silent the Colonies remain and refuse the loud alarm.

On those vast shady hills between America & Albion's shore,
Now barr'd out by the Atlantic sea, call'd Atlantean hills,
Because from their bright summits you may pass to the Golden world,
An ancient palace, archetype of mighty Emperies,
Rears its immortal pinnacles, built in the forest of God
By Ariston, the king of beauty, for his stolen bride.

Here on their magic seats the thirteen Angels sat perturb'd,
For clouds from the Atlantic hover o'er the solemn roof.

Fiery the Angels rose, & as they rose deep thunder roll'd
Around their shores, indignant burning with the fires of Orc;
And Boston's Angel cried aloud as they flew thro' the dark night.

He cried: "Why trembles honesty, and like a murderer
Why seeks he refuge from the frowns of his immortal station?
Must the generous tremble & leave his joy to the idle, to the pestilence,
That mock him? who commanded this? what God? what Angel?
To keep the gen'rous from experience till the ungenerous
Are unrestrain'd performers of the energies of nature;
Till pity is become a trade, and generosity a science
That men get rich by; & the sandy desart is giv'n to the strong?
What God is he writes laws of peace & clothes him in a tempest?
What pitying Angel lusts for tears and fans himself with sighs?
What crawling villain preaches abstinence & wraps himself
In fat of lambs? no more I follow, no more obedience pay!"

So cried he, rending off his robe & throwing down his scepter
In sight of Albion's Guardian; and all the thirteen Angels
Rent off their robes to the hungry wind, & threw their golden scepters
Down on the land of America; indignant they descended
Headlong from out their heav'nly heights, descending swift as fires
Over the land; naked & flaming are their lineaments seen
In the deep gloom; by Washington & Paine & Warren they stood;
And the flame folded, roaring fierce within the pitchy night
Before the Demon red, who burnt towards America,
In black smoke, thunders, and loud winds, rejoicing in its terror,
Breaking in smoky wreaths from the wild deep, & gath'ring thick
In flames as of a furnace on the land from North to South,
What time the thirteen Governors that England sent, convene
In Bernard's house; the flames cover'd the land, they rouze, they cry;
Shaking their mental chains, they rush in fury to the sea
To quench their anguish; at the feet of Washington down fall'n
They grovel on the sand and writhing lie, while all
The British soldiers thro' the thirteen states sent up a howl
Of anguish, threw their swords & muskets to the earth, & ran
From their encampments and dark castles, seeking where to hide
From the grim flames, and from the visions of Orc, in sight
Of Albion's Angel; who, enrag'd, his secret clouds open'd
From north to south and burnt outstretch'd on wings of wrath, cov'ring
The eastern sky, spreading his awful wings across the heavens.
Beneath him roll'd his num'rous hosts, all Albion's Angels camp'd
Darken'd the Atlantic mountains; & their trumpets shook the valleys,
Arm'd with diseases of the earth to cast upon the Abyss,
Their numbers forty millions, must'ring in the eastern sky.

In the flames stood & view'd the armies drawn out in the sky,
Washington, Franklin, Paine, & Warren, Allen, Gates, & Lee,
And heard the voice of Albion's Angel give the thunderous command;
His plagues, obedient to his voice, flew forth out of their clouds,
Falling upon America, as a storm to cut them off,
As a blight cuts the tender corn when it begins to appear.
Dark is the heaven above, & cold & hard the earth beneath:
And as a plague wind fill'd with insects cuts off man & beast,
And as a sea o'erwhelms a land in the day of an earthquake,
Fury! rage! madness! in a wind swept through America;
And the red flames of Orc, that folded roaring, fierce, around
The angry shores; and the fierce rushing of th' inhabitants together!
The citizens of New York close their books & lock their chests;

The mariners of Boston drop their anchors and unlade;
The scribe of Pensylvania casts his pen upon the earth;
The builder of Virginia throws his hammer down in fear.

Then had America been lost, o'erwhelm'd by the Atlantic,
And Earth had lost another portion of the infinite,
But all rush together in the night in wrath and raging fire.
The red fires rag'd! the plagues recoil'd! then roll'd they back with fury
On Albion's Angels: then the Pestilence began in streaks of red
Across the limbs of Albion's Guardian; the spotted plague smote Bristol's
And the Leprosy London's Spirit, sickening all their bands:
The millions sent up a howl of anguish and threw off their hammer'd mail,
And cast their swords & spears to earth, & stood, a naked multitude:
Albion's Guardian writhed in torment on the eastern sky,
Pale, quiv'ring toward the brain his glimmering eyes, teeth chattering,
Howling & shuddering, his legs quivering, convuls'd each muscle & sinew:
Sick'ning lay London's Guardian, and the ancient miterd York,
Their heads on snowy hills, their ensigns sick'ning in the sky.
The plagues creep on the burning winds driven by flames of Orc,
And by the fierce Americans rushing together in the night,
Driven o'er the Guardians of Ireland, and Scotland and Wales.
They, spotted with plagues, forsook the frontiers; & their banners, sear'd
With fires of hell, deform their ancient heavens with shame & woe.
Hid in his caves the Bard of Albion felt the enormous plagues,
And a cowl of flesh grew o'er his head, & scales on his back & ribs;
And, rough with black scales, all his Angels fright their ancient heavens.
The doors of marriage are open, and the Priests in rustling scales
Rush into reptile coverts, hiding from the fires of Orc,
That play around the golden roofs in wreaths of fierce desire,
Leaving the females naked and glowing with the lusts of youth.

For the female spirits of the dead, pining in bonds of religion,
Run from their fetters reddening, & in long drawn arches sitting,
They feel the nerves of youth renew, and desires of ancient times
Over their pale limbs, as a vine when the tender grape appears.

Over the hills, the vales, the cities, rage the red flames fierce:
The Heavens melted from north to south; and Urizen, who sat
Above all heavens, in thunders wrap'd, emerg'd his leprous head
From out his holy shrine, his tears in deluge piteous
Falling into the deep sublime; flag'd with grey-brow'd snows
And thunderous visages, his jealous wings wav'd over the deep;

Weeping in dismal howling woe, he dark descended, howling
Around the smitten bands, clothed in tears & trembling, shudd'ring cold.
His stored snows he poured forth, and his icy magazines
He open'd on the deep, and on the Atlantic sea white shiv'ring
Leprous his limbs, all over white, and hoary was his visage,
Weeping in dismal howlings before the stern Americans,
Hiding the Demon red with clouds & cold mists from the earth;
Till Angels & weak men twelve years should govern o'er the strong;
And then their end should come, when France receiv'd the Demon's light.

Stiff shudderings shook the heav'nly thrones! France, Spain, & Italy
In terror view'd the bands of Albion, and the ancient Guardians,
Fainting upon the elements, smitten with their own plagues.
They slow advance to shut the five gates of their law-built heaven,
Filled with blasting fancies and with mildews of despair,
With fierce disease and lust, unable to stem the fires of Orc.
But the five gates were consum'd, & their bolts and hinges melted;
And the fierce flames burnt round the heavens & round the abodes of men.

AMERICA

Cancelled plates etched about 1793

A PROPHECY

THE Guardian Prince of Albion burns in his nightly tent:
Sullen fires across the Atlantic glow to America's shore,
Piercing the souls of warlike men who rise in silent night.
Washington, Hancock, Paine & Warren, Gates, Franklin & Green
Meet on the coast glowing with blood from Albion's fiery Prince.
Washington spoke: "Friends of America! look over the Atlantic sea;
A bended bow in heaven is lifted, & a heavy iron chain
Descends, link by link, from Albion's cliffs across the sea, to bind
Brothers & sons of America till our faces pale and yellow,
Heads deprest, voices weak, eyes downcast, hands work-bruised,
Feet bleeding on the sultry sands, & the furrows of the whip
Descend to generations that in future times forget."
The strong voice ceas'd, for a terrible blast swept over the heaving sea:
The eastern cloud rent: on his cliffs stood Albion's fiery Prince,
A dragon form, clashing his scales: at midnight he arose,
And flam'd fierce meteors round the band of Albion beneath;

His voice, his locks, his awful shoulders, & his glowing eyes
Reveal the dragon thro' the human; coursing swift as fire
To the close hall of counsel, where his Angel form renews.
In a sweet vale shelter'd with cedars, that eternal stretch
Their unmov'd branches, stood the hall, built when the moon shot forth,
In that dread night when Urizen call'd the stars round his feet;
Then burst the center from its orb, and found a place beneath;
And Earth conglob'd, in narrow room, roll'd round its sulphur Sun.
To this deep valley situated by the flowing Thames,
Where George the third holds council & his Lords & Commons meet,
Shut out from mortal sight the Angel came; the vale was dark
With clouds of smoke from the Atlantic, that in volumes roll'd
Between the mountains; dismal visions mope around the house
On chairs of iron, canopied with mystic ornaments
Of life by magic power condens'd; infernal forms art-bound
The council sat; all rose before the aged apparition,
His snowy beard that streams like lambent flames down his wide breast
Wetting with tears, & his white garments cast a wintry light.
Then as arm'd clouds arise terrific round the northern drum.
The world is silent at the flapping of the folding banners.
So still terrors rent the house, as when the solemn globe
Launch'd to the unknown shore, while Sotha held the northern helm,
Till to that void it came & fell; so the dark house was rent.
The valley mov'd beneath; its shining pillars split in twain,
And its roofs crack across down falling on th' Angelic seats.

Then Albion's Angel rose resolv'd to the cove of armoury:
His shield that bound twelve demons & their cities in its orb
He took down from its trembling pillar; from its cavern deep,
His helm was brought by London's Guardian, & his thirsty spear
By the wise spirit of London's river; silent stood the King breathing
          damp mists,
And on his aged limbs they clasp'd the armour of terrible gold.
Infinite London's awful spires cast a dreadful cold
Even on rational things beneath and from the palace walls
Around Saint James's, chill & heavy, even to the city gate.
On the vast stone whose name is Truth he stood, his cloudy shield
Smote with his scepter, the scale bound orb loud howl'd; the pillar
Trembling sunk, an earthquake roll'd along the mossy pile.
In glitt'ring armour, swift as winds, intelligent as clouds
Four winged heralds mount the furious blasts & blow their trumps;
Gold, silver, brass & iron clangors clamoring rend the shores.

Like white clouds rising from the deeps his fifty-two armies
From the four cliffs of Albion rise, mustering around their Prince;
Angels of cities and of parishes and villages and families,
In armour as the nerves of wisdom, each his station holds.
In opposition dire, a warlike cloud, the myriads stood
In the red air before the Demon seen even by mortal men,
Who call it Fancy, or shut the gates of sense, or in their chambers
Sleep like the dead. But like a constellation ris'n and blazing
Over the rugged ocean, so the Angels of Albion hung
Over the frowning shadow like an aged King in arms of gold,
Who wept over a den, in which his only son outstretch'd
By rebels' hands was slain; his white beard wav'd in the wild wind.
On mountains & cliffs of snow the awful apparition hover'd,
And like the voices of religious dead heard in the mountains
When holy zeal scents the sweet valleys of ripe virgin bliss,
Such was the hollow voice that o'er America lamented.

FRAGMENT

perhaps originally intended for America
Etched about 1793

AS when a dream of Thiralatha flies the midnight hour:
In vain the dreamer grasps the joyful images, they fly
Seen in obscured traces in the Vale of Leutha, So
The British Colonies beneath the woful Princes fade.

And so the Princes fade from earth, scarce seen by souls of men,
But tho' obscur'd, this is the form of the Angelic land.

EUROPE

A Prophecy

Etched 1794

"FIVE windows light the cavern'd Man: thro' one he breathes the air;
Thro' one hears music of the spheres; thro' one the eternal vine
Flourishes, that he may recieve the grapes; thro' one can look
And see small portions of the eternal world that ever groweth;

Thro' one himself pass out what time he please; but he will not,
For stolen joys are sweet & bread eaten in secret pleasant."

So sang a Fairy, mocking, as he sat on a streak'd Tulip,
Thinking none saw him: when he ceas'd I started from the trees
And caught him in my hat, as boys knock down a butterfly.
"How know you this," said I, "small Sir? where did you learn this song?"
Seeing himself in my possession, thus he answer'd me:
"My master, I am yours! command me, for I must obey."

"Then tell me, what is the material world, and is it dead?"
He, laughing, answer'd: "I will write a book on leaves of flowers,
If you will feed me on love-thoughts & give me now and then
A cup of sparkling poetic fancies; so, when I am tipsie,
I'll sing to you to this soft lute, and shew you all alive
The world, where every particle of dust breathes forth its joy."

I took him home in my warm bosom: as we went along
Wild flowers I gather'd, & he shew'd me each eternal flower:
He laugh'd aloud to see them whimper because they were pluck'd.
They hover'd round me like a cloud of incense: when I came
Into my parlour and sat down and took my pen to write,
My Fairy sat upon the table and dictated EUROPE.

PRELUDIUM

T H E nameless shadowy female rose from out the breast of Orc,
Her snaky hair brandishing in the winds of Enitharmon;
And thus her voice arose:

"O mother Enitharmon, wilt thou bring forth other sons?
To cause my name to vanish, that my place may not be found,
For I am faint with travail,
Like the dark cloud disburden'd in the day of dismal thunder.

"My roots are brandish'd in the heavens, my fruits in earth beneath
Surge, foam and labour into life, first born & first consum'd!
Consumed and consuming!
Then why shouldst thou, accursed mother, bring me into life?

"I wrap my turban of thick clouds around my lab'ring head,
And fold the sheety waters as a mantle round my limbs;
Yet the red sun and moon
And all the overflowing stars rain down prolific pains.

"Unwilling I look up to heaven, unwilling count the stars:
Sitting in fathomless abyss of my immortal shrine
I sieze their burning power
And bring forth howling terrors, all devouring fiery kings,

"Devouring & devoured, roaming on dark and desolate mountains,
In forests of eternal death, shrieking in hollow trees.
Ah mother Enitharmon!
Stamp not with solid form this vig'rous progeny of fires.

"I bring forth from my teeming bosom myriads of flames,
And thou dost stamp them with a signet; then they roam abroad
And leave me void as death.
Ah! I am drown'd in shady woe and visionary joy.

"And who shall bind the infinite with an eternal band?
To compass it with swaddling bands? and who shall cherish it
With milk and honey?
I see it smile, & I roll inward, & my voice is past."

              She ceast, & roll'd her shady clouds
              Into the secret place.

A PROPHECY

THE deep of winter came,
What time the secret child
Descended thro' the orient gates of the eternal day:
War ceas'd, & all the troops like shadows fled to their abodes.

Then Enitharmon saw her sons & daughters rise around;
Like pearly clouds they meet together in the crystal house;
And Los, possessor of the moon, joy'd in the peaceful night,
Thus speaking, while his num'rous sons shook their bright fiery wings:

"Again the night is come
That strong Urthona takes his rest;
And Urizen, unloos'd from chains,
Glows like a meteor in the distant north.
Stretch forth your hands and strike the elemental strings!
Awake the thunders of the deep!

"The shrill winds wake,
Till all the sons of Urizen look out and envy Los.
Sieze all the spirits of life, and bind
Their warbling joys to our loud strings!
Bind all the nourishing sweets of earth
To give us bliss, that we may drink the sparkling wine of Los!
And let us laugh at war,
Despising toil and care,
Because the days and nights of joy in lucky hours renew.

"Arise, O Orc, from thy deep den!
First born of Enitharmon, rise!
And we will crown thy head with garlands of the ruddy vine;
For now thou art bound,
And I may see thee in the hour of bliss, my eldest born."

The horrent Demon rose surrounded with red stars of fire
Whirling about in furious circles round the immortal fiend.

Then Enitharmon down descended into his red light,
And thus her voice rose to her children: the distant heavens reply:

"Now comes the night of Enitharmon's joy!
Who shall I call? Who shall I send,
That Woman, lovely Woman, may have dominion?
Arise, O Rintrah, thee I call! & Palamabron, thee!
Go! tell the Human race that Woman's love is Sin;
That an Eternal life awaits the worms of sixty winters
In an allegorical abode where existence hath never come.
Forbid all Joy, & from her childhood shall the little female
Spread nets in every secret path.

"My weary eyelids draw towards the evening; my bliss is yet but new.

"Arise, O Rintrah, eldest born, second to none but Orc!
O lion Rintrah, raise thy fury from thy forests black!
Bring Palamabron, horned priest, skipping upon the mountains,

And silent Elynittria, the silver bowed queen.
Rintrah, where hast thou hid thy bride?
Weeps she in desart shades?
Alas! my Rintrah, bring the lovely jealous Ocalythron.

"Arise, my son! bring all thy brethren, O thou king of fire!
Prince of the sun! I see thee with thy innumerable race,
Thick as the summer stars;
But each, ramping, his golden mane shakes,
And thine eyes rejoice because of strength, O Rintrah, furious king!"

Enitharmon slept
Eighteen hundred years. Man was a Dream!
The night of Nature and their harps unstrung!
She slept in middle of her nightly song
Eighteen hundred years, a female dream.

Shadows of men in fleeting bands upon the winds
Divide the heavens of Europe
Till Albion's Angel, smitten with his own plagues, fled with his bands.
The cloud bears hard on Albion's shore,
Fill'd with immortal demons of futurity:
In council gather the smitten Angels of Albion;
The cloud bears hard upon the council house, down rushing
On the heads of Albion's Angels.

One hour they lay buried beneath the ruins of that hall;
But as the stars rise from the salt lake, they arise in pain,
In troubled mists, o'erclouded by the terrors of strugling times.

In thoughts perturb'd they rose from the bright ruins, silent following
The fiery King, who sought his ancient temple, serpent-form'd,
That stretches out its shady length along the Island white.
Round him roll'd his clouds of war; silent the Angel went
Along the infinite shores of Thames to golden Verulam.
There stand the venerable porches that high-towering rear
Their oak-surrounded pillars, form'd of massy stones, uncut
With tool, stones precious, such eternal in the heavens,
Of colours twelve, few known on earth, give light in the opake,
Plac'd in the order of the stars, when the five senses whelm'd
In deluge o'er the earth-born man; then turn'd the fluxile eyes
Into two stationary orbs, concentrating all things:

The ever-varying spiral ascents to the heavens of heavens
Were bended downward, and the nostrils' golden gates shut,
Turn'd outward, barr'd and petrify'd against the infinite.

Thought chang'd the infinite to a serpent, that which pitieth
To a devouring flame; and man fled from its face and hid
In forests of night: then all the eternal forests were divided
Into earths rolling in circles of space, that like an ocean rush'd
And overwhelmed all except this finite wall of flesh.
Then was the serpent temple form'd, image of infinite
Shut up in finite revolutions, and man became an Angel,
Heaven a mighty circle turning, God a tyrant crown'd.

Now arriv'd the ancient Guardian at the southern porch
That planted thick with trees of blackest leaf & in a vale
Obscure enclos'd the Stone of Night; oblique it stood, o'erhung
With purple flowers and berries red, image of that sweet south
Once open to the heavens, and elevated on the human neck,
Now overgrown with hair and cover'd with a stony roof.
Downward 'tis sunk beneath th' attractive north, that round the feet,
A raging whirlpool, draws the dizzy enquirer to his grave.

    Albion's Angel rose upon the Stone of Night.
    He saw Urizen on the Atlantic;
    And his brazen Book
    That Kings & Priests had copied on Earth,
    Expanded from North to South.

And the clouds & fires pale roll'd round in the night of Enitharmon,
Round Albion's cliffs & London's walls: still Enitharmon slept.
Rolling volumes of grey mist involve Churches, Palaces, Towers;
For Urizen unclasp'd his Book, feeding his soul with pity.
The youth of England, hid in gloom, curse the pain'd heavens, compell'd
Into the deadly night to see the form of Albion's Angel.
Their parents brought them forth, & aged ignorance preaches, canting,
On a vast rock, perciev'd by those senses that are clos'd from thought:
Bleak, dark, abrupt it stands & overshadows London city.
They saw his boney feet on the rock, the flesh consum'd in flames;
They saw the Serpent temple lifted above, shadowing the Island white;
They heard the voice of Albion's Angel howling in flames of Orc,
Seeking the trump of the last doom.

Above the rest the howl was heard from Westminster louder & louder:
The Guardian of the secret codes forsook his ancient mansion,
Driven out by the flames of Orc; his furr'd robes & false locks
Adhered and grew one with his flesh, and nerves & veins shot thro' them.
With dismal torment sick, hanging upon the wind, he fled
Groveling along Great George Street thro' the Park gate: all the soldiers
Fled from his sight: he drag'd his torments to the wilderness.

Thus was the howl thro' Europe!
For Orc rejoic'd to hear the howling shadows; .
But Palamabron shot his lightnings, trenching down his wide back;
And Rintrah hung with all his legions in the nether deep.

Enitharmon laugh'd in her sleep to see (O woman's triumph!)
Every house a den, every man bound: the shadows are fill'd
With spectres, and the windows wove over with curses of iron:
Over the doors "Thou shalt not," & over the chimneys "Fear" is written:
With bands of iron round their necks fasten'd into the walls
The citizens, in leaden gyves the inhabitants of suburbs
Walk heavy; soft and bent are the bones of villagers.

Between the clouds of Urizen the flames of Orc roll heavy
Around the limbs of Albion's Guardian, his flesh consuming:
Howlings & hissings, shrieks & groans, & voices of despair
Arise around him in the cloudy heavens of Albion. Furious,
The red limb'd Angel siez'd in horror and torment
The Trump of the last doom; but he could not blow the iron tube!
Thrice he assay'd presumptuous to awake the dead to Judgment.

A mighty Spirit leap'd from the land of Albion,
Nam'd Newton: he siez'd the trump & blow'd the enormous blast!
Yellow as leaves of Autumn, the myriads of Angelic hosts
Fell thro' the wintry skies seeking their graves,
Rattling their hollow bones in howling and lamentation.

Then Enitharmon woke, nor knew that she had slept;
And eighteen hundred years were fled
As if they had not been.
She call'd her sons & daughters
To the sports of night
Within her crystal house,
And thus her song proceeds:

"Arise, Ethinthus! tho' the earth-worm call,
Let him call in vain,
Till the night of holy shadows
And human solitude is past!

"Ethinthus, queen of waters, how thou shinest in the sky!
My daughter, how do I rejoice! for thy children flock around
Like the gay fishes on the wave, when the cold moon drinks the dew.
Ethinthus! thou art sweet as comforts to my fainting soul,
For now thy waters warble round the feet of Enitharmon.

"Manathu-Varcyon! I behold thee flaming in my halls,
Light of thy mother's soul! I see thy lovely eagles round;
Thy golden wings are my delight, & thy flames of soft delusion.

"Where is my lureing bird of Eden? Leutha, silent love!
Leutha, the many colour'd bow delights upon thy wings:
Soft soul of flowers, Leutha!
Sweet smiling pestilence! I see thy blessing light;
Thy daughters, many changing,
Revolve like sweet perfumes ascending, O Leutha, silken queen!

"Where is the youthful Antamon, prince of the pearly dew?
O Antamon! why wilt thou leave thy mother Enitharmon?
Alone I see thee, crystal form,
Floating upon the bosom'd air
With lineaments of gratified desire.
My Antamon, the seven churches of Leutha seek thy love.

"I hear the soft Oothoon in Enitharmon's tents;
Why wilt thou give up woman's secrecy, my melancholy child?
Between two moments bliss is ripe.
O Theotormon! robb'd of joy, I see thy salt tears flow
Down the steps of my crystal house.

"Sotha & Thiralatha! secret dwellers of dreamful caves,
Arise and please the horrent fiend with your melodious songs;
Still all your thunders, golden-hoof'd, & bind your horses black.
Orc! smile upon my children!
Smile, son of my afflictions.
Arise, O Orc, and give our mountains joy of thy red light!"

She ceas'd; for All were forth at sport beneath the solemn moon
Waking the stars of Urizen with their immortal songs,
That nature felt thro' all her pores the enormous revelry
Till morning oped the eastern gate;
Then every one fled to his station, & Enitharmon wept.

But terrible Orc, when he beheld the morning in the east,
Shot from the heights of Enitharmon,
And in the vineyards of red France appear'd the light of his fury.

The sun glow'd fiery red!
The furious terrors flew around
On golden chariots raging with red wheels dropping with blood!
The Lions lash their wrathful tails!
The Tigers couch upon the prey & suck the ruddy tide,
And Enitharmon groans & cries in anguish and dismay.
Then Los arose: his head he rear'd in snaky thunders clad;
And with a cry that shook all nature to the utmost pole,
Call'd all his sons to the strife of blood.

THE FIRST BOOK OF URIZEN

Etched 1794

PRELUDIUM TO THE FIRST BOOK OF URIZEN

OF the primeval Priest's assum'd power,
When Eternals spurn'd back his religion
And gave him a place in the north,
Obscure, shadowy, void, solitary.

Eternals! I hear your call gladly.
Dictate swift winged words & fear not
To unfold your dark visions of torment.

CHAPTER I

1. Lo, a shadow of horror is risen
In Eternity! Unknown, unprolific,
Self-clos'd, all-repelling; what Demon
Hath form'd this abominable void,
This soul-shudd'ring vacuum? Some said

"It is Urizen." But unknown, abstracted,
Brooding, secret, the dark power hid.

2. Times on times he divided & measur'd
Space by space in his ninefold darkness,
Unseen, unknown; changes appear'd
Like desolate mountains, rifted furious
By the black winds of perturbation.

3. For he strove in battles dire,
In unseen conflictions with shapes
Bred from his forsaken wilderness
Of beast, bird, fish, serpent & element,
Combustion, blast, vapour and cloud.

4. Dark, revolving in silent activity:
Unseen in tormenting passions:
An activity unknown and horrible,
A self-contemplating shadow,
In enormous labours occupied.

5. But Eternals beheld his vast forests;
Age on ages he lay, clos'd, unknown,
Brooding shut in the deep; all avoid
The petrific, abominable chaos.

6. His cold horrors silent, dark Urizen
Prepar'd; his ten thousands of thunders,
Rang'd in gloom'd array, stretch out across
The dread world; & the rolling of wheels,
As of swelling seas, sound in his clouds,
In his hills of stor'd snows, in his mountains
Of hail & ice; voices of terror
Are heard, like thunders of autumn
When the cloud blazes over the harvests.

CHAPTER II

1. Earth was not: nor globes of attraction;
The will of the Immortal expanded
Or contracted his all flexible senses;
Death was not, but eternal life sprung.

2. The sound of a trumpet the heavens
Awoke, & vast clouds of blood roll'd
Round the dim rocks of Urizen, so nam'd
That solitary one in Immensity.

3. Shrill the trumpet: & myriads of Eternity
Muster around the bleak desarts,
Now fill'd with clouds, darkness, & waters,
That roll'd perplex'd, lab'ring; & utter'd
Words articulate bursting in thunders
That roll'd on the tops of his mountains:

4. "From the depths of dark solitude, From
The eternal abode in my holiness,
Hidden, set apart, in my stern counsels,
Reserv'd for the days of futurity,
I have sought for a joy without pain,
For a solid without fluctuation.
Why will you die, O Eternals?
Why live in unquenchable burnings?

5. "First I fought with the fire, consum'd
Inwards into a deep world within:
A void immense, wild, dark & deep,
Where nothing was: Nature's wide womb;
And self balanc'd, stretch'd o'er the void,
I alone, even I! the winds merciless
Bound; but condensing in torrents
They fall & fall; strong I repell'd
The vast waves, & arose on the waters
A wide world of solid obstruction.

6. "Here alone I, in books form'd of metals,
Have written the secrets of wisdom,
The secrets of dark contemplation,
By fightings and conflicts dire
With terrible monsters Sin-bred
Which the bosoms of all inhabit,
Seven deadly Sins of the soul.

7. "Lo! I unfold my darkness, and on
This rock place with strong hand the Book
Of eternal brass, written in my solitude:

8. "Laws of peace, of love, of unity,
Of pity, compassion, forgiveness;
Let each chuse one habitation,
His ancient infinite mansion,
One command, one joy, one desire,
One curse, one weight, one measure,
One King, one God, one Law."

CHAPTER III

1. The voice ended: they saw his pale visage
Emerge from the darkness, his hand
On the rock of eternity unclasping
The Book of brass. Rage seiz'd the strong,

2. Rage, fury, intense indignation,
In cataracts of fire, blood, & gall,
In whirlwinds of sulphurous smoke,
And enormous forms of energy,
All the seven deadly sins of the soul
In living creations appear'd,
In the flames of eternal fury.

3. Sund'ring, dark'ning, thund'ring,
Rent away with a terrible crash,
Eternity roll'd wide apart,
Wide asunder rolling;
Mountainous all around
Departing, departing, departing,
Leaving ruinous fragments of life
Hanging, frowning cliffs & all between,
An ocean of voidness unfathomable.

4. The roaring fires ran o'er the heav'ns
In whirlwinds & cataracts of blood,
And o'er the dark desarts of Urizen
Fires pour thro' the void on all sides
On Urizen's self-begotten armies.

5. But no light from the fires: all was darkness
In the flames of Eternal fury.

6. In fierce anguish & quenchless flames
To the desarts and rocks he ran raging
To hide; but he could not: combining,
He dug mountains & hills in vast strength,
He piled them in incessant labour,
In howlings & pangs & fierce madness,
Long periods in burning fires labouring
Till hoary, and age-broke, and aged,
In despair and the shadows of death.

7. And a roof vast, petrific around
On all sides he fram'd, like a womb,
Where thousands of rivers in veins
Of blood pour down the mountains to cool
The eternal fires, beating without
From Eternals; & like a black globe,
View'd by sons of Eternity standing
On the shore of the infinite ocean,
Like a human heart, strugling & beating,
The vast world of Urizen appear'd.

8. And Los, round the dark globe of Urizen,
Kept watch for Eternals to confine
The obscure separation alone;
For Eternity stood wide apart,
As the stars are apart from the earth.

9. Los wept, howling around the dark Demon,
And cursing his lot; for in anguish
Urizen was rent from his side,
And a fathomless void for his feet,
And intense fires for his dwelling.

10. But Urizen laid in a stony sleep,
Unorganiz'd, rent from Eternity.

11. The Eternals said: "What is this? Death.
Urizen is a clod of clay."

12. Los howl'd in a dismal stupor,
Groaning, gnashing, groaning,
Till the wrenching apart was healed.

13. But the wrenching of Urizen heal'd not.
Cold, featureless, flesh or clay,
Rifted with direful changes,
He lay in a dreamless night,

14. Till Los rouz'd his fires, affrighted
At the formless, unmeasurable death.

CHAPTER IV [a]

1. Los, smitten with astonishment,
Frighten'd at the hurtling bones

2. And at the surging, sulphureous,
Perturbed Immortal, mad raging

3. In whirlwinds & pitch & nitre
Round the furious limbs of Los.

4. And Los formed nets & gins
And threw the nets round about.

5. He watch'd in shudd'ring fear
The dark changes, & bound every change
With rivets of iron & brass.

6. And these were the changes of Urizen:

CHAPTER IV [b]

1. Ages on ages roll'd over him;
In stony sleep ages roll'd over him,
Like a dark waste stretching, chang'able,
By earthquakes riv'n, belching sullen fires:
On ages roll'd ages in ghastly
Sick torment; around him in whirlwinds
Of darkness the eternal Prophet howl'd,
Beating still on his rivets of iron,
Pouring sodor of iron; dividing
The horrible night into watches.

2. And Urizen (so his eternal name)
His prolific delight obscur'd more & more
In dark secresy, hiding in surgeing
Sulphureous fluid his phantasies.

The Eternal Prophet heav'd the dark bellows,
And turn'd restless the tongs, and the hammer
Incessant beat, forging chains new & new,
Numb'ring with links hours, days & years.

3. The Eternal mind, bounded, began to roll
Eddies of wrath ceaseless round & round,
And the sulphureous foam, surgeing thick,
Settled, a lake, bright & shining clear,
White as the snow on the mountains cold.

4. Forgetfulness, dumbness, necessity,
In chains of the mind locked up,
Like fetters of ice shrinking together,
Disorganiz'd, rent from Eternity,
Los beat on his fetters of iron,
And heated his furnaces, & pour'd
Iron sodor and sodor of brass.

5. Restless turn'd the Immortal inchain'd,
Heaving dolorous, anguish'd unbearable;
Till a roof, shaggy wild, inclos'd
In an orb his fountain of thought.

6. In a horrible, dreamful slumber,
Like the linked infernal chain,
A vast Spine writh'd in torment
Upon the winds, shooting pain'd
Ribs, like a bending cavern;
And bones of solidness froze
Over all his nerves of joy.
And a first Age passed over,
And a state of dismal woe.

7. From the caverns of his jointed Spine
Down sunk with fright a red
Round Globe, hot burning, deep,
Deep down into the Abyss;
Panting, Conglobing, Trembling,
Shooting out ten thousand branches
Around his solid bones.
And a second Age passed over,
And a state of dismal woe.

8. In harrowing fear rolling round,
His nervous brain shot branches
Round the branches of his heart
On high into two little orbs,
And fixed in two little caves,
Hiding carefully from the wind,
His Eyes beheld the deep.
And a third Age passed over,
And a state of dismal woe.

9. The pangs of hope began.
In heavy pain, striving, struggling,
Two Ears in close volutions
From beneath his orbs of vision
Shot spiring out and petrified
As they grew. And a fourth Age passed,
And a state of dismal woe.

10. In ghastly torment sick,
Hanging upon the wind,
Two Nostrils bend down to the deep.
And a fifth Age passed over,
And a state of dismal woe.

11. In ghastly torment sick,
Within his ribs bloated round,
A craving Hungry Cavern;
Thence arose his channel'd Throat,
And, like a red flame, a Tongue
Of thirst & of hunger appear'd.
And a sixth Age passed over,
And a state of dismal woe.

12. Enraged & stifled with torment,
He threw his right Arm to the north,
His left Arm to the south
Shooting out in anguish deep,
And his feet stamp'd the nether Abyss
In trembling & howling & dismay.
And a seventh Age passed over,
And a state of dismal woe.

CHAPTER V

1. In terrors Los shrunk from his task:
His great hammer fell from his hand.
His fires beheld, and sickening
Hid their strong limbs in smoke;
For with noises, ruinous, loud,
With hurtlings & clashings & groans,
The Immortal endur'd his chains,
Tho' bound in a deadly sleep.

2. All the myriads of Eternity,
All the wisdom & joy of life
Roll like a sea around him,
Except what his little orbs
Of sight by degrees unfold.

3. And now his eternal life
Like a dream was obliterated.

4. Shudd'ring the Eternal Prophet smote
With a stroke from his north to south region.
The bellows & hammer are silent now;
A nerveless silence his prophetic voice
Siez'd; a cold solitude & dark void
The Eternal Prophet & Urizen clos'd.

5. Ages on ages roll'd over them,
Cut off from life & light, frozen
Into horrible forms of deformity.
Los suffer'd his fires to decay;
Then he look'd back with anxious desire,
But the space, undivided by existence,
Struck horror into his soul.

6. Los wept obscur'd with mourning,
His bosom earthquak'd with sighs;
He saw Urizen deadly black
In his chains bound, & Pity began,

7. In anguish dividing & dividing,
For pity divides the soul

In pangs, eternity on eternity,
Life in cataracts pour'd down his cliffs.
The void shrunk the lymph into Nerves
Wand'ring wide on the bosom of night
And left a round globe of blood
Trembling upon the void.
Thus the Eternal Prophet was divided
Before the death image of Urizen;
For in changeable clouds and darkness,
In a winterly night beneath,
The Abyss of Los stretch'd immense;
And now seen, now obscur'd, to the eyes
Of Eternals the visions remote
Of the dark seperation appear'd:
As glasses discover Worlds
In the endless Abyss of space,
So the expanding eyes of Immortals
Beheld the dark visions of Los
And the globe of life blood trembling.

8. The globe of life blood trembled
Branching out into roots,
Fibrous, writhing upon the winds,
Fibres of blood, milk and tears,
In pangs, eternity on eternity.
At length in tears & cries imbodied,
A female form, trembling and pale,
Waves before his deathy face.

9. All Eternity shudder'd at sight
Of the first female now separate,
Pale as a cloud of snow
Waving before the face of Los.

10. Wonder, awe, fear, astonishment
Petrify the eternal myriads
At the first female form now separate.
They call'd her Pity, and fled.

11. "Spread a Tent with strong curtains **around them**
Let cords & stakes bind in the Void,
That Eternals may no more behold them."

12. They began to weave curtains of darkness,
They erected large pillars round the Void,
With golden hooks fasten'd in the pillars;
With infinite labour the Eternals
A woof wove, and called it Science.

CHAPTER VI

1. But Los saw the Female & pitied;
He embrac'd her; she wept, she refus'd;
In perverse and cruel delight
She fled from his arms, yet he follow'd.

2. Eternity shudder'd when they saw
Man begetting his likeness
On his own divided image.

3. A time passed over: the Eternals
Began to erect the tent,
When Enitharmon, sick,
Felt a Worm within her Womb.

4. Yet helpless it lay like a Worm
In the trembling womb
To be moulded into existence.

5. All day long the worm lay on her bosom;
All night within her womb
The worm lay till it grew to a serpent,
With dolorous hissings & poisons
Round Enitharmon's loins folding.

6. Coil'd within Enitharmon's womb
The serpent grew, casting its scales;
With sharp pangs the hissings began
To change to a grating cry:
Many sorrows and dismal throes,
Many forms of fish, bird & beast
Brought forth an Infant form
Where a worm was before.

7. The Eternals their tent finished
Alarm'd with these gloomy visions,
When Enitharmon groaning
Produc'd a man Child to the light.

8. A shriek ran thro' Eternity,
And a paralytic stroke,
At the birth of the Human shadow.

9. Delving earth in his resistless way,
Howling, the Child with fierce flames
Issu'd from Enitharmon.

10. The Eternals closed the tent;
They beat down the stakes, the cords
Stretch'd for a work of eternity.
No more Los beheld Eternity.

11. In his hands he siez'd the infant,
He bathed him in springs of sorrow,
He gave him to Enitharmon.

CHAPTER VII

1. They named the child Orc; he grew,
Fed with milk of Enitharmon.

2. Los awoke her. O sorrow & pain!
A tight'ning girdle grew
Around his bosom. In sobbings
He burst the girdle in twain;
But still another girdle
Oppress'd his bosom. In sobbings
Again he burst it. Again
Another girdle succeeds.
The girdle was form'd by day,
By night was burst in twain.

3. These falling down on the rock
Into an iron Chain
In each other link by link lock'd.

4. They took Orc to the top of a mountain.
O how Enitharmon wept!
They chain'd his young limbs to the rock
With the Chain of Jealousy
Beneath Urizen's deathful shadow.

5. The dead heard the voice of the child
And began to awake from sleep;
All things heard the voice of the child
And began to awake to life.

6. And Urizen, craving with hunger,
Stung with the odours of Nature,
Explor'd his dens around.

7. He form'd a line & a plummet
To divide the Abyss beneath;
He form'd a dividing rule;

8. He formed scales to weigh,
He formed massy weights;
He formed a brazen quadrant;
He formed golden compasses,
And began to explore the Abyss;
And he planted a garden of fruits.

9. But Los encircled Enitharmon
With fires of Prophecy
From the sight of Urizen & Orc.

10. And she bore an enormous race.

CHAPTER VIII

1. Urizen explor'd his dens,
Mountain, moor & wilderness,
With a globe of fire lighting his journey,
A fearful journey, annoy'd
By cruel enormities, forms
Of life on his forsaken mountains.

2. And his world teemed vast enormities,
Fright'ning, faithless, fawning
Portions of life, similitudes
Of a foot, or a hand, or a head,
Or a heart, or an eye; they swam mischievous.
Dread terrors, delighting in blood.

3. Most Urizen sicken'd to see
His eternal creations appear,
Sons & daughters of sorrow on mountains
Weeping, wailing. First Thiriel appear'd,
Astonish'd at his own existence,
Like a man from a cloud born; & Utha,
From the waters emerging, laments;
Grodna rent the deep earth, howling
Amaz'd; his heavens immense cracks
Like the ground parch'd with heat, then Fuzon
Flam'd out, first begotten, last born;
All his Eternal sons in like manner;
His daughters from green herbs & cattle,
From monsters & worms of the pit.

4. He in darkness clos'd view'd all his race,
And his soul sicken'd! he curs'd
Both sons & daughters; for he saw
That no flesh nor spirit could keep
His iron laws one moment.

5. For he saw that life liv'd upon death:
The Ox in the slaughter house moans,
The Dog at the wintry door;
And he wept & he called it Pity,
And his tears flowed down on the winds.

6. Cold he wander'd on high, over their cities
In weeping & pain & woe;
And wherever he wander'd, in sorrows
Upon the aged heavens,
A cold shadow follow'd behind him
Like a spider's web, moist, cold & dim,
Drawing out from his sorrowing soul,
The dungeon-like heaven dividing,
Where ever the footsteps of Urizen
Walked over the cities in sorrow;

7. Till a Web, a dark & cold, throughout all
The tormented element stretch'd
From the sorrows of Urizen's soul.
And the Web is a Female in embrio.
None could break the Web, no wings of fire,

8. So twisted the cords, & so knotted
The meshes, twisted like to the human **brain**.

9. And all call'd it The Net of Religion.

CHAPTER IX

1. Then the Inhabitants of those Cities
Felt their Nerves change into Marrow,
And hardening Bones began
In swift diseases and torments,
In throbbings & shootings & grindings
Thro' all the coasts; till weaken'd
The Senses inward rush'd, shrinking
Beneath the dark net of infection;

2. Till the shrunken eyes, clouded over,
Discern'd not the woven hipocrisy;
But the streaky slime in their heavens,
Brought together by narrowing perceptions,
Appear'd transparent air; for their eyes
Grew small like the eyes of a man,
And in reptile forms shrinking together,
Of seven feet stature they remain'd.

3. Six days they shrunk up from existence,
And on the seventh day they rested,
And they bless'd the seventh day, in sick hope,
And forgot their eternal life.

4. And their thirty cities divided
In form of a human heart.
No more could they rise at will
In the infinite void, but bound down
To earth by their narrowing perceptions
They lived a period of years;
Then left a noisom body
To the jaws of devouring darkness.

5. And their children wept, & built
Tombs in the desolate places,
And form'd laws of prudence, and call'd **them**
The eternal laws of God.

6. And the thirty cities remain'd,
Surrounded by salt floods, now call'd
Africa: its name was then Egypt.

7. The remaining sons of Urizen
Beheld their brethren shrink together
Beneath the Net of Urizen.
Perswasion was in vain;
For the ears of the inhabitants
Were wither'd & deafen'd & cold,
And their eyes could not discern
Their brethren of other cities.

8. So Fuzon call'd all together
The remaining children of Urizen,
And they left the pendulous earth.
They called it Egypt, & left it.

9. And the salt Ocean rolled englob'd.

THE BOOK OF AHANIA

Etched 1795

CHAPTER I

1. F U Z O N on a chariot iron-wing'd
On spiked flames rose; his hot visage
Flam'd furious; sparkles his hair & beard
Shot down his wide bosom and shoulders.
On clouds of smoke rages his chariot
And his right hand burns red in its cloud
Moulding into a vast Globe his wrath,
As the thunder-stone is moulded.
Son of Urizen's silent burnings:

2. "Shall we worship this Demon of smoke,"
Said Fuzon, "this abstract non-entity,
This cloudy God seated on waters,
Now seen, now obscur'd, King of sorrow?"

3. So he spoke in a fiery flame,
On Urizen frowning indignant,
The Globe of wrath shaking on high;
Roaring with fury he threw
The howling Globe; burning it flew
Length'ning into a hungry beam. Swiftly

4. Oppos'd to the exulting flam'd beam,
The broad Disk of Urizen upheav'd
Across the Void many a mile.

5. It was forg'd in mills where the winter
Beats incessant: ten winters the disk
Unremitting endur'd the cold hammer.

6. But the strong arm that sent it remember'd
The sounding beam: laughing, it tore through
That beaten mass, keeping its direction,
The cold loins of Urizen dividing.

7. Dire shriek's his invisible Lust;
Deep groan'd Urizen! stretching his awful hand,
Ahania (so name his parted soul)
He siez'd on his mountains of Jealousy.
He groan'd anguish'd, & called her Sin,
Kissing her and weeping over her;
Then hid her in darkness, in silence,
Jealous, tho' she was invisible.

8. She fell down a faint shadow wand'ring
In chaos and circling dark Urizen,
As the moon anguish'd circles the earth,
Hopeless! abhorr'd! a death-shadow,
Unseen, unbodied, unknown,
The mother of Pestilence.

9. But the fiery beam of Fuzon
Was a pillar of fire to Egypt
Five hundred years wand'ring on earth,
Till Los siez'd it and beat in a mass
With the body of the sun.

CHAPTER II

1. But the forehead of Urizen gathering,
And his eyes pale with anguish, his lips
Blue & changing, in tears and bitter
Contrition he prepar'd his Bow,

2. Form'd of Ribs, that in his dark solitude,
When obscur'd in his forests, fell monsters
Arose. For his dire Contemplations
Rush'd down like floods from his mountains,
In torrents of mud settling thick,
With Eggs of unnatural production:
Forthwith hatching, some howl'd on his hills,
Some in vales, some aloft flew in air.

3. Of these, an enormous dread Serpent,
Scaled and poisonous horned,
Approach'd Urizen, even to his knees,
As he sat on his dark rooted Oak.

4. With his horns he push'd furious:
Great the conflict & great the jealousy
In cold poisons, but Urizen smote him.

5. First he poison'd the rocks with his blood,
Then polish'd his ribs, and his sinews
Dried, laid them apart till winter;
Then a Bow black prepar'd: on this Bow
A poisoned rock plac'd in silence.
He utter'd these words to the Bow:

6. "O Bow of the clouds of secresy!
O nerve of that lust-form'd monster!
Send this rock swift, invisible thro'
The black clouds on the bosom of Fuzon."

7. So saying, In torment of his wounds
He bent the enormous ribs slowly,
A circle of darkness! then fixed
The sinew in its rest; then the Rock,
Poisonous source, plac'd with art, lifting difficult
Its weighty bulk; silent the rock lay,

8. While Fuzon, his tygers unloosing,
Thought Urizen slain by his wrath.
"I am God!" said he, "eldest of things."

9. Sudden sings the rock; swift & invisible
On Fuzon flew, enter'd his bosom;
His beautiful visage, his tresses
That gave light to the mornings of heaven,
Were smitten with darkness, deform'd
And outstretch'd on the edge of the forest.

10. But the Rock fell upon the Earth,
Mount Sinai in Arabia.

CHAPTER III

1. The Globe shook, and Urizen seated
On black clouds his sore wound anointed;
The ointment flow'd down on the void
Mix'd with blood—here the snake gets her poison.

2. With difficulty & great pain Urizen
Lifted on high the dead corse:
On his shoulders he bore it to where
A Tree hung over the Immensity.

3. For when Urizen shrunk away
From Eternals, he sat on a rock
Barren: a rock which himself
From redounding fancies had petrified.
Many tears fell on the rock,
Many sparks of vegetation.
Soon shot the pained root
Of Mystery under his heel:
It grew a thick tree: he wrote
In silence his book of iron,
Till the horrid plant bending its boughs
Grew to roots when it felt the earth,
And again sprung to many a tree.

4. Amaz'd started Urizen when
He beheld himself compassed round
And high roofed over with trees.

He arose, but the stems stood so thick
He with difficulty and great pain
Brought his Books, all but the Book
Of iron, from the dismal shade.

5. The Tree still grows over the Void
Enrooting itself all around,
An endless labyrinth of woe!

6. The corse of his first begotten
On the accursed Tree of Mystery,
On the topmost stem of this Tree,
Urizen nail'd Fuzon's corse.

CHAPTER IV

1. Forth flew the arrows of pestilence
Round the pale living Corse on the tree.

2. For in Urizen's slumbers of abstraction
In the infinite ages of Eternity,
When his Nerves of Joy melted & flow'd,
A white Lake on the dark blue air
In perturb'd pain and dismal torment
Now stretching out, now swift conglobing,

3. Effluvia vapor'd above
In noxious clouds; these hover'd thick
Over the disorganiz'd Immortal,
Till petrific pain scurf'd o'er the Lakes
As the bones of man, solid & dark.

4. The clouds of disease hover'd wide
Around the Immortal in torment,
Perching around the hurtling bones,
Disease on disease, shape on shape
Winged screaming in blood & torment.

5. The Eternal Prophet beat on his anvils;
Enrag'd in the desolate darkness
He forg'd nets of iron around
And Los threw them around the bones.

6. The shapes screaming flutter'd vain:
Some combin'd into muscles & glands,
Some organs for craving and lust;
Most remain'd on the tormented void,
Urizen's army of horrors.

7. Round the pale living Corse on the Tree
Forty years flew the arrows of pestilence.

8. Wailing and terror and woe
Ran thro' all his dismal world;
Forty years all his sons & daughters
Felt their skulls harden; then Asia
Arose in the pendulous deep.

9. They reptilize upon the Earth.

10. Fuzon groan'd on the Tree.

CHAPTER V

1. The lamenting voice of Ahania
Weeping upon the void!
And round the Tree of Fuzon,
Distant in solitary night,
Her voice was heard, but no form
Had she; but her tears from clouds
Eternal fell round the Tree.

2. And the voice cried: "Ah, Urizen! Love!
Flower of morning! I weep on the verge
Of Non-entity; how wide the Abyss
Between Ahania and thee!

3. "I lie on the verge of the deep;
I see thy dark clouds ascend;
I see thy black forests and floods,
A horrible waste to my eyes!

4. "Weeping I walk over rocks,
Over dens & thro' valleys of death.
Why didst thou despise Ahania
To cast me from thy bright presence
Into the World of Loneness?

5. "I cannot touch his hand,
Nor weep on his knees, nor hear
His voice & bow, nor see his eyes
And joy, nor hear his footsteps and
My heart leap at the lovely sound!
I cannot kiss the place
Whereon his bright feet have trod,
But I wander on the rocks
With hard necessity.

6. "Where is my golden palace?
Where my ivory bed?
Where the joy of my morning hour?
Where the sons of eternity singing

7. "To awake bright Urizen, my king,
To arise to the mountain sport,
To the bliss of eternal valleys;

8. "To awake my king in the morn,
To embrace Ahania's joy
On the bredth of his open bosom?
From my soft cloud of dew to fall
In showers of life on his harvests,

9. "When he gave my happy soul
To the sons of eternal joy,
When he took the daughters of life
Into my chambers of love,

10. "When I found babes of bliss on my beds
And bosoms of milk in my chambers
Fill'd with eternal seed.
O eternal births sung round Ahania
In interchange sweet of their joys!

11. "Swell'd with ripeness & fat with fatness,
Bursting on winds, my odors,
My ripe figs and rich pomegranates
In infant joy at thy feet,
O Urizen, sported and sang.

12. "Then thou with thy lap full of seed,
With thy hand full of generous fire
Walked forth from the clouds of morning,
On the virgins of springing joy,
On the human soul to cast
The seed of eternal science.

13. "The sweat poured down thy temples;
To Ahania return'd in evening,
The moisture awoke to birth
My mothers-joys, sleeping in bliss.

14. "But now alone over rocks, mountains,
Cast out from thy lovely bosom,
Cruel jealousy! selfish fear!
Self-destroying, how can delight
Renew in these chains of darkness,
Where bones of beasts are strown
On the bleak and snowy mountains,
Where bones from the birth are buried
Before they see the light?"

THE BOOK OF LOS

Etched 1795

CHAPTER I

1. E N O, aged Mother,
Who the chariot of Leutha guides
Since the day of thunders in old time,

2. Sitting beneath the eternal Oak
Trembled and shook the steadfast Earth,
And thus her speech broke forth:

3. "O Times remote!
When Love & Joy were adoration,
And none impure were deem'd:
Not Eyeless Covet,

Nor Thin-lip'd Envy,
Nor Bristled Wrath,
Nor Curled Wantonness;

4. "But Covet was poured full,
Envy fed with fat of lambs,
Wrath with lion's gore,
Wantonness lull'd to sleep
With the virgin's lute
Or sated with her love;

5. "Till Covet broke his locks & bars
And slept with open doors;
Envy sung at the rich man's feast;
Wrath was follow'd up and down
By a little ewe lamb,
And Wantonness on his own true love
Begot a giant race."

6. RAGING furious, the flames of desire
Ran thro' heaven & earth, living flames
Intelligent, organiz'd, arm'd
With destruction & plagues. In the midst
The Eternal Prophet, bound in a chain,
Compell'd to watch Urizen's shadow,

7. Rag'd with curses & sparkles of fury:
Round the flames roll, as Los hurls his chains,
Mounting up from his fury, condens'd,
Rolling round & round, mounting on high
Into vacuum, into non-entity
Where nothing was; dashed wide apart,
His feet stamp the eternal fierce-raging
Rivers of wide flame; they roll round
And round on all sides, making their way
Into darkness and shadowy obscurity.

8. Wide apart stood the fires: Los remain'd
In the void between fire and fire:
In trembling and horror they beheld him;
They stood wide apart, driv'n by his hands
And his feet, which the nether abyss
Stamp'd in fury and hot indignation.

9. But no light from the fires! all was
Darkness round Los: heat was not; for bound up
Into fiery spheres from his fury,
The gigantic flames trembled and hid.

10. Coldness, darkness, obstruction, a Solid
Without fluctuation, hard as adamant,
Black as marble of Egypt, impenetrable,
Bound in the fierce raging Immortal;
And the separated fires froze in:
A vast solid without fluctuation
Round in his expanding clear senses.

CHAPTER II

1. The Immortal stood frozen amidst
The vast rock of eternity times
And times, a night of vast durance,
Impatient, stifled, stiffen'd, hard'ned;

2. Till impatience no longer could bear
The hard bondage: rent, rent, the vast solid,
With a crash from immense to immense,

3. Cracked across into numberless fragments.
The Prophetic wrath, strugling for vent,
Hurls apart, stamping furious to dust
And crumbling with bursting sobs, heaves
The black marble on high into fragments.

4. Hurl'd apart on all sides as a falling
Rock, the innumerable fragments away
Fell asunder; and horrible vacuum
Beneath him, & on all sides round,

5. Falling, falling, Los fell & fell,
Sunk precipitant, heavy, down, down,
Times on times, night on night, day on day—
Truth has bounds, Error none—falling, falling,
Years on years, and ages on ages
Still he fell thro' the void, still a void
Found for falling, day & night without end;
For tho' day or night was not, their spaces

Were measur'd by his incessant whirls
In the horrid vacuity bottomless.

6. The Immortal revolving, indignant,
First in wrath threw his limbs like the babe
New born into our world: wrath subsided,
And contemplative thoughts first arose;
Then aloft his head rear'd in the Abyss
And his downward-borne fall chang'd oblique

7. Many ages of groans, till there grew
Branchy forms organizing the Human
Into finite inflexible organs;

8. Till in process from falling he bore
Sidelong on the purple air, wafting
The weak breeze in efforts o'erwearied.

9. Incessant the falling Mind labour'd,
Organizing itself, till the Vacuum
Became element, pliant to rise
Or to fall or to swim or to fly,
With ease searching the dire vacuity.

CHAPTER III

1. The Lungs heave incessant, dull, and heavy;
For as yet were all other parts formless,
Shiv'ring, clinging around like a cloud,
Dim & glutinous as the white Polypus
Driv'n by waves & englob'd on the tide.

2. And the unformed part crav'd repose;
Sleep began; the Lungs heave on the wave:
Weary, overweigh'd, sinking beneath
In a stifling black fluid, he woke.

3. He arose on the waters; but soon
Heavy falling, his organs like roots
Shooting out from the seed, shot beneath,
And a vast world of waters around him
In furious torrents began.

4. Then he sunk, & around his spent **Lungs**
Began intricate pipes that drew in
The spawn of the waters, Outbranching
An immense Fibrous Form, stretching **out**
Thro' the bottoms of immensity raging.

5. He rose on the floods; then he smote
The wild deep with his terrible wrath,
Seperating the heavy and thin.

6. Down the heavy sunk, cleaving **around**
To the fragments of solid: up rose
The thin, flowing round the fierce fires
That glow'd furious in the expanse.

CHAPTER IV

1. Then Light first began: from the fires,
Beams, conducted by fluid so pure,
Flow'd around the Immense. Los beheld
Forthwith, writhing upon the dark **void**,
The Back bone of Urizen appear
Hurtling upon the wind
Like a serpent! like an iron **chain**
Whirling about in the Deep.

2. Upfolding his Fibres together
To a Form of impregnable strength.
Los, astonish'd and terrified, buiit
Furnaces; he formed an Anvil,
A Hammer of adamant: then began
The binding of Urizen day and night.

3. Circling round the dark Demon with **howlings**,
Dismay & sharp blightings, the Prophet
Of Eternity beat on his iron links.

4. And first from those infinite fires,
The light that flow'd down on the winds
He siez'd, beating incessant, condensing
The subtil particles in an Orb.

5. Roaring indignant, the bright sparks
Endur'd the vast Hammer; but unwearied
Los beat on the Anvil, till glorious
An immense Orb of fire he fram'd.

6. Oft he quench'd it beneath in the Deeps,
Then survey'd the all bright mass, Again
Siezing fires from the terrific Orbs,
He heated the round Globe, then beat,
While, roaring, his Furnaces endur'd
The chain'd Orb in their infinite wombs.

7. Nine ages completed their circles
When Los heated the glowing mass, casting
It down into the Deeps: the Deeps fled
Away in redounding smoke: the Sun
Stood self-balanc'd. And Los smil'd with joy.
He the vast Spine of Urizen siez'd,
And bound down to the glowing illusion.

8. But no light! for the Deep fled away
On all sides, and left an unform'd
Dark vacuity: here Urizen lay
In fierce torments on his glowing bed;

9. Till his Brain in a rock & his Heart
In a fleshy slough formed four rivers
Obscuring the immense Orb of fire
Flowing down into night: till a Form
Was completed, a Human Illusion
In darkness and deep clouds involv'd.

THE SONG OF LOS

Etched 1795

AFRICA

I WILL sing you a song of Los, the Eternal Prophet:
He sung it to four harps at the tables of Eternity.
In heart-formed Africa
Urizen faded! Ariston shudder'd!
And thus the Song began:

Adam stood in the garden of Eden
And Noah on the mountains of Ararat;
They saw Urizen give his laws to the Nations
By the hands of the children of Los.

Adam shudder'd! Noah faded! black grew the sunny African
When Rintrah gave Abstract Philosophy to Brama in the East.
(Night spoke to the Cloud:
"Lo these Human form'd spirits, in smiling hipocrisy, War
Against one another; so let them War on, slaves to the eternal Elements.")
Noah shrunk beneath the waters;
Abram fled in fires from Chaldea;
Moses beheld upon Mount Sinai forms of dark delusion.

To Trismegistus, Palamabron gave an abstract Law:
To Pythagoras, Socrates & Plato.

Times rolled on o'er all the sons of Har: time after time
Orc on Mount Atlas howl'd, chain'd down with the Chain of Jealousy;
Then Oothoon hover'd over Judah & Jerusalem,
And Jesus heard her voice (a man of sorrows) he reciev'd
A Gospel from wretched Theotormon.

The human race began to wither, for the healthy built
Secluded places, fearing the joys of Love,
And the diseased only propagated.
So Antamon call'd up Leutha from her valleys of delight
And to Mahomet a loose Bible gave.
But in the North, to Odin, Sotha gave a Code of War,
Because of Diralada, thinking to reclaim his joy.
   These were the Churches, Hospitals, Castles, Palaces,
Like nets & gins & traps to catch the joys of Eternity,
      And all the rest a desart;
Till, like a dream, Eternity was obliterated & erased.

Since that dread day when Har and Heva fled
Because their brethren & sisters liv'd in War & Lust;
And as they fled they shrunk
Into two narrow doleful forms
Creeping in reptile flesh upon
The bosom of the ground;
And all the vast of Nature shrunk
Before their shrunken eyes.

Thus the terrible race of Los & Enitharmon gave
Laws & Religions to the sons of Har, binding them more
And more to Earth, closing and restraining,
Till a Philosophy of Five Senses was complete.
Urizen wept & gave it into the hands of Newton & Locke.

Clouds roll heavy upon the Alps round Rousseau & Voltaire,
And on the mountains of Lebanon round the deceased Gods
Of Asia, & on the desarts of Africa round the Fallen Angels
The Guardian Prince of Albion burns in his nightly tent.

ASIA

THE Kings of Asia heard
The howl rise up from Europe,
And each ran out from his Web,
From his ancient woven Den;
For the darkness of Asia was startled
At the thick-flaming, thought-creating fires of Orc.

And the Kings of Asia stood
And cried in bitterness of soul:

"Shall not the King call for Famine from the heath,
Nor the Priest for Pestilence from the fen,
To restrain, to dismay, to thin
The inhabitants of mountain and plain,
In the day of full-feeding prosperity
And the night of delicious songs?

"Shall not the Councellor throw his curb
Of Poverty on the laborious,
To fix the price of labour,
To invent allegoric riches?

"And the privy admonishers of men
Call for fires in the City,
For heaps of smoking ruins
In the night of prosperity & wantonness?

"To turn man from his path,
To restrain the child from the womb,
To cut off the bread from the city,
That the remnant may learn to obey,

"That the pride of the heart may fail,
That the lust of the eyes may be quench'd,
That the delicate ear in its infancy
May be dull'd, and the nostrils clos'd up,
To teach mortal worms the path
That leads from the gates of the Grave?"

Urizen heard them cry,
And his shudd'ring, waving wings
Went enormous above the red flames,
Drawing clouds of despair thro' the heavens
Of Europe as he went.
And his Books of brass, iron & gold
Melted over the land as he flew,
Heavy-waving, howling, weeping.

And he stood over Judea,
And stay'd in his ancient place,
And stretch'd his clouds over Jerusalem;

For Adam, a mouldering skeleton,
Lay bleach'd on the garden of Eden;
And Noah, as white as snow,
On the mountains of Ararat.

Then the thunders of Urizen bellow'd aloud
From his woven darkness above.
   Orc, raging in European darkness,
Arose like a pillar of fire above the Alps,
Like a serpent of fiery flame!
            The sullen Earth
            Shrunk!

Forth from the dead dust, rattling bones to bones
Join; shaking convuls'd, the shiv'ring clay breathes,
And all flesh naked stands: Fathers and Friends,
Mothers & Infants, Kings & Warriors.

The Grave shrieks with delight & shakes
Her hollow womb & clasps the solid stem:
Her bosom swells with wild desire,
And milk & blood & glandous wine
In rivers rush & shout & dance,
On mountain, dale and plain.

The SONG of LOS is Ended.

Urizen Wept.

THE FOUR ZOAS

Written and Revised 1795-1804
Dated 1797

[*Title, first form*]

VALA

OR

THE DEATH AND JUDGEMENT

OF THE ANCIENT MAN

A DREAM OF NINE NIGHTS

[*Title, second form*]

THE FOUR ZOAS
THE TORMENTS OF LOVE & JEALOUSY IN

THE DEATH AND JUDGEMENT

OF ALBION THE ANCIENT MAN

Rest before Labour

῞Οτι οὐκ ἔστιν ἡμῖν ἡ πάλη πρὸς αἷμα καὶ σάρκα, ἀλλὰ πρὸς τὰς
ἀρχάς, πρὸς τὰς ἐξουσίας, πρὸς τοὺς κοσμοκράτορας τοῦ σκότους τοῦ
αἰῶνος τούτου, πρὸς τὰ πνευματικὰ τῆς πονηρίας ἐν τοῖς ἐπουρανίοις.
Ἐφεσ., 6 κεφ., 12.[1]

---

1 "For our contention is not with the blood and the flesh, but with dominion, with authority,
with the blind world-rulers of this life, with the spirit of evil in things heavenly." Ephes., 6
chap., 12.

VALA

NIGHT THE FIRST

THE Song of the Aged Mother which shook the heavens with wrath,
Hearing the march of long resounding, strong heroic Verse
Marshall'd in order for the day of Intellectual Battle.
The heavens quake, the earth was moved & shudder'd, & the mountains
With all their woods, the streams & valleys wail'd in dismal fear.

Four Mighty Ones are in every Man; a Perfect Unity   John xvii. c.,
Cannot Exist but from the Universal Brotherhood of Eden,   21, 22,
                                                          23, v
The Universal Man, To Whom be Glory Evermore.   John i c., 14 v
        Amen.   Καὶ ἐσκήνωσεν ἐν ἡμῖν.[1]
What are the Natures of those Living Creatures the Heav'nly Father only
Knoweth. No Individual knoweth, nor can know in all Eternity.[2]

Los was the fourth immortal starry one, & in the Earth
Of a bright Universe, Empery attended day & night,
Days & nights of revolving joy. Urthona was his name
In Eden; in the Auricular Nerves of Human Life,
Which is the Earth of Eden, he his Emanations propagated,
Fairies of Albion, afterwards Gods of the Heathen.
        Daughter of Beulah, Sing
His fall into Division & his Resurrection to Unity:
His fall into the Generation of decay & death, & his
Regeneration by the Resurrection from the dead.

Begin with Tharmas, Parent power, dark'ning in the West.

"Lost! Lost! Lost! are my Emanations! Enion, O Enion,
We are become a Victim to the Living. We hide in secret.
I have hidden Jerusalem in silent Contrition, O Pity Me.
I will build thee a Labyrinth also: O pity me. O Enion,
Why hast thou taken sweet Jerusalem from my inmost Soul?
Let her Lay secret in the soft recess of darkness & silence.
It is not Love I bear to Enitharmon. It is Pity.
She hath taken refuge in my bosom & I cannot cast her out.

---

1 "And he dwelt among us."
2 Blake's late additions and corrections in the MS., made in pencil, are printed throughout
in italic.

"The Men have receiv'd their death wounds & their Emanations are fled
To me for refuge & I cannot turn them out for Pity's sake."

Enion said: "Thy fear has made me tremble, thy terrors have surrounded
    me.
All Love is lost: Terror succeeds, & Hatred instead of Love,
And stern demands of Right & Duty instead of Liberty.
Once thou wast to Me the loveliest son of heaven—But now
Why art thou Terrible? and yet I love thee in thy terror till
I am almost Extinct & soon shall be a shadow in Oblivion,
Unless some way can be found that I may look upon thee & live.
Hide me some shadowy semblance, secret whisp'ring in my Ear,
In secret of soft wings, in mazes of delusive beauty.
I have look'd into the secret soul of him I lov'd,
And in the Dark recesses found Sin & cannot return."

Trembling & pale sat Tharmas, weeping in his clouds.

"Why wilt thou Examine every little fibre of my soul,
Spreading them out before the sun like stalks of flax to dry?
The infant joy is beautiful, but its anatomy
Horrible, Ghast & Deadly; nought shalt thou find in it
But Death, Despair & Everlasting brooding Melancholy.
Thou wilt go mad with horror if thou dost Examine thus
Every moment of my secret hours. Yea, I know
That I have sinn'd, & that my Emanations are become harlots.
I am already distracted at their deeds, & if I look
Upon them more, Despair will bring self-murder on my soul.
O Enion, thou art thyself a root growing in hell,
Tho' thus heavenly beautiful to draw me to destruction.
Sometimes I think thou art a flower expanding,
Sometimes I think thou art fruit, breaking from its bud
In dreadful dolor & pain; & I am like an atom,
A Nothing, left in darkness; yet I am an identity:
I wish & feel & weep & groan. Ah, terrible! terrible!"

In Eden, Females sleep the winter in soft silken veils
Woven by their own hands to hide them in the darksom **grave;**
But Males immortal live renew'd by female deaths; in soft
Delight they die, & they revive in spring with music & songs.
Enion said: "Farewell, I die. I hide from thy searching eyes."

So saying, From her bosom weaving soft in sinewy threads
A tabernacle *for Jerusalem,* she sat among the Rocks
Singing her lamentation. Tharmas groan'd among his Clouds
Weeping; then bending from his Clouds, he stoop'd his innocent head,
And stretching out his holy hand in the vast deep sublime,
Turn'd round the circle of Destiny with tears & bitter sighs
And said: "Return, O wanderer, when the day of Clouds is o'er."

So saying, he sunk down into the sea, a pale white corse.
In torment he sunk down & flow'd among her filmy Woof,
His spectre issuing from his feet in flames of fire.
In gnawing pain drawn out by her lov'd fingers, every nerve
She counted, every vein & lacteal, threading them among
Her woof of terror. Terrified & drinking tears of woe
Shudd'ring she wove nine days & nights, sleepless; her food was tears.
Wond'ring she saw her woof begin to animate, & not
As Garments woven subservient to her hands, but having a will
Of its own, perverse & wayward. Enion lov'd & wept.
Nine days she labour'd at her work, & nine dark sleepless nights;
But on the tenth trembling morn, the Circle of Destiny complete,
Round roll'd the sea, Englobing in a wat'ry Globe, self balanc'd.
A Frowning Continent appear'd where Enion in the desart,
Terrified in her own Creation, viewing her woven shadow,
Sat in a dread intoxication of Repentance & Contrition.
He spurn'd Enion with his foot; he sprang aloft in Clouds
Alighting in his drunken joy in a far distant Grove.

There is from Great Eternity a mild & pleasant rest
Nam'd Beulah, a soft Moony Universe, feminine, lovely,
Pure, mild & Gentle, given in mercy to those who sleep,
Eternally Created by the Lamb of God around,
On all sides, within & without the Universal Man.
The daughters of Beulah follow sleepers in all their dreams,
Creating spaces, lest they fall into Eternal Death.
The Circle of Destiny complete, they gave to it a space
And nam'd the space Ulro, & brooded over it in care & love.
They said: "The Spectre is in every man insane & most
Deform'd. Thro' the three heavens descending in fury & fire
We meet it with our songs & loving blandishments, & give
To it a form of vegetation. But this Spectre of Tharmas
Is Eternal Death. What shall we do? O God, pity & help!"
So spoke they, & clos'd the Gate of the Tongue in trembling fear.

"What have I done," said Enion, "accursed wretch! What deed?
Is this a deed of Love? I know what I have done. I know
Too late now to repent. Love is chang'd to deadly Hate,
A life is blotted out, & I alone remain, possess'd with Fears.
I see the shadow of the dead within my soul, wandering
In darkness & solitude, forming Seas of Doubt & rocks of Repentance.
Already are my Eyes reverted; all that I behold
Within my soul has lost its splendor, & a brooding Fear
Shadows me o'er & drives me outward to a world of woe."
So wail'd she, trembling before her own Created Phantasm
Who animating times on times by the force of her sweet song . . .
But standing on the Rocks, her woven shadow glowing bright,
She drew the Spectre forth from Tharmas in her shining loom
Of Vegetation, weeping in wayward infancy & sullen youth.

List'ning to her soft lamentations, soon his tongue began
To lisp out words, & soon, in masculine strength augmenting, he
Rear'd up a form of gold & stood upon the glittering rock
A shadowy human form winged, & in his depths
The dazzlings as of gems shone clear; rapturous in fury,
Glorying in his own eyes, Exalted in terrific Pride,
Searching for glory, wishing that the heavens had eyes to see,
And courting that the Earth would ope her Eyelids & behold
Such wondrous beauty, repining in the midst of all his glory
That nought but Enion could be found to praise, adore, & love.

Three days in self admiring raptures on the rocks he flam'd,
And three dark nights repin'd the solitude, but the third morn
Astonish'd he found Enion hidden in the darksom Cave.

She spoke: "What am I? wherefore was I put forth on these rocks
Among the Clouds to tremble in the wind in solitude?
Where is the voice that lately woke the desart? where the Face
That wept among the clouds, & where the voice that shall reply?
No other living thing is here. The Sea, the Earth, the Heaven,
And Enion, desolate; where art thou, Tharmas? O return."

Three days she wail'd & three dark nights, sitting among the Rocks
While the bright spectre hid himself among the vailing clouds.
Then sleep fell on her eye lids in a Chasm of the Valley.
The sixteenth morn the Spectre stood before her manifest.

The Spectre thus spoke: "Who art thou, Diminutive husk & shell
Broke from my bonds? I scorn my prison, I scorn & yet I love.
Art thou not my slave, & shalt thou dare
To smite me with thy tongue? beware lest I sting also thee.
If thou hast sinn'd & art polluted, know that I am pure
And unpolluted, & will bring to rigid strict account
All thy past deeds; hear what I tell thee! mark it well! remember!
This world is Thine in which thou dwellest; that within thy soul,
That dark & dismal infinite where Thought roams up & down,
Is Mine, & there thou goest when with one Sting of my tongue
Envenom'd thou roll'st inwards to the place *whence I emerg'd*."

She trembling answer'd: "Wherefore was I born, and what am I?
A sorrow & a fear, a living torment, & naked Victim.
I thought to weave a Covering for my Sins from wrath of Tharmas.

"Examining the sins of Tharmas I soon found my own.
O slay me not! thou art his wrath embodied in Deceit.
I thought Tharmas a sinner & I murder'd his Emanations,
His secret loves & Graces. Ah me wretched! What have I done?
For now I find that all those Emanations were my Children's souls,
And I have murder'd these with Cruelty above atonement.
Those that remain have fled from my cruelty into the desarts,
And thou, the delusive tempter to these deeds, sitt'st before me.
And art thou Tharmas? all thy soft delusive beauty cannot
Tempt me to murder my own soul & wipe my tears & smile
In this thy world, not mine: tho' dark I feel my world within.

The Spectre said: "Thou sinful Woman, was it thy desire
That I should hide thee with my power & delight thee with my beauty?
And now thou dark'nest in my presence; never from my sight
Shalt thou depart to weep in secret. In my jealous wings
I evermore will hold thee, when thou goest out or comest in.
'Tis thou hast darken'd all My World, O Woman, lovely bane."

Thus they contended all the day among the Caves of Tharmas,
Twisting in fearful forms & howling, howling, harsh shrieking,
Howling, harsh shrieking; mingling, their bodies join in burning anguish.
Mingling his brightness with her tender limbs, then high she soar'd
Above the ocean; a bright wonder, Nature,
Half Woman & half Spectre; all his lovely changing colours mix
With her fair crystal clearness; in her lips & cheeks his poisons rose

In blushes like the morning, and his scaly armour softening,
A monster lovely in the heavens or wandering on the earth,
With spectre voice incessant wailing, in incessant thirst,
Beauty all blushing with desire, mocking her fell despair.
Wandering desolate, a wonder abhorr'd by Gods & Men,
Till, with fierce pain, she brought forth on the rocks her sorrow & woe:
Behold two little Infants wept upon the desolate wind.

The first state weeping they began, & helpless as a wave
Beaten along its sightless way, growing enormous in its motion to
Its utmost goal, till strength from Enion, like richest summer shining,
Rais'd the *fierce* boy & girl with glories from their heads out-beaming,
Drawing forth drooping mother's pity, drooping mother's sorrow.

But those in Great Eternity Met in the Council of God
As One Man, hovering over Gilead & Hermon.
He is the Good Shepherd, He is the Lord & Master
To Create Man Morning by Morning, to give gifts at Noon day.

Enion brooded o'er the rocks; the rough rocks groaning vegetate.
Such power was given to the Solitary wanderer:
The barked Oak, the long limb'd Beech, the Chestnut tree, the Pine,
The Pear tree mild, the frowning Walnut, the sharp Crab, & Apple sweet,
The rough bark opens; twittering peep forth little beaks & wings,
The Nightingale, the Goldfinch, Robin, Lark, Linnet & Thrush.
The Goat leap'd from the craggy cliff, the Sheep awoke from the mould,
Upon its green stalk rose the Corn, waving innumerable,
Infolding the bright Infants from the desolating winds.

They sulk upon her breast, her hair became like snow on mountains:
Weaker & weaker, weeping woful, wearier and wearier,
Faded, & her bright Eyes decay'd, melted with pity & love.
And then they wander'd far away, she sought for them in vain:
In weeping blindness, stumbling, she follow'd them o'er rocks & mountains,
Rehumanizing from the Spectre in pangs of maternal love.
Ingrate they wander'd, scorning her, drawing her *spectrous Life,*
Repelling her away & away by a dread repulsive power
Into Non Entity, revolving round in dark despair
And drawing in the spectrous life in pride and haughty joy.
Thus Enion gave them all her spectrous life.

Then Eno, a daughter of Beulah, took a Moment of Time
And drew it out to seven thousand years with much care & affliction

And many tears, & in every year made windows into Eden.
She also took an atom of space & open'd its centre
Into Infinitude & ornamented it with wondrous art.
Astonish'd sat her sisters of Beulah to see her soft affection
To Enion & her children, & they ponder'd these things wond'ring,
And they Alternate kept watch over the Youthful terrors.
They saw not yet the Hand Divine, for it was not yet reveal'd,
But they went on in silent Hope & Feminine repose.

But Los & Enitharmon delighted in the Moony spaces of *Eno,*
Nine Times they liv'd among the forests, feeding on sweet fruits,
And nine bright Spaces wander'd, weaving mazes of delight,
Snaring the wild Goats for their milk, they eat the flesh of Lambs:
A male & female, naked & ruddy as the pride of summer.

Alternate Love & Hate his breast: hers Scorn & Jealousy
In embryon passions; they kiss'd not nor embrac'd for shame & fear.
His head beam'd light & in his vigorous voice was prophecy.
He could control the times & seasons & the days & years;
She could controll the spaces, regions, desart, flood & forest,
But had no power to weave the Veil of covering for her sins.
She drave the Females all away from Los,
And Los drave the Males from her away.
They wander'd long, till they sat down upon the margin'd sea,
Conversing with the visions of Beulah in dark slumbrous bliss.
Nine years they view the living spheres, Reading the Visions of Beulah.

But the two youthful wonders wander'd in the world of Tharmas.
"Thy name is Enitharmon," said the fierce prophetic boy.
"While thy mild voice fills all these caverns with sweet harmony,
O how our Parents sit & mourn in their silent secret bowers!"
But Enitharmon answer'd with a dropping tear & frowning
Dark as a dewy morning when the crimson light appears,
"To make us happy *let them* weary their immortal powers
While we draw in their sweet delights, while we return them scorn
On scorn to feed our discontent; for if we grateful prove
They will withhold sweet love, whose food is thorns & bitter roots.
We hear the warlike clarions, we view the burning spheres,
Yet Thou in indolence reposest, holding me in bonds.
Hear! I will sing a Song of Death! it is a Song of Vala!
The Fallen Man takes his repose, Urizen sleeps in the porch,
Luvah and Vala wake & *fly* up from the Human Heart

Into the Brain from thence; upon the pillow Vala slumber'd,
And Luvah seiz'd the Horses of Light & rose into the Chariot of Day.
Sweet laughter seiz'd me in my sleep; silent & close I laugh'd,
For in the visions of Vala I walk'd with the mighty Fallen One,
I heard his voice among the branches & among sweet flowers:
'Why is the light of Enitharmon darken'd in dewy morn?
Why is the silence of Enitharmon a terror, & her smile a whirlwind,
Uttering this darkness in my halls, in the pillars of my Holy-ones?
Why dost thou weep as Vala & wet thy veil with dewy tears,
In slumbers of my night-repose infusing a false morning,
Driving the Female Emanations all away from Los?
I have refus'd to look upon the Universal Vision.
And wilt thou slay with death him who devotes himself to thee,
Once born for the sport & amusement of Man, now born to drink up all
     his Powers?'
I heard the sounding sea, I heard the voice weaker and weaker,
The voice came & went like a dream: I awoke in my sweet bliss."

Then Los smote her upon the Earth; 'twas long e'er she reviv'd.
He answer'd, dark'ning *more,* with indignation hid in smiles:
"I die not, Enitharmon, tho' thou sing'st thy song of Death,
Nor shalt thou me torment; For I behold the Fallen Man
Seeking to comfort Vala: she will not be comforted.
She rises from his throne and seeks the shadows of her garden
Weeping for Luvah lost in bloody beams of your false morning;
Sick'ning lies the Fallen Man, his head sick, his heart faint:
Mighty achievement of your power; Beware the punishment!

"Refusing to behold the Divine Image which all behold
And live thereby, he is sunk down into a deadly sleep.
But we, immortal in our own strength, survive by stern debate
Till we have drawn the Lamb of God into a mortal form.
And that he must be born is certain, for One must be All
And comprehend within himself all things both small & great.
We therefore, for whose sake all things aspire to be & live,
Will so receive the Divine Image that amongst the Reprobate
He may be devoted to destruction from his mother's womb.

"I see, invisible descend into the Gardens of Vala,
Luvah walking on the winds! I see the invisible knife,
I see the shower of blood, I see the swords & spears of futurity.

"Tho' in the Brain of Man we live & in his circling Nerves,
Tho' this bright world of all our joy is in the Human Brain
Where Urizen & all his Hosts hang their immortal lamps,
Thou ne'er shalt leave this cold expanse where wat'ry Tharmas mourns."

So spoke Los. Scorn & Indignation rose upon Enitharmon.

Then Enitharmon, redd'ning fierce, stretch'd her immortal hands:
"Descend, O Urizen, descend with horse & chariot!
Threaten not me, O visionary; thine the punishment.
The Human Nature shall no more remain, nor Human acts
Form the rebellious Spirits of Heaven, but War & Princedom, & Victory
      & Blood."

Night darken'd as she spoke; a shudd'ring ran from East to West;
A Groan was heard on high. The warlike clarions ceast, the Spirits
Of Luvah & Vala shudder'd in their Orb, an orb of blood.

Eternity groan'd & was troubled at the Image of Eternal Death.
The Wandering Man bow'd his faint head and Urizen descended—
And *the one must have murder'd the Man if he had not descended—*
Indignant, muttering low thunders, Urizen descended,
Gloomy, sounding: "Now I am God from Eternity to Eternity."

Sullen sat Los plotting Revenge. Silent he eyed the Prince
Of Light. Silent the Prince of Light view'd Los; at length a brooded
Smile broke from Urizen, for Enitharmon brighten'd more & more.
Sullen he lower'd on Enitharmon, but he smil'd on Los,
Saying: "Thou art the Lord of Luvah: into thine hands I give
The prince of Love, the murderer; his soul is in thine hands.
Pity not Vala, for she pitied not the Eternal Man,
Nor pity thou the cries of Luvah. Lo, these starry hosts,
They are thy servants if thou wilt obey my awful Law."

So spoke the Prince of Light & sat beside the seat of Los.
Upon the sandy shore rested his chariot of fire.

Los answer'd furious: "Art thou one of those who when most complacent
Mean mischief most? If you are such, Lo! I am also such.
One must be master. Try thy Arts. I also will try mine,
For I perceive thou hast Abundance which I claim as mine."

Urizen startled stood, but not Long; Soon he cried:
"Obey my voice, young Demon; I am God from Eternity to Eternity
Art thou a visionary of Jesus, the soft delusion of Eternity?
Lo I am God, the terrible destroyer, & not the Saviour.
Why should the Divine Vision compell the sons of Eden
To forego each his own delight, to war against his spectre?
The Spectre is the Man. The rest is only delusion & fancy."
Thus Urizen spoke, collected in himself in awful pride.
Ten thousand thousand were his hosts of spirits on the wind,
Ten thousand thousand glittering Chariots shining in the sky.
They pour upon the golden shore beside the silent ocean,
Rejoicing in the Victory, & the heavens were fill'd with blood.

The Earth spread forth her table wide; the Night, a silver cup
Fill'd with the wine of anguish, waited at the golden feast.
But the bright Sun was not as yet; he, filling all the expanse,
Slept as a bird in the blue shell that soon shall burst away.

Los saw the wound of his blow: he saw, he pitied, he wept.
Los now repented that he had smitten Enitharmon; he felt love
Arise in all his Veins; he threw his arms around her loins
To heal the wound of his smiting.

They eat the fleshly bread, they drank the nervous wine;
They listened to the Elemental Harps & Sphery Song:
They view'd the dancing Hours quick sporting thro' the sky.
With winged radiance scattering joys thro' the ever changing light.

But Luvah and Vala standing in the bloody sky
On high remain'd alone, forsaken, in fierce jealousy.
They stood above the heavens, forsaken, desolate, suspended in blood
Descend they could not, nor from Each other avert their eyes.
Eternity appear'd above them as One Man infolded
In Luvah's robes of blood & bearing all his afflictions;
As the sun shines down on the misty earth, such was the Vision.

But purple night and crimson morning & golden day descending
Thro' the clear changing atmosphere display'd green fields among
The varying clouds, like paradises stretch'd in the expanse,
With towns & villages and temples, tents, sheepfolds and pastures
Where dwell the children of the elemental worlds in harmony.

Not long in harmony they dwell, their life is drawn away
And wintry woes succeed, successive driven into the Void
Where Enion craves, successive drawn into the golden feast.

And Los & Enitharmon sat in discontent & scorn.
The Nuptial Song arose from all the thousand thousand spirits
Over the joyful Earth & Sea & ascended into the Heavens;
For Elemental Gods their thunderous Organs blew, creating
Delicious Viands. Demons of Waves their wat'ry Eccho's woke.
Bright Souls of vegetative life budding and blossoming
Stretch their immortal hands to smite the gold & silver Wires,
And with immortal Voice soft warbling, fill all Earth & Heaven.
With doubling voices, & loud Horns wound round, sounding,
Cavernous dwellers fill'd the enormous Revelry, Responsing,
And Spirits of Flaming fire on high govern'd the mighty Song.

And This is the Song sung at The Feast of Los & Enitharmon:

"*Ephraim* call'd out to *Zion:* 'Awake, O Brother Mountain!
Let us refuse the Plow & Spade, the heavy Roller & spiked
Harrow; burn all these Corn fields, throw down all these fences!
Fatten'd on Human blood & drunk with wine of life is better far
Than all these labours of the harvest & the vintage. See the river,
Red with the blood of Men, swells lustful round my rocky knees;
My clouds are not the clouds of verdant fields & groves of fruit,
But Clouds of Human Souls: my nostrils drink the lives of Men.'

"The Villages lament: they faint, outstretch'd upon the plain.
Wailing runs round the Valleys from the Mill & from the Barn.
But most the polish'd Palaces, dark, silent, bow with dread,
Hiding their books & pictures underneath the dens of Earth.

"The Cities send to one another saying: 'My sons are Mad
With wine of cruelty. Let us plat a scourge, O Sister City.'
Children are nourish'd for the Slaughter; once the Child was fed
With Milk, but wherefore now are Children fed with blood?
The Horse is of more value than the Man. The Tyger fierce
Laughs as the Human form; the Lion mocks & thirsts for blood.
They cry, 'O Spider, spread thy web! Enlarge thy bones & fill'd
With marrow, sinews & flesh, Exalt thyself, attain a voice.

" 'Call to thy dark arm'd hosts; for all the sons of Men muster together
To desolate their cities! Man shall be no more! Awake, O Hosts!'
The bow string sang upon the hills, 'Luvah & Vala ride
Triumphant in the bloody sky, & the Human form is no more.'

"The list'ning Stars heard, & the first beam of the morning started back:
He cried out to his Father 'depart! depart;' but sudden Siez'd,
And clad in steel, & his Horse proudly neigh'd; he smelt the battle
Afar off. Rushing back, redd'ning with rage, the Mighty Father

"Siez'd his bright sheephook studded with gems & gold; he swung it
    round
His head, shrill sounding in the sky; down rush'd the Sun with noise
Of war; the Mountains fled away; they sought a place beneath.
Vala remain'd in deserts of dark solitude, nor Sun nor Moon

"By night nor day to comfort her; she labour'd in thick smoke.
Tharmas endur'd not; he fled howling: then, a barren waste, sunk down
Conglobing in the dark confusion. Mean time Los was born
And thou, O Enitharmon! Hark, I hear the hammers of Los.

"They melt the bones of Vala & the bones of Luvah into wedges;
The innumerable sons & daughters of Luvah, clos'd in furnaces,
Melt into furrows; winter blows his bellows: Ice & snow
Tend the dire anvils: Mountains mourn, & Rivers faint & fail.

"There is no City, nor Cornfield, nor Orchard; all is Rock & Sand.
There is no Sun, nor Moon, nor Star, but rugged wintry rocks
Justling together in the void, suspended by inward fires.
Impatience now no longer can endure. Distracted Luvah,
Bursting forth from the loins of Enitharmon, Thou fierce Terror,
Go howl in vain! Smite, smite his fetters! smite, O wintry hammers!
Smite, Spectre of Urthona! mock the field who drew us down
From heavens of joy into this deep. Now rage, but rage in vain!"

Thus sang the demons of the deep; the Clarions of war blew loud.
The Feast redounds, & Crown'd with roses & the circling vine
The Enormous Bride & Bridegroom sat; beside them Urizen,
With faded radiance sigh'd, forgetful of the flowing wine
And of Ahania, his Pure Bride; but she was distant far.

But Los & Enitharmon sat in discontent & scorn,
Craving the more, the more enjoying, drawing out sweet bliss
From all the turning wheels of heaven & the chariots of the Slain.

At distance, Far in Night repell'd, in direful hunger craving,
Summers & winters round revolving in the frightful deep,
Enion, blind & age-bent, wept upon the desolate wind:

"Why does the Raven cry aloud and no eye pities her?
Why fall the Sparrow & the Robin in the foodless winter?
Faint, shivering, they sit on leafless bush or frozen stone

"Wearied with seeking food across the snowy waste, the little
Heart cold, and the little tongue consum'd that once in thoughtless joy
Gave songs of gratitude to waving cornfields round their nest.

"Why howl the Lion & the Wolf? why do they roam abroad?
Deluded by summer's heat, they sport in enormous love
And cast their young out to the hungry wilds & sandy desarts.

"Why is the Sheep given to the knife? the Lamb plays in the Sun:
He starts! he hears the foot of Man! he says: Take thou my wool,
But spare my life: *but* he knows not that winter cometh fast.

"The Spider sits in his labour'd Web, eager watching for the Fly.
Presently comes a famish'd Bird & takes away the Spider.
His Web is left all desolate that his little anxious heart
So careful wove & spread it out with sighs and weariness."

This was the Lamentation of Enion round the golden Feast.
Eternity groan'd and was troubled at the image of Eternal Death
Without the body of Man, an Exudation from his sick'ning limbs.

Now Man was come to the Palm tree & to the Oak of Weeping
Which stand upon the Edge of Beulah, & he sunk down
From the supporting arms of the Eternal Saviour who dispos'd
The pale limbs of his Eternal Individuality
Upon The Rock of Ages, Watching over him with Love & Care.

Then those in Great Eternity met in the Council of God
As one Man, for contracting their Exalted Senses
They behold Multitude, or Expanding they behold as one,
As One Man all the Universal family; & that One Man
They call Jesus the Christ, & they in him & he in them
Live in Perfect harmony, in Eden the land of life,
Consulting as One Man above the Mountain of Snowdon Sublime.

For messengers from Beulah come in tears & dark'ning clouds
Saying, "Shiloh is in ruins, our brother is sick: Albion, He
Whom thou lovest, is sick; he wanders from his house of Eternity.
The Daughters of Beulah, terrified, have clos'd the Gate of the Tongue.
Luvah & Urizen contend in war around the holy tent."

So spoke the Ambassadors from Beulah, & with solemn mourning
They were introduc'd to the divine presence, & they kneeled down
In Conway's Vale, thus recounting the Wars of Death Eternal:

"The Eternal Man wept in the holy tent: Our Brother in Eternity,
Even Albion whom thou lovest, wept in pain; his family
Slept round on hills & valleys in the regions of his love.
But Urizen awoke, & Luvah woke, & they conferr'd:
'Thou Luvah,' said the Prince of Light, 'behold our sons & daughters
Repos'd on beds; let them sleep on; do thou alone depart
Into thy wished Kingdom, where in Majesty & Power
We may erect a throne; deep in the North I place my lot,
Thou in the South; listen attentive. In silent of this night
I will infold the Eternal tent in clouds opake, while thou,
Siezing the chariots of the morning, Go, outfleeting ride
Afar into the Zenith high, bending thy furious course
Southward, with half the tents of men inclos'd in clouds
Of Tharmes & Urthona. I, remaining in porches of the brain,
Will lay my scepter on Jerusalem, the Emanation,
On all her sons, & on thy sons, O Luvah, & on mine
Till dawn was wont to wake them; then my trumpet sounding loud,
Ravish'd away in night; my strong command shall be obey'd
For I have plac'd my centinels in stations; each tenth man
Is bought & sold, & in dim night my word shall be their law.'

"Luvah replied: 'Dictate to thy Equals: am not I
The Prince of all the hosts of Men, nor Equal know in Heaven?
If I arise into the Zenith, leaving thee to watch
The Emanation & her Sons, the Satan & the Anak,
Sihon and Og, wilt thou not, rebel to my laws, remain
In darkness building thy strong throne, & in my ancient night
Daring my power wilt arm my sons against me in the Atlantic,
My deep, My night, which thou assuming hast assum'd my Crown?
I will remain as well as thou, & here with hands of blood
Smite this dark sleeper in his tent, then try my strength with thee.'

"While thus he spoke his fires redden'd o'er the holy tent.
Urizen cast deep darkness round him, silent brooding death,
Eternal death to Luvah; raging, Luvah pour'd
The Lances of Urizen from chariots round the holy tent.
Discord began, & yells & cries shook the wide firmament.

"Beside his anvil stood Urthona dark; a mass of iron
Glow'd furious on the anvil prepar'd for spades & coulters. All
His sons fled from his side to join the conflict; pale he heard
The Eternal voice; he stood, the sweat chill'd on his mighty limbs.
He drop'd his hammer: dividing from his aking bosom fled
A portion of his life; shrieking upon the wind she fled,
And Tharmas took her in, pitying. Then Enion in jealous fear
Murder'd her & hid her in her bosom, embalming her for fear
She should arise again to life. Embalm'd in Enion's bosom
Enitharmon remains a corse; such thing was never known
In Eden, that one died a death never to be reviv'd.
Urthona stood in terror, but not long; his spectre fled
To Enion, & his body fell. Tharmas beheld him fall
Endlong, a raging serpent rolling round the holy tent.
The sons of war, astonish'd at the Glitt'ring monster, drove
Him far into the world of Tharmas, into a cavern'd rock.

"But Urizen, with darkness overspreading all the armies,
Sent round his heralds secretly commanding to depart
Into the north. Sudden with thunder's sound his multitudes
Retreat from the fierce conflict, all the sons of Urizen at once
Must'ring together in thick clouds, leaving the rage of Luvah
To pour its fury on himself & on the Eternal Man.

"Sudden down fell they all together into an unknown Space,
Deep, horrible, without End, separated from Beulah, far beneath.
The Man's exteriors are become indefinite, open'd to pain
In a fierce hungry void, & none can visit his regions.

"Jerusalem, his Emanation, *is* become a ruin,
Her little ones *are* slain on the top of every street,
And she herself led captive & scatter'd into the indefinite.
Gird on thy sword, O thou most mighty in glory & misery!
Destroy these opressors of Jerusalem & those who ruin Shiloh."

So spoke the Messengers of Beulah. Silently removing,
The Family Divine drew up the Universal tent
Above High Snowdon, & clos'd the Messengers in clouds around
Till the time of the End. Then they Elected Seven, called the Seven
Eyes of God & the Seven Lamps of the Almighty.
The Seven are one within the other; the Seventh is named Jesus,
The Lamb of God, blessed for ever, & he follow'd the Man
Who wander'd in mount Ephraim seeking a Sepulcher,
His inward eyes closing from the Divine vision, & all
His children wandering outside, from his bosom fleeing away.

END OF THE FIRST NIGHT

The Daughters of Beulah beheld the Emanation; they pitied,
They wept before the Inner gates of Enitharmon's bosom,
And of her fine wrought brain, & of her bowels within her loins.
These gates within, Glorious & bright, open into Beulah
From Enitharmon's inward parts; but the bright female terror
Refus'd to open the bright gates; she clos'd and barr'd them fast
Lest Los should enter into Beulah thro' her beautiful gates.

The Emanation stood before the Gates of Enitharmon,
Weeping; the Daughters of Beulah silent in the Porches
Spread her a couch unknown to Enitharmon; here repos'd
Jerusalem in slumbers soft, lull'd into silent rest.

Terrific rag'd the Eternal wheels of intellect, terrific rag'd
The living creatures of the wheels, in the Wars of Eternal life.
But perverse roll'd the wheels of Urizen & Luvah, back revers'd
Downwards & outwards, consuming in the wars of Eternal Death.
[*Additional lines*]

VALA

NIGHT THE SECOND

Rising upon his Couch of death Albion beheld his sons.
Turning his Eyes outward to Self, losing the Divine Vision,
Albion call'd Urizen & said: "Behold these sick'ning Spheres,
Whence is this voice of Enion that soundeth in my *Porches?*

Take thou possession! take this Scepter! go forth in my might,
For I am weary & must sleep in the dark sleep of Death.
Thy brother Luvah hath smitten me, but pity thou his youth
Tho' thou hast not piti'd my Age, O Urizen, Prince of Light."

Urizen rose from the bright Feast like a star thro' the evening sky,
Exulting at the voice that call'd him from the Feast of envy.
First he beheld the body of Man, pale, cold; the horrors of death
Beneath his feet shot thro' him as he stood in the Human Brain,
And all its golden porches grew pale with his sickening light,
No more exulting, for he saw Eternal Death beneath.
Pale, he beheld futurity: pale, he beheld the Abyss
Where Enion, blind & age bent, wept in direful hunger craving,
All rav'ning like the hungry worm & like the silent grave.
Mighty was the draught of Voidness to draw Existence in.

Terrific Urizen strode above in fear & pale dismay.
He saw the indefinite space beneath & his soul shrunk with horror,
His feet upon the verge of Non Existence; his voice went forth:
Luvah & Vala trembling & shrinking beheld the great Work master
And heard his Word: "Divide, ye bands, influence by influence.
Build we a Bower for heaven's darling in the grizly deep:
Build we the Mundane Shell around the Rock of Albion."

The Bands of Heaven flew thro' the air singing & shouting to Urizen.
Some fix'd the anvil, some the loom erected, some the plow
And harrow form'd & fram'd the harness of silver & ivory,
The golden compasses, the quadrant, & the rule & balance.
They erected the furnaces, they form'd the anvils of gold beaten in mills
Where winter beats incessant, fixing them firm on their base.
The bellows began to blow, & the Lions of Urizen stood round the anvil
And the leopards cover'd with skins of beasts tended the roaring fires,
Sublime, distinct, their lineaments divine of human beauty.
The tygers of wrath called the horses of instruction from their mangers,
They unloos'd them & put on the harness of gold & silver & ivory,
In human forms distinct they stood round Urizen, prince of Light,
Petrifying all the Human Imagination into rock & sand.
Groans ran along Tyburn's brook and along the River of Oxford
Among the Druid Temples. Albion groan'd on Tyburn's brook:
Albion gave his loud death groan. The Atlantic Mountains trembled.
Aloft the Moon fled with a cry: the Sun with streams of blood.

From Albion's Loins fled all Peoples and Nations of the Earth,
Fled with the noise of Slaughter, & the stars of heaven fled.
Jerusalem came down in a dire ruin over all the Earth,
She fell cold from Lambeth's Vales in groans & dewy death—
The dew of anxious souls, the death-sweat of the dying—
In every pillar'd hall & arched roof of Albion's skies.
The brother & the brother bathe in blood upon the Severn,
The Maiden weeping by. The father & the mother with
The Maiden's father & her mother fainting over the body,
And the Young Man, the Murderer, fleeing over the mountains.

Reuben slept on Penmaenmawr & Levi slept on Snowdon.
Their eyes, their ears, nostrils & tongues roll outward, they behold
What is within now seen without; they are raw to the hungry wind.
They become Natures far remote, in a little & dark Land.
The daughters of Albion girded around their garments of Needlework,
Stripping Jerusalem's curtains from mild demons of the hills;
Across Europe & Asia to China & Japan like lightnings
They go forth & return to Albion on his rocky couch:
Gwendolen, Ragan, Sabrina, Gonorill, Mehetabel, Cordella,
Boadicea, Conwenna, Estrild, Gwinefrid, Ignoge, Cambel,
Binding Jerusalem's Children in the dungeons of Babylon;
They play before the Armies, before the hounds of Nimrod,
While the Prince of Light on Salisbury plain among the Druid Stones.

Rattling, the adamantine chains & hooks heave up the ore,
In mountainous masses plung'd in furnaces, & they shut & seal'd
The furnaces a time & times; all the while blew the North
His cloudy bellows, & the South & East & dismal West,
And all the while the plow of iron cut the dreadful furrows
In Ulro, beneath Beulah, where the dead wail Night & Day.
Luvah was cast into the Furnaces of affliction & sealed,
And Vala fed in cruel delight the furnaces with fire.
Stern Urizen beheld, urg'd by necessity to keep
The evil day afar, & if perchance with iron power
He might avert his own despair; in woe & fear he saw
Vala incircle round the furnaces where Luvah was clos'd.
In joy she heard his howlings & forgot he was her Luvah,
With whom she walk'd in bliss in times of innocence & youth.

Hear ye the voice of Luvah from the furnaces of Urizen:

"If I indeed am Vala's King, & ye, O sons of Men,
The workmanship of Luvah's hands in times of Everlasting,
When I call'd forth the Earth-worm from the cold & dark obscure
I nurtur'd her, I fed her with my rains & dews; she grew
A scaled Serpent, yet I fed her tho' she hated me;
Day after day she fed upon the mountains in Luvah's sight,
I brought her thro' the Wilderness, a dry & thirsty land,
And I commanded springs to rise for her in the black desart,
Till she became a Dragon, winged, bright & poisonous.
I open'd all the floodgates of the heavens to quench her thirst,
And I commanded the Great deep to hide her in his hand
Till she became a little weeping Infant a span long.
I carried her in my bosom as a man carries a lamb,
I loved her, I gave her all my soul & my delight,
I hid her in soft gardens & in secret bowers of summer,
Weaving mazes of delight along the sunny paradise,
Inextricable labyrinths. She bore me sons & daughters,
And they have taken her away & hid her from my sight.
They have surrounded me with walls of iron & brass. O Lamb
Of God clothed in Luvah's garments! little knowest thou
Of death Eternal, that we all go to Eternal Death,
To our Primeval Chaos in fortuitous concourse of incoherent
Discordant principles of Love & Hate. I suffer affliction
Because I love, for I was love, but hatred awakes in me
And Urizen, who was Faith & certainty, is chang'd to Doubt;
The hand of Urizen is upon me because I blotted out
That Human delusion to deliver all the sons of God
From bondage of the Human form. O first born Son of Light,
O Urizen my enemy, I weep for thy stern ambition,
But weep in vain. O when will you return, Vala the Wanderer?"

These were the words of Luvah, patient in afflictions,
Reasoning from the loins in the unreal forms of Ulro's night.

And when Luvah, age after age, was quite melted with woe,
The fires of Vala faded like a shadow cold & pale,
An evanescent shadow; last she fell, a heap of Ashes
Beneath the furnaces, a woful heap in living death.

Then were the furnaces unseal'd with spades, & pickaxes
Roaring let out the fluid: the molten metal ran in channels
Cut by the plow of ages held in Urizen's strong hand
In many a valley, for the Bulls of Luvah drag'd the Plow.

With trembling horror pale, aghast the Children of Man
Stood on the infinite Earth & saw these visions in the air,
In waters & in earth beneath; they cried to one another,
"What! are we terrors to one another? Come, O brethren, wherefore
Was this wide Earth spread all abroad? not for wild beasts to roam."
But many stood silent, & busied in their families.
And many said, "We see no Visions in the darksom air.
Measure the course of that sulphur orb that lights the darksom day;
Set stations on this breeding Earth & let us buy & sell."
Others arose & schools erected, forming Instruments
To measure out the course of heaven. Stern Urizen beheld
In woe his brethren & his sons, in dark'ning woe lamenting
Upon the winds in clouds involv'd, Uttering his voice in thunders,
Commanding all the work with care & power & severity.

Then seiz'd the Lions of Urizen their work, & heated in the forge
Roar the bright masses; thund'ring beat the hammers, many a pyramid
Is form'd & thrown down thund'ring into the deeps of Non Entity.
Heated red hot they, hizzing, rend their way down many a league
Till resting, each his basement finds; suspended there they stand
Casting their sparkles dire abroad into the dismal deep.
For, measur'd out in order'd spaces, the Sons of Urizen
With compasses divide the deep; they the strong scales erect
That Luvah rent from the faint Heart of the Fallen Man,
And weigh the massy Cubes, then fix them in their awful stations.

And all the time, in Caverns shut, the golden Looms erected
First spun, then wove the Atmospheres; there the Spider & Worm
Plied the wing'd shuttle, piping shrill thro' all the list'ning threads;
Beneath the Caverns roll the weights of lead & spindles of iron,
The enormous warp & woof rage direful in the affrighted deep.

While far into the vast unknown the strong wing'd Eagles bend
Their venturous flight in Human forms distinct; thro' darkness deep
They bear the woven draperies; on golden hooks they hang abroad
The universal curtains & spread out from Sun to Sun
The vehicles of light; they separate the furious particles
Into mild currents as the water mingles with the wine.

While thus the Spirits of strongest wing enlighten the dark deep,
The threads are spun & the cords twisted & drawn out; then the weak
Begin their work. & many a net is netted, many a net

Spread, & many a Spirit caught: innumerable the nets,
Innumerable the gins & traps, & many a soothing flute
Is form'd, & many a corded lyre outspread over the immense.
In cruel delight they trap the listeners, & in cruel delight
Bind them, condensing the strong energies into little compass.
Some became seed of every plant that shall be planted; some
The bulbous roots, thrown up together into barns & garners.

Then rose the Builders. First the Architect divine his plan
Unfolds. The wondrous scaffold rear'd all round the infinite,
Quadrangular the building rose, the heavens squared by a line,
Trigons & cubes divide the elements in finite bonds.
Multitudes without number work incessant: the hewn stone
Is plac'd in beds of mortar mingled with the ashes of Vala.
Severe the labour; female slaves the mortar trod oppressed.

Twelve halls after the names of his twelve sons compos'd
The wondrous building, & three Central Domes after the Names
Of his three daughters were encompass'd by the twelve bright halls.
Every hall surrounded by bright Paradises of Delight
In which were towns & Cities, Nations, Seas, Mountains & Rivers.
Each Dome open'd toward four halls, & the Three Domes Encompass'd
The Golden Hall of Urizen, whose western side glow'd bright
With ever streaming fires beaming from his awful limbs.
His Shadowy Feminine Semblance here repos'd on a White Couch,
Or hover'd over his starry head; & when he smil'd she brighten'd
Like a bright Cloud in harvest; but when Urizen frown'd she wept
In mists over his carved throne; & when he turned his back
Upon his Golden hall & sought the Labyrinthine porches
Of his wide heaven, Trembling, cold, in jealous fears she sat
A shadow of Despair; therefore toward the West, Urizen form'd
A recess in the wall for fires to glow upon the pale
Female's limbs in his absence, & her Daughters oft upon
A Golden Altar burnt perfumes: with Art Celestial form'd
Foursquare, sculptur'd & sweetly Engrav'd to please their shadowy
    mother.
Ascending into her misty garments the blue smoke roll'd to revive
Her cold limbs in the absence of her Lord. Also her sons,
With lives of Victims sacrificed upon an altar of brass
On the East side, Reviv'd her soul with lives of beasts & birds
Slain on the Altar, up ascending into her cloudy bosom.
Of terrible workmanship the Altar, labour of ten thousand Slaves,

One thousand Men of wondrous power spent their lives in its formation.
It stood on twelve steps nam'd after the names of her twelve sons,
And was erected at the chief entrance of Urizen's hall.

When Urizen return'd from his immense labours & travels,
Descending she repos'd beside him, folding him around
In her bright skirts. Astonish'd & Confounded he beheld
Her shadowy form now separate; he shudder'd & was silent
Till her caresses & her tears reviv'd him to life & joy.
Two wills they had, two intellects, & not as in times of old.
This Urizen perciev'd, & silent brooded in dark'ning Clouds.
To him his Labour was but Sorrow & his Kingdom was Repentance.
He drave the Male Spirits all away from Ahania,
And she drave all the Females from him away.

Los joy'd, & Enitharmon laugh'd, saying, "Let us go down
And see this labour & sorrow." They went down to see the woes
Of Vala & the woes of Luvah, to draw in their delights.

And Vala like a shadow oft appear'd to Urizen.
The King of Light beheld her mourning among the Brick kilns, compell'd
To labour night & day among the fires; her lamenting voice
Is heard when silent night returns & the labourers take their rest.

"O Lord, wilt thou not look upon our sore afflictions
Among these flames incessant labouring? our hard masters laugh
At all our sorrow. We are made to turn the wheel for water,
To carry the heavy basket on our scorched shoulders, to sift
The sand & ashes, & to mix the clay with tears & repentance.
The times are now return'd upon us; we have given ourselves
To scorn, and now are scorned by the slaves of our enemies.
Our beauty is cover'd over with clay & ashes, & our backs
Furrow'd with whips, & our flesh bruised with the heavy basket.
Forgive us, O thou piteous one whom we have offended! forgive
The weak remaining shadow of Vala that returns in sorrow to thee.

*"I see not Luvah as of old, I only see his feet
Like pillars of fire travelling thro' darkness & non entity."*

Thus she lamented day & night, compell'd to labour & sorrow.
Luvah in vain her lamentations heard: in vain his love
Brought him in various forms before her, still she knew him not,
Still she despis'd him, calling on his name & knowing him not,
Still hating, still professing love, still labouring in the smoke.

And Los & Enitharmon joy'd; they drank in tenfold joy
From all the sorrow of Luvah & the labour of Urizen.
And Enitharmon joy'd, Plotting to rend the secret cloud,
To plant divisions in the soul of Urizen & Ahania.
But infinitely beautiful the wondrous work arose
In sorrow and care, a Golden World whose porches round the heavens
And pillar'd halls & rooms reciev'd the eternal wandering stars.
A wondrous golden Building, many a window, many a door
And many a division let in & out the vast unknown.
Circled in infinite orb immoveable, within its walls & cielings
The heavens were clos'd, and spirits mourn'd their bondage night & day,
And the Divine Vision appear'd in Luvah's robes of blood.

Thus was the Mundane shell builded by Urizen's strong Power.

Sorrowing went the Planters forth to plant, the Sowers to sow;
They dug the channels for the rivers, & they pour'd abroad
The seas & lakes; they rear'd the mountains & the rocks & hills
On broad pavilions, on pillar'd roofs & porches & high towers,
In beauteous order; thence arose soft clouds & exhalations
Wandering even to the sunny Cubes of light & heat,
For many a window ornamented with sweet ornaments
Look'd out into the World of Tharmas, where in ceaseless torrents
His billows roll, where monsters wander in the foamy paths.

On clouds the Sons of Urizen beheld Heaven walled round;
They weigh'd & order'd all, & Urizen conforted saw
The wondrous work flow forth like visible out of the invisible;
For the Divine Lamb, Even Jesus who is the Divine Vision,
Permitted all, lest Man should fall into Eternal Death;
For when Luvah sunk down, himself put on the robes of blood
Lest the state call'd Luvah should cease; & the Divine Vision
Walked in robes of blood till he who slept should awake.

Thus were the stars of heaven created like a golden chain
To bind the Body of Man to heaven from falling into the Abyss.
Each took his station & his course began with sorrow & care.

In sevens & ten & fifties, hundreds, thousands, number'd all
According to their various powers, subordinate to Urizen
And to his sons in their degrees & to his beauteous daughters,
Traveling in silent majesty along their order'd ways

In right lined paths outmeasur'd by proportions of number, weight,
And measure, mathematic motion wondrous along the deep,
In fiery pyramid, or Cube, or unornamented pillar square
Of fire, far shining, traveling along even to its destin'd end;
Then falling down a terrible space, recovering in winter dire
Its wasted strength, it back returns upon a nether course,
Till fir'd with ardour fresh recruited in its humble season,
It rises up on high all summer, till its wearied course
Turns into autumn. Such the periods of many worlds.
Others triangular, right angled course maintain. Others obtuse,
Acute, Scalene, in simple paths; but others move
In intricate ways, biquadrate, Trapeziums, Rhombs, Rhomboids,
Paralellograms triple & quadruple, polygonic
In their amazing hard subdu'd course in the vast deep.

And Los & Enitharmon were drawn down by their desires,
Descending sweet upon the wind among soft harps & voices
To plant divisions in the Soul of Urizen & Ahania,
To conduct the Voice of Enion to Ahania's midnight pillow.

Urizen saw & envied, & his imagination was filled.
Repining he contemplated the past in his bright sphere,
Terrified with his heart & spirit at the visions of futurity
That his dread fancy form'd before him in the uniform'd void.

For Los & Enitharmon walk'd forth on the dewy Earth
Contracting or expanding their all flexible senses
At will to murmur in the flowers small as the honey bee,
At will to stretch across the heavens & step from star to star,
Or standing on the Earth erect, or on the stormy waves
Driving the storms before them, or delighting in sunny beams,
While round their heads the Elemental Gods kept harmony.

And Los said: "Lo, the Lilly pale & the rose redd'ning fierce
Reproach thee, & the beamy gardens sicken at thy beauty;
I grasp thy vest in my strong hands in vain, like water springs
In the bright sands of Los evading my embrace; then I alone
Wander among the virgins of the summer. Look, they cry,
The poor forsaken Los, mock'd by the worm, the shelly snail,
The Emmet & the beetle, hark! they laugh, & mock at Los."

Enitharmon answer'd:
"Secure now from the smitings of thy Power, demon of fury,
If the God enraptur'd me infolds
In clouds of sweet obscurity my beauteous form dissolving,
How thou over the body of death; 'tis thine. But if among the virgins
Of summer I have thee sleep & turn thy cheek delighted
Upon the rose or lilly pale, or on a bank where sleep
The beamy daughters of the light, starting, they rise, they flee
From thy fierce love, for tho' I am dissolv'd in the bright God,
My spirit still pursues thy false love over rocks & valleys."

Los answer'd: "Therefore fade I thus dissolv'd in raptur'd trance.
Thou canst repose on clouds of secrecy, while o'er my limbs
Cold dews & hoary frost creep tho' I lie on banks of summer
Among the beauties of the World. Cold & repining Los
Still dies for Enitharmon, nor a spirit springs from my dead corse;
Then I am dead till thou revivest me with thy sweet song.
Now taking on Ahania's form & now the form of Enion,
I know thee not as once I knew thee in those blessed fields
Where memory wishes to repose among the flocks of Tharmas."

Enitharmon answer'd: "Wherefore didst thou throw thine arms around
Ahania's Image? I deciev'd thee & will still decieve.
Urizen saw thy sin & hid his beams in dark'ning clouds.
I still keep watch altho' I tremble & wither across the heavens
In strong vibrations of fierce jealousy; for thou art mine,
Created for my will, my slave, tho' strong, tho' I am weak.
Farewell, the God calls me away. I depart in my sweet bliss."

She fled, vanishing on the wind, And left a dead cold corse
In Los's arms; howlings began over the body of death.
Los spoke. "Thy God in vain shall call thee if by my strong power
I can infuse my dear revenge into his glowing breast.
Then jealousy shall shadow all his mountains & Ahania
Curse thee, thou plague of woful Los, & seek revenge on thee."

So saying in deep sobs he languish'd till dead he also fell.
Night passed, & Enitharmon, e'er the dawn, return'd in bliss.
She sang O'er Los reviving him to Life: his groans were terrible;
But thus she sang:

        "I sieze the sphery harp. I strike the strings.

"At the first sound the Golden sun arises from the deep
And shakes his awful hair,
The Eccho wakes the moon to unbind her silver locks,
The golden sun bears on my song
And nine bright spheres of harmony rise round the fiery king.

"The joy of woman is the death of her most best beloved
Who dies for Love of her
In torments of fierce jealousy & pangs of adoration.
The Lovers' night bears on my song
And the nine spheres rejoice beneath my powerful controll.

"They sing unceasing to the notes of my immortal hand.
The solemn, silent moon
Reverberates the living harmony upon my limbs,
The birds & beasts rejoice & play,
And every one seeks for his mate to prove his inmost joy.

"Furious & terrible they sport & red the nether deep;
The deep lifts up his rugged head,
And lost in infinite humming wings vanishes with a cry.
The fading cry is ever dying,
The living voice is ever living in its inmost joy.

"Arise, you little glancing wings & sing your infant joy!
Arise & drink your bliss!
For every thing that lives is holy; for the source of life
Descends to be a weeping babe;
For the Earthworm renews the moisture of the sandy plain.

"Now my left hand I stretch to earth beneath,
And strike the terrible string.
I wake sweet joy in dens of sorrow & I plant a smile
In forests of affliction,
And wake the bubbling springs of life in regions of dark death

"O, I am weary! lay thine hand upon me or I faint,
I faint beneath these beams of thine,
For thou hast touch'd my five senses & they answer'd thee.
Now I am nothing, & I sink
And on the bed of silence sleep till thou awakest me."

Thus sang the Lovely one in Rapturous delusive trance.
Los heard, reviving; he siez'd her in his arms; delusive hopes
Kindling, she led him into shadows & thence fled outstretch'd
Upon the immense like a bright rainbow, weeping & smiling & fading.

Thus liv'd Los, driving Enion far into the *deathful* infinite [1]
That he may also draw Ahania's spirit into her Vortex.
Ah, happy blindness! Enion sees not the terrors of the uncertain,
And thus she wails from the dark deep; the golden heavens tremble:

"I am made to sow the thistle for wheat, the nettle for a nourishing dainty.
I have planted a false oath in the earth; it has brought forth a poison tree.
I have chosen the serpent for a councellor, & the dog
For a schoolmaster to my children.
I have blotted out from light & living the dove & nightingale,
And I have caused the earth worm to beg from door to door.

"I have taught the thief a secret path into the house of the just.
I have taught pale artifice to spread his nets upon the morning.
My heavens are brass, my earth is iron, my moon a clod of clay,
My sun a pestilence burning at noon & a vapour of death in night.

"What is the price of Experience? do men buy it for a song?
Or wisdom for a dance in the street? No, it is bought with the price
Of all that a man hath, his house, his wife, his children.
Wisdom is sold in the desolate market where none come to buy,
And in the wither'd field where the farmer plows for bread in vain.

"It is an easy thing to triumph in the summer's sun
And in the vintage & to sing on the waggon loaded with corn.
It is an easy thing to talk of patience to the afflicted,
To speak the laws of prudence to the houseless wanderer,
To listen to the hungry raven's cry in wintry season
When the red blood is fill'd with wine & with the marrow of lambs.

"It is an easy thing to laugh at wrathful elements,
To hear the dog howl at the wintry door, the ox in the slaughter house
    moan;
To see a god on every wind & a blessing on every blast;

[1] This line refers back to p. 741, l. 8 from bottom, the intervening passages being an insertion.

To hear sounds of love in the thunder storm that destroys our enemies'
    house;

To rejoice in the blight that covers his field, & the sickness that cuts off
    his children,

While our olive & vine sing & laugh round our door, & our children bring
    fruits & flowers.

Then the groan & the dolor are quite forgotten, & the slave grinding at
    the mill,

And the captive in chains, & the poor in the prison, & the soldier in the
    field

When the shatter'd bone hath laid him groaning among the happier dead.

"It is an easy thing to rejoice in the tents of prosperity:
Thus could I sing & thus rejoice: but it is not so with me."

Ahania heard the Lamentation, & a swift Vibration
Spread thro' her Golden frame. She rose up e'er the dawn of day
When Urizen slept on his couch: drawn thro' unbounded space
On the margin of Non Entity the bright Female came.
There she beheld the *Spectrous* form of Enion in the Void,
And never from that moment could she rest upon her pillow.

END OF THE SECOND NIGHT

VALA

NIGHT THE THIRD

N O W sat the King of Light on high upon his starry throne,
And bright Ahania bow'd herself before his splendid feet.

"O Urizen, look on *Me*; like a mournful stream
I Embrace round thy knees & wet *My* bright hair with *My* tears.
Why sighs my Lord? are not the morning stars thy obedient Sons?
Do they not bow their bright heads at thy voice? at thy command
Do they not fly into their stations & return their light to thee?
The immortal Atmospheres are thine; there thou art seen in glory
Surrounded by the ever changing Daughters of the Light.
Why wilt thou look upon futurity, dark'ning present joy?"

She ceas'd; the Prince his light obscur'd & the splendors of his crown
Infolded in thick clouds from whence his mighty voice burst forth:

"O bright Ahania, a Boy is born of the dark Ocean
Whom Urizen doth serve, with Light replenishing his darkness.
I am set here a King of trouble, commanded here to serve
And do my ministry to those who eat of my wide table.
All this is mine, yet I must serve, & that Prophetic boy
Must grow up to command his Prince; *but hear my determin'd decree:*
Vala shall become a Worm in Enitharmon's Womb,
Laying her seed upon the fibres, soon to issue forth,
And Luvah in the loins of Los a dark & furious death.
Alas for me! what will become of me at that dread time?"

Ahania bow'd her head & wept seven days before the King;
And on the eighth day, when his clouds unfolded from his throne,
She rais'd her bright head sweet perfum'd & thus with heavenly voice:

"O Prince, the Eternal One hath set thee leader of his hosts,
Raise then thy radiant eyes to him, raise thy obedient hands,
And comforts shall descend from heaven into thy dark'ning clouds.
Leave all futurity to him. Resume thy fields of Light.
Why didst thou listen to the voice of Luvah that dread morn
To give the immortal steeds of light to his deceitful hands?
No longer now obedient to thy will, thou art compell'd
To forge the curbs of iron & brass, to build the iron mangers,
To feed them with intoxication from the wine presses of Luvah
Till the Divine Vision & Fruition is quite obliterated.
They call thy lions to the field of blood; they rouze thy tygers
Out of the halls of justice, till these dens thy wisdom fram'd
Golden & beautiful, but O how unlike those sweet fields of bliss
Where liberty was justice, & eternal science was mercy.
Then, O my dear lord, listen to Ahania, listen to the vision,
The vision of Ahania in the slumbers of Urizen
When Urizen slept in the porch & the Ancient Man was smitten.
The Dark'ning Man walk'd on the steps of fire before his halls,
And Vala walk'd with him in dreams of soft deluding slumber.
He looked up & saw thee, Prince of Light, thy splendor faded,
But saw not Los nor Enitharmon for Luvah hid them in shadow
In a soft cloud outstretch'd across, & Luvah dwelt in the cloud.

"Then Man ascended mourning into the splendors of his palace,
Above him rose a Shadow from his wearied intellect
Of living gold, pure, perfect, holy; in white linen pure he hover'd,
A sweet entrancing self delusion, a wat'ry vision of Man
Soft exulting in existence, all the Man absorbing.

"Man fell upon his face prostrate before the wat'ry shadow,
Saying, 'O Lord, whence is this change? thou knowest I am nothing.'
And Vala trembled & cover'd her face, & her locks were spread on the
    pavement.
We heard astonish'd at the Vision, & *our* hearts trembled within *us*.
We heard the voice of the Slumberous Man, & thus he spoke
Idolatrous to his own Shadow, words of Eternity uttering:
'O I am nothing when I enter into judgment with thee.
If thou withdraw thy breath I die & vanish into Hades;
If thou doest lay thine hand upon me, behold I am silent;
If thou withhold thine hand I perish like a fallen leaf.
O I am nothing, & to nothing must return again.
If thou withdraw thy breath, behold I am oblivion.'

"He ceas'd: the shadowy voice was silent, but the cloud hover'd over their
    heads
In golden wreathes, the sorrow of Man, & the balmy drops fell down,
And Lo, that Son of Man, that shadowy Spirit of *Albion*.
Luvah, descended from the cloud. In terror *Albion rose:*
Indignant rose the Awful Man & turn'd his back on Vala.

"We heard the Voice of Albion starting from his sleep:
'Why roll thy clouds in sick'ning mists? I can no longer hide
The dismal vision of mine eyes. O love & life & light!
Prophetic dreads urge me to speak; futurity is before me
Like a dark lamp. Eternal death haunts all my expectation.
Rent from Eternal Brotherhood we die & are no more.

" 'Whence is this voice crying, Enion! that soundeth in my ears?
O cruel pity! O dark deceit! can Love seek for dominion?'

"And Luvah strove to gain dominion over *mighty Albion*.
They strove together above the Body where Vala was inclos'd
And the dark Body of *Albion* left prostrate upon the crystal pavement,
Cover'd with boils from head to foot, the terrible smiting of Luvah.

"Then frown'd *Albion* & put forth Luvah from his presence
(I heard him: frown not, Urizen, but listen to my Vision)
Saying, 'Go & die the Death of Man for Vala the sweet wanderer.
I will turn the volutions of your Ears outward, & bend your Nostrils
Downward, & your fluxile Eyes englob'd roll round in fear;
Your with'ring Lips & Tongue shrink up into a narrow circle

Till into narrow forms you creep. Go take your fiery way
And learn what 'tis to absorb the Man, you Spirits of Pity & Love.'
O Urizen, why art thou pale at the visions of Ahania?
Listen to her who loves thee, lest we also are driven away.
They heard the Voice & fled, swift as the winter's setting sun.
And now the Human Blood foam'd high. I saw that Luvah & Vala
Went down the Human Heart, where Paradise & its joys abounded,
In jealous fears, in fury & rage, & flames roll'd round their fervid feet,
And the vast form of Nature like a Serpent play'd before them;
And as they went, in folding fires & thunders of the deep,
Vala shrunk in like the dark sea that leaves its slimy banks,
And from her bosom Luvah fell far as the east & west
And the vast form of Nature, like a Serpent, roll'd between.
Whether this is Jerusalem or Babylon we know not.
All is Confusion. All is tumult, & we alone are escaped."
She ended, for his wrathful throne burst forth the black hail storm.

(Albion clos'd the Western Gate, & shut America out by the Atlantic, for
a curse, and hidden horror, and an altar of victims to Sin and
Repentance.)

"Am I not God?" said Urizen. "Who is Equal to me?
Do I not stretch the heavens abroad, or fold them up like a garment?"
He spoke, mustering his heavy clouds around him, black, opake.
Then thunders roll'd around & lightnings darted to and fro;
His visage chang'd to darkness, & his strong right hand came forth
To cast Ahania to the Earth; he siez'd her by the hair
And threw her from the steps of ice that froze around his throne,
Saying, "Art thou also become like Vala? thus I cast thee out!
Shall the feminine indolent bliss, the indulgent self of weariness,
The passive idle sleep, the enormous night & darkness of Death
Set herself up to give her laws to the active masculine virtue?
Thou little diminutive portion that dar'st be a counterpart,
Thy passivity, thy laws of obedience & insincerity
Are my abhorrence. Wherefore hast thou taken that fair form?
Whence is this power given to thee? Once thou wast in my breast
A sluggish current of dim waters on whose verdant margin
A cavern shagg'd with horrid shades, dark, cool & deadly, where
I laid my head in the hot noon after the broken clods
Had wearied me; there I laid my plow, & there my horses fed:
And thou hast risen with thy moist locks into a wat'ry image

Reflecting all my indolence, my weakness & my death,
To weigh me down beneath the grave into non Entity
Where Luvah strives, scorned by Vala, age after age wandering,
Shrinking & shrinking from her Lord & calling him the Tempter.
And art thou also become like Vala? thus I cast thee out!"

So loud in thunders spoke the King, folded in dark despair,
And threw Ahania from his bosom obdurate. She fell like lightning.
Then fled the sons of Urizen from his thunderous throne petrific;
They fled to East & West & left the North & South of Heaven.
A crash ran thro' the immense. The bounds of Destiny were broken.
The bounds of Destiny crash'd direful, & the swelling sea
Burst from its bonds in whirlpools fierce, roaring with Human voice,
Triumphing even to the stars at bright Ahania's fall.

Down from the dismal North the Prince in thunders & thick clouds—
As when the thunderbolt down falleth on the appointed place—
Fell down, down rushing, ruining, thundering, shuddering,
Into the Caverns of the Grave & places of Human Seed.
Where the impressions of Despair & Hope enroot for ever:
A world of Darkness. Ahania fell far into Non Entity.

She Continued falling. Loud the Crash continu'd, loud & Hoarse.
From the Crash roared a flame of blue sulphureous fire, from the flame
A dolorous groan that struck with dumbness all confusion,
Swallowing up the horrible din in agony on agony.
Thro' the Confusion, like a crack across from immense to immense,
Loud, strong, a universal groan of death, louder
Than all the wracking elements, deafen'd & rended worse
Than Urizen & all his hosts in curst despair down rushing.
But from the Dolorous Groan one like a shadow of smoke appear'd,
And human bones rattling together in the smoke & stamping
The nether Abyss, & gnashing in fierce despair, panting in sobs,
Thick, short, incessant, bursting, sobbing, deep despairing, stamping,
     struggling,
Struggling to utter the voice of Man, struggling to take the features of
     Man struggling
To take the limbs of Man, at length emerging from the smoke
Of Urizen dashed in pieces from his precipitant fall,
Tharmas rear'd up his hands & stood on the affrighted Ocean:
The dead rear'd up his Voice & stood on the resounding shore,

Crying: "Fury in my limbs! destruction in my bones & marrow!
My skull riven into filaments, my eyes into sea jellies
Floating upon the tide wander bubbling & bubbling,
Uttering my lamentations & begetting little monsters
Who sit mocking upon the little pebbles of the tide
In all my rivers & on dried shells that the fish
Have quite forsaken. O fool! fool! to lose my sweetest bliss.
Where art thou, Enion? ah, too near to cunning, too far off
And yet too near. Dash'd down I send thee into distant darkness
Far as my strength can hurl thee; wander there & laugh & play
Among the frozen arrows; they will tear thy tender flesh.
Fall off afar from Tharmas, come not too near my strong fury.
Scream & fall off & laugh at Tharmas, lovely summer beauty,
Till winter rends thee into Shivers as thou hast rended me."

So Tharmas bellow'd o'er the ocean, thund'ring, sobbing, bursting.
The bounds of Destiny were broken, & hatred now began
Instead of love to Enion. Enion, blind & age bent,
Plung'd into the cold billows, living a life in midst of waters;
In terrors she wither'd away to Entuthon Benithon,
A world of deep darkness where all things in horrors are rooted.

These are the words of Enion, heard from the cold waves of despair:
"O Tharmas, I had lost thee, & when I hoped I had found thee,
O Tharmas, do not thou destroy me quite, but let
A little shadow, but a little showery form of Enion
Be near thee, loved Terror; let me still remain, & then do thou
Thy righteous doom upon me; only let me hear thy voice.
Driven by thy rage I wander like a cloud into the deep
Where never yet Existence came; there losing all my life
I back return weaker & weaker; consume me not away
In thy great wrath; tho' I have sinned, tho' I have rebell'd
Make me not like the things forgotten as they had not been.
Make me not the thing that loveth thee a tear wiped away."

Tharmas replied, riding on storms, his voice of Thunder roll'd:
"Image of grief, thy fading lineaments make my eyelids fail.
What have I done? both rage & mercy are alike to me;
Looking upon thee, Image of faint waters, I recoil
From my fierce rage into thy semblance. Enion, return.
Why does thy piteous face Evanish like a rainy cloud
Melting, a shower of falling tears, nothing but tears! Enion,

Substanceless, voiceless, weeping, vanish'd, nothing but tears! Enion,
Art thou for ever vanish'd from the wat'ry eyes of Tharmas?
Rage, Rage shall never from my bosom: winds & waters of woe
Consuming all, to the end consuming. Love and Hope are ended."

For now no more remain'd of Enion in the dismal air,
Only a voice eternal wailing in the Elements.

Where Enion, blind & age bent, wander'd, Ahania wanders now:
She wanders in Eternal fear of falling into the indefinite,
For her bright eyes behold the Abyss. Sometimes a little sleep
Weighs down her eyelids; then she falls; then starting, wakes in fears
Sleepless to wander round, repell'd on the margin of Non Entity.

END OF THE THIRD NIGHT

VALA

NIGHT THE FOURTH

B U T Tharmas rode on the dark Abyss; the voice of Tharmas roll'd
Over the heaving deluge; he saw Los & Enitharmon Emerge
In strength & brightness from the Abyss; his bowels yearn'd over them.
They rose in strength above the heaving deluge in mighty scorn,
Red as the Sun in the hot morning of the bloody day
Tharmas beheld them; his bowels yearn'd over them.

And he said: "Wherefore do I feel such love & pity?
Ah, Enion! Ah, Enion! Ah, lovely, lovely Enion!
How is this? All my hope is gone! for ever fled!
Like a famish'd Eagle, Eyeless, raging in the vast expanse,
Incessant tears are now my food, incessant rage & tears.
Deathless for ever now I wander seeking oblivion
In torrents of despair: in vain; for if I plunge beneath,
Stifling I live: If dash'd in pieces from a rocky height,
I reunite in endless torment; would I had never risen
From death's cold sleep beneath the bottom of the raging Ocean.
And cannot those who once have lov'd ever forget their Love?
Are love & rage the same passion? they are the same in me.
Are those who love like those who died, risen again from death,
Immortal in immortal torment, never to be deliver'd?

Is it not possible that one risen again from death
Can die? When dark despair comes over, can I not
Flow down into the sea & slumber in oblivion? Ah Enion,
Deform'd I see these lineaments of ungratified desire.
The all powerful curse of an honest man be upon Urizen & Luvah.
But thou, My Son, Glorious in Brightness, comforter of Tharmas,
Go forth, Rebuild this Universe beneath my indignant power,
A Universe of Death & Decay. Let Enitharmon's hands
Weave soft delusive forms of Man above my wat'ry world;
Renew these ruin'd souls of Men thro' Earth, Sea, Air & Fire,
To waste in endless corruption, renew those I will destroy.
Perhaps Enion may resume some little semblance
To ease my pangs of heart & to restore some peace to Tharmas."

Los answer'd in his furious pride, sparks issuing from his hair:
"Hitherto shalt thou come, no further; here thy proud waves cease.
We have drunk up the Eternal Man by our unbounded power,
Beware lest we also drink up thee, rough Demon of the waters.
Our God is Urizen the King, King of the Heavenly hosts;
We have no other God but he, thou father of worms & clay,
And he is fall'n into the Deep, rough Demon of the waters,
And Los remains God over all, weak father of worms & clay.
I know I was Urthona, keeper of the gates of heaven,
But now I am all powerful Los, & Urthona is but my shadow."

Doubting stood Tharmas in the solemn darkness; his dim Eyes
Swam in red tears; he rear'd his waves above the head of Los
In wrath, but pitying back withdrew with many a sigh.
Now he resolv'd to destroy Los, & now his tears flow'd down.

In scorn stood Los, red sparks of blighting from his furious head
Flew over the waves of Tharmas; pitying, Tharmas stayed his Waves,
For Enitharmon shriek'd amain, crying: "O my sweet world
Built by the Architect divine, whose love to Los & Enitharmon
Thou rash abhorred Demon in thy fury hast o'erthrown!"
"What Sovereign Architect," said Tharmas, "dare my will controll?
For if I will, I urge these waters. If I will, they sleep
In peace beneath my awful frown; my will shall be my Law."

So saying, in a Wave he rap'd bright Enitharmon far
Apart from Los, but cover'd her with softest brooding care
On a broad wave in the warm west, balming her bleeding wound.

O how Los howl'd at the rending asunder! All the fibres rent,
Where Enitharmon join'd to his left side, in griding pain.
He, falling on the rocks, bellow'd his dolor till the blood
Stanch'd: then in ululation wail'd his woes upon the wind.

And Tharmas call'd to the Dark Spectre who upon the shores
With dislocated Limbs had fall'n. The Spectre rose in pain,
A shadow blue, obscure & dismal; like a statue of lead,
Bent by its fall from a high tower, the dolorous shadow rose.

"Go forth," said Tharmas, "works of joy are thine: obey & live,
So shall the spungy marrow issuing from thy splinter'd bones
Bonify, & thou shalt have rest when this thy labour is done.
Go forth, bear Enitharmon back to the Eternal Prophet,
Build her a bower in the midst of all my dashing waves;
Make first a resting place for Los & Enitharmon, then
Thou shalt have rest. If thou refusest, dash'd abroad on all
My waves, thy limbs shall separate in stench & rotting, & thou
Become a prey to all my demons of despair & hope."

The Spectre of Urthona seeing Enitharmon, writh'd
His cloudy form in jealous fear, & muttering thunders hoarse
And casting round thick glooms, thus utter'd his fierce pangs of heart:

"Tharmas, I know thee: how are we alter'd, our beauty decay'd!
But still I know thee, tho' in this horrible ruin whelm'd.
Thou, once the mildest son of heaven, art now become a Rage,
A terror to all living things; think not that I am ignorant
That thou art risen from the dead, or that, my power forgot,
I slumber here in weak repose. I well remember the Day,
The day of terror & abhorrence
When fleeing from the battle, thou fleeing like the raven
Of dawn, outstretching an expanse where ne'er expanse had been,
Drew'st all the Sons of Beulah into thy dread vortex, following
Thy Eddying spirit down the hills of Beulah. All my sons
Stood round me at the anvil, where, new heated, the wedge
Of iron glow'd furious, prepar'd for spades & mattocks.
Hearing the symphonies of war loud sounding, All my sons
Fled from my side; then pangs smote me unknown before. I saw
My loins begin to break forth into veiny pipes & writhe
Before me in the wind englobing, trembling with strong vibrations,
The bloody mass began to animate. I, bending over,

Wept bitter tears incessant. Still beholding how the piteous form
Dividing & dividing from my loins, a weak & piteous
Soft cloud of snow, a female pale & weak, I soft embrac'd
My counter part & call'd it Love. I nam'd her Enitharmon,
But found myself and her together issuing down the tide
Which now our rivers were become, delving thro' caverns huge
Of goary blood, struggling to be deliver'd from our bonds.
She strove in vain; not so Urthona strove, for breaking forth,
A shadow blue, obscure & dismal, from the breathing Nostrils
Of Enion I issued into the air, divided from Enitharmon.
I howl'd in sorrow. I beheld thee rotting upon the Rocks.
I, pitying, hover'd over thee; I protected thy ghastly corse
From Vultures of the deep; then wherefore shouldst thou rage
Against me who thee guarded in the night of death from harm?"

Tharmas replied: "Art thou Urthona, My friend, my old companion
With whom I liv'd in happiness before that deadly night
When Urizen gave the horses of Light into the hands of Luvah?
Thou knowest not what Tharmas knows. O I could tell thee tales
That would enrage thee as it has Enraged me, even
From death in wrath & fury. But now, come, bear back
Thy loved Enitharmon. For thou hast her here before thine eyes;
But my sweet Enion is vanish'd, & I never more
Shall see her, unless thou, O Shadow, wilt protect this Son
Of Enion & him assist to bind the fallen King,
Lest he should rise again from death in all his dreary pow'r.
Bind him; take Enitharmon for thy sweet reward, while I
In vain am driven on false hope, hope sister of despair."

Groaning the terror rose & drave his solid rocks before
Upon the tide, till underneath the feet of Los a World
Dark dreadful rose, & Enitharmon lay at Los's feet.
The dolorous shadow joy'd; weak hope appear'd around his head.

Tharmas before Los stood, & thus the Voice of Tharmas roll'd:

"Now all comes into the power of Tharmas. Urizen is fall'n
And Luvah hidden in the Elemental forms of Life & Death.
Urthona is My Son. O Los, thou art Urthona, & Tharmas
Is God, The Eternal Man is seal'd, never to be deliver'd.
I roll my floods over his body, my billows & waves pass over him,
The sea encompasses him & monsters of the deep are his companions.

Dreamer of furious oceans, cold sleeper of weeds & shells,
Thy Eternal form shall never renew, my uncertain prevails against thee.
Yet tho' I rage, God over all, A portion of my Life
That in Eternal fields in comfort wander'd with my flocks
At noon & laid her head upon my wearied bosom at night,
She is divided. She is vanish'd, even like Luvah & Vala.
O why did foul ambition sieze thee, Urizen, Prince of Light?
And thee, O Luvah, prince of Love, till Tharmas was divided?
And I, what can I now behold but an Eternal Death
Before my Eyes, & an Eternal weary work to strive
Against the monstrous forms that breed among my silent waves?
Is this to be A God? far rather would I be a Man,
To know sweet Science, & to do with simple companions
Sitting beneath a tent & viewing sheepfolds & soft pastures.
Take thou the hammer of Urthona: rebuild these furnaces.
Dost thou refuse? mind I the sparks that issue from thy hair?
I will compell thee to rebuild by these my furious waves.
Death choose or life; thou strugglest in my waters; now choose life,
And all the Elements shall serve thee to their soothing flutes:
Their sweet inspiriting lyres thy labours shall administer,
And they to thee; only remit not, faint not thou, my son.
Now thou dost know what 'tis to strive against the God of waters."

So saying, Tharmas on his furious chariots of the Deep
Departed far into the Unknown & left a wondrous void
Round Los; afar his waters bore on all sides round with noise
Of wheels & horses' hoofs, & Trumpets, Horns & Clarions.

Terrified, Los beheld the ruins of Urizen beneath,
A horrible Chaos to his eyes, a formless unmeasurable Death
Whirling up broken rocks on high into the dismal air
And fluctuating all beneath in Eddies of molten fluid.

Then Los with terrible hands seiz'd on the Ruin'd Furnaces
Of Urizen: Enormous work, he builded them anew,
Labour of Ages in the Darkness & the war of Tharmas;
And Los form'd Anvils of Iron petrific, for his blows
Petrify with incessant beating many a rock, many a planet.

But Urizen slept in a stoned stupor in the nether Abyss,
A dreamful, horrible state in tossings on his icy bed
Freezing to solid all beneath: his grev oblivious form,

Stretch'd over the immense, heaves in strong shudders, silent his voice,
In brooding contemplation stretching out from North to South
In mighty power. Round him Los roll'd furious
His thunderous wheels from furnace to furnace, tending diligent
The contemplative terror frighten'd in his scornful sphere,
Frighten'd with cold infectious madness; in his hand the thundering
Hammer of Urthona forming under his heavy hand the hours,
The days & years, in chains of iron round the limbs of Urizen
Link'd hour to hour & day to night & night to day & year to yea;
In periods of pulsative furor; mills he form'd & works
Of many wheels resistless in the power of dark Urthona.

But Enitharmon wrap'd in clouds wail'd loud, for as Los beat
The anvils of Urthona, link by link the chains of sorrow,
Warping upon the winds & whirling round in the dark deep,
Lash'd on the limbs of Enitharmon, & the sulphur fires,
Belch'd from the furnaces, wreath'd round her, chain'd in ceaseless fire.
The lovely female howl'd, & Urizen beneath, deep groan'd
Deadly between the hammer's beating, grateful to the Ears
of Los absorb'd in dire revenge; he drank with joy the cries
Of Enitharmon & the groans of Urizen, fuel for his wrath
And for his pity, secret feeding on thoughts of cruelty.

The Spectre wept at his dire labours when from Ladles huge
He pour'd the molten iron round the limbs of Enitharmon.
But when he pour'd it round the bones of Urizen, he laugh'd
Hollow upon the hollow wind, his shadowy form obeying
The voice of Los; compell'd he labour'd round the Furnaces.

And thus began the binding of Urizen; day & night in fear
Circling round the dark Demon, with howlings, dismay & sharp
    blightings,
The Prophet of Eternity beat on his iron links & links of brass;
And as he beat round the hurtling Demon, terrified at the Shapes
Enslav'd humanity put on, he became what he beheld.
Raging against Tharmas his God, & uttering
Ambiguous words, blasphemous, fill'd with envy, firm resolv'd
On hate Eternal, in his vast disdain he labour'd beating
The Links of fate, link after link, an endless chain of sorrows.

The Eternal Mind, bounded, began to roll eddies of wrath ceaseless
Round & round, & the sulphureous foam surgeing thick,
Settled, a Lake bright & shining clear, White as the snow.

Forgetfulness, dumbness, necessity, in chains of the mind lock'd up,
In fetters of ice shrinking, disorganiz'd, rent from Eternity,
Los beat on his fetters & heated his furnaces,
And pour'd iron sodor & sodor of brass.

Restless the immortal inchain'd, heaving dolorous,
Anguish'd unbearable till a roof, shaggy wild, inclos'd
In an orb his fountain of thought.

In a horrible dreamful slumber, like the linked chain,
A vast spine writh'd in torment upon the wind,
Shooting pain'd ribbs, like a bending Cavern,
And bones of solidness froze over all his nerves of joy.
A first age passed, a state of dismal woe.

From the Caverns of his jointed spine, down sunk with fright
A red round globe, hot burning, deep deep down into the Abyss,
Panting, conglobing, trembling, shooting out ten thousand branches
Around his solid bones, & a second age passed over.

In harrowing fear rolling, his nervous brain shot branches
On high into two little orbs hiding in two little caves,
Hiding carefully from the wind; his eyes beheld the deep,
And a third age passed, a state of dismal woe.

The pangs of hope began; in heavy pain striving, struggling,
Two Ears in close volutions from beneath his orbs of vision
Shot spiring out & petrified as they grew. And a Fourth
Age passed over & a state of dismal woe.

In ghastly torment sick, hanging upon the wind,
Two nostrils bent down to the deeps,
And a fifth age passed & a state of dismal woe.

In ghastly torment sick, within his ribs bloated round,
A craving hungry cavern. Thence arose his channel'd
Throat; then like a red flame a tongue of hunger
And thirst appear'd, and a sixth age pass'd of dismal woe.

Enraged & stifled with torment, he threw his right arm to the north,
His left arm to the south, shooting out in anguish deep,
And his feet stamp'd the nether abyss in trembling, howling & dismay,
And a seventh age passed over & a state of dismal woe.

The Council of God on high watching over the Body
Of Man cloth'd in Luvah's robes of blood, saw & wept.
Descending over Beulah's mild moon cover'd regions,
The daughters of Beulah saw the Divine Vision; they were comforted,
And as a double female form, loveliness & perfection of beauty,
They bow'd the head & worshipp'd, & with mild voice spoke these words:

"Lord Saviour, if thou hadst been here our brother had not died,
And now we know that whatsoever thou wilt ask of God
He will give it thee; for we are weak women & dare not lift
Our eyes to the Divine pavilions; therefore in mercy thou
Appearest cloth'd in Luvah's garments that we may behold thee
And live. Behold Eternal Death is in Beulah. Behold
We perish & shall not be found unless thou grant a place
In which we may be hidden under the shadow of wings.
For if we, who are for but a time & who pass away in winter,
Behold these wonders of Eternity, we shall consume."

Such were the words of Beulah, of the Feminine Emanation.
The Empyrean groan'd throughout. All Eden was darken'd.
The Corse of Albion lay on the Rock; the sea of Time & Space
Beat round the Rock in mighty waves, & as a Polypus
That vegetates beneath the Sea, the limbs of Man vegetated
In monstrous forms of Death, a Human polypus of Death.

The Saviour mild & gentle bent over the corse of Death,
Saying, "If ye will Believe, your brother shall rise again."
And first he found the Limit of Opacity, & nam'd it Satan,
In Albion's bosom, for in every human bosom these limits stand.
And next he found the Limit of Contraction, & nam'd it Adam,
While yet those beings were not born nor knew of good or Evil.

Then wondrously the *Starry Wheels* felt the divine hand. Limit
Was put to Eternal Death. Los felt the Limit & saw
The Finger of God touch the Seventh furnace in terror.
And Los beheld the hand of God over his furnaces
Beneath the Deeps in dismal Darkness beneath immensity.

In terrors Los shrank from his task; his great hammer
Fell from his hand, his fires hid their strong limbs in smoke;
For with noises ruinous, hurtlings & clashings & groans,
The immortal endur'd, tho' bound in a deadly sleep.

Pale terror siez'd the Eyes of Los as he beat round
The hurtling demon; terrified at the shapes
Enslav'd humanity put on, he became what he beheld:
He became what he was doing: he was himself transform'd.

(Bring in here the Globe of Blood as in the Book of Urizen.)

Spasms siez'd his muscular fibres writhing to & fro: his pallid lips
Unwilling mov'd as Urizen howl'd: his loins wav'd like the sea
At Enitharmon's shrieks: his knees each other smote, & then he look'd
With stony Eyes on Urizen, & then swift writh'd his neck
Involuntary to the Couch where Enitharmon lay.
The bones of Urizen hurtle on the wind: the bones of Los
Twinge & his iron sinews bend like lead & fold
Into unusual forms, dancing & howling, stamping the abyss.

END OF THE FOURTH NIGHT

VALA

NIGHT THE FIFTH

INFECTED, Mad, he danc'd on his mountains high & dark as heaven,
Now fix'd into one stedfast bulk his features stonify,
From his mouth curses, & from his eyes sparks of blighting,
Beside the anvil cold he danc'd with the hammer of Urthona.
Terrific pale Enitharmon stretched on the *dreary* earth
Felt her immortal limbs freeze, stiffening, pale, inflexible.
His feet shrink with'ring from the deep, shrinking & withering,
And Enitharmon shrunk up, all their fibres with'ring beneath,
As plants wither'd by winter, leaves & stems & roots decaying
Melt into thin air, while the seed, driv'n by the furious wind,
Rests on the distant Mountain's top. So Los & Enitharmon,
Shrunk into fixed space, stood trembling on a Rocky cliff,
Yet mighty bulk & majesty & beauty remain'd, but unexpansive.
As far as highest Zenith from the lowest Nadir, so far shrunk
Los from the furnaces, a space immense, & left the cold
Prince of Light bound in chains of intellect among the furnaces;
But all the furnaces were out & the bellows had ceast to blow.

He stood trembling & Enitharmon clung around his knees,
Their senses unexpansive in one stedfast bulk remain.
The night blew cold, & Enitharmon shriek'd on the dismal wind.
Her pale hands cling around her husband, & over her weak head
Shadows of Eternal Death sit in the leaden air.

But the soft pipe, the flute, the viol, organ, harp, & cymbal,
And the sweet sound of silver voices calm the weary couch
Of Enitharmon; but her groans drown the immortal harps.
Loud & more loud the living music floats upon the air,
Faint & more faint the daylight wanes; the wheels of turning darkness
Began in solemn revolutions. Earth, convuls'd with rending pangs,
Rock'd to & fro & cried sore at the groans of Enitharmon.
Still the faint harps & silver voices calm the weary couch,
But from the caves of deepest night, ascending in clouds of mist,
The winter spread his wide black wings across from pole to pole:
Grim frost beneath & terrible snow, link'd in a marriage chain,
Began a dismal dance. The winds around on pointed rocks
Settled like bats innumerable, ready to fly abroad.
The groans of Enitharmon shake the skies, the lab'ring Earth,
Till from her heart rending his way, a terrible child sprang forth
In thunder, smoke & sullen flames, & howlings & fury & blood.

Soon as his burning Eyes were open'd on the Abyss,
The horrid trumpets of the deep bellow'd with bitter blasts.
The Enormous Demons woke & howl'd around the new born King,
Crying, "Luvah, King of Love, thou art the King of rage & death."
Urizen cast deep darkness round him; raging, Luvah pour'd
The spears of Urizen from Chariots round the Eternal tent.
Discord began, then yells & cries shook the wide firmament:

"Where is sweet Vala, gloomy prophet? where the lovely form
That drew the body of Man from heaven into this dark Abyss?
Soft tears & sighs, where are you? come forth! shout on bloody fields.
Shew thy soul, Vala! shew thy bow & quiver of secret fires.

"Draw thy bow, Vala! from the depths of hell thy black bow draw,
And twang the bowstring to our howlings; let thine arrows black
Sing in the Sky as once they sang upon the hills of Light
When dark Urthona wept in torment of the secret pain:

"He wept & he divided & he laid his gloomy head
Down on the Rock of Eternity on darkness of the deep,
Torn by black storms & ceaseless torrents of consuming fire,
Within his breast his fiery sons chain'd down & fill'd with cursings.
And breathing terrible blood & vengeance, gnashing his teeth with pain,
Let loose the Enormous Spirit on the darkness of the deep,
And his dark wife, that once fair crystal form divinely clear,
Within his ribs producing serpents whose souls are flames of fire.

"But now the times return upon thee. Enitharmon's womb
Now holds thee, soon to issue forth. Sound, Clarions of war!
Call Vala from her close recess in all her dark deceit,
Then rage on rage shall fierce redound out of her crystal quiver."

So sung the Demons round red Orc & round faint Enitharmon.
Sweat & blood stood on the limbs of Los in globes; his fiery Eyelids
Faded; he rouz'd, he siez'd the wonder in his hands & went
Shudd'ring & weeping thro' the Gloom & down into the deeps.

Enitharmon nurs'd her fiery child in the dark deeps
Sitting in darkness: over her Los mourn'd in anguish fierce
Cover'd with gloom; the fiery boy grew, fed by the milk
Of Enitharmon. Los around her builded pillars of iron
And brass & silver & gold fourfold, in dark prophetic fear,
For now he fear'd Eternal Death & uttermost Extinction:
He builded Golgonooza on the Lake of Udan Adan.
Upon the Limit of Translucence then he builded Luban.
Tharmas laid the Foundation & Los finish'd it in howling woe.

But when fourteen summers & winters had revolved over
Their solemn habitation, Los beheld the ruddy boy
Embracing his bright mother, & beheld malignant fires
In his young eyes, discerning plain that Orc plotted his death.
Grief rose upon his ruddy brows; a tightning girdle grew
Around his bosom like a bloody cord; in secret sobs
He burst it, but next morn another girdle succeeds
Around his bosom. Every day he view'd the fiery youth
With silent fear, & his immortal cheeks grew deadly pale,
Till many a morn & many a night pass'd over in dire woe
Forming a girdle in the day & bursting it at night.
The girdle was form'd by day, by night was burst in twain,
Falling down on the rock, an iron chain link by link lock'd.

Enitharmon beheld the bloody chain of nights & days
Depending from the bosom of Los, & how with *griding* pain
He went each morning to his labours with the spectre dark,
Call'd it the chain of Jealousy. Now Los began to speak
His woes aloud to Enitharmon, since he could not hide
His uncouth plague. He siez'd the boy in his immortal hands,
While Enitharmon follow'd him, weeping in dismal woe,
Up to the iron mountain's top, & there the jealous chain
Fell from his bosom on the mountain. The spectre dark
Held the fierce boy. Los nail'd him down, binding around his limbs
The *accursed* chain. O how bright Enitharmon howl'd & cried
Over her son! Obdurate, Los bound down her loved joy.

The hammer of Urthona smote the rivets in terror, of brass
Tenfold; the Demon's rage flam'd tenfold forth, rending,
Roaring, redounding, Loud, Loud, Louder & Louder, & fir'd
The darkness, warring with the waves of Tharmas & Snows of Urizen.
Crackling the flames went up with fury from the immortal demon.
Surrounded with flames the Demon grew, loud howling in his fires;
Los folded Enitharmon in a cold white cloud in fear,
Then led her down into the deeps & into his labyrinth,
Giving the Spectre sternest charge over the howling fiend,
Concenter'd into Love of Parent, Storgous Appetite, Craving.

His limbs bound down mock at his chains, for over them a flame
Of circling fire unceasing plays; to feed them with life & bring
The virtues of the Eternal worlds, ten thousand thousand spirits
Of life lament around the Demon, going forth & returning.
At his enormous call they flee into the heavens of heavens
And back return with wine & food, or dive into the deeps
To bring the thrilling joys of sense to quell his ceaseless rage.
His eyes, the lights of his large soul, contract or else expand:
Contracted they behold the secrets of the infinite mountains,
The veins of gold & silver & the hidden things of Vala,
Whatever grows from its pure bud or breathes a fragrant soul:
Expanded they behold the terrors of the Sun & Moon,
The Elemental Planets & the orbs of eccentric fire.
His nostrils breathe a fiery flame, his locks are like the forests
Of wild beasts; there the lion glares, the tyger & wolf howl there,
And there the Eagle hides her young in cliffs & precipices.
His bosom is like starry heaven expanded; all the stars
Sing round; there waves the harvest & the vintage rejoices; the springs
Flow into rivers of delight; there the spontaneous flowers

Drink, laugh & sing, the grasshopper, the Emmet and the Fly;
The golden Moth builds there a house & spreads her silken bed.
His loins inwove with silken fires are like a furnace fierce:
As the strong Bull in summer time when bees sing round the heath
Where the herds low after the shadow & after the water spring,
The num'rous flocks cover the mountains & shine along the valley.
His knees are rocks of adament & rubie & emerald:
Spirits of strength in Palaces rejoice in golden armour
Armed with spear & shield they drink & rejoice over the slain.
Such is the Demon, such his terror on the nether deep.

But, when return'd to Golgonooza, Los & Enitharmon
Felt all the sorrow Parents feel, they wept toward one another
And Los repented that he had chain'd Orc upon the mountain.
And Enitharmon's tears prevail'd; parental love return'd,
Tho' terrible his dread of that infernal chain. They rose
At midnight hasting to their much beloved care.
Nine days they travel'd thro' the Gloom of Entuthon Benithon.
Los, taking Enitharmon by the hand, led her along
The dismal vales & up to the iron mountain's top where Orc
Howl'd in the furious wind; he thought to give to Enitharmon
Her son in tenfold joy, & to compensate for her tears
Even if his own death resulted, so much pity him pain'd.

But when they came to the dark rock & to the spectrous cave,
Lo, the young limbs had strucken root into the rock, & strong
Fibres had from the Chain of Jealousy inwove themselves
In a swift vegetation round the rock & round the Cave
And over the immortal limbs of the terrible fiery boy.
In vain they strove now to unchain, In vain with bitter tears
To melt the chain of Jealousy; not Enitharmon's death,
Nor the Consummation of Los could ever melt the chain
Nor unroot the infernal fibres from their rocky bed,
Nor all Urthona's strength, nor all the power of Luvah's Bulls,
Tho' they each morning drag the unwilling Sun out of the deep,
Could uproot the infernal chain, for it had taken root
Into the iron rock & grew a chain beneath the Earth
Even to the Center, wrapping round the Center; & the limbs
Of Orc entering with fibres become one with him, a living Chain
Sustained by the Demon's life. Despair & Terror & Woe & Rage
Inwrap the Parents in cold clouds as they bend howling over
The terrible boy, till fainting by his side, the Parents fell.

Not long they lay; Urthona's spectre found herbs of the pit.
Rubbing their temples, he reviv'd them; all their lamentations
I write not here, but all their after life was lamentation.

When satiated with grief they return'd back to Golgonooza,
Enitharmon on the road of Dranthon felt the inmost gate
Of her bright heart burst open & again close with a deadly pain.
Within her heart Vala began to reanimate in bursting sobs;
And when the Gate was open she beheld that dreary deep
Where bright Ahania wept. She also saw the infernal roots
Of the chain of Jealousy, & felt the rendings of fierce howling Orc
Rending the Caverns like a mighty wind pent in the Earth.
Tho' wide apart as furthest north is from the furthest south,
Urizen trembled where he lay to hear the howling terror.
The rocks shook, the Eternal bars tugg'd to & fro were rifted.
Outstretch'd upon the stones of ice, the ruins of his throne,
Urizen shudd'ring heard, his trembling limbs shook the strong caves.

The Woes of Urizen shut up in the deep dens of Urthona:

"Ah! how shall Urizen the King submit to this dark mansion?
Ah! how is this? Once on the heights I stretch'd my throne sublime;
The mountains of Urizen, once of silver, where the sons of wisdom dwelt,
And on whose tops the Virgins sang, are rocks of desolation.

"My fountains, once the haunt of swans, now breed the scaly tortoise,
The houses of my harpers are become a haunt of crows,
The gardens of wisdom are become a field of horrid graves,
And on the bones I drop my tears & water them in vain.

"Once how I walked from my palace in gardens of delight,
The sons of wisdom stood around, the harpers follow'd with harps,
Nine virgins cloth'd in light compos'd the song to their immortal voices,
And at my banquets of new wine my head was crown'd with joy.

"Then in my ivory pavilions I slumber'd in the noon
And walked in the silent night among sweet smelling flowers,
Till on my silver bed I slept & sweet dreams round me hover'd,
But now my land is darken'd & my wise men are departed.

"My songs are turned into cries of Lamentation
Heard on my Mountains, & deep sighs under my palace roofs,
Because the Steeds of Urizen, once swifter than the light,
Were kept back from my Lord & from his chariot of mercies.

"O did I keep the horses of the day in silver pastures!
O I refus'd the lord of day the horses of his prince!
O did I close my treasures with roofs of solid stone
And darken all my Palace walls with envyings & hate!

"O Fool! to think that I could hide from his all piercing eyes
The gold & silver & costly stones, his holy workmanship!
O Fool! could I forget the light that filled my bright spheres
Was a reflection of his face who call'd me from the deep!

"I well remember, for I heard the mild & holy voice
Saying, 'O light, spring up & shine,' & I sprang up from the deep.
He gave me a silver scepter, & crown'd me with a golden crown,
& said, 'Go forth & guide my Son who wanders on the ocean.'

"I went not forth: I hid myself in black clouds of my wrath;
I call'd the stars around my feet in the night of councils dark;
The stars threw down their spears & fled naked away.
We fell. I siez'd thee, dark Urthona. In my left hand falling

"I siez'd thee, beauteous Luvah; thou art faded like a flower
And like a lilly is thy wife Vala wither'd by winds.
When thou didst bear the golden cup at the immortal tables
Thy children smote their fiery wings, crown'd with the gold of heaven.

"Thy pure feet step'd on the steps divine, too pure for other feet,
And thy fair locks shadow'd thine eyes from the divine effulgence,
Then thou didst keep with Strong Urthona the living gates of heaven,
But now thou art bow'd down with him, even to the gates of hell.

"Because thou gavest Urizen the wine of the Almighty
For Steeds of Light, that they might run in thy golden chariot of pride,
I gave to thee the Steeds, I pour'd the stolen wine
And drunken with the immortal draught fell from my throne sublime.

"I will arise, Explore these dens, & find that deep pulsation
That shakes my cavern with strong shudders; perhaps this is the night
Of Prophecy, & Luvah hath burst his way from Enitharmon.
When Thought is clos'd in Caves Then love shall shew its root in deepest
    Hell."

END OF THE FIFTH NIGHT

VALA

NIGHT THE SIXTH

s o Urizen arose, & leaning on his spear explor'd his dens.
He threw his flight thro' the dark air to where a river flow'd,
And taking off his silver helmet filled it & drank;
But when, unsatiated his thirst, he assay'd to gather more,
Lo, three terrific women at the verge of the bright flood,
Who would not suffer him to approach, but drove him back with storms.

Urizen knew them not, & thus addressed the spirits of darkness:

"Who art thou, Eldest Woman, sitting in thy clouds?
What is that name written on thy forehead? what art thou?
And wherefore dost thou pour this water forth in sighs & care?"

She answer'd not, but fill'd her urn & pour'd it forth abroad.

"Answerest thou not?" said Urizen. "Then thou maist answer me,
Thou terrible woman, clad in blue, whose strong attractive power
Draws all into a fountain at the rock of thy attraction;
With frowning brow thou sittest, mistress of these mighty waters.'

She answer'd not, but stretched her arms & threw her limbs abroad.

"Or wilt thou answer, youngest Woman, clad in shining green?
With labour & care thou dost divide the current into four.
Queen of these dreadful rivers, speak, & let me hear thy voice."

They rear'd up a wall of rocks, *and* Urizen rais'd his spear.
They gave a scream, they knew their father: Urizen knew his daughters.
They shrunk into their channels, dry the rocky strand beneath his feet,
Hiding themselves in rocky forms from the Eyes of Urizen.

Then Urizen wept & thus his lamentation poured forth:

"O horrible, O dreadful state! those whom I loved best,
On whom I pour'd the beauties of my light, adorning them
With jewels & precious ornament labour'd with art divine,
Vests of the radiant colours of heaven & crowns of golden fire.

I gave sweet lillies to their breasts & roses to their hair,
I taught them songs of sweet delight, I gave their tender voices
Into the blue expanse, & I invented with laborious art
Sweet instruments of sound; in pride encompassing my knees
They pour'd their radiance above all; the daughters of Luvah envied
At their exceeding brightness, & the sons of eternity sent them gifts.
Now will I pour my fury on them, & I will reverse
The precious benediction; for their colours of loveliness
I will give blackness; for jewels, hoary frost; for ornament, deformity;
For crowns, wreath'd serpents; for sweet odors, stinking corruptibility;
For voices of delight, hoarse croakings inarticulate thro' frost;
For labour'd fatherly care & sweet instruction, I will give
Chains of dark ignorance & cords of twisted self-conceit
And whips of stern repentance & food of stubborn obstinacy,
That they may curse Tharmas their God, & Los his adopted son;
That they may curse & worship the obscure demon of destruction;
That they may worship terrors & obey the violent.
Go forth, sons of my curse. Go forth, daughters of my abhorrence."

Tharmas heard the deadly scream across his wat'ry world
And Urizen's loud sounding voice lamenting on the wind,
And he came riding in his fury; froze to solid were his waves,
Silent in ridges he beheld them stand round Urizen,
A dreary waste of solid waters; for the King of Light
Darken'd his brows with his cold helmet, & his gloomy spear
Darken'd before him. Silent on the ridgy waves he took
His gloomy way; before him Tharmas fled, & flying fought,
Crying: "What & who art thou, Cold Demon? art thou Urizen?
Art thou, like me, risen again from death? or art thou deathless?
If thou art he, my desperate purpose hear, & give me death,
For death to me is better far than life, death my desire
That I in vain in various paths have sought, but still I live.
The Body of Man is given to me. I seek in vain to destroy,
For still it surges forth in fish & monsters of the deeps,
And in these monstrous forms I Live in an Eternal woe,
And thou, O Urizen, art fall'n, never to be deliver'd.
Withhold thy light from me for ever, & I will withhold
From thee thy food; so shall we cease to be, & all our sorrows
End, & the Eternal Man no more renew beneath our power.
If thou refusest, in eternal flight thy beams in vain
Shall pursue Tharmas, & in vain shalt crave for food. I will
Pour down my flight thro' dark immensity Eternal falling.

Thou shalt pursue me but in vain, till starv'd upon the void
Thou hang'st, a dried skin, shrunk up, weak wailing in the wind."

So Tharmas spoke, but Urizen replied not. On his way
He took, high bounding over hills & desarts, floods & horrible chasms.
Infinite was his labour, without end his travel; he strove
In vain, for hideous monsters of the deeps annoy'd him sore,
Scaled & finn'd with iron & brass, they devour'd the path before him.
Incessant was the conflict. On he bent his weary steps
Making a path toward the dark world of Urthona; he rose
With pain upon the dreary mountains & with pain descended
And saw their grizly fears, & his eyes sicken'd at the sight:
The howlings, gnashings, groanings, shriekings, shudderings, sobbings,
        burstings
Mingle together to create a world for Los. In cruel delight
Los brooded on the darkness, nor saw Urizen with a Globe of fire
Lighting his dismal journey thro' the pathless world of death,
Writing in bitter tears & groans in books of iron & brass
The enormous wonders of the Abysses, once his brightest joy.

For Urizen beheld the terrors of the Abyss wandering among
The ruin'd spirits, once his children & the children of Luvah.
Scar'd at the sound of their own sigh that seems to shake the immense
They wander Moping, in their heart a sun, a dreary moon,
A Universe of fiery constellations in their brain,
An earth of wintry woe beneath their feet, & round their loins
Waters or winds or clouds or brooding lightnings & pestilential plagues.
Beyond the bounds of their own self their senses cannot penetrate:
As the tree knows not what is outside of its leaves & bark
And yet it drinks the summer joy & fears the winter sorrow,
So, in the regions of the grave, none knows his dark compeer
Tho' he partakes of his dire woes & mutual returns the pang,
The throb, the dolor, the convulsion, in soul-sickening woes.

Not so clos'd kept the Prince of Light now darken'd, wand'ring among
The Ruin'd Spirits, once his Children & the Children of Luvah:
For Urizen beheld the terrors of the Abyss, wandering among
The horrid shapes & sights of torment in burning dungeons & in
Fetters of red hot iron; some with crowns of serpents & some
With monsters girding round their bosoms; some lying on beds of sulphur,
On racks & wheels; he beheld women marching o'er burning wastes
Of Sand in bands of hundreds & of fifties & of thousands, strucken with

Lightnings which blazed after them upon their shoulders in their march
In successive volleys with loud thunders: swift flew the King of Light
Over the burning desarts; Then, the desarts pass'd, involv'd in clouds
Of smoke with myriads moping in the stifling vapours, Swift
Flew the King, tho' flag'd his powers, labouring till over rocks
And Mountains faint weary he wander'd where multitudes were shut
Up in the solid mountains & in rocks which heav'd with their torments.
Then came he among fiery cities & castles built of burning steel.
Then he beheld the forms of tygers & of Lions, dishumaniz'd men.
Many in serpents & in worms, stretched out enormous length
Over the sullen mould & slimy tracks, obstruct his way
Drawn out from deep to deep, woven by ribb'd
And scaled monsters or arm'd in iron shell, or shell of brass
Or gold: a glittering torment shining & hissing in eternal pain;
Some, columns of fire or of water, sometimes stretch'd out in heighth,
Sometimes in length, sometimes englobing, wandering in vain seeking for
    ease.
His voice to them was but an inarticulate thunder, for their Ears
Were heavy & dull, & their eyes & nostrils closed up.
Oft he stood by a howling victim Questioning in words
Soothing or Furious; no one answer'd; every one wrap'd up
In his own sorrow howl'd regardless of his words, nor voice
Of sweet response could he obtain, tho' oft assay'd with tears.
He knew they were his Children ruin'd in his ruin'd world.

Oft would he stand & question a fierce scorpion glowing with gold;
In vain, the terror heard not; then a lion he would sieze
By the fierce mane, staying his howling course; in vain the voice
Of Urizen, in vain the Eloquent tongue. A Rock, a Cloud, a Mountain,
Were now not Vocal as in Climes of happy Eternity
Where the lamb replies to the infant voice, & the lion to the man of years
Giving them sweet instructions; where the Cloud, the River & the Field
Talk with the husbandman & shepherd. But these attack'd him sore,
Siezing upon his feet, & rending the sinews, that in Caves
He hid to recure his obstructed powers with rest & oblivion.

Here he had time enough to repent of his rashly threaten'd curse.
He saw them curs'd beyond his Curse: his soul melted with fear.
He could not take their fetters off, for they grew from the soul,
Nor could he quench the fires, for they flam'd out from the heart,
Nor could he calm the Elements, because himself was subject;
So he threw his flight in terror & pain, & in repentant tears.

When he had pass'd these southern terrors he approach'd the East,
Void, pathless, beaten with iron sleet, & eternal hail & ran.
No form was there, no living thing, & yet his way lay thro'
This dismal world; he stood a while & look'd back over his former
Terrific voyage, Hills & Vales of torment & despair!
Sighing, & weeping a fresh tear, then turning round, he threw
Himself into the dismal void; falling he fell & fell,
Whirling in unresistible revolutions down & down
In the horrid bottomless vacuity, falling, falling, falling
Into the Eastern vacuity, the empty world of Luvah.

The ever pitying one who seeth all things, saw his fall,
And in the dark vacuity created a bosom of clay;
When wearied, dead he fell, his limbs repos'd in the bosom of slime;
As the seed falls from the sower's hand, so Urizen fell, & death
Shut up his powers in oblivion; then as the seed shoots forth
In pain & sorrow, so the slimy bed his limbs renew'd.
At first an infant weakness; periods pass'd; he gather'd strength,
But still in solitude he sat; then rising, threw his flight
Onward, tho' falling, thro' the waste of night & ending in death
And in another resurrection to sorrow & weary travel.
But still his books he bore in his strong hands, & his iron pen,
For when he died they lay beside his grave, & when he rose
He siez'd them with a *gloomy* smile; for wrap'd in his death clothes
He hid them when he slept in death, when he reviv'd, the clothes
Were rotted by the winds; the books remain'd still unconsum'd,
Still to be written & interleav'd with brass & iron & gold,
Time after time, for such a journey none but iron pens
Can write And adamantine leaves recieve, nor can the man who goes
The journey obstinate refuse to write time after time.

Endless had been his travel, but the Divine hand him led,
For infinite the distance & obscur'd by Combustions dire,
By rocky masses frowning in the abysses, revolving erratic
Round Lakes of fire in the dark deep, the ruins of Urizen's world.

Oft would he sit in a dark rift & regulate his books,
Or sleep such sleep as spirits eternal, wearied in his dark
Tearful & sorrowful state; then rise, look out & ponder
His dismal voyage, eyeing the next sphere tho' far remote;
Then darting into the Abyss of night his venturous limbs
Thro' lightnings, thunders, earthquakes & concussions, fires & floods

Stemming his downward fall, labouring up against futurity,
Creating many a Vortex, fixing many a Science in the deep,
And thence throwing his venturous limbs into the vast unknown,
Swift, swift from Chaos to chaos, from void to void, a road immense.
For when he came to where a Vortex ceas'd to operate,
Nor down nor up remain'd, then if he turn'd & look'd back
From whence he came, 'twas upward all; & if he turn'd and view'd
The unpass'd void, upward was still his mighty wand'ring,
The midst between, an Equilibrium grey of air serene
Where he might live in peace & where his life might meet repose.

But Urizen said: "Can I not leave this world of Cumbrous wheels,
Circle o'er Circle, nor on high attain a void
Where self sustaining I may view all things beneath my feet?
Or sinking thro' these Elemental wonders, swift to fall,
I thought perhaps to find an End, a world beneath of voidness
Whence I might travel round the outside of this dark confusion.
When I bend downward, bending my head downward into the deep,
'Tis upward all which way soever I my course begin;
But when A Vortex, form'd on high by labour & sorrow & care
And weariness, begins on all my limbs, then sleep revives
My wearied spirits; waking then 'tis downward all which way
Soever I my spirits turn, no end I find of all.
O what a world is here, unlike those climes of bliss
Where my sons gather'd round my knees! O, thou poor ruin'd world!
Thou horrible ruin! once like me thou wast all glorious,
And now like me partaking desolate thy master's lot.
Art thou, O ruin, the once glorious heaven? are these thy rocks
Where joy sang on the trees & pleasure sported in the rivers,
And laughter sat beneath the Oaks, & innocence sported round
Upon the green plains, & sweet friendship met in palaces,
And books & instruments of song & pictures of delight?
Where are they, whelmed beneath these ruins in horrible destruction?
And if, Eternal falling, I repose on the dark bosom
Of winds & waters, or thence fall into a Void where air
Is not, down falling thro' immensity ever & ever,
I lose my powers, weaken'd every revolution, till a death
Shuts up my powers; then a seed in the vast womb of darkness
I dwell in dim oblivion; brooding over me, the Enormous worlds
Reorganize me, shooting forth in bones & flesh & blood,
I am regenerated, to fall or rise at will, or to remain
A labourer of ages, a dire discount, a living woe

Wandering in vain. Here will I fix my foot & here rebuild.
Here Mountains of Brass promise much riches in their dreadful bosoms."

So he began to form of gold, silver & iron
And brass, vast instruments to measure out the immense & fix
The whole into another world better suited to obey
His will, where none should dare oppose his will, himself being King
Of All, & all futurity be bound in his vast chain.
And the Sciences were fix'd & the Vortexes began to operate
On all the sons of men, & every human soul terrified
At the living wheels of heaven shrunk away inward, with'ring away.
Gaining a New dominion over all his Sons & Daughters, & over the Sons
    & Daughters of Luvah in the horrible Abyss.
For Urizen lamented over them in a selfish lamentation
Till a white woof cover'd his cold limbs from head to feet,
Hair white as snow cover'd him in flaky locks terrific
Overspreading his limbs; in pride he wander'd weeping,
Clothed in aged venerableness, obstinately resolv'd,
Travelling thro' darkness; & wherever he travel'd a dire Web
Follow'd behind him, as the Web of a Spider, dusky & cold,
Shivering across from Vortex to Vortex, drawn out from his mantle of
    years:
A living Mantle adjoined to his life & growing from his soul.
And the Web of Urizen stretch'd direful, shiv'ring in clouds,
And uttering such woes, such cries, such thunderings.
The eyelids expansive as morning & the Ears
As a golden ascent winding round to the heavens of heavens
Within the dark horrors of the Abysses, lion or tyger, or scorpion;
For every one open'd within into Eternity at will,
But they refus'd, because their outward forms were in the Abyss;
And the wing-like tent of the Universe, beautiful, surrounding all,
Or drawn up or let down at the will of the immortal man,
Vibrated in such anguish the eyelids quiver'd,
Weak & Weaker their expansive orbs began shrinking;
Pangs smote thro' the brain & a universal shriek
Ran thro' the Abysses rending the web, torment on torment.

Thus Urizen in sorrows wander'd many a dreary way
Warring with monsters of the deeps in his most hideous pilgrimage,
Till, his bright hair scatter'd in snows, his skin bark'd o'er with wrinkles,
Four Caverns rooting downwards their foundations, thrusting forth
The metal, rock & stone in ever painful throes of vegetation.

The Cave of Orc stood to the South, a furnace of dire flames,
Quenchless, unceasing. In the west the Cave of Urizen;
For Urizen fell, as the Midday sun falls down, into the West.
North stood Urthona's stedfast throne, a World of Solid darkness
Shut up in stifling obstruction, rooted in dumb despair.
The East was Void. But Tharmas roll'd his billows in ceaseless eddies,
Void, pathless, beat with Snows eternal & iron hail & rain
All thro' the caverns of fire & air & Earth, Seeking
For Enion's limbs, nought finding but the black sea weed & sick'ning
    slime:
Flying away from Urizen that he might not give him food,
Above, beneath, on all sides round in the vast deep of immensity,
That he might starve the sons & daughters of Urizen on the winds,
Making between, horrible chasms into the vast unknown.
All these around the world of Los cast forth their monstrous births.
But in eternal times the Seat of Urizen is in the South,
Urthona in the North, Luvah in East, Tharmas in West.

And now he came into the Abhorred world of Dark Urthona,
By Providence Divine conducted, not bent from his own will
Lest Death Eternal should be the result, for the Will cannot be violated:
Into the doleful vales where no tree grew nor river flow'd,
Nor man nor beast nor creeping thing, nor sun nor cloud nor star;
Still he, with his globe of fire immense in his venturous hand,
Bore on thro' the Affrighted vales, ascending & descending,
O'erwearied or in cumbrous flight he ventur'd o'er dark rifts,
Or down dark precipices, or climb'd with pain and labours huge
Till he beheld the world of Los from the Peaked rock of Urthona
And heard the howling of red Orc distincter & distincter.

Redoubling his immortal efforts, thro' the narrow vales
With difficulty down descending, guided by his Ear
And by his globe of fire, he went down the Vale of Urthona
Between the enormous iron walls built by the Spectre dark.
Dark grew his globe redd'ning with mists, & full before his path,
Striding across the narrow vale, the Shadow of Urthona
A spectre Vast appear'd, whose feet & legs with iron scaled,
Stamp'd the hard rocks expectant of the unknown wanderer
Whom he had seen wandering his nether world when distant far,
And watch'd his swift approach; collected, dark, the Spectre stood.
Beside him Tharmas stay'd his flight & stood in stern defiance,
Communing with the Spectre who rejoic'd along the vale.

Round his loins a girdle glow'd with many colour'd fires,
In his hand a knotted Club whose knots like mountains frown'd
Desart among the stars, them withering with its ridges cold.
Black scales of iron arm the dread visage; iron spikes instead
Of hair shoot from his orbed scull; his glowing eyes
Burn like two furnaces; he call'd with Voice of Thunder.
Four winged heralds mount the furious blasts & blow their trumps;
Gold, Silver, Brass & iron clangors, clamoring rend the *shores*.
Like white clouds rising from the Vales, his fifty-two armies
From the four Cliffs of Urthona rise glowing around the Spectre.
Four sons of Urizen the Squadrons of Urthona led, in arms
Of gold & silver, brass & iron: he knew his mighty sons.

Then Urizen arose upon the wind, back many a mile
Returning into his dire Web, scattering fleecy snows:
As he ascended, howling loud, the Web vibrated strong,
From heaven to heaven, from globe to globe. In vast excentric paths
Compulsive roll'd the Comets at his dread command, the dreary way
Falling with wheel impetuous down among Urthona's vales
And round red Orc; returning back to Urizen, gorg'd with blood.
Slow roll the massy Globes at his command, & slow o'erwheel
The dismal squadrons of Urthona weaving the dire Web
In their progressions, & preparing Urizen's path before him.

END OF THE SIXTH NIGHT

VALA

NIGHT THE SEVENTH [a][1]

THEN Urizen arose. The Spectre fled, & Tharmas fled;
The dark'ning Spectre of Urthona hid beneath a rock.
Tharmas threw his impetuous flight thro' the deeps of immensity
Revolving round in whirlpools fierce, all round the cavern'd worlds.

But Urizen silent descended to the Caves of Orc & saw
A Cavern'd Universe of flaming fire; the horses of Urizen
Here bound to fiery mangers, furious dash their golden hoofs,
Striking fierce sparkles from their brazen fetters; fierce his lions

---

[1] Blake wrote two versions of "Night the Seventh," but did not finally reject either.
They are here distinguished as *a* and *b*.

Howl in the burning dens; his tygers roam in the redounding smoke
In forests of affliction; the adamantine scales of justice
Consuming in the raging lamps of mercy, pour'd in rivers.
The holy oil rages thro' all the cavern'd rocks; fierce flames
Dance on the rivers & the rocks; howling & drunk with fury
The plow of ages & the golden harrow wade thro' fields
Of goary blood; the immortal seed is nourish'd for the slaughter.
The bulls of Luvah, breathing fire, bellow on burning pastures
Round howling Orc, whose awful limbs cast forth red smoke & fire,
That Urizen approach'd not near but took his seat on a rock
And rang'd his books around him, brooding Envious over Orc.

Howling & rending his dark caves the awful Demon lay:
Pulse after pulse beat on his fetters, pulse after pulse his spirit
Darted & darted higher & higher to the shrine of Enitharmon;
As when the thunder folds himself in thickest clouds,
The wat'ry nations couch & hide in the profoundest deeps,
Then bursting from his troubled head, with terrible visages & flaming
     hair,
His swift wing'd daughters sweep across the vast black ocean.

Los felt the Envy in his limbs like to a blighted tree,
For Urizen fix'd in envy sat brooding & cover'd with snow;
His book of iron on his knees, he trac'd the dreadful letters
While his snows fell & his storms beat to cool the flames of Orc
Age after Age, till underneath his heel a deadly root
Struck thro' the rock, the root of Mystery accursed shooting up
Branches into the heaven of Los: they, pipe form'd, bending down
Take root again where ever they touch, again branching forth
In intricate labyrinths o'erspreading many a grizly deep.

Amaz'd started Urizen when he found himself compass'd round
And high roofed over with trees; he arose, but the stems
Stood so thick he with difficulty & great pain brought
His books out of the dismal shade, all but the book of iron.
Again he took his seat & rang'd his Books around
On a rock of iron frowning over the foaming fires of Orc.
And Urizen hung over Orc & view'd his terrible wrath;
Sitting upon an iron Crag, at length his words broke forth:

"Image of dread, whence art thou? whence is this most woful place?
Whence these fierce fires, but from thyself? No other living thing

In all this Chasm I behold. No other living thing
Dare thy most terrible wrath abide. Bound here to waste in pain
Thy vital substance in these fires that issue new & new
Around thee, sometimes like a flood, & sometimes like a rock
Of living pangs, thy horrible bed glowing with ceaseless fires
Beneath thee & around. Above, a shower of fire now beats,
Moulded to globes & arrowy wedges, rending thy bleeding limbs.
And now a whirling pillar of burning sands to overwhelm thee,
Steeping thy wounds in salts infernal & in bitter anguish.
And now a rock moves on the surface of this lake of fire
To bear thee down beneath the waves in stifling despair.
Pity for thee mov'd me to break my dark & long repose,
And to reveal myself before thee in a form of wisdom.
Yet thou dost laugh at all these tortures, & this horrible place:
Yet throw thy limbs these fires abroad that back return upon thee
While thou reposest, throwing rage on rage, feeding thyself
With visions of sweet bliss far other than this burning clime.
Sure thou art bath'd in rivers of delight, on verdant fields
Walking in joy, in bright Expanses sleeping on bright clouds
With visions of delight so lovely that they urge thy rage
Tenfold with fierce desire to rend thy chain & howl in fury
And dim oblivion of all woe, & desperate repose.
Or is thy joy founded on torment which others bear for thee?"

Orc answer'd: "Curse thy hoary brows! What dost thou in this deep?
Thy Pity I contemn. Scatter thy snows elsewhere.
I rage in the deep, for Lo, my feet & hands are nail'd to the burning rock,
Yet my fierce fires are better than thy snows. Shudd'ring thou sittest.
Thou art not chain'd. Why shouldst thou sit, cold grovelling demon of woe,
In tortures of dire coldness? now a Lake of waters deep
Sweeps over thee freezing to solid; still thou sit'st clos'd up
In that transparent rock as if in joy of thy bright prison,
Till, overburden'd with its own weight drawn out thro' immensity,
With a crash breaking across, the horrible mass comes down
Thund'ring, & hail & frozen iron hail'd from the Element
Rends thy white hair; yet thou dost, fix'd obdurate brooding, sit
Writing thy books. Anon a cloud, fill'd with a waste of snows
Covers thee, still obdurate, still resolv'd & writing still;
Tho' rocks roll o'er thee, tho' floods pour, tho' winds black as the sea
Cut thee in gashes, tho' the blood pours down around thy ankles,
Freezing thy feet to the hard rock, still thy pen obdurate
Traces the wonders of Futurity in horrible fear of the future.

I rage furious in the deep, for lo, my feet & hands are nail'd
To the hard rock, or thou shouldst feel my enmity & hate
In all the diseases of man falling upon thy grey accursed front."

Urizen answer'd: "Read my books, explore my Constellations,
Enquire of my Sons & they shall teach thee how to War.
Enquire of my Daughters, who, accurs'd in the dark depths,
Knead bread of Sorrow by my stern command; for I am God
Of all this dreadful ruin. Rise, O daughters, at my stern command!"

Rending the Rocks, Eleth & Uveth rose, & Ona rose,
Terrific with their iron vessels, driving them across
In the dim air; they took the book of iron & plac'd above
On clouds of death, & sang their songs, kneading the bread of Orc.
Orc listen'd to the song, compell'd, hung'ring on the cold wind
That swagg'd heavy with the accursed dough; the hoar frost rag'd
Thro' Ona's sieve; the torrent rain poured from the iron pail
Of Eleth, & the icy hands of Uveth kneaded the bread.
The heavens bow with terror underneath their iron hands,
Singing at their dire work the words of Urizen's book of iron
While the enormous scrolls roll'd dreadful in the heavens above;
And still the burden of their song in tears was pour'd forth:
"The bread is kneaded, let us rest, O cruel father of children!"

But Urizen remitted not their labours upon his rock,
And Urizen Read in his book of brass in sounding tones:
"Listen, O Daughters, to my voice. Listen to the Words of Wisdom,
So shall [you] govern over all; let Moral Duty tune your tongue,
But be your hearts harder than the nether millstone.
To bring the Shadow of Enitharmon beneath our wondrous tree,
That Los may Evaporate like smoke & be no more,
Draw down Enitharmon to the spectre of Urthona,
And let him have dominion over Los, the terrible shade.
Compell the poor to live upon a Crust of bread, by soft mild arts.
Smile when they frown, frown when they smile; & when a man looks pale
With labour & abstinence, say he looks healthy & happy;
And when his children sicken, let them die; there are enough
Born, even too many, & our Earth will be overrun
Without these arts. If you would make the poor live with temper[ance],
With pomp give every crust of bread you give; with gracious cunning
Magnify small gifts; reduce the man to want a gift, & then give with pomp.
Say he smiles if you hear him sigh. If pale, say he is ruddy.

Preach temperance: say he is overgorg'd & drowns his wit
In strong drink, tho' you know that bread & water are all
He can afford. Flatter his wife, pity his children, till we can
Reduce all to our will, as spaniels are taught with art.
Lo! how the heart & brain are formed in the breeding womb
Of Enitharmon: how it buds with life & forms the bones,
The little heart, the liver, & the red blood in its labyrinths;
By gratified desire, by strong devouring appetite, she fills
Los with ambitious fury that his race shall all devour."

Then Orc cried: "Curse thy Cold hypocrisy! already round thy Tree
In scales that shine with gold & rubies, thou beginnest to weaken
My divided Spirit. Like a worm I rise in peace, unbound
From wrath. Now when I rage, my fetters bind me more.
O torment! O torment! A Worm compell'd! Am I a worm?
Is it in strong deceit that man is born? In strong deceit
Thou dost restrain my fury that the worm may fold the tree.
Avaunt, Cold hypocrite! I am chain'd, or thou couldst not use me thus.
The Man shall rage, bound with this chain, the worm in silence creep.
Thou wilt not cease from rage. Grey demon, silence all thy storms,
Give me example of thy mildness. King of furious hail storms,
Art thou the cold attractive power that holds me in this chain?
I well remember how I stole thy light & it became fire
Consuming. Thou Know'st me now, O Urizen, Prince of Light,
And I know thee; is this the triumph, this the Godlike State,
That lies beyond the bounds of Science in the Grey obscure?"

Terrified Urizen heard Orc, now certain that he was Luvah.
And Orc began to organize a Serpent body,
Despising Urizen's light & turning it into flaming fire,
Recieving as a poison'd cup Recieves the heavenly wine,
And turning affection into fury, & thought into abstraction,
A Self consuming dark devourer rising into the heavens.

Urizen envious brooding sat & saw the secret terror
Flame high in pride & laugh to scorn the source of his deceit,
Nor knew the source of his own, but thought himself the sole author
Of all his wandering Experiments in the horrible Abyss.
He knew that weakness stretches out in breadth & length, he knew
That wisdom reaches high & deep; & therefore he made Orc,
In serpent form compell'd, stretch out & up the mysterious tree.
He suffer'd him to climb that he might draw all human forms
Into submission to his will, nor knew the dread result.

Los sat in showers of Urizen watching cold Enitharmon.
His broodings rush down to his feet, producing Eggs that hatching
Burst forth upon the winds above the tree of Mystery.
Enitharmon lay on his knees. Urizen trac'd his Verses.
In the dark deep the dark tree grew; her shadow was drawn down,
Down to the roots; it wept over Orc, the shadow of Enitharmon.

Los saw her stretch'd, the image of death, upon his wither'd valleys;
Her shadow went forth & return'd. Now she was pale as snow
When the mountains & hills are cover'd over & the paths of Men shut up,
But when her spirit return'd, as ruddy as a morning when
The ripe fruit blushes into joy in heaven's eternal halls,
She secret joy'd to see; she fed herself on his Despair.
She said, "I am aveng'd for all my sufferings of old."
Sorrow shot thro' him from his feet, it shot up to his head
Like a cold night that nips the roots & shatters off the leaves.
Silent he stood o'er Enitharmon, watching her pale face.
He spoke not, he was silent till he felt the cold disease.
Then Los mourn'd on the dismal wind in his jealous lamentation:

"Why can I not Enjoy thy beauty, Lovely Enitharmon?
When I return from clouds of Grief in the wand'ring Elements
Where thou in thrilling joy, in beaming summer loveliness,
Delectable reposest, ruddy in my absence, flaming with beauty,
Cold pale in sorrow at my approach, trembling at my terrific
Forehead & eyes, thy lips decay like roses in the spring.
How art thou shrunk! thy grapes that burst in summer's vast Excess,
Shut up in little purple covering, faintly bud & die.
Thy olive trees that pour'd down oil upon a thousand hills,
Sickly look forth & scarcely stretch their branches to the plain.
Thy roses that expanded in the face of glowing morn,
Hid in a little silken veil scarce breathe & faintly shine.
Thy lillies that gave light what time the morning looked forth,
Hid in the Vales, faintly lament, & no one hears their voice.
All things beside the woful Los enjoy the delights of beauty!
Once how I sang & call'd the beasts & birds to their delight,
Nor knew that I, alone exempted from the joys of love,
Must war with secret monsters of the animating worlds.
O that I had not seen the day! then should I be at rest,
Nor felt the stingings of desire, nor longings after life,
For life is sweet to Los the wretched; to his winged woes
Is given a craving cry, that they may sit at night on barren rocks

And whet their beaks & snuff the air, & watch the opening dawn,
And shriek till, at the smells of blood, they stretch their boney wings
And cut the winds like arrows shot by troops of Destiny."

Thus Los lamented in the night, unheard by Enitharmon.
For the Shadow of Enitharmon descended down the tree of Mystery.
The Spectre saw the Shade Shiv'ring over his gloomy rocks
Beneath the tree of Mystery, which in the dismal Abyss
Began to blossom in fierce pain, shooting its writhing buds
In throes of birth; & now, the blossoms falling, shining fruit
Appear'd of many colours & of various poisonous qualities,
Of Plagues hidden in shining globes that grew on the living tree.

The Spectre of Urthona saw the Shadow of Enitharmon
Beneath the Tree of Mystery among the leaves & fruit.
Redd'ning, the demon strong prepar'd the poison of sweet Love.
He turn'd from side to side in tears; he wept & he embrac'd
The fleeting image, & in whispers mild woo'd the faint shade:

"Loveliest delight of Men! Enitharmon, shady hiding
In secret places where no eye can trace thy wat'ry way,
Have I found thee? have I found thee? tremblest thou in fear
Because of Orc? because he rent his discordant way
From thy sweet loins of bliss? red flow'd thy blood,
Pale grew thy face, lightnings play'd around thee, thunders hover'd
Over thee, & the terrible Orc rent his discordant way;
But the next joy of thine shall be in sweet delusion,
And its birth in fainting & sleep & sweet delusions of Vala."

The Shadow of Enitharmon answer'd: "Art thou, terrible Shade,
Set over this sweet boy of mine to guard him lest he rend
His mother to the winds of heaven? Intoxicated with
The fruit of this delightful tree, I cannot flee away
From thy embrace, else be assur'd so horrible a form
Should never in my arms repose; now listen, I will tell
Thee Secrets of Eternity which ne'er before unlock'd
My golden lips nor took the bar from Enitharmon's breast.
Among the Flowers of Beulah walk'd the Eternal Man & saw
Vala, the lilly of the desart melting in high noon;
Upon her bosom in sweet bliss he fainted. Wonder seiz'd
All heaven; they saw him dark; they built a golden wall
Round Beulah. There he revel'd in delight among the Flowers.

Vala was pregnant & brought forth Urizen, Prince of Light,
First born of Generation. Then behold a wonder to the Eyes
Of the now fallen Man; a double form Vala appear'd, a Male
And female; shudd'ring pale the Fallen Man recoil'd
From the Enormity & call'd them Luvah & Vala, turning down
The vales to find his way back into Heaven, but found none,
For his frail eyes were faded & his ears heavy & dull.
Urizen grew up in the plains of Beulah. Many sons
And many daughters flourish'd round the holy Tent of Man
Till he forgot Eternity, delighted in his sweet joy
Among his family, his flocks & herds & tents & pastures.
But Luvah close conferr'd with Urizen in darksom night
To bind the father & enslave the brethren. Nought he knew
Of sweet Eternity; the blood flow'd round the holy tent & riv'n
From its hinges, uttering its final groan, all Beulah fell
In dark confusion; mean time Los was born & Enitharmon,
But how, I know not; then forgetfulness quite wrap'd me up
A period, nor do I more remember till I stood
Beside Los in the Cavern dark, enslav'd to vegetative forms
According to the Will of Luvah, who assum'd the Place
Of the Eternal Man & smote him. But thou, Spectre dark,
Maist find a way to punish Vala in thy fiery south,
To bring her down subjected to the rage of my fierce boy."

The Spectre said: "Thou lovely Vision, this delightful Tree
Is given us for a Shelter from the tempests of Void & Solid,
Till once again the morn of ages shall renew upon us,
To reunite in those mild fields of happy Eternity
Where thou & I in undivided Essence walk'd about
Imbodied, thou my garden of delight & I the spirit in the garden;
Mutual there we dwelt in one another's joy, revolving
Days of Eternity, with Tharmas mild & Luvah sweet melodious
Upon our waters. This thou well rememberest; listen, I will tell
What thou forgettest. They in us & we in them alternate Liv'd,
Drinking the joys of Universal Manhood. One dread morn—
Listen, O vision of Delight! One dread morn of goary blood
The manhood was divided, for the gentle passions, making way
Thro' the infinite labyrinths of the heart & thro' the nostrils issuing
In odorous stupefaction, stood before the Eyes of Man
A female bright. I stood beside my anvil dark, a mass
Of iron glow'd bright prepar'd for spade & plowshares: sudden down
I sunk with cries of blood issuing downward in the veins

Which now my rivers were become, rolling in tubelike forms
Shut up within themselves descending down. I sunk along
The goary tide even to the place of seed, & there dividing
I was divided in darkness & oblivion; thou an infant woe,
And I an infant terror in the womb of Enion.
My masculine spirit, scorning the frail body, issued forth
From Enion's brain In this deformed form, leaving thee there
Till times pass'd over thee; but still my spirit returning hover'd
And form'd a Male, to be a counterpart to thee, O Love
Darken'd & Lost! In due time issuing forth from Enion's womb
Thou & that demon Los were born. Ah, jealousy & woe!
Ah, poor divided dark Urthona! now a Spectre wand'ring
The deeps of Los, the slave of that Creation I created.
I labour night & day for Los; but listen thou my vision.
I view futurity in thee. I will bring down soft Vala
To the embraces of this terror, & I will destroy
That body I created; then shall we unite again in bliss;
For till these terrors planted round the Gates of Eternal life
Are driven away & annihilated, we never can repass the Gates.
Thou knowest that the Spectre is in Every Man insane, brutish,
Deform'd, that I am thus a ravening devouring lust continually
Craving and devouring; but my Eyes are always upon thee, O lovely
Delusion, & I cannot crave for any thing but thee: not so
The Spectres of the Dead, for I am as the Spectre of the Living."

Astonish'd, fill'd with tears, the spirit of Enitharmon beheld
And heard the Spectre; bitterly she wept, Embracing fervent
Her once lov'd Lord, now but a Shade, herself also a shade,
Conferring times on times among the branches of that Tree.
Thus they conferr'd among the intoxicating fumes of Mystery
Till Enitharmon's shadow, pregnant in the deeps beneath,
Brought forth a wonder horrible. While Enitharmon shriek'd
And trembled, thro' the Worlds above Los wept, his fierce soul was terrified
At the shrieks of Enitharmon, at her tossings, nor could his eyes percieve
The cause of her dire anguish, for she lay the image of death,
Mov'd by strong shudders till her shadow was delivered, then she ran
Raving about the upper Elements in maddening fury.

She burst the Gates of Enitharmon's heart with direful Crash,
Nor could they ever be clos'd again; the golden hinges were broken,
And the gates broke in sunder & their ornaments defac'd
Beneath the tree of Mystery, for the immortal shadow shuddering

Brought forth this wonder horrible: a Cloud; she grew & grew
Till many of the Dead burst forth from the bottoms of their tombs
In male forms without female counterparts, or Emanations,
Cruel and ravening with Enmity & Hatred & War,
In dreams of Ulro, dark delusive, drawn by the lovely shadow.

The Spectre terrified gave her Charge over the howling Orc.
Then took the tree of Mystery root in the World of Los,
Its topmost boughs shooting a fibre beneath Enitharmon's couch,
The double rooted Labyrinth soon wav'd around their heads.

But then the Spectre enter'd Los's bosom. Every sigh & groan
Of Enitharmon bore Urthona's Spectre on its wings.
Obdurate Los felt Pity. Enitharmon told the tale
Of Urthona. Los embrac'd the Spectre, first as a brother,
Then as another Self, astonish'd, humanizing & in tears,
In Self abasement Giving up his Domineering lust.

"Thou never canst embrace sweet Enitharmon, terrible Demon, Till
Thou art united with thy Spectre, Consummating by pains & labours
That mortal body, & by Self annihilation back returning
To Life Eternal; be assur'd I am thy real self,
Tho' thus divided from thee & the slave of Every passion
Of thy fierce Soul. Unbar the Gates of Memory: look upon me
Not as another, but as thy real Self. I am thy Spectre,
Thou didst subdue me in old times by thy Immortal Strength
When I was a ravening hungering & thirsting cruel lust & murder.
Tho' horrible & Ghastly to thine Eyes, tho' buried beneath
The ruins of the Universe, hear what inspir'd I speak, & be silent.
If we unite in one, another better world will be
Open'd within your heart & loins & wondrous brain,
Threefold, as it was in Eternity, & this, the fourth Universe,
Will be Renew'd by the three & consummated in Mental fires;
But if thou dost refuse, Another body will be prepared
For me, & thou, annihilate, evaporate & be no more.
For thou art but a form & organ of life, & of thyself
Art nothing, being Created Continually by Mercy & Love divine."

Los furious answered: "Spectre horrible, thy words astound my Ear
With irresistible conviction. I feel I am not one of those
Who when convinc'd can still persist: tho' furious, controllable
By Reason's power. Even I already feel a World within

Opening its gates, & in it all the real substances
Of which these in the outward World are shadows which pass away.
Come then into my Bosom, & in thy shadowy arms bring with thee
My lovely Enitharmon. I will quell my fury & teach
Peace to the soul of dark revenge, & repentance to Cruelty."

So spoke Los, & Embracing Enitharmon & the Spectre,
Clouds would have folded round in Extacy & Love uniting,
But Enitharmon trembling, fled & hid beneath Urizen's tree.
But mingling together with his Spectre, the Spectre of Urthona
Wondering beheld the Center open'd; by Divine Mercy inspir'd—
He in his turn Gave Tasks to Los, Enormous, to destroy
That body he created; but in vain, for Los perform'd
Wonders of labour—
They Builded Golgonooza, Los labouring builded pillars high
And Domes terrific in the nether heavens, for beneath
Was open'd new heavens & a new Earth beneath & within,
Threefold, within the brain, within the heart, within the loins:
A Threefold Atmosphere Sublime, continuous from Urthona's world,
But yet having a Limit Twofold named Satan & Adam.

But Los stood on the Limit of Translucence, weeping & trembling,
Filled with doubts in self accusation, beheld the fruit
Of Urizen's Mysterious tree. For Enitharmon thus spake:
"When In the Deeps beneath I gather'd of this ruddy fruit,
It was by that I knew that I had Sinn'd, & then I knew
That without a ransom I could not be sav'd from Eternal death:
That Life lives upon death, & by devouring appetite
All things subsist on one another; thenceforth in despair
I spend my glowing time; but thou art strong & mighty
To bear this Self conviction; take then, Eat thou also of
The fruit & give me proof of life Eternal or I die."

Then Los plucked the fruit & Eat & sat down in Despair,
And must have given himself to death Eternal, But
Urthona's spectre in part mingling with him, comforted him,
Being a medium between him & Enitharmon. But This Union
Was not to be Effected without Cares & Sorrows & Troubles
Of six thousand Years of self denial and of bitter Contrition.

Urthona's Spectre terrified beheld the Spectres of the dead:
Each male form'd without a counterpart, without a concentering vision.

The Spectre of Urthona wept before Los, saying, "I am the cause
That this dire state commences. I began the dreadful state
Of Separation, & on my dark head the curse & punishment
Must fall unless a way be found to Ransom & Redeem.
But I have thee my Counterpart miraculous,
These spectres have no Counter [parts], therefore they ravin
Without the food of life. Let us Create them Coun[terparts];
For without a Created body the Spectre is Eternal Death."

Los trembling, answer'd: "Now I feel the weight of stern repentance.
Tremble not so, my Enitharmon, at the awful gates
Of thy poor broken Heart. I see thee like a shadow withering
As on the outside of Existence; but look! behold! take comfort!
Turn inwardly thine Eyes & there behold the Lamb of God
Clothed in Luvah's robes of blood descending to redeem.
O Spectre of Urthona, take comfort! O Enitharmon!
Could'st thou but cease from terror & trembling & affright.
When I appear before thee in forgiveness of ancient injuries,
Why should'st thou remember & be afraid? I surely have died in pain
Often enough to convince thy jealousy & fear & terror.
Come hither; be patient; let us converse together, because
I also tremble at myself & at all my former life."

Enitharmon answer'd: "I behold the Lamb of God descending
To Meet these Spectres of the Dead. I therefore fear that he
Will give us to Eternal Death, fit punishment for such
Hideous offenders: Uttermost extinction in eternal pain:
An ever dying life of stifling & obstruction: shut out
Of existence to be a sign & terror to all who behold,
Lest any should in futurity do as we have done in heaven.
Such is our state; nor will the Son of God redeem us, but destroy."
So Enitharmon spoke trembling & in torrents of tears.

Los sat in Golgonooza, in the Gate of Luban where
He had erected many porches where branched the Mysterious tree,
Where the Spectrous dead wail; & sighing thus he spoke to Enitharmon:

"Lovely delight of Men, Enitharmon, shady refuge from furious war,
Thy bosom translucent is a soft repose for the weeping souls
Of those piteous victims of battle; there they sleep in happy obscurity;
They feed upon our life; we are their victims. Stern desire
I feel to fabricate embodied semblances in which the dead

May live before us in our palaces & in our gardens of labour,
Which now, open'd within the Center, we behold spread abroad
To form a world of sacrifice of brothers & sons & daughters,
To comfort Orc in his dire sufferings; look, my fires enlume afresh
Before my face ascending with delight as in ancient times!"

Enitharmon spread her beamy locks upon the wind & said,
"O Lovely terrible Los, wonder of Eternity, O Los, my defence & guide,
Thy works are all my joy & in thy fires my soul delights;
If mild they burn in just proportion, & in secret night
And silence build their day in shadow of soft clouds & dews,
Then I can sigh forth on the winds of Golgonooza piteous forms
That vanish again into my bosom; but if thou, my Los,
Wilt in sweet moderated fury fabricate forms *sublime,*
Such as the piteous spectres may assimilate themselves into,
They shall be ransoms for our Souls that we may live."

So Enitharmon spoke, & Los, his hands divine inspir'd, began
To modulate his fires; studious the loud roaring flames
He vanquish'd with the strength of Art, bending their iron points
And drawing them forth delighted upon the winds of Golgonooza
From the ranks of Urizen's war & from the fiery lake
Of Orc, bending down as the binder of the sheaves follows
The reaper, in both arms embracing the furious raging flames.
Los drew them forth out of the deeps, planting his right foot firm
Upon the Iron crag of Urizen, thence springing up aloft
Into the heavens of Enitharmon in a mighty circle.

And first he drew a line upon the walls of shining heaven,
And Enitharmon tinctur'd it with beams of blushing love.
It remain'd permanent, a lovely form, inspir'd, divinely human.
Dividing into just proportions, Los unwearied labour'd
The immortal lines upon the heavens, till with sighs of love,
Sweet Enitharmon mild, Entranc'd breath'd forth upon the wind
The spectrous dead. Weeping, the Spectres view'd the immortal works
Of Los, Assimilating to those forms, Embodied & Lovely
In youth & beauty, in the arms of Enitharmon mild reposing.

First Rintrah & then Palamabron, drawn from out the ranks of war,
In infant innocence repos'd on Enitharmon's bosom.
Orc was comforted in the deeps; his soul reviv'd in them:
As the Eldest brother is the father's image, So Orc became

As Los, a father to his brethren, & he joy'd in the dark lake
Tho' bound with chains of Jealousy & in scales of iron & brass.

But Los loved them & refus'd to Sacrifice their infant limbs,
And Enitharmon's smiles & tears prevail'd over self protection.
They rather chose to meet Eternal Death than to destroy
The offspring of their Care & Pity. Urthona's spectre was comforted;
But Tharmas most rejoic'd in hope of Enion's return,
For he beheld new Female forms born forth upon the air
Who wove soft silken veils of covering in sweet raptur'd trance,
Mortal, & not as Enitharmon, without a covering veil.

First his immortal spirit drew Urizen's Spectre away
From out the ranks of war, separating him in sunder,
Leaving his Spectrous form, which could not be drawn away.
Then he divided Tiriel, the Eldest of Urizen's sons:
Urizen became Rintrah, Tiriel became Palamabron.
Thus dividing the power of Every Warrior,
Startled was Los; he found his Enemy Urizen now
In his hands; he wonder'd that he felt love & not hate.
His whole soul loved him; he beheld him an infant
Lovely, breath'd from Enitharmon; he trembled within himself.

END OF THE SEVENTH NIGHT [a]

VALA

NIGHT THE SEVENTH [b]

BUT in the deeps beneath the tree of Mystery in darkest night
When Urizen sat on his rock, the Shadow brooded.
Urizen saw & triumph'd, & he cried to his warriors:
"The time of Prophecy is now revolv'd, & all
The Universal ornament is mine, & in my hands
The ends of heaven; like a Garment will I fold them round me,
Consuming what must be consum'd; then in power & majesty
I will walk forth thro' those wide fields of endless Eternity,
A God & not a Man, a Conqueror in triumphant glory,
And all the Sons of Everlasting shall bow down at my feet."

First Trades & Commerce, ships & armed vessels he builded laborious
To swim the deep; & on the land, children are sold to trades
Of dire necessity, still laboring day & night till all
Their life extinct they took the spectre form in dark despair;
And slaves in myriads, in ship loads, burden the hoarse sounding deep,
Rattling with clanking chains; the Universal Empire groans.

And he commanded his Sons to form a Center in the Deep;
And Urizen laid the first Stone, & all his myriads
Builded a temple in the image of the human heart.
And in the inner part of the Temple, wondrous workmanship,
They form'd the Secret place, reversing all the order of delight,
That whosoever enter'd into the temple might not behold
The hidden wonders, allegoric of the Generations
Of secret lust, when hid in chambers dark the nightly harlot
Plays in Disguise in whisper'd hymn & mumbling prayer. The priests
He ordain'd & Priestesses, cloth'd in disguises beastial,
Inspiring secrecy; & lamps they bore: intoxicating fumes
Roll round the Temple; & they took the Sun that glow'd o'er Los
And, with immense machines down rolling, the terrific orb
Compell'd. The Sun, redd'ning like a fierce lion in his chains,
Descended to the sound of instruments that drown'd the noise
Of the hoarse wheels & the terrific howlings of wild beasts
That drag'd the wheels of the Sun's chariot; & they put the Sun
Into the temple of Urizen to give light to the Abyss,
To light the War by day, to hide his secret beams by night,
For he divided day & night in different order'd portions,
The day for war, the night for secret religion in his temple.

Los rear'd his mighty stature: on Earth stood his feet. Above
The moon his furious forehead, circled with black bursting thunders,
His naked limbs glittering upon the dark blue sky, his knees
Bathed in bloody clouds, his loins in fires of war where spears
And swords rage, where the Eagles cry & the Vultures laugh, saying:
"Now comes the night of Carnage, now the flesh of Kings & Princes
Pampered in palaces for our food, the blood of Captains nurtur'd
With lust & murder for our drink; the drunken Raven shall wander
All night among the slain, & mock the wounded that groan in the field."

Tharmas laugh'd furious among the Banners cloth'd in blood,
Crying: "As I will I rend the Nations all asunder, rending
The People: vain their combinations, I will scatter them.

But thou, O Son, whom I have crowned and inthroned, thee strong
I will preserve tho' Enemies arise around thee numberless.
I will command my winds & they shall scatter them, or call
My Waters like a flood around thee; fear not, trust in me
And I will give thee all the ends of heaven for thy possession.
In war shalt thou bear rule, in blood shalt thou triumph for me,
Because in times of Everlasting I was rent in sunder
And what I loved best was divided among my Enemies.
My little daughters were made captives, & I saw them beaten
With whips along the sultry sands. I heard those whom I lov'd
Crying in secret tents at night, & in the morn compell'd
To labour; & behold, my heart sunk down beneath
In sighs & sobbings, all dividing, till I was divided
In twain; & lo, my Crystal form that lived in my bosom
Follow'd her daughters to the fields of blood: they left me naked,
Alone, & they refus'd to return from the fields of the mighty.
Therefore I will reward them as they have rewarded me.
I will divide them in my anger, & thou, O my King,
Shalt gather them from out their graves, & put thy fetter on them,
And bind them to thee, that my crystal form may come to me."

So cried the Demon of the Waters in the Clouds of Los.
Outstretch'd upon the hills lay Enitharmon; clouds & tempests
Beat round her head all night: all day she riots in Excess.
But night or day Los follows War, & the dismal moon rolls over her,
That when Los warr'd upon the South, reflected the fierce fires
Of his immortal head into the North, upon faint Enitharmon.
Red rage the furies of fierce Orc; black thunders roll round Los;
Flaming his head, like the bright sun seen thro' a mist that magnifies
The disk into a terrible vision to the Eyes of trembling mortals.

And Enitharmon, trembling & in fear, utter'd these words:

"I put not any trust in thee, nor in thy glitt'ring scales;
Thy eyelids are a terror to me; & the flaming of thy crest,
The rushing of thy scales confound me, thy hoarse rushing scales.
And if that Los had not built me a tower upon a rock,
I must have died in the dark desert among noxious worms.
How shall I flee, how shall I flee into the tower of Los?
My feet are turned backward & my footsteps slide in clay,
And clouds are clos'd around my tower; my arms labour in vain.
Does not the God of waters in the wracking Elements

Love those who hate, rewarding with hate the Loving Soul?
And must not I obey the God, thou Shadow of Jealousy?
I cry; the watchman heareth not. I pour my voice in roarings:
Watchman! the night is thick, & darkness choaks my rayie sight.
Lift up! Lift up! O Los! awake my watchman, for he sleepeth.
Lift up! Lift up! Shine forth, O Light! watchman, thy light is out.
O Los! unless thou keep my tower the Watchman will be slain."

So Enitharmon cried upon her terrible Earthy bed
While the broad Oak wreath'd his roots round her, forcing his dark way
Thro' caves of death into Existence. The Beach, long limbed, advanc'd
Terrific into the pain'd heavens. The fruit trees humanizing
Shew'd their immortal energies in warlike desperation,
Rending the heavens & earths & drinking blood in the hot battle
To feed their fruit, to gratify their hidden sons & daughters
That far within the close recesses of their secret palaces
View'd the vast war & joy'd, writhing to vegetate
Into the worlds of Enitharmon. Loud the roaring winds,
Burden'd with clouds, howl round the Couch. Sullen the wooly sheep
Walks thro' the battle. Dark & fierce the Bull his rage
Propagates thro' the warring Earth. The Lions raging in flames,
The Tygers in redounding smoke. The serpent of the woods
And of the waters, & the scorpion of the desart irritate
With harsh songs every living soul. The Prester Serpent runs
Along the ranks, crying, "Listen to the Priest of God, ye warriors;
This Cowl upon my head he plac'd in times of Everlasting,
And said, 'Go forth & guide my battles; like the jointed spine
Of Man I made thee when I blotted Man from life & light.
Take thou the Seven Diseases of Man; store them for times to come
In store houses, in secret places that I will tell thee of,
To be my great & awful curses at the time appointed.'"
The Prester Serpent ceas'd; the War song sounded loud & strong
Thro' all the heavens. Urizen's Web vibrated, torment on torment.

Now in the Caverns of the Graves & Places of human seed
The nameless shadowy Vortex stood before the face of Orc.
The shadow rear'd her dismal head over the flaming youth
With sighs & howlings & deep sobs; that he might lose his rage
And with it lose himself in meekness, she embrac'd his fire.—
As when the Earthquake rouzes from his den, his shoulders huge
Appear above the crumbling Mountain, Silence waits around him
A moment, then astounding horror belches from the Center,

The fiery dogs arise, the shoulders huge appear—
So Orc roll'd round his clouds upon the deeps of dark Urthona,
Knowing the arts of Urizen were Pity & Meek affection
And that by these arts the serpent form exuded from his limbs
Silent as despairing love & strong as jealousy,
Jealous that she was Vala, now become Urizen's harlot
And the Harlot of Los & the deluded harlot of the Kings of the Earth,
His soul was gnawn in sunder.
The hairy shoulders rend the links, free are the wrists of fire.
Red rage redounds, he rouz'd his lions from his forest black,
They howl around the flaming youth, rending the nameless shadow
And running their immortal course thro' solid darkness borne.

Loud sounds the war song round red Orc in his fury
And round the nameless shadowy Female in her howling terror
When all the Elemental Gods join'd in the wondrous Song:

"Sound the War trumpet terrific, souls clad in attractive steel!
Sound the shrill fife, serpents of war! I hear the northern drum.
Awake! I hear the flapping of the folding banners.

"The dragons of the North put on their armour;
Upon the Eastern sea direct they take their course.
The glittering of their horses' trappings stains the vault of night.

"Stop we the rising of the glorious King: spur, spur your clouds
Of death! O northern drum, awake! O hand of iron, sound
The northern drum! Now give the charge! bravely obscur'd
With darts of wintry hail. Again the black bow draw:
Again the Elemental strings to your right breasts draw,
And let the thundering drum speed on the arrows black."

The arrows flew from cloudy bow all day, till blood
From east to west flow'd, like the human veins, in rivers
Of life upon the plains of death & valleys of despair.

"Now sound the clarions of Victory, now strip the slain.
Clothe yourselves in golden arms, brothers of war."
They sound the clarions strong, they chain the howling captives,
They give the Oath of blood, they cast the lots into the helmet,
They vote the death of Luvah & they nail'd him to the tree,
They pierc'd him with a spear & laid him in a sepulcher
To die a death of Six thousand years, bound round with desolation.

The sun was black & the moon roll'd, a useless globe, thro' heaven.

Then left the sons of Urizen the plow & harrow, the loom,
The hammer & the chisel & the rule & compasses.
They forg'd the sword, the chariot of war, the battle ax,
The trumpet fitted to the battle & the flute of summer,
And all the arts of life they chang'd into the arts of death.
The hour glass contemn'd because its simple workmanship
Was as the workmanship of the plowman, & the water wheel
That raises water into Cisterns, broken & burn'd in fire
Because its workmanship was like the workmanship of the shepherd,
And in their stead intricate wheels invented, Wheel without wheel,
To perplex youth in their outgoings & to bind to labours
Of day & night the myriads of Eternity, that they might file
And polish brass & iron hour after hour, laborious workmanship,
Kept ignorant of the use that they might spend the days of wisdom
In sorrowful drudgery to obtain a scanty pittance of bread,
In ignorance to view a small portion & think that All,
And call it demonstration, blind to all the simple rules of life.

·"Now, now the Battle rages round thy tender limbs, O Vala!
Now smile among thy bitter tears, now put on all thy beauty.
Is not the wound of the sword sweet & the broken bone delightful?
Wilt thou now smile among the slain when the wounded groan in the field?

"Lift up thy blue eyes, Vala, & put on thy sapphire shoes.
O Melancholy Magdalen, behold the morning breaks!
Gird on thy flaming Zone, descend into the Sepulchre,
Scatter the blood from thy golden brow, the tears from thy silver locks,
Shake off the water from thy wings & the dust from thy white garments.

"Remember all thy feigned terrors on the secret couch
When the sun rose in glowing morn with arms of mighty hosts
Marching to battle, who was wont to rise with Urizen's harps
Girt as a Sower with his seed to scatter life abroad.

"Arise, O Vala! bring the bow of Urizen, bring the swift arrows of light.
How rag'd the golden horses of Urizen, bound to the chariot of Love,
Compell'd to leave the plow to the Ox, to snuff up the winds of desolation,
To trample the cornfields in boastful neighings; this is no gentle harp,
This no warbling brook, nor Shadow of a Myrtle tree,

"But blood & wounds & dismal cries & clarions of war,
And hearts laid open to the light by the broad grizly sword,
And bowels hidden in hammered steel ripp'd forth upon the ground.
Call forth thy smiles of soft deceit, call forth thy cloudy tears!
We hear thy sighs in trumpets shrill when Morn shall blood renew."

So sung the demons of the deep; the Clarions of war blew loud.
Orc rent her, & his human form consum'd in his own fires
Mingled with her dolorous members strewn thro' the Abyss.
She joy'd in all the Conflict, Gratified & drinking tears of woe.
No more remain'd of Orc but the Serpent round the tree of Mystery.
The form of Orc was gone; he rear'd his serpent bulk among
The stars of Urizen in Power, rending the form of life
Into a formless indefinite & strewing her on the Abyss
Like clouds upon a winter sky, broken with winds & thunders.
This was, to her, Supreme delight. The Warriors mourn'd disappointed.
They go out to war with strong shouts & loud clarions.
O, Pity! They return with lamentations, mourning, & weeping.
Invisible or visible, drawn out in length or stretcht in breadth,
The Shadowy Female Varied in the War in her delight,
Howling in discontent, black & heavy, uttering brute sounds,
Wading thro' fires among the slimy weeds, making Lamentations
To decieve Tharmas in his rage, to soothe his furious soul,
To stay him in his flight that Urizen might live tho' in pain.
He said: "Art thou bright Enion? is the shadow of hope return'd?"

And she said: "Tharmas, I am Vala, bless thy innocent face!
Doth Enion avoid the sight of thy blue wat'ry eyes?
Be not perswaded that the air knows this, or the falling dew."

Tharmas repli'd: "O Vala, once I liv'd in a garden of delight;
I waken'd Enion in the morning, & she turn'd away
Among the apple trees; & all the garden of delight
Swam like a dream before my eyes. I went to seek the steps
Of Enion in the gardens, & the shadows compass'd me
And clos'd me in a wat'ry world of woe when Enion stood
Trembling before me like a shadow, like a mist, like air.
And she is gone, & here alone I war with darkness & death.
I hear thy voice, but not thy form see; thou & all delight
And life appear & vanish, mocking me with shadows of false hope.
Hast thou forgot that the air listens thro' all its districts, telling
The subtlest thoughts shut up from light in chambers of the Moon?"

"Tharmas, The Moon has chambers where the babes of love lie hid,
And whence they never can be brought in all Eternity
Unless expos'd by their vain parents. Lo, him whom I love
Is hidden from me, & I never in all Eternity
Shall see him. Enitharmon & Ahania, combin'd with Enion,
Hid him in that Outrageous form of Orc, which torments me for Sin.
For all my secret faults, which he brings forth upon the light
Of day, in jealousy & blood my Children are led to Urizen's war
Before my eyes, & for every one of these I am condemn'd
To Eternal torment in these flames; for tho' I have the power
To rise on high, Yet love here binds me down, & never, never
Will I arise till him I love is loos'd from this dark chain."

Tharmas replied: "Vala, thy sins have lost us heaven & bliss.
Thou art our Curse, and till I can bring love into the light
I never will depart from my greath wrath."

So Tharmas wail'd wrathful; then rode upon the stormy Deep
Cursing the voice that mock'd him with false hope, in furious mood.
Then she returns, swift as a blight upon the infant bud,
Howling in all the notes of woe to stay his furious rage,
Stamping the hills, wading or swimming, flying furious or falling,
Or like an Earthquake rumbling in the bowels of the earth,
Or like a cloud beneath, & like a fire flaming on high,
Walking in pleasure of the hills or murmuring in the dales
Like to a rushing torrent beneath & a falling rock above,
A thunder cloud in the south & a lulling voice heard in the north.

And she went forth & saw the forms of life & of delight
Walking on Mountains or flying in the open expanse of heaven.
She heard sweet voices in the winds & in the voices of birds
That rose from waters; for the waters were as the voice of Luvah,
Not seen to her like waters or like this dark world of death,
Tho' all those fair perfections, which men know only by name,
In beautiful substantial forms appear'd & served her
As food or drink or ornament, or in delightful works
To build her bowers; for the Elements brought forth abundantly
The living soul in glorious forms, & every one came forth
Walking before her Shadowy face & bowing at her feet.
But in vain delights were poured forth on the howling melancholy.
For her delight the horse his proud neck bow'd & his white mane,
And the strong Lion deign'd in his mouth to wear the golden bit,
While the far beaming Peacock waited on the fragrant wind

To bring her fruits of sweet delight from trees of richest wonders,
And the strong pinion'd Eagle bore the fire of heaven in the night season.
Woo'd & subdu'd into Eternal Death the Demon Lay,
In rage against the dark despair, the howling Melancholy.
For far & wide she stretch'd thro' all the worlds of Urizen's journey,
And was Adjoin'd to Beulah as the Polypus to the Rock.
Mourning the daughters of Beulah saw, nor could they have sustain'd
The horrid sight of death & torment, But the Eternal Promise
They wrote on all their tombs & pillars, & on every Urn
These words: "If ye will believe, your Brother shall rise again,"
In golden letters ornamented with sweet labours of Love,
Waiting with patience for the fulfilment of the Promise Divine.

And all the Songs of Beulah sounded comfortable notes,
Not suffering doubt to rise up from the Clouds of the Shadowy Female
The myriads of the dead burst thro' the bottom of their tombs,
Descending on the shadowy female's clouds in Spectrous terror,
Beyond the Limit of Translucence on the Lake of Udan Adan.
These they nam'd Satans, & in the Aggregate they nam'd them Satan.

END OF THE SEVENTH NIGHT [*b*]

VALA

NIGHT THE EIGHTH

THEN All in Great Eternity Met in the Council of God
As one Man, Even Jesus, upon Gilead & Hermon,
Upon the Limit of Contraction to create the fallen Man.
The Fallen Man stretch'd like a corse upon the oozy Rock,
Wash'd with the tides, pale, overgrown with weeds
That mov'd with horrible dreams; hovering high over his head
Two winged immortal shapes, one standing at his feet
Toward the East, one standing at his head toward the west,
Their wings join'd in the Zenith over head; but other wings
They had which cloth'd their bodies like a garment of soft down,
Silvery white, shining upon the dark blue sky in silver.
Their wings touch'd the heavens; their fair feet hover'd above
The swelling tides; they bent over the dead corse like an arch,
Pointed at top in highest heavens, of precious stones & pearl.
Such is a Vision of All Beulah hov'ring over the Sleeper.

The limit of Contraction now was fix'd & Man began
To wake upon the Couch of Death; he sneez'd seven times;
A tear of blood dropped from either eye; again he repos'd
In the Saviour's arms, in the arms of tender mercy & loving kindness.

Then Los said: "I behold the Divine Vision thro' the broken Gates
Of thy poor broken heart, astonish'd, melted into Compassion & Love."
And Enitharmon said: "I see the Lamb of God upon Mount Zion."
Wondering with love & Awe they felt the divine hand upon them;

For nothing could restrain the dead in Beulah from descending
Unto Ulro's night; tempted by the Shadowy female's sweet
Delusive cruelty, they descend away from the Daughters of Beulah
And Enter Urizen's temple, Enitharmon pitying, & her heart
Gates broken down; they descend thro' the Gate of Pity,
The broken heart Gate of Enitharmon which join'd to Urizen's temple
Which is the Synagogue of Satan. She sighs them forth upon the wind
Of Golgonooza. Los stood recieving them—
For Los could enter into Enitharmon's bosom & explore
Its intricate Labyrinths now the Obdurate heart was broken—
From out the War of Urizen, & Tharmas receiving them
Into his hands. Then Enitharmon erected Looms in Luban's Gate
And call'd the Looms Cathedron; in these Looms she wove the Spectres
Bodies of Vegetation, singing lulling Cadences to drive away
Despair from the poor wondering spectres; and Los loved them
With a parental love, for the Divine hand was upon him
And upon Enitharmon, & the Divine Countenance shone
In Golgonooza. Looking down, the daughters of Beulah saw
With joy the bright Light, & in it a Human form,
And knew he was the Saviour, Even Jesus: & they worshipped.

Astonish'd, comforted, Delighted, in notes of Rapturous Extacy
All Beulah stood astonish'd, looking down to Eternal Death.
They saw the Saviour beyond the Pit of death & destruction;
For whether they look'd upward they saw the Divine Vision,
Or whether they look'd downward still they saw the Divine Vision
Surrounding them on all sides beyond sin & death & hell.

Enitharmon wove in tears, singing songs of Lamentation
And pitying comfort as she sigh'd forth on the wind the Spectres,
Also the Vegetated bodies which Enitharmon wove
Open'd within their hearts & in their loins & in their brain

To Beulah; & the Dead in Ulro descended from the War
Of Urizen & Tharmas & from the Shadowy female's clouds.
And some were woven single, & some twofold, & some threefold
In Head or Heart or Reins, according to the fittest order
Of most merciful pity & compassion to the spectrous dead.

When Urizen saw the Lamb of God clothed in Luvah's robes,
Perplex'd & terrifi'd he stood, tho' well he knew that Orc
Was Luvah. But he now beheld a new Luvah, Or Orc
Who assum'd Luvah's form & stood before him opposite.
But he saw Orc a Serpent form augmenting times on times
In the fierce battle; & he saw the Lamb of God & the World of Los
Surrounded by his dark machines; for Orc augmented swift
In fury, a Serpent wondrous among the Constellations of Urizen.
A crest of fire rose on his forehead, red as the carbuncle,
Beneath, down to his eyelids, scales of pearl, then gold & silver
Immingled with the ruby overspread his Visage down
His furious neck; writhing contortive in dire budding pains
The scaly armour shot out. Stubborn, down his back & bosom
The Emerald, Onyx, Sapphire, jasper, beryl, amethyst
Strove in terrific emulation which should gain a place
Upon the mighty Fiend, the fruit of the mysterious tree
Kneaded in Uveth's kneading trough. Still Orc devour'd the food
In raging hunger. Still the pestilential food, in gems & gold,
Exuded round his awful limbs, Stretching to serpent length
His human bulk, While the dark shadowy female, brooding over,
Measur'd his food morning & evening in cups & baskets of iron.
With tears of sorrow incessant she labour'd the food of Orc,
Compell'd by the iron hearted sisters, Daughters of Urizen,
Gath'ring the fruit of that mysterious tree, circling its root
She spread herself thro' all the branches in the power of Orc.

Thus Urizen, in self deciet, his warlike preparations fabricated;
And when all things were finish'd, sudden wav'd among the stars,
His hurtling hand gave the dire signal; thunderous clarions blow,
And all the hollow deep rebellow'd with the wond'rous war.
But Urizen his mighty rage let loose in the mid deep.
Sparkles of dire affliction issu'd round his frozen limbs.
Horrible hooks & nets he form'd, twisting the cords of iron
And brass, & molten metals cast in hollow globes, & bor'd
Tubes in petrific steel, & ramm'd combustibles, & wheels
And chains & pullies fabricated all round the Heavens of Los;

Communing with the Serpent of Orc in dark dissimulation,
And with the Synagogue of Satan in dark Sanhedrim,
To undermine the World of Los & tear bright Enitharmon
To the four winds, hopeless of future. All futurity
Seems teeming with endless destruction never to be expell'd;
Desperate remorse swallows the present in a quenchless rage.

Terrified & astonish'd, Urizen beheld the battle take a form
Which he intended not: a Shadowy hermaphrodite, black & opake;
The soldiers nam'd it Satan, but he was yet unform'd & vast.
Hermaphroditic it at length became, hiding the Male
Within as in a Tabernacle, Abominable, Deadly.

The battle howls, the terrors fir'd rage in the work of death;—
Enormous Works Los contemplated, inspir'd by the holy Spirit.—
Los builds the Walls of Golgonooza against the stirring battle
That only thro' the Gates of Death they can enter to Enitharmon.
Raging they take the human visage & the human form,
Feeling the hand of Los in Golgonooza & the force
Attractive of his hammer's beating & the silver looms
Of Enitharmon singing lulling cadences on the wind;
They humanize in the fierce battle, where in direful pain
Troop by troop the beastial droves rend one another, sounding loud
The instruments of sound; & troop by troop, in human forms, they urge
The dire confusion till the battle faints; those that remain
Return in pangs & horrible convulsions to their beastial state;
For the monsters of the Elements, Lions or Tygers or Wolves,
Sound loud the howling music Inspir'd by Los & Enitharmon, sounding
    loud; terrific men
They seem to one another, laughing terrible among the banners.
And when, the revolution of their day of battles over,
Relapsing in dire torment they return to forms of woe,
To moping visages returning, inanimate tho' furious,
No more erect, tho' strong, drawn out in length they ravin
For senseless gratification, & their visages thrust forth,
Flatten above & beneath & stretch out into beastial length.
Weaken'd they stretch beyond their power in dire droves till war begins,
Or secret religion in their temples before secret shrines.

And Urizen gave life & sense by his immortal power
To all his Engines of deceit: that linked chains might run
Thro' ranks of war spontaneous: & that hooks & boring screws

Might act according to their forms by innate cruelty.
He formed also harsh instruments of sound
To grate the soul into destruction, or to inflame with fury
The spirits of life, to pervert all the faculties of sense
Into their own destruction, if perhaps he might avert
His own despair even at the cost of every thing that breathes.

Thus in the temple of the Sun his books of iron & brass
And silver & gold he consecrated, reading incessantly
To myriads of perturbed spirits; thro' the universe
They propagated the deadly words, the Shadowy Female absorbing
The enormous Sciences of Urizen, ages after ages exploring
The fell destruction. And she said: "O Urizen, Prince of Light,
What words of dread pierce my faint Ear! what falling snows around
My feeble limbs infold my destin'd misery!
I alone dare the lash abide to sit beneath the blast
Unhurt, & dare the inclement forehead of the King of Light;
From dark abysses of the times remote fated to be
The Sorrower of Eternity; in love, with tears submiss I rear
My Eyes to thy Pavilions; hear my prayer for Luvah's sake.
I see the murderer of my Luvah, cloth'd in robes of blood:
He who assum'd my Luvah's throne in times of Everlasting.
Where hast thou hid him whom I love; in what remote Abyss
Resides that God of my delight? O might my eyes behold
My Luvah, then could I deliver all the sons of God
From Bondage of these terrors, & with influences sweet,
As once in those eternal fields, in brotherhood & Love
United, we should live in bliss as those who sinned not.
The Eternal Man is seal'd by thee, never to be deliver'd.
We are all servants to thy will. O King of Light, relent
Thy furious power; to be our father & our loved King.
But if my Luvah is no more, If thou hast smitten him
And laid him in the Sepulcher, Or if thou wilt revenge
His murder on another, Silent I bow with dread.
But happiness can never [come] to thee, O King, nor me,
For he was source of every joy that this mysterious tree
Unfolds in Allegoric fruit. When shall the dead revive?
Can that which has existed cease, or can love & life expire?"

Urizen heard the Voice & saw the shadow underneath
His woven darkness; & in laws & deceitful religions,
Beginning at the tree of Mystery, circling its root

She spread herself thro' all the branches in the power of Orc:
A shapeless & indefinite cloud, in tears of sorrow incessant
Steeping the direful Web of Religion; swagging heavy, it fell
From heaven to heaven, thro' all its meshes, altering the Vortexes,
Misplacing every Center; hungry desire & lust began
Gathering the fruit of that Mysterious tree, till Urizen,
Sitting within his temple, furious, felt the numbing stupor,
Himself tangled in his own net, in sorrow, lust, repentance.

Enitharmon wove in tears, singing songs of Lamentations
And pitying comfort as she sigh'd forth on the wind the spectres
And wove them bodies, calling them her belov'd sons & daughters,
Employing the daughters in her looms, & Los employ'd the sons
In Golgonooza's Furnaces among the Anvils of time & space,
Thus forming a vast family, wondrous in beauty & love,
And they appear'd a Universal female form created
From those who were dead in Ulro, from the spectres of the dead.

And Enitharmon nam'd the Female, Jerusalem the holy.
Wond'ring, she saw the Lamb of God within Jerusalem's Veil;
The Divine Vision seen within the inmost deep recess
Of fair Jerusalem's bosom in a gently beaming fire.

Then sang the sons of Eden round the Lamb of God, & said,
"Glory, Glory, Glory to the holy Lamb of God
Who now beginneth to put off the dark Satanic body.
Now we behold redemption. Now we know that life Eternal
Depends alone upon the Universal hand, & not in us
Is aught but death In individual weakness, sorrow & pain.
We behold with wonder Enitharmon's Looms & Los's Forges,
And the Spindles of Tirzah & Rahab, and the Mills of Satan & Beelzeboul.
In Golgonooza Los's anvils stand & his Furnaces rage;
The hard dentant hammers are lull'd by the flutes' lula lula,
The bellowing furnaces blown by the long sounding Clarions.
Ten thousand Demons labour at the forges Creating Continually
The times & spaces of Mortal Life, the Sun, the Moon, the Stars,
In periods of Pulsative furor, breaking into wedges & bars,
Then drawing into wires the terrific Passions & Affections
Of Spectrous dead. Thence to the Looms of Cathedron convey'd,
The Daughters of Enitharmon weave the ovarium & the integument
In soft silk, drawn from their own bowels in lascivious delight,
With songs of sweetest cadence to the turning spindle & reel,

Lulling the weeping spectres of the dead, Clothing their limbs
With gifts & gold of Eden. Astonish'd, stupefied with delight,
The terrors put on their sweet clothing on the banks of Arnon,
Whence they plunge into the river of space for a period, till
The dread Sleep of Ulro is past. But Satan, Og & Sihon
Build Mills of resistless wheels to unwind the soft threads & reveal
Naked of their clothing the poor spectres before the accusing heavens,
While Rahab & Tirzah far different mantles prepare; webs of torture,
Mantles of despair, girdles of bitter compunction, shoes of indolence,
Veils of ignorance covering from head to feet with a cold web.
We look down into Ulro; we behold the Wonders of the Grave.
Eastward of Golgonooza stands the Lake of Udan Adan, In
Entuthon Benithon, a Lake not of Waters but of Spaces,
Perturb'd, black & deadly; on its Islands & its Margins
The Mills of Satan and Beelzeboul stand round the roots of Urizen's tree;
For this Lake is form'd from the tears & sighs & death sweat of the
    Victims
Of Urizen's laws, to irrigate the roots of the tree of Mystery.
They unweave the soft threads, then they weave them anew in the forms
Of dark death & despair, & none from Eternity to Eternity could Escape,
But thou, O Universal Humanity—who is One Man, blessed for Ever—
Recievest the Integuments woven. Rahab beholds the Lamb of God.
She smites with her knife of flint. She destroys her own work
Times upon times, thinking to destroy the Lamb blessed for Ever.
He puts off the clothing of blood, he redeems the spectres from their bonds,
He awakes sleepers in Ulro; the Daughters of Beulah praise him;
They anoint his feet with ointment, they wipe them with the hair of their
    head.

"We now behold the Ends of Beulah, & we now behold
Where death Eternal is put off Eternally.
Assume the dark Satanic body in the Virgin's womb,
O Lamb Divine! it cannot thee annoy. O pitying one,
Thy pity is from the foundation of the World, & thy Redemption
Begun Already in Eternity. Come then, O Lamb of God,
Come, Lord Jesus, come quickly."

So sang they in Eternity, looking down into Beulah.
The war roar'd round Jerusalem's Gates; it took a hideous form
Seen in the aggregate, a Vast Hermaphroditic form
Heav'd like an Earthquake lab'ring with convulsive groans
Intolerable: at length an awful wonder burst

From the Hermaphroditic bosom. Satan he was nam'd,
Son of Perdition, terrible his form, dishumaniz'd, monstrous,
A male without a female counterpart, a howling fiend
Forlorn of Eden & repugnant to the forms of life,
Yet hiding the shadowy female Vala as in an ark & Curtains,
Abhorr'd, accursed, ever dying an Eternal death,
Being multitudes of tyrant Men in union blasphemous
Against the Divine image, Congregated assemblies of wicked men.

Los said to Enitharmon, "Pitying I saw."
Pitying, the Lamb of God descended thro' Jerusalem's gates
To put off Mystery time after time; & as a Man
Is born on Earth, so was he born of Fair Jerusalem
In mystery's woven mantle, & in the Robes of Luvah.
He stood in fair Jerusalem to awake up into Eden
The fallen Man, but first to Give his vegetated body
To be cut off & separated, that the Spiritual body may be Reveal'd.

The Lamb of God stood before Satan opposite
In Entuthon Benithon, in the shadows of torment & woe
Upon the heights of Amalek, taking refuge in his arms
The victims fled from punishment, for all his words were peace.
Urizen call'd together the Synagogue of Satan in dire Sanhedrim
To judge the Lamb of God to Death as a murderer & robber:
As it is written, he was number'd among the transgressors.
Cold, dark, opake, the Assembly met twelvefold in Amalek,
Twelve rocky unshap'd forms, terrific forms of torture & woe,
Such seem'd the Synagogue to distant view; amidst them beam'd
A False Feminine Counterpart, of Lovely Delusive Beauty
Dividing & Uniting at will in the Cruelties of Holiness,
Vala, drawn down into a Vegetated body, now triumphant.
The Synagogue of Satan Clothed her with Scarlet robes & Gems,
And on her forehead was her name written in blood, "Mystery."
When view'd remote she is One, when view'd near she divides
To multitude, as it is in Eden, so permitted because
It was the best possible in the State called Satan to save
From Death Eternal & to put off Satan Eternally.
The Synagogue Created her from Fruit of Urizen's tree
By devilish arts, abominable, unlawful, unutterable,
Perpetually vegetating in detestable births
Of femals forms, beautiful thro' poisons hidden in secret
Which give a tincture to false beauty; then was hidden within

The bosom of Satan The false Female, as in an ark & veil
Which Christ must rend & her reveal. Her daughters are call'd
Tirzah; She is named Rahab; their various divisions are call'd
The daughters of Amalek, Canaan & Moab, binding on the stones
Their victims, & with knives tormenting them, singing with tears
Over their victims. Hear ye the song of the Females of Amalek:

"O thou poor human form! O thou poor child of woe!
Why dost thou wander away from Tirzah? why me compell to bind thee?
If thou dost go away from me, I shall consume upon the rocks.
These fibres of thine eyes that used to wander in distant heavens
Away from me, I have bound down with a hot iron.
These nostrils that Expanded with delight in morning skies
I have bent downward with lead molten in my roaring furnaces.
My soul is seven furnaces, incessant roar the bellows
Upon my terribly flaming heart, the molten metal runs
In channels thro' my fiery limbs. O love! O pity! O pain!
O the pangs, the bitter pangs of love forsaken!
Ephraim was a wilderness of joy where all my wild beasts ran.
The river Kanah wander'd by my sweet Manasseh's side.
Go, Noah, fetch the girdle of strong brass, heat it red hot,
Press it around the loins of this expanding cruelty.
Shriek not so, my only love.
Bind him down, sisters, bind him down on Ebal, mount of cursing.
Malah, come forth from Lebanon, & Hoglah from Mount Sinai,
Come circumscribe this tongue of sweets, & with a screw of iron
Fasten this Ear into the Rock. Milcah, the task is thine.
Weep not so, sisters, weep not so; our life depends on this,
Or mercy & truth are fled away from Shechem & Mount Gilead,
Unless my beloved is bound upon the stems of Vegetation."

Such are the songs of Tirzah, such the loves of Amalek.
The Lamb of God descended thro' the twelve portions of Luvah,
Bearing his sorrows & recieving all his cruel wounds.

Thus was the Lamb of God condemn'd to Death.
They nail'd him upon the tree of Mystery, weeping over him
And then mocking & then worshipping, calling him Lord & King.
Sometimes as twelve daughters lovely, & sometimes as five
They stood in beaming beauty, & sometimes as one, even Rahab
Who is Mystery, Babylon the Great, the Mother of Harlots.

Jerusalem saw the Body dead upon the Cross. She fled away,
Saying: "Is this Eternal Death? Where shall I hide from Death?
Pity me, Los! pity me, Urizen! & let us build
A Sepulcher & worship Death in fear while yet we live:
Death! God of All! from whom we rise, to whom we all return:
And Let all Nations of the Earth worship at the Sepulcher
With Gifts & Spices, with lamps rich emboss'd, jewels & gold."

Los took the Body from the Cross, Jerusalem weeping over;
They bore it to the Sepulcher which Los had hewn in the rock
Of Eternity for himself: he hew'd it despairing of Life Eternal.
But when Rahab had cut off the Mantle of Luvah from
The Lamb of God, it roll'd apart, revealing to all in heaven
And all on Earth, the Temple & the Synagogue of Satan, & Mystery
Even Rahab in all her turpitude. Rahab divided herself;
She stood before Los in her Pride among the Furnaces,
Dividing & uniting in Delusive feminine powers, questioning him.
He answer'd her with tenderness & love not uninspired.

Los sat upon his anvil stock; they sat beside the forge.
Los wip'd the sweat from his red brow & thus began
To the delusive female forms shining among his furnaces:
"I am that shadowy Prophet who six thousand years ago
Fell from my station in the Eternal bosom. I divided
To multitude, & my multitudes are children of Care & Labour.
O Rahab, I behold thee. I was once like thee, a Son
Of Pride, and I also have pierc'd the Lamb of God in pride & wrath
Hear me repeat my Generations that thou maist also repent.
And these are the Sons of Los & Enitharmon: Rintrah, Palamabron,
Theotormon, Bromion, Antamon, Ananton, Ozoth, Ohana,
Sotha, Mydon, Ellayol, Natho, Gon, Harhath, Satan,
Har, Ochim, Ijim, Adam, Reuben, Simeon, Levi, Judah, Dan, Naphtali,
Gad, Asher, Issachar, Zebulum, Joseph, Benjamin, David, Solomon,
Paul, Constantine, Charlemaine, Luther, Milton.
These are our daughters: Ocalythron, Elynittria, Oothoon, Leutha,
Elythiria, Enanto, Manathu Vorcyon, Ethinthus, Moab, Midian,
Adah, Zillah, Caina, Naamah, Tamar, Rahab, Tirzah, Mary.
And myriads more of Sons & daughters to whom our love increas'd,
To each according to the multiplication of their multitudes.
But Satan accus'd Palamabron before his brethren, also he madden'd
The horses of Palamabron's harrow, wherefore Rintrah & Palamabron
Cut him off from Golgonooza. But Enitharmon in tears

Wept over him, Created him a Space clos'd with a tender moon
And he roll'd down beneath the fires of Orc, a Globe immense
Crested with snow in a dim void; here, by the Arts of Urizen,
He tempted many of the Sons & daughters of Los to flee
Away from Me; first Reuben fled, then Simeon, then Levi, then Judah,
Then Dan, then Naphtali, then Gad, then Asher, then Issachar,
Then Zebulun, then Joseph, then Benjamin, twelve sons of Los.
And this is the manner in which Satan became the Tempter.
There is a State nam'd Satan; learn distinct to know, O Rahab!
The difference between States & Individuals of those States.
The State nam'd Satan never can be redeem'd in all Eternity;
But when Luvah in Orc became a Serpent, he descended into
That State call'd Satan. Enitharmon breath'd forth on the Winds
Of Golgonooza her well beloved, knowing he was Orc's human remains.
She tenderly lov'd him above all his brethren; he grew up
In mother's tenderness. The Enormous worlds rolling in Urizen's power
Must have given Satan, by these mild arts, dominion over all;
Wherefore Palamabron, being accused by Satan to Los,
Call'd down a Great Solemn assembly. Rintrah in fury & fear
Defended Palamabron, & rage fill'd the Universal Tent—
Because Palamabron was good natur'd, Satan suppos'd he fear'd him—
And Satan, not having the Science of Wrath but only of Pity,
Was soon condemn'd, & wrath was left to wrath, & Pity to Pity:
Rintrah & Palamabron, Cut sheer off from Golgonooza,
Enitharmon's Moony space, & in it, Satan & his companions.
They roll'd down a dim world, crusted with Snow, deadly & dark.
Jerusalem, pitying them, wove them mantles of life & death,
Times after times. And those in Eden sent Lucifer for their Guard.
Lucifer refus'd to die for Satan & in pride he forsook his charge. Then
they sent Molech. Molech was impatient. They sent
Molech impatient. They sent Elohim, who created Adam
To die for Satan. Adam refus'd, but was compell'd to die
By Satan's arts. Then the Eternals sent Shaddai.
Shaddai was angry. Pachad descended. Pachad was terrified.
And then they sent Jehovah, who leprous stretch'd his hand to Eternity.
Then Jesus came & Died willing beneath Tirzah & Rahab.
Thou art that Rahab. Lo the tomb! what can we purpose more?
Lo, Enitharmon, terrible & beautiful in Eternal youth!
Bow down before her, you her children, & set Jerusalem free."

Rahab, burning with pride & revenge, departed from Los.
Los drop'd a tear at her departure, but he wip'd it away in hope.

She went to Urizen in pride; the Prince of Light beheld
Reveal'd before the face of heaven his secret holiness.

Darkness & sorrow cover'd all flesh. Eternity was darken'd.

Urizen sitting in his web of deceitful religion
Felt the female death, a dull & numming stupor, such as ne'er
Before assaulted the bright human form; he felt his pores
Drink in the deadly dull delusion; horrors of Eternal Death
Shot thro' him. Urizen sat stonied upon his rock.
Forgetful of his own Laws, pitying he began to embrace
The shadowy Female; since life cannot be quench'd, Life exuded;
His eyes shot outwards, then his breathing nostrils drawn forth,
Scales cover'd over a cold forehead & a neck outstretch'd
Into the deep to sieze the shadow; scales his neck & bosom
Cover'd & scales his hands & feet; upon his belly falling
Outstretch'd thro' the immense, his mouth wide opening, tongueless.
His teeth a triple row, he strove to sieze the shadow in vain,
And his immense tail lash'd the Abyss; his human form a Stone,
A form of Senseless Stone remain'd in terrors on the rock,
Abominable to the eyes of mortals who explore his books.
His wisdom still remain'd, & all his memory stor'd with woe.

And still his stony form remain'd in the Abyss immense,
Like the pale visage in its sheet of lead that cannot follow—
Incessant stern disdain his scaly form gnaws inwardly,
With deep repentance for the loss of that fair form of Man.
With Envy he saw Los, with Envy Tharmas & the Spectre,
With Envy & in vain he swam around his stony form.

No longer now Erect, the King of Light outstretch'd in fury
Lashes his tail in the wild deep: his eyelids, like the Sun
Arising in his pride, enlighten all the Grizly deeps,
His scales transparent give forth light like windows of the morning,
His neck flames with wrath & majesty, he lashes the Abyss,
Beating the desarts & the rocks; the desarts feel his power,
They shake their slumbers off, they wave in awful fear
Calling the Lion & the Tyger, the horse & the wild stag,
The Elephant, the wolf, the Bear, the Larma, the Satyr.
His Eyelids give their light around; his folding tail aspires
Among the stars; the Earth & all the Abysses feel his fury
When as the snow covers the mountains, oft petrific hardness

Covers the deeps, at his vast fury moaning in his rock,
Hardens the Lion & the Bear; trembling in the solid mountain
They view the light & wonder; crying out in terrible existence,
Up bound the wild stag & the horse: behold the King of Pride!

Oft doth his Eye emerge from the Abyss into the realms
Of his Eternal day, & memory strives to augment his ruthfulness.
Then weeping he descends in wrath, drawing all things in his fury
Into obedience to his will; & now he finds in vain
That not of his own power he bore the human form erect,
Nor of his own will gave his Laws in times of Everlasting,
For now fierce Orc in wrath & fury rises into the heavens,
A King of wrath & fury, a dark enraged horror:
And Urizen, repentant, forgets his wisdom in the abyss,
In forms of priesthood, in the dark delusions of repentance
Repining in his heart & spirit that Orc reign'd over all,
And that his wisdom serv'd but to augment the indefinite lust.

Then Tharmas & Urthona felt the stony stupor rise
Into their limbs. Urthona shot forth a Vast Fibrous form.
Tharmas like a pillar of sand roll'd round by the whirlwind,
An animated Pillar rolling round & round in incessant rage.
Los felt the stony stupor, & his head roll'd down beneath
Into the Abysses of his bosom; the vessels of his blood
Dart forth upon the wind in pipes, writhing about in the Abyss
And Enitharmon, pale & cold, in milky juices flow'd
Into a form of Vegetation, living, having a voice,
Moving in root-like fibres, breathing in fear upon the Earth.

And Tharmas gave his Power to Los, Urthona gave his Strength
Into the youthful Prophet for the Love of Enitharmon
And of the nameless shadowy female in the nether deep,
And for the dread of the dark terrors of Orc & Urizen.

Thus in a living death the nameless shadow all things bound:
All mortal things made permanent that they may be put off
Time after time by the Divine Lamb who died for all,
And all in him died, & he put off all mortality.

Tharmas on high rode furious thro' the afflicted worlds,
Pursuing the Vain Shadow of Hope, fleeing from identity
In abstract false Expanses that he may not hear the Voice

Of Ahania wailing on the winds; in vain he flies, for still
The voice incessant calls on all the children of Men:
For she spoke of all in heaven, & all upon the Earth
Saw not as yet the Divine Vision; her eyes are toward Urizen,
And thus Ahania cries aloud to the Caverns of the Grave:

"Will you keep a flock of wolves & lead them? will you take the wintry
    blast
For a covering to your limbs, or the summer pestilence for a tent to abide
    in?
Will you erect a lasting habitation in the mouldering Church yard?
Or a pillar & palace of Eternity in the jaws of the hungry grave?
Will you seek pleasure from the festering wound, or marry for a Wife
The ancient Leprosy? that the King & Priest may still feast on your decay
And the grave mock & laugh at the plow'd fields, saying,
'I am the nourisher, thou the destroyer; in my bosom is milk & wine,
And a fountain from my breasts; to me come all multitudes;
To my breath they obey; they worship me. I am a goddess & queen.'
But listen to Ahania, O ye sons of the Murder'd one,
Listen to her whose memory beholds your ancient days,
Listen to her whose eyes behold the dark body of corruptible death
Looking for Urizen in vain; in vain I seek for morning.
The Eternal Man sleeps in the Earth, nor feels the vig'rous sun
Nor silent moon, nor all the hosts of heaven move in his body.
His fiery halls are dark, & round his limbs the Serpent Orc
Fold without fold incompasses him, And his corrupting members
Vomit out the scaly monsters of the restless deep.
They come up in the rivers & annoy the nether parts
Of Man who lays upon the Shores, leaning his faded head
Upon the Oozy rock inwrapped with the weeds of death.
His eyes sink hollow in his head, his flesh cover'd with slime
And shrunk up to the bones; alas, that Man should come to this!
His strong bones beat with snows & hid within the caves of night,
Marrowless, bloodless, falling into dust, driven by the winds.
O how the horrors of Eternal Death take hold on Man!
His faint groans shake the caves & issue thro' the desolate rocks,
And the strong Eagle, now with numbing cold blighted of feathers,
Once like the pride of the sun, now flagging on cold night,
Hovers with blasted wings aloft, watching with Eager Eye
Till Man shall leave a corruptible body; he, famish'd, hears him groan,
And now he fixes his strong talons in the pointed rock,
And now he beats the heavy air with his enormous wings.

Beside him lies the Lion dead, & in his belly worms
Feast on his death till universal death devours all,
And the pale horse seeks for the pool to lie him down & die,
But finds the pools filled with serpents devouring one another.
He droops his head & trembling stands, & his bright eyes decay.
These are the Visions of My Eyes, the Visions of Ahania."

Thus cries Ahania. Enion replies from the Caverns of the Grave:

"Fear not, O poor forsaken one! O land of briars & thorns
Where once the olive flourish'd & the Cedar spread his wings!
Once I wail'd desolate like thee; my fallow fields in fear
Cried to the Churchyards & the Earthworm came in dismal state.
I found him in my bosom, & I said the time of love
Appears upon the rocks & hills in silent shades; but soon
A voice came in the night, a midnight cry upon the mountains:
'Awake! the bridegroom cometh!' I awoke to sleep no more;
But an Eternal consummation is dark Enion,
The wat'ry Grave. O thou corn field! O thou vegetater happy!
More happy is the dark consumer; hope drowns all my torment,
For I am surrounded by a shadowy vortex drawing
The spectre quite away from Enion, that I die a death
Of better hope, altho' I consume in these raging waters.
The furrow'd field replies to the grave. I hear her reply to me:
'Behold the time approaches fast that thou shalt be as a thing
Forgotten; when one speaks of thee he will not be believ'd.
When a man gently fades away in his immortality,
When the mortal disappears in improved knowledge, cast away
The former things, so shall the Mortal gently fade away
And so become invisible to those who still remain.
Listen. I will tell thee what is done in the caverns of the grave.
The Lamb of God has rent the Veil of Mystery, soon to return
In Clouds & Fires around the rock & the Mysterious tree.
And as the seed waits Eagerly watching for its flower & fruit,
Anxious its little soul looks out into the clear expanse
To see if hungry winds are abroad with their invisible array,
So Man looks out in tree & herd & fish & bird & beast
Collecting up the scatter'd portions of his immortal body
Into the Elemental forms of every thing that grows.
He tries the sullen north wind, riding on its angry furrows,
The sultry south when the sun rises, & the angry east
When the sun sets; when the clods harden & the cattle stand

Drooping & the birds hide in their silent nests, he stores his thoughts
As in a store house in his memory; he regulates the forms
Of all beneath & all above, & in the gentle West
Reposes where the Sun's heat dwells; he rises to the Sun
And to the Planets of the Night, & to the stars that gild
The Zodiac, & the stars that sullen stand to north & south.
He touches the remotest pole, & in the center weeps
That Man should Labour & sorrow, & learn & forget, & return
To the dark valley whence he came, to begin his labour anew.
In pain he sighs, in pain he labours in his universe,
Sorrowing in birds over the deep, & howling in the wolf
Over the slain, & moaning in the cattle, & in the winds,
And weeping over Orc & Urizen in clouds & *flaming* fires,
And in the cries of birth & in the groans of death his voice
Is heard throughout the Universe; wherever a grass grows
Or a leaf buds, The Eternal Man is seen, is heard, is felt,
And all his sorrows, till he reassumes his ancient bliss.' "

Such are the words of Ahania & Enion. Los hears & weeps.

And Los & Enitharmon took the Body of the Lamb
Down from the Cross & plac'd it in a sepulcher which Los had hewn
For himself in the Rock of Eternity, trembling & in despair.
Jerusalem wept over the Sepulcher two thousand years.

Rahab triumphs over all; she took Jerusalem
Captive, a Willing Captive, by delusive arts impell'd
To worship Urizen's Dragon form, to offer her own Children
Upon the bloody Altar. John saw these things Reveal'd in Heaven
On Patmos Isle, & heard the souls cry out to be deliver'd.
He saw the Harlot of the Kings of Earth, & saw her Cup
Of fornication, food of Orc & Satan, press'd from the fruit of Mystery.
But when she saw the form of Ahania weeping on the Void,
And heard Enion's voice sound from the caverns of the Grave,
No more spirit remain'd in her. She secretly left the Synagogue of Satan,
She commun'd with Orc in secret. She hid him with the flax
That Enitharmon had number'd, away from the Heavens,
She gather'd it together to consume her Harlot Robes
In bitterest contrition; sometimes Self condemning, repentant,
And sometimes kissing her Robes & Jewels & weeping over them;
Sometimes returning to the Synagogue of Satan in Pride,
And sometimes weeping before Orc in humility & trembling.

The Synagogue of Satan therefore, uniting against Mystery,
Satan divided against Satan, resolv'd in open Sanhedrim
To burn Mystery with fire & form another from her ashes,
For God put it into their heart to fulfill all his will.

The Ashes of Mystery began to animate; they call'd it Deism
And Natural Religion; as of old, so now anew began
Babylon again in Infancy, call'd Natural Religion.

END OF THE EIGHTH NIGHT

NIGHT THE NINTH

BEING

THE LAST JUDGMENT

A N D Los & Enitharmon builded Jerusalem, weeping
Over the Sepulcher & over the Crucified body
Which, to their Phantom Eyes, appear'd still in the Sepulcher;
But Jesus stood beside them in the spirit, separating
Their spirit from their body. Terrified at Non Existence,
For such they deem'd the death of the body, Los his vegetable hands
Outstretch'd; his right hand, branching out in fibrous strength,
Siez'd the Sun; His left hand, like dark roots, cover'd the Moon,
And tore them down, cracking the heavens across from immense to immense.
Then fell the fires of Eternity with loud & shrill
Sound of Loud Trumpet thundering along from heaven to heaven
A might sound articulate: "Awake, ye dead, & come
To Judgment from the four winds! Awake & Come away!"
Folding like scrolls of the Enormous volume of Heaven & Earth,
With thunderous noise & dreadful shakings, rocking to & fro,
The heavens are shaken & the Earth removed from its place,
The foundations of the Eternal hills discover'd:
The thrones of Kings are shaken, they have lost their robes & crowns,
The poor smite their oppressors, they awake up to the harvest,
The naked warriors rush together down to the sea shore
Trembling before the multitudes of slaves now set at liberty:
They are become like wintry flocks, like forests strip'd of leaves:
The oppressed pursue like the wind; there is no room for escape.

The Spectre of Enitharmon, let loose on the troubled deep,
Wail'd shrill in the confusion, & the Spectre of Urthona
Reciev'd her in the darkening south; their bodies lost, they stood
Trembling & weak, a faint embrace, a fierce desire, as when
Two shadows mingle on a wall; they wail & shadowy tears
Fell down, & shadowy forms of joy mix'd with despair & grief—
Their bodies buried in the ruins of the Universe—
Mingled with the confusion. Who shall call them from the Grave?

Rahab & Tirzah wail aloud in the wild flames; they give up themselves
    to Consummation.

The books of Urizen unroll with dreadful noise; the folding Serpent
Of Orc began to Consume in fierce raving fire; his fierce flames
Issu'd on all sides, gathering strength in animating volumes,
Roaming abroad on all the winds, raging intense, reddening
Into resistless pillars of fire rolling round & round, gathering
Strength from the Earths consum'd & heavens & all hidden abysses,
Where'er the Eagle has Explor'd, or Lion or Tyger trod,
Or where the Comets of the night or stars of asterial day
Have shot their arrows or long beamed spears in wrath & fury.

And all while the trumpet sounds, "Awake, ye dead, & come
To Judgment!" From the clotted gore & from the hollow den
Start forth the trembling millions into flames of mental fire,
Bathing their limbs in the bright visions of Eternity.
Then, like the doves from pillars of Smoke, the trembling families
Of women & children throughout every nation under heaven
Cling round the men in bands of twenties & of fifties, pale
As snow that falls around a leafless tree upon the green.
Their oppressors are fall'n, they have stricken them, they awake to life.
Yet pale the just man stands erect & looking up to heav'n.
Trembling & strucken by the Universal stroke, the trees unroot,
The rocks groan horrible & run about; the mountains &
Their rivers cry with a dismal cry; the cattle gather together,
Lowing they kneel before the heavens; the wild beasts of the forests
Tremble; the Lion shuddering asks the Leopard: "Feelest thou
The dread I feel, unknown before? My voice refuses to roar,
And in weak moans I speak to thee. This night,
Before the morning's dawn, the Eagle call'd the Vulture,
The Raven call'd the hawk, I heard them from my forests black,
Saying: 'Let us go up far, for soon, I smell upon the wind.

A terror coming from the south.' The Eagle & Hawk fled away
At dawn, & e'er the sun arose, the raven & Vulture follow'd.
Let us flee also to the north." They fled. The Sons of Men
Saw them depart in dismal droves. The trumpet sounded loud
And all the Sons of Eternity Descended into Beulah.

In the fierce flames the limbs of Mystery lay consuming with howling
And deep despair. Rattling go up the flames around the Synagogue
Of Satan. Loud the Serpent Orc rag'd thro' his twenty seven
Folds. The tree of Mystery went up in folding flames.
Blood issu'd out in rushing volumes, pouring in whirlpools fierce
From out the flood gates of the Sky. The Gates are burst; down pour
The torrents black upon the Earth; the blood pours down incessant.
Kings in their palaces lie drown'd. Shepherds, their flocks, their tents,
Roll down the mountains in black torrents. Cities, Villages,
High spires & Castles drown'd in the black deluge; shoal on shoal
Float the dead carcases of Men & Beasts, driven to & fro on waves
Of foaming blood beneath the black incessant sky, till all
Mystery's tyrants are cut off & not one left on Earth.

And when all Tyranny was cut off from the face of the Earth,
Around the dragon form of Urizen, & round his strong form,
The flames rolling intense thro' the wide Universe
Began to enter the Holy City. Ent'ring, the dismal clouds
In furrow'd lightnings break their way, the wild flames licking up
The Bloody Deluge: living flames winged with intellect
And Reason, round the Earth they march in order, flame by flame.
From the clotted gore & from the hollow den
Start forth the trembling millions into flames of mental fire,
Bathing their limbs in the bright visions of Eternity.

Beyond this Universal Confusion, beyond the remotest Pole
Where their vortexes began to operate, there stands
A Horrible rock far in the South; it was forsaken when
Urizen gave the horses of Light into the hands of Luvah.
On this rock lay the faded head of the Eternal Man
Enwrapped round with weeds of death, pale cold in sorrow & woe.
He lifts the blue lamps of his Eyes & cries with heavenly voice:
Bowing his head over the consuming Universe, he cried:
"O weakness & O weariness! O war within my members!
My sons, exiled from my breast, pass to & fro before me.
My birds are silent on my hills, flocks die beneath my branches.

My tents are fallen, my trumpets & the sweet sound of my harp
Is silent on my clouded hills that belch forth storms & fire.
My milk of cows & honey of bees & fruit of golden harvest
Are gather'd in the scorching heat & in the driving rain.
My robe is turned to confusion, & my bright gold to stone.
Where once I sat, I weary walk in misery & pain,
For from within my wither'd breast grown narrow with my woes
The Corn is turncd to thistles & the apples into poison,
The birds of song to murderous crows, My joys to bitter groans,
The voices of children in my tents to cries of helpless infants,
And all exiled from the face of light & shine of morning
In this dark world, a narrow house, I wander up & down.
I hear Mystery howling in these flames of Consummation.
When shall the Man of future times become as in days of old?
O weary life! why sit I here & give up all my powers
To indolence, to the night of death, when indolence & mourning
Sit hovering over my dark threshold? tho' I arise, look out
And scorn the war within my members, yet my heart is weak
And my head faint. Yet will I look again into the morning.
Whence is this sound of rage of Men drinking each other's blood,
Drunk with the smoking gore, & red, but not with nourishing wine?"

The Eternal Man sat on the Rocks & cried with awful voice:
'O Prince of Light, where art thou? I behold thee not as once
In those Eternal fields, in clouds of morning stepping forth
With harps & songs when bright Ahania sang before thy face
And all thy sons & daughters gather'd round my ample table.
See you not all this wracking furious confusion?
Come forth from slumbers of thy cold abstraction! Come forth,
Arise to Eternal births! Shake off thy cold repose,
Schoolmaster of souls, great opposer of change, arise!
That the Eternal worlds may see thy face in peace & joy,
That thou, dread form of Certainty, maist sit in town & village
While little children play around thy feet in gentle awe,
Fearing thy frown, loving thy smile, O Urizen, Prince of Light."

He call'd; the deep buried his voice & answer none return'd.
Then wrath burst round; the Eternal Man was wrath; again he cried:
"Arise, O stony form of death! O dragon of the Deeps!
Lie down before my feet, O Dragon! let Urizen arise.
O how couldst thou deform those beautiful proportions
Of life & person: for as the Person, so is his life proportion'd.

Let Luvah rage in the dark deep, even to Consummation,
For if thou feedest not his rage, it will subside in peace.
But if thou darest obstinate refuse my stern behest,
Thy crown & scepter I will sieze, & regulate all my members
In stern severity, & cast thee out into the indefinite
Where nothing lives, there to wander; & if thou returnest weary,
Weeping at the threshold of Existence, I will steel my heart
Against thee to Eternity, & never recieve thee more.
Thy self-destroying, beast form'd Science shall be thy eternal lot.
My anger against thee is greater than against this Luvah,
For war is energy Enslav'd, but thy religion,
The first author of this war & the distracting of honest minds
Into confused perturbation & strife & horrour & pride,
Is a deciet so detestable that I will cast thee out
If thou repentest not, & leave thee as a rotten branch to be burn'd
With Mystery the Harlot & with Satan for Ever & Ever.
Error can never be redeemed in all Eternity,
But Sin, Even Rahab, is redeem'd in blood & fury & jealousy—
That line of blood that stretch'd across the windows of the morning—
Redeem'd from Error's power. Wake, thou dragon of the deeps!"

Urizen wept in the dark deep, anxious his scaly form
To reassume the human; & he wept in the dark deep,
Saying: "O that I had never drunk the wine nor eat the bread
Of dark mortality, or cast my view into futurity, nor turn'd
My back, dark'ning the present, clouding with a cloud,
And building arches high, & cities, turrets & towers & domes
Whose smoke destroy'd the pleasant gardens, & whose running kennels
Chok'd the bright rivers; burd'ning with my Ships the angry deep;
Thro' Chaos seeking for delight, & in spaces remote
Seeking the Eternal which is always present to the wise;
Seeking for pleasure which unsought falls round the infant's path
And on the fleeces of mild flocks who neither care nor labour;
But I, the labourer of ages, whose unwearied hands
Are thus deform'd with hardness, with the sword & with the spear
And with the chisel & the mallet, I, whose labours vast
Order the nations, separating family by family,
Alone enjoy not. I alone, in misery supreme,
Ungratified give all my joy unto this Luvah & Vala.
Then Go, O dark futurity! I will cast thee forth from these
Heavens of my brain, nor will I look upon futurity more.
I cast futurity away, & turn my back upon that void

Which I have made; for lo! futurity is in this moment.
Let Orc consume, let Tharmas rage, let dark Urthona give
All strength to Los & Enitharmon, & let Los self-curs'd
Rend down this fabric, as a wall ruin'd & family extinct.
Rage Orc! Rage Tharmas! Urizen no longer curbs your rage."

So Urizen spoke; he shook his snows from off his shoulders & arose
As on a Pyramid of mist, his white robes scattering
The fleecy white: renew'd, he shook his aged mantles off
Into the fires. Then, glorious bright, Exulting in his joy,
He sounding rose into the heavens in naked majesty,
In radiant Youth; when Lo! like garlands in the Eastern sky
When vocal may comes dancing from the East, Ahania came
Exulting in her flight, as when a bubble rises up
On the surface of a lake, Ahania rose in joy.
Excess of Joy is worse than grief; her heart beat high, her blood
Burst its bright vessels: she fell down dead at the feet of Urizen
Outstretch'd, a smiling corse: they buried her in a silent cave.
Urizen dropped a tear; the Eternal Man Darken'd with sorrow.

The three daughters of Urizen guard Ahania's death couch;
Rising from the confusion in tears & howling & despair,
Calling upon their father's Name, upon their Rivers dark.

And the Eternal Man said: "Hear my words, O Prince of Light.
Behold Jerusalem in whose bosom the Lamb of God
Is seen; tho' slain before her Gates, he self-renew'd remains
Eternal, & I thro' him awake from death's dark vale.
The times revolve; the time is coming when all these delights
Shall be renew'd, & all these Elements that now consume
Shall reflourish. Then bright Ahania shall awake from death,
A glorious Vision to thine Eyes, a Self-renewing Vision:
The spring, the summer, to be thine; then sleep the wintry days
In silken garments spun by her own hands against her funeral.
The winter thou shalt plow & lay thy stores into thy barns
Expecting to recieve Ahania in the spring with joy.
Immortal thou, Regenerate She, & all the lovely Sex
From her shall learn obedience & prepare for a wintry grave,
That spring may see them rise in tenfold joy & sweet delight
Thus shall the male & female live the life of Eternity,
Because the Lamb of God Creates himself a bride & wife
That we his Children evermore may live in Jerusalem

Which now descendeth out of heaven, a City, yet a Woman,
Mother of myriads redeem'd & born in her spiritual palaces,
By a New Spiritual birth Regenerated from Death."

Urizen said: "I have Erred, & my Error remains with me.
What Chain encompasses? in what Lock is the river of light confin'd
That issues forth in the morning by measure & in the evening by care-
    fulness?
Where shall we take our stand to view the infinite & unbounded?
Or where are human feet? for Lo, our eyes are in the heavens."

He ceas'd, for riv'n link from link, the bursting Universe explodes.
All things revers'd flew from their centers: rattling bones
To bones Join: shaking convuls'd, the shivering clay breathes:
Each speck of dust to the Earth's center nestles round & round
In pangs of an Eternal Birth: in torment & awe & fear,
All spirits deceas'd, let loose from reptile prisons, come in shoals:
Wild furies from the tyger's brain & from the lion's eyes,
And from the ox & ass come moping terrors, from the eagle
And raven: numerous as the leaves of autumn, every species
Flock to the trumpet, mutt'ring over the sides of the grave & crying
In the fierce wind round heaving rocks & mountains fill'd with groans.
On rifted rocks, suspended in the air by inward fires,
Many a woful company & many on clouds & waters,
Fathers & friends, Mothers & Infants, Kings & Warriors,
Priests & chain'd Captives, met together in a horrible fear;
And every one of the dead appears as he had liv'd before,
And all the marks remain of the slave's scourge & tyrant's Crown,
And of the Priest's o'ergorged Abdomen, & of the merchant's thin
Sinewy deception, & of the warrior's outbraving & thoughtlessness
In lineaments too extended & in bones too strait & long.
They shew their wounds: they accuse: they sieze the opressor; howlings
    began
On the golden palace, songs & joy on the desart; the Cold babe
Stands in the furious air; he cries: "the children of six thousand years
Who died in infancy rage furious: a mighty multitude rage furious,
Naked & pale standing in the expecting air, to be deliver'd.
Rend limb from limb the warrior & the tyrant, reuniting in pain."

The furious wind still rends around; they flee in sluggish effort;
They beg, they intreat in vain now; they listened not to intreaty;
They view the flames red rolling on thro' the wide universe

From the dark jaws of death beneath & desolate shores remote,
These covering vaults of heaven & these trembling globes of earth.
One Planet calls to another & one star enquires of another:
"What flames are these, coming from the South? what noise, what dread-
    ful rout
As of a battle in the heavens? hark! heard you not the trumpet
As of fierce battle?" While they spoke, the flames come on intense roaring.
They see him whom they have pierc'd, they wail because of him,
They magnify themselves no more against Jerusalem, Nor
Against her little ones; the innocent, accused before the Judges,
Shines with immortal glory; trembling, the judge springs from his throne
Hiding his face in the dust beneath the prisoner's feet & saying:
"Brother of Jesus, what have I done? intreat thy lord for me:
Perhaps I may be forgiven." While he speaks the flames roll on,
And after the flames appears the Cloud of the Son of Man
Descending from Jerusalem with power and great Glory.
All nations look up to the Cloud & behold him who was crucified.
The Prisoner answers: "You scourg'd my father to death before my face
While I stood bound with cords & heavy chains. Your hipocrisy
Shall now avail you nought." So speaking, he dash'd him with his foot.

The Cloud is Blood, dazling upon the heavens, & in the cloud,
Above upon its volumes, is beheld a throne & a pavement
Of precious stones surrounded by twenty-four venerable patriarchs,
And these again surrounded by four Wonders of the Almighty,
Incomprehensible, pervading all, amidst & round about,
Fourfold, each in the other reflected; they are named Life's—in
    Eternity—
Four Starry Universes going forward from Eternity to Eternity.
And the Fall'n Man who was arisen upon the Rock of Ages
Beheld the Vision of God, & he arose up from the Rock,
And Urizen arose up with him, walking thro' the flames
To meet the Lord coming to Judgment; but the flames repell'd them
Still to the Rock; in vain they strove to Enter the Consummation
Together, for the Redeem'd Man could not enter the Consummation.

Then siez'd the sons of Urizen the Plow: they polish'd it
From rust of ages; all its ornaments of gold & silver & ivory
Reshone across the field immense where all the nations
Darken'd like Mould in the divided fallows where the weed
Triumphs in its own destruction; they took down the harness
From the blue walls of heaven, starry jingling, ornamented

With beautiful art, the study of angels, the workmanship of Demons
When Heaven & Hell in Emulation strove in sports of Glory.

The noise of rural works resounded thro' the heavens of heavens,
The horses neigh from the battle, the wild bulls from the sultry waste,
The tygers from the forests, & the lions from the sandy desarts.
They sing; they sieze the instruments of harmony; they throw away
The spear, the bow, the gun, the mortar; they level the fortifications.
They beat the iron engines of destruction into wedges;
They give them to Urthona's sons; ringing the hammers sound
In dens of death to forge the spade, the mattock & the ax,
The heavy roller to break the clods, to pass over the nations.

The Sons of Urizen shout. Their father rose. The Eternal horses
Harness'd, They call'd to Urizen; the heavens moved at their call.
The limbs of Urizen shone with ardor. He laid his hand on the Plow,
Thro' dismal darkness drave the Plow of ages over Cities
And all their Villages; over Mountains & all their Vallies;
Over the graves & caverns of the dead; Over the Planets
And over the void spaces; over sun & moon & star & constellation.

Then Urizen commanded & they brought the Seed of Men.
The trembling souls of All the dead stood before Urizen,
Weak wailing in the troubled air. East, west & north & south
He turn'd the horses loose & laid his Plow in the northern corner
Of the wide Universal field, then step'd forth into the immense.

Then he began to sow the seed; he girded round his loins
With a bright girdle, & his skirt fill'd with immortal souls.
Howling & Wailing fly the souls from Urizen's strong hand,
For from the hand of Urizen the myriads fall like stars
Into their own appointed places, driven back by the winds.
The naked warriors rush together down to the sea shores:
They are become like wintry flocks, like forests strip'd of leaves;
The Kings & Princes of the Earth cry with a feeble cry,
Driven on the unproducing sands & on the harden'd rocks;
And all the while the flames of Orc follow the vent'rous feet
Of Urizen, & all the while the Trump of Tharmas sounds.
Weeping & wailing fly the souls from Urizen's strong hands—
The daughters of Urizen stand with Cups & measures of foaming wine
Immense upon the heavens with bread & delicate repasts—
Then follows the golden harrow in the midst of Mental fires.

To ravishing melody of flutes & harps & softest voice
The seed is harrow'd in, while flames heat the black mould & cause
The human harvest to begin. Towards the south first sprang
The myriads, & in silent fear they look out from their graves.

Then Urizen sits down to rest, & all his wearied sons
Take their repose on beds; they drink, they sing, they view the flames
Of Orc; in joy they view the human harvest springing up.
A time they give to sweet repose, till all the harvest is ripe.
And Lo, like the harvest Moon, Ahania cast off her death clothes;
She folded them up in care, in silence, & her bright'ning limbs
Bath'd in the clear spring of the rock; then from her darksome cave
Issu'd in majesty divine. Urizen rose up from his couch
On wings of tenfold joy, clapping his hands, his feet, his radiant wings
In the immense: as when the Sun dances upon the mountains
A shout of jubilee in lovely notes responds from daughter to daughter,
From son to son: as if the stars beaming innumerable
Thro' night should sing soft warbling, filling earth & heaven;
And bright Ahania took her seat by Urizen in songs & joy.

The Eternal Man also sat down upon the Couches of Beulah,
Sorrowful that he could not put off his new risen body
In mental flames; the flames refus'd, they drove him back to Beulah.
His body was redeem'd to be permanent thro' Mercy Divine.

And now fierce Orc had quite consum'd himself in Mental flames,
Expending all his energy against the fuel of fire.
The Regenerate Man stoop'd his head over the Universe & in
His holy hands reciev'd the flaming Demon & Demoness of smoke
And gave them to Urizen's hands; the Immortal frown'd, saying,

"Luvah & Vala, henceforth you are Servants; obey & live.
You shall forget your former state; return, & Love in peace,
Into your place, the place of seed, not in the brain or heart.
If Gods combine against Man, setting their dominion above
The Human form Divine, Thrown down from their high station
In the Eternal heavens of Human Imagination, buried beneath
In dark Oblivion, with incessant pangs, ages on ages,
In enmity & war first weaken'd, then in stern repentance
They must renew their brightness, & their disorganiz'd functions
Again reorganize, till they resume the image of the human,
Co-operating in the bliss of Man, obeying his Will,
Servants to the infinite & Eternal of the Human form."

Luvah & Vala descended & enter'd the Gates of Dark Urthona,
And walk'd from the hands of Urizen in the shadows of Vala's Garden
Where the impressions of Despair & Hope for ever vegetate
In flowers, in fruits, in fishes, birds & beasts & clouds & waters,
The land of doubts & shadows, sweet delusions, unform'd hopes.
They saw no more the terrible confusion of the wracking universe.
They heard not, saw not, felt not all the terrible confusion,
For in their orbed senses, within clos'd up, they wander'd at will.
And those upon the Couches view'd them, in the dreams of Beulah,
As they repos'd from the terrible wide universal harvest.
Invisible Luvah in bright clouds hover'd over Vala's head,
And thus their ancient golden age renew'd; for Luvah spoke
With voice mild from his golden Cloud upon the breath of morning:

"Come forth, O Vala, from the grass & from the silent dew,
Rise from the dews of death, for the Eternal Man is Risen."

She rises among flowers & looks toward the Eastern clearness,
She walks yea runs, her feet are wing'd, on the tops of the bending grass,
Her garments rejoice in the vocal wind & her hair glistens with dew.

She answer'd thus: "Whose voice is this, in the voice of the nourishing
    air,
In the spirit of the morning, awaking the Soul from its grassy bed?
Where dost thou dwell? for it is thee I seek, & but for thee
I must have slept Eternally, nor have felt the dew of thy morning.
Look how the opening dawn advances with vocal harmony!
Look how the beams foreshew the rising of some glorious power!
The sun is thine, he goeth forth in his majestic brightness.
O thou creating voice that callest! & who shall answer thee?"

"Where dost thou flee, O fair one? where doth thou seek thy happy
    place?"

"To yonder brightness, there I haste, for sure I came from thence
Or I must have slept eternally, nor have felt the dew of morning."

"Eternally thou must have slept, not have felt the morning dew,
But for yon nourishing sun; 'tis that by which thou art arisen.
The birds adore the sun: the beasts rise up & play in his beams,
And every flower & every leaf rejoices in his light.
Then, O thou fair one, sit thee down, for thou art as the grass,
Thou risest in the dew of morning & at night art folded up."

"Alas! am I but as a flower? then will I sit me down,
Then will I weep, then I'll complain & sigh for immortality,
And chide my maker, thee O sun, that raisedst me to fall."

So saying she sat down & wept beneath the apple trees.

"O be thou blotted out, thou Sun! that raisedst me to trouble,
That gavest me a heart to crave, & raisedst me, thy phantom,
To feel thy heat & see thy light & wander here alone,
Hopeless, if I am like the grass & so shall pass away."

"Rise, sluggish Soul, why sit'st thou here? why dost thou sit & weep?
Yon sun shall wax old & decay, but thou shalt ever flourish.
The fruit shall ripen & fall down, & the flowers consume away,
But thou shalt still survive; arise, O dry thy dewy tears."

"Hah! shall I still survive? whence came that sweet & comforting voice?
And whence that voice of sorrow? O sun! thou art nothing now to me.
Go on thy course rejoicing, & let us both rejoice together.
I walk among his flocks & hear the bleating of his lambs.
O that I could behold his face & follow his pure feet!
I walk by the footsteps of his flocks; come hither, tender flocks.
Can you converse with a pure soul that seeketh for her maker?
You answer not: then am I set your mistress in this garden.
I'll watch you & attend your footsteps; you are not like the birds
That sing & fly in the bright air; but you do lick my feet
And let me touch your woolly backs; follow me as I sing,
For in my bosom a new song arises to my Lord:

"Rise up, O sun, most glorious minister & light of day.
Flow on, ye gentle airs, & bear the voice of my rejoicing.
Wave freshly, clear waters flowing around the tender grass;
And thou, sweet smelling ground, put forth thy life in fruits & flowers.
Follow me, O my flocks, & hear me sing my rapturous song.
I will cause my voice to be heard on the clouds that glitter in the sun.
I will call; & who shall answer me? I will sing; who shall reply?
For from my pleasant hills behold the living, living springs,
Running among my green pastures, delighting among my trees.
I am not here alone: my flocks, you are my brethren;
And you birds that sing & adorn the sky, you are my sisters.
I sing, & you reply to my song; I rejoice, & you are glad.
Follow me, O my flocks; we will now descend into the valley.

O how delicious are the grapes, flourishing in the sun!
How clear the spring of the rock, running among the golden sand!
How cool the breezes of the valley, & the arms of the branching trees!
Cover us from the sun; come & let us sit in the shade.
My Luvah here hath plac'd me in a sweet & pleasant land,
And given me fruits & pleasant waters, & warm hills & cool valleys.
Here will I build myself a house, & here I'll call on his name,
Here I'll return when I am weary & take my pleasant rest."

So spoke the sinless soul, & laid her head on the downy fleece
Of a curl'd Ram who stretch'd himself in sleep beside his mistress,
And soft sleep fell upon her eyelids in the silent noon of day.

Then Luvah passed by, & saw the sinless soul,
And said: "Let a pleasant house arise to be the dwelling place
Of this immortal spirit growing in lower Paradise."
He spoke, & pillars were builded, & walls as white as ivory.
The grass she slept upon was pav'd with pavement as of pearl.
Beneath her rose a downy bed, & a cieling cover'd all.

Vala awoke. "When in the pleasant gates of sleep I enter'd,
I saw my Luvah like a spirit stand in the bright air.
Round him stood spirits like me, who rear'd me a bright house,
And here I see thee, house, remain in my most pleasant world.
My Luvah smil'd: I kneeled down: he laid his hand on my head,
And when he laid his hand upon me, from the gates of sleep I came
Into this bodily house to tend my flocks in my pleasant garden."

So saying, she arose & walked round her beautiful house,
And then from her white door she look'd to see her bleating lambs,
But her flocks were gone up from beneath the trees into the hills.

"I see the hand that leadeth me doth also lead my flocks."
She went up to her flocks & turned oft to see her shining house.
She stop'd to drink of the clear spring & eat the grapes & apples.
She bore the fruits in her lap; she gather'd flowers for her bosom.
She called to her flocks, saying, "Follow me, O my flocks!"

They follow'd her to the silent valley beneath the spreading trees.
And on the river's margin she ungirded her golden girdle;
She stood in the river & view'd herself within the wat'ry glass,
And her bright hair was wet with the waters: she rose up from the river,

And as she rose her eyes were open'd to the world of waters:
She saw Tharmas sitting upon the rocks beside the wavy sea.
He strok'd the water from his beard & mourn'd faint thro' the summer
    vales.

And Vala stood on the rocks of Tharmas & heard his mournful voice:

"O Enion, my weary head is in the bed of death,
For weeds of death have wrap'd around my limbs in the hoary deeps.
I sit in the place of shells & mourn, & thou art clos'd in clouds.
When will the time of Clouds be past, & the dismal night of Tharmas?
Arise, O Enion! Arise & smile upon my head
As thou dost smile upon the barren mountains and they rejoice.
When wilt thou smile on Tharmas, O thou bringer of golden day?
Arise, O Enion, arise, for Lo, I have calm'd my seas."

So saying, his faint head he laid upon the Oozy rock,
And darkness cover'd all the deep; the light of Enion faded
Like a faint flame quivering upon the surface of the darkness.

Then Vala lifted up her hands to heaven to call on Enion.
She call'd, but none could answer her & the eccho her voice return'd:

"Where is the voice of God that call'd me from the silent dew?
Where is the Lord of Vala? dost thou hide in clefts of the rock?
Why shouldst thou hide thyself from Vala, from the soul that wanders
    desolate?"

She ceas'd, & light beamed round her like the glory of the morning,
And she arose out of the river & girded her golden girdle.
And now her feet step on the grassy bosom of the ground
Among her flocks, & she turn'd her eyes toward her pleasant house
And saw in the door way beneath the trees two little children playing
She drew near to her house & her flocks follow'd her footsteps.
The children clung around her knees, she embrac'd them & wept over
    them.

"Thou, little Boy, art Tharmas, & thou, bright Girl, Enion.
How are ye thus renew'd & brought into the Gardens of Vala?"

She embrac'd them in tears, till the sun descended the western hills,
And then she enter'd her bright house, leading her mighty children.

And when night came, the flocks laid round the house beneath the trees.
She laid the children on the beds which she saw prepar'd in the house,
Then last, herself laid down & clos'd her Eyelids in soft slumbers.

And in the morning, when the sun arose in the crystal sky,
Vala awoke & call'd the children from their gentle slumbers;

"Awake, O Enion, awake & let thine innocent Eyes
Enlighten all the Crystal house of Vala! awake! awake!
Awake, Tharmas, awake, awake thou child of dewy tears.
Open the orbs of thy blue eyes & smile upon my gardens."

The Children woke & smil'd on Vala; she kneel'd by the golden couch,
She pres'd them to her bosom & her pearly tears drop'd down.
"O my sweet Children! Enion, let Tharmas kiss thy Cheek.
Why dost thou turn thyself away from his sweet wat'ry eyes?
Tharmas, henceforth in Vala's bosom thou shalt find sweet peace.
O bless the lovely eyes of Tharmas & the Eyes of Enion!"

They rose; they went out wand'ring, sometimes together, sometimes
    alone.
"Why weep'st thou, Tharmas, Child of tears, in the bright house of joy?
Doth Enion avoid the sight of thy blue heavenly Eyes?
And dost thou wander with my lambs & wet their innocent faces
With thy bright tears because the steps of Enion are in the gardens?
Arise, sweet boy, & let us follow the path of Enion."

So saying, they went down into the garden among the fruits.
And Enion sang among the flowers that grew among the trees,
And Vala said: "Go, Tharmas; weep not. Go to Enion."

He said: "O Vala, I am sick, & all this garden of Pleasure
Swims like a dream before my eyes; but the sweet smiling fruit
Revives me to new deaths. I fade, even as a water lilly
In the sun's heat, till in the night on the couch of Enion
I drink new life & feel the breath of sleeping Enion.
But in the morning she arises to avoid my Eyes,
Then my loins fade & in the house I sit me down & weep."

"Chear up thy Countenance, bright boy, & go to Enion.
Tell her that Vala waits her in the shadows of her garden."

He went with timid steps, & Enion, like the ruddy morn
When infant spring appears in swelling buds & opening flowers,
Behind her Veil withdraws; so Enion turn'd her modest head.

But Tharmas spoke: "Vala seeks thee, sweet Enion, in the shades.
Follow the steps of Tharmas, O thou brightness of the gardens."
He took her hand reluctant; she follow'd in infant doubts.
Thus in Eternal Childhood, straying among Vala's flocks
In infant sorrow & joy alternate, Enion & Tharmas play'd
Round Vala in the Gardens of Vala & by her river's margin.
They are the shadows of Tharmas & of Enion in Vala's world.

And the sleepers who rested from their harvest work beheld these visions.
Thus were the sleepers entertain'd upon the Couches of Beulah.

When Luvah & Vala were clos'd up in their world of shadowy forms,
Darkness was all beneath the heavens: only a little light
Such as glows out from sleeping spirits, appear'd in the deeps beneath.
As when the wind sweeps over a corn field, the noise of souls
Thro' all the immense, borne down by Clouds swagging in autumnal heat,
Mutt'ring along from heaven to heaven, hoarse roll the human forms
Beneath thick clouds, dreadful lightnings burst & thunders roll,
Down pour the torrent floods of heaven on all the human harvest.
Then Urizen, sitting at his repose on beds in the bright South,
Cried, "Times are Ended!" he exulted; he arose in joy; he exulted;
He pour'd his light, & all his sons & daughters pour'd their light
To exhale the spirits of Luvah & Vala thro' the the atmosphere.
And Luvah & Vala saw the Light; their spirits were exhal'd
In all their ancient innocence; the floods depart; the clouds
Dissipate or sink into the Seas of Tharmas. Luvah sat
Above on the bright heavens in peace; the Spirits of Men beneath
Cried out to be deliver'd, & the spirit of Luvah wept
Over the human harvest & over Vala, the sweet wanderer.
In pain the human harvest wav'd, in horrible groans of woe.
The Universal Groan went up; the Eternal Man was darken'd.

Then Urizen arose & took his sickle in his hand.
There is a brazen sickle, & a scythe of iron hid
Deep in the South, guarded by a few solitary stars.
This sickle Urizen took; the scythe his sons embrac'd
And went forth & began to reap; & all his joyful sons

Reap'd the wide Universe & bound in sheaves a wondrous harvest.
They took them into the wide barns with loud rejoicings & triumph
Of flute & harp & drum & trumpet, horn & clarion.

The feast was spread in the bright South, & the Regenerate Man
Sat at the feast rejoicing, & the wine of Eternity
Was serv'd round by the flames of Luvah all day & all the Night.
And when Morning began to dawn upon the distant hills,
A whirlwind rose up in the Center, & in the whirlwind a shriek,
And in the shriek a rattling of bones, & in the rattling of bones
A dolorous groan, & from the dolorous groan in tears
Rose Enion like a gentle light; & Enion spoke, saying:

"O Dreams of Death! the human form dissolving, companied
By beasts & worms & creeping things, & darkness & despair.
The clouds fall off from my wet brow, the dust from my cold limbs
Into the sea of Tharmas. Soon renew'd, a Golden Moth,
I shall cast off my death clothes & Embrace Tharmas again.
For Lo, the winter melted away upon the distant hills,
And all the black mould sings." She speaks to her infant race; her milk
Descends down on the sand; the thirsty sand drinks & rejoices
Wondering to behold the Emmet, the Grasshopper, the jointed worm.
The roots shoot thick thro' the solid rocks, bursting their way
They cry out in joys of existence; the broad stems
Rear on the mountains stem after stem; the scaly newt creeps
From the stone, & the armed fly springs from the rocky crevice,
The spider, The bat burst from the harden'd slime, crying
To one another: "What are we, & whence is our joy & delight?
Lo, the little moss begins to spring, & the tender weed
Creeps round our secret nest." Flocks brighten the Mountains,
Herds throng up the Valley, wild beasts fill the forests.

Joy thrill'd thro' all the Furious forms of Tharmas humanizing.
Mild he Embrac'd her whom he sought; he rais'd her thro' the heavens,
Sounding his trumpet to awake the dead, on high her soar'd
Over the ruin'd worlds, the smoking tomb of the Eternal Prophet.

The Eternal Man arose. He welcom'd them to the Feast.
The feast was spread in the bright South, & the Eternal Man
Sat at the feast rejoicing, & the wine of Eternity
Was serv'd round by the flames of Luvah all day & all the night.

And Many Eternal Men sat at the golden feast to see
The female form now separate. They shudder'd at the horrible thing
Not born for the sport and amusement of Man, but born to drink up all
    his powers.
They wept to see their shadows; they said to one another: "This is Sin:
This is the Generative world;" they remember'd the days of old.

And One of the Eternals spoke. All was silent at the feast.

"Man is a Worm; wearied with joy, he seeks the caves of sleep
Among the Flowers of Beulah, in his selfish cold repose
Forsaking Brotherhood & Universal love, in selfish clay
Folding the pure wings of his mind, seeking the places dark
Abstracted from the roots of Science; then inclos'd around
In walls of Gold we cast him like a Seed into the Earth
Till times & spaces have pass'd over him; duly every morn
We visit him, covering with a Veil the immortal seed;
With windows from the inclement sky we cover him, & with walls
And hearths protect the selfish terror, till divided all
In families we see our shadows born, ⎫
    & thence we know   ⎪
That Man subsists by Brotherhood   ⎬ Ephesians iii. c. 10 v.
    & Universal Love.   ⎪
We fall on one another's necks,   ⎪
    more closely we embrace.   ⎭
Not for ourselves, but for the Eternal family we live.
Man liveth not by Self alone, but in his brother's face
Each shall behold the Eternal Father & love & joy abound."

So spoke the Eternal at the Feast; they embrac'd the New born Man,
Calling him Brother, image of the Eternal Father; they sat down
At the immortal tables, sounding loud their instruments of joy,
Calling the Morning into Beulah; the Eternal Man rejoic'd.
When Morning dawn'd, The Eternals rose to labour at the Vintage.
Beneath they saw their sons & daughters, wond'ring inconceivable
At the dark myriads in shadows in the worlds beneath.

The morning dawn'd. Urizen rose, & in his hand the Flail
Sounds on the Floor, heard terrible by all beneath the heavens.
Dismal loud redounding, the nether floor shakes with the sound,
And all Nations were threshed out, & the stars thresh'd from their husks.

Then Tharmas took the Winnowing fan; the winnowing wind furious
Above, veer'd round by violent whirlwind, driven west & south,
Tossed the Nations like chaff into the seas of Tharmas.

"O Mystery," Fierce Tharmas cries, "Behold thy end is come!
Art thou she that made the nations drunk with the cup of Religion?
Go down, ye Kings & Councellors & Giant Warriors,
Go down into the depths, go down & hide yourselves beneath,
Go down with horse & Chariots & Trumpets of hoarse war.

"Lo, how the Pomp of Mystery goes down into the Caves!
Her great men howl & throw the dust, & rend their hoary hair.
Her delicate women & children shriek upon the bitter wind,
Spoil'd of their beauty, their hair rent & their skin shrivel'd up.

"Lo, darkness covers the long pomp of banners on the wind,
And black horses & armed men & miserable bound captives.
Where shall the graves recieve them all, & where shall be their place?
And who shall mourn for Mystery who never loos'd her Captives?

"Let the slave, grinding at the mill, run out into the field;
Let him look up into the heavens & laugh in the bright air.
Let the inchained soul, shut up in darkness & in sighing,
Whose face has never seen a smile in thirty weary years,
Rise & look out: his chains are loose, his dungeon doors are open;
And let his wife & children return from the opressor's scourge.

"They look behind at every step & believe it is a dream.
Are these the slaves that groan'd along the streets of Mystery?
Where are your bonds & task masters? are these the prisoners?
Where are your chains? where are your tears? why do you look around?
If you are thirsty, there is the river: go, bathe your parched limbs,
The good of all the Land is before you, for Mystery is no more."

Then All the Slaves from every Earth in the wide Universe
Sing a New Song, drowning confusion in its happy notes,
While the flail of Urizen sounded loud, & the winnowing wind of Tharmas
So loud, so clear in the wide heavens; & the song that they sung was this,
Composed by an African Black from the little Earth of Sotha:

"Aha! Aha! how came I here so soon in my sweet native land?
How came I here? Methinks I am as I was in my youth
When in my father's house I sat & heard his chearing voice.
Methinks I see his flocks & herds & feel my limbs renew'd,
And Lo, my Brethren in their tents, & their little ones around them!"

The song arose to the Golden feast; the Eternal Man rejoic'd.
Then the Eternal Man said: "Luvah, the Vintage is ripe: arise!
The sons of Urizen shall gather the vintage with sharp hooks,
And all thy sons, O Luvah! bear away the families of Earth.
I hear the flail of Urizen; his barns are full; no room
Remains, & in the Vineyards stand the abounding sheaves beneath
The falling Grapes that odorous burst upon the winds. Arise
My flocks & herds, trample the Corn! my cattle, browze upon
The ripe Clusters! The shepherds shout for Luvah, prince of Love.
Let the Bulls of Luvah tread the Corn & draw the loaded waggon
Into the Barn while children glean the Ears around the door.
Then shall they lift their innocent hands & stroke his furious nose,
And he shall lick the little girl's white neck & on her head
Scatter the perfume of his breath; while from his mountains high
The lion of terror shall come down, & bending his bright mane
And crouching at their side, shall eat from the curl'd boy's white lap
His golden food, and in the evening sleep before the door."

"Attempting to be more than Man We become less," said Luvah
As he arose from the bright feast, drunk with the wine of ages.
His crown of thorns fell from his head, he hung his living Lyre
Behind the seat of the Eternal Man & took his way
Sounding the Song of Los, descending to the Vineyards bright.
His sons, arising from the feast with golden baskets, follow,
A fiery train, as when the Sun sings in the ripe vineyards.
Then Luvah stood before the Wine press; all his fiery sons
Brought up the loaded Waggons with shoutings; ramping tygers play
In the jingling traces; furious lions sound the songs of joy
To the golden wheels circling upon the pavement of heaven, & all
The Villages of Luvah ring; the golden tiles of the villages
Reply to violins & tabors, to the pipe, flute, lyre & cymbal.
Then fell the Legions of Mystery in madd'ning confusion,
Down, down thro' the immense, with outcry, fury & despair,
Into the wine presses of Luvah; howling fell the clusters
Of human families thro' the deep; the wine presses were fill'd;

The blood of life flow'd plentiful. Odors of life arose
All round the heavenly arches, & the Odors rose singing this song:

"O terrible wine presses of Luvah! O caverns of the Grave!
How lovely the delights of those risen again from death!
O trembling joy! excess of joy is like Excess of grief."

So sang the Human Odors round the wine presses of Luvah;

But in the Wine presses is wailing, terror & despair.
Forsaken of their Elements they vanish & are no more,
No more but a desire of Being, a distracted, ravening desire,
Desiring like the hungry worm & like the gaping grave.
They plunge into the Elements; the Elements cast them forth
Or else consume their shadowy semblance. Yet they, obstinate
Tho' pained to distraction, cry, "O let us Exist! for
This dreadful Non Existence is worse than pains of Eternal Birth:
Eternal death who can Endure? let us consume in fires,
In waters stifling, or in air corroding, or in earth shut up.
The Pangs of Eternal birth are better than the Pangs of Eternal death."

How red the sons & daughters of Luvah! how they tread the Grapes!
Laughing & shouting, drunk with odors, many fall o'erwearied:
Drown'd in the wine is many a youth & maiden; those around
Lay them on skins of tygers or the spotted Leopard or wild Ass
Till they revive, or bury them in cool Grots making lamentation.

But in the Wine Presses the Human Grapes sing not nor dance,
They howl & writhe in shoals of torment, in fierce flames consuming,
In chains of iron & in dungeons circled with ceaseless fires,
In pits & dens & shades of death, in shapes of torment & woe;
The Plates, the Screw & Racks & Saws & cords & fires & floods,
The cruel joy of Luvah's daughters, lacerating with knives
And whips their Victims, & the deadly sport of Luvah's sons.
Timbrels & Violins sport round the Wine Presses. The little Seed,
The sportive root, the Earthworm, the small beetle, the wise Emmett,
Dance round the Wine Presses of Luvah; the Centipede is there,
The ground Spider with many eyes, the Mole clothed in Velvet,
The Earwig arm'd, the tender maggot, emblem of Immortality;
The slow slug, the grasshopper that sings & laughs & drinks:
The winter comes; he folds his slender bones without a murmur.
There is the Nettle that stings with soft down; & there

The indignant Thistle whose bitterness is bred in his milk
And who lives on the contempt of his neighbour; there all the idle **weeds**,
That creep about the obscure places, shew their various limbs
Naked in all their beauty, dancing round the Wine Presses.
They dance around the dying & they drink the howl & groan;
They catch the shrieks in cups of gold; they hand them to one **another**.
These are the sports of love & these the sweet delights of amorous **play**:
Tears of the grape, the death sweat of the Cluster, the last sigh
Of the mild youth who listens to the luring songs of Luvah.
The Eternal Man darken'd with sorrow & a wintry mantle
Cover'd the Hills. He said, "O Tharmas, rise! & O Urthona!"
Then Tharmas & Urthona rose from the Golden feast, satiated
With Mirth & Joy: Urthona, limping from his fall, on Tharmas **lean'd**,
In his right hand his hammer. Tharmas held his shepherd's crook
Beset with gold, gold were the ornaments form'd by sons of **Urizen**.
Then Enion & Ahania & Vala & the wife of dark Urthona
Rose from the feast, in joy ascending to their Golden Looms.
There the wing'd shuttle sang, the spindle & the distaff & the **Reel**
Rang sweet the praise of industry. Thro' all the golden rooms
Heaven rang with winged Exultation. All beneath howl'd loud;
With tenfold rout & desolation roar'd the Chasms beneath
Where the wide woof flow'd down & where the Nations are **gather'd**
    together.

Tharmas went down to the Wine presses & beheld the sons & daughters
Of Luvah quite exhausted with the labour & quite fill'd
With new wine, that they began to torment one another and to tread
The weak. Luvah & Vala slept on the floor, o'erwearied.
Urthona call'd his sons around him: Tharmas call'd his sons
Numerous; they took the wine, they separated the Lees,
And Luvah was put for dung on the ground by the Sons of Tharmas &
    Urthona.
They formed the heavens of sweetest woods, of gold & silver & ivory,
Of glass & precious stones. They loaded all the waggons of heaven
And took away the wine of ages with solemn songs & joy.

Luvah & Vala woke, & all the sons & daughters of Luvah
Awoke; they wept to one another & they reascended
To the Eternal Man in woe: he cast them wailing into
The world of shadows, thro' the air; till winter is over & gone;
But the Human Wine stood wondering; in all their delightful Expanses
The elements subside; the heavens roll'd on with vocal harmony.

Then Los, who is Urthona, rose in all his regenerate power.
The Sea that roll'd & foam'd with darkness, & the shadows of death
Vomited out & gave up all; the floods lift up their hands
Singing & shouting to the Man; they bow their hoary heads
And murmuring in their channels flow & circle round his feet.

Then Dark Urthona took the Corn out of the Stores of Urizen;
He ground it in his rumbling Mills. Terrible the distress
Of all the Nations of Earth, ground in the Mills of Urthona.
In his hand Tharmas takes the Storms: he turns the whirlwind loose
Upon the wheels; the stormy seas howl at his dread command
And Eddying fierce rejoice in the fierce agitation of the wheels
Of Dark Urthona. Thunders, Earthquakes, Fires, Water floods,
Rejoice to one another; loud their voices shake the Abyss,
Their dread forms tending the dire mills. The grey hoar frost was there,
And his pale wife, the aged Snow; they watch over the fires,
They build the Ovens of Urthona. Nature in darkness groans
And Men are bound to sullen contemplation in the night:
Restless they turn on beds of sorrow; in their inmost brain
Feeling the crushing Wheels, they rise, they write the bitter words
Of Stern Philosophy & knead the bread of knowledge with tears & groans.

Such are the works of Dark Urthona. Tharmas sifts the corn.
Urthona made the Bread of Ages, & he placed it,
In golden & in silver baskets, in heavens of precious stone
And then took his repose in Winter, in the night of Time.

The Sun has left his blackness & has found a fresher morning,
And the mild moon rejoices in the clear & cloudless night,
And Man walks forth from midst of the fires: the evil is all consum'd.
His eyes behold the Angelic spheres arising night & day;
The stars consum'd like a lamp blown out, & in their stead, behold
The Expanding Eyes of Man behold the depths of wondrous worlds!
One Earth, one sea beneath; nor Erring Globes wander, but Stars
Of fire rise up nightly from the Ocean; & one Sun
Each morning, like a New born Man, issues with songs & joy
Calling the Plowman to his Labour & the Shepherd to his rest.
He walks upon the Eternal Mountains, raising his heavenly voice,
Conversing with the Animal forms of wisdom night & day,
That, risen from the Sea of fire, renew'd walk o'er the Earth;
For Tharmas brought his flocks upon the hills, & in the Vales

Around the Eternal Man's bright tent, the little Children play
Among the wooly flocks. The hammer of Urthona sounds
In the deep caves beneath; his limbs renew'd, his Lions roar
Around the Furnaces & in Evening sport upon the plains.
They raise their faces from the Earth, conversing with the Man:

"How is it we have walk'd thro' fires & yet are not consum'd?
How is it that all things are chang'd, even as in ancient times?"

The Sun arises from his dewy bed, & the fresh airs
Play in his smiling beams giving the seeds of life to grow,
And the fresh Earth beams forth ten thousand thousand springs of life.
Urthona is arisen in his strength, no longer now
Divided from Enitharmon, no longer the Spectre Los.
Where is the Spectre of Prophecy? where is the delusive Phantom?
Departed: & Urthona rises from the ruinous Walls
In all his ancient strength to form the golden armour of science
For intellectual War. The war of swords departed now,
The dark Religions are departed & sweet Science reigns.

 END OF THE DREAM

NOTES WRITTEN ON THE PAGES OF THE FOUR ZOAS

Christ's Crucifix shall be made an excuse for Executing Criminals.

Till thou dost injure the distrest

Thou shalt never have peace within thy breast.

The Christian Religion teaches that No Man is Indifferent to you, but that every one is Either your friend or your enemy; he must necessarily be either the one or the other, And that he will be equally profitable both ways if you treat him as he deserves.

Unorganiz'd Innocence: An Impossibility.
Innocence dwells with Wisdom, but never with Ignorance.

END OF THE FOUR ZOAS

THE FOUR ZOAS

ADDITIONAL FRAGMENTS

BENEATH the veil of Vala rose Tharmas from dewy tears.
The *eternal* man bow'd his bright head, & Urizen, prince of light,
Astonish'd look'd from his bright portals, Luvah, King of Love
Awaken'd Vala. Ariston ran forth with bright Anana,
And dark Urthona rouz'd his shady bride from her deep den.
Pitying, they view'd the new born demon, for they could not love.
Male form'd the demon mild athletic force his shoulders spread,
And his bright feet firm as a brazen altar; but the parts
To love devoted, female; all astonish'd stood the hosts
Of heaven, while Tharmas with wing'd speed flew to the sandy shore,
He rested on the desart wild, & on the raging sea
He stood & stretch'd his wings &c

With printless feet, scorning the concave of the joyful sky,
Female her form, bright as the summer, but the parts of love
Male, & her brow, radiant as day, darted a lovely scorn.
Tharmas beheld from his rock &c

※

The ocean calm, the clouds fold round, & fiery flames of love
Inwrap the immortal limbs, struggling in terrific joy.
Not long; thunders, lightnings swift, rendings & blasting winds
Sweep o'er the struggling copulation, in fell writhing pangs
They lie, in twisting agonies beneath the covering heavens.

※

The womb impress'd, Enion fled & hid in verdant mountains,
Yet here his heavenly orbs &c

※

From Enion pours the seed of life, & death in all her limbs
Froze; in the womb of Tharmas rush the rivers of Enion's pain.
Trembling he lay, swell'd with the deluge, stifling in the anguish.

※

Opening in rifted rocks, mingling *together they* join in burning anguish,
Mingling his horrible *darkness* with her tender limbs; then high she
    soar'd,
Shrieking above the ocean: a bright wonder that nature shudder'd at,
Half Woman & half desart, all his *darkly waving* colours mix
With her fair crystal clearness; in her lips & cheeks his metals rose
In blushes like the morning, & his *rocky features* soft'ning,
A *wonder,* lovely in the heavens or wand'ring on the earth,
With female voice warbling upon the hills & hollow vales,
Beauty all blushing with desire, a self enjoying wonder.
For Enion brooded, groaning loud; the rough seas vegetate.
    Golden rocks rise from the vast . . .
And thus her voice: "Glory, delight & sweet enjoyment born
To mild Eternity, shut in a threefold shape delightful,
To wander in sweet solitude, enraptur'd at every wind."

❊

The Lamb of God stood before Urizen opposite
In Entuthon Benithon, in the shadows of torment & woe
Upon the heights of Amalek, taking refuge in his arms
The victims fled from punishment, for all his words were peace.
Urizen call'd together all the synagogue of Satan in dark Sanhedrim
To judge the lamb of God to death as a murderer & robber:
At it is written, He was number'd among the transgressors.

Cold, dark, opake the Assembly met twelvefold in Amalek,
Twelve rocky unshap'd forms, terrific forms of torture & woe,
Such seem'd the Synagogue to distant view; around them stood
The daughters of Canaan & Moab, binding on the Stones
Their victims, & with knives tormenting them, singing with tears
Over their victims. Thus was the Lamb of God condemn'd to death.
They nailed him upon the tree of Mystery, & weeping over him
And mocking & then worshiping, calling him Lord & King.
Sometimes as twelve daughters lovely, & sometimes as five
They stood in beaming beauty, & sometimes as One, even Rahab
Who is Mystery, Babylon the Great, Mother of Harlots.

And Rahab strip'd off Luvah's robes from off the lamb of God,
Then first she saw his glory, & her harlot form appear'd
In all its turpitude beneath the divine light, & of Luvah's robes

She made herself a Mantle.
Also the Vegetated bodies which Enitharmon wove in her looms
Open'd within the heart & in the loins & in the brain
To Beulah, & the dead in Beulah descended thro' their gates.
And some were woven onefold, some twofold, & some threefold
In head or heart or reins, according to the fittest order
Of most merciful pity & compassion to the spectrous dead.
Darkness & sorrow cover'd all flesh; eternity was darken'd.
Urizen sitting in his web of deceitful religion was tormented.
He felt the female &c

END OF ADDITIONAL FRAGMENTS

MILTON

A Poem in Two Books

To Justify the Ways of God to Men

Written and etched, 1804-1808

PREFACE

T H E Stolen and Perverted Writings of Homer & Ovid, of Plato & Cicero, which all men ought to contemn, are set up by artifice against the Sublime of the Bible; but when the New Age is at leisure to Pronounce, all will be set right, & those Grand Works of the more ancient & consciously & professedly Inspired Men will hold their proper rank, & the Daughters of Memory shall become the Daughters of Inspiration. Shakspeare & Milton were both curb'd by the general malady & infection from the silly Greek & Latin slaves of the Sword.

Rouze up, O Young Men of the New Age! set your foreheads against the ignorant Hirelings! For we have Hirelings in the Camp, the Court & the University, who would, if they could, for ever depress Mental & prolong Corporeal War. Painters! on you I call. Sculptors! Architects! Suffer not the fashonable Fools to depress your powers by the prices they pretend to give for contemptible works, or the expensive advertizing boasts that they make of such works; believe Christ & his Apostles that there is a Class of Men whose whole delight is in Destroying. We do not want either Greek or Roman Models if we are but just & true to our own Imaginations, those Worlds of Eternity in which we shall live for ever in JESUS OUR LORD.

And did those feet in ancient time
Walk upon England's mountains green?
And was the holy Lamb of God
On England's pleasant pastures seen?

And did the Countenance Divine
Shine forth upon our clouded hills?
And was Jerusalem builded here
Among these dark Satanic Mills?

Bring me my Bow of burning gold:
Bring me my Arrows of desire:
Bring me my Spear: O clouds unfold!
Bring me my Chariot of fire.

I will not cease from Mental Fight,
Nor shall my Sword sleep in my hand
Till we have built Jerusalem
In England's green & pleasant Land.

"Would to God that all the Lord's people were Prophets."
NUMBERS, xi. ch., 29 v.

MILTON

BOOK THE FIRST

2

DAUGHTERS of Beulah! Muses who inspire the Poet's Song,
Record the journey of immortal Milton thro' your Realms
Of terror & mild moony lustre in soft sexual delusions
Of varied beauty, to delight the wanderer and repose
His burning thirst & freezing hunger! Come into my hand,
By your mild power descending down the Nerves of my right arm
From out the portals of my Brain, where by your ministry
The Eternal Great Humanity Divine planted his Paradise
And in it caus'd the Spectres of the Dead to take sweet forms
In likeness of himself. Tell also of the False Tongue! vegetated
Beneath your land of shadows, of its sacrifices and
Its offerings: even till Jesus, the image of the Invisible God,

Became its prey, a curse, an offering and an atonement
For Death Eternal in the heavens of Albion & before the Gates
Of Jerusalem his Emanation, in the heavens beneath Beulah.

Say first! what mov'd Milton, who walk'd about in Eternity
One hundred years, pond'ring the intricate mazes of Providence,
Unhappy tho' in heav'n—he obey'd, he murmur'd not, he was silent
Viewing his Sixfold Emanation scatter'd thro' the deep
In torment—To go into the deep her to redeem & himself perish?
That cause at length mov'd Milton to this unexampled deed.
A Bard's prophetic Song! for sitting at eternal tables,
Terrific among the Sons of Albion, in chorus solemn & loud
A Bard broke forth: all sat attentive to the awful man.

Mark well my words! they are of your eternal salvation.

Three Classes are Created by the Hammer of Los & Woven

3

By Enitharmon's Looms when Albion was slain upon his Mountains
And in his Tent, thro' envy of the Living Form, even of the Divine Vision,
And of the sports of Wisdom in the Human Imagination,
Which is the Divine Body of the Lord Jesus, blessed for ever
Mark well my words! they are of your eternal salvation.

Urizen lay in darkness & solitude, in chains of the mind lock'd up
Los siez'd his Hammer & Tongs; he labour'd at his resolute Anvil
Among indefinite Druid rocks & snows of doubt & reasoning.

Refusing all Definite Form, the Abstract Horror roof'd, stony hard;
And a first Age passed over, & a State of dismal woe.

Down sunk with fright a red round Globe, hot burning, deep,
Deep down into the Abyss, panting, conglobing, trembling;
And a second Age passed over, & a State of dismal woe.

Rolling round into two little Orbs, & closed in two little Caves,
The Eyes beheld the Abyss, lest bones of solidness freeze over all;
And a third Age passed over, & a State of dismal woe.

From beneath his Orbs of Vision, Two Ears in close volutions
Shot spiring out in the deep darkness & petrified as they grew;
And a fourth Age passed over, & a State of dismal woe.

Hanging upon the wind, Two Nostrils bent down into the Deep;
And a fifth Age passed over, & a State of dismal woe.

In ghastly torment sick, a Tongue of hunger & thirst flamed out;
And a sixth Age passed over, & a State of dismal woe.

Enraged & stifled without & within, in terror & woe he threw his
Right Arm to the north, his left Arm to the south, & his feet
Stamp'd the nether Abyss in trembling & howling & dismay;
And a seventh Age passed over, & a State of dismal woe.

Terrified, Los stood in the Abyss, & his immortal limbs
Grew deadly pale; he became what he beheld, for a red
Round Globe sunk down from his Bosom into the Deep; in pangs
He hover'd over it trembling & weeping: suspended it shook
The nether Abyss; in tremblings he wept over it, he cherish'd it
In deadly, sickening pain, till separated into a Female pale
As the cloud that brings the snow; all the while from his Back
A blue fluid exuded in Sinews, hardening in the Abyss
Till it separated into a Male Form howling in Jealousy.

Within labouring, beholding Without, from Particulars to Generals
Subduing his Spectre, they Builded the Looms of Generation;
They builded Great Golgonooza Times on Times, Ages on Ages.
First Orc was born, then the shadowy Female: then All Los's family.
At last Enitharmon brought forth Satan, Refusing Form in vain,
The Miller of Eternity made subservient to the Great Harvest
That he may go to his own Place, Prince of the Starry Wheels

4

Beneath the Plow of Rintrah & the Harrow of the Almighty
In the hands of Palamabron, Where the Starry Mills of Satan
Are built beneath the Earth & Waters of the Mundane Shell:
Here the Three Classes of Men take their Sexual texture, Woven;
The Sexual is Threefold, the Human is Fourfold.

"If you account it Wisdom when you are angry to be silent and
Not to shew it, I do not account that Wisdom, but Folly.
Every Man's Wisdom is peculiar to his own Individuality.
O Satan, my youngest born, art thou not Prince of the Starry Hosts
And of the Wheels of Heaven, to turn the Mills day & night?
Art thou not Newton's Pantocrator, weaving the Woof of Locke?

To Mortals thy Mills seem every thing, & the Harrow of Shaddai
A Scheme of Human conduct invisible & incomprehensible.
Get to thy Labours at the Mills & leave me to my wrath."

Satan was going to reply, but Los roll'd his loud thunders.

"Anger me not! thou canst not drive the Harrow in pity's paths:
Thy work is Eternal Death with Mills & Ovens & Cauldrons.
Trouble me no more; thou canst not have Eternal Life."

So Los spoke. Satan trembling obey'd, weeping along the way.
Mark well my words! they are of your eternal Salvation.

Between South Molton Street & Stratford Place, Calvary's foot,
Where the Victims were preparing for Sacrifice their Cherubim;
Around their Loins pour'd forth their arrows, & their bosoms beam
With all colours of precious stones, & their inmost palaces
Resounded with preparation of animals wild & tame,
(Mark well my words: Corporeal Friends are Spiritual Enemies)
Mocking Druidical Mathematical Proportion of Length, Bredth, Highth:
Displaying Naked Beauty, with Flute & Harp & Song.

5

Palamabron with the fiery Harrow in morning returning
From breathing fields, Satan fainted beneath the artillery.
Christ took on Sin in the Virgin's Womb & put it off on the Cross.
All pitied the piteous & was wrath with the wrathful, & Los heard it.

And this is the manner of the Daughters of Albion in their beauty.
Every one is threefold in Head & Heart & Reins, & every one
Has three Gates into the Three Heavens of Beulah, which shine
Translucent in their Foreheads & their Bosoms & their Loins
Surrounded with fires unapproachable: but whom they please
They take up into their Heavens in intoxicating delight;
For the Elect cannot be Redeem'd, but Created continually
By Offering & Atonement in the cruelties of Moral Law.
Hence the three Classes of Men take their fix'd destinations.
They are the Two Contraries & the Reasoning Negative.

While the Females prepare the Victims, the Males at Furnaces
And Anvils dance the dance of tears & pain: loud lightnings
Lash on their limbs as they turn the whirlwinds loose upon
The Furnaces, lamenting around the Anvils, & this their Song:

"Ah weak & wide astray! Ah shut in narrow doleful form,
Creeping in reptile flesh upon the bosom of the ground!
The Eye of Man a little narrow orb, clos'd up & dark,
Scarcely beholding the great light, conversing with the Void;
The Ear a little shell, in small volutions shutting out
All melodies & comprehending only Discord and Harmony;
The Tongue a little moisture fills, a little food it cloys,
A little sound it utters & its cries are faintly heard,
Then brings forth Moral Virtue the cruel Virgin Babylon.

"Can such an Eye judge of the stars? & looking thro' its tubes
Measure the sunny rays that point their spears on Udanadan?
Can such an Ear, fill'd with the vapours of the yawning pit,
Judge of the pure melodious harp struck by a hand divine?
Can such closed Nostrils feel a joy? or tell of autumn fruits
When grapes & figs burst their covering to the joyful air?
Can such a Tongue boast of the living waters? or take in
Ought but the Vegetable Ratio & loathe the faint delight?
Can such gross Lips perceive? alas, folded within themselves
They touch not ought, but pallid turn & tremble at every wind."

Thus they sing Creating the Three Classes among Druid Rocks.
Charles calls on Milton for Atonement. Cromwell is ready.
James calls for fires in Golgonooza, for heaps of smoking ruins
In the night of prosperity and wantonness which he himself Created
Among the Daughters of Albion, among the Rocks of the Druids
When Satan fainted beneath the arrows of Elynittria,
And Mathematic Proportion was subdued by Living Proportion.

6

From Golgonooza the spiritual Four-fold London eternal,
In immense labours & sorrows, ever building, ever falling,
Thro' Albion's four Forests which overspread all the Earth
From London Stone to Blackheath east: to Hounslow west:
To Finchley north: to Norwood south: and the weights
Of Enitharmon's Loom play lulling cadences on the winds of Albion
From Caithness in the north to Lizard-point & Dover in the south.

Loud sounds the Hammer of Los & loud his Bellows is heard
Before London to Hampstead's breadths & Highgate's heights, To
Stratford & old Bow & across to the Gardens of Kensington
On Tyburn's Brook: loud groans Thames beneath the iron Forge

Of Rintrah & Palamabron, of Theotorm & Bromion, to forge the instruments
    ments
Of Harvest, the Plow & Harrow to pass over the Nations.

The Surrey hills glow like the clinkers of the furnace; Lambeth's Vale
Where Jerusalem's foundations began, where they were laid in ruins,
Where they were laid in ruins from every Nation, & Oak Groves rooted,
Dark gleams before the Furnace-mouth a heap of burning ashes.
When shall Jerusalem return & overspread all the Nations?
Return, return to Lambeth's Vale, O building of human souls!
Thence stony Druid Temples overspread the Island white,
And thence from Jerusalem's ruins, from her walls of salvation
And praise, thro' the whole Earth were rear'd from Ireland
To Mexico & Peru west, & east to China & Japan, till Babel
The Spectre of Albion frown'd over the Nations in glory & war.
All things begin & end in Albion's ancient Druid rocky shore:
But now the Starry Heavens are fled from the mighty limbs of Albion.

Loud sounds the Hammer of Los, loud turn the Wheels of Enitharmon:
Her Looms vibrate with soft affections, weaving the Web of Life,
Out from the ashes of the Dead; Los lifts his iron Ladles
With molten ore: he heaves the iron cliffs in his rattling chains
From Hyde Park to the Alms-houses of Mile-end & old Bow.
Here the Three Classes of Mortal Men take their fix'd destinations,
And hence they overspread the Nations of the whole Earth, & hence
The Web of Life is woven & the tender sinews of life created
And the Three Classes of Men regulated by Los's Hammers [and woven

7

By Enitharmon's Looms & Spun beneath the Spindle of Tirzah. *erased*]
The first, The Elect from before the foundation of the World:
The second, The Redeem'd: The Third, The Reprobate & form'd
To destruction from the mother's womb: .   .   .   .
.   .   .   .   .   *[words erased]* follow me with my plow.

Of the first class was Satan: with incomparable mildness,
His primitive tyrannical attempts on Los, with most endearing love
He soft intreated Los to give to him Palamabron's station,
For Palamabron return'd with labour wearied every evening.
Palamabron oft refus'd, and as often Satan offer'd
His service, till by repeated offers and repeated intreaties
Los gave to him the Harrow of the Almighty; alas, blamable,

Palamabron fear'd to be angry lest Satan should accuse him of
Ingratitude & Los believe the accusation thro' Satan's extreme
Mildness. Satan labour'd all day: it was a thousand years:
In the evening returning terrified, overlabour'd & astonish'd,
Embrac'd soft with a brother's tears Palamabron, who also wept.

Mark well my words! they are of your eternal salvation.

 Next morning Palamabron rose; the horses of the Harrow
Were madden'd with tormenting fury, & the servants of the Harrow,
The Gnomes, accus'd Satan with indignation, fury and fire.
Then Palamabron, reddening like the Moon in an Eclipse,
Spoke, saying: "You know Satan's mildness and his self-imposition,
Seeming a brother, being a tyrant, even thinking himself a brother
While he is murdering the just: prophetic I behold
His future course thro' darkness and despair to eternal death.
But we must not be tyrants also: he hath assum'd my place
For one whole day under pretence of pity and love to me.
My horses hath he madden'd and my fellow servants injur'd.
How should he, he, know the duties of another? O foolish forbearance!
Would I had told Los all my heart! but patience, O my friends,
All may be well: silent remain, while I call Los and Satan."

Loud as the wind of Beulah that unroots the rocks & hills
Palamabron call'd, and Los & Satan came before him,
And Palamabron shew'd the horses & the servants. Satan wept
And mildly cursing Palamabron, him accus'd of crimes
Himself had wrought. Los trembled: Satan's blandishments almost
Perswaded the Prophet of Eternity that Palamabron
Was Satan's enemy & that the Gnomes, being Palamabron's friends,
Were leagued together against Satan thro' ancient enmity.
What could Los do? how could he judge, when Satan's self believ'd
That he had not oppres'd the horses of the Harrow nor the servants.

So Los said: "Henceforth, Palamabron, let each his own station
Keep: nor in pity false, nor in officious brotherhood, where
None needs, be active." Mean time Palamabron's horses
Rag'd with thick flames redundant, & the Harrow madden'd with fury.
Trembling Palamabron stood; the strongest of Demons trembled,
Curbing his living creatures; many of the strongest Gnomes
They bit in their wild fury, who also madden'd like wildest beasts.

Mark well my words! they are of your eternal salvation.

8

Mean while wept Satan before Los accusing Palamabron
Himself exculpating with mildest speech, for himself believ'd
That he had not oppress'd nor injur'd the refractory servants.

But Satan returning to his Mills (for Palamabron had serv'd
The Mills of Satan as the easier task) found all confusion,
And back return'd to Los, not fill'd with vengeance but with tears,
Himself convinc'd of Palamabron's turpitude. Los beheld
The servants of the Mills drunken with wine and dancing wild
With shouts and Palamabron's songs, rending the forests green
With ecchoing confusion, tho' the Sun was risen on high.

Then Los took off his left sandal, placing it on his head,
Signal of solemn mourning: when the servants of the Mills
Beheld the signal they in silence stood, tho' drunk with wine.
Los wept! But Rintrah also came, and Enitharmon on
His arm lean'd tremblingly, observing all these things.

And Los said: "Ye Genii of the Mills! the Sun is on high,
Your labours call you: Palamabron is also in sad dilemma:
His horses are mad, his Harrow confounded, his companions enrag'd.
Mine is the fault! I should have remember'd that pity divides the soul
And man unmans; follow with me my Plow: this mournful day
Must be a blank in Nature: follow with me and tomorrow again
Resume your labours, & this day shall be a mournful day."

Wildly they follow'd Los and Rintrah, & the Mills were silent.
They mourn'd all day, this mournful day of Satan & Palamabron:
And all the Elect & all the Redeem'd mourn'd one toward another
Upon the mountains of Albion among the cliffs of the Dead.

They Plow'd in tears; incessant pour'd Jehovah's rain & Molech's
Thick fires contending with the rain thunder'd above, rolling
Terrible over their heads; Satan wept over Palamabron.
Theotormon & Bromion contended on the side of Satan,
Pitying his youth and beauty, trembling at eternal death.
Michael contended against Satan in the rolling thunder:
Thulloh the friend of Satan also reprov'd him: faint their reproof.

But Rintrah who is of the reprobate, of those form'd to destruction,
In indignation for Satan's soft dissimulation of friendship
Flam'd above all the plowed furrows, angry, red and furious,
Till Michael sat down in the furrow, weary, dissolv'd in tears.
Satan, who drave the team beside him, stood angry & red:
He smote Thulloh & slew him, & he stood terrible over Michael
Urging him to arise: he wept: Enitharmon saw his tears.
But Los hid Thulloh from her sight, lest she should die of grief.
She wept, she trembled, she kissed Satan, she wept over Michael:
She form'd a Space for Satan & Michael & for the poor infected.
Trembling she wept over the Space & clos'd it with a tender Moon.

Los secret buried Thulloh, weeping disconsolate over the moony Space.

But Palamabron called down a Great Solemn Assembly,
That he who will not defend Truth, may be compelled to
Defend a Lie, that he may be snared & caught & taken.

9

And all Eden descended into Palamabron's tent
Among Albion's Druids & Bards in the caves beneath Albion's
Death Couch, in the caverns of death, in the corner of the Atlantic.
And in the midst of the Great Assembly Palamabron pray'd:
"O God, protect me from my friends, that they have not power over me.
Thou hast giv'n me power to protect myself from my bitterest enemies."

Mark well my words! they are of your eternal salvation.

Then rose the Two Witnesses, Rintrah & Palamabron:
And Palamabron appeal'd to all Eden and reciev'd
Judgment: and Lo! it fell on Rintrah and his rage,
Which now flam'd high & furious in Satan against Palamabron
Till it became a proverb in Eden: Satan is among the Reprobate.

Los in his wrath curs'd heaven & earth; he rent up Nations,
Standing on Albion's rocks among high-rear'd Druid temples
Which reach the stars of heaven & stretch from pole to pole.
He displac'd continents, the oceans fled before his face:
He alter'd the poles of the world, east, west & north & south,
But he clos'd up Enitharmon from the sight of all these things.

For Satan, flaming with Rintrah's fury hidden beneath his own mildness,
Accus'd Palamabron before the Assembly of ingratitude, of malice.
He created Seven deadly Sins, drawing out his infernal scroll
Of Moral laws and cruel punishments upon the clouds of Jehovah,
To pervert the Divine voice in its entrance to the earth
With thunder of war & trumpet's sound, with armies of disease,
Punishments & deaths muster'd & number'd, Saying: "I am God
    alone:
There is no other! let all obey my principles of moral individuality.
I have brought them from the uppermost, innermost recesses
Of my Eternal Mind: transgressors I will rend off for ever
As now I rend this accursed Family from my covering."

Thus Satan rag'd amidst the Assembly, and his bosom grew
Opake against the Divine Vision: the paved terraces of
His bosom inwards shone with fires, but the stones becoming opake
Hid him from sight in an extreme blackness and darkness.
And there a World of deeper Ulro was open'd in the midst
Of the Assembly. In Satan's bosom, a vast unfathomable Abyss.

Astonishment held the Assembly in an awful silence, and tears
Fell down as dews of night, & a loud solemn universal groan
Was utter'd from the east & from the west & from the south
And from the north; and Satan stood opake immeasurable,
Covering the east with solid blackness round his hidden heart,
With thunders utter'd from his hidden wheels, accusing loud
The Divine Mercy for protecting Palamabron in his tent.

Rintrah rear'd up walls of rocks and pour'd rivers & moats
Of fire round the walls: columns of fire guard around
Between Satan and Palamabron in the terrible darkness.

And Satan not having the Science of Wrath, but only of Pity,
Rent them asunder, and wrath was left to wrath, & pity to pity.
He sunk down, a dreadful Death unlike the slumbers of Beulah.

The Separation was terrible: the Dead was repos'd on his Couch
Beneath the Couch of Albion, on the seven mountains of Rome,
In the whole place of the Covering Cherub, Rome, Babylon & Tyre.
His Spectre raging furious descended into its Space.

11

Then Los & Enitharmon knew that Satan is Urizen,
Drawn down by Orc & the Shadowy Female into Generation.
Oft Enitharmon enter'd weeping into the Space, there appearing
An aged Woman raving along the Streets (the Space is named
Canaan): then she returned to Los, weary, frightened as from dreams.

The nature of a Female Space is this: it shrinks the Organs
Of Life till they become Finite & Itself seems Infinite.

And Satan vibrated in the immensity of the Space, Limited
To those without, but Infinite to those within: it fell down and
Became Canaan, closing Los from Eternity in Albion's Cliffs.
A mighty Fiend against the Divine Humanity, must'ring to War.

"Satan, Ah me! is gone to his own place," said Los: "their God
I will not worship in their Churches, nor King in their Theatres.
Elynittria! whence is this Jealousy running along the mountains?
British Women were not Jealous when Greek & Roman were Jealous.
Every thing in Eternity shines by its own Internal light but thou
Darkenest every Internal light with the arrows of thy quiver,
Bound up in the horns of Jealousy to a deadly fading Moon,
And Ocalythron binds the Sun into a Jealous Globe,
That every thing is fix'd Opake without Internal light."

So Los lamented over Satan who triumphant divided the Nations.

12

He set his face against Jerusalem to destroy the Eon of Albion.

But Los hid Enitharmon from the sight of all these things
Upon the Thames whose lulling harmony repos'd her soul,
Where Beulah lovely terminates in rocky Albion,
Terminating in Hyde Park on Tyburn's awful brook.

And the Mills of Satan were separated into a moony Space
Among the rocks of Albion's Temples, and Satan's Druid sons
Offer the Human Victims throughout all the Earth, and Albion's
Dread Tomb, immortal on his Rock, overshadow'd the whole Earth,
Where Satan, making to himself Laws from his own identity,
Compell'd others to serve him in moral gratitude & submission,

Being call'd God, setting himself above all that is called God;
And all the Spectres of the Dead, calling themselves Sons of God,
In his Synagogues worship Satan under the Unutterable Name.

And it was enquir'd Why in a Great Solemn Assembly
The Innocent should be condemn'd for the Guilty. Then an Eternal rose,

Saying: "If the Guilty should be condemn'd he must be an Eternal Death,
And one must die for another throughout all Eternity.
Satan is fall'n from his station & never can be redeem'd,
But must be new Created continually moment by moment.
And therefore the Class of Satan shall be call'd the Elect, & those
Of Rintrah the Reprobate, & those of Palamabron the Redeem'd:
For he is redeem'd from Satan's Law, the wrath falling on Rintrah.
And therefore Palamabron dared not to call a solemn Assembly
Till Satan had assum'd Rintrah's wrath in the day of mourning,
In a feminine delusion of false pride self-deciev'd."

So spake the Eternal and confirm'd it with a thunderous oath.

But when Leutha (a Daughter of Beulah) beheld Satan's condemnation,
She down descended into the midst of the Great Solemn Assembly,
Offering herself a Ransom for Satan, taking on her his Sin.

Mark well my words! they are of your eternal salvation.

And Leutha stood glowing with varying colours, immortal, heart-piercing
And lovely, & her moth-like elegance shone over the Assembly.

At length, standing upon the golden floor of Palamabron,
She spake: "I am the Author of this Sin! by my suggestion
My Parent power Satan has committed this transgression.
I loved Palamabron & I sought to approach his Tent,
But beautiful Elynittria with her silver arrows repell'd me.

13

"For her light is terrible to me: I fade before her immortal beauty.
O wherefore doth a Dragon-form forth issue from my limbs
To sieze her new born son? Ah me! the wretched Leutha!
This to prevent, entering the doors of Satan's brain night after night
Like sweet perfumes, I stupified the masculine perceptions
And kept only the feminine awake: hence rose his soft

Delusory love to Palamabron, admiration join'd with envy.
Cupidity unconquerable! my fault, when at noon of day
The Horses of Palamabron call'd for rest and pleasant death,
I sprang out of the breast of Satan, over the Harrow beaming
In all my beauty, that I might unloose the flaming steeds
As Elynittria used to do; but too well those living creatures
Knew that I was not Elynittria and they brake the traces.
But me the servants of the Harrow saw not but as a bow
Of varying colours on the hills; terribly rag'd the horses.
Satan astonish'd and with power above his own controll
Compell'd the Gnomes to curb the horses & to throw banks of sand
Around the fiery flaming Harrow in labyrinthine forms,
And brooks between to intersect the meadows in their course.
The Harrow cast thick flames: Jehovah thunder'd above
Chaos & ancient night fled from beneath the fiery Harrow:
The Harrow cast thick flames & orb'd us round in concave fires,
A Hell of our own making; see! its flames still gird me round.
Jehovah thunder'd above; Satan in pride of heart
Drove the fierce Harrow among the constellations of Jehovah,
Drawing a third part in the fires as stubble north & south
To devour Albion and Jerusalem, the Emanation of Albion,
Driving the Harrow in Pity's paths: 'twas then, with our dark fires
Which now gird round us (O eternal torment!) I form'd the Serpent
Of precious stones & gold, turn'd poisons on the sultry wastes.
The Gnomes in all that day spar'd not; they curs'd Satan bitterly
To do unkind things in kindness, with power arm'd to say
The most irritating things in the midst of tears and love:
These are the stings of the Serpent! thus did we by them till thus
They in return retaliated, and the Living Creatures madden'd.
The Gnomes labour'd. I weeping hid in Satan's inmost brain.
But when the Gnomes refus'd to labour more, with blandishments
I came forth from the head of Satan: back the Gnomes recoil'd
And called me Sin and for a sign portentous held me. Soon
Day sunk and Palamabron return'd; trembling I hid myself
In Satan's inmost Palace of his nervous fine wrought Brain:
For Elynittria met Satan with all her singing women,
Terrific in their joy & pouring wine of wildest power.
They gave Satan their wine; indignant at the burning wrath,
Wild with prophetic fury, his former life became like a dream.
Cloth'd in the Serpent's folds, in selfish holiness demanding purity,
Being most impure, self-condemn'd to eternal tears, he drove
Me from his inmost Brain & the doors clos'd with thunder's sound.

O Divine Vision who didst create the Female to repose
The Sleepers of Beulah, pity the repentant Leutha! My

14

"Sick Couch bears the dark shades of Eternal Death infolding
The Spectre of Satan: he furious refuses to repose in sleep.
I humbly bow in all my Sin before the Throne Divine.
Not so the Sick-one. Alas, what shall be done him to restore
Who calls the Individual Law Holy and despises the Saviour,
Glorying to involve Albion's Body in fires of eternal War?"

Now Leutha ceas'd: tears flow'd, but the Divine Pity supported her.

"All is my fault! We are the Spectre of Luvah, the murderer
Of Albion. O Vala! O Luvah! O Albion! O lovely Jerusalem!
The Sin was begun in Eternity and will not rest to Eternity
Till two Eternitys meet together. Ah! lost, lost, lost for ever!"

So Leutha spoke. But when she saw that Enitharmon had
Created a New Space to protect Satan from punishment,
She fled to Enitharmon's Tent & hid herself. Loud raging
Thunder'd the Assembly dark & clouded, and they ratify'd
The kind decision of Enitharmon & gave a Time to the Space,
Even Six Thousand years, and sent Lucifer for its Guard.
But Lucifer refus'd to die & in pride he forsook his charge:
And they elected Molech, and when Molech was impatient
The Divine hand found the Two Limits, first of Opacity, then of Contrac-
    tion.
Opacity was named Satan, Contraction was named Adam.
Triple Elohim came: Elohim wearied fainted: they elected Shaddai:
Shaddai angry, Pahad descended: Pahad terrified, they sent Jehovah,
And Jehovah was leprous; loud he call'd, stretching his hand to Eternity,
For then the Body of Death was perfected in hypocritic holiness,
Around the Lamb, a Female Tabernacle woven in Cathedron's Looms.
He died as a Reprobate, he was Punish'd as a Transgressor.
Glory! Glory! Glory! to the Holy Lamb of God!
I touch the heavens as an instrument to glorify the Lord!

The Elect shall meet the Redeem'd on Albion's rocks, they shall meet
Astonish'd at the Transgressor, in him beholding the Saviour.
And the Elect shall say to the Redeem'd: "We behold it is of Divine
Mercy alone, of Free Gift and Election that we live:

Our Virtues & Cruel Goodnesses have deserv'd Eternal Death."
Thus they weep upon the fatal Brook of Albion's River.

But Elynittria met Leutha in the place where she was hidden
And threw aside her arrows and laid down her sounding Bow.
She sooth'd her with soft words & brought her to Palamabron's bed
In moments new created for delusion, interwoven round about.
In dreams she bore the shadowy Spectre of Sleep & nam'd him Death:
In dreams she bore Rahab, the mother of Tirzah, & her sisters
In Lambeth's vales, in Cambridge & in Oxford, places of Thought,
Intricate labyrinths of Times and Spaces unknown, that Leutha lived
In Palamabron's Tent and Oothoon was her charming guard.

The Bard ceas'd. All consider'd and a loud resounding murmur
Continu'd round the Halls; and much they question'd the immortal
Loud voic'd Bard, and many condemn'd the high toned Song,
Saying: "Pity and Love are too venerable for the imputation
Of Guilt." Others said: "If it is true, if the acts have been perform'd,
Let the Bard himself witness. Where hadst thou this terrible Song?"
The Bard replied: "I am Inspired I know it is Truth! for I Sing

15

"According to the inspiration of the Poetic Genius
Who is the eternal all-protecting Divine Humanity,
To whom be Glory & Power & Dominion Evermore. Amen."

Then there was great murmuring in the Heavens of Albion
Concerning Generation & the Vegetative power & concerning
The Lamb the Saviour. Albion trembled to Italy, Greece & Egypt
To Tartary & Hindostan & China & to Great America,
Shaking the roots & fast foundations of the Earth in doubtfulness.
The loud voic'd Bard terrify'd took refuge in Milton's bosom.

Then Milton rose up from the heavens of Albion ardorous.
The whole Assembly wept prophetic, seeing in Milton's face
And in his lineaments divine the shades of Death & Ulro:
He took off the robe of the promise & ungirded himself from the oath of
   God.

And Milton said: "I go to Eternal Death! The Nations still
Follow after the detestable Gods of Priam, in pomp
Of warlike selfhood contradicting and blaspheming.

When will the Resurrection come to deliver the sleeping body
From corruptibility? O when, Lord Jesus, wilt thou come?
Tarry no longer, for my soul lies at the gates of death.
I will arise and look forth for the morning of the grave:
I will go down to the sepulcher to see if morning breaks:
I will go down to self annihilation and eternal death,
Lest the Last Judgment come & find me unannihilate
And I be siez'd & giv'n into the hands of my own Selfhood.
The Lamb of God is seen thro' mists & shadows, hov'ring
Over the sepulchers in clouds of Jehovah & winds of Elohim,
A disk of blood distant, & heav'ns & earths roll dark between.
What do I here before the Judgment? without my Emanation?
With the daughters of memory & not with the daughters of inspiration?
I in my Selfhood am that Satan: I am that Evil One!
He is my Spectre! in my obedience to loose him from my Hells,
To claim the Hells, my Furnaces, I go to Eternal Death."

And Milton said: "I go to Eternal Death!" Eternity shudder'd,
For he took the outside course among the graves of the dead,
A mournful shade. Eternity shudder'd at the image of eternal death.

Then on the verge of Beulah he beheld his own Shadow,
A mournful form double, hermaphroditic, male & female
In one wonderful body; and he enter'd into it
In direful pain, for the dread shadow twenty-seven fold
Reach'd to the depths of direst Hell & thence to Albion's land,
Which is this earth of vegetation on which now I write.

The Seven Angels of the Presence wept over Milton's Shadow.

17

As when a man dreams he reflects not that his body sleeps,
Else he would wake, so seem'd he entering his Shadow: but
With him the Spirits of the Seven Angels of the Presence
Entering, they gave him still perceptions of his Sleeping Body
Which now arose and walk'd with them in Eden, as an Eighth
Image Divine tho' darken'd and tho' walking as one walks
In sleep, and the Seven comforted and supported him.

Like as a Polypus that vegetates beneath the deep,
They saw his Shadow vegetated underneath the Couch
Of death: for when he enter'd into his Shadow, Himself,

His real and immortal Self, was, as appear'd to those
Who dwell in immortality, as One sleeping on a couch
Of gold, and those in immortality gave forth their Emanations
Like Females of sweet beauty to guard round him & to feed
His lips with food of Eden in his cold and dim repose:
But to himself he seem'd a wanderer lost in dreary night.

Onwards his Shadow kept its course among the Spectres call'd
Satan, but swift as lightning passing them, startled the shades
Of Hell beheld him in a trail of light as of a comet
That travels into Chaos: so Milton went guarded within.

The nature of infinity is this: That every thing has its
Own Vortex, and when once a traveller thro' Eternity
Has pass'd that Vortex, he percieves it roll backward behind
His path, into a globe itself infolding like a sun,
Or like a moon, or like a universe of starry majesty,
While he keeps onwards in his wondrous journey on the earth,
Or like a human form, a friend with whom he liv'd benevolent.
As the eye of man views both the east & west encompassing
Its vortex, and the north & south with all their starry host,
Also the rising sun & setting moon he views surrounding
His corn-fields and his valleys of five hundred acres square,
Thus is the earth one infinite plane, and not as apparent
To the weak traveller confin'd beneath the moony shade.
Thus is the heaven a vortex pass'd already, and the earth
A vortex not yet pass'd by the traveller thro' Eternity.

First Milton saw Albion upon the Rock of Ages,
Deadly pale outstretch'd and snowy cold, storm cover'd,
A Giant form of perfect beauty outstretch'd on the rock
In solemn death: the Sea of Time & Space thunder'd aloud
Against the rock, which was inwrapped with the weeds of death.
Hovering over the cold bosom in its vortex Milton bent down
To the bosom of death: what was underneath soon seem'd above:
A cloudy heaven mingled with stormy seas in loudest ruin;
But as a wintry globe descends precipitant thro' Beulah bursting
With thunders loud and terrible, so Milton's shadow fell
Precipitant, loud thund'ring into the Sea of Time & Space.

Then first I saw him in the Zenith as a falling star
Descending perpendicular, swift as the swallow or swift:

And on my left foot falling on the tarsus, enter'd there:
But from my left foot a black cloud redounding spread over Europe.

Then Milton knew that the Three Heavens of Beulah were beheld
By him on earth in his bright pilgrimage of sixty years

19 [1]

In those three females whom his wives, & those three whom his Daughters
Had represented and contain'd, that they might be resum'd
By giving up Selfhood: & they distant view'd his journey
In their eternal spheres, now Human, tho' their Bodies remain clos'd
In the dark Ulro till the Judgment: also Milton knew they and
Himself was Human, tho' now wandering thro' Death's Vale
In conflict with those Female forms, which in blood & jealousy
Surrounded him, dividing & uniting without end or number.

He saw the Cruelties of Ulro and he wrote them down
In iron tablets; and his Wives' & Daughters' names were these:
Rahab and Tirzah, & Milcah & Malah & Noah & Hoglah.
They sat rang'd round him as the rocks of Horeb round the land
Of Canaan, and they wrote in thunder, smoke and fire
His dictate; and his body was the Rock Sinai, that body
Which was on earth born to corruption; & the six Females
Are Hor & Peor & Bashan & Abarim & Lebanon & Hermon,
Seven rocky masses terrible in the Desarts of Midian.

But Milton's Human Shadow continu'd journeying above
The rocky masses of The Mundane Shell, in the Lands
Of Edom & Aram & Moab & Midian & Amalek.

The Mundane Shell is a vast Concave Earth, an immense
Harden'd shadow of all things upon our Vegetated Earth,
Enlarg'd into dimension & deform'd into indefinite space,
In Twenty-seven Heavens and all their Hells, with Chaos
And Ancient Night & Purgatory. It is a cavernous Earth
Of labyrinthine intricacy, twenty-seven-folds of opakeness,
And finishes where the lark mounts; here Milton journeyed
In that Region call'd Midian among the Rocks of Horeb.
For travellers from Eternity pass outward to Satan's seat,
But travellers to Eternity pass inward to Golgonooza.

[1] *Plate* 18, *a full-page design, bears the legend:* To Annihilate the Self-hood of Deceit & False Forgiveness. *This is probably not part of the text.*

Los, the Vehicular terror, beheld him, & divine Enitharmon
Call'd all her daughters, Saying: "Surely to unloose my bond
Is this Man come! O Satan shall be unloos'd upon Albion!"

Los heard in terror Enitharmon's words; in fibrous strength
His limbs shot forth like roots of trees against the forward path
Of Milton's journey. Urizen beheld the immortal Man

20

And Tharmas, Demon of the Waters, & Orc, who is Luvah.

The Shadowy Female seeing Milton, howl'd in her lamentation
Over the Deeps, outstretching her Twenty-seven Heavens over Albion,

And thus the Shadowy Female howls in articulate howlings:

"I will lament over Milton in the lamentations of the afflicted:
My Garments shall be woven of sighs & heart broken lamentations:
The misery of unhappy Families shall be drawn out into its border,
Wrought with the needle with dire sufferings, poverty, pain & woe
Along the rocky Island & thence throughout the whole Earth;
There shall be the sick Father & his starving Family, there
The Prisoner in the stone Dungeon & the Slave at the Mill.
I will have writings written all over it in Human Words
That every Infant that is born upon the Earth shall read
And get by rote as a hard task of a life of sixty years.
I will have Kings inwoven upon it & Councellors & Mighty Men:
The Famine shall clasp it together with buckles & Clasps,
And the Pestilence shall be its fringe & the War its girdle,
To divide into Rahab & Tirzah that Milton may come to our tents.
For I will put on the Human Form & take the Image of God,
Even Pity & Humanity, but my Clothing shall be Cruelty:
And I will put on Holiness as a breastplate & as a helmet,
And all my ornaments shall be of the gold of broken hearts,
And the precious stones of anxiety & care & desperation & death
And repentance for sin & sorrow & punishment & fear,
To defend me from thy terrors, O Orc, my only beloved!"

Orc answer'd: "Take not the Human Form, O loveliest, Take not
Terror upon thee! Behold how I am & tremble lest thou also
Consume in my Consummation; but thou maist take a Form
Female & lovely, that cannot consume in Man's consummation.

Wherefore dost thou Create & Weave this Satan for a Covering?
When thou attemptest to put on the Human Form, my wrath
Burns to the top of heaven against thee in Jealousy & Fear;
Then I rend thee asunder, then I howl over thy clay & ashes.
When wilt thou put on the Female Form as in times of old,
With a Garment of Pity & Compassion like the Garment of God?
His Garments are long sufferings for the Children of Men;
Jerusalem is his Garment, & not thy Covering Cherub, O lovely
Shadow of my delight, who wanderest seeking for the prey."

So spoke Orc when Oothoon & Leutha hover'd over his Couch
Of fire, in interchange of Beauty & Perfection in the darkness
Opening interiorly into Jerusalem & Babylon, shining glorious
In the Shadowy Female's bosom. Jealous her darkness grew:
Howlings fill'd all the desolate places in accusations of Sin,
In Female beauty shining in the unform'd void; & Orc in vain
Stretch'd out his hands of fire & wooed: they triumph in his pain.

Thus darken'd the Shadowy Female tenfold, & Orc tenfold
Glow'd on his rocky Couch against the darkness: loud thunders
Told of the enormous conflict. Earthquake beneath, around,
Rent the Immortal Females limb from limb & joint from joint,
And moved the fast foundations of the Earth to wake the Dead.

Urizen emerged from his Rocky Form & from his Snows,

21

And he also darken'd his brows, freezing dark rocks between
The footsteps and infixing deep the feet in marble beds,
That Milton labour'd with his journey & his feet bled sore
Upon the clay now chang'd to marble; also Urizen rose
And met him on the shores of Arnon & by the streams of the brooks.

Silent they met and silent strove among the streams of Arnon
Even to Mahanaim, when with cold hand Urizen stoop'd down
And took up water from the river Jordan, pouring on
To Milton's brain the icy fluid from his broad cold palm.
But Milton took of the red clay of Succoth, moulding it with care
Between his palms and filling up the furrows of many years,
Beginning at the feet of Urizen, and on the bones
Creating new flesh on the Demon cold and building him
As with new clay, a Human form in the Valley of Beth Peor.

Four Universes round the Mundane Egg remain Chaotic,
One to the North, named Urthona: One to the South, named Urizen:
One to the East, named Luvah: One to the West, named Tharmas;
They are the Four Zoas that stood around the Throne Divine.
But when Luvah assum'd the World of Urizen to the South
And Albion was slain upon his mountains & in his tent,
All fell towards the Center in dire ruin sinking down.
And in the South remains a burning fire: in the East, a void:
In the West, a world of raging waters: in the North, a solid,
Unfathomable, without end. But in the midst of these
Is built eternally the Universe of Los and Enitharmon,
Towards which Milton went, but Urizen oppos'd his path.

The Man and Demon strove many periods. Rahab beheld,
Standing on Carmel. Rahab and Tirzah trembled to behold
The enormous strife, one giving life, the other giving death
To his adversary, and they sent forth all their sons & daughters
In all their beauty to entice Milton across the river.

The Twofold form Hermaphroditic and the Double-sexed,
The Female-male & the Male-female, self-dividing stood
Before him in their beauty & in cruelties of holiness,
Shining in darkness, glorious upon the deeps of Entuthon,

Saying: "Come thou to Ephraim! behold the Kings of Canaan!
The beautiful Amalekites behold the fires of youth
Bound with the Chain of Jealousy by Los & Enitharmon.
The banks of Cam, cold learning's streams, London's dark frowning
    towers
Lament upon the winds of Europe in Rephaim's Vale,
Because Ahania, rent apart into a desolate night,
Laments, & Enion wanders like a weeping inarticulate voice,
And Vala labours for her bread & water among the Furnaces.
Therefore bright Tirzah triumphs, putting on all beauty
And all perfection in her cruel sports among the Victims.
Come, bring with thee Jerusalem with songs on the Grecian Lyre!
In Natural Religion, in experiments on Men
Let her be Offer'd up to Holiness! Tirzah numbers her:
She numbers with her fingers every fibre ere it grow.
Where is the Lamb of God? where is the promise of his coming?
Her shadowy Sisters form the bones, even the bones of Horeb
Around the marrow, and the orbed scull around the brain.

His Images are born for War, for Sacrifice to Tirzah,
To Natural Religion, to Tirzah, the Daughter of Rahab the Holy!
She ties the knot of nervous fibres into a white brain!
She ties the knot of bloody veins into a red hot heart!
Within her bosom Albion lies embalm'd, never to awake.
Hand is become a rock: Sinai & Horeb is Hyle & Coban:
Scofield is bound in iron armour before Reuben's Gate.
She ties the knot of milky seed into two lovely Heavens,

22

"Two yet but one, each in the other sweet reflected; these
Are our Three Heavens beneath the shades of Beulah, land of rest.
Come then to Ephraim & Manasseh, O beloved-one!
Come to my ivory palaces, O beloved of thy mother!
And let us bind thee in the bands of War, & be thou King
Of Canaan and reign in Hazor where the Twelve Tribes meet."

So spoke they as in one voice. Silent Milton stood before
The darken'd Urizen, as the sculptor silent stands before
His forming image; he walks round it patient labouring.
Thus Milton stood forming bright Urizen, while his Mortal part
Sat frozen in the rock of Horeb, and his Redeemed portion
Thus form'd the Clay of Urizen; but within that portion
His real Human walk'd above in power and majesty,
Tho' darken'd, and the Seven Angels of the Presence attended him.

O how can I with my gross tongue that cleaveth to the dust
Tell of the Four-fold Man in starry numbers fitly order'd,
Or how can I with my cold hand of clay! But thou, O Lord,
Do with me as thou wilt! for I am nothing, and vanity.
If thou chuse to elect a worm, it shall remove the mountains.
For that portion nam'd the Elect, the Spectrous body of Milton,
Redounding from my left foot into Los's Mundane Space,
Brooded over his Body in Horeb against the Resurrection,
Preparing it for the Great Consummation; red the Cherub on Sinai
Glow'd, but in terrors folded round his clouds of blood.

    Now Albion's sleeping Humanity began to turn upon his Couch,
Feeling the electric flame of Milton's awful precipitate descent.
Seest thou the little winged fly, smaller than a grain of sand?
It has a heart like thee, a brain open to heaven & hell,
Withinside wondrous & expansive: its gates are not clos'd:

I hope thine are not: hence it clothes itself in rich array:
Hence thou art cloth'd with human beauty, O thou mortal man.
Seek not thy heavenly father then beyond the skies,
There Chaos dwells & ancient Night & Og & Anak old.
For every human heart has gates of brass & bars of adamant
Which few dare unbar, because dread Og & Anak guard the gates
Terrific: and each mortal brain is wall'd and moated round
Within, and Og & Anak watch here: here is the Seat
Of Satan in its Webs: for in brain and heart and loins
Gates open behind Satan's Seat to the City of Golgonooza,
Which is the spiritual fourfold London in the loins of Albion.

Thus Milton fell thro' Albion's heart, travelling outside of Humanity
Beyond the Stars in Chaos, in Caverns of the Mundane Shell.

But many of the Eternals rose up from eternal tables
Drunk with the Spirit; burning round the couch of death they stood
Looking down into Beulah; wrathful, fill'd with rage
They rend the heavens round the Watchers in a fiery circle
And round the Shadowy Eighth: the Eight close up the Couch
Into a tabernacle and flee with cries down to the Deeps,
Where Los opens his three wide gates surrounded by raging fires.
They soon find their own place & join the Watchers of the Ulro.

Los saw them and a cold pale horror cover'd o'er his limbs.
Pondering he knew that Rintrah & Palamabron might depart,
Even as Reuben & as Gad: gave up himself to tears,
He sat down on his anvil-stock and lean'd upon the trough,
Looking into the black water, mingling it with tears.

At last when desperation almost tore his heart in twain
He recollected an old Prophecy in Eden recorded
And often sung to the loud harp at the immortal feasts:
That Milton of the Land of Albion should up ascend
Forwards from Ulro from the Vale of Felpham, and set free
Orc from his Chain of Jealousy: he started at the thought

23

And down descended into Udan-Adan; it was night,
And Satan sat sleeping upon his Couch in Udan-Adan:
His Spectre slept, his Shadow woke; when one sleeps th'other wakes.

But Milton entering my Foot, I saw in the nether
Regions of the Imagination—also all men on Earth
And all in Heaven saw in the nether regions of the Imagination
In Ulro beneath Beulah—the vast breach of Milton's descent.
But I knew not that it was Milton, for man cannot know
What passes in his members till periods of Space & Time
Reveal the secrets of Eternity: for more extensive
Than any other earthly things are Man's earthly lineaments.
And all this Vegetable World appear'd on my left Foot
As a bright sandal form'd immortal of precious stones & gold.
I stooped down & bound it on to walk forward thro' Eternity.

There is in Eden a sweet River of milk & liquid pearl
Nam'd Ololon, on whose mild banks dwelt those who Milton drove
Down into Ulro: and they wept in long resounding song
For seven days of eternity, and the river's living banks,
The mountains, wail'd, & every plant that grew, in solemn sighs
     lamented.

When Luvah's bulls each morning drag the sulphur Sun out of the Deep
Harness'd with starry harness, black & shining, kept by black slaves
That work all night at the starry harness, Strong and vigorous
They drag the unwilling Orb: at this time all the Family
Of Eden heard the lamentation and Providence began.
But when the clarions of day sounded, they drown'd the lamentations,
And when night came, all was silent in Ololon, & all refus'd to lament
In the still night, fearing lest they should others molest.

Seven mornings Los heard them, as the poor bird within the shell
Hears its impatient parent bird, and Enitharmon heard them
But saw them not, for the blue Mundane Shell inclos'd them in.

And they lamented that they had in wrath & fury & fire
Driven Milton into the Ulro; for now they knew too late
That it was Milton the Awakener: they had not heard the Bard
Whose song call'd Milton to the attempt; and Los heard these laments
He heard them call in prayer all the Divine Family,
And he beheld the Cloud of Milton stretching over Europe.

But all the Family Divine collected as Four Suns
In the Four Points of heaven, East, West & North & South,
Enlarging and enlarging till their Disks approach'd each other,

And when they touch'd, closed together Southward in One Sun
Over Ololon; and as One Man who weeps over his brother
In a dark tomb, so all the Family Divine wept over Ololon,

Saying: "Milton goes to Eternal Death!" so saying they groan'd in spirit
And were troubled; and again the Divine Family groaned in spirit.

And Ololon said: "Let us descend also, and let us give
Ourselves to death in Ulro among the Transgressors.
Is Virtue a Punisher? O no! how is this wondrous thing,
This World beneath, unseen before, this refuge from the wars
Of Great Eternity! unnatural refuge! unknown by us till now?
Or are these the pangs of repentance? let us enter into them."

Then the Divine Family said: "Six Thousand Years are now
Accomplished in this World of Sorrow. Milton's Angel knew
The Universal Dictate, and you also feel this Dictate.
And now you know this World of Sorrow and feel Pity. Obey
The Dictate! Watch over this World, and with your brooding wings
Renew it to Eternal Life. Lo! I am with you alway.
But you cannot renew Milton: he goes to Eternal Death."

So spake the Family Divine as One Man, even Jesus,
Uniting in One with Ololon, & the appearance of One Man,
Jesus the Saviour, appear'd coming in the Clouds of Ololon.

24

Tho' driven away with the Seven Starry Ones into the Ulro,
Yet the Divine Vision remains Every-where For-ever. Amen.
And Ololon lamented for Milton with a great lamentation.

While Los heard indistinct in fear, what time I bound my sandals
On to walk forward thro' Eternity, Los descended to me:
And Los behind me stood, a terrible flaming Sun, just close
Behind my back. I turned round in terror, and behold!
Los stood in that fierce glowing fire, & he also stoop'd down
And bound my sandals on in Udan-Adan; trembling I stood
Exceedingly with fear & terror, standing in the Vale
Of Lambeth; but he kissed me and wish'd me health,
And I became One Man with him arising in my strength.
'Twas too late now to recede. Los had enter'd into my soul:
His terrors now possess'd me whole! I arose in fury & strength.

"I am that Shadowy Prophet who Six Thousand Years ago
Fell from my station in the Eternal bosom. Six Thousand Years
Are finish'd. I return! both Time & Space obey my will.
I in Six Thousand Years walk up and down; for not one Moment
Of Time is lost, nor one Event of Space unpermanent,
But all remain: every fabric of Six Thousand Years
Remains permanent, tho' on the Earth where Satan
Fell and was cut off, all things vanish & are seen no more,
They vanish not from me & mine, we guard them first & last.
The generations of men run on in the tide of Time,
But leave their destin'd lineaments permanent for ever & ever."

So spoke Los as we went along to his supreme abodes.

Rintrah and Palamabron met us at the Gate of Golgonooza,
Clouded with discontent & brooding in their minds terrible things.

They said: "O Father most beloved! O merciful Parent
Pitying and permitting evil, tho' strong & mighty to destroy!
Whence is this Shadow terrible? wherefore dost thou refuse
To throw him into the Furnaces? knowest thou not that he
Will unchain Orc & let loose Satan, Og, Sihon & Anak
Upon the Body of Albion? for this he is come! behold it written
Upon his fibrous left Foot black, most dismal to our eyes.
The Shadowy Female shudders thro' heaven in torment inexpressible,
And all the Daughters of Los prophetic wail; yet in deceit
They weave a new Religion from new Jealousy of Theotormon.
Milton's Religion is the cause: there is no end to destruction.
Seeing the Churches at their Period in terror & despair,
Rahab created Voltaire, Tirzah created Rousseau,
Asserting the Self-righteousness against the Universal Saviour,
Mocking the Confessors & Martyrs, claiming Self-righteousness,
With cruel Virtue making War upon the Lamb's Redeemed
To perpetuate War & Glory, to perpetuate the Laws of Sin.
They perverted Swedenborg's Visions in Beulah & in Ulro
To destroy Jerusalem as a Harlot & her Sons as Reprobates,
To raise up Mystery the Virgin Harlot, Mother of War,
Babylon the Great, the Abomination of Desolation.
O Swedenborg! strongest of men, the Samson shorn by the Churches,
Shewing the Transgressors in Hell, the proud Warriors in Heaven,
Heaven as a Punisher, & Hell as One under Punishment,
With Laws from Plato & his Greeks to renew the Trojan Gods

In Albion, & to deny the value of the Saviour's blood.
But then I rais'd up Whitefield, Palamabron rais'd up Westley,
And these are the cries of the Churches before the two Witnesses.
Faith in God the dear Saviour who took on the likeness of men,
Becoming obedient to death, even the death of the Cross.
The Witnesses lie dead in the Street of the Great City:
No Faith is in all the Earth: the Book of God is trodden under Foot.
He sent his two Servants, Whitefield & Westley: were they Prophets,
Or were they Idiots or Madmen? shew us Miracles!

25

"Can you have greater Miracles than these? Men who devote
Their life's whole comfort to intire scorn & injury & death?
Awake, thou sleeper on the Rock of Eternity! Albion awake!
The trumpet of Judgment hath twice sounded: all Nations are awake,
But thou art still heavy and dull. Awake, Albion awake!
Lo, Orc arises on the Atlantic. Lo, his blood and fire
Glow on America's shore. Albion turns upon his Couch:
He listens to the sounds of War, astonished and confounded:
He weeps into the Atlantic deep, yet still in dismal dreams
Unwaken'd, and the Covering Cherub advances from the East.
How long shall we lay dead in the Street of the great City?
How long beneath the Covering Cherub give our Emanations?
Milton will utterly consume us & thee our beloved Father.
He hath enter'd into the Covering Cherub, becoming one with
Albion's dread Sons: Hand, Hyle & Coban surround him as
A girdle, Gwendolen & Conwenna as a garment woven
Of War & Religion; let us descend & bring him chained
To Bowlahoola, O father most beloved! O mild Parent!
Cruel in thy mildness, pitying and permitting evil,
Tho' strong and mighty to destroy, O Los our beloved Father!"

Like the black storm, coming out of Chaos beyond the stars,
It issues thro' the dark & intricate caves of the Mundane Shell,
Passing the planetary visions & the well adorned Firmament.
The Sun rolls into Chaos & the stars into the Desarts,
And then the storms become visible, audible & terrible,
Covering the light of day & rolling down upon the mountains,
Deluge all the country round. Such is a vision of Los
When Rintrah & Palamabron spake, and such his stormy face
Appear'd as does the face of heaven when cover'd with thick storms,
Pitying and loving tho' in frowns of terrible perturbation.

But Los dispers'd the clouds even as the strong winds of Jehovah,
And Los thus spoke: "O noble Sons, be patient yet a little!
I have embrac'd the falling Death, he is become One with me:
O Sons, we live not by wrath, by mercy alone we live!
I recollect an old Prophecy in Eden recorded in gold and oft
Sung to the harp, That Milton of the land of Albion
Should up ascend forward from Felpham's Vale & break the Chain
Of Jealousy from all its roots; be patient therefore, O my Sons!
These lovely Females form sweet night and silence and secret
Obscurities to hide from Satan's Watch-Fiends Human loves
And graces, lest they write them in their Books & in the Scroll
Of mortal life to condemn the accused, who at Satan's Bar
Tremble in Spectrous Bodies continually day and night,
While on the Earth they live in sorrowful Vegetations.
O when shall we tread our Wine-presses in heaven and Reap
Our wheat with shoutings of joy, and leave the Earth in peace?
Remember how Calvin and Luther in fury premature
Sow'd War and stern division between Papists & Protestants.
Let it not be so now! O go not forth in Martyrdoms & Wars!
We were plac'd here by the Universal Brotherhood & Mercy
With powers fitted to circumscribe this dark Satanic death,
And that the Seven Eyes of God may have space for Redemption.
But how this is as yet we know not, and we cannot know
Till Albion is arisen; then patient wait a little while.
Six Thousand years are pass'd away, the end approaches fast:
This mighty one is come from Eden, he is of the Elect
Who died from Earth & he is return'd before the Judgment. This thing
Was never known, that one of the holy dead should willing return.
Then patient wait a little while till the Last Vintage is over,
Till we have quench'd the Sun of Salah in the Lake of Udan-Adan.
O my dear Sons, leave not your Father as your brethren left me!
Twelve Sons successive fled away in that thousand years of sorrow

26

"Of Palamabron's Harrow & of Rintrah's wrath & fury:
Reuben & Manazzoth & Gad & Simeon & Levi
And Ephraim & Judah were Generated because
They left me, wandering with Tirzah. Enitharmon wept
One thousand years, and all the Earth was in a wat'ry deluge.
We call'd him Menassheh because of the Generations of Tirzah,
Because of Satan: & the Seven Eyes of God continually

Guard round them, but I, the Fourth Zoa, am also set
The Watchman of Eternity: the Three are not, & I am preserved.
Still my four mighty ones are left to me in Golgonooza,
Still Rintrah fierce, and Palamabron mild & piteous,
Theotormon fill'd with care, Bromion loving Science.
You, O my Sons, still guard round Los: O wander not & leave me!
Rintrah, thou well rememberest when Amalek & Canaan
Fled with their Sister Moab into that abhorred Void,
They became Nations in our sight beneath the hands of Tirzah.
And Palamabron, thou rememberest when Joseph, an infant,
Stolen from his nurse's cradle, wrap'd in needle-work
Of emblematic texture, was sold to the Amalekite
Who carried him down into Egypt where Ephraim & Menassheh
Gather'd my Sons together in the Sands of Midian.
And if you also flee away and leave your Father's side
Following Milton into Ulro, altho' your power is great,
Surely you also shall become poor mortal vegetations
Beneath the Moon of Ulro: pity then your Father's tears.
When Jesus rais'd Lazarus from the Grave I stood & saw
Lazarus, who is the Vehicular Body of Albion the Redeem'd,
Arise into the Covering Cherub, who is the Spectre of Albion,
By martyrdoms to suffer, to watch over the Sleeping Body
Upon his Rock beneath his Tomb. I saw the Covering Cherub
Divide Four-foid into Four Churches when Lazarus arose,
Paul, Constantine, Charlemaine, Luther; behold, they stand before us
Stretch'd over Europe & Asia! come O Sons, come, come away!
Arise, O Sons, give all your strength against Eternal Death,
Lest we are vegetated, for Cathedron's Looms weave only Death,
A Web of Death: & were it not for Bowlahoola & Allamanda
No Human Form but only a Fibrous Vegetation,
A Polypus of soft affections without Thought or Vision,
Must tremble in the Heavens & Earths thro' all the Ulro space.
Throw all the Vegetated Mortals into Bowlahoola:
But as to this Elected Form who is return'd again,
He is the Signal that the Last Vintage now approaches,
Nor Vegetation may go on till all the Earth is reap'd."

So Los spoke. Furious they descended to Bowlahoola & Allamanda,
Indignant, unconvinc'd by Los's arguments & thunders rolling:
They saw that wrath now sway'd and now pity absorb'd him.
As it was so it remain'd & no hope of an end.

Bowlahoola is nam'd Law by mortals; Tharmas founded
Because of Satan, before Luban in the City of Golgonooza.
But Goigonooza is nam'd Art & Manufacture by mortal men.

In Bowlahoola Los's Anvils stand & his Furnaces rage;
Thundering the Hammers beat & the Bellows blow loud,
Living, self moving, mourning, lamenting & howling incessantly.
Bowlahoola thro' all its porches feels, tho' too fast founded
Its pillars & porticoes to tremble at the force
Of mortal or immortal arm: and softly lilling flutes,
Accordant with the horrid labours, make sweet melody.
The Bellows are the Animal Lungs: the Hammers the Animal Heart:
The Furnaces the Stomach for digestion: terrible their fury.
Thousands & thousands labour, thousands play on instruments
Stringed or fluted to ameliorate the sorrows of slavery.
Loud sport the dancers in the dance of death, rejoicing in carnage.
The hard dentant Hammers are lull'd by the flutes' lula lula,
The bellowing Furnaces blare by the long sounding clarion,
The double drum drowns howls & groans, the shrill fife shrieks & cries,
The crooked horn mellows the hoarse raving serpent, terrible but har-
     monious:
Bowlahoola is the Stomach in every individual man.

Los is by mortals nam'd Time, Enitharmon is nam'd Space;
But they depict him bald & aged who is in eternal youth
All powerful and his locks flourish like the brows of morning:
He is the Spirit of Prophecy, the ever apparent Elias.
Time is the mercy of Eternity; without Time's swiftness,
Which is the swiftest of all things, all were eternal torment.
All the Gods of the Kingdoms of Earth labour in Los's Halls:
Every one is a fallen Son of the Spirit of Prophecy.
He is the Fourth Zoa that stood around the Throne Divine.

27

Loud shout the Sons of Luvah at the Wine-presses as Los descended
With Rintrah & Palamabron in his fires of resistless fury.

The Wine-press on the Rhine groans loud, but all its central beams
Act more terrific in the central Cities of the Nations
Where Human Thought is crush'd beneath the iron hand of Power:
There Los puts all into the Press, the Opressor & the Opressed
Together, ripe for the Harvest & Vintage & ready for the Loom.

They sang at the Vintage: "This is the Last Vintage, & Seed
Shall no more be sown upon Earth till all the Vintage is over
And all gather'd in, till the Plow has pass'd over the Nations
And the Harrow & heavy thundering Roller upon the mountains."

And loud the Souls howl round the Porches of Golgonooza,
Crying: "O God deliver us to the Heavens or to the Earths,
That we may preach righteousness & punish the sinner with death."
But Los refused, till all the Vintage of Earth was gathered in.

And Los stood & cried to the Labourers of the Vintage in voice of awe:

"Fellow Labourers! The Great Vintage & Harvest is now upon Earth.
The whole extent of the Globe is explored. Every scatter'd Atom
Of Human Intellect now is flocking to the sound of the Trumpet.
All the Wisdom which was hidden in caves & dens from ancient
Time is now sought out from Animal & Vegetable & Mineral.
The Awakener is come outstretch'd over Europe: the Vision of God is
    fulfilled:
The Ancient Man upon the Rock of Albion Awakes,
He listens to the sounds of War astonish'd & ashamed,
He sees his Children mock at Faith and deny Providence.
Therefore you must bind the Sheaves not by Nations or Families,
You shall bind them in Three Classes, according to their Classes
So shall you bind them, Separating What has been Mixed
Since Men began to be Wove into Nations by Rahab & Tirzah,
Since Albion's Death & Satan's Cutting off from our awful Fields,
When under pretence to benevolence the Elect Subdu'd All
From the Foundation of the World. The Elect is one Class: You
Shall bind them separate: they cannot Believe in Eternal Life
Except by Miracle & a New Birth. The other two Classes,
The Reprobate who never cease to Believe, and the Redeem'd
Who live in doubts & fears perpetually tormented by the Elect,
These you shall bind in a twin-bundle for the Consummation:
But the Elect must be saved from fires of Eternal Death,
To be formed into the Churches of Beulah that they destroy not the Earth.
For in every Nation & every Family the Three Classes are born,
And in every Species of Earth, Metal, Tree, Fish, Bird & Beast.
We form the Mundane Egg, that Spectres coming by fury or amity,
All is the same, & every one remains in his own energy.
Go forth Reapers with rejoicing; you sowed in tears,

But the time of your refreshing cometh: only a little moment
Still abstain from pleasure & rest in the labours of eternity,
And you shall Reap the whole Earth from Pole to Pole, from Sea to Sea,
Beginning at Jerusalem's Inner Court, Lambeth, ruin'd and given
To the detestable Gods of Priam, to Apollo, and at the Asylum
Given to Hercules, who labour in Tirzah's Looms for bread,
Who set Pleasure against Duty, who Create Olympic crowns
To make Learning a burden & the Work of the Holy Spirit, Strife:
The Thor & cruel Odin who first rear'd the Polar Caves.
Lambeth mourns, calling Jerusalem: she weeps & looks abroad
For the Lord's coming, that Jerusalem may overspread all Nations.
Crave not for the mortal & perishing delights, but leave them
To the weak, and pity the weak as your infant care. Break not
Forth in your wrath, lest you also are vegetated by Tirzah.
Wait till the Judgement is past, till the Creation is consumed,
And then rush forward with me into the glorious spiritual
Vegetation, the Supper of the Lamb & his Bride, and the
Awaking of Albion our friend and ancient companion."

So Los spoke. But lightnings of discontent broke on all sides round
And murmurs of thunder rolling heavy long & loud over the mountains
While Los call'd his Sons around him to the Harvest & the Vintage.

Thou seest the Constellations in the deep & wondrous Night:
They rise in order and continue their immortal courses
Upon the mountains & in vales with harp & heavenly song,
With flute & clarion, with cups & measures fill'd with foaming wine.
Glitt'ring the streams reflect the Vision of beatitude,
And the calm Ocean joys beneath & smooths his awful waves:

28

These are the Sons of Los, & these the Labourers of the Vintage.
Thou seest the gorgeous clothed Flies that dance & sport in summer
Upon the sunny brooks & meadows: every one the dance
Knows in its intricate mazes of delight artful to weave:
Each one to sound his instruments of music in the dance,
To touch each other & recede, to cross & change & return:
These are the Children of Los; thou seest the Trees on mountains,
The wind blows heavy, loud they thunder thro' the darksom sky,
Uttering prophecies & speaking instructive words to the sons
Of men: These are the Sons of Los: These the Visions of Eternity,

But we see only as it were the hem of their garments
When with our vegetable eyes we view these wondrous Visions.

There are Two Gates thro' which all Souls descend, One Southward
From Dover Cliff to Lizard Point, the other toward the North,
Caithness & rocky Durness, Pentland & John Groat's House.

The Souls descending to the Body wail on the right hand
Of Los, & those deliver'd from the Body on the left hand.
For Los against the east his force continually bends
Along the Valleys of Middlesex from Hounslow to Blackheath,
Lest those Three Heavens of Beulah should the Creation destroy;
And lest they should descend before the north & south Gates,
Groaning with pity, he among the wailing Souls laments.

And these the Labours of the Sons of Los in Allamanda
And in the City of Golgonooza & in Luban & around
The Lake of Udan-Adan in the Forests of Enthuthon Benython,
Where Souls incessant wail, being piteous Passions & Desires
With neither lineament nor form, but like to wat'ry clouds
The Passions & Desires descend upon the hungry winds,

For such alone Sleepers remain, meer passion & appetite.
The Sons of Los clothe them & feed & provide houses & fields.

And every Generated Body in its inward form
Is a garden of delight & a building of magnificence,
Built by the Sons of Los in Bowlahoola & Allamanda:
And the herbs & flowers & furniture & beds & chambers
Continually woven in the Looms of Enitharmon's Daughters,
In bright Cathedron's golden Dome with care & love & tears.
For the various Classes of Men are all mark'd out determinate
In Bowlahoola, & as the Spectres choose their affinities,
So they are born on Earth, & every Class is determinate:
But not by Natural, but by Spiritual power alone, Because
The Natural power continually seeks & tends to Destruction,
Ending in Death, which would of itself be Eternal Death.
And all are Class'd by Spiritual & not by Natural power.

And every Natural Effect has a Spiritual Cause, and Not
A Natural; for a Natural Cause only seems: it is a Delusion
Of Ulro & a ratio of the perishing Vegetable Memory.

29

But the Wine-press of Los is eastward of Golgonooza before the Seat
Of Satan: Luvah laid the foundation & Urizen finish'd it in howling woe.
How red the sons & daughters of Luvah! here they tread the grapes:
Laughing & shouting, drunk with odours many fall o'erwearied,
Drown'd in the wine is many a youth & maiden: those around
Lay them on skins of Tygers & of the spotted Leopard & the Wild Ass
Till they revive, or bury them in cool grots, making lamentation.

This Wine-press is call'd War on Earth: it is the Printing-Press
Of Los, and here he lays his words in order above the mortal brain,
As cogs are form'd in a wheel to turn the cogs of the adverse wheel.

Timbrels & violins sport round the Wine-presses; the little Seed,
The sportive Root, the Earth-worm, the gold Beetle, the wise Emmet
Dance round the Wine-presses of Luvah: the Centipede is there,
The ground Spider with many eyes, the Mole clothed in velvet,
The ambitious Spider in his sullen web, the lucky golden Spinner,
The Earwig arm'd, the tender Maggot, emblem of immortality,
The Flea, Louse, Bug, the Tape-Worm, all the Armies of Disease,
Visible or invisible to the slothful vegetating Man.
The slow Slug, the Grasshopper that sings & laughs & drinks:
Winter comes, he folds his slender bones without a murmur.
The cruel Scorpion is there, the Gnat, Wasp, Hornet & the Honey Bee,
The Toad & venomous Newt, the Serpent cloth'd in gems & gold.
They throw off their gorgeous raiment: they rejoice with loud jubilee
Around the Wine-presses of Luvah, naked & drunk with wine.

There is the Nettle that stings with soft down, and there
The indignant Thistle whose bitterness is bred in his milk,
Who feeds on contempt of his neighbour: there all the idle Weeds
That creep around the obscure places shew their various limbs
Naked in all their beauty dancing round the Wine-presses.

But in the Wine-presses the Human grapes sing not nor dance:
They howl & writhe in shoals of torment, in fierce flames consuming,
In chairs of iron & in dungeons circled with ceaseless fires,
In pits & dens & shades of death, in shapes of torment & woe:
The plates & screws & wracks & saws & cords & fires & cisterns,
The cruel joys of Luvah's Daughters, lacerating with knives
And whips their Victims, & the deadly sport of Luvah's Sons.

They dance around the dying & they drink the howl & groan,
They catch the shrieks in cups of gold, they hand them to one another:
These are the sports of love, & these the sweet delights of amorous play,
Tears of the grape, the death sweat of the cluster, the last sigh
Of the mild youth who listens to the lureing songs of Luvah.

But Allamanda, call'd on Earth Commerce, is the Cultivated land
Around the City of Golgonooza in the Forests of Entuthon:
Here the Sons of Los Labour against Death Eternal, through all
The Twenty-seven Heavens of Beulah in Ulro, Seat of Satan,
Which is the False Tongue beneath Beulah: it is the Sense of Touch.
The Plow goes forth in tempests & lightnings, & the Harrow cruel
In blights of the east, the heavy Roller follows in howlings of woe.

Urizen's sons here labour also, & here are seen the Mills
Of Theotormon on the verge of the Lake of Udan-Adan.
These are the starry voids of night & the depths & caverns of earth.
These Mills are oceans, clouds & waters ungovernable in their fury:
Here are the stars created & the seeds of all things planted,
And here the Sun & Moon recieve their fixed destinations.

But in Eternity the Four Arts, Poetry, Painting, Music
And Architecture, which is Science, are the Four Faces of Man.
Not so in Time & Space: there Three are shut out, and only
Science remains thro' Mercy, & by means of Science the Three
Become apparent in Time & Space in the Three Professions,
[Poetry in Religion: Music, Law: Painting, in Physic & Surgery: *erased*]
That Man may live upon Earth till the time of his awaking.
And from these Three Sciences derives every Occupation of Men,
And Science is divided into Bowlahoola & Allamanda.

30

Some Sons of Los surround the Passions with porches of iron & silver,
Creating form & beauty around the dark regions of sorrow,
Giving to airy nothing a name and a habitation
Delightful, with bounds to the Infinite putting off the Indefinite
Into most holy forms of Thought; such is the power of inspiration.
They labour incessant with many tears & afflictions,
Creating the beautiful House for the piteous sufferer.

Others Cabinets richly fabricate of gold & ivory
For Doubts & fears unform'd & wretched & melancholy.

The little weeping Spectre stands on the threshold of Death
Eternal, and sometimes two Spectres like lamps quivering,
And often malignant they combat; heart-breaking sorrowful & piteous,
Antamon takes them into his beautiful flexible hands:
As the Sower takes the seed or as the Artist his clay
Or fine wax, to mould artful a model for golden ornaments.
The soft hands of Antamon draw the indelible line,
Form immortal with golden pen, such as the Spectre admiring
Puts on the sweet form; then smiles Antamon bright thro' his windows.
The Daughters of beauty look up from their Loom & prepare
The integument soft for its clothing with joy & delight.

But Theotormon & Sotha stand in the Gate of Luban anxious.
Their numbers are seven million & seven thousand & seven hundred.
They contend with the weak Spectres, they fabricate soothing forms.
The Spectre refuses, he seeks cruelty: they create the crested Cock.
Terrified the Spectre screams & rushes in fear into their Net
Of kindness & compassion, & is born a weeping terror.
Or they create the Lion & Tyger in compassionate thunderings:
Howling the Spectres flee: they take refuge in Human lineaments.

The Sons of Ozoth within the Optic Nerve stand fiery glowing,
And the number of his Sons is eight millions & eight.
They give delights to the man unknown; artificial riches
They give to scorn, & their possessors to trouble & sorrow & care,
Shutting the sun & moon & stars & trees & clouds & waters
And hills out from the Optic Nerve, & hardening it into a bone
Opake and like the black pebble on the enraged beach,
While the poor indigent is like the diamond which, tho' cloth'd
In rugged covering in the mine, is open all within
And in his hallow'd center holds the heavens of bright eternity.
Ozoth here builds walls of rocks against the surging sea,
And timbers crampt with iron cramps bar in the joys of life
From fell destruction in the Spectrous cunning or rage. He Creates
The speckled Newt, the Spider & Beetle, the Rat & Mouse.
The Badger & Fox: they worship before his feet in trembling fear.

But others of the Sons of Los build Moments & Minutes & Hours
And Days & Months & Years & Ages & Periods, wondrous buildings;
And every Moment has a Couch of gold for soft repose,
(A Moment equals a pulsation of the artery),
And between every two Moments stands a Daughter of Beulah

To feed the Sleepers on their Couches with maternal care.
And every Minute has an azure Tent with silken Veils:
And every Hour has a bright golden Gate carved with skill:
And every Day & Night has Walls of brass & Gates of adamant,
Shining like precious Stones & ornamented with appropriate signs:
And every Month a silver paved Terrace builded high:
And every Year invulnerable Barriers with high Towers:
And every Age is Moated deep with Bridges of silver & gold:
And every Seven Ages is Incircled with a Flaming Fire.
Now Seven Ages is amounting to Two Hundred Years.
Each has its Guard, each Moment, Minute, Hour, Day, Month & Year.
All are the work of Fairy hands of the Four Elements:
The Guard are Angels of Providence on duty evermore.
Every Time less than a pulsation of the artery
Is equal in its period & value to Six Thousand Years,

31

For in this Period the Poet's Work is Done, and all the Great
Events of Time start forth & are conciev'd in such a Period,
Within a Moment, a Pulsation of the Artery.

The Sky is an immortal Tent built by the Sons of Los:
And every Space that a Man views around his dwelling-place
Standing on his own roof or in his garden on a mount
Of twenty-five cubits in height, such space is his Universe:
And on its verge the Sun rises & sets, the Clouds bow
To meet the flat Earth & the Sea in such an order'd Space:
The Starry heavens reach no further, but here bend and set
On all sides, & the two Poles turn on their valves of gold;
And if he move his dwelling-place, his heavens also move
Where'er he goes, & all his neighbourhood bewail his loss.
Such are the Spaces called Earth & such its dimension.
As to that false appearance which appears to the reasoner
As of a Globe rolling thro' Voidness, it is a delusion of Ulro.
The Microscope knows not of this nor the Telescope: they alter
The ratio of the Spectator's Organs, but leave Objects untouch'd.
For every Space larger than a red Globule of Man's blood
Is visionary, and is created by the Hammer of Los:
And every Space smaller than a Globule of Man's blood opens
Into Eternity of which this vegetable Earth is but a shadow.
The red Globule is the unwearied Sun by Los created
To measure Time and Space to mortal Men every morning.

Bowlahoola & Allamanda are placed on each side
Of that Pulsation & that Globule, terrible their power.

But Rintrah & Palamabron govern over Day & Night
In Allamanda & Entuthon Benython where Souls wail,
Where Orc incessant howls, burning in fires of Eternal Youth,
Within the vegetated mortal Nerves; for every Man born is joined
Within into One mighty Polypus, and this Polypus is Orc.

But in the Optic vegetative Nerves, Sleep was transformed
To Death in old time by Satan the father of Sin & Death:
And Satan is the Spectre of Orc, & Orc is the generate Luvah.

But in the Nerves of the Nostrils, Accident being formed
Into Substance & Principle by the cruelties of Demonstration
It became Opake & Indefinite, but the Divine Saviour
Formed it into a Solid by Los's Mathematic power.
He named the Opake, Satan: he named the Solid, Adam.

And in the Nerves of the Ear (for the Nerves of the Tongue are closed)
On Albion's Rock Los stands creating the glorious Sun each morning,
And when unwearied in the evening, he creates the Moon,
Death to delude, who all in terror at their splendor leaves
His prey, while Los appoints & Rintrah & Palamabron guide
The Souls clear from the Rock of Death, that Death himself may wake
In his appointed season when the ends of heaven meet.

Then Los conducts the Spirits to be Vegetated into
Great Golgonooza, free from the four iron pillars of Satan's Throne,
(Temperance, Prudence, Justice, Fortitude, the four pillars of tyranny)
That Satan's Watch-Fiends touch them not before they Vegetate.

But Enitharmon and her Daughters take the pleasant charge
To give them to their lovely heavens till the Great Judgment Day:
Such is their lovely charge. But Rahab & Tirzah pervert
Their mild influences; therefore the Seven Eyes of God walk round
The Three Heavens of Ulro where Tirzah & her Sisters
Weave the black Woof of Death upon Entuthon Benython,
In the Vale of Surrey where Horeb terminates in Rephaim.
The stamping feet of Zelophehad's Daughters are cover'd with Human
      gore
Upon the treddles of the Loom: they sing to the winged shuttle.

The River rises above his banks to wash the Woof:
He takes it in his arms; he passes it in strength thro' his current;
The veil of human miseries is woven over the Ocean
From the Atlantic to the Great South Sea, the Erythrean.

Such is the World of Los, the labour of six thousand years.
Thus Nature is a Vision of the Science of the Elohim.

END OF THE FIRST BOOK

BOOK THE SECOND

33

THERE is a place where Contrarieties are equally True:
This place is called Beulah. It is a pleasant lovely Shadow
Where no dispute can come, Because of those who Sleep.
Into this place the Sons & Daughters of Ololon descended
With solemn mourning, into Beulah's moony shades & hills
Weeping for Milton: mute wonder held the Daughters of Beulah,
Enraptur'd with affection sweet and mild benevolence.

Beulah is evermore Created around Eternity, appearing
To the Inhabitants of Eden around them on all sides.
But Beulah to its Inhabitants appears within each district
As the beloved infant in his mother's bosom round incircled
With arms of love & pity & sweet compassion. But to
The Sons of Eden the moony habitations of Beulah
Are from Great Eternity a mild & pleasant Rest.

And it is thus Created. Lo, the Eternal Great Humanity,
To whom be Glory & Dominion Evermore, Amen,
Walks among all his awful Family seen in every face:
As the breath of the Almighty such are the words of man to man
In the great Wars of Eternity, in fury of Poetic Inspiration,
To build the Universe stupendous, Mental forms Creating.

But the Emanations trembled exceedingly, nor could they
Live, because the life of Man was too exceeding unbounded.
His joy became terrible to them; they trembled & wept,
Crying with one voice: "Give us a habitation & a place

In which we may be hidden under the shadow of wings:
For if we, who are but for a time & who pass away in winter,
Behold these wonders of Eternity we shall consume:
But you, O our Fathers & Brothers, remain in Eternity.
But grant us a Temporal Habitation, do you speak
To us; we will obey your words as you obey Jesus
The Eternal who is blessed for ever & ever. Amen."

So spake the lovely Emanations, & there appear'd a pleasant
Mild Shadow above, beneath, & on all sides round.

34

Into this pleasant Shadow all the weak & weary
Like Women & Children were taken away as on wings
Of dovelike softness, & shadowy habitations prepared for them.
But every Man return'd & went still going forward thro'
The Bosom of the Father in Eternity on Eternity,
Neither did any lack or fall into Error without
A Shadow to repose in all the Days of happy Eternity.

Into this pleasant Shadow, Beulah, all Ololon descended,
And when the Daughters of Beulah heard the lamentation
All Beulah wept, for they saw the Lord coming in the Clouds.
And the Shadows of Beulah terminate in rocky Albion.

And all Nations wept in affliction, Family by Family:
Germany wept towards France & Italy, England wept & trembled
Towards America, India rose up from his golden bed
As one awaken'd in the night; they saw the Lord coming
In the Clouds of Ololon with Power & Great Glory.

And all the Living Creatures of the Four Elements wail'd
With bitter wailing; these in the aggregate are named Satan
And Rahab: they know not of Regeneration, but only of Generation:
The Fairies, Nymphs, Gnomes & Genii of the Four Elements,
Unforgiving & unalterable, these cannot be Regenerated
But must be Created, for they know only of Generation:
These are the Gods of the Kingdoms of the Earth, in contrarious
And cruel opposition, Element against Element, opposed in War
Not Mental, as the Wars of Eternity, but a Corporeal Strife
In Los's Halls, continual labouring in the Furnaces of Golgonooza.
Orc howls on the Atlantic: Enitharmon trembles: All Beulah weeps.

Thou hearest the Nightingale begin the Song of Spring.
The Lark sitting upon his earthy bed, just as the morn
Appears, listens silent; then springing from the waving Cornfield, loud
He leads the Choir of Day: trill, trill, trill, trill,
Mounting upon the wings of light into the Great Expanse,
Reecchoing against the lovely blue & shining heavenly Shell,
His little throat labours with inspiration; every feather
On throat & breast & wings vibrates with the effluence Divine.
All Nature listens silent to him, & the awful Sun
Stands still upon the Mountain looking on this little Bird
With eyes of soft humility & wonder, love & awe,
Then loud from their green covert all the Birds begin their Song:
The Thrush, the Linnet & the Goldfinch, Robin & the Wren
Awake the Sun from his sweet reverie upon the Mountain.
The Nightingale again assays his song, & thro' the day
And thro' the night warbles luxuriant, every Bird of Song
Attending his loud harmony with admiration & love.
This is a Vision of the lamentation of Beulah over Ololon.

Thou perceivest the Flowers put forth their precious Odours,
And none can tell how from so small a center comes such sweets,
Forgetting that within that Center Eternity expands
Its ever during doors that Og & Anak fiercely guard.
First, e'er the morning breaks, joy opens in the flowery bosoms,
Joy even to tears, which the Sun rising dries; first the Wild Thyme
And Meadow-sweet, downy & soft waving among the reeds,
Light springing on the air, lead the sweet Dance: they wake
The Honeysuckle sleeping on the Oak; the flaunting beauty
Revels along upon the wind; the White-thorn, lovely May,
Opens her many lovely eyes listening; the Rose still sleeps,
None dare to wake her; soon she bursts her crimson curtain'd bed
And comes forth in the majesty of beauty; every Flower,
The Pink, the Jessamine, the Wall-flower, the Carnation,
The Jonquil, the mild Lilly, opes her heavens; every Tree
And Flower & Herb soon fill the air with an innumerable Dance,
Yet all in order sweet & lovely. Men are sick with Love,
Such is a Vision of the lamentation of Beulah over Ololon.

35

And Milton oft sat upon the Couch of Death & oft conversed
In vision & dream beatific with the Seven Angels of the Presence.

"I have turned my back upon these Heavens builded on cruelty;
My Spectre still wandering thro' them follows my Emanation,
He hunts her footsteps thro' the snow & the wintry hail & rain.
The idiot Reasoner laughs at the Man of Imagination,
And from laughter proceeds to murder by undervaluing calumny."

Then Hillel, who is Lucifer, replied over the Couch of Death,
And thus the Seven Angels instructed him, & thus they converse:

"We are not Individuals but States, Combinations of Individuals.
We were Angels of the Divine Presence, & were Druids in Annandale,
Compell'd to combine into Form by Satan, the Spectre of Albion,
Who made himself a God & destroyed the Human Form Divine.
"But the Divine Humanity & Mercy gave us a Human Form
Because we were combin'd in Freedom & holy Brother-
    hood,
While those combin'd by Satan's Tyranny, first in the blood
    of War
And Sacrifice & next in Chains of imprisonment, are Shapeless Rocks

                                          כירבים
                                       as multitudes
                                       Vox Populi.

Retaining only Satan's Mathematic Holiness, Length, Bredth & Highth,
Calling the Human Imagination, which is the Divine Vision & Fruition
In which Man liveth eternally, madness & blasphemy against
Its own Qualities, which are Servants of Humanity, not Gods or Lords.
Distinguish therefore States from Individuals in those States.
States Change, but Individual Identities never change nor cease.
You cannot go to Eternal Death in that which can never Die.
Satan & Adam are States Created into Twenty-seven Churches,
And thou, O Milton, art a State about to be Created,
Called Eternal Annihilation, that none but the Living shall
Dare to enter, & they shall enter triumphant over Death
And Hell & the Grave: States that are not, but ah! Seem to be.

"Judge then of thy Own Self: thy Eternal Lineaments explore,
What is Eternal & what Changeable, & what Annihilable.
The Imagination is not a State: it is the Human Existence itself.
Affection or Love becomes a State when divided from Imagination.
The Memory is a State always, & the Reason is a State
Created to be Annihilated & a new Ratio Created.
Whatever can be Created can be Annihilated: Forms cannot:
The Oak is cut down by the Ax, the Lamb falls by the Knife,
But their Forms Eternal Exist For-ever. Amen. Hallelujah!"

Thus they converse with the Dead, watching round the Couch of Death;
For God himself enters Death's Door always with those that enter
And lays down in the Grave with them, in Visions of Eternity,
Till they awake & see Jesus & the Linen Clothes lying
That the Females had Woven for them, & the Gates of their Father's
House.

36

And the Divine Voice was heard in the Songs of Beulah, Saying:

"When I first Married you, I gave you all my whole Soul.
I thought that you would love my loves & joy in my delights,
Seeking for pleasures in my pleasures, O Daughter of Babylon.
Then thou wast lovely, mild & gentle; now thou art terrible
In jealousy & unlovely in my sight, because thou hast cruelly
Cut off my loves in fury till I have no love left for thee.
Thy loves depends on him thou lovest, & on his dear loves
Depend thy pleasures, which thou hast cut off by jealousy.
Therefore I shew my Jealousy & set before you Death.
Behold Milton descended to Redeem the Female Shade
From Death Eternal; such your lot, to be continually Redeem'd
By death & misery of those you love & by Annihilation.
When the Sixfold Female perceives that Milton annihilates
Himself, that seeing all his loves by her cut off, he leaves
Her also, intirely abstracting himself from Female loves,
She shall relent in fear of death; She shall begin to give
Her maidens to her husband, delighting in his delight.
And then & then alone begins the happy Female joy
As it is done in Beulah, & thou, O Virgin Babylon, Mother of Whoredoms,
Shalt bring Jerusalem in thine arms in the night watches, and
No longer turning her a wandering Harlot in the streets,
Shalt give her into the arms of God your Lord & Husband."

Such are the Songs of Beulah in the Lamentations of Ololon.

38

And all the Songs of Beulah sounded comfortable notes
To comfort Ololon's lamentation, for they said:
"Are you the Fiery Circle that late drove in fury & fire
The Eight Immortal Starry-Ones down into Ulro dark
Rending the Heavens of Beulah with your thunders & lightnings?
And can you thus lament & can you pity & forgive?
Is terror chang'd to pity? O wonder of Eternity!"

And the Four States of Humanity in its Repose
Were shewed them. First of Beulah, a most pleasant Sleep
On Couches soft with mild music, tended by Flowers of Beulah,
Sweet Female forms, winged or floating in the air spontaneous:
The Second State is Alla, & the third State Al-Ulro:
But the Fourth State is dreadful, it is named Or-Ulro.
The First State is in the Head, the Second is in the Heart,
The Third in the Loins & Seminal Vessels, & the Fourth
In the Stomach & Intestines terrible, deadly, unutterable.
And he whose Gates are open'd in those Regions of his Body
Can from those Gates view all these wondrous Imaginations.

But Ololon sought the Or-Ulro & its fiery Gates
And the Couches of the Martyrs, & many Daughters of Beulah
Accompany them down to the Ulro with soft melodious tears,
A long journey & dark thro' Chaos in the track of Milton's course,
To where the Contraries of Beulah War beneath Negation's Banner.

Then view'd from Milton's Track they see the Ulro a vast Polypus
Of living fibres down into the Sea of Time & Space growing
A self-devouring monstrous Human Death Twenty-seven fold.
Within it sit Five Females & the nameless Shadowy Mother,
Spinning it from their bowels with songs of amorous delight
And melting cadences that lure the Sleepers of Beulah down
The River Storge (which is Arnon) into the Dead Sea.
Around this Polypus Los continual builds the Mundane Shell.
Four Universes round the Universe of Los remain Chaotic,
Four intersectiong Globes, & the Egg form'd World of Los
In midst, stretching from Zenith to Nadir in midst of Chaos.
One of these Ruin'd Universes is to the North, named Urthona:
One to the South, this was the glorious World of Urizen:
One to the East, of Luvah: One to the West, of Tharmas.
But when Luvah assumed the World of Urizen in the South
All fell towards the Center sinking downward in dire Ruin.

Here in these Chaoses the Sons of Ololon took their abode,
In Chasms of the Mundane Shell which open on all sides round,
Southward & by the East within the Breach of Milton's descent,
To watch the time, pitying, & gentle to awaken Urizen.
They stood in a dark land of death, of fiery corroding waters,
Where lie in evil death the Four Immortals pale and cold
And the Eternal Man, even Albion, upon the Rock of Ages.

Seeing Milton's Shadow, some Daughters of Beulah trembling
Return'd, but Ololon remain'd before the Gates of the Dead.

And Ololon looked down into the Heavens of Ulro in fear.
They said: "How are the Wars of man, which in Great Eternity
Appear around in the External Spheres of Visionary Life,
Here render'd Deadly within the Life & Interior Vision?
How are the Beasts & Birds & Fishes & Plants & Minerals
Here fix'd into a frozen bulk subject to decay & death?
Those Visions of Human Life & Shadows of Wisdom & Knowledge

39

"Are here frozen to unexpansive deadly destroying terrors,
And War & Hunting, the Two Fountains of the River of Life,
Are become Fountains of bitter Death & of corroding Hell,
Till Brotherhood is chang'd into a Curse & a Flattery
By Differences between Ideas, that Ideas themselves (which are
The Divine Members) may be slain in offerings for sin.
O dreadful Loom of Death! O piteous Female forms compell'd
To weave the Woof of Death! On Camberwell Tirzah's Courts,
Malah's on Blackheath, Rahab & Noah dwell on Windsor's heights:
Where once the Cherubs of Jerusalem spread to Lambeth's Vale
Milcah's Pillar's shine from Harrow to Hampstead, where Hoglah
On Highgate's heights magnificent Weaves over trembling Thames
To Shooters' Hill and thence to Blackheath, the dark Woof. Loud,
Loud roll the Weights & Spindles over the whole Earth, let down
On all sides round to the Four Quarters of the World, eastward on
Europe to Euphrates & Hindu to Nile, & back in Clouds
Of Death across the Atlantic to America North & South."

So spake Ololon in reminiscence astonish'd, but they
Could not behold Golgonooza without passing the Polypus,
A wondrous journey not passable by Immortal feet, & none
But the Divine Saviour can pass it without annihilation.
For Golgonooza cannot be seen till having pass'd the Polypus
It is viewed on all sides round by a Four-fold Vision,
Or till you become Mortal & Vegetable in Sexuality,
Then you behold its mighty Spires & Domes of ivory & gold.

And Ololon examined all the Couches of the Dead,
Even of Los & Enitharmon & all the Sons of Albion
And his Four Zoas terrified & on the verge of Death.

In midst of these was Milton's Couch, & when they saw Eight
Immortal Starry-Ones guarding the Couch in flaming fires,
They thunderous utter'd all a universal groan, falling down
Prostrate before the Starry Eight asking with tears forgiveness,
Confessing their crime with humiliation and sorrow.

O how the Starry Eight rejoic'd to see Ololon descended,
And now that a wide road was open to Eternity
By Ololon's descent thro' Beulah to Los & Enitharmon!
For mighty were the multitudes of Ololon, vast the extent
Of their great sway reaching from Ulro to Eternity,
Surrounding the Mundane Shell outside in its Caverns
And through Beulah, and all silent forbore to contend
With Ololon, for they saw the Lord in the Clouds of Ololon.

There is a Moment in each Day that Satan cannot find,
Nor can his Watch Fiends find it: but the Industrious find
This Moment & it multiply, & when it once is found
It renovates every Moment of the Day if rightly placed.
In this Moment Ololon descended to Los & Enitharmon
Unseen beyond the Mundane Shell, Southward in Milton's track.

Just in this Moment, when the morning odours rise abroad
And first from the Wild Thyme, stands a Fountain in a rock
Of crystal flowing into two Streams: one flows thro' Golgonooza
And thro' Beulah to Eden beneath Los's western Wall:
The other flows thro' the Aerial Void & all the Churches,
Meeting again in Golgonooza beyond Satan's Seat.

The Wild Thyme is Los's Messenger to Eden, a mighty Demon,
Terrible, deadly & poisonous his presence in Ulro dark;
Therefore he appears only a small Root creeping in grass
Covering over the Rock of Odours his bright purple mantle
Beside the Fount above the Lark's nest in Golgonooza.
Luvah slept here in death & here is Luvah's empty Tomb.
Ololon sat beside this Fountain on the Rock of Odours.

Just at the place to where the Lark mounts is a Crystal Gate:
It is the entrance of the First Heaven, named Luther; for
The Lark is Los's Messenger thro' the Twenty-seven Churches

That the Seven Eyes of God, who walk even to Satan's Seat
Thro' all the Twenty-seven Heavens, may not slumber nor sleep.
But the Lark's Nest is at the Gate of Los, at the eastern
Gate of wide Golgonooza, & the Lark is Los's Messenger.

40

When on the highest lift of his light pinions he arrives
At that bright Gate, another Lark meets him, & back to back
They touch their pinions, tip tip, and each descend
To their respective Earths & there all night consult with Angels
Of Providence & with the eyes of God all night in slumbers
Inspired, & at the dawn of day send out another Lark
Into another Heaven to carry news upon his wings.
Thus are the Messengers dispatch'd till they reach the Earth again
In the East Gate of Golgonooza, & the Twenty-eighth bright
Lark met the Female Ololon descending into my Garden.
Thus it appears to Mortal eyes & those of the Ulro Heavens,
But not thus to Immortals: the Lark is a mighty Angel.

For Ololon step'd into the Polypus within the Mundane Shell.
They could not step into Vegetable Worlds without becoming
The enemies of Humanity, except in a Female Form,
And as One Female Ololon and all its mighty Hosts
Appear'd, a Virgin of twelve years: nor time nor space was
To the perception of the Virgin Ololon, but as the
Flash of lightning, but more quick the Virgin in my Garden
Before my Cottage stood, for the Satanic Space is delusion.

For when Los join'd with me he took me in his fi'ry whirlwind:
My Vegetated portion was hurried from Lambeth's shades,
He set me down in Felpham's Vale & prepar'd a beautiful
Cottage for me, that in three years I might write all these Visions
To display Nature's cruel holiness, the deceits of Natural Religion.
Walking in my Cottage Garden, sudden I beheld
The Virgin Ololon & addres'd her as a Daughter of Beulah:

'Virgin of Providence, fear not to enter into my Cottage.
What is thy message to thy friend? What am I now to do?
Is it again to plunge into deeper affliction? behold me
Ready to obey, but pity thou my Shadow of Delight:
Enter my Cottage, comfort her, for she is sick with fatigue."

41

The Virgin answer'd: "Knowest thou of Milton who descended
Driven from Eternity? him I seek, terrified at my Act
In Great Eternity which thou knowest: I come him to seek."

So Ololon utter'd in words distinct the anxious thought:
Mild was the voice but more distinct than any earthly.
That Milton's Shadow heard, & condensing all his Fibres
Into a strength impregnable of majesty & beauty infinite,
I saw he was the Covering Cherub & within him Satan
And Rahab in an outside which is fallacious, within,
Beyond the outline of Identity, in the Selfhood deadly;
And he appear'd the Wicker Man of Scandinavia, in whom
Jerusalem's children consume in flames among the Stars.

Descending down into my Garden, a Human Wonder of God
Reaching from heaven to earth, a Cloud, & Human Form,
I beheld Milton with astonishment & in him beheld
The Monstrous Churches of Beulah, the Gods of Ulro dark,
Twelve monstrous dishumaniz'd terrors, Synagogues of Satan,
A Double Twelve & Thrice Nine: such their divisions.

And these their Names & their Places within the Mundane Shell:

In Tyre & Sidon I saw Baal & Ashtaroth: In Moab Chemosh:
In Ammon Molech, loud his Furnaces rage among the Wheels
Of Og, & pealing loud the cries of the Victims of Fire,
And pale his Priestesses infolded in Veils of Pestilence border'd
With War, Woven in Looms of Tyre & Sidon by beautiful Ashtaroth:
In Palestine Dagon, Sea Monster, worship'd o'er the Sea:
Thammuz in Lebanon & Rimmon in Damascus curtain'd:
Osiris, Isis, Orus in Egypt, dark their Tabernacles on Nile
Floating with solemn songs & on the Lakes of Egypt nightly
With pomp even till morning break & Osiris appear in the sky:
But Belial of Sodom & Gomorrha, obscure Demon of Bribes
And secret Assasinations, not worship'd nor ador'd, but
With a finger on the lips & the back turn'd to the light:
And Saturn, Jove & Rhea of the Isles of the Sea remote.
These Twelve Gods are the Twelve Spectre Sons of the Druid Albion.

And these the names of the Twenty-seven Heavens & their Churches:
Adam, Seth, Enos, Cainan, Mahalaleel, Jared, Enoch,
Methuselah, Lamech, these are Giants Mighty, Hermaphroditic;
Noah, Shem, Arphaxad, Cainan the second, Salah, Heber,
Peleg, Reu, Serug, Nahor, Terah, these are the Female-Males,
A Male within a Female hid as in an Ark & Curtains;
Abraham, Moses, Solomon, Paul, Constantine, Charlemaine,
Luther, these seven are the Male-Females, the Dragon Forms,
Religion hid in War, a Dragon red & hidden Harlot.

All these are seen in Milton's Shadow, who is the Covering Cherub,
The Spectre of Albion in which the Spectre of Luvah inhabits
In the Newtonian Voids between the Substances of Creation.

For the Chaotic Voids outside of the Stars are measured by
The Stars, which are the boundaries of Kingdoms, Provinces
And Empires of Chaos invisible to the Vegetable Man.
The Kingdom of Og is in Orion: Sihon is in Ophiucus.
Og has Twenty-seven Districts: Sihon's Districts Twenty-one.
From Star to Star, Mountains & Valleys, terrible dimension
Stretch'd out, compose the Mundane Shell, a mighty Incrustation
Of Forty-eight deformed Human Wonders of the Almighty,
With Caverns whose remotest bottoms meet again beyond
The Mundane Shell in Golgonooza; but the Fires of Los rage
In the remotest bottoms of the Caves, that none can pass
Into Eternity that way, but all descend to Los,
To Bowlahoola & Allamanda & to Entuthon Benython.

The Heavens are the Cherub: the Twelve Gods are Satan,

43

And the Forty-eight Starry Regions are Cities of the Levites,
The Heads of the Great Polypus, Four-fold twelve enormity,
In mighty & mysterious comingling, enemy with enemy,
Woven by Urizen into Sexes from his mantle of years.
And Milton collecting all his fibres into impregnable strength
Descended down a Paved work of all kinds of precious stones
Out from the eastern sky; descending down into my Cottage
Garden, clothed in black, severe & silent he descended.

The Spectre of Satan stood upon the roaring sea & beheld
Milton within his sleeping Humanity; trembling & shudd'ring

He stood upon the waves a Twenty-seven fold mighty Demon
Georgeous & beautiful; loud roll his thunders against Milton.
Loud Satan thunder'd, loud & dark upon mild Felpham shore
Not daring to touch one fibre he howl'd round upon the Sea.

I also stood in Satan's bosom & beheld its desolations:
A ruin'd Man, a ruin'd building of God, not made with hands:
Its plains of burning sand, its mountains of marble terrible:
Its pits & declivities flowing with molten ore & fountains
Of pitch & nitre: its ruin'd palaces & cities & mighty works:
Its furnaces of affliction, in which his Angels & Emanations
Labour with blacken'd visages among its stupendous ruins,
Arches & pyramids & porches, colonades & domes,
In which dwells Mystery, Babylon; here is her secret place,
From hence she comes forth on the Churches in delight;
Here is her Cup fill'd with its poisons in these horried vales,
And here her scarlet Veil woven in pestilence & war;
Here is Jerusalem bound in chains in the Dens of Babylon.

In the Eastern porch of Satan's Universe Milton stood & said:

"Satan! my Spectre! I know my power thee to annihilate
And be a greater in thy place & be thy Tabernacle,
A covering for thee to do thy will, till one greater comes
And smites me as I smote thee & becomes my covering.
Such are the Laws of thy false Heav'ns; but Laws of Eternity
Are not such; know thou, I come to Self Annihilation.
Such are the Laws of Eternity, that each shall mutually
Annihilate himself for others' good, as I for thee.
Thy purpose & the purpose of thy Priests & of thy Churches
Is to impress on men the fear of death, to teach
Trembling & fear, terror, constriction, abject selfishness.
Mine is to teach Men to despise death & to go on
In fearless majesty annihilating Self, laughing to scorn
Thy Laws & terrors, shaking down thy Synagogues as webs.
I come to discover before Heav'n & Hell the Self righteousness
In all its Hypocritic turpitude, opening to every eye
These wonders of Satan's holiness, shewing to the Earth
The Idol Virtues of the Natural Heart, & Satan's Seat
Explore in all its Selfish Natural Virtue, & put off
In Self annihilation all that is not of God alone,
To put off Self & all I have, ever & ever. Amen."

Satan heard, Coming in a cloud, with trumpets & flaming fire,
Saying: "I am God the judge of all, the living & the dead.
Fall therefore down & worship me, submit thy supreme
Dictate to my eternal Will, & to my dictate bow.
I hold the Balances of Right & Just & mine the Sword.
Seven Angels bear my Name & in those Seven I appear,
But I alone am God & I alone in Heav'n & Earth
Of all that live dare utter this, others tremble & bow,

44

"Till All Things become One Great Satan, in Holiness
Oppos'd to Mercy, and the Divine Delusion, Jesus, be no more."

Suddenly around Milton on my Path the Starry Seven
Burn'd terrible; my Path became a solid fire, as bright
As the clear Sun, & Milton silent came down on my Path.
And there went forth from the Starry limbs of the Seven, Forms
Human, with Trumpets, innumerable, sounding articulate
As the Seven spake; and they stood in a mighty Column of Fire
Surrounding Felpham's Vale, reaching to the Mundane Shell, Saying:

"Awake, Albion awake! reclaim thy Reasoning Spectre, Subdue
Him to the Divine Mercy. Cast him down into the Lake
Of Los that ever burneth with fire ever & ever, Amen!
Let the Four Zoas awake from Slumbers of Six Thousand Years."

Then loud the Furnaces of Los were heard, & seen as Seven Heavens
Stretching from south to north over the mountains of Albion.

Satan heard; trembling round his Body, he incircled it:
He trembled with exceeding great trembling & astonishment,
Howling in his Spectre round his Body, hung'ring to devour
But fearing for the pain, for if he touches a Vital
His torment is unendurable: therefore he cannot devour
But howls round it as a lion round his prey continually.
Loud Satan thunder'd, loud & dark upon mild Felpham's Shore,
Coming in a Cloud with Trumpets & with Fiery Flame,
An awful Form eastward from midst of a bright Paved-work
Of precious stones by Cherubim surrounded, so permitted
(Lest he should fall apart in his Eternal Death) to imitate
The Eternal Great Humanity Divine surrounded by

His Cherubim & Seraphim in ever happy Eternity.
Beneath sat Chaos: Sin on his right hand, Death on his left,
And Ancient Night spread over all the heav'n his Mantle of Laws.
He trembled with exceeding great trembling & astonishment.

Then Albion rose up in the Night of Beulah on his Couch
Of dread repose; seen by the visionary eye, his face is toward
The east, toward Jerusalem's Gates; groaning he sat above
His rocks. London & Bath & Legions & Edinburgh
Are the four pillars of his Throne: his left foot near London
Covers the shades of Tyburn: his instep from Windsor
To Primrose Hill stretching to Highgate & Holloway.
London is between his knees, its basements fourfold;
His right foot stretches to the sea on Dover's cliffs, his heel
On Canterbury's ruins; his right hand covers lofty Wales,
His left Scotland; his bosom girt with gold involves
York, Edinburgh, Durham & Carlisle, & on the front
Bath, Oxford, Cambridge, Norwich; his right elbow
Leans on the Rocks of Erin's Land, Ireland, ancient nation;
His head bends over London; he sees his embodied Spectre
Trembling before him with exceeding great trembling & fear.
He views Jerusalem & Babylon, his tears flow down.
He mov'd his right foot to Cornwall, his left to the Rocks of Bognor.
He strove to rise to walk into the Deep, but strength failing
For bad, & down with dreadful groans he sunk upon his Couch
In moony Beulah. Los, his strong Guard, walks round beneath the Moon.

Urizen faints in terror striving among the Brooks of Arnon
With Milton's Spirit; as the Plowman or Artificer or Shepherd
While in the labours of his Calling sends his Thought abroad
To labour in the ocean or in the starry heaven, So Milton
Labour'd in Chasms of the Mundane Shell, tho' here before
My Cottage midst the Starry Seven where the Virgin Ololon
Stood trembling in the Porch; loud Satan thunder'd on the stormy Sea
Circling Albion's Cliffs, in which the Four-fold World resides,
Tho' seen in fallacy outside, a fallacy of Satan's Churches.

46

Before Ololon Milton stood & perceiv'd the Eternal Form
Of that mild Vision; wondrous were their acts, by me unknown
Except remotely, and I heard Ololon say to Milton:

"I see thee strive upon the Brooks of Arnon: there a dread
And awful Man I see, o'ercover'd with the mantle of years.
I behold Los & Urizen, I behold Orc & Tharmas,
The Four Zoas of Albion, & thy Spirit with them striving,
In Self annihilation giving thy life to thy enemies.
Are those who contemn Religion & seek to annihilate it
Become in their Feminine portions the causes & promoters
Of these Religions? how is this thing, this Newtonian Phantasm,
This Voltaire & Rousseau, this Hume & Gibbon & Bolingbroke,
This Natural Religion, this impossible absurdity?
Is Ololon the cause of this? O where shall I hide my face?
These tears fall for the little ones, the Children of Jerusalem,
Lest they be annihilated in thy annihilation."

No sooner had she spoke but Rahab Babylon appear'd
Eastward upon the Paved work across Europe & Asia,
Glorious as the midday Sun in Satan's bosom glowing,
A Female hidden in a Male, Religion hidden in War,
Nam'd Moral Virtue, cruel two-fold Monster shining bright,
A Dragon red & hidden Harlot which John in Patmos saw.

And all beneath the Nations innumerable of Ulro
Appear'd: the Seven Kingdoms of Canaan & Five Baalim
Of Philistea into Twelve divided, call'd after the Names
Of Israel, as they are in Eden, Mountain, River & Plain,
City & sandy Desart intermingled beyond mortal ken.

But turning toward Ololon in terrible majesty Milton
Replied: "Obey thou the Words of the Inspired Man.
All that can be annihilated must be annihilated
That the Children of Jerusalem may be saved from slavery.
There is a Negation, & there is a Contrary:
The Negation must be destroy'd to redeem the Contraries.
The Negation is the Spectre, the Reasoning Power in Man:
This is a false Body, in Incrustation over my Immortal
Spirit, a Selfhood which must be put off & annihilated alway.
To cleanse the Face of my Spirit by Self-examination,

48

"To bathe in the Waters of Life; to wash off the Not Human,
I come in Self-annihilation & the grandeur of Inspiration,
To cast off Rational Demonstration by Faith in the Saviour,

To cast off the rotten rags of Memory by Inspiration,
To cast off Bacon, Locke & Newton from Albion's covering,
To take off his filthy garments & clothe him with Imagination,
To cast aside from Poetry all that is not Inspiration,
That it no longer shall dare to mock with the aspersion of Madness
Cast on the Inspired by the tame high finisher of paltry Blots
Indefinite, or paltry Rhymes, or paltry Harmonies,
Who creeps into State Government like a catterpiller to destroy;
To cast off the idiot Questioner who is always questioning
But never capable of answering, who sits with a sly grin
Silent plotting when to question, like a thief in a cave,
Who publishes doubt & calls it knowledge, whose Science is Despair,
Whose pretence to knowledge is Envy, whose whole Science is
To destroy the wisdom of ages to gratify ravenous Envy
That rages round him like a Wolf day & night without rest:
He smiles with condescension, he talks of Benevolence & Virtue,
And those who act with Benevolence & Virtue they murder time on time.
These are the destroyers of Jerusalem, these are the murderers
Of Jesus, who deny the Faith & mock at Eternal Life,
Who pretend to Poetry that they may destroy Imagination
By imitation of Nature's Images drawn from Remembrance.
These are the Sexual Garments, the Abomination of Desolation,
Hiding the Human Lineaments as with an Ark & Curtains
Which Jesus rent & now shall wholly purge away with Fire
Till Generation is swallow'd up in Regeneration."

Then trembled the Virgin Ololon & reply'd in clouds of despair:

"Is this our Feminine Portion, the Six-fold Miltonic Female?
Terribly this Portion trembles before thee, O awful Man.
Altho' our Human Power can sustain the severe contentions
Of Friendship, our Sexual cannot, but flies into the Ulro.
Hence arose all our terrors in Eternity; & now remembrance
Returns upon us; are we Contraries, O Milton, Thou & I?
O Immortal, how were we led to War the Wars of Death?
Is this the Void Outside of Existence, which if enter'd into

49

"Becomes a Womb? & is this the Death Couch of Albion?
Thou goest to Eternal Death & all must go with thee."

So saying, the Virgin divided Six-fold, & with a shriek
Dolorous that ran thro' all Creation, a Double Six-fold Wonder

Away from Ololon she divided & fled into the depths
Of Milton's Shadow, as a Dove upon the stormy Sea.

Then as a Moony Ark Ololon descended to Felpham's Vale
In clouds of blood, in streams of gore, with dreadful thunderings
Into the Fires of Intellect that rejoic'd in Felpham's Vale
Around the Starry Eight; with one accord the Starry Eight became
One Man, Jesus the Saviour, wonderful! round his limbs
The Clouds of Ololon folded as a Garment dipped in blood,
Written within & without in woven letters, & the Writing
Is the Divine Revelation in the Litteral expression,
A Garment of War. I heard it nam'd the Woof of Six Thousand Years.

And I beheld the Twenty-four Cities of Albion
Arise upon their Thrones to Judge the Nations of the Earth;
And the Immortal Four in whom the Twenty-four appear Four-fold
Arose around Albion's body. Jesus wept & walked forth
From Felpham's Vale clothed in Clouds of blood, to enter into
Albion's Bosom, the bosom of death, & the Four surrounded him
In the Column of Fire in Felpham's Vale; then to their mouths the Four
Applied their Four Trumpets & them sounded to the Four winds.

Terror struck in the Vale I stood at that immortal sound.
My bones trembled, I fell outstretch'd upon the path
A moment, & my Soul return'd into its mortal state
To Resurrection & Judgment in the Vegetable Body,
And my sweet Shadow of Delight stood trembling by my side.

Immediately the Lark mounted with a loud trill from Felpham's Vale,
And the Wild Thyme from Wimbleton's green & impurpled Hills,
And Los & Enitharmon rose over the Hills of Surrey:
Their clouds roll over London with a south wind; soft Oothoon
Pants in the Vale of Lambeth, weeping o'er her Human Harvest.
Los listens to the Cry of the Poor Man, his Cloud
Over London in volume terrific low bended in anger.

Rintrah & Palamabron view the Human Harvest beneath.
Their Wine-presses & Barns stand open, the Ovens are prepar'd,
The Waggons ready; terrific Lions & Tygers sport a play.
All Animals upon the Earth are prepar'd in all their strength

50

To go forth to the Great Harvest & Vintage of the Nations

JERUSALEM

The Emanation of the Giant Albion
Written and etched 1804-1820

3

SHEEP   TO THE PUBLIC   GOATS

AFTER my three years slumber on the banks of the Ocean, I again display my Giant forms to the Public. My former Giants & Fairies having reciev'd the highest reward possible, the *love* [1] and *friendship* of those with whom to be connected is to be *blessed*, I cannot doubt that this more consolidated & extended work will be as kindly recieved. The Enthusiasm of the following Poem, the Author hopes *that all will think* . . . *or engraving when he* . . . *and the Ancients* . . . *to their* . . . *I have* . . . *acknowledge mine for my* . . . *and* . . . *for they were wholly accursed in their ideas.* I also hope the Reader will be with me, wholly One in Jesus our Lord, who is the God *of Fire* and Lord *of Love* to whom the Ancients look'd and saw his day afar off, with trembling & amazement.

The Spirit of Jesus is continual forgiveness of Sin: he who waits to be righteous before he enters into the Saviour's kingdom, the Divine Body, will never enter there. I am perhaps the most sinful of men. I pretend not to holiness: yet I pretend to love, to see, to converse with daily as man with man, & the more to have an interest in the Friend of Sinners. Therefore, *dear* Reader, *forgive* what you do not approve, & *love* me for this energetic exertion of my talent.

> Reader! *lover* of books! *lover* of heaven,
> And of that God from whom *all things are given,*
> Who in mysterious Sinai's awful cave
> To Man the wondrous art of writing gave:
> Again he speaks in thunder and in fire!
> Thunder of Thought, flames of fierce desire:
> Even from the depths of Hell his voice I hear
> Within the unfathom'd caverns of my Ear.
> Therefore I print; nor vain my types shall be:
> Heaven, Earth & Hell henceforth shall live in harmony.

[1] All the words on this plate here printed in italic have been partially erased from the copper together with others which cannot be recovered.

Of the Measure in which
the following Poem is written.

We who dwell on Earth can do nothing of ourselves; every thing is
conducted by Spirits, no less than Digestion or Sleep. *I fear the best
. . . in Jesus whom we . . .* When this Verse was first dictated to me,
I consider'd a Monotonous Cadence, like that used by Milton & Shakespeare & all writers of English Blank Verse, derived from the modern
bondage of Rhyming, to be a necessary and indispensible part of Verse.
But I soon found that in the mouth of a true Orator such monotony was
not only awkward, but as much a bondage as rhyme itself. I therefore
have produced a variety in every line, both of cadences & number of syllables. Every word and every letter is studied and put into its fit place;
the terrific numbers are reserved for the terrific parts, the mild & gentle
for the mild & gentle parts, and the prosaic for inferior parts; all are
necessary to each other. Poetry Fetter'd Fetters the Human Race. Nations are Destroy'd or Flourish in proportion as Their Poetry, Painting
and Music are Destroy'd or Flourish! The Primeval State of Man was
Wisdom, Art and Science.

4

Μονος ὁ Ιεσους

JERUSALEM

CHAPTER I

OF the Sleep of Ulro! and of the passage through
Eternal Death! and of the awaking to Eternal Life.

This theme calls me in sleep night after night, & ev'ry morn
Awakes me at sun-rise; then I see the Saviour over me
Spreading his beams of love & dictating the words of this mild song.

"Awake! awake O sleeper of the land of shadows, wake! expand!
I am in you and you in me, mutual in love divine:
Fibres of love from man to man thro' Albion's pleasant land.
In all the dark Atlantic vale down from the hills of Surrey
A black water accumulates; return Albion! return!
Thy brethren call thee, and thy fathers and thy sons,
Thy nurses and thy mothers, thy sisters and thy daughters
Weep at thy soul's disease, and the Divine Vision is darken'd,

Thy Emanation that was wont to play before thy face,
Beaming forth with her daughters into the Divine bosom:

"Where hast thou hidden thy Emanation, lovely Jerusalem,
From the vision and fruition of the Holy-one?
I am not a God afar off, I am a brother and friend:
Within your bosoms I reside, and you reside in me:
Lo! we are One, forgiving all Evil, Not seeking recompense.
Ye are my members, O ye sleepers of Beulah, land of shades!"

But the perturbed Man away turns down the valleys dark:
"Phantom of the over heated brain! shadow of immortality!
Seeking to keep my soul a victim to thy Love! which binds
Man, the enemy of man, into deceitful friendships,
Jerusalem is not! her daughters are indefinite:
By demonstration man alone can live, and not by faith.
My mountains are my own, and I will keep them to myself:
The Malvern and the Cheviot, the Wolds, Plinlimmon & Snowdon
Are mine: here will I build my Laws of Moral Virtue.
Humanity shall be no more, but war & princedom & victory!"

So spoke Albion in jealous fears, hiding his Emanation
Upon the Thames and Medway, rivers of Beulah, dissembling
His jealousy before the throne divine, darkening, cold!

5

The banks of the Thames are clouded! the ancient porches of Albion are
Darken'd! they are drawn thro' unbounded space, scatter'd upon
The Void in incoherent despair! Cambridge & Oxford & London
Are driven among the starry Wheels, rent away and dissipated
In Chasms & Abysses of sorrow, enlarg'd without dimension, terrible.
Albion's mountains run with blood, the cries of war & of tumult
Resound into the unbounded night, every Human perfection
Of mountain & river & city are small & wither'd & darken'd.
Cam is a little stream! Ely is almost swallow'd up!
Lincoln & Norwich stand trembling on the brink of Udan-Adan!
Wales and Scotland shrink themselves to the west and to the north!
Mourning for fear of the warriors in the Vale of Entuthon-Benython
Jerusalem is scatter'd abroad like a cloud of smoke thro' non-entity.
Moab & Ammon & Amalek & Canaan & Egypt & Aram
Recieve her little-ones for sacrifices and the delights of cruelty.

Trembling I sit day and night, my friends are astonish'd at me,
Yet they forgive my wanderings. I rest not from my great task!
To open the Eternal Worlds, to open the immortal Eyes
Of Man inwards into the Worlds of Thought, into Eternity
Ever expanding in the Bosom of God, the Human Imagination.
O Saviour pour upon me thy Spirit of meekness & love!
Annihilate the Selfhood in me: be thou all my life!
Guide thou my hand, which trembles exceedingly upon the rock of ages,
While I write of the building of Golgonooza, & of the terrors of Entuthon,
Of Hand & Hyle & Coban, of Kwantok, Peachey, Brereton, Slayd &
    Hutton,
Of the terrible sons & daughters of Albion, and their Generations.

Scofield, Kox, Kotope and Bowen revolve most mightily upon
The Furnace of Los; before the eastern gate bending their fury
They war to destroy the Furnaces, to desolate Golgonooza,
And to devour the Sleeping Humanity of Albion in rage & hunger.
They revolve into the Furnaces Southward & are driven forth Northward,
Divided into Male and Female forms time after time.
From these Twelve all the Families of England spread abroad.

The Male is a Furnace of beryll; the Female is a golden Loom.
I behold them, and their rushing fires overwhelm my Soul
In London's darkness, and my tears fall day and night
Upon the Emanations of Albion's Sons, the Daughters of Albion,
Names anciently remember'd, but now contemn'd as fictions
Although in every bosom they controll our Vegetative powers.

These are united into Tirzah and her Sisters on Mount Gilead,
Cambel & Gwendolen & Conwenna & Cordella & Ignoge.
And these united into Rahab in the Covering Cherub on Euphrates,
Gwiniverra & Gwinefred & Gonorill & Sabrina beautiful,
Estrild, Mehetabel & Ragan, lovely Daughters of Albion,
They are the beautiful Emanations of the Twelve Sons of Albion.

The Starry Wheels revolv'd heavily over the Furnaces,
Drawing Jerusalem in anguish of maternal love
Eastward, a pillar of cloud with Vala upon the mountains
Howling in pain, redounding from the arms of Beulah's Daughters!
Out from the Furnaces of Los above the head of Los.
A pillar of smoke writhing afar into Non-Entity, redounding
Till the cloud reaches afar outstretch'd among the starry Wheels
Which revolve heavily in the mighty Void above the Furnaces.

O what avail the loves & tears of Beulah's lovely Daughters!
They hold the Immortal Form in gentle bands & tender tears,
But all within is open'd into the deeps of Entuthon Benython,
A dark and unknown night, indefinite, unmeasurable, without end,
Abstract Philosophy warring in enmity against Imagination
(Which is the Divine Body of the Lord Jesus, blessed for ever),
And there Jerusalem wanders with Vala upon the mountains.
Attracted by the revolutions of those Wheels, the Cloud of smoke
Immense and Jerusalem & Vala weeping in the Cloud
Wander away into the Chaotic Void, lamenting with her Shadow
Among the Daughters of Albion, among the Starry Wheels,
Lamenting for her children, for the sons & daughters of Albion.

Los heard her lamentations in the deeps afar! his tears fall
Incessant before the Furnaces, and his Emanation divided in pain
Eastward toward the Starry Wheels. But Westward, a black Horror,

6

His Spectre driv'n by the Starry Wheels of Albion's sons, black and
Opake divided from his back; he labours and he mourns!

For as his Emanation divided, his Spectre also divided
In terror of those starry wheels: and the Spectre stood over Los
Howling in pain, a black'ning Shadow, black'ning dark & opake,
Cursing the terrible Los, bitterly cursing him for his friendship
To Albion, suggesting murderous thoughts against Albion.

Los rag'd and stamp'd the earth in his might & terrible wrath!
He stood and stamp'd the earth; then he threw down his hammer in
    rage &
In fury; then he sat down and wept, terrified! Then arose
And chaunted his song, labouring with the tongs and hammer;
But still the Spectre divided, and still his pain increas'd!

In pain the Spectre divided, in pain of hunger and thirst
To devour Los's Human Perfection; but when he saw that Los

7

Was living, panting like a frighted wolf and howling
He stood over the Immortal in the solitude and darkness
Upon the dark'ning Thames, across the whole Island westward,
A horrible Shadow of Death among the Furnaces beneath

The pillar of folding smoke; and he sought by other means
To lure Los, by tears, by arguments of science & by terrors,
Terrors in every Nerve, by spasms & extended pains,
While Los answer'd unterrified to the opake blackening Fiend.

And thus the Spectre spoke: "Wilt thou still go on to destruction?
Till thy life is all taken away by this deceitful Friendship?
He drinks thee up like water, like wine he pours thee
Into his tuns; thy Daughters are trodden in his vintage.
He makes thy Sons the trampling of his bulls, they are plow'd.
And harrow'd for his profit; lo! thy stolen Emanation
Is his garden of pleasure! all the Spectres of his Sons mock thee;
Look how they scorn thy once admired palaces, now in ruins
Because of Albion! because of deceit and friendship! For Lo!
Hand has peopled Babel & Nineveh: Hyle, Ashur & Aram:
Coban's son is Nimrod: his son Cush is adjoin'd to Aram
By the Daughter of Babel in a woven mantle of pestilence & war.
They put forth their spectrous cloudy sails which drive their immense
Constellations over the deadly deeps of indefinite Udan-Adan.
Kox is the Father of Shem & Ham & Japheth, he is the Noah
Of the Flood of Udan-Adan: Hut'n is the Father of the Seven
From Enoch to Adam: Schofield is Adam who was New-
Created in Edom. I saw it indignant, & thou are not moved!
This has divided thee in sunder, and wilt thou still forgive?
O! thou seest not what I see, what is done in the Furnaces.
Listen, I will tell thee what is done in moments to thee unknown:
Luvah was cast into the Furnaces of affliction and sealed,
And Vala fed in cruel delight the Furnaces with fire.
Stern Urizen beheld, urg'd by necessity to keep
The evil day afar, and if perchance with iron power
He might avert his own despair, in woe & fear he saw
Vala incircle round the Furnaces where Luvah was clos'd.
With joy she heard his howlings & forgot he was her Luvah,
With whom she liv'd in bliss in times of innocence & youth.
Vala comes from the Furnace in a cloud, but wretched Luvah
Is howling in the Furnaces, in flames among Albion's Spectres,
To prepare the Spectre of Albion to reign over thee, O Los,
Forming the Spectres of Albion according to his rage:
To prepare the Spectre sons of Adam, who is Scofield, the Ninth
Of Albion's sons & the father of all his brethren in the Shadowy
Generation. Cambel & Gwendolen wove webs of war & of
Religion to involve all Albion's sons, and when they had

Involv'd Eight, their webs roll'd outwards into darkness,
And Scofield the Ninth remain'd on the outside of the Eight,
And Kox, Kotope & Bowen, One in him, a Fourfold Wonder,
Involv'd the Eight. Such are the Generations of the Giant Albion,
To separate a Law of Sin, to punish thee in thy members."

Los answer'd: "Altho' I know not this, I know far worse than this:
I know that Albion hath divided me, and that thou, O my Spectre,
Hast just cause to be irritated; but look stedfastly upon me;
Comfort thyself in my strength; the time will arrive
When all Albion's injuries shall cease, and when we shall
Embrace him, tenfold bright, rising from his tomb in immortality.
They have divided themselves by Wrath, they must be united by
Pity; let us therefore take example & warning, O my Spectre.
O that I could abstain from wrath! O that the Lamb
Of God would look upon me and pity me in my fury,
In anguish of regeneration, in terrors of self annihilation!
Pity must join together those whom wrath has torn in sunder,
And the Religion of Generation, which was meant for the destruction
Of Jerusalem, become her covering till the time of the End.
O holy Generation, Image of regeneration!
O point of mutual forgiveness between Enemies!
Birthplace of the Lamb of God incomprehensible!
The Dead despise & scorn thee & cast thee out as accursed,
Seeing the Lamb of God in thy gardens & thy palaces
Where they desire to place the Abomination of Desolation.
Hand sits before his furnace: scorn of others & furious pride
Freeze round him to bars of steel & to iron rocks beneath
His feet; indignant self-righteousness like whirlwinds of the north

8

"Rose up against me thundering, from the Brook of Albion's River,
From Ranelagh & Strumbolo, from Cromwell's gardens & Chelsea,
The place of wounded Soldiers; but when he saw my Mace
Whirl'd round from heaven to earth, trembling he sat: his cold
Poisons rose up, & his sweet deceits cover'd them all over
With a tender cloud. As thou art now, such was he, O Spectre.
I know thy deceit & thy revenges, and unless thou desist
I will certainly create an eternal Hell for thee. Listen!
Be attentive! be obedient! Lo, the Furnaces are ready to recieve thee!
I will break thee into shivers & melt thee in the furnaces of death.
I will cast thee into forms of abhorrence & torment if thou

Desist not from thine own will & obey not my stern command.
I am clos'd up from my children: my Emanation is dividing,
And thou my Spectre art divided against me. But mark,
I will compell thee to assist me in my terrible labours: To beat
These hypocritic Selfhoods on the Anvils of bitter Death.
I am inspired. I act not for myself; for Albion's sake
I now am what I am! a horror and an astonishment,
Shudd'ring the heavens to look upon me. Behold what cruelties
Are practised in Babel & Shinar, & have approached to Zion's Hill."

While Los spoke the terrible Spectre fell shudd'ring before him,
Watching his time with glowing eyes to leap upon his prey.
Los open'd the Furnaces in fear, the Spectre saw to Babel & Shinar
Across all Europe & Asia, he saw the tortures of the Victims.
He saw now from the outside what he before saw & felt from within;
He saw that Los was the sole, uncontroll'd Lord of the Furnaces.
Groaning he kneel'd before Los's iron-shod feet on London Stone,
Hung'ring & thirsting for Los's life, yet pretending obedience,
While Los pursu'd his speech in threat'nings loud & fierce:

"Thou art my Pride & Self-righteousness: I have found thee out.
Thou art reveal'd before me in all thy magnitude & power.
Thy Uncircumcised pretences to Chastity must be cut in sunder.
Thy holy wrath & deep deceit cannot avail against me,
Nor shalt thou ever assume the triple-form of Albion's Spectre,
For I am one of the living: dare not to mock my inspired fury.
If thou wast cast forth from my life, if I was dead upon the mountains,
Thou mightest be pitied & lov'd; but now I am living, unless
Thou abstain ravening I will create an eternal Hell for thee.
Take thou this Hammer & in patience heave the thundering Bellows;
Take thou these Tongs, strike thou alternate with me, labour obedient.
Hand & Hyle & Koban, Skofeld, Kox & Kotope labour mightily
In the Wars of Babel & Shinar; all their Emanations were
Condens'd. Hand has absorb'd all his Brethren in his might;
All the infant Loves & Graces were lost, for the mighty Hand

9

"Condens'd his Emanations into hard opake substances,
And his infant thoughts & desires into cold dark cliffs of death.
His hammer of gold he siez'd, and his anvil of adamant;
He siez'd the bars of condens'd thoughts to forge them

Into the sword of war, into the bow and arrow,
Into the thundering cannon and into the murdering gun.
I saw the limbs form'd for exercise, contemn'd, & the beauty of
Eternity look'd upon as deformity, & loveliness as a dry tree.
I saw disease forming a Body of Death around the Lamb
Of God to destroy Jerusalem & to devour the body of Albion,
By war and stratagem to win the labour of the husbandman.
Awkwardness arm'd in steel, folly in a helmet of gold,
Weakness with horns & talons, ignorance with a rav'ning beak,
Every Emanative joy forbidden as a Crime
And the Emanations buried alive in the earth with pomp of religion,
Inspiration deny'd, Genius forbidden by laws of punishment,
I saw terrified. I took the sighs & tears & bitter groans,
I lifted them into my Furnaces to form the spiritual sword
That lays open the hidden heart. I drew forth the pang
Of sorrow red hot: I work'd it on my resolute anvil:
I heated it in the flames of Hand & Hyle & Coban
Nine times. Gwendolen & Cambel & Gwineverra

"Are melted into the gold, the silver, the liquid ruby,
The crysolite, the topaz, the jacinth & every precious stone.
Loud roar my Furnaces and loud my hammer is heard.
I labour day and night. I behold the soft affections
Condense beneath my hammer into forms of cruelty,
But still I labour in hope, tho' still my tears flow down:
That he who will not defend Truth may be compell'd to defend
A Lie: that he may be snared and caught and snared and taken:
That Enthusiasm and Life may not cease; arise Spectre, arise!"

Thus they contended among the Furnaces with groans & tears.
Groaning the Spectre heav'd the billows, obeying Los's frowns,
Till the Spaces of Erin were perfected in the furnaces
Of affliction and Los drew them forth, compelling the harsh Spectre

10

Into the Furnaces & into the valleys of the Anvils of Death
And into the mountains of the Anvils & of the heavy Hammers,
Till he should bring the Sons & Daughters of Jerusalem to be
The Sons & Daughters of Los, that he might protect them from
Albion's dread Spectres; storming, loud, thunderous & mighty
The Bellows & the Hammers move compell'd by Los's hand.

And this is the manner of the Sons of Albion in their strength:
They take the Two Contraries which are call'd Qualities, with which
Every Substance is clothed: they name them Good & Evil
From them they make an Abstract, which is a Negation
Not only of the Substance from which it is derived,
A murderer of its own Body, but also a murderer
Of every Divine Member: it is the Reasoning Power,
An Abstract objecting power that Negatives every thing.
This is the Spectre of Man, the Holy Reasoning Power,
And in its Holiness is closed the Abomination of Desolation.

Therefore Los stands in London building Golgonooza,
Compelling his Spectre to labours mighty; trembling in fear
The Spectre weeps, but Los unmov'd by tears or threats remains.

"I must Create a System or be enslav'd by another Man's.
I will not Reason & Compare: my business is to Create."

So Los in fury & strength, in indignation & burning wrath.
Shudd'ring the Spectre howls, his howlings terrify the night,
He stamps around the Anvil, beating blows of stern despair,
He curses Heaven & Earth, Day & Night & Sun & Moon,
He curses Forest, Spring & River, Desart & sandy Waste,
Cities & Nations, Families & Peoples, Tongues & Laws,
Driven to desperation by Los's terrors & threatening fears.

Los cries, "Obey my voice & never deviate from my will
And I will be merciful to thee! be thou invisible to all
To whom I make thee invisible, but chief to my own Children.
O Spectre of Urthona! Reason not against their dear approach
Nor them obstruct with thy temptations of doubt & despair.
O Shame, O strong & mighty Shame, I break thy brazen fetters!
If thou refuse, thy present torments will seem southern breezes
To what thou shalt endure if thou obey not my great will."

The Spectre answer'd: "Art thou not asham'd of those thy Sins
That thou callest thy Children? lo, the Law of God commands
That they be offered upon his Altar! O cruelty & torment,
For thine are also mine! I have kept silent hitherto
Concerning my chief delight, but thou hast broken silence.
Now I will speak my mind! Where is my lovely Enitharmon?
O thou my enemy, where is my Great Sin? She is also thine.

I said: now is my grief at worst, incapable of being
Surpassed; but every moment it accumulates more & more,
It continues accumulating to eternity; the joys of God advance,
For he is Righteous, he is not a Being of Pity & Compassion,
He cannot feel Distress, he feeds on Sacrifice & Offering,
Delighting in cries & tears & clothed in holiness & solitude;
But my griefs advance also, for ever & ever without end.
O that I could cease to be! Despair! I am Despair,
Created to be the great example of horror & agony; also my
Prayer is vain. I called for compassion; compassion mock'd;
Mercy & pity threw the grave stone over me, & with lead
And iron bound it over me for ever. Life lives on my
Consuming, & the Almighty hath made me his Contrary
To be all evil, all reversed & for ever dead, knowing
And seeing life, yet living not; how can I then behold
And not tremble? how can I be beheld & not abhorr'd?"

So spoke the Spectre shudd'ring, & dark tears ran down his shadowy face,
Which Los wiped off, but comfort none could give, or beam of hope.
Yet ceas'd he not from labouring at the roarings of his Forge,
With iron & brass Building Golgonooza in great contendings,
Till his Sons & Daughters came forth from the Furnaces
At the sublime Labours: for Los compell'd the invisible Spectre

11

To labours mighty with vast strength, with his mighty chains,
In pulsations of time, & extensions of space like Urns of Beulah,
With great labour upon his anvils, & in his ladles the Ore
He lifted, pouring it into the clay ground prepar'd with art,
Striving with Systems to deliver Individuals from those Systems,
That whenever any Spectre began to devour the Dead,
He might feel the pain as if a man gnaw'd his own tender nerves.

Then Erin came forth from the Furnaces, & all the Daughters of Beulah
Came from the Furnaces, by Los's mighty power for Jerusalem's
Sake, walking up and down among the Spaces of Erin.
And the Sons and Daughters of Los came forth in perfection lovely,
And the Spaces of Erin reach'd from the starry heighth to the starry
    depth.

Los wept with exceeding joy & all wept with joy together.
They fear'd they never more should see their Father who
Was built in from Eternity in the Cliffs of Albion.

But when the joy of meeting was exhausted in loving embrace,
Again they lament: "O what shall we do for lovely Jerusalem
To protect the Emanations of Albion's mighty ones from cruelty?
Sabrina & Ignoge begin to sharpen their beamy spears
Of light and love; their little children stand with arrows of gold.
Ragan is wholly cruel, Scofield is bound in iron armour,
He is like a mandrake in the earth before Reuben's gate,
He shoots beneath Jerusalem's walls to undermine her foundations
Vala is but thy shadow, O thou loveliest among women!
A shadow animated by thy tears, O mournful Jerusalem!

12

"Why wilt thou give to her a Body whose life is but a Shade?
Her joy and love, a shade, a shade of sweet repose:
But animated and vegetated she is a devouring worm,
What shall we do for thee, O lovely mild Jerusalem?"

And Los said, "I behold the finger of God in terrors!
Albion is dead! his Emanation is divided from him!
But I am living! yet I feel my Emanation also dividing.
Such thing was never known! O pity me, thou all-piteous-one!
What shall I do, or how exist, divided from Enitharmon?
Yet why despair? I saw the finger of God go forth
Upon my Furnaces from within the Wheels of Albion's Sons,
Fixing their Systems permanent, by mathematic power
Giving a body to Falsehood that it may be cast off for ever,
With Demonstrative Science piercing Apollyon with his own bow
God is within & without: he is even in the depths of Hell!"

Such were the lamentations of the Labourers in the Furnaces.

And they appear'd within & without, incircling on both sides
The Starry Wheels of Albion's Sons, with Spaces for Jerusalem
And for Vala the shadow of Jerusalem, the ever mourning Shade,
On both sides, within & without beaming gloriously.

Terrified at the sublime Wonder, Los stood before his Furnaces.
And they stood around, terrified with admiration at Erin's Spaces,
For the Spaces reach'd from the starry heighth to the starry depth:
And they builded Golgonooza: terrible eternal labour!

What are those golden builders doing? where was the burying-place
Of soft Ethinthus? near Tyburn's fatal Tree? is that
Mild Zion's hill's most ancient promontory, near mournful
Ever weeping Paddington? is that Calvary and Golgotha
Becoming a building of pity and compassion? Lo!
The stones are pity, and the bricks, well wrought affections
Enamel'd with love & kindness, & the tiles engraven gold,
Labour of merciful hands: the beams & rafters are forgiveness:
The mortar & cement of the work, tears of honesty: the nails
And the screws & iron braces are well wrought blandishments
And well contrived words, firm fixing, never forgotten,
Always comforting the remembrance: the floors, humility:
The cielings, devotion: the hearths, thanksgiving.
Prepare the furniture, O Lambeth, in thy pitying looms,
The curtains, woven tears & sighs wrought into lovely forms
For comfort; there the secret furniture of Jerusalem's chamber
Is wrought. Lambeth! the Bride, the Lamb's Wife, loveth thee.
Thou art one with her & knowest not of self in thy supreme joy.
Go on, builders in hope, tho' Jerusalem wanders far away
Without the gate of Los, among the dark Satanic wheels.

Fourfold the Sons of Los in their divisions, and fourfold
The great City of Golgonooza: fourfold toward the north,
And toward the south fourfold, & fourfold toward the east & west,
Each within other toward the four points: that toward
Eden, and that toward the World of Generation,
And that toward Beulah, and that toward Ulro.
Ulro is the space of the terrible starry wheels of Albion's sons,
But that toward Eden is walled up till time of renovation,
Yet it is perfect in its building, ornaments & perfection.

And the Four Points are thus beheld in Great Eternity:
West, the Circumference: South, the Zenith: North,
The Nadir: East, the Center, unapproachable for ever.
These are the four Faces towards the Four Worlds of Humanity
In every Man. Ezekiel saw them by Chebar's flood.
And the Eyes are the South, and the Nostrils are the East,
And the Tongue is the West, and the Ear is the North.

And the North Gate of Golgonooza, toward Generation
Has four sculptur'd Bulls, terrible, before the Gate of iron,
And iron the Bulls; and that which looks towards Ulro,

Clay bak'd & enamel'd, eternal glowing as four furnaces,
Turning upon the Wheels of Albion's sons with enormous power:
And that toward Beulah four, gold, silver, brass & iron;

13

And that toward Eden, four, form'd of gold, silver, brass & iron.

The South, a golden Gate, has four Lions terrible, living:
That toward Generation, four, of iron carv'd wondrous:
That toward Ulro, four, clay bak'd, laborious workmanship:
That toward Eden, four, immortal gold, silver, brass & iron.

The Western Gate fourfold is clos'd, having four Cherubim
Its guards, living, the work of elemental hands, laborious task,
Like Men hermaphroditic, each winged with eight wings.
That toward Generation, iron: that toward Beulah, stone:
That toward Ulro, clay: that toward Eden, metals:
But all clos'd up till the last day, when the graves shall yield their dead.

The Eastern Gate fourfold, terrible & deadly its ornaments,
Taking their forms from the Wheels of Albion's sons, as cogs
Are form'd in a wheel to fit the cogs of the adverse wheel.

That toward Eden, eternal ice frozen in seven folds
Of forms of death: and that toward Beulah, stone,
The seven diseases of the earth are carved terrible:
And that toward Ulro, forms of war, seven enormities:
And that toward Generation, seven generative forms.

And every part of the City is fourfold; & every inhabitant, fourfold.
And every pot & vessel & garment & utensil of the houses,
And every house, fourfold; but the third Gate in every one
Is clos'd as with a threefold curtain of ivory & fine linen & ermine.
And Luban stands in the middle of the City; a moat of fire
Surrounds Luban, Los's Palace & the golden Looms of Cathedron.

And sixty-four thousand Genii guard the Eastern Gate,
And sixty-four thousand Gnomes guard the Northern Gate,
And sixty-four thousand Nymphs guard the Western Gate,
And sixty-four thousand Fairies guard the Southern Gate.

Around Golgonooza lies the land of death eternal, a Land
Of pain and misery and despair and ever brooding melancholy
In all the Twenty-seven Heavens, number'd from Adam to Luther,
From the blue Mundane Shell, reaching to the Vegetative Earth.

The Vegetative Universe opens like a flower from the Earth's center
In which is Eternity. It expands in Stars to the Mundane Shell
And there it meets Eternity again, both within and without,
And the abstract Voids between the Stars are the Satanic Wheels.

There is the Cave, the Rock, the Tree, the Lake of Udan-Adan,
The Forest and the Marsh and the Pits of bitumen deadly,
The Rocks of solid fire, the Ice valleys, the Plains
Of burning sand, the rivers, cataract & Lakes of Fire,
The Islands of the fiery Lakes, the Trees of Malice, Revenge
And black Anxiety, and the Cities of the Salamandrine men,
(But whatever is visible to the Generated Man
Is a Creation of mercy & love from the Satanic Void).
The land of darkness flamed, but no light & no repose:
The land of snows of trembling & of iron hail incessant:
The land of earthquakes, and the land of woven labyrinths:
The land of snares & traps & wheels & pit-falls & dire mills:
The Voids, the Solids, & the land of clouds & regions of waters
With their inhabitants, in the Twenty-seven Heavens beneath Beulah:
Self-righteousness conglomerating against the Divine Vision:
A Concave Earth wondrous, Chasmal, Abysmal, Incoherent,
Forming the Mundane Shell: above, beneath, on all sides surrounding
Golgonooza. Los walks round the walls night and day.

He views the City of Golgonooza & its smaller Cities,
The Looms & Mills & Prisons & Work-houses of Og & Anak,
The Amalekite, the Canaanite, the Moabite, the Egyptian,
And all that has existed in the space of six thousand years,
Permanent & not lost, not lost nor vanish'd, & every little act,
Word, work & wish that has existed, all remaining still
In those Churches ever consuming & ever building by the Spectres
Of all the inhabitants of the Earth wailing to be Created,
Shadowy to those who dwell not in them, meer possibilities,
But to those who enter into them they seem the only substances;
For every thing exists & not one sigh nor smile nor tear,

14

One hair nor particle of dust, not one can pass away.

He views the Cherub at the Tree of Life, also the Serpent
Orc, the first born, coil'd in the south, the Dragon Urizen,
Tharmas the Vegetated Tongue, even the Devouring Tongue,
A threefold region, a false brain, a false heart
And false bowels, altogether composing the False Tongue,
Beneath Beulah as a wat'ry flame revolving every way,
And as dark roots and stems, a Forest of affliction, growing
In seas of sorrow. Los also views the Four Females,
Ahania and Enion and Vala and Enitharmon lovely,
And from them, all the lovely beaming Daughters of Albion.
Ahania & Enion & Vala are three evanescent shades:
Enitharmon is a vegetated mortal Wife of Los,
His Emanation, yet his Wife till the sleep of Death is past.

Such are the Buildings of Los, & such are the Woofs of Enitharmon.

And Los beheld his Sons and he beheld his Daughters,
Every one a translucent Wonder, a Universe within,
Increasing inwards into length and breadth and heighth,
Starry & glorious; and they every one in their bright loins
Have a beautiful golden gate, which opens into the vegetative world;
And every one a gate of rubies & all sorts of precious stones
In their translucent hearts, which opens into the vegetative world;
And every one a gate of iron dreadful and wonderful
In their translucent heads, which opens into the vegetative world;
And every one has the three regions, Childhood, Manhood & Age;
But the gate of the tongue, the western gate, in them is closed,
Having a wall builded against it, and thereby the gates
Eastward & Southward & Northward are incircled with flaming fires.
And the North is Breadth, the South is Heighth & Depth,
The East is Inwards, & the West is Outwards every way.

And Los beheld the mild Emanation, Jerusalem, eastward bending
Her revolutions toward the Starry Wheels in maternal anguish,
Like a pale cloud, arising from the arms of Beulah's Daughters
In Entuthon Benython's deep Vales beneath Golgonooza.

15

And Hand & Hyle rooted into Jerusalem by a fibre
Of strong revenge, & Skofeld Vegetated by Reuben's Gate
In every Nation of the Earth, till the Twelve Sons of Albion
Enrooted into every nation, a mighty Polypus growing
From Albion over the whole Earth: such is my awful Vision.

I see the Four-fold Man, The Humanity in deadly sleep
And its fallen Emanation, The Spectre & its cruel Shadow.
I see the Past, Present & Future existing all at once
Before me. O Divine Spirit, sustain me on thy wings,
That I may awake Albion from his long & cold repose;
For Bacon & Newton, sheath'd in dismal steel, their terrors hang
Like iron scourges over Albion: Reasonings like vast Serpents
Infold around my limbs, bruising my minute articulations.

I turn my eyes to the Schools & Universities of Europe
And there behold the Loom of Locke, whose Woof rages dire,
Wash'd by the Water-wheels of Newton: black the cloth
In heavy wreathes folds over every Nation: cruel Works
Of many Wheels I view, wheel without wheel, with cogs tyrannic
Moving by compulsion each other, not as those in Eden, which,
Wheel within Wheel, in freedom revolve in harmony & peace.

I see in deadly fear in London Los raging round his Anvil
Of death, forming an Ax of gold; the Four Sons of Los
Stand round him cutting the Fibres from Albion's hills
That Albion's Sons may roll apart over the Nations,
While Reuben enroots his brethren in the narrow Canaanite
From the Limit Noah to the Limit Abram, in whose Loins
Reuben in his Twelve-fold majesty & beauty shall take refuge
As Abraham flees from Chaldea shaking his goary locks.
But first Albion must sleep, divided from the Nations.

I see Albion sitting upon his Rock in the first Winter,
And thence I see the Chaos of Satan & the World of Adam
When the Divine Hand went forth on Albion in the mid Winter
And at the place of Death, when Albion sat in Eternal Death
Among the Furnaces of Los in the Valley of the Son of Hinnom.

16

Hampstead, Highgate, Finchley, Hendon, Muswell hill rage loud
Before Bromion's iron Tongs & glowing Poker reddening fierce;
Hertfordshire glows with fierce Vegetation; in the Forests
The Oak frowns terrible, the Beech & Ash & Elm enroot
Among the Spiritual fires; loud the Corn-fields thunder along,
The Soldier's fife, the Harlot's shriek, the Virgin's dismal groan,
The Parent's fear, the Brother's jealousy, the Sister's curse,
Beneath the Storms of Theotormon, & the thund'ring Bellows
Heaves in the hand of Palamabron, who in London's darkness
Before the Anvil watches the bellowing flames: thundering
The Hammer loud rages in Rintrah's strong grasp, swinging loud
Round from heaven to earth, down falling with heavy blow
Dead on the Anvil, where the red hot wedge groans in pain.
He quenches it in the black trough of his Forge: London's River
Feeds the dread Forge, trembling & shuddering along the Valleys.

Humber & Trent roll dreadful before the Seventh Furnace,
And Tweed & Tyne anxious give up their Souls for Albion's sake.
Lincolnshire, Derbyshire, Nottinghamshire, Leicestershire,
From Oxfordshire to Norfolk on the Lake of Udan-Adan,
Labour within the Furnaces, walking among the Fires
With Ladles huge & iron Pokers over the Island white.

Scotland pours out his Sons to labour at the Furnaces;
Wales gives his Daughters to the Looms; England, nursing Mothers
Gives to the Children of Albion & to the Children of Jerusalem.
From the blue Mundane Shell even to the Earth of Vegetation,
Throughout the whole Creation, which groans to be deliver'd,
Albion groans in the deep slumbers of Death upon his Rock.

Here Los fix'd down the Fifty-two Counties of England & Wales,
The Thirty-six of Scotland & the Thirty-four of Ireland,
With mighty power, when they fled out at Jerusalem's Gates
Away from the Conflict of Luvah & Urizen, fixing the Gates
In the Twelve Counties of Wales, & thence Gates looking every way
To the Four Points conduct to England & Scotland & Ireland,
And thence to all the Kingdoms & Nations & Families of the Earth.
The Gate of Reuben in Carmarthenshire: the Gate of Simeon in
Cardiganshire, & the Gate of Levi in Montgomeryshire:
The Gate of Judah, Merionethshire: the Gate of Dan, Flintshire:

The Gate of Napthali, Radnorshire: the Gate of Gad, Pembrokeshire:
The Gate of Asher, Carnarvonshire: the Gate of Issachar, Brecknokshire:
The Gate of Zebulun, in Anglesea & Sodor; so is Wales divided:
The Gate of Joseph, Denbighshire: the Gate of Benjamin, Glamorgan-
    shire:
For the protection of the Twelve Emanations of Albion's Sons.

And the Forty Counties of England are thus divided in the Gates:
Of Reuben: Norfolk, Suffolk, Essex; Simeon: Lincoln, York, Lancashire;
Levi: Middlesex, Kent, Surrey; Judah: Somerset, Glouster, Wiltshire;
Dan: Cornwal, Devon, Dorset; Napthali: Warwick, Leicester, Worcester;
Gad: Oxford, Bucks, Harford; Asher: Sussex, Hampshire, Berkshire;
Issachar: Northampton, Rutland, Nottgham; Zebulun: Bedford, Huntgn,
    Camb;
Joseph: Stafford, Shrops, Heref; Benjamin: Derby, Cheshire, Monmouth;
And Cumberland, Northumberland, Westmoreland & Durham are
Divided in the Gates of Reuben, Judah, Dan & Joseph.

And the Thirty-six Counties of Scotland, divided in the Gates:
Of Reuben: Kincard, Haddntn, Forfar; Simeon: Ayr, Argyll, Banff;
Levi: Edinburgh, Roxbro, Ross; Judah: Aberdeen, Berwik, Dumfries;
Dan: Bute, Caitnes, Clakmanan; Napthali: Nairn, Invernes, Linlithgo;
Gad: Peebles, Perth, Renfru; Asher: Sutherlan, Sterling, Wigtoun;
Issachar: Selkirk, Dumbartn, Glasgo; Zebulun: Orkney, Shetland, Skye;
Joseph: Elgin, Lanerk, Kinros; Benjamin: Kromarty, Murra, Kirku-
    briht;
Governing all by the sweet delights of secret amorous glances
In Enitharmon's Halls builded by Los & his mighty Children.

All things acted on Earth are seen in the bright Sculptures of
Los' Halls, & every Age renews its powers from these Works
With every pathetic story possible to happen from Hate or
Wayward Love; & every sorrow & distress is carved here,
Every Affinity of Parents, Marriages & Friendships are here
In all their various combinations wrought with wondrous Art,
All that can happen to Man in his pilgrimage of seventy years.
Such is the Divine Written Law of Horeb & Sinai,
And such the Holy Gospel of Mount Olivet & Calvary.

17

His Spectre divides & Los in fury compells it to divide,
To labour in the fire, in the water, in the earth, in the air, '
To follow the Daughters of Albion as the hound follows the scent

Of the wild inhabitant of the forest to drive them from his own,
To make a way for the Children of Los to come from the Furnaces.
But Los himself against Albion's Sons his fury bends, for he
Dare not approach the Daughters openly, lest he be consumed
In the fires of their beauty & perfection & be Vegetated beneath
Their Looms in a Generation of death & resurrection to forgetfulness.
They wooe Los continually to subdue his strength; he continually
Shews them his Spectre, sending him abroad over the four points of heaven
In the fierce desires of beauty & in the tortures of repulse. He is
The Spectre of the Living pursuing the Emanations of the Dead.
Shudd'ring they flee: they hide in the Druid Temples in cold chastity,
Subdued by the Spectre of the Living & terrified by the undisguis'd desire.

For Los said: "Tho' my Spectre is divided, as I am a Living Man
I must compell him to obey me wholly, that Enitharmon may not
Be lost, & lest he should devour Enitharmon. Ah me!
Piteous image of my soft desires & loves, O Enitharmon!
I will compell my Spectre to obey. I will restore to thee thy Children.
No one bruises or starves himself to make himself fit for labour!

"Tormented with sweet desire for these beauties of Albion,
They would never love my power if they did not seek to destroy
Enitharmon. Vala would never have sought & loved Albion
If she had not sought to destroy Jerusalem; such is that false
And Generating Love, a pretence of love to destroy love,
Cruel hipocrisy, unlike the lovely delusions of Beulah,
And cruel forms unlike the merciful forms of Beulah's Night.

"They know not why they love nor wherefore they sicken & die,
Calling that Holy Love which is Envy, Revenge & Cruelty,
Which separated the stars from the mountains, the mountains from Man
And left Man, a little grovelling Root outside of Himself.
Negations are not Contraries: Contraries mutually Exist;
But Negations Exist Not. Exceptions & Objections & Unbeliefs
Exist not, nor shall they ever be Organized for ever & ever.
If thou separate from me, thou art a Negation, a meer
Reasoning & Derogation from me, an Objecting & cruel Spite
And Malice & Envy; but my Emanation, Alas! will become
My Contrary. O thou Negation, I will continually compell
Thee to be invisible to any but whom I please, & when
And where & how I please, and never! never! shalt thou be Organized
But as a distorted & reversed Reflexion in the Darkness

And in the Non Entity: nor shall that which is above
Ever descend into thee, but thou shalt be a Non Entity for ever;
And if any enter into thee, thou shall be an Unquenchable Fire,
And he shall be a never dying Worm, mutually tormented by
Those that thou tormentest: a Hell & Despair for ever & ever."

So Los in secret with himself communed, & Enitharmon heard
In her darkness & was comforted; yet still she divided away
In gnawing pain from Los's bosom in the deadly Night;
First as a red Globe of blood trembling beneath his bosom
Suspended over her he hung: he infolded her in his garments
Of wool: he hid her from the Spectre in shame & confusion of
Face, in terrors & pains of Hell & Eternal Death; the
Trembling Globe shot forth Self-living, & Los howl'd over it
Feeding it with his groans & tears, day and night without ceasing:
And the Spectrous Darkness from his back divided in temptations
And in grinding agonies, in threats, stiflings & direful strugglings.

"Go thou to Skofield: ask him if he is Bath or if he is Canterbury.
Tell him to be no more dubious; demand explicit words.
Tell him I will dash him into shivers where & at what time
I please: tell Hand & Skofield they are my ministers of evil
To those I hate, for I can hate also as well as they!"

18

From every-one of the Four Regions of Human Majesty
There is an Outside spread Without & an Outside spread Within,
Beyond the Outline of Identity both ways, which meet in One,
An orbed Void of doubt, despair, hunger & thirst & sorrow.
Here the Twelve Sons of Albion, join'd in dark Assembly,
Jealous of Jerusalem's children, asham'd of her little-ones,
(For Vala produc'd the Bodies, Jerusalem gave the Souls)
Became as Three Immense Wheels turning upon one-another
Into Non-Entity, and their thunders hoarse appall the Dead
To murder their own Souls, to build a Kingdom among the Dead.

"Cast, Cast ye Jerusalem forth! The Shadow of delusions!
The Harlot daughter! Mother of pity and dishonourable forgiveness!
Our Father Albion's sin and shame! But father now no more,
Nor sons, nor hateful peace & love, nor soft complacencies,
With transgressors meeting in brotherhood around the table
Or in the porch or garden. No more the sinful delights

Of age and youth, and boy and girl, and animal and herb,
And river and mountain, and city & village, and house & family,
Beneath the Oak & Palm, beneath the Vine and Fig-tree,
In self-denial!—But War and deadly contention Between
Father and Son, and light and love! All bold asperities
Of Haters met in deadly strife, rending the house & garden,
The unforgiving porches, the tables of enmity, and beds
And chambers of trembling & suspition, hatreds of age & youth,
And boy & girl, & animal & herb, & river & mountain,
And city & village, and house & family, That the Perfect
May live in glory, redeem'd by Sacrifice of the Lamb
And of his children before sinful Jerusalem, to build
Babylon the City of Vala, the Goddess Virgin-Mother.
She is our Mother! Nature! Jerusalem is our Harlot-Sister
Return'd with Children of pollution to defile our House
With Sin and Shame. Cast her into the Potter's field!
Her little-ones She must slay upon our Altars, and her aged
Parents must be carried into captivity: to redeem her Soul,
To be for a Shame & a Curse, and to be our Slave for ever."

So cry Hand & Hyle, the eldest of the fathers of Albion's
Little-ones, to destroy the Divine Saviour, the Friend of Sinners,
Building Castles in desolated places and strong Fortifications.
Soon Hand mightily devour'd & absorb'd Albion's Twelve Sons.
Out from his bosom a mighty Polypus, vegetating in darkness;
And Hyle & Coban were his two chosen ones for Emissaries
In War: forth from his bosom they went and return'd,
Like Wheels from a great Wheel reflected in the Deep.
Hoarse turn'd the Starry Wheels rending a way in Albion's Loins:
Beyond the Night of Beulah, In a dark & unknown Night
Outstretch'd his Giant beauty on the ground in pain & tears:

19

His Children exil'd from his breast pass to and fro before him,
His birds are silent on his hills, flocks die beneath his branches,
His tents are fall'n; his trumpets and the sweet sound of his harp
Are silent on his clouded hills that belch forth storms & fire.
His milk of Cows & honey of Bees & fruit of golden harvest
Is gather'd in the scorching heat & in the driving rain.
Where once he sat, he weary walks in misery and pain,
His Giant beauty and perfection fallen into dust,
Till, from within his wither'd breast, grown narrow with his woes,

The corn is turn'd to thistles & the apples into poison,
The birds of song to murderous crows, his joys to bitter groans,
The voices of children in his tents to cries of helpless infants,
And self-exiled from the face of light & shine of morning,
In the dark world, a narrow house! he wanders up and down
Seeking for rest and finding none! and hidden far within,
His Eon weeping in the cold and desolated Earth.

All his Affections now appear withoutside; all his Sons,
Hand, Hyle & Coban, Guantok, Peachey, Brereton, Slayd & Hutton,
Scofield, Kox, Kotupe & Bowen: his Twelve Sons, Satanic Mill,
Who are the Spectres of the Twenty-four, each Double-form'd,
Revolve upon his mountains groaning in pain beneath
The dark incessant sky, seeking for rest and finding none,
Raging against their Human natures, rav'ning to gormandize
The Human majesty and beauty of the Twenty-four,
Condensing them into solid rocks with cruelty and abhorrence,
Suspition & revenge; & the seven diseases of the Soul
Settled around Albion and around Luvah in his secret cloud.
Willing the Friends endur'd for Albion's sake and for
Jerusalem, his Emanation, shut within his bosom,
Which harden'd against them more and more as he builded onwards
On the Gulph of Death in self-righteousness that roll'd
Before his awful feet, in pride of virtue for victory:
And Los was roof'd in from Eternity in Albion's Cliffs
Which stand upon the ends of Beulah, and withoutside all
Appear'd a rocky form against the Divine Humanity.

Albion's Circumference was clos'd: his Center began dark'ning
Into the Night of Beulah, and the Moon of Beulah rose
Clouded with storms. Los, his strong Guard, walk'd round beneath the
    Moon,
And Albion fled inward among the currents of his rivers.

He found Jerusalem upon the River of his City, soft repos'd
In the arms of Vala, assimilating in one with Vala,
The Lily of Havilah; and they sang soft thro' Lambeth's vales
In a sweet moony night & silence that they had created
With a blue sky spread over with wings and a mild moon,
Dividing & uniting into many female forms, Jerusalem
Trembling; then in one comingling in eternal tears,
Sighing to melt his Giant beauty on the moony river.

20

But when they saw Albion fall'n upon mild Lambeth's vale,
Astonish'd, Terrified, they hover'd over his Giant limbs.
Then thus Jerusalem spoke, while Vala wove the veil of tears,
Weeping in pleadings of Love, in the web of despair:

"Wherefore hast thou shut me into the winter of human life,
And clos'd up the sweet regions of youth and virgin innocence
Where we live forgetting error, not pondering on evil,
Among my lambs & brooks of water, among my warbling birds:
Where we delight in innocence before the face of the Lamb,
Going in and out before him in his love and sweet affection?"

Vala replied weeping & trembling, hiding in her veil:

"When winter rends the hungry family and the snow falls
Upon the ways of men hiding the paths of man and beast,
Then mourns the wanderer: then he repents his wanderings & eyes
The distant forest: then the slave groans in the dungeon of stone,
The captive in the mill of the stranger, sold for scanty hire.
They view their former life: they number moments over and over,
Stringing them on their remembrance as on a thread of sorrow.
Thou art my sister and my daughter: thy shame is mine also:
Ask me not of my griefs! thou knowest all my griefs."

Jerusalem answer'd with soft tears over the valleys:

"O Vala, what is Sin, that thou shudderest and weepest
At sight of thy once lov'd Jerusalem? What is Sin but a little
Error & fault that is soon forgiven? but mercy is not a Sin,
Nor pity nor love nor kind forgiveness. O, if I have Sinned
Forgive & pity me! O, unfold thy Veil in mercy & love!
Slay not my little ones, beloved Virgin daughter of Babylon,
Slay not my infant loves & graces, beautiful daughter of Moab!
I cannot put off the human form. I strive but strive in vain.
When Albion rent thy beautiful net of gold and silver twine,
Thou hadst woven it with art, thou hadst caught me in the bands
Of love, thou refusedst to let me go: Albion beheld thy beauty,
Beautiful thro' our Love's comeliness, beautiful thro' pity.
The Veil shone with thy brightness in the eyes of Albion
Because it inclos'd pity & love, because we lov'd one-another.

Albion lov'd thee: he rent thy Veil: he embrac'd thee: he lov'd thee!
Astonish'd at his beauty & perfection, thou forgavest his furious love.
I redounded from Albion's bosom in my virgin loveliness:
The Lamb of God receiv'd me in his arms, he smil'd upon us:
He made me his Bride & Wife: he gave thee to Albion.
Then was a time of love. O why is it passed away!"

Then Albion broke silence and with groans reply'd:

21

"O Vala! O Jerusalem! do you delight in my groans!
You, O lovely forms, you have prepared my death-cup.
The disease of Shame covers me from head to feet. I have no hope.
Every boil upon my body is a separate & deadly Sin.
Doubt first assail'd me, then Shame took possession of me.
Shame divides Families, Shame hath divided Albion in sunder.
First fled my Sons & then my Daughters, then my Wild Animations,
My Cattle next, last ev'n the Dog of my Gate; the Forests fled,
The Corn-fields & the breathing Gardens outside separated,
The Sea, the Stars, the Sun, the Moon, driv'n forth by my disease.
All is Eternal Death unless you can weave a chaste
Body over an unchaste Mind! Vala! O that thou wert pure!
That the deep wound of Sin might be clos'd up with the Needle
And with the Loom, to cover Gwendolen & Ragan with costly Robes
Of Natural Virtue, for their Spiritual forms without a Veil
Wither in Luvah's Sepulcher. I thrust him from my presence,
And all my Children follow'd his loud howlings into the Deep.
Jerusalem! dissembler Jerusalem! I look into thy bosom:
I discover thy secret places. Cordella! I behold
Thee whom I thought pure as the heavens in innocence & fear,
Thy Tabernacle taken down, thy secret Cherubim disclosed.
Art thou broken? Ah me, Sabrina, running by my side,
In childhood what wert thou? unutterable anguish! Conwenna!
Thy cradled infancy is most piteous. O hide, O hide!
Their secret gardens were made paths to the traveller.
I knew not of their secret loves with those I hated most,
Nor that their every thought was Sin & secret appetite.
Hyle sees in fear, he howls in fury over them. Hand sees
In jealous fear: in stern accusation with cruel stripes
He drives them thro' the Streets of Babylon before my face.
Because they taught Luvah to rise into my clouded heavens,
Battersea and Chelsea mourn for Cambel & Gwendolen.

Hackney and Holloway sicken for Estrild & Ignoge:
Because the Peak, Malvern & Cheviot Reason in Cruelty,
Penmaenmawr & Dhinas-bran Demonstrate in Unbelief,
Manchester & Liverpool are in tortures of Doubt and Despair,
Malden & Colchester Demonstrate. I hear my Children's voices,
I see their piteous faces gleam out upon the cruel winds
From Lincoln & Norwich, from Edinburgh & Monmouth:
I see them distant from my bosom scourg'd along the roads,
Then lost in clouds. I hear their tender voices! clouds divide:
I see them die beneath the whips of the Captains; they are taken
In solemn pomp into Chaldea across the bredths of Europe.
Six months they lie embalm'd in silent death, worshipped,
Carried in Arks of Oak before the armies in the spring.
Bursting their Arks they rise again to life: they play before
The Armies. I hear their loud cymbals & their deadly cries.
Are the Dead cruel? are those who are infolded in moral Law
Revengeful? O that Death & Annihilation were the same!"

Then Vala answer'd spreading her scarlet Veil over Albion:

2 2

"Albion thy fear has made me tremble; thy terrors have surrounded me:
Thy Sons have nail'd me on the Gates, piercing my hands & feet,
Till Skofield's Nimrod, the mighty Huntsman Jehovah, came
With Cush his Son & took me down. He in a golden Ark
Bears me before his Armies, tho' my shadow hovers here.
The flesh of multitudes fed & nourish'd me in my childhood,
My morn & evening food were prepar'd in Battles of Men.
Great is the cry of the Hounds of Nimrod along the Valley
Of Vision, they scent the odor of War in the Valley of Vision.
All Love is lost! terror succeeds, & Hatred instead of Love,
And stern demands of Right & Duty instead of Liberty.
Once thou wast to me the loveliest Son of heaven, but now
Where shall I hide from thy dread countenance & searching eyes?
I have looked into the secret Soul of him I loved,
And in the dark recesses found Sin & can never return."

Albion again utter'd his voice beneath the silent Moon:

"I brought Love into light of day, to pride in chaste beauty,
I brought Love into light, & fancied Innocence is no more."

Then spoke Jerusalem: "O Albion! my Father Albion!
Why wilt thou number every little fibre of my Soul,
Spreading them out before the Sun like stalks of flax to dry?
The Infant Joy is beautiful, but its anatomy
Horrible, ghast & deadly! nought shall thou find in it
But dark despair & everlasting brooding melancholy!"

Then Albion turn'd his face toward Jerusalem & spoke:

"Hide thou, Jerusalem, in impalpable voidness, not to be
Touch'd by the hand nor seen with the eye. O Jerusalem,
Would thou wert not & that thy place might never be found!
But come, O Vala, with knife & cup, drain my blood
To the last drop, then hide me in thy Scarlet Tabernacle;
For I see Luvah whom I slew, I behold him in my Spectre
As I behold Jerusalem in thee, O Vala, dark and cold."

Jerusalem then stretch'd her hand toward the Moon & spoke:

"Why should Punishment Weave the Veil with Iron Wheels of War
When Forgiveness might it Weave with Wings of Cherubim?"

Loud groan'd Albion from mountain to mountain & replied:

23

"Jerusalem! Jerusalem! deluding shadow of Albion!
Daughter of my phantasy! unlawful pleasure! Albion's curse!
I came here with intention to annihilate thee, But
My soul is melted away, inwoven within the Veil.
Hast thou again knitted the Veil of Vala which I for thee
Pitying rent in ancient times? I see it whole and more
Perfect and shining with beauty" "But thou! O wretched Father?"

Jerusalem reply'd, like a voice heard from a sepulcher,
"Father once piteous! Is Pity a Sin? Embalm'd in Vala's bosom
In an Eternal Death for Albion's sake, our best beloved,
Thou art my Father & my Brother. Why hast thou hidden me
Remote from the divine Vision my Lord and Saviour?"

Trembling stood Albion at her words in jealous dark despair;
He felt that Love and Pity are the same, a soft repose,
Inward complacency of Soul, a Self-annihilation.

"I have erred! I am ashamed! and will never return more.
I have taught my children sacrifices of cruelty: what shall I answer?
I will hide it from Eternals! I will give myself for my Children!
Which way soever I turn, I behold Humanity and Pity!"

He recoil'd: he rush'd outwards: he bore the Veil whole away.
His fires redound from his Dragon Altars in Errors returning.
He drew the Veil of Moral Virtue, woven for Cruel Laws,
And cast it into the Atlantic Deep to catch the Souls of the Dead.
He stood between the Palm tree & the Oak of weeping
Which stand upon the edge of Beulah, and there Albion sunk
Down in sick pallid languor. These were his last words, relapsing
Hoarse from his rocks, from caverns of Derbyshire & Wales
And Scotland, utter'd from the Circumference into Eternity:

"Blasphemous Sons of Feminine delusion! God in the dreary Void
Dwells from Eternity, wide separated from the Human Soul.
But thou, deluding Image, by whom imbu'd the Veil I rent,
Lo, here is Vala's Veil whole, for a Law, a Terror & a Curse!
And therefore God takes vengeance on me: from my clay-cold bosom
My children wander, trembling victims of his Moral Justice:
His snows fall on me and cover me, while in the Veil I fold
My dying limbs. Therefore O Manhood, if thou art aught
But a meer Phantasy, hear dying Albion's Curse!
May God, who dwells in the dark Ulro & voidness, vengeance take,
And draw thee down into this Abyss of sorrow and torture,
Like me thy Victim. O that Death & Annihilation were the same!

24

"What have I said? What have I done? O all-powerful Human Words!
You recoil back upon me in the blood of the Lamb slain in his Children.
Two bleeding Contraries, equally true, are his Witnesses against me.
We reared mighty Stones, we danced naked around them,
Thinking to bring Love into light of day, to Jerusalem's shame
Displaying our Giant limbs to all the winds of heaven. Sudden
Shame siez'd us, we could not look on one-another for abhorrence: the
    Blue
Of our immortal Veins & all their Hosts fled from our Limbs
And wander'd distant in a dismal Night clouded & dark.
The Sun fled from the Briton's forehead, the Moon from his mighty loins,
Scandinavia fled with all his mountains fill'd with groans.

"O what is Life & what is Man? O what is Death? Wherefore
Are you, my Children, natives in the Grave to where I go?
Or are you born to feed the hungry ravenings of Destruction,
To be the sport of Accident, to waste in Wrath & Love a weary
Life, in brooding cares & anxious labours that prove but chaff?
O Jerusalem, Jerusalem, I have forsaken thy Courts,
Thy Pillars of ivory & gold, thy Curtains of silk & fine
Linen, thy Pavements of precious stones, thy Walls of pearl
And gold, thy Gates of Thanksgiving, thy Windows of Praise,
Thy Clouds of Blessing, thy Cherubims of Tender-mercy
Stretching their Wings sublime over the Little-ones of Albion!
O Human Imagination, O Divine Body I have Crucified,
I have turned my back upon thee into the Wastes of Moral Law.
There Babylon is builded in the Waste, founded in Human desolation.
O Babylon, thy Watchman stands over thee in the night,
Thy severe Judge all the day long proves thee, O Babylon,
With provings of destruction, with giving thee thy heart's desire;
But Albion is cast forth to the Potter, his Children to the Builders
To build Babylon because they have forsaken Jerusalem.
The Walls of Babylon are Souls of Men, her Gates the Groans
Of Nations, her Towers are the Miseries of once happy Families,
Her Streets are paved with Destruction, her Houses built with Death,
Her Palaces with Hell & the Grave, her Synagogues with Torments
Of ever-hardening Despair, squar'd & polish'd with cruel skill.
Yet thou wast lovely as the summer cloud upon my hills
When Jerusalem was thy heart's desire, in times of youth & love.
Thy Sons came to Jerusalem with gifts; she sent them away
With blessings on their hands & on their feet, blessings of gold
And pearl & diamond: thy Daughters sang in her Courts.
They came up to Jerusalem: they walked before Albion:
In the Exchanges of London every Nation walk'd,
And London walk'd in every Nation, mutual in love & harmony.
Albion cover'd the whole Earth, England encompass'd the Nations,
Mutual each within other's bosom in Visions of Regeneration.
Jerusalem cover'd the Atlantic Mountains & the Erythrean
From bright Japan & China to Hesperia, France & England.
Mount Zion lifted his head in every Nation under heaven,
And the Mount of Olives was beheld over the whole Earth.
The footsteps of the Lamb of God were there; but now no more,
No more shall I behold him; he is clos'd in Luvah's Sepulcher.
Yet why these smitings of Luvah, the gentlest mildest Zoa?
If God was Merciful, this could not be. O Lamb of God,

Thou art a delusion and Jerusalem is my Sin! O my Children,
I have educated you in the crucifying cruelties of Demonstration
Till you have assum'd the Providence of God & slain your Father.
Dost thou appear before me, who liest dead in Luvah's Sepulcher?
Dost thou forgive me, thou who wast Dead & art Alive?
Look not so merciful upon me, O thou Slain Lamb of God!
I die! I die in thy arms, tho' Hope is banish'd from me."

Thund'ring the Veil rushes from his hand, Vegetating Knot by
Knot, Day by Day, Night by Night; loud roll the indignant Atlantic
Waves & the Erythrean, turning up the bottoms of the Deeps.

25

And there was heard a great lamenting in Beulah; all the Regions
Of Beulah were moved as the tender bowels are moved, and they said:

"Why did you take Vengeance, O ye Sons of the mighty Albion,
Planting these Oaken Groves, Erecting these Dragon Temples?
Injury the Lord heals, but Vengeance cannot be healed.
As the Sons of Albion have done to Luvah, so they have in him
Done to the Divine Lord & Saviour, who suffers with those that suffer;
For not one sparrow can suffer & the whole Universe not suffer also
In all its Regions, & its Father & Saviour not pity and weep.
But Vengeance is the destroyer of Grace & Repentance in the bosom
Of the Injurer, in which the Divine Lamb is cruelly slain.
Descend, O Lamb of God, & take away the imputation of Sin
By the Creation of States & the deliverance of Individuals Evermore.
    Amen."

Thus wept they in Beulah over the Four Regions of Albion;
But many doubted & despair'd & imputed Sin & Righteousness
To Individuals & not to States, and these Slept in Ulro.

END OF CHAPTER I

27

TO THE JEWS

JERUSALEM the Emanation of the Giant Albion! Can it be? Is it a
Truth that the Learned have explored? Was Britain the Primitive Seat
of the Patriarchal Religion? If it is true, my title-page is also True, that

Jerusalem was & is the Emanation of the Giant Albion. It is True and cannot be controverted. Ye are united, O ye Inhabitants of Earth, in One Religion, The Religion of Jesus, the most Ancient, the Eternal & the Everlasting Gospel. The Wicked will turn it to Wickedness, the Righteous to Righteousness. Amen! Huzza! Selah!

"All things Begin & End in Albion's Ancient Druid Rocky Shore."

Your Ancestors derived their origin from Abraham, Heber, Shem and Noah, who were Druids, as the Druid Temples (which are the Patriarchal Pillars & Oak Groves) over the whole Earth witness to this day.

You have a tradition, that Man anciently contain'd in his mighty limbs all things in Heaven & Earth: this you received from the Druids.

"But now the Starry Heavens are fled from the mighty limbs of Albion."

Albion was the Parent of the Druids, & in his Chaotic State of Sleep, Satan & Adam & the whole World was Created by the Elohim.

> The fields from Islington to Marybone,
> To Primrose Hill and Saint John's Wood,
>   Were builded over with pillars of gold,
> And there Jerusalem's pillars stood.
>
> Her Little-ones ran on the fields,
> The Lamb of God among them seen,
>   And fair Jerusalem his Bride,
> Among the little meadows green.
>
> Pancrass & Kentish-town repose
> Among her golden pillars high,
>   Among her golden arches which
> Shine upon the starry sky.
>
> The Jew's-harp-house & the Green Man,
> The Ponds where Boys to bathe delight,
>   The fields of Cows by Willan's farm,
> Shine in Jerusalem's pleasant sight.
>
> She walks upon our meadows green,
> The Lamb of God walks by her side,
>   And every English Child is seen
> Children of Jesus & his Bride.

Forgiving trespasses and sins
Lest Babylon with Cruel Og
With Moral & Self-righteous Law
Should Crucify in Satan's Synagogue!

What are those golden Builders doing
Near Mournful ever-weeping Paddington,
    Standing above that mighty Ruin
Where Satan the first victory won,

Where Albion slept beneath the Fatal Tree,
And the Druids' golden Knife
    Rioted in human gore,
In Offerings of Human Life?

They groan'd aloud on London Stone
They groan'd aloud on Tyburn's Brook,
    Albion gave his deadly groan,
And all the Atlantic Mountains shook.

Albion's Spectre from his Loins
Tore forth in all the pomp of War:
    Satan his name: in flames of fire
He stretch'd his Druid Pillars far.

Jerusalem fell from Lambeth's Vale
Down thro' Poplar & Old Bow,
    Thro' Malden & across the Sea,
In War & howling, death & woe.

The Rhine was red with human blood,
The Danube roll'd a purple tide,
    On the Euphrates Satan stood,
And over Asia stretch'd his pride.

He wither'd up sweet Zion's Hill
From every Nation of the Earth;
    He wither'd up Jerusalem's Gates,
And in a dark Land gave her birth.

He wither'd up the Human Form
By laws of sacrifice for sin,
    Till it became a Mortal Worm,
But O! translucent all within.

The Divine Vision still was seen,
Still was the Human Form Divine,
Weeping in weak & mortal clay,
O Jesus, still the Form was thine.

And thine the Human Face, & thine
The Human Hands & Feet & Breath,
Entering thro' the Gates of Birth
And passing thro' the Gates of Death.

And O thou Lamb of God, whom I
Slew in my dark self-righteous pride,
Art thou return'd to Albion's Land?
And is Jerusalem thy Bride?

Come to my arms & never more
Depart, but dwell for ever here:
Create my Spirit to thy Love:
Subdue my Spectre to thy Fear.

Spectre of Albion! warlike Fiend!
In clouds of blood & ruin roll'd,
I here reclaim thee as my own,
My Selfhood! Satan! arm'd in gold

Is this thy soft Family-Love,
Thy cruel Patriarchal pride,
Planting thy Family alone,
Destroying all the World beside?

A man's worst enemies are those
Of his own house & family;
And he who makes his law a curse,
By his own law shall surely die.

In my Exchanges every Land
Shall walk, & mine in every Land,
Mutual shall build Jerusalem,
Both heart in heart & hand in hand.

If Humility is Christianity, you, O Jews, are the true Christians. If
your tradition that Man contained in his Limbs all Animals is True, &
they were separated from him by cruel Sacrifices, and when compulsory

cruel Sacrifices had brought Humanity into a Feminine Tabernacle in
the loins of Abraham & David, the Lamb of God, the Saviour became
apparent on Earth as the Prophets had foretold, The Return of Israel is
a Return to Mental Sacrifice & War. Take up the Cross, O Israel, &
follow Jesus.

28

JERUSALEM

CHAPTER 2

E V E R Y ornament of perfection and every labour of love
In all the Garden of Eden & in all the golden mountains
Was become an envied horror and a remembrance of jealousy,
And every Act a Crime, and Albion the punisher & judge.

And Albion spoke from his secret seat and said:

"All these ornaments are crimes, they are made by the labours
Of loves, of unnatural consanguinities and friendships
Horrid to think of when enquired deeply into; and all
These hills & valleys are accursed witnesses of Sin.
I therefore condense them into solid rocks, stedfast,
A foundation and certainty and demonstrative truth,
That Man be separated from Man, & here I plant my seat."

Cold snows drifted around him: ice cover'd his loins around.
He sat by Tyburn's brook, and underneath his heel shot up
A deadly Tree: he nam'd it Moral Virtue and the Law
Of God who dwells in Chaos hidden from the human sight.

The Tree spread over him its cold shadows, (Albion groan'd)
They bent down, they felt the earth, and again enrooting
Shot into many a Tree, an endless labyrinth of woe.

From willing sacrifice of Self, to sacrifice of (miscall'd) Enemies
For Atonement. Albion began to erect twelve Altars
Of rough unhewn rocks, before the Potter's Furnace.
He nam'd them Justice and Truth. And Albion's Sons
Must have become the first Victims, being the first transgressors,
But they fled to the mountains to seek ransom, building A Strong
Fortification against the Divine Humanity and Mercy,
In Shame & Jealousy to annihilate Jerusalem.

29

Then the Divine Vision like a silent Sun appear'd above
Albion's dark rocks, setting behind the Gardens of Kensington
On Tyburn's River in clouds of blood, where was mild Zion Hill's
Most ancient promontory; and in the Sun a Human Form appear'd,
And thus the Voice Divine went forth upon the rocks of Albion:

"I elected Albion for my glory: I gave to him the Nations
Of the whole Earth. He was the Angel of my Presence, and all
The Sons of God were Albion's Sons, and Jerusalem was my joy.
The Reactor hath hid himself thro' envy. I behold him,
But you cannot behold him till he be reveal'd in his System.
Albion's Reactor must have a Place prepar'd. Albion must Sleep
The Sleep of Death till the Man of Sin & Repentance be reveal'd.
Hidden in Albion's Forests he lurks: he admits of no Reply
From Albion, but hath founded his Reaction into a Law
Of Action, for Obedience to destroy the Contraries of Man.
He hath compell'd Albion to become a Punisher & hath possess'd
Himself of Albion's Forests & Wilds, and Jerusalem is taken,
The City of the Woods in the Forest of Ephratah is taken!
London is a stone of her ruins, Oxford is the dust of her walls,
Sussex & Kent are her scatter'd garments, Ireland her holy place,
And the murder'd bodies of her little ones are Scotland and Wales.
The Cities of the Nations are the smoke of her consummation,
The Nations are her dust, ground by the chariot wheels
Of her lordly conquerors, her palaces levell'd with the dust.
I come that I may find a way for my banished ones to return.
Fear not, O little Flock, I come. Albion shall rise again."

So saying, the mild Sun inclos'd the Human Family.

Forthwith from Albion's dark'ning locks came two Immortal forms,
Saying: "We alone are escaped, O merciful Lord and Saviour,
We flee from the interiors of Albion's hills and mountains,
From his Valleys Eastward from Amalek, Canaan & Moab,
Beneath his vast ranges of hills surrounding Jerusalem.

"Albion walk'd on the steps of fire before his Halls,
And Vala walk'd with him in dreams of soft deluding slumber;
He looked up & saw the Prince of Light with splendor faded.
Then Albion ascended mourning into the porches of his Palace,

Above him rose a Shadow from his wearied intellect,
Of living gold, pure, perfect, holy; in white linen pure he hover'd,
A sweet entrancing self-delusion, a wat'ry vision of Albion,
Soft exulting in existence, all the Man absorbing.

"Albion fell upon his face prostrate before the wat'ry Shadow,
Saying: 'O Lord, whence is this change? thou knowest I am nothing!'
And Vala trembled & cover'd her face, & her locks were spread on the
      pavement.

"We heard, astonish'd at the Vision, & our hearts tremble within us;
We heard the voice of slumberous Albion, and thus he spake,
Idolatrous to his own Shadow, words of eternity uttering:

" 'O I am nothing when I enter into judgment with thee!
If thou withdraw thy breath, I die & vanish into Hades;
If thou dost lay thine hand upon me, behold I am silent;
If thou withhold thine hand, I perish like a fallen leaf.
O I am nothing, and to nothing must return again!
If thou withdraw thy breath, Behold, I am oblivion.'

"He ceas'd: the shadowy voice was silent: but the cloud hover'd over their
      heads
In golden wreathes, the sorrow of Man, & the balmy drops fell down.
And lo! that son of Man, that Shadowy Spirit of mild Albion,
Luvah, descended from the cloud; in terror Albion rose:
Indignant rose the awful Man & turn'd his back on Vala.

"We heard the voice of Albion starting from his sleep:

" 'Whence is this voice crying, Enion! that soundeth in my ears?
O cruel pity! O dark deceit! can love seek for dominion?'

"And Luvah strove to gain dominion over Albion:
They strove together above the Body where Vala was inclos'd
And the dark Body of Albion left prostrate upon the crystal pavement,
Cover'd with boils from head to foot, the terrible smitings of Luvah.

"Then frown'd the fallen Man and put forth Luvah from his presence,
Saying, 'Go and Die the Death of Man for Vala the sweet wanderer.
I will turn the volutions of your ears outward, and bend your nostrils
Downward, and your fluxile eyes englob'd roll round in fear;

Your with'ring lips and tongue shrink up into a narrow circle,
Till into narrow forms you creep: go take your fiery way,
And learn what 'tis to absorb the Man, you Spirits of Pity & Love.'

"They heard the voice and fled swift as the winter's setting sun.
And now the human blood foam'd high; the Spirits Luvah & Vala
Went down the Human Heart, where Paradise & its joys abounded,
In jealous fears & fury & rage, & flames roll round their fervid feet,
And the vast form of Nature like a serpent play'd before them.
And as they fled in folding fires & thunders of the deep,
Vala shrunk in like the dark sea that leaves its slimy banks;
And from her bosom Luvah fell far as the east and west,
And the vast form of Nature like a serpent roll'd between,
Whether of Jerusalem's or Vala's ruins congenerated, we know not:
All is confusion, all is tumult, & we alone are escaped."
So spoke the fugitives; they join'd the Divine Family, trembling.

30

And the Two that escaped were the Emanation of Los & his
Spectre; for where ever the Emanation goes, the Spectre
Attends her as her Guard, & Los's Emanation is named
Enitharmon, & his Spectre is named Urthona; they knew
Not where to flee: they had been on a visit to Albion's Children,
And they strove to weave a Shadow of the Emanation
To hide themselves, weeping & lamenting for the Vegetation
Of Albion's Children, fleeing thro' Albion's vales in streams of gore.

Being not irritated by insult, bearing insulting benevolences,
They percieved that corporeal friends are spiritual enemies:
They saw the Sexual Religion in its embryon Uncircumcision,
And the Divine hand was upon them, bearing them thro' darkness
Back safe to their Humanity, as doves to their windows.
Therefore the Sons of Eden praise Urthona's Spectre in Songs,
Because he kept the Divine Vision in time of trouble.

They wept & trembled, & Los put forth his hand & took them in,
Into his Bosom, from which Albion shrunk in dismal pain,
Bending the fibres of Brotherhood & in Feminine Allegories
Inclosing Los; but the Divine Vision appear'd with Los
Following Albion into his Central Void among his Oaks.

And Los prayed and said, "O Divine Saviour, arise
Upon the Mountains of Albion as in ancient time! Behold!
The Cities of Albion seek thy face: London groans in pain

From Hill to Hill, & the Thames laments along the Valleys:
The little Villages of Middlesex & Surrey hunger & thirst:
The Twenty-eight Cities of Albion stretch their hands to thee
Because of the Opressors of Albion in every City & Village.
They mock at the Labourer's limbs: they mock at his starv'd Children:
They buy his Daughters that they may have power to sell his Sons:
They compell the Poor to live upon a crust of bread by soft mild arts:
They reduce the Man to want, then give with pomp & ceremony:
The praise of Jehovah is chaunted from lips of hunger & thirst.
Humanity knows not of Sex: wherefore are Sexes in Beulah?
In Beulah the Female lets down her beautiful Tabernacle
Which the Male enters magnificent between her Cherubim
And becomes One with her, mingling, condensing in Self-love
The Rocky Law of Condemnation & double Generation & Death.
Albion hath enter'd the Loins, the place of the Last Judgment,
And Luvah hath drawn the Curtains around Albion in Vala's bosom.
The Dead awake to Generation! Arise O Lord, & rend the Veil!"

So Los in lamentations follow'd Albion. Albion cover'd

31

His western heaven with rocky clouds of death & despair.

Fearing that Albion should turn his back against the Divine Vision,
Los took his globe of fire to search the interiors of Albion's
Bosom, in all the terrors of friendship entering the caves
Of despair & death to search the tempters out, walking among
Albion's rocks & precipices, caves of solitude & dark despair,
And saw every Minute Particular of Albion degraded & murder'd,
But saw not by whom; they were hidden within in the minute particulars
Of which they had possess'd themselves, and there they take up
The articulations of a man's soul and laughing throw it down
Into the frame, then knock it out upon the plank, & souls are bak'd
In bricks to build the pyramids of Heber & Terah. But Los
Search'd in vain; clos'd from the minutia, he walk'd difficult.
He came down from Highgate thro' Hackney & Holloway towards London
Till he came to old Stratford, & thence to Stepney & the Isle
Of Leutha's Dogs, thence thro' the narrows of the River's side,
And saw every minute particular: the jewels of Albion running down
The kennels of the streets & lanes as if they were abhorr'd:
Every Universal Form was become barren mountains of Moral
Virtue, and every Minute Particular harden'd into grains of sand,

And all the tendernesses of the soul cast forth as filth & mire:
Among the winding places of deep contemplation intricate,
To where the Tower of London frown'd dreadful over Jerusalem,
A building of Luvah, builded in Jerusalem's eastern gate, to be
His secluded Court: thence to Bethlehem, where was builded
Dens of despair in the house of bread, enquiring in vain
Of stones and rocks, he took his way, for human form was none;
And thus he spoke, looking on Albion's City with many tears:

"What shall I do? what could I do if I could find these Criminals?
I could not dare to take vengeance, for all things are so constructed
And builded by the Divine hand that the sinner shall always escape,
And he who takes vengeance alone is the criminal of Providence.
If I should dare to lay my finger on a grain of sand
In way of vengeance, I punish the already punish'd. O whom
Should I pity if I pity not the sinner who is gone astray?
O Albion, if thou takest vengeance, if thou revengest thy wrongs,
Thou art for ever lost! What can I do to hinder the Sons
Of Albion from taking vengeance? or how shall I them perswade?"

So spoke Los, travelling thro' darkness & horrid solitude;
And he beheld Jerusalem in Westminster & Marybone
Among the ruins of the Temple, and Vala who is her Shadow,
Jerusalem's Shadow, bent northward over the Island white.
At length he sat on London Stone & heard Jerusalem's voice:

"Albion, I cannot be thy Wife; thine own Minute Particulars
Belong to God alone, and all thy little ones are holy;
They are of Faith & not of Demonstration; wherefore is Vala
Cloth'd in black mourning upon my river's currents? Vala awake!
I hear thy shuttles in the sky, and round my limbs
I feel the iron threads of love & jealousy & despair."

Vala reply'd: "Albion is mine! Luvah gave me to Albion
And now recieves reproach & hate. Was it not said of old,
'Set your Son before a man & he shall take you & your sons
For slaves; but set your Daughter before a man & She
Shall make him & his sons & daughters your slaves for ever?'
And is this Faith? Behold the strife of Albion & Luvah
Is great in the east, their spears of blood rage in the eastern heaven.
Urizen is the champion of Albion; they will slay my Luvah,
And thou, O harlot daughter, daughter of despair, art all

This cause of these shakings of my towers on Euphrates.
Here is the House of Albion & here is thy secluded place,
And here we have found thy sins; & hence we turn thee forth
For all to avoid thee, to be astonish'd at thee for thy sins,
Because thou art the impurity & the harlot, & thy children,
Children of whoredoms, born for Sacrifice, for the meat & drink
Offering, to sustain the glorious combat & the battle & war,
That Man may be purified by the death of thy delusions."

So saying she her dark threads cast over the trembling River
And over the valleys, from the hills of Hertfordshire to the hills
Of Surrey across Middlesex, & across Albion's House
Of Eternity; pale stood Albion at his eastern gate,

32

Leaning against the pillars, & his disease rose from his skirts:
Upon the Precipice he stood, ready to fall into Non-Entity.

Los was all astonishment & terror, he trembled sitting on the Stone
Of London; but the interiors of Albion's fibres & nerves were hidden
From Los, astonish'd he beheld only the petrified surfaces
And saw his Furnaces in ruins, for Los is the Demon of the Furnaces;
He saw also the Four Points of Albion revers'd inwards.
He siez'd his Hammer & Tongs, his iron Poker & his Bellows,
Upon the valleys of Middlesex, Shouting loud for aid Divine.

In stern defiance came from Albion's bosom Hand, Hyle, Koban,
Gwantok, Peachy, Brertun, Slaid, Huttn, Skofeld, Kock, Kotope,
Bowen, Albion's Sons; they bore him a golden couch into the porch
And on the Couch repos'd his limbs trembling from the bloody field,
Rearing their Druid Patriarchal rocky Temples around his limbs.
(All things begin & end in Albion's Ancient Druid Rocky Shore.)

33

Turning his back to the Divine Vision, his Spectrous
Chaos before his face appear'd, an Unformed Memory.

Then spoke the Spectrous Chaos to Albion, dark'ning cold,
From the back & loins where dwell the Spectrous Dead:

"I am your Rational Power, O Albion, & that Human Form
You call Divine is but a Worm seventy inches long
That creeps forth in a night & is dried in the morning sun,

In fortuitous concourse of memorys accumulated & lost.
It plows the Earth in its own conceit, it overwhelms the Hills
Beneath its winding labyrinths, till a stone of the brook
Stops it in midst of its pride among its hills & rivers.
Battersea & Chelsea mourn, London & Canterbury tremble:
Their place shall not be found as the wind passes over.
The ancient Cities of the Earth remove as a traveller,
And shall Albion's Cities remain when I pass over them
With my deluge of forgotten remembrances over the tablet?"

So spoke the Spectre to Albion: he is the Great Selfhood,
Satan, Worship'd as God by the Mighty Ones of the Earth,
Having a white Dot call'd a Center, from which branches out
A Circle in continual gyrations: this became a Heart
From which sprang numerous branches varying their motions,
Producing many Heads, three or seven or ten, & hands & feet
Innumerable at will of the unfortunate contemplator
Who becomes his food: such is the way of the Devouring Power.

And this is the cause of the appearance in the frowning Chaos:
Albion's Emanation, which he had hidden in Jealousy,
Appear'd now in the frowning Chaos, prolific upon the Chaos,
Reflecting back to Albion in Sexual Reasoning Hermaphroditic.

Albion spoke: "Who art thou that appearest in gloomy pomp
Involving the Divine Vision in colours of autumn ripeness?
I never saw thee till this time, nor beheld life abstracted,
Nor darkness immingled with light on my furrow'd field.
Whence camest thou? who art thou, O loveliest? the Divine Vision
Is as nothing before thee: faded is all life and joy."

Vala replied in clouds of tears, Albion's garment embracing:

"I was a City & a Temple built by Albion's Children.
I was a Garden planted with beauty. I allured on hill & valley
The River of Life to flow against my walls & among my trees.
Vala was Albion's Bride & Wife in great Eternity,
The loveliest of the daughters of Eternity when in daybreak
I emanated from Luvah over the Towers of Jerusalem,
And in her Courts among her little Children offering up
The Sacrifice of fanatic love! why loved I Jerusalem?
Why was I one with her, embracing in the Vision of Jesus?

Wherefore did I, loving, create love, which never yet
Immingled God & Man, when thou & I hid the Divine Vision
In cloud of secret gloom which, behold, involves me round about?
Know me now Albion: look upon me. I alone am Beauty.
The Imaginative Human Form is but a breathing of Vala:
I breathe him forth into the Heaven from my secret Cave,
Born of the Woman, to obey the Woman, O Albion the mighty,
For the Divine appearance is Brotherhood, but I am love

34

"Elevate into the Region of Brotherhood with my red fires."

"Art thou Vala?" replied Albion, "image of my repose!
O how I tremble! how my members pour down milky fear!
A dewy garment covers me all over, all manhood is gone!
At thy word & at thy look, death enrobes me about
From head to feet, a garment of death & eternal fear.
Is not that Sun thy husband & that Moon thy glimmering Veil?
Are not the Stars of heaven thy Children? art thou not Babylon?
Art thou Nature, Mother of all? is Jerusalem thy Daughter?
Why have thou elevate inward, O dweller of outward chambers,
From grot & cave beneath the Moon, dim region of death
Where I laid my Plow in the hot noon, where my hot team fed,
Where implements of War are forged, the Plow to go over the Nations,
In pain girding me round like a rib of iron in heaven? O Vala!
In Eternity they neither marry nor are given in marriage.
Albion, the high Cliff of the Atlantic, is become a barren Land."

Los stood at his Anvil: he heard the contentions of Vala;
He heav'd his thund'ring Bellows upon the valleys of Middlesex,
He open'd his Furnaces before Vala; then Albion frown'd in anger
On his Rock, ere yet the Starry Heavens were fled away
From his awful Members; and thus Los cried aloud
To the Sons of Albion & to Hand the eldest Son of Albion:

"I hear the screech of Childbirth loud pealing, & the groans
Of Death in Albion's clouds dreadful utter'd over all the Earth.
What may Man be? who can tell! but what may Woman be
To have power over Man from Cradle to corruptible Grave?
There is a Throne in every Man, it is the Throne of God;
This, Woman has claim'd as her own, & Man is no more!
Albion is the Tabernacle of Vala & her Temple,
And not the Tabernacle & Temple of the Most High.

O Albion, why wilt thou Create a Female Will?
To hide the most evident God in a hidden covert, even
In the shadows of a Woman & a secluded Holy Place,
That we may pry after him as after a stolen treasure,
Hidden among the Dead & mured up from the paths of life.
Hand! art thou not Reuben enrooting thyself into Bashan
Till thou remainest a vaporous Shadow in a Void? O Merlin!
Unknown among the Dead where never before Existence came,
Is this the Female Will, O ye lovely Daughters of Albion, To
Converse concerning Weight & Distance in the Wilds of Newton &
    Locke?"

So Los spoke, standing on Mam-Tor, looking over Europe & Asia.
The Graves thunder beneath his feet from Ireland to Japan.

Reuben slept in Bashan like one dead in the valley
Cut off from Albion's mountains & from all the Earth's Summits
Between Succoth & Zaretan beside the Stone of Bohan,
While the Daughters of Albion divided Luvah into three Bodies.
Los bended his Nostrils down to the Earth, then sent him over
Jordan to the Land of the Hittite; every-one that saw him
Fled! they fled at his horrible Form: they hid in caves
And dens; they looked on one-another & became what they beheld.

Reuben return'd to Bashan; in despair he slept on the Stone.
Then Gwendolen divided into Rahab & Tirza in Twelve Portions.
Los rolled his Eyes into two narrow circles, then sent him
Over Jordan; all terrified fled: they became what they beheld.

If Perceptive Organs vary, Objects of Perception seem to vary:
If the Perceptive Organs close, their Objects seem to close also.
"Consider this, O mortal Man, O worm of sixty winters," said Los,
"Consider Sexual Organization & hide thee in the dust."

35

Then the Divine hand found the Two Limits, Satan and Adam,
In Albion's bosom, for in every Human bosom those Limits stand,
And the Divine voice came from the Furnaces, as multitudes without
Number, the voices of the innumerable multitudes of Eternity!
And the appearance of a Man was seen in the Furnaces
Saving those who have sinned from the punishment of the Law
(In pity of the punisher whose state is eternal death)
And keeping them from Sin by the mild counsels of his love;

"Albion goes to Eternal Death. In Me all Eternity

Must pass thro' condemnation and awake beyond the Grave.
No individual can keep these Laws, for they are death
To every energy of man and forbid the springs of life.
Albion hath enter'd the State Satan! Be permanent, O State!
And be thou for ever accursed! that Albion may arise again.
And be thou created into a State! I go forth to Create
States, to deliver Individuals evermore! Amen."

So spoke the voice from the Furnaces, descending into Non-Entity.

36

Reuben return'd to his place; in vain he sought beautiful Tirzah,
For his Eyelids were narrow'd & his Nostrils scented the ground.
And Sixty Winters Los raged in the Divisions of Reuben,
Building the Moon of Ulro plank by plank & rib by rib.
Reuben slept in the Cave of Adam, and Los folded his Tongue
Between Lips of mire & clay, then sent him forth over Jordan.
In the love of Tirzah he said: "Doubt is my food day & night."
All that beheld him fled howling and gnawed their tongues
For pain: they became what they beheld. In reasonings Reuben returned
To Heshbon: disconsolate he walk'd thro' Moab & he stood
Before the Furnaces of Los in a horrible dreamful slumber
On Mount Gilead looking toward Gilgal: and Los bended
His Ear in a spiral circle outward, then sent him over Jordan.

The Seven Nations fled before him; they became what they beheld.
Hand, Hyle & Coban fled: they became what they beheld.
Gwantock & Peachy hid in Damascus beneath Mount Lebanon,
Brereton & Slade in Egypt: Hutton & Skofeld & Kox
Fled over Chaldea in terror, in pains in every nerve.
Kotope & Bowen became what they beheld, fleeing over the Earth,
And the Twelve Female Emanations fled with them, agonising.

Jerusalem trembled seeing her Children driv'n by Los's Hammer
In the visions of the dreams of Beulah on the edge of Non-Entity.
Hand stood between Reuben & Merlin, as the Reasoning Spectre
Stands between the Vegetative Man & his Immortal Imagination.

And the Four Zoas clouded rage East & West & North & South;
They change their situations in the Universal Man.
Albion groans, he sees the Elements divide before his face,
And England, who is Brittannia, divided into Jerusalem & Vala;
And Urizen assumes the East, Luvah assumes the South,
In his dark Spectre ravening from his open Sepulcher.

And the Four Zoas, who are the Four Eternal Senses of Man,
Became Four Elements separating from the Limbs of Albion:
These are their names in the Vegetative generation:
[*one line erased from the plate*]
And Accident & Chance were found hidden in Length, Bredth & Highth,
And they divided into Four ravening deathlike Forms,
Fairies & Genii & Nymphs & Gnomes of the Elements:
These are States Permanently Fixed by the Divine Power.
The Atlantic Continent sunk round Albion's cliffy shore,
And the Sea poured in amain upon the Giants of Albion
As Los bended the Senses of Reuben. Reuben is Merlin
Exploring the Three States of Ulro: Creation, Redemption & Judgment.

And many of the Eternal Ones laughed after their manner:

"Have you known the Judgment that is arisen among the
Zoas of Albion, where a Man dare hardly to embrace
His own Wife for the terrors of Chastity that they call
By the name of Morality? their Daughters govern all
In hidden deceit! they are Vegetable, only fit for burning.
Art & Science cannot exist but by Naked Beauty display'd."

Then those in Great Eternity who contemplate on Death
Said thus: "What seems to Be, Is, To those to whom
It seems to Be, & is productive of the most dreadful
Consequences to those to whom it seems to Be, even of
Torments, Despair, Eternal Death; but the Divine Mercy
Steps beyond and Redeems Man in the Body of Jesus. Amen.
And Length, Bredth, Highth again Obey the Divine Vision.
 Hallelujah."

37

And One stood forth from the Divine family & said:
"I feel my Spectre rising upon me! Albion! arouze thyself!
Why dost thou thunder with frozen Spectrous wrath against us?
The Spectre is, in Giant Man, insane and most deform'd.
Thou wilt certainly provoke my Spectre against thine in fury!
He has a Sepulcher hewn out of a Rock ready for thee,
And a Death of Eight thousand years, forg'd by thyself, upon
The point of his Spear, if thou persistest to forbid with Laws
Our Emanations and to attack our secret supreme delights."

So Los spoke. But when he saw blue death in Albion's feet
Again he join'd the Divine Body, following merciful,
While Albion fled more indignant, revengeful covering

38

His face and bosom with petrific hardness, and his hands
And feet, lest any should enter his bosom & embrace
His hidden heart; his Emanation wept & trembled within him,
Uttering not his jealousy but hiding it as with
Iron and steel, dark and opake, with clouds & tempests brooding;
His strong limbs shudder'd upon his mountains high and dark.

Turning from Universal Love, petrific as he went,
His cold against the warmth of Eden rag'd with loud
Thunders of deadly war (the fever of the human soul)
Fires and clouds of rolling smoke! but mild, the Saviour follow'd him,
Displaying the Eternal Vision, the Divine Similitude,
In loves and tears of brothers, sisters, sons, fathers and friends,
Which if Man ceases to behold, he ceases to exist,

Saying, "Albion! Our wars are wars of life, & wounds of love
With intellectual spears, & long winged arrows of thought.
Mutual in one another's love and wrath all renewing
We live as One Man; for contracting our infinite senses
We behold multitude, or expanding, we behold as one,
As One Man all the Universal Family, and that One Man
We call Jesus the Christ; and he in us, and we in him
Live in perfect harmony in Eden, the land of life,
Giving, recieving, and forgiving each other's trespasses.
He is the Good shepherd, he is the Lord and master,
He is the Shepherd of Albion, he is all in all,
In Eden, in the garden of God, and in heavenly Jerusalem.
If we have offended, forgive us; take not vengeance against us."

Thus speaking, the Divine Family follow Albion.
I see them in the Vision of God upon my pleasant valleys.

I behold London, a Human awful wonder of God!
He says: "Return, Albion, return! I give myself for thee.
My Streets are my Ideas of Imagination.
Awake Albion, awake! and let us awake up together.
My Houses are Thoughts: my Inhabitants, Affections,

The children of my thoughts walking within my blood-vessels,
Shut from my nervous form which sleeps upon the verge of Beulah
In dreams of darkness, while my vegetating blood in veiny pipes
Rolls dreadful thro' the Furnaces of Los and the Mills of Satan.
For Albion's sake and for Jerusalem thy Emanation
I give myself, and these my brethren give themselves for Albion."

So spoke London, immortal Guardian! I heard in Lambeth's shades.
In Felpham I heard and saw the Visions of Albion.
I write in South Molton Street what I both see and hear
In regions of Humanity, in London's opening streets.

I see thee, awful Parent Land in light, behold I see!
Verulam! Canterbury! venerable parent of men,
Generous immortal Guardian, golden clad! for Cities
Are Men, fathers of multitudes, and Rivers & Mountains
Are also Men; every thing is Human, mighty! sublime!
In every bosom a Universe expands as wings,
Let down at will around and call'd the Universal Tent.
York, crown'd with loving kindness, Edinburgh, cloth'd
With fortitude, as with a garment of immortal texture
Woven in looms of Eden, in spiritual deaths of mighty men
Who give themselves in Golgotha, Victims to Justice, where
There is in Albion a Gate of precious stones and gold
Seen only by Emanations, by vegetations viewless:
Bending across the road of Oxford Street, it from Hyde Park
To Tyburn's deathful shades admits the wandering souls
Of multitudes who die from Earth: this Gate cannot be found

39

By Satan's Watch-fiends, tho' they search numbering every grain
Of sand on Earth every night, they never find this Gate.
It is the Gate of Los. Withoutside is the Mill, intricate, dreadful
And fill'd with cruel tortures; but no mortal man can find the Mill
Of Satan in his mortal pilgrimage of seventy years,
For Human beauty knows it not, nor can Mercy find it! But
In the Fourth region of Humanity, Urthona nam'd,
Mortality begins to roll the billows of Eternal Death
Before the Gate of Los. Urthona here is named Los,
And here begins the System of Moral Virtue named Rahab.
Albion fled thro' the Gate of Los and he stood in the Gate.

Los was the friend of Albion who most lov'd him. In Cambridgeshire
His eternal station, he is the twenty-eighth & is four-fold.
Seeing Albion had turn'd his back against the Divine Vision,
Los said to Albion: "Whither fleest thou?" Albion reply'd:

"I die! I go to Eternal Death! the shades of death
Hover within me & beneath, and spreading themselves outside
Like rocky clouds, build me a gloomy monument of woe.
Will none accompany me in my death, or be a Ransom for me
In that dark Valley? I have girded round my cloke, and on my feet
Bound these black shoes of death, & on my hands, death's iron gloves.
God hath forsaken me & my friends are become a burden,
A weariness to me, & the human footstep is a terror to me."

Los answered troubled, and his soul was rent in twain:
"Must the Wise die for an Atonement? does Mercy endure Atonement?
No! It is Moral Severity & destroys Mercy in its Victim."
So speaking, not yet infected with the Error & Illusion,

40

Los shudder'd at beholding Albion, for his disease
Arose upon him pale and ghastly, and he call'd around
The Friends of Albion; trembling at the sight of Eternal Death
The four appear'd with their Emanations in fiery
Chariots: black their fires roll, beholding Albion's House of Eternity:
Damp couch the flames beneath and silent sick, stand shuddering
Before the Porch of sixteen pillars; weeping every one
Descended and fell down upon their knees round Albion's knees,
Swearing the Oath of God with awful voice of thunders round
Upon the hills & valleys, and the cloudy Oath roll'd far and wide.

"Albion is sick!" said every Valley, every mournful Hill
And every River: "our brother Albion is sick to death.
He hath leagued himself with robbers: he hath studied the arts
Of unbelief. Envy hovers over him: his Friends are his abhorrence:
Those who give their lives for him are despised:
Those who devour his soul are taken into his bosom:
To destroy his Emanation is their intention.
Arise! awake, O Friends of the Giant Albion!
They have perswaded him of horrible falshoods:
They have sown errors over all his fruitful fields!"

The Twenty-four heard! they came trembling on wat'ry chariots
Borne by the Living Creatures of the third procession
Of Human Majesty: the Living Creatures wept aloud, as they
Went along Albion's roads, till they arriv'd at Albion's House.

O! how the torments of Eternal death waited on Man,
And the loud-rending bars of the Creation ready to burst,
That the wide world might fly from its hinges & the immortal **mansion**
Of Man for ever be possess'd by monsters of the deeps,
And Man himself become a Fiend, wrap'd in an endless **curse**,
Consuming and consum'd for-ever in flames of Moral Justice.

For had the Body of Albion fall'n down and from its dreadful **ruins**
Let loose the enormous Spectre on the darkness of the deep
At enmity with the Merciful & fill'd with devouring fire,
A nether-world must have reciev'd the foul enormous spirit
Under pretence of Moral Virtue, fill'd with Revenge and **Law,**
There to eternity chain'd down and issuing in red flames
And curses, with his mighty arms brandish'd against the heavens,
Breathing cruelty, blood & vengeance, gnashing his teeth with pain.
Torn with black storms & ceaseless torrents of his own consuming **fire,**
Within his breast his mighty Sons chain'd down & fill'd with **cursings,**
And his dark Eon, that once fair crystal form divinely clear,
Within his ribs producing serpents whose souls are flames of fire.
But glory to the Merciful One, for he is of tender mercies!
And the Divine Family wept over him as One Man.

And these the Twenty-four in whom the Divine Family
Appear'd; and they were One in Him. A Human Vision!
Human Divine, Jesus the Saviour, blessed for ever and **ever.**

Selsey, true friend! who afterwards submitted to be devour'd
By the waves of Despair, whose Emanation rose above
The flood and was nam'd Chichester, lovely mild and gentle! Lo!
Her lambs bleat to the sea-fowls' cry, lamenting still for Albion.

Submitting to be call'd the son of Los, the terrible vision
Winchester stood devoting himself for Albion, his tents
Outspread with abundant riches, and his Emanations
Submitting to be call'd Enitharmon's daughters and be **born**
In vegetable mould, created by the Hammer and Loom
In Bowlahoola & Allamanda where the Dead wail night & day.

(I call them by their English names: English, the rough basement.
Los built the stubborn structure of the Language, acting against
Albion's melancholy, who must else have been a Dumb despair.)

Gloucester and Exeter and Salisbury and Bristol, and benevolent Bath,

41

Bath who is Legions; he is the Seventh, the physician and
The poisoner, the best and worst in Heaven and Hell,
Whose Spectre first assimilated with Luvah in Albion's mountains,
A triple octave he took, to reduce Jerusalem to twelve,
To cast Jerusalem forth upon the wilds to Poplar & Bow,
To Malden & Canterbury in the delights of cruelty.
The Shuttles of death sing in the sky to Islington & Pancrass,
Round Marybone to Tyburn's River, weaving black melancholy as a net,
And despair as meshes closely wove over the west of London
Where mild Jerusalem sought to repose in death & be no more.
She fled to Lambeth's mild Vale and hid herself beneath
The Surrey Hills where Rephaim terminates: her Sons are siez'd
For victims of sacrifice; but Jerusalem cannot be found, Hid
By the Daughters of Beulah, gently snatch'd away and hid in Beulah.

There is a Grain of Sand in Lambeth that Satan cannot find,
Nor can his Watch Fiends find it; 'tis translucent & has many Angles,
But he who finds it will find Oothoon's palace; for within
Opening into Beulah, every angle is a lovely heaven.
But should the Watch Fiends find it, they would call it Sin
And lay its Heavens & their inhabitants in blood of punishment.
Here Jerusalem & Vala were hid in soft slumberous repose,
Hid from the terrible East, shut up in the South & West.

The Twenty-eight trembled in Death's dark caves; in cold despair
They kneel'd around the Couch of Death, in deep humiliation
And tortures of self condemnation, while their Spectres rag'd within.
The Four Zoas in terrible combustion clouded rage,
Drinking the shuddering fears & loves of Albion's Families,
Destroying by selfish affections the things that they most admire,
Drinking & eating, & pitying & weeping as at a trajic scene
The soul drinks murder & revenge & applauds its own holiness.

They saw Albion endeavouring to destroy their Emanations.

42

Thus Albion sat, studious of others in his pale disease,
Brooding on evil; but when Los open'd the Furnaces before him
He saw that the accursed things were his own affections
And his own beloveds; then he turn'd sick: his soul died within him.
Also Los, sick & terrified, beheld the Furnaces of Death
And must have died, but the Divine Saviour descended
Among the infant loves & affections, and the Divine Vision wept
Like evening dew on every herb upon the breathing ground.

Albion spoke in his dismal dreams: "O thou deceitful friend,
Worshipping mercy & beholding thy friend in such affliction!
Los! thou now discoverest thy turpitude to the heavens.
I demand righteousness & justice. O thou ingratitude!
Give me my Emanations back, food for my dying soul.
My daughters are harlots: my sons are accursed before me.
Enitharmon is my daughter, accursed with a father's curse.
O! I have utterly been wasted. I have given my daughters to devils."

So spoke Albion in gloomy majesty, and deepest night
Of Ulro roll'd round his skirts from Dover to Cornwall.

Los answer'd: "Righteousness & justice I give thee in return
For thy righteousness, but I add mercy also and bind
Thee from destroying these little ones; am I to be only
Merciful to thee and cruel to all that thou hatest?
Thou wast the Image of God surrounded by the four Zoas.
Three thou hast slain. I am the Fourth; thou canst not destroy me.
Thou art in Error; trouble me not with thy righteousness.
I have innocence to defend and ignorance to instruct:
I have no time for seeming and little arts of compliment
In morality and virtue, in self-glorying and pride.
There is a limit of Opakeness and a limit of Contraction
In every Individual Man, and the limit of Opakeness
Is named Satan, and the limit of Contraction is named Adam.
But when Man sleeps in Beulah, the Saviour in Mercy takes
Contraction's Limit, and of the Limit he forms Woman, That
Himself may in process of time be born Man to redeem.
But there is no Limit of Expansion; there is no Limit of Translucence
In the bosom of Man for ever from eternity to eternity.
Therefore I break thy bonds of righteousness. I crush thy messengers,

That they may not crush me and mine; do thou be righteous
And I will return it; otherwise I defy thy worst revenge.
Consider me as thine enemy: on me turn all thy fury;
But destroy not these little ones, nor mock the Lord's anointed:
Destroy not by Moral Virtue the little ones whom he hath chosen,
The little ones whom he hath chosen in preference to thee.
He hath cast thee off for ever: the little ones he hath anointed!
Thy Selfhood is for ever accursed from the Divine presence."

So Los spoke, then turn'd his face & wept for Albion.

Albion replied: "Go, Hand & Hyle! sieze the abhorred friend
As you have siez'd the Twenty-four rebellious ingratitudes
To atone for you, for spiritual death. Man lives by deaths of Men.
Bring him to justice before heaven here upon London stone,
Between Blackheath & Hounslow, between Norwood & Finchley.
All that they have is mine: from my free gen'rous gift
They now hold all they have; ingratitude to me,
To me their benefactor, calls aloud for vengeance deep."

Los stood before his Furnaces awaiting the fury of the Dead,
And the Divine hand was upon him, strengthening him mightily.

The Spectres of the Dead cry out from the deeps beneath
Upon the hills of Albion; Oxford groans in his iron furnace,
Winchester in his den & cavern; they lament against
Albion: they curse their human kindness & affection:
They rage like wild beasts in the forests of affliction:
In the dreams of Ulro they repent of their human kindness.

"Come up, build Babylon, Rahab is ours & all her multitudes
With her, in pomp and glory of victory. Depart,
Ye twenty-four, into the deeps; let us depart to glory!"

Their Human majestic Forms sit up upon their Couches
Of death; they curb their Spectres as with iron curbs:
They enquire after Jerusalem in the regions of the dead
With the voices of dead men, low, scarcely articulate,
And with tears cold on their cheeks they weary repose.

"O when shall the morning of the grave appear, and when
Shall our salvation come? we sleep upon our watch,
We cannot awake, and our Spectres rage in the forests.
O God of Albion, where art thou? pity the watchers!"

Thus mourn they. Loud the Furnaces of Los thunder upon
The clouds of Europe & Asia among the Serpent Temples.

And Los drew his Seven Furnaces around Albion's Altars;
And as Albion built his frozen Altars, Los built the Mundane Shell
In the Four Regions of Humanity, East & West & North & South,
Till Norwood & Finchley & Blackheath & Hounslow cover'd the whole
    Earth.
This is the Net & Veil of Vala among the Souls of the Dead.

43

They saw their Wheels rising up poisonous against Albion:
Urizen cold & scientific, Luvah pitying & weeping,
Tharmas indolent & sullen, Urthona doubting & despairing,
Victims to one another & dreadfully plotting against each other
To prevent Albion walking about in the Four Complexions.

They saw America clos'd out by the Oaks of the western shore,
And Tharmas dash'd on the Rocks of the Altars of Victims in Mexico.
"If we are wrathful, Albion will destroy Jerusalem with rooty Groves:
If we are merciful, ourselves must suffer destruction on his Oaks.
Why should we enter into our Spectres to behold our own corruptions?
O God of Albion, descend! deliver Jerusalem from the Oaken Groves!"

Then Los grew furious, raging: "Why stand we here trembling around
Calling on God for help, and not ourselves, in whom God dwells,
Stretching a hand to save the falling Man? are we not Four
Beholding Albion upon the Precipice ready to fall into Non-Entity?
Seeing these Heavens & Hells conglobing in the Void, Heavens over Hells
Brooding in holy hypocritic lust, drinking the cries of pain
From howling victims of Law, building Heavens Twenty-seven-fold,
Swell'd & bloated General Forms repugnant to the Divine-
Humanity who is the Only General and Universal Form,
To which all Lineaments tend & seek with love & sympathy.
All broad & general principles belong to benevolence
Who protects minute particulars every one in their own identity;
But here the affectionate touch of the tongue is clos'd in by deadly teeth,
And the soft smile of friendship & the open dawn of benevolence
Become a net & a trap, & every energy render'd cruel,
Till the existence of friendship & benevolence is denied:
The wine of the Spirit & the vineyards of the Holy-One
Here turn into poisonous stupor & deadly intoxication.
That they may be condemn'd by Law & the Lamb of God be slain;

And the two Sources of Life in Eternity, Hunting and War,
Are become the Sources of dark & bitter Death & of corroding Hell.
The open heart is shut up in integuments of frozen silence
That the spear that lights it forth may shatter the ribs & bosom.
A pretence of Art to destroy Art; a pretence of Liberty
To destroy Liberty; a pretence of Religion to destroy Religion.
Oshea and Caleb fight: they contend in the valleys of Peor,
In the terrible Family Contentions of those who love each other.
The Armies of Balaam weep—no women come to the field:
Dead corses lay before them, & not as in Wars of old;
For the Soldier who fights for Truth calls his enemy his brother:
They fight & contend for life & not for eternal death;
But here the Soldier strikes, & a dead corse falls at his feet,
Nor Daughter nor Sister nor Mother come forth to embosom the Slain;
But Death, Eternal Death, remains in the Valleys of Peor.
The English are scatter'd over the face of the Nations: are these
Jerusalem's children? Hark! hear the Giants of Albion cry at night:
'We smell the blood of the English! we delight in their blood on our Altars.
The living & the dead shall be ground in our rumbling Mills
For bread of the Sons of Albion, of the Giants Hand & Scofield.'
Scofeld & Kox are let loose upon my Saxons! they accumulate
A World in which Man is by his Nature the Enemy of Man,
In pride of Selfhood unwieldy stretching out into Non Entity,
Generalizing Art & Science till Art & Science is lost.
Bristol & Bath, listen to my words, & ye Seventeen, give ear!
It is easy to acknowledge a man to be great & good while we
Derogate from him in the trifles & small articles of that goodness.
Those alone are his friends who admire his minutest powers.
Instead of Albion's lovely mountains & the curtains of Jerusalem,
I see a Cave, a Rock, a Tree deadly and poisonous, unimaginative.
Instead of the Mutual Forgivenesses, the Minute Particulars, I see
Pits of bitumen ever burning, artificial Riches of the Canaanite
Like Lakes of liquid lead: instead of heavenly Chapels built
By our dear Lord, I see Worlds crusted with snows & ice.
I see a Wicker Idol woven round Jerusalem's children. I see
The Canaanite, the Amalekite, the Moabite, the Egyptian,
By Demonstrations the cruel Sons of Quality & Negation,
Driven on the Void in incoherent despair into Non Entity.
I see America clos'd apart, & Jerusalem driven in terror
Away from Albion's mountains, far away from London's spires.
I will not endure this thing! I alone withstand to death
This outrage! Ah me! how sick & pale you all stand round me!

Ah me! pitiable ones! do you also go to death's vale?
All you my friends & Brothers, all you my beloved Companions
Have you also caught the infection of Sin & stern Repentance?
I see Disease arise upon you! yet speak to me and give
Me some comfort! why do you all stand silent? I alone
Remain in permanent strength. Or is all this goodness & pity only
That you may take the greater vengeance in your Sepulcher?"

So Los spoke. Pale they stood around the House of Death,
In the midst of temptations & despair, among the rooted Oaks,
Among reared Rocks of Albion's Sons; at length they rose

44

With one accord in love sublime, &, as on Cherub's wings,
They Albion surround with kindest violence to bear him back
Against his will thro' Los's Gate to Eden. Four-fold, loud,
Their Wings waving over the bottomless Immense, to bear
Their awful charge back to his native home; but Albion dark,
Repugnant, roll'd his Wheels backward into Non-Entity.
Loud roll the Starry Wheels of Albion into the World of Death,
And all the Gate of Los, clouded with clouds redounding from
Albion's dread Wheels, stretching out spaces immense between,
That every little particle of light & air became Opake,
Black & immense, a Rock of difficulty & a Cliff
Of black despair, that the immortal Wings labour'd against
Cliff after cliff & over Valleys of despair & death.
The narrow Sea between Albion & the Atlantic Continent,
Its waves of pearl became a boundless Ocean bottomless,
Of grey obscurity, fill'd with clouds & rocks & whirling waters,
And Albion's Sons ascending & descending in the horrid Void.

But as the Will must not be bended but in the day of Divine
Power, silent calm & motionless in the mid-air sublime
The Family Divine hover around the darken'd Albion.

Such is the nature of the Ulro, that whatever enters
Becomes Sexual & is Created and Vegetated and Born.
From Hyde Park spread their vegetating roots beneath Albion,
In dreadful pain the Spectrous Uncircumcised Vegetation
Forming a Sexual Machine, an Aged Virgin Form,
In Erin's Land toward the north, joint after joint, & burning
In love & jealousy immingled, & calling it Religion.

And feeling the damps of death, they with one accord delegated Los,
Conjuring him by the Highest that he should Watch over them
Till Jesus shall appear; & they gave their power to Los
Naming him the Spirit of Prophecy, calling him Elijah.

Strucken with Albion's disease, they become what they behold.
They assimilate with Albion in pity & compassion.
Their Emanations return not: their Spectres rage in the Deep.
The Slumbers of Death came over them around the Couch of Death.
Before the Gate of Los & in the depths of Non Entity,
Among the Furnaces of Los, among the Oaks of Albion.

Man is adjoin'd to Man by his Emanative portion
Who is Jerusalem in every individual Man, and her
Shadow is Vala, builded by the Reasoning power in Man.
O search & see: turn your eyes upward: open, O thou World
Of Love & Harmony in Man: expand thy ever lovely Gates!

They wept into the deeps a little space; at length was heard
The voice of Bath, faint as the voice of the Dead in the House of Death,

45

Bath, healing City! whose wisdom, in midst of Poetic
Fervor, mild spoke thro' the Western Porch in soft gentle tears:

"O Albion, mildest Son of Eden! clos'd is thy Western Gate.
Brothers of Eternity, this Man whose great example
We all admir'd & loved, whose all benevolent countenance seen
In Eden, in lovely Jerusalem, drew even from envy
The tear, and the confession of honesty open & undisguis'd
From mistrust and suspition: The Man is himself become
A piteous example of oblivion, To teach the Sons
Of Eden that however great and glorious, however loving
And merciful the Individuality, however high
Our palaces and cities and however fruitful are our fields,
In Selfhood, we are nothing, but fade away in morning's breath.
Our mildness is nothing: the greatest mildness we can use
Is incapable and nothing: none but the Lamb of God can heal
This dread disease, none but Jesus. O Lord, descend and save!
Albion's Western Gate is clos'd: his death is coming apace.
Jesus alone can save him; for alas, we none can know
How soon his lot may be our own. When Africa in sleep
Rose in the night of Beulah and bound down the Sun & Moon,

His friends cut his strong chains & overwhelm'd his dark
Machines in fury & destruction, and the Man reviving repented:
He wept before his wrathful brethren, thankful & considerate
For their well timed wrath. But Albion's sleep is not
Like Africa's, and his machines are woven with his life.
Nothing but mercy can save him! nothing but mercy interposing
Lest he should slay Jerusalem in his fearful jealousy.
O God, descend! gather our brethren: deliver Jerusalem!
But that we may omit no office of the friendly spirit,
Oxford, take thou these leaves of the Tree of Life; with eloquence
That thy immortal tongue inspires, present them to Albion:
Perhaps he may recieve them, offer'd from thy loved hands."

So spoke, unheard by Albion, the merciful Son of Heaven
To those whose Western Gates were open, as they stood weeping
Around Albion; but Albion heard him not: obdurate, hard,
He frown'd on all his Friends, counting them enemies in his sorrow.

And the Seventeen conjoining with Bath, the Seventh
In whom the other Ten shone manifest a Divine Vision,
Assimilated and embrac'd Eternal Death for Albion's sake.

And these the names of the Eighteen combining with those Ten:

46

Bath, mild Physician of Eternity, mysterious power
Whose springs are unsearchable & knowledge infinite:
Hereford, ancient Guardian of Wales, whose hands
Builded the mountain palaces of Eden, stupendous works!
Lincoln, Durham & Carlisle, Councellors of Los,
And Ely, Scribe of Los, whose pen no other hand
Dare touch: Oxford, immortal Bard, with eloquence
Divine he wept over Albion speaking the words of God
In mild perswasion, bringing leaves of the Tree of Life:

"Thou art in Error, Albion, the land of Ulro.
One Error not remov'd will destroy a human Soul.
Repose in Beulah's night till the Error is remov'd.
Reason not on both sides. Repose upon our bosoms
Till the Plow of Jehovah and the Harrow of Shaddai
Have passed over the Dead to awake the Dead to Judgment."
But Albion turn'd away refusing comfort.

Oxford trembled while he spoke, then fainted in the arms
Of Norwich, Peterboro, Rochester, Chester awful, Worcester,
Litchfield, Saint David's, Landaff, Asaph, Bangor, Sodor,
Bowing their heads devoted: and the Furnaces of Los
Began to rage; thundering loud the storms began to roar
Upon the Furnaces, and loud the Furnaces rebellow beneath.

And these the Four in whom the twenty-four appear'd four-fold:
Verulam, London, York, Edinburgh, mourning one towards another.
Alas!—The time will come when a man's worst enemies
Shall be those of his own house and family, in a Religion
Of Generation to destroy, by Sin and Atonement, happy Jerusalem,
The Bride and Wife of the Lamb. O God, thou art Not an Avenger!

47

From Camberwell to Highgate where the mighty Thames shudders along,
Where Los's Furnaces stand, where Jerusalem & Vala howl,
Luvah tore forth from Albion's Loins in fibrous veins, in rivers
Of blood over Europe: a Vegetating Root, in grinding pain
Animating the Dragon Temples, soon to become that Holy Fiend
The Wicker Man of Scandinavia, in which, cruelly consumed,
The Captives rear'd to heaven howl in flames among the stars.
Loud the cries of War on the Rhine & Danube with Albion's Sons:
Away from Beulah's hills & vales break forth the Souls of the Dead,
With cymbal, trumpet, clarion & the scythed chariots of Britain.

And the Veil of Vala is composed of the Spectres of the Dead.

Hark! the mingling cries of Luvah with the Sons of Albion.
Hark! & Record the terrible wonder! that the Punisher
Mingles with his Victim's Spectre, enslaved & tormented
To him whom he has murder'd, bound in vengeance & enmity.
Shudder not, but Write, & the hand of God will assist you!
Therefore I write Albion's last words: "Hope is banish'd from me."

48

These were his last words; and the merciful Saviour in his arms
Reciev'd him, in the arms of tender mercy, and repos'd
The pale limbs of his Eternal Individuality
Upon the Rock of Ages. Then, surrounded with a Cloud,
In silence the Divine Lord builded with immortal labour
Of gold & jewels. a sublime Ornament, a Couch of repose

With Sixteen pillars, canopied with emblems & written verse,
Spiritual Verse, order'd & measur'd: from whence time shall reveal
The Five books of the Decalogue: the books of Joshua & Judges,
Samuel, a double book, & Kings, a double book, the Psalms & Prophets,
The Four-fold Gospel, and the Revelations everlasting.
Eternity groan'd & was troubled at the image of Eternal Death!

Beneath the bottoms of the Graves, which is Earth's central joint,
There is a place where Contrarieties are equally true:
(To protect from the Giant blows in the sports of intellect,
Thunder in the midst of kindness, & love that kills its beloved:
Because Death is for a period, and they renew tenfold.)
From this sweet Place Maternal Love awoke Jerusalem;
With pangs she forsook Beulah's pleasant lovely shadowy Universe
Where no dispute can come, created for those who Sleep.

Weeping was in all Beulah, and all the Daughters of Beulah
Wept for their Sister, the Daughter of Albion, Jerusalem,
When out of Beulah the Emanation of the Sleeper descended
With solemn mourning, out of Beulah's moony shades and hills
Within the Human Heart, whose Gates closed with solemn sound.

And this the manner of the terrible Separation.
The Emanations of the grievously afflicted Friends of Albion
Concenter in one Female form, an Aged pensive Woman.
Astonish'd, lovely, embracing the sublime shade, the Daughters of
    Beulah
Beheld her with wonder! With awful hands she took
A Moment of Time, drawing it out with many tears & afflictions
And many sorrows, oblique across the Atlantic Vale,
Which is the Vale of Rephaim dreadful from East to West
Where the Human Harvest waves abundant in the beams of Eden.
Into a Rainbow of jewels and gold, a mild Reflection from
Albion's dread Tomb: Eight thousand and five hundred years
In its extension. Every two hundred years has a door to Eden.
She also took an Atom of Space, with dire pain opening it a Center
Into Beulah; trembling the Daughters of Beulah dried
Her tears; she ardent embrac'd her sorrows, occupied in labours
Of sublime mercy in Rephaim's Vale. Perusing Albion's Tomb
She sat: she walk'd among the ornaments solemn mourning.
The Daughters attended her shudderings, wiping the death sweat.
Los also saw her in his seventh Furnace; he also, terrified,

Saw the finger of God go forth upon his seventh Furnace
Away from the Starry Wheels to prepare Jerusalem a place,
When with a dreadful groan the Emanation mild of Albion
Burst from his bosom in the Tomb like a pale snowy cloud,
Female and lovely, struggling to put off the Human form,
Writhing in pain. The Daughters of Beulah in kind arms reciev'd
Jerusalem, weeping over her among the Spaces of Erin
In the Ends of Beulah, where the Dead wail night & day.

And thus Erin spoke to the Daughters of Beulah in soft tears:

"Albion the Vortex of the Dead! Albion the Generous!
Albion the mildest son of Heaven! The Place of Holy Sacrifice
Where Friends Die for each other, will become the Place
Of Murder & Unforgiving, Never-awaking Sacrifice of Enemies
The Children must be sacrific'd! (a horror never known
Till now in Beulah) unless a Refuge can be found
To hide them from the wrath of Albion's Law that freezes sore
Upon his Sons & Daughters, self-exiled from his bosom.
Draw ye Jerusalem away from Albion's Mountains
To give a Place for Redemption, let Sihon and Og
Remove Eastward to Bashan and Gilead, and leave

49

'The secret coverts of Albion & the hidden places of America.
Jerusalem! Jerusalem! why wilt thou turn away?
Come ye, O Daughters of Beulah, lament for Og & Sihon
Upon the Lakes of Ireland from Rathlin to Baltimore.
Stand ye upon the Dargle from Wicklow to Drogheda.
Come & mourn over Albion, the White Cliff of the Atlantic,
The Mountain of Giants: all the Giants of Albion are become
Weak, wither'd, darken'd, & Jerusalem is cast forth from Albion.
They deny that they ever knew Jerusalem, or ever dwelt in Shiloh.
The Gigantic roots & twigs of the vegetating Sons of Albion,
Fill'd with the little-ones, are consumed in the Fires of their Altars.
The vegetating Cities are burned & consumed from the Earth,
And the Bodies in which all Animals & Vegetations, the Earth & Heaven
Were contain'd in the All Glorious Imagination, are wither'd & darken'd.
The golden Gate of Havilah and all the Garden of God
Was caught up with the Sun in one day of fury and war.
The Lungs, the Heart, the Liver, shrunk away far distant from Man
And left a little slimy substance floating upon the tides.

In one night the Atlantic Continent was caught up with the moon
And became an Opake Globe far distant, clad with moony beams.
The Visions of Eternity, by reason of narrowed perceptions,
Are become weak Visions of Time & Space, fix'd into furrows of death,
Till deep dissimulation is the only defence an honest man has left.
O Polypus of Death! O Spectre over Europe and Asia,
Withering the Human Form by Laws of Sacrifice for Sin!
By Laws of Chastity & Abhorrence I am wither'd up:
Striving to create a Heaven in which all shall be pure & holy
In their Own Selfhoods: in Natural Selfish Chastity to banish Pity
And dear Mutual Forgiveness, & to become One Great Satan
Inslav'd to the most powerful Selfhood: to murder the Divine Humanity
In whose sight all are as the dust & who chargeth his Angels with folly!
Ah! weak & wide astray! Ah! shut in narrow doleful form!
Creeping in reptile flesh upon the bosom of the ground!
The Eye of Man, a little narrow orb, clos'd up & dark,
Scarcely beholding the Great Light, conversing with the ground:
The Ear, a little shell, in small volutions shutting out
True Harmonies & comprehending great as very small:
The Nostrils, bent down to the earth & clos'd with senseless flesh
That odours cannot them expand, nor joy on them exult:
The Tongue, a little moisture fills, a little food it cloys,
A little sound it utters, & its cries are faintly heard.
Therefore they are removed: therefore they have taken root
In Egypt & Philistea, in Moab & Edom & Aram:
In the Erythrean Sea their Uncircumcision in Heart & Loins
Be lost for ever & ever; then they shall arise from Self
By Self Annihilation into Jerusalem's Courts & into Shiloh,
Shiloh, the Masculine Emanation among the Flowers of Beulah.
Lo, Shiloh dwells over France, as Jerusalem dwells over Albion.
Build & prepare a Wall & Curtain for America's shore!
Rush on! Rush on! Rush on, ye vegetating Sons of Albion!
The Sun shall go before you in Day, the Moon shall go
Before you in Night. Come on! Come on! Come on! The Lord
Jehovah is before, behind, above, beneath, around.
He has builded the arches of Albion's Tomb, binding the Stars
In merciful Order, bending the Laws of Cruelty to Peace.
He hath placed Og & Anak, the Giants of Albion, for their Guards,
Building the Body of Moses in the Valley of Poor, the Body
Of Divine Analogy; and Og & Sihon in the tears of Balaam
The Son of Beor, have given their power to Joshua & Caleb.
Remove from Albion, far remove these terrible surfaces:

They are beginning to form Heavens & Hells in immense
Circles, the Hells for food to the Heavens, food of torment,
Food of despair: they drink the condemn'd Soul & rejoice
In cruel holiness in their Heavens of Chastity & Uncircumcision;
Yet they are blameless, & Iniquity must be imputed only
To the State they are enter'd into, that they may be deliver'd.
Satan is the State of Death & not a Human existence;
But Luvah is named Satan because he has enter'd that State:
A World where Man is by Nature the enemy of Man,
Because the Evil is Created into a State, that Men
May be deliver'd time after time, evermore. Amen.
Learn therefore, O Sisters, to distinguish the Eternal Human
That walks about among the stones of fire in bliss & woe
Alternate, from those States or Worlds in which the Spirit travels.
This is the only means to Forgiveness of Enemies.
Therefore remove from Albion these terrible Surfaces
And let wild seas & rocks close up Jerusalem away from

50

"The Atlantic Mountains where Giants dwelt in Intellect,
Now given to stony Druids and Allegoric Generation,
To the Twelve Gods of Asia, the Spectres of those who Sleep
Sway'd by a Providence oppos'd to the Divine Lord Jesus:
A murderous Providence! A Creation that groans, living on Death,
Where Fish & Bird & Beast & Man & Tree & Metal & Stone
Live by Devouring, going into Eternal Death continually!
Albion is now possess'd by the War of Blood! the Sacrifice
Of envy Albion is become, and his Emanation cast out.
Come Lord Jesus, Lamb of God descend! for if, O Lord!
If thou hadst been here, our brother Albion had not died.
Arise sisters! Go ye & meet the Lord, while I remain.
Behold the foggy mornings of the Dead on Albion's cliffs!
Ye know that if the Emanation remains in them
She will become an Eternal Death, an Avenger of Sin,
A Self-righteousness, the proud Virgin-Harlot! Mother of War!
And we also & all Beulah consume beneath Albion's curse."

So Erin spoke to the Daughters of Beulah. Shuddering
With their wings, they sat in the Furnace, in a night
Of stars, for all the Sons of Albion appear'd distant stars
Ascending and descending into Albion's sea of death.
And Erin's lovely Bow enclos'd the Wheels of Albion's Sons.

Expanding on wing, the Daughters of Beulah replied in sweet response:

"Come, O thou Lamb of God, and take away the remembrance of Sin.
To Sin & to hide the Sin in sweet deceit is lovely!
To Sin in the open face of day is cruel & pitiless! But
To record the Sin for a reproach, to let the Sun go down
In a remembrance of the Sin, is a Woe & a Horror,
A brooder of an Evil Day and a Sun rising in blood!
Come then, O Lamb of God, and take away the remembrance of Sin."

END OF CHAPTER 2

52

Rahab is an }   TO THE DEISTS.   The Spiritual
Eternal State. }   States of the Soul
                                         are all Eternal.
                                         Distinguish be-
                                         tween the Man &
                                         his present State.

HE never can be a Friend to the Human Race who is the Preacher of Natural Morality or Natural Religion; he is a flatterer who means to betray, to perpetuate Tyrant Pride & the Laws of that Babylon which he foresees shall shortly be destroyed, with the Spiritual and not the Natural Sword. He is in the State named Rahab, which State must be put off before he can be the Friend of Man.

You, O Deists, profess yourselves the Enemies of Christianity, and you are so: you are also the Enemies of the Human Race & of Universal Nature. Man is born a Spectre or Satan & is altogether an Evil, & requires a New Selfhood continually, & must continually be changed into his direct Contrary. But your Greek Philosophy (which is a remnant of Druidism) teaches that Man is Righteous in his Vegetated Spectre: an Opinion of fatal & accursed consequence to Man, as the Ancients saw plainly by Revelation, to the intire abrogation of Experimental Theory; and many believed what they saw and Prophecied of Jesus.

Man must & will have Some Religion: if he has not the Religion of Jesus, he will have the Religion of Satan & will erect the Synagogue of Satan, calling the Prince of this World, God, and destroying all who do not worship Satan under the Name of God. Will any one say, "Where are those who worship Satan under the Name of God?" Where are they? Listen! Every Religion that Preaches Vengeance for Sin is the Religion of the Enemy & Avenger and not of the Forgiver of Sin, and their God is Satan, Named by the Divine Name. Your Religion, O Deists! Deism, is the Worship of the God of this World by the means of what you call Natural Religion and Natural Philosophy, and of Natural Morality or Self-Righteousness, the Selfish Virtues of the Natural Heart. This was the Religion of the Pharisees who murder'd Jesus. Deism is the same & ends in the same.

Voltaire, Rousseau, Gibbon, Hume, charge the Spiritually Religious with Hypocrisy; but how a Monk, or a Methodist either, can be a Hypocrite, I cannot conceive. We are Men of like passions with others & pretend not to be holier than others; therefore, when a Religious Man falls into Sin, he ought not to be call'd a Hypocrite; this title is more properly to be given to a Player who falls into Sin, whose profession is Virtue & Morality & the making Men Self-Righteous. Foote in calling Whitefield, Hypocrite, was himself one; for Whitefield pretended not to be holier than others, but confessed his Sins before all the World. Voltaire! Rousseau! You cannot escape my charge that you are Pharisees & Hypocrites, for you are constantly talking of the Virtues of the Human Heart and particularly of your own, that you may accuse others, & especially the Religious, whose errors you, by this display of pretended Virtue, chiefly design to expose. Rousseau thought Men Good by Nature: he found them Evil & found no friend. Friendship cannot exist without Forgiveness of Sins continually. The Book written by Rousseau call'd his Confessions, is an apology & cloke for his sin & not a confession.

But you also charge the poor Monks & Religious with being the causes of War, while you acquit & flatter the Alexanders & Caesars, the Lewis's & Fredericks, who alone are its causes & its actors. But the Religion of Jesus, Forgiveness of Sin, can never be the cause of a War nor of a single Martyrdom.

Those who Martyr others or who cause War are Deists, but never can be Forgivers of Sin. The Glory of Christianity is To Conquer by Forgiveness. All the Destruction, therefore, in Christian Europe has arisen from Deism, which is Natural Religion.

I saw a Monk of Charlemaine
Arise before my sight:
I talk'd with the Grey Monk as we stood
In beams of infernal light.

Gibbon arose with a lash of steel,
And Voltaire with a wracking wheel:
    The Schools, in clouds of learning roll'd,
Arose with War in iron & gold.

"Thou lazy Monk," they sound afar,
"In vain condemning glorious War;
    And in your Cell you shall ever dwell:
Rise, War, & bind him in his Cell!"

The blood red ran from the Grey Monk's side,
His hands & feet were wounded wide,
    His body bent, his arms & knees
Like to the roots of ancient trees.

When Satan first the black bow bent
And the Moral Law from the Gospel rent,
    He forg'd the Law into a Sword
And spill'd the blood of mercy's Lord.

Titus! Constantine! Charlemaine!
O Voltaire! Rousseau! Gibbon! Vain
    Your Grecian Mocks & Roman Sword
Against this image of his Lord!

For a Tear is an Intellectual thing,
And a Sigh is the Sword of an Angel King,
    And the bitter groan of a Martyr's woe
Is an Arrow from the Almightie's Bow.

JERUSALEM

CHAPTER 3

BUT Los, who is the Vehicular Form of strong Urthona,
Wept vehemently over Albion where Thames' currents spring
From the rivers of Beulah; pleasant river! soft, mild parent stream.
And the roots of Albion's Tree enter'd the Soul of Los
As he sat before his Furnaces clothed in sackcloth of hair,
In gnawing pain dividing him from his Emanation,
Inclosing all the Children of Los time after time,

Their Giant forms condensing into Nations & Peoples & Tongues.
Translucent the Furnaces, of Beryll & Emerald immortal
And Seven-fold each within other, incomprehensible
To the Vegetated Mortal Eye's perverted & single vision.
The Bellows are the Animal Lungs, the Hammers the Animal Heart,
The Furnaces the Stomach for Digestion; terrible their fury
Like seven burning heavens rang'd from South to North.

Here, on the banks of the Thames, Los builded Golgonooza,
Outside of the Gates of the Human Heart beneath Beulah
In the midst of the rocks of the Altars of Albion. In fears
He builded it, in rage & in fury. It is the Spiritual Four-fold
London, continually building & continually decaying desolate.
In eternal labours loud the Furnaces & loud the Anvils
Of Death thunder incessant around the flaming Couches of
The Twenty-four Friends of Albion and round the awful Four
For the protection of the Twelve Emanations of Albion's Sons,
The Mystic Union of the Emanation in the Lord. Because
Man divided from his Emanation is a dark Spectre,
His Emanation is an ever-weeping melancholy Shadow;
But she is made receptive of Generation thro' mercy
In the Potter's Furnace among the Funeral Urns of Beulah,
From Surrey hills thro' Italy and Greece to Hinnom's vale.

54

In Great Eternity every particular Form gives forth or Emanates
Its own peculiar Light, & the Form is the Divine Vision
And the Light is his Garment. This is Jerusalem in every Man,
A Tent & Tabernacle of Mutual Forgiveness, Male & Female Clothings.
And Jerusalem is called Liberty among the Children of Albion.

But Albion fell down, a Rocky fragment from Eternity hurl'd
By his own Spectre, who is the Reasoning Power in every Man,
Into his own Chaos, which is the Memory between Man & Man.

The silent broodings of deadly revenge springing from the
All powerful parental affection, fills Albion from head to foot.
Seeing his Sons assimilate with Luvah, bound in the bonds
Of spiritual Hate, from which springs Sexual Love as iron chains,
He tosses like a cloud outstretch'd among Jerusalem's Ruins
Which overspread all the Earth; he groans among his ruin'd porches.
But the Spectre, like a hoar frost & a Mildew, rose over Albion,
Saying, "I am God, O Sons of Men! I am your Rational Power!

Am I not Bacon & Newton & Locke who teach Humility to Man,
Who teach Doubt & Experiment? & my two Wings, Voltaire, Rousseau?
Where is that Friend of Sinners? that Rebel against my Laws
Who teaches Belief to the Nations & an unknown Eternal Life?
Come hither into the Desart & turn these stones to bread.
Vain foolish Man! wilt thou believe without Experiment
And build a World of Phantasy upon my Great Abyss,
A World of Shapes in craving lust & devouring appetite?"

So spoke the hard cold constrictive Spectre: he is named Arthur,
Constricting into Druid Rocks round Canaan, Agag & Aram & Pharoh.
Then Albion drew England into his bosom in groans & tears,
But she stretch'd out her starry Night in Spaces against him like
A long Serpent in the Abyss of the Spectre, which augmented
The Night with Dragon wings cover'd with stars, & in the Wings
Jerusalem & Vala appear'd; & above, between the Wings magnificent,
The Divine Vision dimly appear'd in clouds of blood weeping.

55

When those who disregard all Mortal Things saw a Mighty-One
Among the Flowers of Beulah still retain his awful strength,
They wonder'd, checking their wild flames; & Many gathering
Together into an Assembly, they said, "let us go down
And see these changes." Others said, "If you do so, prepare
For being driven from our fields; what have we to do with the Dead?
To be their inferiors or superiors we equally abhor:
Superior, none we know: inferior, none: all equal share
Divine Benevolence & joy; for the Eternal Man
Walketh among us, calling us his Brothers & his Friends,
Forbidding us that Veil which Satan puts between Eve & Adam,
By which the Princes of the Dead enslave their Votaries
Teaching them to form the Serpent of precious stones & gold,
To sieze the Sons of Jerusalem & plant them in One Man's Loins,
To make One Family of Contraries, that Joseph may be sold
Into Egypt for Negation, a Veil the Saviour born & dying rends."

But others said: "Let us to him, who only Is & who
Walketh among us, give decision: bring forth all your fires!"

So saying, an eternal deed was done: in fiery flames
The Universal Concave raged such thunderous sounds as never
Were sounded from a mortal cloud, nor on Mount Sinai old,
Nor in Havilah where the Cherub roll'd his redounding flame.

Loud! loud! the Mountains lifted up their voices, loud the Forests:
Rivers thunder'd against their banks, loud Winds furious fought:
Cities & Nations contended in fires & clouds & tempests:
The Seas rais'd up their voices & lifted their hands on high:
The Stars in their courses fought, the Sun, Moon, Heaven, Earth,
Contending for Albion & for Jerusalem his Emanation,
And for Shiloh the Emanation of France, & for lovely Vala.

Then far the greatest number were about to make a Separation;
And they Elected Seven, call'd the Seven Eyes of God,
Lucifer, Molech, Elohim, Shaddai, Pahad, Jehovah, Jesus.
They nam'd the Eighth: he came not, he hid in Albion's Forests.
But first they said: (& their Words stood in Chariots in array
Curbing their Tygers with golden bits & bridles of silver & ivory)

"Let the Human Organs be kept in their perfect integrity,
At will Contracting into Worms or Expanding into Gods,
And then, behold! what are these Ulro Visions of Chastity?
Then as the moss upon the tree, or dust upon the plow,
Or as the sweat upon the labouring shoulder, or as the chaff
Of the wheat-floor, or as the dregs of the sweet winepress:
Such are these Ulro Visions; for tho' we sit down within
The plowed furrow, list'ning to the weeping clods till we
Contract or Expand Space at will, or if we raise ourselves
Upon the chariots of the morning, Contracting or Expanding Time,
Every one knows we are One Family, One Man blessed for ever."

Silence remain'd & every one resum'd his Human Majesty.
And many conversed on these things as they labour'd at the furrow,
Saying: "It is better to prevent misery than to release from misery:
It is better to prevent error than to forgive the criminal.
Labour well the Minute Particulars, attend to the Little-ones,
And those who are in misery cannot remain so long
If we do but our duty: labour well the teeming Earth."

They Plow'd in tears, the trumpets sounded before the golden Plow,
And the voices of the Living Creatures were heard in the clouds of heaven,
Crying: "Compell the Reasoner to Demonstrate with unhewn Demon-
   strations.
Let the Indefinite be explored, and let every Man be Judged
By his own Works. Let all Indefinites be thrown into Demonstrations,
To be pounded to dust & melted in the Furnaces of Affliction.

He who would do good to another must do it in Minute Particulars:
General Good is the plea of the scoundrel, hypocrite & flatterer,
For Art & Science cannot exist but in minutely organized Particulars
And not in generalizing Demonstrations of the Rational Power.
The Infinite alone resides in Definite & Determinate Identity;
Establishment of Truth depends on destruction of Falshood continually,
On Circumcision, not on Virginity, O Reasoners of Albion!"

So cried they at the Plow. Albion's Rock frowned above,
And the Great Voice of Eternity rolled above terrible in clouds,
Saying "Who will go forth for us, & Who shall we send before our face?"

56

Then Los heaved his thund'ring Bellows on the Valley of Middlesex,
And thus he chaunted his Song: the Daughters of Albion reply:

"What may Man be? who can tell! But what may Woman be
To have power over Man from Cradle to corruptible Grave?
He who is an Infant and whose Cradle is a Manger
Knoweth the Infant sorrow, whence it came and where it goeth
And who weave it a Cradle of the grass that withereth away.
This World is all a Cradle for the erred wandering Phantom,
Rock'd by Year, Month, Day & Hour; and every two Moments
Between dwells a Daughter of Beulah to feed the Human Vegetable.
Entune, Daughters of Albion, your hymning Chorus mildly,
Cord of affection thrilling extatic on the iron Reel
To the golden Loom of Love, to the moth-labour'd Woof,
A Garment and Cradle weaving for the infantine Terror,
For fear, at entering the gate into our World of cruel
Lamentation, it flee back & hide in Non-Entity's dark wild
Where dwells the Spectre of Albion, destroyer of Definite Form.
The Sun shall be a Scythed Chariot of Britain: the Moon, a Ship
In the British Ocean, Created by Los's Hammer, measured out
Into Days & Nights & Years & Months, to travel with my feet
Over these desolate rocks of Albion. O daughters of despair!
Rock the Cradle, and in mild melodies tell me where found
What you have enwoven with so much tears & care, so much
Tender artifice, to laugh, to weep, to learn, to know:
Remember! recollect! what dark befel in wintry days."

"O it was lost for ever, and we found it not; it came
And wept at our wintry Door. Look! look! behold! Gwendolen
Is become a Clod of Clay! Merlin is a Worm of the Valley!"

Then Los utter'd with Hammer & Anvil: "Chaunt! revoice!
I mind not your laugh, and your frown I not fear, and
You must my dictate obey; from your gold-beam'd Looms trill
Gentle to Albion's Watchman; on Albion's mountains reecho,
And rock the Cradle while, Ah me! Of that Eternal Man
And of the cradled Infancy in his bowels of compassion
Who fell beneath his instruments of husbandry & became
Subservient to the clods of the furrow; the cattle and even
The emmet and earth-Worm are his superiors & his lords."

Then the response came warbling from trilling Looms in Albion:
'We Women tremble at the light, therefore hiding fearful
The Divine Vision with Curtain & Veil & flashly Tabernacle."
Los utter'd, swift as the rattling thunder upon the mountains:
"Look back into the Church Paul! Look! Three Women around
The Cross! O Albion, why didst thou a Female Will Create?"

57

And the voices of Bath & Canterbury & York & Edinburgh Cry
Over the Plow of Nations in the strong hand of Albion, thundering along
Among the Fires of the Druid & the deep black rethundering Waters
Of the Atlantic which poured in, impetuous, loud, loud, louder & louder.
And the Great Voice of the Atlantic howled over the Druid Altars,
Weeping over his Children in Stone-henge, in Malden & Colchester,
Round the Rocky Peak of Derbyshire, London Stone & Rosamond's
    Bower:

"What is a Wife & what is a Harlot? What is a Church & What
Is a Theatre? are they Two & not One? can they Exist Separate?
Are not Religion & Politics the Same Thing? Brotherhood is Religion,
O Demonstrations of Reason Dividing Families in Cruelty & Pride!"

But Albion fled from the Divine Vision; with the Plow of Nations enflam-
    ing,
The Living Creatures madden'd, and Albion fell into the Furrow; and
The Plow went over him & the Living was Plowed in among the Dead.
But his Spectre rose over the starry Plow. Albion fled beneath the Plow
Till he came to the Rock of Ages, & he took his Seat upon the Rock.

Wonder siez'd all in Eternity, to behold the Divine Vision open
The Center into an Expanse, & the Center rolled out into an Expanse.

58

In beauty the Daughters of Albion divide & unite at will,
Naked & drunk with blood. Gwendolen dancing to the timbrel
Of War, reeling up the Street of London, she divides in twain
Among the Inhabitants of Albion: the People fall around.
The Daughters of Albion divide & unite in jealousy & cruelty.
The Inhabitants of Albion at the Harvest & the Vintage
Feel their Brain cut round beneath the temples, shrieking,
Bonifying into a Scull, the Marrow exuding in dismal pain.
They flee over the rocks bonifying. Horses, Oxen feel the knife.
And while the Sons of Albion by severe War & Judgment bonify,
The Hermaphroditic Condensations are divided by the Knife:
The obdurate Forms are cut asunder by Jealousy & Pity.

Rational Philosophy and Mathematic Demonstration
Is divided in the intoxications of pleasure & affection.
Two Contraries War against each other in fury & blood,
And Los fixes them on his Anvil, incessant his blows:
He fixes them with strong blows, placing the stones & timbers
To Create a World of Generation from the World of Death,
Dividing the Masculine & Feminine, for the comingling
Of Albion's & Luvah's Spectres was Hermaphroditic.

Urizen wrathful strode above, directing the awful Building
As a Mighty Temple, delivering Form out of confusion.
Jordan sprang beneath its threshold, bubbling from beneath
Its pillars: Euphrates ran under its arches: white sails
And silver oars reflect on its pillars & sound on its ecchoing
Pavements, where walk the Sons of Jerusalem who remain Ungenerate.
But the revolving Sun and Moon pass thro' its porticoes:
Day & night in sublime majesty & silence they revolve
And shine glorious within. Hand & Koban arch'd over the Sun
In the hot noon as he travel'd thro' his journey. Hyle & Skofield
Arch'd over the Moon at midnight, & Los Fix'd them there
With his thunderous Hammer: terrified the Spectres rage & flee.
Canaan is his portico. Jordan is a fountain in his porch,
A fountain of milk & wine to relieve the traveller.
Egypt is the eight steps within. Ethiopia supports his pillars.
Lybia & the Lands unknown are the ascent without;
Within is Asia & Greece, ornamented with exquisite art.
Persia & Media are his halls: his inmost hall is Great Tartary.

China & India & Siberia are his temples for entertainment.
Poland & Russia & Sweden, his soft retired chambers.
France & Spain & Italy & Denmark & Holland & Germany
Are the temples among his pillars: Britain is Los's Forge.
America North & South are his baths of living waters.

Such is the Ancient World of Urizen in the Satanic Void,
Created from the Valley of Middlesex by London's River,
From Stone-henge and from London Stone, from Cornwall to Cathnes
The Four Zoas rush around on all sides in dire ruin:
Furious in pride of Selfhood the terrible Spectres of Albion
Rear their dark Rocks among the Stars of God, stupendous
Works! A World of Generation continually Creating out of
The Hermaphroditic Satanic World of rocky destiny,

59

And formed into Four precious stones for enterance from Beulah.

For the Veil of Vala, which Albion cast into the Atlantic Deep
To catch the Souls of the Dead, began to Vegetate & Petrify
Around the Earth of Albion among the Roots of his Tree.
This Los formed into the Gates & mighty Wall between the Oak
Of Weeping & the Palm of Suffering beneath Albion's Tomb.
Thus in process of time it became the beautiful Mundane Shell,
The Habitation of the Spectres of the Dead, & the Place
Of Redemption & of awaking again into Eternity.

For Four Universes round the Mundane Egg remain Chaotic:
One to the North, Urthona: One to the South, Urizen:
One to the East, Luvah: One to the West, Tharmas.
They are the Four Zoas that stood around the Throne Divine,
Verulam, London, York & Edinburgh, their English names.
But when Luvah assumed the World of Urizen Southward
And Albion was slain upon his Mountains & in his Tent,
All fell towards the Centre, sinking downwards in dire ruin.
In the South remains a burning Fire: in the East, a Void:
In the West, a World of raging Waters: in the North, solid Darkness
Unfathomable without end; but in the midst of these
Is Built eternally the sublime Universe of Los & Enitharmon.

And in the North Gate, in the West of the North, toward Beulah,
Cathedron's Looms are builded, and Los's Furnaces in the South.
A wondrous golden Building immense with ornaments sublime
Is bright Cathedron's golden Hall, its Courts, Towers & Pinnacles.

And one Daughter of Los sat at the fiery Reel, & another
Sat at the shining Loom with her Sisters attending round;
Terrible their distress, & their sorrow cannot be utter'd;
And another Daughter of Los sat at the Spinning Wheel,
Endless their labour, with bitter food, void of sleep;
Tho' hungry, they labour: they rouze themselves anxious
Hour after hour labouring at the whirling Wheel,
Many Wheels & as many lovely Daughters sit weeping.

Yet the intoxicating delight that they take in their work
Obliterates every other evil; none pities their tears,
Yet they regard not pity & they expect no one to pity,
For they labour for life & love regardless of any one
But the poor Spectres that they work for always, incessantly.

They are mock'd by every one that passes by; they regard not,
They labour, & when their Wheels are broken by scorn & malice
They mend them sorrowing with many tears & afflictions.

Other Daughters Weave on the Cushion & Pillow Network fine
That Rahab & Tirzah may exist & live & breathe & love.
Ah, that it could be as the Daughters of Beulah wish!

Other Daughters of Los, labouring at Looms less fine,
Create the Silk-worm & the Spider & the Catterpiller
To assist in their most grievous work of pity & compassion;
And others Create the wooly Lamb & the downy Fowl
To assist in the work; the Lamb bleats, the Sea-fowl cries:
Men understand not the distress & the labour & sorrow
That in the Interior Worlds is carried on in fear & trembling,
Weaving the shudd'ring fears & loves of Albion's Families.
Thunderous rage the Spindles of iron, & the iron Distaff
Maddens in the fury of their hands, weaving in bitter tears
The Veil of Goats-hair & Purple & Scarlet & fine twined Linen.

60

The clouds of Albion's Druid Temples rage in the eastern heaven
While Los sat terrified beholding Albion's Spectre, who is Luvah,
Spreading in bloody veins in torments over Europe & Asia,
Not yet formed, but a wretched torment unformed & abyssal
In flaming fire; within the Furnaces the Divine Vision appear'd
On Albion's hills, often walking from the Furnaces in clouds

And flames among the Druid Temples & the Starry Wheels,
Gather'd Jerusalem's Children in his arms & bore them like
A Shepherd in the night of Albion which overspread all the Earth.

"I gave thee liberty and life, O lovely Jerusalem,
And thou hast bound me down upon the Stems of Vegetation.
I gave thee Sheep-walks upon the Spanish Mountains, Jerusalem,
I gave thee Priam's City and the Isles of Grecia lovely.
I gave thee Hand & Scofield & the Counties of Albion,
They spread forth like a lovely root into the Garden of God,
They were as Adam before me, united into One Man,
They stood in innocence & their skiey tent reach'd over Asia
To Nimrod's Tower, to Ham & Canaan, walking with Mizraim
Upon the Egyptian Nile, with solemn songs to Grecia
And sweet Hesperia, even to Great Chaldea & Tesshina,
Following thee as a Shepherd by the Four Rivers of Eden.
Why wilt thou rend thyself apart, Jerusalem,
And build this Babylon & sacrifice in secret Groves
Among the Gods of Asia, among the fountains of pitch & nitre?
Therefore thy Mountains are become barren, Jerusalem,
Thy Valleys, Plains of burning sand; thy Rivers, waters of death;
Thy Villages die of the Famine, and thy Cities
Beg bread from house to house, lovely Jerusalem.
Why wilt thou deface thy beauty & the beauty of thy little-ones
To please thy Idols in the pretended chastities of Uncircumcision?
Thy Sons are lovelier than Egypt or Assyria; wherefore
Dost thou blacken their beauty by a Secluded place of rest,
And a peculiar Tabernacle to cut the integuments of beauty
Into veils of tears and sorrows, O lively Jerusalem?
They have perswaded thee to this; therefore their end shall come,
And I will lead thee thro' the Wilderness in shadow of my cloud,
And in my love I will lead thee, lovely Shadow of Sleeping Albion."

This is the Song of the Lamb, sung by Slaves in evening time.

But Jerusalem faintly saw him; clos'd in the Dungeons of Babylon
Her Form was held by Beulah's Daughters; but all within unseen
She sat at the Mills, her hair unbound, her feet naked
Cut with the flints, her tears run down, her reason grows like
The Wheel of Hand incessant turning day & night without rest,
Insane she raves upon the winds, hoarse, inarticulate.
All night Vala hears, she triumphs in pride of holiness
To see Jerusalem deface her lineaments with bitter blows

Of despair, while the Satanic Holiness triumph'd in Vala
In a Religion of Chastity & Uncircumcised Selfishness
Both of the Head & Heart & Loins, clos'd up in Moral Pride.

But the Divine Lamb stood beside Jerusalem; oft she saw
The lineaments Divine & oft the Voice heard, & oft she said:

* "O Lord & Saviour, have the Gods of the Heathen pierced thee,
Or hast thou been pierced in the House of thy Friends?
Art thou alive, & livest thou for evermore? or art thou
Not [Nought] but a delusive shadow, a thought that liveth **not**?
Babel mocks, saying there is no God nor Son of God,
That thou, O Human Imagination, O Divine Body, art all
A delusion; but I know thee, O Lord, when thou arisest upon
My weary eyes, even in this dungeon & this iron mill.
The Stars of Albion cruel rise; thou bindest to sweet influences,
For thou also sufferest with me, altho' I behold thee not;
And altho' I sin & blaspheme thy holy name, **thou** pitiest me
Because thou knowest I am deluded by the turning mills
And by these visions of pity & love because of Albion's **death**."

Thus spake Jerusalem, & thus the Divine Voice replied:

"Mild Shade of Man, pitiest thou these Visions of terror & woe?
Give forth thy pity & love; fear not! lo, I am with thee always.
Only believe in me, that I have power to raise from death
Thy Brother who Sleepeth in Albion; fear not, trembling Shade,

61

"Behold, in the Visions of Elohim Jehovah, behold Joseph & Mary
And be comforted, O Jerusalem, in the Visions of Jehovah Elohim."

She looked & saw Joseph the Carpenter in Nazareth & Mary
His espoused Wife. And Mary said, "If thou put me away from thee
Dost thou not murder me?" Joseph spoke in anger & fury, "Should I
Marry a Harlot & an Adulteress?" Mary answer'd, "Art thou more pure
Than thy Maker who forgiveth Sins & calls again Her that is Lost?
Tho' She hates, he calls her again in love. I love my dear Joseph,
But he driveth me away from his presence; yet I hear the voice of God
In the voice of my Husband: tho' he is angry for a moment, he will not
Utterly cast me away; if I were pure, never could I taste the sweets
Of the Forgiveness of Sins; if I were holy, I never could behold the tears
Of love of him who loves me in the midst of his anger in furnace of fire."

"Ah my Mary!" said Joseph, weeping over & embracing her closely in
His arms: "Doth he forgive Jerusalem, & not exact Purity from her who is
Polluted? I heard his voice in my sleep & his Angel in my dream,
Saying, 'Doth Jehovah Forgive a Debt only on condition that it shall
Be Payed? Doth he Forgive Pollution only on conditions of Purity?
That Debt is not Forgiven! That Pollution is not Forgiven!
Such is the Forgiveness of the Gods, the Moral Virtues of the
Heathen whose tender Mercies are Cruelty. But Jehovah's Salvation
Is without Money & without Price, in the Continual Forgiveness of Sins,
In the Perpetual Mutual Sacrifice in Great Eternity; for behold,
There is none that liveth & Sinneth not! And this is the Covenant
Of Jehovah: If you Forgive one-another, so shall Jehovah Forgive You,
That He Himself may Dwell among You. Fear not then to take
To thee Mary thy Wife, for she is with Child by the Holy Ghost.'"

Then Mary burst forth into a Song: she flowed like a River of
Many Streams in the arms of Joseph & gave forth her tears of joy
Like many waters, and Emanating into gardens & palaces upon
Euphrates, & to forests & floods & animals wild & tame from
Gihon to Hiddekel, & to corn fields & villages & inhabitants
Upon Pison & Arnon & Jordan. And I heard the voice among
The Reapers, Saying, "Am I Jerusalem the lost Adulteress? or am I
Babylon come up to Jerusalem?" And another voice answer'd, Saying,

"Doth the voice of my Lord call me again? am I pure thro' his Mercy
And Pity? Am I become lovely as a Virgin in his sight, who am
Indeed a Harlot drunken with the Sacrifice of Idols? does he
Call her pure as he did in the days of her Infancy when She
Was cast out to the loathing of her person? The Chaldean took
Me from my Cradle. The Amalekite stole me away upon his Camels
Before I had ever beheld with love the Face of Jehovah, or known
That there was a God of Mercy. O Mercy, O Divine Humanity!
O Forgiveness & Pity & Compassion! If I were Pure I should never
Have known Thee: If I were Unpolluted I should never have
Glorified thy Holiness or rejoiced in thy great Salvation."

Mary leaned her side against Jerusalem: Jerusalem recieved
The Infant into her hands in the Visions of Jehovah. Times passed on.
Jerusalem fainted over the Cross & Sepulcher. She heard the voice:
"Wilt thou make Rome thy Patriarch Druid & the Kings of Europe his
Horsemen? Man in the Resurrection changes his Sexual Garments at
   Will.
Every Harlot was once a Virgin: every Criminal an Infant Love.

62

"Repose on me till the morning of the Grave. I am thy life."

Jerusalem replied: "I am an outcast: Albion is dead:
I am left to the trampling foot & the spurning heel:
A Harlot I am call'd: I am sold from street to street:
I am defaced with blows & with the dirt of the Prison,
And wilt thou become my Husband, O my Lord & Saviour?
Shall Vala bring thee forth? shall the Chaste be ashamed also?
I see the Maternal Line, I behold the Seed of the Woman:
Cainah & Ada & Zillah, & Naamah, Wife of Noah,
Shuah's daughter & Tamar & Rahab the Canaanites,
Ruth the Moabite, & Bathsheba of the daughters of Heth,
Naamah the Ammonite, Zibeah the Philistine, & Mary:
These are the Daughters of Vala, Mother of the Body of death;
But I, thy Magdalen, behold thy Spiritual Risen Body.
Shall Albion arise? I know he shall arise at the Last Day!
I know that in my flesh I shall see God; but Emanations
Are weak, they know not whence they are nor wither tend."

Jesus replied, "I am the Resurrection & the Life.
I Die & pass the limits of possibility as it appears
To individual perception. Luvah must be Created
And Vala, for I cannot leave them in the gnawing Grave
But will prepare a way for my banished-ones to return.
Come now with me into the villages, walk thro' all the cities;
Tho' thou are taken to prison & judgment, starved in the streets,
I will command the cloud to give thee food & the hard rock
To flow with milk & wine; tho' thou seest me not a season,
Even a long season, & a hard journey & a howling wilderness,
Tho' Vala's cloud hide thee & Luvah's fires follow thee,
Only believe & trust in me. Lo, I am always with thee!"

So spoke the Lamb of God while Luvah's Cloud reddening above
Burst forth in streams of blood upon the heavens, & dark night
Involv'd Jerusalem, & the Wheels of Albion's Sons turn'd hoarse
Over the Mountains, & the fires blaz'd on Druid Altars,
And the Sun set in Tyburn's Brook where Victims howl & cry.

But Los beheld the Divine Vision among the flames of the Furnaces.
Therefore he lived & breathed in hope; but his tears fell incessant
Because his Children were clos'd from him apart & Enitharmon

Dividing in fierce pain; also the Vision of God was clos'd in clouds
Of Albion's Spectres, that Los in despair oft sat & often ponder'd
On Death Eternal, in fierce shudders upon the mountains of Albion
Walking, & in the vales in howlings fierce; then to his Anvils
Turning, anew began his labours, tho' in terrible pains.

63

Jehovah stood among the Druids in the Valley of Annandale
When the Four Zoas of Albion, the Four Living Creatures, the Cherubim
Of Albion tremble before the Spectre in the starry Harness of the Plow
Of Nations. And their Names are Urizen & Luvah & Tharmas & Urthona.
Luvah slew Tharmas, the Angel of the Tongue, & Albion brought him
To Justice in his own City of Paris, denying the Resurrection.
Then Vala, the Wife of Albion, who is the Daughter of Luvah,
Took vengeance Twelve-fold among the Chaotic Rocks of the Druids
Where the Human Victims howl to the Moon, & Thor & Friga
Dance the dance of death, contending with Jehovah among the Cherubim.
The Chariot Wheels filled with Eyes rage along the howling Valley
In the Dividing of Reuben & Benjamin bleeding from Chester's River.

The Giants & the Witches & the Ghosts of Albion dance with
Thor & Friga, & the Fairies lead the Moon along the Valley of Cherubim
Bleeding in torrents from Mountain to Mountain, a lovely Victim.
And Jehovah stood in the Gates of the Victim, & he appeared
A weeping Infant in the Gates of Birth in the midst of Heaven.

The Cities & Villages of Albion became Rock & Sand Unhumanized,
The Druid Sons of Albion; & the Heavens a Void around, unfathomable;
No Human Form but Sexual, & a little weeping Infant pale reflected
Multitudinous in the Looking Glass of Enitharmon, on all sides
Around in the clouds of the Female, on Albion's Cliffs of the Dead.

Such the appearance in Cheviot, in the Divisions of Reuben,
When the Cherubim hid their heads under their wings in deep slumbers,
When the Druids demanded Chastity from Woman & all was lost.

"How can the Female be Chaste, O thou stupid Druid," Cried Los,
"Without the Forgiveness of Sins in the merciful clouds of Jehovah
And without the Baptism of Repentance to wash away Calumnies and
The Accusations of Sin, that each may be Pure in their Neighbours' sight?
O when shall Jehovah give us Victims from his Flocks & Herds
Instead of Human Victims by the Daughters of Albion & Canaan?"

Then laugh'd Gwendolen, & her laughter shook the Nations & Familys of
The Dead beneath Beulah from Tyburn to Golgotha and from
Ireland to Japan: furious her Lions & Tygers & Wolves sport before
Los on the Thames & Medway: London & Canterbury groan in pain.

Los knew not yet what was done: he thought it was all in Vision,
In Visions of the Dreams of Beulah among the Daughters of Albion;
Therefore the Murder was put apart in the Looking-Glass of Enitharmon.

He saw in Vala's hand the Druid Knife of Revenge & the Poison Cup
Of Jealousy, and thought it a Poetic Vision of the Atmospheres,
Till Canaan roll'd apart from Albion across the Rhine, along the Danube.

And all the Land of Canaan suspended over the Valley of Cheviot,
From Bashan to Tyre & from Troy to Gaza of the Amalekite.
And Reuben fled with his head downwards among the Caverns

64

Of the Mundane Shell which froze on all sides round Canaan on
The vast Expanse, where the Daughters of Albion Weave the Web
Of Ages & Generations, folding & unfolding it like a Veil of Cherubim;
And sometimes it touches the Earth's summits & sometimes spreads
Abroad into the Indefinite Spectre, who is the Rational Power.

Then All the Daughters of Albion became One before Los, even Vala.
And she put forth her hand upon the Looms in dreadful howlings
Till she vegetated into a hungry Stomach & a devouring Tongue.
Her Hand is a Court of Justice: her Feet two Armies in Battle:
Storms & Pestilence in her Locks, & in her Loins Earthquake
And Fire & the Ruin of Cities & Nations & Families & Tongues.

She cries: "The Human is but a Worm, & thou, O Male! Thou art
Thyself Female, a Male, a breeder of Seed, a Son & Husband: & Lo,
The Human Divine is Woman's Shadow, a Vapor in the summer's heat.
Go assume Papal dignity, thou Spectre, thou Male Harlot! Arthur,
Divide into the Kings of Europe in times remote, O Woman-born
And Woman-nourish'd & Woman-educated & Woman-scorn'd!"

"Wherefore art thou living," said Los, "& Man cannot live in thy pres-
ence?
Art thou Vala the Wife of Albion, O thou lovely Daughter of Luvah?
All Quarrels arise from Reasoning: the secret Murder and

The violent Man-slaughter, these are the Spectre's double Cave,
The Sexual Death living on accusation of Sin & Judgment,
To freeze Love & Innocence into the gold & silver of the Merchant.
Without Forgiveness of Sin, Love is Itself Eternal Death."

Then the Spectre drew Vala into his bosom, magnificent, terrific,
Glittering with precious stones & gold, with Garments of blood & fire.
He wept in deadly wrath of the Spectre, in self-contradicting agony,
Crimson with Wrath & green with Jealousy, dazling with Love
And Jealousy immingled, & the purple of the violet darken'd deep,
Over the Plow of Nations thund'ring in the hand of Albion's Spectre.

A dark Hermaphrodite they stood frowning upon London's River;
And the Distaff & Spindle in the hands of Vala, with the Flax of
Human Miseries, turn'd fierce with the Lives of Men along the Valley
As Reuben fled before the Daughters of Albion, Taxing the Nations.

Derby Peak yawn'd a horrid Chasm at the Cries of Gwendolen & at
The stamping feet of Ragan upon the flaming Treddles of her Loom
That drop with crimson gore with the Loves of Albion & Canaan,
Opening along the Valley of Rephaim, weaving over the Caves of Machpelah,

65

To decide Two Worlds with a great decision, a World of Mercy and
A World of Justice, the World of Mercy for Salvation:
To cast Luvah into the Wrath and Albion into the Pity,
In the Two Contraries of Humanity & in the Four Regions.

For in the depths of Albion's bosom in the eastern heaven
They sound the clarions strong, they chain the howling Captives,
They cast the lots into the helmet, they give the oath of blood in Lambeth,
They vote the death of Luvah & they nail'd him to Albion's Tree in Bath,
They stain'd him with poisonous blue, they inwove him in cruel roots
To die a death of Six thousand years bound round with vegetation.
The sun was black & the moon roll'd a useless globe thro' Britain.

Then left the Sons of Urizen the plow & harrow, the loom,
The hammer & the chisel & the rule & compasses; from London fleeing,
They forg'd the sword on Cheviot, the chariot of war & the battleax,
The trumpet fitted to mortal battle, & the flute of summer in Annandale;
And all the Arts of Life they chang'd into the Arts of Death in Albion.
The hour-glass contemn'd because its simple workmanship

Was like the workmanship of the plowman, & the water wheel
That raises water into cisterns, broken & burn'd with fire
Because its workmanship was like the workmanship of the shepherd;
And in their stead, intricate wheels invented, wheel without wheel,
To perplex youth in their outgoings & to bind to labours in Albion
Of day & night the myriads of eternity: that they may grind
And polish brass & iron hour after hour, laborious task,
Kept ignorant of its use: that they might spend the days of wisdom
In sorrowful drudgery to obtain a scanty pittance of bread,
In ignorance to view a small portion & think that All,
And call it Demonstration, blind to all the simple rules of life.

"Now, now the battle rages round thy tender limbs, O Vala!
Now smile among thy bitter tears, now put on all thy beauty.
Is not the wound of the sword sweet & the broken bone delightful?
Wilt thou now smile among the scythes when the wounded groan in the
    field?
We were carried away in thousands from London & in tens
Of thousands from Westminster & Marybone, in ships clos'd up,
Chain'd hand & foot, compell'd to fight under the iron whips
Of our captains, fearing our officers more than the enemy.
Lift up thy blue eyes, Vala, & put on thy sapphire shoes!
O melancholy Magdalen, behold the morning over Malden break!
Gird on thy flaming zone, descend into the sepulcher of Canterbury.
Scatter the blood from thy golden brow, the tears from thy silver locks;
Shake off the waters from thy wings & the dust from thy white garments.
Remember all thy feigned terrors on the secret couch of Lambeth's Vale
When the sun rose in glowing morn, with arms of mighty hosts
Marching to battle, who was wont to rise with Urizen's harps
Girt as a sower with his seed to scatter life abroad over Albion.
Arise, O Vala, bring the bow of Urizen, bring the swift arrows of light.
How rag'd the golden horses of Urizen, compell'd to the chariot of love!
Compell'd to leave the plow to the ox, to snuff up the winds of desolation,
To trample the corn fields in boastful neighings; this is no gentle harp,
This is no warbling brook nor shadow of a mirtle tree,
But blood and wounds and dismal cries and shadows of the oak,
And heats laid open to the light by the broad grizly sword,
And bowels, hid in hammer'd steel, rip'd quivering on the ground.
Call forth thy smiles of soft deceit: call forth thy cloudy tears.
We hear thy sighs in trumpets shrill when morn shall blood renew."

So sang the Spectre Sons of Albion round Luvah's Stone of Trial,
Mocking and deriding at the writhings of their Victim on Salisbury,
Drinking his Emanations in intoxicating bliss, rejoicing in Giant dance;
For a Spectre has no Emanation but what he imbibes from decieving
A Victim: Then he becomes her Priest & she his Tabernacle
And his Oak Grove, till the Victim rend the woven Veil
In the end of his sleep when Jesus calls him from his grave.

Howling the Victims on the Druid Altars yield their souls
To the stern Warriors; lovely sport the Daughters round their Victims,
Drinking their lives in sweet intoxication; hence arose from Bath
Self deluding odours, in spiral volutions intricately winding
Over Albion's mountains a feminine indefinite cruel delusion.
Astonish'd, terrified & in pain & torment, Sudden they behold
Their own Parent, the Emanation of their murder'd Enemy
Become their Emanation and their Temple and Tabernacle.
They knew not this Vala was their beloved Mother Vala, Albion's Wife.

Terrified at the sight of the Victim, at his distorted sinews,
The tremblings of Vala vibrate thro' the limbs of Albion's Sons
While they rejoice over Luvah in mockery & bitter scorn.
Suddenly they become like what they behold, in howlings & deadly pain:
Spasms smite their features, sinews & limbs: pale they look on one an-
     other;
They turn, contorted: their iron necks bend unwilling towards
Luvah: their lips tremble: their muscular fibres are cramp'd & smitten:
They become like what they behold! Yet immense in strength & power,

66

In awful pomp & gold, in all the previous unhewn stones of Eden
They build a stupendous Building on the Plain of Salisbury, with chains
Of rocks round London Stone, of Reasonings, of unhewn Demonstrations
In labyrinthine arches (Mighty Urizen the Architect) thro' which
The Heavens might revolve & Eternity be bound in their chain.
Labour unparallell'd! a wondrous rocky World of cruel destiny,
Rocks piled on rocks reaching the stars, stretching from pole to pole.
The Building is Natural Religion & its Altars Natural Morality,
A building of eternal death, whose proportions are eternal despair.
Here Vala stood turning the iron Spindle of destruction
From heaven to earth, howling invisible; but not invisible
Her two Covering Cherubs, afterwards named Voltaire & Rousseau,
Two frowning Rocks on each side of the Cove & Stone of Torture,

Frozen Sons of the feminine Tabernacle of Bacon, Newton & Locke;
For Luvah is France, the Victim of the Spectres of Albion.
Los beheld in terror; he pour'd his loud storms on the Furnaces.
The Daughters of Albion clothed in garments of needle work
Strip them off from their shoulders and bosoms, they lay aside
Their garments, they sit naked upon the Stone of trial.
The Knife of flint passes over the howling Victim: his blood
Gushes & stains the fair side of the fair Daughters of Albion.
They put aside his curls, they divide his seven locks upon
His forehead, they bind his forehead with thorns of iron,
They put into his hand a reed, they mock, Saying: "Behold
The King of Canaan whose are seven hundred chariots of iron!"
They take off his vesture whole with their Knives of flint,
But they cut asunder his inner garments, searching with
Their cruel fingers for his heart, & there they enter in pomp,
In many tears, & there they erect a temple & an altar.
They pour cold water on his brain in front, to cause
Lids to grow over his eyes in veils of tears, and caverns
To freeze over his nostrils, while they feed his tongue from cups
And dishes of painted clay. Glowing with beauty & cruelty
They obscure the sun & the moon: no eye can look upon them.

Ah! alas! at the sight of the Victim & at sight of those who are smitten
All who see become what they behold; their eyes are cover'd
With veils of tears and their nostrils & tongues shrunk up,
Their ear bent outwards; as their Victim, so are they, in the pangs
Of unconquerable fear amidst delights of revenge Earth-shaking.
And as their eye & ear shrunk, the heavens shrunk away:
The Divine Vision became first a burning flame, then a column
Of fire, then an awful fiery wheel surrounding earth & heaven,
And then a globe of blood wandering distant in an unknown night.
Afar into the unknown night the mountains fled away,
Six months of mortality, a summer, & six months of mortality, a winter.
The Human form began to be alter'd by the Daughters of Albion
And the perceptions to be dissipated into the Indefinite, Becoming
A mighty Polypus nam'd Albion's Tree; they tie the Veins
And Nerves into two knots & the Seed into a double knot.
They look forth: the Sun is shrunk: the Heavens are shrunk
Away into the far remote, and the Trees & Mountains wither'd
Into indefinite cloudy shadows in darkness & separation.
By Invisible Hatreds adjoin'd, they seem remote and separate
From each other, and yet are a Mighty Polypus in the Deep!

As the Misletoe grows on the Oak, so Albion's Tree on Eternity. Lo!
He who will not comingle in Love must be adjoin'd by Hate.

They look forth from Stone-henge: from the Cove round London Stone
They look on one another: the mountain calls out to the mountain.
Plinlimmon shrunk away: Snowdon trembled: the mountains
Of Wales & Scotland beheld the descending War, the routed flying.
Red run the streams of Albion: Thames is drunk with blood
As Gwendolen cast the shuttle of war, as Cambel return'd the beam,
The Humber & the Severn are drunk with the blood of the slain.
London feels his brain cut round: Edinburgh's heart is circumscribed:
York & Lincoln hide among the flocks because of the griding Knife.
Worcester & Hereford, Oxford & Cambridge reel & stagger
Overwearied with howling. Wales & Scotland alone sustain the fight!
The inhabitants are sick to death: they labour to divide into Days
And Nights the uncertain Periods, and into Weeks & Months. In vain
They send the Dove & Raven & in vain the Serpent over the mountains
And in vain the Eagle & Lion over the four-fold wilderness:
They return not, but generate in rocky places desolate:
They return not, but build a habitation separate from Man.
The Sun forgets his course like a drunken man; he hesitates
Upon the Cheselden hills, thinking to sleep on the Severn.
In vain: he is hurried afar into an unknown Night:
He bleeds in torrents of blood as he rolls thro' heaven above.
He chokes up the paths of the sky; the Moon is leprous as snow,
Trembling & descending down, seeking to rest on high Mona,
Scattering her leprous snows in flakes of disease over Albion.
The Stars flee remote; the heaven is iron, the earth is sulphur,
And all the mountains & hills shrink up like a withering gourd
As the Senses of Men shrink together under the Knife of flint
In the hands of Albion's Daughters among the Druid Temples,

67

By those who drink their blood & the blood of their Covenant.

And the Twelve Daughters of Albion united in Rahab & Tirzah,
A Double Female; and they drew out from the Rocky Stones
Fibres of Life to Weave, for every Female is a Golden Loom,
The Rocks are opake hardnesses covering all Vegetated things;
And as they Wove & Cut from the Looms, in various divisions
Stretching over Europe & Asia from Ireland to Japan,
They divided into many lovely Daughters, to be counterparts

To those they Wove; for when they Wove a Male, they divided
Into a Female to the Woven Male: in opake hardness
They cut the Fibres from the Rocks: groaning in pain they Weave,
Calling the Rocks Atomic Origins of Existence, denying Eternity
By the Atheistical Epicurean Philosophy of Albion's Tree.
Such are the Feminine & Masculine when separated from Man.
They call the Rocks Parents of Men, & adore the frowning Chaos,
Dancing around in howling pain, clothed in the bloody Veil,
Hiding Albion's Sons within the Veil, closing Jerusalem's
Sons without, to feed with their Souls the Spectres of Albion,
Ashamed to give Love openly to the piteous & merciful Man,
Counting him an imbecile mockery, but the Warrior
They adore & his revenge cherish with the blood of the Innocent.
They drink up Dan & Gad to feed with milk Skofeld & Kotope;
They strip off Joseph's Coat & dip it in the blood of battle.

Tirzah sits weeping to hear the shrieks of the dying: her Knife
Of flint is in her hand: she passes it over the howling Victim.
The Daughters Weave their Work in loud cries over the Rock
Of Horeb, still eyeing Albion's Cliffs, eagerly siezing & twisting
The threads of Vala & Jerusalem running from mountain to mountain
Over the whole Earth; loud the Warriors rage in Beth Peor
Beneath the iron whips of their Captains & consecrated banners:
Loud the Sun & Moon rage in the conflict: loud the Stars
Shout in the night of battle, & their spears grow to their hands,
With blood weaving the deaths of the Mighty into a Tabernacle
For Rahab & Tirzah, till the Great Polypus of Generation covered the
    Earth.

In Verulam the Polypus's Head, winding around his bulk
Thro' Rochester and Chichester & Exeter & Salisbury
To Bristol, & his Heart beat strong on Salisbury Plain
Shooting out Fibres round the Earth thro' Gaul & Italy
And Greece & along the Sea of Rephaim into Judea
To Sodom & Gomorrha: thence to India, China & Japan

The Twelve Daughters in Rahab & Tirzah have circumscrib'd the Brain
Beneath & pierced it thro' the midst with a golden pin.
Blood hath stain'd her fair side beneath her bosom.

"O thou poor Human Form!" said she. "O thou poor child of woe!
Why wilt thou wander away from Tirzah? why me compel to bind thee?

If thou dost go away from me I shall consume upon these Rocks.
These fibres of thine eyes that used to beam in distant heavens
Away from me, I have bound down with a hot iron.
These nostrils that expanded with delight in morning skies
I have bent downward with lead melted in my roaring furnaces
Of affliction, of love, of sweet despair, of torment unendurable.
My soul is seven furnaces; incessant roars the bellows
Upon my terribly flaming heart, the molten metal runs
In channels thro' my fiery limbs. O love, O pity, O fear,
O pain! O the pangs, the bitter pangs of love forsaken!
Ephraim was a wilderness of joy where all my wild beasts ran.
The River Kanah wander'd by my sweet Manasseh's side
To see the boy spring into heavens sounding from my sight!
Go Noah, fetch the girdle of strong brass, heat it red-hot,
Press it around the loins of this ever expanding cruelty.
Shriek not so my only love. I refuse thy joys: I drink
Thy shrieks because Hand & Hyle are cruel & obdurate to me.

68

O Skofield, why art thou cruel? Lo, Joseph is thine! to make
You One, to weave you both in the same mantle of skin.
Bind him down, Sisters, bind him down on Ebal, Mount of cursing.
Malah, come forth from Lebanon, & Hoglah, from Mount Sinai!
Come, circumscribe this tongue of sweets, & with a screw of iron
Fasten this ear into the rock. Milcah, the task is thine!
Weep not so, Sisters, weep not so: our life depends on this,
Or mercy & truth are fled away from Shechem & Mount Gilead,
Unless my beloved is bound upon the Stems of Vegetation."

And thus the Warriors cry, in the hot day of Victory, in Songs:

"Look! the beautiful Daughter of Albion sits naked upon the Stone,
Her panting Victim beside her: her heart is drunk with blood
Tho' her brain is not drunk with wine: she goes forth from Albion
In pride of beauty, in cruelty of holiness, in the brightness
Of her tabernacle & her ark & secret place: the beautiful Daughter
Of Albion delights the eyes of the Kings: their hearts & the
Hearts of their Warriors glow hot before Thor & Friga. O Molech!
O Chemosh! O Bacchus! O Venus! O Double God of Generation!
The Heavens are cut like a mantle around from the Cliffs of Albion
Across Europe, across Africa: in howling & deadly War,
A sheet & veil & curtain of blood is let down from Heaven

Across the hills of Ephraim & down Mount Olivet to
The Valley of the Jebusite. Molech rejoices in heaven,
He sees the Twelve Daughters naked upon the Twelve Stones
Themselves condensing to rocks & into the Ribs of a Man.
Lo, they shoot forth in tender Nerves across Europe & Asia.
Lo, they rest upon the Tribes, where their panting Victims lie.
Molech rushes into the Kings, in love to the beautiful Daughters,
But they frown & delight in cruelty, refusing all other joy.
Bring your Offerings, your first begotten, pamper'd with milk & blood,
Your first born of seven years old, be they Males or Females,
To the beautiful Daughters of Albion! they sport before the Kings
Clothed in the skin of the Victim! blood, human blood is the life
And delightful food of the Warrior; the well fed Warrior's flesh
Of him who is slain in War fills the Valleys of Ephraim with
Breeding Women walking in pride & bringing forth under green trees
With pleasure, without pain, for their food is blood to the Captive.
Molech rejoices thro' the Land from Havilah to Shur: he rejoices
In moral law & its severe penalties; loud Shaddai & Jehovah
Thunder above, when they see the Twelve panting Victims
On the Twelve Stones of Power, & the beautiful Daughters of Albion:
'If you dare rend their Veil with your spear, you are healed of Love.'
From the Hills of Camberwell & Wimbledon, from the Valleys
Of Walton & Esher, from Stone-henge & from Malden's Cove,
Jerusalem's Pillars fall in the rendings of fierce War.
Over France & Germany, upon the Rhine & Danube,
Reuben & Benjamin flee: they hide in the Valley of Rephaim.
Why trembles the Warrior's limbs when he beholds thy beauty
Spotted with Victims' Blood? by the fires of thy secret tabernacle
And thy ark & holy place, at thy frowns, at thy dire revenge,
Smitten as Uzzah of old, his armour is soften'd, his spear
And sword faint in his hand from Albion across Great Tartary.
O beautiful Daughter of Albion! cruelty is thy delight.
O Virgin of terrible eyes who dwellest by Valleys of springs
Beneath the Mountains of Lebanon in the City of Rehob in Hamath,
Taught to touch the harp, to dance in the Circle of Warriors
Before the Kings of Canaan, to cut the flesh from the Victim,
To roast the flesh in fire, to examine the Infant's limbs
In cruelties of holiness, to refuse the joys of love, to bring
The Spies from Egypt, to raise jealousy in the bosoms of the Twelve
Kings of Canaan, then let the Spies depart to Meribah Kadesh,
To the place of the Amalekite: I am drunk with unsatiated love,
I must rush again to War, for the Virgin has frown'd & refus'd.

Sometimes I curse & sometimes bless thy fascinating beauty.
Once Man was occupied in intellectual pleasures & energies,
But now my Soul is harrow'd with grief & fear & love & desire,
And now I hate & now I love, & Intellect is no more.
There is no time for anything but the torments of love & desire.
The Feminine & Masculine Shadows, soft, mild & ever varying
In beauty, are Shadows now no more, but Rocks in Horeb."

69

Then all the Males conjoined into One Male, & every one
Became a ravening eating Cancer growing in the Female,
A Polypus of Roots, of Reasoning, Doubt, Despair & Death,
Going forth & returning from Albion's Rocks to Canaan,
Devouring Jerusalem from every Nation of the Earth.

Envying stood the enormous Form, at variance with Itself
In all its Members, in eternal torment of love & jealousy,
Driv'n forth by Los time after time from Albion's cliffy shore,
Drawing the free loves of Jerusalem into infernal bondage
That they might be born in contentions of Chastity & in
Deadly Hate between Leah & Rachel, Daughters of Deceit & Fraud
Bearing the Images of various Species of Contention
And Jealousy & Abhorrence & Revenge & deadly Murder,
Till they refuse liberty to the Male, & not like Beulah
Where every Female delights to give her maiden to her husband:
The Female searches sea & land for gratifications to the
Male Genius, who in return clothes her in gems & gold
And feeds her with the food of Eden; hence all her beauty beams.
She Creates at her will a little moony night & silence
With Spaces of sweet gardens & a tent of elegant beauty,
Closed in by a sandy desart & a night of stars shining
And a little tender moon & hovering angels on the wing;
And the Male gives a Time & Revolution to her Space
Till the time of love is passed in ever varying delights.
For All Things Exist in the Human Imagination,
And thence in Beulah they are stolen by secret amorous theft
Till they have had Punishment enough to make them commit Crimes.
Hence rose the Tabernacle in the Wilderness & all its Offerings,
From Male & Female Loves in Beulah & their Jealousies;
But no one can consummate Female bliss in Los's World without
Becoming a Generated Mortal, a Vegetating Death.

And now the Spectres of the Dead awake in Beulah; all
The Jealousies become Murderous, uniting together in Rahab
A Religion of Chastity, forming a Commerce to sell Loves,
With Moral Law an Equal Balance not going down with decision.
Therefore the Male severe & cruel, fill'd with stern Revenge,
Mutual Hate returns & mutual Deceit & mutual Fear.

Hence the Infernal Veil grows in the disobedient Female,
Which Jesus rends & the whole Druid Law removes away
From the Inner Sanctuary, a False Holiness hid within the Center.
For the Sanctuary of Eden is in the Camp, in the Outline,
In the Circumference, & every Minute Particular is Holy:
Embraces are Cominglings from the Head even to the Feet,
And not a pompous High Priest entering by a Secret Place.

Jerusalem pined in her inmost soul over Wandering Reuben
As she slept in Beulah's Night, hid by the Daughters of Beulah.

70

And this the form of mighty Hand sitting on Albion's cliffs
Before the face of Albion, a mighty threat'ning Form:

His bosom wide & shoulders huge, overspreading wondrous,
Bear Three strong sinewy Necks & Three awful & terrible Heads,
Three Brains, in contradictory council brooding incessantly,
Neither daring to put in act its councils, fearing each-other,
Therefore rejecting Ideas as nothing & holding all Wisdom
To consist in the agreements & disagreements of Ideas,
Plotting to devour Albion's Body of Humanity & Love.

Such Form the aggregate of the Twelve Sons of Albion took, & such
Their appearance when combin'd; but often by birth-pangs & loud groans
They divide to Twelve; the key-bones & the chest dividing in pain
Disclose a hideous orifice; thence issuing, the Giant-brood
Arise, as the smoke of the furnace, shaking the rocks from sea to sea,
And there they combine into Three Forms named Bacon & Newton &
   Locke
In the Oak Groves of Albion which overspread all the Earth.

Imputing Sin & Righteousness to Individuals, Rahab
Sat, deep within him hid, his Feminine Power unreveal'd,
Brooding Abstract Philosophy to destroy Imagination, the Divine-

Humanity: A Three-fold Wonder, feminine, most beautiful, Three-fold
Each within other. On her white marble & even Neck, her Heart,
Inorb'd and bonified, with locks of shadowing modesty, shining
Over her beautiful Female features soft flourishing in beauty,
Beams mild, all love and all perfection, that when the lips
Recieve a kiss from Gods or Men, a three-fold kiss returns
From the press'd loveliness; so her whole immortal form three-fold,
Three-fold embrace returns, consuming lives of Gods & Men,
In fires of beauty melting them as gold & silver in the furnace.
Her Brain enlabyrinths the whole heaven of her bosom & loins
To put in act what her Heart wills. O who can withstand her power!
Her name is Vala in Eternity: in Time her name is Rahab.

The Starry Heavens all were fled from the mighty limbs of Albion,

71

And above Albion's Land was seen the Heavenly Canaan
As the Substance is to the Shadow, and above Albion's Twelve Sons
Were seen Jerusalem's Sons and all the Twelve Tribes spreading
Over Albion. As the Soul is to the Body, so Jerusalem's Sons
Are to the Sons of Albion, and Jerusalem is Albion's Emanation.

What is Above is Within, for every-thing in Eternity is translucent:
The Circumference is Within, Without is formed the Selfish Center,
And the Circumference still expands going forward to Eternity,
And the Center has Eternal States; these States we now explore.

And these the Names of Albion's Twelve Sons & of his Twelve Daughters
With their Districts: Hand dwelt in Selsey & had Sussex & Surrey
And Kent & Middlesex, all their Rivers & their Hills of flocks & herds,
Their Villages, Towns, Cities, Sea-Ports, Temples, sublime Cathedrals,
All were his Friends, & their Sons & Daughters intermarry in Beulah;
For all are Men in Eternity, Rivers, Mountains, Cities, Villages,
All are Human, & when you enter into their Bosoms you walk
In Heavens & Earths, as in your own Bosom you bear your Heaven
And Earth & all you behold; tho' it appears Without, it is Within,
In your Imagination, of which this World of Mortality is but a Shadow.

Hyle dwelt in Winchester, comprehending Hants, Dorset, Devon,
    Cornwall,
Their Villages, Cities, Sea Ports, their Corn fields & Gardens spacious,
Palaces, Rivers & Mountains; and between Hand & Hyle arose

Gwendolen & Cambel who is Boadicea: they go abroad & return
Like lovely beams of light from the mingled affections of the Brothers.
The Inhabitants of the whole Earth rejoice in their beautiful light.

Coban dwelt in Bath: Somerset, Wiltshire, Gloucestershire
Obey'd his awful voice: Ignoge is his lovely Emanation;
She adjoin'd with Gwantoke's Children; soon lovely Cordella arose;
Gwantoke forgave & joy'd over South Wales & all its Mountains.

Peachey had North Wales, Shropshire, Cheshire & the Isle of Man;
His Emanation is Mehetabel, terrible & lovely upon the Mountains

Brertun had Yorkshire, Durham, Westmoreland, & his Emanation
Is Ragan; she adjoin'd to Slade, & produced Gonorill far beaming.

Slade had Lincoln, Stafford, Derby, Nottingham, & his lovely
Emanation, Gonorill, rejoices over hills & rocks & woods & rivers.

Huttn had Warwick, Northampton, Bedford, Buckingham,
Leicester & Berkshire, & his Emanation is Gwinefred beautiful.

Skofeld had Ely, Rutland, Cambridge, Huntingdon, Norfolk,
Suffolk, Hartford & Essex, & his Emanation is Gwinevera
Beautiful; she beams towards the east, all kinds of precious stones
And pearl, with instruments of music in holy Jerusalem.

Kox had Oxford, Warwick, Wilts; his Emanation is Estrild;
Join'd with Cordella she shines southward over the Atlantic.

Kotope had Hereford, Stafford, Worcester, & his Emanation
Is Sabrina; join'd with Mehetabel she shines west over America.

Bowen had all Scotland, the Isles, Northumberland & Cumberland;
His Emanation is Conwenna; she shines a triple form
Over the north with peariy beams gorgeous & terrible.
Jerusalem & Vala rejoice in Bowen & Conwenna.

But the Four Sons of Jerusalem that never were Generated
Are Rintrah and Palamabron and Theotormon and Bromion. They
Dwell over the Four Provinces of Ireland in heavenly light,
The Four Universities of Scotland, & in Oxford & Cambridge &
    Winchester.

But now Albion is darkened & Jerusalem lies in ruins
Above the Mountains of Albion, above the head of Los.

And Los shouted with ceaseless shoutings, & his tears poured down
His immortal cheeks, rearing his hands to heaven for aid Divine!
But he spoke not to Albion, fearing lest Albion should turn his Back
Against the Divine Vision & fall over the Precipice of Eternal Death;
But he receded before Albion & before Vala weaving the Veil
With the iron shuttle of War among the rooted Oaks of Albion,
Weeping & shouting to the Lord day & night; and his Children
Wept round him as a flock silent Seven Days of Eternity.

72

And the Thirty-two Counties of the Four Provinces of Ireland
Are thus divided: The Four Counties are in the Four Camps,
Munster South in Reuben's Gate, Connaut West in Joseph's Gate,
Ulster North in Dan's Gate, Leinster East in Judah's Gate;

For Albion in Eternity has Sixteen Gates among his Pillars,
But the Four towards the West were Walled up, & the Twelve
That front the Four other Points were turned Four Square
By Los for Jerusalem's sake & called the Gates of Jerusalem,
Because Twelve Sons of Jerusalem fled successive thro' the Gates.
But the Four Sons of Jerusalem who fled not but remain'd,
Are Rintrah & Palamabron & Theotormon & Bromion,
The Four that remain with Los to guard the Western Wall;
And these Four remain to guard the Four Walls of Jerusalem
Whose foundations remain in the Thirty-two Counties of Ireland
And in Twelve Counties of Wales & in the Forty Counties
Of England & in the Thirty-six Counties of Scotland.

And the names of the Thirty-two Counties of Ireland are these:
Under Judah & Issachar & Zebulun are Lowth, Longford,
Eastmeath, Westmeath, Dublin, Kildare, King's County,
Queen's County, Wicklow, Catherloh, Wexford, Kilkenny.
And those under Reuben & Simeon & Levi are these:
Waterford, Tipperary, Cork, Limerick, Kerry, Clare.
And those under Ephraim, Manasseh & Benjamin are these:
Galway, Roscommon, Mayo, Sligo, Leitrim.
And those under Dan, Asher & Napthali are these:
Donnegal, Antrim, Tyrone, Fermanagh, Armagh, Londonderry,
Down, Managhan, Cavan. These are the Land of Erin.

All these Center in London & in Golgonooza, from whence
They are Created continually, East & West & North & South,
And from them are Created all the Nations of the Earth,
Europe & Asia & Africa & America, in fury Fourfold.

And Thirty-two the Nations to dwell in Jerusalem's Gates.
O Come ye Nations! Come ye People! Come up to Jerusalem!
Return, Jerusalem, & dwell together as of old! Return,
Return, O Albion! let Jerusalem overspread all Nations
As in the times of old! O Albion awake! Reuben wanders,
The Nations wait for Jerusalem, they look up for the Bride.

France, Spain, Italy, Germany, Poland, Russia, Sweden, Turkey,
Arabia, Palestine, Persia, Hindostan, China, Tartary, Siberia,
Egypt, Lybia, Ethiopia, Guinea, Caffraria, Negroland, Morocco,
Congo, Zaara, Canada, Greenland, Carolina, Mexico,
Peru, Patagonia, Amazonia, Brazil: Thirty-two Nations,
And under these Thirty-two Classes of Islands in the Ocean
All the Nations, Peoples & Tongues throughout all the Earth.

And the Four Gates of Los surround the Universe Within and
Without; & whatever is visible in the Vegetable Earth, the same
Is visible in the Mundane Shell revers'd, in mountain & vale.
And a Son of Eden was set over each Daughter of Beulah to guard
In Albion's Tomb the wondrous Creation, & the Four-fold Gate
Towards Beulah is to the South. Fenelon, Guion, Teresa,
Whitefield & Hervey guard that Gate, with all the gentle Souls
Who guide the great Wine-press of Love. Four precious Stones that
    Gate.

73

Such are Cathedron's golden Halls in the City of Golgonooza.

And Los's Furnaces howl loud, living, self-moving, lamenting
With fury & despair, & they stretch from South to North
Thro' all the Four Points. Lo! the Labourers at the Furnaces,
Rintrah & Palamabron, Theotormon & Bromion, loud lab'ring
With the innumerable multitudes of Golgonooza round the Anvils
Of Death! But how they came forth from the Furnaces, & how long
Vast & severe the anguish e'er they knew their Father, were
Long to tell; & of the iron rollers, golden axle-trees & yokes
Of brass, iron chains & braces, & the gold, silver & brass,

Mingled or separate, for swords, arrows, cannons, mortars,
The terrible ball, the wedge, the loud sounding hammer of destruction,
The sounding flail to thresh, the winnow to winnow kingdoms,
The water wheel & mill of many innumerable wheels resistless,
Over the Four-fold Monarchy from Earth to the Mundane Shell:

Perusing Albion's Tomb in the starry characters of Og & Anak,
To Create the lion & wolf, the bear, the tyger & ounce,
To Create the wooly lamb & downy fowl & scaly serpent,
The summer & winter, day & night, the sun & moon & stars,
The tree, the plant, the flower, the rock, the stone, the metal
Of Vegetative Nature by their hard restricting condensations.

Where Luvah's World of Opakeness grew to a period, It
Became a Limit, a Rocky hardness without form & void,
Accumulating without end; here Los, who is of the Elohim,
Opens the Furnaces of affliction in the Emanation,
Fixing the Sexual into an ever-prolific Generation,
Naming the Limit of Opakeness, Satan, & the Limit of Contraction,
Adam, who is Peleg & Joktan, & Esau & Jacob, & Saul & David.

Voltaire insinuates that these Limits are the cruel work of God,
Mocking the Remover of Limits & the Resurrection of the Dead,
Setting up Kings in wrath, in holiness of Natural Religion:
Which Los with his mighty Hammer demolishes time on time
In miracles & wonders in the Four-fold Desart of Albion:
Permanently Creating, to be in Time Reveal'd & Demolish'd,
Satan, Cain, Tubal, Nimrod, Pharoh, Priam, Bladud, Belin,
Arthur, Alfred, the Norman Conqueror, Richard, John,
And all the Kings & Nobles of the Earth & all their Glories:
These are Created by Rahab & Tirzah in Ulro; but around
These, to preserve them from Eternal Death, Los Creates
Adam, Noah, Abraham, Moses, Samuel, David, Ezekiel,
Dissipating the rocky forms of Death by his thunderous Hammer.
As the Pilgrim passes while the Country permanent remains,
So Men pass on, but States remain permanent for ever.

The Spectres of the Dead howl round the porches of Los
In the terrible Family feuds of Albion's cities & villages,
To devour the Body of Albion, hung'ring & thirsting & rav'ning.
The Sons of Los clothe them & feed, & provide houses & gardens,
And every Human Vegetated Form in its inward recesses
Is a house of pleasantness & a garden of delight Built by the
Sons & Daughters of Los in Bowlahoola & in Cathedron.

From London to York & Edinburgh the Furnaces rage terrible.
Primrose Hill is the mouth of the Furnace & the Iron Door.

74

The Four Zoas clouded rage. Urizen stood by Albion
With Rintrah and Palamabron and Theotormon and Bromion:
These Four are Verulam & London & York & Edinburgh.
And the Four Zoas are Urizen & Luvah & Tharmas & Urthona:
In opposition deadly, and their Wheels in poisonous
And deadly stupor turn'd against each other, loud & fierce,
Entering into the Reasoning Power, forsaking Imagination,
They became Spectres, & their Human Bodies were reposed
In Beulah by the Daughters of Beulah with tears & lamentations.

The Spectre is the Reasoning Power in Man, & when separated
From Imagination and closing itself as in steel in a Ratio
Of the Things of Memory, It thence frames Laws & Moralities
To destroy Imagination, the Divine Body, by Martyrdoms & Wars.

Teach me, O Holy Spirit, the Testimony of Jesus! let me
Comprehend wonderous things out of the Divine Law!
I behold Babylon in the opening Streets of London. I behold
Jerusalem in ruins wandering about from house to house.
This I behold: the shudderings of death attend my steps.
I walk up and down in Six Thousand Years: their Events are present
    before me
To tell how Los in grief & anger, whirling round his Hammer on high,
Drave the Sons & Daughters of Albion from their ancient mountains.
They became the Twelve Gods of Asia Opposing the Divine Vision.

The Sons of Albion are Twelve, the Sons of Jerusalem Sixteen.
I tell how Albion's Sons, by Harmonies of Concords & Discords
Opposed to Melody, and by Lights & Shades opposed to Outline,
And by Abstraction opposed to the Visions of Imagination,
By cruel Laws, divided Sixteen into Twelve Divisions:
How Hyle roof'd Los in Albion's Cliffs by the Affections rent
Asunder & opposed to Thought, to draw Jerusalem's Sons
Into the Vortex of his Wheels, therefore Hyle is called Gog,
Age after age drawing them away towards Babylon,
Babylon, the Rational Morality, deluding to death the little ones
In strong temptations of stolen beauty. I tell how Reuben slept
On London Stone, & the Daughters of Albion ran around admiring

His awful beauty; with Moral Virtue, the fair deciever, offspring
Of Good & Evil, they divided him in love upon the Thames & sent
Him over Europe, in streams of gore, out of Cathedron's Looms:
How Los drave them from Albion & they became Daughters of Canaan;
Hence Albion was call'd the Canaanite & all his Giant Sons.
Hence is my Theme. O Lord my Saviour, open thou the Gates
And I will lead forth thy Words! telling how the Daughters
Cut the Fibres of Reuben, how he roll'd apart & took Root
In Bashan: terror-struck Albion's Sons look toward Bashan.
They have divided Simeon: he also roll'd apart in blood
Over the Nations till he took Root beneath the shining Looms
Of Albion's Daughters in Philistea by the side of Amalek.
They have divided Levi: he hath shot out into Forty-eight Roots
Over the Land of Canaan; they have divided Judah:
He hath took Root in Hebron, in the Land of Hand & Hyle.
Dan, Napthali, Gad, Asher, Issachar, Zebulun roll apart
From all the Nations of the Earth to dissipate into Non Entity.

I see a Feminine Form arise from the Four terrible Zoas,
Beautiful but terrible, struggling to take a form of beauty,
Rooted in Shechem: this is Dinah, the youthful form of Erin.
The Wound I see in South Molton Street & Stratford place,
Whence Joseph & Benjamin roll'd apart away from the Nations.
In vain they roll'd apart: they are fix'd into the Land of Cabul.

75

And Rahab, Babylon the Great, hath destroyed Jerusalem.
Bath stood upon the Severn with Merlin & Bladud & Arthur,
The Cup of Rahab in his hand, her Poisons Twenty-seven-fold.

And all her Twenty-seven Heavens, now hid & now reveal'd,
Appear in strong delusive light of Time & Space, drawn out
In shadowy pomp, by the Eternal Prophet created evermore.
For Los in Six Thousand Years walks up & down continually
That not one Moment of Time be lost, & every revolution
Of Space he makes permanent in Bowlahoola & Cathedron.

And these the names of the Twenty-seven Heavens & their Churches:
Adam, Seth, Enos, Cainan, Mahalaleel, Jared, Enoch,
Methuselah, Lamech: these are the Giants mighty, Hermaphroditic.
Noah, Shem, Arphaxad, Cainan the Second, Salah, Heber,

Peleg, Reu, Serug, Nahor, Terah: these are the Female Males,
A Male within a Female hid as in an Ark & Curtains.
Abraham, Moses, Solomon, Paul, Constantine, Charlemaine,
Luther: these Seven are the Male Females, the Dragon Forms,
The Female hid within a Male; thus Rahab is reveal'd,
Mystery, Babylon the Great, the Abomination of Desolation,
Religion hid in War, a Dragon red & hidden Harlot.
But Jesus, breaking thro' the Central Zones of Death & Hell,
Opens Eternity in Time & Space, triumphant in Mercy.

Thus are the Heavens form'd by Los within the Mundane Shell.
And where Luther ends Adam begins again in Eternal Circle
To awake the Prisoners of Death, to bring Albion again
With Luvah into light eternal in his eternal day.

But now the Starry Heavens are fled from the mighty limbs of Albion.

END OF CHAPTER 3

77

TO THE CHRISTIANS

Devils are   I give you the end of a golden
False Religions.   string,
    "Saul, Saul,   Only wind it into a ball,
"Why persecutest thou me?"   It will lead you in at Heaven's gate
                                Built in Jerusalem's wall.

WE are told to abstain from fleshly desires that we may lose no time
from the Work of the Lord: Every moment lost is a moment that cannot
be redeemed; every pleasure that intermingles with the duty of our
station is a folly unredeemable, & is planted like the seed of a wild flower
among our wheat: All the tortures of repentance are tortures of self-
reproach on account of our leaving the Divine Harvest to the Enemy,
the struggles of intanglement with incoherent roots. I know of no other
Christianity and of no other Gospel than the liberty both of body &
mind to exercise the Divine Arts of Imagination, Imagination, the real

& eternal World of which this Vegetable Universe is but a faint shadow, & in which we shall live in our Eternal or Imaginative Bodies when these Vegetable Mortal Bodies are no more. The Apostles knew of no other Gospel. What were all their spiritual gifts? What is the Divine Spirit? is the Holy Ghost any other than an Intellectual Fountain? What is the Harvest of the Gospel & its Labours? What is that Talent which it is a curse to hide? What are the Treasures of Heaven which we are to lay up for ourselves, are they any other than Mental Studies & Performances? What are all the Gifts of the Gospel, are they not all Mental Gifts? Is God a Spirit who must be worshipped in Spirit & in Truth, and are not the Gifts of the Spirit Every-thing to Man? O ye Religious, discountenance every one among you who shall pretend to despise Art & Science! I call upon you in the Name of Jesus! What is the Life of Man but Art & Science? is it Meat & Drink? is not the Body more than Raiment? What is Mortality but the things relating to the Body which Dies? What is Immortality but the things relating to the Spirit which Lives Eternally? What is the Joy of Heaven but Improvement in the things of the Spirit? What are the Pains of Hell but Ignorance, Bodily Lust, Idleness & devastation of the things of the Spirit? Answer this to yourselves, & expel from among you those who pretend to despise the labours of Art & Science, which alone are the labours of the Gospel. Is not this plain & manifest to the thought? Can you think at all & not pronounce heartily That to Labour in Knowledge is to Build up Jerusalem, and to Despise Knowledge is to Despise Jerusalem & her Builders. And remember: He who despises & mocks a Mental Gift in another, calling it pride & selfishness & sin, mocks Jesus the giver of every Mental Gift, which always appear to the ignorance-loving Hypocrite as Sins; but that which is a Sin in the sight of cruel Man is not so in the sight of our kind God. Let every Christian, as much as in him lies, engage himself openly & publicly before all the World in some Mental pursuit for the Building up of Jerusalem.

> I stood among my valleys of the south
> And saw a flame of fire, even as a Wheel
> Of fire surrounding all the heavens: it went
> From west to east, against the current of
> Creation, and devour'd all things in its loud
> Fury & thundering course round heaven & earth.
> By it the Sun was roll'd into an orb,
> By it the Moon faded into a globe
> Travelling thro' the night; for, from its dire

And restless fury, Man himself shrunk up
Into a little root a fathom long.
And I asked a Watcher & a Holy-One
Its Name; he answered: "It is the Wheel of Religion."
I wept & said: "Is this the law of Jesus,
This terrible devouring sword turning every way?"
He answer'd: "Jesus died because he strove
Against the current of this Wheel; its Name
Is Caiaphas, the dark preacher of Death,
Of sin, of sorrow & of punishment:
Opposing Nature! It is Natural Religion;
But Jesus is the bright Preacher of Life
Creating Nature from this fiery Law
By self-denial & forgiveness of Sin.
Go therefore, cast out devils in Christ's name,
Heal thou the sick of spiritual disease,
Pity the evil, for thou art not sent
To smite with terror & with punishments
Those that are sick, like to the Pharisees
Crucifying & encompassing sea & land
For proselytes to tyranny & wrath;
But to the Publicans & Harlots go,
Teach them True Happiness, but let no curse
Go forth out of thy mouth to blight their peace;
For Hell is open'd to Heaven: thine eyes beheld
The dungeons burst & the Prisoners set free."

  England! awake! awake! awake!
   Jerusalem thy Sister calls!
  Why wilt thou sleep the sleep of death
   And close her from thy ancient walls?

  Thy hills & valleys felt her feet
   Gently upon their bosoms move:
  Thy gates beheld sweet Zion's ways:
   Then was a time of joy and love.

  And now the time returns again:
   Our souls exult, & London's towers
  Recieve the Lamb of God to dwell
   In England's green & pleasant bowers.

78

JERUSALEM

CHAPTER 4

THE Spectres of Albion's Twelve Sons revolve mightily
Over the Tomb & over the Body, rav'ning to devour
The Sleeping Humanity. Los with his mace of iron
Walks round; loud his threats, loud his blows fall
On the rocky Spectres, as the Potter breaks the potsherds,
Dashing in pieces Self-righteousnesses, driving them from Albion's
Cliffs, dividing them into Male & Female forms in the Furnaces
And on his Anvils; lest they destroy the Feminine Affections
They are broken. Loud howl the Spectres in his iron Furnace.

While Los laments at his dire labours, viewing Jerusalem,
Sitting before his Furnaces clothed in sackcloth of hair,
Albion's Twelve Sons surround the Forty-two Gates of Erin
In terrible armour, raging against the Lamb & against Jerusalem,
Surrounding them with armies to destroy the Lamb of God.
They took their Mother Vala and they crown'd her with gold;
They nam'd her Rahab & gave her power over the Earth,
The Concave Earth round Golgonooza in Entuthon Benython,
Even to the stars exalting her Throne, to build beyond the Throne
Of God and the Lamb, to destroy the Lamb & usurp the Throne of God,
Drawing their Ulro Voidness round the Four-fold Humanity.

Naked Jerusalem lay before the Gates upon Mount Zion
The Hill of Giants, all her foundations levell'd with the dust,

Her Twelve Gates thrown down, her children carried into captivity,
Herself in chains; this from within was seen in a dismal night
Outside, unknown before in Beulah; & the twelve gates were fill'd
With blood, from Japan eastward to the Giants causway west
In Erin's Continent; and Jerusalem wept upon Euphrates' banks
Disorganiz'd: an evanescent shade scarce seen or heard among
Her children's Druid Temples, dropping with blood, wander'd weeping!
And thus her voice went forth in the darkness of Philisthea:

"My brother & my father are no more! God hath forsaken me!
The arrows of the Almighty pour upon me & my children!
I have sinned and am an outcast from the Divine Presence!

79

"My tents are fall'n! my pillars are in ruins! my children dash'd
Upon Egypt's iron floors & the marble pavements of Assyria!
I melt my soul in reasonings among the towers of Heshbon.
Mount Zion is become a cruel rock, & no more dew
Nor rain, no more the spring of the rock appears, but cold
Hard & obdurate are the furrows of the mountain of wine & oil;
The mountain of blessing is itself a curse & an astonishment.
The hills of Judea are fallen with me into the deepest hell.
Away from the Nations of the Earth & from the Cities of the Nations
I walk to Ephraim. I seek for Shiloh. I walk like a lost sheep
Among precipices of despair; in Goshen I seek for light
In vain, and in Gilead for a physician and a comforter.
Goshen hath follow'd Philistea. Gilead hath join'd with Og.
They are become narrow places in a little and dark land,
How distant far from Albion! his hills & his valleys no more
Recieve the feet of Jerusalem: they have cast me quite away,
And Albion is himself shrunk to a narrow rock in the midst of the sea!
The plains of Sussex & Surrey, their hills of flocks & herds
No more seek to Jerusalem nor to the sound of my Holy-ones.
The Fifty-two Counties of England are harden'd against me
As if I was not their Mother; they despise me & cast me out.
London cover'd the whole Earth: England encompass'd the Nations,
And all the Nations of the Earth were seen in the Cities of Albion.
My pillars reach'd from sea to sea. London beheld me come
From my east & from my west: he blessed me and gave
His children to my breasts, his sons & daughters to my knees.
His aged parents sought me out in every city & village;
They discern'd my countenance with joy, they shew'd me to their sons,
Saying, 'Lo Jerusalem is here! she sitteth in our secret chambers.
Levi and Judah & Issachar, Ephraim, Manasseh, Gad and Dan
Are seen in our hills & valleys: they keep our flocks & herds:
They watch them in the night, and the Lamb of God appears among us.'
The river Severn stay'd his course at my command:
Thames poured his waters into my basons and baths:
Medway mingled with Kishon: Thames reciev'd the heavenly Jordan.
Albion gave me to the whole Earth to walk up & down, to pour
Joy upon every mountain, to teach songs to the shepherd & plowman.
I taught the ships of the sea to sing the songs of Zion.
Italy saw me in sublime astonishment: France was wholly mine

As my garden & as my secret bath: Spain was my heavenly couch,
I slept in his golden hills; the Lamb of God met me there,
There we walked as in our secret chamber among our little ones,
They looked upon our loves with joy, they beheld our secret joys
With holy raptures of adoration, rap'd sublime in the Visions of God.
Germany, Poland & the North wooed my footsteps, they found
My gates in all their mountains & my curtains in all their vales;
The furniture of their houses was the furniture of my chamber.
Turkey & Grecia saw my instruments of music; they arose,
They siez'd the harp, the flute, the mellow horn of Jerusalem's joy;
They sounded thanksgivings in my courts. Egypt & Lybia heard,
The swarthy sons of Ethiopia stood round the Lamb of God
Enquiring for Jerusalem: he led them up my steps to my altar.
And thou, America! I once beheld thee, but now behold no more
Thy golden mountains where my Cherubim & Seraphim rejoic'd
Together among my little-ones. But now my Altars run with blood,
My fires are corrupt, my incense is a cloudy pestilence
Of seven diseases! Once a continual cloud of salvation rose
From all my myriads, once the Four-fold World rejoic'd among
The pillars of Jerusalem between my winged Cherubim;
But now I am clos'd out from them in the narrow passages
Of the valleys of destruction into a dark land of pitch & bitumen,
From Albion's Tomb afar and from the four-fold wonders of God
Shrunk to a narrow doleful form in the dark land of Cabul.
There is Reuben & Gad & Joseph & Judah & Levi clos'd up
In narrow vales. I walk & count the bones of my beloveds
Along the Valley of Destruction, among these Druid Temples
Which overspread all the Earth in patriarchal pomp & cruel pride.
Tell me, O Vala, thy purposes; tell me wherefore thy shuttles
Drop with the gore of the slain, why Euphrates is red with blood,
Wherefore in dreadful majesty & beauty outside appears
Thy Masculine from thy Feminine, hardening against the heavens
To devour the Human! Why dost thou weep upon the wind among
These cruel Druid Temples? O Vala! Humanity is far above
Sexual organization & the Visions of the Night of Beulah
Where Sexes wander in dreams of bliss among the Emanations,
Where the Masculine & Feminine are nurs'd into Youth & Maiden
By the tears & smiles of Beulah's Daughters till the time of Sleep is past,
Wherefore then do you realize these nets of beauty & delusion
In open day, to draw the souls of the Dead into the light
Till Albion is shut out from every Nation under Heaven?

80

"Encompass'd by the frozen Net and by the rooted Tree
I walk weeping in pangs of a Mother's torment for her Children.
I walk in affliction. I am a worm and no living soul!
A worm going to eternal torment, rais'd up in a night
To an eternal night of pain, lost! lost! lost! for ever!"

Beside her Vala howl'd upon the winds in pride of beauty,
Lamenting among the timbrels of the Warriors, among the Captives
In cruel holiness, and her lamenting songs were from Arnon
And Jordan to Euphrates. Jerusalem follow'd trembling
Her children in captivity, listening to Vala's lamentation
In the thick cloud & darkness, & the voice went forth from
The cloud: "O rent in sunder from Jerusalem the Harlot daughter!
In an eternal condemnation, in fierce burning flames
Of torment unendurable! and if once a Delusion be found
Woman must perish & the Heavens of Heavens remain no more.

"My Father gave to me command to murder Albion
In unreviving Death; my Love, my Luvah, order'd me in night
To murder Albion, the King of Men; he fought in battles fierce,
He conquer'd Luvah, my beloved, he took me and my Father,
He slew them. I revived them to life in my warm bosom.
He saw them issue from my bosom dark in Jealousy.
He burn'd before me. Luvah fram'd the Knife & Luvah gave
The Knife into his daughter's hand; such thing was never known
Before in Albion's land, that one should die a death never to be reviv'd!
For, in our battles, we the Slain men view with pity and love,
We soon revive them in the secret of our tabernacles;
But I, Vala, Luvah's daughter, keep his body, embalm'd in moral laws
With spices of sweet odours of lovely jealous stupefaction,
Within my bosom, lest he arise to life & slay my Luvah.
Pity me then, O Lamb of God! O Jesus pity me!
Come into Luvah's Tents and seek not to revive the Dead!"

So sang she, and the Spindle turn'd furious as she sang.
The Children of Jerusalem, the Souls of those who sleep,
Were caught into the flax of her Distaff & in her Cloud
To weave Jerusalem a body according to her will,
A Dragon form on Zion Hill's most ancient promontory.

The Spindle turn'd in blood & fire: loud sound the trumpets
Of war: cymbals play loud before the Captains
With Cambel & Gwendolen in dance and solemn song.
The Cloud of Rahab vibrating with the Daughters of Albion
Los saw terrified, melted with pity & divided in wrath
He sent them over the narrow seas in pity and love
Among the Four Forests of Albion which overspread all the Earth.
They go forth & return swift as a flash of lightning
Among the tribes of warriors, among the Stones of power;
Against Jerusalem they rage thro' all the Nations of Europe,
Thro' Italy & Grecia to Lebanon & Persia & India.

The Serpent Temples thro' the Earth, from the wide Plain of Salisbury,
Resound with cries of Victims, shouts & songs & dying groans
And flames of dusky fire, to Amalek, Canaan and Moab.
And Rahab, like a dismal and indefinite hovering Cloud,
Refus'd to take a definite form; she hover'd over all the Earth
Calling the definite, sin, defacing every definite form
Invisible or Visible, stretch'd out in length or spread in breadth
Over the Temples, drinking groans of victims, weeping in pity
And joying in the pity, howling over Jerusalem's walls.

Hand slept on Skiddaw's top, drawn by the love of beautiful
Cambel, his bright beaming Counterpart, divided from him;
And her delusive light beam'd fierce above the Mountain,
Soft, invisible, drinking his sighs in sweet intoxication,
Drawing out fibre by fibre, returning to Albion's Tree
At night and in the morning to Skiddaw; she sent him over
Mountainous Wales into the Loom of Cathedron fibre by fibre.
He ran in tender nerves across Europe to Jerusalem's Shade
To weave Jerusalem a Body repugnant to the Lamb.

Hyle on East Moor in rocky Derbyshire rav'd to the Moon
For Gwendolen; she took up in bitter tears his anguish'd heart
That, apparent to all in Eternity, glows like the Sun in the breast:
She hid it in his ribs & back; she hid his tongue with teeth.
In terrible convulsions, pitying & gratified, drunk with pity,
Glowing with loveliness before him, becoming apparent
According to his changes, she roll'd his kidneys round
Into two irregular forms, and looking on Albion's dread Tree,
She wove two vessels of seed, beautiful as Skiddaw's snow,
Giving them bends of self interest & selfish natural virtue.

She hid them in his loins; raving he ran among the rocks,
Compell'd into a shape of Moral Virtue against the Lamb,
The invisible lovely one giving him a form according to
His Law, a form against the Lamb of God, oppos'd to Mercy
And playing in the thunderous Loom in sweet intoxication,
Filling cups of silver & crystal with shrieks & cries, with groans
And dolorous sobs, the wine of lovers in the Wine-press of Luvah.

"O sister Cambel," said Gwendolen, as their long beaming light
Mingled above the Mountain, "what shall we do to keep
These awful forms in our soft bands distracted with trembling?

81

"I have mock'd those who refused cruelty, & I have admired
The cruel Warrior. I have refused to give love to Merlin the piteous.
He brings to me the Images of his Love & I reject in chastity
And turn them out into the streets for Harlots, to be food
To the stern Warrior. I am become perfect in beauty over my Warrior;
For Men are caught by Love: Woman is caught by Pride,
That Love may only be obtain'd in the passages of Death.
Let us look: let us examine: is the Cruel become an Infant,
Or is he still a cruel Warrior? look Sisters, look! O piteous!
I have destroy'd Wand'ring Reuben who strove to bind my Will.
I have strip'd off Joseph's beautiful integument for my Beloved,
The Cruel-one of Albion, to clothe him in gems of my Zone.
I have named him Jehovah of Hosts. Humanity is become
A weeping Infant in ruin'd lovely Jerusalem's folding Cloud.

82

"I have heard Jerusalem's groans; from Vala's cries & lamentations
I gather our eternal fate. Outcasts from life and love,
Unless we find a way to bind these awful Forms to our
Embrace, we shall perish annihilate; discover'd our Delusions.
Look! I have wrought without delusion. Look! I have wept,
And given soft milk mingled together with the spirits of flocks
Of lambs and doves, mingled together in cups and dishes
Of painted clay; the mighty Hyle is become a weeping infant.
Soon shall the Spectres of the Dead follow my weaving threads."

The Twelve Daughters of Albion attentive listen in secret shades,
On Cambridge and Oxford beaming soft, uniting with Rahab's cloud,
While Gwendolen spoke to Cambel, turning soft the spinning reel,

Or throwing the wing'd shuttle, or drawing the cords with softest songs.
The golden cords of the Looms animate beneath their touches soft
Along the Island white, among the Druid Temples, while Gwendolen
Spoke to the Daughters of Albion standing on Skiddaw's top.

So saying she took a Falshood & hid it in her left hand
To entice her Sisters away to Babylon on Euphrates.
And thus she closed her left hand and utter'd her Falshood,
Forgetting that Falshood is prophetic: she hid her hand behind her,
Upon her back behind her loins, & thus utter'd her Deceit:

"I heard Enitharmon say to Los: 'Let the Daughters of Albion
Be scatter'd abroad and let the name of Albion be forgotten.
Divide them into three; name them Amalek, Canaan & Moab.
Let Albion remain a desolation without an inhabitant,
And let the Looms of Enitharmon & the Furnaces of Los
Create Jerusalem & Babylon & Egypt & Moab & Amalek
And Helle & Hesperia & Hindostan & China & Japan;
But hide America, for a Curse, an Altar of Victims & a Holy Place.'
See Sisters, Canaan is pleasant, Egypt is as the Garden of Eden,
Babylon is our chief desire, Moab our bath in summer.
Let us lead the stems of this Tree, let us plant it before Jerusalem,
To judge the Friend of Sinners to death without the Veil,
To cut her off from America, to close up her secret Ark
And the fury of Man exhaust in War, Woman permanent remain.
See how the fires of our loins point eastward to Babylon!
Look, Hyle is become an infant Love! look! behold! see him lie
Upon my bosom; look! here is the lovely wayward form
That gave me sweet delight by his torments beneath my Veil!
By the fruit of Albion's Tree I have fed him with sweet milk.
By contentions of the mighty for Sacrifice of Captives,
Humanity, the Great Delusion, is chang'd to War & Sacrifice:
I have nail'd his hands on Beth Rabbim & his hands on Heshbon's Wall.
O that I could live in his sight! O that I could bind him to my arm!"

So saying, She drew aside her Veil, from Mam-Tor to Dovedale,
Discovering her own perfect beauty to the Daughters of Albion
And Hyle a winding Worm beneath . . .
                              . . . & not a weeping Infant
Trembling & pitying she scream'd & fled upon the wind.
Hyle was a winding Worm and herself perfect in beauty.
The desarts tremble at his wrath, they shrink themselves in fear.

Cambel trembled with jealousy: she trembled! she envied!
The envy ran thro' Cathedron's Looms into the Heart
Of mild Jerusalem to destroy the Lamb of God. Jerusalem
Languish'd upon Mount Olivet, East of mild Zion's Hill.

Los saw the envious blight above his Seventh Furnace
On London's Tower on the Thames; he drew Cambel in wrath
Into his thundering Bellows, heaving it for a loud blast,
And with the blast of his Furnace upon fishy Billingsgate,
Beneath Albion's fatal Tree before the Gate of Los,
Shew'd her the fibres of her beloved to ameliorate
The envy; loud she labour'd in the Furnace of fire
To form the mighty form of Hand according to her will
In the Furnaces of Los & in the Wine-press, treading day & night
Naked among the human clusters, bringing wine of anguish
To feed the afflicted in the Furnaces; she minded not
The raging flames, tho' she return'd . . .
                                    . . . instead of beauty
Deformity; she gave her beauty to another, bearing abroad
Her struggling torment in her iron arms, and like a chain
Binding his wrists & ankles with the iron arms of love.

Gwendolen saw the Infant in her sister's arms; she howl'd
Over the forests with bitter tears and over the winding Worm
Repentant, and she also in the eddying wind of Los's Bellows
Began her dolorous task of love in the Wine-press of Luvah
To form the Worm into a form of love by tears & pain.
The Sisters saw: trembling ran thro' their Looms, softening mild
Towards London: then they saw the Furnaces open'd & in tears
Began to give their souls away in the Furnaces of affliction.
Los saw & was comforted at his Furnaces, uttering thus his voice:
"I know I am Urthona, keeper of the Gates of Heaven,
And that I can at will expatiate in the Gardens of bliss;
But pangs of love draw me down to my loins, which are
Become a fountain of veiny pipes. O Albion! my brother!

83

"Corruptability appears upon thy limbs, and never more
Can I arise and leave thy side, but labour here incessant
Till thy awaking: yet alas, I shall forget Eternity!
Against the Patriarchal pomp and cruelty labouring incessant,

I shall become an Infant horror. Enion! Tharmas! friends
Absorb me not in such dire grief. O Albion, my brother!
Jerusalem hungers in the desart; affection to her children!
The scorn'd and contemn'd youthful girl, where shall she fly?
Sussex shuts up her Villages: Hants, Devon & Wilts,
Surrounded with masses of stone in order'd forms: determine then
A form for Vala and a form for Luvah, here on the Thames
Where the Victim nightly howls beneath the Druid's knife,
A Form of Vegetation; nail them down on the stems of Mystery.
O when shall the Saxon return with the English, his redeemed brother?
O when shall the Lamb of God descend among the Reprobate?
I woo to Amalek to protect my fugitives: Amalek trembles.
I call to Canaan & Moab in my night watches: they mourn,
They listen not to my cry, they rejoice among their warriors.
Woden and Thor and Friga wholly consume my Saxons
On their enormous Altars built in the terrible north
From Ireland's rocks to Scandinavia, Persia and Tartary,
From the Atlantic Sea to the universal Erythrean.
Found ye London! enormous City! weeps thy River?
Upon his parent bosom lay thy little ones, O Land
Forsaken! Surrey and Sussex are Enitharmon's Chamber
Where I will build her a Couch of repose, & my pillars
Shall surround her in beautiful labyrinths. Oothoon!
Where hides my child? in Oxford hidest thou with Antamon?
In graceful hidings of error, in merciful deceit
Lest Hand the terrible destroy his Affection, thou hidest her;
In chaste appearances for sweet deceits of love & modesty
Immingled, interwoven, glistening to the sickening sight.
Let Cambel and her Sisters sit within the Mundane Shell
Forming the fluctuating Globe according to their will:
According as they weave the little embryon nerves & veins,
The Eye, the little Nostrils & the delicate Tongue, & Ears
Of labyrinthine intricacy, so shall they fold the World,
That whatever is seen upon the Mundane Shell, the same
Be seen upon the Fluctuating Earth woven by the Sisters.
And sometimes the Earth shall roll in the Abyss & sometimes
Stand in the Center & sometimes stretch flat in the Expanse,
According to the will of the lovely Daughters of Albion;
Sometimes it shall assimilate with mighty Golgonooza,
Touching its summits, & sometimes divided roll apart.
As a beautiful Veil, so these Females shall fold & unfold,
According to their will, the outside surface of the Earth,

An outside shadowy Surface superadded to the real Surface
Which is unchangeable for ever & ever. Amen: so be it!
Separate Albion's Sons gently from their Emanations,
Weaving bowers of delight on the current of infant Thames,
Where the old Parent still retains his youth, as I alas!
Retain my youth eight thousand and five hundred years,
The labourer of ages in the Valleys of Despair!
The land is mark'd for desolation & unless we plant
The seeds of Cities & of Villages in the Human bosom
Albion must be a rock of blood; mark ye the points
Where Cities shall remain & where Villages; for the rest,
It must lie in confusion till Albion's time of awaking.
Place the Tribes of Llewellyn in America for a hiding place
Till sweet Jerusalem emanates again into Eternity.
The night falls thick: I go upon my watch: be attentive.
The Sons of Albion go forth; I follow from my Furnaces
That they return no more, that a place be prepar'd on Euphrates.
Listen to your Watchman's voice: sleep not before the Furnaces,
Eternal Death stands at the door. O God, pity our labours."

So Los spoke to the Daughters of Beulah while his Emanation
Like a faint rainbow waved before him in the awful gloom
Of London City on the Thames from Surrey Hills to Highgate.
Swift turn the silver spindles & the golden weights play soft
And lulling harmonies beneath the Looms from Caithness in the north
To Lizard-point & Dover in the south; his Emanation
Joy'd in the many weaving threads in bright Cathedron's Dome,
Weaving the Web of life for Jerusalem; the Web of life,
Down flowing into Entuthon's Vales, glistens with soft affections.

While Los arose upon his Watch and down from Golgonooza,
Putting on his golden sandals to walk from mountain to mountain,
He takes his way, girding himself with gold & in his hand
Holding his iron mace, The Spectre remains attentive.
Alternate they watch in night, alternate labour in day,
Before the Furnaces labouring, while Los all night watches
The stars rising & setting & the meteors & terrors of night.
With him went down the Dogs of Leutha; at his feet
They lap the water of the trembling Thames, then follow swift,
And thus he heard the voice of Albion's daughters on Euphrates:

"Our Father Albion's land, O it was a lovely land! & the Daughters of
  Beulah
Walked up and down in its green mountains; but Hand is fled
Away & mighty Hyle, & after them Jerusalem is gone. Awake

84

"Highgate's heights & Hampstead's, to Poplar, Hackney & Bow,
To Islington & Paddington & the Brook of Albion's River.
We builded Jerusalem as a City & a Temple; from Lambeth
We began our Foundations, lovely Lambeth. O lovely Hills
Of Camberwell, we shall behold you no more in glory & pride,
For Jerusalem lies in ruins & the Furnaces of Los are builded there.
You are now shrunk up to a narrow Rock in the midst of the Sea;
But here we build Babylon on Euphrates, compell'd to build
And to inhabit, our Little-ones to clothe in armour of the gold
Of Jerusalem's Cherubims & to forge them swords of her Altars.
I see London, blind & age bent, begging thro' the Streets
Of Babylon, led by a child; his tears run down his beard.
The voice of Wandering Reuben ecchoes from street to street
In all the Cities of the Nations, Paris, Madrid, Amsterdam.
The Corner of Broad Street weeps; Poland Street languishes;
To Great Queen Street & Lincoln's Inn all is distress & woe.
The night falls thick. Hand comes from Albion in his strength:
He combines into a Mighty-one, the Double Molech & Chemosh,
Marching thro' Egypt in his fury: the East is pale at his course.
The Nations of India, the Wild Tartar that never knew Man
Starts from his lofty places & casts down his tents & flees away;
But we woo him all the night in songs. O Los come forth, O Los
Divide us from these terrors & give us power them to subdue.
Arise upon thy Watches, let us see thy Globe of fire
On Albion's Rocks & let thy voice be heard upon Euphrates."

Thus sang the Daughters in lamentation, uniting into One
With Rahab as she turn'd the iron Spindle of destruction.
Terrified at the Sons of Albion they took the Falshood which
Gwendolen hid in her left hand: it grew & grew till it

85

Became a Space & an Allegory around the Winding Worm.
They nam'd it Canaan & built for it a tender Moon.
Los smil'd with joy, thinking on Enitharmon, & he brought
Reuben from his twelvefold wand'rings & led him into it,

Planting the Seeds of the Twelve Tribes & Moses & David,
And gave a Time & Revolution to the Space, Six Thousand Years.
He call'd it Divine Analogy, for in Beulah the Feminine
Emanations Create Space, the Masculine Create Time & plant
The Seeds of Beauty in the Space; list'ning to their lamentation
Los walks upon his ancient Mountains in the deadly darkness,
Among his Furnaces directing his laborious Myriads, watchful
Looking to the East, & his voice is heard over the whole Earth
As he watches the Furnaces by night & directs the labourers.

And thus Los replies upon his Watch: the Valleys listen silent,
The Stars stand still to hear: Jerusalem & Vala cease to mourn:
His voice is heard from Albion: the Alps & Appenines
Listen: Hermon & Lebanon bow their crowned heads:
Babel & Shinar look toward the Western Gate, they sit down
Silent at his voice: they view the red Globe of fire in Los's hand
As he walks from Furnace to Furnace directing the Labourers.
And this is the Song of Los, the Song that he sings on his Watch:

"O lovely mild Jerusalem! O Shiloh of Mount Ephraim!
I see thy Gates of precious stones, thy Walls of gold & silver.
Thou art the soft reflected Image of the Sleeping Man
Who, stretch'd on Albion's rocks, reposes amidst his Twenty-eight
Cities, where Beulah lovely terminates in the hills & valleys of Albion,
Cities not yet embodied in Time and Space; plant ye
The Seeds, O Sisters, in the bosom of Time & Space's womb,
To spring up for Jerusalem, lovely Shadow of Sleeping Albion.
Why wilt thou rend theyself apart & build an Earthly Kingdom
To reign in pride & to opress & to mix the Cup of Delusion?
O thou that dwellest with Babylon! Come forth, O lovely-one!

86

"I see thy Form, O lovely mild Jerusalem, Wing'd with Six Wings
In the opacous Bosom of the Sleeper, lovely Three-fold
In Head & Heart & Reins, three Universes of love & beauty.
Thy forehead bright, Holiness to the Lord, with Gates of pearl
Reflects Eternity; beneath, thy azure wings of feathery down
Ribb'd delicate & cloth'd with feather'd gold & azure & purple,
From thy white shoulders shadowing purity in holiness!
Thence, feather'd with soft crimson of the ruby, bright as fire,
Spreading into the azure, Wings which like a canopy
Bends over thy immortal Head in which Eternity dwells.

Albion, beloved Land! I see thy mountains & thy hills
And valleys & thy pleasant Cities, Holiness to the Lord.
I see the Spectres of thy Dead, O Emanation of Albion.

"Thy Bosom white, translucent, cover'd with immortal gems,
A sublime ornament not obscuring the outlines of beauty,
Terrible to behold for thy extreme beauty & perfection;
Twelve-fold here all the Tribes of Israel I behold
Upon the Holy Land. I see the River of Life & Tree of Life,
I see the New Jerusalem descending out of Heaven,
Between thy Wings of gold & silver, feather'd, immortal,
Clear as the rainbow, as the cloud of the Sun's tabernacle.

"Thy Reins, cover'd with Wings translucent, sometimes covering
And sometimes spread abroad, reveal the flames of holiness
Which like a robe covers & like a Veil of Seraphim
In flaming fire unceasing burns from Eternity to Eternity.
Twelvefold I there behold Israel in her Tents;
A Pillar of a Cloud by day, a Pillar of fire by night
Guides them; there I behold Moab & Ammon & Amalek.
There, Bells of silver round thy knees living articulate
Comforting sounds of love & harmony, & on thy feet
Sandals of gold & pearl, & Egypt & Assyria before me,
The Isles of Javan, Philistea, Tyre and Lebanon."

Thus Los sings upon his Watch, walking from Furnace to Furnace.
He siezes his Hammer every hour; flames surround him as
He beats, seas roll beneath his feet, tempests muster
Around his head, the thick hail stones stand ready to obey
His voice in the black cloud, his Sons labour in thunders
At his Furnaces, his Daughters at their Looms sing woes,
His Emanation separates in milky fibres agonizing
Among the golden Looms of Cathedron, sending fibres of love
From Golgonooza with sweet visions for Jerusalem, wanderer.

Nor can any consummate bliss without being Generated
On Earth, of those whose Emanations weave the loves
Of Beulah for Jerusalem & Shiloh in immortal Golgonooza,
Concentering in the majestic form of Erin in eternal tears,
Viewing the Winding Worm on the Desarts of Great Tartary,
Viewing Los in his shudderings, pouring balm on his sorrows:
So dread is Los's fury that none dare him to approach
Without becoming his Children in the Furnaces of affliction.

And Enitharmon like a faint rainbow waved before him
Filling with Fibres from his loins which redden'd with desire
Into a Globe of blood beneath his bosom trembling in darkness
Of Albion's clouds; he fed it with his tears & bitter groans,
Hiding his Spectre in invisibility from the timorous Shade,
Till it became a separated cloud of beauty, grace & love
Among the darkness of his Furnaces, dividing asunder till
She separated stood before him, a lovely Female weeping,
Even Enitharmon separated outside; & his Loins closed
And heal'd after the separation; his pains he soon forgot,
Lured by her beauty outside of himself in shadowy grief.
Two Wills they had, Two Intellects, & not as in times of old.

Silent they wander'd hand in hand, like two Infants wand'ring,
From Enion in the desarts, terrified at each other's beauty,
Envying each other, yet desiring in all devouring Love,

87

Repelling weeping Enion, blind & age-bent, into the four-fold
Desarts, Los first broke silence & began to utter his love:

"O lovely Enitharmon! I behold thy graceful forms
Moving beside me till, intoxicated with the woven labyrinth
Of beauty & perfection, my wild fibres shoot in veins
Of blood thro' all my nervous limbs; soon overgrown in roots
I shall be closed from thy sight; sieze therefore in thy hand
The small fibres as they shoot around me, draw out in pity
And let them run on the winds of thy bosom: I will fix them
With pulsations; we will divide them into Sons & Daughters
To live in thy Bosom's translucence as in an eternal morning."

Enitharmon answer'd: "No! I will sieze thy Fibres & weave
Them, not as thou wilt, but as I will; for I will Create
A round Womb beneath my bosom, lest I also be overwoven
With Love; be thou assured I never will be thy slave.
Let Man's delight be Love, but Woman's delight be Pride.
In Eden our Loves were the same; here they are opposite.
I have Loves of my own; I will weave them in Albion's Spectre.
Cast thou in Jerusalem's shadows thy Loves, silk of liquid
Rubies, Jacinths, Crysolites, issuing from thy Furnaces. While
Jerusalem divides thy care, while thou carest for Jerusalem,

Know that I never will be thine; also thou hidest Vala:
From her these fibres shoot to shut me in a Grave.
You are Albion's Victim; he has set his Daughter in your path."

88

Los answer'd, sighing like the Bellows of his Furnaces:

"I care not! the swing of my Hammer shall measure the starry round.
When in Eternity Man converses with Man, they enter
Into each other's Bosom (which are Universes of delight)
In mutual interchange, and first their Emanations meet
Surrounded by their Children; if they embrace & comingle
The Human Four-fold Forms mingle also in thunders of Intellect;
But if the Emanations mingle not, with storms & agitations
Of earthquakes & consuming fires they roll apart in fear;
For Man cannot unite with Man but by their Emanations
Which stand both Male & Female at the Gates of each Humanity.
How then can I ever again be united as Man with Man
While thou, my Emanation, refusest my Fibres of dominion?
When Souls mingle & join thro' all the Fibres of Brotherhood
Can there be any secret joy on Earth greater than this?"

Enitharmon answer'd: "This is Woman's World, nor need she any
Spectre to defend her from Man. I will Create secret places,
And the masculine names of the places, Merlin & Arthur.
A triple Female Tabernacle for Moral Law I weave,
That he who loves Jesus may loathe, terrified, Female love,
Till God himself become a Male subservient to the Female."

She spoke in scorn & jealousy, alternate torments; and
So speaking she sat down on Sussex shore, singing lulling
Cadences & playing in sweet intoxication among the glistening
Fibres of Los, sending them over the Ocean eastward into
The realms of dark death. O perverse to thyself, contrarious
To thy own purposes! for when she began to weave,
Shooting out in sweet pleasure, her bosom in milky Love
Flow'd into the aching fibres of Los, yet contending against him,
In pride sending his Fibres over to her objects of jealousy
In the little lovely Allegoric Night of Albion's Daughters
Which stretch'd abroad, expanding east & west & north & south,
Thro' all the World of Erin & of Los & all their Children.

A sullen smile broke from the Spectre in mockery & scorn;
Knowing himself the author of their divisions & shrinkings, gratified
At their contentions, he wiped his tears, he wash'd his visage.

"The Man who respects Woman shall be despised by Woman,
And deadly cunning & means abjectness only shall enjoy them.
For I will make their places of joy & love excrementitious,
Continually building, continually destroying in Family feuds.
While you are under the dominion of a jealous Female,
Unpermanent for ever because of love & jealousy,
You shall want all the Minute Particulars of Life."

Thus joy'd the Spectre in the dusky fires of Los's Forge, eyeing
Enitharmon who at her shining Looms sings lulling cadences
While Los stood at his Anvil in wrath, the victim of their love
And hate, dividing the Space of Love with brazen Compasses
In Golgonooza & in Udan-Adan & in Entuthon of Urizen.

The blow of his Hammer is Justice, the swing of his Hammer Mercy,
The force of Los's Hammer is eternal Forgiveness; but
His rage or his mildness were vain, she scatter'd his love on the wind
Eastward into her own Center, creating the Female Womb
In mild Jerusalem around the Lamb of God. Loud howl
The Furnaces of Los! loud roll the Wheels of Enitharmon!
The Four Zoas in all their faded majesty burst out in fury
And fire. Jerusalem took the Cup which foam'd in Vala's hand
Like the red Sun upon the mountains in the bloody day
Upon the Hermaphroditic Wine-presses of Love & Wrath.

89

Tho' divided by the Cross & Nails & Thorns & Spear
In cruelties of Rahab & Tirzah, permanent endure
A terrible indefinite Hermaphroditic form,
A Wine-press of Love & Wrath, double, Hermaphroditic,
Twelvefold in Allegoric pomp, in selfish holiness:
The Pharisaion, the Grammateis, the Presbuterion,
The Archiereus, the Iereus, the Saddusaion: double
Each withoutside of the other, covering eastern heaven.

Thus was the Covering Cherub reveal'd, majestic image
Of Selfhood, Body put off, the Antichrist accursed,
Cover'd with precious stones: a Human Dragon terrible
And bright stretch'd over Europe & Asia gorgeous.
In three nights he devour'd the rejected corse of death.

His Head, dark, deadly, in its Brain incloses a reflexion
Of Eden all perverted: Egypt on the Gihon, many tongued
And many mouth'd, Ethiopia, Lybia, the Sea of Rephaim.
Minute Particulars in slavery I behold among the brick-kilns
Disorganiz'd; & there is Pharoh in his iron Court
And the Dragon of the River & the Furnaces of iron.
Outwoven from Thames & Tweed & Severn, awful streams,
Twelve ridges of Stone frown over all the Earth in tyrant pride,
Frown over each River, stupendous Works of Albion's Druid Sons,
And Albion's Forests of Oaks cover'd the Earth from Pole to Pole.

His Bosom wide reflects Moab & Ammon on the River
Pison, since call'd Arnon: there is Heshbon beautiful,
The Rocks of Rabbath on the Arnon & the Fish-pools of Heshbon
Whose currents flow into the Dead Sea by Sodom & Gomorra.
Above his Head high arching Wings, black, fill'd with Eyes,
Spring upon iron sinews from the Scapulæ & Os Humeri:
There Israel in bondage to his Generalizing Gods,
Molech & Chemosh; & in his left breast is Philistea,
In Druid Temples over the whole Earth with Victim's Sacrifice
From Gaza to Damascus, Tyre & Sidon, & the Gods
Of Javan thro' the Isles of Grecia & all Europe's Kings,
Where Hiddekel pursues his course among the rocks.
Two Wings spring from his ribs of brass, starry, black as night,
But translucent their blackness as the dazling of gems.

His Loins inclose Babylon on Euphrates beautiful
And Rome in sweet Hesperia: there Israel scatter'd abroad
In martyrdoms & slavery I behold, ah vision of sorrow!
Inclosed by eyeless Wings, glowing with fire as the iron
Heated in the Smith's forge, but cold the wind of their dread fury.

But in the midst of a devouring Stomach, Jerusalem
Hidden within the Covering Cherub, as in a Tabernacle
Of threefold workmanship, in allegoric delusion & woe:
There the Seven Kings of Canaan & Five Baalim of Philistea,
Sihon & Og, the Anakim & Emim, Nephilim & Gibborim,
From Babylon to Rome; & the Wings spread from Japan,
Where the Red Sea terminates the World of Generation & Death,
To Ireland's farthest rocks, where Giants builded their Causeway,
Into the Sea of Raphaim, but the Sea o'erwhelm'd them all.

A Double Female now appear'd within the Tabernacle,
Religion hid in War, a Dragon red & hidden Harlot
Each within other, but without, a Warlike Mighty-one
Of dreadful power sitting upon Horeb, pondering dire
And mighty preparations, mustering multitudes innumerable
Of warlike sons among the sands of Midian & Aram.
For multitudes of those who sleep in Alla descend,
Lured by his warlike symphonies of tabret, pipe & harp,
Burst the bottoms of the Graves & Funeral Arks of Beulah.
Wandering in that unknown Night beyond the silent Grave
They become One with the Antichrist & are absorb'd in him.

90

The Feminine separates from the Masculine & both from Man,
Ceasing to be His Emanations, Life to Themselves assuming:
And while they circumscribe his Brain & while they circumscribe
His Heart & while they circumscribe his Loins, a Veil & Net
Of Veins of red Blood grows around them like a scarlet robe
Covering them from the sight of Man, like the woven Veil of Sleep
Such as the Flowers of Beulah weave to be their Funeral Mantles;
But dark, opake, tender to touch, & painful & agonizing
To the embrace of love & to the mingling of soft fibres
Of tender affection, that no more the Masculine mingles
With the Feminine, but the Sublime is shut out from the Pathos
In howling torment, to build stone walls of separation, compelling
The Pathos to weave curtains of hiding secresy from the torment.

Bowen & Conwenna stood on Skiddaw cutting the Fibres
Of Benjamin from Chester's River; loud the River, loud the Mersey
And the Ribble thunder into the Irish sea as the Twelve Sons
Of Albion drank & imbibed the Life & eternal Form of Luvah;
Cheshire & Lancashire & Westmoreland groan in anguish
As they cut the fibres from the Rivers; he sears them with hot
Iron of his Forge & fixes them into Bones of chalk & Rock.
Conwenna sat above; with solemn cadences she drew
Fibres of life out from the Bones into her golden Loom.
Hand had his Furnace on Highgate's heights & it reach'd
To Brockley Hills across the Thames; he with double Boadicea
In cruel pride cut Reuben apart from the Hills of Surrey,
Comingling with Luvah & with the Sepulcher of Luvah.
For the Male is a Furnace of beryll, the Female is a golden Loom.

Los cries: "No Individual ought to appropriate to Himself
Or to his Emanation any of the Universal Characteristics
Of David or of Eve, of the Woman or of the Lord,
Of Reuben or of Benjamin, of Joseph or Judah or Levi.
Those who dare appropriate to themselves Universal Attributes
Are the Blasphemous Selfhoods, & must be broken asunder.
A Vegetated Christ & a Virgin Eve are the Hermaphroditic
Blasphemy; by his Maternal Birth he is that Evil-One
And his Maternal Humanity must be put off Eternally,
Lest the Sexual Generation swallow up Regeneration.
Come Lord Jesus, take on thee the Satanic Body of Holiness!"

So Los cried in the Valleys of Middlesex in the Spirit of Prophecy,
While in Selfhood & Hyle & Bowen & Skofeld appropriate
The Divine Names, seeking to Vegetate the Divine Vision
In a corporeal & ever dying Vegetation & Corruption;
Mingling with Luvah in One, they become One Great Satan.

Loud scream the Daughters of Albion beneath the Tongs & Hammer,
Dolorous are their lamentations in the burning Forge.
They drink Reuben & Benjamin as the iron drinks the fire:
They are red hot with cruelty, raving along the Banks of Thames
And on Tyburn's Brook among the howling Victims in loveliness,
While Hand & Hyle condense the Little-ones & erect them into
A mighty Temple even to the stars; but they Vegetate
Beneath Los's Hammer, that Life may not be blotted out.

For Los said: "When the Individual appropriates Universality
He divides into Male & Female, & when the Male & Female
Appropriate Individuality they become an Eternal Death.
Hermaphroditic worshippers of a God of cruelty & law,
Your Slaves & Captives you compel to worship a God of Mercy!
These are the Demonstrations of Los & the blows of my mighty Hammer.'

So Los spoke. And the Giants of Albion, terrified & ashamed
With Los's thunderous Words, began to build trembling rocking Stones
For his Words roll in thunders & lightnings among the Temples
Terrified rocking to and fro upon the earth, & sometimes
Resting in a Circle in Malden or in Strathness or Dura,
Plotting to devour Albion & Los the friend of Albion,
Denying in private, mocking God & Eternal Life, & in Public
Collusion calling themselves Deists, Worshipping the Maternal
Humanity, calling it Nature and Natural Religion.

But still the thunder of Los peals loud, & thus the thunders cry:
"These beautiful Witchcrafts of Albion are gratifyd by Cruelty.

91

"It is easier to forgive an Enemy than to forgive a Friend.
The man who permits you to injure him deserves your vengeance:
He also will recieve it; go Spectre! obey my most secret desire
Which thou knowest without my speaking. Go to these Fiends of Right-
    eousness,
Tell them to obey their Humanities & not pretend Holiness
When they are murderers as far as my Hammer & Anvil permit.
Go, tell them that the Worship of God is honouring his gifts
In other men & loving the greatest men best, each according
To his Genius which is the Holy Ghost in Man; there is no other
God than that God who is the intellectual fountain of Humanity.
He who envies or calumniates, which is murder & cruelty,
Murders the Holy-one. Go, tell them this, & overthrow their cup,
Their bread, their altar-table, their incense & their oath,
Their marriage & their baptism, their burial & consecration.
I have tried to make friends by corporeal gifts but have only
Made enemies. I never made friends but by spiritual gifts,
By severe contentions of friendship & the burning fire of thought.
He who would see the Divinity must see him in his Children,
One first, in friendship & love, then a Divine Family, & in the midst
Jesus will appear; so he who wishes to see a Vision, a perfect Whole
Must see it in its Minute Particulars, Organized, & not as thou,
O Fiend of Righteousness, pretendest; thine is a Disorganized
And snowy cloud, brooder of tempests & destructive War.
You smile with pomp & rigor, you talk of benevolence & virtue;
I act with benevolence & Virtue & get murder'd time after time.
You accumulate Particulars & murder by analyzing, that you
May take the aggregate, & you call the aggregate Moral Law,
And you call that swell'd & bloated Form a Minute Particular;
But General Forms have their vitality in Particulars, & every
Particular is a Man, a Divine Member of the Divine Jesus."

So Los cried at his Anvil in the horrible darkness weeping.

The Spectre builded stupendous Works, taking the Starry Heavens
Like to a curtain & folding them according to his will,
Repeating the Smaragdine Table of Hermes to draw Los down
Into the Indefinite, refusing to believe without demonstration.

Los reads the Stars of Albion, the Spectre reads the Voids
Between the Stars among the arches of Albion's Tomb sublime,
Rolling the Sea in rocky paths, forming Leviathan
And Behemoth, the War by Sea enormous & the War
By Land astounding, erecting pillars in the deepest Hell
To reach the heavenly arches. Los beheld undaunted, furious,
His heav'd Hammer; he swung it round & at one blow
In unpitying ruin driving down the pyramids of pride,
Smiting the Spectre on his Anvil & the integuments of his Eye
And Ear unbinding in dire pain, with many blows
Of strict severity self-subduing, & with many tears labouring.

Then he sent forth the Spectre: all his pyramids were grains
Of sand, & his pillars dust on the fly's wing, & his starry
Heavens a moth of gold & silver, mocking his anxious grasp.
Thus Los alter'd his Spectre, & every Ratio of his Reason
He alter'd time after time with dire pain & many tears
Till he had completely divided him into a separate space.

Terrified Los sat to behold, trembling & weeping & howling:
"I care not whether a Man is Good or Evil; all that I care
Is whether he is a Wise Man or a Fool. Go, put off Holiness
And put on Intellect, or my thund'rous Hammer shall drive thee
To wrath which thou condemnest, till thou obey my voice."

So Los terrified cries, trembling & weeping & howling: "Beholding,

92

"What do I see! The Briton, Saxon, Roman, Norman amalgamating
In my Furnaces into One Nation, the English, & taking refuge
In the Loins of Albion. The Canaanite united with the fugitive
Hebrew, whom she divided into Twelve & sold into Egypt,
Then scatter'd the Egyptian & Hebrew to the four Winds.
This sinful Nation Created in our Furnaces & Looms is Albion."

So Los spoke. Enitharmon answer'd in great terror in Lambeth's Vale:

"The Poet's Song draws to its period, & Enitharmon is no more;
For if he be that Albion, I can never weave him in my Looms,
But when he touches the first fibrous thread, like filmy dew
My Looms will be no more & I annihilate vanish for ever.
Then thou wilt Create another Female according to thy Will."

Los answer'd swift as the shuttle of gold: "Sexes must vanish & cease
To be when Albion arises from his dread repose, O lovely Enitharmon:
When all their Crimes, their Punishments, their Accusations of Sin,
All their Jealousies, Revenges, Murders, hidings of Cruelty in Deceit
Appear only in the Outward Spheres of Visionary Space and Time,
In the shadows of Possibility, by Mutual Forgiveness for evermore,
And in the Vision & in the Prophecy, that we may Foresee & Avoid
The terrors of Creation & Redemption & Judgment: Beholding them
Display'd in the Emanative Visions of Canaan, in Jerusalem & in Shiloh
And in the Shadows of Remembrance & in the Chaos of the Spectre,
Amalek, Edom, Egypt, Moab, Ammen, Ashur, Philistea, around Jerusa-
lem,
Where the Druids rear'd their Rocky Circles to make permanent Remem-
brance
Of Sin, & the Tree of Good & Evil from the Rocky Circle & Snake
Of the Druid, along the Valley of Rephaim from Camberwell to Golgotha,
And framed the Mundane Shell Cavernous in Length, Bredth & Highth."

93

Enitharmon heard. She rais'd her head like the mild Moon:

"O Rintrah! O Palamabron! What are your dire & awful purposes?
Enitharmon's name is nothing before you; you forget all my Love.
The Mother's love of obedience is forgotten, & you seek a Love
Of the pride of dominion that will Divorce Ocalythron & Elynittria
Upon East Moor in Derbyshire & along the Valleys of Cheviot.
Could you Love me, Rintrah, if you Pride not in my Love?
As Reuben found Mandrakes in the field & gave them to his Mother,
Pride meets with Pride upon the Mountains in the stormy day,
In that terrible Day of Rintrah's Plow & of Satan's driving the Team.
Ah! then I heard my little ones weeping along the Valley.
Ah! then I saw my beloved ones fleeing from my Tent.
Merlin was like thee, Rintrah, among the Giants of Albion,
Judah was like Palamabron. O Simeon! O Levi! ye fled away!
How can I hear my little ones weeping along the Valley,
Or how upon the distant Hills see my beloveds' Tents?"

Then Los again took up his speech as Enitharmon ceast:

"Fear not, my Sons, this Waking Death; he is become One with me.
Behold him here! We shall not Die! we shall be united in Jesus.
Will you suffer this Satan, this Body of Doubt that Seems but Is Not,

To occupy the very threshold of Eternal Life? if Bacon, Newton, Locke
Deny a Conscience in Man & the Communion of Saints & Angels,
Contemning the Divine Vision & Fruition, Worshiping the Deus
Of the Heathen, the God of This World, & the Goddess Nature,
Mystery, Babylon the Great, The Druid Dragon & hidden Harlot,
Is it not that Signal of the Morning which was told us in the Beginning?"

Thus they converse upon Mam-Tor, the Graves thunder under their feet.

94

Albion cold lays on his Rock: storms & snows beat round him,
Beneath the Furnaces & the starry Wheels & the Immortal Tomb:
Howling winds cover him: roaring seas dash furious against him:
In the deep darkness broad lightnings glare, long thunders roll.

The weeds of Death inwrap his hands & feet, blown incessant
And wash'd incessant by the for-ever restless sea-waves foaming abroad
Upon the white Rock. England, a Female Shadow, as deadly damps
Of the Mines of Cornwall & Derbyshire, lays upon his bosom heavy,
Moved by the wind in volumes of thick cloud, returning, folding round
His loins & bosom, unremovable by swelling storms & loud rending
Of enraged thunders. Around them the Starry Wheels of their Giant Sons
Revolve, & over them the Furnaces of Los, & the Immortal Tomb around,
Erin sitting in the Tomb to watch them unceasing night and day:
And the Body of Albion was closed apart from all Nations.

Over them the famish'd Eagle screams on boney Wings, and around
Them howls the Wolf of famine; deep heaves the Ocean black, thundering
Around the wormy Garments of Albion, then pausing in deathlike silence.

Time was Finished! The Breath Divine Breathed over Albion
Beneath the Furnaces & starry Wheels and in the Immortal Tomb,
And England, who is Brittannia, awoke from Death on Albion's bosom:
She awoke pale & cold; she fainted seven times on the Body of Albion.

"O pitious Sleep, O pitious Dream! O God, O God awake! I have slain
In Dreams of Chastity & Moral Law: I have Murdered Albion! Ah!
In Stone-henge & on London Stone & in the Oak Groves of Malden
I have Slain him in my Sleep with the Knife of the Druid. O England!
O all ye Nations of the Earth, behold ye the Jealous Wife!
The Eagle & the Wolf & Monkey & Owl & the King & Priest were there."

95

Her voice pierc'd Albion's clay cold ear; he moved upon the Rock.
The Breath Divine went forth upon the morning hills. Albion mov'd
Upon the Rock, he open'd his eyelids in pain, in pain he mov'd
His stony members, he saw England. Ah! shall the Dead live again?

The Breath Divine went forth over the morning hills. Albion rose
In anger, the wrath of God breaking, bright flaming on all sides around
His awful limbs; into the Heavens he walked, clothed in flames,
Loud thund'ring, with broad flashes of flaming lightning & pillars,
Of fire, speaking the Words of Eternity in Human Forms, in direful
Revolutions of Action & Passion, thro' the Four Elements on all sides
Surrounding his awful Members. Thou seest the Sun in heavy clouds
Struggling to rise above the Mountains; in his burning hand
He takes his Bow, then chooses out his arrows of flaming gold;
Murmuring the Bowstring breathes with ardor! clouds roll round the
Horns of the wide Bow, loud sounding winds sport on the mountain brows,
Compelling Urizen to his Furrow & Tharmas to his Sheepfold
And Luvah to his Loom. Urthona he beheld, mighty labouring at
His Anvil, in the Great Spectre Los unwearied labouring & weeping:
Therefore the Sons of Eden praise Urthona's Spectre in songs,
Because he kept the Divine Vision in time of trouble.

As the Sun & Moon lead forward the Visions of Heaven & Earth,
England, who is Brittannia, entered Albion's bosom rejoicing.
Rejoicing in his indignation, adoring his wrathful rebuke.
She who adores not your frowns will only loathe your smiles.

96

As the Sun & Moon lead forward the Visions of Heaven & Earth,
England, who is Brittannia, entered Albion's bosom rejoicing.

Then Jesus appeared standing by Albion as the Good Shepherd
By the lost Sheep that he hath found, & Albion knew that it
Was the Lord, the Universal Humanity; & Albion saw his Form
A Man, & they conversed as Man with Man in Ages of Eternity.
And the Divine Appearance was the likeness & similitude of Los.

Albion said: "O Lord, what can I do? my Selfhood cruel
Marches against thee, deceitful, from Sinai & from Edom
Into the Wilderness of Judah, to meet thee in his pride.

I behold the Visions of my deadly Sleep of Six Thousand Years
Dazling around thy skirts like a Serpent of precious stones & gold.
I know it is my Self, O my Divine Creator & Redeemer."

Jesus replied: "Fear not Albion: unless I die thou canst not live;
But if I die I shall arise again & thou with me.
This is Friendship & Brotherhood: without it Man Is Not."

So Jesus spoke: the Covering Cherub coming on in darkness
Overshadow'd them, & Jesus said, "Thus do Men in Eternity
One for another to put off, by forgiveness, every sin."

Albion reply'd: "Cannot Man exist without Mysterious
Offering of Self for Another? is this Friendship & Brotherhood?
I see thee in the likeness & similitude of Los my Friend."

Jesus said: "Wouldest thou love one who never died
For thee, or ever die for one who had not died for thee?
And if God dieth not for Man & giveth not himself
Eternally for Man, Man could not exist; for Man is Love
As God is Love: every kindness to another is a little Death
In the Divine Image, nor can Man exist but by Brotherhood."

So saying the Cloud overshadowing divided them asunder.
Albion stood in terror, not for himself but for his Friend
Divine; & Self was lost in the contemplation of faith
And wonder at the Divine Mercy & at Los's sublime honour.

"Do I sleep amidst danger to Friends? O my Cities & Counties,
Do you sleep? rouze up, rouze up. Eternal Death is abroad!"

So Albion spoke & threw himself into the Furnace of affliction.
All was a Vision, all a Dream: the Furnaces became
Fountains of Living Waters flowing from the Humanity Divine.
And all the Cities of Albion rose from their Slumbers, and All
The Sons & Daughters of Albion on soft clouds, waking from Sleep.
Soon all around remote the Heavens burnt with flaming fires,
And Urizen & Luvah & Tharmas & Urthona arose into
Albion's Bosom. Then Albion stood before Jesus in the Clouds
Of Heaven, Fourfold among the Visions of God in Eternity.

97

"Awake, Awake, Jerusalem! O lovely Emanation of Albion,
Awake and overspread all Nations as in Ancient Time;
For lo! the Night of Death is past and the Eternal Day
Appears upon our Hills. Awake, Jerusalem, and come away!"

So spake the Vision of Albion, & in him so spake in my hearing
The Universal Father. Then Albion stretch'd his hand into Infinitude
And took his Bow. Fourfold the Vision; for bright beaming Urizen
Lay'd his hand on the South & took a breathing Bow of carved Gold:
Luvah his hand stretch'd to the East & bore a Silver Bow, bright shining:
Tharmas Westward a Bow of Brass, pure flaming, richly wrought:
Urthona Northward in thick storms a Bow of Iron, terrible thundering.

And the Bow is a Male & Female, & the Quiver of the Arrows of Love
Are the Children of this Bow, a Bow of Mercy & Loving kindness laying
Open the hidden Heart in Wars of mutual Benevolence, Wars of Love:
And the Hand of Man grasps firm between the Male & Female
And he Clothed himself in Bow & Arrows, in awful state, Fourfold,
In the midst of his Twenty-eight Cities, each with his Bow breathing.

98

Then each an Arrow flaming from his Quiver fitted carefully;
They drew fourfold the unreprovable String, bending thro' the wide
    Heavens
The horned Bow Fourfold; loud sounding flew the flaming Arrow fourfold.

Murmuring the Bowstring breathes with ardor. Clouds roll round the
    horns
Of the wide Bow; loud sounding Winds sport on the Mountains' Brows.
The Druid Spectre was Annihilate, loud thund'ring, rejoicing terrific,
    vanishing,
Fourfold Annihilation; & at the clangor of the Arrows of Intellect
The innumerable Chariots of the Almighty appear'd in Heaven,
And Bacon & Newton & Locke, & Milton & Shakspear & Chaucer,
A Sun of blood red wrath surrounding heaven, on all sides around,
Glorious, incomprehensible by Mortal Man, & each Chariot was Sexual
    Threefold.

And every Man stood Fourfold; each Four Faces had: One to the West,
One toward the East, One to the South, One to the North, the Horses
    Fourfold.

And the dim Chaos brighten'd beneath, above, around: Eyed as the Peacock,
According to the Human Nerves of Sensation, the Four Rivers of the Water of Life.

South stood the Nerves of the Eye; East, in Rivers of bliss, the Nerves of the
Expansive Nostrils; West flow'd the Parent Sense, the Tongue; North stood
The labyrinthine Ear: Circumscribing & Circumcising the excrementitious
Husk & Covering, into Vacuum evaporating, revealing the lineaments of Man,
Driving outward the Body of Death in an Eternal Death & Resurrection,
Awaking it to Life among the Flowers of Beulah, rejoicing in Unity
In the Four Senses, in the Outline, the Circumference & Form, for ever
In Forgiveness of Sins which is Self Annihilation; it is the Covenant of Jehovah.

The Four Living Creatures, Chariots of Humanity Divine Incomprehensible,
In beautiful Paradises expand. These are the Four Rivers of Paradise
And the Four Faces of Humanity, fronting the Four Cardinal Points
Of Heaven, going forward, forward irresistible from Eternity to Eternity.

And they conversed together in Visionary forms dramatic which bright
Redounded from their Tongues in thunderous majesty, in Visions
In new Expanses, creating exemplars of Memory and of Intellect,
Creating Space, Creating Time, according to the wonders Divine
Of Human Imagination throughout all the Three Regions immense
Of Childhood, Manhood & Old Age; & the all tremendous unfathomable Non Ens
Of Death was seen in regenerations terrific or complacent, varying
According to the subject of discourse; & every Word & every Character
Was Human according to the Expansion or Contraction, the Translucence or
Opakeness of Nervous fibres: such was the variation of Time & Space
Which vary according as the Organs of Perception vary; & they walked
To & fro in Eternity as One Man, reflecting each in each & clearly seen
And seeing, according to fitness & order. And I heard Jehovah speak
Terrific from his Holy Place, & saw the Words of the Mutual Covenant Divine

On Chariots of gold & jewels, with Living Creatures, starry & flaming
With every Colour, Lion, Tyger, Horse, Elephant, Eagle, Dove, Fly,
   Worm
And the all wondrous Serpent clothed in gems & rich array, Humanize
In the Forgiveness of Sins according to thy Covenant, Jehovah. They Cry:

"Where is the Covenant of Priam, the Moral Virtues of the Heathen?
Where is the Tree of Good & Evil that rooted beneath the cruel heel
Of Albions Spectre, the Patriarch Druid? where are all his Human Sac-
   rifice
For Sin in War & in the Druid Temples of the Accuser of Sin, beneath
The Oak Groves of Albion that cover'd the whole Earth beneath his
   Spectre?
Where are the Kingdoms of the World & all their glory that grew on
   Desolation,
The Fruit of Albion's Poverty Tree, when the Triple Headed Gog-Magog
   Giant
Of Albion Taxed the Nations into Desolation & then gave the Spectrous
   Oath?"

Such is the Cry from all the Earth, from the Living Creatures of the Earth
And from the great City of Golgonooza in the Shadowy Generation,
And from the Thirty-two Nations of the Earth among the Living Crea
   tures.

99

All Human Forms identified, even Tree, Metal, Earth & Stone: all
Human Forms identified, living, going forth & returning wearied
Into the Planetary lives of Years, Months, Days & Hours; reposing,
And then Awaking into his Bosom in the Life of Immortality.

And I heard the Name of their Emanations: they are named Jerusalem

THE END OF THE SONG OF JERUSALEM

FOR THE SEXES:
THE GATES OF PARADISE

PROLOGUE

MUTUAL Forgiveness of each Vice,
Such are the Gates of Paradise.
Against the Accuser's chief desire,
Who walk'd among the Stones of Fire,
Jehovah's Finger Wrote the Law:
Then Wept! then rose in Zeal & Awe,
And the Dead Corpse from Sinai's heat
Buried beneath his Mercy Seat.
O Christians, Christians! tell me Why
You rear it on your Altars high.

THE KEYS

THE Catterpiller on the Leaf
Reminds thee of thy Mother's Grief.

OF THE GATES

1 MY Eternal Man set in Repose,
  The Female from his darkness rose
  And she found me beneath a Tree,
  A Mandrake, & in her Veil hid me.
  Serpent Reasonings us entice
  Of Good & Evil, Virtue & Vice.
2 Doubt Self Jealous, Wat'ry folly,
3 Struggling thro' Earth's Melancholy.
4 Naked in Air, in Shame & Fear,
5 Blind in Fire with shield & spear,
  Two Horn'd Reasoning, Cloven Fiction,
  In Doubt, which is Self contradiction,
  A dark Hermaphrodite We stood,
  Rational Truth, Root of Evil & Good.

Round me flew the Flaming Sword;
Round her snowy Whirlwinds roar'd,
Freezing her Veil, the Mundane Shell.
6 I rent the Veil where the Dead dwell:
When weary Man enters his Cave
He meets his Saviour in the Grave.
Some find a Female Garment there,
And some a Male, woven with care,
Lest the Sexual Garments sweet
Should grow a devouring Winding sheet.
7 One Dies! Alas! the Living & Dead,
One is slain & One is fled.
8 In Vain-glory hatcht & nurst,
By double Spectres Self Accurst,
My Son! my Son! thou treatest me
But as I have instructed thee.
9 On the shadows of the Moon
Climbing thro' Night's highest noon.
10 In Time's Ocean falling drown'd.
In Aged Ignorance profound,
11 Holy & cold, I clip'd the Wings
Of all Sublunary Things,
12 And in depths of my Dungeons
Closed the Father & the Sons.
13 But when once I did descry
The Immortal Man that cannot Die,
14 Thro' evening shades I haste away
To close the Labours of my Day.
15 The Door of Death I open found
And the Worm Weaving in the Ground:
16 Thou'rt my Mother from the Womb,
Wife, Sister, Daughter, to the Tomb,
Weaving to Dreams the Sexual strife
And weeping over the Web of Life.

EPILOGUE

To The Accuser who is
The God of This World

TRULY, My Satan, thou art but a Dunce,
And dost not know the Garment from the Man.
Every Harlot was a Virgin once,
Nor can'st thou ever change Kate into Nan.

Tho' thou art Worship'd by the Names Divine.
Of Jesus & Jehovah, thou art still
The Son of Morn in weary Night's decline,
The lost Traveller's Dream under the Hill.

THE LAOCOON GROUP

Engraved about 1820 *and entitled:*

יה [1] & his two Sons, Satan & Adam, as they were copied from the
Cherubim of Solomon's Temple by three Rhodians & applied to Natural
Fact, or History of Ilium.

Above the head of the central figure is engraved:

The Angel of the Divine Presence

מלאך יהוה [2]

οφιουχος [3]

Above his right arm:

The Gods of Priam are the Cherubim of Moses & Solomon, The Hosts
of Heaven.

The serpent on the right is called: Evil.

The serpent on the left is called: Good and לילית. [4]

Sentences engraved about the plate:

IF Morality was Christianity, Socrates was the Saviour.

Art Degraded, Imagination Denied, War Governed the Nations.

---

[1] Jah, for Jehovah.   [2] Angel of Jehovah.
[3] The Serpent-bearer.   [4] Lilith (Adam's first wife).

Spiritual War: Israel deliver'd from Egypt, is Art deliver'd from Nature & Imitation.

A Poet, a Painter, a Musician, an Architect: the Man Or Woman who is not one of these is not a Christian.

You must leave Fathers & Mothers & Houses & Lands if they stand in the way of Art.

Prayer is the Study of Art.

Praise is the Practise of Art.

Fasting &c., all relate to Art.

The outward Ceremony is Antichrist.

The Eternal Body of Man is The Imagination, that is,
God himself ⎫
The Divine Body ⎬ ישוע, Jesus: we are his Members.

It manifests itself in his Works of Art (in Eternity All is Vision).

The True Christian Charity not dependent on Money (the life's blood of Poor Families), that is, on Caesar or Empire or Natural Religion: Money, which is The Great Satan or Reason, the Root of Good & Evil In The Accusation of Sin.

Good & Evil are Riches & Poverty, a Tree of Misery, propagating Generation & Death.

Where any view of Money exists, Art cannot be carried on, but War only (Read Matthew, c. x: 9 & 10 v.) by pretences to the Two Impossibilities, Chastity & Abstinence, Gods of the Heathen.

He repented that he had made Adam (of the Female, the Adamah) & it grieved him at his heart.

What can be Created Can be Destroyed.

Adam is only The Natural Man & not the Soul or Imagination.

Hebrew Art is called Sin by the Deist Science.

All that we See is Vision, from Generated Organs gone as soon as come, Permanent in The Imagination, Consider'd as Nothing by the Natural Man.

Art can never exist without Naked Beauty displayed.

The Gods of Greece & Egypt were Mathematical Diagrams—See Plato's Works.

Divine Union Deriding, And Denying Immediate Communion with God, The Spoilers say, "Where are his Works That he did in the Wilderness? Lo, what are these? Whence came they?" These are not the Works Of Egypt nor Babylon, Whose Gods are the Powers Of this World, Goddess Nature, Who first spoil & then destroy Imaginative Art; For their Glory is War and Dominion.

Empire against Art—See Virgil's Eneid, Lib. VI, v. 848.[1]

Satan's Wife, The Goddess Nature, is War & Misery, & Heroism a Miser.

For every Pleasure Money Is Useless.

There are States in which all Visionary Men are accounted Mad Men; such are Greece & Rome: Such is Empire or Tax—See Luke, Ch. 2, v. 1.

Without Unceasing Practise nothing can be done. Practise is Art. If you leave off you are Lost.

Jesus & his Apostles & Disciples were all Artists. Their Works were destroy'd by the Seven Angels of the Seven Churches in Asia, Antichrist Science.

The Old & New Testaments are the Great Code of Art.

Art is the Tree of Life. God is Jesus.

Science is the Tree of Death.

The Whole Business of Man Is The Arts, & All Things Common. No Secresy in Art.

The unproductive Man is not a Christian, much less the Destroyer.

Christianity is Art & not Money. Money is its Curse.

What we call Antique Gems are the Gems of Aaron's Breast Plate.

Is not every Vice possible to Man described in the Bible openly?

All is not Sin that Satan calls so: all the Loves & Graces of Eternity.

---

[1] Excudent alii spirantia mollius aera, "Others shall more softly fashion the breathing brass" (Page).

ON HOMER'S POETRY & ON VIRGIL

Etched about 1820

ON HOMER'S POETRY

EVERY Poem must necessarily be a perfect Unity, but why Homer's is peculiarly so, I cannot tell; he has told the story of Bellerophon & omitted the Judgment of Paris, which is not only a part, but a principal part, of Homer's subject.

But when a Work has Unity, it is as much in a Part as in the Whole: the Torso is as much a Unity as the Laocoon.

As Unity is the cloke of folly, so Goodness is the cloke of knavery. Those who will have Unity exclusively in Homer come out with a Moral like a sting in the tail. Aristotle says Characters are either Good or Bad; now Goodness or Badness has nothing to do with Character: an Apple tree, a Pear tree, a Horse, a Lion are Characters, but a Good Apple tree or a Bad is an Apple tree still; a Horse is not more a Lion for being a Bad Horse: that is its Character: its Goodness or Badness is another consideration.

It is the same with the Moral of a whole Poem as with the Moral Goodness of its parts. Unity & Morality are secondary considerations, & belong to Philosophy & not to Poetry, to Exception & not to Rule, to Accident & not to Substance; the Ancients call'd it eating of the tree of good & evil.

The Classics! it is the Classics, & not Goths nor Monks, that Desolate Europe with Wars.

ON VIRGIL

SACRED Truth has pronounced that Greece & Rome, as Babylon & Egypt, so far from being parents of Arts & Sciences as they pretend, were destroyers of all Art. Homer, Virgil & Ovid confirm this opinion & make us reverence The Word of God, the only light of antiquity that remains unperverted by War. Virgil in the Eneid, Book vi, line 848, says "Let others study Art: Rome has somewhat better to do, namely War & Dominion."

Rome & Greece swept Art into their maw & destroy'd it; a Warlike State never can produce Art. It will Rob & Plunder & accumulate into one place, & Translate & Copy & Buy & Sell & Criticise, but not Make. Grecian is Mathematic Form: Gothic is Living Form. Mathematic Form is Eternal in the Reasoning Memory: Living Form is Eternal Existence.

THE GHOST OF ABEL

A Revelation in the Visions of Jehovah Seen by William Blake

Etched 1822

TO LORD BYRON in the Wilderness:

What doest thou here, Elijah?
Can a Poet doubt the Visions of Jehovah? Nature has no Outline, but
Imagination has. Nature has no Tune, but Imagination has. Nature has
no Supernatural & dissolves: Imagination is Eternity.

SCENE—*A rocky Country.* EVE *fainted over the dead body of* ABEL, *which
lays near a Grave.* ADAM *kneels by her.* JEHOVAH *stands above.*
Jehovah. Adam!
Adam.   I will not hear thee more, thou Spiritual Voice.
   Is this Death?
Jehovah.   Adam!
Adam.   It is in vain. I will not hear thee
   Henceforth! Is this thy Promise, that the Woman's Seed
   Should bruise the Serpent's head? Is this the Serpent? Ah!
   Seven times, O Eve, thou hast fainted over the Dead. Ah! Ah!
                    EVE *revives.*
Eve. Is this the Promise of Jehovah! O, it is all a vain delusion,
   This Death & this Life and this Jehovah!
Jehovah.   Woman, lift thine eyes!

          A Voice is heard coming on.
Voice. O Earth, cover not thou my Blood! cover not thou my Blood!

          Enter the Ghost *of* ABEL.
Eve. Thou Visionary Phantasm, thou art not the real Abel.
Abel. Among the Elohim, a Human Victim I wander: I am their House,
   Prince of the Air, & our dimensions compass Zenith & Nadir.
   Vain is thy Covenant, O Jehovah! I am the Accuser & Avenger
   Of Blood. O Earth, Cover not thou the Blood of Abel.
Jehovah. What Vengeance dost thou require?
Abel.   Life for Life! Life for Life!
Jehovah. He who shall take Cain's life must also Die, O Abel!
   And who is he! Adam, wilt thou, or Eve, thou do this?

Adam. It is all a Vain delusion of the all creative Imagination.
    Eve, come away, & let us not believe these vain delusions.
    Abel is dead, & Cain slew him. We shall also Die a Death,
    And then, what then? be, as poor Abel, a Thought, or as
    This! O, what shall I call thee, Form Divine, Father of Mercies,
    That appearest to my Spiritual Vision? Eve, seest thou also?
Eve. I see him plainly with my Mind's Eye. I see also Abel living,
    Tho' terribly afflicted, as We also are, yet Jehovah sees him
    Alive & not Dead; were it not better to believe Vision
    With all our might & strength, tho' we are fallen & lost?
Adam. Eve, thou hast spoken truly: let us kneel before his feet.
                They Kneel before JEHOVAH.
Abel. Are these the Sacrifices of Eternity, O Jehovah, a Broken Spirit
    And a Contrite Heart? O, I cannot Forgive! the Accuser hath
    Enter'd into Me as into his House, & I loathe thy Tabernacles.
    As thou hast said, so is it come to pass: My desire is unto Cain,
    And He doth rule over Me; therefore My Soul in fumes of Blood
    Cries for Vengeance, Sacrifice on Sacrifice, Blood on Blood!
Jehovah. Lo, I have given you a Lamb for an Atonement instead
    Of the Transgressor, or no Flesh or Spirit could ever Live.
Abel. Compelled I cry, O Earth, cover not the Blood of Abel!

      ABEL *sinks down into the Grave, from which arises* SATAN,
         Armed in glittering scales, with a Crown & a Spear.

Satan. I will have Human Blood & not the blood of Bulls or Goats,
    And no Atonement, O Jehovah! the Elohim live on Sacrifice
    Of Men: hence I am God of Men: Thou Human, O Jehovah!
    By the Rock & Oak of the Druid, creeping Misletoe & Thorn,
    Cain's City built with Human Blood, not Blood of Bulls & Goats,
    Thou shalt Thyself be Sacrificed to Me, thy God, on Calvary.
Jehovah. Such is My Will   *Thunders.*
           that Thou Thyself go to Eternal Death
  In Self Annihilation, even till Satan, Self-subdu'd, Put off Satan
  Into the Bottomless Abyss, whose torment arises for ever & ever.

    On each side a Chorus of Angels entering Sing the following:

The Elohim of the Heathen Swore Venegeance for Sin! Then Thou
    stood'st
Forth, O Elohim Jehovah! in the midst of the darkness of the Oath, All
    Clothed

In Thy Covenant of the Forgiveness of Sins: Death, O Holy! Is this
Brotherhood.
The Elohim saw their Oath Eternal Fire: they rolled apart trembling
over The
Mercy Seat, each in his station fixt in the Firmament by Peace, Brother-
hood and Love.

THE CURTAIN FALLS.

Epigrams, Verses, and Fragments

Written about 1808-1811

*

YOU don't believe—I won't attempt to make ye:
You are asleep—I won't attempt to wake ye.
Sleep on, Sleep on! while in your pleasant dreams
Of Reason you may drink of Life's clear streams.
Reason and Newton, they are quite two things;
For so the Swallow & the Sparrow sings.
Reason says "Miracle": Newton says "Doubt."
Aye! that's the way to make all Nature out.
"Doubt, Doubt, & don't believe without experiment":
That is the very thing that Jesus meant,
When he said, "Only Believe! Believe & try!
Try, Try, and never mind the Reason why."

*

AND his legs carried it like a long fork,
Reach'd all the way from Chichester to York,
From York all across Scotland to the Sea;
This was a Man of Men, as seems to me.
Not only in his Mouth his own Soul lay,
But my Soul also would he bear away.
Like as a Pedlar bears his weary Pack,
So Stewhard's Soul he buckl'd to his Back.
But once, alas! committing a Mistake,
He bore the wretched Soul of William Blake
That he might turn it into Eggs of Gold;
But neither Back nor mouth those Eggs could hold.

His under jaw drop'd as those Eggs he laid,
And Stewhard's Eggs are addled & decay'd.
The Examiner, whose very name is Hunt,
Call'd Death a Madman, trembling for the affront,
Like trembling Hare sits on his weakly paper
On which he us'd to dance & sport & caper.
Yorkshire Jack Hemp & gentle, blushing Daw
Clap'd Death into the corner of their jaw,
And Felpham Billy rode out every morn
Horseback with Death over the fields of corn,
Who with iron hand cuff'd in the afternoon
The Ears of Billy's Lawyer & Dragoon.
And Cur, my Lawyer, & Dady, Jack Hemp's Parson,
Both went to Law with Death to keep our Ears on.
For how to starve Death we had laid a plot
Against his Price—but Death was in the Pot.
He made them pay his Price, alack a day!
He knew both Law & Gospel better than they.
O' that I ne'er had seen that William Blake,
Or could from death Assassinetti wake!
We thought—Alas, that such a thought should be!—
That Blake would Etch for him & draw for me.
For 'twas a kind of Bargain Screwmuch made
That Blake's designs should be by us display'd,
Because he makes designs so very cheap.
Then Screwmuch at Blake's soul took a long leap.
'Twas not a Mouse—'twas Death in a disguise,
And I, alas! live to weep out mine Eyes.
And Death sits laughing on their Monuments,
On which he's written, "Reciev'd the Contents."
But I have writ—so sorrowful my thought is—
His Epitaph, for my tears are aqua fortis:
"Come Artists, knock your heads against this stone
For Sorrow that our friend Bob Screwmuch's gone."
And now, the Muses upon me smile & Laugh,
I'll also write my own dear Epitaph,
And I'll be buried near a Dike
That my friends may weep as much as they like:
"Here lies Stewhard the Friend of All, &c."

WAS I angry with Hayley who us'd me so ill,
Or can I be angry with Felpham's old Mill?
Or angry with Flaxman or Cromek or Stothard,
Or poor Schiavonetti, whom they to death bother'd?
Or angry with Macklin or Boydel or Bowyer,
Because they did not say, "O what a Beau ye are"?
At a Friend's Errors Anger shew,
Mirth at the Errors of a Foe.

❧

ANGER & Wrath my bosom rends:
I thought them the Errors of friends.
But all my limbs with warmth glow:
I find them the Errors of the foe.

❧

THE Sussex Men are Noted Fools,
And weak is their brain pan:
I wonder if H[aines] the painter
Is not a Sussex Man?

❧

"MADMAN" I have been call'd: "Fool" they call **thee**
I wonder which they Envy, Thee or Me?

TO H[UNT]

YOU think Fuseli is not a Great Painter. I'm glad:
This is one of the best compliments he ever had.

TO F[LAXMAN]

I MOCK thee not, tho' I by thee am Mocked.
Thou call'st me Madman, but I call thee Blockhead.
❧

s [TOTHARD] in Childhood on the Nursery floor
Was extreme Old & most extremely poor.
He is grown old & rich & what he will:
He is extreme old & extreme poor still.

TO NANCY F[LAXMAN]

HOW can I help thy Husband's copying Me?
Should that make difference 'twixt me & Thee?

❋

OF H[ayley]'s birth this was the happy lot,
His Mother on his Father him begot.

❋

HE'S a Blockhead who wants a proof of what he can't Percieve,
And he's a Fool who tries to make such a Blockhead believe.

❋

CR[OMEK] loves artists as he loves his Meat.
He loves the Art, but 'tis the Art to Cheat.

❋

A PETTY Sneaking Knave I knew—
O Mr. Cr[omek], how do ye do?

❋

HE has observ'd the Golden Rule
Till he's become the Golden Fool.

TO S[TOTHAR]D

YOU all your Youth observ'd the Golden Rule
Till you're at last become the golden fool.
I sport with Fortune, Merry, Blithe & Gay,

Like to the Lion Sporting with his Prey.
Take you the hide & horns which you may wear:
Mine is the flesh——the bones may be your Share.

MR. STOTHARD TO MR. CROMEK

FOR Fortune's favours you your riches bring,
But Fortune says she gave you no such thing.
Why should you be ungrateful to your friends,
Sneaking & Backbiting & Odds & Ends?

MR. CROMEK TO MR. STOTHARD

FORTUNE favours the Brave, old Proverbs say;
But not with Money: that is not the way.
Turn back, turn back: you travel all in vain.
Turn thro' the iron gate down Sneaking lane.

❊

I AM no Homer's Hero, you all know;
I profess not Generosity to a Foe.
My Generosity is to my Friends,
That for their Friendship I may make amends.
The Generous to Enemies promotes their Ends
And becomes the Enemy & Betrayer of his Friends.

ON F[LAXMAN] & S[TOTHARD]

I FOUND them blind: I taught them how to see;
And now they know neither themselves nor me.
'Tis Excellent to turn a thorn to a pin,
A Fool to a bolt, a Knave to a glass of gin.

❊

P[HILLIPS] loved me not as he lov'd his Friends,
For he lov'd them for gain to serve his Ends.
He loved me and for no Gain at all
But to rejoice & triumph in my fall.

❊

T O forgive Enemies H [ayley] does pretend,
Who never in his Life forgave a friend.

TO F [LAXMAN]

Y O U call me Mad: 'tis Folly to do so—
To seek to turn a Madman to a Foe.
If you think as you speak, you are an Ass.
If you do not, you are but what you was.

ON H [AYLEY]'S FRIENDSHIP

W H E N H [ayley] finds out what you cannot do,
That is the very thing he'll set you to.
If you break not your Neck, 'tis not his fault,
But pecks of poison are not pecks of salt.
And when he could not act upon my wife
Hired a Villain to bereave my Life.

❧

S O M E Men, created for destruction, come
Into the World & make the World their home.
Be they as Vile & Base as E'er they can,
They'll still be called "The World's honest man."

ON S [TOTHARD]

Y O U say reserve & modesty he has,
Whose heart is iron, his head wood, & his face brass.
The Fox, the Owl, the Beetle & the Bat
By sweet reserve & modesty get Fat.

IMITATION OF POPE: A COMPLIMENT
TO THE LADIES

W O N D R O U S the Gods, more wondrous are the Men,
More Wondrous Wondrous still the Cock & Hen,
More Wondrous still the Table, Stool & Chair;
But Ah! More wondrous still the Charming Fair.

TO H[ALEY]

THY Friendship oft has made my heart to ake:
Do be my Enemy for Friendship's sake.

❧

COSWAY, Frazer & Baldwin of Egypt's Lake
Fear to associate with Blake.
This Life is a Warfare against Evils;
They heal the sick; he casts out devils.
Hayley, Flaxman & Stothard are also in doubt
Lest their Virtue should be put to the rout.
One grins, t'other spits & in corners hides,
And all the Virtuous have shewn their backsides.

AN EPITAPH

COME knock you heads against this stone
For sorrow that poor John Thompson's gone.

ANOTHER

I WAS buried near this Dike,
That my Friends may weep as much as they like.

ANOTHER

HERE lies John Trot, the Friend of all mankind:
He has not left one Enemy behind.
Friends were quite hard to find, old authors say;
But now they stand in every bodies way.

❧

MY title as a Genius thus is prov'd:
Not Prais'd by Hayley nor by Flaxman lov'd.

❧

I, RUBENS, am a Statesman & a Saint.
Deceptions? And so I'll learn to Paint.

TO ENGLISH CONNOISSEURS

YOU must agree that Rubens was a Fool,
And yet you make him master of your School
And give more money for his slobberings
Than you will give for Rafael's finest Things.
I understood Christ was a Carpenter
And not a Brewer's Servant, my good Sir.

❋

SWELL'D limbs, with no outline that you can descry,
That Stink in the Nose of a Stander-by.
But all the Pulp wash'd, painted, finish'd with labour
Of an hundred Journeymen's "how d'ye do, Neighbour."

A PRETTY EPIGRAM FOR THE ENTERTAIN-MENT OF THOSE WHO HAVE PAID GREAT SUMS IN THE VENETIAN & FLEMISH OOZE

NATURE & Art in this together Suit:
What is Most Grand is always most Minute.
Rubens thinks Tables, Chairs & Stools are Grand,
But Rafael thinks A Head, a foot, a hand.

❋

THESE are the Idiot's chiefest arts,
To blend & not define the Parts.
The Swallow sings in Courts of Kings
That Fools have their high finishings,
And this the Princes' golden rule,
The Laborious stumble of a Fool.
To make out the parts is the wise man's aim.
But to lose them the Fool makes his foolish Game.

❋

RAFAEL Sublime, Majestic, Graceful, Wise,
His Executive Power must I despise?
Rubens Low, Vulgar, Stupid, Ignorant,

His power of Execution I must grant?
Learn the Laborious stumble of a Fool,
And from an Idiot's Actions form my rule?
Go send your Children to the Slobbering School!

✢

IF I e'er Grow to Man's Estate,
O, Give to me a Woman's fate!
May I govern all, both great & small,
Have the last word & take the wall.

ON THE GREAT ENCOURAGEMENT GIVEN BY ENGLISH NOBILITY & GENTRY TO CORREGGIO, RUBENS, REMBRANDT, REYNOLDS, GAINSBOR-OUGH, CATALANI, DU CROWE, & DILBURY DOODLE

AS the Ignorant Savage will sell his own Wife
For a Sword or a Cutlass, a dagger or Knife,
So the Taught, Savage Englishman spends his whole Fortune
On a smear or a squall to destroy Picture or Tune,
And I call upon Colonel Wardle
To give these Rascals a dose of Cawdle.

✢

GIVE pensions to the Learned Pig
Or the Hare playing on a Tabor;
Anglus can never see Perfection
But in the Journeyman's Labour.

✢

THE Cunning-sures & the aim-at-yours . . .

✢

ALL Pictures that's Painted with Sense & with Thought
Are Painted by Madmen as sure as a Groat;
For the Greater the Fool in the Pencil more blest.

And when they are drunk they always paint best.
They never can Rafael it, Fuseli it, nor Blake it;
If they can't see an outline, pray how can they make it?
When Men will draw outlines begin you to jaw them;
Madmen see outlines & therefore they draw them.

ON H[AYLEY] THE PICK THANK

I WRITE the Rascal Thanks till he & I
With Thanks & Compliments are quite drawn dry.

CROMEK SPEAKS

I ALWAYS take my judgment from a Fool
Because his judgment is so very Cool,
Not prejudic'd by feelings great or small.
Amiable state! he cannot feel at all.

ENGLISH ENCOURAGEMENT OF ART:
CROMEK'S OPINIONS PUT INTO RHYME

IF you mean to Please Every body you will
Set to work both Ignorance & skill;
For a great multitude are Ignorant,
And skill to them seems raving & rant;
Like putting oil & water into a lamp,
'Twill make a great splutter with smoke & damp;
For there is no use, as it seems to me,
Of Lighting a Lamp when you don't wish to see.
And, when it smells of the Lamp, we can
Say all was owing to the Skilful Man.
For the smell of water is but small,
So e'en let Ignorance do it all.

❧

WHEN you look at a picture, you always can see
If a Man of Sense has Painted he.
They never flinch, but keep up a Jaw
About freedom & Jenny suck awa'.

❧

Y O U say their Pictures well Painted be,
And yet they are Blockheads you all agree.
Thank God, I never was sent to school
To be Flog'd into following the Style of a Fool.

The Errors of a Wise Man make your Rule
Rather than the Perfections of a Fool.

THE WASHERWOMAN'S SONG

I W A S H ' D them out & wash'd them in,
And they told me it was a great Sin.

❦

W H E N I see a Rubens, Rembrandt, Correggio,
I think of the Crippled Harry & Slobbering Joe;
And then I question thus: are artists' rules
To be drawn from the works of two manifest fools?
Then God defend us from the Arts I say!
Send Battle, Murder, Sudden death, O pray!
Rather than be such a blind Human Fool
I'd be an Ass, a Hog, a worm, a Chair, a Stool!

❦

G R E A T things are done when Men & Mountains meet;
This is not done by Jostling in the Street.

❦

I F you play a Game of Chance, know, before you begin,
If you are benevolent you will never win.

WILLIAM COWPER, ESQ.

[*The first stanza erased and illegible*]

F O R this is being a Friend just in the nick,
Not when he's well, but waiting till he's sick.
He calls you to his help: be you not mov'd
Untill, by being Sick, his wants are prov'd.

You see him spend his Soul in Prophecy.
Do you believe it a confounded lie
Till some Bookseller & the Public Fame
Proves there is truth in his extravagant claim.

For 'tis atrocious in a Friend you love
To tell you any thing that he can't prove,
And 'tis most wicked in a Christian Nation
For any Man to pretend to Inspiration.

❊

THE only Man that e'er I knew
Who did not make me almost spew
Was Fuseli: he was both Turk & Jew—
And so, dear Christian Friends, how do you do?

❊

GREAT Men & Fools do often me Inspire,
But the Greater Fool, the Greater Liar.

BLAKE'S APOLOGY FOR HIS CATALOGUE

HAVING given great offence by writing in Prose,
I'll write in Verse as soft as Bartolloze.
Some blush at what others can see no crime in,
But nobody sees any harm in Rhyming.
Dryden in Rhyme cries, "Milton only plann'd!"
Every Fool shook his bells throughout the land.
Tom Cooke cut Hogarth down with his clean graving.
Thousands of Connoisseurs with joy ran raving.
Thus Hayley on his Toilette seeing the sope,
Cries, "Homer is very much improv'd by Pope."
Some say I've given great Provision to my foes,
And that now I lead my false friends by the nose.
Flaxman & Stothard smelling a sweet savour
Cry, "Blakified drawing spoils painter & Engraver,"
While I, looking up to my Umbrella,
Resolv'd to be a very contrary fellow,
Cry, looking quite from Skumference to Center,

"No one can finish so high as the original Inventor."
Thus Poor Schiavonetti died of the Cromek,
A thing that's tied around the Examiner's neck.
This is my sweet apology to my friends,
That I may put them in mind of their latter ends.

❋

IF Men will act like a maid smiling over a Churn,
They ought not, when it comes to another's turn,
To grow sower at what a friend may utter,
Knowing & feeling that we all have need of Butter.
False Friends! fie! fie! our Friendship you shan't severe,
In spite we will be greater friends than ever.

❋

SOME people admire the work of a Fool,
For it's sure to keep your judgment cool;
It does not reproach you with want of wit;
It is not like a lawyer serving a writ.

TO GOD

IF you have form'd a Circle to go into,
Go into it yourself & see how you would do.

❋

"NOW Art has lost its mental Charms
France shall subdue the World in Arms."
So spoke an Angel at my birth,
Then said, "Descend thou upon Earth.
Renew the Arts on Britain's Shore,
And France shall fall down & adore.
With works of Art their Armies meet,
And War shall sink beneath thy feet.
But if thy Nation Arts refuse,
And if they scorn the immortal Muse,
France shall the arts of Peace restore,
And save thee from the Ungrateful shore."

Spirit, who lov'st Brittannia's Isle
Round which the Fiends of Commerce smile . . .

Marginalia

MS. EPIGRAMS AND VERSES CONCERNING SIR JOSHUA REYNOLDS

Written about 1808-1811

❧

No real Style of Colouring ever appears,
But advertising in the News Papers.
Look there—you'll see Sir Joshua's Colouring.
Look at his Pictures—All has taken Wing.

❧

CAN there be any thing more mean,
More Malice in disguise,
Than Praise a Man for doing what
That Man does most despise?
Reynolds Lectures Exactly so
When he praises Michael Angelo.

❧

SIR JOSHUA Praises Michael Angelo:
'Tis Christian Mildness when Knaves Praise a Foe:
But 'Twould be Madness all the World would say
Should Michael Angelo praise Sir Joshua—
Christ us'd the Pharisees in a rougher way.

❧

SIR JOSHUA praised Rubens with a Smile
By calling his the ornamental Style;
And yet his praise of Flaxman was the smartest

When he call'd him the Ornamental Artist.
But sure such ornaments we well may spare,
As Crooked limbs & louzy heads of hair.

FLORENTINE INGRATITUDE

SIR JOSHUA sent his own Portrait to
The birth Place of Michael Angelo,
And in the hand of the simpering fool
He put a dirty paper scroll,
And on the paper, to be polite,
Did "Sketches by Michael Angelo" write.
The Florentines said, " 'Tis a Dutch English bore,
Michael Angelo's Name writ on Rembrandt's door."
The Florentines call it an English Fetch,
For Michael Angelo did never sketch.
Every line of his has Meaning
And needs neither Suckling nor Weaning.
'Tis the trading English Venetian cant
To speak Michael Angelo & Act Rembrandt.
It will set his Dutch friends all in a roar
To write "Mich. Ang." on Rembrandt's Door.
But You must not bring in your hand a Lie
If you mean the Florentines should buy.

Ghiotto's Circle or Apelles' Line
Were not the Work of Sketchers drunk with Wine,
Nor of the City Clark's warm hearted Fashion,
Nor of Sir Isaac Newton's Calculation,
Nor of the City Clark's Idle Facilities
Which sprang from Sir Isaac Newton's great Abilities.

These Verses were written by a very Envious Man,
Who, whatever likeness he may have to Michael Angelo,
Never can have any to Sir Jehoshuan.

A PITIFUL CASE

THE Villain at the Gallows tree
When he is doom'd to die,
To assuage his misery
In Virtue's praise does cry.

So Reynolds when he came to die,
To assuage his bitter woe
Thus aloud does howl & cry:
"Michael Angelo! Michael Angelo!"

TO THE ROYAL ACADEMY

A STRANGE Erratum in all the Editions
Of Sir Joshua Reynolds' Lectures
Should be corrected by the Young Gentlemen
And the Royal Academy's directors.

Instead of "Michael Angelo"
Read "Rembrandt," for it is fit
To make meer common honesty
In all that he has writ.

❋

THE Cripple every Step Drudges & labours,
And says: "come, learn to walk of me, Good Neighbours."
Sir Joshua in astonishment cries out:
"See, what Great Labour! Pain in Modest Doubt!"

Newton & Bacon cry, being badly Nurst:
"He is all Experiments from last to first.
He walks & stumbles as if he crep,
And how high labour'd is every step!"

❋

I ASK'D my dear Friend, Orator Prig:
"What's the first part of Oratory?" he said: "a great wig."
"And what is the second?" then dancing a jig
And bowing profoundly he said: "a great wig."
"And what is the third?" then he snor'd like a pig,
And puffing his cheeks he replied: "a Great wig."
So if a Great Painter with Questions you push,
"What's the first Part of Painting?" he'll say: "a Paint Brush."
"And what is the second?" with most modest blush,
He'll smile like a Cherub & say: "a paint Brush."

"And what is the third?" he'll bow like a rush,
With a lear in his Eye, he'll reply: "a Paint Brush."
Perhaps this is all a Painter can want;
But look yonder—that house is the house of Rembrandt, &c.

TO VENETIAN ARTISTS

THAT God is Colouring Newton does shew,
And the devil is a Black outline, all of us know.
Perhaps this little Fable may make us merry:
A dog went over the water without a wherry:
A bone which he had stolen he had in his mouth;
He cared not whether the wind was north or south.
As he swam he saw the reflection of the bone.
"This is quite Perfection, one Generalizing Tone!
Outline! There's no outline! There's no such thing!
All is Chiaro Scuro, Poco Pen, it's all colouring."

Snap, Snap! he has lost shadow & substance too.
He had them both before: now how do ye do?
"A great deal better than I was before.
Those who taste colouring love it more & more."
[Then Reynolds said: "O woman most sage!" *del.*]
"O dear Mother outline, of knowledge most sage,
What's the First Part of Painting?" she said: "Patronage.
"And what is the second?" to please & Engage,
She frown'd like a Fury & said: "Patronage."
"And what is the Third?" she put off Old Age,
And smil'd like a Syren & said: "Patronage."